Elements of Literature

Fiction • Poetry • Drama

Fourth Canadian Edition

Elements of Literature

Fiction • Poetry • Drama

Edited by

Robert Scholes

Nancy R. Comley

Carl H. Klaus

David Staines

OXFORD

UNIVERSITY PRESS

OXFORD
UNIVERSITY PRESS

8 Sampson Mews, Suite 204, Don Mills, Ontario M3C 0H5
www.oupcanada.com

Oxford University Press is a department of the University of Oxford.
It furthers the University's objective of excellence in research, scholarship,
and education by publishing worldwide in

Oxford   New York

Auckland   Cape Town   Dar es Salaam   Hong Kong   Karachi
Kuala Lumpur   Madrid   Melbourne   Mexico City   Nairobi
New Delhi   Shanghai   Taipei   Toronto

With offices in

Argentina   Austria   Brazil   Chile   Czech Republic   France   Greece
Guatemala   Hungary   Italy   Japan   Poland   Portugal   Singapore
South Korea   Switzerland   Thailand   Turkey   Ukraine   Vietnam

Oxford is a trade mark of Oxford University Press
in the UK and in certain other countries

Published in Canada
by Oxford University Press

Copyright © Oxford University Press Canada 2010

Original edition published by Oxford University Press, Inc.,
198 Madison Avenue, New York, NY 10016–4314, USA
Copyright © Oxford University Press, Inc.

Library and Archives Canada Cataloguing in Publication

Elements of literature / [edited by] Robert
Scholes ... [et al.]. — 4th Canadian ed.

Includes bibliographical references and index.

ISBN 978-0-19-543097-4

1. English literature.   2. American literature.
3. Canadian literature (English).   I. Scholes, Robert, 1929–

PN6014.E44 2009   820.8   C2009-902801-8

MIX
Paper from
responsible sources
FSC
www.fsc.org   FSC® C004071

Printed in Canada

11 12 13 – 16 15 14

Contents

FROM THE PUBLISHER xi

PREFACE xiii

FICTION

The Elements of Fiction 3

A Collection of Modern Fiction

NATHANIEL HAWTHORNE 21
My Kinsman, Major Molineux 21

EDGAR ALLAN POE 34
The Purloined Letter 34

HERMAN MELVILLE 47
Bartleby, the Scrivener 47

KATE CHOPIN 72
The Story of an Hour 73

CHARLOTTE PERKINS GILMAN 75
The Yellow Wallpaper 75

CHARLES G.D. ROBERTS 87
Strayed 87

STEPHEN LEACOCK 90
The Marine Excursion of the Knights
     of Pythias 90

STEPHEN CRANE 102
The Bride Comes to Yellow Sky 102

JAMES JOYCE 110
Araby 111

D.H. LAWRENCE 115
The Rocking-Horse Winner 115

KATHERINE MANSFIELD 126
The Garden Party 126

F. SCOTT FITZGERALD 137
Babylon Revisited 137

WILLIAM FAULKNER 151
A Rose for Emily 152

ELIZABETH BOWEN 159
The Demon Lover 159

ERNEST HEMINGWAY 164
A Clear, Well-Lighted Place 164

MORLEY CALLAGHAN 168
A Cap for Steve 168

SINCLAIR ROSS 176
The Painted Door 176

SHEILA WATSON 189
Antigone 190

EUDORA WELTY 196
Why I live at the P.O. 196

JOHN CHEEVER 205
The Swimmer 205

BERNARD MALAMUD 213
The Magic Barrel 213

DORIS LESSING 225
A Sunrise on the Veld 225

MAVIS GALLANT 231
The Ice Wagon Going Down
     the Street 231

FLANNERY O'CONNOR 247
Everything That Rises Must Converge 248

MARGARET LAURENCE 259
A Bird in the House 259

JOHN BARTH 272
Lost in the Funhouse 272

ALICE MUNRO 288
Family Furnishings 288

ALISTAIR MACLEOD 308
The Boat 309

BHARATI MUKHERJEE 321
The Lady from Lucknow 321

THOMAS KING 328
Borders 328

ROHINTON MISTRY 336
The Collectors 336

LOUISE ERDRICH 353
Fleur 353

POETRY

The Elements of Poetry 365

A Selection of Poets

GEOFFREY CHAUCER 401
From *The Canterbury Tales*
The Miller's Prologue and Tale 401

WILLIAM SHAKESPEARE 427
Sonnets
18 [Shall I compare thee] 427
29 [When, in disgrace] 428
35 [No more be grieved at that which thou
hast done] 428
55 [Not marble nor the gilded
monuments] 429
65 [Since brass, nor stone, nor earth] 429
73 [That time of year thou mayst in me
behold] 429
130 [My mistress' eyes are nothing like
the sun] 430

JOHN DONNE 430
The Good Morrow 431
The Sun Rising 431
The Canonization 432
The Flea 434
The Relic 435

Holy Sonnets
10 [Death, be not proud] 436
14 [Batter my heart] 436

ROBERT HERRICK 437
Delight in Disorder 437

Upon Julia's Clothes 438
To the Virgins, to Make Much of Time 438

JOHN MILTON 439
On Shakespeare 439
How Soon Hath Time 440
Lycidas 440
When I Consider How My Light is Spent 445

ANDREW MARVELL 446
To His Coy Mistress 446
The Garden 447
The Fair Singer 449
The Coronet 450

ALEXANDER POPE 451
The Rape of the Lock 451
Epistle IV To Richard Boyle, Earl of
Burlington 470

WILLIAM BLAKE 477
From *Songs of Innocence*
The Lamb 478

From *Songs of Experience*
The Clod and the Pebble 478
The Chimney-Sweeper 479
The Sick Rose 479
The Tyger 480
London 480

Auguries of Innocence 481

WILLIAM WORDSWORTH 484
I Wandered Lonely as a Cloud 485
Ode: Intimations of Immortality 486

Sonnets
4 Composed upon Westminster Bridge 492
14 [The World is too much with us] 492

Lines Composed a Few Miles Above
    Tintern Abbey 493

JOHN KEATS 497
Ode to a Nightingale 497
Ode on a Grecian Urn 500
Ode to Autumn 502
La Belle Dame sans Merci 503
Bright Star 505
On the Sonnet 506

ALFRED, LORD TENNYSON 506
The Lady of Shalott 507
Ulysses 512
Tears, Idle Tears 513

From *In Memoriam*
7 [Dark House, by which more I stand] 514
8 [A happy lover] 515
115 [Now fades the last long streak] 515

ROBERT BROWNING 516
Soliloquy of the Spanish Cloister 517
My Last Duchess 519
The Bishop Orders His Tomb 520
Porphyria's Lover 523

WALT WHITMAN 525
Crossing Brooklyn Ferry 525
I Hear America Singing 530
A Sight in Camp in the Daybreak Gray
    and Dim 531
The Ox-Tamer 531
The Dalliance of the Eagles 532

EMILY DICKINSON 532
[Success Is Counted Sweetest] 533
[I'm 'Wife'— I've Finished That] 533
[The Heart Asks Pleasure — First] 534
[Because I could not stop for Death] 534
[What Is — 'Paradise'] 535
[I Never Hear the Word] 535
[I Heard a Fly Buzz] 536

THOMAS HARDY 537
Hap 537
The Darkling Thrush 538
The Convergence of the Twain 539
The Oxen 541
During Wind and Rain 541
In Time of 'The Breaking of Nations' 542

GERARD MANLEY HOPKINS 543
God's Grandeur 543
The Windhover 544
Pied Beauty 544
Spring and Fall: To a Young Child 545
Thou Art Indeed Just, Lord 545

ARCHIBALD LAMPMAN 546
The Railway Station 546
The Death of Tennyson 547
The City of the End of Things 547
Winter-Solitude 549
At the Long Sault: May 1660 550

WILLIAM BUTLER YEATS 553
The Lake Isle of Innisfree 553
The Dolls 554
The Wild Swans at Coole 554
The Second Coming 555
Leda and the Swan 556
Among School Children 556
Sailing to Byzantium 559
After Long Silence 560
The Circus Animals' Desertion 560

ROBERT FROST 562
Mending Wall 562
After Apple-Picking 563
Birches 564
Design 566
Stopping by Woods on a Snowy
    Evening 566
Provide, Provide 567

WALLACE STEVENS 568
Sunday Morning 568
Anecdote of the Jar 572
Thirteen Ways of Looking at a
    Blackbird 572
The Snow Man 575
A High-Toned Old Christian Woman 575
Of Modern Poetry 576

E.J. PRATT 577
The Shark 577
One Hour of Life 578
Erosion 578
Silences 579
The Deed 580

WILLIAM CARLOS WILLIAMS 581
The Widow's Lament in Springtime 582
Spring and All 582
The Red Wheelbarrow 583
Flowers by the Sea 584
The Last Words of My English
    Grandmother 584
The Yachts 585
Landscape with the Fall of Icarus 586

MARIANNE MOORE 587
Poetry 588
The Fish 589
Nevertheless 590
A Jellyfish 591

T.S. ELIOT 591
The Love Song of J. Alfred Prufrock 592
The Hollow Men 596
Journey of the Magi 599
Marina 600

E.E. CUMMINGS 602
Buffalo Bill 's 602
Spring is like a perhaps hand 602
somewhere i have never travelled 603
my father moved through dooms
    of love 604
pity this busy monster 606

W.H. AUDEN 607
Who's Who 607
As I Walked Out One Evening 608
Lullaby 609
Musée des Beaux Arts 610
In Memory of W.B. Yeats 611
The Unknown Citizen 613

A.M. KLEIN 614
Soirée of Velvel Kleinburger 615
The Rocking Chair 618
Portrait of the Poet as Landscape 619

ELIZABETH BISHOP 624
The Map 624
First Death in Nova Scotia 625
In the Waiting Room 626
One Art 629

IRVING LAYTON 630
The Cold Green Element 630
Berry Picking 631
Whatever Else Poetry Is Freedom 632
Keine Lazarovitch 1870–1959 634

DYLAN THOMAS 635
The Force that through the Green Fuse
    Drives the Flower 635
A Refusal to Mourn the Death, by Fire,
    of a Child in London 636
Do Not Go Gentle into That Good
    Night 637
Fern Hill 637

P.K. PAGE 639
The Stenographers 639
Photos of a Salt Mine 641
Arras 642
The New Bicycle 644
Deaf-Mute in the Pear Tree 645

ROBERT LOWELL 646
'To Speak of Woe That is in Marriage' 646
Skunk Hour 647
Water 649
For the Union Dead 650

MARGARET AVISON 652
Snow 652
New Year's Poem 652
The Swimmer's Moment 653
Butterfly Bones; or Sonnet against
    Sonnets 654
In a Season of Unemployment 654
We are the Poor Who Are Always
    with Us 655

ROBERT KROETSCH 656
The Poet's Mother 656

From *The Hornbooks of Rita K.*
Hornbook #43 659
Hornbook #45 659

PHYLLIS WEBB 660
Marvell's Garden 660
Lament 662
To Friends Who Have Also Considered
    Suicide 662
The Days of the Unicorns 663

ADRIENNE RICH 665
The Afterwake 665
Moving in Winter 666
Novella 666
Night-Pieces: For a Child 667
Rape 668

SYLVIA PLATH 669
Sheep in Fog 669
Daddy 670
Kindness 672
Edge 673
Words 673

MARGARET ATWOOD 674
At the Tourist Centre in Boston 675
Death of a Young Son by Drowning 676
Variations on the Word *Love* 677
Variations on the Word *Sleep* 678
Interlunar 678
The Door 680

ROY MIKI 681
make it new 681

attractive 682
subversion in tokyo 684
on the sublime 686

MICHAEL ONDAATJE 687
Bearhug 688
Letters & Other Worlds 688
Elizabeth 690
The Cinnamon Peeler 692

ROBERT BRINGHURST 693
Essay on Adam 694
The Stonecutter's Horses 694
Leda and the Swan 699

DIONNE BRAND 701
Islands Vanish 701

From *thirsty*
Poem I 703
Poem II 704
Poem III 705

GEORGE ELLIOTT CLARKE 706
From *Whylah Falls*
Look Homeward, Exile 707
Bees' Wings 708
Blank Sonnet 708

Le Tombeau de Bishop 709
Paris Annapolis 710
Burning Poems 711

DRAMA

The Elements of Drama 715

A Collection of Plays

SOPHOCLES 737
Oedipus Rex 737

WILLIAM SHAKESPEARE 779
King Lear 780

ROBERT BRINSLEY SHERIDAN 894
The School for Scandal 895

HENRIK IBSEN 960
Hedda Gabler 961

OSCAR WILDE 1022
The Importance of Being Earnest 1022

GEORGE BERNARD SHAW 1065
Pygmalion 1066

SAMUEL BECKETT 1141
Krapp's Last Tape 1142

ARTHUR MILLER 1148
The Price 1149

EDWARD ALBEE 1207
The Zoo Story 1208

SHARON POLLOCK 1224
Doc 1225

MICHEL TREMBLAY 1281
For the Pleasure of Seeing Her Again 1281

TOMSON HIGHWAY 1312
The Rez Sisters 1312

GLOSSARY OF CRITICAL TERMS 1355

ACKNOWLEDGEMENTS 1361

INDEX 1365

From the Publisher

◆

Oxford University Press is proud to publish the fourth Canadian edition of *Elements of Literature*, edited by Robert Scholes, Nancy Comley, Carl Klaus, and David Staines. Like its predecessors, the new edition is designed to introduce students to the greatest works of short fiction, poetry, and drama written in (or translated into) English from the Golden Age of classical Greek theatre to the twenty-first century. Each writer is introduced by a short biocritical headnote to set his or her work within the context of the literary canon. In addition, each of the three major sections begins with an essay that introduces students to the key characteristics of the genre—fiction, poetry, or drama—while providing an overview of approaches to critical analysis. The selections we have added for this new edition, from Charles G.D. Roberts, Archibald Lampman, John Donne, Alexander Pope, and William Butler Yeats, reflect our commitment to refining the selection of artists and works with a view to assembling the broadest spectrum of English literature that can be achieved in a single volume. We believe that together with the strengths of the previous edition—its comprehensive treatment of each author and genre and its outstanding coverage of Canadian writers—these changes give *Elements of Literature* a depth of coverage that is unmatched in any single-volume anthology on the market.

Reviewers

We would like to thank the following reviewers, whose thoughtful comments and suggestions have helped to shape this and earlier editions of the anthology:

Bert Almon, University of Alberta
Anne Blott, Vanier College
Stewart Blott, Vanier College
Roy Campbell, University of Manitoba
Rhiannon Don, Nipissing University
Candace Fertile, Camosun College
Debbie Hlady, Camosun College
Kathleen James-Cavan, University of Saskatchewan
Mike Matthews, Vancouver Island University
Robert J. Merrett, University of Alberta
David J. Parkinson, University of Saskatchewan
Barry Popowich, University of Saskatchewan

Preface

◈

This fourth edition of *Elements of Literature* brings together outstanding works of fiction, poetry, and drama in a collection designed to aid those who want to learn how to understand and appreciate works of literature. There are introductory discussions for each of the literary forms represented, genre-specific glossaries of critical terms, and biographical headnotes for each author.

The stories, poems, and plays presented here have been chosen for their suitability in introducing the work of their authors. Fiction writers, poets, and playwrights are presented chronologically by date of birth. They range in time and place from Sophocles and the world of classical Greek tragedy to such contemporary writers as Rohinton Mistry and Louise Erdrich, Adrienne Rich and George Elliott Clarke, and Edward Albee and Michel Tremblay. The date of its earliest publication follows each story, poem, and play. The collection is not a history of literature in English. It is a textbook of significant fiction, poetry, and drama of American, British, and Canadian literatures.

I wish to take this occasion to thank four people from Oxford University Press who stand behind this new edition. Phyllis Wilson invited me to rethink the original text, Eric Sinkins provided his careful editorial suggestions, Ryan Chynces marshalled from across the country critical commentaries for this new edition, and Peter Chambers oversaw the final production of the edition with authority. My thanks to them for their advice and unfailing support.

David Staines
Ottawa, Ontario
May 2009

FICTION

FICTION

The Elements of Fiction

FICTION, FACT, AND TRUTH

A fiction is a made-up story. This definition covers a lot of territory. It includes the 'white' lies we tell to protect ourselves from scrutiny and the jokes and anecdotes we hear and re-tell in casual conversation. It also covers great visionary works of literature like John Milton's *Paradise Lost* and even the Bible. To call something a fiction does not mean that it necessarily lacks truth, or that it may not contain fact. The relationship between fact and fiction is by no means simple, and, since it is important to an understanding of fiction, it must be considered with some care.

Fact and fiction are old acquaintances. Both derive from Latin words: 'fact' comes from *facere*, 'to make or do'; 'fiction' comes from *fingere*, 'to make or shape'. Plain enough words, one would think—not necessarily loaded with overtones of approval or disapproval. But their fortunes in the world of words have not been equal. In ordinary use, fact is associated with those pillars of verbal society 'reality' and 'truth'. Fiction, on the other hand, is known to consort with such suspicious characters as 'unreality' and 'falsehood'. But if we look deeper into the matter, we can see that the relation of fact and fiction to 'the real' and 'the untrue' is not exactly what it appears on the surface. Fact still means literally 'a thing done', and fiction has never lost its meaning of 'a thing made'. But in what sense do things done or things made partake of truth or reality?

We can observe the relationship between fact and fiction clearly if we consider one place where the two come together: in history. The word 'history' itself hides a double meaning. It comes from a Greek word that originally meant 'inquiry' or 'investigation', but it soon acquired the two meanings that interest us here. On the one hand, history can mean 'things that have happened'; on the other, it can refer to 'a recorded version of things that are supposed to have happened'. In other words, history can mean both the events of the past and the story of those events: fact—or fiction. The word 'story' lurks in the word 'history' and is derived from it. Fact, in order to survive, must become fiction. Seen in this way, fiction is not the opposite of fact but its complement: it gives a more lasting shape to the vanishing deeds of women and men.

This is just one aspect of fiction. We *do* think of it also as something different from historical records or mere data. We think of it not just as made but made up, a product of the imagination. It is helpful to see fiction in both ways outlined here: it can be factual, maintaining the closest possible correspondence between its story and events that have actually happened, or it can be fanciful, defying our sense of life's ordinary possibilities.

If we take these two extremes of fiction as opposite ends of a spectrum—the infrared of pure history and the ultra-violet of pure imagination—we can distinguish many shades of coloration. All are fragments of the white radiance of truth, which is present in both history books and fairy tales—though only partly present in each—fragmented by the prism of fiction, without which we could not see it at all. For truth is like ordinary light, present everywhere but invisible, and we must break it to behold it. To fracture truth in a purposeful and pleasing way—that is the job of the writer of fiction, with whatever shades from the spectrum he or she chooses to work.

THE SPECTRUM OF FICTION

The fictional spectrum can be a useful way to analyze fiction as long as we remember that it is just a metaphor, a handy linguistic tool to be discarded when it becomes more of a hindrance to understanding than a help. In terms of this metaphor, we may think of fiction as resembling the spectrum of colour found in ordinary light, with history and fantasy as its ends. Of course, only a recording angel, taking notes of all the deeds of humankind without distorting or omitting anything, could be called a 'pure' historian. All recorded history becomes fictional, just as all human fantasy involves some resemblance—however far-fetched—to real life. For the student of fiction, then, the way historical and imaginative materials are combined becomes crucial. This is because our understanding of fiction depends on our grasping the way in which any particular work is related to life.

Life itself is neither tragic nor comic, neither sentimental nor ironic. It is a sequence of sensations, actions, thoughts, and events that we try to tame with language. Every time we say a word about our existence, we are engaged in this taming process. The art of fiction is like a highly developed method of domestication, in which life is not merely brought under control but asked to perform tricks as well. The tricks, if well done, please us in a complicated way. In the first place, they please us because their order and intelligibility are a welcome relief from the confusions and pressures of daily life. In the second place, this artificial order may be mastered and used to help us make sense of our own experience. We recognize aspects of ourselves and our situations in the more ordered perspectives of fiction, and having read Flannery O'Connor or Alice Munro, we begin to recognize certain situations in our existence as having a family resemblance to situations these authors describe. At the same time, fiction presents us with ideal and debased extremes of existence—both possible and impossible—that are interesting in themselves and interestingly different from our own experience. In this way, literature offers us an 'escape' from life, but also provides us with new equipment for our inevitable return. It also offers us an 'imitation' of life that helps us to understand it, just as life helps us to understand fiction. Our experience of fiction, then, involves both pleasure and understanding. We may think of understanding either as a result of the pleasurable experience of fiction or as a necessary preliminary to that pleasure. But no matter how we view the complicated relationship between pleasure and understanding, we must recognize that the two are inseparable in the reading of fiction.

Understanding a work of fiction begins with recognizing what kind of fiction it is. Here, again, the notion of fiction as a spectrum may be useful: we can adjust to the special qualities of any given work more easily if we begin with a clear and flexible view of fictional possibilities. Any attempt to give *every* shade of fiction its own place would be cumbersome and misleading, but we can imagine the 'spectrum of fiction' as a rough scale, showing the primary possibilities located in relation to one another. Between the extremes of history and fantasy on such a scale we might locate two major points of reference: *realism* and *romance*. Realism and romance represent the two principal ways that fiction can be related to life.

Realism is a matter of perception. The realist presents impressions of the world of experience. A part of the vocabulary and other technical instruments the realist shares with social scientists—especially psychologists and sociologists. The realistic writer sets out to give the reader a sense of the way things are, but feels that a made-up structure of character and event can do better justice to the way things are than any attempt to copy real life directly. The realist's truth is a bit more general and typical than the reporter's 'fact'. It may also be more vivid and memorable.

Romance is a matter of vision. The writer of romance presents not so much impressions of the world as ideas about it. The ordinary world is seen at a greater distance, and its shape and colour are deliberately altered by the lenses and filters of philosophy and fantasy. In the world of romance, ideas are given freedom to play without being encumbered by data. Yet although 'what is' often gives way in romance to 'what ought to be' or 'what might be', *ought* and *might* always hint at what is by their distortion of it.

Realism and romance are not absolutely different: they have some qualities in common. Realism itself is more romantic than history or journalism. (It is not reality, after all, but real*ism*.) And romance is more realistic than fantasy. Many important works of fiction are rich and complicated blends of romance and realism. In fact, it is possible to say that the greatest works are those that successfully blend the realist's perception and the romance writer's vision, giving us fictional worlds remarkably close to our sense of the actual, but skilfully shaped to make us intensely aware of the meaningful potential of existence.

FICTIONAL MODES AND PATTERNS

The usefulness of the concept of a fictional spectrum depends on our ability to adapt it to different works of fiction. Before we can begin to do this, we need to add to our scale certain fictional modes and patterns.

The spectrum assumes that romance diverges from realism in one way only along the line that leads from history to fantasy. But we gain a fuller view of this divergence by recognizing that there are two different modes of what we have been calling romance. These two modes represent two obvious ways that reality can be distorted by fiction: it can be made to appear better or worse than we believe it to be. These distortions are ways of seeing certain aspects of reality more clearly at the expense of others. A fictional work that presents a world better than the real world is in the mode of romance; a work that presents a fictional world worse than the real world is in the mode of 'anti-romance', or satire. Because they represent certain potentialities that we recognize as present in our world, both views depend on our sense of the actual to achieve their effects.

The world of romance emphasizes beauty and order. The world of satire emphasizes ugliness and disorder. The ways in which individual characters relate to their distorted worlds constitute a crucial element of fiction, for these relations determine certain patterns, or master plots, that affect the shaping of the particular plot of every story. One of these master plots deals with the kind of character who begins out of harmony with his world and is gradually educated or initiated into a harmonious situation in it. This pattern may operate in either the ordered world of romance or the chaotic world of satire, but the same pattern will have quite a different effect on us when we observe it working out in such different situations. Education that adapts the inept or foolish character for a role in the orderly world presents a comic rise that we observe with approval and pleasure. An initiation into a world of ugliness and disorder amounts to corruption, an ironic rise to what Milton called a 'bad eminence', and we react with disapproval or even disgust.

Another master plot reverses this process of accommodation and presents us with a character who begins in harmony with his world but is ultimately rejected or destroyed by it. Our reaction again depends on our view of the world presented. The heroic figure who falls from a lofty position in the orderly world through some flaw in character is *tragic*. The lowly creature whose doom is the result of his unfortunate virtue or delicacy is *pathetic*. The latter's fall is, ironically, a kind of rise.

The *comic* rise and the *tragic* fall are straightforward, because the values of the orderly world represent human virtue raised to a heroic power. The *satiric* rise and *pathetic* fall are ironic because of the inverted values of the debased world. Satire and pathos debase the world in order to criticize it; tragedy and comedy elevate it to make it acceptable. The two romantic patterns promote resignation, the two satiric patterns opposition.

One other pair of fictional patterns may be added to the two already considered. When characters begin and end in a harmonious relation to their worlds, the fictional pattern is one not of change but of movement. These characters will have adventures or encounters, but they will not make any fundamental change in themselves or in their relation to the world around them. In this kind of story the hero will not be as important as the things he or she meets. In the romantic world the adventures of the (traditionally male) hero will take the form of a quest or voyage that ends with his triumphant return and/or his marriage to the heroine. This pattern moves us to admiration of the wonderful, offering us more an escape from the actual than a criticism of it. In the satiric world, the adventures of a born anti-hero or rogue will parody the quest pattern, typically reflecting the chaos of the debased world by becoming endless themselves. Stories of this kind are likely to end when the rogue heads for new territory or another tour of the familiar chaos. This picaresque pattern moves us to recognition and acceptance of the chaotic.

We have, then, distinguished three pairs of fictional patterns, or six kinds in all: the comic and the satiric rise; the tragic and the pathetic fall; the heroic (romantic) and the anti-heroic (picaresque) quest. But we have done this only with regard to the fantasy worlds of romance and satire. When these patterns are applied to a more realistic fictional world, the results become complicated: the neat, schematic distinctions fade; the various patterns combine and interact; and values themselves are called into question. Rise and fall, success and failure, all become problematic. This problematic quality is one of the great sources of interest in realistic fiction. Realism uses the familiar patterns of education, expulsion, and quest, but often in such a way as to call into question the great issues of whether the education is beneficial, the expulsion or death justified, the quest worthwhile. Our recognition of the traces of traditional patterns in realistic fiction is useful mainly in helping us to see what questions are being raised.

Viewed historically, realism developed later than romance and satire, and it is useful to see realistic fiction as combining elements of its predecessors in various ways. It would be a mistake, though, to think of realism as superseding the earlier forms just because it uses some of their elements in a new way. In fact, the rise of realism led to a kind of counterflow of realistic elements into the older forms of fiction, reinvigorating them with its problematical qualities. The reader of contemporary fiction in particular will require the flexibility of response that can be attained through careful attention to the workings of traditional patterns in modern fiction. But our ability to identify these patterns in any work of fiction will depend on our grasp of the specific elements of that work. We must be alert to the way that its plots, its characters, and its point of view adapt the traditional elements we have been considering.

Plot

Fiction is movement. A story is a story because it tells about a process of change: a character changes, or his or her situation changes, or our understanding of the character changes. These are the essential movements of fiction. Before we can begin to interpret what we are reading, we must be able to recognize these movements and follow them. The points below offer some advice about how to perceive and follow fictional plotting. Keep in mind that not all stories follow a linear chronology. For instance, a story could begin with a character speaking in the present and recounting an event through a series of flashbacks. Nevertheless, although the movement may appear to be disjointed, the story still traces a process of change.

1. *Look at beginnings and endings.* Movement in fiction is always movement *from* and *to.* A good grasp of a story's start and finish should give you a sense of its overall direction.

2. *Isolate the central characters.* The things that happen in fiction happen to somebody. A few major characters or even a single central character may be the real focus of our concern. Consider the situation of each of the central characters at the start and at the end of the story. The changes the characters have undergone will give a good indication of what the story is about.

3. *Note the stages in all important changes.* If a character has moved from one situation to another, or from one state of mind to another, the steps leading to the completed change should be illuminating. By examining each step in the process, the reader can get to the 'hows' and 'whys' of the change.

4. *Note the things working against the movement of the story.* The interest generated in a story is often the product of two forces: the things that work to move a story toward its end, and those that work against that movement, delaying its completion. If the main characters in a story are advancing towards a particular destination, for

example, consider what things delay the journey. When we see the obstacles clearly, we gain a better sense of the direction of the plot itself.

5. *In a long story or novel, consider the various lines of action.* A complex fiction is likely to involve a number of actions, each with its own central character or characters. The actions may not interact, and the central character in one line of action may be insignificant in another. But by isolating the various lines of action, we should gain a better sense of those things that connect them. Often these connections will lead us to related themes that cast light on the meaning of the fiction as a whole.

6. *Take note of characters or events that seem to make no contribution to plot or movement.* This advice is a way of moving from the story's plot to its meaning. Elements that are not important in the plot often have a special thematic importance.

Some of the strategies suggested here can be applied either during or following a first reading. It is worth remembering that a good story may be experienced pleasurably many times, and that a second or third reading will often be more satisfying in every respect than the first.

Character

No character in a book is a real person. Characters in fiction are *like* real people, but they are also unlike them. In realistic fiction, which includes most novels and short stories, writers emphasize the lifelikeness of their characters. They do this by surrounding these characters with details drawn from contemporary life, and by trying to restrict the events of their narrative to things likely to happen in ordinary life. As a result, writers of realistic fiction have to abandon certain kinds of plots that are too fanciful for characters supposed to typify ordinary life. In this way, they try to draw the reader away from an interest in the movement of fiction and toward an interest in character for its own sake.

Realistic writers draw on psychology and sociology to offer instruction in human nature. The motivation of characters, the workings of conscience and consciousness, are the focal point of most novels and short stories. The best example of this is writing based on a stream-of-consciousness narrative, through which fiction writers offer us a version of mental process at the level where impressions of things seen and heard converge with confused thoughts and longings arising from the subconscious mind. In reading this kind of fiction we must check the validity of its characterization against our own sense of the way people behave. The best realists always offer us a shock of recognition through which we share their perception of human behaviour.

It may be useful to think of character as a function of two impulses: the impulse to individualize and the impulse to typify. Great and memorable characters are the result of a powerful combination of these two impulses. We remember the special, individualizing quirks—habitual patterns of speech, action, or appearance—and we remember the way the character represents something larger than herself. These individualizing touches are part of the storyteller's art. They amuse us or engage our sympathy for the character. The typifying touches are part of a story's meaning. In realistic fiction a character is likely to be representative of a social class, a race, a profession. Or the character may be a recognizable psychological type, who can be analyzed in terms of a particular complex or syndrome. The character may even be a mixture of social and psychological qualities. In allegorical fiction the characters are more likely to represent philosophical positions. In a story of adventure we will encounter types belonging to the traditional pattern of romantic quest: hero, heroine, villain, monster.

The important thing for a reader to remember about characterization is that there are many varieties—and many combinations of the varieties. An adventure story may have an important realistic or allegorical dimension that can be observed in its characterizations. Characters in realistic novels may also be meaningful as illustrations of philosophical ideas or attitudes. As readers, we must be alert and ready to respond to different kinds of characterization on their own terms. A story by James Joyce and a story by Rohinton Mistry are not likely to yield equally to the same kind of reading. It is the reader's business to adapt to whatever fictional world is being entered; it is the writer's business to make the reader's business worthwhile.

Themes

More often than not, when we discuss a story after reading it, we talk about its meaning. In the classroom, 'What are the themes of this work?' is a favourite question. This interpretive aspect of literary analysis is the most difficult, because in order to attempt it we must look carefully not only at the work but also away from the work to the world of ideas and experiences. Discovering themes in a story involves making connections between the work and the world outside it. These connections *are* the meaning. The great problem for the reader, then, surrounds the validity of the thematic elements he or she discovers. *Are these ideas really there?* we want to know. Are they being 'read out' of the story or 'read into' it? Is any given set of connections between story and world necessarily implied by the story itself? Or are they arbitrarily imposed by an over-zealous reader?

A story is always particular, always an instance. How do we properly move from any given instance to a general notion? When, for example, is it legitimate to conclude from the presence of a husband and wife in a story that the story is 'about' marriage— that it makes a statement or raises a question about this aspect of human relations? It is impossible to provide a single method that will always work, but there are certain procedures that will frequently prove helpful.

If we isolate everything that is not just narration, description, or dialogue, some clues are likely to appear. The title of a work is a good example. Sometimes it will point our thinking about the work in a particular direction, or else it may emphasize the importance of a particular element in the work. Like the title, passages in the writing that are themselves commentary or interpretation are of particular importance for thematic discussion. Often interpretive passages will not be presented directly by omniscient and objective narrators with all their authority behind them. They may be spoken instead by a narrator who is also a participant in the action described, and who is therefore not objective, or they may be presented by another character in speech reported by the narrator. In this case, we must assess the reliability of the character before we decide to accept the character's interpretation as valid. Sometimes the narrator herself will be characterized to the extent that we must question her reliability. In similar ways narration and description may also be coloured by thematic materials. The author may present a character or a scene in a manner that leads us to think about the materials presented in a particular way. A character called 'Dean Drone' is introduced to us with a name that carries some not too subtle advice about how we are to understand the presentation.

In less obvious cases, where the author refrains from direct commentary, we must look for subtler clues. Patterns of repetition, ironic juxtaposition, the tone of the narration—devices such as these must lead us to the connections between the particular world of the book and the generalized world of ideas. And the more delicate and subtle the story is, the more delicate our interpretation must be. Thus, taking care that our interpretation is rooted in the work itself is only one aspect of the problem.

The other aspect involves the outside knowledge that the reader brings to the work. If the story is realistic, it will be understood best by those readers whose experience has equipped them with information about the aspect of reality the story points to. This does not mean that one must be the transplanted son of a Cape Breton fisherman to understand Alistair MacLeod's 'The Boat'. But interpreting the story depends on the reader's having some understanding of family ties and cultural displacement and some sense of the way nature can act destructively upon individuals or even whole groups of human beings.

Often a realistic story may point to an aspect of life we have encountered but never understood, and the fiction may help us clarify and organize that experience. D.H. Lawrence's 'The Rocking-Horse Winner' can teach us something about personal relations, but Lawrence requires us to bring some experience of family life to that story, for without that it must remain meaningless for the reader. Fantasy and adventure are the principal ingredients of children's literature, since children lack the experience that would make realism meaningful to them and the learning required to interpret complex allegorical fiction.

Often allegorical fiction takes the form of fantasy or adventure, so that it can be read by the child on one level and by the adult on another. 'The Rocking-Horse Winner' is an exciting story about a boy with a kind of magical power, but it is also a criticism of an excessively materialistic society. Modern allegories of this kind are called 'fabulation', and they trace their roots to the simple fable and the homely parable. Modern fabulation may contain many realistic details, but in such modern fables as Nathaniel Hawthorne's 'My Kinsman, Major Molineux' or John Cheever's 'The Swimmer' there is at least one break with what we recognize as normal or probable; there is some moving away from realism for the sake of ideas that may ordinarily be concealed by the surface of reality. Modern fables try to unsettle, to disturb patterns of thought and action that have become so habitual they conceal important dimensions of existence. In studying such tales we must ask what ideas are being called into question. Often the best way to do this is to locate the most fabulous elements in each work and ask why the author chose to break with ordinary probabilities or possibilities where they occur. With this question in mind, it should be possible to examine the way any given feature of a fable relates to the larger concerns of the whole story.

Fiction generates its meanings in innumerable ways, but always in terms of some movement from the particular characters and events of the story to general ideas or human situations suggested by them. Readers come to an understanding of a fictional work by sifting their store of general notions drawn from experience or systematic thought to find those appropriate to the particular materials of the story, then applying these general notions to the story in order to test their relevance. In this way, readers look for the ways the story refines, qualifies, questions, or reinforces those notions. This process—performed not a single time but in rapid oscillation into the work and back out—should leave readers with an understanding of the story and with an enriched store of general notions they have been led to develop in order to understand. In addition to acquiring new notions, readers may have refined their attitudes toward their old notions and toward experience itself. Fiction is justified not as a means of conveying ideas but as a means of generating attitudes toward ideas. The meaning of fiction must finally be seen in terms of emotions directed toward impressions of experience or toward ideas about life.

Point of View: Perspective and Language

Point of view is a technical term for the way a story is told. A stage play normally has no particular point of view: no one stands between the audience and the action. But if we *read* a play, the stage directions—the words of someone who is not a character—offer a special point of view. Similarly, a story told entirely through dialogue would be without a point of view, but as soon as a descriptive phrase is added—such as 'he said *cruelly*' or 'she *complained bitterly*'—we as readers begin to have access to a special viewpoint. A voice outside the action is shaping our attitude toward the events being presented. In our experience of fiction, the attitude we develop toward the events, and our understanding of those events, will usually be controlled by the author through his or her technical management of point of view.

The concept of fictional viewpoint can be conveniently divided into two related parts: one dealing with the storyteller in any given fiction, the other dealing with language. Obviously the two are not really separate. Certain kinds of narration require certain kinds of language—the narrator of Thomas King's 'Borders', for instance, must talk like an Aboriginal Canadian—but we may consider them apart for analytical purposes.

The nature of the storyteller is far from a simple matter. We need to consider such things as the extent to which the storyteller is presenting a character whose personality affects our understanding of the storyteller's statements, and the extent to which the storyteller's view of events is limited in time and space or in the storyteller's ability to see into the minds of various characters. The reader's problem comes down to knowing how to take the things presented. This means paying special attention to any limitations in the narrator's viewpoint. If the viewpoint in the story is 'partial'—if it is either incomplete or biased—the reader must be ready to compensate in appropriate ways.

The language of narration presents a similar problem for the reader—that is, a problem of adjustment and compensation. Of all the dimensions of language that can be considered, two are especially important for the reader of fiction. Both may be seen as ways in which wit—or artistic intelligence—operates through language. One has to do with *tone*, or the way unstated attitudes are conveyed through language. The other has to do with *metaphor*, or the way language can convey the richest and most delicate kinds of understanding by bringing together different images and ideas. Consider first this short passage from 'The Marine Excursion of the Knights of Pythias', from Stephen Leacock's *Sunshine Sketches of a Little Town*:

> Dr Gallagher, who knew Canadian history, said to Dean Drone that it was strange to think that Champlain had landed there with his French explorers three hundred years ago; and Dean Drone, who didn't know Canadian history, said it was stranger still to think that the hand of the Almighty had piled up the hills and rocks long before that; and Dr Gallagher said it was wonderful how the French had found their way through such a pathless wilderness; and Dean Drone said that it was wonderful also to think that the Almighty had placed even the smallest shrub in its appointed place. Dr Gallagher said it filled him with admiration. Dean Drone said it filled him with awe. Dr Gallagher said he'd been full of it ever since he was a boy and Dean Drone said so had he.

The tone of this passage is clearly sarcastic. The paragraph asks us to be critical of the two characters, but it does not do so directly. It uses the indirection of verbal irony, in which the real meaning is different from the apparent sense of the words. The last sentence might be read aloud with a particular emphasis on the phrase 'full of it', accompanied by a knowing smirk. How do we know this? How do we supply the appropriate tone of voice for words that we see on the page but do not hear pronounced? We pay attention to the clues given. Dean Drone and Dr Gallagher appear in a similar light several times in this story. For example, when confronted with a report that the *Mariposa Belle* is sinking, Dr Gallagher 'said no, that he had thought so earlier in the day but that he didn't now think that she was.' To the same fact, 'Dean Drone, of course, and some others were quieter about it, and said that one must make allowances and that naturally there were two sides to everything.' Both men are befuddled, clearly out of touch with reality. Their responses to the sinking parallel their responses in their conversation: they speak at cross-purposes to each other, each trying to show off knowledge and expertise with inaccurate information that is meaningless to the other. The 'He said . . . He said . . .' sentence pattern of the first passage shows that neither is interested in what the other has to say. The final statement, if read literally, conflicts both with the actions narrated and with the tone of the narration. It is difficult to believe that Dean Drone's or Dr Gallagher's comments have anything to do with awe or admiration. On the contrary, the two characters seem motivated by one-upmanship. We resolve the conflict by reading the sentence as *ironic*, meaning something other than what it seems to say, and acquiring thereby a sarcastic tone. The additional connotations of the phrase 'full of it' show that Dean Drone and Dr Gallagher are equally objects of the author's sympathetic but nonetheless real irony.

Catching the tone of this passage is a matter of paying attention to clues in sentence pattern and choice of words, and also of keeping in mind the whole context of the story we are reading. The more we read a particular author, the better we become at catching his tone—at perceiving the emotional shades that colour the sense of his words. In *Sunshine Sketches of a Little Town*, Dean Drone and Dr Gallagher are presented in a similar way often enough that by this appearance, we have been prepared to regard them unsympathetically. But on the strength of these sentences we should be able to catch the tone.

The second key dimension of the language of narration, *metaphor*, is illustrated well in Sinclair Ross's 'The Painted Door'. In the following passage, Ann watches her husband set off to visit his father on a prairie winter morning:

> From the bedroom window she watched him nearly a mile along the road. The fire had gone down when at last she turned away, and already through the house there was an encroaching chill. A blaze sprang up again when the drafts were opened, but as she went on clearing the table her movements were furtive and constrained. It was the silence weighing upon her—the frozen silence of the bitter fields and sun-chilled sky—lurking outside as if alive, relentlessly in wait, mile-deep between her now and John. She listened to it, suddenly tense, motionless. The fire crackled and the clock ticked. Always it was there. 'I'm a fool,' she whispered hoarsely, rattling the dishes in defiance, going back to the stove to put in another fire. 'Warm and safe—I'm a fool. It's a good chance when he's away to paint. The day will go quickly. I won't have time to brood.'
>
> Since November now the paint had been waiting warmer weather. The frost in the walls on a day like this would crack and peel it as it dried, but she needed something to keep her hands occupied, something to stave off the gathering cold and loneliness. 'First of all,' she said aloud, opening the paint and mixing it with a little turpentine, 'I must get the house warmer. Fill up the stove and open the oven door so that all the heat comes out. Wad something along the window sills to keep out the drafts. Then I'll feel brighter. It's the cold that depresses.'

The word 'depress' has been used so often to mean 'dispirit' or 'sadden' that it is possible to use it without any sense that it is metaphorical. But the notion of pressing or pushing down is present in the expression. A writer who, like Ross, is sensitive to metaphor can pick up the implications of such an expression and use them to strengthen his meaning. The somewhat uncharacteristic syntax of the final line—it would be more common to say 'It's the cold that depresses people' or 'It's the cold people find depressing'—draws our attention to this word and lets us know that the author wants us to notice it. Throughout the passage, the cold outside is associated with the quiet of the small house. The 'frozen silence', which represents Ann's fear and loneliness, is characterized as 'encroaching', 'gathering', 'lurking'. In the line, 'It was the silence weighing upon her', the author uses another metaphor for depression—'weighing upon'—that, like 'depresses', has as its literal meaning the idea of pressing or forcing down. In a paragraph that comes shortly after this passage, we read the following:

Suddenly her movements became precise, deliberate, her posture self-conscious, as if someone had entered the room and were watching her. It was the silence again, aggressive, hovering.

Here the 'frozen silence' of the earlier line returns as something 'hovering' over Ann, reinforcing the idea that fear and loneliness are depressing or 'weighing upon her'.

The combined effect of these lines is a powerful metaphor that presents intangible ideas—loneliness and fear—as something physical, a sort of malevolent being waiting to pounce. The image, however, takes on added significance, by way of contrast, later in the same story. The following passage recounts Ann's reaction to the arrival of a family friend, Steven:

. . . suddenly at the assurance of his touch and voice the fear that had been gripping her gave way to an hysteria of relief. Scarcely aware of herself she seized his arm and sobbed against it. He remained still a moment, unyielding, then slipped his other arm around her shoulder. It was comforting and she relaxed against it, hushed by a sudden sense of lull and safety. Her shoulders trembled with the easing of the strain, then fell limp and still. 'You're shivering,'—he drew her gently towards the stove. 'There's nothing to be afraid of now, though. . . .'

Note the contrasts between this passage and the one cited previously. No longer is Ann's 'posture self-conscious': now she is 'scarcely aware of herself', and her shoulders are now 'limp'. Her fear, once again described metaphorically as 'gripping', gives way to relief, and the last line, in which Steven addresses Ann's cold and fear, confirms that his arrival represents a brief end to the 'frozen silence' that has been 'weighing upon her'.

Design: Juxtaposition and Repetition in the Structure of Fiction

When we look at a painting up close, we can see clearly its details and the texture of its brush strokes, but we cannot see it as a whole. When we back away, we lose our perception of these minute qualities but gain, with this new perspective, a sense of its design. Similarly, as we read a story, we are involved in its details. And in a story we are involved especially because we experience it as a flow of words in time, bringing us impressions and ideas, moving us emotionally and stirring us intellectually. It is natural to back away from a painting and see it as a whole. But it is less natural and more difficult to gain a similar perspective on a book. We can never 'see' it all at once. Yet design is an important part of the writer's art, and a sense of design is essential to a thorough assessment of the text.

Design in fiction takes many forms, but these may be seen as mainly of two kinds. One has to do with *juxtaposition*, with what is put next to what in the arrangement of the story. The other has to do with *repetition*, with images, ideas, or situations that are repeated—often with interesting variations—in the course of the narrative. Juxtaposition is more important in some kinds of fiction than it is in others. If a single action is presented in a simple, chronological arrangement, the order of events is not likely to assume any special significance. But if the action is rearranged in time so that we encounter events out of their chronological sequence—through flashbacks, for example—the order should be given some attention. We must look for reasons behind the author's manipulation of chronology. Why has the author chosen to place this particular scene from the narrative past next to this particular scene in the narrative present? Similarly, if we are following two actions in one story, we should look for reasons why an incident from one plot line has been placed next to a particular incident in the other.

This method of examination often uncovers interesting parallels: similar situations that amount to a kind of repetition with variation. If character A gets into a situation and takes one kind of action, while character B, in a similar situation, takes a different action, we should compare the two and contrast their distinctive behaviour, which will help us learn more about both. This kind of comparison can also lead us to generalizations about the meaning of a work as a whole.

Significant kinds of repetition occur also in sections of a story that are not placed next to one another. This kind of repetition, an important element of design, serves to tie separate parts of a story together, enriching and strengthening the whole structure. Structure in fiction is a complicated notion because it involves so many factors. We can think of structure in one sense as the elements that shape our experience as we move through the story; in this sense structure is close to plot. We can also think of structure as the elements that enable us to see a meaningful pattern in the whole work; in this sense structure is close to design. If plot has to do with the *dynamics*, or movement, of fiction, design has to do with the *statics* of fiction—the way we see a whole story after we have stopped moving through it. When we become aware of design in reading, so that one part of a story reminds us of parts we have read earlier, we are involved in a movement counter to our progress from beginning to end. Plot wants to move us along; design wants to delay our movement, to make us pause and 'see'. The opposition of these two forces is one of the things that enrich our experience of fiction.

Design is often a matter of repeating images or metaphors. In considering the metaphors in 'The Painted Door', we have already begun an examination of the way metaphoric design can tie together different characters and situations. The following example is a striking illustration of a rather different use of repetition in the design of a story. This is a case in which two episodes in the life of the same character—separated both by pages of our reading and by weeks in the life of the character—are brought together into powerful contrasts by means of repetition with variation.

At the end of the second chapter of James Joyce's first published novel, *A Portrait of the Artist as a Young Man*, the young man of the title, Stephen Dedalus, has been led by the urgings of physical desire into the arms of a prostitute. This is the last paragraph of that chapter:

> With a sudden movement she bowed his head and joined her lips to his and he read the meaning of her movements in her frank uplifted eyes. It was too much for him. He closed his eyes, surrendering himself to her, body and mind, conscious of nothing in the world but the dark pressure of her softly parting lips. They pressed upon his brain as upon his lips as though they were the

vehicle of vague speech; and between them he felt an unknown and timid pressure, darker than the swoon of sin, softer than sound or odour.

By the end of the third chapter, Joyce has taken Stephen Dedalus through a period of disgust, remorse, and repentance. In the last paragraphs of the chapter we find Stephen receiving Holy Communion:

He knelt before the altar with his classmates, holding the altar cloth with them over a living rail of hands. His hands were trembling, and his soul trembled as he heard the priest pass with the ciborium from communicant to communicant.

—*Corpus Domini nostri.*

Could it be? He knelt there sinless and timid: and he would hold upon his tongue the host and God would enter his purified body.

—*In vitam eternam. Amen.*

Another life! A life of grace and virtue and happiness! It was true.

—*Corpus Domini nostri.*

The ciborium had come to him.

In the last sentence of the second chapter, Stephen felt the woman's tongue, pressing through her kiss—'an unknown and timid pressure'. In the last lines of the third chapter, his tongue receives the body of Christ, making a contrast that is striking and rich in emotional and intellectual implications. Design here is carrying out Joyce's intention, which is to make us see Stephen poised between the extremes of sin and redemption, both of which attract him powerfully but neither of which can hold him finally—as the later chapters demonstrate. The focus on tongues in these two episodes is the crucial repeated element that makes the contrast Joyce wishes. And in the context of the whole story, it reminds us that tongues are not only for kissing or receiving the sacrament. They are also instruments of expression. Stephen ultimately must strive to express himself as an artist of languages, using his gift of tongues. In these two episodes, Stephen has been passive, the receiver. Later he will learn to speak out.

What we have been considering is the way that an object—in this case the tongue—can by its use in a fictional design acquire a metaphorical value that points in the direction of meaning. When this happens, the object becomes a symbol.

A fiction, we noted at the beginning, is a made-up story, and this anthology reveals a myriad of fascinating stories that will challenge you, disturb you, and entertain you. All fiction invites and demands your complete involvement in the story, and what you must bring to your careful reading is a flexibility of response. As you examine the designs of the individual stories, you are entering the worlds of contemporary fiction.

A GUIDE TO OUR SELECTIONS

So when I write a story I want to make a certain kind of structure, and I know the feeling I want to get from being inside that structure. This is the hard part of the explanation, where I have to use a word like 'feeling', which is not very precise, because if I attempt to be more intellectually respectable I will have to be dishonest. 'Feeling' will have to do.

So states Alice Munro, one of the preeminent writers of short fiction in the English-speaking world. To write a short story is to create a structure for this 'feeling'. But as Munro goes on to say, there is no blueprint, no plan, for the structure of a story.

> It's not a question of, 'I'll make this kind of house because if I do it right it will have this effect.' I've got to make, I've got to build up, a house, a story, to fit around the indescribable 'feeling' that is like the soul of a story, and which I must insist upon in a dogged, embarrassed way, as being no more definable than that. And I don't know where it comes from. It seems to be already there, and some unlikely clue, such as a shop window or a bit of conversation, makes me aware of it. Then I start accumulating the material and putting it together. Some of the material I may have lying around already, in memories and obser-vations, and some I invent, and some I have to go diligently looking for (factual details), while some is dumped in my lap (anecdotes, bits of speech). I see how this material might go together to make the shape I need, and I try it. I keep trying and seeing where I went wrong and trying again.[1]

For a writer to talk about the structure of the writing, there are many handicaps. A writer can talk about the craft of writing, yet no sense emerges of just what the writer is doing, apart from piecing together the fragments that ultimately become the completed story.

The word *novel* comes from a word meaning 'new', a word that, in the plural, is used to mean 'news', news of the day or news of the period. The English novel begins with the august figure of Daniel Defoe, the author of such books as *Robinson Crusoe* (1719), a work of fiction based on 'a real life story' of a round-the-world voyage described to him by the returned traveller. Defoe stitched this together with material he had gathered from another written account. All of Defoe's novels pretend to be factual accounts or factual documents, and so the English novel, by his hand, came into being as a long prose account of true happenings. It is then not surprising that many novel-ists were first of all journalists, newspaper people who specialized in reporting. Defoe was a journalist, and so were other celebrated novelists, people like Charles Dickens, William Faulkner, Ernest Hemingway, and Morley Callaghan. For this reason, the novel has its roots in a love of fact, and we speak of the novel's penchant for realism, its commitment to mirroring its society and the realities of its time.

The short story begins with Edgar Allan Poe, who never wrote a novel but wrote many stories where brevity and a sense of mystery are the dominant features of his style. He conceived of the mystery story as his own creation, and he became a sem-inal influence on the writing of detective fiction.

For Herman Melville, fiction was a true story, rooted closely in the world it was meant to depict. His classic novel *Moby-Dick*, the gruesome tale of Captain Ahab and his maniacal pursuit of the great white whale, includes a compendium on whaling, com-plete with many chapters that contain truths 'stranger than fiction'. These chapters of verifiable fact are a bridge to the credibility of the pursuit. In Melville's short story 'Bartleby the Scrivener: A Story of Wall Street', we encounter in a downtown New York office 'a rather elderly man', who tells us the story of Bartleby. We believe what we read because the narrator describes what he has seen and heard. At the same time, Nathaniel Hawthorne, also rooting his stories in a fixed time and place, strove to create what he called 'tales', stories that move well beyond the surface reality to explore the hidden inner life of his characters.

In Canada the short story first emerged in the animal stories of Charles G.D. Roberts and Ernest Thompson Seton. This was the medium in which these writers, for the first time, described their world in fictional form, and in their hands it differed markedly from the animal story of contemporary American and British writers. American animal stories are confrontations between human beings and animals, where the latter symbolize nature's hostility. British animal stories are thinly disguised fables, acted out by animals to illuminate human problems. Canadian animal stories, on the other hand, focus on animals, and we are often invited to sympathize with their plight.

In the writings of Kate Chopin and Charlotte Perkins Gilman, the female voice produces stories that are deliberately strong and pointed, in Chopin through a third-person narrator, in Gilman through a first-person narrator who introduces an autobiographical dimension to the fiction. Their contemporary, Stephen Crane, made the American southwest the background for his depiction of the people dwelling on American's newest frontier. Together, the stories of three writers represent the fiction of the 1890s.

Stephen Leacock ushers in the new century with his classic comic story 'The Marine Excursion of the Knights of Pythias'. It is perhaps the finest illustration of his talent as a humorist. Leacock wrote almost a volume of comic stories and sketches every year from 1910 until his death in 1944; he never wrote a novel.

James Joyce introduced the concept of the 'epiphany', or 'moment of illumination', in his fiction. A moment like the appearance of Mangan's sister to the thirteen-year-old narrator in 'Araby' is a revelatory incident that suggests the nature of their encounter and its aftermath. Joyce's contemporary, D.H. Lawrence, portrays his young protagonist through an omniscient, third-person narrator, who describes a struggling family and the young boy who goes to his death fixated on his shining, modern rocking-horse. So, too, does Katherine Mansfield employ an objective narrator, though hers indulges in terse irony as she dissects the relationships of her main characters.

For the American writers, F. Scott Fitzgerald and Ernest Hemingway, the short story was a vehicle for conveying much of the tension and the regret that are also present in their novels. In their selections here, Fitzgerald paints the dreary world of an exile during the Depression, while Hemingway casts his eye on the equally dreary world of cafés and bodegas. Both writers use the omniscient third-person narrator to illuminate their depictions of their individualistic worlds.

The Irish writer Elizabeth Bowen harkens back to Poe and Hawthorne in her attempt to find the supernatural in the relative calm of the everyday. In 'The Demon Lover', the third-person narrator manages to capture the horror of the unexpected and the consequent jeopardy into which Mrs Drover's life is placed.

The literature of the American South comes to especial prominence in the short stories and novels of William Faulkner. A chronicler of his imaginary Yoknapatawpha

County in his native Mississippi, he reveals the glories and the prejudices that undermine the surface reality of the South. Another Mississippian, Eudora Welty, takes a more humorous view of her fellow Southerners. And Flannery O'Connor, from Georgia, looks with her concentrated and Catholic vision on the prejudices of the people around her.

Canadian writer Morley Callaghan fashioned short stories out of his highly objective style. In his autobiographical *That Summer in Paris*, he states his own artistic purpose: 'Strip the language, and make the style, the method, all the psychological ramifications, the ambience of the relationships, all the one thing, so the reader couldn't make separations. Cézanne's apples. The appleness of apples. Yet just apples.' He sent a short story to *The New Yorker*, and it became the first piece of fiction the magazine printed. At the same time, Sinclair Ross was writing, as he does in 'The Painted Door', about the windswept plains, the drought of the Depression, and the lives of people caught in this immensely forbidding landscape of the Prairies.

Sheila Watson's 'Antigone' marks a dramatic change from the short story worlds of, for example, Fitzgerald, Bowen, and Callaghan. Her novel *The Double Hook* marks the beginning of modern Canadian fiction, and her short story here is mythic in its structure, employing classical mythology—the story of Antigone and her sister Ismene—to organize contemporary reality and to endow seemingly homely actions with the significance usually associated with myth. So, too, does John Cheever's 'The Swimmer' turn the story of one man's homeward journey into a mythic return through the grass-lined suburbs of New York City. And John Barth's 'Lost in the Funhouse' mixes realism and surrealism to look back on his academic exercises as a writing student.

More recent writers have continued to fashion their stories to reflect their own real or imagined worlds. Doris Lessing paints an astonishing sunrise on her African landscape, and Mavis Gallant, like Fitzgerald and Hemingway earlier in the century, records with penetrating insight the pathetic lives of exiled North Americans in Europe.

Margaret Laurence paints the threatening world of Manawaka, Manitoba for the young Vanessa MacLeod, the narrator of 'A Bird in the House'; Alice Munro depicts, in a more complex way, the many views of Alfrida that confront her first-person narrator; and Alistair MacLeod looks back, again through a first-person narrator, on the summer long ago when he was only fifteen. These three Canadian authors write of distant incidents through the prism of their carefully delineated narrators.

In the contemporary world, we meet many writers from many worlds who bring their ethnic roots to bear on their fiction. Bernard Malamud brings Jewish characters into the mainstream of American fiction, Bharati Mukherjee and Rohinton Mistry bring their Indian backgrounds to their stories of an interracial affair and a young boy's seeming obsession with stamp collecting, and Aboriginal authors Thomas King and Louise Erdrich bring their roots to the surface of their writings.

The stories presented in this anthology run the gamut from the comic to the tragic. All of them reflect the time, locations, and cultural backgrounds of their authors, and in doing so they also represent the variegated short story itself, taking on many forms all under the single term of 'the short story'.

Just as we began this brief tour through the stories with Alice Munro, we will close with the words of the same writer. Reflecting on her purpose in writing, she concludes:

It seems to me this is what writing is, when it's real—a straining of something immense and varied, a whole dense vision of the world, into whatever confines the writer has learned to make for it, and this process, unless you are Shakespeare or Tolstoy, must be accompanied by regret; fortunately it is often accompanied by gleeful satisfactions as well.[2]

Notes

1. 'What Is Real?' in *Making it New: Contemporary Canadian Stories*, edited by John Metcalf (Toronto: Methuen, 1982), p. 224.

2. 'Author's Commentary', in *Sixteen by Twelve: Short Stories by Canadian Writers*, edited by John Metcalf (Toronto: The Ryerson Press, 1970), p. 126.

Nathaniel Hawthorne
1804–1864

Born in Salem, Massachusetts, at a time when the American Revolution was still living history and the Puritan heritage of Salem was very much alive, Nathaniel Hawthorne absorbed its preoccupation with sin and its remembrance of witch hunts. Four years at Bowdoin College in Maine, a job at the Boston Custom House, and a short stay at Brook Farm—an idealistic commune that ran into practical problems—broadened his horizons, but his best work came from brooding over the past more than from observation of his own time. He called his short fiction 'tales' and his longer works 'romances', insisting that his imagination have a certain latitude in which to work. *The Scarlet Letter* (1850) has become a classic of world literature, and many of his shorter tales, such as the one reprinted here, have proven equally durable.

'My Kinsman, Major Molineux', which was first published in 1832 but not collected until *The Snow-Image, and Other Tales* (1851), pushes beyond surface reality to focus intently on the complex inner life of the individual. The story probes this inner life and becomes a warning against simplistic moral judgments.

My Kinsman, Major Molineux

After the kings of Great Britain had assumed the right of appointing the colonial governors, the measures of the latter seldom met with the ready and generous approbation which had been paid to those of their predecessors, under the original charters. The people looked with most jealous scrutiny to the exercise of power which did not emanate from themselves, and they usually rewarded their rulers with slender gratitude for the compliances by which, in softening their instructions from beyond the sea, they had incurred the reprehension of those who gave them. The annals of Massachusetts Bay will inform us, that of six governors in the space of about forty years from the surrender of the old charter, under James II, two were imprisoned by a popular insurrection; a third, as Hutchinson inclines to believe, was driven from the province by the whizzing of a musket-ball; a fourth, in the opinion of the same historian, was hastened to his grave by continual bickerings with the House of Representatives; and the remaining two, as well as their successors, till the Revolution, were favoured with few and brief intervals of peaceful sway. The inferior members of the court party, in times of high political excitement, led scarcely a more desirable life. These remarks may serve as a preface to the following adventures, which chanced upon a summer night, not far from a hundred years ago.[1] The reader, in order to avoid a long and dry detail of colonial affairs, is requested to dispense with an account of the train of circumstances that had caused much temporary inflammation of the popular mind.

1 The time of this tale is the eve of the American Revolution. The place is Boston.

It was near nine o'clock of a moonlight evening, when a boat crossed the ferry with a single passenger, who had obtained his conveyance at that unusual hour by the promise of an extra fare. While he stood on the landing-place, searching in either pocket for the means of fulfilling his agreement, the ferryman lifted a lantern, by the aid of which, and the newly risen moon, he took a very accurate survey of the stranger's figure. He was a youth of barely eighteen years, evidently country-bred, and now, as it should seem, upon his first visit to town. He was clad in a coarse grey coat, well worn, but in excellent repair; his under garments were durably constructed of leather, and fitted tight to a pair of serviceable and well-shaped limbs; his stockings of blue yarn were the incontrovertible work of a mother or a sister; and on his head was a three-cornered hat, which in its better days had perhaps sheltered the graver brow of the lad's father. Under his left arm was a heavy cudgel formed of an oak sapling, and retaining a part of the hardened root; and his equipment was completed by a wallet, not so abundantly stocked as to incommode the vigorous shoulders on which it hung. Brown, curly hair, well-shaped features, and bright, cheerful eyes were nature's gifts, and worth all that art could have done for his adornment.

The youth, one of whose names was Robin, finally drew from his pocket the half of a little province bill of five shillings, which, in the depreciation in that sort of currency, did but satisfy the ferryman's demand, with the surplus of a sexangular piece of parchment, valued at three pence. He then walked forward into town, with as light a step as if his day's journey had not already exceeded thirty miles, and with as eager an eye as if he were entering London city, instead of the little metropolis of a New England colony. Before Robin had proceeded far, however, it occurred to him that he knew not whither to direct his steps; so he paused, and looked up and down the narrow street, scrutinizing the small and mean wooden buildings that were scattered on either side.

'This low hovel cannot be my kinsman's dwelling,' thought he, 'nor yonder old house, where the moonlight enters at the broken casement; and truly I see none hereabouts that might be worthy of him. It would have been wise to inquire my way of the ferryman, and doubtless he would have gone with me, and earned a shilling from the Major for his pains. But the next man I meet will do as well.'

He resumed his walk, and was glad to perceive that the street now became wider, and the houses more respectable in their appearance. He soon discerned a figure moving on moderately in advance, and hastened his steps to overtake it. As Robin drew nigh, he saw that the passenger was a man in years, with a full periwig of grey hair, a wide-skirted coat of dark cloth, and silk stockings rolled above his knees. He carried a long and polished cane, which he struck down perpendicularly before him at every step; and at regular intervals he uttered two successive hems, of a peculiarly solemn and sepulchral intonation. Having made these observations, Robin laid hold of the skirt of the old man's coat, just when the light from the open door and windows of a barber's shop fell upon both their figures.

'Good evening to you, honoured sir,' said he, making a low bow, and still retaining his hold of the skirt. 'I pray you tell me whereabouts is the dwelling of my kinsman, Major Molineux.'

The youth's question was uttered very loudly; and one of the barbers, whose razor was descending on a well-soaped chin, and another who was dressing a Ramillies wig, left their occupations, and came to the door. The citizen, in the mean time, turned a long-favoured countenance upon Robin, and answered him in a tone of excessive anger and annoyance. His two sepulchral hems, however, broke into the very centre of his rebuke, with most singular effect, like a thought of the cold grave obtruding among wrathful passions.

'Let go my garment, fellow! I tell you, I know not the man you speak of. What! I have authority, I have—hem, hem—authority; and if this be the respect you show for your betters, your feet shall be brought acquainted with the stocks[2] by daylight, tomorrow morning!'

Robin released the old man's skirt, and hastened away, pursued by an ill-mannered roar of laughter from the barber shop. He was at first considerably surprised by the result of his question, but, being a shrewd youth, soon thought himself able to account for the mystery.

'This is some country representative', was his conclusion, 'who has never seen the inside of my kinsman's door, and lacks the breeding to answer a stranger civilly. The man is old, or verily—I might be tempted to turn back and smite him on the nose. Ah, Robin, Robin! even the barber's boys laugh at you for choosing such a guide! You will be wiser in time, friend Robin.'

He now became entangled in a succession of crooked and narrow streets, which crossed each other, and meandered at no great distance from the water-side. The smell of tar was obvious to his nostrils, the masts of vessels pierced the moonlight above the tops of the buildings, and the numerous signs, which Robin paused to read, informed him that he was near the centre of business. But the streets were empty, the shops were closed, and lights were visible only in the second storeys of a few dwelling-houses. At length, on the corner of a narrow lane, through which he was passing, he beheld the broad countenance of a British hero swinging before the door of an inn, whence proceeded the voices of many guests. The casement of one of the lower windows was thrown back, and a very thin curtain permitted Robin to distinguish a party at supper, round a well-furnished table. The fragrance of the good cheer steamed forth into the outer air, and the youth could not fail to recollect that the last remnant of his travelling stock of provision had yielded to his morning appetite, and that noon had found and left him dinnerless.

'Oh, that a parchment three-penny might give me a right to sit down at yonder table!' said Robin, with a sigh. 'But the Major will make me welcome to the best of his victuals; so I will even step boldly in, and inquire my way to his dwelling.'

He entered the tavern, and was guided by the murmur of voices and the fumes of tobacco to the public-room. It was a long and low apartment, with oaken walls, grown dark in the continual smoke, and a floor which was thickly sanded, but of no immaculate purity. A number of persons—the larger part of whom appeared to be mariners, or in some way connected with the sea—occupied the wooden benches, or leather-bottomed chairs, conversing on various matters, and occasionally lending their attention to some topic of general interest. Three or four little groups were draining as many bowls of punch, which the West India trade had long since made a familiar drink in the

2 The stocks were an outdoor engine of imprisonment.

colony. Others, who had the appearance of men who lived by regular and laborious handicraft, preferred the insulated bliss of an unshared potation, and became more taciturn under its influence. Nearly all, in short, evinced a predilection for the Good Creature in some of its various shapes, for this is a vice to which, as Fast Day sermons of a hundred years ago will testify, we have a long hereditary claim. The only guests to whom Robin's sympathies inclined him were two or three sheepish countrymen, who were using the inn somewhat after the fashion of a Turkish caravansary; they had gotten themselves into the darkest corner of the room, and heedless of the Nicotian atmosphere, were supping on the bread of their own ovens, and the bacon cured in their own chimney-smoke. But though Robin felt a sort of brotherhood with these strangers, his eyes were attracted from them to a person who stood near the door, holding a whispered conversation with a group of ill-dressed associates. His features were separately striking almost to grotesqueness, and the whole face left a deep impression on the memory. The forehead bulged out into a double prominence, with a vale between; the nose came boldly forth in an irregular curve, and its bridge was of more than a finger's breadth; the eyebrows were deep and shaggy, and the eyes glowed beneath them like fire in a cave.

While Robin deliberated of whom to inquire respecting his kinsman's dwelling, he was accosted by the innkeeper, a little man in a stained white apron, who had come to pay his professional welcome to the stranger. Being in the second generation from a French Protestant, he seemed to have inherited the courtesy of his parent nation; but no variety of circumstances was ever known to change his voice from the one shrill note in which he now addressed Robin.

'From the country, I presume, sir?' said he, with a profound bow. 'Beg leave to congratulate you on your arrival, and trust you intend a long stay with us. Fine town here, sir, beautiful buildings, and much that may interest a stranger. May I hope for the honour of your commands in respect to supper?'

'The man sees a family likeness! the rogue has guessed that I am related to the Major!' thought Robin, who had hitherto experienced little superfluous civility.

All eyes were now turned on the country lad, standing at the door, in his worn three-cornered hat, grey coat, leather breeches, and blue yarn stockings, leaning on an oaken cudgel, and bearing a wallet on his back.

Robin replied to the courteous innkeeper, with such an assumption of confidence as befitted the Major's relative. 'My honest friend,' he said, 'I shall make it a point to patronize your house on some occasion, when'—here he could not help lowering his voice—'when I may have more than a parchment three-pence in my pocket. My present business', continued he, speaking with lofty confidence, 'is merely to inquire my way to the dwelling of my kinsman, Major Molineux.'

There was a sudden and general movement in the room, which Robin interpreted as expressing the eagerness of each individual to become his guide. But the innkeeper turned his eyes to a written paper on the wall, which he read, or seemed to read, with occasional recurrences to the young man's figure.

'What have we here?' said he, breaking his speech into little dry fragments. ' "Left the house of the subscriber, bounden servant, Hezekiah Mudge,—had on, when he went away, grey coat, leather breeches, master's third-best hat. One pound currency reward to whosoever shall lodge him in any jail of the province." Better trudge, boy; better trudge!'

Robin had begun to draw his hand towards the lighter end of the oak cudgel, but a strange hostility in every countenance induced him to relinquish his purpose of breaking the courteous innkeeper's head. As he turned to leave the room, he encountered a sneering glance from the bold-featured personage whom he had before noticed; and no sooner was he beyond the door, than he heard a general laugh, in which the innkeeper's voice might be distinguished, like the dropping of small stones into a kettle.

'Now, is it not strange,' thought Robin, with his usual shrewdness,—'is it not strange that the confession of an empty pocket should outweigh the name of my kinsman, Major Molineux? Oh, if I had one of those grinning rascals in the woods, where I and my oak sapling grew up together, I would teach him that my arm is heavy though my purse be light!'

On turning the corner of the narrow lane, Robin found himself in a spacious street, with an unbroken line of lofty houses on each side, and a steepled building at the upper end, whence the ringing of a bell announced the hour of nine. The light of the moon, and the lamps from the numerous shop-windows, discovered people promenading on the pavement, and amongst them Robin had hoped to recognize his hitherto inscrutable relative. The result of his former inquiries made him unwilling to hazard another, in a scene of such publicity, and he determined to walk slowly and silently up the street, thrusting his face close to that of every elderly gentleman, in search of the Major's lineaments. In his progress, Robin encountered many gay and gallant figures. Embroidered garments of showy colours, enormous periwigs, gold-laced hats, and silver-hilted swords glided past him and dazzled his optics. Travelled youths, imitators of the European fine gentlemen of the period, trod jauntily along, half dancing to the fashionable tunes which they hummed, and making poor Robin ashamed of his quiet and natural gait. At length, after many pauses to examine the gorgeous display of goods in the shop-windows, and after suffering some rebukes for the impertinence of his scrutiny into people's faces, the Major's kinsman found himself near the steepled building, still unsuccessful in his search. As yet, however, he had seen only one side of the thronged street; so Robin crossed, and continued the same sort of inquisition down the opposite pavement, with stronger hopes than the philosopher seeking an honest man, but with no better fortune. He had arrived about midway towards the lower end, from which his course began, when he overheard the approach of someone who struck down a cane on the flagstones at every step, uttering at regular intervals, two sepulchral hems.

'Mercy on us!' quoth Robin, recognizing the sound.

Turning a corner, which chanced to be close at his right hand, he hastened to pursue his researches in some other part of town. His patience now was wearing low, and he seemed to feel more fatigue from his rambles since he crossed the ferry, than from his journey of several days on the other side. Hunger also pleaded loudly within him, and Robin began to balance the propriety of demanding, violently, and with lifted cudgel, the necessary guidance from the first solitary passenger whom he should meet. While a resolution to this effect was gaining strength, he entered a street of mean appearance, on either side of which a row of ill-built houses was straggling towards the harbour. The moonlight fell upon no passenger along the whole extent, but in the third domicile which Robin passed there was a half-opened door, and his keen glance detected a woman's garment within.

'My luck may be better here,' said he to himself.

Accordingly, he approached the door, and beheld it shut closer as he did so; yet an open space remained, sufficing for the fair occupant to observe the stranger, without a corresponding display on her part. All that Robin could discern was a strip of scarlet petticoat, and the occasional sparkle of an eye, as if the moonbeams were trembling on some bright thing.

'Pretty mistress,' for I may call her so with a good conscience, thought the shrewd youth, since I know nothing to the contrary,—'my sweet pretty mistress, will you be kind enough to tell me whereabouts I must seek the dwelling of my kinsman, Major Molineux?'

Robin's voice was plaintive and winning, and the female, seeing nothing to be shunned in the handsome country youth, thrust open the door, and came forth into the moonlight. She was a dainty little figure, with a white neck, round arms, and a slender waist, at the extremity of which her scarlet petticoat jutted out over a hoop, as if she were standing in a balloon. Moreover, her face was oval and pretty, her hair dark beneath the little cap, and her bright eyes possessed a sly freedom, which triumphed over those of Robin.

'Major Molineux dwells here,' said this fair woman.

Now, her voice was the sweetest Robin had heard that night, yet he could not help doubting whether that sweet voice spoke Gospel truth. He looked up and down the mean street, and then surveyed the house before which they stood. It was a small, dark edifice of two storeys, the second of which projected over the lower floor, and the front apartment had the aspect of a shop for pretty commodities.

'Now, truly, I am in luck,' replied Robin, cunningly, 'and so indeed is my kinsman, the Major, in having so pretty a housekeeper. But I prithee trouble him to step to the door; I will deliver him a message from his friends in the country, and then go back to my lodgings at the inn.'

'Nay, the Major has been abed this hour or more,' said the lady of the scarlet petticoat; 'and it would be to little purpose to disturb him tonight, seeing his evening draught was of the strongest. But he is a kind-hearted man, and it would be as much as my life's worth to let a kinsman of his turn away from the door. You are the good old gentleman's very picture, and I could swear that was his rainy-weather hat. Also he has garments very much resembling those leather small-clothes. But come in, I pray, for I bid you hearty welcome in his name.'

So saying, the fair and hospitable dame took our hero by the hand; and the touch was light, and the force was gentleness, and though Robin read in her eyes what he did not hear in her words, yet the slender-waisted woman in the scarlet petticoat proved stronger than the athletic country youth. She had drawn his half-willing footsteps nearly to the threshold, when the opening of a door in the neighbourhood startled the Major's housekeeper, and, leaving the Major's kinsman, she vanished speedily into her own domicile. A heavy yawn preceded the appearance of a man, who, like the Moonshine of Pyramus and Thisbe, carried a lantern, needlessly aiding his sister luminary in the heavens. As he walked sleepily up the street, he turned his broad, dull face on Robin, and displayed a long staff, spiked at the end.

'Home, vagabond, home!' said the watchman, in accents that seemed to fall asleep as soon as they were uttered. 'Home, or we'll set you in the stocks by peep of day!'

'This is the second hint of the kind,' thought Robin. 'I wish they would end my difficulties, by setting me there tonight.'

Nevertheless, the youth felt an instinctive antipathy towards the guardian of midnight order, which at first prevented him from asking his usual question. But just when the man was about to vanish behind the corner, Robin resolved not to lose the opportunity, and shouted lustily after him,—

'I say, friend! will you guide me to the house of my kinsman, Major Molineux?'

The watchman made no reply, but turned the corner and was gone; yet Robin seemed to hear the sound of drowsy laughter stealing along the solitary street. At that moment, also, a pleasant titter saluted him from the open window above his head; he looked up, and caught the sparkle of a saucy eye; a round arm beckoned to him, and next he heard light footsteps descending the staircase within. But Robin, being of the household of a New England clergyman, was a good youth, as well as a shrewd one; so he resisted temptation, and fled away.

He now roamed desperately, and at random, through the town, almost ready to believe that a spell was on him, like that by which a wizard of his country had once kept three pursuers wandering, a whole winter night, within twenty paces of the cottage which they sought. The streets lay before him, strange and desolate, and the lights were extinguished in almost every house. Twice, however, little parties of men, among whom Robin distinguished individuals in outlandish attire, came hurrying along; but, though on both occasions, they paused to address him, such intercourse did not at all enlighten his perplexity. They did but utter a few words in some language of which Robin knew nothing, and perceiving his inability to answer, bestowed a curse upon him in plain English and hastened away. Finally, the lad determined to knock at the door of every mansion that might appear worthy to be occupied by his kinsman, trusting that perseverance would overcome the fatality that had hitherto thwarted him. Firm in this resolve, he was passing beneath the walls of a church, which formed the corner of two streets, when, as he turned into the shade of its steeple, he encountered a bulky stranger, muffled in a cloak. The man was proceeding with the speed of earnest business, but Robin planted himself full before him, holding the oak cudgel with both hands across his body as a bar to further passage.

'Halt, honest man, and answer me a question,' said he, very resolutely. 'Tell me, this instant, whereabouts is the dwelling of my kinsman, Major Molineux!'

'Keep your tongue between your teeth, fool, and let me pass!' said a deep, gruff voice, which Robin partly remembered. 'Let me pass, I say, or I'll strike you to the earth!'

'No, no, neighbour!' cried Robin, flourishing his cudgel, and then thrusting its larger end close to the man's muffled face. 'No, no, I'm not the fool you take me for, nor do you pass till I have an answer to my question. Whereabouts is the dwelling of my kinsman, Major Molineux?'

The stranger, instead of attempting to force his passage, stepped back into the moonlight, unmuffled his face, and stared full into that of Robin.

'Watch here an hour, and Major Molineux will pass by,' said he.

Robin gazed with dismay and astonishment on the unprecedented physiognomy of the speaker. The forehead with its double prominence, the broad hooked nose, the shaggy eyebrows, and fiery eyes were those which he had noticed at the inn, but the man's complexion had undergone a singular, or more properly, a twofold change. One side of the face blazed an intense red, while the other was black as midnight, the division line being in the broad bridge of the nose; and a mouth which seemed to extend from ear to ear was black or red, in contrast to the colour of the cheek.[3] The effect was as if two individual devils, a fiend of fire and a fiend of darkness, had united themselves to form this infernal visage. The stranger grinned in Robin's face, muffled his party-coloured features, and was out of sight in a moment.

'Strange things we travellers see!' ejaculated Robin.

He seated himself, however, upon the steps of the church-door, resolving to wait the appointed time for his kinsman. A few moments were consumed in philosophical speculations upon the species of man who had just left; but having settled this point shrewdly, rationally, and satisfactorily, he was compelled to look elsewhere for his amusement. And first he threw his eyes along the street. It was of more respectable appearance than most of those into which he had wandered; and the moon, creating, like the imaginative power, a beautiful strangeness in familiar objects, gave something of romance to a scene that might not have possessed it in the light of day. The irregular and often quaint architecture of the houses, some of whose roofs were broken into numerous little peaks, while others ascended, steep and narrow, into a single point, and others again were square; the pure snow-white of some of their complexions, the aged darkness of others, and the thousand sparklings, reflected from bright substances in the walls of many; these matters engaged Robin's attention for a while, and then began to grow wearisome. Next he endeavoured to define the forms of distant objects, starting away, with almost ghostly indistinctness, just as his eye appeared to grasp them; and finally he took a minute survey of an edifice which stood on the opposite side of the street, directly in front of the church-door, where he was stationed. It was a large, square mansion, distinguished from its neighbours by a balcony, which rested on tall pillars, and by an elaborate Gothic window, communicating therewith.

'Perhaps this is the very house I have been seeking,' thought Robin.

Then he strove to speed away the time, by listening to a murmur which swept continually along the street, yet was scarcely audible, except to an unaccustomed ear like his; it was a low, dull, dreamy sound, compounded of many noises, each of which was at too great a distance to be separately heard. Robin marvelled at this snore of a sleeping town, and marvelled more whenever its continuity was broken by now and then a distant shout, apparently loud where it originated. But altogether it was a sleep-inspiring sound, and, to shake off its drowsy influence, Robin arose, and climbed a window-frame, that he might view the interior of the church. There the moonbeams

3 The disguise of an Indian in war paint was much used by the early revolutionaries, as in the Boston Tea Party.

came trembling in, and fell down upon the deserted pews, and extended along the quiet aisles. A fainter yet more awful radiance was hovering around the pulpit, and one solitary ray had dared to rest upon the open page of the great Bible. Had nature, in that deep hour, become a worshipper in the house which man had builded? Or was that heavenly light the visible sanctity of the place,—visible because no earthly and impure feet were within the walls? The scene made Robin's heart shiver with a sensation of loneliness stronger than he had ever felt in the remotest depths of his native woods; so he turned away and sat down again before the door. There were graves around the church, and now an uneasy thought obtruded into Robin's breast. What if the object of his search, which had been so often and so strangely thwarted, were all the time mouldering in his shroud? What if his kinsman should glide through yonder gate, and nod and smile to him in dimly passing by?

'Oh that any breathing thing were here with me!' said Robin.

Recalling his thoughts from this uncomfortable track, he sent them over forest, hill, and stream, and attempted to imagine how that evening of ambiguity and weariness had been spent by his father's household. He pictured them assembled at the door, beneath the tree, the great old tree, which had been spared for its huge twisted trunk and venerable shade, when a thousand leafy brethren fell. There, at the going down of the summer sun, it was his father's custom to perform domestic worship, that the neighbours might come and join with him like brothers of the family, and that the wayfaring man might pause to drink at that fountain, and keep his heart pure by freshening the memory of home. Robin distinguished the seat of every individual of the little audience; he saw the good man in the midst, holding the Scriptures in the golden light that fell from the western clouds; he beheld him close the book and all rise up to pray. He heard the old thanksgivings for daily mercies, the old supplications for their continuance, to which he had so often listened in weariness, but which were now among his dear remembrances. He perceived the slight inequality of his father's voice when he came to speak of the absent one; he noted how his mother turned her face to the broad and knotted trunk; how his elder brother scorned, because the beard was rough upon his upper lip, to permit his features to be moved; how the younger sister drew down a low hanging branch before her eyes; and how the little one of all, whose sports had hitherto broken the decorum of the scene, understood the prayer for her playmate, and burst into clamorous grief. Then he saw them go in at the door; and when Robin would have entered also, the latch tinkled into its place, and he was excluded from his home.

'Am I here, or there?' cried Robin, starting; for all at once, when his thoughts had become visible and audible in a dream, the long, wide, solitary street shone out before him.

He aroused himself, and endeavoured to fix his attention steadily upon the large edifice which he had surveyed before. But still his mind kept vibrating between fancy and reality; by turns, the pillars of the balcony lengthened into the tall, bare stems of pines, dwindled down to human figures, settled again into their true shape and size, and then commenced a new succession of changes. For a single moment, when he deemed himself awake, he could have sworn that a visage—one which he seemed to remember, yet could not absolutely name as his kinsman's—was looking towards him from the Gothic window. A deeper sleep wrestled with and nearly overcame him, but fled at the sound of footsteps along the opposite pavement. Robin rubbed his eyes, discerned a man passing at the foot of the balcony, and addressed him in a loud, peevish, and lamentable cry.

'Hallo, friend! must I wait here all night for my kinsman, Major Molineux?'

The sleeping echoes awoke, and answered the voice; and the passenger, barely able to discern a figure sitting in the oblique shade of the steeple, traversed the street to obtain a nearer view. He was himself a gentleman in his prime, of open, intelligent, cheerful, and altogether prepossessing countenance. Perceiving a country youth, apparently homeless and without friends, he accosted him in a tone of real kindness, which had become strange to Robin's ears.

'Well, my good lad, why are you sitting here?' inquired he. 'Can I be of service to you in any way?'

'I am afraid not, sir,' replied Robin, despondingly; 'yet I shall take it kindly, if you'll answer me a single question. I've been searching, half the night, for one Major Molineux; now, sir, is there really such a person in these parts, or am I dreaming?'

'Major Molineux! The name is not altogether strange to me,' said the gentleman, smiling. 'Have you any objection to telling me the nature of your business with him?'

Then Robin briefly related that his father was a clergyman, settled on a small salary, at a long distance back in the country, and that he and Major Molineux were brothers' children. The Major, having inherited riches, and acquired civil and military rank, had visited his cousin, in great pomp, a year or two before; had manifested much interest in Robin and an elder brother, and, being childless himself, had thrown out hints respecting the future establishment of one of them in life. The elder brother was destined to succeed to the farm which his father cultivated in the interval of sacred duties; it was therefore determined that Robin should profit by his kinsman's generous intentions, especially as he seemed to be rather the favourite, and was thought to possess other necessary endowments.

'For I have the name of being a shrewd youth,' observed Robin, in this part of the story.

'I doubt not you deserve it,' replied his new friend, good-naturedly; 'but pray proceed.'

'Well, sir, being nearly eighteen years old, and well grown, as you see,' continued Robin, drawing himself up to his full height, 'I thought it high time to begin in the world. So my mother and sister put me in handsome trim, and my father gave me half the remnant of his last year's salary, and five days ago I started for this place, to pay the Major a visit. But, would you believe it, sir! I crossed the ferry a little after dark, and have yet found nobody that would show me the way to his dwelling; only, an hour or two since, I was told to wait here, and Major Molineux would pass by.'

'Can you describe the man who told you this?' inquired the gentleman.

'Oh, he was a very ill-favoured fellow, sir,' replied Robin, 'with two great bumps on his forehead, a hook nose, fiery eyes; and, what struck me as the strangest, his face was of two different colours. Do you happen to know such a man, sir?'

'Not intimately,' answered the stranger, 'but I chanced to meet him a little time previous to your stopping me. I believe you may trust his word, and that the Major will very shortly pass through this street. In the mean time, as I have a singular curiosity to witness your meeting, I will sit down here upon the steps and bear you company.'

He seated himself accordingly, and soon engaged his companion in animated discourse. It was but of brief continuance, however, for a noise of shouting, which had long been remotely audible, drew so much nearer that Robin inquired its cause.

'What may be the meaning of this uproar?' asked he. 'Truly, if your town be always as noisy, I shall find little sleep while I am an inhabitant.'

'Why, indeed, friend Robin, there do appear to be three or four riotous fellows abroad tonight,' replied the gentleman. 'You must not expect all the stillness of your native woods here in our streets. But the watch will shortly be at the heels of these lads and'—

'Ay, and set them in the stocks by peep of day,' interrupted Robin, recollecting his own encounter with the drowsy lantern-bearer. 'But, dear sir, if I may trust my ears, an army of watchmen would never make head against such a multitude of rioters. There were at least a thousand voices went up to make that one shout.'

'May not a man have several voices, Robin, as well as two complexions?' said his friend.

'Perhaps a man may; but Heaven forbid that a woman should!' responded the shrewd youth, thinking of the seductive tones of the Major's housekeeper.

The sounds of a trumpet in some neighbouring street now became so evident and continual, that Robin's curiosity was strongly excited. In addition to the shouts, he heard frequent bursts from many instruments of discord, and a wild and confused laughter filled up the intervals. Robin rose from the steps, and looked wistfully towards the point whither people seemed to be hastening.

'Surely some prodigious merry-making is going on,' exclaimed he. 'I have laughed very little since I left home, sir, and should be sorry to lose an opportunity. Shall we step round the corner by that darkish house, and take our share of the fun?'

'Sit down again, sit down, good Robin,' replied the gentleman, laying his hand on the skirt of the grey coat. 'You forget that we must wait here for your kinsman; and there is reason to believe that he will pass by, in the course of a very few moments.'

The near approach of the uproar had now disturbed the neighbourhood; windows flew open on all sides; and many heads, in the attire of the pillow, and confused by sleep suddenly broken, were protruded to the gaze of whoever had leisure to observe them. Eager voices hailed each other from house to house, all demanding the explanation, which not a soul could give. Half-dressed men hurried towards the unknown commotion, stumbling as they went over the stone steps that thrust themselves into the narrow foot-walk. The shouts, the laughter, and the tuneless bray, the antipodes of music, came onwards with increasing din, till scattered individuals, and then denser bodies, began to appear round a corner at a distance of a hundred yards.

'Will you recognize your kinsman, if he passed in this crowd?' inquired the gentleman.

'Indeed, I can't warrant it, sir; but I'll take my stand here, and keep a bright lookout,' answered Robin, descending to the outer edge of the pavement.

A mighty stream of people now emptied into the street, and came rolling slowly towards the church. A single horseman wheeled the corner in the midst of them, and close behind him came a band of fearful wind-instruments, sending forth a fresher discord now that no intervening buildings kept it from the ear. Then a redder light disturbed the moonbeams, and a dense multitude of torches shone along the street, concealing, by their glare, whatever object they illuminated. The single horseman, clad in a military dress, and bearing a drawn sword, rode onward as the leader, and, by his fierce and variegated countenance, appeared like war personified; the red of one cheek was an emblem of fire and sword; the blackness of the other betokened the mourning that attends them. In his train were wild figures in the Indian dress, and many fantastic shapes without a model, giving the whole march a visionary air, as if a dream had broken forth from some feverish brain, and were sweeping visibly through the midnight streets. A mass of people, inactive, except as applauding spectators, hemmed the procession in; and several women ran along the sidewalk, piercing the confusion of heavier sounds with their shrill voices of mirth or terror.

'The double-faced fellow has his eye upon me,' muttered Robin, with an indefinite but an uncomfortable idea that he was himself to bear a part in the pageantry.

The leader turned himself in the saddle, and fixed his glance full upon the country youth, as the steed went slowly by. When Robin had freed his eyes from those fiery ones, the musicians were passing before him, and the torches were close at hand; but the unsteady brightness of the latter formed a veil which he could not penetrate. The rattling of wheels over the stones sometimes found its way to his ear, and the confused traces of a human form appeared at intervals, and then melted into the vivid light. A moment more, and the leader thundered a command to halt: the trumpets vomited a horrid breath, and then held their peace; the shouts and laughter of the people died away, and there remained only a universal hum, allied to silence. Right before Robin's eyes was an uncovered cart. There the torches blazed the brightest, there the moon shone out like day, and there, in tar-and-feathery dignity,[4] sat his kinsman, Major Molineux!

He was an elderly man, of large and majestic person, and strong, square features, betokening a steady soul; but steady as it was, his enemies had found means to shake it. His face was pale as death, and far more ghastly; the broad forehead was contracted in his agony, so that his eyebrows formed one grizzled line; his eyes were red and wild, and the foam hung white upon his quivering lip. His whole frame was agitated by a quick and continual tremor, which his pride strove to quell, even in those circumstances of overwhelming humiliation. But perhaps the bitterest pang of all was when his eyes met those of Robin; for he evidently knew him on the instant, as the youth stood witnessing the foul disgrace of a head grown grey in honour. They stared at each other in silence, and Robin's knees shook, and his hair bristled, with a mixture of pity and terror. Soon, however, a bewildering excitement began to seize upon his mind; the preceding adventures of the night, the unexpected appearance of the crowd, the

4 In this rough punishment a man was stripped naked, covered with hot tar, and sprinkled with feathers. It was frequently visited upon those suspected of resisting the Revolution.

torches, the confused din and the hush that followed, the spectre of his kinsman reviled by that great multitude,—all this, and more than all, a perception of tremendous ridicule in the whole scene, affected him with a sort of mental inebriety. At that moment a voice of sluggish merriment saluted Robin's ears; he turned instinctively, and just behind the corner of the church stood the lantern-bearer, rubbing his eyes, and drowsily enjoying the lad's amazement. Then he heard a peal of laughter like the ringing of silvery bells; a woman twitched his arm, a saucy eye met his, and he saw the lady of the scarlet petticoat. A sharp, dry cachinnation appealed to his memory, and, standing on tiptoe in the crowd, with his white apron over his head, he beheld the courteous little innkeeper. And lastly, there sailed over the heads of the multitude a great, broad laugh, broken in the midst by two sepulchral hems; thus, 'haw, haw, haw,—hem, hem,—haw, haw, haw, haw!'

The sound proceeded from the balcony of the opposite edifice, and thither Robin turned his eyes. In front of the Gothic window stood the old citizen, wrapped in a wide gown, his grey periwig exchanged for a nightcap, which was thrust back from his forehead, and his silk stockings hanging about his legs. He supported himself on his polished cane in a fit of convulsive merriment, which manifested itself on his solemn old features like a funny inscription on a tombstone. Then Robin seemed to hear the voices of the barbers, of the guests of the inn, and of all who had made sport of him that night. The contagion was spreading among the multitude, when all at once, it seized upon Robin, and he sent forth a shout of laughter that echoed through the street,—every man shook his sides, every man emptied his lungs, but Robin's shout was the loudest there. The cloud-spirits peeped from their silvery islands, as the congregated mirth went roaring up the sky! The Man in the Moon heard the far bellow. 'Oho,' quoth he, 'the old earth is frolicsome tonight!'

When there was a momentary calm in that tempestuous sea of sound, the leader gave the sign, the procession resumed its march. On they went, like fiends that throng in mockery around some dead potentate, mighty no more, but majestic still in his agony. On they went, in counterfeited pomp, in senseless uproar, in frenzied merriment, trampling all on an old man's heart. On swept the tumult, and left a silent street behind.

'Well, Robin, are you dreaming?' inquired the gentleman, laying his hand on the youth's shoulder.

Robin started, and withdrew his arm from the stone post to which he had instinctively clung, as the living stream rolled by him. His cheek was somewhat pale, and his eye not quite as lively as in the earlier part of the evening.

'Will you be kind enough to show me the way to the ferry?' said he, after a moment's pause.

'You have, then, adopted a new subject of inquiry?' observed his companion, with a smile.

'Why, yes, sir,' replied Robin, rather dryly. 'Thanks to you, and to my other friends, I have at last met my kinsman, and he will scarce desire to see my face again. I begin to grow weary of a town life, sir. Will you show me the way to the ferry?'

'No, my good friend Robin,—not tonight, at least,' said the gentleman. 'Some few days hence, if you wish it, I will speed you on your journey. Or, if you prefer to remain with us, perhaps, as you are a shrewd youth, you may rise in the world without the help of your kinsman, Major Molineux.'

1832

Edgar Allan Poe
1809–1849

◆

Born in Boston into a theatrical family, Edgar Allan Poe became an orphan at an early age and was adopted and raised by John Allan, a Virginia tobacco exporter. He began his schooling in England but returned to the United States to attend the University of Virginia. Expelled for drinking and gambling, he entered the army for two years and later attended the United States Military Academy at West Point, from which he was also expelled.

Poet and short-story writer, critic and editor, he aimed for a 'unity of effect' in all his writings. In his essay 'The Poetic Principle', he suggests that brevity, a sense of mystery, some degree of verbal magic, and immediate emotional effect are the qualities he seeks in poetry. These are also the qualities he brings to his own short fiction. In 'The Purloined Letter', he makes the mystery story his own unique creation. He became a major influence on the detective story.

The Purloined Letter

Nil sapientiae odiosius acumine nimio.[1]

—Seneca

At Paris, just after dark one gusty evening in the autumn of 18—, I was enjoying the twofold luxury of meditation and a meerschaum, in company with my friend, C. Auguste Dupin, in his little back library, or book-closet, *au troisième*, No. 33 *Rue Dunôt, Faubourg St Germain*.[2] For one hour at least we had maintained a profound silence; while each, to any casual observer, might have seemed intently and exclusively occupied with the curling eddies of smoke that oppressed the atmosphere of the chamber. For myself, however, I was mentally discussing certain topics which had formed matter for conversation between us at an earlier period of the evening; I mean the affair of the Rue Morgue, and the mystery attending the murder of Marie Rogêt.[3] I looked upon it, therefore, as something of a coincidence, when the door of our apartment was

1 Nothing is more offensive to the wise than an excess of trickery.
2 On the third floor in a fashionable district in Paris.
3 These are the subjects of previous detective stories by Poe.

thrown open and admitted our old acquaintance, Monsieur G——, the Prefect of the Parisian police.

We gave him a hearty welcome; for there was nearly half as much of the entertaining as of the contemptible about the man, and we had not seen him for several years. We had been sitting in the dark, and Dupin now rose for the purpose of lighting a lamp, but sat down again, without doing so, upon G.'s saying that he had called to consult us, or rather to ask the opinion of my friend, about some official business which had occasioned a great deal of trouble.

'If it is any point requiring reflection,' observed Dupin, as he forbore to enkindle the wick, 'we shall examine it to better purpose in the dark.'

'That is another of your odd notions,' said the Prefect, who had the fashion of calling everything 'odd' that was beyond his comprehension, and thus lived amid an absolute legion of 'oddities'.

'Very true,' said Dupin, as he supplied his visitor with a pipe, and rolled toward him a comfortable chair.

'And what is the difficulty now?' I asked. 'Nothing more in the assassination way I hope?'

'Oh, no; nothing of that nature. The fact is, the business is *very* simple indeed, and I make no doubt that we can manage it sufficiently well ourselves; but then I thought Dupin would like to hear the details of it because it is so excessively *odd*.'

'Simple and odd,' said Dupin.

'Why, yes; and not exactly that either. The fact is, we have all been a good deal puzzled because the affair *is* so simple, and yet baffles us altogether.'

'Perhaps it is the very simplicity of the thing which puts you at fault,' said my friend.

'What nonsense you *do* talk!' replied the Prefect, laughing heartily.

'Perhaps the mystery is a little *too* plain,' said Dupin.

'Oh, good heavens! who ever heard of such an idea?'

'A little *too* self-evident.'

'Ha! ha! ha!—ha! ha! ha!—ho! ho! ho!' roared our visitor, profoundly amused, 'oh, Dupin, you will be the death of me yet!'

'And what, after all, *is* the matter on hand?' I asked.

'Why, I will tell you,' replied the Prefect, as he gave a long, steady, and contemplative puff, and settled himself in his chair. 'I will tell you in a few words; but, before I begin, let me caution you that this is an affair demanding the greatest secrecy, and that I should most probably lose the position I now hold, were it known that I confided it to anyone.'

'Proceed,' said I.

'Or not,' said Dupin.

'Well, then; I have received personal information, from a very high quarter, that a certain document of the last importance has been purloined from the royal apartments. The individual who purloined it is known; this beyond a doubt; he was seen to take it. It is known, also, that it still remains in his possession.'

'How is this known?' asked Dupin.

'It is clearly inferred', replied the Prefect, 'from the nature of the document, and from the non-appearance of certain results which would at once arise from its passing *out* of the robber's possession—that is to say, from his employing it as he must design in the end to employ it.'

'Be a little more explicit,' I said.

'Well, I may venture so far as to say that the paper gives its holder a certain power in a certain quarter where such power is immensely valuable.' The Prefect was fond of the cant of diplomacy.

'Still I do not quite understand,' said Dupin.

'No? Well; the disclosure of the document to a third person, who shall be name-less, would bring in question the honour of a personage of most exalted station; and this fact gives the holder of the document an ascendancy over the illustrious personage whose honour and peace are so jeopardized.'

'But this ascendancy', I interposed, 'would depend upon the robber's knowledge of the loser's knowledge of the robber. Who would dare—'

'The thief', said G., 'is the Minister D——, who dares all things, those unbe-coming as well as becoming a man. The method of the theft was not less ingenious than bold. The document in question—a letter, to be frank—had been received by the personage robbed while in the royal *boudoir*. During its perusal she was suddenly inter-rupted by the entrance of the other exalted personage from whom especially it was her wish to conceal it. After a hurried and vain endeavour to thrust it in a drawer, she was forced to place it, open as it was, upon a table. The address, however, was uppermost, and, the contents thus unexposed, the letter escaped notice. At this juncture enters the Minister D——. His lynx eye immediately perceives the paper, recognizes the hand-writing of the address, observes the confusion of the personage addressed, and fathoms her secret. After some business transactions, hurried through in his ordinary manner, he produces a letter somewhat similar to the one in question, opens it, pretends to read it, and then places it in close juxtaposition to the other. Again he converses, for some fifteen minutes, upon the public affairs. At length, in taking leave, he takes also from the table the letter to which he had no claim. Its rightful owner saw, but, of course, dared not call attention to the act, in the presence of the third personage who stood at her elbow. The Minister decamped; leaving his own letter—one of no importance—upon the table.'

'Here, then,' said Dupin to me, 'you have precisely what you demand to make the ascendancy complete—the robber's knowledge of the loser's knowledge of the robber.'

'Yes,' replied the Prefect; 'and the power thus attained has, for some months past, been wielded, for political purposes, to a very dangerous extent. The personage robbed is more thoroughly convinced, every day, of the necessity of reclaiming her letter. But this, of course, cannot be done openly. In fine, driven to despair, she has committed the matter to me.'

'Than whom', said Dupin, amid a perfect whirlwind of smoke, 'no more sagacious agent could, I suppose, be desired, or even imagined.'

'You flatter me,' replied the Prefect; 'but it is possible that some such opinion may have been entertained.'

'It is clear,' said I, 'as you observe, that the letter is still in the possession of the Minister; since it is this possession, and not any employment of the letter, which bestows the power. With the employment the power departs.'

'True,' said G.; 'and upon this conviction I proceeded. My first care was to make thorough search of the Minister's hotel;[4] and here my chief embarrassment lay in the necessity of searching without his knowledge. Beyond all things, I have been warned of the danger which would result from giving him reason to suspect our design.'

'But,' said I, 'you are quite *au fait* in these investigations. The Parisian police have done this thing often before.'

'Oh, yes; and for this reason I did not despair. The habits of the Minister gave me, too, a great advantage. He is frequently absent from home at night. His servants are by no means numerous. They sleep at a distance from their master's apartment, and, being chiefly Neapolitans, are readily made drunk. I have keys, as you know, with which I can open any chamber or cabinet in Paris. For three months a night has not passed, during the greater part of which I have not been engaged, personally, in ransacking the D—— Hotel. My honour is interested, and, to mention a great secret, the reward is enormous. So I did not abandon the search until I had become fully satisfied that the thief is a more astute man than myself. I fancy that I have investigated every nook and corner of the premises in which it is possible that the paper can be concealed.'

'But is it not possible', I suggested, 'that although the letter may be in possession of the Minister, as it unquestionably is, he may have concealed it elsewhere than upon his own premises?'

'This is barely possible,' said Dupin. 'The present peculiar condition of affairs at court, and especially of those intrigues in which D—— is known to be involved, would render the instant availability of the document—its susceptibility of being produced at a moment's notice—a point of nearly equal importance with its possession.'

'Its susceptibility of being produced?' said I.

'That is to say, of being *destroyed*,' said Dupin.

'True,' I observed; 'the paper is clearly then upon the premises. As for its being upon the person of the Minister, we may consider that as out of the question.'

'Entirely,' said the Prefect. 'He has been twice waylaid, as if by footpads, and his person rigidly searched under my own inspection.'

'You might have spared yourself this trouble,' said Dupin. 'D——, I presume, is not altogether a fool, and, if not, must have anticipated these waylayings, as a matter of course.'

'Not *altogether* a fool,' said G., 'but then he is a poet, which I take to be only one remove from a fool.'

'True,' said Dupin, after a long and thoughtful whiff from his meerschaum, 'although I have been guilty of certain doggerel myself.'

'Suppose you detail', said I, 'the particulars of your search.'

'Why, the fact is, we took our time, and we searched *everywhere*. I have had long experience in these affairs. I took the entire building, room by room; devoting the

---

4 'hotel' in the French sense: a large building; in this case a private house in the city

nights of a whole week to each. We examined, first, the furniture of each apartment. We opened every possible drawer; and I presume you know that, to a properly trained police agent, such a thing as a "*secret*" drawer is impossible. Any man is a dolt who permits a "secret" drawer to escape him in a search of this kind. The thing is so plain. There is a certain amount of bulk—of space—to be accounted for in every cabinet. Then we have accurate rules. The fiftieth part of a line could not escape us. After the cabinets we took the chairs. The cushions we probed with the fine long needles you have seen me employ. From the table we removed the tops.'

'Why so?'

'Sometimes the top of a table, or other similarly arranged piece of furniture, is removed by the person wishing to conceal an article; then the leg is excavated, the article deposited within the cavity, and the top replaced. The bottoms and tops of bedposts are employed in the same way.'

'But could not the cavity be detected by sounding?' I asked.

'By no means, if, when the article is deposited, a sufficient wadding of cotton be placed around it. Besides, in our case, we were obliged to proceed without noise.'

'But you could not have removed—you could not have taken to pieces *all* the articles of furniture in which it would have been possible to make a deposit in the manner you mention. A letter may be compressed into a thin spiral roll, not differing much in shape or bulk from a large knitting needle, and in this form it might be inserted into the rung of a chair, for example. You did not take to pieces all the chairs?'

'Certainly not; but we did better—we examined the rungs of every chair in the hotel, and, indeed, the jointings of every description of furniture, by the aid of a most powerful microscope. Had there been any traces of recent disturbance we should not have failed to detect it instantly. A single grain of gimlet dust, for example, would have been as obvious as an apple. Any disorder in the gluing—any unusual gaping in the joints—would have sufficed to insure detection.'

'I presume you looked to the mirrors, between the boards and the plates, and you probed the beds and the bedclothes, as well as the curtains and carpets.'

'That of course; and when we had absolutely completed every particle of furniture in this way, then we examined the house itself. We divided its entire surface into compartments, which we numbered, so that none might be missed; then we scrutinized each individual square inch throughout the premises, including the two houses immediately adjoining, with the microscope, as before.'

'The two houses adjoining!' I exclaimed; 'you must have had a great deal of trouble.'

'We had; but the reward offered is prodigious.'

'You included the *grounds* about the houses?'

'All the grounds are paved with brick. They gave us comparatively little trouble. We examined the moss between the bricks, and found it undisturbed.'

'You looked among D——'s papers, of course, and into the books of the library?'

'Certainly; we opened every package and parcel; we not only opened every book, but we turned over every leaf in each volume, not contenting ourselves with a mere shake, according to the fashion of some of our police officers. We also measured the thickness of every book *cover*, with the most accurate admeasurement, and applied to each the most jealous scrutiny of the microscope. Had any of the bindings been recently meddled with, it would have been utterly impossible that the fact should have escaped observation. Some five or six volumes, just from the hands of the binder, we carefully probed, longitudinally, with needles.'

'You explored the floors beneath the carpets?'

'Beyond a doubt. We removed every carpet, and examined the boards with the microscope.'

'And the paper on the walls?'

'Yes.'

'You looked into the cellars?'

'We did.'

'Then', I said, 'you have been making a miscalculation, and the letter is *not* upon the premises, as you suppose.'

'I fear you are right there,' said the Prefect. 'And now, Dupin, what would you advise me to do?'

'To make a thorough research of the premises.'

'That is absolutely needless,' replied G., 'I am not more sure that I breathe than I am that the letter is not at the hotel.'

'I have no better advice to give you,' said Dupin. 'You have, of course, an accurate description of the letter?'

'Oh, yes!'—And here the Prefect, producing a memorandum book, proceeded to read aloud a minute account of the internal, and especially of the external, appearance of the missing document. Soon after finishing the perusal of this description, he took his departure, more entirely depressed in spirits than I had ever known the good gentleman before.

In about a month afterward he paid us another visit, and found us occupied very nearly as before. He took a pipe and a chair and entered into some ordinary conversation. At length I said:

'Well, but G., what of the purloined letter? I presume you have at last made up your mind that there is no such thing as overreaching the Minister?'

'Confound him, say I—yes; I made the re-examination, however, as Dupin suggested—but it was all labour lost, as I knew it would be.'

'How much was the reward offered, did you say?' asked Dupin.

'Why, a very great deal—a *very* liberal reward—I don't like to say how much, precisely; but one thing I *will* say, that I wouldn't mind giving my individual cheque for fifty thousand francs to any one who could obtain me that letter. The fact is, it is becoming of more and more importance every day; and the reward has been lately doubled. If it were trebled, however, I could do no more than I have done.'

'Why, yes,' said Dupin, drawlingly, between the whiffs of his meerschaum, 'I really—think, G., you have not exerted yourself—to the utmost in this matter. You might—do a little more, I think, eh?'

'How?—in what way?'

'Why—puff, puff—you might—puff, puff—employ counsel in the matter, eh?— puff, puff, puff. Do you remember the story they tell of Abernethy?'

'No; hang Abernethy!'

'To be sure! hang him and welcome. But, once upon a time, a certain rich miser conceived the design of spunging upon this Abernethy for a medical opinion. Getting up, for this purpose, an ordinary conversation in a private company, he insinuated his case to the physician, as that of an imaginary individual.

' "We will suppose", said the miser, "that his symptoms are such and such; now, doctor, what would you have directed him to take?"

' "Take!" said Abernethy, "why, take *advice*, to be sure." '

'But,' said the Prefect, a little discomposed, '*I* am *perfectly* willing to take advice, and to pay for it. I would *really* give fifty thousand francs to anyone who would aid me in the matter.'

'In that case,' replied Dupin, opening a drawer, and producing a chequebook, 'you may as well fill me up a cheque for the amount mentioned. When you have signed it, I will hand you the letter.'

I was astounded. The Prefect appeared absolutely thunder-stricken. For some minutes he remained speechless and motionless, looking incredulously at my friend with open mouth, and eyes that seemed starting from their sockets; then apparently recovering himself in some measure, he seized a pen, and after several pauses and vacant stares, finally filled up and signed a cheque for fifty thousand francs, and handed it across the table to Dupin. The latter examined it carefully and deposited it in his pocketbook; then, unlocking an *escritoire*, took thence a letter and gave it to the prefect. This functionary grasped it in a perfect agony of joy, opened it with a trembling hand, cast a rapid glance at its contents, and then, scrambling and struggling to the door, rushed at length unceremoniously from the room and from the house, without having uttered a syllable since Dupin had requested him to fill up the cheque.

When he had gone, my friend entered into some explanations.

'The Parisian police', he said, 'are exceedingly able in their way. They are persevering, ingenious, cunning, and thoroughly versed in the knowledge which their duties seem chiefly to demand. Thus, when G. detailed to us his mode of searching the premises at the Hotel D———, I felt entire confidence in his having made a satisfactory investigation—so far as his labours extended.'

'So far as his labours extended?' said I.

'Yes,' said Dupin, 'The measures adopted were not only the best of their kind, but carried out to absolute perfection. Had the letter been deposited within the range of their search, these fellows would, beyond a question, have found it.'

I merely laughed—but he seemed quite serious in all that he said.

'The measures, then,' he continued, 'were good in their kind, and well executed; their defect lay in their being inapplicable to the case and to the man. A certain set of highly ingenious resources are, with the Prefect, a sort of Procrustean bed, to which he forcibly adapts his designs. But he perpetually errs by being too deep or too shallow for the matter at hand; and many a schoolboy is a better reasoner than he. I knew one about eight years of age, whose success at guessing in the game of "even and odd" attracted universal admiration. This game is simple, and is played with marbles. One player holds in his hand a number of these toys, and demands of another whether that number is even or odd. If the guess is right, the guesser wins one; if wrong, he loses one. The boy to whom I allude won all the marbles at school. Of course he had some principle of guessing; and this lay in mere observation and admeasurements of the astuteness of his opponents. For example, an arrant simpleton is his opponent, and holding up his closed hand, asks, "Are they even or odd?" Our schoolboy replies, "Odd," and loses; but upon the second trial he wins, for he then says to himself: "The simpleton had them even upon the first trial, and his amount of cunning is just sufficient to make him have them odd upon the second; I will therefore guess odd";—he guesses odd, and wins. Now, with a simpleton a degree above the first, he would have reasoned thus: "This fellow finds that in the first instance I guessed odd, and, in the second, he will propose to himself, upon the first impulse, a simple variation from even to odd, as did the first simpleton; but then a second thought will suggest that this is too simple a variation, and finally he will decide upon putting it even as before. I will therefore guess even";—he guesses even, and wins. Now this mode of reasoning in the schoolboy, whom his fellows termed "lucky",—what, in its last analysis, is it?'

'It is merely', I said, 'an identification of the reasoner's intellect with that of his opponent.'

'It is,' said Dupin; 'and, upon inquiring of the boy by what means he effected the *thorough* identification in which his success consisted, I received answer as follows; "When I wish to find out how wise, or how stupid, or how good, or how wicked is anyone, or what are his thoughts at the moment, I fashion the expression of my face, as accurately as possible, in accordance with the expression of his, and then wait to see what thoughts or sentiments arise in my mind or heart, as if to match or correspond with the expression." This response of the schoolboy lies at the bottom of all the spurious profundity which has been attributed to Rochefoucault, to La Bougive, to Machiavelli, and to Campanella.'

'And the identification', I said, 'of the reasoner's intellect with that of his opponent, depends, if I understand you aright, upon the accuracy with which the opponent's intellect is admeasured.'

'For its practical value it depends upon this,' replied Dupin; 'and the Prefect and his cohort fail so frequently, first, by default of this identification and, secondly, by ill-admeasurement, or rather through non-admeasurement, of the intellect with which they are engaged. They consider only their *own* ideas of ingenuity; and, in searching for anything hidden, advert only to the modes in which *they* would have hidden it. They are right in this much—that their own ingenuity is a faithful representative of that of the *mass*; but when the cunning of the individual felon is diverse in character from their own, the felon foils them, of course. This always happens when it is above their own, and very usually when it is below. They have no variation of principle in their investigations; at best, when urged by some unusual emergency—by some extraordinary reward—they extend or exaggerate their old modes of *practice*, without touching their principles. What, for example, in this case of D——, has been done to vary the principle of action? What is all this boring, and probing, and sounding, and scrutinizing with the microscope, and dividing the surface of the building into registered square inches—what is it all but an exaggeration *of the application* of the one principle or set of principles of search, which are based upon the one set of notions regarding human ingenuity, to which the Prefect, in the long routine of his duty, has been accustomed? Do you not see he has taken it for granted that *all* men proceed to conceal a letter, not exactly in a gimlet-hole bored in a chair leg, but, at least, in *some* out-of-the-way hole or corner suggested by the same tenor of thought which would urge a man to secrete a letter in a gimlet-hole bored in a chair leg? And do you not see also, that such *recherchés* nooks for concealment are adapted only for ordinary occasions, and would be adopted only by ordinary intellects; for, in all cases of concealment, a disposal of the article concealed—a disposal of it in this *recherché* manner,—is, in the very first instance, presumable and presumed; and thus its discovery depends, not at all upon the acumen, but altogether upon the mere care, patience, and determination of the seekers; and where the case is of importance—or, what amounts to the same thing in the political eyes, when the reward is of magnitude,—the qualities in question have *never* been known to fail. You will now understand what I mean in suggesting that, had the purloined letter been hidden anywhere within the limits of the Prefect's examination—in other words, had the principle of its concealment been comprehended within the principles of the Prefect—its discovery would have been a matter altogether without question. This functionary, however, has been thoroughly mystified; and the remote source of his defeat lies in the supposition that the Minister is a fool, because he has acquired renown as a poet. All fools are poets; this the Prefect *feels*; and he is merely guilty of a *non distributio medii* in thence inferring that all poets are fools.'

'But is this really the poet?' I asked. 'There are two brothers, I know; and both have attained reputation in letters. The Minister I believe has written learnedly on the Differential Calculus. He is a mathematician, and no poet.'

'You are mistaken; I know him well; he is both. As poet *and* mathematician, he would reason well; as mere mathematician, he could not have reasoned at all, and thus would have been at the mercy of the Prefect.'

'You surprise me', I said, 'by these opinions, which have been contradicted by the voice of the world. You do not mean to set at naught the well-digested idea of centuries. The mathematical reason has long been regarded as the reason *par excellence.*'

'"*Il y a à parier*"', replied Dupin, quoting from Chamfort, '"*que toute idée publique, toute convention reçue, est une sottise, car elle a convenu au plus grand nombre.*"[5] The mathematicians, I grant you, have done their best to promulgate the popular error to which you allude, and which is none the less an error for its promulgation as truth. With an art worthy a better cause, for example, they have insinuated the term "analysis" into application to algebra. The French are the originators of this particular deception; but if a term is of any importance—if words derive any value from applicability—then "analysis" conveys "algebra" about as much as, in Latin, "ambitus" implies "*ambition*", "*religio*" "*religion*", or "*hommes honesti*" a set of *honourable* men.'

'You have a quarrel on hand, I see,' said I, 'with some of the algebraists of Paris; but proceed.'

5 'The odds are that any public idea or accepted opinion is stupid, because it has suited the majority of people.'

'I dispute the availability, and thus the value, of that reason which is cultivated in any especial form other than the abstractly logical. I dispute, in particular, the reason educed by mathematical study. The mathematics are the science of form and quantity; mathematical reasoning is merely logic applied to observation upon form and quantity. The great error lies in supposing that even the truths of what is called *pure* algebra are abstract or general truths. And this error is so egregious that I am confounded at the universality with which it has been received. Mathematical axioms are *not* axioms of general truth. What is true of *relation*—of form and quantity—is often grossly false in regard to morals, for example. In this latter science it is very usually *un*true that the aggregated parts are equal to the whole. In chemistry also the axiom fails. In the consideration of motive it fails; for two motives, each of a given value, have not, necessarily, a value when united, equal to the sum of their values apart. There are numerous other mathematical truths which are only truths within the limits of *relation*. But the mathematician argues from his *finite truths*, through habit, as if they were of an absolutely general applicability—as the world indeed imagines them to be. Bryant, in his very learned "Mythology", mentions an analogous source of error, when he says that "although the pagan fables are not believed, yet we forget ourselves continually, and make inferences from them as existing realities." With the algebraists, however, who are pagans themselves, the "pagan fables" *are* believed and the inferences are made, not so much through lapse of memory as through an unaccountable addling of the brains. In short, I never yet encountered the mere mathematician who would be trusted out of equal roots, or one who did not clandestinely hold it as a point of his faith that $x2 + px$ was absolutely and unconditionally equal to q. Say to one of these gentlemen, by way of experiment, if you please, that you believe occasions may occur where $x2 + px$ is *not* altogether equal to q, and, having made him understand what you mean, get out of his reach as speedily as convenient, for, beyond doubt, he will endeavour to knock you down.

'I mean to say', continued Dupin, while I merely laughed at his last observations, 'that if the Minister had been no more than a mathematician, the Prefect would have been under no necessity of giving me this cheque. I knew him, however, as both mathematician and poet, and my measures were adapted to his capacity, with reference to the circumstances by which he was surrounded. I knew him as a courtier, too, and as a bold *intriguant*. Such a man, I considered, could not fail to be aware of the ordinary police modes of action. He could not have failed to anticipate—and events have proved that he did not fail to anticipate—the waylayings to which he was subjected. He must have foreseen, I reflected, the secret investigations of his premises. His frequent absences from home at night, which were hailed by the Prefect as certain aids to his success, I regarded only as ruses, to afford opportunity for thorough search to the police, and thus the sooner to impress them with the conviction to which G., in fact, did finally arrive—the conviction that the letter was not upon the premises. I felt, also, that the whole train of thought, which I was at some pains in detailing to you just now, concerning the invariable principle of policial action in searches for articles concealed—I felt that this whole train of thought would necessarily pass through the mind of the Minister. It would imperatively lead him to despise all the ordinary *nooks* of concealment. *He* could not, I reflected, be so weak as not to see that the most intricate and remote recess of his hotel would be as open as his commonest closets to the eyes, to the probes, to the gimlets, and to the microscopes of the Prefect. I saw, in fine, that he would be driven, as a matter of course, to *simplicity*, if not deliberately induced to it as a matter of choice. You will remember, perhaps, how desperately the Prefect laughed when I suggested, upon our first interview, that it was just possible this mystery troubled him so much on account of its being so *very* self-evident.'

'Yes,' said I, 'I remember his merriment well. I really thought he would have fallen into convulsions.'

'The material world', continued Dupin, 'abounds with very strict analogies to the immaterial; and thus some colour of truth has been given to the rhetorical dogma, that metaphor, or simile, may be made to strengthen an argument as well as to embellish a description. The principle of the *vis inertiae*, for example, seems to be identical in physics and metaphysics. It is not more true in the former, that a large body is with more difficulty set in motion than a smaller one, and that its subsequent *momentum* is commensurate with this difficulty, than it is, in the latter, that intellects of the vaster capacity, while more forcible, more constant, and more eventful in their movements than those of inferior grade, are yet the less readily moved, and more embarrassed, and full of hesitation in the first few steps of their progress. Again: have you ever noticed which of the street signs, over the shop doors, are the most attractive of attention?'

'I have never given the matter a thought,' I said.

'There is a game of puzzles,' he resumed, 'which is played upon a map. One party playing requires another to find a given word—the name of a town, river, state, or empire—any word, in short, upon the motley and perplexed surface of the chart. A novice in the game generally seeks to embarrass his opponents by giving them the most minutely lettered names; but the adept selects such words as stretch, in large characters, from one end of the chart to the other. These, like the over-largely lettered signs and placards of the street, escape observation by dint of being excessively obvious; and here the physical oversight is precisely analogous with the moral inapprehension by which the intellect suffers to pass unnoticed those considerations which are too obtrusively and too palpably self-evident. But this is a point, it appears, somewhat above or beneath the understanding of the Prefect. He never once thought it probable, or possible, that the Minister had deposited the letter immediately beneath the nose of the whole world, by way of best preventing any portion of that world from perceiving it.

'But the more I reflected upon the daring, dashing, and discriminating ingenuity of D——; upon the fact that the document must always have been *at hand*, if he intended to use it to good purpose; and upon the decisive evidence, obtained by the Prefect, that it was not hidden within the limits of the dignitary's ordinary search—the more satisfied I became that, to conceal this letter, the Minister had resorted to the comprehensive and sagacious expedient of not attempting to conceal it at all.

'Full of these ideas, I prepared myself with a pair of green spectacles, and called one fine morning, quite by accident, at the Ministerial hotel. I found D—— at home, yawning, lounging, and dawdling, as usual, and pretending to be in the last extremity of *ennui*. He is, perhaps, the most really energetic human being now alive—but that is only when nobody sees him.

'To be even with him, I complained of my weak eyes, and lamented the necessity of the spectacles, under cover of which I cautiously and thoroughly surveyed the whole apartment, while seemingly intent only upon the conversation of my host.

'I paid especial attention to a large writing-table near which he sat, and upon which lay confusedly, some miscellaneous letters and other papers, with one or two musical instruments and a few books. Here, however, after a long and very deliberate scrutiny, I saw nothing to excite particular suspicion.

'At length my eyes, in going the circuit of the room, fell upon a trumpery filigree card-rack of pasteboard, that hung dangling by a dirty blue ribbon, from a little brass knob just beneath the middle of the mantelpiece. In this rack, which had three or four compartments, were five or six visiting cards and a solitary letter. This last was much soiled and crumpled. It was torn nearly in two, across the middle—as if a design, in the first instance, to tear it entirely up as worthless, had been altered, or stayed, in the second. It had a large black seal, bearing the D—— cipher *very* conspicuously, and was addressed, in a diminutive female hand, to D——, the Minister himself. It was thrust carelessly, and even, as it seemed, contemptuously, into one of the uppermost divisions of the rack.

'No sooner had I glanced at this letter than I concluded it to be that of which I was in search. To be sure, it was, to all appearance, radically different from the one of which the Prefect had read us so minute a description. Here the seal was large and black, with the D—— cipher; there it was small and red, with the ducal arms of the S—— family. Here, the address, to the Minister, was diminutive and feminine; there the superscription, to a certain royal personage, was markedly bold and decided; the size alone formed a point of correspondence. But, then, the *radicalness* of these differences, which was excessive; the dirt; the soiled and torn condition of the paper, so inconsistent with the *true* methodical habits of D——, and so suggestive of a design to delude the beholder into an idea of the worthlessness of the document;—these things, together with the hyperobtrusive situation of this document, full in the view of every visitor, and thus exactly in accordance with the conclusions to which I had previously arrived; these things, I say, were strongly corroborative of suspicion, in one who came with the intention to suspect.

'I protracted my visit as long as possible, and, while I maintained a most animated discussion with the Minister, upon a topic which I knew well had never failed to interest and excite him, I kept my attention really riveted upon the letter. In this examination, I committed to memory its external appearance and arrangement in the rack; and also fell, at length, upon a discovery which set at rest whatever trivial doubt I might have entertained. In scrutinizing the edges of the paper, I observed them to be more *chafed* than seemed necessary. They presented the *broken* appearance which is manifested when a stiff paper, having been once folded and pressed with a folder, is refolded in a reversed direction, in the same creases or edges which had formed the original fold. This discovery was sufficient. It was clear to me that the letter had been turned, as a glove, inside out, re-directed and re-sealed. I bade the Minister good-morning, and took my departure at once, leaving a gold snuff-box upon the table.

'The next morning I called for the snuff-box, when we resumed, quite eagerly, the conversation of the preceding day. While thus engaged, however, a loud report, as if of a pistol, was heard immediately beneath the windows of the hotel, and was succeeded by a series of fearful screams, and the shoutings of a terrified mob. D—— rushed to a casement, threw it open, and looked out. In the meantime I stepped to the card-rack, took the letter, put it in my pocket, and replaced it by a *facsimile*, (so far as regards externals) which I had carefully prepared at my lodgings—imitating the D—— cipher, very readily, by means of a seal formed of bread.

'The disturbance in the street had been occasioned by the frantic behaviour of a man with a musket. He had fired it among a crowd of women and children. It proved, however, to have been without ball, and the fellow was suffered to go his way as a lunatic or a drunkard. When he had gone, D—— came from the window, whither I had followed him immediately upon securing the object in view. Soon afterward I bade him farewell. The pretended lunatic was a man in my own pay.'

'But what purpose had you', I asked, 'in replacing the letter by a *facsimile*? Would it not have been better, at the first visit, to have seized it openly, and departed?'

'D——', replied Dupin, 'is a desperate man, and a man of nerve. His hotel, too, is not without attendants devoted to his interests. Had I made the wild attempt you suggest, I might never have left the Ministerial presence alive. The good people of Paris might have heard of me no more. But I had an object apart from these considerations. You know my political prepossessions. In this matter, I act as a partisan of the lady concerned. For eighteen months the Minister has had her in his power. She has now him in hers—since, being unaware that the letter is not in his possession, he will proceed with his exactions as if it was. Thus will he inevitably commit himself, at once, to his political destruction. His downfall, too, will not be more precipitate than awkward. It is all very well to talk about the *facilis descensus Averni*;[6] but in all kinds of climbing, as Catalani said of singing, it is far more easy to get up than to come down. In the present instance I have no sympathy—at least no pity—for him who descends. He is that *monstrum horrendum*, an unprincipled man of genius. I confess, however, that I should like very well to know the precise character of his thoughts, when, being defied by her whom the Prefect terms "a certain personage", he is reduced to opening the letter which I left for him in the card-rack.'

'How? did you put any thing particular in it?'

'Why—it did not seem altogether right to leave the interior blank—that would have been insulting. D——, at Vienna once, did me an evil turn, which I told him, quite good-humouredly, that I should remember. So, as I knew he would feel some curiosity in regard to the identity of the person who had outwitted him, I thought it

6 'the easy descent to Hell' as described by Virgil in *The Aeneid*

a pity not to give him a clue. He is well acquainted with my MS.,[7] and I just copied into the middle of the blank sheet the words—

"——Un dessein si funeste,
   S'il n'est digne d'Atrée, est digne de Thyeste."[8]

They are to be found in Crébillon's "Atrée".'

1845

7 MS—handwriting.
8 'A scheme so horrible, / If it is unworthy of Atreus, is worthy of Thyestes.' The allusion is to a particularly revolting episode of revenge in Greek mythology.

Herman Melville
1819–1891

A native of New York City, Herman Melville attended the Albany Academy and the Albany Classical School, then worked as a bank clerk and as a schoolteacher before deciding to seek his fortune at sea. He signed on a packet ship bound for Liverpool in 1839; the experience, however, proved disillusioning, and he went back to teaching. But in 1841 he returned to life on the sea, signing on the whaler Acushnet, bound for the South Seas. There he jumped ship to live in Tahiti before ultimately returning as a sailor to the United States.

In his fiction, Melville often sought to record and recreate his experiences at sea; among his novels of the sea are *White-Jacket* (1850), *Moby-Dick* (1851), and the posthumously published novella *Billy Budd* (1924). Deeply distressed, like his contemporary Walt Whitman, by the American Civil War, he turned to poetry to record his reflections in the collection *Battle-Pieces* (1866); it was the first of four volumes of poetry he would write.

In his own lifetime Melville's writings met with little critical and even less popular success, and he never made enough money to support himself and his family.

Bartleby, the Scrivener: A Story of Wall Street

I am a rather elderly man. The nature of my avocations, for the last thirty years, has brought me into more than ordinary contact with what would seem an interesting and somewhat singular set of men, of whom, as yet, nothing, that I know of, has ever been written—I mean, the law-copyists, or scriveners. I have known very many of them professionally and privately, and, if I pleased, could relate divers histories, at which good-natured gentlemen might smile, and sentimental souls might weep. But I waive the biographies of all other scriveners, for a few passages in the life of Bartleby, who was a scrivener, the strangest I ever saw, or heard of. While, of other law-copyists, I might write the complete life, of Bartleby nothing of that sort can be done. I believe that no materials exist for a full and satisfactory biography of this man. It is an irreparable loss to literature. Bartleby was one of those beings of whom nothing is ascertainable, except from the original sources, and, in his case, those are very small. What my own astonished eyes saw of Bartleby, *that* is all I know of him, except, indeed, one vague report, which will appear in the sequel.

Ere introducing the scrivener, as he first appeared to me, it is fit I make some mention of myself, my *employés*, my business, my chambers, and general surroundings; because some such description is indispensable to an adequate understanding of the chief character about to be presented. Imprimis: I am a man who, from his youth upwards, has been filled with a profound conviction that the easiest way of life is the best. Hence, though I belong to a profession proverbially energetic and nervous, even to turbulence, at times, yet nothing of that sort have I ever suffered to invade my peace. I am one of those unambitious lawyers who never address a jury, or in any way draw down public applause; but, in the cool tranquility of a snug retreat, do a snug business among rich men's bonds, and mortgages, and title deeds. All who know me, consider me an eminently *safe* man. The late John Jacob Astor, a personage little given to poetic enthusiasm, had no hesitation in pronouncing my first grand point to be prudence; my next, method. I do not speak it in vanity, but simply record the fact, that I was not unemployed in my profession by the late John Jacob Astor; a name which, I admit, I love to repeat; for it hath a rounded and orbicular sound to it, and rings like unto bullion. I will freely add, that I was not insensible to the late John Jacob Astor's good opinion.

Some time prior to the period at which this little history begins, my avocations had been largely increased. The good old office, now extinct in the State of New York, of a Master in Chancery, had been conferred upon me. It was not a very arduous office, but very pleasantly remunerative. I seldom lose my temper; much more seldom indulge in dangerous indignation at wrongs and outrages; but I must be permitted to be rash here and declare, that I consider the sudden and violent abrogation of the office of Master in Chancery, by the new Constitution, as a—premature act; inasmuch as I had counted upon a life-lease of the profits, whereas I only received those of a few short years. But this is by the way.

My chambers were upstairs, at No. — Wall Street. At one end, they looked upon the white wall of the interior of a spacious skylight shaft, penetrating the building from top to bottom.

This view might have been considered rather tame than otherwise, deficient in what landscape painters call 'life'. But, if so, the view from the other end of my chambers offered, at least, a contrast, if nothing more. In that direction, my windows commanded an unobstructed view of a lofty brick wall, black by age and everlasting shade; which wall required no spy-glass to bring out its lurking beauties, but, for the benefit of all near-sighted spectators, was pushed up to within ten feet of my window panes. Owing to the great height of the surrounding buildings, and my chambers being on the second floor, the interval between this wall and mine not a little resembled a huge square cistern.

At the period just preceding the advent of Bartleby, I had two persons as copyists in my employment, and a promising lad as an office-boy. First, Turkey; second,

Nippers; third, Ginger Nut. These may seem names, the like of which are not usually found in the Directory. In truth, they were nicknames, mutually conferred upon each other by my three clerks, and were deemed expressive of their respective persons or characters. Turkey was a short, pursy Englishman, of about my own age—that is, somewhere not far from sixty. In the morning, one might say, his face was of a fine florid hue, but after twelve o'clock, meridian—his dinner hour—it blazed like a grate full of Christmas coals; and continued blazing—but, as it were, with a gradual wane—till six o'clock, p.m., or thereabouts; after which, I saw no more of the proprietor of the face, which, gaining its meridian with the sun, seemed to set with it, to rise, culminate, and decline the following day, with the like regularity and undiminished glory. There are many singular coincidences I have known in the course of my life, not the least among which was the fact, that, exactly when Turkey displayed his fullest beams from his red and radiant countenance, just then, too, at that critical moment, began the daily period when I considered his business capacities as seriously disturbed for the remainder of the twenty-four hours. Not that he was absolutely idle, or averse to business then; far from it. The difficulty was, he was apt to be altogether too energetic. There was a strange, inflamed, flurried, flighty recklessness of activity about him. He would be incautious in dipping his pen into his inkstand. All his blots upon my documents were dropped there after twelve o'clock, meridian. Indeed, not only would he be reckless, and sadly given to making blots in the afternoon, but, some days, he went further, and was rather noisy. At such times, too, his face flamed with augmented blazonry, as if canned coal had been heaped on anthracite. He made an unpleasant racket with his chair; spilled his sand-box; in mending his pens, impatiently split them all to pieces, and threw them on the floor in a sudden passion; stood up, and leaned over his table, boxing his papers about in a most indecorous manner, very sad to behold in an elderly man like him. Nevertheless, as he was in many ways a most valuable person to me, and all the time before twelve o'clock, meridian, was the quickest, steadiest creature, too, accomplishing a great deal of work in a style not easily to be matched—for these reasons, I was willing to overlook his eccentricities, though, indeed, occasionally, I remonstrated with him. I did this very gently, however, because, though the civilest, nay, the blandest and most reverential of men in the morning, yet, in the afternoon, he was disposed, upon provocation, to be slightly rash with his tongue—in fact, insolent. Now, valuing his morning services as I did, and resolved not to lose them—yet, at the same time, made uncomfortable by his inflamed ways after twelve o'clock—and being a man of peace, unwilling by my admonitions to call forth unseemly retorts from him, I took upon me, one Saturday noon (he was always worse on Saturdays) to hint to him, very kindly, that, perhaps, now that he was growing old, it might be well to abridge his labours; in short, he need not come to my chambers after twelve o'clock, but, dinner over, had best go home to his lodgings, and rest himself till tea-time. But no; he insisted upon his afternoon devotions. His countenance became intolerably fervid, as he oratorically assured me—gesticulating with a long ruler at the other end of the room—that if his services in the morning were useful, how indispensable, then, in the afternoon?

'With submission, sir,' said Turkey, on this occasion, 'I consider myself your right-hand man. In the morning I but marshal and deploy my columns; but in the afternoon

I put myself at their head, and gallantly charge the foe, thus'—and he made a violent thrust with the ruler.

'But the blots, Turkey,' intimated I.

'True; but, with submission, sir, behold these hairs! I am getting old. Surely, sir, a blot or two of a warm afternoon is not to be severely urged against grey hairs. Old age—even if it blot the page—is honourable. With submission, sir, we *both* are getting old.'

This appeal to my fellow-feeling was hardly to be resisted. At all events, I saw that go he would not. So, I made up my mind to let him stay, resolving, nevertheless, to see to it that, during the afternoon, he had to do with my less important papers.

Nippers, the second on my list, was a whiskered, sallow, and, upon the whole, rather piratical-looking young man, of about five-and-twenty. I always deemed him the victim of two evil powers—ambition and indigestion. The ambition was evinced by a certain impatience of the duties of a mere copyist, an unwarrantable usurpation of strictly professional affairs, such as the original drawing up of legal documents. The indigestion seemed betokened in an occasional nervous testiness and grinning irritability, causing the teeth to audibly grind together over mistakes committed in copying; unnecessary maledictions, hissed, rather than spoken, in the heat of business; and especially by a continual discontent with the height of the table where he worked. Though of a very ingenious mechanical turn, Nippers could never get this table to suit him. He put chips under it, blocks of various sorts, bits of pasteboard, and at last went so far as to attempt an exquisite adjustment, by final pieces of folded blotting-paper. But no invention would answer. If, for the sake of easing his back, he brought the table lid at a sharp angle well up towards his chin, and wrote there like a man using the steep roof of a Dutch house for his desk, then he declared that it stopped the circulation in his arms. If now he lowered the table to his waistbands, and stooped over it in writing, then there was a sore aching in his back. In short, the truth of the matter was, Nippers knew not what he wanted. Or, if he wanted anything, it was to be rid of a scrivener's table altogether. Among the manifestations of his diseased ambition was a fondness he had for receiving visits from certain ambiguous-looking fellows in seedy coats, whom he called his clients. Indeed, I was aware that not only was he, at times, considerable of a ward-politician, but he occasionally did a little business at the Justices' courts, and was not unknown on the steps of the Tombs. I have good reason to believe, however, that one individual who called upon him at my chambers, and who, with a grand air, he insisted was his client, was no other than a dun, and the alleged title-deed, a bill. But, with all his failings, and the annoyances he caused me, Nippers, like his compatriot Turkey, was a very useful man to me; wrote a neat, swift hand; and, when he chose, was not deficient in a gentlemanly sort of deportment. Added to this, he always dressed in a gentlemanly sort of way; and so, incidentally, reflected credit upon my chambers. Whereas, with respect to Turkey, I had much ado to keep him from being a reproach to me. His clothes were apt to look oily, and smell of eating-houses. He wore his pantaloons very loose and baggy in summer. His coats were execrable; his hat not to be handled. But while the hat was a thing of indifference to me, inasmuch as his natural civility and deference, as a dependent Englishman, always led him to doff it the moment he entered the room, yet his coat was another matter. Concerning his coats, I reasoned with him; but with no effect. The truth was, I suppose, that a man with so small an income could not afford to sport such a lustrous face and a lustrous coat at one and the same time. As Nippers once observed, Turkey's money went chiefly for red ink. One winter day, I presented Turkey with a highly respectable-looking coat of my own—a padded grey coat, of a most comfortable warmth, and which buttoned straight up from the knee to the neck. I thought Turkey would appreciate the favour, and abate his rashness and obstreperousness of afternoons. But no; I verily believe that buttoning himself up in so downy and blanket-like a coat had a pernicious effect upon him—upon the same principle that too much oats are bad for horses. In fact, precisely as a rash, restive horse is said to feel his oats, so Turkey felt his coat. It made him insolent. He was a man whom prosperity harmed.

Though, concerning the self-indulgent habits of Turkey, I had my own private surmises, yet, touching Nippers, I was well persuaded that, whatever might be his faults in other respects, he was, at least, a temperate young man. But, indeed, nature herself seemed to have been his vintner, and, at his birth, charged him so thoroughly with an irritable, brandy-like disposition, that all subsequent potations were needless. When I consider how, amid the stillness of my chambers, Nippers would sometimes impatiently rise from his seat, and stopping over his table, spread his arms wide apart, seize the whole desk, and move it, and jerk it, with a grim, grinding motion on the floor, as if the table were a perverse voluntary agent, intent on thwarting and vexing him, I plainly perceive that, for Nippers, brandy-and-water were altogether superfluous.

It was fortunate for me that, owing to its peculiar cause—indigestion—the irritability and consequent nervousness of Nippers were mainly observable in the morning, while in the afternoon he was comparatively mild. So that, Turkey's paroxysms only coming on about twelve o'clock, I never had to do with their eccentricities at one time. Their fits relieved each other, like guards. When Nippers's was on, Turkey's was off; and *vice versa*. This was a good natural arrangement under the circumstances.

Ginger Nut, the third on my list, was a lad, some twelve years old. His father was a carman, ambitious of seeing his son on the bench instead of a cart, before he died. So he sent him to my office, as student at law, errand-boy, cleaner, and sweeper, at the rate of one dollar a week. He had a little desk to himself, but he did not use it much. Upon inspection, the drawer exhibited a great array of the shells of various sorts of nuts. Indeed, to this quick-witted youth, the whole noble science of the law was contained in a nut-shell. Not the least among the employments of Ginger Nut, as well as one which he discharged with the most alacrity, was his duty as cake and apple purveyor for Turkey and Nippers. Copying law papers being proverbially a dry, husky sort of business, my two scriveners were fain to moisten their mouths very often with Spitzenbergs, to be had at the numerous stalls nigh the Custom House and Post Office. Also, they sent Ginger Nut very frequently for that peculiar cake—small, flat, round, and very spicy—after which he had been named by them. Of a cold morning, when business was but dull, Turkey would gobble up scores of these cakes, as if they were mere wafers—indeed, they sell them at the rate of six or eight for a penny—the scrape of his pen blending with the crunching of the crisp particles in his mouth. Of

all the fiery afternoon blunders and flurried rashnesses of Turkey, was his once moistening a ginger-cake between his lips, and clapping it on to a mortgage, for a seal.
I came within an ace of dismissing him then. But he mollified me by making an oriental bow, and saying—

'With submission, sir, it was generous of me to find you in stationery on my account.'

Now my original business—that of a conveyancer and title hunter, and drawer-up
of recondite documents of all sorts—was considerably increased by receiving the
Master's office. There was now great work for scriveners. Not only must I push the
clerks already with me, but I must have additional help.

In answer to my advertisement, a motionless young man one morning stood upon
my office threshold, the door being open, for it was summer. I can see that figure
now—pallidly neat, pitiably respectable, incurably forlorn! It was Bartleby.

After a few words touching his qualifications, I engaged him, glad to have among
my corps of copyists a man of so singularly sedate an aspect, which I thought might
operate beneficially upon the flighty temper of Turkey, and the fiery one of Nippers.

I should have stated before that ground-glass folding doors divided my premises
into two parts, one of which was occupied by my scriveners, the other by myself.
According to my humour, I threw open these doors, or closed them. I resolved to
assign Bartleby a corner by the folding doors, but on my side of them, so as to have
this quiet man within easy call, in case any trifling thing was to be done. I placed his
desk close up to a small side-window in that part of the room, a window which originally had afforded a lateral view of certain grimy back-yards and bricks, but which,
owing to subsequent erections, commanded at present no view at all, though it gave
some light. Within three feet of the panes was a wall, and the light came down from
far above, between two lofty buildings, as from a very small opening in a dome. Still
further to a satisfactory arrangement, I procured a high green folding screen, which
might entirely isolate Bartleby from my sight, though not remove him from my voice.
And thus, in a manner, privacy and society were conjoined.

At first, Bartleby did an extraordinary quantity of writing. As if long famishing for
something to copy, he seemed to gorge himself on my documents. There was no pause
for digestion. He ran a day and night line copying by sunlight and by candle-light. I
should have been quite delighted with his application, had he been cheerfully industrious. But he wrote on silently, palely, mechanically.

It is, of course, an indispensable part of a scrivener's business to verify the accuracy of his copy, word by word. Where there are two or more scriveners in an office,
they assist each other in this examination, one reading from the copy, the other holding the original. It is a very dull, wearisome, and lethargic affair. I can readily imagine
that, to some sanguine temperaments, it would be altogether intolerable. For example,
I cannot credit that the mettlesome poet, Byron, would have contentedly sat down
with Bartleby to examine a law document of, say five hundred pages, closely written
in a crimpy hand.

Now and then, in the haste of business, it had been my habit to assist in comparing some brief document myself, calling Turkey or Nippers for this purpose. One
object I had, in placing Bartleby so handy to me behind the screen, was, to avail myself

of his services on such trivial occasions. It was on the third day, I think, of his being with me, and before any necessity had arisen for having his own writing examined, that, being much hurried to complete a small affair I had in hand, I abruptly called to Bartleby. In my haste and natural expectancy of instant compliance, I sat with my head bent over the original on my desk, and my right hand sideways, and somewhat nervously extended with the copy, so that, immediately upon emerging from his retreat, Bartleby might snatch it and proceed to business without the least delay.

In this very attitude did I sit when I called to him, rapidly stating what it was I wanted him to do—namely, to examine a small paper with me. Imagine my surprise, nay, my consternation, when, without moving from his privacy, Bartleby, in a singularly mild, firm voice, replied, 'I would prefer not to.'

I sat awhile in perfect silence, rallying my stunned faculties. Immediately it occurred to me that my ears had deceived me, or Bartleby had entirely misunderstood my meaning. I repeated my request in the clearest tone I could assume; but in quite as clear a one came the previous reply, 'I would prefer not to.'

'Prefer not to,' echoed I, rising in high excitement, and crossing the room with a stride. 'What do you mean? Are you moon-stuck? I want you to help me compare this sheet here—take it,' and I thrust it towards him.

'I would prefer not to,' said he.

I looked at him steadfastly. His face was leanly composed; his grey eye dimly calm. Not a wrinkle of agitation rippled him. Had there been the least uneasiness, anger, impatience, or impertinence in his manner; in other words, had there been anything ordinarily human about him, doubtless I should have violently dismissed him from the premises. But as it was, I should have soon thought of turning my pale plaster-of-paris bust of Cicero out of doors. I stood gazing at him awhile, as he went on with his own writing, and then reseated myself at my desk. This is very strange, thought I. What had one best do? But my business hurried me. I concluded to forget the matter for the present, reserving it for my future leisure. So, calling Nippers from the other room, the paper was speedily examined.

A few days after this, Bartleby concluded four lengthy documents, being quadruplicates of a week's testimony taken before me in my High Court of Chancery. It became necessary to examine them. It was an important suit, and great accuracy was imperative. Having all things arranged, I called Turkey, Nippers, and Ginger Nut, from the next room, meaning to place the four copies in the hands of my four clerks, while I should read from the original. Accordingly, Turkey, Nippers, and Ginger Nut had taken their seats in a row, each with his document in his hand, when I called to Bartleby to join this interesting group.

'Bartleby! quick, I am waiting.'

I heard a slow scrape of his chair legs on the uncarpeted floor, and soon he appeared standing at the entrance of his hermitage.

'What is wanted?' said he, mildly.

'The copies, the copies,' said I, hurriedly. 'We are going to examine them. There'—and I held towards him the fourth quadruplicate.

'I would prefer not to,' he said, and gently disappeared behind the screen.

For a few moments I was turned into a pillar of salt, standing at the head of my seated column of clerks. Recovering myself, I advanced towards the screen, and demanded the reason for such extraordinary conduct.

'*Why* do you refuse?'

'I would prefer not to.'

With any other man I should have flown outright into a dreadful passion, scorned all further words, and thrust him ignominiously from my presence. But there was something about Bartleby that not only strangely disarmed me, but, in a wonderful manner, touched and disconcerted me. I began to reason with him.

'These are your own copies we are about to examine. It is labour saving to you, because one examination will answer for your four papers. It is common usage. Every copyist is bound to help examine his copy. Is it not so? Will you not speak? Answer!'

'I prefer not to,' he replied in a flute-like tone. It seemed to me that, while I had been addressing him, he carefully revolved every statement that I made; fully comprehended the meaning; could not gainsay the irresistible conclusion; but, at the same time, some paramount consideration prevailed with him to reply as he did.

'You are decided, then, not to comply with my request—a request made according to common usage and common sense?'

He briefly gave me to understand, that on that point my judgment was sound. Yes: his decision was irreversible.

It is not seldom the case that, when a man is browbeaten in some unprecedented and violently unreasonable way, he begins to stagger in his own plainest faith. He begins, as it were, vaguely to surmise that, wonderful as it may be, all the justice and all the reason is on the other side. Accordingly, if any disinterested persons are present, he turns to them for some reinforcement for his own faltering mind.

'Turkey,' said I, 'what do you think of this? Am I not right?'

'With submission, sir,' said Turkey, in his blandest tone, 'I think you are.'

'Nippers,' said I, 'what do *you* think of it?'

'I think I should kick him out of the office.'

(The reader of nice perceptions will here perceive that, it being morning, Turkey's answer is couched in polite and tranquil terms, but Nippers's replies in ill-tempered ones. Or, to repeat a previous sentence, Nippers's ugly mood was on duty, and Turkey's off.)

'Ginger Nut,' said I, willing to enlist the smallest suffrage in my behalf, 'what do *you* think of it?'

'I think, sir, he's a little *luny*,' replied Ginger Nut, with a grin.

'You hear what they say,' said I, turning towards the screen, 'come forth and do your duty.'

But he vouchsafed no reply. I pondered a moment in sore perplexity. But once more business hurried me. I determined again to postpone the consideration of this dilemma to my future leisure. With a little trouble we made out to examine the papers without Bartleby, though at every page or two Turkey deferentially dropped his opinion, that this proceeding was quite out of the common; while Nippers, twitching in his chair with a dyspeptic nervousness, ground out, between his set teeth, occasional hissing maledictions against the stubborn oaf behind the screen. And for his (Nippers's) part, this was the first and the last time he would do another man's business without pay.

Meanwhile Bartleby sat in his hermitage, oblivious to everything but his own peculiar business there.

Some days passed, the scrivener being employed upon another lengthy work. His late remarkable conduct led me to regard his ways narrowly. I observed that he never went to dinner; indeed, that he never went anywhere. As yet I had never, of my personal knowledge, known him to be outside of my office. He was a perpetual sentry in the corner. At about eleven o'clock though, in the morning, I noticed that Ginger Nut would advance toward the opening in Bartleby's screen, as if silently beckoned thither by a gesture invisible to me where I sat. The boy would then leave the office, jingling a few pence, and reappear with a handful of ginger-nuts, which he delivered in the hermitage, receiving two of the cakes for his trouble.

He lives, then, on ginger-nuts, thought I; never eats a dinner, properly speaking; he must be a vegetarian, then, but no; he never eats even vegetables, he eats nothing but ginger-nuts. My mind then ran on in reveries concerning the probable effects upon the human constitution of living entirely on ginger-nuts. Ginger-nuts are so called, because they contain ginger as one of their peculiar constituents and the final flavoring one. Now, what was ginger? A hot, spicy thing. Was Bartleby hot and spicy? Not at all. Ginger, then, had no effect upon Bartleby. Probably he preferred it should have none.

Nothing so aggravates an earnest person as a passive resistance. If the individual so resisted be of a not inhumane temper, and the resisting one perfectly harmless in his passivity, then, in the better moods of the former, he will endeavour charitably to construe to his imagination what proves impossible to be solved by his judgment. Even so, for the most part, I regarded Bartleby and his ways. Poor fellow! thought I, he means no mischief; it is plain he intends no insolence; his aspect sufficiently evinces that his eccentricities are involuntary. He is useful to me. I can get along with him. If I turn him away, the chances are he will fall in with some less indulgent employer, and then he will be rudely treated, and perhaps driven forth miserably to starve. Yes. Here I can cheaply purchase a delicious self-approval. To befriend Bartleby; to humour him in his strange wilfulness, will cost me little or nothing, while I lay up in my soul what will eventually prove a sweet morsel for my conscience. But this mood was invariable with me. The passiveness of Bartleby sometimes irritated me. I felt strangely goaded on to encounter him in a new opposition—to elicit some angry spark from him answerable to my own. But, indeed, I might as well have essayed to strike fire with my knuckles against a bit of Windsor soap. But one afternoon the evil impulse in me mastered me, and the following little scene ensued:

'Bartleby,' said I, 'when those papers are all copied, I will compare them with you.'

'I would prefer not to.'

'How? Surely you do not mean to persist in that mulish vagary?'

No answer.

I threw open the folding doors near by, and, turning upon Turkey and Nippers, exclaimed:

'Bartleby a second time says, he won't examine his papers. What do you think of it, Turkey?'

It was afternoon, be it remembered. Turkey sat glowing like a brass boiler; his bald head steaming; his hands reeling among his blotted papers.

'Think of it?' roared Turkey. 'I think I'll just step behind his screen, and black his eyes for him!'

So saying, Turkey rose to his feet and threw his arms into a pugilistic position. He was hurrying away to make good his promise, when I detained him, alarmed at the effect of incautiously rousing Turkey's combativeness after dinner.

'Sit down, Turkey,' said I, 'and hear what Nippers has to say. What do you think of it, Nippers? Would I not be justified in immediately dismissing Bartleby?'

'Excuse me, that is for you to decide, sir. I think his conduct quite unusual, and, indeed, unjust, as regards to Turkey and myself. But it may only be a passing whim.'

'Ah,' exclaimed I, 'you have strangely changed your mind, then—you speak very gently of him now.'

'All beer,' cried Turkey; 'gentleness is effects of beer—Nippers and I dined together today. You see how gentle I am, sir. Shall I go and black his eyes?'

'You refer to Bartleby, I suppose. No, not today, Turkey,' I replied; 'pray, put up your fists.'

I closed the doors, and again advanced towards Bartleby. I felt additional incentives tempting me to my fate. I burned to be rebelled against again. I remembered that Bartleby never left the office.

'Bartleby,' said I, 'Ginger Nut is away; just step around to the Post Office, won't you?' (it was but a three minutes' walk) 'and see if there is anything for me.'

'I would prefer not to.'

'You *will* not?'

'I *prefer* not.'

I staggered to my desk, and sat there in a deep study. My blind inveteracy returned. Was there any other thing in which I could procure myself to be ignominiously repulsed by this lean, penniless wight?—my hired clerk? What added thing is there, perfectly reasonable, that he will be sure to refuse to do?

'Bartleby!'

No answer.

'Bartleby,' in a louder tone.

No answer.

'Bartleby,' I roared.

Like a very ghost, agreeably to the laws of magical invocation, at the third summons, he appeared at the entrance of his hermitage.

'Go to the next room, and tell Nippers to come to me.'

'I prefer not to,' he respectfully and slowly said, and mildly disappeared.

'Very good, Bartleby,' said I, in a quiet sort of serenely severe self-possessed tone, intimating the unalterable purpose of some terrible retribution very close at hand. At the moment I half intended something of the kind. But upon the whole, as it was drawing towards my dinner-hour, I thought it best to put on my hat and walk home for the day, suffering much from perplexity and distress of mind.

Shall I acknowledge it? The conclusion of this whole business was, that it soon became a fixed fact of my chambers, that a pale young scrivener, by the name of Bartleby, had a desk there; that he copied for me at the usual rate of four cents a folio (one hundred words); but he was permanently exempt from examining the work done by him, that duty being transferred to Turkey and Nippers, out of compliment, doubtless, to their superior acuteness; moreover, said Bartleby was never, on any account, to be dispatched on the most trivial errand of any sort; and that even if entreated to take upon him such a matter, it was generally understood that he would 'prefer not to'—in other words, that he would refuse point-blank.

As days passed on, I became considerably reconciled to Bartleby. His steadiness, his freedom from all dissipation, his incessant industry (except when he chose to throw himself into a standing reverie behind his screen) his great stillness, his unalterableness of demeanour under all circumstances, made him a valuable acquisition. One prime thing was this—*he was always there*—first in the morning, continually through the day, and the last at night. I had a singular confidence in his honesty. I felt my most precious papers perfectly safe in his hands. Sometimes, to be sure, I could not, for the very soul of me, avoid falling into sudden spasmodic passions with him. For it was exceeding difficult to bear in mind all the time those strange peculiarities, privileges, and unheard-of exemptions, forming the tacit stipulations on Bartleby's part under which he remained in my office. Now and then, in the eagerness of dispatching pressing business, I would inadvertently summon Bartleby, in a short, rapid tone, to put his finger, say, on the incipient tie of a bit of red tape with which I was about compressing some papers. Of course, from behind the screen the usual answer, 'I prefer not to,' was sure to come; and then, how could a human creature, with the common infirmities of our nature, refrain from bitterly exclaiming upon such perverseness—such unreasonableness? However, every added repulse of this sort which I received only tended to lessen the probability of my repeating the inadvertence.

Here it must be said, that, according to the custom of most legal gentlemen occupying chambers in densely populated law buildings, there were several keys to my door. One was kept by a woman residing in the attic, which person weekly scrubbed and daily swept and dusted my apartments. Another was kept by Turkey for convenience sake. The third I sometimes carried in my own pocket. The fourth I knew not who had.

Now, one Sunday morning I happened to go to Trinity Church, to hear a celebrated preacher, and finding myself rather early on the ground I thought I would walk round to my chambers for a while. Luckily I had my key with me; but upon applying it to the lock, I found it resisted by something inserted from the inside. Quite surprised, I called out; when to my consternation a key was turned from within; and thrusting his lead visage at me, and holding the door ajar, the apparition of Bartleby appeared, in his shirt-sleeves, and otherwise in a strangely tattered déshabillé, saying quietly that he was sorry, but he was deeply engaged just then, and—preferred not admitting me at present. In a brief word or two, he moreover added, that perhaps I had better walk round the block two or three times, and by that time he would probably have concluded his affairs.

Now, the utterly unsurmised appearance of Bartleby, tenanting my law-chambers of a Sunday morning, with his cadaverously gentlemanly *nonchalance*, yet withal firm and self-possessed, had such a strange effect upon me, that incontinently I slunk away from my own door, and did as desired. But not without sundry twinges of impotent rebellion against the mild effrontery of this unaccountable scrivener. Indeed, it was his wonderful mildness chiefly, which not only disarmed me, but unmanned me, as it were. For I consider that one, for the time, is a sort of unmanned when he tranquilly permits his hired clerk to dictate to him, and order him away from his own premises. Furthermore, I was full of uneasiness as to what Bartleby could possibly be doing in my office in his shirt-sleeves, and in an otherwise dismantled condition of a Sunday morning. Was anything amiss going on? Nay, that was out of the question. It was not to be thought of for a moment that Bartleby was an immoral person. But what could he be doing there—copying? Nay again, whatever might be his eccentricities, Bartleby was an eminently decorous person. He would be the last man to sit down to his desk in any state approaching to nudity. Besides, it was Sunday; and there was something about Bartleby that forbade the supposition that he would by any secular occupation violate the proprieties of the day.

Nevertheless, my mind was not pacified; and full of a restless curiosity, at last I returned to the door. Without hindrance I inserted my key, opened it, and entered. Bartleby was not to be seen. I looked round anxiously, peeped behind his screen; but it was very plain that he was gone. Upon more closely examining the place, I surmised that for an indefinite period Bartleby must have ate, dressed, and slept in my office, and that too without plate, mirror, or bed. The cushioned seat of a rickety old sofa in one corner bore the faint impress of a lean, reclining form. Rolled away under his desk, I found a blanket; under the empty grate, a blacking box and brush; on a chair, a tin basin, with soap and a ragged towel; in a newspaper a few crumbs of ginger-nuts and a morsel of cheese. Yes, thought I, it is evident enough that Bartleby had been making his home here, keeping bachelor's hall all by himself. Immediately then the thought came sweeping across me, what miserable friendlessness and loneliness are here revealed? His poverty is great; but his solitude, how horrible! Think of it. Of a Sunday, Wall Street is deserted as Petra; and every night of every day it is an emptiness. This building, too, which of weekdays hums with industry and life, at nightfall echoes with sheer vacancy, and all through Sunday is forlorn. And there Bartleby makes his home; sole spectator of a solitude which he has seen all populous—a sort of innocent and transformed Marius brooding among the ruins of Carthage!

For the first time in my life a feeling of overpowering stinging melancholy seized me. Before, I had never experienced aught but a not unpleasing sadness. The bond of a common humanity now drew me irresistibly to gloom. A fraternal melancholy! For both I and Bartleby were sons of Adam. I remembered the bright silks and sparkling faces I had seen that day, in gala trim, swan-like sailing down the Mississippi of Broadway; and I contrasted them with the pallid copyist, and thought to myself, Ah, happiness courts the light, so we deem the world is gay; but misery hides aloof, so we deem that misery there is none. These sad fancyings—chimeras, doubtless of a sick and silly brain—led on to other and more special thoughts, concerning the eccentricities of Bartleby. Presentiments of strange discoveries hovered round me. The scrivener's pale form appeared to me laid out, among uncaring strangers, in its shivering winding-sheet.

Suddenly I was attracted by Bartleby's closed desk, the key in open sight left in the lock.

I mean no mischief, seek the gratification of no heartless curiosity, thought I; besides, the desk is mine, and its contents, too, so I will make bold to look within. Everything was methodically arranged, the papers smoothly placed. The pigeon-holes were deep, and removing the files of documents, I groped into their recesses. Presently I felt something there, and dragged it out. It was an old bandanna handkerchief, heavy and knotted. I opened it, and saw it was a saving's bank.

I now recalled all the quiet mysteries which I had noted in the man. I remembered that he never spoke but to answer; that, though at intervals he had considerable time to himself, yet I had never seen him reading—no, not even a newspaper; that for long periods he would stand looking out, at his pale window behind the screen, upon the dead brick wall; I was quite sure he never visited any refectory or eating-house; while his pale face clearly indicated that he never drank beer like Turkey, or tea and coffee even, like other men; that he never went anywhere in particular that I could learn; never went out for a walk, unless, indeed, that was the case at present; that he had declined telling who he was or whence he came, or whether he had any relatives in the world; that though so thin and pale, he never complained of ill-health. And more than all, I remembered a certain unconscious air of pallid—how shall I call it?—of pallid haughtiness, say, or rather an austere reserve about him which had positively awed me into my tame compliance with his eccentricities, when I had feared to ask him to do the slightest incidental thing for me, even though I might know, from his long-continued motionlessness, that behind his screen he must be standing in one of those dead-wall reveries of his.

Revolving all these things, and coupling them with the recently discovered fact, that he made my office his constant abiding place and home, and not forgetful of his morbid moodiness; revolving all these things, a prudential feeling began to steal over me. My first emotions had been those of pure melancholy and sincerest pity; but just in proportion as the forlornness of Bartleby grew and grew to my imagination, did that same melancholy merge into fear, that pity into repulsion. So true it is, and so terrible, too, that up to a certain point the thought or sight of misery enlists our best affections; but, in certain special cases, beyond that point it does not. They err who would assert that invariably this is owing to the inherent selfishness of the human heart. It rather proceeds from a certain hopelessness of remedying excessive and organic ill. To a sensitive being, pity is not seldom pain. And when at last it is perceived that such pity cannot lead to effectual succour, common sense bids the soul be rid of it. What I saw that morning persuaded me that the scrivener was the victim of innate and incurable disorder. I might give alms to his body; but his body did not pain him; it was his soul that suffered, and his soul I could not reach.

I did not accomplish the purpose of going to Trinity Church that morning. Somehow, the things I had seen disqualified me for the time from church-going. I walked homeward, thinking what I would do with Bartleby. Finally, I resolved upon this—I would put certain calm questions to him the next morning, touching his history, etc., and if he declined to answer them openly and unreservedly (and I supposed he would prefer not), then to give him a twenty dollar bill over and above whatever I might owe him, and tell him his services are no longer required; but that if in any other way I could assist him, I would be happy to do so, especially if he desired to return to his native place, wherever that might be, I would willingly help to defray the expenses. Moreover, if, after reaching home, he found himself at any time in want of aid, a letter from him would be sure of reply.

The next morning came.

'Bartleby,' said I, gently calling to him behind his screen.

No reply.

'Bartleby,' said I, in a still gentler tone, 'come here; I am not going to ask you to do anything you would prefer not to do—I simply wish to speak to you.'

Upon this he noiselessly slid into view.

'Will you tell me, Bartleby, where you were born?'

'I would prefer not to.'

'Will you tell me *anything* about yourself?'

'I would prefer not to.'

'But what reasonable objection can you have to speak to me? I feel friendly towards you.'

He did not look at me while I spoke, but kept his glance fixed upon my bust of Cicero, which, as I then sat, was directly behind me, some six inches above my head.

'What is your answer, Bartleby?' said I, after waiting a considerable time for a reply, during which his countenance remained immovable, only there was the faintest conceivable tremor of the white attenuated mouth.

'At present I prefer to give no answer,' he said, and retired into his hermitage.

It was rather weak of me I confess, but his manner, on this occasion, nettled me. Not only did there seem to lurk in it a certain calm disdain, but his perverseness seemed ungrateful, considering the undeniable good usage and indulgence he had received from me.

Again I sat ruminating what I should do. Mortified as I was at his behaviour, and resolved as I had been to dismiss him when I entered my office, nevertheless I strangely felt something superstitious knocking at my heart, and forbidding me to carry out my purpose, and denouncing me for a villain if I dared to breathe one bitter word against this forlornest of mankind. At last, familiarly drawing my chair behind his screen, I sat down and said: 'Bartleby, never mind, then, about revealing your history; but let me entreat you, as a friend, to comply as far as may be with the usages of this office. Say now, you will help to examine papers tomorrow or next day: in short, say now, that in a day or two you will begin to be a little reasonable:—say so, Bartleby.'

'At present I would prefer not to be a little reasonable,' was his mildly cadaverous reply.

Just then the folding doors opened, and Nippers approached. He seemed suffering from an unusually bad night's rest, induced by severer indigestion than common. He overhead those final words of Bartleby.

'*Prefer not*, eh?' gritted Nippers—'I'd *prefer* him, if I were you, sir,' addressing me—'I'd *prefer* him; I'd give him preferences, the stubborn mule! What is it, sir, pray, that he *prefers* not to do now?'

Bartleby moved not a limb.

'Mr Nippers,' said I, 'I'd prefer that you would withdraw for the present.'

Somehow, of late, I had got into the way of involuntarily using this word 'prefer' upon all sorts of not exactly suitable occasions. And I trembled to think that my contact with the scrivener had already and seriously affected me in a mental way. And what further and deeper aberration might it not yet produce? This apprehension had not been without efficacy in determining me to summary measures.

As Nippers, looking very sour and sulky, was departing, Turkey blandly and deferentially approached.

'With submission, sir,' said he, 'yesterday I was thinking about Bartleby here, and I think that if he would but prefer to take a quart of good ale every day it would do much towards mending him, and enabling him to assist in examining his papers.'

'So you have got the word, too,' said I, slightly excited.

'With submission, what word, sir?' asked Turkey, respectfully crowding himself into the contracted space behind the screen, and by so doing, making me jostle the scrivener. 'What word, sir?'

'I would prefer to be left alone here,' said Bartleby, as if offended at being mobbed in his privacy.

'*That's* the word, Turkey,' said I—'*that's* it.'

'Oh, *prefer*? oh yes—queer word. I never use it myself. But, sir, as I was saying, if he would but prefer—'

'Turkey,' interrupted I, 'you will please withdraw.'

'Oh certainly, sir, if you prefer that I should.'

As he opened the folding door to retire, Nippers at his desk caught glimpse of me, and asked whether I would prefer to have certain paper copied on blue paper or white. He did not in the least roguishly accent the word 'prefer'. It was plain that it involuntarily rolled from his tongue. I thought to myself, surely I must get rid of a demented man, who already has in some degree turned the tongues, if not the heads of myself and clerks. But I thought it prudent not to break the dismission at once.

The next day I noticed that Bartleby did nothing but stand at his window in his dead-wall revery. Upon asking him why he did not write, he said that he had decided upon doing no more writing.

'Why, how now? what next?' exclaimed I, 'do no more writing?'

'No more.'

'And what is the reason?'

'Do you not see the reason for yourself?' he indifferently replied.

I looked steadfastly at him, and perceived that his eyes looked dull and glazed. Instantly it occurred to me, that his unexampled diligence in copying by his dim window for the first few weeks of his stay with me might have temporarily impaired his vision.

I was touched. I said something in condolence with him. I hinted that of course he did wisely in abstaining from writing for a while; and urged him to embrace that opportunity of taking wholesome exercise in the open air. This, however, he did not do. A few days after this, my other clerks being absent, and being in a great hurry to dispatch certain letters by the mail, I thought that, having nothing else earthly to do, Bartleby would surely be less inflexible than usual, and carry these letters to the post office. But he blankly declined. So, much to my inconvenience, I went myself.

Still added days went by. Whether Bartleby's eyes improved or not, I could not say. To all appearance, I thought they did. But when I asked him if they did, he vouchsafed no answer. At all events, he would do no copying. At last, in reply to my urgings, he informed me that he had permanently given up copying.

'What!' exclaimed I; 'suppose your eyes should get entirely well—better than ever before—would you copy then?'

'I have given up copying,' he answered, and slid aside.

He remained as ever, a fixture in my chamber. Nay—if that were possible—he became still more of a fixture than before. What was to be done? He would do nothing in the office; why should he stay there? In plain fact, he had now become a millstone to me, not only useless as a necklace, but afflictive to bear. Yet I was sorry for him. I speak less than truth when I say that, on his own account, he occasioned me uneasiness. If he would but have named a single relative or friend, I would instantly have written, and urged their taking the poor fellow away to some convenient retreat. But he seemed alone, absolutely alone in the universe. A bit of wreck in the mid-Atlantic. At length, necessities connected with my business tyrannized over all other considerations. Decently as I could, I told Bartleby that in six days' time he must unconditionally leave the office. I warned him to take measures, in the interval, for procuring some other abode. I offered to assist him in this endeavour, if he himself would but take the first step towards a removal. 'And when you finally quit me, Bartleby,' added I, 'I shall see that you go not away entirely unprovided. Six days from this hour, remember.'

At the expiration of that period, I peeped behind the screen, and lo! Bartleby was there.

I buttoned up my coat, balanced myself; advanced slowly towards him, touched his shoulder, and said, 'The time has come; you must quit this place; I am sorry for you; here is money; but you must go.'

'I would prefer not,' he replied, with his back still towards me.

'You *must*.'

He remained silent.

Now I had an unbounded confidence in this man's common honesty. He had frequently restored to me sixpences and shillings carelessly dropped upon the floor, for I am apt to be very reckless in such shirt-button affairs. The proceeding, then, which followed will not be deemed extraordinary.

'Bartleby,' said I, 'I owe you twelve dollars on account; here are thirty-two, the odd twenty are yours—Will you take it?' and I handed the bills towards him.

But he made no motion.

'I will leave them here, then,' putting them under a weight on the table. Then taking my hat and cane and going to the door, I tranquilly turned and added—'After you have removed your things from these offices, Bartleby, you will of course lock the door—since everyone is now gone for the day but you—and if you please, slip your key underneath the mat, so that I may have it in the morning. I shall not see you again; so good-bye to you. If, hereafter, in your new place of abode, I can be of any service to you, do not fail to advise me by letter. Good-bye, Bartleby, and fare you well.'

But he answered not a word; like the last column of some ruined temple, he remained standing mute and solitary in the middle of the otherwise deserted room.

As I walked home in a pensive mood, my vanity got the better of my pity. I could not but highly plume myself on my masterly management in getting rid of Bartleby. Masterly I call it, and such it must appear to any dispassionate thinker. The beauty of my procedure seemed to consist in its perfect quietness. There was no vulgar bullying, no bravado of any sort, no choleric hectoring, and striding to and fro across the apartment, jerking out vehement commands for Bartleby to bundle himself off with his beggarly traps. Nothing of the kind. Without loudly bidding Bartleby depart—as an inferior genius might have done—I *assumed* the ground that depart he must; and upon that assumption built all I had to say. The more I thought over my procedure, the more I was charmed with it. Nevertheless, next morning, upon awakening, I had my doubts—I had somehow slept off the fumes of vanity. One of the coolest and wisest hours a man has, is just after he awakes in the morning. My procedure seemed as sagacious as ever—but only in theory. How it would prove in practice—there was the rub. It was truly a beautiful thought to have assumed Bartleby's departure; but, after all, that assumption was simply my own, and none of Bartleby's. The great point was, not whether I had assumed that he would quit me, but whether he would prefer so to do. He was more a man of preferences than assumptions.

After breakfast, I walked downtown, arguing the probabilities *pro* and *con*. One moment I thought it would prove a miserable failure, and Bartleby would be found all alive at my office as usual; the next moment it seemed certain that I should find his chair empty. And so I kept veering about. At the corner of Broadway and Canal Street, I saw quite an excited group of people standing in earnest conversation.

'I'll take odds he doesn't,' said a voice as I passed.

'Doesn't go?—done!' said I, 'put up your money.'

I was instinctively putting my hand in my pocket to produce my own, when I remembered that this was an election day. The words I had overheard bore no reference to Bartleby, but to the success or non-success of some candidate for the mayoralty. In my intent frame of mind, I had, as it were, imagined that all Broadway shared in my excitement, and were debating the same question with me. I passed on, very thankful that the uproar of the street screened my momentary absent-mindedness.

As I had intended, I was earlier than usual at my office door. I stood listening for a moment. All was still. He must be gone. I tried the knob. The door was locked. Yes, my procedure had worked to a charm; he indeed must be vanished. Yet a certain melancholy mixed with this: I was almost sorry for my brilliant success. I was fumbling under the door mat for the key, which Bartleby was to have left there for me, when accidentally my knee knocked against a panel, producing a summoning sound, and in response a voice came to me from within— 'Not yet; I am occupied.'

It was Bartleby.

I was thunderstruck. For an instant I stood like the man who, pipe in mouth, was killed one cloudless afternoon long ago in Virginia, by summer lightning; at his own warm open window he was killed, and remained leaning out there upon the dreamy afternoon, till someone touched him, when he fell.

'Not gone!' I murmured at last. But again obeying that wondrous ascendancy which the inscrutable scrivener had over me, and from which ascendancy, for all my chafing, I could not completely escape, I slowly went downstairs and out into the street, and while walking round the block, considered what I should next do in this unheard-of perplexity. Turn the man out by an actual thrusting I could not; to drive him away by calling him hard names would not do; calling in the police was an unpleasant idea; and yet, permit him to enjoy his cadaverous triumph over me—this, too, I could not think of. What was to be done? or, if nothing could be done, was there anything further that I could *assume* in the matter? Yes, as before I had prospectively assumed that Bartleby would depart, so now I might retrospectively assume that departed he was. In the legitimate carrying out of this assumption, I might enter my office in a great hurry, and pretending not to see Bartleby at all, walk straight against him as if he were air. Such a proceeding would in a singular degree have the appearance of a home-thrust. It was hardly possible that Bartleby could withstand such an application of the doctrine of assumptions. But upon second thoughts the success of the plan seemed rather dubious. I resolved to argue the matter over with him again.

'Bartleby,' said I, entering the office, with a quietly severe expression, 'I am seriously displeased. I am pained, Bartleby. I had thought better of you. I had imagined you of such a gentlemanly organization, that in any delicate dilemma a slight hint would suffice—in short, an assumption. But it appears I am deceived. Why,' I added, unaffectedly starting, 'you have not even touched that money yet,' pointing to it, just where I had left it the evening previous.

He answered nothing.

'Will you, or will you not, quit me?' I now demanded in a sudden passion, advancing close to him.

'I would prefer *not* to quit you,' he replied, gently emphasizing the *not*.

'What earthly right have you to stay here? Do you pay rent? Do you pay taxes? Or is this property yours?'

He answered nothing.

'Are you ready to go on and write now? Are your eyes recovered? Could you copy a small paper for me this morning? or help examine a few lines? or step round to the post office? In a word, will you do anything at all, to give a colouring to your refusal to depart the premises?'

He silently returned into his hermitage.

I was now in such a state of nervous resentment that I thought it but prudent to check myself at present from further demonstrations. Bartleby and I were alone.

I remembered the tragedy of the unfortunate Adams and the still more unfortunate Colt in the solitary office of the latter; and how poor Colt, being dreadfully incensed by Adams, and imprudently permitting himself to get wildly excited, was at unawares hurried into his fatal act—an act which certainly no man could possibly deplore more than the actor himself. Often it had occurred to me in my ponderings upon the subject that had that altercation taken place in the public street, or at a private residence, it would not have terminated as it did. It was the circumstances of being alone in a solitary office, upstairs, or a building entirely unhallowed by humanizing domestic associations—an uncarpeted office, doubtless, of a dusty, haggard sort of appearance—this it must have been, which greatly helped to enhance the irritable desperation of the harmless Colt.

But when this old Adam of resentment rose in me and tempted me concerning Bartleby, I grappled him and threw him. How? Why, simply by recalling the divine injunction: 'A new commandment give I unto you, that ye love one another.' Yes, this it was that saved me. Aside from higher considerations, charity often operates as a vastly wise and prudent principle—a great safeguard to its possessor. Men have committed murder for jealousy's sake, and anger's sake, and hatred's sake, and selfishness' sake, and spiritual pride's sake; but no man, that ever I heard of, ever committed a diabolical murder for sweet charity's sake. Mere self-interest, then, if no better motive can be enlisted, should, especially with high-tempered men, prompt all beings to charity and philanthropy. At any rate, upon the occasion in question, I strove to drown my exasperated feelings towards the scrivener by benevolently construing his conduct. Poor fellow, poor fellow! thought I, he don't mean anything; and besides, he has seen hard times, and ought to be indulged.

I endeavoured, also, immediately to occupy myself, and at the same time to comfort my despondency. I tried to fancy, that in the course of the morning, at such time as might prove agreeable to him, Bartleby, of his own free accord, would emerge from his hermitage and take up some decided line of march in the direction of the door. But no. Half-past twelve o'clock came; Turkey began to glow in the face, overturn his inkstand, and become generally obstreperous; Nippers abated down into quietude and courtesy; Ginger Nut munched his noon apple; and Bartleby remained standing at his window in one of his profoundest dead-wall reveries. Will it be credited? Ought I to acknowledge it? That afternoon I left the office without saying one further word to him.

Some days now passed, during which, at leisure intervals, I looked a little into 'Edwards on the Will', and 'Priestley on Necessity'. Under the circumstances, those books induced a salutary feeling. Gradually I slid into the persuasion that these troubles of mine, touching the scrivener, had been all predestinated from eternity, and Bartleby was billeted upon me for some mysterious purpose of an all-wise Providence, which it was not for a mere mortal like me to fathom. Yes, Bartleby, stay there behind your screen, thought I; I shall persecute you no more; you are harmless and noiseless as any of these old chairs; in short, I never feel so private as when I know you are here. At last I see it, I feel it; I penetrate to the predestinated purpose of my life. I am content. Others may have loftier parts to enact; but my mission in this world, Bartleby, is to furnish you with office-room for such period as you may see fit to remain.

I believe that this wise and blessed frame of mind would have continued with me, had it not been for the unsolicited and uncharitable remarks obtruded upon me by my professional friends who visited the rooms. But thus it often is, that the constant friction of illiberal minds wears out at last the best resolves of the more generous. Though to be sure, when I reflected upon it, it was not strange that people entering my office should be struck by the peculiar aspect of the unaccountable Bartleby, and so be tempted to throw out some sinister observations concerning him. Sometimes an attorney, having business with me, and calling at my office, and finding no one but the scrivener there, would undertake to obtain some sort of precise information from him touching my whereabouts; but without heeding his idle talk, Bartleby would remain standing immovable in the middle of the room. So after contemplating him in that position for a time, the attorney would depart, no wiser than he came.

Also, when a reference was going on, and the room full of lawyers and witnesses, and business driving fast, some deeply occupied legal gentleman present, seeing Bartleby wholly unemployed, would request him to run round to his (the legal gentleman's) office and fetch some papers for him. Thereupon, Bartleby would tranquilly decline, and yet remain idle as before. Then the lawyer would give a great stare, and turn to me. And what could I say? At last I was made aware that all through the circle of my professional acquaintance, a whisper of wonder was running round, having reference to the strange creature I kept at my office. This worried me very much. And as the idea came upon me of his possibly turning out a long-lived man, and keep occupying my chambers, and denying my authority; and perplexing my visitors; and scandalizing my professional reputation; and casting a general gloom over the premises; keeping soul and body together to the last upon his savings (for doubtless he spent but half a dime a day), and in the end perhaps outlive me, and claim possession of my office by right of his perpetual occupancy: as all these dark anticipations crowded upon me more and more, and my friends continually intruded their relentless remarks upon the apparition in my room; a great change was wrought in me. I resolved to gather all my faculties together, and forever rid me of this intolerable incubus.

Ere revolving any complicated project, however, adapted to this end, I first simply suggested to Bartleby the propriety of his permanent departure. In a calm and serious tone, I commended the idea to his careful and mature consideration. But, having taken three days to meditate upon it, he apprised me, that his original determination remained the same; in short, that he still preferred to abide with me.

What shall I do? I now said to myself, buttoning up my coat to the last button. What shall I do? what ought I to do? What does conscience say I *should* do with this man, or, rather, ghost. Rid myself of him, I must; go, he shall. But how? You will not thrust him, the poor, pale, passive mortal—you will not thrust such a helpless creature out of your door? you will not dishonour yourself by such cruelty? No, I will not, I cannot do that. Rather would I let him live and die here, and then mason up his remains in the wall. What, then, will you do? For all your coaxing, he will not budge. Bribes he leaves under your own paper-weight on your table; in short, it is quite plain that he prefers to cling to you.

Then something severe, something unusual must be done. What! surely you will not have him collared by a constable, and commit his innocent pallor to the common jail? And upon what ground could you procure such a thing to be done?—a vagrant, is he? What! he a vagrant, a wanderer, who refuses to budge? It is because he will *not* be a vagrant, then, that you seek to count him *as* a vagrant. That is too absurd. No visible means of support: there I have him. Wrong again: for indubitably he *does* support himself, and that is the only unanswerable proof that any man can show of his possessing the means so to do. No more then. Since he will not quit me, I must quit him. I will change my offices; I will move elsewhere, and give him fair notice, that if I find him on my new premises I will then proceed against him as a common trespasser.

Acting accordingly, next day I thus addressed him: 'I find these chambers too far from the City Hall; the air is unwholesome. In a word, I propose to remove my offices next week, and shall no longer require your services. I tell you this now, in order that you may seek another place.'

He made no reply, and nothing more was said.

On the appointed day I engaged carts and men, proceeded to my chambers, and, having but little furniture, everything was removed in a few hours. Throughout, the scrivener remained standing behind the screen, which I directed to be removed the last thing. It was withdrawn; and, being folded up like a huge folio, left him the motionless occupant of a naked room. I stood in the entry watching him a moment, while something from within me upbraided me.

I re-entered, with my hand in my pocket—and—and my heart in my mouth.

'Good-bye, Bartleby; I am going—good-bye, and God some way bless you; and take that,' slipping something in his hand. But it dropped upon the floor, and then—strange to say—I tore myself from him whom I had so longed to be rid of.

Established in my new quarters, for a day or two I kept the door locked, and started at every footfall in the passages. When I returned to my rooms, after any little absence, I would pause at the threshold for an instant, and attentively listen, ere applying my key. But these fears were needless. Bartleby never came nigh me.

I thought all was going well, when a perturbed-looking stranger visited me, inquiring whether I was the person who had recently occupied rooms at No. — Wall Street.

Full of forebodings, I replied that I was.

'Then, sir,' said the stranger, who proved a lawyer, 'you are responsible for the man you left there. He refuses to do any copying; he refuses to do anything; he says he prefers not to; and he refuses to quit the premises.'

'I am very sorry, sir,' said I, with assumed tranquility, but an inward tremor, 'but, really, the man you allude to is nothing to me—he is no relation or apprentice of mine, that you should hold me responsible for him.'

'In mercy's name, who is he?'

'I certainly cannot inform you. I know nothing about him. Formerly I employed him as a copyist; but he has done nothing for me now for some time past.'

'I shall settle him, then—good morning, sir.'

Several days passed, and I heard nothing more; and, though I often felt a charitable prompting to call at the place and see poor Bartleby, yet a certain squeamishness, of I know not what, withheld me.

All is over with him, by this time, thought I, at last, when, through another week, no further intelligence reached me. But, coming to my room the day after, I found several persons waiting at my door in a high state of nervous excitement.

'That's the man—here he comes,' cried the foremost one, whom I recognized as the lawyer who had previously called upon me alone.

'You must take him away, sir, at once,' cried a portly person among them, advancing upon me, and whom I knew to be the landlord of No. — Wall Street. 'These gentlemen, my tenants, cannot stand it any longer; Mr B——', pointing to the lawyer, 'has turned him out of his room, and he now persists in haunting the building generally, sitting upon the banisters of the stairs by day, and sleeping in the entry by night. Everybody is concerned; clients are leaving the offices; some fears are entertained of a mob; something you must do, and that without delay.'

Aghast at this torrent, I fell back before it, and would fain have locked myself in my new quarters. In vain I persisted that Bartleby was nothing to me—no more than to anyone else. In vain—I was the last person known to have anything to do with him, and they held me to the terrible account. Fearful, then, of being exposed in the papers (as one person present obscurely threatened), I considered the matter, and, at length, said, that if the lawyer would give me a confidential interview with the scrivener, in his (the lawyer's) own room, I would, that afternoon, strive my best to rid them of the nuisance they complained of.

Going upstairs to my old haunt, there was Bartleby silently sitting upon the banister at the landing.

'What are you doing here, Bartleby?' said I.

'Sitting upon the banister,' he mildly replied.

I motioned him into the lawyer's room, who then left us.

'Bartleby,' said I, 'are you aware that you are the cause of a great tribulation to me, by persisting in occupying the entry after being dismissed from the office?'

No answer.

'Now one of two things must take place. Either you must do something, or something must be done to you. Now what sort of business would you like to engage in? Would you like to re-engage in copying for someone?'

'No; I would prefer not to make any change.'

'Would you like a clerkship in a dry-goods store?'

'There is too much confinement about that. No, I would not like a clerkship; but I am not particular.'

'Too much confinement,' I cried, 'why, you keep yourself confined all the time!'

'I would prefer not to take a clerkship,' he rejoined, as if to settle that little item at once.

'How would a bartender's business suit you? There is no trying of the eyesight in that.'

'I would not like it at all; though, as I said before, I am not particular.'

His unwonted wordiness inspired me. I returned to the charge.

'Well, then, would you like to travel through the country collecting bills for the merchants? That would improve your health.'

'No, I would prefer to be doing something else.'

'How, then, would going as a companion to Europe, to entertain some young gentleman with your conversation—how would that suit you?'

'Not at all. It does not strike me that there is anything definite about that. I like to be stationary. But I am not particular.'

'Stationary you shall be, then,' I cried, now losing all patience, and, for the first time in all my exasperating connection with him, fairly flying into a passion. 'If you do not go away from these premises before night, I shall feel bound—indeed, I *am* bound—to—to—to quit the premises myself!' I rather absurdly concluded, knowing not with what possible threat to try to frighten his immobility into compliance. Despairing of all further efforts, I was precipitately leaving him, when a final thought occurred to me—one which had not been wholly unindulged before.

'Bartleby,' said I, in the kindest tone I could assume under such exciting circumstances, 'will you go home with me now—not to my office, but my dwelling—and remain there till we can conclude upon some convenient arrangement for you at our leisure? Come, let us start now, right away.'

'No: at present I would prefer not to make any change at all.'

I answered nothing; but, effectually dodging everyone by the suddenness and rapidity of my flight, rushed from the building, ran up Wall Street towards Broadway, and, jumping into the first omnibus, was soon removed from pursuit. As soon as tranquility returned, I distinctly perceived that I had now done all that I possibly could, both in respect to the demands of the landlord and his tenants, and with regard to my own desire and sense of duty, to benefit Bartleby, and shield him from rude persecution. I now strove to be entirely care-free and quiescent; and my conscience justified me in the attempt; though, indeed, it was not so successful as I could have wished. So fearful was I of being again hunted out by the incensed landlord and his exasperated tenants, that, surrendering my business to Nippers, for a few days, I drove about the upper part of the town and through the suburbs, in my rockaway; crossed over to Jersey City and Hoboken, and paid fugitive visits to Manhattanville and Astoria. In fact, I almost lived in my rockaway for the time.

When again I entered my office, lo, a note from the landlord lay upon the desk. I opened it with trembling hands. It informed me that the writer had sent to the police, and had Bartleby removed to the Tombs as a vagrant. Moreover, since I knew more about him than anyone else, he wished me to appear at that place, and make a suitable statement of the facts. These tidings had a conflicting effect upon me. At first I was indignant; but, at last, almost approved. The landlord's energetic, summary disposition, had led him to adopt a procedure which I do not think I would have decided upon myself; and yet, as a last resort, under such peculiar circumstances, it seemed the only plan.

As I afterwards learned, the poor scrivener, when told that he must be conducted to the Tombs, offered not the slightest obstacle, but, in his pale, unmoving way, silently acquiesced.

Some of the compassionate and curious bystanders joined the party; and headed by one of the constables arm-in-arm with Bartleby, the silent procession filed its way through all the noise, and heat, and joy of the roaring thoroughfares at noon.

The same day I received the note, I went to the Tombs, or, to speak more properly, the Halls of Justice. Seeking the right officer, I stated the purpose of my call, and was informed that the individual I described was, indeed, within. I then assured the functionary that Bartleby was a perfectly honest man, and greatly to be compassionated, however unaccountably eccentric. I narrated all I knew, and closed by suggesting the idea of letting him remain in as indulgent confinement as possible, till something less harsh might be done—though, indeed, I hardly knew what. At all events, if nothing else could be decided upon, the alms-house must receive him. I then begged to have an interview.

Being under no disgraceful charge, and quite serene and harmless in all his ways, they had permitted him freely to wander about the prison, and, especially, in the inclosed grass-platted yards thereof. And so I found him there, standing all alone in the quietest of the yards, his face towards a high wall, while all around, from the narrow slits of the jail windows, I thought I saw peering out upon him the eyes of murderers and thieves.

'Bartleby!'

'I know you,' he said, without looking round—'and I want nothing to say to you.'

'It was not I that brought you here, Bartleby,' said I, keenly pained at his implied suspicion. 'And to you, this should not be so vile a place. Nothing reproachful attaches to you by being here. And see, it is not so sad a place as one might think. Look, there is the sky, and here is the grass.'

'I know where I am,' he replied, but would say nothing more, and so I left him.

As I entered the corridor again, a broad meat-like man, in an apron accosted me, and, jerking his thumb over his shoulder, said—'Is that your friend?'

'Yes.'

'Does he want to starve? If he does, let him live on the prison fare, that's all.'

'Who are you?' asked I, not knowing what to make of such an unofficially speaking person in such a place.

'I am the grub-man. Such gentlemen as have friends here, hire me to provide them with something good to eat.'

'Is this so?' said I, turning to the turnkey.

He said it was.

'Well, then,' said I, slipping some silver into the grub-man's hand (for so they called him), 'I want you to give particular attention to my friend there; let him have the best dinner you can get. And you must be as polite to him as possible.'

'Introduce me, will you?' said the grub-man, looking at me with an expression which seemed to say he was all impatience for an opportunity to give a specimen of his breeding.

Thinking it would prove of benefit to the scrivener, I acquiesced; and, asking the grub-man his name, went up with him to Bartleby.

'Bartleby, this is a friend; you will find him very useful to you.'

'Your sarvant, sir, your sarvant,' said the grub-man, making a low salutation behind his apron. 'Hope you find it pleasant here, sir, nice grounds—cool apartments—hope you'll stay with us some time—try to make it agreeable. What will you have for dinner today?'

'I prefer not to dine today,' said Bartleby, turning away. 'It would disagree with me; I am unused to dinners.' So saying, he slowly moved to the other side of the enclosure, and took up a position fronting the dead-wall.

'How's this?' said the grub-man, addressing me with a stare of astonishment. 'He's odd, ain't he?'

'I think he is a little deranged,' said I, sadly.

'Deranged? deranged is it? Well, now, upon my word, I thought that friend of yourn was a gentleman forger; they are always pale and genteel-like, them forgers. I can't help pity 'em—can't help it, sir. Did you know Monroe Edwards?' he added, touchingly, and paused. Then, laying his hand piteously on my shoulder, sighed, 'He died of consumption at Sing-Sing. So you weren't acquainted with Monroe?'

'No, I was never socially acquainted with any forgers. But I can not stop longer. Look to my friend yonder. You will not lose by it. I will see you again.'

Some few days after this, I again obtained admission to the Tombs, and went through the corridors in quest of Bartleby; but without finding him.

'I saw him coming from his cell not long ago,' said a turnkey, 'maybe he's gone to loiter in the yards.'

So I went in that direction.

'Are you looking for the silent man?' said another turnkey, passing me. 'Yonder he lies—sleeping in the yard there. 'Tis not twenty minutes since I saw him lie down.'

The yard was entirely quiet. It was not accessible to the common prisoners. The surrounding walls, of amazing thickness, kept off all sounds behind them. The Egyptian character of the masonry weighed upon me with its gloom. But a soft imprisoned turf grew under foot. The heart of the eternal pyramids, it seemed, wherein, by some strange magic, through the clefts, grass-seed, dropped by birds, had sprung.

Strangely huddled at the base of the wall, his knees drawn up, and lying on his side, his head touching the cold stones, I saw the wasted Bartleby. But nothing stirred. I paused; then went close up to him; stooped over, and saw that his dim eyes were open; otherwise he seemed profoundly sleeping. Something prompted me to touch him. I felt his hand, when a tingling shiver ran up my arm and down my spine to my feet.

The round face of the grub-man peered upon me now. 'His dinner is ready. Won't he dine today, either? Or does he live without dining?'

'Lives without dining,' said I, and closed the eyes.

'Eh!—He's asleep, ain't he?'

'With kings and counsellors,' murmured I.

There would seem little need for proceeding further in this history. Imagination will readily supply the meagre recital of poor Bartleby's interment. But, ere parting with the reader, let me say, that if this little narrative has sufficiently interested him to awaken curiosity as to who Bartleby was, and what manner of life he led prior to the present narrator's making his acquaintance, I can only reply, that in such curiosity I fully share, but am wholly unable to gratify it. Yet here I hardly know whether I should divulge one little item of rumour, which came to my ear a few months after the scrivener's decease. Upon what basis it rested, I could never ascertain; and hence, how true it is I cannot tell. But, inasmuch as this vague report has not been without a certain suggestive interest to me, however sad, it may prove the same with some others, and so I will briefly mention it. The report was this: that Bartleby had been a subordinate clerk in the Dead Letter Office at Washington, from which he had been suddenly removed by a change in the administration. When I think over this rumour, hardly can I express the emotions which seize me. Dead letters! does it not sound like dead men? Conceive a man by nature and misfortune prone to a pallid hopelessness, can any business seem more fitted to heighten it than that of continually handling these dead letters, and assorting them for the flames? For by the cart-load they are annually burned. Sometimes from out of the folded paper the pale clerks take a ring—the finger it was meant for, perhaps, moulders in the grave; a bank-note sent in swiftest charity—he whom it would relieve, nor eats nor hungers anymore; pardon for those who died despairing; hope for those who died unhoping; good tidings for those who died stifled by unrelieved calamities. On errands of life, these letters speed to death.

Ah, Bartleby! Ah, humanity!

1856

Kate Chopin
1851–1904

Kate O'Flaherty was born in St Louis, Missouri, to an Irish immigrant father and a French mother. She was educated in a Catholic convent school in St Louis, and married Oscar Chopin, a Louisiana banker, when she was nineteen. In Louisiana she had six children before her husband's death in 1882, after which she returned to St Louis and began writing to help support herself and her family. Her fine novel *The Awakening*, which has been called an American *Madame Bovary*, was published in 1899 and instantly became the target of attacks by reviewers. It was actually removed from the shelves of the Mercantile Library in St Louis, and Chopin was denied membership in the Fine Arts Club because the book was, as a local magazine said, 'too strong drink for moral babes and should be labelled "poison".' Like so many writers, Chopin began to get her due appreciation only after her death. Although the story reprinted here, which first appeared in *Vogue* (6 December 1894), is the shortest one of Chopin's works, it is, if not 'poison', strong medicine.

The Story of an Hour

Knowing that Mrs Mallard was afflicted with a heart trouble, great care was taken to break to her as gently as possible the news of her husband's death.

It was her sister Josephine who told her, in broken sentences; veiled hints that revealed in half concealing. Her husband's friend Richards was there, too, near her. It was he who had been in the newspaper office when intelligence of the railroad disaster was received, with Brently Mallard's name leading the list of 'killed'. He had only taken the time to assure himself of its truth by a second telegram, and had hastened to forestall any less careful, less tender friend in bearing the sad message.

She did not hear the story as many have heard the same, with a paralyzed inability to accept its significance. She wept at once, with sudden, wild abandonment, in her sister's arms. When the storm of grief had spent itself she went away to her room alone. She would have no one follow her.

There stood, facing the open window, a comfortable, roomy armchair. Into this she sank, pressed down by a physical exhaustion that haunted her body and seemed to reach into her soul.

She could see in the open square before her house the tops of trees that were all aquiver with the new spring life. The delicious breath of rain in the air. In the street below a peddler was crying his wares. The notes of a distant song which someone was singing reached her faintly, and countless sparrows were twittering in the eaves.

There were patches of blue sky showing here and there through the clouds that had met and piled one above the other in the west facing her window.

She sat with her head thrown back upon the cushion of the chair, quite motionless, except when a sob came up into her throat and shook her, as a child who has cried itself to sleep continues to sob in its dreams.

She was young, with a fair, calm face, whose lines bespoke repression and even a certain strength. But now there was a dull stare in her eyes, whose gaze was fixed away off yonder on one of those patches of blue sky. It was not a glance of reflection, but rather indicated a suspension of intelligent thought.

There was something coming to her and she was waiting for it, fearfully. What was it? She did not know; it was too subtle and elusive to name. But she felt it, creeping out of the sky, reaching toward her through the sounds, the scents, the colour that filled the air.

Now her bosom rose and fell tumultuously. She was beginning to recognize this thing that was approaching to possess her, and she was striving to beat it back with her will—as powerless as her two white slender hands would have been.

When she abandoned herself a little whispered word escaped her slightly parted lips. She said it over and over under her breath: 'free, free, free!' The vacant stare and the look of terror that had followed it went from her eyes. They stayed keen and bright. Her pulses beat fast, and the coursing blood warmed and relaxed every inch of her body.

She did not stop to ask if it were or were not a monstrous joy that held her. A clear and exalted perception enabled her to dismiss the suggestion as trivial.

She knew that she would weep again when she saw the kind, tender hands folded in death; the face that had never looked save with love upon her, fixed and grey and dead. But she saw beyond that bitter moment a long procession of years to come that would belong to her absolutely. And she opened and spread her arms out to them in welcome.

There would be no one to live for her during those coming years; she would live for herself. There would be no powerful will bending hers in that blind persistence with which men and women believe they have a right to impose a private will upon a fellow creature. A kind intention or a cruel intention made the act seem no less a crime as she looked upon it in that brief moment of illumination.

And yet she had loved him—sometimes. Often she had not. What did it matter! What could love, the unsolved mystery, count for in face of this possession of self-assertion which she suddenly recognized as the strongest impulse of her being!

'Free! Body and soul free!' she kept whispering.

Josephine was kneeling before the closed door with her lips to the keyhole, imploring for admission. 'Louise, open the door! I beg; open the door—you will make yourself ill. What are you doing, Louise? For heaven's sake open the door.'

'Go away. I am not making myself ill.' No; she was drinking in a very elixir of life through that open window.

Her fancy was running riot along those days ahead of her. Spring days, and summer days, and all sorts of days that would be her own. She breathed a quick prayer that life might be long. It was only yesterday she had thought with a shudder that life might be long.

She arose at length and opened the door to her sister's importunities. There was a feverish triumph in her eyes, and she carried herself unwittingly like a goddess of Victory. She clasped her sister's waist, and together they descended the stairs. Richards stood waiting for them at the bottom.

Someone was opening the front door with a latchkey. It was Brently Mallard who entered, a little travel-stained, composedly carrying his grip-sack and umbrella. He had been far from the scene of accident, and did not even know there had been one. He stood amazed at Josephine's piercing cry; at Richards' quick motion to screen him from the view of his wife.

But Richards was too late.

When the doctors came they said she had died of heart disease—of joy that kills.

1894

Charlotte Perkins Gilman
1860–1935

Born in Hartford, Connecticut, Charlotte Anna Perkins was the grandniece of Harriet Beecher Stowe, author of *Uncle Tom's Cabin*. She grew up in an unstable family environment that her father abandoned soon after her birth. She attended many different schools and ended her formal education when she was fifteen. Her first marriage ended in 1892, when she filed for divorce; she relinquished custody of her daughter, Katharine, to her husband and his new wife. In 1900 she married Houghton Gilman in a relationship founded on her beliefs in an equal partnership between the woman and the man.

In her autobiography Gilman wrote that her heredity included 'the Beecher urge to social service, the Beecher wit and gift of words,

and such small sense of art as I have'. A journalist, she edited the monthly liberal journal *The Forerunner* and wrote and lectured on topics concerning women, social rights, and the labour movement. Her non-fiction works include *Women and Economics* (1898), which described the subordinate role of women and proposed social and labour reform. Later in her life she wrote novels, utopian in nature, that presented social evils and feminist remedies. A Gothic tale of a personal descent into insanity, 'The Yellow Wallpaper' is a semi-autobiographical story. Written after Gilman's institutionalization as a consequence of post-natal depression following Katharine's birth, it is a devastating indictment of the restricting bonds of marriage and motherhood.

The Yellow Wallpaper

It is very seldom that mere ordinary people like John and myself secure ancestral halls for the summer.

A colonial mansion, a hereditary estate, I would say a haunted house, and reach the height of romantic felicity—but that would be asking too much of fate!

Still I will proudly declare that there is something queer about it.

Else, why should it be let so cheaply? And why have stood so long untenanted?

John laughs at me, of course, but one expects that in marriage.

John is practical in the extreme. He has no patience with faith, an intense horror of superstition, and he scoffs openly at any talk of things not to be felt and seen and put down in figures.

John is a physician, and *perhaps*—(I would not say it to a living soul, of course, but this is dead paper and a great relief to my mind—) *perhaps* that is one reason I do not get well faster.

You see he does not believe I am sick!

And what can one do?

If a physician of high standing, and one's own husband, assures friends and relatives that there is really nothing the matter with one but temporary nervous depression—a slight hysterical tendency—what is one to do?

My brother is also a physician, and also of high standing, and he says the same thing.

So I take phosphates or phosphites—whichever it is, and tonics, and journeys, and air, and exercise, and am absolutely forbidden to 'work' until I am well again.

Personally, I disagree with their ideas.

Personally, I believe that congenial work, with excitement and change, would do me good.

But what is one to do?

I did write for a while in spite of them; but it *does* exhaust me a good deal—having to be so sly about it, or else meet with heavy opposition.

I sometimes fancy that in my condition if I had less opposition and more society and stimulus—but John says the very worst thing I can do is think about my condition, and I confess it always makes me feel bad.

So I will let it alone and talk about the house.

The most beautiful place! It is quite alone, standing well back from the road, quite three miles from the village. It makes me think of English places that you read about, for there are hedges and walls and gates that lock, and lots of separate little houses for the gardeners and people.

There is a *delicious* garden! I never saw such a garden—large and shady, full of box-bordered paths, and lined with long grape-covered arbours with seats under them.

There were greenhouses, too, but they are all broken now.

There was some legal trouble, I believe, something about the heirs and co-heirs; anyhow, the place has been empty for years.

That spoils my ghostliness, I am afraid, but I don't care—there is something strange about the house—I can feel it.

I even said so to John one moonlight evening, but he said what I felt was a *draft*, and shut the window.

I get unreasonably angry with John sometimes. I'm sure I never used to be so sensitive. I think it is due to this nervous condition.

But John says if I feel so, I shall neglect proper self-control; so I take pains to control myself—before him, at least, and that makes me very tired.

I don't like our room a bit. I wanted one downstairs that opened on the piazza and had roses all over the window, and such pretty old-fashioned chintz hangings! but John would not hear of it.

He said there was only one window and not room for two beds, and no near room for him if he took another.

He is very careful and loving, and hardly lets me stir without special direction.

I have a schedule prescription for each hour in the day; he takes all care from me, and so I feel basely ungrateful not to value it more.

He said we came here solely on my account, that I was to have perfect rest and all the air I could get. 'Your exercise depends on your strength, my dear,' said he, 'and your food somewhat on your appetite; but air you can absorb all the time.' So we took the nursery at the top of the house.

It is a big, airy room, the whole floor nearly, with windows that look all ways, and air and sunshine galore. It was nursery first and then playroom and gymnasium, I should judge; for the windows are barred for little children, and there are rings and things in the walls.

The paint and paper look as if a boys' school had used it. It is stripped off—the paper—in great patches all around the head of my bed, about as far as I can reach, and in a great place on the other side of the room low down. I never saw a worse paper in my life.

One of those sprawling flamboyant patterns committing every artistic sin.

It is dull enough to confuse the eye in following, pronounced enough to constantly irritate and provoke study, and when you follow the lame uncertain curves for a little distance they suddenly commit suicide—plunge off at outrageous angles, destroy themselves in unheard of contradictions.

The colour is repellant, almost revolting; a smouldering unclean yellow, strangely faded by the slow-turning sunlight.

It is a dull yet lurid orange in some places, a sickly sulphur tint in others.

No wonder the children hated it! I should hate it myself if I had to live in this room long.

There comes John, and I must put this away,—he hates to have me write a word.

We have been here two weeks, and I haven't felt like writing before, since that first day.

I am sitting by the window now, up in this atrocious nursery, and there is nothing to hinder my writing as much as I please, save lack of strength.

John is away all day, and even some nights when his cases are serious.

I am glad my case is not serious!

But these nervous troubles are dreadfully depressing.

John does not know how much I really suffer. He knows there is no *reason* to suffer, and that satisfies him.

Of course it is only nervousness. It does weigh on me so not to do my duty in any way!

I meant to be such a help to John, such a real rest and comfort, and here I am a comparative burden already!

Nobody would believe what an effort it is to do what little I am able,—to dress and entertain, and order things.

It is fortunate Mary is so good with the baby. Such a dear baby!

And yet I *cannot* be with him, it makes me so nervous.

I suppose John never was nervous in his life. He laughs at me so about this wallpaper!

At first he meant to repaper the room, but afterwards he said that I was letting it get the better of me, and that nothing was worse for a nervous patient than to give way to such fancies.

He said that after the wallpaper was changed it would be the heavy bedstead, and then the barred windows, and then that gate at the head of the stairs, and so on.

'You know the place is doing you good,' he said, 'and really, dear, I don't care to renovate the house just for a three months' rental.'

'Then do let us go downstairs,' I said, 'there are such pretty rooms there.'

Then he took me in his arms and called me a blessed little goose, and said he would go down cellar, if I wished, and have it whitewashed into the bargain.

But he is right enough about the beds and windows and things.

It is an airy and comfortable room as anyone need wish, and, of course, I would not be so silly as to make him uncomfortable just for a whim.

I'm really getting quite fond of the big room, all but that horrid paper.

Out of one window I can see the garden, those mysterious deep-shaded arbours, the riotous old-fashioned flowers, and bushes and gnarly trees.

Out of another I get a lovely view of the bay and a little private wharf belonging to the estate. There is a beautiful shaded lane that runs down there from the house. I always fancy I see people walking in these numerous paths and arbours, but John has cautioned me not to give way to fancy in the least. He says that with my imaginative power and habit of story-making, a nervous weakness like mine is sure to lead to all manner of excited fancies, and that I ought to use my will and good sense to check the tendency. So I try.

I think sometimes that if I were only well enough to write a little it would relieve the press of ideas and rest me.

But I find I get pretty tired when I try.

It is so discouraging not to have any advice and companionship about my work. When I get really well, John says he will ask Cousin Henry and Julia down for a long visit; but he says he would as soon put fireworks in my pillowcase as to let me have those stimulating people about now.

I wish I could get well faster.

But I must not think about that. This paper looks to me as if it *knew* what a vicious influence it had!

There is a recurrent spot where the pattern lolls like a broken neck and two bulbous eyes stare at you upside down.

I get positively angry with the impertinence of it and the everlastingness. Up and down and sideways they crawl, and those absurd, unblinking eyes are everywhere. There is one place where two breadths didn't match, and the eyes go all up and down the line, one a little higher than the other.

I never saw so much expression in an inanimate thing before, and we all know how much expression they have! I used to lie awake as a child and get more entertainment and terror out of blank walls and plain furniture than most children could find in a toy-store.

I remember what a kindly wink the knobs of our big, old bureau used to have, and there was one chair that always seemed like a strong friend.

I used to feel that if any of the other things looked too fierce I could always hop into that chair and be safe.

The furniture in this room is no worse than inharmonious, however, for we had to bring it all from downstairs. I suppose when this was used as a playroom they had to take the nursery things out, and no wonder! I never saw such ravages as the children have made here.

The wallpaper, as I said before, is torn off in spots, and it sticketh closer than a brother—they must have had perseverance as well as hatred.

Then the floor is scratched and gouged and splintered, the plaster itself is dug out here and there, and this great heavy bed which is all we found in the room, looks as if it had been through the wars.

But I don't mind a bit—only the paper.

There comes John's sister. Such a dear girl as she is, and so careful of me! I must not let her find me writing.

She is a perfect and enthusiastic housekeeper, and hopes for no better profession. I verily believe she thinks it is the writing which made me sick!

But I can write when she is out, and see her a long way off from these windows.

There is one that commands the road, a lovely shaded winding road, and one that just looks off over the country. A lovely country, too, full of great elms and velvet meadows.

This wallpaper has a kind of subpattern in a different shade, a particularly irritating one, for you can only see it in certain lights, and not clearly then.

But in the places where it isn't faded and where the sun is just so—I can see a strange, provoking, formless sort of figure, that seems to skulk about behind that silly conspicuous front design.

There's sister on the stairs!

Well, the Fourth of July is over! The people are all gone and I am tired out. John thought it might do me good to see a little company, so we just had mother and Nellie and the children down for a week.

Of course I didn't do a thing. Jennie sees to everything now.

But it tired me all the same.

John says if I don't pick up faster he shall send me to Weir Mitchell in the fall.

But I don't want to go there at all. I had a friend who was in his hands once, and she says he is just like John and my brother, only more so!

Besides, it is such an undertaking to go so far.

I don't feel as if it was worth while to turn my hand over for anything, and I'm getting dreadfully fretful and querulous.

I cry at nothing, and cry most of the time.

Of course, I don't when John is here, or anybody else, but when I am alone.

And I am alone a good deal just now. John is kept in town very often by serious cases, and Jennie is good and lets me alone when I want her to.

So I walk a little in the garden or down that lovely lane, sit on the porch under the roses, and lie down here a good deal.

I'm getting really fond of the room in spite of the wallpaper. Perhaps *because* of the wallpaper.

It dwells in my mind so!

I lie here on this great immovable bed—it is nailed down, I believe—and follow that pattern about by the hour. It is as good as gymnastics, I assure you. I start, we'll say, at the bottom, down in the corner over there where it has not been touched, and I determine for the thousandth time that I *will* follow that pointless pattern to some sort of conclusion.

I know a little of the principle of design, and I know this thing was not arranged on any laws of radiation, or alternation, or repetition, or symmetry, or anything else that I ever heard of.

It is repeated, of course, by the breadths, but not otherwise.

Looked at in one way each breadth stands alone, the bloated curves and flourishes—a kind of 'debased Romanesque' with *delirium tremens*—go waddling up and down in isolated columns of fatuity.

But, on the other hand, they connect diagonally, and the sprawling outlines run off in great slanting waves of optic horror, like a lot of wallowing seaweeds in full chase.

The whole thing goes horizontally, too, at least it seems so, and I exhaust myself in trying to distinguish the order of its going in that direction.

They have used a horizontal breadth for a frieze, and that adds wonderfully to the confusion.

There is one end of the room where it is almost intact, and there, when the crosslights fade and the low sun shines directly upon it, I can almost fancy radiation after all,—the interminable grotesques seem to form around a common centre and rush off in headlong plunges of equal distraction.

It makes me tired to follow it. I will take a nap I guess.

I don't know why I should write this.

I don't want to.

I don't feel able.

And I know John would think it absurd. But I *must* say what I feel and think in some way—it is such a relief!

But the effort is getting to be greater than the relief.

Half the time now I am awfully lazy, and lie down ever so much.

John says I mustn't lose my strength, and has me take cod liver oil and lots of tonics and things, to say nothing of ale and wine and rare meat.

Dear John! He loves me very dearly, and hates to have me sick. I tried to have a real earnest reasonable talk with him the other day, and tell him how I wish he would let me go and make a visit to Cousin Henry and Julia.

But he said I wasn't able to go, nor able to stand it after I got there; and I did not make out a very good case for myself, for I was crying before I had finished.

It is getting to be a great effort for me to think straight. Just this nervous weakness I suppose.

And dear John gathered me up in his arms, and just carried me upstairs and laid me on the bed, and sat by me and read to me till it tired my head.

He said I was his darling and his comfort and all he had, and that I must take care of myself for his sake, and keep well.

He says no one but myself can help me out of it, that I must use my will and self-control and not let any silly fancies run away with me.

There's one comfort, the baby is well and happy, and does not have to occupy this nursery with the horrid wallpaper.

If we had not used it, that blessed child would have! What a fortunate escape! Why, I wouldn't have a child of mine, an impressionable little thing, live in such a room for worlds.

I never thought of it before, but it is lucky that John kept me here after all, I can stand it so much easier than a baby, you see.

Of course I never mention it to them anymore—I am too wise,—but I keep watch of it all the same.

There are things in that paper that nobody knows but me, or ever will.

Behind that outside pattern the dim shapes get clearer every day.

It is always the same shape, only very numerous.

And it is like a woman stooping down and creeping about behind that pattern. I don't like it a bit. I wonder—I begin to think—I wish John would take me away from here!

It is so hard to talk with John about my case because he is so wise, and because he loves me so.

But I tried it last night.

It was moonlight. The moon shines in all around just as the sun does.

I hate to see it sometimes, it creeps so slowly, and always comes in by one window or another.

John was asleep and I hated to waken him, so I kept still and watched the moonlight on that undulating wallpaper till I felt creepy.

The faint figure behind seemed to shake the pattern, just as if she wanted to get out.

I got up softly and went to feel and see if the paper *did* move, and when I came back John was awake.

'What is it, little girl?' he said. 'Don't go walking about like that—you'll get cold.'

I thought it was a good time to talk, so I told him that I really was not gaining here, and that I wished he would take me away.

'Why, darling!' said he, 'our lease will be up in three weeks, and I can't see how to leave before.

'The repairs are not done at home, and I cannot possibly leave town just now. Of course if you were in any danger, I could and would, but you really are better, dear, whether you can see it or not. I am a doctor, dear, and I know. You are gaining flesh and colour, your appetite is better, I feel really much easier about you.'

'I don't weigh a bit more,' said I, 'nor as much; and my appetite may be better in the evening when you are here, but it is worse in the morning when you are away!'

'Bless her little heart!' said he with a big hug, 'she shall be as sick as she pleases! But now let's improve the shining hours by going to sleep, and talk about it in the morning!'

'And you won't go away?' I asked gloomily.

'Why, how can I, dear? It is only three weeks more and then we will take a nice little trip of a few days while Jennie is getting the house ready. Really dear you are better!'

'Better in body perhaps—' I began, and stopped short, for he sat up straight and looked at me with such a stern, reproachful look that I could not say another word.

'My darling,' said he, 'I beg of you, for my sake and for our child's sake, as well as for your own, that you will never for one instant let that idea enter your mind! There is nothing so dangerous, so fascinating, to a temperament like yours. It is a false and foolish fancy. Can you not trust me as a physician when I tell you so?'

So of course I said no more on that score, and we went to sleep before long. He thought I was asleep first, but I wasn't, and lay there for hours trying to decide whether that front pattern and the back pattern really did move together or separately.

On a pattern like this, by daylight, there is a lack of sequence, a defiance of law, that is a constant irritant to a normal mind.

The colour is hideous enough, and unreliable enough, and infuriating enough, but the pattern is torturing.

You think you have mastered it, but just as you get well underway in following, it turns a back-somersault and there you are. It slaps you in the face, knocks you down, and tramples upon you. It is like a bad dream.

The outside pattern is a florid arabesque, reminding one of a fungus. If you can imagine a toadstool in joints, an interminable string of toadstools, budding and sprouting in endless convolutions—why, that is something like it.

That is, sometimes!

There is one marked peculiarity about this paper, a thing nobody seems to notice but myself, and that is that it changes as the light changes.

When the sun shoots in through the east window—I always watch for that first long, straight ray—it changes so quickly that I never can quite believe it.

That is why I watch it always.

By moonlight—the moon shines in all night when there is a moon—I wouldn't know it was the same paper.

At night in any kind of light, in twilight, candlelight, lamplight, and worst of all by moonlight, it becomes bars! The outside pattern I mean, and the woman behind it is as plain as can be.

I didn't realize for a long time what the thing was that showed behind, that dim sub-pattern, but now I am quite sure it is a woman.

By daylight she is subdued, quiet. I fancy it is the pattern that keeps her so still. It is so puzzling. It keeps me quiet by the hour.

I lie down ever so much now. John says it is good for me, and to sleep all I can.

Indeed he started the habit by making me lie down for an hour after each meal.

It is a very bad habit I am convinced, for you see I don't sleep.

And that cultivates deceit, for I don't tell them I'm awake—O no!

The fact is I am getting a little afraid of John.

He seems very queer sometimes, and even Jennie has an inexplicable look.

It strikes me occasionally, just as a scientific hypothesis,—that perhaps it is the paper!

I have watched John when he did not know I was looking, and come into the room suddenly on the most innocent excuses, and I've caught him several times *looking at the paper*! And Jennie too. I caught Jennie with her hand on it once.

She didn't know I was in the room, and when I asked her in a quiet, a very quiet voice, with the most restrained manner possible, what she was doing with the paper— she turned around as if she had been caught stealing, and looked quite angry—asked me why I should frighten her so!

Then she said that the paper stained everything it touched, that she had found yellow smooches on all my clothes and John's, and she wished we would be more careful!

Did not that sound innocent? But I know she was studying that pattern, and I am determined that nobody shall find it out but myself!

Life is very much more exciting now than it used to be. You see I have something more to expect, to look forward to, to watch. I really do eat better, and am more quiet than I was.

John is so pleased to see me improve! He laughed a little the other day, and said I seemed to be flourishing in spite of my wallpaper.

I turned it off with a laugh. I had no intention of telling him it was *because* of the wallpaper—he would make fun of me. He might even want to take me away.

I don't want to leave now until I have found it out. There is a week more, and I think that will be enough.

I'm feeling ever so much better! I don't sleep much at night, for it is so interesting to watch developments; but I sleep a good deal in the daytime.

In the daytime it is tiresome and perplexing.

There are always new shoots on the fungus, and new shades of yellow all over it. I cannot keep count of them, though I have tried conscientiously.

It is the strangest yellow, that wallpaper! It makes me think of all the yellow things I ever saw—not beautiful ones like buttercups, but old foul, bad yellow things.

But there is something else about that paper—the smell! I noticed it the moment we came into the room, but with so much air and sun it was not bad. Now we have had a week of fog and rain, and whether the windows are open or not, the smell is here.

It creeps all over the house.

I find it hovering in the dining room, skulking in the parlour, hiding in the hall, lying in wait for me on the stairs.

It gets into my hair.

Even when I go to ride, if I turn my head suddenly and surprise it—there is that smell!

Such a peculiar odour, too! I have spent hours in trying to analyze it, to find what it smelled like.

It is not bad—at first, and very gentle, but quite the subtlest, most enduring odour I ever met.

In this damp weather it is awful, I wake up in the night and find it hanging over me.

It used to disturb me at first. I thought seriously of burning the house—to reach the smell.

But now I am used to it. The only thing I can think of that it is like is the *colour* of the paper! A yellow smell.

There is a very funny mark on this wall, low down, near the mopboard. A streak that runs around the room. It goes behind every piece of furniture, except the bed, a long, straight, even *smooch*, as if it had been rubbed over and over.

I wonder how it was done and who did it, and what they did it for. Round and round and round—round and round and round—it makes me dizzy!

I really have discovered something at last.

Through watching so much at night, when it changes so, I have finally found out. The front pattern *does* move—and no wonder! The woman behind shakes it!

Sometimes I think there are a great many women behind, and sometimes only one, and she crawls around fast, and her crawling shakes it all over.

Then in the very bright spots she keeps still, and in the very shady spots she just takes hold of the bars and shakes them hard.

And she is all the time trying to climb through. But nobody could climb through that pattern—it strangles so; I think that is why it has so many heads.

They get through, and then the pattern strangles them off and turns them upside down, and makes their eyes white!

If those heads were covered or taken off it would not be half so bad.

I think that woman gets out in the daytime!

And I'll tell you why—privately—I've seen her!

I can see her out of every one of my windows!

It is the same woman, I know, for she is always creeping, and most women do not creep by daylight.

I see her in that long shaded lane, creeping up and down. I see her in those dark grape arbours, creeping all around the garden.

I see her on that long road under the trees, creeping along, and when a carriage comes she hides under the blackberry vines.

I don't blame her a bit. It must be very humiliating to be caught creeping by daylight!

I always lock the door when I creep by daylight. I can't do it at night, for I know John would suspect something at once.

And John is so queer now, that I don't want to irritate him. I wish he would take another room! Besides, I don't want anybody to get that woman out at night but myself.

I often wonder if I could see her out of all the windows at once.

But, turn as fast as I can, I can only see out of one at one time.

And though I always see her, she *may* be able to creep faster than I can turn!

I have watched her sometimes away off in the open country, creeping as fast as a cloud shadow in a high wind.

If only that top pattern could be gotten off from the under one! I mean to try it, little by little.

I have found out another funny thing, but I shan't tell it this time! It does not do to trust people too much.

There are only two more days to get this paper off, and I believe John is beginning to notice. I don't like the look in his eyes.

And I heard him ask Jennie a lot of professional questions about me. She had a very good report to give.

She said I slept a good deal in the daytime.

John knows I don't sleep well at night, for all I'm so quiet!

He asked me all sorts of questions, too, and pretended to be very loving and kind.

As if I couldn't see through him!

Still, I don't wonder he acts so, sleeping under this paper for three months.

It only interests me, but I feel sure John and Jennie are secretly affected by it.

Hurrah! This is the last day, but it is enough. John had to stay in town over night, and won't be out until this evening.

Jennie wanted to sleep with me—the sly thing! But I told her I should undoubtedly rest better for a night all alone.

That was clever, for really I wasn't alone a bit! As soon as it was moonlight and that poor thing began to crawl and shake the pattern, I got up and ran to help her.

I pulled and she shook, I shook and she pulled, and before morning we had peeled off yards of that paper.

A strip about as high as my head and half around the room.

And then when the sun came and that awful pattern began to laugh at me, I declared I would finish it today!

We go away tomorrow, and they are moving all my furniture down again to leave things as they were before.

Jennie looked at the wall in amazement, but I told her merrily that I did it out of pure spite at the vicious thing.

She laughed and said she wouldn't mind doing it herself, but I must not get tired.

How she betrayed herself that time!

But I am here, and no person touches this paper but me,—not *alive*!

She tried to get me out of the room—it was too patent! But I said it was so quiet and empty and clean now that I believed I would lie down again and sleep all I could; and not to wake me even for dinner—I would call when I woke.

So now she is gone, and the servants are gone, and the things are gone, and there is nothing left but that great bedstead nailed down, with the canvas mattress we found on it.

We shall sleep downstairs tonight, and take the boat home tomorrow.

I quite enjoy the room, now it is bare again.

How those children did tear about here!

This bedstead is fairly gnawed!

But I must get to work.

I have locked the door and thrown the key down into the front path.

I don't want to go out, and I don't want to have anybody come in, till John comes.

I want to astonish him.

I've got a rope up here that even Jennie did not find. If that woman does get out, and tries to get away, I can tie her!

But I forgot I could not reach far without anything to stand on!

This bed will *not* move!

I tried to lift and push it until I was lame, and then I got so angry I bit off a little piece at one corner—but it hurt my teeth.

Then I peeled off all the paper I could reach standing on the floor. It sticks horribly and the pattern just enjoys it! All those strangled heads and bulbous eyes and waddling fungus growths just shriek with derision!

I am getting angry enough to do something desperate. To jump out of the window would be admirable exercise, but the bars are too strong even to try.

Besides I wouldn't do it. Of course not. I know well enough that a step like that is improper and might be misconstrued.

I don't like to *look* out of the windows even—there are so many of those creeping women, and they creep so fast.

I wonder if they all come out of that wallpaper as I did?

But I am securely fastened now by my well-hidden rope—you don't get *me* out in the road there!

I suppose I shall have to get back behind the pattern when it comes night, and that is hard!

It is so pleasant to be out in this great room and creep around as I please!

I don't want to go outside. I won't, even if Jennie asks me to.

For outside you have to creep on the ground, and everything is green instead of yellow.

But here I can creep smoothly on the floor, and my shoulder just fits in that long smooch around the wall, so I cannot lose my way.

Why there's John at the door!

It is no use, young man, you can't open it!

How he does call and pound!

Now he's crying for an axe.

It would be a shame to break down that beautiful door!

'John dear!' said I in the gentlest voice, 'the key is down by the front steps, under a plantain leaf!'

That silenced him for a few moments.

Then he said—very quietly indeed, 'Open the door, my darling!'

'I can't,' said I. 'The key is down by the front door under a plantain leaf!'

And then I said it again, several times, very gently and slowly, and said it so often that he had to go and see, and he got it of course, and came in. He stopped short by the door.

'What is the matter?' he cried. 'For God's sake, what are you doing!'

I kept on creeping just the same, but I looked at him over my shoulder.

'I've got out at last,' said I, 'in spite of you and Jane! And I've pulled off most of the paper, so you can't put me back!'

Now why should that man have fainted? But he did, and right across my path by the wall, so that I had to creep over him every time!

1892

◆

Charles G.D. Roberts
1860–1935

◆

Born in Douglas, New Brunswick, Charles G.D. Roberts was educated at the University of New Brunswick and taught English, French, and economics at King's College, Nova Scotia, from 1885 until 1895. It was during this time that he edited the literary journal *The Week* and wrote the poems that would establish his position as the father of Canadian poetry. He gave up his teaching career to devote himself to his writing and to promoting the literature of his own country. From 1896 until 1907 he worked as a freelance writer in New York, where he wrote some of his best-known fiction, including his animal stories. He then went abroad to live in Europe and to serve in the Great War before returning in 1925 to Canada, settling in Toronto.

Roberts's poetry is recognized as one of the first flowerings of the poetic voice in Canada, and his remarkable prose — in both short stories and novels — set the standard for his contemporaries and for future generations of writers. In 'Strayed', his first published short story, the animals are indeed animals, and the reader is invited to sympathize with them and their plight.

Strayed

In the Cabineau Camp, of unlucky reputation, there was a young ox of splendid build, but of a wild and restless nature.

He was one of a yoke, of part Devon blood, large, dark-red, all muscle and nerve, and with wide, magnificent horns. His yoke-fellow was a docile steady worker, the pride of his owner's heart; but he himself seemed never to have been more than half broken in. The woods appeared to draw him by some spell. He wanted to get back to the pastures where he had roamed untrammelled of old with his fellow-steers. The remembrance was in his heart of the dewy mornings when the herd used to feed together on the sweet grassy hillocks, and of the clover-smelling heats of June when they would gather hock-deep in the pools under the green willow-shadows. He hated the yoke, he hated the winter; and he imagined that in the wild pastures he remembered it would be for ever summer. If only he could get back to those pastures!

One day there came the longed-for opportunity; and he seized it. He was standing unyoked beside his mate, and none of the teamsters were near. His head went up in the air, and with a snort of triumph he dashed away through the forest.

For a little while there was a vain pursuit. At last the lumbermen gave it up. 'Let him be!' said his owner, 'an' I rayther guess he'll turn up agin when he gits peckish. He kaint browse on spruce buds an' lung-wort.'

Plunging on with long gallop through the snow he was soon miles from camp. Growing weary he slackened his pace. He came down to a walk. As the lonely red of the winter sunset began to stream through the openings of the forest, flushing the snows of the tiny glades and swales, he grew hungry, and began to swallow unsatisfying mouthfuls of the long moss which roughened the tree-trunks. Ere the moon got up he had filled himself with this fodder, and then he lay down in a little thicket for the night.

But some miles back from his retreat a bear had chanced upon his foot-prints. A strayed steer! That would be an easy prey. The bear started straightway in pursuit. The moon was high in heaven when the crouched ox heard his pursuer's approach. He had no idea what was coming, but he rose to his feet and waited.

The bear plunged boldly into the thicket, never dreaming of resistance. With a muffled roar the ox charged upon him and bore him to the ground. Then he wheeled, and charged again, and the astonished bear was beaten at once. Gored by those keen horns he had no stomach for further encounter, and would fain have made his escape; but as he retreated the ox charged him again, dashing him against a huge trunk. The bear dragged himself up with difficulty, beyond his opponent's reach; and the ox turned scornfully back to his lair.

At the first yellow of dawn the restless creature was again upon the march. He pulled more mosses by the way, but he disliked them the more intensely now because he thought he must be nearing his ancient pastures with their tender grass and their streams. The snow was deeper about him, and his hatred of the winter grew apace. He came out upon a hill-side, partly open, whence the pine had years before been stripped, and where now grew young birches thick together. Here he browsed on the aromatic twigs, but for him it was harsh fare.

As his hunger increased he thought a little longingly of the camp he had deserted, but he dreamed not of turning back. He would keep on till he reached his pastures, and the glad herd of his comrades licking salt out of the trough beside the accustomed pool. He had some blind instinct as to his direction, and kept his course to the south very strictly, the desire in his heart continually leading him aright.

That afternoon he was attacked by a panther, which dropped out of a tree and tore his throat. He dashed under a low branch and scraped his assailant off, then, wheeling about savagely, put the brute to flight with his first mad charge. The panther sprang back into his tree, and the ox continued his quest.

Soon his steps grew weaker, for the panther's cruel claws had gone deep into his neck, and his path was marked with blood. Yet the dream in his great wild eyes was not dimmed as his strength ebbed away. His weakness he never noticed or heeded. The desire that was urging him absorbed all other thoughts—even, almost, his sense of hunger. This, however, it was easy for him to assuage, after a fashion, for the long, grey, unnourishing mosses were abundant.

By and by his path led him into the bed of a stream, whose waters could be heard faintly tinkling on thin pebbles beneath their coverlet of ice and snow. His slow steps conducted him far along this open course. Soon after he had disappeared, around a curve in the distance there came the panther, following stealthily upon his crimsoned trail. The crafty beast was waiting till the bleeding and the hunger should do its work, and the object of its inexorable pursuit should have no more heart left for resistance.

This was late in the afternoon. The ox was now possessed with his desire, and would not lie down for any rest. All night long, through the gleaming silver of the open spaces, through the weird and checkered gloom of the deep forest, heedless even of this hunger, or perhaps driven the mores by it as he thought of the wild clover bunches and tender timothy awaiting him, the solitary ox strove on. And all night, lagging far behind in his unabating caution, the panther followed him.

At sunrise the worn and stumbling animal came out upon the borders of the great lake, stretching its leagues of unshadowed snow away to the south before him. There was his path, and without hesitation he followed it. The wide and frost-bound water here and there had been swept clear of its snows by the wind, but for the most part its covering lay unruffled; and the pale dove-colours, and saffrons, and rose-lilacs of the dawn were sweetly reflected on its surface.

The doomed ox was now journeying very slowly, and with the greatest labour. He staggered at every step, and his beautiful head drooped almost to the snow. When he had got a great way out upon the lake, at the forest's edge appeared the pursuing panther, emerging cautiously from the coverts. The round tawny face and malignant green eyes were raised to peer out across the expanse. The labouring progress of the ox was promptly marked. Dropping its nose again to the ensanguined snow, the beast resumed his pursuit, first at a slow trot, and then at a long, elastic gallop. By this time the ox's quest was nearly done. He plunged forward upon his knees, rose again with difficulty, stood still, and looked around him. His eyes were clouding over, but he saw, dimly, the tawny brute that was now hard upon his steps. Back came a flash of the old courage, and he turned, horns lowered, to face the attack. With the last of his strength he charged, and the panther paused irresolutely; but the wanderer's knees gave way beneath his own impetus, and his horns ploughed the snow. With a deep bellowing groan he rolled over on his side, and the longing, and the dream of the pleasant pastures, faded from his eyes. With a great spring the panther was upon him, and the eager teeth were at his throat—but he knew nought of it. No wild beast, but his own desire, had conquered him.

When the panther had slaked his thirst for blood, he raised his head, and stood with his fore-paws resting on the dead ox's side, and gazed all about him.

To one watching from the lake shore, had there been anyone to watch in that solitude, the wild beast and his prey would have seemed but a speck of black on the gleaming waste. At the same hour league upon league back in the depth of the ancient forest, a lonely ox was lowing in his stanchions, restless, refusing to eat, grieving for the absence of his yoke-fellow.

1888

Stephen Leacock
1869–1944

Humorist and humanist, professor and pundit, Stephen Leacock was born in the village of Swanmore, Hampshire, in England. His family emigrated in 1876 to a farm north of Toronto. Educated at the University of Toronto, he pursued graduate studies in economics at the University of Chicago, where he studied under Thorstein Veblen, author of *The Theory of the Leisure Class*. After completing his PhD in 1903, Leacock moved to McGill University to teach economics; he chaired the Department of Political Science and Economics from 1908 until his retirement in 1936. His most profitable work, the textbook *Elements of Political Science* (1906), was translated into seventeen languages.

The author of nineteen books and count-less articles on economics, history, and political science, Leacock turned to writing humour as his beloved avocation. He approached it, like he approached his other writing, with professionalism and a shrewd business sense. His first collection of humorous stories, *Literary Lapses*, appeared in 1910, and from that time until his death he published a volume of humour almost every year. The two finest are the complementary volumes *Sunshine Sketches of a Little Town* (1912), with its now classic account of 'The Marine Excursion of the Knights of Pythias', and the urban satire *Arcadian Adventures with the Idle Rich* (1914). He also wrote popular biographies of his two favourite writers, *Mark Twain* (1932) and *Charles Dickens* (1933).

The Marine Excursion of the Knights of Pythias

Half-past six on a July morning! The *Mariposa Belle* is at the wharf, decked in flags, with steam up ready to start.

Excursion day!

Half-past six on a July morning, and Lake Wissanotti lying in the sun as calm as glass. The opal colours of the morning light are shot from the surface of the water.

Out on the lake the last thin threads of the mist are clearing away like flecks of cotton wool.

The long call of the loon echoes over the lake. The air is cool and fresh. There is in it all the new life of the land of the silent pine and the moving waters. Lake Wissanotti in the morning sunlight! Don't talk to me of the Italian lakes, or the Tyrol or the Swiss Alps. Take them away. Move them somewhere else. I don't want them.

Excursion day, at half-past six of a summer morning! With the boat all decked in flags and all the people in Mariposa on the wharf, and the band in peaked caps with big cornets tied to their bodies ready to play at any minute! I say! Don't tell me about the Carnival of Venice and the Delhi Durbar. Don't! I wouldn't look at them. I'd shut my eyes! For light and colour give me every time an excursion out of Mariposa down the lake to the Indian's Island out of sight in the morning mist. Talk of your Papal Zouaves and your Buckingham Palace Guard! I want to see the Mariposa band in uniform and the Mariposa Knights of Pythias with their aprons and their insignia and their picnic baskets and their five-cent cigars!

Half-past six in the morning, and all the crowd on the wharf and the boat due to leave in half an hour. Notice it!—in half an hour. Already she's whistled twice (at six, and at six fifteen), and at any minute now, Christie Johnson will step into the pilot house and pull the string for the warning whistle that the boat will leave in half an hour. So keep ready. Don't think of running back to Smith's Hotel for the sandwiches. Don't be fool enough to try to go up to the Greek Store, next to Netley's, and buy fruit. You'll be left behind for sure if you do. Never mind the sandwiches and the fruit! Anyway, here comes Mr Smith himself with a huge basket of provender that would feed a factory. There must be sandwiches in that. I think I can hear them clinking. And behind Mr Smith is the German waiter from the caff with another basket—undubitably lager beer; and behind him, the bartender of the hotel, carrying nothing, as far as one can see. But of course if you know Mariposa you will understand that why he looks so nonchalant and empty-handed is because he has two bottles of rye whisky under his linen duster. You know, I think, the peculiar walk of a man with two bottles of whisky in the inside pockets of a linen coat. In Mariposa, you see, to bring beer to an excursion is quite in keeping with public opinion. But, whisky—well, one has to be a little careful.

Do I say that Mr Smith is here? Why, everybody's here. There's Hussell, the editor of the *Newspacket*, wearing a blue ribbon on his coat, for the Mariposa Knights of Pythias are, by their constitution, dedicated to temperance; and there's Henry Mullins, the manager of the Exchange Bank, also a Knight of Pythias, with a small flask of Pogram's Special in his hip pocket as a sort of amendment to the constitution. And there's Dean Drone, the Chaplain of the Order, with a fishing rod (you never saw such green bass as lie among the rocks at Indian's Island), and with a trolling line in case of maskinonge, and a landing-net in case of pickerel, and with his eldest daughter, Lilian Drone, in case of young men. There never was such a fisherman as the Rev. Rupert Drone.

Perhaps I ought to explain that when I speak of the excursion as being of the Knights of Pythias, the thing must not be understood in any narrow sense. In Mariposa practically everybody belongs to the Knights of Pythias just as they do to everything else. That's the great thing about the town and that's what makes it so different from the city. Everybody is in everything.

You should see them on the seventeenth of March, for example, when everybody wears a green ribbon and they're all laughing and glad—you know what the Celtic nature is—and talking about Home Rule.

On St Andrew's Day every man in town wears a thistle and shakes hands with everybody else, and you see the fine old Scotch honesty beaming out of their eyes.

And on St George's Day!—well, there's no heartiness like the good old English spirit, after all; why shouldn't a man feel glad that he's an Englishman?

Then on the Fourth of July there are stars and stripes flying over half the stores in town, and suddenly all the men are seen to smoke cigars, and to know all about Roosevelt and Bryan and the Philippine Islands. Then you learn for the first time that Jeff Thorpe's people came from Massachusetts and that his uncle fought at Bunker Hill (anyway Jefferson will swear it was in Dakota all right enough); and you find that George Duff has a married sister in Rochester and that her husband is all right; in fact, George was down there as recently as eight years ago. Oh, it's the most American town imaginable is Mariposa—on the Fourth of July.

But wait, just wait, if you feel anxious about the solidity of the British connexion, till the twelfth of the month, when everybody is wearing an orange streamer in his coat and the Orangemen (every man in town) walk in the big procession. Allegiance! Well, perhaps you remember the address they gave to the Prince of Wales on the platform of the Mariposa station as he went through on his tour to the west. I think that pretty well settled that question.

So you will easily understand that of course everybody belongs to the Knights of Pythias and the Masons and Oddfellows, just as they all belong to the Snow Shoe Club and the Girls' Friendly Society.

And meanwhile the whistle of the steamer has blown again for a quarter to seven—loud and long this time, for anyone not here now is late for certain, unless he should happen to come down in the last fifteen minutes.

What a crowd upon the wharf and how they pile onto the steamer! It's a wonder that the boat can hold them all. But that's just the marvellous thing about the *Mariposa Belle*.

I don't know—I have never known—where the steamers like the *Mariposa Belle* come from. Whether they are built by Harland and Wolff of Belfast, or whether, on the other hand, they are not built by Harland and Wolff of Belfast, is more than one would like to say offhand.

The *Mariposa Belle* always seems to me to have some of those strange properties that distinguish Mariposa itself. I mean, her size seems to vary so. If you see her there in the winter, frozen in the ice beside the wharf with a snowdrift against the windows of the pilot house, she looks a pathetic little thing the size of a butternut. But in the summer time, especially after you've *been* in Mariposa for a month or two, and have paddled alongside of her in a canoe, she gets larger and taller, and with a great sweep of black sides, till you see no difference between the *Mariposa Belle* and the *Lusitania*. Each one is a big steamer and that's all you can say.

Nor do her measurements help you much. She draws about eighteen inches forward, and more than that—at least half an inch more, astern, and when she's loaded down with an excursion crowd she draws a good two inches more. And above the water—why, look at all the decks on her! There's the deck you walk onto, from the wharf, all shut in, with windows along it, and the after cabin with the long table, and above that the deck with all the chairs piled upon it, and the deck in front where the band stand round in a circle, and the pilot house is higher than that, and above the pilot house is the board with the gold name and the flag pole and the steel ropes and the flags; and fixed in somewhere on the different levels is the lunch counter where they sell the sandwiches, and the engine room, and down below the deck level, beneath the water line, is the place where the crew sleep. What with steps and stairs and passages and piles of cordwood for the engine— oh, no, I guess Harland and Wolff didn't build her. They couldn't have.

Yet even with a huge boat like the *Mariposa Belle*, it would be impossible for her to carry all of the crowd that you see in the boat and on the wharf. In reality, the crowd is made up of two classes—all of the people in Mariposa who are going on the excursion and all those who are not. Some come for the one reason and some for the other.

The two tellers of the Exchange Bank are both there standing side by side. But one of them—the one with the cameo pin and the long face like a horse—is going, and the other—with the other cameo pin and the face like another horse—is not. In the same way, Hussell of the *Newspacket* is going, but his brother, beside him, isn't. Lilian Drone is going, but her sister can't; and so on all through the crowd.

And to think that things should look like that on the morning of a steamboat accident.

How strange life is!

To think of all these people so eager and anxious to catch the steamer, and some of them running to catch it, and so fearful that they might miss it—the morning of a steamboat accident. And the captain blowing his whistle, and warning them so severely that he would leave them behind—leave them out of the accident! And everybody crowding so eagerly to be in the accident.

Perhaps life is like that all through.

Strangest of all to think, in a case like this, of the people who were left behind, or in some way or other prevented from going, and always afterwards told of how they had escaped being on board the *Mariposa Belle* that day!

Some of the instances were certainly extraordinary.

Nivens, the lawyer, escaped from being there merely by the fact that he was away in the city.

Towers, the tailor, only escaped owing to the fact that, not intending to go on the excursion he had stayed in bed till eight o'clock and so had not gone. He narrated afterwards that waking up that morning at half-past five, he had thought of the excursion and for some unaccountable reason had felt glad that he was not going.

The case of Yodel, the auctioneer, was even more inscrutable. He had been to the Oddfellows' excursion on the train the week before and to the Conservative picnic the week before that, and had decided not to go on this trip. In fact, he had not the least intention of going. He narrated afterwards how the night before someone had stopped him on the corner of Nippewa and Tecumseh Streets (he indicated the very spot) and asked: 'Are you going to take in the excursion tomorrow?' and he had said, just as simply as he was talking when narrating it: 'No.' And ten minutes after that, at the corner of Dalhousie and Brock Streets (he offered to lead a party of verification to the precise place) somebody else had stopped him and asked: 'Well, are you going on the steamer trip tomorrow?' Again he had answered: 'No,' apparently almost in the same tone as before.

He said afterwards that when he heard the rumour of the accident it seemed like the finger of Providence, and he fell on his knees in thankfulness.

There was the similar case of Morison (I mean the one in Glover's hardware store that married one of the Thompsons). He said afterwards that he had read so much in the papers about accidents lately—mining accidents, and aeroplanes and gasoline—that he had grown nervous. The night before his wife had asked him at supper: 'Are you going on the excursion?' He had answered: 'No, I don't think I feel like it,' and had added: 'Perhaps your mother might like to go.' And the next evening just at dusk, when the news ran through the town, he said the first thought that flashed through his head was: 'Mrs Thompson's on that boat.'

He told this right as I say it—without the least doubt or confusion. He never for a moment imagined she was on the *Lusitania* or the *Olympic* or any other boat. He knew she was on this one. He said you could have knocked him down where he stood. But no one had. Not even when he got halfway down—on his knees, and it would have been easier still to knock him down or kick him. People do miss a lot of chances.

Still, as I say, neither Yodel nor Morison nor anyone thought about there being an accident until just after sundown when they—

Well, have you ever heard the long booming whistle of a steamboat two miles out on the lake in the dusk, and while you listen and count and wonder, seen the crimson rockets going up against the sky and then heard the fire bell ringing right there beside you in the town, and seen the people running to the town wharf?

That's what the people of Mariposa saw and felt that summer evening as they watched the Mackinaw lifeboat go plunging out into the lake with seven sweeps to a side and the foam clear to the gunwale with the lifting stroke of fourteen men!

But, dear me, I am afraid that this is no way to tell a story. I suppose the true art would have been to have said nothing about the accident till it happened. But when you write about Mariposa, or hear of it, if you know the place, it's all so vivid and real, that a thing like the contrast between the excursion crowd in the morning and the scene at night leaps into your mind and you must think of it.

But never mind about the accident—let us turn back again to the morning.

The boat was due to leave at seven. There was no doubt about the hour—not only seven, but seven sharp. The notice in the *Newspacket* said: 'The boat will leave sharp at seven'; and the advertising posters on the telegraph poles on Missinaba Street that began, 'Ho, for Indian's Island!' ended up with the words: 'Boat leaves at seven sharp.' There was a big notice on the wharf that said: 'Boat leaves sharp on time.'

So at seven, right on the hour, the whistle blew loud and long, and then at seven-fifteen three short peremptory blasts, and at seven-thirty one quick angry call—just one—and very soon after that they cast off the last of the ropes and the *Mariposa Belle* sailed off in her cloud of flags, and the band of the Knights of Pythias, timing it to a nicety, broke into the 'Maple Leaf for Ever!'

I suppose that all excursions when they start are much the same. Anyway, on the *Mariposa Belle* everybody went running up and down all over the boat with deck chairs and camp stools and baskets, and found places, splendid places to sit, and then got scared that there might be better ones and chased off again. People hunted for places out of the sun and when they got them swore that they weren't going to freeze to please anybody; and the people in the sun said that they hadn't paid fifty cents to get roasted. Others said that they hadn't paid fifty cents to get covered with cinders, and there were still others who hadn't paid fifty cents to get shaken to death with the propeller.

Still, it was all right presently. The people seemed to get sorted out into the places on the boat where they belonged. The women, the older ones, all gravitated into the cabin on the lower deck and by getting round the table with needlework, and with all the windows shut, they soon had it, as they said themselves, just like being at home.

All the young boys and the toughs and the men in the band got down on the lower deck forward, where the boat was dirtiest and where the anchor was and the coils of rope.

And upstairs on the after deck there were Lilian Drone and Miss Lawson, the high-school teacher, with a book of German poetry—Gothey I think it was—and the bank teller and the young men.

In the centre, standing beside the rail, were Dean Drone and Dr Gallagher, looking through binocular glasses at the shore.

Up in front on the little deck forward of the pilot house was a group of the older men, Mullins and Duff and Mr Smith in a deck chair, and beside him Mr Golgotha Gingham, the undertaker of Mariposa, on a stool. It was part of Mr Gingham's principles to take in an outing of this sort, a business matter, more or less—for you never know what may happen at these water parties. At any rate, he was there in a neat suit of black, not, of course, his heavier or professional suit, but a soft clinging effect as of burnt paper that combined gaiety and decorum to a nicety.

'Yes,' said Mr Gingham, waving his black glove in a general way towards the shore, 'I know the lake well, very well. I've been pretty much all over it in my time.'

'Canoeing?' asked somebody.

'No,' said Mr Gingham, 'not in a canoe.' There seemed a peculiar and quiet meaning in his tone.

'Sailing, I suppose,' said somebody else.

'No,' said Mr Gingham. 'I don't understand it.'

'I never knowed that you went onto the water at all, Gol,' said Mr Smith, breaking in.

'Ah, not now,' explained Mr Gingham; 'it was years ago, the first summer I came to Mariposa. I was on the water practically all day. Nothing like it to give a man an appetite and keep him in shape.'

'Was you camping?' asked Mr Smith.

'We camped at night,' assented the undertaker, 'but we put in practically the whole day on the water. You see, we were after a party that had come up here from the city on his vacation and gone out in a sailing canoe. We were dragging. We were up every morning at sunrise, lit a fire on the beach and cooked breakfast, and then we'd light our pipes and be off with the net for a whole day. It's great life,' concluded Mr Gingham wistfully.

'Did you get him?' asked two or three together.

There was a pause before Mr Gingham answered.

'We did,' he said '—down in the reeds past Horseshoe Point. But it was no use. He turned blue on me right away.'

After which Mr Gingham fell into such a deep reverie that the boat had steamed another half-mile down the lake before anybody broke the silence again. Talk of this sort—and after all what more suitable for a day on the water?—beguiled the way.

Down the lake, mile by mile over the calm water, steamed the *Mariposa Belle*. They passed Poplar Point where the high sand-banks are with all the swallows' nests in them, and Dean Drone and Dr Gallagher looked at them alternately through the binocular glasses, and it was wonderful how plainly one could see the swallows and the banks and the shrubs—just as plainly as with the naked eye.

And a little farther down they passed the Shingle Beach, and Dr Gallagher, who knew Canadian history, said to Dean Drone that it was strange to think that Champlain had landed there with his French explorers three hundred years ago; and Dean Drone, who didn't know Canadian history, said it was stranger still to think that the hand of the Almighty had piled up the hills and rocks long before that; and Dr Gallagher said it was wonderful how the French had found their way through such a pathless wilderness; and Dean Drone said that it was wonderful also to think that the Almighty had placed even the smallest shrub in its appointed place. Dr Gallagher said it filled him with admiration. Dean Drone said it filled him with awe. Dr Gallagher said he'd been full of it ever since he was a boy and Dean Drone said so had he.

Then a little further, as the *Mariposa Belle* steamed on down the lake, they passed the Old Indian Portage where the great grey rocks are; and Dr Gallagher drew Dean Drone's attention to the place where the narrow canoe track wound up from the shore to the woods, and Dean Drone said he could see it perfectly well without the glasses.

Dr Gallagher said that it was just here that a party of five hundred French had made their way with all their baggage and accoutrements across the rocks of the divide and down to the Great Bay. And Dean Drone said that it reminded him of Xenophon leading his ten thousand Greeks over the hill passes of Armenia down to the sea. Dr Gallagher said that he had often wished he could have seen and spoken to Champlain, and Dean Drone said how much he regretted to have never known Xenophon.

And then after that they fell to talking of relics and traces of the past, and Dr Gallagher said that if Dean Drone would come round to his house some night he would show him some Indian arrow heads that he had dug up in his garden. And Dean Drone said that if Dr Gallagher would come round to the rectory any afternoon he would show him a map of Xerxes' invasion of Greece. Only he must come some time between the Infant Class and the Mothers' Auxiliary.

So presently they both knew that they were blocked out of one another's houses for some time to come, and Dr Gallagher walked forward and told Mr Smith, who had never studied Greek, about Champlain crossing the rock divide.

Mr Smith turned his head and looked at the divide for half a second and then said he had crossed a worse one up north back of the Wahnipitae and that the flies were Hades—and then went on playing freezeout poker with the two juniors in Duff's bank.

So Dr Gallagher realized that that's always the way when you try to tell people things, and that as far as gratitude and appreciation goes one might as well never read books or travel anywhere or do anything.

In fact, it was at this very moment that he made up his mind to give the arrows to the Mariposa Mechanics' Institute—they afterwards became, as you know, the Gallagher Collection. But, for the time being, the doctor was sick of them and wandered off round the boat and watched Henry Mullins showing George Duff how to make a John Collins without lemons, and finally went and sat down among the Mariposa band and wished that he hadn't come.

So the boat steamed on and the sun rose higher and higher, and the freshness of the morning changed into the full glare of noon, and pretty soon the *Mariposa Belle* had floated out onto the lake again and they went on to where the lake began to narrow in at its foot, just where the Indian's Island is—all grass and trees and with a log wharf running into the water. Below it the Lower Ossawippi runs out of the lake, and quite near are the rapids, and you can see down among the trees the red brick of the power house and hear the roar of the leaping water.

The Indian's Island itself is all covered with trees and tangled vines, and the water about it is so still that it's all reflected double and looks the same either way up. Then when the steamer's whistle blows as it comes into the wharf, you hear it echo among the trees of the island, and reverberate back from the shores of the lake.

The scene is all so quiet and still and unbroken, that Miss Cleghorn—the sallow girl in the telephone exchange, that I spoke of—said she'd like to be buried there. But all the people were so busy getting their baskets and gathering up their things that no one had time to attend to it.

I mustn't even try to describe the landing and the boat crunching against the wooden wharf and all the people running to the same side of the deck and Christie Johnson calling out to the crowd to keep to the starboard and nobody being able to find it. Everyone who has been on a Mariposa excursion knows all about that.

Nor can I describe the day itself and the picnic under the trees. There were speeches afterwards, and Judge Pepperleigh gave such offence by bringing in Conservative politics that a man called Patriotus Canadiensis wrote and asked for some of the invaluable space of the *Mariposa Times-Herald* and exposed it.

I should say that there were races too, on the grass on the open side of the island, graded mostly according to ages—races for boys under thirteen and girls over nineteen and all that sort of thing. Sports are generally conducted on that plan in Mariposa. It is realized that a woman of sixty has an unfair advantage over a mere child.

Dean Drone managed the races and decided the ages and gave out the prizes; the Wesleyan minister helped, and he and the young student, who was relieving in the Presbyterian Church, held the string at the winning point.

They had to get mostly clergymen for the races because all the men had wandered off, somehow, to where they were drinking lager beer out of two kegs stuck on pine logs among the trees.

But if you've ever been on a Mariposa excursion you know all about these details anyway.

So the day wore on and presently the sun came through the trees on a slant and the steamer whistle blew with a great puff of white steam and all the people came straggling down to the wharf and pretty soon the *Mariposa Belle* had floated out onto the lake again and headed for the town, twenty miles away.

I suppose you have often noticed the contrast there is between an excursion on its way out in the morning and what it looks like on the way home.

In the morning everybody is so restless and animated and moves to and from all over the boat and asks questions. But coming home, as the afternoon gets later and later and the sun sinks beyond the hills, all the people seem to get so still and quiet and drowsy.

So it was with the people on the *Mariposa Belle*. They sat there on the benches and the deck chairs in little clusters, and listened to the regular beat of the propeller and almost dozed off asleep as they sat. Then when the sun set and the dusk drew on, it grew almost dark on the deck and so still that you could hardly tell there was anyone on board.

And if you had looked at the steamer from the shore or from one of the islands, you'd have seen the row of lights from the cabin windows shining on the water and the red glare of the burning hemlock from the funnel, and you'd have heard the soft thud of the propeller miles away over the lake.

Now and then, too, you could have heard them singing on the steamer—the voices of the girls and the men blended into unison by the distance, rising and falling in long-drawn melody: '*O—Can-a-da—O—Can-a-da*.'

You may talk as you will about the intoning choirs of your European cathedrals, but the sound of '*O—Can-a-da*', borne across the waters of a silent lake at evening is good enough for those of us who know Mariposa.

I think that it was just as they were singing like this: '*O—Can-a-da*', that word went round that the boat was sinking.

If you have ever been in any sudden emergency on the water, you will understand the strange psychology of it—the way in which what is happening seems to become known all in a moment without a word being said. The news is transmitted from one to the other by some mysterious process.

At any rate, on the *Mariposa Belle* first one and then the other heard that the steamer was sinking. As far as I could ever learn the first of it was that George Duff, the bank manager, came very quietly to Dr Gallagher and asked him if he thought that the boat was sinking. The doctor said no, that he had thought so earlier in the day but that he didn't now think that she was.

After that Duff, according to his own account, had said to Macartney, the lawyer, that the boat was sinking, and Macartney said that he doubted it very much.

Then somebody came to Judge Pepperleigh and woke him up and said that there was six inches of water in the steamer and that she was sinking. And Pepperleigh said it was perfect scandal and passed the news on to his wife and she said that they had no business to allow it and that if the steamer sank that was the last excursion she'd go on.

So the news went all round the boat and everywhere the people gathered in groups and talked about it in the angry and excited way that people have when a steamer is sinking on one of the lakes like Lake Wissanotti.

Dean Drone, of course, and some others were quieter about it, and said that one must make allowances and that naturally there were two sides to everything. But most of them wouldn't listen to reason at all. I think, perhaps, that some of them were frightened. You see the last time but one that the steamer had sunk, there had been a man drowned and it made them nervous.

What? Hadn't I explained about the depth of Lake Wissanotti? I had taken it for granted that you knew; and in any case parts of it are deep enough, though I don't suppose in this stretch of it from the big reed beds up to within a mile of the town wharf, you could find six feet of water in it if you tried. Oh, pshaw! I was not talking about a steamer sinking in the ocean and carrying down its screaming crowds of people into the hideous depths of green water. Oh, dear me, no! That kind of thing never happens on Lake Wissanotti.

But what does happen is that the *Mariposa Belle* sinks every now and then, and sticks there on the bottom till they get things straightened up.

On the lakes round Mariposa, if a person arrives late anywhere and explains that the steamer sank, everybody understands the situation.

You see when Harland and Wolff built the *Mariposa Belle*, they left some cracks in between the timbers that you fill up with cotton waste every Sunday. If this is not attended to, the boat sinks. In fact, it is part of the law of the province that all the steamers like the *Mariposa Belle* must be properly corked—I think that is the word—every season. There are inspectors who visit all the hotels in the province to see that it is done.

So you can imagine now that I've explained it a little straighter, the indignation of the people when they knew that the boat had come uncorked and that they might be stuck out there on a shoal or a mud-bank half the night.

I don't say either that there wasn't any danger; anyway, it doesn't feel very safe when you realize that the boat is settling down with every hundred yards that she goes, and you look over the side and see only the black water in the gathering night.

Safe! I'm not sure now that I come to think of it that it isn't worse thank sinking in the Atlantic. After all, in the Atlantic there is wireless telegraphy, and a lot of trained sailors and stewards. But out on Lake Wissanotti—far out, so that you can only just see the lights of the town away off to the south—when the propeller comes to a stop—and you can hear the hiss of steam as they start to rake out the engine fires to prevent explosion—and when you turn from the red glare that comes from the furnace doors as they open them, to the black dark that is gathering over the lake—and there's a night wind beginning to run among the rushes—and you see the men going forward to the roof of the pilot house to send up the rockets to rouse the town—safe? Safe yourself, if you like; as for me, let me once get back to Mariposa again, under the night shadow of the maple trees, and this shall be the last, last time I'll go on Lake Wissanotti.

Safe! Oh, yes! Isn't it strange how safe other people's adventures seem after they happen? But you'd have been scared, too, if you'd been there just before the steamer sank, and seen them bringing up all the women onto the top deck.

I don't see how some of the people took it so calmly; how Mr Smith, for instance, could have gone on smoking and telling how he'd had a steamer 'sink on him' on Lake Nipissing and a still bigger one, a side-wheeler, sink on him in Lake Abbitibbi.

Then, quite suddenly, with a quiver, down she went. You could feel the boat sink, sink—down, down—would it never get to the bottom? The water came flush up to the lower deck, and then—thank heaven—the sinking stopped and there was the *Mariposa Belle* safe and tight on a reed bank.

Really, it made one positively laugh! It seemed so queer and, anyway, if a man has a sort of natural courage, danger makes him laugh. Danger? pshaw! fiddlesticks! everybody scouted the idea. Why, it is just the little things like this that give zest to a day on the water.

Within half a minute they were all running round looking for sandwiches and cracking jokes and talking of making coffee over the remains of the engine fires.

I don't need to tell at length how it all happened after that.

I suppose the people on the *Mariposa Belle* would have had to settle down there all night or till help came from the town, but some of the men who had gone forward and were peering out into the dark said that it couldn't be more than a mile across the water to Miller's Point. You could almost see it over there to the left—some of them, I think, said 'off on the port bow', because you know when you get mixed up in these marine disasters, you soon catch the atmosphere of the thing.

So pretty soon they had the davits swung out over the side and were lowering the old lifeboat from the top deck into the water.

There were men leaning out over the rail of the *Mariposa Belle* with lanterns that threw the light as they let her down, and the glare fell on the water and the reeds. But when they got the boat lowered, it looked such a frail, clumsy thing as one saw it from the rail above, that the cry was raised: 'Women and children first!' For what was the sense, if it should turn out that the boat wouldn't even hold women and children, of trying to jam a lot of heavy men into it?

So they put in mostly women and children and the boat pushed out into the darkness so freighted down it would hardly float.

In the bow of it was the Presbyterian student who was relieving the minister, and he called out that they were in the hands of Providence. But he was crouched and ready to spring out of them at the first moment.

So the boat went and was lost in the darkness except for the lantern in the bow that you could see bobbing on the water. Then presently it came back and they sent another load, till pretty soon the decks began to thin out and everybody got impatient to be gone.

It was about the time that the third boat-load put off that Mr Smith took a bet with Mullins for twenty-five dollars, that he'd be home in Mariposa before the people in the boats had walked round the shore.

No one knew just what he meant, but pretty soon they saw Mr Smith disappear down below the lowest part of the steamer with a mallet in one hand and a big bundle of marline in the other.

They might have wondered more about it, but it was just at this time that they heard the shouts from the rescue boat—the big Mackinaw lifeboat—that had put out from the town with fourteen men at the sweeps when they saw the first rockets go up.

I suppose there is always something inspiring about a rescue at sea, or on the water.

After all, the bravery of the lifeboat man is the true bravery—expended to save life, not to destroy it.

Certainly they told for months after of how the rescue boat came out to the *Mariposa Belle*.

I suppose that when they put her in the water the lifeboat touched it for the first time since the old Macdonald Government placed her on Lake Wissanotti.

Anyway, the water poured in at every seam. But not for a moment—even with two miles of water between them and the steamer—did the rowers pause for that.

By the time they were halfway there the water was almost up to the thwarts, but they drove her on. Panting and exhausted (for mind you, if you haven't been in a fool boat like that for years, rowing takes it out of you), the rowers stuck to their task. They threw the ballast over and chucked into the water the heavy cork jackets and lifebelts that encumbered their movements. There was no thought of turning back. They were nearer to the steamer than the shore.

'Hang to it, boys,' called the crowd from the steamer's deck, and hang they did.

They were almost exhausted when they got them; men leaning from the steamer threw them ropes and one by one every man was hauled aboard just as the lifeboat sank under their feet.

Saved! by heaven, saved by one of the smartest pieces of rescue work ever seen on the lake.

There's no use describing it; you need to see rescue work of this kind by lifeboats to understand it.

Nor were the lifeboat crew the only ones that distinguished themselves.

Boat after boat and canoe after canoe had put out from Mariposa to the help of the steamer. They got them all.

Pupkin, the other bank teller with a face like a horse, who hadn't gone on the excursion—as soon as he knew that the boat was signalling for help and that Miss Lawson was sending up rockets—rushed for a row boat, grabbed an oar (two would have hampered him)—and paddled madly out into the lake. He struck right out into the dark with the crazy skiff almost sinking beneath his feet. But they got him. They rescued him. They watched him, almost dead with exhaustion, make his way to the steamer, where he was hauled up with ropes. Saved! Saved!

They might have gone on that way half the night, picking up the rescuers, only, at the very moment when the tenth load of people left for the shore—just as suddenly and saucily as you please, up came the *Mariposa Belle* from the mud bottom and floated.

Floated?

Why, of course she did. If you take a hundred and fifty people off a steamer that has sunk, and if you get a man as shrewd as Mr Smith to plug the timber seams with mallet and marline, and if you turn ten bandsmen of the Mariposa band onto your hand pump on the bow of the lower decks—float? why, what else can she do?

Then, if you stuff in hemlock into the embers of the fire that you were raking out, till it hums and crackles under the boiler, it won't be long before you hear the propeller thud—thudding at the stern again, and before the long roar of the steam whistle echoes over to the town.

And so the *Mariposa Belle*, with all steam up again and with the long train of sparks careering from the funnel, is heading for the town.

But no Christie Johnson at the wheel in the pilot house this time.

'Smith! Get Smith!' is the cry.

Can he take her in? Well, now! Ask a man who has had steamers sink on him in half the lakes from Temiscaming to the Bay, if he can take her in? Ask a man who has run a York boat down the rapids of the Moose when the ice is moving, if he can grip the steering wheel of the *Mariposa Belle*? So there she steams safe and sound to the town wharf!

Look at the lights and the crowds! If only the federal census taker could count us now! Hear them calling and shouting back and forward from the deck to the shore! Listen! There is the rattle of the shore ropes as they get them ready, and there's the Mariposa band—actually forming in a circle on the upper deck just as she docks, and the leader with his baton—one—two—ready now—

'O CAN-A-DA!'

1912

Stephen Crane
1871–1900

Born in Newark, New Jersey, Stephen Crane was the fourteenth child of a Methodist minister, who named him after an ancestor who had signed the Declaration of Independence. He was a delicate child, whose health improved when his family moved to Port Jervis, New York, in 1879. After his father died he went to the Hudson River Institute at Caverack, New York, and then to Lafayette College and Syracuse University, where his interests shifted from engineering to literature. While in school he began work as a journalist, a profession he pursued for most of his life. But his reporting always suffered from an excess of art: a poetic image would distract him from journalistic details. He wrote an ironic novel (*Maggie: A Girl of the Streets*, 1893) when he was twenty-two, and a masterful novel of the Civil War (*The Red Badge of Courage*, 1895) two years later. He had not been to war but based his writings on the accounts of soldiers he had heard and on his reading of Tolstoy. He later became a war correspondent and confirmed his guesses firsthand.

Like many of America's best writers, Crane was cynical and sentimental at the same time. His blunt manner and indifference to public opinion offended many of his contemporaries, but Henry James and Joseph Conrad admired his work and came to pay their respects to the younger man as he was dying in Europe of tuberculosis. Written after Crane's travels to the picturesque landscape of the American southwest, 'The Bride Comes to Yellow Sky' centres on the figure of Jack Potter, the marshal of Yellow Sky, and his failure to inform his town of his marriage to a young woman from San Antonio. In contrast to him stands Scratchy Wilson, the town drunk and a throwback to the earlier days of the Wild West. Wilson's violent behaviour leads to his glimpse of a social order in the two newlyweds.

The Bride Comes to Yellow Sky

I

The great Pullman was whirling onward with such dignity of motion that a glance from the window seemed simply to prove that the plains of Texas were pouring eastward. Vast flats of green grass, dull-hued spaces of mesquite and cactus, little groups of frame houses, woods of light and tender trees, all were sweeping into the east, sweeping over the horizon, a precipice.

A newly married pair had boarded this coach at San Antonio. The man's face was reddened from many days in the wind and sun, and a direct result of his new black clothes was that his brick-coloured hands were constantly performing in a most conscious fashion. From time to time he looked down respectfully at his attire. He sat with a hand on each knee, like a man waiting in a barber's shop. The glances he devoted to other passengers were furtive and shy.

The bride was not pretty, nor was she very young. She wore a dress of blue cashmere, with small reservations of velvet here and there, and with steel buttons abounding. She continually twisted her head to regard her puff sleeves, very stiff, straight, and high. They embarrassed her. It was quite apparent that she had cooked, and that she expected to cook, dutifully. The blushes caused by the careless scrutiny of some passengers as she had entered the car were strange to see upon this plain, under-class countenance, which was drawn in placid, almost emotionless lines.

They were evidently very happy. 'Ever been in a parlour-car before?' he asked, smiling with delight.

'No,' she answered; 'I never was. It's fine, ain't it?'

'Great! And then after a while we'll go forward to the diner, and get a big lay-out. Finest meal in the world. Charge a dollar.'

'Oh, do they?' cried the bride. 'Charge a dollar? Why, that's too much—for us—ain't it, Jack?'

'Not this trip, anyhow,' he answered bravely. 'We're going to go the whole thing.'

Later he explained to her about the trains. 'You see, it's a thousand miles from one end of Texas to the other; and this train runs right across it, and never stops but four times.' He had the pride of an owner. He pointed out to her the dazzling fittings of the coach; and in truth her eyes opened wider as she contemplated the sea-green figured velvet, the shining brass, silver, and glass, the wood that gleamed as darkly brilliant as the surface of a pool of oil. At one end a bronze figure sturdily held a support for a separated chamber, and at convenient places on the ceiling were frescos in olive and silver.

To the minds of the pair, their surroundings reflected the glory of their marriage that morning in San Antonio; this was the environment of their new estate; and the man's face in particular beamed with an elation that made him appear ridiculous to the Negro porter. This individual at times surveyed them from afar with an amused and superior grin. On other occasions he bullied them with skill in ways that did not make it exactly plain to them that they were being bullied. He subtly used all the manners of the most unconquerable kind of snobbery. He oppressed them; but of this oppression they had small knowledge, and they speedily forgot that infrequently a number of travellers covered them with stares of derisive enjoyment. Historically there was supposed to be something infinitely humorous in their situation.

'We are due in Yellow Sky at 3:42,' he said looking tenderly into her eyes.

'Oh, are we?' she said, as if she had not been aware of it. To evince surprise at her husband's statement was part of her wifely amiability. She took from a pocket a little silver watch; and as she held it before her, and stared at it with a frown of attention, the new husband's face shone.

'I bought it in San Anton' from a friend of mine,' he told her gleefully.

'It's seventeen minutes past twelve,' she said, looking up at him with a kind of shy and clumsy coquetry. A passenger, noting this play, grew excessively sardonic, and winked at himself in one of the numerous mirrors.

At last they went to the dining car. Two rows of Negro waiters, in glowing white suits, surveyed their entrance with the interest, and also the equanimity, of men who had been forewarned. The pair fell to the lot of a waiter who happened to feel pleasure in steering them through their meal. He viewed them with the manner of a fatherly pilot, his countenance radiant with benevolence. The patronage, entwined with the ordinary deference, was not plain to them. And yet, as they returned to their coach, they showed in their faces a sense of escape.

To the left, miles down a long purple slope, was a little ribbon of mist where moved the keening Rio Grande. The train was approaching it at an angle, and the apex was Yellow Sky. Presently it was apparent that, as the distance from Yellow Sky grew shorter, the husband became commensurately restless. His brick-red hands were more insistent in their prominence. Occasionally he was even rather absent-minded and faraway when the bride leaned forward and addressed him.

As a matter of truth, Jack Potter was beginning to find the shadow of a deed weigh upon him like a leaden slab. He, the town marshal of Yellow Sky, a man known, liked, and feared in his corner, a prominent person, had gone to San Antonio to meet a girl he believed he loved, and there, after the usual prayers, had actually induced her to marry him, without consulting Yellow Sky for any part of the transaction. He was now bringing his bride before an innocent and unsuspecting community.

Of course people in Yellow Sky married as it pleased them in accordance with a general custom; but such was Potter's thought of his duty to his friends, or of their idea of his duty, or of an unspoken form which does not control men in these matters, that he felt he was heinous. He had committed an extraordinary crime. Face to face with this girl in San Antonio, and spurred by his sharp impulse, he had gone headlong over all the social hedges. At San Antonio he was like a man hidden in the dark. A knife to sever any friendly duty, any form, was easy to his hand in that remote city. But the hour of Yellow Sky—the hour of daylight—was approaching.

He knew full well that his marriage was an important thing to his town. It could only be exceeded by the burning of the new hotel. His friends could not forgive him. Frequently he had reflected on the advisability of telling them by telegraph, but a new cowardice had been upon him. He feared to do it. And now the train was hurrying him toward a scene of amazement, glee, and reproach. He glanced out of the window at the line of haze swinging slowly in toward the train.

Yellow Sky had a kind of brass band, which played painfully, to the delight of the populace. He laughed without heart as he thought of it. If the citizens could dream of his prospective arrival with his bride, they would parade the band at the station and escort them, amid cheers and laughing congratulations, to his adobe home.

He resolved that he would use all the devices of speed and plains-craft in making the journey from the station to his house. Once within that safe citadel, he could issue some sort of vocal bulletin, and then not go among the citizens until they had time to wear off a little of their enthusiasm.

The bride looked anxiously at him. 'What's worrying you, Jack?'

He laughed again. 'I'm not worrying, girl; I'm only thinking of Yellow Sky.'

She flushed in comprehension.

A sense of mutual guilt invaded their minds and developed a finer tenderness. They looked at each other with eyes softly aglow. But Potter often laughed the same nervous laugh; the flush upon the bride's face seemed quite permanent.

The traitor to the feelings of Yellow Sky narrowly watched the speeding landscape. 'We're nearly there,' he said.

Presently the porter came and announced the proximity of Potter's home. He held a brush in his hand, and, with all his airy superiority gone, he brushed Potter's new clothes as the latter slowly turned this way and that way. Potter fumbled out a coin and gave it to the porter, as he had seen others do. It was a heavy and muscle-bound business, as that of a man shoeing his first horse.

The porter took their bag, and as the train began to slow they moved forward to the hooded platform of the car. Presently the two engines and their long string of coaches rushed into the station of Yellow Sky.

'They have to take water here,' said Potter, from a constricted throat and in mournful cadence, as one announcing death. Before the train stopped his eye had swept the length of the platform, and he was glad and astonished to see there was none upon it but the station agent, who, with a slightly hurried and anxious air, was walking toward the water tanks. When the train had halted, the porter alighted first, and placed in position a little temporary step.

'Come on, girl,' said Potter, hoarsely. As he helped her down they each laughed on a false note. He took the bag from the Negro, and bade his wife cling to his arm. As they slunk rapidly away, his hang-dog glance perceived that they were unloading the two trunks, and also that the station agent, far ahead near the baggage car, had turned and was running toward him, making gestures. He laughed, and groaned as he laughed, when he noted the first effect of his marital bliss upon Yellow Sky. He gripped his wife's arm firmly to his side, and they fled. Behind them the porter stood, chuckling fatuously.

II

The California express on the Southern Railway was due at Yellow Sky in twenty-one minutes. There were six men at the bar of the Weary Gentleman saloon. One was a drummer who talked a great deal and rapidly; three were Texans who did not care to talk at that time; and two were Mexican sheep-herders, who did not talk as a general practice in the Weary Gentleman saloon. The barkeeper's dog lay on the boardwalk that crossed in front of the door. His head was on his paws, and he glanced drowsily here and there with the constant vigilance of a dog that is kicked on occasion. Across the sandy street were some vivid green grass-plots, so wonderful in appearance, amid the sands that burned near them in a blazing sun, that they caused a doubt in the mind. They exactly resembled the grass mats used to represent lawns on the stage. At the cooler end of the railway station, a man without a coat sat in a tilted chair and smoked his pipe. The fresh-cut bank of the Rio Grande circled near the town, and there could be seen beyond it a great plum-coloured plain of mesquite.

Save for the busy drummer and his companions in the saloon, Yellow Sky was dozing. The newcomer leaned gracefully upon the bar, and recited many tales with the confidence of a bard who has come upon a new field.

'—and at the moment that the old man fell downstairs with the bureau in his arms, the old woman was coming up with two scuttles of coal, and of course—'

The drummer's tale was interrupted by a young man who suddenly appeared in the open door. He cried: 'Scratchy Wilson's drunk, and has turned loose with both hands.' The two Mexicans at once set down their glasses and faded out of the rear entrance of the saloon.

The drummer, innocent and jocular, answered: 'All right, old man. S'pose he has? Come in and have a drink, anyhow.'

But the information had made such an obvious cleft in every skull in the room that the drummer was obliged to see its importance. All had become instantly solemn. 'Say,' said he, mystified, 'what is this?' His three companions made the introductory gesture of eloquent speech; but the young man at the door forestalled them.

'It means, my friend,' he answered, as he came into the saloon, 'that for the next two hours this town won't be a health resort.'

The barkeeper went to the door, and locked and barred it; reaching out of the window, he pulled in heavy wooden shutters, and barred them. Immediately a solemn, chapel-like gloom was upon the place. The drummer was looking from one to another.

'But say,' he cried, 'what is this, anyhow? You don't mean there is going to be a gunfight?'

'Don't know whether there'll be a fight or not,' answered one man, grimly; 'but there'll be some shootin'—some good shootin'.'

The young man who had warned them waved his hand. 'Oh, there'll be a fight fast enough, if anyone wants it. Anybody can get a fight out there in the street. There's a fight just waiting.'

The drummer seemed to be swayed between the interest of a foreigner and a perception of personal danger.

'What did you say his name was?' he asked.

'Scratchy Wilson,' they answered in chorus.

'And will he kill anybody? What are you going to do? Does this happen often? Does he rampage around like this once a week or so? Can he break in that door?'

'No; he can't break down that door,' replied the barkeeper. 'He's tried it three times. But when he comes you'd better lay down on the floor, stranger. He's dead sure to shoot at it, and a bullet may come through.'

Thereafter the drummer kept a strict eye upon the door. The time had not yet called for him to hug the floor, but, as a minor precaution, he sidled near the wall. 'Will he kill anybody?' he said again.

The men laughed low and scornfully at the question.

'He's out to shoot, and he's out for trouble. Don't see any good in experimentin' with him.'

'But what do you do in a case like this? What do you do?'

A man responded: 'Why, he and Jack Potter—'

'But', in chorus the other men interrupted, 'Jack Potter's in San Anton'.'

'Well, who is he? What's he got to do with it?'

'Oh, he's the town marshal. He goes out and fights Scratchy when he gets on one of these tears.'

'Wow!' said the drummer, mopping his brow. 'Nice job he's got.'

The voices had toned away to mere whisperings. The drummer wished to ask further questions, which were born of an increasing anxiety and bewilderment; but when he attempted them, the men merely looked at him in irritation and motioned him to remain silent. A tense waiting hush was upon them. In the deep shadows of the room their eyes shone as they listened for sounds from the street. One man made three gestures at the barkeeper; and the latter, moving like a ghost, handed him a glass and a bottle. The man poured a full glass of whisky, and set down the bottle noiselessly. He gulped the whisky in a swallow, and turned again toward the door in immovable silence. The drummer saw that the barkeeper, without a sound, had taken a Winchester from beneath the bar. Later he saw this individual beckoning to him, so he tiptoed across the room.

'You better come with me back of the bar.'

'No, thanks,' said the drummer, perspiring; 'I'd rather be where I can make a break for the back door.'

Whereupon the man of bottles made a kindly but peremptory gesture. The drummer obeyed it, and, finding himself seated on a box with his head below the level of the bar, balm was laid upon his soul at sight of various zinc and copper fittings that bore a resemblance to armour-plate. The barkeeper took a seat comfortably upon an adjacent box.

'You see,' he whispered, 'this here Scratchy Wilson is a wonder with a gun—a perfect wonder; and when he goes on the war-trail, we hunt our holes—naturally. He's about the last one of the old gang that used to hang out along the river here. He's a terror when he's drunk. When he's sober he's all right—kind of simple—wouldn't hurt a fly—nicest fellow in town. But when he's drunk—whoo!'

There were periods of stillness. 'I wish Jack Potter was back from San Anton',' said the barkeeper. 'He shot Wilson up once—in the leg—and he would sail in and pull out the kinks in this thing.'

Presently they heard from the distance the sound of a shot, followed by three wild yowls. It instantly removed a bond from the men in the darkened saloon. There was a shuffling of feet. They looked at each other. 'Here he comes,' they said.

III

A man in a maroon-coloured flannel shirt, which had been purchased for purposes of decoration, and made principally by some Jewish women on the East Side of New York, rounded a corner and walked into the middle of the main street of Yellow Sky. In either hand the man held a long, heavy, blue-black revolver. Often he yelled, and these cries rang through a semblance of a deserted village, shrilly flying over the roofs in a volume that seemed to have no relation to the ordinary vocal strength of a man. It was as if the surrounding stillness formed the arch of a tomb over him. These cries of ferocious challenge rang against walls of silence. And his boots had red tops with gilded imprints, of the kind beloved in winter by little sledding boys on the hillsides of New England.

The man's face flamed in a rage begot of whisky. His eyes, rolling, and yet keen for ambush, hunted the still doorways and windows. He walked with the creeping movement of the midnight cat. As it occurred to him, he roared menacing information. The long revolvers in his hands were as easy as straws; they were removed with an electric swiftness. The little fingers of each hand played sometimes in a musician's way. Plain from the low collar of the shirt, the cords of his neck straightened and sank, straightened and sank, as passion moved him. The only sounds were his terrible invitations. The calm adobes preserved their demeanour at the passing of this small thing in the middle of the street.

There was no offer of fight—no offer of fight. The man called to the sky. There were no attractions. He bellowed and fumed and swayed his revolvers here and everywhere.

The dog of the barkeeper of the Weary Gentleman saloon had not appreciated the advance of events. He yet lay dozing in front of his master's door. At sight of the dog, the man paused and raised his revolver humorously. At sight of the man, the dog sprang up and walked diagonally away, with a sullen head, and growling. The man yelled, and the dog broke into a gallop. As it was about to enter the alley, there was a loud noise, a whistling, and something spat the ground directly before it. The dog screamed, and, wheeling in terror, galloped headlong in a new direction. Again there was a noise, a whistling, and sand was kicked viciously before it. Fear-stricken, the dog turned and flurried like an animal in a pen. The man stood laughing, his weapons at his hips.

Ultimately the man was attracted by the closed door of the Weary Gentleman saloon. He went to it and, hammering with a revolver, demanded drink.

The door remaining imperturbable, he picked a bit of paper from the walk, and nailed it to the framework with a knife. He then turned his back contemptuously upon this popular resort and, walking to the opposite side of the street and spinning there on his heel quickly and lithely, fired at the bit of paper. He missed it by a half inch. He swore at himself, and went away. Later he comfortably fusilladed the windows of his most intimate friend. The man was playing with this town; it was a toy for him.

But still there was no offer of fight. The name of Jack Potter, his ancient antagonist, entered his mind, and he concluded that it would be a glad thing if he should go to Potter's house, and by bombardment induce him to come out and fight. He moved in the direction of his desire, chanting Apache scalp-music.

When he arrived at it, Potter's house presented the same still front as had the other adobes. Taking up a strategic position, the man howled a challenge. But this house regarded him as might a great stone god. It gave no sign. After a decent wait, the man howled further challenges, mingling with them wonderful epithets.

Presently there came the spectacle of a man churning himself into deepest rage over the immobility of a house. He fumed at it as the winter wind attacks a prairie cabin in the North. To the distance there should have gone the sound of tumult like the fighting of two hundred Mexicans. As necessity bade him, he paused for breath or to reload his revolvers.

IV

Potter and his bride walked sheepishly and with speed. Sometimes they laughed together shamefacedly and low.

'Next corner, dear,' he said finally.

They put forth the efforts of a pair walking bowed against a strong wind. Potter was about to raise a finger to point the first appearance of the new home when, as they circled the corner, they came face to face with a man in a maroon-coloured shirt, who was feverishly pushing cartridges into a large revolver. Upon the instant the man dropped his revolver to the ground and, like lightning, whipped another from its holster. The second weapon was aimed at the bridegroom's chest.

There was a silence. Potter's mouth seemed to be merely a grave for his tongue. He exhibited an instinct to at once loosen his arm from the woman's grip, and he dropped the bag to the sand. As for the bride, her face had gone as yellow as old cloth. She was a slave to hideous rites, gazing at the apparitional snake.

The two men faced each other at a distance of three paces. He of the revolver smiled with a new and quiet ferocity.

'Tried to sneak up on me,' he said. 'Tried to sneak up on me!' His eyes grew more baleful. As Potter made a slight movement, the man thrust his revolver venomously forward 'No; don't you do it, Jack Potter. Don't you move a finger toward a gun just yet. Don't you move an eyelash. The time has come for me to settle with you and I'm goin' to do it my own way, and loaf along with no interferin'. So if you don't want a gun bent on you, just mind what I tell you.'

Potter looked at his enemy. 'I ain't got a gun on me Scratchy,' he said. 'Honest, I ain't.' He was stiffening and steadying, but yet somewhere at the back of his mind a vision of the Pullman floated: the sea-green figured velvet, the shining brass, silver, and glass, the wood that gleamed as darkly brilliant as the surface of a pool of oil—all the glory of marriage, the environment of the new estate. 'You know I fight when it comes to fighting, Scratchy Wilson; but I ain't got a gun on me. You'll have to do all the shootin' yourself.'

His enemy's face went livid. He stepped forward, and lashed weapon to and fro before Potter's chest. 'Don't you tell me you ain't got no gun on you, you whelp. Don't tell me no lie like that. There ain't a man in Texas ever seen you without no gun. Don't take me for no kid.' His eyes blazed with light, and his throat worked like a pump.

'I ain't takin' you for no kid,' answered Potter. His heels had not moved an inch backward. 'I'm takin' you for a damn fool. I tell you I ain't got a gun, and I ain't. If you're goin' to shoot me up, you better begin now; you'll never get a chance like this again.'

So much enforced reasoning had told on Wilson's rage; he was calmer. 'If you ain't got a gun, why ain't you got a gun?' he sneered. 'Been to Sunday school?'

'I ain't got a gun because I've just come from San Anton' with my wife. I'm married,' said Potter. 'And if I'd thought there was going to be any galoots like you prowling around when I brought my wife home, I'd had a gun, and don't you forget it.'

'Married!' said Scratchy, not at all comprehending.

'Yes, married. I'm married,' said Potter, distinctly.

'Married?' said Scratchy. Seemingly for the first time, he saw the drooping, drowning woman at the other man's side. 'No!' he said. He was like a creature allowed a glimpse of another world. He moved a pace backward, and his arm, with the revolver, dropped to his side. 'Is this the lady?' he asked.

'Yes; this is the lady,' answered Potter.

There was another period of silence.

'Well,' said Wilson at last, slowly, 'I s'pose it's all off now.'

'It's all off if you say so, Scratchy. You know I didn't make the trouble.' Potter lifted his valise.

'Well, I 'low it's off, Jack,' said Wilson. He was looking at the ground. 'Married!' He was not a student of chivalry; it was merely that in the presence of this foreign condition he was a simple child of the earlier plains. He picked up his starboard revolver, and, placing both weapons in their holsters, he went away. His feet made funnel-shaped tracks in the heavy sand.

1898

James Joyce
1882–1941

James Joyce was born near Dublin, Ireland, and educated at the Jesuit school Belvedere College and at University College, Dublin. He went into self-imposed exile in 1904, taking with him a young woman named Nora Barnacle. 'She'll never leave him,' said Joyce's father, and she did not. In Italy and in Switzerland Joyce earned a precarious living teaching English while trying to become a great writer. His short stories were all designed for a collection called *Dubliners*, fifteen stories set in middle-class, Catholic Dublin, which waited ten years before finally being published and then sold fewer than five hundred copies in 1914; 'Araby', the third story, is the first-person account of a young boy's fascination with a girl down the street.

Joyce's autobiographical novel *A Portrait of the Artist as a Young Man* (1916) attracted the attention of T.S. Eliot and Ezra Pound, who helped him get support for his major project, *Ulysses* (1922), which took realism to its logical conclusion and beyond. *Finnegan's Wake* (1939) is all beyond—a book to keep the critics busy, as Joyce observed. Together these works had an immense influence on the form and structure of the modern novel and on the development of stream-of-consciousness narration. Just as remarkable, though less noticeable, as these technical breakthroughs are Joyce's comic spirit and humanity.

Araby *kids*

North Richmond Street, being blind, was a quiet street except at the hour when the Christian Brothers' School set the boys free. An uninhabited house of two storeys stood at the blind end, detached from its neighbours in a square ground. The other houses of the street, conscious of decent lives within them, gazed at one another with brown imperturbable faces.

The former tenant of our house, a priest, had died in the back drawing room. Air, musty from having been long enclosed, hung in all the rooms, and the waste room behind the kitchen was littered with old useless papers. Among these I found a few paper-covered books, the pages of which were curled and damp: *The Abbot*, by Walter Scott, *The Devout Communicant*, and *The Memoirs of Vidocq*. I liked the last best because its leaves were yellow. The wild garden behind the house contained a central apple tree and a few straggling bushes under one of which I found the late tenant's rusty bicycle pump. He had been a very charitable priest; in his will he had left all his money to institutions and the furniture of his house to his sister.

When the short days of winter came dusk fell before we had well eaten our dinners. When we met in the street the houses had grown sombre. The space of the sky above us was the colour of ever-changing violet and towards it the lamps of the street lifted their feeble lanterns. The cold air stung us and we played till our bodies glowed. Our shouts echoed in the silent street. The career of our play brought us through the dark muddy lanes behind the houses where we ran the gauntlet of the rough tribes from the cottages, to the back doors of the dark dripping gardens where odours arose from the ashpits, to the dark odorous stables where a coachman smoothed and combed the horse or shook music from the buckled harness. When we returned to the street light from the kitchen windows had filled the areas. If my uncle was seen turning the corner we hid in the shadows until we had seen him safely housed. Or if Mangan's sister came out on the doorstep to call her brother in to his tea we watched her from our shadow peer up and down the street. We waited to see whether she would remain or go in and, if she remained, we left our shadow and walked up to Mangan's steps resignedly. She was waiting for us, her figure defined by the light from the half-opened door. Her brother always teased her before he obeyed and I stood by the railings looking at her. Her dress swung as she moved her body and the soft rope of her hair tossed from side to side.

Every morning I lay on the floor in the front parlour watching her door. The blind was pulled down to within an inch of the sash so that I could not be seen. When she came out on the doorstep my heart leaped. I ran to the hall, seized my books, and followed her. I kept her brown figure always in my eye and, when we came near the point at which our ways diverged, I quickened my pace and passed her. This happened morning after morning. I had never spoken to her, except for a few casual words, and yet her name was like a summons to all my foolish blood.

Her image accompanied me even in places the most hostile to romance. On Saturday evenings when my aunt went marketing I had to go to carry some of the parcels. We walked through the flaring streets, jostled by drunken men and bargaining women, amid the curse of labourers, the shrill litanies of shop-boys who stood on guard by the barrels of pigs' cheeks, the nasal chanting of street-singers, who sang a *come-all-you* about O'Donovan Rossa, or a ballad about the troubles in our native land. These noises converged in a single sensation of life for me: I imagined that I bore my chalice safely through a throng of foes. Her name sprang to my lips at moments in strange prayers and praises which I myself did not understand. My eyes were often full of tears (I could not tell why) and at times a flood from my heart seemed to pour itself out into my bosom. I thought little of the future. I did not know whether I would ever speak to her or not or, if I spoke to her, how I could tell her of my confused adoration. But my body was like a harp and her words and gestures were like fingers running upon the wires.

One evening I went into the back drawing room in which the priest had died. It was a dark rainy evening and there was no sound in the house. Through one of the broken panes I heard the rain impinge upon the earth, the fine incessant needles of water playing in the sodden beds. Some distant lamp or lighted window gleamed below me. I was thankful that I could see so little. All my senses seemed to desire to veil themselves and, feeling that I was about to slip from them, I pressed the palms of my hands together until they trembled, murmuring: '*O love! O love!*' many times.

At last she spoke to me. When she addressed the first words to me I was so confused that I did not know what to answer. She asked me was I going to *Araby*. I forgot whether I answered yes or no. It would be a splendid bazaar, she said she would love to go.

'And why can't you?' I asked.

While she spoke she turned a silver bracelet round and round her wrist. She could not go, she said, because there would be a retreat that week in her convent. Her brother and two other boys were fighting for their caps and I was alone at the railings. She held one of the spikes, bowing her head towards me. The light from the lamp opposite our door caught the white curve of her neck, lit up her hair that rested there and, falling, lit up the hand upon the railing. It fell over one side of her dress and caught the white border of a petticoat just visible as she stood at ease.

'It's well for you,' she said.

'If I go,' I said, 'I will bring you something.'

What innumerable follies laid waste my waking and sleeping thoughts after that evening! I wished to annihilate the tedious intervening days. I chafed against the work of school. At night in my bedroom and by day in the classroom her image came between me and the page I strove to read. The syllables of the word *Araby* were called to me through the silence in which my soul luxuriated and cast an Eastern enchantment over me. I asked for leave to go to the bazaar on Saturday night. My aunt was surprised and hoped it was not some Freemason affair. I answered few questions in class. I watched my master's face pass from amiability to sternness; he hoped I was not beginning to idle. I could not call my wandering thoughts together. I had hardly any patience with the serious work of life which, now that it stood between me and my desire, seemed to me child's play, ugly monotonous child's play.

On Saturday morning I reminded my uncle that I wished to go to the bazaar in the evening. He was fussing at the hallstand, looking for the hat-brush, and answered me curtly:

'Yes, boy, I know.'

As he was in the hall I could not go into the front parlour and lie at the window. I left the house in bad humour and walked slowly towards the school. The air was pitilessly raw and already my heart misgave me.

When I came home to dinner my uncle had not yet been home. Still it was early. I sat staring at the clock for some time and, when its ticking began to irritate me, I left the room. I mounted the staircase and gained the upper part of the house. The high cold empty gloomy rooms liberated me and I went from room to room singing. From the front window I saw my companions playing below in the street. Their cries reached me weakened and indistinct and, leaning my forehead against the cool glass, I looked over at the dark house where she lived. I may have stood there for an hour, seeing nothing but the brown-clad figure cast by my imagination, touched discreetly by the lamplight at the curved neck, at the hand upon the railings and at the border below the dress.

When I came downstairs again I found Mrs Mercer sitting at the fire. She was an old garrulous woman, a pawnbroker's widow, who collected used stamps for some pious purpose. I had to endure the gossip of the tea-table. The meal was prolonged beyond an hour and still my uncle did not come. Mrs Mercer stood up to go: she was very sorry she couldn't wait any longer, but it was after eight o'clock and she did not like to be out late, as the night air was bad for her. When she had gone I began to walk up and down the room, clenching my fists. My aunt said:

'I'm afraid you may put off your bazaar for this night of Our Lord.'

At nine o'clock I heard my uncle's latchkey in the halldoor. I heard him talking to himself and heard the hallstand rocking when it had received the weight of his overcoat. I could interpret these signs. When he was midway through his dinner I asked him to give me the money to go to the bazaar. He had forgotten.

'The people are in bed and after their first sleep now,' he said.

I did not smile. My aunt said to him energetically:

'Can't you give him the money and let him go? You've kept him late enough as it is.'

My uncle said he was very sorry he had forgotten. He said he believed in the old saying: 'All work and no play makes Jack a dull boy.' He asked me where I was going and, when I had told him a second time he asked me did I know *The Arab's Farewell to his Steed*. When I left the kitchen he was about to recite the opening lines of the piece to my aunt.

I held a florin tightly in my hand as I strode down Buckingham Street towards the station. The sight of the streets thronged with buyers and glaring with gas recalled to me the purpose of my journey. I took my seat in a third-class carriage of a deserted train. After an intolerable delay the train moved out of the station slowly. It crept onward among ruinous houses and over the twinkling river. At Westland Row Station a crowd of people pressed to the carriage doors; but the porters moved them back, saying that it was a special train for the bazaar. I remained alone in the bare carriage. In a few minutes the train drew up beside an improvised wooden platform. I passed out on to the road and saw by the lighted dial of a clock that it was ten minutes to ten. In front of me was a large building which displayed the magical name.

I could not find any sixpenny entrance and, fearing that the bazaar would be closed, I passed quickly through the turnstile, handing a shilling to a weary-looking man. I found myself in a big hall girdled at half its height by a gallery. Nearly all the stalls were closed and the greater part of the hall was in darkness. I recognized a silence like that which pervades a church after a service. I walked into the centre of the bazaar timidly. A few people were gathered about the stalls which were still open. Before a curtain, over which the words *Café Chantant* were written in coloured lamps, two men were counting money on a salver. I listened to the fall of the coins.

Remembering with difficulty why I had come I went over to one of the stalls and examined porcelain vases and flowered tea-sets. At the door of the stall a young lady was talking and laughing with two young gentlemen. I remarked their English accents and listened vaguely to their conversation.

'O, I never said such a thing!'

'O, but you did!'

'O, but I didn't!'

'Didn't she say that?'

'Yes. I heard her.'

'O, there's a . . . fib!'

Observing me the young lady came over and asked me did I wish to buy anything. The tone of her voice was not encouraging; she seemed to have spoken to me out of a sense of duty. I looked humbly at the great jars that stood like eastern guards at either side of the dark entrance to the stall and murmured:

'No, thank you.'

The young lady changed the position of one of the vases and went back to the two young men. They began to talk on the same subject. Once or twice the young lady glanced at me over her shoulder.

I lingered before her stall, though I knew my stay was useless, to make my interest in her wares seem the more real. Then I turned away slowly and walked down the middle of the bazaar. I allowed the two pennies to fall against the sixpence in my pocket. I heard a voice call from one end of the gallery that the light was out. The upper part of the hall was now completely dark.

Gazing up into the darkness I saw myself as a creature driven and derided by vanity; and my eyes burned with anguish and anger.

1914

D.H. Lawrence

1885–1930

David Herbert Lawrence was born in Eastwood, a coal-mining village in the English Midlands. His father was a miner, his mother a woman from the middle class who never accepted her husband's way of life. Lawrence was torn between them: close to his mother during her life, appreciating his father only after his death. The story of this family struggle is told in one of Lawrence's finest works, his novel *Sons and Lovers* (1913). In 1901 Lawrence nearly died of pneumonia, and his health was delicate from this point until his death at the age of forty-five. In 1904 he took the King's Scholarship examination and came first in all England and Wales. He began a career as a teacher, but trouble with his health and his early success as a writer took him away from that profession. In 1912 he ran off with the wife of a former professor of his at Nottingham University, and in 1914, when her divorce became final, he married her. Together they travelled, spending time in Germany, Italy, Ceylon (Sri Lanka), Australia, the United States, and Mexico, until Lawrence's death from tuberculosis in southern France.

Lawrence's personality has drawn almost as much attention as his books. He spoke and wrote informally with the same vitality that animates his literary work, and some of the informality of talk and personal correspondence is found in his poetry and fiction. For a time censorship of his works and controversy over the supposed immorality of his views on sex obscured the seriousness and beauty of his work. Now such stories as 'The Rocking-Horse Winner' are recognized as classic short stories, depicting with sensuous immediacy the delights and obsessions of his characters.

The Rocking-Horse Winner

There was a woman who was beautiful, who started with all the advantages, yet she had no luck. She married for love, and the love turned to dust. She had bonny children, yet she felt they had been thrust upon her, and she could not love them. They looked at her coldly, as if they were finding fault with her. And hurriedly she felt she must cover up some fault in herself. Yet what it was that she must cover up she never knew. Nevertheless, when her children were present, she always felt the centre of her heart go hard. This troubled her, and in her manner she was all the more gentle and anxious for her children, as if she loved them very much. Only she herself knew that at the centre of her heart was a hard little place that could not feel love, no, not for anybody. Everybody else said of her: 'She is such a good mother. She adores her children.' Only she herself, and her children themselves, knew it was not so. They read it in each other's eyes.

There were a boy and two little girls. They lived in a pleasant house, with a garden, and they had discreet servants, and felt themselves superior to anyone in the neighbourhood.

Although they lived in style, they felt always an anxiety in the house. There was never enough money. The mother had a small income, and the father had a small income, but not nearly enough for the social position which they had to keep up. The father went into town to some office. But though he had good prospects, these prospects never materialized. There was always the grinding sense of the shortage of money, though the style was always kept up.

At last the mother said: 'I will see if *I* can't make something.' But she did not know where to begin. She racked her brains, and tried this thing and the other, but could not find anything successful. The failure made deep lines come into her face. Her children were growing up, they would have to go to school. There must be more money, there must be more money. The father, who was always very handsome and expensive in his tastes, seemed as if he never *would* be able to do anything worth doing. And the mother, who had a great belief in herself, did not succeed any better, and her tastes were just as expensive.

And so the house came to be haunted by the unspoken phrase: *There must be more money! There must be more money!* The children could hear it all the time, though nobody said it aloud. They heard it at Christmas, when the expensive and splendid toys filled the nursery. Behind the shining modern rocking-horse, behind the smart doll's house, a voice would start whispering: 'There *must* be more money! There *must* be more money!' And the children would stop playing, to listen for a moment. They would look into each other's eyes, to see if they had all heard. And each one saw in the eyes of the other two that they too had heard. 'There *must* be more money! There *must* be more money!'

It came whispering from the springs of the still-swaying rocking-horse, and even the horse, bending his wooden, champing head, heard it. The big doll, sitting so pink and smirking in her new pram, could hear it quite plainly, and seemed to be smirking all the more self-consciously because of it. The foolish puppy, too, that took the place of the teddy-bear, he was looking so extraordinarily foolish for no other reason but that he heard the secret whisper all over the house: 'There *must* be more money!'

Yet nobody ever said it aloud. The whisper was everywhere, and therefore no one spoke it. Just as no one ever says: 'We are breathing!' in spite of the fact that breath is coming and going all the time.

'Mother,' said the boy Paul one day, 'why don't we keep a car of our own? Why do we always use uncle's, or else a taxi?'

'Because we're the poor members of the family,' said the mother.

'But why *are* we, mother?'

'Well—I suppose', she said slowly and bitterly, 'it's because your father has no luck.'

The boy was silent for some time.

'Is luck money, mother?' he asked, rather timidly.

'No, Paul. Not quite. It's what causes you to have money.'

'Oh!' said Paul vaguely. 'I thought when Uncle Oscar said *filthy lucker*, it meant money.'

'*Filthy lucre* does mean money,' said the mother. 'But it's lucre, not luck.'

'Oh!' said the boy. 'Then what *is* luck, mother?'

'It's what causes you to have money. If you're lucky you have money. That's why it's better to be born lucky than rich. If you're rich, you may lose your money. But if you're lucky, you will always get more money.'

'Oh! Will you? And is father not lucky?'

'Very unlucky, I should say,' she said bitterly.

The boy watched her with unsure eyes.

'Why?' he asked.

'I don't know. Nobody ever knows why one person is lucky and another unlucky.'

'Don't they? Nobody at all? Does *nobody* know?'

'Perhaps God. But He never tells.'

'He ought to, then. And aren't you lucky either, mother?'

'I can't be, if I married an unlucky husband.'

'But by yourself, aren't you?'

'I used to think I was, before I married. Now I think I am very unlucky indeed.'

'Why?'

'Well—never mind! Perhaps I'm not really,' she said.

The child looked at her to see if she meant it. But he saw, by the lines of her mouth, that she was only trying to hide something from him.

'Well, anyhow,' he said stoutly, 'I'm a lucky person.'

'Why?' said his mother, with a sudden laugh.

He stared at her. He didn't even know why he had said it.

'God told me,' he asserted, brazening it out.

'I hope He did, dear!' she said, again with a laugh, but rather bitter.

'He did, mother!'

'Excellent!' said the mother, using one of her husband's exclamations.

The boy saw she did not believe him; or rather, that she paid no attention to his assertion. This angered him somewhere, and made him want to compel her attention.

He went off by himself, vaguely, in a childish way, seeking for the clue to 'luck'. Absorbed, taking no heed of other people, he went about with a sort of stealth, seeking inwardly for luck. He wanted luck, he wanted it, he wanted it. When the two girls were playing dolls in the nursery, he would sit on his big rocking-horse, charging madly into space, with a frenzy that made the little girls peer at him uneasily. Wildly the horse careered, the waving dark hair of the boy tossed, his eyes had a strange glare in them. The little girls dared not speak to him.

When he had ridden to the end of his mad little journey, he climbed down and stood in front of his rocking-horse, staring fixedly into its lowered face. Its red mouth was slightly open, its big eye was wide and glassy-bright.

'Now!' he would silently command the snorting steed. 'Now, take me to where there is luck! Now take me!'

And he would slash the horse on the neck with the little whip he had asked Uncle Oscar for. He *knew* the horse could take him to where there was luck, if only he forced it. So he would mount again and start on his furious ride, hoping at last to get there. He knew he could get there.

'You'll break your horse, Paul!' said the nurse.

'He's always riding like that! I wish he'd leave off!' said his elder sister Joan.

But he only glared down on them in silence. Nurse gave him up. She could make nothing of him. Anyhow, he was growing beyond her.

One day his mother and his Uncle Oscar came in when he was on one of his furious rides. He did not speak to them.

'Hallo, you young jockey! Riding a winner?' said his uncle.

'Aren't you growing too big for a rocking-horse? You're not a very little boy any longer, you know,' said his mother.

But Paul only gave a blue glare from his big, rather close-set eyes. He would speak to nobody when he was in full tilt. His mother watched him with an anxious expression on her face.

At last he suddenly stopped forcing his horse into the mechanical gallop and slid down.

'Well, I got there!' he announced fiercely, his blue eyes still flaring, and his sturdy long legs straddling apart.

'Where did you get to?' asked his mother.

'Where I wanted to go,' he flared back at her.

'That's right, son!' said Uncle Oscar. 'Don't you stop till you get there. What's the horse's name?'

'He doesn't have a name,' said the boy.

'Gets on without all right?' asked the uncle.

'Well, he had different names. He was called Sansovino last week.'

'Sansovino, eh? Won the Ascot. How did you know this name?'

'He always talks about horse races with Bassett,' said Joan.

The uncle was delighted to find that his small nephew was posted with all the racing news. Bassett, the young gardener, who had been wounded in the left foot in the war and had got his present job through Oscar Cresswell, whose batman he had been, was a perfect blade of the 'turf'. He lived in the racing events, and the small boy lived with him.

Oscar Cresswell got it all from Bassett.

'Master Paul comes and asks me, so I can't do more than tell him, sir,' said Bassett, his face terribly serious, as if he were speaking of religious matters.

'And does he ever put anything on a horse he fancies?'

'Well—I don't want to give him away—he's a young sport, a fine sport, sir. Would you mind asking him himself? He sort of takes a pleasure in it, and perhaps he'd feel I was giving him away, sir, if you don't mind.'

Bassett was serious as a church.

The uncle went back to his nephew and took him off for a ride in the car.

'Say, Paul, old man, do you ever put anything on a horse?' the uncle asked.

The boy watched the handsome man closely.

'Why, do you think I oughtn't to?' he parried.

'Not a bit of it! I thought perhaps you might give me a tip for the Lincoln.'

The car sped on into the country, going down to Uncle Oscar's place in Hampshire.

'Honour bright?' said the nephew.

'Honour bright, son!' said the uncle.

'Well, then, Daffodil.'

'Daffodil! I doubt it, sonny. What about Mirza?'

'I only know the winner,' said the boy. 'That's Daffodil.'

'Daffodil, eh?'

There was a pause. Daffodil was an obscure horse comparatively.

'Uncle!'

'Yes, son?'

'You won't let it go any further, will you? I promised Bassett.'

'Bassett be damned, old man! What's he got to do with it?'

'We're partners. We've been partners from the first. Uncle, he lent me my first five shillings, which I lost. I promised him, honour bright, it was only between me and him; only you gave me that ten-shilling note I started winning with, so I thought you were lucky. You won't let it go any further, will you?'

The boy gazed at his uncle from those big, hot, blue eyes, set rather close together. The uncle stirred and laughed uneasily.

'Right you are, son! I'll keep your tip private. Daffodil, eh? How much are you putting on him?'

'All except twenty pounds,' said the boy. 'I keep that in reserve.'

The uncle thought it a good joke.

'You keep twenty pounds in reserve, do you, you young romancer? What are you betting, then?'

'I'm betting three hundred,' said the boy gravely. 'But it's between you and me, Uncle Oscar! Honour bright?'

The uncle burst into a roar of laughter.

'It's between you and me all right, you young Nat Gould,' he said, laughing. 'But where's your three hundred?'

'Bassett keeps it for me. We're partners.'

'You are, are you! And what is Bassett putting on Daffodil?'

'He won't go quite as high as I do, I expect. Perhaps he'll go a hundred and fifty.'

'What, pennies?' laughed the uncle.

'Pounds,' said the child, with a surprised look at his uncle. 'Bassett keeps a bigger reserve than I do.'

Between wonder and amusement Uncle Oscar was silent. He pursued the matter no further, but he determined to take his nephew with him to the Lincoln races.

'Now, son,' he said, 'I'm putting twenty on Mirza, and I'll put five on for you on any horse you fancy. What's your pick?'

'Daffodil, uncle.'

'No, not the fiver on Daffodil!'

'I should if it was my own fiver,' said the child.

'Good! Good! Right you are! A fiver for me and a fiver for you on Daffodil.'

The child had never been to a race-meeting before, and his eyes were blue fire. He pursed his mouth tight and watched. A Frenchman just in front had put his money on Lancelot. Wild with excitement, he flayed his arms up and down, yelling 'Lancelot! Lancelot!' in his French accent.

Daffodil came in first, Lancelot second, Mirza third. The child, flushed and with eyes blazing, was curiously serene. His uncle brought him four five-pound notes, four to one.

'What am I to do with these?' he cried, waving them before the boy's eyes.

'I suppose we'll talk to Bassett,' said the boy. 'I expect I have fifteen hundred now; and twenty in reserve; and this twenty.'

His uncle studied him for some moments.

'Look here, son!' he said. 'You're not serious about Bassett and that fifteen hundred, are you?'

'Yes, I am. But it's between you and me, uncle. Honour bright?'

'Honour bright all right, son! But I must talk to Bassett.'

'If you'd like to be a partner, uncle, with Bassett and me, we could all be partners. Only, you'd have to promise, honour bright, uncle, not to let it go beyond us three. Bassett and I are lucky, and you must be lucky, because it was your ten shillings I started winning with. . . .'

Uncle Oscar took both Bassett and Paul into Richmond Park for an afternoon, and there they talked.

'It's like this, you see, sir,' Bassett said. 'Master Paul would get me talking about racing events, spinning yarns, you know, sir. And he was always keen on knowing if I'd made or if I'd lost. It's about a year since, now, that I put five shillings on Blush of Dawn for him: and we lost. Then the luck turned, with that ten shillings he had from you: that we put on Singhalese. And since that time, it's been pretty steady, all things considering. What do you say, Master Paul?'

'We're all right when we're sure,' said Paul. 'It's when we're not quite sure that we go down.'

'Oh, but we're careful then,' said Bassett.

'But when are you *sure*?' smiled Uncle Oscar.

'It's Master Paul, sir,' said Bassett in a secret, religious voice. 'It's as if he had it from heaven. Like Daffodil, now, for the Lincoln. That was as sure as eggs.'

'Did you put anything on Daffodil?' asked Oscar Cresswell.

'Yes, sir. I made my bit.'

'And my nephew?'

Bassett was obstinately silent, looking at Paul.

'I made twelve hundred, didn't I, Bassett? I told uncle I was putting three hundred on Daffodil.'

'That's right,' said Bassett, nodding.

'But where's the money?' asked the uncle.

'I keep it safe locked up, sir. Master Paul he can have it any minute he likes to ask for it.'

'What, fifteen hundred pounds?'

'And twenty! And *forty*, that is, with the twenty he made on the course.'

'It's amazing!' said the uncle.

'If Master Paul offers you to be partners, sir, I would, if I were you: if you'll excuse me,' said Bassett.

Oscar Cresswell thought about it.

'I'll see the money,' he said.

They drove home again, and, sure enough, Bassett came round to the garden-house with fifteen hundred pounds in notes. The twenty pounds reserve was left with Joe Glee, in the Turf Commission deposit.

'You see, it's all right, uncle, when I'm *sure*! Then we go strong, for all we're worth. Don't we Bassett?'

'We do that, Master Paul.'

'And when are you sure?' said the uncle, laughing.

'Oh, well, sometimes I'm *absolutely* sure, like about Daffodil,' said the boy, 'and sometimes I have an idea; and sometimes I haven't even an idea, have I, Bassett? Then we're careful, because we mostly go down.'

'You do, do you! And when you're sure, like about Daffodil, what makes you sure, sonny?'

'Oh, well, I don't know,' said the boy uneasily. 'I'm sure, you know, uncle; that's all.'

'It's as if he had it from heaven, sir,' Bassett reiterated.

'I should say so!' said the uncle.

But he became a partner. And when the Leger was coming on Paul was 'sure' about Lively Spark, which was a quite inconsiderable horse. The boy insisted on putting a thousand on the horse, Bassett was for five hundred, and Oscar Cresswell two hundred. Lively Spark came in first, and the betting had been ten to one against him. Paul had made ten thousand.

'You see,' he said, 'I was absolutely sure of him.'

Even Oscar Cresswell had cleared two thousand.

'Look here, son,' he said, 'this sort of thing makes me nervous.'

'It needn't, uncle! Perhaps I shan't be sure again for a long time.'

'But what are you going to do with your money?' asked the uncle.

'Of course,' said the boy, 'I started it for mother. She said she had no luck, because father is unlucky, so I thought if *I* was lucky, it might stop whispering.'

'What might stop whispering?'

'Our house. I *hate* our house for whispering.'

'What does it whisper?'

'Why—why'—the boy fidgeted—'why, I don't know. But it's always short of money, you know, uncle.'

'I know it, son, I know it.'

'You know people send mother writs, don't you, uncle?'

'I'm afraid I do,' said the uncle.

'And then the house whispers, like people laughing at you behind your back. It's awful, that is! I thought if I was lucky——'

'You might stop it,' added the uncle.

The boy watched him with big blue eyes, that had an uncanny cold fire in them, and he said never a word.

'Well, then!' said the uncle. 'What are we doing?'

'I shouldn't like mother to know I was lucky,' said the boy.

'Why not, son?'

'She'd stop me.'

'I don't think she would.'

'Oh!'—and the boy writhed in an odd way—'I *don't* want her to know, uncle.'

'All right, son! We'll manage it without her knowing.'

They managed it very easily. Paul, at the other's suggestion, handed over five thousand pounds to his uncle, who deposited it with the family lawyer, who was then to inform Paul's mother that a relative had put five thousand pounds into his hands, which sum was to be paid out a thousand pounds at a time, on the mother's birthday, for the next five years.

'So she'll have a birthday present of a thousand pounds for five successive years,' said Uncle Oscar. 'I hope it won't make it all the harder for her later.'

Paul's mother had her birthday in November. The house had been 'whispering' worse than ever lately, and, even in spite of his luck, Paul could not bear up against it. He was very anxious to see the effect of the birthday letter telling his mother about the thousand pounds.

When there were no visitors, Paul now took his meals with his parents, as he was beyond the nursery control. His mother went into town nearly every day. She had discovered that she had an odd knack of sketching furs and dress materials, so she worked secretly in the studio of a friend who was the chief 'artist' for the leading drapers. She drew the figures of ladies in furs and ladies in silks and sequins for the newspaper advertisements. This young woman artist earned several thousand pounds a year, but Paul's mother only made several hundreds, and she was again dissatisfied. She so wanted to be first in something, and she did not succeed, even in making sketches for drapery advertisements.

She was down to breakfast on the morning of her birthday. Paul watched her face as she read her letters. He knew the lawyer's letter. As his mother read it, her face hardened and became more expressionless. Then a cold, determined look came on her mouth. She hid the letter under the pile of others, and said not a word about it.

'Didn't you have anything nice in the post for your birthday, mother?' said Paul.

'Quite moderately nice,' she said, her voice cold and absent.

She went away to town without saying more.

But in the afternoon Uncle Oscar appeared. He said Paul's mother had had a long interview with the lawyer, asking if the whole five thousand could not be advanced at once, as she was in debt.

'What do you think, uncle?' said the boy.

'I leave it to you, son.'

'Oh, let her have it, then! We can get some more with the other,' said the boy.

'A bird in the hand is worth two in the bush, laddie!' said Uncle Oscar.

'But I'm sure to *know* for the Grand National; or the Lincolnshire; or else the Derby. I'm sure to know for *one* of them,' said Paul.

So Uncle Oscar signed the agreement, and Paul's mother touched the whole five thousand. Then something very curious happened. The voices in the house suddenly went mad, like a chorus of frogs on a spring evening. There were certain new furnishings, and Paul had a tutor. He was *really* going to Eton, his father's school, in the following autumn. There were flowers in the winter, and a blossoming of the luxury Paul's mother had been used to. And yet the voices in the house, behind the sprays of mimosa and almond blossom, and from under the piles of iridescent cushions, simply trilled and screamed in a sort of ecstasy: 'There *must* be more money! Oh-h-h; there *must* be more money. Oh, now, now-w! Now-w-w—there *must* be more money!— more than ever! More than ever!'

It frightened Paul terribly. He studied away at his Latin and Greek with his tutor. But his intense hours were spent with Bassett. The Grand National had gone by: he had not 'known', and had lost a hundred pounds. Summer was at hand. He was in agony for the Lincoln. But even for the Lincoln he didn't 'know', and he lost fifty pounds. He became wild-eyed and strange, as if something were going to explode in him.

'Let it alone, son! Don't you bother about it!' urged Uncle Oscar. But it was as if the boy couldn't really hear what his uncle was saying.

'I've got to know for the Derby! I've got to know for the Derby!' the child reiterated, his big blue eyes blazing with a sort of madness.

His mother noticed how overwrought he was.

'You'd better go to the seaside. Wouldn't you like to go now to the seaside, instead of waiting? I think you'd better,' she said, looking down at him anxiously, her heart curiously heavy because of him.

But the child lifted his uncanny blue eyes.

'I couldn't possibly go before the Derby, mother!' he said. 'I couldn't possibly!'

'Why not!' she said, her voice becoming heavy when she was opposed. 'Why not? You can still go from the seaside to see the Derby with your Uncle Oscar, if that's what you wish. No need for you to wait here. Besides, I think you care too much about these races. It's a bad sign. My family has been a gambling family, and you won't know till you grow up how much damage it has done. But it has done damage. I shall have to send Bassett away, and ask Uncle Oscar not to talk racing to you, unless you promise to be reasonable about it: go away to the seaside and forget it. You're all nerves!'

'I'll do what you like, mother, so long as you don't send me away till after the Derby,' the boy said.

'Send you away from where? Just from this house?'

'Yes,' he said, gazing at her.

'Why, you curious child, what makes you care about this house so much, suddenly? I never knew you loved it.'

He gazed at her without speaking. He had a secret within a secret, something he had not divulged, even to Bassett or to his Uncle Oscar.

But his mother, after standing undecided and a little bit sullen for some moments, said:

'Very well, then! Don't go to the seaside till after the Derby, if you don't wish it. But promise me you won't let your nerves go to pieces. Promise you won't think so much about horse-racing and *events*, as you call them!'

'Oh no,' said the boy casually. 'I won't think much about them, mother. You needn't worry. I wouldn't worry, mother, if I were you.'

'If you were me and I were you,' said his mother, 'I wonder what we *should* do!'

'But you know you needn't worry, mother, don't you?' the boy repeated.

'I should be awfully glad to know it,' she said wearily.

'Oh, well, you *can*, you know. I mean, you *ought* to know you needn't worry,' he insisted.

'Ought I? Then I'll see about it,' she said.

Paul's secret of secrets was his wooden horse, that which had no name. Since he was emancipated from a nurse and a nursery-governess, he had had his rocking-horse removed to his own bedroom at the top of the house.

'Surely you're too big for a rocking-horse!' his mother had remonstrated.

'Well, you see, mother, till I can have a *real* horse, I like to have *some* sort of animal about,' had been his quaint answer.

'Do you feel he keeps you company?' she laughed.

'Oh yes! He's very good, he always keeps me company, when I'm there,' said Paul.

So the horse, rather shabby, stood in an arrested prance in the boy's bedroom.

The Derby was drawing near, and the boy grew more and more tense. He hardly heard what was spoken to him, he was very frail, and his eyes were really uncanny. His mother had sudden strange seizures of uneasiness about him. Sometimes, for half an hour, she would feel a sudden anxiety about him that was almost anguish. She wanted to rush to him at once, and know he was safe.

Two nights before the Derby, she was at a big party in town, when one of her rushes of anxiety about her boy, her first-born, gripped her heart till she could hardly speak. She fought with the feeling, might and main, for she believed in common sense. But it was too strong. She had to leave the dance and go downstairs to telephone to the country. The children's nursery-governess was terribly surprised and startled at being rung up in the night.

'Are the children all right, Miss Wilmot?'

'Oh yes, they are quite all right.'

'Master Paul? Is he all right?'

'He went to bed as right as a trivet. Shall I run up and look at him?'

'No,' said Paul's mother reluctantly. 'No! Don't trouble. It's all right. Don't sit up. We shall be home fairly soon.' She did not want her son's privacy intruded upon.

'Very good,' said the governess.

It was about one o'clock when Paul's mother and father drove up to their house. All was still. Paul's mother went to her room and slipped off her white fur cloak. She had told her maid not to wait up for her. She heard her husband downstairs, mixing a whisky and soda.

And then, because of the strange anxiety at her heart, she stole upstairs to her son's room. Noiselessly she went along the upper corridor. Was there a faint noise? What was it?

She stood, with arrested muscles, outside his door, listening. There was a strange, heavy, and yet not loud noise. Her heart stood still. It was a soundless noise, yet rushing and powerful. Something huge, in violent, hushed motion. What was it? What in God's name was it? She ought to know. She felt that she knew the noise. She knew what it was.

Yet she could not place it. She couldn't say what it was. And on and on it went, like a madness.

Softly, frozen with anxiety and fear, she turned the doorhandle.

The room was dark. Yet in the space near the window, she heard and saw something plunging to and fro. She gazed in fear and amazement.

Then suddenly she switched on the light, and saw her son, in his green pyjamas, madly surging on the rocking-horse. The blaze of light suddenly lit him up, as he urged the wooden horse, and lit her up, as she stood, blonde, in her dress of pale green and crystal, in the doorway.

'Paul!' she cried. 'Whatever are you doing?'

'It's Malabar!' he screamed in a powerful, strange voice. 'It's Malabar!'

His eyes blazed at her for one strange and senseless second, as he ceased urging his wooden horse. Then he fell with a crash to the ground, and she, all her tormented motherhood flooding upon her, rushed to gather him up.

But he was unconscious, and unconscious he remained, with some brain-fever. He talked and tossed, and his mother sat stonily by his side.

'Malabar! It's Malabar! Bassett, Bassett, I *know*! It's Malabar!'

So the child cried, trying to get up and urge the rocking-horse that gave him his inspiration.

'What does he mean by Malabar?' asked the heart-frozen mother.

'I don't know,' said the father stonily.

'What does he mean by Malabar?' she asked her brother Oscar.

'It's one of the horses running for the Derby,' was the answer.

And, in spite of himself, Oscar Cresswell spoke to Bassett, and himself put a thousand on Malabar: at fourteen to one.

The third day of the illness was critical: they were waiting for a change. The boy, with his rather long, curly hair, was tossing ceaselessly on the pillow. He neither slept nor regained consciousness, and his eyes were like blue stones. His mother sat, feeling her heart had gone, turned actually into a stone.

In the evening, Oscar Cresswell did not come, but Bassett sent a message, saying could he come up for one moment, just one moment? Paul's mother was very angry at the intrusion, but on second thoughts she agreed. The boy was the same. Perhaps Bassett might bring him to consciousness.

The gardener, a shortish fellow with a little brown moustache and sharp little brown eyes, tiptoed into the room, touched his imaginary cap to Paul's mother, and stole to the bedside, staring with glittering, smallish eyes at the tossing, dying child.

'Master Paul!' he whispered. 'Master Paul! Malabar came in first all right, a clean win. I did as you told me. You've made over seventy thousand pounds, you have; you've got over eighty thousand. Malabar came in all right, Master Paul.'

'Malabar! Malabar! Did I say Malabar, mother? Did I say Malabar? Do you think I'm lucky, mother? I knew Malabar, didn't I? Over eighty thousand pounds! I call that lucky, don't you, mother? Over eighty thousand pounds! I knew, didn't I know I knew? Malabar came in all right. If I ride my horse till I'm sure, then I tell you, Bassett, you can go as high as you like. Did you go for all you were worth, Bassett?'

'I went a thousand on it, Master Paul.'

'I never told you, mother, that if I can ride my horse, and *get there*, then I'm absolutely sure—oh, absolutely! Mother, did I ever tell you? I *am* lucky!'

'No, you never did,' said his mother.

But the boy died in the night.

And even as he lay dead, his mother heard her brother's voice saying to her: 'My God, Hester, you're eighty-odd thousand to the good, and a poor devil of a son to the bad. But, poor devil, poor devil, he's best gone out of a life where he rides his rocking-horse to find a winner.'

1926

Katherine Mansfield
1888–1923

◆

Born in Wellington, New Zealand, Kathleen Mansfield Beauchamp spent her early years in the nearby village of Karoi. In 1903 she went to Queen's College in London, where she studied to become a cellist. When she returned to New Zealand in 1906, she found the country oppressive and stifling and convinced her parents in 1908 to allow her to go back to London. She spent the rest of her life in Europe, always restlessly in search of a cure for the consumption that had first afflicted her a few years after her return to London. Her first book of stories, *In a German Pension*, was published in 1911 under the pseudonym Katherine Mansfield, and was followed by four more books of stories during her lifetime.

Although she made attempts at writing a novel, it was the short story that proved to be Mansfield's chosen form, accommodating her terse irony, her dissections of class, family, and relationships, and her evocations of natural settings. These features are evident in 'The Garden Party', in which the rituals of the upper-class family as they prepare for the afternoon's festivities seem to provide the context for the ironic presentation of Laura's responses to the workmen setting up the marquee. The story's complex perspective is reflected in the reactions of Laura and her family to the report of a fatal accident, particularly in Laura's inarticulate comments to her brother following her visit to the bereaved family.

The Garden Party

And after all the weather was ideal. They could not have had a more perfect day for a garden party if they had ordered it. Windless, warm, the sky without a cloud. Only the blue was veiled with a haze of light gold, as it is sometimes in early summer. The gardener had been up since dawn, mowing the lawns and sweeping them, until the grass and the dark flat rosettes where the daisy plants had been seemed to shine. As for the roses, you could not help feeling they understood that roses are the only flowers that impress people at garden parties; the only flowers that everybody is certain of knowing. Hundreds, yes, literally hundreds, had come out in a single night; the green bushes bowed down as though they had been visited by archangels.

Breakfast was not yet over before the men came to put up the marquee.

'Where do you want the marquee put, mother?'

'My dear child, it's no use asking me. I'm determined to leave everything to you children this year. Forget I am your mother. Treat me as an honoured guest.'

But Meg could not possibly go and supervise the men. She had washed her hair before breakfast, and she sat drinking her coffee in a green turban, with a dark wet curl stamped on each cheek. Jose, the butterfly, always came down in a silk petticoat and a kimono jacket.

'You'll have to go, Laura, you're the artistic one.'

Away Laura flew, still holding her piece of bread-and-butter. It's so delicious to have an excuse for eating out of doors and, besides, she loved having to arrange things; she always felt she could do it so much better than anybody else.

Four men in their shirt-sleeves stood grouped together on the garden path. They carried staves covered with rolls of canvas, and they had big tool-bags slung on their backs. They looked impressive. Laura wished now that she was not holding that piece of bread-and-butter, but there was nowhere to put it, and she couldn't possibly throw it away. She blushed and tried to look severe and even a little bit short-sighted as she came up to them.

'Good morning,' she said, copying her mother's voice. But that sounded so fearfully affected that she was ashamed, and stammered like a little girl, 'Oh—er—have you come—is it about the marquee?'

'That's right, miss,' said the tallest of the men, a lanky, freckled fellow, and he shifted his tool-bag, knocked back his straw hat, and smiled down at her. 'That's about it.'

His smile was so easy, so friendly, that Laura recovered. What nice eyes he had, small, but such a dark blue! And now she looked at the others, they were smiling too. 'Cheer up, we won't bite,' their smile seemed to say. How very nice workmen were! And what a beautiful morning! She mustn't mention the morning; she must be business-like. The marquee.

'Well, what about the lily-lawn? Would that do?'

And she pointed to the lily-lawn with the hand that didn't hold the bread-and-butter. They turned, they stared in the direction. A little fat chap thrust out his underlip, and the tall fellow frowned.

'I don't fancy it,' said he. 'Not conspicuous enough. You see, with a thing like a marquee,' and he turned to Laura in his easy way, 'you want to put it somewhere where it'll give you a bang slap in the eye, if you follow me.'

Laura's upbringing made her wonder for a moment whether it was quite respectful of a workman to talk to her of bangs slap in the eye. But she did quite follow him.

'A corner of the tennis court,' she suggested. 'But the band's going to be in one corner.'

'H'm, going to have a band, are you?' said another of the workmen. He was pale. He had a haggard look as his dark eyes scanned the tennis court. What was he thinking?

'Only a very small band,' said Laura gently. Perhaps he wouldn't mind so much if the band was quite small. But the tall fellow interrupted.

'Look here, miss, that's the place. Against those trees. Over there. That'll do fine.'

Against the karakas. Then the karaka trees would be hidden. And they were so lovely, with their broad, gleaming leaves, and their clusters of yellow fruit. They were like trees you imagined growing up on a desert island, proud, solitary, lifting their leaves and fruits to the sun in a kind of silent splendour. Must they be hidden by a marquee?

They must. Already the men had shouldered their staves and were making for the place. Only the tall fellow was left. He bent down, pinched a sprig of lavender, put his thumb and forefinger to his nose and snuffed up the smell. When Laura saw that gesture she forgot all about the karakas in her wonder at him caring for things like that—caring for the smell of lavender. How many men that she knew would have done such a thing. *Oh, how extraordinarily nice workmen were*, she thought. Why couldn't she have workmen for friends rather than the silly boys she danced with and who came to Sunday night supper? She would get on much better with men like these.

It's all the fault, she decided, as the tall fellow drew something on the back of an envelope, something that was to be looped up or left to hang, of these absurd class distinctions. Well, for her part, she didn't feel them. Not a bit, not an atom. . . . And now there came the chock-chock of wooden hammers. Someone whistled, someone sang out, 'Are you right there, matey?' 'Matey!' The friendliness of it, the—the— Just to prove how happy she was, just to show the tall fellow how at home she felt, and how she despised stupid conventions, Laura took a big bite of her bread-and-butter as she stared at the little drawing. She felt just like a work-girl.

'Laura, Laura, where are you? Telephone, Laura!' a voice cried from the house.

'Coming!' Away she skimmed, over the lawn, up the path, up the steps, across the veranda, and into the porch. In the hall her father and Laurie were brushing their hats ready to go to the office.

'I say, Laura,' said Laurie very fast, 'you might just give a squiz at my coat before this afternoon. See if it wants pressing.'

'I will,' said she. Suddenly she couldn't stop herself. She ran at Laurie and gave him a small, quick squeeze. 'Oh, I do love parties, don't you?' gasped Laura.

'Ra-ther,' said Laurie's warm, boyish voice, and he squeezed his sister too, and gave her a gentle push. 'Dash off to the telephone, old girl.'

The telephone. 'Yes, yes; oh yes. Kitty? Good morning, dear. Come to lunch? Do, dear. Delighted of course. It will only be a very scratch meal—just the sandwich crusts and broken meringue-shells and what's left over. Yes, isn't it a perfect morning? Your white? Oh, I certainly should. One moment—hold the line. Mother's calling.' And Laura sat back. 'What, mother? Can't hear.'

Mrs Sheridan's voice floated down the stairs. 'Tell her to wear that sweet hat she had on last Sunday.'

'Mother says you're to wear that *sweet* hat you had on last Sunday. Good. One o'clock. Bye-bye.'

Laura put back the receiver, flung her arms over her head, took a deep breath, stretched, and let them fall. 'Huh,' she sighed, and the moment after the sigh she sat up quickly. She was still, listening. All the doors in the house seemed to be open. The house was alive with soft, quick steps and running voices. The green baize door that led to the kitchen regions swung open and shut with a muffled thud. And now there came a long, chuckling absurd sound. It was the heavy piano being moved on its stiff castors. But the air! If you stopped to notice, was the air always like this? Little faint winds were playing chase in at the tops of the windows, out at the doors. And there were two tiny spots of sun, one on the inkpot, one on a silver photograph frame, playing too. Darling little spots. Especially the one on the inkpot lid. It was quite warm. A warm little silver star. She could have kissed it.

The front door bell pealed, and there sounded the rustle of Sadie's print skirt on the stairs. A man's voice murmured; Sadie answered, careless, 'I'm sure I don't know. Wait. I'll ask Mrs Sheridan.'

'What is it, Sadie?' Laura came into the hall.

'It's the florist, Miss Laura.'

It was, indeed. There, just inside the door, stood a wide, shallow tray full of pots of pink lilies. No other kind. Nothing but lilies—canna lilies, big pink flowers, wide open, radiant, almost frighteningly alive on bright crimson stems.

'O-oh, Sadie!' said Laura, and the sound was like a little moan. She crouched down as if to warm herself at that blaze of lilies; she felt they were in her fingers, on her lips, growing in her breast.

'It's some mistake,' she said faintly. 'Nobody ever ordered so many. Sadie, go and find mother.'

But at that moment Mrs Sheridan joined them.

'It's quite right,' she said calmly. 'Yes, I ordered them. Aren't they lovely?' She pressed Laura's arm. 'I was passing the shop yesterday, and I saw them in the window, and I suddenly thought for once in my life I shall have enough canna lilies. The garden party will be a good excuse.'

'But I thought you said you didn't mean to interfere,' said Laura. Sadie had gone. The florist's man was still outside at his van. She put her arm round her mother's neck and gently, very gently, she bit her mother's ear.

'My darling child, you wouldn't like a logical mother, would you? Don't do that. Here's the man.'

He carried more lilies still, another whole tray.

'Bank them up, just inside the door, on both sides of the porch, please,' said Mrs Sheridan. 'Don't you agree, Laura?'

'Oh, I *do*, mother.'

In the drawing room Meg, Jose, and good little Hans had at last succeeded in moving the piano.

'Now, if we put this chesterfield against the wall and move everything out of the room except the chairs, don't you think?'

'Quite.'

'Hans, move these tables into the smoking room, and bring a sweeper to take these marks off the carpet and—one moment, Hans—' Jose loved giving orders to the servants, and they loved obeying her. She always made them feel they were taking part in some drama. 'Tell Mother and Miss Laura to come here at once.'

'Very good, Miss Jose.'

She turned to Meg. 'I want to hear what the piano sounds like, just in case I'm asked to sing this afternoon. Let's try over "This Life is Weary".'

Pom! Ta-ta-ta *Tee*-ta! The piano burst out so passionately that Jose's face changed. She clasped her hands. She looked mournfully and enigmatically at her mother and Laura as they came in.

> This Life is *Wee*-ary,
> A Tear—a Sigh.
> A Love that *Chan*-ges,
>   This Life is *Wee*-ary,
> A Tear—a Sigh.
> A Love that *Chan*-ges,
>   And then . . . Good-bye!

But at the word 'Good-bye', and although the piano sounded more desperate than ever, her face broke into a brilliant, dreadfully unsympathetic smile.

'Aren't I in good voice, mummy?' she beamed.

> This Life is *Wee*-ary,
> Hope comes to Die,
> A Dream—a *Wa*-kening.

But now Sadie interrupted them. 'What is it, Sadie?'

'If you please, m'm, cook says have you got the flags for the sandwiches?'

'The flags for the sandwiches, Sadie?' echoed Mrs Sheridan dreamily. And the children knew by her face that she hadn't got them. 'Let me see.' And she said to Sadie firmly, 'Tell cook I'll let her have them in ten minutes.'

Sadie went.

'Now, Laura,' said her mother quickly, 'come with me into the smoking room. I've got the names somewhere on the back of an envelope. You'll have to write them out for me. Meg, go upstairs this minute and take that wet thing off your head. Jose, run and finish dressing this instant. Do you hear me, children, or shall I have to tell your father when he comes home tonight? And—and, Jose, pacify cook if you do go into the kitchen, will you? I'm terrified of her this morning.'

The envelope was found at last behind the dining-room clock, though how it had got there Mrs Sheridan could not imagine.

'One of you children must have stolen it out of my bag, because I remember vividly—cream-cheese and lemon-curd. Have you done that?'

'Yes.'

'Egg and—' Mrs Sheridan held the envelope away from her. 'It looks like mice. It can't be mice, can it?'

'Olive, pet,' said Laura, looking over her shoulder.

'Yes, of course, olive. What a horrible combination it sounds. Egg and olive.'

They were finished at last, and Laura took them off to the kitchen. She found Jose there pacifying the cook, who did not look at all terrifying.

'I have never seen such exquisite sandwiches,' said Jose's rapturous voice. 'How many kinds did you say there were, cook? Fifteen?'

'Fifteen, Miss Jose.'

'Well, cook, I congratulate you.'

Cook swept up crusts with the long sandwich knife, and smiled broadly.

'Godber's has come,' announced Sadie, issuing out of the pantry. She had seen the man pass the window.

That meant that cream puffs had come. Godber's were famous for their cream puffs. Nobody ever thought of making them at home.

'Bring them in and put them on the table, my girl,' ordered cook.

Sadie brought them in and went back to the door. Of course Laura and Jose were far too grown-up to really care about such things. All the same, they couldn't help agreeing that the puffs looked very attractive. Very. Cook began arranging them, shaking off the extra icing sugar.

'Don't they carry one back to all one's parties?' said Laura.

'I suppose they do,' said practical Jose, who never liked to be carried back. 'They look beautifully light and feathery, I must say.'

'Have one each, my dears,' said cook in her comfortable voice. 'Yer ma won't know.'

Oh, impossible. Fancy cream puffs so soon after breakfast. The very idea made one shudder. All the same, two minutes later Jose and Laura were licking their fingers with that absorbed inward look that only comes from whipped cream.

'Let's go into the garden, out by the back way,' suggested Laura. 'I want to see how the men are getting on with the marquee. They're such awfully nice men.'

But the back door was blocked by cook, Sadie, Godber's man and Hans.

Something had happened.

'Tuk-tuk-tuk,' clucked cook like an agitated hen. Sadie had her hand clapped to her cheek as though she had a toothache. Hans's face was screwed up in the effort to understand. Only Godber's man seemed to be enjoying himself; it was his story.

'What's the matter? What happened?'

'There's been a horrible accident,' said cook. 'A man killed.'

'A man killed! Where? How? When?'

But Godber's man wasn't going to have his story snatched from under his very nose.

'Know those little cottages just below here, miss?' Know them? Of course, she knew them. 'Well, there's a young chap living there, name of *Scott*, a carter. His horse shied at a traction-engine, corner of Hawke Street this morning, and he was thrown out on the back of his head. Killed.'

'Dead!' Laura stared at Godber's man.

'Dead when they picked him up,' said Godber's man with relish. 'They were taking the body home as I come up here.' And he said to the cook, 'He's left a wife and five little ones.'

'Jose, come here.' Laura caught hold of her sister's sleeve and dragged her through the kitchen to the other side of the green baize door. There she paused and leaned against it. 'Jose!' she said, horrified, 'however are we going to stop everything?'

'Stop everything, Laura!' cried Jose in astonishment. 'What do you mean?'

'Stop the garden party, of course.' Why did Jose pretend?

But Jose was still more amazed. 'Stop the garden party? My dear Laura, don't be so absurd. Of course we can't do anything of the kind. Nobody expects us to. Don't be so extravagant.'

'But we can't possibly have a garden party with a man dead just outside the front gate.'

That really was extravagant, for the little cottages were in a lane to themselves at the very bottom of a steep rise that led up to the house. A broad road ran between. True, they were far too near. They were the greatest possible eyesore and they had no right to be in that neighbourhood at all. They were little mean dwellings painted a chocolate brown. In the garden patches there was nothing but cabbage stalks, sick hens and tomato cans. The very smoke coming out of their chimneys was poverty-stricken. Little rags and shreds of smoke, so unlike the great silvery plumes that uncurled from the Sheridans' chimneys. Washerwomen lived in the lane and sweeps and a cobbler and a man whose house-front was studded all over with minute bird-cages. Children swarmed. When the Sheridans were little they were forbidden to set foot there because of the revolting language and of what they might catch. But since they were grown up, Laura and Laurie on their prowls sometimes walked through. It was disgusting and sordid. They came out with a shudder. But still one must go everywhere; one must see everything. So through they went.

'And just think of what the band would sound like to that poor woman,' said Laura.

'Oh, Laura!' Jose began to be seriously annoyed. 'If you're going to stop a band playing every time someone has an accident, you'll lead a very strenuous life. I'm every bit as sorry about it as you. I feel just as sympathetic.' Her eyes hardened. She looked at her sister just as she used to when they were little and fighting together. 'You won't bring a drunken workman back to life by being sentimental,' she said softly.

'Drunk! Who said he was drunk?' Laura turned furiously on Jose. She said just as they had used to say on those occasions, 'I'm going straight up to tell mother.'

'Do, dear,' cooed Jose.

'Mother, can I come into your room?' Laura turned the big glass doorknob.

'Of course, child. Why, what's the matter? What's given you such a colour?' And Mrs Sheridan turned round from her dressing-table. She was trying on a new hat.

'Mother, a man's been killed,' began Laura.

'*Not* in the garden?' interrupted her mother.

'No, no!'

'Oh, what a fright you gave me!' Mrs Sheridan sighed with relief, and took off the big hat and held it on her knees.

'But listen, mother,' said Laura. Breathless, half-choking, she told the dreadful story. 'Of course, we can't have our party, can we?' she pleaded. 'The band and everybody arriving. They'd hear us, mother; they're nearly neighbours!'

To Laura's astonishment her mother behaved just like Jose; it was harder to bear because she seemed amused. She refused to take Laura seriously.

'But, my dear child, use your common sense. It's only by accident we've heard of it. If someone had died there normally—and I can't understand how they keep alive in those poky little holes—we should still be having our party, shouldn't we?'

Laura had to say 'yes' to that, but she felt it was all wrong. She sat down on her mother's sofa and pinched the cushion frill.

'Mother, isn't it really terribly heartless of us?' she asked.

'Darling!' Mrs Sheridan got up and came over to her, carrying the hat. Before Laura could stop her she had popped it on. 'My child!' said her mother, 'the hat is yours. It's made for you. It's much too young for me. I have never seen you look such a picture. Look at yourself!' And she held up her hand-mirror.

'But, mother,' Laura began again. She couldn't look at herself; she turned aside.

This time Mrs Sheridan lost patience just as Jose had done.

'You are being very absurd, Laura,' she said coldly. 'People like that don't expect sacrifices from us. And it's not very sympathetic to spoil everybody's enjoyment as you're doing now.'

'I don't understand,' said Laura, and she walked quickly out of the room into her own bedroom. There, quite by chance, the first thing she saw was this charming girl in the mirror, in her black hat trimmed with gold daisies and a long black velvet ribbon. Never had she imagined she could look like that. Is mother right? she thought. And now she hoped her mother was right. Am I being extravagant? Perhaps it was extravagant. Just for a moment she had another glimpse of that poor woman and those little children, and the body being carried into the house. But it all seemed blurred, unreal, like a picture in the newspaper. I'll remember it again after the party's over, she decided. And somehow that seemed quite the best plan. . . .

Lunch was over by half-past one. By half-past two they were all ready for the fray. The green-coated band had arrived and was established in a corner of the tennis court.

'My dear!' trilled Kitty Maitland, 'aren't they too like frogs for words? You ought to have arranged them round the pond with the conductor in the middle on a leaf.'

Laurie arrived and hailed them on his way to dress. At the sight of him Laura remembered the accident again. She wanted to tell him. If Laurie agreed with the others, then it was bound to be all right. And she followed him into the hall.

'Laurie!'

'Hallo!' He was halfway upstairs, but when he turned round and saw Laura he suddenly puffed out his cheeks and goggled his eyes at her. 'My word, Laura! You do look stunning,' said Laurie. 'What an absolutely topping hat!'

Laura said faintly 'Is it?' and smiled up at Laurie, and didn't tell him after all.

Soon after that people began coming in streams. The band struck up; the hired waiters ran from the house to the marquee. Wherever you looked there were couples strolling, bending to the flowers, greeting, moving on over the lawn. They were like bright birds that had alighted in the Sheridans' garden for this one afternoon, on their way to—where? Ah, what happiness it is to be with people who all are happy, to press hands, press cheeks, smile into eyes.

'Darling Laura, how well you look!'

'What a becoming hat, child!'

'Laura, you look quite Spanish. I've never seen you look so striking.'

And Laura, glowing, answered softly, 'Have you had tea? Won't you have an ice? The passion-fruit ices really are rather special.' She ran to her father and begged him: 'Daddy darling, can't the band have something to drink?'

And the perfect afternoon slowly ripened, slowly faded, slowly its petals closed.

'Never a more delightful garden party . . .' 'The greatest success . . .' 'Quite the most . . .'

Laura helped her mother with the good-byes. They stood side by side on the porch till it was all over.

'All over, all over, thank heaven,' said Mrs Sheridan. 'Round up the others, Laura. Let's go and have some fresh coffee. I'm exhausted. Yes, it's been very successful. But oh, these parties, these parties! Why will you children insist on giving parties!' And they all of them sat down in the deserted marquee.

'Have a sandwich, daddy dear. I wrote the flag.'

'Thanks.' Mr Sheridan took a bite and the sandwich was gone. He took another. 'I suppose you didn't hear of a beastly accident that happened today?' he said.

'My dear,' said Mrs Sheridan, holding up her hand, 'we did. It nearly ruined the party. Laura insisted we should put it off.'

'Oh, mother!' Laura didn't want to be teased about it.

'It was a horrible affair all the same,' said Mr Sheridan. 'The chap was married too. Lived just below in the lane, and leaves a wife and half a dozen kiddies, so they say.'

An awkward little silence fell. Mrs Sheridan fidgeted with her cup. Really, it was very tactless of father. . . .

Suddenly she looked up. There on the table were all those sandwiches, cakes, puffs, all uneaten, all going to be wasted. She had one of her brilliant ideas.

'I know,' she said. 'Let's make up a basket. Let's send that poor creature some of this perfectly good food. At any rate, it will be the greatest treat for the children. Don't you agree? And she's sure to have neighbours calling in and so on. What a point to have it all ready prepared. Laura!' She jumped up. 'Get me the big basket out of the stairs cupboard.'

'But, mother, do you really think it's a good idea?' said Laura.

Again, how curious, she seemed to be different from them all. To take scraps from their party. Would the poor woman really like that?

'Of course! What's the matter with you today? An hour or two ago you were insisting on us being sympathetic.'

Oh well! Laura ran for the basket. It was filled, it was now heaped by her mother.

'Take it yourself, darling,' said she. 'Run down just as you are. No, wait, take the arum lilies too. People of that class are so impressed by arum lilies.'

'The stems will ruin her lace frock,' said practical Jose.

So they would. Just in time. 'Only the basket, then. And, Laura!'—her mother followed her out of the marquee—'don't on any account—'

'What, mother?'

No, better not put such ideas into the child's head! 'Nothing! Run along.'

It was just growing dusky as Laura shut their garden gates. A big dog ran by like a shadow. The road gleamed white, and down below in the hollow the little cottages were in deep shade. How quiet it seemed after the afternoon. Here she was going down the hill to somewhere where a man lay dead, and she couldn't realize it. Why couldn't she? She stopped a minute. And it seemed to her that kisses, voices, tinkling spoons, laughter, the smell of crushed grass were somehow inside her. She had no room for anything else. How strange! She looked up at the pale sky, and all she thought was, 'Yes, it was the most successful party.'

Now the broad road was crossed. The lane began, smoky and dark. Women in shawls and men's tweed caps hurried by. Men hung over the palings; the children played in the doorways. A low hum came from the mean little cottages. In some of them there was a flicker of light, and a shadow, crab-like, moved across the window. Laura bent her head and hurried on. She wished now she had put on a coat. How her frock shone! And the big hat with the velvet streamer—if only it was another hat! Were the people looking at her? They must be. It was a mistake to have come; she knew all along it was a mistake. Should she go back even now?

No, too late. This was the house. It must be. A dark knot of people stood outside. Beside the gate an old, old woman with a crutch sat in a chair, watching. She had her feet on a newspaper. The voices stopped as Laura drew near. The group parted. It was as though she was expected, as though they had known she was coming here.

Laura was terribly nervous. Tossing the velvet ribbon over her shoulder, she said to a woman standing by, 'Is this Mrs Scott's house?' and the woman, smiling queerly, said, 'It is, my lass.'

Oh, to be away from this! She actually said, 'Help me, God,' as she walked up the tiny path and knocked. To be away from those staring eyes, or to be covered up in anything, one of those women's shawls even. I'll just leave the basket and go, she decided. I shan't even wait for it to be emptied.

Then the door opened. A little woman in black showed in the gloom.

Laura said, 'Are you Mrs Scott?' But to her horror the woman answered, 'Walk in, please, miss,' and she was shut in the passage.

'No,' said Laura, 'I don't want to come in. I only want to leave this basket. Mother sent—'

The little woman in the gloomy passage seemed not to have heard her. 'Step this way, please, miss,' she said in an oily voice, and Laura followed her.

She found herself in a wretched little low kitchen, lighted by a smoky lamp. There was a woman sitting before the fire.

'Em,' said the little creature who had let her in. 'Em! It's a young lady.' She turned to Laura. She said meaningly, 'I'm 'er sister, miss. You'll excuse 'er, won't you?'

'Oh, but of course!' said Laura. 'Please, please don't disturb her. I—I only want to leave—'

But at that moment the woman at the fire turned round. Her face, puffed up, red, with swollen eyes and swollen lips, looked terrible. She seemed as though she couldn't understand why Laura was there. What did it mean? Why was this stranger standing in the kitchen with a basket? What was it all about? And the poor face puckered up again.

'All right, my dear,' said the other. 'I'll thenk the young lady.'

And again she began, 'You'll excuse her, miss, I'm sure,' and her face, swollen too, tried an oily smile.

Laura only wanted to get out, to get away. She was back in the passage. The door opened. She walked straight through into the bedroom where the dead man was lying.

'You'd like a look at 'im, wouldn't you?' said Em's sister, and she brushed past Laura over to the bed. 'Don't be afraid, my lass,'—and now her voice sounded fond and sly, and fondly she drew down the sheet—' 'e looks a picture. There's nothing to show. Come along, my dear.'

Laura came.

There lay a young man, fast asleep—sleeping so soundly, so deeply, that he was far, far away from them both. Oh, so remote, so peaceful. He was dreaming. Never wake him up again. His head was sunk in the pillows, his eyes were closed; they were blind under the closed eyelids. He was given up to his dream. What did garden parties and baskets and lace frocks matter to him? He was far from all those things. He was wonderful, beautiful. While they were laughing and while the band was playing, this marvel had come to the lane. Happy . . . happy. . . . All is well, said that sleeping face. This is just as it should be. I am content.

But all the same you had to cry, and she couldn't go out of the room without saying something to him. Laura gave a loud childish sob.

'Forgive my hat,' she said.

And this time she didn't wait for Em's sister. She found her way out of the door, down the path, past all those dark people. At the corner of the lane she met Laurie.

He stepped out of the shadow. 'Is that you, Laura?'

'Yes.'

'Mother was getting anxious. Was it all right?'

'Yes, quite. Oh, Laurie!' She took his arm, she pressed up against him.

'I say, you're not crying, are you?' asked her brother.

Laura shook her head. She was.

Laurie put his arm round her shoulder. 'Don't cry,' he said in his warm, loving voice. 'Was it awful?'

'No,' sobbed Laura. 'It was simply marvellous. But, Laurie—' She stopped, she looked at her brother. 'Isn't life,' she stammered, 'isn't life—' But what life was she couldn't explain. No matter. He quite understood.

'*Isn't* it, darling?' said Laurie.

F. Scott Fitzgerald
1896–1940

Francis Scott Key Fitzgerald was born in St Paul, Minnesota, to a genteel but ineffectual father and a doting, eccentric mother. A delicate child, he was reluctant to go to school but finally went to a small Catholic school, then to St Paul Academy, to Newman, and finally to Princeton. He was unpopular at most of these places for most of the time, and unhappy as well, but his talent for writing and his remarkable good looks began to count for more as he grew up, so that at college he received much of the adulation for which he hungered so deeply. He was concerned to the point of obsession with social standing and prestige. Only his gift for writing and his capacity for ruthless self-criticism prevented him from sliding into a life of empty snobbery.

Shortly after the publication of his first novel, *This Side of Paradise* (1920), which brought him immediate fame, Fitzgerald married the strikingly beautiful Zelda Sayre, who shared his zest for high living. But Zelda's mental health was precarious, and the fame and riches garnered from his writing were more than he could handle. After a breakdown and painful recovery, which he described with a typical lack of self-protectiveness, he lived and worked in Hollywood, never quite recapturing the grace and beauty of his early work. He was the poet laureate of the Jazz Age, and in his finest novels (*The Great Gatsby*, 1925, and *Tender Is the Night*, 1934) and his remarkable short stories, we can find the best epitaph for that era as well as for Fitzgerald himself.

In the Depression-era story 'Babylon Revisited', Charlie Watts, now a widower, returns to Paris to reclaim his nine-year-old daughter Honoria. While some people, like his sister-in-law Marion Peters, cannot forget the past, Charlie, in the pain of the present, still hopes for a future that will bring him contentment.

Babylon Revisited

I

'And where's Mr Campbell?' Charlie asked.

'Gone to Switzerland. Mr Campbell's a pretty sick man, Mr Wales.'

'I'm sorry to hear that. And George Hardt?' Charlie inquired.

'Back in America, gone to work.'

'And where is the Snow Bird?'

'He was in here last week. Anyway, his friend, Mr Schaeffer, is in Paris.'

Two familiar names from the long list of a year and a half ago. Charlie scribbled an address in his notebook and tore out the page.

'If you see Mr Schaeffer, give him this,' he said. 'It's my brother-in-law's address. I haven't settled on a hotel yet.'

He was not really disappointed to find Paris was so empty. But the stillness in the Ritz bar was strange and portentous. It was not an American bar anymore—he felt polite in it, and not as if he owned it. It had gone back into France. He felt the stillness from the moment he got out of the taxi and saw the doorman, usually in a frenzy of activity at this hour, gossiping with a *chasseur* by the servants' entrance.

Passing through the corridor, he heard only a single, bored voice in the once clamorous women's room. When he turned into the bar he travelled the twenty feet of green carpet with his eyes fixed straight ahead by old habit; and then, with his foot firmly on the rail, he turned and surveyed the room, encountering only a single pair of eyes that fluttered up from a newspaper in the corner. Charlie asked for the head barman, Paul, who in the latter days of the bull market had come to work in his own custom-built car—disembarking, however, with due nicety at the nearest corner. But Paul was at his country house today and Alix giving him information.

'No, no more,' Charlie said, 'I'm going slow these days.'

Alix congratulated him: 'You were going pretty strong a couple of years ago.'

'I'll stick to it all right,' Charlie assured him. 'I've stuck to it for over a year and a half now.'

'How do you find conditions in America?'

'I haven't been to America for months. I'm in business in Prague, representing a couple of concerns there. They don't know about me down there.'

Alix smiled.

'Remember the night of George Hardt's bachelor dinner here?' said Charlie. 'By the way, what's become of Claude Fessenden?'

Alix lowered his voice confidentially: 'He's in Paris, but he doesn't come here anymore. Paul doesn't allow it. He ran up a bill of thirty thousand francs, charging all his drinks and his lunches, and usually his dinner, for more than a year. And when Paul finally told him he had to pay, he gave him a bad cheque.'

Alix shook his head sadly.

'I don't understand it, such a dandy fellow. Now he's all bloated up—' He made a plump apple of his hands.

Charlie watched a group of strident queens installing themselves in a corner.

'Nothing affects them,' he thought. 'Stocks rise and fall, people loaf or work, but they go on forever.' The place oppressed him. He called for the dice and shook with Alix for the drink.

'Here for long, Mr Wales?'

'I'm here for four or five days to see my little girl.'

'Oh-h! You have a little girl?'

Outside, the fire-red, gas-blue, ghost-green signs shone smokily through the tranquil rain. It was late afternoon and the streets were in movement; the *bistros* gleamed. At the corner of the Boulevard des Capucines he took a taxi. The Place de la Concorde moved by in pink majesty; they crossed the logical Seine, and Charlie felt the sudden provincial quality of the Left Bank.

Charlie directed his taxi to the Avenue de l'Opera, which was out of his way. But he wanted to see the blue hour spread over the magnificent façade, and imagine that the cab horns, playing endlessly the first few bars of *Le Plus que Lent*, were the trumpets of the Second Empire. They were closing the iron grille in front of Brentano's Book-store, and people were already at dinner behind the trim little bourgeois hedge of Duval's. He had never eaten at a really cheap restaurant in Paris. Five-course dinner, four francs fifty, eighteen cents, wine included. For some odd reason he wished that he had.

As they rolled on to the Left Bank and he felt its sudden provincialism, he thought, 'I spoiled this city for myself. I didn't realize it, but the days came along one after another, and then two years were gone, and everything was gone, and I was gone.'

He was thirty-five, and good to look at. The Irish mobility of his face was sobered by a deep wrinkle between his eyes. As he rang his brother-in-law's bell in the Rue Palatine, the wrinkle deepened till it pulled down his brows; he felt a cramping sensation in his belly. From behind the maid who opened the door darted a lovely little girl of nine who shrieked 'Daddy!' and flew up, struggling like a fish, into his arms. She pulled his head around by one ear and set her cheek against his.

'My old pie,' he said.

'Oh, daddy, daddy, daddy, daddy, dads, dads, dads!'

She drew him into the salon, where the family waited, a boy and a girl his daughter's age, his sister-in-law, and her husband. He greeted Marion with his voice pitched carefully to avoid either feigned enthusiasm or dislike, but the response was more frankly tepid, though she minimized her expression of unalterable distrust by directing her regard toward his child. The two men clasped hands in a friendly way and Lincoln Peters rested his for a moment on Charlie's shoulder.

The room was warm and comfortably American. The three children moved intimately about, playing through the yellow oblongs that led to other rooms; the cheer of six o'clock spoke in the eager smacks of the fire and the sounds of French activity in the kitchen. But Charlie did not relax; his heart sat up rigidly in his body and he drew confidence from his daughter, who from time to time came close to him, holding in her arms the doll he had brought.

'Really extremely well,' he declared in answer to Lincoln's question. 'There's a lot of business there that isn't moving at all, but we're doing even better than ever. In fact, damn well. I'm bringing my sister over from America next month to keep house for me. My income last year was bigger than it was when I had money. You see, the Czechs—'

His boasting was for a specific purpose; but after a moment, seeing a faint restiveness in Lincoln's eye, he changed the subject:

'Those are fine children of yours, well brought up, good manners.'

'We think Honoria's a great little girl too.'

Marion Peters came back from the kitchen. She was a tall woman with worried eyes, who had once possessed a fresh American loveliness. Charlie had never been sensitive to it and was always surprised when people spoke of how pretty she had been. From the first there had been an instinctive antipathy between them.

'Well, how do you find Honoria?' she asked.

'Wonderful. I was astonished how much she's grown in ten months. All the children are looking well.'

'We haven't had a doctor for a year. How do you like being back in Paris?'

'It seems very funny to see so few Americans around.'

'I'm delighted,' Marion said vehemently. 'Now at least you can go into a store without their assuming you're a millionaire. We've suffered like everybody, but on the whole it's a good deal pleasanter.'

'But it was nice while it lasted,' Charlie said. 'We were sort of royalty, almost infallible, with a sort of magic around us. In the bar this afternoon'—he stumbled, seeing his mistake—'there wasn't a man I knew.'

She looked at him keenly. 'I should think you'd have had enough of bars.'

'I only stayed a minute. I take one drink every afternoon, and no more.'

'Don't you want a cocktail before dinner?' Lincoln asked.

'I take only one drink every afternoon, and I've had that.'

'I hope you keep to it,' said Marion.

Her dislike was evident in the coldness with which she spoke, but Charlie only smiled; he had larger plans. Her very aggressiveness gave him an advantage, and he knew enough to wait. He wanted them to initiate the discussion of what they knew had brought him to Paris.

At dinner he couldn't decide whether Honoria was most like him or her mother. Fortunate if she didn't combine the traits of both that had brought them to disaster. A great wave of protectiveness went over him. He thought he knew what to do for her. He believed in character; he wanted to jump back a whole generation and trust in character again as the eternally valuable element. Everything else wore out.

He left soon after dinner, but not to go home. He was curious to see Paris by night with clearer and more judicious eyes than those of other days. He bought a *strapontin* for the Casino and watched Josephine Baker go through her chocolate arabesques.

After an hour he left and strolled toward Montmartre, up the Rue Pigalle into the Place Blanche. The rain had stopped and there were a few people in evening clothes disembarking from taxis in front of cabarets, and *cocottes* prowling singly or in pairs, and many Negroes. He passed a lighted door from which issued music, and stopped with the sense of familiarity; it was Bricktop's, where he had parted with so many hours and so much money. A few doors farther on he found another ancient rendezvous and incautiously put his head inside. Immediately an eager orchestra burst into sound, a pair of professional dancers leaped to their feet, and a maître d'hôtel swooped toward him, crying, 'Crowd just arriving, sir!' But he withdrew quickly.

'You have to be damn drunk,' he thought.

Zelli's was closed, the bleak and sinister cheap hotels surrounding it were dark; up the Rue Blanche there was more light and a local, colloquial French crowd. The Poet's Cave had disappeared, but the two great mouths of the Café of Heaven and the Café of Hell still yawned—even devoured, as he watched, the meagre contents of a tourist bus—a German, a Japanese, and an American couple who glanced at him with frightened eyes.

So much for the effort and ingenuity of Montmartre. All the catering to vice and waste was on an utterly childish scale, and he suddenly realized the meaning of the word 'dissipate'—to dissipate into thin air; to make nothing out of something. In the little hours of the night every move from place to place was an enormous human jump, an increase of paying for the privilege of slower and slower motion.

He remembered thousand-franc notes given to an orchestra for playing a single number, hundred-franc notes tossed to a doorman for calling a cab.

But it hadn't been given for nothing.

It had been given, even the most wildly squandered sum, as an offering to destiny that he might not remember the things most worth remembering, the things that now he would always remember—his child taken from his control, his wife escaped to a grave in Vermont.

In the glare of a *brasserie* a woman spoke to him. He bought her some eggs and coffee, and then, eluding her encouraging stare, gave her a twenty-franc note and took a taxi to his hotel.

II

He woke upon a fine fall day—football weather. The depression of yesterday was gone and he liked the people on the streets. At noon he sat opposite Honoria at Le Grand Vatel, the only restaurant he could think of not reminiscent of champagne dinners and long luncheons that began at two and ended in a blurred and vague twilight.

'Now, how about vegetables? Oughtn't you to have some vegetables?'

'Well, yes.'

'Here's *épinards* and *chou-fleur* and *carrots* and *haricots*.'

'I'd like *chou-fleur*.'

'Wouldn't you like to have two vegetables?'

'I usually only have one at lunch.'

The waiter was pretending to be inordinately fond of children. '*Qu'elle est mignonne la petite! Elle parle exactement comme une Française.*'

'How about dessert? Shall we wait and see?'

The waiter disappeared. Honoria looked at her father expectantly.

'What are we going to do?'

'First, we're going to that toy store in the Rue Saint-Honoré and buy you anything you like. And then we're going to the vaudeville at the Empire.'

She hesitated. 'I like it about the vaudeville, but not the toy store.'

'Why not?'

'Well, you brought me this doll.' She had it with her. 'And I've got lots of things. And we're not rich anymore, are we?'

'We never were. But today you are to have anything you want.'

'All right,' she agreed resignedly.

When there had been her mother and a French nurse he had been inclined to be strict; now he extended himself, reached out for a new tolerance; he must be both parents to her and not shut any of her out of communication.

'I want to get to know you,' he said gravely. 'First let me introduce myself. My name is Charles J. Wales, of Prague.'

'Oh, daddy!' her voice cracked with laughter.

'And who are you, please?' he persisted, and she accepted a rôle immediately: 'Honoria Wales, Rue Palatine, Paris.'

'Married or single?'

'No, not married. Single.'

He indicated the doll. 'But I see you have a child, madame.'

Unwilling to disinherit it, she took it to her heart and thought quickly: 'Yes, I've been married, but I'm not married now. My husband is dead.'

He went on quickly, 'And the child's name?'

'Simone. That's after my best friend at school.'

'I'm very pleased that you're doing so well at school.'

'I'm third this month,' she boasted. 'Elsie'—that was her cousin—'is only about eighteenth, and Richard is about at the bottom.'

'You like Richard and Elsie, don't you?'

'Oh, yes. I like Richard quite well and I like her all right.'

Cautiously and casually he asked: 'And Aunt Marion and Uncle Lincoln—which do you like best?'

'Oh, Uncle Lincoln, I guess.'

He was increasingly aware of her presence. As they came in, a murmur of '. . . adorable' followed them, and now the people at the next table bent all their silences upon her, staring as if she were something no more conscious than a flower.

'Why don't I live with you?' she asked suddenly. 'Because mamma's dead?'

'You must stay here and learn more French. It would have been hard for daddy to take care of you so well.'

'I don't really need much taking care of any more. I do everything for myself.'

Going out of the restaurant, a man and a woman unexpectedly hailed him.

'Well, the old Wales!'

'Hello there, Lorraine. . . . Dunc.'

Sudden ghosts out of the past: Duncan Schaeffer, a friend from college. Lorraine Quarrles, a lovely, pale blonde of thirty; one of a crowd who had helped them make months into days in the lavish times of three years ago.

'My husband couldn't come this year,' she said, in answer to his question. 'We're poor as hell. So he gave me two hundred a month and told me I could do my worst on that. . . . This your little girl?'

'What about coming back and sitting down?' Duncan asked.

'Can't do it.' He was glad for an excuse. As always, he felt Lorraine's passionate, provocative attraction, but his own rhythm was different now.

'Well, how about dinner?' she asked.

'I'm not free. Give me your address and let me call you.'

'Charlie, I believe you're sober,' she said judicially. 'I honestly believe he's sober, Dunc. Pinch him and see if he's sober.'

Charlie indicated Honoria with his head. They both laughed.

'What's your address?' said Duncan skeptically.

He hesitated, unwilling to give the name of his hotel.

'I'm not settled yet. I'd better call you. We're going to the vaudeville at the Empire.'

'There! That's what I want to do,' Lorraine said. 'I want to see some clowns and acrobats and jugglers. That's just what we'll do, Dunc.'

'We've got to do an errand first,' said Charlie. 'Perhaps we'll see you there.'

'All right, you snob. . . . Good-bye, beautiful little girl.'

'Good-bye.'

Honoria bobbed politely.

Somehow, an unwelcome encounter. They liked him because he was functioning, because he was serious; they wanted to see him, because he was stronger than they were now, because they wanted to draw a certain sustenance from his strength.

At the Empire, Honoria proudly refused to sit upon her father's folded coat. She was already an individual with a code of her own, and Charlie was more and more absorbed by the desire of putting a little of himself into her before she crystallized utterly. It was hopeless to try to know her in so short a time.

Between the acts they came upon Duncan and Lorraine in the lobby where the band was playing.

'Have a drink?'

'All right, but not up at the bar. We'll take a table.'

'The perfect father.'

Listening abstractedly to Lorraine, Charlie watched Honoria's eyes leave their table, and he followed them wistfully about the room, wondering what they saw. He met her glance and she smiled.

'I liked that lemonade,' she said.

What had she said? What had he expected? Going home in a taxi afterward, he pulled her over until her head rested against his chest.

'Darling, do you ever think about your mother?'

'Yes, sometimes,' she answered vaguely.

'I don't want you to forget her. Have you got a picture of her?'

'Yes, I think so. Anyhow, Aunt Marion has. Why don't you want me to forget her?'

'She loved you very much.'

'I loved her too.'

They were silent for a moment.

'Daddy, I want to come and live with you,' she said suddenly.

His heart leaped; he had wanted it to come like this.

'Aren't you perfectly happy?'

'Yes, but I love you better than anybody. And you love me better than anybody, don't you, now that mummy's dead?'

'Of course I do. But you won't always like me best, honey. You'll grow up and meet somebody your own age and go marry him and forget you ever had a daddy.'

'Yes, that's true,' she agreed tranquilly.

He didn't go in. He was coming back at nine o'clock and he wanted to keep himself fresh and new for the thing he must say then.

'When you're safe inside, just show yourself in that window.'

'All right. Good-bye, dads, dads, dads, dads.'

He waited in the dark street until she appeared, all warm and glowing, in the window above and kissed her fingers out into the night.

III

They were waiting. Marion sat behind the coffee service in a dignified black dinner dress that just faintly suggested mourning. Lincoln was walking up and down with the animation of one who had already been talking. They were as anxious as he was to get into the question. He opened it almost immediately:

'I suppose you know what I want to see you about—why I really came to Paris.'

Marion played with the black stars on her necklace and frowned.

'I'm awfully anxious to have a home,' he continued. 'And I'm awfully anxious to have Honoria in it. I appreciate your taking in Honoria for her mother's sake, but things have changed now'—he hesitated and then continued more forcibly—'changed radically with me, and I want to ask you to reconsider the matter. It would be silly for me to deny that about three years ago I was acting badly—'

Marion looked up a him with hard eyes.

'—but all that's over. As I told you, I haven't had more than a drink a day for over a year, and I take that drink deliberately, so that the idea of alcohol won't get too big in my imagination. You see the idea?'

'No,' said Marion succinctly.

'It's a sort of stunt I set myself. It keeps the matter in proportion.'

'I get you,' said Lincoln. 'You don't want to admit it's got any attraction for you.'

'Something like that. Sometimes I forget and don't take it. But I try to take it. Anyway, I couldn't afford to drink in my position. The people I represent are more than satisfied with what I've done, and I'm bringing my sister over from Burlington to keep house for me, and I want awfully to have Honoria too. You know that even when her mother and I weren't getting along well we never let anything that happened touch Honoria. I know she's fond of me and I know I'm able to take care of her and—well, there you are. How do you feel about it?'

He knew that now he would have to take a beating. It would last an hour or two hours, and it would be difficult, but if he modulated his inevitable resentment to the chastened attitude of the reformed sinner, he might win his point in the end.

Keep your temper, he told himself. You don't want to be justified. You want Honoria.

Lincoln spoke first: 'We've been talking it over ever since we got your letter last month. We're happy to have Honoria here. She's a dear little thing, and we're glad to be able to help her, but of course that isn't the question—'

Marion interrupted suddenly. 'How long are you going to stay sober, Charlie?' she asked.

'Permanently, I hope.'

'How can anybody count on that?'

'You know I never did drink heavily until I gave up business and came over here with nothing to do. Then Helen and I began to run around with—'

'Please leave Helen out of it. I can't bear to hear you talk about her like that.'

He stared at her grimly; he had never been certain how fond of each other the sisters were in life.

'My drinking only lasted about a year and a half—from the time we came over until I—collapsed.'

'It was time enough.'

'It was time enough,' he agreed.

'My duty is entirely to Helen,' she said. 'I try to think what she would have wanted me to do. Frankly, from the night you did that terrible thing you haven't really existed for me. I can't help that. She was my sister.'

'Yes.'

'When she was dying she asked me to look out for Honoria. If you hadn't been in a sanitarium then, it might have helped matters.'

He had no answer.

'I'll never in my life be able to forget that morning when Helen knocked at my door, soaked to the skin and shivering and said you'd locked her out.'

Charlie gripped the sides of his chair. This was more difficult than he expected; he wanted to launch out into a long expostulation and explanation, but he only said: 'The night I locked her out—' and she interrupted, 'I don't feel up to going over that again.'

After a moment's silence Lincoln said: 'We're getting off the subject. You want Marion to set aside her legal guardianship and give you Honoria. I think the main point for her is whether she has confidence in you or not.'

'I don't blame Marion,' Charlie said slowly, 'but I think she can have entire confidence in me. I had a good record up to three years ago. Of course, it's within human possibilities I might go wrong any time. But if we wait much longer I'll lose Honoria's childhood and my chance for a home.' He shook his head, 'I'll simply lose her, don't you see?'

'Yes, I see,' said Lincoln.

'Why didn't you think of all this before?' Marion asked.

'I suppose I did, from time to time, but Helen and I were getting along badly. When I consented to the guardianship, I was flat on my back in a sanitarium and the market had cleaned me out. I knew I'd acted badly, and I thought if it would bring any peace to Helen, I'd agree to anything. But now it's different. I'm functioning, I'm behaving damn well, so far as—'

'Please don't swear at me,' Marion said.

He looked at her, startled. With each remark the force of her dislike became more and more apparent. She had built up all her fear of life into one wall and faced it toward him. This trivial reproof was possibly the result of some trouble with the cook several hours before. Charlie became increasingly alarmed at leaving Honoria in this atmosphere of hostility against himself; sooner or later it would come out, in a word here, a shake of the head there, and some of that distrust would be irrevocably implanted on Honoria. But he pulled his temper down out of his face and shut it up inside him; he had won a point, for Lincoln realized the absurdity of Marion's remark and asked her lightly since when she had objected to the word 'damn'.

'Another thing,' Charlie said: 'I'm able to give her certain advantages now. I'm going to take a French governess to Prague with me. I've got a lease on a new apartment—'

He stopped, realizing that he was blundering. They couldn't be expected to accept with equanimity the fact that his income was again twice as large as their own.

'I suppose you can give her more luxuries than we can,' said Marion. 'When you were throwing away money we were living along watching every ten francs. . . . I suppose you'll start doing it again.'

'Oh, no,' he said. 'I've learned. I worked hard for ten years, you know—until I got lucky in the market, like so many people. Terribly lucky. It won't happen again.'

There was a long silence. All of them felt their nerves straining, and for the first time in a year Charlie wanted a drink. He was sure now that Lincoln Peters wanted him to have his child.

Marion shuddered suddenly; part of her saw that Charlie's feet were planted on the earth now, and her own maternal feeling recognized the naturalness of his desire; but she had lived for a long time with a prejudice—a prejudice founded on a curious disbelief in her sister's happiness, and which, in the shock of one terrible night, had turned to hatred for him. It had all happened at a point in her life where the discouragement of ill health and adverse circumstances made it necessary for her to believe in tangible villainy and a tangible villain.

'I can't help what I think!' she cried out suddenly. 'How much you were responsible for Helen's death, I don't know. It's something you'll have to square with your own conscience.'

An electric current of agony surged through him; for a moment he was almost on his feet, an unuttered sound echoing from his throat. He hung on to himself for a moment, another moment.

'Hold on there,' said Lincoln uncomfortably. 'I never thought you were responsible for that.'

'Helen died of heart trouble,' Charlie said dully.

'Yes, heart trouble.' Marion spoke as if the phrase had another meaning for her.

Then, in the flatness that followed her outburst, she saw him plainly and she knew he had somehow arrived at control over the situation. Glancing at her husband, she found no help from him, and as abruptly as if it were a matter of no importance, she threw up the sponge.

'Do what you like!' she cried, springing up from her chair. 'She's your child. I'm not the person to stand in your way. I think if it were my child I'd rather see her—' She managed to check herself. 'You two decide it. I can't stand this. I'm sick. I'm going to bed.'

She hurried from the room; after a moment Lincoln said:

'This has been a hard day for her. You know how strongly she feels—' His voice was almost apologetic: 'When a woman gets an idea in her head.'

'Of course.'

'It's going to be all right. I think she sees now that you—can provide for the child, and so we can't very well stand in your way or Honoria's way.'

'Thank you, Lincoln.'

'I'd better go along and see how she is.'

'I'm going.'

He was still trembling when he reached the street, but a walk down the Rue Bonaparte to the *quais* set him up, and as he crossed the Seine, fresh and new by the *quai* lamps, he felt exultant. But back in his room he couldn't sleep. The image of Helen haunted him. Helen whom he had loved so until they had senselessly begun to abuse each other's love, tear it into shreds. On that terrible February night that Marion remembered so vividly, a slow quarrel had gone on for hours. There was a scene at the Florida, and then he attempted to take her home, and then she kissed young Webb at a table; after that there was what she had hysterically said. When he arrived home alone he turned the key in the lock in wild anger. How could he know she would arrive an hour later alone, that there would be a snowstorm in which she wandered about in slippers, too confused to find a taxi? Then the aftermath, her escaping pneumonia by a miracle, and all the attendant horror. They were 'reconciled', but that was the beginning of the end, and Marion, who had seen with her own eyes and who imagined it to be one of many scenes from her sister's martyrdom, never forgot.

Going over it again brought Helen nearer, and in the white, soft light that steals upon half sleep near morning he found himself talking to her again. She said that he was perfectly right about Honoria and that she wanted Honoria to be with him. She said she was glad he was being good and doing better. She said a lot of other things—very friendly things—but she was in a swing in a white dress, and swinging faster and faster all the time, so that at the end he could not hear clearly all that she said.

IV

He woke up feeling happy. The door of the world was open again. He made plans, vistas, futures for Honoria and himself, but suddenly he grew sad, remembering all the plans he and Helen had made. She had not planned to die. The present was the thing—work to do and someone to love. But not to love too much, for he knew the injury that a father can do to a daughter or a mother to a son by attaching them too closely: afterward, out in the world, the child would seek in the marriage partner the same blind tenderness and, failing probably to find it, turn against love and life.

It was another bright, crisp day. He called Lincoln Peters at the bank where he worked and asked if he could count on taking Honoria when he left for Prague. Lincoln agreed that there was no reason for delay. One thing—the legal guardianship. Marion wanted to retain that a while longer. She was upset by the whole matter, and it would oil things if she felt that the situation was still in her control for another year. Charlie agreed, wanting only the tangible, visible child.

Then the question of a governess. Charlie sat in a gloomy agency and talked to a cross Béarnaise and to a buxom Breton peasant, neither of whom he could have endured. There were others whom he would see tomorrow.

He lunched with Lincoln Peters at Griffons, trying to keep down his exultation.

'There's nothing quite like your own child,' Lincoln said. 'But you understand how Marion feels too.'

'She's forgotten how hard I worked for seven years there,' Charlie said. 'She just remembers one night.'

'There's another thing.' Lincoln hesitated. 'While you and Helen were tearing around Europe throwing money away, we were just getting along. I didn't touch any of the prosperity because I never got ahead enough to carry anything but my insurance. I think Marion felt there was some kind of injustice in it—you not even working toward the end, and getting richer and richer.'

'It went just as quick as it came,' said Charlie.

'Yes, a lot of it stayed in the hands of *chasseurs* and saxophone players and maîtres d'hôtel—well, the big party's over now. I just said that to explain Marion's feelings about those crazy years. If you drop in about six o'clock tonight before Marion's too tired, we'll settle the details on the spot.'

Back at his hotel, Charlie found a *pneumatique*[1] that had been redirected from the Ritz bar where Charlie had left his address for the purpose of finding a certain man.

DEAR CHARLIE: You were so strange when we saw you the other day that I wondered if I did something to offend you. If so, I'm not conscious of it. In fact, I have thought about you too much for the last year, and it's always been in the back of my mind that I might see you if I came over here. We *did* have such good times that crazy spring, like the night you and I stole the butcher's tricycle, and the time we tried to call on the president and you had the old derby rim and the wire cane. Everybody seems so old lately, but I don't feel old a bit. Couldn't we get together some time today for old time's sake? I've got a vile hangover for the moment, but will be feeling better this afternoon and will look for you about five in the sweatshop at the Ritz.

Always devotedly,
LORRAINE.

His first feeling was one of awe that he had actually, in his mature years, stolen a tricycle and pedalled Lorraine all over the étoile between the small hours and dawn. In retrospect it was a nightmare. Locking out Helen didn't fit in with any other act of his life, but the tricycle incident did—it was one of many. How many weeks or months of dissipation to arrive at the condition of utter irresponsibility?

He tried to picture how Lorraine had appeared to him then—very attractive; Helen was unhappy about it, though she said nothing. Yesterday, in the restaurant, Lorraine had seemed trite, blurred, worn away. He emphatically did not want to see her, and he was glad Alix had not given away his hotel address. It was a relief to think, instead, of Honoria, to think of Sundays spent with her and of saying good morning to her and of knowing she was there in his house at night, drawing her breath in the darkness.

At five he took a taxi and bought presents for all the Peters—a piquant cloth doll, a box of Roman soldiers, flowers for Marion, big linen handkerchiefs for Lincoln.

He saw, when he arrived in the apartment, that Marion had accepted the inevitable. She greeted him now as though he were a recalcitrant member of the family, rather than a menacing outsider. Honoria had been told she was going; Charlie was glad to see that her tact made her conceal her excessive happiness. Only on his lap did she whisper her delight and the question 'When?' before she slipped away with the other children.

He and Marion were alone for a minute in the room, and on an impulse he spoke out boldly:

'Family quarrels are bitter things. They don't go according to any rules. They're not aches or wounds; they're more like splits in the skin that won't heal because there's not enough material. I wish you and I could be on better terms.'

'Some things are hard to forget,' she answered. 'It's a question of confidence.' There was no answer to this and presently she asked, 'When do you propose to take her?'

'As soon as I can get a governess. I hoped the day after tomorrow.'

'That's impossible. I've got to get her things in shape. Not before Saturday.'

1 a message conveyed by *pneumatique*, a system of sending mail along tubes by air pressure

He yielded. Coming back into the room, Lincoln offered him a drink.

'I'll take my daily whisky,' he said.

It was warm here, it was a home, people together by a fire. The children felt very safe and important; the mother and father were serious, watchful. They had things to do for the children more important than his visit here. A spoonful of medicine was, after all, more important than the strained relations between Marion and himself. They were not dull people, but they were very much in the grip of life and circumstances. He wondered if he couldn't do something to get Lincoln out of his rut at the bank.

A long peal at the doorbell; the *bonne à tout faire* passed through and went down the corridor. The door opened upon another long ring, and then voices, and the three in the salon looked up expectantly; Richard moved to bring the corridor within his range of vision, and Marion rose. Then the maid came back along the corridor, closely followed by the voices, which developed under the light into Duncan Schaeffer and Lorraine Quarrles.

They were gay, they were hilarious, they were roaring with laughter. For a moment Charlie was astounded; unable to understand how they ferreted out the Peters' address.

'Ah-h-h-!' Duncan wagged his finger roguishly at Charlie. 'Ah-h-h!'

They both slid down another cascade of laughter. Anxious and at a loss, Charlie shook hands with them quickly and presented them to Lincoln and Marion. Marion nodded, scarcely speaking. She had drawn back a step toward the fire; her little girl stood beside her, and Marion put an arm about her shoulder.

With growing annoyance at the intrusion, Charlie waited for them to explain themselves. After some concentration Duncan said:

'We came to invite you out to dinner. Lorraine and I insist that all this shishi, cagey business 'bout your address got to stop.'

Charlie came closer to them, as if to force them backward down the corridor.

'Sorry, but I can't. Tell me where you'll be and I'll phone you in half an hour.'

This made no impression. Lorraine sat down suddenly on the side of a chair, and focusing her eyes on Richard, cried, 'Oh, what a nice little boy! Come here, little boy.' Richard glanced at his mother, but did not move. With a perceptible shrug of her shoulders, Lorraine turned back to Charlie:

'Come and dine. Sure your cousins won' mine. See you so sel'om. Or solemn.'

'I can't,' said Charlie sharply. 'You two have dinner and I'll phone you.'

Her voice became suddenly unpleasant. 'All right, we'll go. But I remember once when you hammered on my door at four a.m. I was enough of a good sport to give you a drink. Come on, Dunc.'

Still in slow motion, with blurred, angry faces, with uncertain feet, they retired along the corridor.

'Good night,' Charlie said.

'Good night!' responded Lorraine emphatically.

When he went back into the salon Marion had not moved, only now her son was standing in the circle of her other arm. Lincoln was still swinging Honoria back and forth like a pendulum from side to side.

'What an outrage!' Charlie broke out. 'What an absolute outrage!'

Neither of them answered. Charlie dropped into an armchair, picked up his drink, set it down again and said:

'People I haven't seen for two years having the colossal nerve—'

He broke off. Marion had made the sound 'Oh!' in one swift, furious breath, turned her body from him with a jerk and left the room.

Lincoln set down Honoria carefully.

'You children go in and start your soup,' he said, and when they obeyed, he said to Charlie:

'Marion's not well and she can't stand shocks. That kind of people make her really physically sick.'

'I didn't tell them to come here. They wormed your name out of somebody. They deliberately—'

'Well, it's too bad. It doesn't help matters. Excuse me a minute.'

Left alone, Charlie sat tense in his chair. In the next room he could hear the children eating, talking in monosyllables, already oblivious to the scene between their elders. He heard a murmur of conversation from a farther room and then the ticking bell of a telephone receiver picked up, and in a panic he moved to the other side of the room and out of earshot.

In a minute Lincoln came back. 'Look here, Charlie. I think we'd better call off dinner for tonight. Marion's in bad shape.'

'Is she angry with me?'

'Sort of,' he said, almost roughly. 'She's not strong and—'

'You mean she's changed her mind about Honoria?'

'She's pretty bitter right now. I don't know. You phone me at the bank tomorrow.'

'I wish you'd explain to her I never dreamed these people would come here. I'm just as sore as you are.'

'I couldn't explain anything to her now.'

Charlie got up. He took his coat and hat and started down the corridor. Then he opened the door of the dining room and said in a strange voice, 'Good night, children.'

Honoria rose and ran around the table to hug him.

'Good night, sweetheart,' he said vaguely, and then trying to make his voice more tender, trying to conciliate something, 'Good night, dear children.'

V

Charlie went directly to the Ritz bar with the furious idea of finding Lorraine and Duncan, but they were not there, and he realized that in any case there was nothing he could do. He had not touched his drink at the Peters', and now he ordered a whisky-and-soda. Paul came over to say hello.

'It's a great change,' he said sadly. 'We do about half the business we did. So many fellows I hear about back in the States lost everything, maybe not in the first crash, but then in the second. Your friend George Hardt lost every cent, I hear. Are you back in the States?'

'No, I'm in business in Prague.'

'I heard that you lost a lot in the crash.'

'I did,' and he added grimly, 'but I lost everything I wanted in the boom.'

'Selling short.'

'Something like that.'

Again the memory of those days swept over him like a nightmare—the people they met travelling; then people who couldn't add a row of figures or speak a coherent sentence. The little man Helen had consented to dance with at the ship's party, who had insulted her ten feet from the table; the women and girls carried screaming with drink or drugs out of public places—

—The men who locked their wives out in the snow, because the snow of twenty-nine wasn't real snow. If you didn't want it to be snow, you just paid some money.

He went to the phone and called the Peters' apartment; Lincoln answered.

'I called up because this thing is on my mind. Has Marion said anything definite?'

'Marion's sick,' Lincoln answered shortly. 'I know this thing isn't altogether your fault, but I can't have her go to pieces about it. I'm afraid we'll have to let it slide for six months; I can't take the chance of working her up to this state again.'

'I see.'

'I'm sorry, Charlie.'

He went back to his table. His whisky glass was empty, but he shook his head when Alix looked at it questioningly. There wasn't much he could do now except send Honoria some things; he would send her a lot of things tomorrow. He thought rather angrily that this was just money—he had given so many people money. . . .

'No, no more,' he said to another waiter. 'What do I owe you?'

He would come back some day; they couldn't make him pay forever. But he wanted his child, and nothing was much good now, beside that fact. He wasn't young anymore, with a lot of nice thoughts and dreams to have by himself. He was absolutely sure Helen wouldn't have wanted him to be so alone.

1931

William Faulkner
1897–1962

William Faulkner was born in Union County, Mississippi. His family had been important in the political, economic, and cultural life of northern Mississippi for three generations, but their power and influence were declining, and for a time it looked as though young William might be its least distinguished member. He spent most of his youth hunting, fishing, and playing baseball. But he was gifted at drawing and telling stories, and he maintained from an early age that he wanted to be a writer like his great-grandfather, William Cuthbert Faulkner, whose *White Rose of Memphis* had gone through thirty-five editions after its publication in 1880.

During World War I Faulkner was turned

down by the United States Army Air Corps because he was too short, but he was accepted for flight training in the Canadian Air Force. He had hoped to fly in combat, but the war ended too soon, and he was injured when he and a friend celebrated Armistice Day by stunting over the field and crashing through a hangar roof. He returned to Oxford, Mississippi, where he continued to read and to write, and took courses at the University of Mississippi. But he was neither a regular nor a successful student, nor did he have any luck trying to place his fiction and poetry with magazines until a friend subsidized a private printing of a volume of his poetry, *The Marble Faun*, in 1924. In later life Faulkner spoke of himself as a 'failed poet' who had turned to fiction only because his poetry was not good enough.

In 1925 he moved to New Orleans, where he was admitted to the circle of writers that gathered around Sherwood Anderson. He began to publish sketches in the Sunday feature section of the New Orleans *Times-Picayune*, and, with Anderson's help, he was able to get his first novel, *Soldier's Pay*, published in 1926. In his third novel, *Sartoris* (1929), he began to find his proper material and realize his strength as a writer. With this work he began his immense chronicle of an imaginary Mississippi county, based on the history of the area around his home in Oxford, Mississippi. In 'A Rose for Emily', Miss Emily Grierson represents the old southern world in contrast to the newer generation that engulfs her. His Yoknapatawpha County has become a permanent feature in the international literary landscape. Among his highly regarded works are *Light in August* (1932) and *Absalom, Absalom!* (1936), and two collections of short fiction that have the shape and movement of a novel: *The Unvanquished* (1938) and *Go Down, Moses* (1942). In 1950 he received the Nobel Prize for Literature.

A Rose for Emily

I

When Miss Emily Grierson died, our whole town went to her funeral: the men through a sort of respectful affection for a fallen monument, the women mostly out of curiosity to see the inside of her house, which no one save an old manservant—a combined gardener and cook—had seen in at least ten years.

It was a big, squarish frame house that had once been white, decorated with cupolas and spires and scrolled balconies in the heavily lightsome style of the seventies, set on what had once been our most select street. But garages and cotton gins had encroached and obliterated even the august names of that neighbourhood; only Miss Emily's house was left, lifting its stubborn and coquettish decay above the cotton wagons and the gasoline pumps—an eyesore among eyesores. And now Miss Emily had gone to join the representatives of those august names where they lay in the cedar-bemused cemetery among the ranked and anonymous graves of Union and Confederate soldiers who fell at the battle of Jefferson.

Alive, Miss Emily had been a tradition, a duty, and a care; a sort of hereditary obligation upon the town, dating from that day in 1894 when Colonel Sartoris, the mayor—he who fathered the edict that no Negro woman should appear on the streets without an apron—remitted her taxes, the dispensation dating from the death of her father on into perpetuity. Not that Miss Emily would have accepted charity. Colonel Sartoris invented an involved tale to the effect that Miss Emily's father had loaned money to the town, which the town, as a matter of business, preferred this way of repaying. Only a man of Colonel Sartoris' generation and thought could have invented it, and only a woman could have believed it.

When the next generation, with its more modern ideas, became mayors and aldermen, this arrangement created some little dissatisfaction. On the first of the year they mailed her a tax notice. February came, there was no reply. They wrote her a formal letter, asking her to call at the sheriff's office at her convenience. A week later the mayor wrote her himself, offering to call or to send his car for her, and received in reply a note on paper of an archaic shape, in a thin, flowing calligraphy in faded ink, to the effect that she no longer went out at all. The tax notice was also enclosed, without comment.

They called a special meeting of the Board of Aldermen. A deputation waited upon her, knocked at the door through which no visitor had passed since she ceased giving china-painting lessons eight or ten years earlier. They were admitted by the old Negro into a dim hall from which a stairway mounted into still more shadow. It smelled of dust and disuse—a close, dank smell. The Negro led them into the parlour. It was furnished in heavy, leather-covered furniture. When the Negro opened the blinds of one window, they could see that the leather was cracked; and when they sat down, a faint dust rose sluggishly about their thighs, spinning with slow motions in the single sun-ray. On a tarnished gilt easel before the fireplace stood a crayon portrait of Miss Emily's father.

They rose when she entered—a small, fat woman in black, with a thin gold chain descending to her waist and vanishing into her belt, leaning on an ebony cane with a tarnished gold head. Her skeleton was small and spare; perhaps that was why what would have been merely plumpness in another was obesity in her. She looked bloated, like a body long submerged in motionless water, and of that pallid hue. Her eyes, lost in the fatty ridges of her face, looked like two small pieces of coal pressed into a lump of dough as they moved from one face to another while the visitors stated their errand.

She did not ask them to sit. She just stood in the door and listened quietly until the spokesman came to a stumbling halt. Then they could hear the invisible watch ticking at the end of the gold chain.

Her voice was dry and cold. 'I have no taxes in Jefferson. Colonel Sartoris explained it to me. Perhaps one of you can gain access to the city records and satisfy yourselves.'

'But we have. We are the city authorities, Miss Emily. Didn't you get a notice from the sheriff, signed by him?'

'I received a paper, yes,' Miss Emily said. 'Perhaps he considers himself the sheriff . . . I have no taxes in Jefferson.'

'But there is nothing on the books to show that, you see. We must go by the—'

'See Colonel Sartoris.' (Colonel Sartoris had been dead almost ten years.) 'I have no taxes in Jefferson. Tobe!' The Negro appeared. 'Show these gentlemen out.'

II

So she vanquished them, horse and foot, just as she had vanquished their fathers thirty years before about the smell. That was two years after her father's death and a short time after her sweetheart—the one we believed would marry her—had deserted her. After her father's death she went out very little; after her sweetheart went away, people hardly saw her at all. A few of the ladies had the temerity to call, but were not received, and the only sign of life about the place was the Negro man—a young man then— going in and out with a market basket.

'Just as if a man—any man—could keep a kitchen properly,' the ladies said; so they were not surprised when the smell developed. It was another link between the gross, teeming world and the high and mighty Griersons.

A neighbour, a woman, complained to the mayor, Judge Stevens, eighty years old.

'But what will you have me do about it, madam?' he said.

'Why, send her word to stop it,' the woman said. 'Isn't there a law?'

'I'm sure that won't be necessary,' Judge Stevens said. 'It's probably just a snake or a rat that nigger of hers killed in the yard. I'll speak to him about it.'

The next day he received two more complaints, one from a man who came in diffident deprecation. 'We really must do something about it, Judge. I'd be the last one in the world to bother Miss Emily, but we've got to do something.' That night the Board of Aldermen met—three greybeards and one younger man, a member of the rising generation.

'It's simple enough,' he said. 'Send her word to have her place cleaned up. Give her a certain time to do it in, and if she don't . . .'

'Dammit, sir,' Judge Stevens said, 'will you accuse a lady to her face of smelling bad?'

So the next night, after midnight, four men crossed Miss Emily's lawn and slunk about the house like burglars, sniffing along the base of the brickwork and at the cellar openings while one of them performed a regular sowing motion with his hand out of a sack slung from his shoulder. They broke open the cellar door and sprinkled lime there, and in all the outbuildings. As they recrossed the lawn, a window that had been dark was lighted and Miss Emily sat in it, the light behind her, and her upright torso motionless as that of an idol. They crept quietly across the lawn and into the shadow of the locusts that lined the street. After a week or two the smell went away.

That was when people had begun to feel really sorry for her. People in our town, remembering how old lady Wyatt, her great-aunt, had gone completely crazy at last, believed that the Griersons held themselves a little too high for what they really were. None of the young men were quite good enough for Miss Emily and such. We had long thought of them as a tableau, Miss Emily a slender figure in white in the background, her father a spraddled silhouette in the foreground, his back to her and clutching a horsewhip, the two of them framed by the back-flung front door. So when she got to be thirty and was still single, we were not pleased exactly, but vindicated; even with insanity in the family she wouldn't have turned down all of her chances if they had really materialized.

When her father died, it got about that the house was all that was left to her; and in a way, people were glad. At last they could pity Miss Emily. Being left alone, and a pauper, she had become humanized. Now she too would know the old thrill and the old despair of a penny more or less.

The day after his death all the ladies prepared to call at the house and offer condolence and aid, as is our custom. Miss Emily met them at the door, dressed as usual and with no trace of grief on her face. She told them that her father was not dead. She did that for three days, with the ministers calling on her, and the doctors, trying to persuade her to let them dispose of the body. Just as they were about to resort to law and force, she broke down, and they buried her father quickly.

We did not say she was crazy then. We believed she had to do that. We remembered all the young men her father had driven away, and we knew that with nothing left, she would have to cling to that which had robbed her, as people will.

III

She was sick for a long time. When we saw her again, her hair was cut short, making her look like a girl, with a vague resemblance to those angels in coloured church windows—sort of tragic and serene.

The town had just let the contracts for paving the sidewalks, and in the summer after her father's death they began the work. The construction company came with niggers and mules and machinery, and a foreman named Homer Barron, a Yankee—a big, dark, ready man, with a big voice and eyes lighter than his face. The little boys would follow in groups to hear him cuss the niggers, and the niggers singing in time to the rise and fall of picks. Pretty soon he knew everybody in town. Whenever you heard a lot of laughing anywhere about the square, Homer Barron would be in the centre of the group. Presently we began to see him and Miss Emily on Sunday afternoons driving in the yellow-wheeled buggy and the matched team of bays from the livery stable.

And first we were glad that Miss Emily would have an interest, because the ladies all said, 'Of course a Grierson would not think seriously of a Northerner, a day labourer.' But there were still others, older people, who said that even grief could not cause a real lady to forget *noblesse oblige*—without calling it *noblesse oblige*. They just said, 'Poor Emily. Her kinsfolk should come to her.' She had some kin in Alabama; but years ago her father had fallen out with them over the estate of old lady Wyatt, the crazy woman, and there was no communication between the two families. They had not even been represented at the funeral.

And as soon as the old people said, 'Poor Emily,' the whispering began. 'Do you suppose it's really so?' they said to one another. 'Of course it is. What else could . . .' This behind their hands; rustling of craned silk and satin behind jalousies closed upon the sun of Sunday afternoon as the thin, swift clop-clop-clop of the matched team passed: 'Poor Emily.'

She carried her head high enough—even when we believed that she was fallen. It was as if she demanded more than ever the recognition of her dignity as the last Grierson; as if it had wanted that touch of earthiness to reaffirm her imperviousness. Like when she bought the rat poison, the arsenic. That was over a year after they had begun to say 'Poor Emily,' and while the two female cousins were visiting her.

'I want some poison,' she said to the druggist. She was over thirty then, still a slight woman, though thinner than usual, with cold, haughty eyes in a face the flesh of which was strained across the temples and about the eye-sockets as you imagine a lighthouse-keeper's face ought to look. 'I want some poison,' she said.

'Yes, Miss Emily. What kind? For rats and such? I'd recom—'

'I want the best you have. I don't care what kind.'

The druggist named several. 'They'll kill anything up to an elephant. But what you want is—'

'Arsenic,' Miss Emily said. 'Is that a good one?'

'Is . . . arsenic? Yes, ma'am. But what you want—'

'I want arsenic.'

The druggist looked down at her. She looked back at him, erect, her face like a strained flag. 'Why, of course,' the druggist said. 'If that's what you want. But the law requires you to tell what you are going to use it for.'

Miss Emily just stared at him, her head tilted back in order to look him eye for eye, until he looked away and went and got the arsenic and wrapped it up. The Negro delivery boy brought her the package; the druggist didn't come back. When she opened the package at home there was written on the box, under the skull and bones: 'For rats.'

IV

So the next day we all said, 'She will kill herself'; and we said it would be the best thing. When she had first begun to be seen with Homer Barron, we had said, 'She will marry him.' Then we said, 'She will persuade him yet,' because Homer himself had remarked—he liked men, and it was known that he drank with the younger men in the Elks' Club—that he was not a marrying man. Later we said, 'Poor Emily' behind the jalousies as they passed on Sunday afternoon in the glittering buggy, Miss Emily with her head high and Homer Barron with his hat cocked and a cigar in his teeth, reins and whip in a yellow glove.

Then some of the ladies began to say that it was a disgrace to the town and a bad example to the young people. The men did not want to interfere, but at last the ladies forced the Baptist minister—Miss Emily's people were Episcopal—to call upon her. He would never divulge what happened during that interview, but he refused to go back again. The next Sunday they again drove about the streets, and the following day the minister's wife wrote to Miss Emily's relations in Alabama.

So she had blood-kin under her roof again and we sat back to watch developments. At first nothing happened. Then we were sure that they were to be married. We learned that Miss Emily had been to the jeweller's and ordered a man's toilet set in silver, with the letters H.B. on each piece. Two days later we learned that she had bought a complete outfit of men's clothing, including a nightshirt, and we said, 'They are married.' We were really glad. We were glad because the two female cousins were even more Grierson than Emily had ever been.

So we were not surprised when Homer Barron—the streets had been finished some time since—was gone. We were a little disappointed that there was not a public blowing-off, but we believed that he had gone on to prepare for Miss Emily's coming, or to give her a chance to get rid of the cousins. (By that time it was a cabal, and we were all Miss Emily's allies to help circumvent the cousins.) Sure enough, after another week they departed. And, as we had expected all along, within three days

Homer Barron was back in town. A neighbour saw the Negro man admit him at the kitchen door at dusk one evening.

And that was the last we saw of Homer Barron. And of Miss Emily for some time. The Negro man went in and out with the market basket, but the front door remained closed. Now and then we would see her at a window for a moment, as the men did that night when they sprinkled the lime, but for almost six months she did not appear on the streets. Then we knew that this was to be expected too; as if that quality of her father which had thwarted her woman's life so many times had been too virulent and too furious to die.

When we next saw Miss Emily, she had grown fat and her hair was turning grey. During the next few years it grew greyer and greyer until it attained an even pepper-and-salt iron-grey, when it ceased turning. Up to the day of her death at seventy-four it was still that vigorous iron-grey, like the hair of an active man.

From that time on her front door remained closed, save for a period of six or seven years, when she was about forty, during which she gave lessons in china-painting. She fitted up a studio in one of the downstairs rooms, where the daughters and grand-daughters of Colonel Sartoris' contemporaries were sent to her with the same regularity and in the same spirit that they were sent to church on Sundays with a twenty-five-cent piece for the collection plate. Meanwhile her taxes had been remitted.

Then the newer generation became the backbone and the spirit of the town, and the painting pupils grew up and fell away and did not send their children to her with boxes of colours and tedious brushes and pictures cut from the ladies' magazines. The front door closed upon the last one and remained closed for good. When the town got free postal delivery, Miss Emily alone refused to let them fasten the metal numbers above her door and attach a mailbox to it. She would not listen to them.

Daily, monthly, yearly we watched the Negro grow greyer and more stooped, going in and out with the market basket. Each December we sent her a tax notice, which would be returned by the post office a week later, unclaimed. Now and then we would see her in one of the downstairs windows—she had evidently shut up the top floor of the house—like the carven torso of an idol in a niche, looking or not looking at us, we could never tell which. Thus she passed from generation to generation—dear, inescapable, impervious, tranquil, and perverse.

And so she died. Fell ill in the house filled with dust and shadows, with only a doddering Negro man to wait on her. We did not even know she was sick; we had long since given up trying to get any information from the Negro. He talked to no one, probably not even to her, for his voice had grown harsh and rusty, as if from disuse.

She died in one of the downstairs rooms, in a heavy walnut bed with a curtain, her grey head propped on a pillow yellow and mouldy with age and lack of sunlight.

V

The Negro met the first of the ladies at the front door and let them in, with their hushed, sibilant voices and their quick, curious glances, and then he disappeared. He walked right through the house and out the back and was not seen again.

The two female cousins came at once. They held the funeral on the second day, with the town coming to look at Miss Emily beneath a mass of bought flowers, with the crayon face of her father musing profoundly above the bier and the ladies sibilant and macabre; and the very old men—some in their brushed Confederate uniforms—on the porch and the lawn, talking of Miss Emily as if she had been a contemporary of theirs, believing that they had danced with her and courted her perhaps, confusing time with its mathematical progression, as the old do, to whom all the past is not a diminishing road but, instead, a huge meadow which no winter ever quite touches, divided from them now by the narrow bottle-neck of the most recent decade of years.

Already we knew that there was one room in that region above stairs which no one had seen in forty years, and which would have to be forced. They waited until Miss Emily was decently in the ground before they opened it.

The violence of breaking down the door seemed to fill this room with pervading dust. A thin, acrid pall as of the tomb seemed to lie everywhere upon this room decked and furnished as for a bridal: upon the valance curtains of faded rose colour, upon the rose-shaded lights, upon the dressing table, upon the delicate array of crystal and the man's toilet things backed with tarnished silver, silver so tarnished that the monogram was obscured. Among them lay a collar and tie, as if they had just been removed, which, lifted, left upon the surface a pale crescent in the dust. Upon a chair hung the suit, carefully folded; beneath it the mute shoes and the discarded socks.

The man himself lay in the bed.

For a long while we just stood there, looking down at the profound and fleshless grin. The body had apparently once lain in the attitude of an embrace, but now the long sleep that outlasts love, that conquers even the grimace of love, had cuckolded him. What was left of him, rotten beneath what was left of the nightshirt, had become inextricable from the bed in which he lay; and upon him and upon the pillow beside him lay that even coating of the patient and biding dust.

Then we noticed that in the second pillow was the indentation of a head. One of us lifted something from it, and leaning forward, that faint and invisible dust dry and acrid in the nostrils, we saw a long strand of iron-grey hair.

1930

Elizabeth Bowen

1899–1973

The only child of Henry and Isabel Bowen, of County Cork, Ireland, Elizabeth Bowen was raised at the family mansion, Bowen's Court, until her father went insane and she moved with her mother to East Kent, England. From childhood she was handicapped by a pronounced stammer. She went to school at Downe House in Westerham (West Kent), where she was quite happy. She began writing fiction early, publishing her first collection of stories in 1923, the year in which she married. She travelled in Europe and the United States, building a reputation for sensitive, witty fiction in novels like *The House in Paris* (1938) and *The Death of the Heart* (1938) and in stories with a subtle touch of the supernatural, like those in *The Demon Lover* collection of 1945.

The Demon Lover

Towards the end of her day in London Mrs Drover went round to her shut-up house to look for several things she wanted to take away. Some belonged to herself, some to her family, who were by now used to their country life. It was late August; it had been a steamy, showery day: at the moment the trees down the pavement glittered in an escape of humid yellow afternoon sun. Against the next batch of clouds, already piling up ink-dark, broken chimneys and parapets stood out. In her once familiar street, as in any unused channel, an unfamiliar queerness had silted up; a cat wove itself in and out of railings, but no human eye watched Mrs Drover's return. Shifting some parcels under her arm, she slowly forced round her latchkey in an unwilling lock, then gave the door, which had warped, a push with her knee. Dead air came out to meet her as she went in.

The staircase window having been boarded up, no light came down into the hall. But one door, she could just see, stood ajar, so she went quickly through into the room and unshuttered the big window in there. Now the prosaic woman, looking about her, was more perplexed than she knew by everything that she saw, by traces of her long former habit of life—the yellow smoke-stain up the white marble mantelpiece, the ring left by a vase on the top of the escritoire; the bruise in the wallpaper where, on the door being thrown open widely, the china handle had always hit the wall. The piano, having gone away to be stored, had left what looked like claw-marks on its part of the parquet. Though not much dust had seeped in, each object wore a film of another kind; and, the only ventilation being the chimney, the whole drawing room smelled of the cold hearth. Mrs Drover put down her parcels on the escritoire and left the room to proceed upstairs; the things she wanted were in a bedroom chest.

She had been anxious to see how the house was—the part-time caretaker she shared with some neighbours was away this week on his holiday, known to be not yet back. At the best of times he did not look in often, and she was never sure that she trusted him. There were some cracks in the structure, left by the last bombing, on which she was anxious to keep an eye. Not that one could do anything—

A shaft of refracted daylight now lay across the hall. She stopped dead and stared at the hall table—on this lay a letter addressed to her.

She thought first—then the caretaker *must* be back. All the same, who, seeing the house shuttered, would have dropped a letter in at the box? It was not a circular, it was not a bill. And the post office redirected, to the address in the country, everything for her that came through the post. The caretaker (even if he *were* back) did not know she was due in London today—her call here had been planned to be a surprise—so his negligence in the manner of this letter, leaving it to wait in the dusk and the dust, annoyed her. Annoyed, she picked up the letter, which bore no stamp. But it cannot be important, or they would know . . . She took the letter rapidly upstairs with her, without a stop to look at the writing till she reached what had been her bedroom, where she let in light. The room looked over the garden and other gardens: the sun had gone in; as the clouds sharpened and lowered, the trees and rank lawns seemed already to smoke with dark. Her reluctance to look again at the letter came from the fact that she felt intruded upon—and by someone contemptuous of her ways. However, in the tenseness preceding the fall of rain she read it: it was a few lines.

DEAR KATHLEEN,

You will not have forgotten that today is our anniversary, and the day we said. The years have gone by at once slowly and fast. In view of the fact that nothing has changed, I shall rely upon you to keep your promise. I was sorry to see you leave London, but was satisfied that you would be back in time. You may expect me, therefore, at the hour arranged.

Until then . . .

K.

Mrs Drover looked for the date: it was today's. She dropped the letter onto the bedsprings, then picked it up to see the writing again—her lips, beneath the remains of lipstick, beginning to go white. She felt so much the change in her own face that she went to the mirror, polished a clear patch in it, and looked at once urgently and stealthily in. She was confronted by a woman of forty-four, with eyes starting out under a hat-brim that had been rather carelessly pulled down. She had not put on any more powder since she left the shop where she ate her solitary tea. The pearls her husband had given her on their marriage hung loose round her now rather thinner throat, slipping into the V of the pink wool jumper her sister knitted last autumn as they sat round the fire. Mrs Drover's most normal expression was one of controlled worry, but of assent. Since the birth of the third of her little boys, attended by a quite serious illness, she had had an intermittent muscular flicker to the left of her mouth, but in spite of this she could always sustain a manner that was at once energetic and calm.

Turning from her own face as precipitately as she had gone to meet it, she went to the chest where the things were, unlocked it, threw up the lid, and knelt to search. But as rain began to come crashing down she could not keep from looking over her shoulder at the stripped bed on which the letter lay. Behind the blanket of rain the clock of the church that still stood struck six—with rapidly heightening apprehension, she counted each of the slow strokes. 'The hour arranged . . . My God,' she said, 'what hour? How should I . . . ? After twenty-five years. . . .'

The young girl talking to the soldier in the garden had not ever completely seen his face. It was dark; they were saying good-bye under a tree. Now and then—for it felt, from not seeing him at this intense moment, as though she had never seen him at all—she verified his presence for these few moments longer by putting out a hand, which he each time pressed, without very much kindness, and painfully, onto one of the breast buttons of his uniform. That cut of the button on the palm of her hand was, principally, what she was to carry away. This was so near the end of a leave from France that she could only wish him already gone. It was August 1916. Being not kissed, being drawn away from and looked at intimidated Kathleen till she imagined spectral glitters in the place of his eyes. Turning away and looking back up the lawn she saw, through branches of trees, the drawing-room window alight: she caught a breath for the moment when she could go running back there into the safe arms of her mother and sister, and cry: 'What shall I do, what shall I do? He has gone.'

Hearing her catch her breath, her fiancé said, without feeling: 'Cold?'

'You're going away such a long way.'

'Not so far as you think.'

'I don't understand?'

'You don't have to,' he said. 'You will. You know what we said.'

'But that was—suppose you—I mean, suppose.'

'I shall be with you,' he said, 'sooner or later. You won't forget that. You need do nothing but wait.'

Only a little more than a minute later she was free to run up the silent lawn. Looking in through the window at her mother and sister, who did not for the moment perceive her, she already felt that unnatural promise drive down between her and the rest of all human kind. No other way of having given herself could have made her feel so apart, lost and foresworn. She cold not have plighted a more sinister troth.

Kathleen behaved well when, some months later, her fiancé was reported missing, presumed killed. Her family not only supported her but were able to praise her courage without stint because they could not regret, as a husband for her, the man they knew almost nothing about. They hoped she would, in a year or two, console herself—and had it been only a question of consolation things might have gone much straighter ahead. But her trouble, behind just a little grief, was a complete dislocation from everything. She did not reject other lovers, for these failed to appear: for years she failed to attract men—and with the approach of her thirties she became natural enough to share her family's anxiousness on this score. She began to put herself out, to wonder; and at thirty-two she was very greatly relieved to find herself being courted by William Drover. She married him, and the two of them settled down in this quiet, arboreal part of Kensington: in this house the years piled up, her children were born and they all lived till they were driven out by the bombs of the next war. Her movements as Mrs Drover were circumscribed, and she dismissed any idea that they were still watched.

As things were—dead or living the letter-writer sent her only a threat. Unable, for some minutes, to go on kneeling with her back exposed to the empty room, Mrs Drover rose from the chest to sit on an upright chair whose back was firmly against the wall. The desuetude of her former bedroom, her married London home's whole air of being a cracked cup from which memory, with its reassuring power, had either evaporated or leaked away, made a crisis—and at just this crisis the letter-writer had, knowledgeably, struck. The hollowness of the house this evening cancelled years on years of voices, habits, and steps. Through the shut windows she only heard rain fall on the roofs around. To rally herself, she said she was in a mood—and, for two or three seconds shutting her eyes, told herself that she had imagined the letter. But she opened them—there it lay on the bed.

On the supernatural side of the letter's entrance she was not permitting her mind to dwell. Who, in London, knew she meant to call at the house today? Evidently, however, this had been known. The caretaker, *had* he come back, had had no cause to expect her: he would have taken the letter in his pocket, to forward it, at his own time, through the post. There was no other sign the caretaker had been in—but, if not? Letters dropped in at doors of deserted houses do not fly or walk to tables in halls. They do not sit on the dust of empty tables with the air of certainty that they will be found. There is indeed some human hand—but nobody but the caretaker had a key. Under circumstances she did not care to consider, a house can be entered without a key. It was possible that she was not alone now. She might be being waited for, downstairs. Waited for—until when? Until 'the hour arranged'. At least that was not six o'clock: six has struck.

She rose from the chair and went over and locked the door.

The thing was, to get out. To fly? No, not that: she had to catch her train. As a woman whose utter dependability was the keystone of her family life she was not willing to return to the country, to her husband, her little boys and her sister, without the objects she had come up to fetch. Resuming work at the chest she set about making up a number of parcels in a rapid, fumbling-decisive way. These, with her shopping parcels, would be too much to carry; these meant a taxi—at the thought of the taxi her heart went up and her normal breathing resumed. I will ring up the taxi now; the taxi cannot come too soon: I shall hear the taxi out there running its engine, till I walk calmly down to it through the hall. I'll ring up—But no: the telephone is cut off. . . . She tugged at a knot she had tied wrong.

The idea of flight . . . He was never kind to me, not really. I don't remember him kind at all. Mother said he never considered me. He was set on me, that was what it was—not love. Not love, not meaning a person well. What did he do, to make me promise like that? I can't remember—But she found that she could.

She remembered with such dreadful acuteness that the twenty-five years since then dissolved like smoke and she instinctively looked for the weal left by the button on the palm of her hand. She remembered not only all that he said and did but the complete suspension of *her* existence during that August week. I was not myself—they all told me so at the time. She remembered—but with one white burning blank as where acid has dropped on a photograph: *under no conditions* could she remember his face.

So, wherever he may be waiting, I shall not know him. You have no time to run from a face you do not expect.

The thing was to get to the taxi before any clock struck what could be the hour. She would slip down the street and round the side of the square to where the square gave on the main road. She would return in the taxi, safe, to her own door, and bring the solid driver into the house with her to pick up the parcels from room to room. The idea of the taxi driver made her decisive, bold: she unlocked her door, went to the top of the staircase, and listened down.

She heard nothing—but while she was hearing nothing the *passé* air of the staircase was disturbed by a draft that travelled up to her face. It emanated from the basement: down there a door or window was being opened by someone who chose this moment to leave the house.

The rain had stopped; the pavements steamily shone as Mrs Drover let herself out by inches from her own front door into the empty street. The unoccupied houses opposite continued to meet her look with their damaged stare. Making towards the thoroughfare and the taxi, she tried not to keep looking behind. Indeed, the silence was so intense—one of those creeks of London silence exaggerated this summer by the damage of war—that no tread could have gained on hers unheard. Where her street debouched on the square where people went on living she grew conscious of and checked her unnatural pace. Across the open end of the square two buses impassively passed each other; women, a perambulator, cyclists, a man wheeling a barrow signalized, once again, the ordinary flow of life. At the square's most populous corner should be—and was—the short taxi rank. This evening, only one taxi—but this, although it presented its blank rump, appeared already to be alertly waiting for her. Indeed, without looking round the driver started his engine as she panted up from behind and put her hand on the door. As she did so, the clock struck seven. The taxi faced the main road: to make the trip back to her house it would have to turn—she had settled back on the seat and the taxi *had* turned before she, surprised by its knowing movement, recollected that she had not 'said where'. She leaned forward to scratch at the glass panel that divided the driver's head from her own.

The driver braked to what was almost a stop, turned round and slid the glass panel back: the jolt of this flung Mrs Drover forward till her face was almost into the glass. Through the aperture driver and passenger, not six inches between them, remained for an eternity eye to eye. Mrs Drover's mouth hung open for some seconds before she could issue her first scream. After that she continued to scream freely and to beat with her gloved hands on the glass all round as the taxi, accelerating without mercy, made off with her into the hinterland of deserted streets.

"hell"

1941

Ernest Hemingway
1899–1961

Born in Oak Park, Illinois, the son of a doctor and music teacher, Ernest Hemingway spent his summer holidays in the upper peninsula of Michigan, where his father taught him early to hunt and fish. He was a physically active and popular boy, good at writing but bored with school. A couple of times he simply left and went on the road, but he worked on the school newspaper, graduated, and tried to enlist in the army for the First World War. A bad eye prevented this attempt, but he was able to enlist as an ambulance driver for the Red Cross in Italy, where he saw plenty of combat, was badly wounded, and showed genuine heroism under fire. When the war ended he returned to North America and did newspaper work in Chicago and in Toronto, where for four years he was employed as a staff writer and foreign correspondent for the *Toronto Star*.

In 1924 Hemingway moved to Europe, where he lived with his first wife, mostly in Paris. It was there that he met Ezra Pound and Gertrude Stein, who christened Hemingway and his young friends a 'lost generation'. There, too, Hemingway began to write the stories and novels that made his reputation, beginning with *In Our Time* (1925) and *The Sun Also Rises* (1926). In later years he became more of a public figure and less of a writer, as he hardened into a symbol of patriarchal machismo known as 'Papa'. But he had a fine success with *The Old Man and the Sea* (1952) and won the Nobel Prize for Literature in 1954. In 1961, in ill health and unable to write, he use his silver-inlaid, double-barrelled shotgun to end his life.

A Clean, Well-Lighted Place

It was late and everyone had left the café except an old man who sat in the shadow the leaves of the tree made against the electric light. In the daytime the street was dusty, but at night the dew settled the dust and the old man liked to sit late because he was deaf and now at night it was quiet and he felt the difference. The two waiters inside the café knew the old man was a little drunk, and while he was a good client they knew that if he became too drunk he would leave without paying, so they kept watch on him.

'Last week he tried to commit suicide,' one waiter said.

'Why?'

'He was in despair.'

'What about?'

'Nothing.'

'How do you know it was nothing?'

'He has plenty of money.'

They sat together at a table that was close against the wall near the door of the café and looked at the terrace where the tables were all empty except where the old man sat in the shadow of the leaves of the tree that moved slightly in the wind. A girl and a soldier went by in the street. The street light shone on the brass number on his collar. The girl wore no head covering and hurried beside him.

'The guard will pick him up,' one waiter said.

'What does it matter if he gets what he's after?'

'He had better get off the street now. The guard will get him. They went by five minutes ago.'

The old man sitting in the shadow rapped on his saucer with his glass. The younger waiter went over to him.

'What do you want?'

The old man looked at him. 'Another brandy,' he said.

'You'll be drunk,' the waiter said. The old man looked at him. The waiter went away.

'He'll stay all night,' he said to his colleague. 'I'm sleepy now. I never get into bed before three o'clock. He should have killed himself last week.'

The waiter took the brandy bottle and another saucer from the counter inside the café and marched out to the old man's table. He put down the saucer and poured the glass full of brandy.

'You should have killed yourself last week,' he said to the deaf man. The old man motioned with his finger. 'A little more,' he said. The waiter poured on into the glass so that the brandy slopped over and ran down the stem into the top saucer of the pile. 'Thank you,' the old man said. The waiter took the bottle back inside the café. He sat down at the table with his colleague again.

'He's drunk now,' he said.

'He's drunk every night.'

'What did he want to kill himself for?'

'How should I know.'

'How did he do it?'

'He hung himself with a rope.'

'Who cut him down?'

'His niece.'

'Why did they do it?'

'Fear for his soul.'

'How much money has he got?'

'He's got plenty.'

'He must be eighty years old.'

'Anyway I should say he was eighty.'

'I wish he would go home. I never get to bed before three o'clock. What kind of hour is that to go to bed?'

'He stays up because he likes it.'

'He's lonely. I'm not lonely. I have a wife waiting in bed for me.'

'He had a wife once too.'

'A wife would be no good to him now.'

'You can't tell. He might be better with a wife.'

'His niece looks after him.'

'I know. You said she cut him down.'

'I wouldn't want to be that old. An old man is a nasty thing.'

'Not always. This old man is clean. He drinks without spilling. Even now, drunk. Look at him.'

'I don't want to look at him. I wish he would go home. He has no regard for those who must work.'

The old man looked from his glass across the square, then over at the waiters.

'Another brandy,' he said, pointing to his glass. The waiter who was in a hurry came over.

'Finished,' he said, speaking with that omission of syntax stupid people employ when talking to drunken people or foreigners. 'No more tonight. Close now.'

'Another,' said the old man.

'No. Finished.' The waiter wiped the edge of the table with a towel and shook his head.

The old man stood up, slowly counted the saucers, took a leather coin purse from his pocket and paid for the drinks, leaving half a peseta tip.

The waiter watched him go down the street, a very old man walking unsteadily but with dignity.

'Why didn't you let him stay and drink?' the unhurried waiter asked. They were putting up the shutters. 'It is half-past two.'

'I want to go home to bed.'

'What is an hour?'

'More to me than to him.'

'An hour is the same.'

'You talk like an old man yourself. He can buy a bottle and drink at home.'

'It's not the same.'

'No, it is not,' agreed the waiter with a wife. He did not wish to be unjust. He was only in a hurry.

'And you? You have no fear of going home before your usual hour?'

'Are you trying to insult me?'

'No, hombre, only to make a joke.'

'No,' the waiter who was in a hurry said, rising from pulling down the metal shutters. 'I have confidence. I am all confidence.'

'You have youth, confidence, and a job,' the older waiter said. 'You have everything.'

'And what do you lack?'

'Everything but work.'

'You have everything I have.'

'No. I have never had confidence and I am not young.'

'Come on. Stop talking nonsense and lock up.'

'I am of those who like to stay late at the café,' the older waiter said. 'With all those who do not want to go to bed. With all those who need a light for the night.'

'I want to go home and into bed.'

'We are of two different kinds,' the older waiter said. He was now dressed to go home. 'It is not only a question of youth and confidence although those things are very beautiful. Each night I am reluctant to close up because there may be someone who needs the café.'

'Hombre, there are bodegas open all night long.'

'You do not understand. This is a clean and pleasant café. It is well lighted. The light is very good and also, now, there are shadows of the leaves.'

'Good night,' said the younger waiter.

'Good night,' the other said. Turning off the electric light he continued the conversation with himself. It is the light of course but it is necessary that the place be clean and pleasant. You do not want music. Certainly you do not want music. Nor can you stand before a bar with dignity although that is all that is provided for these hours. What did he fear? It was not fear or dread. It was a nothing that he knew too well. It was all a nothing and a man was nothing too. It was only that and light was all it needed and a certain cleanness and order. Some lived in it and never felt it but he knew it all was nada y pues nada y nada y pues nada. Our nada who art in nada, nada be thy name thy kingdom nada thy will be nada in nada as it is in nada. Give us this nada our daily nada and nada us our nada as we nada our nadas and nada us not into nada but deliver us from nada; pues nada. Hail nothing full of nothing, nothing is with thee. He smiled and stood before a bar with a shining steam pressure coffee machine.

'What's yours?' asked the barman.

'Nada.'

'Otro loco mas,' said the barman and turned away.

'A little cup,' said the waiter.

The barman poured it for him.

'The light is very bright and pleasant but the bar is unpolished,' the waiter said.

The barman looked at him but did not answer. It was too late at night for conversation.

'You want another copita?' the barman asked.

'No, thank you,' said the waiter and went out. He disliked bars and bodegas. A clean, well-lighted café was a very different thing. Now, without thinking further, he would go home to his room. He would lie in the bed and finally, with daylight, he would go to sleep. After all, he said to himself, it is probably only insomnia. Many must have it.

1933

Morley Callaghan

1903–1990

Canada's first professional writer, the first to devote his life to the vocation of writing, Toronto-born Morley Callaghan was a graduate of the University of Toronto and Osgoode Hall Law School. His first novel, *Strange Fugitive*, was published in 1928, the same year he was called to the bar. Fiction, however, commanded his complete attention, and he never practised law. In April 1929 he travelled with his wife to Paris, where their literary circle of friends included Ernest Hemingway—with whom Callaghan had already worked as a journalist at the *Toronto Star*—F. Scott Fitzgerald, James Joyce, and many others. The following autumn he returned to Toronto, which had been and which would remain his physical and literary home. His sojourn in Paris is the subject of his beautiful memoir, *That Summer in Paris* (1963).

The author of twenty novels and more than a hundred shorter pieces of fiction, Callaghan focused his writing on individual lives, often exploring the moral courage and innate dignity of his characters as they confront adverse and demeaning social situations.

A Cap for Steve

Dave Diamond, a poor man, a carpenter's assistant, was a small, wiry, quick-tempered individual who had learned how to make every dollar count in his home. His wife, Anna, had been sick a lot, and his twelve-year-old son, Steve, had to be kept in school. Steve, a big-eyed, shy kid, ought to have known the value of money as well as Dave did. It had been ground into him.

But the boy was crazy about baseball, and after school, when he could have been working as a delivery boy or selling papers, he played ball with the kids. His failure to appreciate that the family needed a few extra dollars disgusted Dave. Around the house he wouldn't let Steve talk about baseball, and he scowled when he saw him hurrying off with his glove after dinner.

When the Phillies came to town to play an exhibition game with the home team and Steve pleaded to be taken to the ballpark, Dave, of course, was outraged. Steve knew they couldn't afford it. But he had got his mother on his side. Finally Dave made a bargain with them. He said that if Steve came home after school and worked hard helping to make some kitchen shelves he would take him that night to the ballpark.

Steve worked hard, but Dave was still resentful. They had to coax him to put on his good suit. When they started out Steve held aloof, feeling guilty, and they walked down the street like strangers; then Dave glanced at Steve's face and, half-ashamed, took his arm more cheerfully.

As the game went on, Dave had to listen to Steve's recitation of the batting average of every Philly that stepped up to the plate; the time the boy must have wasted learning these averages began to appall him. He showed it so plainly that Steve felt guilty again and was silent.

After the game Dave let Steve drag him onto the field to keep him company while he tried to get some autographs from the Philly players, who were being hemmed in by gangs of kids blocking the way to the clubhouse. But Steve, who was shy, let the other kids block him off from the players. Steve would push his way in, get blocked out, and come back to stand mournfully beside Dave. And Dave grew impatient. He was wasting valuable time. He wanted to get home; Steve knew it and was worried.

Then the big, blond Philly outfielder, Eddie Condon, who had been held up by a gang of kids tugging at his arm and thrusting their scorecards at him, broke loose and made a run for the clubhouse. He was jostled, and his blue cap with the red peak, tilted far back on his head, fell off. It fell at Steve's feet, and Steve stooped quickly and grabbed it. 'Okay, son,' the outfielder called, turning back. But Steve, holding the hat in both hands, only stared at him.

'Give him his cap, Steve,' Dave said, smiling apologetically at the big outfielder who towered over them. But Steve drew the hat closer to his chest. In an awed trance he looked up at big Eddie Condon. It was an embarrassing moment. All the other kids were watching. Some shouted. 'Give him his cap.'

'My cap, son,' Eddie Condon said, his hand out.

'Hey, Steve,' Dave said, and he gave him a shake. But he had to jerk the cap out of Steve's hands.

'Here you are,' he said.

The outfielder, noticing Steve's white, worshipping face and pleading eyes, grinned and then shrugged. 'Aw, let him keep it,' he said.

'No, Mister Condon, you don't need to do that,' Steve protested.

'It's happened before. Forget it,' Eddie Condon said, and he trotted away to the clubhouse.

Dave handed the cap to Steve; envious kids circled around them and Steve said, 'He said I could keep it, Dad. You heard him, didn't you?'

'Yeah, I heard him,' Dave admitted. The wonder in Steve's face made him smile. He took the boy by the arm and they hurried off the field.

On the way home Dave couldn't get him to talk about the game; he couldn't get him to take his eyes off the cap. Steve could hardly believe in his own happiness. 'See,' he said suddenly, and he showed Dave that Eddie Condon's name was printed on the sweatband. Then he went on dreaming. Finally he put the cap on his head and turned to Dave with a slow, proud smile. The cap was too big for him; it fell down over his ears. 'Never mind,' Dave said. 'You can get your mother to take a tuck in the back.'

When they got home Dave was tired and his wife didn't understand the cap's importance, and they couldn't get Steve to go to bed. He swaggered around wearing the cap and looking in the mirror every ten minutes. He took the cap to bed with him.

Dave and his wife had a cup of coffee in the kitchen, and Dave told her again how they had got the cap. They agreed that their boy must have an attractive quality that showed in his face and that Eddie Condon must have been drawn to him—why else would he have singled Steve out from all the kids?

But Dave got tired of the fuss Steve made over that cap and of the way he wore it from the time he got up in the morning until the time he went to bed. Some kid was always coming in, wanting to try on the cap. It was childish, Dave said, for Steve to go around assuming that the cap made him important in the neighbourhood, and to keep telling them how he had become a leader in the park a few blocks away where he played ball in the evenings. And Dave wouldn't stand for Steve's keeping the cap on while he was eating. He was always scolding his wife for accepting Steve's explanation that he'd forgotten he had it on. Just the same, it was remarkable what a little thing like a ball cap could do for a kid, Dave admitted to his wife as he smiled to himself.

One night Steve was late coming home from the park. Dave didn't realize how late it was until he put down his newspaper and watched his wife at the window. Her restlessness got on his nerves. 'See what comes from encouraging the boy to hang around with those park loafers,' he said. 'I don't encourage him,' she protested. 'You do,' he insisted irritably, for he was really worried now. A gang hung around the park until midnight. It was a bad park. It was true that on one side there was a good district with fine, expensive apartment houses, but the kids from that neighbourhood left the park to the kids from the poorer homes. When his wife went out and walked down to the corner it was his turn to wait and worry and watch at the open window. Each waiting moment tortured him. At last he heard his wife's voice and Steve's voice, and he relaxed and sighed; then he remembered his duty and rushed angrily to meet them.

'I'll fix you, Steve, once and for all,' he said. 'I'll show you you can't start coming into the house at midnight.'

'Hold your horses, Dave,' his wife said. 'Can't you see the state he's in?' Steve looked utterly exhausted and beaten.

'What's the matter?' Dave asked quickly.

'I lost my cap,' Steve whispered; he walked past his father and threw himself on the couch in the living room and lay with his face hidden.

'Now, don't scold him, Dave,' his wife said.

'Scold him. Who's scolding him?' Dave asked, indignantly. 'It's his cap, not mine. If it's not worth his while to hang on to it, why should I scold him?' But he was implying resentfully that he alone recognized the cap's value.

'So you are scolding him,' his wife said. 'It's his cap. Not yours. What happened, Steve?'

Steve told them he had been playing ball and he found that when he ran the bases the cap fell off; it was still too big despite the tuck his mother had taken in the band. So the next time he came to bat he tucked the cap in his hip pocket. Someone had lifted it, he was sure.

'And he didn't even know whether it was still in his pocket,' Dave said sarcastically.

'I wasn't careless, Dad,' Steve said. For the last three hours he had been wandering around to the homes of the kids who had been in the park at the time; he wanted to go on, but he was too tired. Dave knew the boy was apologizing to him, but he didn't know why it made him angry.

'If he didn't hang on to it, it's not worth worrying about now,' he said, and he sounded offended.

After that night they knew that Steve didn't go to the park to play ball; he went to look for the cap. It irritated Dave to see him sit around listlessly, or walk in circles, trying to force his memory to find a particular incident which would suddenly recall to him the moment when the cap had been taken. It was no attitude for a growing, healthy boy to take, Dave complained. He told Steve firmly once and for all he didn't want to hear any more about the cap.

One night, two weeks later, Dave was walking home with Steve from the shoemaker's. It was a hot night. When they passed an ice-cream parlour Steve slowed down. 'I guess I couldn't have a soda, could I?' Steve said. 'Nothing doing,' Dave said firmly. 'Come on now,' he added as Steve hung back, looking in the window.

'Dad, look!' Steve cried suddenly, pointing at the window. 'My cap! There's my cap! He's coming out!'

A well-dressed boy was leaving the ice-cream parlour; he had on a blue ball cap with a red peak, just like Steve's cap. 'Hey, you!' Steve cried, and he rushed at the boy, his small face fierce and his eyes wild. Before the boy could back away Steve had snatched the cap from his head. 'That's my cap!' he shouted.

'What's this!' the bigger boy said. 'Hey, give me my cap or I'll give you a poke on the nose.'

Dave was surprised that his own shy boy did not back away. He watched him clutch the cap in his left hand, half crying with excitement as he put his head down and drew back his right fist: he was willing to fight. And Dave was proud of him.

'Wait, now,' Dave said. 'Take it easy, son,' he said to the other boy, who refused to back away.

'My boy says it's his cap,' Dave said.

'Well, he's crazy. It's my cap.'

'I was with him when he got this cap. When the Phillies played here. It's a Philly cap.'

'Eddie Condon gave it to me,' Steve said. 'And you stole it from me, you jerk.'

'Don't call me a jerk, you little squirt. I never saw you before in my life.'

'Look,' Steve said, pointing to the printing on the cap's sweatband. 'It's Eddie Condon's cap. See? See, Dad?'

'Yeah. You're right, son. Ever see this boy before, Steve?'

'No,' Steve said reluctantly.

The other boy realized he might lose the cap. 'I bought it from a guy,' he said. 'I paid him. My father knows I paid him.' He said he got the cap at the ballpark. He groped for some magically impressive words and suddenly found them. 'You'll have to speak to my father,' he said.

'Sure, I'll speak to your father,' Dave said. 'What's your name? Where do you live?'

'My name's Hudson. I live about ten minutes away on the other side of the park.' The boy appraised Dave, who wasn't any bigger than he was and who wore a faded blue windbreaker and no tie. 'My father is a lawyer,' he said boldly. 'He wouldn't let me keep the cap if he didn't think I should.'

'Is that a fact?' Dave asked belligerently. 'Well, we'll see. Come on. Let's go.' And he got between the two boys and they walked along the street. They didn't talk to each other. Dave knew the Hudson boy was waiting to get to the protection of his home, and Steve knew it, too, and he looked up apprehensively at Dave. Dave, reaching for his hand, squeezed it encouragingly and strode along, cocky and belligerent, knowing that Steve relied on him.

The Hudson boy lived in that row of fine apartment houses on the other side of the park. At the entrance to one of these houses Dave tried not to hang back and show he was impressed, because he could feel Steve hanging back. When they got into the small elevator Dave didn't know why he took off his hat. In the carpeted hall on the fourth floor the Hudson boy said, 'Just a minute,' and entered his own apartment. Dave and Steve were left alone in the corridor, knowing that the other boy was preparing his father for the encounter. Steve looked anxiously at his father, and Dave said, 'Don't worry, son,' and he added resolutely, 'No one's putting anything over on us.'

A tall, balding man in a brown velvet smoking-jacket suddenly opened the door. Dave had never seen a man wearing one of these jackets, although he had seen them in department-store windows. 'Good evening,' he said, making a deprecatory gesture at the cap Steve still clutched tightly in his left hand. 'My boy didn't get your name. My name is Hudson.'

'Mine's Diamond.'

'Come on in,' Mr Hudson said, putting out his hand and laughing good-naturedly. He led Dave and Steve into his living room. 'What's this about a cap?' he asked. 'The way kids can get excited about a cap. Well, it's understandable, isn't it?'

'So it is,' Dave said, moving closer to Steve, who was awed by the broadloom rug and the fine furniture. He wanted to show Steve he was at ease himself, and he wished Mr Hudson wouldn't be so polite. That meant Dave had to be polite and affable, too, and it was hard to manage when he was standing in the middle of the floor in his old windbreaker.

'Sit down, Mr Diamond,' Mr Hudson said. Dave took Steve's arm and sat him down beside him on the chesterfield. The Hudson boy watched his father. And Dave looked at Steve and saw that he wouldn't face Mr Hudson or the other boy; he kept looking up at Dave, putting all his faith in him.

'Well, Mr Diamond, from what I gathered from my boy, you're able to prove this cap belonged to your boy.'

'That's a fact,' Dave said.

'Mr Diamond, you'll have to believe my boy bought that cap from some kid in good faith.'

'I don't doubt it,' Dave said. 'But no kid can sell something that doesn't belong to him. You know that's a fact, Mr Hudson.'

'Yes, that's a fact,' Mr Hudson agreed. 'But that cap means a lot to my boy, Mr Diamond.'

'It means a lot to my boy, too, Mr Hudson.'

'Sure it does. But supposing we called in a policeman. You know what he'd say? He'd ask you if you were willing to pay my boy what he paid for the cap. That's usually the way it works out,' Mr Hudson said, friendly and smiling, as he eyed Dave shrewdly.

'But that's not right. It's not justice,' Dave protested. 'Not when it's my boy's cap.'

'I know it isn't right. But that's what they do.'

'All right. What did you say your boy paid for the cap?' Dave said reluctantly.

'Two dollars.'

'Two dollars!' Dave repeated. Mr Hudson's smile was still kindly, but his eyes were shrewd, and Dave knew that the lawyer was counting on his not having the two dollars; Mr Hudson thought he had Dave sized up; he had looked at him and decided he was broke. Dave's pride was hurt, and he turned to Steve. What he saw in Steve's face was more powerful than the hurt to his pride; it was the memory of how difficult it had been to get an extra nickel, the talk he heard about the cost of food, the worry on his mother's face as she tried to make ends meet, and the bewildered embarrassment that he was here in a rich man's home, forcing his father to confess that he couldn't afford to spend two dollars. Then Dave grew angry and reckless. 'I'll give you the two dollars,' he said.

Steve looked at the Hudson boy and grinned brightly. The Hudson boy watched his father.

'I suppose that's fair enough,' Mr Hudson said. 'A cap like this can be worth a lot to a kid. You know how it is. Your boy might want to sell—I mean be satisfied. Would he take five dollars for it?'

'Five dollars?' Dave repeated, 'Is it worth five dollars, Steve?' he asked uncertainly.

Steve shook his head and looked frightened.

'No thanks, Mr Hudson,' Dave said firmly.

'I'll tell you what I'll do,' Mr Hudson said. 'I'll give you ten dollars. The cap has a sentimental value for my boy, a Philly cap, a big-leaguer's cap. It's only worth about a buck and a half really,' he added. But Dave shook his head again. Mr Hudson frowned. He looked at his own boy with indulgent concern, but now he was embarrassed. 'I'll tell you what I'll do,' he said. 'This cap—well, it's worth as much as a day at the circus to my boy. Your boy should be recompensed. I want to be fair. Here's twenty dollars,' and he held out two ten-dollar bills to Dave.

That much money for a cap, Dave thought, and his eyes brightened. But he knew what the cap had meant to Steve; to deprive him of it now that it was within his reach would be unbearable. All the things he needed in his life gathered around him; his wife was there, saying he couldn't afford to reject the offer, he had no right to do it; and he turned to Steve to see if Steve thought it wonderful that the cap could bring them twenty dollars.

'What do you say, Steve?' he asked uneasily.

'I don't know,' Steve said. He was in a trance. When Dave smiled, Steve smiled too, and Dave believed that Steve was as impressed as he was, only more bewildered, and maybe even more aware that they could not possibly turn away that much money for a ball cap.

'Well, here you are,' Mr Hudson said, and he put the two bills in Steve's hand. 'It's a lot of money. But I guess you had a right to expect as much.'

With a dazed, fixed smile Steve handed the money slowly to his father, and his face was white.

Laughing jovially, Mr Hudson led them to the door. His own boy followed a few paces behind.

In the elevator Dave took the bills out of his pocket. 'See, Stevie,' he whispered eagerly. 'That windbreaker you wanted! And ten dollars for your bank! Won't Mother be surprised?'

'Yeah,' Steve whispered, the little smile still on his face. But Dave had to turn away quickly so their eyes wouldn't meet, for he saw it was a scared smile.

Outside, Dave said, 'Here, you carry the money home, Steve. You show it to your mother.'

'No, you keep it,' Steve said, and then there was nothing to say. They walked in silence.

'It's a lot of money,' Dave said finally. When Steve didn't answer him, he added angrily, 'I turned to you, Steve. I asked you, didn't I?'

'That man knew how much his boy wanted that cap,' Steve said.

'Sure. But he recognized how much it was worth to us.'

'No, you let him take it away from us,' Steve blurted.

'That's unfair,' Dave said. 'Don't dare say that to me.'

'I don't want to be like you,' Steve muttered, and he darted across the road and walked along on the other side of the street.

'It's unfair,' Dave said angrily, only now he didn't mean that Steve was unfair, he meant that what had happened in the prosperous Hudson home was unfair, and he didn't know quite why. He had been trapped, not just by Mr Hudson, but by his own life. Across the road Steve was hurrying along with his head down, wanting to be alone. They walked most of the way home on opposite sides of the street, until Dave could stand it no longer. 'Steve,' he called, crossing the street. 'It was very unfair. I mean, for you to say . . .' but Steve started to run. Dave walked as fast as he could and Steve was getting beyond him, and he felt enraged and suddenly yelled, 'Steve!' and he started to chase his son. He wanted to get hold of Steve and pound him, and he didn't know why. He gained on him, he gasped for breath and he almost got him by the shoulder. Turning, Steve saw his father's face in the street light and was terrified; he circled away, got to the house, and rushed in, yelling, 'Mother!'

'Son, son!' she cried, rushing from the kitchen. As soon as she threw her arms around Steve, shielding him, Dave's anger left him and he felt stupid. He walked past them into the kitchen.

'What happened?' she asked anxiously. 'Have you both gone crazy? What did you do, Steve?'

'Nothing,' he said sullenly.

'What did your father do?'

'We found the boy with my ball cap, and he let the boy's father take it from us.'

'No, no,' Dave protested. 'Nobody pushed us around. The man didn't put anything over us.' He felt tired and his face was burning. He told what had happened; then he slowly took the two ten-dollar bills out of his wallet and tossed them on the table and looked up guiltily at his wife.

It hurt him that she didn't pick up the money, and that she didn't rebuke him. 'It is a lot of money, son,' she said slowly. 'Your father was only trying to do what he knew was right, and it'll work out, and you'll understand.' She was soothing Steve, but Dave knew she felt that she needed to be gentle with him, too, and he was ashamed.

When she went with Steve to his bedroom, Dave sat by himself. His son had contempt for him, he thought. His son, for the first time, had seen how easy it was for another man to handle him, and he had judged him and had wanted to walk alone on the other side of the street. He looked at the money and he hated the sight of it.

His wife returned to the kitchen, made a cup of tea, talked soothingly, and said it was incredible that he had forced the Hudson man to pay him twenty dollars for the cap, but all Dave could think of was how scared Steve was of him.

Finally, he got up and went into Steve's room. The room was in darkness, but he could see the outlines of Steve's body on the bed, and he sat down beside him and whispered, 'Look, son, it was a mistake. I know why. People like us—in circumstances where money can scare us. No, no,' he said, feeling ashamed and shaking his head apologetically; he was taking the wrong way of showing the boy they were together; he was covering up his own failure. For the failure had been his, and it had come out of being so separated from his son that he had been blind to what was beyond the price in a boy's life. He longed now to show Steve he could be with him from day to day. His hand went out hesitantly to Steve's shoulder. 'Steve, look,' he said eagerly. 'The trouble was I didn't realize how much I enjoyed it that night at the ballpark. If I had watched you playing for your own team—the kids around here say you could be a great pitcher. We could take that money and buy a new pitcher's glove for you, and a catcher's mitt. Steve, Steve, are you listening? I could catch you, work with you in the lane. Maybe I could be your coach . . . watch you become a great pitcher.' In the half-darkness he could see the boy's pale face turn to him.

Steve, who had never heard his father talk like this, was shy and wondering. All he knew was that his father, for the first time, wanted to be with him in his hopes and adventures. He said, 'I guess you do know how important that cap was.' His hand went out to his father's arm. 'With that man the cap—well it was just something he could buy, eh Dad?' Dave gripped his son's hand hard. The wonderful generosity of childhood—the price a boy was willing to pay to be able to count on his father's admiration and approval—made him feel humble, then strangely exalted.

1952

Sinclair Ross

1908–1996

Born on a homestead near Shellbrook in northern Saskatchewan, Sinclair Ross dropped out of school after grade eleven to work in a bank. His banking career took him to many small-town banks in Saskatchewan before he transferred to a bank in Winnipeg in 1933. Apart from wartime service with the Canadian army in London, England, he remained in banking until his retirement in 1968. In 1941 he published his first novel, *As for Me and My House*, with its stunning depiction of small-town prairie life during the Depression. The prairie is also the principal setting for his two collections of short fiction, *The Lamp at Noon and Other Stories* (1968) and *The Race and Other Stories* (1982), which explore the landscape's unique ability to sustain, to suffocate, or to challenge its inhabitants.

In 1984 the National Film Board of Canada made a faithful film adaptation of the selection reprinted here, 'The Painted Door'.

The Painted Door

Straight across the hills it was five miles from John's farm to his father's. But in winter, with the roads impassable, a team had to make a wide detour and skirt the hills, so that from five the distance was more than trebled to seventeen.

'I think I'll walk,' John said at breakfast to his wife. 'The drifts in the hills wouldn't hold a horse, but they'll carry me all right. If I leave early I can spend a few hours helping him with his chores, and still be back by suppertime.'

Moodily she went to the window, and thawing a clear place in the frost with her breath, stood looking across the snowswept farmyard to the huddle of stables and sheds. 'There was a double wheel around the moon last night,' she countered presently. 'You said yourself we could expect a storm. It isn't right to leave me here alone. Surely I'm as important as your father.'

He glanced up uneasily, then drinking off his coffee tried to reassure her. 'But there's nothing to be afraid of—even supposing it does start to storm. You won't need to go near the stable. Everything's fed and watered now to last till night. I'll be back at the latest by seven or eight.'

She went on blowing against the frosted pane, carefully elongating the clear place until it was oval-shaped and symmetrical. He watched her a moment or two longer, then more insistently repeated, 'I say you won't need to go near the stable. Everything's fed and watered, and I'll see that there's plenty of wood in. That will be all right, won't it?'

'Yes—of course—I heard you—' It was a curiously cold voice now, as if the words were chilled by their contact with the frosted pane. 'Plenty to eat—plenty of wood to keep me warm—what more could a woman ask for?'

'But he's an old man—living there all alone. What is it, Ann? You're not like your-self this morning.'

She shook her head without turning. 'Pay no attention to me. Seven years a farmer's wife—it's time I was used to staying alone.'

Slowly the clear place on the glass enlarged: oval, then round, then oval again. The sun was risen above the frost mists now, so keen and hard a glitter on the snow that instead of warmth its rays seemed shedding cold. One of the two-year-old colts that had cantered away when John turned the horses out for water stood covered with rime at the stable door again, head down and body hunched, each breath a little plume of steam against the frosty air. She shivered, but did not turn. In the clear, bitter light the long white miles of prairie landscape seemed a region strangely alien to life. Even the distant farmsteads she could see served only to intensify a sense of isolation. Scattered across the face of so vast and bleak a wilderness it was difficult to conceive them as a testimony of human hardihood and endurance. Rather they seemed futile, lost. Rather they seemed to cower before the implacability of snow-swept earth and clear pale sun-chilled sky.

And when at last she turned from the window there was a brooding stillness in her face as if she had recognized this mastery of snow and cold. It troubled John. 'If you're really afraid,' he yielded, 'I won't go today. Lately it's been so cold, that's all. I just wanted to make sure he's all right in case we do have a storm.'

'I know—I'm not really afraid.' She was putting in a fire now, and he could no longer see her face. 'Pay no attention. It's ten miles there and back, so you'd better get started.'

'You ought to know by now I wouldn't stay away,' he tried to brighten her. 'No matter how it stormed. Twice a week before we were married I never missed—and there were bad blizzards that winter too.'

He was a slow, unambitious man, content with his farm and cattle, naively proud of Ann. He had been bewildered by it once, her caring for a dull-witted fellow like him; then assured at last of her affection he had relaxed against it gratefully, unsus-pecting it might ever be less constant than his own. Even now, listening to the restless brooding in her voice, he felt only a quick, unformulated kind of pride that after seven years his absence for a day should still concern her. While she, his trust and earnest-ness controlling her again:

'I know. It's just that sometimes when you're away I get lonely. . . . . There's a long cold tramp in front of you. You'll let me fix a scarf around your face.'

He nodded. 'And on my way I'll drop in at Steven's place. Maybe he'll come over tonight for a game of cards. You haven't seen anybody but me for the last two weeks.'

She glanced up sharply, then busied herself clearing the table. 'It will mean another two miles if you do. You're going to be cold and tired enough as it is. When you're gone I think I'll paint the kitchen woodwork. White this time—you remember we got the paint last fall. It's going to make the room a lot lighter. I'll be too busy to find the day long.'

'I will though,' he insisted, 'and if a storm gets up you'll feel safer, knowing that he's coming. That's what you need, Ann—someone to talk to besides me.'

She stood at the stove motionless a moment, then turned to him uneasily. 'Will you shave then, John—now—before you go?'

He glanced at her questioningly, and avoiding his eyes she tried to explain, 'I mean—he may be here before you're back—and you won't have a chance then.'

'But it's only Steven—he's seen me like this—'

'He'll be shaved, though—that's what I mean—and I'd like you too to spend a little time on yourself.'

He stood up, stroking the heavy stubble on his chin. 'Maybe I should all right, but it makes the skin too tender. Especially when I've got to face the wind.'

She nodded and began to help him dress, bringing heavy socks and a big woollen sweater from the bedroom, wrapping a scarf around his face and forehead. 'I'll tell Steven to come early,' he said, as he went out. 'In time for supper. Likely there'll be chores for me to do, so if I'm not back by six don't wait.'

From the bedroom window she watched him nearly a mile along the road. The fire had gone down when at last she turned away, and already through the house there was an encroaching chill. A blaze sprang up again when the drafts were opened, but as she went on clearing the table her movements were furtive and constrained. It was the silence weighing upon her—the frozen silence of the bitter fields and sun-chilled sky—lurking outside as if alive, relentlessly in wait, mile-deep between her now and John. She listened to it, suddenly tense, motionless. The fire crackled and the clock ticked. Always it was there. 'I'm a fool,' she whispered hoarsely, rattling the dishes in defiance, going back to the stove to put in another fire. 'Warm and safe—I'm a fool. It's a good chance when he's away to paint. The day will go quickly. I won't have time to brood.'

Since November now the paint had been waiting warmer weather. The frost in the walls on a day like this would crack and peel it as it dried, but she needed something to keep her hands occupied, something to stave off the gathering cold and loneliness. 'First of all,' she said aloud, opening the paint and mixing it with a little turpentine, 'I must get the house warmer. Fill up the stove and open the oven door so that all the heat comes out. Wad something along the window sills to keep out the drafts. Then I'll feel brighter. It's the cold that depresses.'

She moved briskly, performing each little task with careful and exaggerated absorption, binding her thoughts to it, making it a screen between herself and the surrounding snow and silence. But when the stove was filled and the windows sealed it was more difficult again. Above the quiet, steady swishing of her brush against the bedroom door the clock began to tick. Suddenly her movements became precise, deliberate, her posture self-conscious, as if someone had entered the room and were watching her. It was the silence again, aggressive, hovering. The fire spit and crackled at it. Still it was there. 'I'm a fool,' she repeated. 'All farmers' wives have to stay alone. I mustn't give in this way. I mustn't brood. A few hours now and they'll be here.'

The sound of her voice reassured her. She went on: 'I'll get them a good supper—and for coffee tonight after cards bake some of the little cakes with raisins that he likes. . . . Just three of us, so I'll watch, and let John play. It's better with four, but at least we can talk. That's all I need—someone to talk to. John never talks. He's stronger—he doesn't understand. But he likes Steven—no matter what the neighbours say. Maybe he'll have him come again, and some other young people too. It's what we need, both of us, to help keep young ourselves. . . . And then before we know it we'll be into March. It's cold still in March sometimes, but you never mind the same. At least you're beginning to think about spring.'

She began to think about it now. Thoughts that outstripped her words, that left her alone again with herself and the ever-lurking silence. Eager and hopeful first; then clenched, rebellious, lonely. Windows open, sun and thawing earth again, the urge of growing, living things. Then the days that began in the morning at half-past four and lasted till ten at night; the meals at which John gulped his food and scarcely spoke a word; the brute-tired stupid eyes he turned on her if ever she mentioned town or visiting.

For spring was drudgery again. John never hired a man to help him. He wanted a mortgage-free farm; then a new house and pretty clothes for her. Sometimes, because with the best of crops it was going to take so long to pay off anyway, she wondered whether they mightn't better let the mortgage wait a little. Before they were worn out, before their best years were gone. It was something of life she wanted, not just a house and furniture; something of John, not pretty clothes when she would be too old to wear them. But John of course couldn't understand. To him it seemed only right that she should have the clothes—only right that he, fit for nothing else, should slave away fifteen hours a day to give them to her. There was in his devotion a baffling, insurmountable humility that made him feel the need of sacrifice. And when his muscles ached, when his feet dragged stolidly with weariness, then it seemed that in some measure at least he was making amends for his big hulking body and simple mind. That by his sacrifice he succeeded only in the extinction of his personality never occurred to him. Year after year their lives went on in the same little groove. He drove his horses in the field; she milked cows and hoed potatoes. By dint of his drudgery he saved a few months' wages, added a few dollars more each fall to his payments on the mortgage; but the only real difference that it all made was to deprive her of his companionship, to make him a little duller, older, uglier than he might otherwise have been. He never saw their lives objectively. To him it was not what he actually accomplished by means of the sacrifice that mattered, but the sacrifice itself, the gesture—something done for her sake.

And she, understanding, kept her silence. In such a gesture, however futile, there was a graciousness not to be shattered lightly. 'John,' she would begin sometimes, 'you're doing too much. Get a man to help you—just for a month—' but smiling down at her he would answer simply, 'I don't mind. Look at the hands on me. They're made for work.' While in his voice there would be a stalwart ring to tell her that by her thoughtfulness she had made him only the more resolved to serve her, to prove his devotion and fidelity.

They were useless, such thoughts. She knew. It was his very devotion that made him useless, that forbade her to rebel. Yet over and over, sometimes hunched still before their bleakness, sometimes her brush making swift sharp strokes to pace the chafe and rancour that they brought, she persisted in them.

This now, the winter, was their slack season. She could sleep sometimes till eight, and John till seven. They could linger over their meals a little, read, play cards, go visiting the neighbours. It was the time to relax, to indulge and enjoy themselves; but instead, fretful and impatient, they kept on waiting for the spring. They were compelled now, not by labour, but by the spirit of labour. A spirit that pervaded their lives and brought with idleness a sense of guilt. Sometimes they did sleep late, sometimes they did play cards, but always uneasily, always reproached by the thought of more important things that might be done. When John got up at five to attend to the fire he wanted to stay up and go out to the stable. When he sat down to a meal he hurried his food and pushed his chair away again, from habit, from sheer work-instinct, even though it was only to put more wood on the stove, or go down cellar to cut up beets and turnips for the cows.

And anyway, sometimes she asked herself, why sit trying to talk with a man who never talked? Why talk when there was nothing to talk about but crops and cattle, the weather and the neighbours? The neighbours, too—why go visiting them when still it was the same—crops and cattle, the weather and the other neighbours? Why go to the dances in the schoolhouse to sit among the older women, one of them now, married seven years, or to waltz with the work-bent, tired old farmers to a squeaky fiddle tune? Once she had danced with Steven six or seven times in the evening, and they had talked about it for as many months. It was easier to stay home. John never danced or enjoyed himself. He was always uncomfortable in his good suit and shoes. He didn't like shaving in the cold weather oftener than once or twice a week. It was easier to stay at home, to stand at the window staring out across the bitter fields, to count the days and look forward to another spring.

But now, alone with herself in the winter silence, she saw the spring for what it really was. This spring—next spring—all the springs and summers to come. While they grew old, while their bodies warped, while their minds kept shrivelling dry and empty like their lives. 'I mustn't,' she said aloud again. 'I married him—and he's a good man. I mustn't keep on this way. It will be noon before long, and then time to think about supper. . . . Maybe he'll come early—and as soon as John is finished at the stable we can all play cards.'

It was getting cold again, and she left her painting to put in more wood. But this time the warmth spread slowly. She pushed a mat up to the outside door, and went back to the window to pat down the woollen shirt that was wadded along the sill. Then she paced a few times round the room, then poked the fire and rattled the stove lids, then paced again. The fire crackled, the clock ticked. The silence now seemed more intense than ever, seemed to have reached a pitch where it faintly moaned. She began to pace on tiptoe, listening, her shoulders drawn together, not realizing for a while that it was the wind she heard, thin-strained and whimpering through the eaves.

Then she wheeled to the window, and with quick short breaths thawed the frost to see again. The glitter was gone. Across the drifts sped swift and snakelike little tongues of snow. She could not follow them, where they sprang from, or where they disappeared. It was as if all across the yard the snow were shivering awake—roused by the warnings of the wind to hold itself in readiness for the impending storm. The sky had become sombre, whitish grey. It, too, as if in readiness, had shifted and lay close to earth. Before her as she watched a mane of powdery snow reared up breast-high against the darker background of the stable, tossed for a moment angrily, and then subsided again as if whipped down to obedience and restraint. But another followed, more reckless and impatient than the first. Another reeled and dashed itself against the window where she watched. Then ominously for a while there were only the angry little snakes of snow. The wind rose, creaking the troughs that were wired beneath the eaves. In the distance, sky and prairie now were merged into one another linelessly. All round her it was gathering; already in its press and whimpering there strummed a boding of eventual fury. Again she saw a mane of snow spring up, so dense and high this time that all the sheds and stables were obscured. Then others followed, whirling fiercely out of hand; and, when at last they cleared, the stables seemed in dimmer outline than before. It was the snow beginning, long lancet shafts of it, straight from the north, borne almost level by the straining wind. 'He'll be there soon,' she whispered, 'and coming home it will be in his back. He'll leave again right away. He saw the double wheel—he knows the kind of storm there'll be.'

She went back to her painting. For a while it was easier, all her thoughts half-anxious ones of John in the blizzard, struggling his way across the hills; but petulantly again she soon began, 'I knew we were going to have a storm—I told him so—but it doesn't matter what I say. Big stubborn fool—he goes his own way anyway. It doesn't matter what becomes of me. In a storm like this he'll never get home. He won't even try. And while he sits keeping his father company I can look after his stable for him, go ploughing through snowdrifts up to my knees—nearly frozen—'

Not that she meant or believed her words. It was just an effort to convince herself that she did have a grievance, to justify her rebellious thoughts, to prove John responsible for her unhappiness. She was young still, eager for excitement and distractions; and John's steadfastness rebuked her vanity, made her complaints seem weak and trivial. Fretfully she went on, 'If he'd listen to me sometimes and not be so stubborn we wouldn't still be living in a house like this. Seven years in two rooms—seven years and never a new stick of furniture. . . . There—as if another coat of paint could make it different anyway.'

She cleaned her brush, filled up the stove again, and went back to the window. There was a void white moment that she thought must be frost formed on the window pane; then, like a fitful shadow through the whirling snow, she recognized the stable roof. It was incredible. The sudden, maniac raging of the storm struck from her face all its pettishness. Her eyes glazed with fear a little; her lips blanched. 'If he starts for home now,' she whispered silently—'But he won't—he knows I'm safe—he knows Steven's coming. Across the hills he would never dare.'

She turned to the stove, holding out her hands to the warmth. Around her now there seemed a constant sway and tremor, as if the air were vibrating with the violent shudderings of the walls. She stood quite still, listening. Sometimes the wind struck with sharp, savage blows. Sometimes it bore down in a sustained, minute-long blast, silent with effort and intensity; then with a foiled shriek of threat wheeled away to gather and assault again. Always the eavestroughs creaked and sawed. She stared towards the window again, then detecting the morbid trend of her thoughts, prepared fresh coffee and forced herself to drink a few mouthfuls. 'He would never dare,' she whispered again. 'He wouldn't leave the old man anyway in such a storm. Safe in here—there's nothing for me to keep worrying about. It's after one already. I'll do my baking now, and then it will be time to get supper ready for Steven.'

Soon, however, she began to doubt whether Steven would come. In such a storm even a mile was enough to make a man hesitate. Especially Steven, who, for all his attractive qualities, was hardly the one to face a blizzard for the sake of someone else's chores. He had a stable of his own to look after anyway. It would be only natural for him to think that when the storm rose John had turned again for home. Another man would have—would have put his wife first.

But she felt little dread or uneasiness at the prospect of spending the night alone. It was the first time she had been left like this on her own resources, and her reaction, now that she could face and appraise her situation calmly, was gradually to feel it a kind of adventure and responsibility. It stimulated her. Before nightfall she must go to the stable and feed everything. Wrap up in some of John's clothes—take a ball of string in her hand, one end tied to the door, so that no matter how blinding the storm she could at least find her way back to the house. She had heard of people having to do that. It appealed to her now because suddenly it made life dramatic. She had not felt the storm yet, only watched it for a minute through the window.

It took nearly an hour to find enough string, to choose the right socks and sweaters. Long before it was time to start out she tried on John's clothes, changing and rechanging, striding around the room to make sure there would be play enough for pitching hay and struggling over snowdrifts; then she took them off again, and for a while busied herself baking the little cakes with raisins that he liked.

Night came early. Just for a moment on the doorstep she shrank back, uncertain. The slow dimming of the light clutched her with an illogical sense of abandonment. It was like the covert withdrawal of an ally, leaving the alien miles unleashed and unrestrained. Watching the hurricane of writhing snow rage past the little house she forced herself, 'They'll never stand the night unless I get them fed. It's nearly dark already, and I've work to last an hour.'

Timidly, unwinding a little of the string, she crept out from the shelter of the doorway. A gust of wind spun her forward a few yards, then plunged her headlong against a drift that in the dense white whirl lay invisible across her path. For nearly a minute she huddled still, breathless and dazed. The snow was in her mouth and nostrils, inside her scarf and up her sleeves. As she tried to straighten a smothering scud flung itself against her face, cutting off her breath a second time. The wind struck from all sides, blustering and furious. It was as if the storm had discovered her, as if all its forces were concentrated upon her extinction. Seized with panic suddenly she threshed out a moment with her arms, then stumbled back and sprawled her length across the drift.

But this time she regained her feet quickly, roused by the whip and batter of the storm to retaliative anger. For a moment her impulse was to face the wind and strike back blow for blow; then, as suddenly as it had come, her frantic strength gave way to limpness and exhaustion. Suddenly, a comprehension so clear and terrifying that it struck all thoughts of the stable from her mind, she realized in such a storm her puny insignificance. And the realization gave her new strength, stilled this time to a desperate persistence. Just for a moment the wind held her, numb and swaying in its vise; then slowly, buckled far forward, she groped her way again towards the house.

Inside, leaning against the door, she stood tense and still a while. It was almost dark now. The top of the stove glowed a deep, dull red. Heedless of the storm, self-absorbed and self-satisfied, the clock ticked on like a glib little idiot. 'He shouldn't have gone,' she whispered silently. 'He saw the double wheel—he knew. He shouldn't have left me here alone.'

For so fierce now, so insane and dominant did the blizzard seem, that she could not credit the safety of the house. The warmth and lull around her was not real yet, not to be relied upon. She was still at the mercy of the storm. Only her body pressing hard like this against the door was staving it off. She didn't dare move. She didn't dare ease the ache and strain. 'He shouldn't have gone,' she repeated, thinking of the stable again, reproached by her helplessness. 'They'll freeze in their stalls—and I can't reach them. He'll say it's all my fault. He won't believe I tried.'

Then Steven came. Quickly, startled to quietness and control, she let him in and lit the lamp. He stared at her a moment, then flinging off his cap crossed to where she stood by the table and seized her arms. 'You're so white—what's wrong? Look at me—' It was like him in such little situations to be masterful. 'You should have known better than to go out on a day like this. For a while I thought I wasn't going to make it here myself—'

'I was afraid you wouldn't come—John left early, and there was the stable—'

But the storm had unnerved her, and suddenly at the assurance of his touch and voice the fear that had been gripping her gave way to an hysteria of relief. Scarcely aware of herself she seized his arm and sobbed against it. He remained still a moment unyielding, then slipped his other arm around her shoulder. It was comforting and she relaxed against it, hushed by a sudden sense of lull and safety. Her shoulders trembled with the easing of the strain, then fell limp and still. 'You're shivering,'—he drew her gently towards the stove. 'There's nothing to be afraid of now, though. I'm going to do the chores for you.'

It was a quiet, sympathetic voice, yet with an undertone of insolence, a kind of mockery even, that made her draw away quickly and busy herself putting in a fire. With his lips drawn in a little smile he watched her till she looked at him again. The smile too was insolent, but at the same time companionable; Steven's smile, and therefore difficult to reprove. It lit up his lean, still-boyish face with a peculiar kind of arrogance; features and smile that were different from John's, from other men's—wilful and derisive, yet naively so—as if it were less the difference itself he was conscious of, than the long-accustomed privilege that thereby fell his due. He was erect, tall, square-shouldered. His hair was dark and trim, his lips curved soft and full. While John, she made the comparison swiftly, was thick-set, heavy-jowled, and stooped. He always stood before her helpless, a kind of humility and wonderment in his attitude. And Steven now smiled on her appraisingly with the worldly-wise assurance of one for whom a woman holds neither mystery nor illusion.

'It was good of you to come, Steven,' she responded, the words running into a sudden, empty laugh. 'Such a storm to face—I suppose I should feel flattered.'

For his presumption, his misunderstanding of what had been only a momentary weakness, instead of angering quickened her, roused from latency and long disuse all the instincts and resources of her femininity. She felt eager, challenged. Something was at hand that hitherto had always eluded her, even in the early days with John, something vital, beckoning, meaningful. She didn't understand, but she knew. The texture of the moment was satisfyingly dreamlike: an incredibility perceived as such, yet acquiesced in. She was John's wife—she knew—but also she knew that Steven standing here was different from John. There was no thought of motive, no understanding of herself as the knowledge persisted. Wary and poised round a sudden little core of blind excitement she evaded him, 'But it's nearly dark—hadn't you better hurry if you're going to do the chores? Don't trouble—I can get them off myself—'

An hour later when he returned from the stable she was in another dress, hair rearranged, a little flush of colour in her face. Pouring warm water for him from the kettle into the basin she said evenly, 'By the time you're washed supper will be ready. John said we weren't to wait for him.'

He looked at her a moment, 'But in a storm like this you're not expecting John?'

'Of course.' As she spoke she could feel the colour deepening in her face. 'We're going to play cards. He was the one that suggested it.'

He went on washing, and then as they took their places at the table, resumed, 'So John's coming. When are you expecting him?'

'He said it might be seven o'clock—or a little later.' Conversation with Steven at other times had always been brisk and natural, but now suddenly she found it strained. 'He may have work to do for his father. That's what he said when he left. Why do you ask, Steven?'

'I was just wondering—it's a rough night.'

'He always comes. There couldn't be a storm bad enough. It's easier to do the chores in the daylight, and I knew he'd be tired—that's why I started out for the stable.'

She glanced up again and he was smiling at her. The same insolence, the same little twist of mockery and appraisal. It made her flinch suddenly, and ask herself why she was pretending to expect John—why there should be this instinct of defence to force her. This time, instead of poise and excitement, it brought a reminder that she had changed her dress and rearranged her hair. It crushed in a sudden silence, through which she heard the whistling wind again, and the creaking saw of the eaves. Neither spoke now. There was something strange, almost terrifying, about this Steven and his quiet, unrelenting smile; but strangest of all was the familiarity: the Steven she had never seen or encountered, and yet had always known, always expected, always waited for. It was less Steven himself that she felt than his inevitability. Just as she had felt the snow, the silence and the storm. She kept her eyes lowered, on the window past his shoulder, on the stove, but his smile now seemed to exist apart from him, to merge and hover with the silence. She clinked a cup—listened to the whistle of the storm—always it was there. He began to speak, but her mind missed the meaning of his words. Swiftly she was making comparisons again; his face so different to John's, so handsome and young and clean-shaven. Swiftly, helplessly, feeling the imperceptible and relentless ascendancy that thereby he was gaining over her, sensing sudden menace in this new, more vital life, even as she felt drawn towards it.

The lamp between them flickered as an onslaught of the storm sent shudderings through the room. She rose to build up the fire again and he followed her. For a long time they stood close to the stove, their arms almost touching. Once as the blizzard creaked the house she spun around sharply, fancying it was John at the door; but quietly he intercepted her. 'Not tonight—you might as well make up your mind to it. Across the hills in a storm like this—it would be suicide to try.'

Her lips trembled suddenly in an effort to answer, to parry the certainty in his voice, then set thin and bloodless. She was afraid now. Afraid of his face so different from John's—of his smile, of her own helplessness to rebuke it. Afraid of the storm, isolating her here alone with him in its impenetrable fastness. They tried to play cards, but she kept starting up at every creak and shiver of the walls. 'It's too rough a night,' he repeated. 'Even for John. Just relax a few minutes—stop worrying and pay a little attention to me.'

But in his tone there was a contradiction to his words. For it implied that she was not worrying—that her only concern was lest it really might be John at the door.

And the implication persisted. He filled up the stove for her, shuffled the cards— won—shuffled—still it was there. She tried to respond to his conversation, to think of the game, but helplessly into her cards instead she began to ask, Was he right? Was that why he smiled? Why he seemed to wait, expectant and assured?

The clock ticked, the fire crackled. Always it was there. Furtively for a moment she watched him as he deliberated over his hand. John, even in the days before they were married, had never looked like that. Only this morning she had asked him to shave. Because Steven was coming—because she had been afraid to see them side by side—because deep within herself she had known even then. The same knowledge, furtive and forbidden, that was flaunted now in Steven's smile. 'You look cold,' he said at last, dropping his cards and rising from the table. 'We're not playing, anyway. Come over to the stove for a few minutes and get warm.'

'But first I think we'll hang blankets over the door. When there's a blizzard like this we always do.' It seemed that in sane, commonplace activity there might be release, a moment or two in which to recover herself. 'John has nails in to put them on. They keep out a little of the draft.'

He stood on a chair for her, and hung the blankets that she had carried from the bedroom. Then for a moment they stood silent, watching the blankets sway and tremble before the blade of wind that spurted around the jamb. 'I forgot', she said at last, 'that I painted the bedroom door. At the top there, see—I've smeared the blankets coming through.'

He glanced at her curiously, and went back to the stove. She followed him, trying to imagine the hills in such a storm, wondering whether John would come. 'A man couldn't live in it,' suddenly he answered her thoughts, lowering the oven door and drawing up their chairs one on each side of it. 'He knows you're safe. It isn't likely that he'd leave his father, anyway.'

'The wind will be in his back,' she persisted. 'The winter before we were married—all the blizzards that we had that year—and he never missed—'

'Blizzards like this one? Up in the hills he wouldn't be able to keep his direction for a hundred yards. Listen to it a minute and ask yourself.'

His voice seemed softer, kindlier now. She met his smile a moment, its assured little twist of appraisal, then for a long time sat silent, tense, careful again to avoid his eyes.

Everything now seemed to depend on this. It was the same as a few hours ago when she braced the door against the storm. He was watching her, smiling. She dared not move, unclench her hands, or raise her eyes. The flames crackled, the clock ticked. The storm wrenched the walls as if to make them buckle in. So rigid and desperate were all her muscles set, withstanding, that the room around her seemed to swim and reel. So rigid and strained that for relief at last, despite herself, she raised her head and met his eyes again.

Intending that it should be for only an instant, just to breathe again, to ease the tension that had grown unbearable—but in his smile now, instead of the insolent appraisal that she feared, there seemed a kind of warmth and sympathy. An understanding that quickened and encouraged her—that made her wonder why but a moment ago she had been afraid. It was as if the storm had lulled, as if she had suddenly found calm and shelter.

Or perhaps, the thought seized her, perhaps instead of his smile it was she that had changed. She who, in the long, wind-creaked silence, had emerged from the increment of codes and loyalties to her real, unfettered self. She who now felt his air of appraisal as nothing more than understanding of the unfulfilled woman that until this moment had lain within her brooding and unadmitted, reproved out of consciousness by the insistence of an outgrown, routine fidelity.

For there had always been Steven. She understood now. Seven years—almost as long as John—ever since the night they first danced together.

The lamp was burning dry, and through the dimming light, isolated in the fastness of silence and storm, they watched each other. Her face was white and struggling still. His was handsome, clean-shaven, young. Her eyes were fanatic, believing desperately, fixed upon him as if to exclude all else, as if to find justification. His were cool, bland, drooped a little with expectancy. The light kept dimming, gathering the shadows round them, hushed, conspiratorial. He was smiling still. Her hands again were clenched up white and hard.

'But he always came,' she persisted. 'The wildest, coldest nights—even such a night as this. There was never a storm—'

'Never a storm like this one.' There was a quietness in his smile now, a kind of simplicity almost, as if to reassure her. 'You were out in it yourself for a few minutes. He would have five miles, across the hills. . . . I'd think twice myself, on such a night, before risking even one.'

Long after he was asleep she lay listening to the storm. As a check on the draft up the chimney they had left one of the stovelids partly off, and through the open bedroom door she could see the flickerings of flame and shadow on the kitchen wall. They leaped and sank fantastically. The longer she watched the more alive they seemed to be. There was one great shadow that struggled towards her threateningly, massive and black and engulfing all the room. Again and again it advanced, about to spring, but each time a little whip of light subdued it to its place among the others on the wall. Yet though it never reached her still she cowered, feeling that gathered there was all the frozen wilderness, its heart of terror and invincibility.

Then she dozed a while, and the shadow was John. Interminably he advanced. The whips of light still flickered and coiled, but now suddenly they were the swift little snakes that this afternoon she had watched twist and shiver across the snow. And they too were advancing. They writhed and vanished and came again. She lay still, paralyzed. He was over her now, so close that she could have touched him. Already it seemed that a deadly tightening hand was on her throat. She tried to scream but her lips were locked. Steven beside her slept on heedlessly.

Until suddenly as she lay staring up at him a gleam of light revealed his face. And in it was not a trace of threat or anger—only calm, and stonelike hopelessness.

That was like John. He began to withdraw, and frantically she tried to call him back. 'It isn't true—not really true—listen, John—' but the words clung frozen to her lips. Already there was only the shriek of wind again, the sawing eaves, the leap and twist of shadow on the wall.

She sat up, startled now and awake. And so real had he seemed there, standing close to her, so vivid the sudden age and sorrow in his face, that at first she could not make herself understand she had been only dreaming. Against the conviction of his presence in the room it was necessary to insist over and over that he must still be with his father on the other side of the hills. Watching the shadows she had fallen asleep. It was only her mind, her imagination, distorted to a nightmare by the illogical and unadmitted dread of his return. But he wouldn't come. Steven was right. In such a storm he would never try. They were safe, alone. No one would ever know. It was only fear, morbid and irrational; only the sense of guilt that even her new-found and challenged womanhood could not entirely quell.

She knew now. She had not let herself understand or acknowledge it as guilt before, but gradually through the wind-torn silence of the night his face compelled her. The face that had watched her from the darkness with its stonelike sorrow—the face that was really John—John more than his features of mere flesh and bone could ever be.

She wept silently. The fitful gleam of light began to sink. On the ceiling and wall at last there was only a faint dull flickering glow. The little house shuddered and quailed, and a chill crept in again. Without wakening Steven she slipped out to build up the fire. It was burned to a few spent embers now, and the wood she put on seemed a long time catching light. The wind swirled through the blankets they had hung around the door, and struck her flesh like laps of molten ice. Then hollow and moaning it roared up the chimney again, as if against its will drawn back to serve still longer with the onrush of the storm.

For a long time she crouched over the stove, listening. Earlier in the evening, with the lamp lit and the fire crackling, the house had seemed a stand against the wilderness, against its frozen, blizzard-breathed implacability, a refuge of feeble walls wherein persisted the elements of human meaning and survival. Now, in the cold, creaking darkness, it was strangely extinct, looted by the storm and abandoned again. She lifted the stove lid and fanned the embers till at last a swift little tongue of flame began to lick around the wood. Then she replaced the lid, extending her hands, and as if frozen in that attitude stood waiting.

It was not long now. After a few minutes she closed the drafts, and as the flames whirled back upon each other, beating against the top of the stove and sending out flickers of light again, a warmth surged up to relax her stiffened limbs. But shivering and numb it had been easier. The bodily well-being that the warmth induced gave play again to an ever more insistent mental suffering. She remembered the shadow that was John. She saw him bent towards her, then retreating, his features pale and overcast with unaccusing grief. She re-lived their seven years together and, in retrospect, found them to be years of worth and dignity. Until crushed by it all at last, seized by a sudden need to suffer and atone, she crossed to where the draft was bitter, and for a long time stood unflinching on the icy floor.

The storm was close here. Even through the blankets she could feel a sift of snow against her face. The eaves sawed, the walls creaked. Above it all, like a wolf in howling flight, the wind shrilled lone and desolate.

And yet, suddenly she asked herself, hadn't there been other storms, other blizzards? And through the worst of them hadn't he always reached her?

Clutched by the thought she stood rooted a minute. It was hard now to understand how she could have so deceived herself—how a moment of passion could have quieted within her not only conscience, but reason and discretion too. John always came. There could never be a storm to stop him. He was strong, inured to the cold. He had crossed the hills since his boyhood, knew every creek-bed and gully. It was madness to go on like this—to wait. While there was still time she must waken Steven, and hurry him away.

But in the bedroom again, standing at Steven's side, she hesitated. In his detachment from it all, in his quiet, even breathing, there was such sanity, such realism. For him nothing had happened; nothing would. If she wakened him he would only laugh and tell her to listen to the storm. Already it was long past midnight; either John had lost his way or not set out at all. And she knew that in his devotion there was nothing foolhardy. He would never risk a storm beyond his endurance, never permit himself a sacrifice likely to endanger her lot or future. They were both safe. No one would ever know. She must control herself—be sane like Steven.

For comfort she let her hand rest a while on Steven's shoulder. It would be easier were he awake now, with her, sharing her guilt; but gradually as she watched his handsome face in the glimmering light she came to understand that for him no guilt existed. Just as there had been no passion, no conflict. Nothing but the sane appraisal of their situation, nothing but the expectant little smile, and the arrogance of features that were different from John's. She winced deeply, remembering how she had fixed her eyes on those features, how she had tried to believe that so handsome and young, so different from John's, they must in themselves be her justification.

In the flickering light they were still young, still handsome. No longer her justification—she knew now—John was the man—but wistfully still, wondering sharply at their power and tyranny, she touched them a moment with her fingertips again.

She could not blame him. There had been no passion, no guilt; therefore there could be no responsibility. Looking down at him as he slept, half-smiling still, his lips relaxed in the conscienceless complacency of his achievement, she understood that thus he was revealed in his entirety—all there ever was or ever could be. John was the man. With him lay all the future. For tonight, slowly and contritely through the day and years to come, she would try to make amends.

Then she stole back to the kitchen, and without thought, impelled by over-whelming need again, returned to the door where the draft was bitter still. Gradually towards morning the storm began to spend itself. Its terror blast became a feeble, worn-out moan. The leap of light and shadow sank, and a chill crept in again. Always the eaves creaked, tortured with wordless prophecy. Heedless of it all the clock ticked on in idiot content.

They found him the next day, less than a mile from home. Drifting with the storm he had run against his own pasture fence and overcome had frozen there, erect still, both hands clasping fast the wire.

'He was south of here,' they said wonderingly when she told them how he had come across the hills. 'Straight south—you'd wonder how he could have missed the buildings. It was the wind last night, coming every way at once. He shouldn't have tried. There was a double wheel around the moon.'

She looked past them a moment, then as if to herself said simply, 'If you knew him, though—John would try.'

It was later, when they had left her a while to be alone with him, that she knelt and touched his hand. Her eyes dimmed, still it was such a strong and patient hand; then, transfixed, they suddenly grew wide and clear. On the palm, white even against its frozen whiteness, was a little smear of paint.

1942

Sheila Watson
1909–1998

Born in New Westminster, British Columbia, where her father was the superintendent of a mental hospital, Sheila Watson, the second of four children, lived with her family in one wing of the institution until her father died in 1920. After graduating from the University of British Columbia, she taught in elementary and sec-ondary schools on the BC mainland and on Vancouver Island. Watson drew on her teaching experience in the Cariboo region of the British Columbia interior in writing her first novel,

Deep Hollow Creek, which she did not publish until 1992. After World War II she moved east to undertake part-time graduate studies in English at the University of Toronto. In 1951 she began a two-year residence in Calgary, where she wrote much of *The Double Hook* (1959), the novel now regarded as the beginning of modern Canadian fiction. In the same decade she com-pleted her graduate studies and began a doc-toral dissertation on Wyndham Lewis. In 1961 she joined the Department of English at the

University of Alberta, where she taught until her retirement in 1975.

In addition to her novel, Watson published six short stories. 'Antigone' (1959) employs classical myth to organize contemporary reality, to distance that reality, and to endow seemingly homely actions with the significance usually associated with myth.

Antigone

My father ruled a kingdom on the right bank of the river. He ruled it with a firm hand and a stout heart though he was often more troubled than Moses, who was simply trying to bring a stubborn and moody people under God's yoke. My father ruled men who thought they were gods or the instruments of gods or, at very least, god-afflicted and god-pursued. He ruled Atlas who held up the sky, and Hermes who went on endless messages, and Helen who'd been hatched from an egg, and Pan the gardener, and Kallisto the bear, and too many others to mention by name. Yet my father had no thunderbolt, no trident, no helmet of darkness. His subjects were delivered bound into his hands. He merely watched over them as the hundred-handed ones watched over the dethroned Titans so that they wouldn't bother Hellas again.

Despite the care which my father took to maintain an atmosphere of sober common sense in his whole establishment, there were occasional outbursts of self-indulgence which he could not control. For instance, I have seen Helen walking naked down the narrow cement path under the chestnut trees for no better reason, I suppose, than that the day was hot and the white flowers themselves lay naked and expectant in the sunlight. And I have seen Atlas forget the sky while he sat eating the dirt which held him up. These were things which I was not supposed to see.

If my father had been as sensible through and through as he was thought to be, he would have packed me off to boarding school when I was old enough to be disciplined by men. Instead he kept me at home with my two cousins who, except for the accident of birth, might as well have been my sisters. Today I imagine people concerned with our welfare would take such an environment into account. At the time I speak of most people thought us fortunate—especially the girls whose father's affairs had come to an unhappy issue. I don't like to revive old scandal and I wouldn't except to deny it; but it takes only a few impertinent newcomers in any community to force open cupboards which have been decently sealed by time. However, my father was so busy setting his kingdom to rights that he let weeds grow up in his own garden.

As I said, if my father had had all his wits about him he would have sent me to boarding school—and Antigone and Ismene too. I might have fallen in love with the headmaster's daughter and Antigone might have learned that no human being can be right always. She might have found out besides that from the seeds of eternal justice grow madder flowers than any which Pan grew in the gardens of my father's kingdom.

Between the kingdom which my father ruled and the wilderness flows a river. It is this river which I am crossing now. Antigone is with me.

How often can we cross the same river, Antigone asks.

Her persistence annoys me. Besides, Heraklitos made nonsense of her question years ago. He saw a river too—the Inachos, the Kephissos, the Lethaios. The name doesn't matter. He said: See how quickly the water flows. However agile a man is, however nimbly he swims, or runs, or flies, the water slips away before him. See, even as he sets down his foot the water is displaced by the stream which crowds along in the shadow of its flight.

But after all, Antigone says, one must admit that it is the same kind of water. The oolichans run in it as they ran last year and the year before. The gulls cry above the same banks. Boats drift towards the Delta and circle back against the current to gather up the catch.

At any rate, I tell her, we're standing on a new bridge. We are standing so high that the smell of mud and river weeds passes under us out to the straits. The unbroken curve of the bridge protects the eye from details of river life. The bridge is foolproof as a clinic's passport to happiness.

The old bridge still spans the river, but the cat-walk with its cracks and knot-holes, with its gap between planking and handrail has been torn down. The centre arch still grinds open to let boats up and down the river, but a child can no longer be walked on it or swung out on it beyond the water-gauge at the very centre of the flood.

I've known men who scorned any kind of bridge, Antigone says. Men have walked into the water, she says, or, impatient, have jumped from the bridge into the river below.

But these, I say, didn't really want to cross the river. They went Persephone's way, cradled in the current's arms, down the long halls under the pink feet of the gulls, under the booms and towlines, under the soft bellies of the fish.

Antigone looks at me.

There's no coming back, she says, if one goes far enough.

I know she's going to speak of her own misery and I won't listen. Only a god has the right to say: Look what I suffer. Only a god should say: What more ought I to have done for you that I have not done?

Once in winter, she says, a man walked over the river.

Taking advantage of nature, I remind her, since the river had never frozen before.

Yet he escaped from the penitentiary, she says. He escaped from the guards walking round the walls or standing with their guns in the sentry-boxes at the four corners of the enclosure. He escaped.

Not without risk, I say. He had to test the strength of the ice himself. Yet safer perhaps than if he had crossed by the old bridge where he might have slipped through a knot-hole or tumbled out through the railing.

He did escape, she persists, and lived forever on the far side of the river in the Alaska tea and bulrushes. For where, she asks, can a man go farther than to the outermost edge of the world?

The habitable world, as I've said, is on the right bank of the river. Here is the market with its market stalls—the coops of hens, the long-tongued geese, the haltered calf, the bearded goat, the shoving pigs, and the empty bodies of cows and sheep and rabbits hanging on iron hooks. My father's kingdom provides asylum in the suburbs. Near it are the convent, the churches, and the penitentiary. Above these on the hill the cemetery looks down on the people and on the river itself.

It is a world spread flat, tipped up into the sky so that men and women bend forward, walking as men walk when they board a ship at high tide. This is the world I feel with my feet. It is the world I see with my eyes.

I remember standing once with Antigone and Ismene in the square just outside the gates of my father's kingdom. Here from a bust set high on a cairn the stone eyes of Simon Fraser look from his stone face over the river that he found.

It is the head that counts, Ismene said.

It's no better than an urn, Antigone said, one of the urns we see when we climb to the cemetery above.

And all I could think was that I didn't want an urn, only a flat green grave with a chain about it.

A chain won't keep out the dogs, Antigone said.

But his soul could swing on it, Ismene said, like a bird blown on a branch in the wind.

And I remembered Antigone's saying: The cat drags its belly on the ground and the rat sharpens its tooth in the ivy.

I should have loved Ismene, but I didn't. It was Antigone I loved. I should have loved Ismene because, although she walked the flat world with us, she managed somehow to see it round.

The earth is an oblate spheroid, she'd say. And I knew that she saw it there before her comprehensible and whole like a tangerine spiked through and held in place while it rotated on the axis of one of Nurse's steel sock needles. The earth was a tangerine and she saw the skin peeled off and the world parcelled out into neat segments, each segment sweet and fragrant in its own skin.

It's the head that counts, she said.

In her own head she made diagrams to live by, cut and fashioned after the eternal patterns spied out by Plato as he rummaged about in the sewing basket of the gods.

I should have loved Ismene. She would live now in some prefabricated and perfect chrysolite by some paradigm which made love round and whole. She would simply live and leave destruction in the purgatorial ditches outside her own walled paradise.

Antigone is different. She sees the world flat as I do and feels it tip beneath her feet. She has walked in the market and seen the living animals penned and the dead hanging stiff on their hooks. Yet she defies what she sees with a defiance which is almost denial. Like Atlas she tries to keep the vaulted sky from crushing the flat earth. Like Hermes she brings a message that there is life if one can escape to it in the brush and bulrushes in some dim Hades beyond the river. It is defiance not belief and I tell her that this time we walk the bridge to a walled cave where we can deny death no longer.

Yet she asks her question still. And standing there I tell her that Heraklitos has made nonsense of her question. I should have loved Ismene for she would have taught me what Plato meant when he said in all earnest that the union of the soul with the body is in no way better than dissolution. I expect that she understood things which Antigone is too proud to see.

I turn away from her and flatten my elbows on the high wall of the bridge. I look back at my father's kingdom. I see the terraces rolling down from the red-brick buildings with their barred windows. I remember hands shaking the bars and hear fingers tearing up paper and stuffing it through the meshes. Diktynna, mother of nets and high leaping fear. O Artemis, mistress of wild beasts and wild men.

The inmates are beginning to come out on the screened verandas. They pace up and down in straight lines or stand silent like figures which appear at the same time each day from some depths inside a clock.

On the upper terrace Pan the gardener is shifting sprinklers with a hooked stick. His face is shadowed by the brim of his hat. He moves as economically as an animal between the beds of lobelia and geranium. It is high noon.

Antigone has cut out a piece of sod and has scooped out a grave. The body lies in a coffin in the shade of the magnolia tree. Antigone and I are standing. Ismene is sitting between two low angled branches of the monkey puzzle tree. Her lap is filled with daisies. She slits the stem of one daisy and pulls the stem of another through it. She is making a chain for her neck and a crown for her hair.

Antigone reaches for a branch of the magnolia. It is almost beyond her grip. The buds flame above her. She stands on a small fire of daisies which smoulder in the roots of the grass.

I see the magnolia buds. They brood above me, whiteness feathered on whiteness. I see Antigone's face turned to the light. I hear the living birds call to the sun. I speak private poetry to myself: Between four trumpeting angels at the four corners of the earth a bride stands before the altar in a gown as white as snow.

Yet I must have been speaking aloud because Antigone challenges me: You're mistaken. It's the winds the angels hold, the four winds of the earth. After the just are taken to paradise the winds will destroy the earth. It's a funeral, she says, not a wedding.

She looks towards the building.

Someone is coming down the path from the matron's house, she says.

I notice that she has pulled one of the magnolia blossoms from the branch. I take it from her. It is streaked with brown where her hands have bruised it. The sparrow which she has decided to bury lies on its back. Its feet are clenched tight against the feathers of its breast. I put the flower in the box with it.

Someone is coming down the path. She is wearing a blue cotton dress. Her cropped head is bent. She walks slowly carrying something in a napkin.

It's Kallisto the bear, I say. Let's hurry. What will my father say if he sees us talking to one of his patients?

If we live here with him, Antigone says, what can he expect? If he spends his life trying to tame people he can't complain if you behave as if they were tame. What would your father think, she says, if he saw us digging in the Institution lawn?

Pan comes closer. I glower at him. There's no use speaking to him. He's deaf and dumb.

Listen, I say to Antigone, my father's not unreasonable. Kallisto thinks she's a bear and he thinks he's a bear tamer, that's all. As for the lawn, I say quoting my father without conviction, a man must have order among his own if he is to keep order in the state.

Kallisto has come up to see us. She is smiling and laughing to herself. She gives me her bundle.

Fish, she says.

I open the napkin.

Pink fish sandwiches, I say.

For the party, she says.

But it isn't a party, Antigone says. It's a funeral.

For the funeral breakfast, I say.

Ismene is twisting two chains of daisies into a rope. Pan has stopped pulling the sprinkler about. He is standing beside Ismene resting himself on his hooked stick. Kallisto squats down beside her. Ismene turns away, preoccupied, but she can't turn far because of Pan's legs.

Father said we never should
Play with madmen in the wood.

I look at Antigone.

It's my funeral, she says.

I go over to Ismene and gather up a handful of loose daisies from her lap. The sun reaches through the shadow of the magnolia tree.

It's my funeral, Antigone says. She moves possessively toward the body.

An ant is crawling into the bundle of sandwiches which I've put on the ground. A file of ants is marching on the sparrow's box.

I go over and drop daisies on the bird's stiff body. My voice speaks ritual words: Deliver me, O Lord, from everlasting death on this dreadful day. I tremble and am afraid.

The voice of a people comforts me. I look at Antigone. I look her in the eye.

It had better be a proper funeral then, I say.

Kallisto is crouched forward on her hands. Tears are running down her cheeks and she is licking them away with her tongue.

My voice rises again: I said in the midst of my days, I shall not see—

Antigone just stands there. She looks frightened, but her eyes defy me with their assertion.

It's my funeral, she says. It's my bird. I was the one who wanted to bury it.

She is looking for reason. She will say something which sounds eternally right.

Things have to be buried, she says. They can't be left lying around anyhow for people to see.

Birds shouldn't die, I tell her. They have wings. Cats and rats haven't wings.

Stop crying, she says to Kallisto. It's only a bird.

It has a bride's flower in its hand, Kallisto says.

We shall rise again, I mutter, but we shall not all be changed.

Antigone does not seem to hear me.

Behold, I say in a voice she must hear, in a moment, in the twinkling of an eye, the trumpet shall sound.

Ismene turns to Kallisto and throws the daisy chain about her neck.

Shall a virgin forget her adorning or a bride the ornament of her breast?

Kallisto is lifting her arms towards the tree.

The bridegroom has come, she says, white as a fall of snow. He stands above me in a great ring of fire.

Antigone looks at me now.

Let's cover the bird up, she says. Your father will punish us all for making a disturbance.

He has on his garment, Kallisto says, and on his thigh is written King of Kings.

I look at the tree. If I could see with Kallisto's eyes I wouldn't be afraid of death, or punishment, or the penitentiary guards. I wouldn't be afraid of my father's belt or his honing strap or his bedroom slipper. I wouldn't be afraid of falling into the river through a knot-hole in the bridge.

But, as I look, I see the buds falling like burning lamps and I hear the sparrow twittering in its box: Woe, woe, woe because of the three trumpets which are yet to sound.

Kallisto is on her knees. She is growling like a bear. She lumbers over to the sandwiches and mauls them with her paw.

Ismene stands alone for Pan the gardener has gone.

Antigone is fitting a turf in place above the coffin. I go over and press the edge of the turf with my feet. Ismene has caught me by the hand.

Go away, Antigone says.

I see my father coming down the path. He has an attendant with him. In front of them walks Pan holding the sprinkler hook like a spear.

What are you doing here? my father asks.

Burying a bird, Antigone says.

Here? my father asks again.

Where else could I bury it? Antigone says.

My father looks at her.

This ground is public property, he says. No single person has any right to an inch of it.

I've taken six inches, Antigone says. Will you dig up the bird again?

Some of his subjects my father restrained since they were moved to throw themselves from high places or to tear one another to bits from jealousy or rage. Others who disturbed the public peace he taught to walk in the airing courts or to work in the kitchen or the garden.

If men live at all, my father said, it is because discipline saves their life for them.

From Antigone he simply turned away.

1959

Eudora Welty

1909–2001

Born in Jackson, Mississippi, where her father was president of an insurance company, Eudora Welty attended school in that city before going to the Mississippi College for Women. She left her home region to finish college at the University of Wisconsin in 1929, and she spent the next two years studying at the Columbia University School of Advertising. Returning to Mississippi, Welty worked for various radio stations and newspapers and took a job as a photographer documenting Depression-era life in her home state for the United States Works Progress Administration.

Welty began writing fiction in the 1930s, publishing her first collection, *A Curtain of Green*, in 1941. From that time until her death she led a quiet life in Mississippi, writing and publishing her uniquely perceptive and humorous stories and novels at regular intervals. In a masterful evocation of idiosyncratic southern speech, 'Why I Live at the P.O.' is an extended dramatic monologue in which Sister gives her account of the family confrontation that prompted her move to the local post office.

Why I Live at the P.O.

I was getting along fine with Mama, Papa-Daddy, and Uncle Rondo until my sister Stella-Rondo just separated from her husband and came back home again. Mr Whitaker! Of course I went with Mr Whitaker first, when he first appeared here in China Grove, taking 'Pose Yourself' photos, and Stella-Rondo broke us up. Told him I was one-sided. Bigger on one side than the other, which is a deliberate, calculated falsehood: I'm the same. Stella-Rondo is exactly twelve months to the day younger than I am and for that reason she's spoiled.

She's always had anything in the world she wanted and then she'd throw it away. Papa-Daddy gave her this gorgeous Add-a-Pearl necklace when she was eight years old and she threw it away playing baseball when she was nine, with only two pearls.

So as soon as she got married and moved away from home the first thing she did was separate! From Mr Whitaker! This photographer with the popeyes she said she trusted. Came home from one of those towns up in Illinois and to our complete surprise brought this child of two.

Mama said she like to made her drop dead for a second. 'Here you had this marvellous blond child and never so much as wrote your mother a word about it,' says Mama. 'I'm thoroughly ashamed of you.' But of course she wasn't.

Stella-Rondo just calmly takes off this *hat*, I wish you could see it. She says, 'Why, Mama, Shirley-T.'s adopted, I can prove it.'

'How?' says Mama, but all I says was, 'H'm!' There I was over the hot stove, trying to stretch two chickens over five people and a completely unexpected child into the bargain, without one moment's notice.

'What do you mean—"H'm!"?' says Stella-Rondo, and Mama says, 'I heard that, Sister.'

I said that oh, I didn't mean a thing, only that whoever Shirley-T. was, she was the spit-image of Papa-Daddy if he'd cut off his beard, which of course he'd never do in the world. Papa-Daddy's Mamma's papa and sulks.

Stella-Rondo got furious! She said, 'Sister, I don't need to tell you you got a lot of nerve and always did have and I'll thank you to make no future reference to my adopted child whatsoever.'

'Very well,' I said. 'Very well, very well. Of course I noticed at once she looks like Mr Whitaker's side too. That frown. She looks like a cross between Mr Whitaker and Papa-Daddy.'

'Well, all I can say is she isn't.'

'She looks exactly like Shirley Temple to me,' says Mama, but Shirley-T. just ran away from her.

So the first thing Stella-Rondo did at the table was turn Papa-Daddy against me.

'Papa-Daddy,' she says. He was trying to cut up his meat. 'Papa-Daddy!' I was taken completely by surprise. Papa-Daddy is about a million years old and's got this long-long beard. 'Papa Daddy, Sister says she fails to understand why you don't cut off your beard.'

So Papa-Daddy l-a-y-s down his knife and fork! He's real rich. Mama says he is, he says he isn't. So he says, 'Have I heard correctly? You don't understand why I don't cut off my beard?'

'Why,' I says, 'Papa-Daddy, of course I understand, I did not say any such of a thing, the idea!'

He says, 'Hussy!'

I says, 'Papa-Daddy, you know I wouldn't any more want you to cut off your beard than the man in the moon. It was the farthest thing from my mind! Stella-Rondo sat there and made that up while she was eating breast of chicken.'

But he says, 'So the postmistress fails to understand why I don't cut off my beard. Which job I got you through my influence with the government. "Bird's nest"—is that what you call it?'

Not that it isn't the next to smallest P.O. in the entire state of Mississippi.

I says, 'Oh, Papa-Daddy,' I says, 'I didn't say any such of a thing, I never dreamed it was a bird's nest, I have always been grateful though this is the next to smallest P.O. in the state of Mississippi, and I do not enjoy being referred to as a hussy by my own grandfather.'

But Stella-Rondo says, 'Yes, you did say it too. Anybody in the world could of heard you, that had ears.'

'Stop right there,' says Mama, looking at *me*.

So I pulled my napkin straight back through the napkin ring and left the table.

As soon as I was out of the room Mama says, 'Call her back, or she'll starve to death,' but Papa-Daddy says, 'This is the beard I started growing on the Coast when I was fifteen years old.' He would of gone on till nightfall if Shirley-T. hadn't lost the Milky Way she ate in Cairo.

So Papa-Daddy says, 'I am going out and lie in the hammock, and you can all sit here and remember my words: I'll never cut off my beard as long as I live, even one inch, and I don't appreciate it in you at all.' Passed right by me in the hall and went straight out and got in the hammock.

It would be a holiday. It wasn't five minutes before Uncle Rondo suddenly appeared in the hall in one of Stella-Rondo's flesh-coloured kimonos, all cut on the bias, like something Mr Whitaker probably thought was gorgeous.

'Uncle Rondo!' I says. 'I didn't know who that was! Where are you going?'

'Sister,' he says, 'get out of my way, I'm poisoned.'

'If you're poisoned stay away from Papa-Daddy,' I says. 'Keep out of the hammock, Papa-Daddy will certainly beat you on the head if you come within forty miles of him. He thinks I deliberately said he ought to cut off his beard after he got me the P.O., and I've told him and told him and told him, and he acts like he just don't hear me. Papa-Daddy must of gone stone deaf.'

'He picked a fine day to do it then,' says Uncle Rondo, and before you could say 'Jack Robinson' flew out in the yard.

What he'd really done, he'd drunk another bottle of that prescription. He does it every single Fourth of July as sure as shooting, and it's horribly expensive. Then he falls over in the hammock and snores. So he insisted on zigzagging right on out to the hammock, looking like a half-wit.

Papa-Daddy woke up with this horrible yell and right there without moving an inch he tried to turn Uncle Rondo against me. I heard every word he said. Oh, he told Uncle Rondo I didn't learn to read till I was eight years old and he didn't see how in the world I ever got the mail put up at the P.O., much less read it all, and he said if Uncle Rondo could only fathom the lengths he had gone to to get me that job! And he said on the other hand he thought Stella-Rondo had a brilliant mind and deserved credit for getting out of town. All the time he was just lying there swinging as pretty as you please and looping out his beard, and poor Uncle Rondo was *pleading* with him to slow down the hammock, it was making him dizzy as a witch to watch it. But that's what Papa-Daddy likes about a hammock. So Uncle Rondo was too dizzy to get turned against me for the time being. He's Mama's only brother and is a good case of a one-track mind. Ask anybody. A certified pharmacist.

Just then I heard Stella-Rondo raising the upstairs window. While she was married she got this peculiar idea that it's cooler with the windows shut and locked. So she has to raise the window before she can make a soul hear her outdoors.

So she raises the window and says, '*Oh!*' You would have thought she was mortally wounded.

Uncle Rondo and Papa-Daddy didn't even look up, but kept right on with what they were doing. I had to laugh.

I flew up the stairs and threw the door open! I says, 'What in the wide world's the matter, Stella-Rondo? You mortally wounded?'

'No,' she says, 'I'm not mortally wounded but I wish you would do me the favour of looking out that window there and telling me what you see.'

So I shade my eyes and look out the window.

'I see the front yard,' I says.

'Don't you see any human beings?' she says.

'I see Uncle Rondo trying to run Papa-Daddy out of the hammock,' I says. 'Nothing more. Naturally, it's so suffocating-hot in the house, with all the windows shut and locked, everybody who cares to stay in their right mind will have to go out and get in the hammock before the Fourth of July is over.'

'Don't you notice anything different about Uncle Rondo?' asks Stella-Rondo.

'Why, no, except he's got on some terrible-looking flesh-coloured contraption I wouldn't be found dead in, is all I can see,' I says.

'Never mind, you won't be found dead in it, because it happens to be part of my trousseau, and Mr Whitaker took several dozen photographs of me in it,' says Stella-Rondo. 'What on earth could Uncle Rondo *mean* by wearing part of my trousseau out in the broad open daylight without saying so much as "Kiss my foot," *knowing* I only got home this morning after my separation and hung my negligee up on the bathroom door, just as nervous as I could be?'

'I'm sure I don't know, and what do you expect me to do about it?' I says. 'Jump out the window?'

'No, I expect nothing of the kind. I simply declare that Uncle Rondo looks like a fool in it, that's all,' she says. 'It makes me sick to my stomach.'

'Well, he looks as good as he can,' I says. 'As good as anybody in reason could.' I stood up for Uncle Rondo, please remember. And I said to Stella-Rondo, 'I think I would do well not to criticize so freely if I were you and came home with a two-year-old child I had never said a word about, and no explanation whatever about the separation.'

'I asked you the instant I entered this house not to refer one more time to my adopted child, and you gave me your word of honour you would not,' was all Stella-Rondo would say, and started pulling out every one of her eyebrows with some cheap Kress tweezers.

So I merely slammed the door behind me and went downstairs and made some green-tomato pickle. Somebody had to do it. Of course Mama had turned the both niggers loose; she always said no earthly power could hold one anyway on the Fourth of July, so she wouldn't even try. It turned out that Jaypan fell in the lake and came within a very narrow limit of drowning.

So Mama trots in. Lifts up the lid and says, 'H'm! Not very good for your Uncle Rondo in his precarious condition, I must say. Or poor little adopted Shirley-T. Shame on you!'

That made me tired. I says, 'Well, Stella-Rondo had better thank her lucky stars it was her instead of me came trotting in with that very peculiar-looking child. Now if it had been me that trotted in from Illinois and brought a peculiar-looking child of two, I shudder to think of the reception I'd of got, much less controlled the diet of an entire family.'

'But you must remember, Sister, that you were never married to Mr Whitaker in the first place and didn't go up to Illinois to live,' says Mama, shaking a spoon in my face. 'If you had I would of been just as overjoyed to see you and your little adopted girl as I was to see Stella-Rondo, when you wound up with your separation and came on back home.'

'You would not,' I says.

'Don't contradict me, I would,' says Mama.

But I said she couldn't convince me though she talked till she was blue in the face. Then I said, 'Besides, you know as well as I do that that child is not adopted.'

'She most certainly is adopted,' says Mama, stiff as a poker.

I says, 'Why Mama, Stella-Rondo had her just as sure as anything in this world, and just too stuck up to admit it.'

'Why, Sister,' said Mama. 'Here I thought we were going to have a pleasant Fourth of July, and you start right out not believing a word your own baby sister tells you!'

'Just like Cousin Annie Flo. Went to her grave denying the facts of life,' I remind Mama.

'I told you if you ever mentioned Annie Flo's name I'd slap your face,' says Mama, and slaps my face.

'All right, you wait and see,' I says.

'I,' says Mama, 'I prefer to take my children's word for anything when it's humanly possible.' You ought to see Mama, she weighs two hundred pounds and has real tiny feet.

Just then something perfectly horrible occurred to me.

'Mama,' I says, 'can that child talk?' I simply had to whisper! 'Mama, I wonder if that child can be—you know—in any way? Do you realize,' I says, 'that she hasn't spoken one single, solitary word to a human being up to this minute? This is the way she looks,' I says, and I looked like this.

Well, Mama and I just stood there and stared at each other. It was horrible!

'I remember well that Joe Whitaker frequently drank like a fish,' says Mama. 'I believed to my soul he drank *chemicals*.' And without another word she marches to the foot of the stairs and calls Stella-Rondo.

'Stella-Rondo? O-o-o-o-o! Stella-Rondo!'

'What?' says Stella-Rondo from upstairs. Not even the grace to get up off the bed.

'Can that child of yours talk?' asks Mama.

Stella-Rondo says, 'Can she what?'

'Talk! Talk!' says Mama. 'Burdyburdyburdyburdy!'

So Stella-Rondo yells back, 'Who says she can't talk?'

'Sister says so,' says Mama.

'You didn't have to tell me, I know whose word of honour don't mean a thing in this house,' says Stella-Rondo.

And in a minute the loudest Yankee voice I ever heard in my life yells out, 'OE'm Pop-OE the Sailor-r-r-r Ma-a-an!' and then somebody jumps up and down in the upstairs hall. In another second the house would of fallen down.

'Not only talks, she can tap-dance!' calls Stella-Rondo. 'Which is more than some people I won't name can do.'

'Why, the little precious darling thing!' Mama says, so surprised. 'Just as smart as she can be!' Starts talking baby talk right there. Then she turns on me. 'Sister, you ought to be thoroughly ashamed! Run upstairs this instant and apologize to Stella-Rondo and Shirley-T.'

'Apologize for what?' I says. 'I merely wondered if the child was normal, that's all. Now that she's proved she is, why, I have nothing further to say.'

But Mama just turned on her heels and flew out, furious. She ran right upstairs and hugged the baby. She believed it was adopted. Stella-Rondo hadn't done a thing but turn her against me from upstairs while I stood there helpless over the hot stove. So that made Mama, Papa-Daddy, and the baby all on Stella-Rondo's side.

Next, Uncle Rondo.

I must say that Uncle Rondo has been marvellous to me at various times in the past and I was completely unprepared to be made to jump out of my skin, the way it turned out. Once Stella-Rondo did something perfectly horrible to him—broke a chain letter from Flanders Field—and he took the radio back he had given her and gave it to me. Stella-Rondo was furious! For six months we all had to call her Stella instead of Stella-Rondo, or she wouldn't answer. I always thought Uncle Rondo had all the brains in the entire family. Another time he sent me to Mammoth Cave, with all expenses paid.

But this would be the day he was drinking that prescription, the Fourth of July.

So at supper Stella-Rondo speaks up and says she thinks Uncle Rondo ought to try to eat a little something. So finally Uncle Rondo said he would try a little cold biscuits and ketchup, but that was all. So *she* brought it to him.

'Do you think it wise to disport with ketchup in Stella-Rondo's flesh-coloured kimono?' I says. Trying to be considerate! If Stella-Rondo couldn't watch out for her trousseau, somebody had to.

'Any objections?' asks Uncle Rondo, just about to pour out all the ketchup.

'Don't mind what she says, Uncle Rondo,' says Stella-Rondo. 'Sister has been devoting this solid afternoon to sneering out my bedroom window at the way you look.'

'What's that?' says Uncle Rondo. Uncle Rondo has got the most terrible temper in the world. Anything is liable to make him tear the house down if it comes at the wrong time.

So Stella-Rondo says, 'Sister says, "Uncle Rondo certainly does look like a fool in that pink kimono!"'

Do you remember who really said that?

Uncle Rondo spills out all the ketchup and jumps out of his chair and tears off the kimono and throws it down on the dirty floor and puts his foot on it. It had to be sent all the way to Jackson to the cleaners and re-pleated.

'So that's your opinion of your Uncle Rondo, is it?' he says. 'I look like a fool, do I? Well, that's the last straw. A whole day in this house with nothing to do, and then to hear you come out with a remark like that behind my back!'

'I didn't say any such of a thing, Uncle Rondo,' I says, 'and I'm not saying who did, either. Why, I think you look all right. Just try to take care of yourself and not talk and eat at the same time,' I says. 'I think you better go lie down.'

'Lie down my foot,' says Uncle Rondo. I ought to of known by that he was fixing to do something perfectly horrible.

So he didn't do anything that night in the precarious state he was in—just played Casino with Mama and Stella-Rondo and Shirley T. and gave Shirley-T. a nickel with a head on both sides. It tickled her nearly to death, and she called him 'Papa'. But at 6:30 a.m. the next morning, he threw a whole five-cent package of some unsold one-inch firecrackers from the store as hard as he could into my bedroom, and they every one went off. Not one bad one in the string. Anybody else, there'd be one that wouldn't go off.

Well, I'm just terribly susceptible to noise of any kind, the doctor has always told me I was the most sensitive person he had ever seen in his whole life, and I was simply prostrated. I couldn't eat! People tell me they heard it as far as the cemetery, and old Aunt Jep Patterson, that had been holding her own so good, thought it was Judgment Day and she was going to meet her whole family. It's usually so quiet here.

And I'll tell you it didn't take me any longer than a minute to make up my mind what to do. There I was with the whole entire house on Stella-Rondo's side and turned against me. If I have anything at all I have pride.

So I just decided I'd go straight down to the P.O. There's plenty of room there in the back, I says to myself.

Well! I made no bones about letting the family catch on to what I was up to. I didn't try to conceal it.

The first thing they knew, I marched in where they were all playing Old Maid and pulled the electric oscillating fan out by the plug, and everything got real hot. Next I snatched the pillow I'd done the needlepoint on right off the davenport from behind Papa-Daddy. He went 'Ugh!' I beat Stella-Rondo up the stairs and finally found my charm bracelet in her bureau drawer under a picture of Nelson Eddy.

'So that's the way the land lies,' says Uncle Rondo. There he was, piecing on the ham. 'Well, Sister, I'll be glad to donate my army cot if you got any place to set it up, providing you'll leave right this minute and let me get some peace.' Uncle Rondo was in France.

'Thank you kindly for the cot and "peace" is hardly the word I would select if I had to resort to firecrackers at 6:30 a.m. in a young girl's bedroom,' I says back to him. 'And as to where I intend to go, you seem to forget my position as postmistress of China Grove, Mississippi,' I says. 'I've always got the P.O.'

Well, that made them all sit up and take notice.

I went out front and started digging up some four-o'clocks to plant around the P.O. 'Ah-ah-ah!' says Mama, raising the window. 'Those happen to be my four-o'clocks. Everything planted in that star is mine. I've never known you to make anything grow in your life.'

'Very well,' I says. 'But I take the fern. Even you, Mama, can't stand there and deny that I'm the one watered that fern. And I happen to know where I can send in a box top and get a packet of one thousand mixed seeds, no two the same kind, free.'

'Oh, where?' Mama wants to know.

But I says, 'Too late. You 'tend to your house, and I'll 'tend to mine. You hear things like that all the time if you know how to listen to the radio. Perfectly marvellous offers. Get anything you want free.'

So I hope to tell you I marched in and got that radio, and they could of all bit a nail in two, especially Stella-Rondo, that it used to belong to, and she well knew she couldn't get it back, I'd sue for it like a shot. And I very politely took the sewing-machine motor I helped pay the most on to give Mama for Christmas back in 1929, and a good big calendar, with the first-aid remedies on it. The thermometer and the

Hawaiian ukulele certainly were rightfully mine, and I stood on the step-ladder and got all my watermelon-rind preserves and every fruit and vegetable I'd put up, every jar. Then I began to pull the tacks out of the bluebird wall vases on the archway to the dining room.

'Who told you you could have those, Miss Priss?' says Mama, fanning as hard as she could.

'I bought 'em and I'll keep track of 'em,' I says. 'I'll tack 'em up one on each side of the post-office window, and you can see 'em when you come to ask me for your mail, if you're so dead to see 'em.'

'Not I! I'll never darken the door to that post office again if I live to be a hundred,' Mama says. 'Ungrateful child! After all the money we spent on you at the Normal.'

'Me either,' says Stella-Rondo. 'You can just let my mail lie there and *rot*, for all I care. I'll never come and relieve you of a single, solitary piece.'

'I should worry,' I says. 'And who you think's going to sit down and write you all those big fat letters and postcards, by the way? Mr Whitaker? Just because he was the only man ever dropped down in China Grove and you got him—unfairly—is he going to sit down and write you a lengthy correspondence after you come home giving no rhyme nor reason whatsoever for your separation and no explanation for the presence of that child? I may not have your brilliant mind, but I fail to see it.'

So Mama says, 'Sister, I've told you a thousand times that Stella-Rondo simply got homesick, and this child is far too big to be hers,' and she says, 'Now, why don't you all just sit down and play Casino?'

Then Shirley-T. sticks out her tongue at me in this perfectly horrible way. She has no more manners than the man in the moon. I told her she was going to cross her eyes like that some day and they'd stick.

'It's too late to stop me now,' I says. 'You should have tried that yesterday. I'm going to the P.O. and the only way you can possibly see me is to visit me there.'

So Papa-Daddy says, 'You'll never catch me setting foot in that post office, even if I should take a notion into my head to write a letter some place.' He says, 'I won't have you reachin' out of that little old window with a pair of shears and cuttin' off any beard of mine. I'm too smart for you!'

'We all are,' says Stella-Rondo.

But I said, 'If you're so smart, where's Mr Whitaker?'

So then Uncle Rondo says, 'I'll thank you from now on to stop reading all the orders I get on postcards and telling everyone in China Grove what you think is the matter with them,' but I says, 'I draw my own conclusions and will continue in the future to draw them.' I says, 'If people want to write their inmost secrets on penny postcards, there's nothing in the wide world you can do about it, Uncle Rondo.'

'And if you think we'll ever *write* another postcard you're sadly mistaken,' says Mama.

'Cutting off your nose to spite your face then,' I says. 'But if you're all determined to have no more to do with the US mail, think of this: What will Stella-Rondo do now, if she wants to tell Mr Whitaker to come after her?'

'Wah!' says Stella-Rondo. I knew she'd cry. She had a conniption fit right there in the kitchen.

'It will be interesting to see how long she holds out,' I says. 'And now—I am leaving.'

'Good-bye,' says Uncle Rondo.

'Oh, I declare,' says Mama, 'to think that a family of mine should quarrel on the Fourth of July, or the day after, over Stella-Rondo leaving old Mr Whitaker and having the sweetest little adopted child! It looks like we'd all be glad!'

'Wah!' says Stella-Rondo, and has a fresh conniption fit.

'*He* left *her*—you mark my words,' I says. 'That's Mr Whitaker. I know Mr Whitaker. After all, I knew him first. I said from the beginning he'd up and leave her. I foretold every single thing that's happened.'

'Where did he go?' asks Mama.

'Probably to the North Pole, if he knows what's good for him,' I says.

But Stella-Rondo just bawled and wouldn't say another word. She flew to her room and slammed the door.

'Now look what you've gone and done, Sister,' says Mama. 'You go apologize.'

'I haven't got time, I'm leaving,' I says.

'Well, what are you waiting around for?' asks Uncle Rondo.

So I just picked up the kitchen clock and marched off, without saying 'Kiss my foot' or anything, and never did tell Stella-Rondo good-bye.

There was a nigger girl going along on a little wagon right in front.

'Nigger girl,' I says, 'come help me haul these things down the hill, I'm going to live in the post office.'

Took her nine trips in her express wagon. Uncle Rondo came out on the porch and threw her a nickel.

And that's the last I've laid eyes on any of my family or my family laid eyes on me for five solid days and nights. Stella-Rondo may be telling the most horrible tales in the world about Mr Whitaker, but I haven't heard them. As I tell everybody, I draw my own conclusions.

But oh, I like it here. It's ideal, as I've been saying. You see, I've got everything cater-cornered, the way I like it. Hear the radio? All the war news. Radio, sewing machine, book ends, ironing board, and that great big piano lamp—peace, that's what I like. Butter-bean vines planted all along the front where the strings are.

Of course, there's not much mail. My family are naturally the main people in China Grove, and if they prefer to vanish from the face of the earth, for all the mail they get or the mail they write, why, I'm not going to open my mouth. Some of the folks here in town are taking up for me and some turned against me. I know which is which. There are always people who will quit buying stamps just to get on the right side of Papa-Daddy.

But here I am, and here I'll stay. I want the world to know I'm happy. And if Stella-Rondo should come to me this minute, on bended knees, and *attempt* to explain the incidents of her life with Mr Whitaker, I'd simply put my fingers in both my ears and refuse to listen.

1941

John Cheever
1912–1982

John Cheever was born in Quincy, Massachusetts, where his father owned a shoe factory until the economic disaster of 1929 wiped him out. After the crash his mother opened a gift shop that was quite successful. He went to school in Massachusetts until he was expelled from Thayer Academy for 'bad behaviour'—smoking. His first story, 'Expelled', appeared in the *New Republic* a few months later, in 1930.

Cheever was a writer from the beginning, living and working in Boston, New York, and the Yaddo writers' colony in Saratoga Springs, surviving with help from his brother and by doing odd jobs. He had published almost forty stories when he joined the United States Army in the Second World War. His first collection of stories was published during the war, but his first real success came with the publication of his second collection, *The Enormous Radio*, in 1953. By then he was writing for *The New Yorker*, where he placed well over one hundred stories following his first acceptance in 1940. His reputation as a writer grew steadily, so that the publication of his collected *Stories of John Cheever* in 1979 was a major literary event.

Although he also wrote novels, the short story was Cheever's form. With a mixture of realism and surrealism, 'The Swimmer' follows Neddy Merrill's quest to return home from a cocktail party by following the series of public and private swimming pools in his affluent neighbourhood. In its representation of all the neighbours he meets, the story is a commentary on the precarious relationship between personal wealth and genuine happiness.

The Swimmer

It was one of those midsummer Sundays when everyone sits around saying, 'I *drank* too much last night.' You might have heard it whispered by the parishioners leaving church, heard it from the lips of the priest himself, struggling with his cassock in the *vestiarium*, heard it from the golf links and the tennis courts, heard it from the wildlife preserve where the leader of the Audubon group was suffering from a terrible hangover. 'I *drank* too much,' said Donald Westerhazy. 'We all *drank* too much,' said Lucinda Merrill. 'It must have been the wine,' said Helen Westerhazy. 'I *drank* too much of that claret.'

This was at the edge of the Westerhazys' pool. The pool, fed by an artesian well with a high iron content, was a pale shade of green. It was a fine day. In the west there was a massive stand of cumulus cloud so like a city seen from a distance—from the bow of an approaching ship—that it might have had a name. Lisbon. Hackensack. The sun was hot. Neddy Merrill sat by the green water, one hand in it, one around a glass of gin. He was a slender man—he seemed to have the especial slenderness of youth— and while he was far from young he had slid down his banister that morning and given the bronze backside of Aphrodite on the hall table a smack, as he jogged toward the smell of coffee in his dining room. He might have been compared to a summer's day, particularly the last hours of one, and while he lacked a tennis racket or a sail bag the impression was definitely one of youth, sport, and clement weather. He had been swimming and now he was breathing deeply, stertorously as if he could gulp into his lungs the components of that moment, the heat of the sun, the intenseness of his pleasure. It all seemed to flow into his chest. His own house stood in Bullet Park, eight miles to the south, where his four beautiful daughters would have had their lunch and might be playing tennis. Then it occurred to him that by taking a dogleg to the southwest he could reach his home by water.

His life was not confining and the delight he took in this observation could not be explained by its suggestion of escape. He seemed to see, with a cartographer's eye, that string of swimming pools, that quasi-subterranean stream that curved across the county. He had made a discovery, a contribution to modern geography; he would name the stream Lucinda after his wife. He was not a practical joker nor was he a fool but he was determinedly original and had a vague and modest idea of himself as a legendary figure. The day was beautiful and it seemed to him that a long swim might enlarge and celebrate its beauty.

He took off a sweater that was hung over his shoulders and dove in. He had an inexplicable contempt for men who did not hurl themselves into pools. He swam a choppy crawl, breathing either with every stroke or every fourth stroke and counting somewhere well in the back of his mind the one-two one-two of a flutter kick. It was not a serviceable stroke for long distances but the domestication of swimming had saddled the sport with some customs and in his part of the world a crawl was customary. To be embraced and sustained by the light green water was less a pleasure, it seemed, than the resumption of a natural condition, and he would have liked to swim without trunks, but this was not possible, considering his project. He hoisted himself up on the far curb—he never used the ladder—and started across the lawn. When Lucinda asked where he was going he said he was going to swim home.

The only maps and charts he had to go by were remembered or imaginary but these were clear enough. First there were the Grahams, the Hammers, the Lears, the Howlands, and the Crosscups. He would cross Ditmar Street to the Bunkers and come, after a short portage, to the Levys, the Welchers, and the public pool in Lancaster. Then there were the Hallorans, the Sachses, the Biswangers, Shirley Adams, the Gilmartins, and the Clydes. The day was lovely, and that he lived in a world so generously supplied with water seemed like a clemency, a beneficence. His heart was high and he ran across the grass. Making his way home by an uncommon route gave him the feeling that he was a pilgrim, an explorer, a man with a destiny, and he knew that he would find friends all along the way; friends would line the banks of the Lucinda River.

He went through a hedge that separated the Westerhazys' land from the Grahams', walked under some flowering apple trees, passed the shed that housed their pump and filter, and came out at the Grahams' pool. 'Why, Neddy,' Mrs Graham said, 'what a marvellous surprise. I've been trying to get you on the phone all morning. Here, let me get you a drink.' He saw then, like any explorer, that the hospitable customs and traditions of the natives would have to be handled with diplomacy if he was ever going to reach his destination. He did not want to mystify or seem rude to the Grahams nor did he have time to linger there. He swam the length of their pool and joined them in the sun and was rescued, a few minutes later, by the arrival of two carloads of friends from Connecticut. During the uproarious reunions he was able to slip away. He went down by the front of the Grahams' house, stepped over a thorny hedge, and crossed a vacant lot to the Hammers'. Mrs Hammer, looking up from her roses, saw him swim by although she wasn't quite sure who it was. The Lears heard him splashing past the open windows of their living room. The Howlands and the Crosscups were away. After leaving the Howlands' he crossed Ditmar Street and started for the Bunkers', where he could hear, even at that distance, the noise of a party.

The water refracted the sound of voices and laughter and seemed to suspend it in midair. The Bunkers' pool was on a rise and he climbed some stairs to a terrace where twenty-five or thirty men and women were drinking. The only person in the water was Rusty Towers, who floated there on a rubber raft. Oh, how bonny and lush were the banks of the Lucinda River! Prosperous men and women gathered by the sapphire-coloured waters while caterer's men in white coats passed them cold gin. Overhead a red de Havilland trainer was circling around and around and around in the sky with something like the glee of a child in a swing. Ned felt a passing affection for the scene, a tenderness for the gathering, as if it was something he might touch. In the distance he heard thunder. As soon as Enid Bunker saw him she began to scream. 'Oh, look who's here! What a marvellous surprise! When Lucinda said that you couldn't come I thought I'd *die*.' She made her way to him through the crowd, and when they had finished kissing she led him to the bar, a progress that was slowed by the fact that he stopped to kiss eight or ten other women and shake the hands of as many men. A smiling bartender he had seen at a hundred parties gave him a gin and tonic and he stood by the bar for a moment, anxious not to get stuck in any conversation that would delay his voyage. When he seemed about to be surrounded he dove in and swam close to the side to avoid colliding with Rusty's raft. At the far end of the pool he bypassed the Tomlinsons with a broad smile and jogged up the garden path. The gravel cut his feet but this was the only unpleasantness. The party was confined to the pool, and as he went toward the house he heard the brilliant, watery sound of voices fade, heard the noise of a radio from the Bunkers' kitchen, where someone was listening to a ball game. Sunday afternoon. He made his way through the parked cars and down the grassy border of their driveway to Alewives Lane. He did not want to be seen on the road in his bathing trunks but there was no traffic and he made the short distance to the Levys' driveway, marked with a PRIVATE PROPERTY sign and a green tube for the *New York Times*. All the doors and windows of the big house were open but there were no signs of life; not even a dog barked. He went around the side of the house to the pool and saw that the Levys had only recently left. Glasses and bottles and dishes of nuts were on a table at the deep end, where there was a bathhouse or gazebo, hung with Japanese lanterns. After swimming the pool he got himself a glass and poured a drink. It was his fourth or fifth drink and he had swum nearly half the length of the Lucinda River. He felt tired, clean, and pleased at that moment to be alone; pleased with everything.

It would storm. The stand of cumulus cloud—that city—had risen and darkened, and while he sat there he heard the percussiveness of thunder again. The de Havilland trainer was still circling overhead and it seemed to Ned that he could almost hear the pilot laugh with pleasure in the afternoon; but when there was another peal of thunder he took off for home. A train whistle blew and he wondered what time it had gotten to be. Four? Five? He thought of the provincial station at that hour, where a waiter, his tuxedo concealed by a raincoat, a dwarf with some flowers wrapped in newspaper, and a woman who had been crying would be waiting for the local. It was suddenly growing dark; it was that moment when the pinheaded birds seemed to organize their song into some acute and knowledgeable recognition of the storm's approach. Then there was a fine noise of rushing water from the crown of an oak at his back, as if a spigot there had been turned. Then the noise of fountains came from the crowns of all the tall trees. Why did he love storms, what was the meaning of his excitement when the door sprang open and the rain wind fled rudely up the stairs, why had the simple task of shutting the windows of an old house seemed fitting and urgent, why did the first watery notes of a storm wind have for him the unmistakable sound of good news, cheer, glad tidings? Then there was an explosion, a smell of cordite, and rain lashed the Japanese lanterns that Mrs Levy had bought in Kyoto the year before last, or was it the year before that?

He stayed in the Levys' gazebo until the storm had passed. The rain had cooled the air and he shivered. The force of the wind had stripped a maple of its red and yellow leaves and scattered them over the grass and the water. Since it was midsummer the tree must be blighted, and yet he felt a peculiar sadness at this sign of autumn. He braced his shoulders, emptied his glass, and started for the Welchers' pool. This meant crossing the Lindleys' riding ring and he was surprised to find it overgrown with grass and all the jumps dismantled. He wondered if the Lindleys had sold their horses or gone away for the summer and put them out to board. He seemed to remember having heard something about the Lindleys and their horses but the memory was unclear. On he went, barefoot through the wet grass, to the Welchers', where he found their pool was dry.

This breach in his chain of water disappointed him absurdly, and he felt like some explorer who seeks a torrential headwater and finds a dead stream. He was disappointed and mystified. It was common enough to go away for the summer but no one ever drained his pool. The Welchers had definitely gone away. The pool furniture was folded, stacked, and covered with a tarpaulin. The bathhouse was locked. All the windows of the house were shut, and when he went around to the driveway in front he saw a FOR SALE sign nailed to a tree. When had he last heard from the Welchers— when, that is, had he and Lucinda last regretted an invitation to dine with them? It seemed only a week or so ago. Was his memory failing or had he so disciplined it in the repression of unpleasant facts that he had damaged his sense of truth? Then in the distance he heard the sound of a tennis game. This cheered him, cleared away all his apprehensions and let him regard the overcast sky and the cold air with indifference. This was the day that Neddy Merrill swam across the country. That was the day! He started off then for his most difficult portage.

Had you gone for a Sunday afternoon ride that day you might have seen him, close to naked, standing on the shoulders of Route 424, waiting for a chance to cross. You might have wondered if he was the victim of foul play, had his car broken down, or was he merely a fool. Standing barefoot in the deposits of the highway—beer cans, rags, and blowout patches—exposed to all kinds of ridicule, he seemed pitiful. He had known when he started that this was a part of his journey—it had been on his maps— but confronted with the lines of traffic, worming through the summery light, he found himself unprepared. He was laughed at, jeered at, a beer can was thrown at him, and he had no dignity or humour to bring to the situation. He could have gone back, back to the Westerhazys', where Lucinda would still be sitting in the sun. He had signed nothing, vowed nothing, pledged nothing, not even to himself. Why, believing as he did, that all human obduracy was susceptible to common sense, was he unable to turn back? Why was he determined to complete his journey even if it meant putting his life in danger? At what point had this prank, this joke, this piece of horseplay become seri- ous? He could not go back, he could not even recall with any clearness the green water at the Westerhazys', the sense of inhaling the day's components, the friendly and relaxed voices saying that they had *drunk* too much. In the space of an hour, more or less, he had covered a distance that made his return impossible.

An old man, tooling down the highway at fifteen miles an hour, let him get to the middle of the road, where there was a grass divider. Here he was exposed to the ridicule of the northbound traffic, but after ten or fifteen minutes he was able to cross. From here he had only a short walk to the Recreation Centre at the edge of the village of Lancaster, where there were some handball courts and a public pool.

The effect of the water on voices, the illusion of brilliance and suspense, was the same here as it has been at the Bunkers' but the sounds here were louder, harsher, and more shrill, and as soon as he entered the crowded enclosure he was confronted with regimentation. 'ALL SWIMMERS MUST TAKE A SHOWER BEFORE USING THE POOL. ALL SWIMMERS MUST USE THE FOOTBATH. ALL SWIMMERS MUST WEAR THEIR IDENTIFI- CATION DISCS.' He took a shower, washed his feet in a cloudy and bitter solution, and made his way to the edge of the water. It stank of chlorine and looked to him like a sink. A pair of lifeguards in a pair of towers blew police whistles at what seemed to be regular intervals and abused the swimmers through a public address system. Neddy remembered the sapphire water at the Bunkers' with longing and thought that he might contaminate himself—damage his own prosperousness and charm—by swim- ming in this murk, but he reminded himself that he was an explorer, a pilgrim, and that this was merely a stagnant bend in the Lucinda River. He dove, scowling with dis- taste, into the chlorine and had to swim with his head above water to avoid collisions, but even so he was bumped into, splashed, and jostled. When he got to the shallow end both lifeguards were shouting at him? 'Hey, you, you without the identification disc, get outa the water.' He did, but they had no way of pursuing him and he went through the reek of suntan oil and chlorine out through the hurricane fence and passed the handball courts. By crossing the road he entered the wooded part of the Halloran estate. The woods were not cleared and the footing was treacherous and difficult until he reached the lawn and the clipped beech hedge that encircled their pool.

The Hallorans were friends, an elderly couple of enormous wealth who seemed to bask in the suspicion that they might be Communists. They were zealous reformers but they were not Communists, and yet when they were accused, as they sometimes were, of subversion, it seemed to gratify and excite them. Their beech hedge was yellow and he guessed this had been blighted like the Levys' maple. He called hullo, hullo, to warn the Hallorans of his approach, to palliate his invasion of their privacy. The Hallorans, for reasons that had never been explained to him, did not wear bathing suits. No explanations were in order, really. Their nakedness was a detail in their uncompromising zeal to reform and he stepped politely out of his trunks before he went through the opening in the hedge.

Mrs Halloran, a stout woman with white hair and a serene face, was reading the *Times*. Mr Halloran was taking beech leaves out of the water with a scoop. They seemed not surprised or displeased to see him. Their pool was perhaps the oldest in the country, a fieldstone rectangle, fed by a brook. It had no filter or pump and its waters were the opaque gold of the stream.

'I'm swimming across the county,' Ned said.

'Why, I didn't know one could,' exclaimed Mrs Halloran.

'Well, I've made it from the Westerhazys',' Ned said. 'That must be about four miles.'

He left his trunks at the deep end, walked to the shallow end, and swam this stretch. As he was pulling himself out of the water he heard Mrs Halloran say, 'We've been *terribly* sorry to hear about all your misfortunes, Neddy.'

'My misfortunes?' Ned asked. 'I don't know what you mean.'

'Why, we heard that you'd sold the house and that your poor children . . .'

'I don't recall having sold the house,' Ned said, 'and the girls are at home.'

'Yes,' Mrs Halloran sighed. 'Yes . . .' Her voice filled the air with an unseasonable melancholy and Ned spoke briskly. 'Thank you for the swim.'

'Well, have a nice trip,' said Mrs Halloran.

Beyond the hedge he pulled on his trunks and fastened them. They were loose and he wondered if, during the space of an afternoon, he could have lost some weight. He was cold and he was tired and the naked Hallorans and their dark water had depressed him. The swim was too much for his strength but how could he have guessed this, sliding down the banister that morning and sitting in the Westerhazys' sun? His arms were lame. His legs felt rubbery and ached at the joints. The worst of it was the cold in his bones and the feeling that he might never be warm again. Leaves were falling down around him and he smelled wood smoke on the wind. Who would be burning wood at this time of year?

He needed a drink. Whiskey would warm him, pick him up, carry him through the last of his journey, refresh his feeling that it was original and valorous to swim across the county. Channel swimmers took brandy. He needed a stimulant. He crossed the lawn in front of the Hallorans' house and went down a little path to where they had built a house for their only daughter, Helen, and her husband, Eric Sachs. The Sachses' pool was small and he found Helen and her husband there.

'Oh, *Neddy*,' Helen said. 'Did you lunch at Mother's?'

'Not *really*,' Ned said. 'I *did* stop to see your parents.' This seemed to be explanation enough. 'I'm terribly sorry to break in on you like this but I've taken a chill and I wonder if you'd give me a drink.'

'Why, I'd *love* to,' Helen said, 'but there hasn't been anything in this house to drink since Eric's operation. That was three years ago.'

Was he losing his memory, had his gift for concealing painful facts let him forget that he had sold his house, that his children were in trouble, and that his friend had been ill? His eyes slipped from Eric's face to his abdomen, where he saw three pale, sutured scars, two of them at least a foot long. Gone was his navel, and what, Neddy thought, would the roving hand, bed-checking one's gifts at 3 a.m., make of a belly with no navel, no link to birth, this breach in the succession?

'I'm sure you can get a drink at the Biswangers',' Helen said. 'They're having an enormous do. You can hear it from here. Listen!'

She raised her head and from across the road, the lawns, the gardens, the woods, the fields, he heard again the brilliant noise of voices over water. 'Well, I'll get wet,' he said, still feeling that he had no freedom of choice about his means of travel. He dove into the Sachses' cold water and, gasping, close to drowning, made his way from one end of the pool to the other. 'Lucinda and I want *terribly* to see you,' he said over his shoulder, his face set toward the Biswangers'. 'We're sorry it's been so long and we'll call you *very* soon.'

He crossed some fields to the Biswangers' and the sounds of revelry there. They would be honoured to give him a drink, they would be happy to give him a drink. The Biswangers invited him and Lucinda for dinner four times a year, six weeks in advance. They were always rebuffed and yet they continued to send out their invitations, unwilling to comprehend the rigid and undemocratic realities of their society. They were the sort of people who discussed the price of things at cocktails, exchanged market tips during dinner, and after dinner told dirty stories to mixed company. They did not belong to Neddy's set—they were not even on Lucinda's Christmas card list. He went toward the pool with feelings of indifference, charity, and some unease, since it seemed to be getting dark and these were the longest days of the year. The party when he joined it was noisy and large. Grace Biswanger was the kind of hostess who asked the optometrist, the veterinarian, the real-estate dealer, and the dentist. No one was swimming and the twilight, reflected on the water of the pool, had a wintry gleam. There was a bar and he started for this. When Grace Biswanger saw him she came toward him, not affectionately as he had every right to expect, but bellicosely.

'Why, this party has everything,' she said loudly, 'including a gate crasher.'

She could not deal him a social blow—there was no question about this and he did not flinch. 'As a gate crasher,' he asked politely, 'do I rate a drink?'

'Suit yourself,' she said. 'You don't seem to pay much attention to invitations.'

She turned her back on him and joined some guests, and he went to the bar and ordered a whiskey. The bartender served him but he served him rudely. His was a world in which the caterer's men kept the social score, and to be rebuffed by a part-time barkeep meant that he had suffered some loss of social esteem. Or perhaps the man was new and uninformed. Then he heard Grace at his back say: 'They went for broke overnight—nothing but income—and he showed up drunk one Sunday and asked us to loan him five thousand dollars. . . .' She was always talking about money. It was worse then eating your peas off a knife. He dove into the pool, swam its length and went away.

The next pool on his list, the last but two, belonged to his old mistress, Shirley Adams. If he had suffered any injuries at the Biswangers' they would be cured here. Love—sexual roughhouse in fact—was the supreme elixir, the pain killer, the brightly coloured pill that would put the spring back into his step, the joy of life in his heart. They had had an affair last week, last month, last year. He couldn't remember. It was he who had broken it off, his was the upper hand, and he stepped through the gate of the wall that surrounded her pool with nothing so considered as self-confidence. It seemed in a way to be his pool, as the lover, particularly the illicit lover, enjoys the possessions of his mistress with an authority unknown to holy matrimony. She was there, her hair the colour of brass, but her figure, at the edge of the lighted, cerulean water, excited in him no profound memories. It had been, he thought, a lighthearted affair, although she had wept when he broke it off. She seemed confused to see him and he wondered if she was still wounded. Would she, God forbid, weep again?

'What do you want?' she asked.

'I'm swimming across the county.'

'Good Christ. Will you ever grow up?'

'What's the matter?'

'If you've come here for money,' she said, 'I won't give you another cent.'

'You could give me a drink.'

'I could but I won't. I'm not alone.'

'Well, I'm on my way.'

He dove in and swam the pool, but when he tried to haul himself up onto the curb he found that the strength in his arms and shoulders had gone, and he paddled to the ladder and climbed out. Looking over his shoulder he saw, in the lighted bathhouse, a young man. Going out onto the dark lawn he smelled chrysanthemums or marigolds—some stubborn autumnal fragrance—on the night air, strong as gas. Looking overhead he saw that the stars had come out, but why should he seem to see Andromeda, Cepheus, and Cassiopeia? What had become of the constellations of midsummer? He began to cry.

It was probably the first time in his adult life that he had ever cried, certainly the first time in his life that he had ever felt so miserable, cold, tired, and bewildered. He could not understand the rudeness of the caterer's barkeep or the rudeness of a mistress who had come to him on her knees and showered his trousers with tears. He had swum too long, he had been immersed too long, and his nose and his throat were sore from the water. What he needed then was a drink, some company, and some clean, dry clothes, and while he could have cut directly across the road to his home he went on to the Gilmartins' pool. Here, for the first time in his life, he did not dive but went down the steps into the icy water and swam a hobbled side-stroke that he might have learned as a youth. He staggered with fatigue on his way to the Clydes' and paddled the length of their pool, stopping again and again with his hand on the curb to rest. He climbed up the ladder and wondered if he had the strength to get home. He had done what he wanted, he had swum the county, but he was so stupefied with exhaustion that his triumph seemed vague. Stooped, holding on to the gateposts for support, he turned up the driveway of his own house.

The place was dark. Was it so late that they had all gone to bed? Had Lucinda stayed at the Westerhazys' for supper? Had the girls joined her there or gone someplace else? Hadn't they agreed, as they usually did on Sunday, to regret all their invitations and stay at home? He tried the garage doors to see what cars were in but the doors were locked and rust came off the handles onto his hands. Going toward the house, he saw that the force of the thunderstorm had knocked one of the rain gutters loose. It hung down over the front door like an umbrella rib, but it could be fixed in the morning. The house was locked, and he thought that the stupid cook or the stupid maid must have locked the place up until he remembered that it had been some time since they had employed a maid or a cook. He shouted, pounded on the door, tried to force it with his shoulder, and then, looking in at the windows, saw that the place was empty.

1964

Bernard Malamud
1914–1986

A city boy, the son of Russian Jewish immigrants, Bernard Malamud was born and raised in Brooklyn, New York. He went to City College for his BA and Columbia University for his MA, then taught night school for almost ten years before taking a job at Oregon State University. His experiences in Oregon from 1949 to 1961 became the basis for his novel *A New Life* (1961). From 1961 he taught at Bennington College in Vermont. Among his most admired works are the novels *The Assistant* (1957) and *The Fixer* (1966) and the stories in *The Magic Barrel* (1958). A leader of the post–Second World War Jewish literary renaissance, Malamud introduced into American fiction Jewish immigrants and their urban locales, thus helping to ensure that marginal ethnic figures would become part of mainstream American fiction. In 'The Magic Barrel', Leo Finkle, a rabbinical student, learns the fundamental importance of his own humanity.

The Magic Barrel

Not long ago there lived in uptown New York, in a small, almost meagre room, though crowded with books, Leo Finkle, a rabbinical student in the Yeshivah University. Finkle, after six years of study, was to be ordained in June and had been advised by an acquaintance that he might find it easier to win himself a congregation if he were married. Since he had no present prospects of marriage, after two tormented days of turning it over in his mind, he called in Pinye Salzman, a marriage broker whose two-line advertisement he had read in the *Forward*.

The matchmaker appeared one night out of the dark fourth-floor hallway of the greystone rooming house where Finkle lived, grasping a black, strapped portfolio that had been worn thin with use. Salzman, who had been long in the business, was of slight but dignified build, wearing an old hat, and an overcoat too short and tight for him. He smelled frankly of fish, which he loved to eat, and although he was missing a few teeth, his presence was not displeasing, because of an amiable manner curiously contrasted with mournful eyes. His voice, his lips, his wisp of beard, his bony fingers were animated, but give him a moment of repose and his mild blue eyes revealed a depth of sadness, a characteristic that put Leo a little at ease although the situation, for him, was inherently tense.

He at once informed Salzman why he had asked him to come, explaining that his home was in Cleveland, and that but for his parents, who had married comparatively late in life, he was alone in the world. He had for six years devoted himself almost entirely to his studies, as a result of which, understandably, he had found himself without time for a social life and the company of young women. Therefore he thought it the better part of trial and error—of embarrassing fumbling—to call in an experienced person to advise him on these matters. He remarked in passing that the function of the marriage broker was ancient and honourable, highly approved in the Jewish community, because it made practical the necessary without hindering joy. Moreover, his own parents had been brought together by a matchmaker. They had made, if not a financially profitable marriage—since neither had possessed any worldly goods to speak of—at least a successful one in the sense of their everlasting devotion to each other. Salzman listened in embarrassed surprise, sensing a sort of apology. Later, however, he experienced a glow of pride in his work, an emotion that had left him years ago, and he heartily approved of Finkle.

The two went to their business. Leo had led Salzman to the only clear place in the room, a table near a window that overlooked the lamp-lit city. He seated himself at the matchmaker's side but facing him, attempting by an act of will to suppress the unpleasant tickle in his throat. Salzman eagerly unstrapped his portfolio and removed a loose rubber band from a thin packet of much-handled cards. As he flipped through them, a gesture and sound that physically hurt Leo, the student pretended not to see and gazed steadfastly out the window. Although it was still February, winter was on its last legs, signs of which he had for the first time in years begun to notice. He now observed the round white moon, moving high in the sky through a cloud menagerie, and watched with half-open mouth as it penetrated a huge hen, and dropped out of her like an egg laying itself. Salzman, though pretending through eyeglasses he had just slipped on to be engaged in scanning the writing on the cards, stole occasional glances at the young man's distinguished face, noting with pleasure the long, severe scholar's nose, brown eyes heavy with learning, sensitive yet ascetic lips, and a certain, almost hollow quality of the dark cheeks. He gazed around at shelves upon shelves of books and let out a soft, contented sigh.

When Leo's eyes fell upon the cards, he counted six spread out in Salzman's hand.

'So few?' he asked in disappointment.

'You wouldn't believe me how much cards I got in my office,' Salzman replied. 'The drawers are already filled to the top, so I keep them now in a barrel, but is every girl good for a new rabbi?'

Leo blushed at this, regretting all he had revealed of himself in a curriculum vitae he had sent to Salzman. He had thought it best to acquaint him with his strict standards and specifications, but in having done so, felt he had told the marriage broker more than was absolutely necessary.

He hesitantly inquired, 'Do you keep photographs of your clients on file?'

'First comes family, amount of dowry, also what kind promises,' Salzman replied, unbuttoning his tight coat and settling himself in the chair. 'After comes pictures, rabbi.'

'Call me Mr Finkle. I'm not yet a rabbi.'

Salzman said he would, but instead called him doctor, which he changed to rabbi when Leo was not listening too attentively.

Salzman adjusted his horn-rimmed spectacles, gently cleared his throat, and read in an eager voice the contents of the top card:

'Sophie P. Twenty-four years. Widow one year. No children. Educated high school and two years college. Father promises eight thousand dollars. Has wonderful whole-sale business. Also real estate. On the mother's side comes teachers, also one actor. Well known on Second Avenue.'

Leo gazed up in surprise. 'Did you say a widow?'

'A widow don't mean spoiled, rabbi. She lived with her husband maybe four months. He was a sick boy she made a mistake to marry him.'

'Marrying a widow has never entered my mind.'

'This is because you have no experience. A widow, especially if she is young and healthy like this girl, is a wonderful person to marry. She will be thankful to you the rest of her life. Believe me, if I was looking now for a bride, I would marry a widow.'

Leo reflected, then shook his head.

Salzman hunched his shoulders in an almost imperceptible gesture of disappoint-ment. He placed the card down on the wooden table and began to read another.

'Lily H. High-school teacher. Regular. Not a substitute. Has savings and new Dodge car. Lived in Paris one year. Father is successful dentist thirty-five years. Interested in a professional man. Well Americanized family. Wonderful opportunity.'

'I knew her personally,' said Salzman. 'I wish you could see this girl. She is a doll. Also very intelligent. All day you could talk to her about books and theyater and what not. She also knows current events.'

'I don't believe you mentioned her age?'

'Her age?' Salzman said, raising his brow. 'Her age is thirty-two years.'

Leo said after a while, 'I'm afraid that seems a little too old.'

Salzman let out a laugh. 'So how old are you, rabbi?'

'Twenty-seven.'

'So what is the difference, tell me, between twenty-seven and thirty-two? My own wife is seven years older than me. So what did I suffer?—Nothing. If Rothschild's daughter wants to marry you, would you say on account her age, no?'

'Yes,' Leo said dryly.

Salzman shook off the no in the yes. 'Five years don't mean a thing. I give you my word that when you will live with her for one week you will forget her age. What does it mean five years—that she lived more and knows more than somebody who is younger? On this girl, God bless her, years are not wasted. Each one that it comes makes better the bargain.'

'What subject does she teach in high school?'

'Languages. If you heard the way she speaks French, you will think it is music. I am in the business twenty-five years, and I recommend her with my whole heart. Believe me, I know what I'm talking, rabbi.'

'What's on the next card?' Leo said abruptly.

Salzman reluctantly turned up the third card:

'Ruth K. Nineteen years. Honour student. Father offers thirteen thousand cash to the right bridegroom. He is a medical doctor. Stomach specialist with marvellous practice. Brother-in-law owns own garment business. Particular people.'

Salzman looked as if he had read his trump card.

'Did you say nineteen?' Leo asked with interest.

'On the dot.'

'Is she attractive?' He blushed. 'Pretty?'

Salzman kissed his finger tips. 'A little doll. On this I give you my word. Let me call the father tonight and you will see what means pretty.'

But Leo was troubled. 'You're sure she's that young?'

'This I am positive. The father will show you the birth certificate.'

'Are you positive there isn't something wrong with her?' Leo insisted.

'Who says there is wrong?'

'I don't understand why an American girl her age should go to a marriage broker.'

A smile spread over Salzman's face.

'So for the same reason you went, she comes.'

Leo flushed. 'I am pressed for time.'

Salzman, realizing he had been tactless, quickly explained. 'The father came, not her. He wants she should have the best, so he looks around himself. When we will locate the right boy he will introduce him and encourage. This makes a better marriage than if a young girl without experience takes for herself. I don't have to tell you this.'

'But don't you think this young girl believes in love?' Leo spoke uneasily.

Salzman was about to guffaw but caught himself and said soberly, 'Love comes with the right person, not before.'

Leo parted dry lips but did not speak. Noticing that Salzman had snatched a glance at the next card, he cleverly asked, 'How is her health?'

'Perfect,' Salzman said, breathing with difficulty. 'Of course, she is a little lame on her right foot from an auto accident that it happened to her when she was twelve years, but nobody notices on account she is so brilliant and also beautiful.'

Leo got up heavily and went to the window. He felt curiously bitter and upbraided himself for having called in the marriage broker. Finally, he shook his head.

'Why not?' Salzman persisted, the pitch of his voice rising.

'Because I detest stomach specialists.'

'So what do you care what is his business? After you marry her do you need him? Who says he must come every Friday night in your house?'

Ashamed of the way the talk was going, Leo dismissed Salzman, who went home with heavy, melancholy eyes.

Though he had felt only relief at the marriage broker's departure, Leo was in low spirits the next day. He explained it as arising from Salzman's failure to produce a suitable bride for him. He did not care for his type of clientele. But when Leo found himself hesitating whether to seek out another matchmaker, one more polished than Pinye, he wondered if it could be—his protestations to the contrary, and although he honoured his father and mother—that he did not, in essence, care for the matchmaking institution? This thought he quickly put out of his mind yet found himself still upset. All day he ran around in the woods—missed an important appointment, forgot to give out his laundry, walked out of a Broadway cafeteria without paying and had to run back with the ticket in his hand; had even not recognized his landlady in the street when she passed with a friend and courteously called out, 'A good evening to you, Doctor Finkle.' By nightfall, however, he had regained sufficient calm to sink his nose into a book and there found peace from his thoughts.

Almost at once there came a knock on the door. Before Leo could say enter, Salzman, commercial cupid, was standing in the room. His face was grey and meagre, his expression hungry, and he looked as if he would expire on his feet. Yet the marriage broker managed, by some trick of the muscles, to display a broad smile.

'So good evening. I am invited?'

Leo nodded, disturbed to see him again, yet unwilling to ask the man to leave.

Beaming still, Salzman laid his portfolio on the table. 'Rabbi, I got for you tonight good news.'

'I've asked you not to call me rabbi. I'm still a student.'

'Your worries are finished. I have for you a first-class bride.'

'Leave me in peace concerning this subject.' Leo pretended lack of interest.

'The world will dance at your wedding.'

'Please, Mr Salzman, no more.'

'But first must come back my strength,' Salzman said weakly. He fumbled with the portfolio straps and took out of the leather case an oily paper bag, from which he extracted a hard, seeded roll and a small, smoked white fish. With a quick motion of his hand he stripped the fish out of its skin and began ravenously to chew. 'All day in a rush,' he muttered.

Leo watched him eat.

'A sliced tomato you have maybe?' Salzman hesitantly inquired.

'No.'

The marriage broker shut his eyes and ate. When he had finished he carefully cleaned up the crumbs and rolled up the remains of the fish, in the paper bag. His spectacled eyes roamed the room until he discovered, amid some piles of books, a one-burner gas stove. Lifting his hat he humbly asked, 'A glass tea you got, rabbi?'

Conscience-stricken, Leo rose and brewed the tea. He served it with a chunk of lemon and two cubes of lump sugar, delighting Salzman.

After he had drunk his tea, Salzman's strength and good spirits were restored.

'So tell me, rabbi,' he said amiably, 'you considered some more the three clients I mentioned yesterday?'

'There was no need to consider.'

'Why not?'

'None of them suits me.'

'What then suits you?'

Leo let it pass because he could give only a confused answer.

Without waiting for a reply, Salzman asked, 'You remember this girl I talked to you—the high school teacher?'

'Age thirty-two?'

But, surprisingly, Salzman's face lit in a smile. 'Age twenty-nine.'

Leo shot him a look. 'Reduced from thirty-two?'

'A mistake,' Salzman avowed. 'I talked today with the dentist. He took me to his safety deposit box and showed me the birth certificate. She was twenty-nine years last August. They made her a party in the mountains where she went for her vacation. When her father spoke to me the first time I forgot to write the age and I told you thirty-two, but now I remember this was a different client, a widow.'

'The same one you told me about? I thought she was twenty-four?'

'A different. Am I responsible that the world is filled with widows?'

'No, but I'm not interested in them, nor for that matter, in school teachers.'

Salzman pulled his clasped hands to his breast. Looking at the ceiling he devoutly exclaimed, 'Yiddishe kinder, what can I say to somebody that he is not interested in high-school teachers? So what then you are interested?'

Leo flushed but controlled himself.

'In what else will you be interested,' Salzman went on, 'if you not interested in this fine girl that she speaks four languages and has personally in the bank ten thousand dollars? Also her father guarantees further twelve thousand. Also she has a new car, wonderful clothes, talks on all subjects, and she will give you a first-class home and children. How near do we come in our life to paradise?'

'If she's so wonderful, why wasn't she married ten years ago?'

'Why?' said Salzman with a heavy laugh. '—Why? Because she is *partikiler*. This is why. She wants the *best*.'

Leo was silent, amused at how he had entangled himself. But Salzman had aroused his interest in Lily H., and he began seriously to consider calling on her. When the marriage broker observed how intently Leo's mind was at work on the facts he had supplied, he felt certain they would soon come to an agreement.

Late Saturday afternoon, conscious of Salzman, Leo Finkle walked with Lily Hirschorn along Riverside Drive. He walked briskly and erectly, wearing with distinction the black fedora he had that morning taken with trepidation out of the dusty hat box on his closet shelf, and the heavy black Saturday coat he had thoroughly whisked clean. Leo also owned a walking stick, a present from a distant relative, but quickly put temptation aside and did not use it. Lily, petite and not unpretty, had on something signifying the approach of spring. She was au courant, animatedly, with all sorts of subjects, and he weighed her words and found her surprisingly sound—score another for Salzman, whom he uneasily sensed to be somewhere around, hiding perhaps high in a tree along the street, flashing the lady signals with a pocket mirror; or perhaps a cloven-hoofed Pan, piping nuptial ditties as he danced his invisible way before them, strewing wild buds on the walk and purple grapes in their path, symbolizing fruit of a union, though there was of course still none.

Lily startled Leo by remarking, 'I was thinking of Mr Salzman, a curious figure, wouldn't you say?'

Not certain what to answer, he nodded.

She bravely went on, blushing, 'I for one am grateful for his introducing us. Aren't you?'

He courteously replied, 'I am.'

'I mean,' she said with a little laugh—and it was all in good taste, or at least gave the effect of being not in bad—'do you mind that we came together so?'

He was not displeased with her honesty, recognizing that she meant to set the relationship aright, and understanding that it took a certain amount of experience in life, and courage, to want to do it quite that way. One had to have some sort of past to make that kind of beginning.

He said that he did not mind. Salzman's function was traditional and honourable—valuable for what it might achieve, which, he pointed out, was frequently nothing.

Lily agreed with a sigh. They walked on for a while and she said after a long silence, again with a nervous laugh, 'Would you mind if I asked you something a little bit personal? Frankly, I find the subject fascinating.' Although Leo shrugged, she went on half embarrassedly, 'How was it that you came to your calling? I mean was it a sudden passionate inspiration?'

Leo after a time, slowly replied, 'I was always interested in the Law.'

'You saw revealed in it the presence of the Highest?'

He nodded and changed the subject. 'I understand that you spent a little time in Paris, Miss Hirschorn?'

'Oh, did Mr Salzman tell you, Rabbi Finkle?' Leo winced but she went on, 'It was ages ago and almost forgotten. I remember I had to return for my sister's wedding.'

And Lily would not be put off. 'When', she asked in a trembly voice, 'did you become enamoured of God?'

He stared at her. Then it came to him that she was talking not about Leo Finkle, but of a total stranger, some mystical figure, perhaps even passionate prophet that Salzman had dreamed up for her—no relation to the living or dead. Leo trembled with rage and weakness. The trickster had obviously sold her a bill of goods, just as he had him, who'd expected to become acquainted with a young lady of twenty-nine, only to behold, the moment he laid eyes upon her strained and anxious face, a woman past thirty-five and aging rapidly. Only his self-control had kept him this long in her presence.

'I am not', he said gravely, 'a talented religious person,' and in seeking words to go on, found himself possessed by shame and fear. 'I think', he said in a strained manner, 'that I came to God not because I loved Him, but because I did not.'

This confession he spoke harshly because its unexpectedness shook him.

Lily wilted. Leo saw a profusion of loaves of bread go flying like ducks high over his head, not unlike the winged loaves by which he had counted himself to sleep last night. Mercifully, then, it snowed, which he would not put past Salzman's machinations.

He was infuriated with the marriage broker and swore he would throw him out of the room the minute he reappeared. But Salzman did not come that night, and when Leo's anger had subsided, an unaccountable despair grew in its place. At first he thought this was caused by his disappointment in Lily, but before long it became evident that he had involved himself with Salzman without a true knowledge of his own intent. He gradually realized—with an emptiness that seized him with six hands—that he had called in the broker to find him a bride because he was incapable of doing it himself. This terrifying insight he had derived as a result of his meeting and conversation with Lily Hirschorn. Her probing questions had somehow irritated him into revealing—to himself more than her—the true nature of his relationship to God, and from that it had come upon him, with shocking force, that apart from his parents, he had never loved anyone. Or perhaps it went the other way, that he did not love God so well as he might, because he had not loved man. It seemed to Leo that his whole life stood starkly revealed and he saw himself for the first time as he truly was—unloved and loveless. This bitter but somehow not fully unexpected revelation brought him to a point of panic, controlled only by extraordinary effort. He covered his face with his hands and cried.

The week that followed was the worst of his life. He did not eat and lost weight. His beard darkened and grew ragged. He stopped attending seminars and almost never opened a book. He seriously considered leaving the Yeshivah, although he was deeply troubled at the thought of the loss of all his years of study—saw them like pages torn from a book, strewn over the city—and at the devastating effect of this decision upon his parents. But he had lived without knowledge of himself, and never in the Five Books and all the Commentaries—mea culpa—had the truth been revealed to him. He did not know where to turn, and in all this desolating loneliness there was no *to whom*, although he often thought of Lily but not once could bring himself to go downstairs and make the call. He became touchy and irritable, especially with his landlady, who asked him all manner of personal questions; on the other hand, sensing his own disagreeableness, he waylaid her on the stairs and apologized abjectly, until mortified, she ran from him. Out of this, however, he drew the consolation that he was a Jew and that a Jew suffered. But gradually, as the long and terrible week drew to a close, he regained his composure and some idea of purpose in life: to go on as planned. Although he was imperfect, the ideal was not. As for his quest of a bride, the thought of continuing afflicted him with anxiety and heartburn, yet perhaps with this new knowledge of himself he would be more successful than in the past. Perhaps love would now come to him and a bride to that love. And for this sanctified seeking who needed a Salzman?

The marriage broker, a skeleton with haunted eyes, returned that very night. He looked, withal, the picture of frustrated expectancy—as if he had steadfastly waited the week at Miss Lily Hirschorn's side for a telephone call that never came.

Casually coughing, Salzman came immediately to the point: 'So how did you like her?'

Leo's anger rose and he could not refrain from chiding the matchmaker: 'Why did you lie to me, Salzman?'

Salzman's pale face went dead white, the world had snowed on him.

'Did you not state that she was twenty-nine?' Leo insisted.

'I give you my word—'

'She was thirty-five, if a day. At *least* thirty-five.'

'Of this don't be too sure. Her father told me—'

'Never mind. The worst of it was that you lied to her.'

'How did I lie to her, tell me?'

'You told her things about me that weren't true. You made me out to be more, consequently less than I am. She had in mind a totally different person, a sort of semi-mystical Wonder Rabbi.'

'All I said, you was a religious man.'

'I can imagine.'

Salzman sighed. 'This is my weakness that I have,' he confessed. 'My wife says to me I shouldn't be a salesman, but when I have two fine people that they would be wonderful to be married, I am so happy that I talk too much.' He smiled wanly. 'This is why Salzman is a poor man.'

Leo's anger left him. 'Well, Salzman, I'm afraid that's all.'

The marriage broker fastened hungry eyes on him.

'You don't want any more a bride?'

'I do,' said Leo, 'but I have decided to seek her in a different way. I am no longer interested in an arranged marriage. To be frank, I now admit the necessity of premarital love. That is, I want to be in love with the one I marry.'

'Love?' said Salzman, astounded. After a moment he remarked, 'For us, our love is our life, not for the ladies. In the ghetto they——'

'I know, I know,' said Leo. 'I've thought of it often. Love, I have said to myself, should be a by-product of living and worship rather than its own end. Yet for myself I find it necessary to establish the level of my need and fulfill it.'

Salzman shrugged but answered, 'Listen, rabbi, if you want love, this I can find for you also. I have such beautiful clients that you will love them the minute your eyes will see them.'

Leo smiled unhappily. 'I'm afraid you don't understand.'

But Salzman hastily unstrapped his portfolio and withdrew a manila packet from it.

'Pictures,' he said, quickly laying the envelope on the table.

Leo called after him to take the pictures away, but as if on the wings of the wind, Salzman had disappeared.

March came. Leo had returned to his regular routine. Although he felt not quite himself yet—lacked energy—he was making plans for a more active social life. Of course it would cost something, but he was an expert in cutting corners; and when there were no corners left he would make circles rounder. All the while Salzman's pictures had lain on the table, gathering dust. Occasionally as Leo sat studying, or enjoying a cup of tea, his eyes fell on the manila envelope, but he never opened it.

The days went by and no social life to speak of developed with a member of the opposite sex—it was difficult, given the circumstances of his situation. One morning Leo toiled up the stairs to his room and stared out the window at the city. Although the day was bright his view of it was dark. For some time he watched the people in the street below hurrying along and then turned with a heavy heart to his little room. On the table was the packet. With a sudden relentless gesture he tore it open. For a half-hour he stood by the table in a state of excitement, examining the photographs of the ladies Salzman had included. Finally, with a deep sigh he put them down. There were six, of varying degrees of attractiveness, but look at them long enough and they all became Lily Hirschorn: all past their prime, all starved behind bright smiles, not a true personality in the lot. Life, despite their frantic yoohooings, had passed them by; they were pictures in a brief case that stank of fish. After a while, however, as Leo attempted to return the photographs into the envelope, he found in it another, a snapshot of the type taken by a machine for a quarter. He gazed at it a moment and let out a cry.

Her face moved him. Why, he could at first not say. It gave him the impression of youth—spring flowers, yet age—a sense of having been used to the bone, wasted; this came from the eyes, which were hauntingly familiar, yet absolutely strange. He had a vivid impression that he had met her before, but try as he might he could not place her although he could almost recall her name, as if he had read it in her own handwriting. No, this couldn't be; he would have remembered her. It was not, he affirmed, that she had an extraordinary beauty—no, though her face was attractive enough; it was that *something* about her moved him. Feature for feature, even some of the ladies of the photographs could do better; but she leaped forth to his heart—had *lived,* or wanted to—more than just wanted, perhaps regretted how she had lived—had somehow deeply suffered: it could be seen in the depths of those reluctant eyes, and from the way the light enclosed and shone from her, and within her, opening realms of possibility: this was her own. Her he desired. His head ached and eyes narrowed with the intensity of his gazing, then as if an obscure fog had blown up in the mind, he experienced fear of her and was aware that he had received an impression, somehow, of evil. He shuddered, saying softly, it is thus with us all. Leo brewed some tea in a small pot and sat sipping it without sugar, to calm himself. But before he had finished drinking, again with excitement he examined the face and found it good: good for Leo Finkle. Only such a one could understand him and help him seek whatever he was seeking. She might, perhaps, love him. How she had happened to be among the discards in Salzman's barrel he could never guess, but he knew he must urgently go find her.

Leo rushed downstairs, grabbed up the Bronx telephone book, and searched for Salzman's home address. He was not listed, nor was his office. Neither was he in the Manhattan book. But Leo remembered having written down the address on a slip of paper after he had read Salzman's advertisement in the 'personals' column of the *Forward.* He ran up to his room and tore through his papers, without luck. It was exasperating. Just when he needed the matchmaker he was nowhere to be found. Fortunately Leo remembered to look in his wallet. There on a card he found his name written and a Bronx address. No phone number was listed, the reason—Leo now recalled—he had originally communicated with Salzman by letter. He got on his coat, put a hat on over his skull cap and hurried to the subway station. All the way to the far end of the Bronx he sat on the edge of his seat. He was more than once tempted to take out the picture and see if the girl's face was as he remembered it, but he refrained, allowing the snapshot to remain in his inside coat pocket, content to have her so close. When the train pulled into the station he was waiting at the door and bolted out. He quickly located the street Salzman had advertised.

The building he sought was less than a block from the subway, but it was not an office building, nor even a loft, nor a store in which one could rent office space. It was a very old tenement house. Leo found Salzman's name in pencil on a soiled tag under the bell and climbed three dark flights to his apartment. When he knocked, the door was opened by a thin, asthmatic, grey-haired woman, in felt slippers.

'Yes?' she said, expecting nothing. She listened without listening. He could have sworn he had seen her, too, before but knew it was an illusion.

'Salzman—does he live here? Pinye Salzman,' he said, 'the matchmaker?'

She stared at him a long minute. 'Of course.'

He felt embarrassed. 'Is he in?'

'No.' Her mouth, though left open, offered nothing more.

'The matter is urgent. Can you tell me where his office is?'

'In the air.' She pointed upward.

'You mean he has no office?' Leo asked.

'In his socks.'

He peered into the apartment. It was sunless and dingy, one large room divided by a half-open curtain, beyond which he could see a sagging metal bed. The near side of a room was crowded with rickety chairs, old bureaus, a three-legged table, racks of cooking utensils, and all the apparatus of a kitchen. But there was no sign of Salzman or his magic barrel, probably also a figment of the imagination. An odour of frying fish made Leo weak to the knees.

'Where is he?' he insisted. 'I've got to see your husband.'

At length she answered, 'So who knows where he is? Every time he thinks a new thought he runs to a different place. Go home, he will find you.'

'Tell him Leo Finkle.'

She gave no sign she had heard.

He walked downstairs, depressed.

But Salzman, breathless, stood waiting at his door.

Leo was astounded and overjoyed. 'How did you get here before me?'

'I rushed.'

'Come inside.'

They entered. Leo fixed tea, and a sardine sandwich for Salzman. As they were drinking he reached behind him for the packet of pictures and handed them to the marriage broker.

Salzman put down his glass and said expectantly, 'You found somebody you like?'

'Not among these.'

The marriage broker turned away.

'Here is the one I want.' Leo held forth the snapshot.

Salzman slipped on his glasses and took the picture into his trembling hand. He turned ghastly and let out a groan.

'What's the matter?' cried Leo.

'Excuse me. Was an accident this picture. She isn't for you.'

Salzman frantically shoved the manila packet into his portfolio. He thrust the snapshot into his pocket and fled down the stairs.

Leo, after momentary paralysis, gave chase and cornered the marriage broker in the vestibule. The landlady made hysterical outcries but neither of them listened.

'Give me back the picture, Salzman.'

'No.' The pain in his eyes was terrible.

'Tell me who she is then.'

'This I can't tell you. Excuse me.'

He made to depart, but Leo, forgetting himself, seized the matchmaker by his tight coat and shook him frenziedly.

'Please,' sighed Salzman. '*Please.*'

Leo ashamedly let him go. 'Tell me who she is,' he begged. 'It's very important for me to know.'

'She is not for you. She is a wild one—wild, without shame. This is not a bride for a rabbi.'

'What do you mean wild?'

'Like an animal. Like a dog. For her to be poor was a sin. This is why to me she is dead now.'

'In God's name, what do you mean?'

'Her I can't introduce to you,' Salzman cried.

'Why are you so excited?'

'Why, he asks,' Salzman said, bursting into tears. 'This is my baby, my Stella, she should burn in hell.'

Leo hurried up to bed and hid under the covers. Under the covers he thought his life through. Although he soon fell asleep he could not sleep her out of his mind. He woke, beating his breast. Though he prayed to be rid of her, his prayers went unanswered. Through days of torment he endlessly struggled not to love her; fearing success, he escaped it. He then concluded to convert her to goodness, himself to God. The idea alternately nauseated and exalted him.

He perhaps did not know that he had come to a final decision until he encountered Salzman in a Broadway cafeteria. He was sitting alone at a rear table, sucking the bony remains of a fish. The marriage broker appeared haggard, and transparent to the point of vanishing.

Salzman looked up at first without recognizing him. Leo had grown a pointed beard and his eyes were weighted with wisdom.

'Salzman,' he said, 'love has at last come to my heart.'

'Who can love from a picture?' mocked the marriage broker.

'It is not impossible.'

'If you can love her, than you can love anybody. Let me show you some new clients that they just sent me their photographs. One is a little doll.'

'Just her I want,' Leo murmured.

'Don't be a fool, doctor. Don't bother with her.'

'Put me in touch with her, Salzman,' Leo said humbly. 'Perhaps I can be of service.'

Salzman had stopped eating and Leo understood with emotion that it was now arranged.

Leaving the cafeteria, he was, however, afflicted by a tormenting suspicion that Salzman had planned it all to happen this way.

Leo was informed by letter that she would meet him on a certain corner, and she was there one spring night, waiting under a street lamp. He appeared, carrying a small bouquet of violets and rosebuds. Stella stood by the lamp post, smoking. She wore white with red shoes, which fitted his expectations, although in a troubled moment he had imagined the dress red, and only the shoes white. She waited uneasily and shyly. From afar he saw that her eyes—clearly her father's—were filled with desperate innocence. He pictured, in her, his own redemption. Violins and lit candles revolved in the sky. Leo ran forward with flowers outthrust.

Around the corner, Salzman, leaning against a wall, chanted prayers for the dead.

1954

Doris Lessing
b. 1919

Doris Taylor was born in Kermanshah, Persia (now Iran), where her father held a managerial post in the Imperial Bank of Persia. He was an Englishman who had lost a leg in the Great War and married his nurse. In 1925 the family moved to southern Rhodesia (now Zimbabwe), where Alfred Taylor got a loan from the government land bank to buy 3,000 acres of land recently taken away from Africans, who had been put onto reservations. With cheap native labour the Taylors raised corn on the land but never made enough money to get off it. Doris Taylor went to a Catholic convent school and Girls' High School in the small city of Salisbury, leaving school at fourteen and working as a nursemaid and then as a secretary. She was married twice (acquiring the name of Lessing), but left Rhodesia for England with her youngest child in 1949, after the breakup of her second marriage. She had been writing for some time, producing some stories and the manuscript for her first novel, *The Grass Is Singing* (1950). In England, she joined the Communist Party briefly and began her five-volume sequence of autobiographical novels, *Children of Violence*. Her most ambitious book, *The Golden Notebook* (1962), is considered one of the key texts of the feminist movement in the 1960s. Her concern with the future led her to write science fiction, including the ambitious series *Canopus in Argos: Archives* (1979–83). She has also completed two volumes of autobiography, *Under My Skin* (1994) and *Waiting in the Shade: 1949–1962* (1997), and won the Nobel Prize for Literature in 2007.

'Sunrise on the Veld' recounts the joys of a fifteen-year-old boy as he awakens to the delights—and the horrors—of a new morning on the veld.

A Sunrise on the Veld

Every night that winter he said aloud into the dark of the pillow: Half-past four! Half-past four! till he felt his brain had gripped the words and held them fast. Then he fell asleep at once, as if a shutter had fallen; and lay with his face turned to the clock so that he could see it first thing when he woke.

It was half-past four to the minute, every morning. Triumphantly pressing down the alarm-knob of the clock, which the dark of his mind had outwitted, remaining vigilant all night and counting the hours as he lay relaxed in sleep, he huddled down for a last warm moment under the clothes, playing with the idea of lying abed for this once only. But he played with it for the fun of knowing that it was a weakness he could defeat without effort; just as he set the alarm each night for the delight of the moment when he woke and stretched his limbs, feeling the muscles tighten, and thought: Even my brain—even that! I can control every part of myself.

Luxury of warm rested body, with the arms and legs and fingers waiting like soldiers for a word of command! Joy of knowing that the precious hours were given to sleep voluntarily!—for he had once stayed awake three nights running, to prove that he could, and then worked all day, refusing to admit that he was tired; and now sleep seemed to him a servant to be commanded and refused.

The boy stretched his frame full-length, touching the wall at his head with his hands, and the bedfoot with his toes; then he sprang out, like a fish leaping from water. And it was cold, cold.

He always dressed rapidly, so as to try and conserve his night-warmth till the sun rose two hours later; but by the time he had on his clothes his hands were numbed and he could scarcely hold his shoes. These he could not put on for fear of waking his parents, who never came to know how early he rose.

As soon as he stepped over the lintel, the flesh of his soles contracted on the chilled earth, and his legs began to ache with cold. It was night: the stars were glittering, the trees standing black and still. He looked for signs of day, for the greying of the edge of a stone, or a lightening in the sky where the sun would rise, but there was nothing yet. Alert as an animal he crept past the dangerous window, standing poised with his hand on the sill for one proudly fastidious moment, looking in at the stuffy blackness of the room where his parents lay.

Feeling for the grass-edge of the path with his toes, he reached inside another window further along the wall, where his gun had been set in readiness the night before. The steel was icy, and numbed fingers slipped along it, so that he had to hold it in the crook of his arm for safety. Then he tiptoed to the room where the dogs slept, and was fearful that they might have been tempted to go before him; but they were waiting, their haunches crouched in reluctance at the cold, but ears and swinging tails greeting the gun ecstatically. His warning undertone kept them secret and silent till the house was a hundred yards back: then they bolted off into the bush, yelping excitedly. The boy imagined his parents turning in their beds and muttering: Those dogs again! before they were dragged back in sleep; and he smiled scornfully. He always looked back over his shoulder at the house before he passed a wall of trees that shut it from sight. It looked so low and small, crouching there under a tall and brilliant sky. Then he turned his back on it, and on the frowsting sleepers, and forgot them.

He would have to hurry. Before the light grew strong he must be four miles away; and already a tint of green stood in the hollow of a leaf, and the air smelled of morning and the stars were dimming.

He slung the shoes over his shoulder, veld *skoen*[1] that were crinkled and hard with the dews of a hundred mornings. They would be necessary when the ground became too hot to bear. Now he felt the chilled dust push up between his toes, and he let the muscles of his feet spread and settle into the shapes of the earth; and he thought: I could walk a hundred miles on feet like these! I could walk all day, and never tire!

He was walking swiftly through the dark tunnel of foliage that in daytime was a road. The dogs were invisibly ranging the lower travelways of the bush, and he heard them panting. Sometimes he felt a cold muzzle on his leg before they were off again, scouting for a trail to follow. They were not trained, but free-running companions of the hunt, who often tired of the long stalk before the final shots, and went off on their own pleasure. Soon he could see them, small and wild-looking in a wild strange light, now that the bush stood trembling on the verge of colour, waiting for the sun to paint earth and grass afresh.

The grass stood to his shoulders; and the trees were showering a faint silver rain. He was soaked; his whole body was clenched in a steady river.

Once he bent to the road that was newly scored with animal trails, and regretfully straightened, reminding himself that the pleasure of tracking must wait till another day.

He began to run along the edge of a field, noting jerkily how it was filmed over with fresh spiderweb, so that the long reaches of great black clods seemed netted in glistening grey. He was using the steady lope he had learned by watching the natives, the run that is a dropping of the weight of the body from one foot to the next in a slow balancing movement that never tires, nor shortens the breath; and he felt the blood pulsing down his legs and along his arms, and the exultation and pride of body mounted in him till he was shutting his teeth hard against a violent desire to shout his triumph.

Soon he had left the cultivated part of the farm. Behind him the bush was low and black. In front was a long *vlei*,[2] acres of long grass that sent back a hollowing gleam of light to a satiny sky. Near him thick swathes of grass were bent with the weight of water, and diamond drops sparkled on each frond.

The first bird woke at his feet and at once a flock of them sprang into the air calling shrilly that day had come; and suddenly, behind him, the bush woke into song, and he could hear the guinea fowl calling far ahead of him. That meant they would now be sailing down from their trees into thick grass, and it was for them he had come: he was too late. But he did not mind. He forgot he had come to shoot. He set his legs wide, and balanced from foot to foot, and swung his gun up and down in both hands horizontally, in kind of improvised exercise, and let his head sink back till it was pillowed in his neck muscles, and watched how above him small rosy clouds floated in a lake of gold.

Suddenly it all rose in him: it was unbearable. He leapt up into the air, shouting and yelling wild, unrecognizable noises. Then he began to run, not carefully, as he had before, but madly, like a wild thing. He was clean crazy, yelling mad with the joy of living and a superfluity of youth. He rushed down the *vlei* under a tumult of crimson and gold, while all the birds of the world sang about him. He ran in great leaping strides,

1 Afrikaans for 'shoes'
2 a low-lying marshy ground, covered with water during the rainy season

and shouted as he ran, feeling his body rise into the crisp rushing air and fall back surely on to sure feet; and thought briefly, not believing that such a thing could happen to him, that he could break his ankle any moment, in this thick tangled grass. He cleared bushes like a *duiker*,[3] leapt over rocks; and finally came to a dead stop at a place where the ground fell abruptly away below him to the river. It had been a two-mile-long dash through waist-high growth, and he was breathing hoarsely and could no longer sing. But he poised on a rock and looked down at stretches of water that gleamed through stooping trees, and thought suddenly, I am fifteen! Fifteen! The words came new to him; so that he kept repeating them wonderingly, with swelling excitement; and he felt the years of his life with his hands, as if he were counting marbles, each one hard and separate and compact, each one a wonderful shining thing. That was what he was: fifteen years of this rich soil, and this slow-moving water, and air that smelt like a challenge whether it was warm and sultry at noon, or as brisk as cold water, like it was now.

There was nothing he couldn't do, nothing! A vision came to him, as he stood there, like when a child hears the word 'eternity' and tries to understand it, and time takes possession of the mind. He felt his life ahead of him as a great and wonderful thing, something that was his; and he said aloud, with the blood rising to his head: all the great men of the world have been as I am now, and there is nothing I can't become, nothing I can't do; there is no country in the world I cannot make part of myself, if I choose. I contain the world. I can make of it what I want. If I choose, I can change everything that is going to happen: it depends on me, and what I decide now.

The urgency, and the truth and the courage of what his voice was saying exulted him so that he began to sing again, at the top of his voice, and the sound went echoing down the river gorge. He stopped for the echo, and sang again: stopped and shouted. That was what he was!—he sang, if he chose; and the world had to answer him.

And for minutes he stood there, shouting and singing and waiting for the lovely eddying sound of the echo; so that his own new strong thoughts came back and washed round his head, as if someone were answering him and encouraging him; till the gorge was full of soft voices clashing back and forth from rock to rock over the river. And then it seemed as if there was a new voice. He listened, puzzled, for it was not his own. Soon he was leaning forward, all his nerves alert, quite still: somewhere close to him there was a noise that was no joyful bird, nor tinkle of falling water, nor ponderous movement of cattle.

There it was again. In the deep morning hush that held his future and his past, was a sound of pain, and repeated over and over: it was a kind of shortened scream, as if someone, something, had no breath to scream. He came to himself, looked about him, and called for the dogs. They did not appear: they had gone off on their own business, and he was alone. Now he was clean sober, all the madness gone. His heart beating fast, because of that frightened screaming, he stepped carefully off the rock and went towards a belt of trees. He was moving cautiously, for not so long ago he had seen a leopard in just this spot.

At the edge of the trees he stopped and peered, holding his gun ready; he advanced, looking steadily about him, his eyes narrowed. Then, all at once, in the middle of a step,

---

3 a small antelope found in southern Africa

he faltered, and his face was puzzled. He shook his head impatiently, as if he doubted his own sight.

There, between two trees, against a background of gaunt black rocks, was a figure from a dream, a strange beast that was horned and drunken-legged, but like something he had never even imagined. It seemed to be ragged. It looked like a small buck that had black ragged tufts of fur standing up irregularly all over it, with patches of raw flesh beneath . . . but the patches of rawness were disappearing under moving black and came again elsewhere; and all the time the creature screamed, in small gasping screams, and leaped drunkenly from side to side, as if it were blind.

Then the boy understood: it *was* a buck. He ran closer, and again stood still, stopped by a new fear. Around him the grass was whispering and alive. He looked wildly about, and then down. The ground was black with ants, great energetic ants that took no notice of him, but hurried and scurried towards the fighting shape, like glistening black water flowing through the grass.

And, as he drew in his breath and pity and terror seized him, the beast fell and the screaming stopped. Now he could hear nothing but one bird singing, and the sound of the rustling, whispering ants.

He peered over at the writhing blackness that jerked convulsively with the jerking nerves. It grew quieter. There were small twitches from the mass that still looked vaguely like the shape of a small animal.

It came into his mind that he should shoot it and end its pain; and he raised the gun. Then he lowered it again. The buck could no longer feel; its fighting was a mechanical protest of the nerves. But it was not that which made him put down the gun. It was a swelling feeling of rage and misery and protest that expressed itself in the thought: if I had not come it would have died like this: so why should I interfere? All over the bush things like this happen; they happen all the time; this is how life goes on, by living things dying in anguish. He gripped the gun between his knees and felt in his own limbs the myriad swarming pain of the twitching animal that could no longer feel, and set his teeth, and said over and over again under his breath: I can't stop it. I can't stop it. There is nothing I can do.

He was glad that the buck was unconscious and had gone past suffering so that he did not have to make a decision to kill it even when he was feeling with his whole body: this is what happens, this is how things work.

It was right—that was what he was feeling. *It was right and nothing could alter it.*

The knowledge of fatality, of what has to be, had gripped him and for the first time in his life; and he was left unable to make any movement of brain or body, except to say: 'Yes, yes. That is what living is.' It had entered his flesh and his bones and grown in to the furthest corners of his brain and would never leave him. And at that moment he could not have performed the smallest action of mercy, knowing as he did, having lived on it all his life, the vast unalterable, cruel veld, where at any moment one might stumble over a skull or crush the skeleton of some small creature.

Suffering, sick, and angry, but also grimly satisfied with his new stoicism, he stood there leaning on his rifle, and watched the seething black mound grow smaller. At his feet, now, were ants trickling back with pink fragments in their mouths, and there was a fresh acid smell in his nostrils. He sternly controlled the uselessly convulsing muscles of his empty stomach, and reminded himself: the ants must eat too! At the same time he found that the tears were streaming down his face, and his clothes were soaked with the sweat of that other creature's pain.

The shape had grown small. Now it looked like nothing recognizable. He did not know how long it was before he saw the blackness thin, and bits of white showed through, shining in the sun—yes, there was the sun, just up, glowing over the rocks. Why, the whole thing could not have taken longer than a few minutes.

He began to swear, as if the shortness of the time was in itself unbearable, using the words he had heard his father say. He strode forward, crushing ants with each step, and brushing them off his clothes, till he stood above the skeleton, which lay sprawled under a small bush. It was clean-picked. It might have been lying there years, save that on the white bone were pink fragments of gristle. About the bones ants were ebbing away, their pincers full of meat.

The boy looked at them, big black ugly insects. A few were standing and gazing up at him with small glittering eyes.

'Go away!' he said to the ants, very coldly. 'I am not for you—not just yet, at any rate. Go away.' And he fancied that the ants turned and went away.

He bent over the bones and touched the sockets in the skull; that was where the eyes were, he thought incredulously, remembering the liquid dark eyes of a buck. And then he bent the slim foreleg bone, swinging it horizontally in his palm.

That morning, perhaps an hour ago, this small creature had been stepping proud and free through the bush, feeling the chill on its hide even as he himself had done, exhilarated by it. Proudly stepping the earth, tossing its horns, frisking a pretty white tail, it had sniffed the cold morning air. Walking like kings and conquerors it had moved through this free-held bush, where each blade of grass grew for it alone, and where the river ran pure sparkling water for its slaking.

And then—what had happened? Such a swift surefooted thing could surely not be trapped by a swarm of ants?

The boy bent curiously to the skeleton. Then he saw that the back leg that lay uppermost and strained out in the tension of death was snapped midway in the thigh, so that broken bones jutted over each other uselessly. So that was it! Limping into the ant-masses it could not escape, once it had sensed danger. Yes, but how had the leg been broken? Had it fallen, perhaps? Impossible, a buck was too light and graceful. Had some jealous rival horned it?

What could possibly have happened? Perhaps some Africans had thrown stones at it, as they do, trying to kill it for meat, and had broken its leg. Yes, that must be it.

Even as he imagined the crowd of running, shouting natives, and the flying stones, and the leaping buck, another picture came into his mind. He saw himself, on any one of these bright ringing mornings, drunk with excitement, taking a snap shot at some half-seen buck. He saw himself with the gun lowered, wondering whether he had missed or not; and thinking at last that it was late, and he wanted his breakfast, and it was not worth while to track miles after an animal that would very likely get away from him in any case.

For a moment he would not face it. He was a small boy again, kicking sulkily at the skeleton, hanging his head, refusing to accept the responsibility.

Then he straightened up, and looked down at the bones with an odd expression of dismay, all the anger gone out of him. His mind went quite empty: all around him he could see trickles of ants disappearing into the grass. The whispering noise was faint and dry, like the rustling of a cast snakeskin.

At last he picked up his gun and walked homewards. He was telling himself half defiantly that he wanted his breakfast. He was telling himself that it was getting very hot, much too hot to be out roaming the bush.

Really, he was tired. He walked heavily, not looking where he put his feet. When he came within sight of his home he stopped, knitting his brows. There was something he had to think out. The death of that small animal was a thing that concerned him, and he was by no means finished with it. It lay at the back of his mind uncomfortably.

Soon, the very next morning, he would get clear of everybody and go to the bush and think about it.

1951

Mavis Gallant
b. 1922

Born in Montreal and educated in many schools in Canada and the eastern United States, Mavis Gallant is a distinguished journalist, novelist, dramatist, and, above all, short-story writer. She published her first two stories in 1944, the year she began work as a journalist with the *Montreal Standard*. Over the next six years she wrote more than sixty feature articles for the *Standard* before leaving, in 1950, for Europe. Since that time Paris has been her home, although she retains her Canadian citizenship.

Gallant has devoted herself primarily to the writing of fiction. Her first collection of short stories, *The Other Paris* (1959), explores the lives of exiles and expatriates; here as elsewhere in her fiction Gallant, an acute observer of social customs, examines men and women trapped in exiled lives that fail to satisfy them. She has published two novels, *Green Water, Green Sky* (1959) and *A Fairly Good Time* (1970), seven more collections of short fiction, a play (*What Is to Be Done?*, 1982), and a collection of essays and review articles, *Paris Notebooks* (1986). She is a frequent contributor to *The New Yorker*, where 'The Ice Wagon Going Down the Street' first appeared, in 1963. Her most recent collection of short fiction is *Going Ashore* (2009).

The Ice Wagon Going Down the Street

Now that they are out of world affairs and back where they started, Peter Frazier's wife says, 'Everybody else did well in the international thing except us.'

'You have to be crooked,' he tells her.

'Or smart. Pity we weren't.'

It is Sunday morning. They sit in the kitchen, drinking their coffee, slowly, remembering the past. They say the names of people as if they were magic. Peter thinks, *Agnes Brusen*, but there are hundreds of other names. As a private married joke, Peter and Sheilah wear the silk dressing gowns they bought in Hong Kong. Each thinks the other a peacock, rather splendid, but they pretend the dressing gowns are silly and worn in fun.

Peter and Sheilah and their two daughters, Sandra and Jennifer, are visiting Peter's unmarried sister, Lucille. They have been Lucille's guests seventeen weeks, ever since they returned to Toronto from the Far East. Their big old steamer trunk blocks a corner of the kitchen, making a problem of the refrigerator door; but even Lucille says the trunk may as well stay where it is, for the present. The Fraziers' future is so unsettled; everything is still in the air.

Lucille has given her bedroom to her two nieces, and sleeps on a camp cot in the hall. The parents have the living-room divan. They have no privileges here; they sleep after Lucille has seen the last television show that interests her. In the hall closet their clothes are crushed by winter overcoats. They know they are being judged for the first time. Sandra and Jennifer are waiting for Sheilah and Peter to decide. They are waiting to learn where these exotic parents will fly to next. What sort of climate will Sheilah consider? What job will Peter consent to accept? When the parents are ready, the children will make a decision of their own. It is just possible that Sandra and Jennifer will choose to stay with their aunt.

The peacock parents are watched by wrens. Lucille and her nieces are much the same—sandy-coloured, proudly plain. Neither of the girls has the father's insouciance or the mother's appearance—her height, her carriage, her thick hair, and sky-blue eyes. The children are more cautious than their parents; more Canadian. When they saw their aunt's apartment they had been away from Canada nine years, ever since they were two and four; and Jennifer, the elder, said, 'Well, now we're home.' Her voice is nasal and flat. Where did she learn that voice? And why should this be home? Peter's answer to anything about his mystifying children is, 'It must be in the blood.'

On Sunday morning Lucille takes her nieces to church. It seems to be the only condition she imposes on her relations: the children must be decent. The girls go willingly, with their new hats and purses and gloves and coral bracelets and strings of pearls. The parents, ramshackle, sleepy, dim in the brain because it is Sunday, sit down to their coffee and privacy and talk of the past.

'We weren't crooked,' says Peter. 'We weren't even smart.'

Sheilah's head bobs up; she is no drowner. It is wrong to say they have nothing to show for time. Sheilah has the Balenciaga. It is a black afternoon dress, stiff and boned at the waist, long for the fashions of now, but neither Sheilah nor Peter would change a thread. The Balenciaga is their talisman, their treasure; and after they remember it they touch hands and think that the years are not behind them but hazy and marvellous and still to be lived.

The first place they went to was Paris. In the early 'fifties the pick of the international jobs was there. Peter had inherited the last scrap of money he knew he was ever likely to see, and it was enough to get them over: Sheilah and Peter and the babies and the steamer trunk. To their joy and astonishment they had money in the bank. They said to each other, 'It should last a year.' Peter was fastidious about the new job; he hadn't come all this distance to accept just anything. In Paris he met Hugh Taylor, who was earning enough smuggling gasoline to keep his wife in Paris and a girl in Rome. That impressed Peter, because he remembered Taylor as a sour scholarship student without the slightest talent for life. Taylor had a job, of course. He hadn't said to himself, I'll go over to Europe and smuggle gasoline. It gave Peter an idea; he saw the shape of things. First you catch your fish. Later, at an international party, he met Johnny Hertzberg, who told him Germany was the place. Hertzberg said that anyone who came out of Germany broke now was too stupid to be here, and deserved to be back home at a desk. Peter nodded, as if he had already thought of that. He began to think about Germany. Paris was fine for a holiday, but it had been picked clean. Yes, Germany. His money was running low. He thought about Germany quite a lot.

That winter was moist and delicate; so fragile that they daren't speak of it now. There seemed to be plenty of everything and plenty of time. They were living the dream of marriage, the fabric uncut, nothing slashed or spoiled. All winter they spent their money, and went to parties, and talked about Peter's future job. It lasted four months. They spent their money, lived in the future, and were never as happy again.

After four months they were suddenly moved away from Paris, but not to Germany—to Geneva. Peter thinks it was because of the incident at the Trudeau wedding at the Ritz. Paul Trudeau was a French-Canadian Peter had known at school and in the Navy. Trudeau had turned into a snob, proud of his career and his Paris connections. He tried to make the difference felt, but Peter thought the difference was only for strangers. At the wedding reception Peter lay down on the floor and said he was dead. He held a white azalea in a brass pot on his chest, and sang, 'Oh, hear us when we cry to Thee for those in peril on the sea.' Sheilah bent over him and said, 'Peter, darling, get up. Pete, listen, every single person who can do something for you is in this room. If you love me, you'll get up.'

'I do love you,' he said, ready to engage in a serious conversation. 'She's so beautiful,' he told a second face. 'She's nearly as tall as I am. She was a model in London. I met her over in London in the war. I met her there in the war.' He lay on his back with the azalea on his chest, explaining their history. A waiter took the brass pot away, and after Peter had been hauled to his feet he knocked the waiter down. Trudeau's bride, who was freshly out of an Ursuline[1] convent, became hysterical; and even though Paul Trudeau and Peter were old acquaintances, Trudeau never spoke to him again. Peter says now that French-Canadians always have that bit of spite. He says Trudeau asked the Embassy to interfere. Luckily, back home there were still a few people to whom the name 'Frazier' meant something, and it was to these people that Peter appealed. He wrote letters saying that a French-Canadian combine was preventing his getting a decent job, and could anything be done? No one answered directly, but it was clear that what they settled for was exile to Geneva: a season of meditation and remorse, as he explained to Sheilah, and it was managed tactfully, through Lucille.

1 The Ursuline Sisters are an order of Catholic nuns dedicated to the education of young girls.

Lucille wrote that a friend of hers, May Fergus, now a secretary in Geneva, had heard about a job. The job was filing pictures in the information services of an international agency in the Palais des Nations. The pay was so-so, but Lucille thought Peter must be getting fed up doing nothing.

Peter often asks his sister now who put her up to it—what important person told her to write that letter suggesting Peter go to Geneva?

'Nobody,' says Lucille. 'I mean, nobody in the way *you* mean. I really did have this girlfriend working there, and I knew you must be running through your money pretty fast in Paris.'

'It must have been somebody pretty high up,' Peter says. He looks at his sister admiringly, as he has often looked at his wife.

Peter's wife had loved him in Paris. Whatever she wanted in marriage she found that winter, there. In Geneva, where Peter was a file clerk and they lived in a furnished flat, she pretended they were in Paris and life was still the same. Often, when the children were at supper, she changed as though she and Peter were dining out. She wore the Balenciaga, and put candles on the card table where she and Peter ate their meal. The neckline of the dress was soiled with make-up. Peter remembers her dabbing on the make-up with a wet sponge. He remembers her in the kitchen, in the soiled Balenciaga, patting on the make-up with a filthy sponge. Behind her, at the kitchen table, Sandra and Jennifer, in buttonless pajamas and bunny slippers, ate their supper of marmalade sandwiches and milk. When the children were asleep, the parents dined solemnly, ritually, Sheilah sitting straight as a queen.

It was a mysterious period of exile, and he had to wait for signs, or signals, to know when he was free to leave. He never saw the job any other way. He forgot he had applied for it. He thought he had been sent to Geneva because of a misdemeanour and had to wait to be released. Nobody pressed him at work. His immediate boss had resigned, and he was alone for months in a room with two desks. He read the *Herald-Tribune*, and tried to discover how things were here—how the others ran their lives on the pay they were officially getting. But it was a closed conspiracy. He was not dealing with adventurers now but civil servants waiting for pension day. No one ever answered his questions. They pretended to think his questions were a form of wit. His only solace in exile was the few happy weekends he had in the late spring and early summer. He had met another old acquaintance, Mike Burleigh. Mike was a serious liberal who had married a serious heiress. The Burleighs had two guest lists. The first was composed of stuffy people they felt obliged to entertain, while the second was made up of their real friends, the friends they wanted. The real friends strove hard to become stuffy and dull and thus achieve the first guest list, but few succeeded. Peter went on the first list straight away. Possibly Mike didn't understand, at the beginning, why Peter was pretending to be a file clerk. Peter had such an air—he might have been sent by a universal inspector to see how things in Geneva were being run.

Every Friday in May and June and part of July, the Fraziers rented a sky-blue Fiat and drove forty miles east of Geneva to the Burleighs' summer house. They brought the children, a suitcase, the childrens' tattered picture books, and a token bottle of gin.

This, in memory, is a period of water and water birds; swans, roses, and singing birds. The children were small and still belonged to them. If they remember too much, their mouths water, their stomachs hurt. Peter says, 'It was fine while it lasted.' Enough. While it lasted Sheilah and Madge Burleigh were close. They abandoned their husbands and spent long summer afternoons comparing their mothers and praising each other's skin and hair. To Madge, and not to Peter, Sheilah opened her Liverpool childhood with the words 'rat poor'. Peter heard about it later, from Mike. The women's friendship seemed to Peter a bad beginning. He trusted women but not with each other. It lasted ten weeks. One Sunday, Madge said she needed the two bedrooms the Fraziers usually occupied for a party of sociologists from Pakistan, and that was the end. In November, the Fraziers heard that the summer house had been closed, and that the Burleighs were in Geneva, in their winter flat; they gave no sign. There was no help for it, and no appeal.

Now Peter began firing letters to anyone who had ever known his late father. He was living in a mild yellow autumn. Why does he remember the streets of the city dark, and the windows everywhere black with rain? He remembers being with Sheilah and the children as if they clung together while just outside their small shelter it rained and rained. The children slept in the bedroom of the flat because the window gave on the street and they could breathe air. Peter and Sheilah had the living-room couch. Their window was not a real window but a square on a wall of cement. The flat seemed damp as a cave. Peter remembers steam in the kitchen, pools under the sink, sweat on the pipes. Water streamed on him from the children's clothes, washed and dripping overhead. The trunk, upended in the children's room, was not quite unpacked. Sheilah had not signed her name to this life; she had not given in. Once Peter heard her drop her aitches. 'You kids are lucky,' she said to the girls. 'I never 'ad so much as a sit-down meal. I ate chips out of a paper or I 'ad a butty out on the stairs.' He never asked her what a butty was. He thinks it means bread and cheese.

The day he heard 'You kids are lucky' he understood they were becoming in fact something they had only *appeared* to be until now—the shabby civil servant and his brood. If he had been European he would have ridden to work on a bicycle, in the uniform of his class and condition. He would have worn a tight coat, a turned collar, and a dirty tie. He wondered then if coming here had been a mistake, and if he should not, after all, still be in a place where his name meant something. Surely Peter Frazier should live where 'Frazier' counts? In Ontario even now when he says 'Frazier' an absent look comes over his hearer's face, as if its owner were consulting an interior guide. What is Frazier? What does it mean? Oil? Power? Politics? Wheat? Real estate? The creditors had the house sealed when Peter's father died. His aunt collapsed with a heart attack in somebody's bachelor apartment, leaving three sons and a widower to surmise they had never known her. Her will was a disappointment. None of that generation left enough. One made it: the granite Presbyterian immigrants from Scotland. Their children, a generation of daunted women and maiden men, held still. Peter's father's crowd spent: they were not afraid of their fathers, and their grandfathers were old. Peter and his sister and his cousins lived on the remains. They were left the rinds of income, of notions, and the memories of ideas rather than ideas intact. If Peter can choose his reincarnation, let him be the oppressed son of a Scottish parson. Let Peter grow up on cuffs and iron principles. Let him make the fortune! Let him flee the manse! When he was small his patrimony was squandered under his nose. He remembers people dancing in his father's house. He remembers seeing and nearly understanding adultery in a guest room, among a pile of wraps. He thought he had seen a murder; he never told. He remembers licking glasses wherever he found them—on window sills, on stairs, in the pantry. In his room he listened while Lucille read Beatrix Potter. The bad rabbit stole the carrot from the good rabbit without saying please, and downstairs was the noise of the party—the roar of the crouched lion. When his father died he saw the chairs upside down and the bailiff's chalk marks. Then the doors were sealed.

He has often tried to tell Sheilah why he cannot be defeated. He remembers his father saying, 'Nothing can touch us,' and Peter believed it and still does. It has prevented his taking his troubles too seriously. 'Nothing can be as bad as this,' he will tell himself. 'It is happening to me.' Even in Geneva, where his status was file clerk, where he sank and stopped on the level of the men who never emigrated, the men on the bicycles—even there he had a manner of strolling to work as if his office were a pastime, and his real life a secret so splendid he could share it with no one except himself.

In Geneva Peter worked for a woman—a girl. She was a Norwegian from a small town in Saskatchewan. He supposed they had been put together because they were Canadian; but they were as strange to each other as if 'Canadian' meant any number of things, or had no real meaning. Soon after Agnes Brusen came to the office she hung her framed university degree on the wall. It was one of the gritty, prideful gestures that stand for push, toil, and family sacrifice. He thought, then, that she must be one of a family of immigrants for whom education is everything. Hugh Taylor had told him that in some families the older children never marry until the youngest have finished school. Sometimes every second child is sacrificed and made to work for the education of the next born. Those who finish college spend years paying back. They are white-hot Protestants, and they live with a load of work and debt and obligation. Peter placed his new colleague on scraps of information. He had never been in the West.

She came to the office on a Monday morning in October. The office was overheated and painted cream. It contained two desks, the filing cabinets, a map of the world as it had been in 1945, and the Charter of the United Nations left behind by Agnes Brusen's predecessor. (She took down the Charter without asking Peter if he minded, with the impudence of gesture you find in women who wouldn't say boo to a goose; and then she hung her college degree on the nail where the Charter had been.) Three people brought her in—a whole committee. One of them said, 'Agnes, this is Pete Frazier. Pete, Agnes Brusen. Pete's Canadian, too, Agnes. He knows all about the office, so ask him anything.'

Of course he knew all about the office: he knew the exact spot where the cord of the venetian blind was frayed, obliging one to give an extra tug to the right.

The girl might have been twenty-three: no more. She wore a brown tweed suit with bone buttons, and a new silk scarf and new shoes. She clutched an unscratched brown purse. She seemed dressed in going-away presents. She said, 'Oh, I never smoke,' with a convulsive movement of her hand, when Peter offered his case. He was courteous, hiding his disappointment. The people he worked with had told him a Scandinavian girl was arriving, and he had expected a stunner. Agnes was a mole: she was small and brown, and round-shouldered as if she had always carried parcels or younger children in her arms. A mole's profile was turned when she said goodbye to her committee. If she had been foreign, ill-favoured though she was, he might have flirted a little, just to show that he was friendly; but their being Canadian, and suddenly left together, was a sexual damper. He sat down and lit his own cigarette. She smiled at him, questioningly, he thought, and sat as if she had never seen a chair before. He wondered if his smoking was annoying her. He wondered if she was fidgety about drafts, or allergic to anything, and whether she would want the blind up or down. His social compass was out of order because the others couldn't tell Peter and Agnes apart. There was a world of difference between them, yet it was she who had been brought in to sit at the larger of the two desks.

While he was thinking this she got up and walked around the office, almost on tiptoe, opening the doors of closets and pulling out the filing trays. She looked inside everything except the drawers of Peter's desk. (In any case, Peter's desk was locked. His desk is locked wherever he works. In Geneva he went into Personnel one morning, early, and pinched his application form. He had stated on the form that he had seven years' experience in public relations and could speak French, German, Spanish, and Italian. He has always collected anything important about himself—anything useful. But he can never get on with the final act, which is getting rid of the information. He has kept papers about for years, a constant source of worry.)

'I know this looks funny, Mr Ferris,' said the girl. 'I'm not really snooping or anything. I just can't feel easy in a new place unless I know where everything is. In a new place everything seems so hidden.'

If she had called him 'Ferris' and pretended not to know he was Frazier, it could only be because they had sent her here to spy on him and see if he had repented and was fit for a better place in life. 'You'll be all right here,' he said. 'Nothing's hidden. Most of us haven't got brains enough to have secrets. This is Rainbow Valley.' Depressed by the thought that they were having him watched now, he passed his hand over his hair and looked outside to the lawn and the parking lot and the peacocks someone gave the Palais des Nations years ago. The peacocks love no one. They wander about the parked cars looking elderly, bad-tempered, mournful, and lost.

Agnes had settled down again. She folded her silk scarf and placed it just so, with her gloves beside it. She opened her new purse and took out a notebook and a shiny gold pencil. She may have written

Duster for desk
Kleenex
Glass jar for flowers
Air-Wick because he smokes
Paper for lining drawers

because the next day she brought each of these articles to work. She also brought a large black Bible, which she unwrapped lovingly and placed on the left-hand corner of her desk. The flower vase—empty—stood in the middle, and the Kleenex made a counterpoise for the Bible on the right.

When he saw the Bible he knew she had not been sent to spy on his work. The conspiracy was deeper. She might have been dispatched by ghosts. He knew everything about her, all in a moment: he saw the ambition, the terror, the dry pride. She was the true heir of the men from Scotland; she was at the start. She had been sent to tell him, 'You can begin, but not begin again.' She never opened the Bible, but she dusted it as she dusted her desk, her chair, and any surface the cleaning staff had overlooked. And Peter, the first days, watching her timid movements, her insignificant little face, felt, as you feel the approach of a storm, the charge of moral certainty round her, the belief in work, the faith in undertakings, the bread of the Black Sunday. He recognized and tasted all of it: ashes in the mouth.

After five days their working relations were settled. Of course, there was the Bible and all that went with it, but his tongue had never held the taste of ashes long. She was an inferior girl of poor quality. She had nothing in her favour except the degree on the wall. In the real world, he would not have invited her to his house except to mind the children. That was what he said to Sheilah. He said that Agnes was a mole, and a virgin, and that her tics and mannerisms were sending him round the bend. She had an infuriating habit of covering her mouth when she talked. Even at the telephone she put up her hand as if afraid of losing anything, even a word. Her voice was nasal and flat. She had two working costumes, both dull as the wall. One was the brown suit, the other a navy-blue dress with changeable collars. She dressed for no one; she dressed for her desk, her jar of flowers, her Bible, and her box of Kleenex. One day she crossed the space between the two desks and stood over Peter, who was reading a newspaper. She could have spoken to him from her desk, but she may have felt that being on her feet gave her authority. She had plenty of courage, but authority was something else.

'I thought—I mean, they told me you were the person . . .' She got on with it bravely: 'If you don't want to do the filing or any work, all right, Mr Frazier. I'm not saying anything about that. You might have poor health or your personal reasons. But it's got to be done, so if you'll kindly show me about the filing I'll do it. I've worked in Information before, but it was a different office, and every office is different.'

'My dear girl,' said Peter. He pushed back his chair and looked at her, astonished. 'You've been sitting there fretting, worrying. How insensitive of me. How trying for you. Usually I file on the last Wednesday of the month, so you see, you just haven't been around long enough to see a last Wednesday. Not another word, please. And let us not waste another moment.' He emptied the heaped baskets of photographs so swiftly, pushing 'Iran—Smallpox Control' into 'Irish Red Cross' (close enough), that the girl looked frightened, as if she had raised a whirlwind. She said slowly, 'If you'll only show me, Mr Frazier, instead of doing it so fast, I'll gladly look after it, because you might want to be doing other things, and I feel the filing should be done every day.' But Peter was too busy to answer, and so she sat down, holding the edge of her desk.

'There,' he said, beaming. 'All done.' His smile, his sunburst, was wasted, for the girl was staring round the room as if she feared she had not inspected everything the first day after all; some drawer, some cupboard, hid a monster. That evening Peter unlocked one of the drawers of his desk and took away the application form he had stolen from Personnel. The girl had not finished her search.

'How could you *not* know?' wailed Sheilah. 'You sit looking at her every day. You must talk about *something*. She must have told you.'

'She did tell me,' said Peter, 'and I've just told you.'

It was this: Agnes Brusen was on the Burleighs' guest list. How had the Burleighs met her? What did they see in her? Peter could not reply. He knew that Agnes lived in a bed-sitting room with a Swiss family and had her meals with them. She had been in Geneva three months, but no one had ever seen her outside the office. 'You *should* know,' said Sheilah. 'She must have something, more than you can see. Is she pretty? Is she brilliant? What is it?'

'We don't really talk,' Peter said. They talked in a way: Peter teased her and she took no notice. Agnes was not a sulker. She had taken her defeat like a sport. She did her work and a good deal of his. She sat behind her Bible, her flowers, and her Kleenex, and answered when Peter spoke. That was how he learned about the Burleighs—just by teasing and being bored. It was a January afternoon. He said, '*Miss* Brusen. Talk to me. Tell me everything. Pretend we have perfect rapport. Do you like Geneva?'

'It's a nice clean town,' she said. He can see to this day the red and blue anemones in the glass jar, and her bent head, and her small untended hands.

'Are you learning beautiful French with your Swiss family?'

'They speak English.'

'Why don't you take an apartment of your own?' he said. Peter was not usually impertinent. He was bored. 'You'd be independent then.'

'I am independent,' she said. 'I earn my living. I don't think it proves anything if you live by yourself. Mrs Burleigh wants me to live alone, too. She's looking for something for me. It mustn't be dear. I send money home.'

Here was the extraordinary thing about Agnes Brusen: she refused the use of Christian names and never spoke to Peter unless he spoke first, but she would tell anything, as if to say, 'Don't waste time fishing. Here it is.'

He learned all in one minute that she sent her salary home, and that she was a friend of the Burleighs. The first he had expected; the second knocked him flat.

'She's got to come to dinner.' Sheilah said. 'We should have had her right from the beginning. If only I'd known! But *you* were the one. You said she looked like—oh, I don't even remember. A Norwegian mole.'

She came to dinner one Saturday night in January, in her navy-blue dress, to which she had pinned an organdy gardenia. She sat upright on the edge of the sofa. Sheilah had ordered the meal from a restaurant. There was lobster, good wine, and a *pièce-montée* full of kirsch and cream. Agnes refused the lobster; she had never eaten anything from the sea unless it had been sterilized and tinned, and said so. She was afraid of skin poisoning. Someone in her family had skin poisoning after having eaten oysters. She touched her cheeks and neck to show where the poisoning had erupted. She sniffed her wine and put the glass down without tasting it. She could not eat the cake because of the alcohol it contained. She ate an egg, bread and butter, a sliced tomato, and drank a glass of ginger ale. She seemed unaware she was creating disaster and pain. She did not help clear away the dinner plates. She sat, adequately nourished, decently dressed, and waited to learn why she had been invited here—that was the feeling Peter had. He folded the card table on which they had dined, and opened the window to air the room.

'It's not the same cold as Canada, but you feel it more,' he said, for something to say.

'Your blood has gotten thin,' said Agnes.

Sheilah returned from the kitchen and let herself fall into an armchair. With her eyes closed she held out her hand for a cigarette. She was performing the haughty-lady act that was a family joke. She flung her head back and looked at Agnes through half-closed lids; then she suddenly brought her head forward, widening her eyes.

'Are you skiing madly?' she said.

'Well, in the first place there hasn't been any snow,' said Agnes. 'So nobody's doing any skiing so far as I know. All I hear is people complaining because there's no snow. Personally, I don't ski. There isn't much skiing in the part of Canada I come from. Besides, my family never had that kind of leisure.'

'Heavens,' said Sheilah, as if her family had every kind.

I'll bet they had, thought Peter. On the dole.

Sheilah was wasting her act. He had a suspicion that Agnes knew it was an act but did not know it was a joke. If so, it made Sheilah seem a fool, and he loved Sheilah too much to enjoy it.

'The Burleighs have been wonderful to me,' said Agnes. She seemed to have divined why she was here, and decided to give them all the information they wanted, so that she could put on her coat and go home to bed. 'They had me out to their place on the lake every weekend until the weather got cold and they moved back to town. They've rented a chalet for the winter, and they want me to come there, too. But I don't know if I will or not. I don't ski, and, oh, I don't know—I don't drink, either, and I don't always see the point. Their friends are too rich and I'm too Canadian.'

She had delivered everything Sheilah wanted and more: Agnes was on the first guest list and didn't care. No, Peter corrected; doesn't know. Doesn't care and doesn't know.

'I thought with you Norwegians it was in the blood, skiing. And drinking,' Sheilah murmured.

'Drinking, maybe,' said Agnes. She covered her mouth and said behind her spread fingers, 'In our family we were religious. We didn't drink or smoke. My brother was in Norway in the war. He saw some cousins. 'Oh,' she said, unexpectedly loud, 'Harry said it was just terrible. They were so poor. They had flies in their kitchen. They gave him something to eat a fly had been on. They didn't have a real toilet, and they'd been in the same house about two hundred years. We've only recently built our own home, and we have a bathroom and two toilets. I'm from Saskatchewan,' she said. 'I'm not from any other place.'

Surely one winter here had been punishment enough? In the spring they would remember him and free him. He wrote Lucille, who said he was lucky to have a job at all. The Burleighs had sent the Fraziers a second-guest-list Christmas card. It showed a Moslem refugee child weeping outside a tent. They treasured the card and left it standing long after the others had been given the children to cut up. Peter had discovered by now what had gone wrong in the friendship—Sheilah had charged a skirt at a dressmaker to Madge's account. Madge had told her she might, and then changed her mind. Poor Sheilah! She was new to this part of it—to the changing humours of independent friends. Paris was already a year in the past. At Mardi Gras, the Burleighs gave their annual party. They invited everyone, the damned and the dropped, with the prodigality of a child at prayers. The invitation said 'in costume', but the Fraziers were too happy to wear a disguise. They might not be recognized. Like many of the guests they expected to meet at the party, they had been disgraced, forgotten, and rehabilitated. They would be anxious to see one another as they were.

On the night of the party, the Fraziers rented a car they had never seen before and drove through the first snowstorm of the year. Peter had not driven since last summer's blissful trips in the Fiat. He could not find the switch for the windshield wiper in this car. He leaned over the wheel. 'Can you see on your side?' he asked. 'Can I make a left turn here? Does it look like a one-way?'

'I can't imagine why you took a car with a right-hand drive,' said Sheilah.

He had trouble finding a place to park; they crawled up and down unknown streets whose curbs were packed with snow-covered cars. When they stood at last on the pavement, safe and sound, Peter said, 'This is the first snow.'

'I can see that,' said Sheilah. 'Hurry, darling. My hair.'

'It's the first snow.'

'You're repeating yourself,' she said. 'Please hurry, darling. Think of my poor shoes. My *hair*.'

She was born in an ugly city, and so was Peter, but they have this difference: she does not know the importance of the first snow—the first clean thing in a dirty year. He would have told her that this storm, which was wetting her feet and destroying her hair, was like the first day of the English spring, but she made a frightened gesture, trying to shield her head. The gesture told him he did not understand her beauty.

'Let me,' she said. He was fumbling with the key, trying to lock the car. She took the key without impatience and locked the door on the driver's side; and then, to show Peter she treasured him and was not afraid of wasting her life or her beauty, she took his arm and they walked in the snow down a street and around a corner to the apartment house where the Burleighs lived. They were, and are, a united couple. They were afraid of the party, and each of them knew it. When they walk together, holding arms, they give each other whatever each can spare.

Only six people had arrived in costume. Madge Burleigh was disguised as Manet's 'Lola de Valence', which everyone mistook for Carmen. Mike was an Impressionist painter, with a straw hat and a glued-on beard. 'I am all of them,' he said. He would rather have dressed as a dentist, he said, welcoming the Fraziers as if he had parted from them the day before, but Madge wanted him to look as if he had created her. 'You know?' he said.

'Perfectly,' said Sheilah. Her shoes were stained and the snow had softened her lacquered hair. She was not wasted; she was the most beautiful woman here.

About an hour after their arrival, Peter found himself with no one to talk to. He had told about the Trudeau wedding in Paris and the pot of azaleas, and after he mislaid his audience he began to look around for Sheilah. She was on a window seat, partly concealed by a green velvet curtain. Facing her, so that their profiles were neat and perfect against the night, was a man. Their conversation was private and enclosed, as if they had in minutes covered leagues of time and arrived at a place where everything was implied, understood. Peter began working his way across the room, toward his wife, when he saw Agnes. He was granted the sight of her drowning face. She had dressed with comic intention, obviously with care, and now she was a ragged hobo, half tramp, half clown. Her hair was tucked up under a bowler hat. The six costumed guests who had made the same mistake—the ghost, the gypsy, the Athenian maiden, the geisha, the Martian, and the apache—were delighted to find a seventh; but Agnes was not amused; she was gasping for life. When a waiter passed with a crowded tray, she took a glass without seeing it; then a wave of the party took her away.

Sheilah's new friend was named Simpson. After Simpson said he thought perhaps he'd better circulate, Peter sat down where he had been. 'Now look, Sheilah,' he began. Their most intimate conversations have taken place at parties. Once at a party she told him she was leaving him; she didn't, of course. Smiling, blue-eyed, she gazed lovingly at Peter and said rapidly, 'Pete, shut up and listen. That man. The man you scared away. He's a big wheel in a company out in India or someplace like that. It's gorgeous out there. Pete, the *servants*. And it's warm. It never snows. He says there's heaps of jobs. You pick them off the trees like . . . orchids. He says it's even easier now than when we owned all those places, because now the poor pets can't run anything and they'll pay *fortunes*. Pete, he says it's warm, it's heaven, and Pete, they pay.'

A few minutes later, Peter was alone again and Sheilah part of a closed, laughing group. Holding her elbow was the man from the place where jobs grew like orchids. Peter edged into the group and laughed at a story he hadn't heard. He heard only the last line, which was, 'Here comes another tunnel.' Looking out from the tight laughing ring, he saw Agnes again, and he thought, I'd be like Agnes if I didn't have Sheilah. Agnes put her glass down on a table and lurched toward the doorway, head forward. Madge Burleigh, who never stopped moving around the room and smiling, was still smiling when she paused and said in Peter's ear, 'Go with Agnes, Pete. See that she gets home. People will notice if Mike leaves.'

'She probably just wants to walk around the block,' said Peter. 'She'll be back.'

'Oh, stop thinking about yourself, for once, and see that that poor girl gets home,' said Madge. 'You've still got your Fiat, haven't you?'

He turned away as if he had been pushed. Any command is a release, in a way. He may not want to go in that particular direction, but at least he is going somewhere. And now Sheilah, who had moved inches nearer to hear what Madge and Peter were murmuring, said, 'Yes, go, darling,' as if he were leaving the gates of Troy.

Peter was to find Agnes and see that she reached home: this he repeated to himself as he stood on the landing, outside the Burleighs' flat, ringing for the elevator. Bored with waiting for it, he ran down the stairs, four flights, and saw that Agnes had stalled the lift by leaving the door open. She was crouched on the floor, propped on her fingertips. Her eyes were closed.

'Agnes,' said Peter. '*Miss* Brusen, I mean. That's no way to leave a party. Don't you know you're supposed to curtsy and say thanks? My God, Agnes, anybody going by here just now might have seen you! Come on, be a good girl. Time to go home.'

She got up without his help and, moving between invisible crevasses, shut the elevator door. Then she left the building and Peter followed, remembering he was to see that she got home. They walked along the snowy pavement, Peter a few steps behind her. When she turned right for no reason, he turned, too. He had no clear idea where they were going. Perhaps she lived close by. He had forgotten where the hired car was parked, or what it looked like; he could not remember its make or its colour. In any case, Sheilah had the key. Agnes walked on steadily, as if she knew her destination, and he thought, Agnes Brusen is drunk in the street in Geneva and dressed like a tramp. He wanted to say, 'This is the best thing that ever happened to you, Agnes; it will help you understand how things are for some of the rest of us.' But she stopped and turned and, leaning over a low hedge, retched on a frozen lawn. He held her clammy forehead and rested his hand on her arched back, on muscles as tight as a fist. She straightened up and drew a breath but the cold air made her cough. 'Don't breath too deeply,' he said. 'It's the worst thing you can do. Have you got a handkerchief?' He passed his own handkerchief over her wet weeping face, upturned like the face of one of his little girls. 'I'm out without a coat,' he said, noticing it. 'We're a pair.'

'I never drink,' said Agnes. 'I'm just not used to it.' Her voice was sweet and quiet. He had never seen her so peaceful, so composed. He thought she must surely be all right, now, and perhaps he might leave her there. The trust in her tilted face had perplexed him. He wanted to get back to Sheilah and have her explain something. He had forgotten what it was, but Sheilah would know. 'Do you live around here?' he said. As he spoke, she let herself fall. He had wiped her face and now she trusted him to pick her up, set her on her feet, take her wherever she ought to be. He pulled her up and she stood, wordless, humble, as he brushed the snow from her tramp's clothes. Snow horizontally crossed the lamplight. The street was silent. Agnes had lost her hat. Snow, which he tasted, melted on her hands. His gesture of licking snow from her hands was formal as a handshake. He tasted snow on her hands and then they walked on.

'I never drink,' she said. They stood on the edge of a broad avenue. The wrong turning now could lead them anywhere; it was the changeable avenue at the edge of towns that loses its houses and becomes a highway. She held his arm and spoke in a gentle voice. She said, 'In our house we didn't smoke or drink. My mother was ambitious for me, more than for Harry and the others.' She said, 'I've never been alone before. When I was a kid I would get up in the summer before the others, and I'd see the ice wagon going down the street. I'm alone now. Mrs Burleigh's found me an apartment. It's only one room. She likes it because it's in an old part of town. I don't like old houses. Old houses are dirty. You don't know who was there before.'

'I should have a car somewhere,' Peter said. 'I'm not sure where we are.'

He remembers that on this avenue they climbed into a taxi, but nothing about the drive. Perhaps he fell asleep. He does remember that when he paid the driver Agnes clutched his arm, trying to stop him. She pressed extra coins into the driver's palm. The driver was paid twice.

'I'll tell you one thing about us,' said Peter. 'We pay everything twice.' This was part of a much longer theory concerning North American behaviour, and it was not Peter's own. Mike Burleigh had held forth about it on summer afternoons.

Agnes pushed open a door between a stationer's shop and a grocery, and led the way up a narrow inside stair. They climbed one flight, frightening beetles. She had to search every pocket for the latchkey. She was shaking with cold. Her apartment seemed little warmer than the street. Without speaking to Peter she turned on all the lights. She looked inside the kitchen and the bathroom and then got down on her hands and knees and looked under the sofa. The room was neat and belonged to no one. She left him standing in this unclaimed room—she had forgotten him—and closed a door behind her. He looked for something to do—some useful action he could repeat to Madge. He turned on the electric radiator in the fireplace. Perhaps Agnes wouldn't thank him for it; perhaps she would rather undress in the cold. 'I'll be on my way,' he called to the bathroom door.

She had taken off the tramp's clothes and put on a dressing gown of orphanage wool. She came out of the bathroom and straight toward him. She pressed her face and rubbed her cheek on his shoulder as if hoping the contact would leave a scar. He saw her back and her profile and his own face in the mirror over the fireplace. He thought, This is how disasters happen. He saw floods of sea water moving with perfect punitive justice over reclaimed land; he saw lava covering vineyards and overtaking of dogs and stragglers. A bridge over an abyss snapped in two and the long express train, suddenly V-shaped, floated like snow. He thought amiably of every kind of disaster and thought, This is how they occur.

Her eyes were closed. She said, 'I shouldn't be over here. In my family we didn't drink or smoke. My mother wanted a lot from me, more than from Harry and the others.' But he knew that; he had known from the day of the Bible, and because once, at the beginning, she had made him afraid. He was not afraid of her now.

She said, 'It's no use staying here, is it?'

'If you mean what I think, no.'

'It wouldn't be better anywhere.'

She let him see full on her blotched face. He was not expected to do anything. He was not required to pick her up when she fell or wipe her tears. She was poor quality, really—he remembered having thought that once. She left him and went quietly in to the bathroom and locked the door. He heard taps running and supposed it was a hot bath. He was pretty certain there would be no more tears. He looked at his watch: Sheilah must be home, now, wondering what had become of him. He descended the beetle's staircase and for forty minutes crossed the city under a windless fall of snow.

The neighbour's child who had stayed with Peter's children was asleep on the living room sofa. Peter woke her and sent her, sleepwalking, to her own door. He sat down, wet to the bone, thinking. I'll call the Burleighs. In half an hour I'll call the police. He heard a car stop and the engine running and a confusion of two voices laughing and calling goodnight. Presently Sheilah let herself in, rosy-faced, smiling. She carried his trenchcoat over her arm. She said, 'How's Agnes?'

'Where were you?' he said. 'Whose car was that?'

Sheilah had gone into the children's room. He heard her shutting their window. She returned, undoing her dress, and said, 'Was Agnes all right?'

'Agnes is all right. Sheilah, this is about the worst . . .'

She stepped out of the Balcenciaga and threw it over a chair. She stopped and looked at him and said, 'Poor old Pete, are you in love with Agnes?' And then, as if the answer were of so little importance she hadn't time for it, she locked her arms around him and said, 'My love, we're going to Ceylon.'

Two days later, when Peter strolled into his office, Agnes was at her desk. She wore the blue dress, with a spotless collar. White and yellow freesias were symmetrically arranged in the glass jar. The room was hot, and the spring snow, glued for a second when it touched the window, blurred the view of parked cars.

'Quite a party,' Peter said.

She did not look up. He sighed, sat down, and thought if the snow held he would be skiing at the Burleighs' very soon. Impressed by his kindness to Agnes, Madge had invited the family for the first possible weekend.

Presently Agnes said, 'I'll never drink again or go to a house where people are drinking. And I'll never bother anyone the way I bothered you.'

'You didn't bother me,' he said. 'I took you home. You were alone and it was late. It's normal.'

'Normal for you, maybe, but I'm used to getting myself home by myself. Please never tell what happened.'

He stared at her. He can still remember the freesias and the Bible and the heat in the room. She looked as if the elements had no power. She felt neither heat nor cold. 'Nothing *happened*,' he said.

'I behaved in a silly way. I had no right to. I led you to think I might do something wrong.'

'I might have tried something,' he said gallantly. 'But that would be my fault and not yours.'

She put her knuckle to her mouth and he could scarcely hear. 'It was because of you. I was afraid you might be blamed, or else you'd blame yourself.'

'There's no question of any blame,' he said. 'Nothing happened. We'd both had a lot to drink. Forget about it. Nothing happened. You'd remember if it had.'

She put down her hand. There was an expression on her face. Now she sees me, he thought. She had never looked at him after the first day. (He has since tried to put a name to the look on her face; but how can he, now, after so many voyages, after Ceylon, and Hong Kong, and Sheilah's nearly leaving him, and all their difficulties—the money owed, the rows with hotel managers, the lost and found steamer trunk, the children throwing up the foreign food?) She sees me now, he thought. What does she see?

She said, 'I'm from a big family. I'm not used to being alone. I'm not a suicidal person, but I could have done something after that party, just not to see any more, or think or listen or expect anything. What can I think when I see these people? All my life I heard, Educated people don't do this, educated people don't do that. And now I'm here, and you're all educated people, and you're nothing but pigs. You're educated and you drink and do everything wrong and you know what you're doing, and that makes you worse than pigs. My family worked to make me an educated person, but they didn't know you. But what if I didn't see and hear and expect anything any more? It wouldn't change anything. You'd all be still the same. Only *you* might have thought it was your fault. You might have thought you were to blame. It could worry you all your life. It would have been wrong for me to worry you.'

He remembered that the rented car was still along a snowy curb somewhere in Geneva. He wondered if Sheilah had the key in her purse and if she remembered where they'd parked.

'I told you about the ice wagon,' Agnes said. 'I don't remember everything, so you're wrong about remembering. But I remember telling you that. That was the best. It's the best you can hope to have. In a big family, if you want to be alone, you have to get up before the rest of them. You get up early in the morning in the summer and it's you, you, once in your life alone in the universe. You think you know everything that can happen . . . Nothing is ever like that again.'

He looked at the smeared window and wondered if this day could end without disaster. In his mind he saw her falling in the snow wearing a tramp's costume, and he saw her coming to him in the orphanage dressing gown. He saw her drowning face at the party. He was afraid for himself. The story was still unfinished. It had to come to a climax, something threatening to him. But there was no climax. They talked that day, and afterward nothing else was said. They went on in the same office for a short time, until Peter left for Ceylon; until somebody read the right letter, passed it on for the right initials, and the Fraziers began the Oriental tour that should have made their fortune. Agnes and Peter were too tired to speak after that morning. They were like a married couple in danger, taking care.

But what were they talking about that day, so quietly, such old friends? They talked about dying, about being ambitious, about being religious, about different kinds of love. What did she see when she looked at him—taking her knuckle slowly from her mouth, bringing her hand down to the desk, letting it rest there? They were both Canadians, so they had this much together—the knowledge of the little you dare admit. Death, near-death, the best thing, the wrong thing—God knows what they were telling each other. Anyway, nothing happened.

When, on Sunday mornings, Sheilah and Peter talk about those times, they take on the glamour of something still to come. It is then he remembers Agnes Brusen. He never says her name. Sheilah wouldn't remember Agnes. Agnes is the only secret Peter has from his wife, the only puzzle he pieces together without her help. He thinks about families in the West as they were fifteen, twenty years ago—the iron-cold ambition, and every member pushing the next one on. He thinks of his father's parties. When he thinks of his father he imagines him with Sheilah, in a crowd. Actually, Sheilah and Peter's father never met, but they might have liked each other. His father admired good-looking women. Peter wonders what they were doing over there in Geneva—not Sheila and Peter, *Agnes* and Peter. It is almost as if they had once run away together, silly as children, irresponsible as lovers. Peter and Sheilah are back where they started. While they were out in world affairs picking up microbes and debts, always on the fringe of disaster, the fringe of a fortune, Agnes went on and did—what? They lost each other. He thinks of the ice wagon going down the street. He sees something he had never seen in his life—a Western town that belongs to Agnes. Here is Agnes—small, mole-faced, round-shouldered because she has always carried a younger child. She watches the ice wagon and the trail of ice water in a morning invented for her: hers. He sees the weak prairie trees and the shadows on the sidewalk. Nothing moves except the shadows and the ice wagon and the changing amber of the child's eyes. The child is Peter. He has seen the grain of the cement sidewalk and the grass in the cracks, and the dust, and the dandelions at the edge of the road. He is there. He has taken the morning that belongs to Agnes, he is up before the others, and he knows everything. There is nothing he doesn't know. He could keep the morning, if he wanted to, but what can Peter do with the start of a summer day? Sheilah is here, it is a true Sunday morning, with its dimness and headache and remorse and regrets and this is life. He says, 'We have the Balenciaga.' He touches Sheilah's hand. The children have their aunt now, and he and Sheilah have each other. Everything works out, somehow or other. Let Agnes have the start of the day. Let Agnes think it was invented for her. Who wants to be alone in the universe? No, begin at the beginning: Peter lost Agnes. Agnes says to herself somewhere, Peter is lost.

1963

Flannery O'Connor
1925–1964

Mary Flannery O'Connor was born in Savannah, Georgia, to Roman Catholic parents whose families had lived in the South for generations. In Savannah she was educated at parochial schools. When she was thirteen her father developed disseminated lupus, a fatal disease in which antibodies attack the blood vessels, joints, and internal organs. The family moved to Milledgeville, Georgia, to live with relatives, and Mary went to Peabody High School and then Georgia State College for Women. She edited the college's literary maga-

zine and won a fellowship to the Writers' Workshop at the University of Iowa, where she received encouragement to publish her fiction. After earning her MFA she went to the writers' colony Yaddo, where she met people who supported her ambition to write and helped her arrange publication for more of her work.

In 1950 O'Connor was diagnosed with the disease that had killed her father nine years earlier. She moved to a farm near Milledgeville and continued writing there until her death in 1964, with her reputation growing steadily, even after her death. Most of her fiction can be found in *Collected Stories* (1971), which includes early versions of her two novels.

The setting for 'Everything That Rises Must Converge' is the recently integrated American South, where Julian, a university graduate, is escorting his mother to a weight loss class at the YWCA. The events that unfold on their bus ride expose their innate fears and prejudices.

Everything That Rises Must Converge

Her doctor had told Julian's mother that she must lose twenty pounds on account of her blood pressure, so on Wednesday nights Julian had to take her downtown on the bus for a reducing class at the Y. The reducing class was designed for working girls over fifty, who weighed from 165 to 200 pounds. His mother was one of the slimmer ones, but she said ladies did not tell their age or weight. She would not ride the buses by herself at night since they had been integrated, and because the reducing class was one of her few pleasures, necessary for her health, and *free*, she said Julian could at least put himself out to take her, considering all she did for him. Julian did not like to consider all she did for him, but every Wednesday night he braced himself and took her.

She was almost ready to go, standing before the hall mirror, putting on her hat, while he, his hands behind him, appeared pinned to the door frame, waiting like Saint Sebastian for the arrows to begin piercing him. The hat was new and had cost her seven dollars and a half. She kept saying, 'Maybe I shouldn't have paid that for it. No, I shouldn't have. I'll take it off and return it tomorrow. I shouldn't have bought it.'

Julian raised his eyes to heaven. 'Yes, you should have bought it,' he said. 'Put it on and let's go.' It was a hideous hat. A purple velvet flap came down on one side of it and stood up on the other; the rest of it was green and looked like a cushion with the stuffing out. He decided it was less comical than jaunty and pathetic. Everything that gave her pleasure was small and depressed him.

She lifted the hat one more time and set it down slowly on top of her head. Two wings of grey protruded on either side of her florid face, but her eyes, sky-blue, were as innocent and untouched by experience as they must have been when she was ten. Were it not that she was a widow who had struggled fiercely to feed and clothe and put him through school and who was supporting him still, 'until he got on his feet', she might have been a little girl that he had to take to town.

'It's all right, it's all right,' he said. 'Let's go.' He opened the door himself and started down the walk to get her going. The sky was a dying violet and the houses stood out darkly against it, bulbous liver-coloured monstrosities of a uniform ugliness though no two were alike. Since this had been a fashionable neighbourhood forty years ago, his mother persisted in thinking they did well to have an apartment in it. Each house had a narrow collar of dirt around it in which sat, usually, a grubby child. Julian walked with his hands in his pockets, his head down and thrust forward, and his eyes glazed with the determination to make himself completely numb during the time he would be sacrificed to her pleasure.

The door closed and he turned to find the dumpy figure, surmounted by the atrocious hat, coming toward him. 'Well,' she said, 'you only live once and paying a little more for it, I at least won't meet myself coming and going.'

'Some day I'll start making money,' Julian said gloomily—he knew he never would—'and you can have one of those jokes whenever you take the fit.' But first they would move. He visualized a place where the nearest neighbours would be three miles away on either side.

'I think you're doing fine,' she said, drawing on her gloves. 'You've only been out of school a year. Rome wasn't built in a day.'

She was one of the few members of the Y reducing class who arrived in hat and gloves and who had a son who had been to college. 'It takes time,' she said, 'and the world is in such a mess. This hat looked better on me than any of the others, though when she brought it out I said, "Take that thing back. I wouldn't have it on my head," and she said, "Now wait till you see it on," and when she put it on me, I said, "We-ull," and she said, "If you ask me, that hat does something for you and you do something for the hat, and besides," she said, "with that hat, you won't meet yourself coming and going."'

Julian thought he could have stood his lot better if she had been selfish, if she had been an old hag who drank and screamed at him. He walked along, saturated in depression, as if in the midst of his martyrdom he had lost his faith. Catching sight of his long, hopeless, irritated face, she stopped suddenly with a grief-stricken look, and pulled back on his arm. 'Wait on me,' she said. 'I'm going back to the house and take this thing off and tomorrow I'm going to return it. I was out of my head. I can pay the gas bill with the seven-fifty.'

He caught her arm in a vicious grip. 'You are not going to take it back,' he said. 'I like it.'

'Well,' she said, 'I don't think I ought . . .'

'Shut up and enjoy it,' he muttered, more depressed than ever.

'With the world in the mess it's in', she said, 'it's a wonder we can enjoy anything. I tell you, the bottom rail is on the top.'

Julian sighed.

'Of course,' she said, 'if you know who you are, you can go anywhere.' She said this every time he took her to the reducing class. 'Most of them in it are not our kind of people,' she said, 'but I can be gracious to anybody. I know who I am.'

'They don't give a damn for your graciousness,' Julian said savagely. 'Knowing who you are is good for one generation only. You haven't the foggiest idea where you stand now or who you are.'

She stopped and allowed her eyes to flash at him. 'I most certainly do know who I am,' she said, 'and if you don't know who you are, I'm ashamed of you.'

'Oh hell,' Julian said.

'Your great-grandfather was a former governor of this state,' she said. 'Your grandfather was a prosperous landowner. Your grandfather was a Godhigh.'

'Will you look around you,' he said tensely, 'and see where you are now?' and he swept his arm jerkily out to indicate the neighbourhood, which the growing darkness at least made less dingy.

'You remain what you are,' she said. 'Your great-grandfather had a plantation and two hundred slaves.'

'There are no more slaves,' he said irritably.

'They were better off when they were,' she said. He groaned to see that she was off on that topic. She rolled onto it every few days like a train on an open track. He knew every stop, every junction, every swamp along the way, and knew the exact point at which her conclusion would roll majestically into the station: 'It's ridiculous. It's simply not realistic. They should rise, yes, but on their own side of the fence.'

'Let's skip it,' Julian said.

'The ones I feel sorry for,' she said, 'are the ones that are half white. They're tragic.'

'Will you skip it?'

'Suppose we were half white. We would certainly have mixed feelings.'

'I have mixed feelings now,' he groaned.

'Well let's talk about something pleasant,' she said. 'I remember going to Grandpa's when I was a little girl. Then the house had double stairways that went up to what was really the second floor—all the cooking was done on the first. I used to like to stay down in the kitchen on account of the way the walls smelled. I would sit with my nose pressed against the plaster and take deep breaths. Actually the place belonged to the Godhighs but your grandfather Chestny paid the mortgage and saved it for them. They were in reduced circumstances,' she said, 'but reduced or not, they never forgot who they were.'

'Doubtless that decayed mansion reminded them,' Julian muttered. He never spoke of it without contempt or thought of it without longing. He had seen it once when he was a child before it had been sold. The double stairways had rotted and been torn down. Negroes were living in it. But it remained in his mind as his mother had known it. It appeared in his dreams regularly. He would stand on the wide porch, listening to the rustle of oak leaves, then wander through the high-ceilinged hall into the parlour that opened onto it and gaze at the worn rugs and faded draperies. It occurred to him that it was he, not she, who could have appreciated it. He preferred its threadbare elegance to anything he could name and it was because of it that all the neighbourhoods they had lived in had been a torment to him—whereas she had hardly known the difference. She called her insensitivity 'being adjustable'.

'And I remember the old darky who was my nurse, Caroline. There was no better person in the world. I've always had a great respect for my coloured friends,' she said. 'I'd do anything in the world for them and they'd . . .'

'Will you for God's sake get off that subject?' Julian said. When he got on a bus by himself, he made it a point to sit down beside a Negro, in reparation as it were for his mother's sins.

'You're mighty touchy tonight,' she said. 'Do you feel all right?'

'Yes I feel all right,' he said. 'Now lay off.'

She pursed her lips. 'Well, you certainly are in a vile humour,' she observed. 'I just won't speak to you at all.'

They had reached the bus stop. There was no bus in sight and Julian, his hands still jammed in his pockets and his head thrust forward, scowled down the empty street. The frustration of having to wait on the bus as well as ride on it began to creep up his neck like a hot hand. The presence of his mother was borne in upon him as she gave a pained sigh. He looked at her bleakly. She was holding herself very erect under the preposterous hat, wearing it like a banner of her imaginary dignity. There was in him an evil urge to break her spirit. He suddenly unloosened his tie and pulled it off and put it in his pocket.

She stiffened. 'Why must you look like that when you take me to town?' she said. 'Why must you deliberately embarrass me?'

'If you'll never learn where you are,' he said, 'you can at least learn where I am.'

'You look like a—thug,' she said.

'Then I must be one,' he murmured.

'I'll just go home,' she said. 'I will not bother you. If you can't do a little thing like that for me . . .'

Rolling his eyes upward, he put his tie back on. 'Restored to my class,' he muttered. He thrust his face toward her and hissed, 'True culture is in the mind, the *mind*,' he said, and tapped his head, 'the mind.'

'It's in the heart,' she said, 'and in how you do things and how you do things is because of who you *are*.'

'Nobody in the damn bus cares who you are.'

'I care who I am,' she said icily.

The lighted bus appeared on top of the next hill and as it approached, they moved out into the street to meet it. He put his hand under her elbow and hoisted her up on the creaking step. She entered with a little smile, as if she were going into a drawing room where everyone had been waiting for her. While he put in the tokens, she sat down in one of the broad front seats for three which faced the aisle. A thin woman with protruding teeth and long yellow hair was sitting on the end of it. His mother moved up beside her and left room for Julian beside herself. He sat down and looked at the floor across the aisle where a pair of thin feet in red and white canvas sandals were planted.

His mother immediately began a general conversation meant to attract anyone who felt like talking. 'Can it get any hotter?' she said and removed from her purse a folding fan, black with a Japanese scene on it, which she began to flutter before her.

'I reckon it might could,' the woman with the protruding teeth said, 'but I know for a fact my apartment couldn't get no hotter.'

'It must get the afternoon sun,' his mother said. She sat forward and looked up and down the bus. It was half filled. Everybody was white. 'I see we have the bus to ourselves,' she said. Julian cringed.

'For a change,' said the woman across the aisle, the owner of the red and white canvas sandals. 'I come on the other day and they were thick as fleas—up front and all through.'

'The world is in a mess everywhere,' his mother said. 'I don't know how we've let it get in this fix.'

'What gets my goat is all those boys from good families stealing automobile tires,' the woman with the protruding teeth said. 'I told my boy, I said you may not be rich but you been raised right and if I ever catch you in any such mess, they can send you on to the reformatory. Be exactly where you belong.'

'Training tells,' his mother said. 'Is your boy in high school?'

'Ninth grade,' the woman said.

'My son just finished college last year. He wants to write but he's selling typewriters until he gets started,' his mother said.

The woman leaned forward and peered at Julian. He threw her such a malevolent look that she subsided against the seat. On the floor across the aisle there was an abandoned newspaper. He got up and got it and opened it out in front of him. His mother discreetly continued the conversation in a lower tone but the woman across the aisle said in a loud voice, 'Well that's nice. Selling typewriters is close to writing. He can go right from one to the other.'

'I tell him', his mother said, 'that Rome wasn't built in a day.'

Behind the newspaper Julian was withdrawing into the inner compartment of his mind where he spent most of his time. This was a kind of mental bubble in which he established himself when he could not bear to be a part of what was going on around him. From it he could see out and judge but in it he was safe from any kind of penetration from without. It was the only place where he felt free of the general idiocy of his fellows. His mother had never entered it but from it he could see her with absolute clarity.

The old lady was clever enough and he thought that if she had started from any of the right premises, more might have been expected of her. She lived according to the laws of her own fantasy world, outside of which he had never seen her set foot. The law of it was to sacrifice herself for him after she had first created the necessity to do so by making a mess of things. If he had permitted her sacrifices, it was only because her lack of foresight had made them necessary. All of her life had been a struggle to act like a Chestny without the Chestny goods, and to give him everything she thought a Chestny ought to have; but since, said she, it was fun to struggle, why complain? And when you had won, as she had won, what fun to look back on the hard times! He could not forgive her that she had enjoyed the struggle and that she thought *she* had won.

What she meant when she said she had won was that she had brought him up successfully and had sent him to college and that he had turned out so well—good looking (her teeth had gone unfilled so that his could be straightened), intelligent (he realized he was too intelligent to be a success), and with a future ahead of him (there was of course no future ahead of him). She excused his gloominess on the grounds that he was still growing up and his radical ideas on his lack of practical experience. She said he didn't yet know a thing about 'life', that he hadn't even entered the real world—when already he was as disenchanted with it as a man of fifty.

The further irony of all this was that in spite of her, he had turned out so well. In spite of going to only a third-rate college, he had, on his own initiative, come out with a first-rate education; in spite of growing up dominated by a small mind, he had ended up with a large one; in spite of all her foolish views, he was free of prejudice and unafraid to face facts. Most miraculous of all, instead of being blinded by love for her as she was for him, he had cut himself emotionally free of her and could see her with complete objectivity. He was not dominated by his mother.

The bus stopped with a sudden jerk and shook him from his meditation. A woman from the back lurched forward with little steps and barely escaped falling in his newspaper as she righted herself. She got off and a large Negro got on. Julian kept his paper lowered to watch. It gave him a certain satisfaction to see injustice in daily operation. It confirmed his view that with a few exceptions there was no one worth knowing within a radius of three hundred miles. The Negro was well dressed and carried a briefcase. He looked around and then sat down on the other end of the seat where the woman with the red and white canvas sandals was sitting. He immediately unfolded a newspaper and obscured himself behind it. Julian's mother's elbow at once prodded insistently into his ribs. 'Now you see why I won't ride on these buses by myself,' she whispered.

The woman with the red and white canvas sandals had risen at the same time the Negro sat down and had gone further back in the bus and taken the seat of the woman who had got off. His mother leaned forward and cast her an approving look.

Julian rose, crossed the aisle, and sat down in the place of the woman with the canvas sandals. From this position, he looked serenely across at his mother. Her face had turned an angry red. He stared at her, making his eyes the eyes of a stranger. He felt the tension suddenly lift as if he had openly declared war on her.

He would have liked to get in conversation with the Negro and to talk with him about art or politics or any subject that would be above the comprehension of those around them, but the man remained entrenched behind his paper. He was either ignoring the change of seating or had never noticed it. There was no way for Julian to convey his sympathy.

His mother kept her eyes fixed reproachfully on his face. The woman with the protruding teeth was looking at him avidly as if he were a type of monster new to her.

'Do you have a light?' he asked the Negro.

Without looking away from his paper, the man reached in his pocket and handed him a packet of matches.

'Thanks,' Julian said. For a moment he held the matches foolishly. A NO SMOKING sign looked down upon him from over the door. This alone would not have deterred him; he had no cigarettes. He had quit smoking some months before because he could not afford it. 'Sorry,' he muttered and handed back the matches. The Negro lowered the paper and gave him an annoyed look. He took the matches and raised the paper again.

His mother continued to gaze at him but she did not take advantage of his momentary discomfort. Her eyes retained their battered look. Her face seemed to be unnaturally red, as if her blood pressure had risen. Julian allowed no glimmer of sympathy to show on his face. Having got the advantage, he wanted desperately to keep it and carry it through. He would have liked to teach her a lesson that would last her a while, but there seemed no way to continue to point. The Negro refused to come out from behind his paper.

Julian folded his arms and looked stolidly before him, facing her but as if he did not see her, as if he had ceased to recognize her existence. He visualized a scene in which, the bus having reached their stop, he would remain in his seat and when she said, 'Aren't you going to get off?' he would look at her as at a stranger who had rashly addressed him. The corner they got off on was usually deserted, but it was well lighted and it would not hurt her to walk by herself the four blocks to the Y. He decided to wait until the time came and then decide whether or not he would let her get off by herself. He would have to be at the Y at ten to bring her back, but he could leave her wondering if he was going to show up. There was no reason for her to think she could always depend on him.

He retired again into the high-ceilinged room sparsely settled with large pieces of antique furniture. His soul expanded momentarily but then he became aware of his mother across from him and the vision shrivelled. He studied her coldly. Her feet in little pumps dangled like a child's and did not quite reach the floor. She was training on him an exaggerated look of reproach. He felt completely detached from her. At that moment he could with pleasure have slapped her as he would have slapped a particularly obnoxious child in his charge.

He began to imagine various unlikely ways by which he could teach her a lesson. He might make friends with some distinguished Negro professor or lawyer and bring him home to spend the evening. He would be entirely justified but her blood pressure would rise to 300. He could not push her to the extent of making her have a stroke, and moreover, he had never been successful at making any Negro friends. He had tried to strike up an acquaintance on the bus with some of the better types, with ones that looked like professors or ministers or lawyers. One morning he had sat down next to a distinguished-looking dark brown man who had answered his questions with a sonorous solemnity but who had turned out to be an undertaker. Another day he had sat down beside a cigar-smoking Negro with a diamond ring on his finger, but after a few stilted pleasantries, the Negro had rung the buzzer and risen, slipping two lottery tickets into Julian's hand as he climbed over him to leave.

He imagined his mother lying desperately ill and his being able to secure only a Negro doctor for her. He toyed with that idea for a few minutes and then dropped it for a momentary vision of himself participating as a sympathizer in a sit-in demonstration. This was possible but he did not linger with it. Instead, he approached the ultimate horror. He brought home a beautiful suspiciously Negroid woman. Prepare yourself, he said. There is nothing you can do about it. This is the woman I've chosen. She's intelligent, dignified, even good, and she's suffered and she hasn't thought it *fun*. Now persecute us, go ahead and persecute us. Drive her out of here, but remember, you're driving me too. His eyes were narrowed and through the indignation he had generated, he saw his mother across the aisle, purple faced, shrunken to the dwarf-like proportions of her moral nature, sitting like a mummy beneath the ridiculous banner of her hat.

He was tilted out of his fantasy again as the bus stopped. The door opened with a sucking hiss and out of the dark a large, gaily dressed, sullen-looking coloured woman got on with a little boy. The child, who might have been four, had on a short plaid suit and a tyrolean hat with a blue feather in it. Julian hoped that he would sit down beside him and that the woman would push in beside his mother. He could think of no better arrangement.

As she waited for her tokens, the woman was surveying the seating possibilities—he hoped with the idea of sitting where she was least wanted. There was something familiar-looking about her but Julian could not place what it was. She was a giant of a woman. Her face was set not only to meet opposition but to seek it out. The downward tilt of her large lower lip was like a warning sign: DON'T TAMPER WITH ME. Her bulging figure was encased in a green crepe dress and her feet overflowed in red shoes. She had on a hideous hat. A purple velvet flap came down on one side of it and stood up on the other; the rest of it was green and looked like a cushion with the stuffing out. She carried a mammoth red pocketbook that bulged throughout as if it were stuffed with rocks.

To Julian's disappointment, the little boy climbed up on the empty seat beside his mother. His mother lumped all children, black and white, into a common category, 'cute', and she thought little Negroes were on the whole cuter than little white children. She smiled at the little boy as he climbed on the seat.

Meanwhile the woman was bearing down upon the empty seat beside Julian. To his annoyance, she squeezed herself into it. He saw his mother's face change as the woman settled herself next to him and he realized with satisfaction that this was more objectionable to her than it was to him. Her face seemed almost grey and there was a look of dull recognition in her eyes, as if suddenly she had sickened at some awful confrontation. Julian saw that it was because she and the woman had, in a sense, swapped sons. Though his mother would not realize the symbolic significance of this, she would feel it. His amusement showed plainly on his face.

The woman next to him muttered something unintelligible to herself. He was conscious of a kind of bristling next to him, muted growling like that of an angry cat. He could not see anything but the red pocketbook upright on the bulging green thighs. He visualized the woman as she had stood waiting for her tokens—the ponderous figure, rising from the red shoes upward over the solid hips, the mammoth bosom, the haughty face, to the green and purple hat.

His eyes widened.

The vision of the two hats, identical, broke upon him with the radiance of a brilliant sunrise. His face was suddenly lit with joy. He could not believe that Fate had thrust upon his mother such a lesson. He gave a loud chuckle so that she would look at him and see that he saw. She turned her eyes on him slowly. The blue in them seemed to have turned a bruised purple. For a moment he had an uncomfortable sense of her innocence, but it lasted only a second before principle rescued him. Justice entitled him to laugh. His grin hardened until it said to her as plainly as if he were saying aloud: Your punishment exactly fits your pettiness. This should teach you a permanent lesson.

Her eyes shifted to the woman. She seemed unable to bear looking at him and to find the woman preferable. He became conscious again of the bristling presence at his side. The woman was rumbling like a volcano about to become active. His mother's mouth began to twitch slightly at one corner. With a sinking heart, he saw incipient signs of recovery on her face and realized that this was going to strike her suddenly as funny and was going to be no lesson at all. She kept her eyes on the woman and an amused smile came over her face as if the woman were a monkey that had stolen her hat. The little Negro was looking up at her with large fascinated eyes. He had been trying to attract her attention for some time.

'Carver!' the woman said suddenly. 'Come heah!'

When he saw that the spotlight was on him at last, Carver drew his feet up and turned himself toward Julian's mother and giggled.

'Carver!' the woman said. 'You heah me? Come heah!'

Carver slid down from the seat but remained squatting with his back against the base of it, his head turned slyly around toward Julian's mother, who was smiling at him. The woman reached a hand across the aisle and snatched him to her. He righted himself and hung backwards on her knees, grinning at Julian's mother. 'Isn't he cute?' Julian's mother said to the woman with the protruding teeth.

'I reckon he is,' the woman said without conviction.

The Negress yanked him upright but he eased out of her grip and shot across the aisle and scrambled, giggling wildly, onto the seat beside his love.

'I think he likes me,' Julian's mother said, and smiled at the woman. It was the smile she used when she was being particularly gracious to an inferior. Julian saw everything lost. The lesson had rolled off her like rain on a roof.

The woman stood up and yanked the little boy off the seat as if she were snatching him from contagion. Julian could feel the rage in her at having no weapon like his mother's smile. She gave the child a sharp slap across his leg. He howled once and then thrust his head into her stomach and kicked his feet against her shins. 'Behave,' she said vehemently.

The bus stopped and the Negro who had been reading the newspaper got off. The woman moved over and set the little boy down with a thump between herself and Julian. She held him firmly by the knee. In a moment he put his hands in front of his face and peeped at Julian's mother through his fingers.

'I see yoooooooo!' she said and put her hand in front of her face and peeped at him.

The woman slapped his hand down. 'Quit yo' foolishness,' she said, 'before I knock the living Jesus out of you!'

Julian was thankful the next stop was theirs. He reached up and pulled the cord. The woman reached up and pulled it at the same time. Oh my God, he thought. He had the terrible intuition that when they got off the bus together, his mother would open her purse and give the little boy a nickel. The gesture would be as natural to her as breathing. The bus stopped and the woman got up and lunged to the front, dragging the child, who wished to stay on, after her. Julian and his mother got up and followed. As they neared the door, Julian tried to relieve her of her pocketbook.

'No,' she murmured, 'I want to give the little boy a nickel.'

'No!' Julian hissed. 'No!'

She smiled down at the child and opened her bag. The bus door opened and the woman picked him up by the arm and descended with him, hanging at her hip. Once in the street she set him down and shook him.

Julian's mother had to close her purse while she got down the bus step but as soon as her feet were on the ground, she opened it again and began to rummage inside. 'I can't find but a penny,' she whispered, 'but it looks like a new one.'

'Don't do it!' Julian said fiercely between his teeth. There was a streetlight on the corner and she hurried to get under it so that she could better see into her pocketbook.

The woman was heading off rapidly down the street with the child still hanging backward on her hand.

'Oh little boy!' Julian's mother called and took a few quick steps and caught up with them just beyond the lamppost. 'Here's a bright new penny for you,' and she held out the coin, which shone bronze in the dim light.

The huge woman turned and for a moment stood, her shoulders lifted and her face frozen with frustrated rage, and stared at Julian's mother. Then all at once she seemed to explode like a piece of machinery that had been given one ounce of pressure too much. Julian saw the black fist swing out with the red pocketbook. He shut his eyes and cringed as he heard the woman shout, 'He don't take nobody's pennies!' When he opened his eyes, the woman was disappearing down the street with the little boy staring wide-eyed over her shoulder. Julian's mother was sitting on the sidewalk.

'I told you not to do that,' Julian said angrily. 'I told you not to do that!'

He stood over her for a minute, gritting his teeth. Her legs were stretched out in front of her and her hat was on her lap. He squatted down and looked her in the face. It was totally expressionless. 'You got exactly what you deserved,' he said. 'Now get up.'

He picked up her pocketbook and put what had fallen out back in it. He picked the hat up off her lap. The penny caught his eye on the sidewalk and he picked that up and let it drop before her eyes into the purse. Then he stood up and leaned over and held his hands out to pull her up. She remained immobile. He sighed. Rising about them on either side were black apartment buildings, marked with irregular rectangles of light. At the end of the block a man came out of a door and walked off in the opposite direction. 'All right,' he said, 'suppose somebody happens by and wants to know why you're sitting on the sidewalk?'

She took the hand and, breathing hard, pulled heavily up on it and then stood for a moment, swaying slightly as if the spots of light in the darkness were circling around her. Her eyes, shadowed and confused, finally settled on his face. He did not try to conceal his irritation. 'I hope this teaches you a lesson,' he said. She leaned forward and her eyes raked his face. She seemed trying to determine his identity. Then, as if she found nothing familiar about him, started off with a headlong movement in the wrong direction.

'Aren't you going on to the Y'? he asked.

'Home,' she muttered.

'Well, are we walking?'

For answer she kept going. Julian followed along, his hands behind him. He saw no reason to let the lesson she had had go without backing it up with an explanation of its meaning. She might as well be made to understand what had happened to her. 'Don't think that was just an uppity Negro woman,' he said. 'That was the whole coloured race which will no longer take your condescending pennies. That was your black double. She can wear the same hat as you, and to be sure,' he added gratuitously (because he thought it was funny), 'it looked better on her than it did on you. What all this means', he said, 'is that the old world has gone. The old manners are obsolete and your graciousness is not worth a damn.' He thought bitterly of the house that had been lost for him. 'You aren't who you think you are,' he said.

She continued to plow ahead, paying no attention to him. Her hair had come undone on one side. She dropped her pocketbook and took no notice. He stooped and picked it up and handed it to her but she did not take it.

'You needn't act as if the world had come to an end,' he said, 'because it hasn't. From now on, you've got to live in a new world and face a few realities for a change. Buck up,' he said, 'it won't kill you.'

She was breathing fast.

'Let's wait on the bus,' he said.

'Home,' she said thickly.

'I hate to see you behave like this,' he said. 'Just like a child. I should be able to expect more of you.' He decided to stop where he was and make her stop and wait for a bus. 'I'm not going any farther,' he said, stopping. 'We're going on the bus.'

She continued to go on as if she had not heard him. He took a few steps and caught her arm and stopped her. He looked into her face and caught his breath. He was looking into a face he had never seen before. 'Tell Grandpa to come get me,' she said.

He stared, stricken.

'Tell Caroline to come get me,' she said.

Stunned, he let her go and she lurched forward again, walking as if one leg were shorter than the other. A tide of darkness seemed to be sweeping her from him. 'Mother!' he cried. 'Darling, sweetheart, wait!' Crumpling, she fell to the pavement. He dashed forward and fell at her side, crying, 'Mamma, Mamma!' He turned her over. Her face was fiercely distorted. One eye, large and staring, moved slightly on the left as if it had become unmoored. The other remained fixed on him, raked his face again, found nothing and closed.

'Wait here, wait here!' he cried and jumped up and began to run for help toward a cluster of lights he saw in the distance ahead of him. 'Help, help!' he shouted, but his voice was thin, scarcely a thread of sound. The lights drifted farther away the faster he ran and his feet moved numbly as if they carried him nowhere. The tide of darkness seemed to sweep him back to her, postponing from moment to moment his entry into the world of guilt and sorrow.

1961

Margaret Laurence

1926–1987

The most distinguished Canadian novelist of her generation, Jean Margaret Wemys was born in the small prairie town of Neepawa, Manitoba, of Scottish Presbyterian ancestry. She attended United College in Winnipeg, now the University of Winnipeg, where she developed her interest in fiction writing. In 1947 she married Jack Laurence, a civil engineer. She spent the early 1950s with her husband in Africa, first in Somaliland (now Somalia) and later in the Gold Coast (now Ghana). Her stay in these countries introduced her to African culture and art, and she translated some Nigerian literature, wrote critical studies of African writings, and set

her first novel, *This Side Jordan* (1960), and her first collection of short stories, *The Tomorrow-Tamer* (1963), in Africa. Even though she returned to Canada in 1957, she continued for five years to set her fiction in Africa. In 1962 Laurence moved to England, where she completed *The Stone Angel* (1964), her first novel set in the fictional prairie town of Manawaka. Three more novels, *A Jest of God* (1966), *The Fire-Dwellers* (1969), and *The Diviners* (1974), as well as the short-story sequence *A Bird in the House* (1970), continued Laurence's chronicling of Manawaka, each a close examination of the life of one woman in the town.

A Bird in the House

The parade would be almost over by now, and I had not gone. My mother had said in a resigned voice, 'All right, Vanessa, if that's the way you feel,' making me suffer twice as many jabs of guilt as I would have done if she had lost her temper. She and Grandmother MacLeod had gone off, my mother pulling the low box-sleigh with Roddie all dolled up in his new red snowsuit, just the sort of little kid anyone would want people to see. I sat on the lowest branch of the birch tree in our yard, not minding the snowy wind, even welcoming its punishment. I went over my reasons for not going, trying to believe they were good and sufficient, but in my heart I felt I was betraying my father. This was the first time I had stayed away from the Remembrance Day parade. I wondered if he would notice that I was not there, standing on the sidewalk at the corner of River and Main while the parade passed, and then following to the Court House grounds where the service was held.

    I could see the whole thing in my mind. It was the same every year. The Manawaka Civic Band always led the way. They had never been able to afford full uniforms, but they had peaked navy-blue caps and sky-blue chest ribbons. They were joined on Remembrance Day by the Salvation Army band, whose uniforms seemed too ordinary for a parade, for they were the same ones the bandsmen wore every Saturday night when they played 'Nearer My God to Thee' at the foot of River Street. The two bands never managed to practise quite enough together, so they did not keep in time too well. The Salvation Army band invariably played faster, and afterwards my father would say irritably, 'They play those marches just like they do hymns, blast them, as though they wouldn't get to heaven if they didn't hustle up.' And my mother, who had great respect for the Salvation Army because of the good work they did, would respond chidingly, 'Now, now, Ewen—' I vowed I would never say 'Now, now' to my husband or children, not that I ever intended having the latter, for I had been put off by my brother Roderick, who was now two years old with wavy hair, and everyone said what a beautiful child. I was twelve, and no one in their right mind would have said what a beautiful child, for I was big-boned like my Grandfather Connor and had straight lanky black hair like a Blackfoot or Cree.

After the bands would come the veterans. Even thinking of them at this distance, in the white and withdrawn quiet of the birch tree, gave me a sense of painful embarrassment. I might not have minded so much if my father had not been among them. How could he go? How could he not see how they all looked? It must have been a long time since they were soldiers, for they had forgotten how to march in step. They were old—that was the thing. My father was bad enough, being almost forty, but he wasn't a patch on Howard Tully from the drugstore, who was completely grey-haired and also fat, or Stewart MacMurchie, who was bald at the back of his head. They looked to me like imposters, plump or spindly caricatures of past warriors. I almost hated them for walking in that limping column down Main. At the Court House, everyone would sing *Lord God of Hosts, be with us yet, lest we forget, lest we forget.* Will Masterson would pick up his old Army bugle and blow the Last Post. Then it would be over and everyone could start gabbling once more and go home.

I jumped down from the birch bough and ran to the house, yelling, making as much noise as I could.

> I'm a poor lonesome cowboy
> An' a long way from home—

I stepped inside the front hall and kicked off my snow boots. I slammed the door behind me, making the dark ruby and emerald glass shake in the small leaded panes. I slid purposely on the hall rug, causing it to bunch and crinkle on the slippery polished oak of the floor. I seized the newel post, round as a head, and spun myself to and fro on the bottom stair.

> I ain't got no father
> To buy the clothes I wear,
> I'm a poor lonesome—

At this moment my shoulders were firmly seized and shaken by a pair of hands, white and delicate and old, but strong as talons.

'Just what do you think you're doing, young lady?' Grandmother MacLeod enquired, in a voice like frost on a windowpane, infinitely cold and clearly etched.

I went limp and in a moment she took her hands away. If you struggled, she would always hold on longer.

'Gee, I never knew you were home yet.'

'I would have thought that on a day like this you might have shown a little respect and consideration,' Grandmother MacLeod said, 'even if you couldn't make the effort to get cleaned up enough to go to the parade.'

I realized with surprise that she imagined this to be my reason for not going. I did not try to correct her impression. My real reason would have been even less acceptable.

'I'm sorry,' I said quickly.

In some families, *please* is described as the magic word. In our house, however, it was sorry.

'This isn't an easy day for any of us,' she said.

Her younger son, my Uncle Roderick, had been killed in the Great War. When my father marched, and when the hymn was sung, and when that unbearably lonely tune was sounded by the one bugle and everyone forced themselves to keep absolutely still, it would be that boy of whom she was thinking. I felt the enormity of my own offence.

'Grandmother—I'm sorry.'

'So you said.'

I could not tell her I had not really said it before at all. I went into the den and found my father there. He was sitting in the leather-cushioned armchair beside the fireplace. He was not doing anything, just sitting and smoking. I stood beside him, wanting to touch the light-brown hairs on his forearm, but thinking he might laugh at me or pull his arm away if I did.

'I'm sorry,' I said, meaning it.

'What for, honey?'

'For not going.'

'Oh—that. What was the matter?'

I did not want him to know, and yet I had to tell him, make him see.

'They look silly,' I blurted. 'Marching like that.'

For a minute I thought he was going to be angry. It would have been a relief to me if he had been. Instead, he drew his eyes away from mine and fixed them above the mantelpiece where the sword hung, the handsome and evil-looking crescent in its carved bronze sheath that some ancestor had once brought from the Northern Frontier of India.

'Is that the way it looks to you?' he said.

I felt in his voice some hurt, something that was my fault. I wanted to make everything all right between us, to convince him that I understood, even if I did not. I prayed that Grandmother MacLeod would stay put in her room, and that my mother would take a long time in the kitchen, giving Roddie his lunch. I wanted my father to myself, so I could prove to him that I cared more about him than any of the others did. I wanted to speak in some way that would be more poignant and comprehending than anything of which my mother could possibly be capable. But I did not know how.

'You were right there when Uncle Roderick got killed, weren't you?' I began uncertainly.

'Yes.'

'How old was he, Dad?'

'Eighteen,' my father said.

Unexpectedly, that day came into intense being for me. He had had to watch his own brother die, not in the antiseptic calm of some hospital, but out in the open, the stretches of mud I had seen in his snapshots. He would not have known what to do. He would just have had to stand there and look at it, whatever that might mean. I looked at my father with a kind of horrified awe, and then I began to cry. I had forgotten about impressing him with my perception. Now I needed him to console me for this unwanted glimpse of the pain he had once known.

'Hey, cut it out, honey,' he said, embarrassed. 'It was bad, but it wasn't all as bad as that part. There were a few other things.'

'Like what?' I said, not believing him.

'Oh—I don't know,' he replied evasively. 'Most of us were pretty young, you know, I and the boys I joined up with. None of us had ever been away from Manawaka before. Those of us who came back mostly came back here, or else went no further away from town than Winnipeg. So when we were overseas—that was the only time most of us were ever a long way from home.'

'Did you want to be?' I asked, shocked.

'Oh well—' my father said uncomfortably. 'It was kind of interesting to see a few other places for a change, that's all.'

Grandmother MacLeod was standing in the doorway.

'Beth's called you twice for lunch, Ewen. Are you deaf, you and Vanessa?'

'Sorry,' my father and I said simultaneously.

Then we went upstairs to wash our hands.

That winter my mother returned to her old job as nurse in my father's medical practice. She was able to do this only because of Noreen.

'Grandmother MacLeod says we're getting a maid,' I said to my father, accusingly, one morning. 'We're not, are we?'

'Believe you me, on what I'm going to be paying her,' my father growled, 'she couldn't be called anything as classy as a maid. Hired girl would be more like it.'

'Now, now, Ewen,' my mother put in, 'it's not as if we were cheating her or anything. You know she wants to live in town, and I can certainly see why, stuck out there on the farm, and her father hardly ever letting her come in. What kind of life is that for a girl?'

'I don't like the idea of your going back to work, Beth,' my father said. 'I know you're fine now, but you're not exactly the robust type.'

'You can't afford to hire a nurse any longer. It's all very well to say the Depression won't last forever—probably it won't, but what else can we do for now?'

'I'm damned if I know,' my father admitted. 'Beth—'

'Yes?'

They both seemed to have forgotten about me. It was at breakfast, which we always ate in the kitchen, and I sat rigidly on my chair, pretending to ignore and thus snub their withdrawal from me. I glared at the window, but it was so thickly plumed and scrolled with frost that I could not see out. I glanced back to my parents. My father had not replied, and my mother was looking at him in that anxious and half-frowning way she had recently developed.

'What is it, Ewen?' Her voice had the same nervous sharpness it bore sometimes when she would say to me, 'For mercy's sake, Vanessa, what is it *now*?' as though whatever was the matter, it was bound to be the last straw.

My father spun his sterling silver serviette ring, engraved with his initials, slowly around on the table.

'I never thought things would turn out like this, did you?'

'Please—' my mother said in a low strained voice, 'please, Ewen, let's not start all this again. I can't take it.'

'All right,' my father said. 'Only—'

'The MacLeods used to have money and now they don't,' my mother cried. 'Well, they're not alone. Do you think all that matters to me, Ewen? What I can't bear is to see you forever reproaching yourself. As if it were your fault.'

'I don't think it's the comedown,' my father said. 'If I were somewhere else, I don't suppose it would matter to me, either, except where you're concerned. But I suppose you'd work too hard wherever you were—it's bred into you. If you haven't got anything to slave away at, you'll sure as hell invent something.'

'What do you think I should do, let the house go to wrack and ruin? That would go over well with your mother, wouldn't it?'

'That's just it,' my father said. 'It's the damned house all the time. I haven't only taken on my father's house, I've taken on everything that goes with it, apparently. Sometimes I really wonder—'

'Well, it's a good thing I've inherited some practicality even if you haven't,' my mother said. 'I'll say that for the Connors—they aren't given to brooding, thank you Lord. Do you want your egg poached or scrambled?'

'Scrambled,' my father said. 'All I hope is that this Noreen doesn't get married straightaway, that's all.'

'She won't,' my mother said. 'Who's she going to meet who could afford to marry?'

'I marvel at you, Beth,' my father said. 'You look as though a puff of wind would blow you away. But underneath, by God, you're all hardwood.'

'Don't talk stupidly,' my mother said. 'All I hope is that she doesn't object to taking your mother's breakfast up on a tray.'

'That's right,' my father said angrily. 'Rub it in.'

'Oh Ewen, I'm sorry!' my mother cried, her face suddenly stricken. 'I don't know why I say these things. I didn't mean to.'

'I know,' my father said. 'Here, cut it out, honey. Just for God's sake please don't cry.'

'I'm sorry,' my mother repeated, blowing her nose.

'We're both sorry,' my father said. 'Not that that changes anything.'

After my father had gone, I got down from my chair and went to my mother.

'I don't want you to go back to the office. I don't want a hired girl here. I'll hate her.'

My mother sighed, making me feel that I was placing an intolerable burden on her, and yet making me resent having to feel this weight. She looked tired, as she often did these days. Her tiredness bored me, made me want to attack her for it.

'Catch me getting along with a dumb old hired girl,' I threatened.

'Do what you like,' my mother said abruptly. 'What can I do about it?'

And then, of course, I felt bereft, not knowing which way to turn.

My father need not have worried about Noreen getting married. She was, as it turned out, interested not in boys but in God. My mother was relieved about the boys but alarmed about God.

'It isn't natural,' she said, 'for a girl of seventeen. Do you think she's all right mentally, Ewen?'

When my parents, along with Grandmother MacLeod, went to the United Church every Sunday, I was made to go to Sunday school in the church basement, where there were small red chairs which humiliatingly resembled kindergarten furniture, and pictures of Jesus wearing a white sheet and surrounded by a whole lot of well-dressed kids whose mothers obviously had not suffered them to come unto Him until every face and ear was properly scrubbed. Our religious observances also included grace at meals, when my father would mumble 'For what we are about to receive the Lord make us truly thankful Amen,' running the words together as though they were one long word. My mother approved of these rituals, which seemed decent and moderate to her. Noreen's religion, however, was a different matter. Noreen belonged to the Tabernacle of the Risen and Reborn, and she had got up to testify no less than seven times in the past two years, she told us. My mother, who could not imagine anyone's voluntarily making a public spectacle of themselves, was profoundly shocked by this revelation.

'Don't worry,' my father soothed her. 'She's all right. She's just had kind of a dull life, that's all.'

My mother shrugged and went on worrying and trying to help Noreen without hurting her feelings, by tactful remarks about the advisability of modulating one's voice when singing hymns, and the fact that there was plenty of hot water so Noreen didn't need to hesitate about taking a bath. She even bought a razor and a packet of blades and whispered to Noreen that any girl who wore transparent blouses so much would probably like to shave under her arms. None of these suggestions had the slightest effect on Noreen. She did not cease belting out hymns at the top of her voice, she bathed once a fortnight, and the sorrel-coloured hair continued to bloom like a thicket of Indian paintbrush in her armpits.

Grandmother MacLeod refused to speak to Noreen. This caused Noreen a certain amount of bewilderment until she finally hit on an answer.

'Your poor grandma,' she said. 'She is deaf as a post. These things are sent to try us here on earth, Vanessa. But if she makes it into Heaven, I'll bet you anything she will hear clear as a bell.'

Noreen and I talked about Heaven quite a lot, and also Hell. Noreen had an intimate and detailed knowledge of both places. She not only knew what they looked like—she even knew how big they were. Heaven was seventy-seven thousand miles square and it had four gates, each one made out of a different kind of precious jewel. The Pearl Gate, the Topaz Gate, the Amethyst Gate, the Ruby Gate—Noreen would reel them off, all the gates of Heaven. I told Noreen they sounded like poetry, but she was puzzled by my reaction and said I shouldn't talk that way. If you said poetry, it sounded like it was just made up and not really so, Noreen said.

Hell was larger than Heaven, and when I asked why, thinking of it as something of a comedown for God, Noreen said naturally it had to be bigger because there were a darn sight more people there than in Heaven. Hell was one hundred and ninety million miles deep and was in perpetual darkness, like a cave or under the sea. Even the flames (this was the awful thing) *did not give off any light.*

I did not actually believe in Noreen's doctrines, but the images which they conjured up began to inhabit my imagination. Noreen's fund of exotic knowledge was not limited to religion, although in a way it all seemed related. She could do many things which had a spooky tinge to them. Once when she was making a cake, she found we had run out of eggs. She went outside and gathered a bowl of fresh snow and used it instead. The cake rose like a charm, and I stared at Noreen as though she were a sorceress. In fact, I began to think of her as a sorceress, someone not quite of this earth. There was nothing unearthly about her broad shoulders and hips and her forest of dark red hair, but even these features took on a slightly sinister significance to me. I no longer saw her through the eyes of the expressed opinions of my mother and father, as a girl who had quit school at grade eight and whose life on the farm had been endlessly drab. I knew the truth—Noreen's life had not been drab at all, for she dwelt in a world of violent splendours, a world filled with angels whose wings of delicate light bore real feathers, and saints shining like the dawn, and prophets who spoke in ancient tongues, and the ecstatic souls of the saved, as well as denizens of the lower regions—mean-eyed imps and crooked cloven-hoofed monsters and beasts with the bodies of swine and the human heads of murderers, and lovely depraved jezebels torn by dogs through all eternity. The middle layer of Creation, our earth, was equally full of grotesque presences, for Noreen believed strongly in the visitation of ghosts and the communication with spirits. She could prove this with her Ouija board. We would both place our fingers lightly on the indicator, and it would skim across the board and spell out answers to our questions. I did not believe wholeheartedly in the Ouija board, either, but I was cautious about the kind of question I asked, in case the answer would turn out unfavourable and I would be unable to forget it.

One day Noreen told me she could also make a table talk. We used the small table in my bedroom, and sure enough, it lifted very slightly under our fingertips and tapped once for *Yes*, twice for *No*. Noreen asked if her Aunt Ruthie would get better from the kidney operation, and the table replied No. I withdrew my hands.

'I don't want to do it any more.'

'Gee, what's the matter, Vanessa?' Noreen's plain placid face creased in a frown. 'We only just begun.'

'I have to do my homework.'

My heart lurched as I said this. I was certain Noreen would know I was lying, and that she would know not by any ordinary perception, either. But her attention had been caught by something else, and I was thankful, at least until I saw what it was.

My bedroom window was not opened in the coldest weather. The storm window, which was fitted outside as an extra wall against the winter, had three small circular holes in its frame so that some fresh air could seep into the house. The sparrow must have been floundering in the new snow on the roof, for it had crawled in through one of these holes and was now caught between the two layers of glass. I could not bear the panic of the trapped bird, and before I realized what I was doing, I had thrown open the bedroom window. I was not releasing the sparrow into any better a situation, I soon saw, for instead of remaining quiet and allowing us to catch it in order to free it, it began flying blindly around the room, hitting the lampshade, brushing against the walls, its wings seeming to spin faster and faster.

I was petrified. I thought I would pass out if those palpitating wings touched me. There was something in the bird's senseless movements that revolted me. I also thought it was going to damage itself, break one of those thin wing-bones, perhaps, and then it would be lying on the floor, dying, like the pimpled and horribly feath-erless baby birds we saw sometimes on the sidewalks in the spring when they had fallen out of their nests. I was not any longer worried about the sparrow. I wanted only to avoid the sight of it lying broken on the floor. Viciously, I thought that if Noreen said, *God sees the little sparrow fall*, I would kick her in the shins. She did not, however, say this.

'A bird in the house means a death in the house,' Noreen remarked.

Shaken, I pulled my glance away from the whirling wings and looked at Noreen. 'What?'

'That's what I've heard said, anyhow.'

The sparrow had exhausted itself. It lay on the floor, spent and trembling. I could not bring myself to touch it. Noreen bent and picked it up. She cradled it with great gentleness between her cupped hands. Then we took it downstairs, and when I had opened the back door, Noreen set the bird free.

'Poor little scrap,' she said, and I felt struck to the heart, knowing she had been concerned all along about the sparrow, while I, perfidiously, in the chaos of the moment, had been concerned only about myself.

'Wanna do some with the Ouija board, Vanessa?' Noreen asked.

I shivered a little, perhaps only because of the blast of cold air which had come into the kitchen when the door was opened.

'No thanks, Noreen. Like I said, I got my homework to do. But thanks all the same.'

'That's okay,' Noreen said in her guileless voice. 'Any time.'

But whenever she mentioned the Ouija board or the talking table, after that, I always found some excuse not to consult these oracles.

'Do you want to come to church with me this evening, Vanessa?' my father asked.

'How come you're going to the evening service?' I enquired.

'Well, we didn't go this morning. We went snowshoeing instead, remember? I think your grandmother was a little bit put out about it. She went alone this morning. I guess it wouldn't hurt you and me, to go now.'

We walked through the dark, along the white streets, the snow squeaking dryly under our feet. The streetlights were placed at long intervals along the sidewalks, and around each pole the circle of flimsy light created glistening points of blue and crystal on the crusted snow. I would have liked to take my father's hand, as I used to do, but

I was too old for that now. I walked beside him, taking long steps so he would not have to walk more slowly on my account.

The sermon bored me, and I began leafing through the Hymnary for entertainment. I must have drowsed, for the next thing I knew, my father was prodding me and we were on our feet for the closing hymn.

> Near the Cross, near the Cross,
> Be my glory ever,
> Till my ransomed soul shall find
> Rest beyond the river.

I knew the tune well, so I sang loudly for the first verse. But the music to that hymn is sombre, and all at once the words themselves seemed too dreadful to be sung. I stopped singing, my throat knotted. I thought I was going to cry, but I did not know why, except that the song recalled to me my Grandmother Connor, who had been dead only a year now. I wondered why her soul needed to be ransomed. If God did not think she was good enough just as she was, then I did not have much use for His opinion. *Rest beyond the river*—was that what had happened to her? She had believed in Heaven, but I did not think that rest beyond the river was quite what she had in mind. To think of her in Noreen's flashy Heaven, though—that was even worse. Someplace where nobody ever got annoyed or had to be smoothed down and placated, someplace where there were never any family scenes—that would have suited my Grandmother Connor. Maybe she wouldn't have minded a certain amount of rest beyond the river, at that.

When we had the silent prayer, I looked at my father. He sat with his head bowed and his eyes closed. He was frowning deeply, and I could see the pulse in his temple. I wondered then what he believed. I did not have any real idea what it might be. When he raised his head, he did not look uplifted or anything like that. He merely looked tired. Then Reverend McKee pronounced the benediction, and we could go home.

'What do you think about all that stuff, Dad?' I asked hesitantly, as we walked.

'What stuff, honey?'

'Oh, Heaven and Hell, and like that.'

My father laughed. 'Have you been listening to Noreen too much? Well, I don't know. I don't think they're actual places. Maybe they stand for something that happens all the time here, or else doesn't happen. It's kind of hard to explain. I guess I'm not so good at explanations.'

Nothing seemed to have been made any clearer to me. I reached out and took his hand, not caring that he might think this a babyish gesture.

'I hate that hymn!'

'Good Lord,' my father said in astonishment. 'Why, Vanessa?'

But I did not know and so could not tell him.

Many people in Manawaka had flu that winter, so my father and Dr Cates were kept extremely busy. I had flu myself, and spent a week in bed, vomiting only the first day and after that enjoying poor health, as my mother put it, with Noreen bringing me ginger ale and orange juice, and each evening my father putting a wooden tongue-depressor into my mouth and peering down my throat, then smiling and saying he thought I might live after all.

Then my father got sick himself, and had to stay at home and go to bed. This was such an unusual occurrence that it amused me.

'Doctors shouldn't get sick,' I told him.

'You're right,' he said. 'That was pretty bad management.'

'Run along now, dear,' my mother said.

That night I woke and heard voices in the upstairs hall. When I went out, I found my mother and Grandmother MacLeod, both in their dressing gowns. With them was Dr Cates. I did not go immediately to my mother, as I would have done only a year before. I stood in the doorway of my room, squinting against the sudden light.

'Mother—what is it?'

She turned, and momentarily I saw the look on her face before she erased it and put on a contrived calm.

'It's all right,' she said. 'Dr Cates has just come to have a look at Daddy. You go on back to sleep.'

The wind was high that night, and I lay and listened to it rattling the storm windows and making the dry and winter-stiffened vines of the Virginia creeper scratch like small persistent claws against the red brick. In the morning, my mother told me that my father had developed pneumonia.

Dr Cates did not think it would be safe to move my father to the hospital. My mother began sleeping in the spare bedroom, and after she had been there for a few nights, I asked if I could sleep in there too. I thought she would be bound to ask me why, and I did not know what I would say, but she did not ask. She nodded, and in some way her easy agreement upset me.

That night Dr Cates came again, bringing with him one of the nurses from the hospital. My mother stayed upstairs with them. I sat with Grandmother MacLeod in the living room. That was the last place in the world I wanted to be, but I thought she would be offended if I went off. She sat as straight and rigid as a totem pole, and embroidered away at the needlepoint cushion cover she was doing. I perched on the edge of the chesterfield and kept my eyes fixed on *The White Company* by Conan Doyle, and from time to time I turned a page. I had already read it three times before, but luckily Grandmother MacLeod did not know that. At nine o'clock she looked at her gold brooch watch, which she always wore pinned to her dress, and told me to go to bed, so I did that.

I wakened in darkness. At first, it seemed to me that I was in my own bed, and everything was a usual, with my parents in their room, and Roddie curled up in the crib in his room, and Grandmother MacLeod sleeping with her mouth open in her enormous spool bed, surrounded by a half a dozen framed photos of Uncle Roderick and only one of my father, and Noreen snoring fitfully in the room next to mine, with the dark flames of her hair spreading out across the pillow, and the pink and silver motto cards from the Tabernacle stuck with adhesive tape onto the wall beside her bed—*Lean on Him, Emmanuel Is My Refuge, Rock of Ages Cleft for Me.*

Then in the total night around me, I heard a sound. It was my mother, and she was crying, not loudly at all, but from somewhere very deep inside her. I sat up in bed. Everything seemed to have stopped, not only time but my own heart and blood as well. Then my mother noticed that I was awake.

I did not ask her, and she did not tell me anything. There was no need. She held me in her arms, or I held her, I am not certain which. And after a while the first mourning stopped, too, as everything does sooner or later, for when the limits of endurance have been reached, then people must sleep.

In the days following my father's death, I stayed close beside my mother, and this was only partly for my own consoling. I also had the feeling that she needed my protection. I did not know from what, nor what I could possibly do, but something held me there. Reverend McKee called, and I sat with my grandmother and my mother in the living room. My mother told me I did not need to stay unless I wanted to, but I refused to go. What I thought chiefly was that he would speak of the healing power of prayer, and all that, and it would be bound to make my mother cry again. And in fact, it happened in just that way, but when it actually came, I could not protect her from this assault. I could only sit there and pray my own prayer, which was that he would go away quickly.

My mother tried not to cry unless she was alone or with me. I also tried, but neither of us was entirely successful. Grandmother MacLeod, on the other hand, was never seen crying, not even the day of my father's funeral. But that day, when we had returned to the house and she had taken off her black velvet overshoes and her heavy sealskin coat with its black fur that was the softest thing I had ever touched, she stood in the hallway and for the first time she looked unsteady. When I reached out instinctively towards her, she sighed.

'That's right,' she said. 'You might just take my arm while I go upstairs, Vanessa.'

That was the most my Grandmother MacLeod ever gave in, to anyone's sight. I left her in her bedroom, sitting on the straight chair beside her bed and looking at the picture of my father that had been taken when he graduated from medical college. Maybe she was sorry now that she had only the one photograph of him, but whatever she felt, she did not say.

I went down to the kitchen. I had scarcely spoken to Noreen since my father's death. This had not been done on purpose. I simply had not seen her. I had not really seen anyone except my mother. Looking at Noreen now, I suddenly recalled the sparrow. I felt physically sick, remembering the fearful darting and plunging of those wings, and the fact that it was I who had opened the window and let it in. Then an inexplicable fury took hold of me, some terrifying need to hurt, burn, destroy. Absolutely without warning, either to her or to myself, I hit Noreen as hard as I could. When she swung around, appalled, I hit out at her once more, my arms and legs flailing. Her hands snatched at my wrists, and she held me, but still I continued to struggle, fighting blindly, my eyes tightly closed, as though she were a prison all around me and I was battling to get out. Finally, too shocked at myself to go on, I went limp in her grasp and she let me drop to the floor.

'Vanessa! I never done one single solitary thing to you, and here you go hitting and scratching me like that! What in the world has got into you?'

I began to say I was sorry, which was certainly true, but I did not say it. I could not say anything.

'You're not yourself, what with your dad and everything,' she excused me. 'I been praying every night that your dad is with God, Vanessa. I know he wasn't actually saved in the regular way, but still and all—'

'Shut up,' I said.

Something in my voice made her stop talking. I rose from the floor and stood in the kitchen doorway.

'He didn't need to be saved,' I went on coldly, distinctly. 'And he is not in Heaven, because there is no Heaven. And it doesn't matter, see? *It doesn't matter!*'

Noreen's face looked peculiarly vulnerable now, her high wide cheekbones and puzzled childish eyes, and the thick russet tangle of her hair. I had not hurt her much before, when I hit her. But I had hurt her now, hurt her in some inexcusable way. Yet I sensed, too, that already she was gaining some satisfaction out of feeling sorrowful about my disbelief.

I went upstairs to my room. Momentarily I felt a sense of calm, almost of acceptance. *Rest beyond the river*. I knew now what that meant. It meant Nothing. It meant only silence, forever.

Then I lay down on my bed and spent the last of my tears, or what seemed then to be the last. Because, despite what I had said to Noreen, it did matter. It mattered, but there was no help for it.

Everything changed after my father's death. The MacLeod house could not be kept up any longer. My mother sold it to a local merchant who subsequently covered the deep red of the brick over with yellow stucco. Something about the house had always made me uneasy—that tower room where Grandmother MacLeod's potted plants drooped in a lethargic and lime-green confusion, those long stairways and hidden places, the attic which I had always imagined to be dwelt in by the spirits of the family dead, that gigantic portrait of the Duke of Wellington at the top of the stairs. It was never an endearing house. And yet when it was no longer ours, and when the Virginia creeper had been torn down and the dark walls turned to a light marigold, I went out of my way to avoid walking past, for it seemed to me that the house had lost the stern dignity that was its very heart.

Noreen went back to the farm. My mother and brother and myself moved into Grandmother Connor's house. Grandmother MacLeod went to live with Aunt Morag in Winnipeg. It was harder for her than for anyone, because so much of her life was bound up with the MacLeod house. She was fond of Aunt Morag, but that hardly counted. Her men were gone, her husband and her sons, and a family whose men are gone is no family at all. The day she left, my mother and I did not know what to say. Grandmother MacLeod looked even smaller than usual in her fur coat and her black velvet toque. She became extremely agitated about trivialities, and fussed about the possibility of the taxi not arriving on time. She had forbidden us to accompany her to the station. About my father, or the house, or anything important, she did not say a word. Then, when the taxi had finally arrived, she turned to my mother.

'Roddie will have Ewen's seal ring, of course, with the MacLeod crest on it,' she said. 'But there is another seal as well, don't forget, the larger one with the crest and motto. It's meant to be worn on a watch chain. I keep it in my jewel-box. It was Roderick's. Roddie's to have that, too, when I die. Don't let Morag talk you out of it.'

During the Second World War, when I was seventeen and in love with an airman who did not love me, and desperately anxious to get away from Manawaka and from my grandfather's house, I happened one day to be going through the old mahogany desk that had belonged to my father. It had a number of small drawers inside, and I accidentally pulled one of these all the way out. Behind it there was another drawer, one I had not known about. Curiously, I opened it. Inside there was a letter written on almost transparent paper in a cramped angular handwriting. It began—*Cher Monsieur Ewen*—That was all I could make out, for the writing was nearly impossible to read and my French was not good. It was dated 1919. With it, there was a picture of a girl, looking absurdly old-fashioned to my eyes, like the faces on long-discarded calendars or chocolate boxes. But beneath the dated quality of the photograph, she seemed neither expensive nor cheap. She looked like what she probably had been—an ordinary middle-class girl, but in another country. She wore her hair in long ringlets, and her mouth was shaped into a sweetly sad posed smile like Mary Pickford's. That was all. There was nothing else in the drawer.

I looked for a long time at the girl, and hoped she had meant some momentary and unexpected freedom. I remembered what he had said to me, after I hadn't gone to the Remembrance Day parade.

'What are you doing, Vanessa?' my mother called from the kitchen.

'Nothing,' I replied.

I took the letter and picture outside and burned them. That was all I could do for him. Now that we might have talked together, it was many years too late. Perhaps it would not have been possible anyway. I did not know.

As I watched the smile of the girl turn into scorched paper, I grieved for my father as though he had just died now.

1970

John Barth
b. 1930

John Barth and his twin sister, Jill, were born in Cambridge, on the eastern shore of Maryland. As a boy he was a serious musician, organizing his own band and starting study at the Julliard School of Music. His interest shifted to literature, and he transferred to Johns Hopkins, where he received his MA in 1952. He supported himself, his wife, and his children by his music until he got his first teaching job in 1953. He taught for the next forty years, publishing his first novel in 1956 and establishing himself as a major writer with *The Sot-Weed Factor* in 1960 and his collection of short fiction *Lost in the Funhouse* in 1968.

In 'Lost in the Funhouse', Barth shows his postmodern tendencies by freeing himself from the absolute boundaries of memory and history in exploring a thirteen-year-old boy's coming of age. This piece of self-referential metafiction explores the hidden thoughts of a blocked writer attempting to adhere to the formulaic rules of a creative writing course.

Lost in the Funhouse

For whom is the funhouse fun? Perhaps for lovers. For Ambrose it is *a place of fear and confusion.* He has come to the seashore with his family for the holiday, *the occasion of their visit is Independence Day, the most important secular holiday of the United States of America.* A single straight underline is the manuscript mark for italic type, *which in turn* is the printed equivalent to oral emphasis of words and phrases as well as the customary type for titles of complete works, not to mention. Italics are also employed, in fiction stories especially, for 'outside', intrusive, or artificial voices, such as radio announcements, the texts of telegrams and newspaper articles, et cetera. They should be used *sparingly.* If passages originally in roman type are italicized by someone repeating them, it's customary to acknowledge the fact. *Italics mine.*

Ambrose was 'at that awkward age'. His voice came out high-pitched as a child's if he let himself get carried away; to be on the safe side, therefore, he moved and spoke with *deliberate calm* and *adult gravity.* Talking soberly of unimportant or irrelevant matters and listening consciously to the sound of our own voice are useful habits for maintaining control in this difficult interval. *En route* to Ocean City he sat in the back seat of the family car with his brother Peter, age fifteen, and Magda G——, age fourteen, a pretty girl and exquisite young lady, who lived not far from them on B—— Street in the town of D——, Maryland. Initials, blanks, or both were often substituted for proper names in nineteenth-century fiction to enhance the illusion of reality. It is as if the author felt it necessary to delete the names for reasons of tact or legal liability. Interestingly, as with other aspects of realism, it is an *illusion* that is being enhanced, by purely artificial means. Is it likely, does it violate the principle of verisimilitude, that a thirteen-year-old boy could make such a sophisticated observation? A girl of fourteen is *the psychological coeval* of a boy of fifteen or sixteen; a thirteen-year-old boy, therefore, even one precocious in some other respects, might be three years her emotional junior.

Thrice a year—on Memorial, Independence, and Labor Days—the family visits Ocean City for the afternoon and evening. When Ambrose and Peter's father was their age, the excursion was made by train, as mentioned in the novel *The 42nd Parallel* by John Dos Passos. Many families from the same neighbourhood used to travel together, with dependent relatives and often with Negro servants; schoolfuls of children swarmed through the railway cars; everyone shared everyone else's Maryland fried chicken, Virginia ham, devilled eggs, potato salad, beaten biscuits, iced tea. Nowadays (that is, in 19—, the year of our story) the journey is made by automobile—more comfortably and quickly though without the extra fun though without the *camaraderie* of a general excursion. It's all part of the deterioration of American life, their father declares; Uncle Karl supposes that when the boys take *their* families to Ocean City for the holidays they'll fly in Autogiros. Their mother, sitting in the middle of the front seat like Magda in the second, only with her arms on the seat-back behind the men's shoulders, wouldn't want the good old days back again, the steaming trains and stuffy long dresses; on the other hand she can do without Autogiros, too, if she has to become a grandmother to fly in them.

Description of physical appearance and mannerisms is one of several standard methods of characterization used by writers of fiction. It is also important to 'keep the senses operating'; when a detail from one of the five senses, say visual, is 'crossed' with a detail from another, say auditory, the reader's imagination is oriented to the scene, perhaps unconsciously. This procedure may be compared to the way surveyors and navigators determine their positions by two or more compass bearings, a process known as triangulation. The brown hair on Ambrose's mother's forearms gleamed in the sun like. Though right-handed, she took her left arm from the seat-back to press the dashboard cigar lighter for Uncle Karl. When the glass bead in its handle glowed red, the lighter was ready for use. The smell of Uncle Karl's cigar smoke reminded one of. The fragrance of the ocean came strong to the picnic ground where they always stopped for lunch, two miles inland from Ocean City. Having to pause for a full hour almost within sound of the breakers was difficult for Peter and Ambrose when they were younger; even at their present age it was not easy to keep their anticipation, *stimulated by the briny spume,* from turning into short temper. The Irish author James Joyce, in his unusual novel entitled *Ulysses,* now available in this country, uses the adjectives *snot-green* and *scrotum-tightening* to describe the sea. Visual; auditory; tactile; olfactory; gustatory. Peter and Ambrose's father, while steering their black 1936 LaSalle sedan with one hand, could with the other remove the first cigarette from a white pack of Lucky Strikes and, more remarkably, light it with a match forefingered from its book and thumbed against the flint paper without being detached. The matchbook cover merely advertised US War Bonds and Stamps. A fine metaphor, simile, or other figure of speech, in addition to its obvious 'first-order' relevance to the thing it describes, will be seen upon reflection to have a second order of significance: it may be drawn from the *milieu* of the action, for example, or be particularly appropriate to the sensibility of the narrator, even hinting to the reader things of which the narrator is unaware; or it may cast further and subtler lights upon the things it describes, sometimes ironically qualifying the more evident sense of the comparison.

To say that Ambrose's and Peter's mother was *pretty* is to accomplish nothing; the reader may acknowledge the proposition, but his imagination is not engaged. Besides, Magda was also pretty, yet in an altogether different way. Although she lived on B—— Street she had very good manners and did better than average in school. Her figure was very well developed for her age. Her right hand lay casually on the plush upholstery of the seat, very near Ambrose's left leg, on which his own hand rested. The space between their legs, between her right and his left leg, was out of the line of sight of anyone sitting on the other side of Magda, as well as anyone glancing into the rear-view mirror. Uncle Karl's face resembled Peter's—rather, vice versa. Both had dark hair and eyes, short husky statures, deep voices. Magda's left hand was probably in a similar position on her left side. The boys' father is difficult to describe; no particular feature of his appearance or manner stood out. He wore glasses and was principal of a T—— County grade school. Uncle Karl was a masonry contractor.

Although Peter must have known as well as Ambrose that the latter, because of his position in the car, would be the first to see the electrical towers of the power plant at V——, the halfway point of their trip, he leaned forward and slightly toward the centre of the car and pretended to be looking for them through the flat pinewoods and tuckahoe creeks along the highway. For as long as the boys could remember, 'looking for the Towers' had been a feature of the first half of their excursions to Ocean City, 'looking for the standpipe' of the second. Though the game was childish, their mother preserved the tradition of rewarding the first to see the Towers with a candy-bar or piece of fruit. She insisted now that Magda play the game; the prize, she said, was 'something hard to get nowadays'. Ambrose decided not to join in; he sat far back in his seat. Magda, like Peter, leaned forward. Two sets of straps were discernible through the shoulders of her sun dress; the inside right one, a brassiere-strap, was fastened or shortened with a small safety pin. The right armpit of her dress, presumably the left as well, was damp with perspiration. The simple strategy for being first to espy the Towers, which Ambrose had understood by the age of four, was to sit on the right-hand side of the car. Whoever sat there, however, had also to put up with the worst of the sun, and so Ambrose, without mentioning the matter, chose sometimes the one and sometimes the other. Not impossibly Peter had never caught on to the trick, or thought that his brother hadn't simply because Ambrose on occasion preferred shade to a Baby Ruth or tangerine.

The shade–sun situation didn't apply to the front seat, owing to the windshield; if anything the driver got more sun, since the person on the passenger side not only was shaded below by the door and dashboard but might swing down his sunvisor all the way too.

'Is that them?' Magda asked. Ambrose's mother teased the boys for letting Magda win, insinuating that 'somebody [had] a girlfriend'. Peter and Ambrose's father reached a long thin arm across their mother to butt his cigarette in the dashboard ashtray, under the lighter. The prize this time for seeing the Towers first was a banana. Their mother bestowed it after chiding their father for wasting a half-smoked cigarette when everything was so scarce. Magda, to take the prize, moved her hand from so near Ambrose's that he could have touched it as though accidentally. She offered to share the prize, things like that were so hard to find; but everyone insisted it was hers alone. Ambrose's mother sang an iambic trimeter couplet from a popular song, femininely rhymed:

> *'What's good is in the Army;*
> *What's left will never harm me.'*

Uncle Karl tapped his cigar ash out the ventilator window; some particles were sucked by the slipstream back into the car through the rear window on the passenger side. Magda demonstrated her ability to hold a banana in one hand and peel it with her teeth. She still sat forward; Ambrose pushed his glasses back onto the bridge of his nose with his left hand, which he then negligently let fall to the seat cushion immediately behind her. He even permitted the single hair, gold, on the second joint of his thumb to brush the fabric of her skirt. Should she have sat back at that instant, his hand would have been caught under her.

Plush upholstery prickles uncomfortably through gabardine slacks in the July sun. The function of the *beginning* of a story is to introduce the principal characters, establish their initial relationships, set the scene for the main action, expose the background of the situation if necessary, plant motifs and foreshadowings where appropriate, and initiate the first complication or whatever of the 'rising action'. Actually, if one imagines a story called 'The Funhouse', or 'Lost in the Funhouse', the details of the drive to Ocean City don't seem especially relevant. The *beginning* should recount the events between Ambrose's first sight of the funhouse early in the afternoon and his entering it with Magda and Peter in the evening. The *middle* would narrate all relevant events from the time he goes in to the time he loses his way; middles have the double and contradictory function of delaying the climax while at the same time preparing the reader for it and fetching him to it. Then the *ending* would tell what Ambrose does while he's lost, how he finally finds his way out, and what everybody makes of the experience. So far there's been no real dialogue, very little sensory detail, and nothing in the way of a *theme*. And a long time has gone by already without anything happening; it makes a person wonder. We haven't even reached Ocean City yet: we will never get out of the funhouse.

The more closely the author identifies with the narrator, literally or metaphorically, the less advisable it is, as a rule, to use the first-person narrative viewpoint. Once three years previously the young people *aforementioned* played Niggers and Masters in the backyard; when it was Ambrose's turn to be Master and theirs to be Niggers Peter had to go serve his evening papers; Ambrose was afraid to punish Magda alone, but she led him to the whitewashed Torture Chamber between the woodshed and the privy in the Slaves Quarters; there she knelt sweating among bamboo rakes and dusty Mason jars, pleadingly embraced his knees, and while bees droned in the lattice as if on an ordinary summer afternoon, purchased clemency at a surprising price set by herself. Doubtless she remembered nothing of this event; Ambrose on the other hand seemed unable to forget the least detail of his life. He even recalled how, standing beside himself with awed impersonality in the reeky heat, he'd stared the while at an empty cigar box in which Uncle Karl kept stone-cutting chisels: beneath the words *El Producto* a laureled, loose-toga'd lady regarded the sea from a marble bench; beside her, forgotten or not yet turned to, was a five-stringed lyre. Her chin reposed on the back of her right hand; her left depended negligently from the bench-arm. The lower half of the scene and lady was peeled away; the words EXAMINED BY _____ were inked there into the wood. Nowadays cigar boxes are made of pasteboard. Ambrose wondered what Magda would have done, Ambrose wondered what Magda would do when she sat back on his hand as he resolved she should. Be angry. Make a teasing joke of it. Give no sign at all. For a long time she leaned forward, playing cow-poker with Peter against Uncle Karl and Mother and watching for the first sign of Ocean City. At nearly the same instant, picnic ground and Ocean City standpipe hove into view; an Amoco filling station on their side of the road cost Mother and Uncle Karl fifty cows and the game; Magda bounced back, clapping her right hand on Mother's right arm; Ambrose moved clear 'in the nick of time'.

At this rate our hero, at this rate our protagonist will remain in the funhouse forever. Narrative ordinarily consists of alternating dramatization and summarization. One symptom of nervous tension, paradoxically, is repeated and violent yawning; neither Peter nor Magda nor Uncle Karl nor Mother reacted in this manner. Although they were no longer small children, Peter and Ambrose were each given a dollar to spend on boardwalk amusements in addition to what money of their own they'd brought along. Magda too, though she protested she had ample spending money. The boys' mother made a little scene out of distributing the bills; she pretended that her sons and Magda were small children and cautioned them not to spend the sum too quickly or in one place. Magda promised with a merry laugh and, having both hands free, took the bill with her left. Peter laughed also and pledged in a falsetto to be a good boy. His imitation of a child was not clever. The boys' father was tall and thin, balding, fair-complexioned. Assertions of that sort are not effective; the reader may acknowledge the proposition, *but*. We should be much farther along than we are; something has gone wrong; not much of this preliminary rambling seems relevant. Yet everyone begins in the same place; how is it that most go along without difficulty but a few lose their way?

'Stay out from under the boardwalk,' Uncle Karl growled from the side of his mouth. The boys' mother pushed his shoulder *in mock annoyance*. They were all standing before Fat May the Laughing Lady who advertised the funhouse. Larger than life, Fat May mechanically shook, rocked on her heels, slapped her thighs, while recorded laughter—uproarious, female—came amplified from a hidden loudspeaker. It chuckled, wheezed, wept; tried in vain to catch its breath, tittered, groaned, exploded raucous and anew. You couldn't hear it without laughing yourself, no matter how you felt. Father came back from talking to a Coast-Guardsman on duty and reported that the surf was spoiled with crude oil from tankers recently torpedoed offshore. Lumps of it, difficult to remove, made tarry tidelines on the beach and stuck on swimmers. Many bathed in the surf nevertheless and came out speckled; others paid to use a municipal pool and only sunbathed on the beach. We would do the latter. We would do the latter. We would do the latter.

Under the boardwalk, matchbook covers, grainy other things. What is the story's theme? Ambrose is ill. He perspires in the dark passages; candied apples-on-a-stick, delicious-looking, disappointing to eat. Funhouses need men's and ladies' rooms at intervals. Others perhaps have also vomited in corners and corridors; may even have had bowel movements liable to be stepped in in the dark. The word *fuck* suggests suction and or and or flatulence. Mother and Father; grandmothers and grandfathers on both sides; great-grandmothers and great-grandfathers on four sides, et cetera. Count a generation as thirty years: in approximately the year when Lord Baltimore was granted charter to the province of Maryland by Charles I, five hundred twelve women—English, Welsh, Bavarian, Swiss—of every class and character, received into themselves the penises the intromittent organs of five hundred twelve men, ditto, in every circumstance and posture, to conceive the five hundred twelve ancestors of the two hundred fifty-six ancestors of the et cetera et cetera et cetera et cetera et cetera et cetera et cetera et cetera of the author, of the narrator, of this story, *Lost in the Funhouse*. In alleyways, ditches, canopy beds, pinewoods, bridal suites, ship's cabins, coach-and-fours, coaches-and-four, sultry toolsheds; on the cold sand under boardwalks, littered with *El Producto* cigar butts, treasured with Lucky Strike cigarette stubs, Coca-Cola caps, gritty turds, cardboard lollipop sticks, matchbook covers warning that A Slip of the Lip Can Sink a Ship. The shluppish whisper, continuous as seawash round the globe, tidelike falls and rises with the circuit of dawn and dusk.

Magda's teeth. She *was* left-handed. Perspiration. They've gone all the way, through, Magda and Peter, they've been waiting for hours with Mother and Uncle Karl while Father searches for his lost son; they draw french-fried potatoes from a paper cup and shake their heads. They've named the children they'll one day have and bring to Ocean City on holidays. Can spermatozoa properly be thought of as male animalcules when there are no female spermatozoa? They grope through hot, dark windings, past Love's Tunnel's fearsome obstacles. Some perhaps lose their way.

Peter suggested then and there that they do the funhouse; he had been through it before, so had Magda, Ambrose hadn't and suggested, his voice cracking on account of Fat May's laugher, that they swim first. All were chuckling, couldn't help it; Ambrose's father, Ambrose's and Peter's father came up grinning like a lunatic with two boxes of syrup-coated popcorn, one for Mother, one for Magda; the men were to help themselves. Ambrose walked on Magda's right; being by nature left-handed, she carried the box in her left hand. Up front the situation was reversed.

'What are you limping for?' Magda inquired of Ambrose. He supposed in a husky tone that his foot had gone to sleep in the car. Her teeth flashed. 'Pins and needles?' It was the honeysuckle on the lattice of the former privy that drew the bees. Imagine being stung there. How long is this going to take?

The adults decided to forgo the pool; but Uncle Karl insisted they change into swimsuits and do the beach. 'He wants to watch the pretty girls,' Peter teased, and ducked behind Magda from Uncle Karl's pretended wrath. 'You've got all the pretty girls you need right here,' Magda declared, and Mother said: 'Now that's the gospel truth.' Magda scolded Peter, who reached over her shoulder to sneak some popcorn. 'Your brother and father aren't getting any.' Uncle Karl wondered if they were going to have fireworks that night, what with the shortages. It wasn't the shortages, Mr M—— replied; Ocean City had fireworks from pre-war. But it was too risky on account of the enemy submarines, some people thought.

'Don't seem like Fourth of July without fireworks,' said Uncle Karl. The inverted tag in dialogue writing is still considered permissible with proper names or epithets, but sounds old-fashioned with personal pronouns. 'We'll have 'em again soon enough,' predicted the boys' father. Their mother declared she could do without fireworks: they reminded her too much of the real thing. Their father said all the more reason to shoot off a few now and again. Uncle Karl asked *rhetorically* who needed reminding, just look at people's hair and skin.

'The oil, yes,' said Mrs M——.

Ambrose had a pain in his stomach and so didn't swim but enjoyed watching the others. He and his father burned red easily. Magda's figure was exceedingly well developed for her age. She too declined to swim, and got mad, and became angry when Peter attempted to drag her into the pool. She always swam, he insisted; what did she mean not swim? Why did a person come to Ocean City?

'Maybe I want to lay here with Ambrose,' Magda teased.

Nobody likes a pedant.

'Aha,' said Mother. Peter grabbed Magda by one ankle and ordered Ambrose to grab the other. She squealed and rolled over on the beach blanket. Ambrose pretended to help hold her back. Her tan was darker than even Mother's and Peter's. 'Help out, Uncle Karl!' Peter cried. Uncle Karl went to seize the other ankle. Inside the top of her swimsuit, however, you could see the line where the sunburn ended and, when she hunched her shoulders and squealed again, one nipple's auburn edge. Mother made them behave themselves. '*You* should certainly know,' she said to Uncle Karl. Archly. 'That when a lady says she doesn't feel like swimming, a gentleman doesn't ask questions.' Uncle Karl said excuse *him*; Mother winked at Magda; Ambrose blushed; stupid Peter kept saying 'Phooey on *feel like*!' and tugging at Magda's ankle; then even he got the point, and cannon-balled with a holler into the pool.

'I swear,' Magda said, in mock *in feigned* exasperation.

The diving would make a suitable literary symbol. To go off the high board you had to wait in a line along the poolside and up the ladder. Fellows tickled girls and goosed one another and shouted to the ones at the top the hurry up, or razzed them for bellyfloppers. Once on the springboard some took a great while posing or clowning or deciding on a dive or getting up their nerve; others ran right off. Especially among the younger fellows the idea was to strike the funniest pose or do the craziest stunt as you fell; a thing that got harder to do as you kept on and kept on. But whether you hollered *Geronimo!* or *Sieg heil!*, held your nose or 'rode a bicycle', pretended to be shot or did a perfect jacknife or changed your mind halfway down and ended up with nothing, it was over in two seconds, after all that wait. Spring, pose, splash. Spring, neat-o, splash. Spring, aw fooey, splash.

The grown-ups had gone on; Ambrose wanted to converse with Magda; she was remarkably well developed for her age; it was said that that came from rubbing with a turkish towel, and there were other theories. Ambrose could think of nothing to say except how good a diver Peter was, who was showing off for her benefit. You could pretty well tell by looking at their bathing suits and arm muscles how far along the different fellows were. Ambrose was glad he hadn't gone in swimming, the cold water shrank you up so. Magda pretended to be uninterested in the diving; she probably weighed as much as he did. If you know your way around in the funhouse like your own bedroom, you could wait until a girl came along and then slip away without ever getting caught, even if her boyfriend was right with her. She'd think *he* did it! It would be better to be the boyfriend, and act outraged, and tear the funhouse apart.

Not act; *be*.

'He's a master diver,' Ambrose said. In feigned admiration. 'You really have to slave away at it to get that good.' What would it matter anyhow if he asked her right out whether she remembered, even teased her with it as Peter would have?

There's no point in going farther; this isn't getting anybody anywhere; they haven't even come to the funhouse yet. Ambrose is off the track, in some new or old part of the place that's not supposed to be used; he strayed into it by some one-in-a-million chance, like the time the roller coaster car left the tracks in the nineteen-teens against all the laws of physics and sailed over the boardwalk in the dark. And they can't locate him because they don't know where to look. Even the designer and operator have forgotten this other part, that winds around on itself like a whelk shell. That winds around the right part like the snakes on Mercury's caduceus. Some people, perhaps, don't 'hit their stride' until their twenties, when the growing-up business is over and women appreciate other things besides wisecracks and teasing and strutting. Peter didn't have one-tenth the imagination *he* had, not one-tenth. Peter did this naming-their-children thing as a joke, making up names like Aloysius and Murgatroyd, but Ambrose knew *exactly* how it would feel to be married and have children of your own, and be a loving husband and father, and go comfortably to work in the morning and to bed with your wife at night, and wake up with her there. With a breeze coming through the sash and birds and mocking birds singing in the Chinese-cigar trees. His eyes watered, there aren't enough ways to say that. He would be quite famous in his line of work. Whether Magda was his wife or not, one evening when he was wise-lined and grey at the temples he'd smile gravely, at a fashionable dinner party, and remind her of his youthful passion. The time they went with his family to Ocean City; the *erotic fantasies* he used to have about her. How long ago it seemed, and childish! Yet tender, too, *n'est-ce pas?* Would she have imagined that the world-famous whatever remembered how many strings were on the lyre on the bench beside the girl on the label of the cigar box he'd stared at in the toolshed at age ten while she, age eleven. Even then he had felt *wise beyond his years*; he'd stroked her hair and said in his deepest voice and correctest English, as to a dear child: 'I shall never forget this moment.'

But though he had breathed heavily, groaned as if ecstatic, what he'd really felt throughout was an odd detachment, as though someone else were Master. Strive as he might to be transported, he heard his mind take notes upon the scene: *This is what they call* passion. *I am experiencing it.* Many of the digger machines were out of order in the penny arcades and could not be repaired or replaced for the duration. Moreover the prizes, made now in USA, were less interesting than formerly, pasteboard items for the most part, and some of the machines wouldn't work on white pennies. The gypsy fortune-teller machine might have provided a foreshadowing of the climax of this story if Ambrose had operated it. It was even dilapidateder than most: the silver coating was worn off the brown metal handles, the glass windows around the dummy were cracked and taped, her kerchiefs and silks long-faded. If a man lived by himself, he could take a department-store mannequin with flexible joints and modify her in certain ways. *However*: by the time he was that old he'd have a real woman. There was a machine that stamped your name around a white-metal coin with a star in the middle: *A_____*. His son would be the second, and when the lad reached thirteen or so he would put a strong arm around his shoulder and tell him calmly: 'It is perfectly normal. We have all been through it. It will not last forever.' Nobody knew how to be what they were right. He'd smoke a pipe, teach his son how to fish and softcrab, assure him he needn't worry about himself. Magda would certainly give, Magda would certainly yield a great deal of milk, although guilty of occasional solecisms. It don't taste so bad. Suppose the lights came on now!

The day wore on. You think you're yourself, but there are other persons in you. Ambrose gets hard when Ambrose doesn't want to, *and obversely*. Ambrose watches them disagree; Ambrose watches him watch. In the funhouse mirror-room you can't see yourself go on forever, because no matter how you stand, your head gets in the way. Even if you had a glass periscope, the image of your eye would cover up the thing you really wanted to see. The police will come; there'll be a story in the papers. That must be where it happened. Unless he can find a surprise exit, an unofficial backdoor or escape hatch opening on an alley, say, and then stroll up to the family in front of the funhouse and ask where everybody's been; *he's* been out of the place for ages. That's just where it happened, in that last lighted room: Peter and Magda found the right exit; he found one that you weren't supposed to find and strayed off into the works somewhere. In a perfect funhouse you'd be able to go only one way, like the divers off the high-board; getting lost would be impossible; the doors and halls would work like minnow traps or the valves in veins.

On account of German U-boats, Ocean City was 'browned out': streetlights were shaded on the seaward side; shop-windows and boardwalk amusement places were kept dim, not to silhouette tankers and Liberty-ships for torpedoing. In a short story about Ocean City, Maryland, during World War II, the author could make use of the image of sailors on leave in the penny arcades and shooting galleries, sighting through the crosshairs of toy machine guns at swastika'd subs, while out in the black Atlantic a U-boat skipper squints through his periscope at real ships outlined by the glow of penny arcades. After dinner the family strolled back to the amusement end of the boardwalk. The boy's father had burnt red as always and was masked with Noxema, a minstrel in reverse. The grown-ups stood at the end of the boardwalk where the Hurricane of '33 had cut an inlet from the ocean to Assawoman Bay.

'Pronounced with a long *o*,' Uncle Karl reminded Magda with a wink. His shirt sleeves were rolled up; Mother punched his brown biceps with the arrowed heart on it and said his mind was naughty. Fat May's laugh came suddenly from the funhouse, as if she'd just got the joke; the family laughed too at the coincidence. Ambrose went under the boardwalk to search for out-of-town matchbook covers with the aid of his pocket flashlight; he looked out from the edge of the North American continent and wondered how far their laughter carried over the water. Spies in rubber rafts; survivors in lifeboats. If the joke had been beyond his understanding, he could have said: '*The laughter was over his head.*' And let the reader see the serious wordplay on second reading.

He turned the flashlight on and then off at once even before the woman whooped. He sprang away, heart athud, dropping the light. What had the man grunted? Perspiration drenched and chilled him by the time he scrambled up to the family. 'See anything?' his father asked. His voice wouldn't come; he shrugged and violently brushed sand from his pants legs.

'Let's ride the old flying horses!' Magda cried. I'll never be an author. It's been forever already, everybody's gone home, Ocean City's deserted, the ghost-crabs are tickling across the beach and down the littered cold streets. And the empty halls of clapboard hotels and abandoned funhouses. A tidal wave; an enemy air raid; a monster-crab swelling like an island from the sea. *The inhabitants fled in terror.* Magda clung to his trouser leg; he alone knew the maze's secret. 'He gave his life that we might live,' said Uncle Karl with a scowl of pain, as he. The fellow's hands had been tattooed; the woman's legs, the woman's fat white legs had. *An astonishing coincidence.* He yearned to tell Peter. He wanted to throw up for excitement. They hadn't even chased him. He wished he were dead.

One possible ending would be to have Ambrose come across another lost person in the dark. They'd match their wits together against the funhouse, struggle like Ulysses past obstacle after obstacle, help and encourage each other. Or a girl. By the time they found the exit they'd be closest friends, sweethearts if it were a girl; they'd know each other's inmost souls, be bound together *by the cement of shared adventure;* then they'd emerge into the light and it would turn out that his friend was a Negro. A blind girl. President Roosevelt's son. Ambrose's former archenemy.

Shortly after the mirror room he'd groped along a musty corridor, his heart already misgiving him at the absence of phosphorescent arrows and other signs. He'd found a crack of light—not a door, it turned out, but a seam between the plyboard wall panels—and squinting up to it, espied a small old man, *in appearance not unlike* the photographs at home of Ambrose's late grandfather, nodding upon a stool beneath a bare, speckled bulb. A crude panel of toggle- and knife-switches hung beside the open fuse box near his head; elsewhere in the little room were wooden levers and ropes belayed to boat cleats. At the time, Ambrose wasn't lost enough to rap or call; later he couldn't find that crack. Now it seemed to him that he'd possibly dozed off for a few minutes somewhere along the way; certainly he was exhausted from the afternoon's sunshine and the evening's problems; he couldn't be sure he hadn't dreamed part or all of the sight. Had an old black wall fan droned like bees and shimmied two flypaper streamers? Had the funhouse operator—gentle, somewhat sad and tired-appearing, in expression not unlike the photographs at home of Ambrose's late Uncle Konrad—murmured in his sleep? Is there really such a person as Ambrose, or is he a figment of the author's imagination? Was it Assawoman Bay or Sinepuxent? Are there other errors of fact in this fiction? Was there another sound besides the little slap slap of thigh on ham, like water sucking at the chine-boards of a skiff?

When you're lost, the smartest thing to do is stay put till you're found, hollering if necessary. But to holler guarantees humiliation as well as rescue; keeping silent permits some saving of face—you can act surprised at the fuss when your rescuers find you and swear you weren't lost, if they do. What's more you might find your own way yet, *however belatedly.*

'Don't tell me your foot's still asleep!' Magda exclaimed as the three young people walked from the inlet to the area set aside for ferris wheels, carousels, and other carnival rides, they having decided in favour of the vast and ancient merry-go-round instead of the funhouse. What a sentence, everything was wrong from the outset. People don't know what to make of him, he doesn't know what to make of himself, he's only thirteen, *athletically and socially inept*, not astonishingly bright, but there are antennae; he has . . . some sort of receivers in his head; things speak to him, he understands more than he should, the world winks at him through its objects, grabs grinning at his coat. Everybody else is in on some secret he doesn't know; they've forgotten to tell him. Through simple *procrastination* his mother put off his baptism until this year. Everyone else had it done as a baby; he'd assumed the same of himself, as had his mother, so she claimed, until it was time for him to join Grace Methodist-Protestant and the oversight came out. He was mortified, but pitched sleepless through his private catechizing, intimidated by the ancient mysteries, a thirteen year old would never say that, resolved to experience conversion like St Augustine. When the water touched his brow and Adam's sin left him, he contrived by a strain like defecation to bring tears into his eyes—but felt nothing. There was some simple, radical difference about him; he hoped it was genius, feared it was madness, devoted himself to amiability and inconspicuousness. Alone on the seawall near his house he was seized by the terrifying transports he'd thought to find in toolshed, in Communion-cup. The grass was alive! The town, the river, himself, were not imaginary; time roared in his ears like wind; the world was *going on*! This part ought to be dramatized. The Irish author James Joyce once wrote. Ambrose M—— is going to scream.

There is no *texture of rendered sensory detail*, for one thing. The faded distorting mirrors beside Fat May; the impossibility of choosing a mount when one had but a single ride on the great carousel; the *vertigo attendant on his recognition* that Ocean City was worn out, the place of fathers and grandfathers, straw-boatered men and parasoled ladies survived by their amusements. Money spent, the three paused at Peter's insistence beside Fat May to watch the girls get their skirts blown up. The object was to tease Magda, who said: 'I swear, Peter M——, you've got a one-track mind! Amby and me aren't *interested* in such things.' In the tumbling-barrel, too, just inside the Devil's-mouth entrance to the funhouse, the girls were upended and their boyfriends and others could see up their dresses if they cared to. Which was the whole point, Ambrose realized. Of the entire funhouse! If you looked around, you noticed that almost all the people on the boardwalk were paired off into couples except the small children; in a way, that was the whole point of Ocean City! If you had X-ray eyes and could see everything going on at that instant under the boardwalk and in all the hotel rooms and cars and alleyways, you'd realize that all that normally *showed*, like restaurants and dance halls and clothing and test-your-strength machines, was merely preparation and intermission. Fat May screamed.

Because he watched the goings-on from the corner of his eye, it was Ambrose who spied the half-dollar on the boardwalk near the tumbling-barrel. Losers weepers. The first time he'd heard some people moving through a corridor not far away, just after he'd lost sight of the crack of light, he'd decided not to call to them, for fear they'd guess he was scared and poke fun; it sounded like roughnecks; he'd hoped they'd come by and he could follow in the dark without their knowing. Another time he'd heard just one person, unless he imagined it, bumping along as if on the other side of the plywood; perhaps Peter coming back for him, or Father, or Magda lost too. Or the owner and operator of the funhouse. He'd called out once, as though merrily: 'Anybody know where the heck we are?' But the query was too stiff, his voice cracked, when the sounds stopped he was terrified: maybe it was a queer who waited for fellows to get lost, or a longhaired filthy monster that lived in some cranny of the funhouse. He stood rigid for hours it seemed like, scarcely respiring. His future was shockingly clear, in outline. He tried holding his breath to the point of unconsciousness. There ought to be a button you could push to end your life absolutely without pain; disappear in a flick, like turning out a light. He would push it instantly! He despised Uncle Karl. But he despised his father too, for not being what he was supposed to be. Perhaps his father hated *his* father, and so on, and his son would hate him, and so on. Instantly!

Naturally he didn't have nerve enough to ask Magda to go through the funhouse with him. With incredible nerve and to everyone's surprise he invited Magda, quietly and politely, to go through the funhouse with him. 'I warn you, I've never been through it before,' he added, *laughing easily*; 'but I reckon we can manage somehow. The important thing to remember, after all, is that it's meant to be a *fun*house; that is, a place of amusement. If people really got lost or injured or too badly frightened in it, the owner'd go out of business. There'd even be lawsuits. No character in a work of fiction can make a speech this long without interruption or acknowledgement from the other characters.'

Mother teased Uncle Karl: 'Three's a crowd, I always heard.' But actually Ambrose was relieved that Peter now had a quarter too. Nothing was what it looked like. Every instant, under the surface of the Atlantic Ocean, millions of living animals devoured one another. Pilots were falling in flames over Europe; women were being forcibly raped in the South Pacific. His father should have taken him aside and said: 'There is a simple secret to getting through the funhouse, as simple as being first to see the Towers. Here it is. Peter does not know it; neither does your Uncle Karl. You and I are different. Not surprisingly, you've often wished you weren't. Don't think I haven't noticed how unhappy your childhood has been! But you'll understand, when I tell you, why it had to be kept secret until now. And you won't regret not being like your brother and your uncle. *On the contrary*!' If you knew all the stories behind all the people on the boardwalk, you'd see that *nothing* was what it looked like. Husbands and wives often hated each other; parents didn't necessarily love their children; et cetera. A child took things for granted because he had nothing to compare his life to and everybody acted as if things were as they should be. Therefore each saw himself as the hero of the story, when the truth might turn out to be that he's the villain, or the coward. And there wasn't one thing you could do about it!

Hunchbacks, fat ladies, fools—that no one chose what he was was unbearable. In the movies he'd meet a beautiful young girl in the funhouse; they'd have hairs-breadth escapes from real dangers; he'd do and say the right things; she also; in the end they'd be lovers; their dialogue lines would match up; he'd be perfectly at ease; she'd not only like him well enough, she'd think he was *marvellous*; she'd lie awake thinking about him, instead of vice versa—the way *his* face looked in different lights and how he stood and exactly what he'd said—and yet that would be only one small episode in his wonderful life, among many many others. Not a *turning point* at all. What had happened in the toolshed was nothing. He hated, he loathed his parents! One reason for not writing a lost-in-the-funhouse story is that either everybody felt what Ambrose feels, in which case it goes without saying, or else no normal person feels such things, in which case Ambrose is a freak. 'Is anything more tiresome, in fiction, than the problems of sensitive adolescents?' And it's all too long and rambling, as if the author. For all a person knows the first time through, the end could be just around the corner; perhaps, *not impossibly* it's been within reach any number of times. On the other hand he may be scarcely past the start, with everything yet to get through, an intolerable idea.

Fill in: His father's raised eyebrows when he announced his decision to do the funhouse with Magda. Ambrose understands now, but didn't then, that his father was wondering whether he knew what the funhouse was *for*—especially since he didn't object, as he should have, when Peter decided to come along too. The ticket-woman, witchlike, mortifying him when inadvertently he gave her his name-coin instead of the half-dollar, then unkindly calling Magda's attention to the birthmark on his temple: 'Watch out for him, girlie, he's a marked man!' She wasn't even cruel, he understood, only vulgar and insensitive. Somewhere in the world there was a young woman with such splendid understanding that she'd see him entire, like a poem or story, and find his words so valuable after all that when he confessed his apprehensions she would explain why they were in fact the very things that made him precious to her . . . and to Western Civilization! There was no such girl, the simple truth being. Violent yawns as they approached the mouth. Whispered advice from an old-timer on a bench near the barrel: 'Go crabwise and ye'll get an eyeful without upsetting!' Composure vanished at the first pitch: Peter hollered joyously, Magda tumbled, shrieked, clutched her skirt; Ambrose scrambled crabwise, tight-lipped with terror, was soon out, watched his dropped name-coin slide among the couples. Shamefaced he saw that to get through expeditiously was not the point; Peter feigned assistance in order to trip Magda up, shouted 'I see Christmas!' when her legs went flying. The old man, his latest betrayer, cackled approval. A dim hall then of black-thread cobwebs and recorded gibber: he took Magda's elbow to steady her against revolving discs set in the slanted floor to throw your feet out from under, and explained to her in a calm, deep voice his theory that each phase of the funhouse was triggered either automatically, by a series of photoelectric devices, or else manually by operators stationed at peepholes. But he lost his voice thrice as the discs unbalanced him; Magda was anyhow squealing; but at one point she clutched him about the waist to keep from falling, and her right cheek pressed for a moment against his belt-buckle. Heroically he drew her up, it was his chance to clutch her close as if for support and say: 'I love you.' He even put an arm lightly about the small of her back before a sailor-and-girl pitched into them from behind, sorely treading his left big toe and knocking Magda asprawl with them. The sailor's girl was a string-haired hussy with a loud laugh and light blue drawers; Ambrose realized that he wouldn't have said 'I love you' anyhow, and was smitten with self-contempt. How much better it would be to be that common sailor!

A wiry little Seaman 3rd, the fellow squeezed a girl to each side and stumbled hilarious into the mirror room, closer to Magda in thirty seconds than Ambrose had got in thirteen years. She giggled at something the fellow said to Peter; she drew her hair from her eyes with a movement so womanly it struck Ambrose's heart; Peter's smacking her backside then seemed particularly coarse. But Magda made a pleased indignant face and cried, 'All right for *you*, mister!' and pursued Peter into the maze without a backward glance. The sailor followed after, leisurely, drawing his girl against his hip; Ambrose understood not only that they were all so relieved to be rid of his burdensome company that they didn't even notice his absence, but that he himself shared their relief. Stepping from the treacherous passage at last into the mirror-maze, he saw once again, more clearly than ever, how readily he deceived himself into supposing he was a person. He even foresaw, wincing at his dreadful self-knowledge, that he would repeat the deception, at ever-rarer intervals, all his wretched life, so fearful were the alternatives. Fame, madness, suicide; perhaps all three. It's not believable that so young a boy could articulate that reflection, and in fiction the merely true must always yield to the plausible. Moreover, the symbolism is in places heavy-footed. Yet Ambrose M—— understood, as few adults do, that the famous loneliness of the great was no popular myth but a general truth—furthermore, that it was as much cause as effect.

All the preceding except the last few sentences is exposition that should've been done earlier or interspersed with the present action instead of lumped together. No reader would put up with so much with such *prolixity*. It's interesting that Ambrose's father, though presumably an intelligent man (as indicated by his role as grade-school principal), neither encouraged nor discouraged his sons at all in any way—as if he either didn't care about them or cared all right but didn't know how to act. If this fact should contribute to one of them's becoming a celebrated but wretchedly unhappy scientist, was it a good thing or not? He too might someday face the question; it would be useful to know whether it had tortured his father for years, for example, or never once crossed his mind.

In the maze two important things happened. First, our hero found a name-coin someone else had lost or discarded: *AMBROSE*, suggestive of the famous lightship and of his late grandfather's favourite dessert, which his mother used to prepare on special occasions out of coconut, oranges, grapes, and what else. Second, as he wondered at the endless replication of his image in the mirrors, second, as he *lost himself in the reflection* that the necessity for an observer makes perfect observation impossible, better make him eighteen at least, yet that would render other things unlikely, he heard Peter and Magda chuckling somewhere together in the maze. 'Here!' 'No, here!' they shouted to each other; Peter said, 'Where's Amby?' Magda murmured. 'Amb?' Peter called. In a pleased, friendly voice. He didn't reply. The truth was, his brother was a *happy-go-lucky youngster* who'd've been better off with a regular brother of his own, but who seldom complained of his lot and was generally cordial. Ambrose's throat ached; there aren't enough different ways to say that. He stood quietly while the two young people giggled and thumped through the glittering maze, hurrah'd their discovery of its exit, cried out in joyful alarm at what next beset them. Then he set his mouth and followed after, as he supposed, took a wrong turn, strayed into the pass *wherein he lingers yet*.

The action of conventional dramatic narrative may be represented by a diagram called Freitag's Triangle:

or more accurately by a variant of that diagram:

in which *AB* represents the exposition, *B* the introduction of conflict, *BC* the 'rising action', complication, or development of the conflict, *C* the climax, or turn of the action, *CD* the dénouement, or resolution of the conflict. While there is no reason to regard this pattern as an absolute necessity, like many other conventions it became conventional because great numbers of people over many years learned by trial and error that it was effective; one ought not to forsake it, therefore, unless one wishes to forsake as well the effect of drama or has clear cause to feel that deliberate violation of the 'normal' pattern can better can better effect that effect. This can't go on much longer; it can go on forever. He died telling stories to himself in the dark; years later, when that vast unsuspected area of the funhouse came to light, the first expedition found his skeleton in one of its labyrinthine corridors and mistook it for part of the entertainment. He died of starvation telling himself stories in the dark; but unbeknownst unbeknownst to him, an assistant operator of the funhouse, happening to overhear him, crouched just behind the plyboard partition and wrote down his every word. The operator's daughter, an exquisite young woman with a figure unusually well developed for her age, crouched just behind the partition and transcribed his every word. Though she had never laid eyes on him, she recognized that here was one of Western Culture's truly great imaginations, the eloquence of whose suffering would be an inspiration to unnumbered. And her heart was torn between her love for the misfortunate young man (yes, she loved him, though she had never laid though she knew him only—but how well!—through his words, and the deep, calm voice in which he spoke them) between her love et cetera and her womanly intuition that only in suffering and isolation could he give voice et cetera. Lone dark dying. Quietly she kissed the rough plyboard, and a tear fell upon the page. Where she had written in shorthand *Where she had written in shorthand* Where she had written in shorthand *Where she* et cetera. A long time ago we should have passed the apex of Freitag's Triangle and made brief work of the *dénouement*; the plot doesn't rise by meaningful steps but winds upon itself, digresses, retreats, hesitates, sighs, collapses, expires. The climax of the story must be its protagonist's discovery of a way to get through the funhouse. But he has found none, may have ceased to search.

What relevance does the war have to the story? Should there be fireworks outside or not?

Ambrose wandered, languished, dozed. Now and then he fell into his habit of rehearsing to himself the unadventurous story of his life, narrated from the third-person point of view, from his earliest memory parenthesis of maple leaves stirring in the summer breath of tidewater Maryland end of parenthesis to the present moment. Its principal events, on this telling, would appear to have been *A, B, C,* and *D.*

He imagined himself years hence, successful, married, at ease in the world, the trials of his adolescence far behind him. He has come to the seashore with his family for the holiday: how Ocean City has changed! But at one seldom at one ill-frequented end of the boardwalk a few derelict amusements survive from times gone by: the great carousel from the turn of the century, with its monstrous griffins and mechanical concert band; the roller coaster rumoured since 1916 to have been condemned; the mechanical shooting gallery in which only the image of our enemies changed. His own son laughs with Fat May and wants to know what a funhouse is; Ambrose hugs the sturdy lad close and smiles around his pipestem at his wife.

The family's going home. Mother sits between Father and Uncle Karl, who teases him good-naturedly who chuckles over the fact that the comrade with whom he'd fought his way shoulder to shoulder through the funhouse had turned out to be a blind Negro girl—to their mutual discomfort, as they'd opened their souls. But such are the walls of custom, which even. Whose arm is where? How must it feel. He dreams of a funhouse vaster by far than any yet constructed; but by then they may be out of fashion, like steamboats and excursion trains. Already quaint and seedy: the draperied ladies of the frieze of the carousel are his father's father's mooncheeked dreams; if he thinks of it more he will vomit his apple-on-a-stick.

He wonders: will he become a regular person? Something has gone wrong; his vaccination didn't take; at the Boy-Scout initiation campfire he only pretended to be deeply moved, as he pretends to this hour that it is not so bad after all in the funhouse, and that he has a little limp. How long will it last? He envisions a truly astonishing funhouse, incredibly complex yet utterly controlled from a great central switchboard like the console of a pipe organ. Nobody had enough imagination. He could design such a place himself, wiring and all, and he's only thirteen years old. He would be its operator: panel lights would show what was up in every cranny of its cunning of its multifarious vastness; a switch-flick would ease this fellow's way, complicate that's, to balance things out; if anyone seemed lost or frightened, all the operator had to do was.

He wishes he had never entered the funhouse. But he has. Then he wishes he were dead. But he's not. Therefore he will construct funhouses for others and be their secret operator—though he would rather be among the lovers for whom funhouses are designed.

1968

Alice Munro
b. 1931

Alice Laidlaw was born and raised in the rural community of Wingham in south-western Ontario. After two years of study at the University of Western Ontario she moved to the West Coast, living first in Vancouver, where she worked as an assistant in the Vancouver Public Library, and then in Victoria, where she and her first husband, James Munro, opened a bookstore. She has generally set her thirteen volumes of fiction in the rural area of south-western Ontario where she was born and where she now resides. A prevailing theme of her stories is a young girl coming of age, searching for her identity as a woman. Her early short-story sequence *Lives of Girls and Women* (1971), which centres around a young heroine, Del Jordan,

who must learn that true fiction is rooted in the factual and tactile world that surrounds her, is typical in this regard. In 'Family Furnishings', which comes from Munro's collection *Hateship, Friendship, Courtship, Loveship, Marriage* (2001), we meet Alfrida at various times in her life. Her complex and developing relationship with the narrator forms the basis of the story.

Acknowledging the fiction of Flannery O'Connor and Eudora Welty among the major influences on her own work, Munro writes out of the world she knows well, taking the ordinary, everyday reality around her and transforming it into fiction. She is now regarded as one of the finest short-story writers in the English language.

Family Furnishings

Alfrida. My father called her Freddie. The two of them were first cousins and lived for a while on adjoining farms. One day they were out in the fields of stubble playing with my father's dog, whose name was Mack. That day the sun shone, but did not melt the ice in the furrows. They stomped on the ice and enjoyed its crackle underfoot.

How could she remember a thing like that? my father said. She made it up, he said.
'I did not,' she said.
'You did so.'
'I did not.'

All of a sudden they heard bells pealing, whistles blowing. The town bell and the church bells were ringing. The factory whistles were blowing in the town three miles away. The world had burst its seams for joy, and Mack tore out to the road, because he was sure a parade was coming. It was the end of the First World War.

Three times a week, we could read Alfrida's name in the paper. Just her first name— Alfrida. It was printed as if written by hand, a flowing, fountain-pen signature. Round and About the Town, with Alfrida. The town mentioned was not the one close by, but the city to the south, where Alfrida lived, and which my family visited perhaps every two or three years.

Now is the time for all you future June brides to start registering your preferences at the China Cabinet, and I must tell you that if I were a bride-to-be—which alas I am not—

I might resist all the patterned dinner sets, exquisite as they are, and go for the pearly-white, the ultra-modern Rosenthal . . .

Beauty treatments may come and beauty treatments may go, but the masques they slather on you at Fantine's Salon are guaranteed—speaking of brides—to make your skin bloom like orange blossoms. And to make the bride's mom—and the bride's aunts and for all I know her grandmom—feel as if they'd just taken a dip in the Fountain of Youth . . .

You would never expect Alfrida to write in this style, from the way she talked.

She was also one of the people who wrote under the name of Flora Simpson, on the Flora Simpson Housewives' Page. Women from all over the countryside believed that they were writing their letters to the plump woman with the crimped grey hair and the forgiving smile who was pictured at the top of the page. But the truth—which I was not to tell—was that the notes that appeared at the bottom of each of their letters were produced by Alfrida and a man she called Horse Henry, who otherwise did the obituaries. The women gave themselves such names as Morning Star and Lily-of-the-Valley and Green Thumb and Little Annie Rooney and Dishmop Queen. Some names were so popular that numbers had to be assigned to them—Goldilocks 1, Goldilocks 2, Goldilocks 3.

Dear Morning Star, Alfrida or Horse Henry would write,

Eczema is a dreadful pest, especially in this hot weather we're having, and I hope the baking soda does some good. Home treatments certainly ought to be respected, but it never hurts to seek out your doctor's advice. It's splendid news to hear your hubby is up and about again. It can't have been any fun with both of you under the weather . . .

In all the small towns of that part of Ontario, housewives who belonged to the Flora Simpson Club would hold an annual summer picnic. Flora Simpson always sent her special greetings but explained that there were just too many events for her to show up at all of them and she did not like to make distinctions. Alfrida said that there had been talk of sending Horse Henry done up in a wig and pillow bosoms, or perhaps herself leering like the Witch of Babylon (not even she, at my parents' table, could quote the Bible accurately and say 'Whore') with a ciggie-boo stuck to her lipstick. But, oh, she said, the paper would kill us. And anyway, it would be too mean.

She always called her cigarettes ciggie-boos. When I was fifteen or sixteen she leaned across the table and asked me, 'How would you like a ciggie-boo, too?' The meal was finished, and my younger brother and sister had left the table. My father was shaking his head. He had started to roll his own.

I said thank you and let Alfrida light it and smoked for the first time in front of my parents.

They pretended that it was a great joke.

'Ah, will you look at your daughter?' said my mother to my father. She rolled her eyes and clapped her hands to her chest and spoke in an artificial, languishing voice. 'I'm like to faint.'

'Have to get the horsewhip out,' my father said, half rising in his chair.

This moment was amazing, as if Alfrida had transformed us into new people. Ordinarily, my mother would say that she did not like to see a woman smoke. She did not say that it was indecent, or unladylike—just that she didn't like it. And when she said in a certain tone that she did not like something it seemed that she was not making a confession of irrationality but drawing on a private source of wisdom, which was unassailable and almost sacred. It was when she reached for this tone, with its accompanying expression of listening to inner voices, that I particularly hated her.

As for my father, he had beaten me, in this very room, not with a horsewhip but his belt, for running afoul of my mother's rules and wounding my mother's feelings, and for answering back. Now it seemed that such beatings could occur only in another universe.

My parents had been put in a corner by Alfrida—and also by me—but they had responded so gamely and gracefully that it was really as if the three of us—my mother and my father and myself—had been lifted to a new level of ease and aplomb. In that instant I could see them—particularly my mother—as being capable of a kind of light-heartedness that was scarcely ever on view.

All due to Alfrida.

Alfrida was always referred to as a career girl. This made her seem to be younger than my parents, though she was known to be about the same age. It was also said that she was a city person. And the city, when it was spoken of in this way, meant the one she lived and worked in. But it meant something else as well—not just a distinct configuration of buildings and sidewalks and streetcar lines or even a crowding together of individual people. It meant something more abstract that could be repeated over and over, something like a hive of bees, stormy but organized, not useless or deluded exactly, but disturbing and sometimes dangerous. People went into such a place when they had to and were glad when they got out. Some, however, were attached to it—as Alfrida must have been, long ago, and as I was now, puffing on my cigarette and trying to hold it in a nonchalant way, though it seemed to have grown to the size of a baseball bat between my fingers.

My family did not have a regular social life—people did not come to the house for dinner, let alone to parties. It was a matter of class, maybe. The parents of the boy I married, about five years after this scene at the dinner table, invited people who were not related to them to dinner, and they went to afternoon parties that they spoke of, unselfconsciously, as cocktail parties. It was a life such as I had read of in magazine stories, and it seemed to me to place my in-laws in a world of storybook privilege.

What our family did was put boards in the dining-room table two or three times a year to entertain my grandmother and my aunts—my father's older sisters—and their husbands. We did this at Christmas or Thanksgiving, when it was our turn, and perhaps also when a relative from another part of the province showed up on a visit. This visitor would always be a person rather like the aunts and their husbands and never the least bit like Alfrida.

My mother and I would start preparing for such dinners a couple of days ahead. We ironed the good tablecloth, which was as heavy as a bed quilt, and washed the good dishes, which had been sitting in the china cabinet collecting dust, and wiped the legs of the dining-room chairs, as well as making jellied salads, the pies and cakes, that had to accompany the central roast turkey or baked ham and bowls of vegetables. There had to be far too much to eat, and most of the conversation at the table had to do with the food, with the company saying how good it was and being urged to have more, and saying that they couldn't, they were stuffed, and then the aunts' husbands relenting, taking more, and the aunts taking just a little more and saying that they shouldn't, they were ready to bust.

And dessert still to come.

There was hardly any idea of a general conversation, and in fact there was a feeling that conversation that passed beyond certain understood limits might be a disruption, a showing-off. My mother's understanding of the limits was not reliable, and she sometimes could not wait out the pauses or honour the aversion to follow-up. So when somebody said, 'Seen Harley upstreet yesterday,' she was liable to say, perhaps, 'Do you think a man like Harley is a confirmed bachelor? Or he just hasn't met the right person?'

As if, when you mentioned seeing a person you were bound to have something further to say, something *interesting*.

Then there might be a silence, not because the people at the table meant to be rude but because they were flummoxed. Till my father would say with embarrassment, and oblique reproach, 'He seems to get on all right by hisself.'

If his relatives had not been present, he would more likely have said 'himself'.

And everybody went on cutting, spooning, swallowing, in the glare of the fresh tablecloth, with the bright light pouring in through the newly washed windows. These dinners were always in the middle of the day.

The people at that table were quite capable of talk. Washing and drying the dishes, in the kitchen, the aunts would talk about who had a tumor, a septic throat, a bad mess of boils. They would tell about how their own digestions, kidneys, nerves were functioning. Mention of intimate bodily matters seemed never to be so out of place, or suspect, as the mention of something read in a magazine, or an item in the news—it was improper somehow to pay attention to anything that was not close at hand. Meanwhile, resting on the porch, or during a brief walk out to look at the crops, the aunts' husbands might pass on information that somebody was in a tight spot with the bank, or still owed money on an expensive piece of machinery, or had invested in a bull that was a disappointment on the job.

It could have been that they felt clamped down by the formality of the dining room, the presence of bread-and-butter plates and dessert spoons, when it was the custom, at other times, to put a piece of pie right onto a dinner plate that had been cleaned up with bread. (It would have been an offence, however, not to set things out in this proper way. In their own houses, on like occasions, they would put their guests through the same paces.) It may have been just that eating was one thing, and talking was something else.

When Alfrida came it was altogether another story. The good cloth would be spread and the good dishes would be out. My mother would have gone to a lot of trouble with the food and she would be nervous about the results—probably she would have abandoned the usual turkey-and-stuffing-and-mashed-potatoes menu and made something like chicken salad surrounded by mounds of moulded rice with cut-up pimientos, and this would be followed by a dessert involving gelatin and egg white and whipped cream, taking a long, nerve-racking time to set because we had no refrigerator and it had to be chilled on the cellar floor. But the constraint, the pall over the table, was quite absent. Alfrida not only accepted second helpings, she asked for them. And she did this almost absentmindedly, and tossed off her compliments in the same way, as if the food, the eating of the food, was a secondary though agreeable thing, and she was really there to talk, and make other people talk, and anything you wanted to talk about—almost anything—would be fine.

She always visited in summer, and usually she wore some sort of striped, silky sundress, with a halter top that left her back bare. Her back was not pretty, being sprinkled with little dark moles, and her shoulders were bony and her chest nearly flat. My father would always remark on how much she could eat and remain thin. Or he turned truth on its head by noting that her appetite was as picky as ever, but she still hadn't been prevented from larding on the fat. (It was not considered out of place in our family to comment about fatness or skinniness or pallor or ruddiness or baldness.)

Her dark hair was done up in rolls above her face and at the sides, in the style of the time. Her skin was brownish-looking, netted with fine wrinkles, and her mouth wide, the lower lip rather thick, almost drooping, painted with a hearty lipstick that left a smear on the teacup and water tumbler. When her mouth was opened wide—as it nearly always was, talking or laughing—you could see that some of her teeth had been pulled at the back. Nobody could say that she was good-looking—any woman over twenty-five seemed to me to have pretty well passed beyond the possibility of being good-looking, anyway, to have lost the right to be so, and perhaps even the desire—but she was fervent and dashing. My father said thoughtfully that she had zing.

Alfrida talked to my father about things that were happening in the world, about politics. My father read the paper, he listened to the radio, he had opinions about these things but rarely got a chance to talk about them. The aunts' husbands had opinions too, but theirs were brief and unvaried and expressed an everlasting distrust of all public figures and particularly all foreigners, so that most of the time all that could be gotten out of them were grunts of dismissal. My grandmother was deaf—nobody could tell how much she knew or what she thought about anything, and the aunts themselves seemed fairly proud of how much they didn't know or didn't have to pay attention to. My mother had been a schoolteacher, and she could readily have pointed out all the countries of Europe on the map, but she saw everything through a personal haze, with the British Empire and the royal family looming large and everything else diminished, thrown into a jumble-heap that was easy for her to disregard.

Alfrida's views were not really so far away from those of the uncles. Or so it appeared. But instead of grunting and letting the subject go, she gave her hooting laugh, and told stories about prime ministers and the American president and John L. Lewis and the mayor of Montreal—stories in which they all came out badly. She told stories about the royal family too, but there she made a distinction between the good ones like the king and queen and the beautiful Duchess of Kent and the dreadful ones like the Windsors and old King Eddy, who—she said—had a certain disease and had marked his wife's neck by trying to strangle her, which was why she always had to wear her pearls. This distinction coincided pretty well with one my mother made but seldom spoke about, so she did not object—though the reference to syphilis made her wince.

I smiled at it, knowingly, with a foolhardy composure.

Alfrida called the Russians funny names. Mikoyan-sky. Uncle Joe-sky. She believed that they were pulling the wool over everybody's eyes, and that the United Nations was a farce that would never work and that Japan would rise again and should have been finished off when there was the chance. She didn't trust Quebec either. Or the pope. There was a problem for her with Senator McCarthy—she would have liked to be on his side, but his being a Catholic was a stumbling block. She called the pope the poop. She relished the thought of all the crooks and scoundrels to be found in the world.

Sometimes it seemed as if she was putting on a show—a display, maybe to tease my father. To rile him up, as he himself would have said, to get his goat. But not because she disliked him or even wanted to make him uncomfortable. Quite the opposite. She might have been tormenting him as young girls torment boys at school, when arguments are a peculiar delight to both sides and insults are taken as flattery. My father argued with her, always in a mild steady voice, and yet it was clear that he had the intention of goading her on. Sometimes he would do a turnaround, and say that maybe she was right—that with her work on the newspaper, she must have sources of information that he couldn't have. You've put me straight, he would say, if I had any sense I'd be obliged to you. And she would say, Don't give me that load of baloney.

'You two,' said my mother, in mock despair and perhaps in real exhaustion, and Alfrida told her to go and have a lie-down, she deserved it after this splendiferous dinner, she and I would manage the dishes. My mother was subject to a tremor in her right arm, a stiffness in her fingers, that she believed came when she got overtired.

While we worked in the kitchen Alfrida talked to me about celebrities—actors, even minor movie stars, who had made stage appearances in the city where she lived. In a lowered voice still broken by wildly disrespectful laughter she told me stories of their bad behaviour, the rumours of private scandals that had never made it into the magazines. She mentioned queers, man-made bosoms, household triangles—all things that I had found hints of in my reading but felt giddy to hear about, even at third or fourth hand, in real life.

Alfrida's teeth always got my attention, so that even in these confidential recitals I sometimes lost track of what was being said. Those teeth that were left, across the front, were each of a slightly different colour, no two alike. Some with a fairly strong enamel tended towards shades of dark ivory, others were opalescent, shadowed with lilac, and giving out fish-flashes of silver rims, occasionally a gleam of gold. People's teeth in those days seldom made such a solid, handsome show as they do now, unless they were false. But these teeth of Alfrida's were unusual in their individuality, clear separation, and large size. When Alfrida let out some jibe that was especially, knowingly outrageous, they seemed to leap to the fore like a palace guard, like jolly spear-fighters.

'She always did have trouble with her teeth,' the aunts said. 'She had that abscess, remember, the poison went all through her system.'

How like them, I thought, to toss aside Alfrida's wit and style and turn her teeth into a sorry problem.

'Why doesn't she just have them all out and be done with it?' they said.

'Likely she couldn't afford it,' said my grandmother, surprising everybody as she sometimes did, by showing that she had been keeping up with the conversation all along.

And surprising me with the new, everyday sort of light this shed on Alfrida's life. I had believed that Alfrida was rich—rich at least in comparison with the rest of the family. She lived in an apartment—I had never seen it, but to me that fact conveyed at least the idea of a very civilized life—and she wore clothes that were not homemade, and her shoes were not Oxfords like the shoes of practically all the other grown-up women I knew—they were sandals made of bright strips of the new plastic. It was hard to know whether my grandmother was simply living in the past, when getting your false teeth was the solemn, crowning expense of a lifetime, or whether she really knew things about Alfrida's life that I never would have guessed.

The rest of the family was never present when Alfrida had dinner at our house. She did go to see my grandmother, who was her aunt, her mother's sister. My grandmother no longer lived at her own house but lived alternately with one or the other of the aunts, and Alfrida went to whichever house she was living in at the time, but not to the other house, to see the other aunt who was as much her cousin as my father was. And the meal she took was never with any of them. Usually she came to our house first and visited awhile, and then gathered herself up, as if reluctantly, to make the other visit. When she came back later and we sat down to eat, nothing derogatory was said outright against the aunts and their husbands, and certainly nothing disrespectful about my grandmother. In fact, it was the way that my grandmother would be spoken of by Alfrida—a sudden sobriety and concern in her voice, even a touch of fear (what about her blood pressure, had she been to the doctor lately, what did he have to say?)—that made me aware of the difference, the coolness or possibly unfriendly restraint, with which she asked after the others. Then there would be a similar restraint in my mother's reply, and an extra gravity in my father's—a caricature of gravity, you might say—that showed how they all agreed about something they could not say.

On the day when I smoked the cigarette Alfrida decided to take this a bit further, and she said solemnly, 'How about Asa, then? Is he still as much of a conversation grabber as ever?'

My father shook his head sadly, as if the thought of his uncle's garrulousness must weigh us all down.

'Indeed,' he said. 'He is indeed.'

Then I took my chance.

'Looks like the roundworms have got into the hogs,' I said. 'Yup.'

Except for the 'yup', this was just what my uncle had said, and he had said it at this very table, being overcome by an uncharacteristic need to break the silence or to pass on something important that had just come to mind. And I said it with just his stately grunts, his innocent solemnity.

Alfrida gave a great, approving laugh, showing her festive teeth. 'That's it, she's got him to a *T*.'

My father bent over his plate, as if to hide how he was laughing too, but of course not really hiding it, and my mother shook her head, biting her lips, smiling. I felt a keen triumph. Nothing was said to put me in my place, no reproof for what was sometimes called my sarcasm, my being smart. The word 'smart' when it was used about me, in the family, might mean intelligent, and then it was used rather grudgingly—'oh, she's smart enough some ways'—or it might be used to mean pushy, attention-seeking, obnoxious. *Don't be so smart.*

Sometimes my mother said sadly, 'You have a cruel tongue.'

Sometimes—and this was a great deal worse—my father was disgusted with me. 'What makes you think you have the right to run down decent people?'

This day nothing like that happened—I seemed to be as free as a visitor at the table, almost as free as Alfrida, and flourishing under the banner of my own personality.

But there was a gap about to open, and perhaps that was the last time, the very last time, that Alfrida sat at our table. Christmas cards continued to be exchanged, possibly even letters—as long as my mother could manage a pen—and we still read Alfrida's name in the paper, but I cannot recall any visits during the last couple of years I lived at home.

It may have been that Alfrida asked if she could bring her friend and had been told that she could not. If she was already living with him, that would have been one reason, and if he was the same man she had later, the fact that he was married would have been another. My parents would have been united in this. My mother had a horror of irregular sex or flaunted sex—of any sex, you might say, for the proper married kind was not acknowledged at all—and my father too judged these matters strictly at that time in his life. He might have had a special objection, also, to a man who could get a hold over Alfrida.

She would have made herself cheap in their eyes. I can imagine either one of them saying it. *She didn't need to go and make herself cheap.*

But she may not have asked at all, she may have known enough not to. During the time of those earlier, lively visits there may have been no man in her life, and then when there was one, her attention may have shifted entirely. She may have become a different person then, as she certainly was later on.

Or she may have been wary of the special atmosphere of a household where there is a sick person who will go on getting sicker and never get better. Which was the case with mother, whose symptoms joined together, and turned a corner, and instead of a worry and an inconvenience became her whole destiny.

'The poor thing,' the aunts said.

And as my mother was changed from a mother into a stricken presence around the house, these other, formerly so restricted females in the family seemed to gain some little liveliness and increased competence in the world. My grandmother got herself a hearing aid—something nobody would have suggested to her. One of the aunts' husbands—not Asa, but the one called Irvine—died, and the aunt who had been married to him learned to drive the car and got a job doing alterations in a clothing store and no longer wore a hairnet.

They called to see my mother, and saw always the same thing—that the one who had been better-looking, who had never quite let them forget she was a schoolteacher, was growing month by month more slow and stiff in the movements of her limbs and more thick and importunate in her speech, and that nothing was going to help her.

They told me to take good care of her.

'She's your mother,' they reminded me.

'The poor thing.'

Alfrida would not have been able to say those things, and she might not have been able to find anything to say in their place.

Her not coming to see us was all right with me. I didn't want people coming. I had no time for them, I had become a furious housekeeper—waxing the floors and ironing even the dish towels, and this was all done to keep some sort of disgrace (my mother's deterioration seemed to be a unique disgrace that infected us all) at bay. It was done to make it seem as if I lived with my parents and my brother and my sister in a normal family in an ordinary house, but the moment somebody stepped in our door and saw my mother they saw that this was not so and they pitied us. A thing I could not stand.

I won a scholarship. I didn't stay home to take care of my mother or of anything else. I went off to college. The college was in the city where Alfrida lived. After a few months she asked me to come for supper, but I could not go, because I worked every evening of the week except on Sundays. I worked in the city library, downtown, and in the college library, both of which stayed open until nine o'clock. Some time later, during the winter, Alfrida asked me again, and this time the invitation was for a Sunday. I told her that I could not come because I was going to a concert.

'Oh—a date?' she said, and I said yes, but at the time it was not true. I would go to the free Sunday concerts in the college auditorium with another girl, or two or three other girls, for something to do and in the faint hope of meeting some boys there.

'Well you'll have to bring him around sometime,' Alfrida said. 'I'm dying to meet him.'

Towards the end of the year I did have someone to bring, and I had actually met him at the concert. At least, he had seen me at a concert and had phoned me up and asked me to go out with him. But I would never have brought him to meet Alfrida. I would never have brought any of my new friends to meet her. My new friends were people who said, 'Have you read *Look Homeward Angel*? Oh, you have to read that. Have you read *Buddenbrooks*?' They were people with whom I went to see *Forbidden Games* and *Les Enfants du Paradis* when the Film Society brought them in. The boy I went out with, and later became engaged to, had taken me to the Music Building, where you could listen to records at lunch hour. He introduced me to Gounod and because of Gounod I loved opera, and because of opera I loved Mozart.

When Alfrida left a message at my rooming house, asking me to call back, I never did. After that she didn't call again.

She still wrote for the paper—occasionally I glanced at one of her rhapsodies about Royal Doulton figurines or imported ginger biscuits or honeymoon negligees. Very likely she was still answering the letters from the Flora Simpson housewives, and still laughing at them. Now that I was living in that city I seldom looked at the paper that had once seemed to me the centre of city life—and even, in a way, the centre of our life at home, sixty miles away. The jokes, the compulsive insincerity, of people like Alfrida and Horse Henry now struck me as tawdry and boring.

I did not worry about running into her, even in this city that was not, after all, so very large. I never went into the shops that she mentioned in her column. I had no reason to walk past the newspaper building, and she lived far away from my rooming house, somewhere on the south side of town.

Nor did I think that Alfrida was the kind of person to show up at the library. The very word, 'library', would probably make her turn down her big mouth in a parody of consternation, as she used to do at the books in the bookcase in our house—those books not bought in my time, some of them won as school prizes by my teenaged parents (there was my mother's maiden name, in her beautiful lost handwriting), books that seemed to me not like things bought in a store at all, but like presences in the house just as the trees outside the window were not plants but presences rooted in the ground. *The Mills on the Floss, The Call of the Wild, The Heart of Midlothian.* 'Lots of hotshot reading in there,' Alfrida had said. 'Bet you don't crack those very often.' And my father had said no, he didn't, falling in with her comradely tone of dismissal or even contempt and to some extent telling a lie, because he did look into them, once in a long while, when he had the time.

That was the kind of lie that I hoped never to have to tell again, the contempt I hoped never to have to show, about the things that really mattered to me. And in order not to have to do that, I would pretty well have to stay clear of the people I used to know.

At the end of my second year I was leaving college—my scholarship had covered only two years there. It didn't matter—I was planning to be a writer anyway. And I was getting married.

Alfrida had heard about this, and she got in touch with me again.

'I guess you must've been too busy to call me, or maybe nobody ever gave you my messages,' she said.

I said that maybe I had been, or maybe they hadn't.

This time I agreed to visit. A visit would not commit me to anything, since I was not going to be living in this city in the future. I picked a Sunday, just after my final exams were over, when my fiancé was going to be in Ottawa for a job interview. The day was bright and sunny—it was around the beginning of May. I decided to walk. I had hardly ever been south of Dundas Street or east of Adelaide, so there were parts of the city that were entirely strange to me. The shade trees along the northern streets had just come out in leaf, and the lilacs, the ornamental crab apple trees, the beds of tulips were all in flower, the lawns like fresh carpets. But after a while I found myself walking along streets where there were no shade trees, streets where the houses were hardly an arm's reach from the sidewalk, and where such lilacs as there were—lilacs will grow anywhere—were pale, as if sun-bleached, and their fragrance did not carry. On these streets, as well as houses there were narrow apartment buildings, only two or three stories high—some with the utilitarian decoration of a rim of bricks around their doors, and some with raised windows and limp curtains falling out over their sills.

Alfrida lived in a house, not in an apartment building. She had the whole upstairs of a house. The downstairs, at least the front part of the downstairs, had been turned into a shop, which was closed, because of Sunday. It was a secondhand shop—I could see through the dirty front windows a lot of nondescript furniture with stacks of old dishes and utensils set everywhere. The only thing that caught my eye was a honey pail, exactly like the honey pail with a blue sky and a golden beehive in which I had carried my lunch to school when I was six or seven years old. I could remember reading over and over the words on its side.

All pure honey will granulate.

I had no idea then what 'granulate' meant, but I liked the sound of it. It seemed ornate and delicious.

I had taken longer to get there than I had expected and I was very hot. I had not thought that Alfrida, inviting me to lunch, would present me with a meal like the Sunday dinners at home, but it was cooked meat and vegetables I smelled as I climbed the outdoor stairway.

'I thought you'd got lost,' Alfrida called out above me. 'I was about to get up a rescue party.'

Instead of a sundress she was wearing a pink blouse with a floppy bow at the neck, tucked into a pleated brown skirt. Her hair was no longer done up in smooth rolls but cut short and frizzed around her face, its dark brown colour now harshly touched with red. And her face, which I remembered as lean and summer-tanned, had got fuller and somewhat pouchy. Her makeup stood out on her skin like orange-pink paint in the noon light.

But the biggest difference was that she had gotten false teeth, of a uniform colour, slightly overfilling her mouth and giving an anxious edge to her old expression of slap-dash eagerness.

'Well—haven't you plumped out,' she said. 'You used to be so skinny.'

This was true, but I did not like to hear it. Along with all the girls at the rooming house, I ate cheap food—copious meals of Kraft dinners and packages of jam-filled cookies. My fiancé, so sturdily and possessively in favour of everything about me, said that he liked full-bodied women and that I reminded him of Jane Russell. I did not mind his saying that, but usually I was affronted when people had anything to say about my appearance. Particularly when it was somebody like Alfrida—somebody who had lost all importance in my life. I believed that such people had no right to be look-ing at me, or forming any opinions about me, let alone stating them.

This house was narrow across the front, but long from front to back. There was a living room whose ceiling sloped at the sides and whose windows overlooked the street, a hall-like dining room with no windows at all because side bedrooms with dormers opened off it, a kitchen, a bathroom also without windows that got its daylight through a pebbled-glass pane in its door, and across the back of the house a glassed-in sunporch.

The sloping ceilings made the rooms look makeshift, as if they were only pretend-ing to be anything but bedrooms. But they were crowded with serious furniture—din-ing-room table and chairs, kitchen table and chairs, living-room sofa and recliner—all meant for larger, proper rooms. Doilies on the tables, squares of embroidered white cloth protecting the backs and arms of sofa and chairs, sheer curtains across the windows and heavy flowered drapes at the sides—it was all more like the aunts' houses than I would have thought possible. And on the dining-room wall—not in the bathroom or bedroom but in the dining room—there hung a picture that was the silhouette of a girl in a hoopskirt, all constructed of pink satin ribbon.

A strip of tough linoleum was laid down on the dining-room floor, or the path from the kitchen to the living room.

Alfrida seemed to guess something of what I was thinking.

'I know I've got far too much stuff in here,' she said. 'But it's my parents' stuff. It's family furnishings, and I couldn't let them go.'

I had never thought of her as having parents. Her mother had died long ago, and she had been brought up by my grandmother, who was her aunt.

'My dad and mother's,' Alfrida said. 'When Dad went off, your grandma kept it because she said it ought to be mine when I grew up, and so here it is. I couldn't turn it down, when she went to that trouble.'

Now it came back to me—the part of Alfrida's life that I had forgotten about. Her father had married again. He had left the farm and got a job working for the railway. He had some other children, the family moved from one town to another, and sometimes Alfrida used to mention them, in a joking way that had something to do with how many children there had been and how close they came together and how much the family had to move around.

'Come and meet Bill,' Alfrida said.

Bill was out on the sunporch. He sat, as if waiting to be summoned, on a low couch or daybed that was covered with a brown plaid blanket. The blanket was rumpled—he must have been lying on it recently—and the blinds on the windows were all pulled down to their sills. The light in the room—the hot sunlight coming through the rain-marked yellow blinds—and the rumpled rough blanket and faded, dented cushion, even the smell of the blanket, and of the masculine slippers, old scuffed slippers that had lost their shape and pattern, reminded me—just as much as the doilies and the heavy polished furniture in the inner rooms had done, and the ribbon-girl on the wall—of my aunts' houses. There, too, you could come upon a shabby male hideaway with its furtive yet insistent odours, its shamefaced but stubborn look of contradicting the female domain.

Bill stood up and shook my hand, however, as the uncles would never have done with a strange girl. Or with any girl. No specific rudeness would have held them back, just a dread of appearing ceremonious.

He was a tall man with wavy, glistening grey hair and a smooth but not young-looking face. A handsome man, with the force of his good looks somehow drained away—by indifferent health, or some bad luck, or lack of gumption. But he had still a worn courtesy, a way of bending towards a woman, that suggested the meeting would be a pleasure, for her and for himself.

Alfrida directed us into the windowless dining room where the lights were on in the middle of this bright day. I got the impression that the meal had been ready some time ago, and that my late arrival had delayed their usual schedule. Bill served the roast chicken and dressing, Alfrida the vegetables. Alfrida said to Bill, 'Honey, what do you think that is beside your plate?' and then he remembered to pick up his napkin.

He had not much to say. He offered the gravy, he inquired as to whether I wanted mustard relish or salt and pepper, he followed the conversation by turning his head towards Alfrida or towards me. Every so often he made a little whistling sound between his teeth, a shivery sound that seemed meant to be genial and appreciative and that I thought at first might be a prelude to some remark. But it never was, and Alfrida never paused for it. I have since seen reformed drinkers who behaved somewhat as he did—chiming in agreeably but unable to carry things beyond that, helplessly preoccupied. I never knew whether that was true of Bill, but he did seem to carry around a history of defeat, of troubles borne and lessons learned. He had an air too of gallant accommodation towards whatever choices had gone wrong or chances hadn't panned out.

These were frozen peas and carrots, Alfrida said. Frozen vegetables were fairly new at this time.

'They beat the canned,' she said. 'They're practically as good as fresh.'

Then Bill made a whole statement. He said they were better than fresh. The colour, the flavour, everything was better than fresh. He said it was remarkable what they could do now and what would be done by way of freezing things in the future.

Alfrida leaned forward, smiling. She seemed almost to hold her breath, as if he was her child taking unsupported steps, or a first lone wobble on a bicycle.

There was a way they could inject something into a chicken, he told us, there was a new process that would have every chicken coming out the same, plump and tasty. No such thing as taking a risk on getting an inferior chicken anymore.

'Bill's field is chemistry,' Alfrida said.

When I had nothing to say to this she added, 'He worked for Gooderhams.'

Still nothing.

'The distillers,' she said. 'Gooderhams Whisky.'

The reason I had nothing to say was not that I was rude or bored (or anymore rude than I was naturally at that time, or more bored than I had expected to be) but that I did not understand that I should ask questions—almost any questions at all, to draw a shy male into conversation, to shake him out of his abstraction and set him up as a man of a certain authority, therefore the man of the house. I did not understand why Alfrida looked at him with such a fiercely encouraging smile. All of my experience of a woman with men, of a woman listening to her man, hoping and hoping that he will establish himself as somebody she can reasonably be proud of, was in the future. The only observation I had made of couples was of my aunts and uncles and of my mother and father, and those husbands and wives seemed to have remote and formalized connections and no obvious dependence on each other.

Bill continued eating as if he had not heard this mention of his profession and his employer, and Alfrida began to question me about my courses. She was still smiling, but her smile had changed. There was a little twitch of impatience and unpleasantness in it, as if she was just waiting for me to get to the end of my explanations so that she could say—as she did say—'You couldn't get me to read that stuff for a million dollars.'

'Life's too short,' she said. 'You know, down at the paper we sometimes get some-body that's been through all that. Honours English. Honours Philosophy. You don't know what to do with them. They can't write worth a nickel. I've told you that, haven't I?' she said to Bill, and Bill looked up and gave her his dutiful smile.

She let this settle.

'So what do you do for fun?' she said.

A Streetcar Named Desire was being done in a theatre in Toronto at that time, and I told her that I had gone down on the train with a couple of friends to see it.

Alfrida let the knife and fork clatter onto her plate.

'That filth,' she cried. Her face leapt out at me, carved with disgust. Then she spoke more calmly but still with a virulent displeasure.

'You went *all the way to Toronto* to see that filth.'

We had finished the dessert, and Bill picked that moment to ask if he might be excused. He asked Alfrida, then with the slightest bow he asked me. He went back to the sunporch and in a little while we could smell his pipe. Alfrida, watching him go, seemed to forget about me and the play. There was a look of such stricken tenderness on her face that when she stood up I thought she was going to follow him. But she was only going to get her cigarettes.

She held them out to me, and when I took one she said, with a deliberate effort at jollity, 'I see you kept up the bad habit I got you started on.' She might have remem-bered that I was not a child anymore and I did not have to be in her house and that there was no point in making an enemy of me. And I wasn't going to argue—I did not care what Alfrida thought about Tennessee Williams. Or what she thought about any-thing else.

'I guess it's your business,' Alfrida said. 'You can go where you want to go.' And she added, 'After all—you'll pretty soon be a married woman.'

By her tone, this could mean either 'I have to allow that you're grown up now' or 'Pretty soon you'll have to toe the line.'

We got up and started to collect the dishes. Working close to each other in the small space between the kitchen table and counter and the refrigerator, we soon devel-oped without speaking about it a certain order and harmony of scraping and stacking and putting the leftover food into smaller containers for storage and filling the sink with hot, soapy water and pouncing on any piece of cutlery that hadn't been touched and slipping it into the baize-lined drawer in the dining-room buffet. We brought the ashtray out to the kitchen and stopped every now and then to take a restorative, busi-nesslike drag on our cigarettes. There are things women agree on or don't agree on when they work together in this way—whether it is all right to smoke, for instance, or preferable not to smoke because some migratory ash might find its way onto a clean dish, or whether every single thing that has been on the table has to be washed even if it has not been used—and it turned out that Alfrida and I agreed. Also, the thought that I could get away, once the dishes were done, made me feel more relaxed and gen-erous. I had already said that I had to meet a friend that afternoon.

'These are pretty dishes,' I said. They were creamy-coloured, slightly yellowish, with a rim of blue flowers.

'Well—they were my mother's wedding dishes,' Alfrida said. 'That was one other good thing your grandma did for me. She packed up all my mother's dishes and put them away until the time came when I could use them. Jeanie never knew they existed. They wouldn't have lasted long, with that bunch.'

Jeanie. That bunch. Her stepmother and the half brothers and sisters.

'You know about that, don't you?' Alfrida said. 'You know what happened to my mother?'

Of course I knew. Alfrida's mother had died when a lamp exploded in her hands—that is, she died of burns she got when a lamp exploded in her hands—and my aunts and my mother had spoken of this regularly. Nothing could be said about Alfrida's mother or about Alfrida's father, and very little about Alfrida herself—without that death being dragged in and tacked onto it. It was the reason that Alfrida's father left the farm (always somewhat of a downward step morally if not financially). It was a reason to be desperately careful with coal oil, and a reason to be grateful for electricity, whatever the cost. And it was a dreadful thing for a child of Alfrida's age, whatever. (That is—whatever she had done with herself since.)

If it hadn't've been for the thunderstorm she wouldn't ever have been lighting a lamp in the middle of the afternoon.

She lived all that night and the next day and the next night and it would have been the best thing in the world for her if she hadn't've.

And just the year after that the Hydro came down their road, and they didn't have a need of the lamps anymore.

The aunts and my mother seldom felt the same way about anything, but they shared a feeling about this story. The feeling was in their voices whenever they said Alfrida's mother's name. The story seemed to be a horrible treasure to them, something our family could claim that nobody else could, a distinction that would never be let go. To listen to them had always made me feel as if there was some obscene connivance going on, a fond fingering of whatever was grisly or disastrous. Their voices were like worms slithering around in my insides.

Men were not like this, in my experience. Men looked away from frightful happenings as soon as they could and behaved as if there was no use, once things were over with, in mentioning them or thinking about them ever again. They didn't want to stir themselves up, or stir other people up.

So if Alfrida was going to talk about it, I thought, it was a good thing that my fiancé had not come. A good thing that he didn't have to hear about Alfrida's mother, on top of finding out about my mother and my family's relative or maybe considerable poverty. He admired opera and Laurence Olivier's *Hamlet*, but he had no time for tragedy—for the squalor of tragedy—in ordinary life. His parents were healthy and good-looking and prosperous (though he said of course that they were dull), and it seemed he had not had to know anybody who did not live in fairly sunny circumstances. Failure in life—failures of luck, of health, of finances—all struck him as lapses, and his resolute approval of me did not extend to my ramshackle background.

'They wouldn't let me in to see her, at the hospital,' Alfrida said, and at least she was saying this in her normal voice, not preparing the way with any special piety, or greasy excitement. 'Well, I probably wouldn't have let me in either, if I'd been in their shoes. I've no idea what she looked like. Probably all bound up like a mummy. Or if she wasn't she should have been. I wasn't there when it happened, I was at school. It got very dark and the teacher turned the lights on—we had lights, at school—and we all had to stay till the thunderstorm was over. Then my aunt Lily—well, your grandmother—she came to meet me and took me to her place. And I never got to see my mother again.'

I thought that was all she was going to say but in a moment she continued, in a voice that had actually brightened up a bit, as if she was preparing for a laugh.

'I yelled and yelled my fool head off that I wanted to see her, carried on and carried on, and finally when they couldn't shut me up your grandmother said to me, "You're just better off not to see her. You would not want to see her, if you knew what she looks like now. You wouldn't want to remember her this way."

'But you know what I said? I remember saying it. I said, But she would want to see me. *She would want to see me.*'

Then she really did laugh, or make a snorting sound that was evasive and scornful.

'I must've thought I was a pretty big cheese, mustn't I? *She would want to see me.*'

This was a part of the story I had never heard.

And the minute I heard it, something happened. It was as if a trap had snapped shut, to hold these words in my head. I did not exactly understand what use I would have for them. I only knew how they jolted me and released me, right away, to breathe a different kind of air, available only to myself,

She would want to see me.

The story I wrote, with this in it, would not be written till years later, not until it had become quite unimportant to think about what had put the idea in my head in the first place.

I thanked Alfrida and said that I had to go. Alfrida went to call Bill to say goodbye to me, but came back to report that he had fallen asleep.

'He'll be kicking himself when he wakes up,' she said. 'He enjoyed meeting you.'

She took off her apron and accompanied me all the way down the outside steps. At the bottom of the steps was a gravel path leading around to the sidewalk. The gravel crunched under our feet and she stumbled in her thin-soled house shoes.

She said, 'Ouch! Goldarn it,' and caught hold of my shoulder.

'How's your dad?' she said.

'He's all right.'

'He works too hard.'

I said, 'He has to.'

'Oh, I know. And how's your mother?'

'She's about the same.'

She turned aside towards the shop window.

'Who do they think is ever going to buy this junk? Look at that honey pail. Your dad and I used to take our lunch to school in pails just like that.'

'So did I,' I said.

'Did you?' She squeezed me. 'You tell your folks I'm thinking about them, will you do that?'

Alfrida did not come to my father's funeral. I wondered if that was because she did not want to meet me. As far as I knew she had never made public what she held against me; nobody else would know about it. But my father had known. When I was home visiting him and learned that Alfrida was living not far away—in my grandmother's house, in fact, which she had finally inherited—I had suggested that we go to see her. This was in the flurry between my two marriages, when I was in an expansive mood, newly released and able to make contact with anyone I chose.

My father said, 'Well, you know, Alfrida was a bit upset.'

He was calling her Alfrida now. When had that started?

I could not even think, at first, what Alfrida might be upset about. My father had to remind me of the story, published several years ago, and I was surprised, even impatient and a little angry, to think of Alfrida's objecting to something that seemed now to have so little to do with her.

'It wasn't Alfrida at all,' I said to my father. 'I changed it, I wasn't even thinking about her. It was a character. Anybody could see that.'

But as a matter of fact there was still the exploding lamp, the mother in her charnel wrappings, the staunch, bereft child.

'Well,' my father said. He was in general quite pleased that I had become a writer, but there were reservations he had about what might be called my character. About the fact that I had ended my marriage for personal—that is, wanton—reasons, and the way I went around justifying myself—or perhaps, as he would have said, weaseling out of things. He would not say so—it was not his business anymore.

I asked him how he knew that Alfrida felt this way.

He said, 'A letter.'

A letter, though they lived not far apart. I did feel sorry to think that he had had to bear the brunt of what could be taken as my thoughtlessness, or even my wrongdoing. Also that he and Alfrida seemed now to be on such formal terms. I wondered what he was leaving out. Had he felt compelled to defend me to Alfrida, as he had to defend my writing to other people? He would do that now, though it was never easy for him. In his uneasy defence he might have said something harsh.

Through me, peculiar difficulties had developed for him.

There was a danger whenever I was on home ground. It was the danger of seeing my life through other eyes than my own. Seeing it as an ever-increasing roll of words like barbed wire, intricate, bewildering, uncomforting—set against the rich productions, the food, flowers, and knitted garments, of other women's domesticity. It became harder to say that it was worth the trouble.

Worth my trouble, maybe, but what about anyone else's?

My father had said that Alfrida was living alone now. I asked him what had become of Bill. He said that all of that was outside of his jurisdiction. But he believed there had been a bit of a rescue operation.

'Of Bill? How come? Who by?'

'Well, I believe there was a wife.'

'I met him at Alfrida's once. I liked him.'

'People did. Women.'

I had to consider that the rupture might have had nothing to do with me. My stepmother had urged my father into a new sort of life. They went bowling and curling and regularly joined other couples for coffee and doughnuts at Tim Horton's. She had been a widow for a long time before she married him, and she had many friends from those days who became new friends for him. What had happened with him and Alfrida might have been simply one of the changes, the wearing-out of old attachments, that I understood so well in my own life but did not expect to happen in the lives of older people—particularly, as I would have said, in the lives of people at home.

My stepmother died just a little before my father. After their short, happy marriage they were sent to separate cemeteries to lie beside their first, more troublesome, partners. Before either of those deaths Alfrida had moved back to the city. She didn't sell the house, she just went away and left it. My father wrote to me, 'That's a pretty funny way of doing things.'

There were a lot of people at my father's funeral, a lot of people I didn't know. A woman came across the grass in the cemetery to speak to me—I thought at first she must be a friend of my stepmother's. Then I saw that the woman was only a few years past my own age. The stocky figure and crown of grey-blond curls and floral-patterned jacket made her look older.

'I recognized you by your picture,' she said. 'Alfrida used to always be bragging about you.'

I said, 'Alfrida's not dead?'

'Oh, no,' the woman said, and went on to tell me that Alfrida was in a nursing home in a town just north of Toronto.

'I moved her down there so's I could keep an eye on her.'

Now it was easy to tell—even by her voice—that she was somebody of my own generation, and it came to me that she must be one of the other family, a half sister of Alfrida's, born when Alfrida was almost grown up.

She told me her name, and it was of course not the same as Alfrida's—she must have married. And I couldn't recall Alfrida's ever mentioning any of her half family by their first names.

I asked how Alfrida was, and the woman said her own eyesight was so bad that she was legally blind. And she had a serious kidney problem, which meant that she had to be on dialysis twice a week.

'Other than that—?' she said, and laughed. I thought, yes, a sister, because I could hear something of Alfrida in that reckless, tossed laugh.

'So she doesn't travel too good,' she said. 'Or else I would've brought her. She still gets the paper from here and I read it to her sometimes. That's where I saw about your dad.'

I wondered out loud, impulsively, if I should go to visit, at the nursing home. The emotions of the funeral—all the warm and relieved and reconciled feelings opened up in me by the death of my father at a reasonable age—prompted this suggestion. It would have been hard to carry out. My husband—my second husband—and I had only two days here before we were flying to Europe on an already delayed holiday.

'I don't know if you'd get so much out of it,' the woman said. 'She has her good days. Then she has her bad days. You never know. Sometimes I think she's putting it on. Like, she'll sit there all day and whatever anybody says to her, she'll just say the same thing. *Fit as a fiddle and ready for love.* That's what she'll say all day long. *Fit-as-a-fiddle-and-ready-for-love.* She'll drive you crazy. Then other days she can answer all right.'

Again, her voice and laugh—this time half submerged—reminded me of Alfrida, and I said, 'You know I must have met you, I remember once when Alfrida's stepmother and her father dropped in, or maybe it was only her father and some of the children—'

'Oh, that's not who I am,' the woman said. 'You thought I was Alfrida's sister? Glory. I must be looking my age.'

I started to say that I could not see her very well, and it was true. In October the afternoon sun was low, and it was coming straight into my eyes. The woman was standing against the light, so that it was hard to make out her features or her expression.

She twitched her shoulders nervously and importantly. She said, 'Alfrida was my birth mom.'

Mawm. Mother.

Then she told me, at not too great length, the story that she must have told often, because it was about an emphatic event in her life and an adventure she had embarked on alone. She had been adopted by a family in eastern Ontario; they were the only family she had ever known ('and I love them dearly'), and she had married and had her children, who were grown up before she got the urge to find out who her own mother was. It wasn't too easy, because of the way records used to be kept, and the secrecy ('It was kept one hundred per cent secret that she had me'), but a few years ago she had tracked down Alfrida.

'Just in time too,' she said. 'I mean, it was time somebody came along to look after her. As much as I can.'

I said, 'I never knew.'

'No. Those days, I don't suppose too many did. They warn you, when you start out to do this, it could be a shock when you show up. Older people, it's still heavy-duty. However. I don't think she minded. Earlier on, maybe she would have.'

There was some sense of triumph about her, which wasn't hard to understand. If you have something to tell that will stagger someone, and you've told it, and it has done so, there has to be a balmy moment of power. In this case it was so complete that she felt a need to apologize.

'Excuse me talking all about myself and not saying how sorry I am about your dad.'

I thanked her.

'You know Alfrida told me that your dad and her were walking home from school one day, this was in high school. They couldn't walk all the way together because, you know, in those days, a boy and a girl, they would just get teased something terrible. So if he got out first he'd wait just where their road went off the main road, outside of town, and if she got out first she would do the same, wait for him. And one day they were walking together and they heard all the bells starting to ring and you know what it was? It was the end of the First World War.'

I said that I had heard that story too.

'Only I thought they were just children.'

'Then how could they be coming home from high school, if they were just children?'

I said that I had thought they were out playing in the fields. 'They had my father's dog with them. He was called Mack.'

'Maybe they had a dog all right. Maybe he came to meet them. I wouldn't think she'd get mixed up on what she was telling me. She was pretty good on remembering anything involved your dad.'

Now I was aware of two things. First, that my father was born in 1902, and that Alfrida was close to the same age. So it was much more likely that they were walking home from high school than that they were playing in the fields, and it was odd that I had never thought of that before. Maybe they had said they were in the fields, that is, walking home across the fields. Maybe they had never said 'playing'.

Also, that the feeling of apology or friendliness, the harmlessness that I had felt in this woman a little while before, was not there now.

I said, 'Things get changed around.'

'That's right,' the woman said. 'People change things around. Do you want to know what Alfrida said about you?'

Now. I knew it was coming now.

'What?'

'She said you were smart, but you weren't ever quite as smart as you thought you were.'

I made myself keep looking into the dark face against the light. Smart, too smart, not smart enough.

I said. 'Is that all?'

'She said you were kind of a cold fish. That's her talking, not me. I haven't got anything against you.'

That Sunday, after the noon dinner at Alfrida's, I set out to walk all the way back to my rooming house. If I walked both ways, I reckoned that I would have covered about ten miles, which ought to offset the effects of the meal I had eaten. I felt overfull, not just of food but of everything that I had seen and sensed in the apartment. The crowded, old-fashioned furnishings. Bill's silences. Alfrida's love stubborn as sludge, and inappropriate, and hopeless—as far as I could see—on the grounds of age alone.

After I had walked for a while, my stomach did not feel so heavy. I made a vow not to eat anything for the next twenty-four hours. I walked north and west, north and west, on the streets of the tidily rectangular small city. On a Sunday afternoon there was hardly any traffic, except on the main thoroughfares. Sometimes my route coincided with a bus route for a few blocks. A bus might go by with only two or three people in it. People I did not know and who did not know me. What a blessing.

I had lied, I was not meeting any friends. My friends had mostly all gone home to wherever they lived. My fiancé would be away until the next day—he was visiting his parents, in Cobourg, on the way home from Ottawa. There would be nobody in the rooming house when I got there—nobody I had to bother talking to or listening to. I had nothing to do.

When I had walked for over an hour, I saw a drugstore that was open. I went in and had a cup of coffee. The coffee was reheated, black and bitter—its taste was medicinal, exactly what I needed. I was already feeling relieved, and now I began to feel happy. Such happiness, to be alone. To see the hot late-afternoon light on the sidewalk outside, the branches of a tree just out in leaf, throwing their skimpy shadows. To hear from the back of the shop the sounds of the ball game that the man who had served me was listening to on the radio. I did not think of the story I would make about Alfrida—not of that in particular—but of the work I wanted to do, which seemed more like grabbing something out of the air than constructing stories. The cries of the crowd came to me like big heartbeats, full of sorrows. Lovely formal-sounding waves, with their distant, almost inhuman assent and lamentation.

This is what I wanted, this was what I thought I had to pay attention to, this was how I wanted my life to be.

2001

◆

Alistair MacLeod
b. 1936

◆

Born in North Battleford, Saskatchewan, Alistair MacLeod grew up in a coal-mining area of Alberta until he was ten, when his parents moved back to the family farm in Inverness County, Cape Breton. After obtaining his teacher's certificate from the Nova Scotia Teachers College, he took his BA and his BEd (1960) from Saint Francis Xavier University, his MA (1961) from the University of New Brunswick, and his PhD (1968) from the University of Notre Dame. He taught at Indiana University from 1966 until 1969, then moved to the University of Windsor, where he was a professor of English literature and creative writing until his retirement in 2000.

Most of the stories of MacLeod's two collections of short fiction, *The Lost Salt Gift of Blood* (1976) and *As Birds Bring Forth the Sun* (1986), are set on the usually rugged and turbulent terrain of Cape Breton, where characters tend to be stern individualists who make their living from the sea and find solace in their deep-rooted traditions. These collections, along with two additional stories, were gathered together in *Island: The Collected Stories* (2000). In 1999 MacLeod published a novel, *No Great Mischief*, which examines the pains and the endurance of the Cape Breton people; it won the International IMPAC Dublin Literary Award.

In 'The Boat', from *The Lost Salt Gift of Blood*, the narrator looks back on the winter when he was fifteen. As he reflects on his Cape Breton childhood, he comes to know and appreciate his feelings for his parents and to understand the emotional price he has paid for leaving the scene of his upbringing to pursue an advanced education.

The Boat

There are times even now, when I awake at four o'clock in the morning with the terrible fear that I have overslept; when I imagine that my father is waiting for me in the room below the darkened stairs or that the shorebound men are tossing pebbles against my window while blowing their hands and stomping their feet impatiently on the frozen steadfast earth. There are times when I am half out of bed and fumbling for socks and mumbling for words before I realize that I am foolishly alone, that no one waits at the base of the stairs and no boat rides restlessly in the waters by the pier.

At such times only the grey corpses on the overflowing ashtray beside my bed bear witness to the extinction of the latest spark and silently await the crushing out of the most recent of their fellows. And then because I am afraid to be alone with death, I dress rapidly, make a great to-do about clearing my throat, turn on both faucets in the sink, and proceed to make loud splashing ineffectual noises. Later I go out and walk the mile to the all-night restaurant.

In the winter it is a very cold walk, and there are often tears in my eyes when I arrive. The waitress usually gives a sympathetic little shiver and says, 'Boy, it must be really cold out there; you got tears in your eyes.'

'Yes,' I say, 'it sure is; it really is.'

And then the three or four of us who are always in such places at such times make uninteresting little protective chit-chat until the dawn reluctantly arrives. Then I swallow the coffee, which is always bitter, and leave with a great busy rush because by that time I have to worry about being late and whether I have a clean shirt and whether my car will start and about all the other countless things one must worry about when one teaches at a great Midwestern university. And I know then that that day will go by as have all the days of the past ten years, for the call and the voices and the shapes and the boat were not really there in the early morning's darkness and I have all kinds of comforting reality to prove it. They are only shadows and echoes, the animals a child's hands make on the wall by lamplight, and the voices from the rain barrel; the cuttings from an old movie made in the black and white of long ago.

I first became conscious of the boat in the same way and at almost the same time that I became aware of the people it supported. My earliest recollection of my father is a view from the floor of gigantic rubber boots and then of being suddenly elevated and having my face pressed against the stubble of his cheek, and of how it tasted of salt and of how he smelled of salt from his red-soled rubber boots to the shaggy whiteness of his hair.

When I was very small, he took me for my first ride in the boat. I rode the half-mile from our house to the wharf on his shoulders and I remember the sound of his rubber boots galumphing along the gravel beach, the tune of the indecent little song he used to sing, and the odour of the salt.

The floor of the boat was permeated with the same odour and in its constancy I was not aware of change. In the harbour we made our little circle and returned. He tied the boat by its painter, fastened the stern to its permanent anchor, and lifted me high over his head to the solidity of the wharf. Then he climbed up the little iron ladder that led to the wharf's cap, placed me once more upon his shoulders, and galumphed off again.

When we returned to the house everyone made a great fuss over my precocious excursion and asked, 'How did you like the boat?' 'Were you afraid in the boat?' 'Did you cry in the boat?' They repeated 'the boat' at the end of all their questions and I knew it must be very important to everyone.

My earliest recollection of my mother is of being alone with her in the mornings while my father was away in the boat. She seemed to be always repairing clothes that were 'torn in the boat', preparing food 'to be eaten in the boat', or looking for 'the boat' through our kitchen window which faced upon the sea. When my father returned about noon, she would ask, 'Well, how did things go in the boat today?' It was the first question I remember asking: 'Well, how did things go in the boat today?' 'Well, how did things go in the boat today?'

The boat in our lives was registered at Port Hawkesbury. She was what Nova Scotians called a Cape Island boat and was designed for the small inshore fishermen who sought the lobsters of the spring and the mackerel of summer and later the cod and haddock and hake. She was thirty-two feet long and nine wide, and was powered by an engine from a Chevrolet truck. She had a marine clutch and a high-speed reverse gear and was painted light green with the name *Jenny Lynn* stencilled in black letters on her bow and painted on an oblong plate across her stern. Jenny Lynn had been my mother's maiden name and the boat was called after her as another link in the chain of tradition. Most of the boats that berthed at the wharf bore the names of some female member of their owner's household.

I say this now as if I knew it all then. All at once, all about boat dimensions and engines, and as if on the day of my first childish voyage I noticed the difference between a stencilled name and a painted name. But of course it was not that way at all, for I learned it all very slowly and there was not time enough.

I learned first about our house, which was one of about fifty that marched around the horseshoe of our harbour and the wharf that was its heart. Some of them were so close to the water that during a storm the sea spray splashed against their windows while others were built farther along the beach, as was the case with ours. The houses and their people, like those of the neighbouring towns and villages, were the result of Ireland's discontent and Scotland's Highland Clearances and America's War of Independence. Impulsive, emotional Catholic Celts who could not bear to live with England and shrewd, determined Protestant Puritans who, in the years after 1776, could not bear to live without.

The most important room in our house was one of those oblong old-fashioned kitchens heated by a wood- and coal-burning stove. Behind the stove was a box of kindlings and beside it a coal scuttle. A heavy wooden table with leaves that expanded or reduced its dimensions stood in the middle of the floor. There were five wooden homemade chairs which had been chipped and hacked by a variety of knives. Against the east wall, opposite the stove, there was a couch which sagged in the middle and had a cushion for a pillow, and above it a shelf which contained matches, tobacco, pencils, odd fish-hooks, bits of twine, and a tin can filled with bills and receipts. The south wall was dominated by a window which faced the sea and on the north there was a five-foot board which bore a variety of clothes hooks and the burdens of each. Beneath the board there was a jumble of odd footwear, mostly of rubber. There was also, on this wall, a barometer, a map of the marine area, and a shelf which held a tiny radio. The kitchen was shared by all of us and was a buffer zone between the immaculate order of ten other rooms and the disruptive chaos of the single room that was my father's.

My mother ran her house as her brothers ran their boats. Everything was clean and spotless and in order. She was tall and dark and powerfully energetic. In later years she reminded me of the women of Thomas Hardy, particularly Eustacia Vye, in a physical way. She fed and clothed a family of seven children, making all of the meals and most of the clothes. She grew miraculous gardens and magnificent flowers and raised broods of hens and ducks. She would walk miles on berry-picking expeditions and hoist her skirts to dig for clams when the tide was low. She was fourteen years younger then my father, whom she had married when she was twenty-six and had been a local beauty for a period of ten years. My mother was of the sea, as were all of her people, and her horizons were the very literal ones she scanned with her dark and fearless eyes.

Between the kitchen clothes rack and barometer, a door opened into my father's bedroom. It was a room of disorder and disarray. It was as if the wind which so often clamoured about the house succeeded in entering this single room and after whipping it into turmoil stole quietly away to renew its knowing laughter from without.

My father's bed was against the south wall. It always looked rumpled and unmade because he lay on top of it more than he slept within any folds it might have had. Beside it, there was a little brown table. An archaic goose-necked reading light, a battered table radio, a mound of wooden matches, one or two packages of tobacco, a deck of cigarette papers, and an overflowing ashtray cluttered its surface. The brown larvae of tobacco shreds and the grey flecks of ash covered both the table and the floor beneath it. The once-varnished surface of the table was disfigured by numerous black scars and gashes inflicted by the neglected burning cigarettes of many years. They had tumbled from the ashtray unnoticed and branded their statements permanently and quietly into the wood until the odour of their burning caused the snuffing out of their lives. At the bed's foot there was a single window which looked upon the sea.

Against the adjacent wall there was a battered bureau and beside it there was a closet which held his single ill-fitting serge suit, the two or three white shirts that strangled him and the square black shoes that pinched. When he took off his more friendly clothes, the heavy woollen sweaters, mitts, and socks which my mother knitted for him and the woollen and doeskin shirts, he dumped them unceremoniously on a single chair. If a visitor entered the room while he was lying on the bed, he would be told to throw the clothes on the floor and take their place upon the chair.

Magazines and books covered the bureau and competed with the clothes for domination of the chair. They further overburdened the heroic little table and lay on top of the radio. They filled a baffling and unknowable cave beneath the bed, and in the corner by the bureau they spilled from the walls and grew up from the floor.

The magazines were the most conventional: *Time, Newsweek, Life, Maclean's, The Family Herald, The Reader's Digest.* They were the result of various cut-rate subscriptions or of the gift subscriptions associated with Christmas, 'the two whole years for only $3.50'.

The books were more varied. There were a few hardcover magnificents and bygone Book-of-the-Month wonders and some were Christmas or birthday gifts. The majority of them, however, were used paperbacks which came from those second-hand bookstores that advertise in the backs of magazines: 'Miscellaneous Used Paperbacks 10¢ Each'. At first he sent for them himself, although my mother resented the expense, but in later years they came more and more often from my sisters who had moved to the cities. Especially at first they were very weird and varied. Mickey Spillane and Ernest Haycox vied with Dostoyevsky and Faulkner, and the Penguin Poets edition of Gerard Manley Hopkins arrived in the same box as a little book on sex technique called *Getting the Most Out of Love.* The former had been assiduously annotated by a very fine hand using a very blue-inked fountain pen while the latter had been studied by someone with very large thumbs, the prints of which were still visible in the margins. At the slightest provocation it would open almost automatically to particularly graphic and well-smudged pages.

When he was not in the boat, my father spent most of his time lying on the bed in his socks, the top two buttons of his trousers undone, his discarded shirt on the ever-ready chair and the sleeves of the woollen Stanfield underwear, which he wore both summer and winter, drawn half way up to his elbows. The pillows propped up the whiteness of his head and the goose-necked lamp illuminated the pages in his hands. The cigarettes smoked and smouldered on the ashtray and on the table and the radio played constantly, sometimes low and sometimes loud. At midnight and at one, two, three, and four, one could sometimes hear the radio, his occasional cough, the rustling thud of a completed book being tossed to the corner heap, or the movement necessitated by his sitting on the edge of the bed to roll the thousandth cigarette. He seemed never to sleep, only to doze, and the light shone constantly from his window to the sea.

My mother despised the room and all it stood for and she had stopped sleeping in it after I was born. She despised disorder in rooms and in houses and in hours and in lives, and she had not read a book since high school. There she had read *Ivanhoe* and considered it a colossal waste of time. Still the room remained, like a rock of opposition in the sparkling waters of clear deep harbour, opening off the kitchen where we really lived our lives, with its door always open and its contents visible to all.

The daughters of the room and of the house were very beautiful. They were tall and willowy like my mother and had her fine facial features set off by the reddish copper-coloured hair that had apparently once been my father's before it turned to white. All of them were very clever in school and helped my mother a great deal about the house. When they were young they sang and were very happy and very nice to me because I was the youngest, and the family's only boy.

My father never approved of their playing about the wharf like the other children, and they went there only when my mother sent them on an errand. At such times they almost always overstayed, playing screaming games of tag or hide-and-seek in and about the fishing shanties, the piled traps and tubs of trawl, shouting down to the perch that swam languidly about the wharf's algae-covered piles, or jumping in and out of the boats that tugged gently at their lines. My mother was never uneasy about them at such times, and when her husband criticized her she would say, 'Nothing will happen to them there,' or 'They could be doing worse things in worse places.'

By about the ninth or tenth grade my sisters one by one discovered my father's bedroom, and then the change would begin. Each would go into the room one morning when he was out. She would go with the ideal hope of imposing order or with the more practical objective of emptying the ashtray, and later she would be found spellbound by the volume in her hand. My mother's reaction was always abrupt, bordering on the angry. 'Take your nose out of that trash and come and do your work,' she would say, and once I saw her slap my youngest sister so hard that the print of her hand was scarletly emblazoned upon her daughter's cheek while the broken-spined paperback fluttered uselessly to the floor.

Thereafter my mother would launch a campaign against what she had discovered but could not understand. At times, although she was not overly religious, she would bring in God to bolster her arguments, saying, 'In the next world God will see to those who waste their lives reading useless books when they should be about their work.' Or without theological aid, 'I would like to know how books help anyone to live a life.' If my father were in, she would repeat the remarks louder than necessary, and her voice would carry into his room where he lay upon his bed. His usual reaction was to turn up the volume of the radio, although that action in itself betrayed the success of the initial thrust.

Shortly after my sisters began to read books, they grew restless and lost interest in darning socks and baking bread, and all of them eventually went to work as summer waitresses in the Sea Food Restaurant. The restaurant was run by a big American concern from Boston and catered to the tourists that flooded the area during July and August. My mother despised the whole operation. She said the restaurant was not run by 'our people', and 'our people' did not eat there, and that it was run by outsiders for outsiders.

'Who are these people anyway?' she would ask, tossing back her dark hair, 'and what do they, though they go about with their cameras for a hundred years, know about the way it is here, and what do they care about me and mine, and why should I care about them?'

She was angry that my sisters should even conceive of working in such a place, and more angry when my father made no move to prevent it, and she was worried about herself and about her family and about her life. Sometimes she would say softly to her sisters, 'I don't know what's the matter with my girls. It seems none of them are interested in any of the right things.' And sometimes there would be bitter savage arguments. One afternoon I was coming in with three mackerel I'd been given at the wharf when I heard her say, 'Well, I hope you'll be satisfied when they come home knocked up and you'll have had your way.'

It was the most savage thing I'd ever heard my mother say. Not just the words but the way she said them, and I stood there in the porch afraid to breathe for what seemed like the years from ten to fifteen, feeling the damp, moist mackerel with their silver glassy eyes growing clammy against my leg.

Through the angle in the screen door I saw my father, who had been walking into his room, wheel around on one of his rubber-booted heels and look at her with his blue eyes flashing like clearest ice beneath the snow that was his hair. His usually ruddy face was drawn and grey, reflecting the exhaustion of a man of sixty-five who had been working in those rubber boots for eleven hours on an August day, and for a fleeting moment I wondered what I would do if he killed my mother while I stood there in the porch with those three foolish mackerel in my hand. Then he turned and went into his room and the radio blared forth the next day's weather forecast and I retreated under the noise and returned again, stamping my feet and slamming the door too loudly to signal my approach. My mother was busy at the stove when I came in, and did not raise her head when I threw the mackerel in a pan. As I looked into my father's room, I said, 'Well, how did things go in the boat today?' and he replied, 'Oh, not too badly, all things considered.' He was lying on his back and lighting the first cigarette and the radio was talking about the Virginia coast.

All of my sisters made good money on tips. They bought my father an electric razor, which he tried to use for a while, and they took out even more magazine subscriptions. They bought my mother a great many clothes of the type she was very fond of, the wide-brimmed hats and the brocaded dresses, but she locked them all in trunks and refused to wear any of them.

On one August day my sisters prevailed upon my father to take some of their restaurant customers for an afternoon ride in the boat. The tourists with their expensive clothes and cameras and sun glasses awkwardly backed down the iron ladder at the wharf's side to where my father waited below, holding the rocking *Jenny Lynn* in snug against the wharf with one hand on the iron ladder and steadying his descending passengers with the other. They tried to look both prim and wind-blown like the girls in the Pepsi-Cola ads and did the best they could, sitting on the thwarts where the newspapers were spread to cover the splattered blood and fish entrails, crowding to one side so that they were in danger of capsizing the boat, taking the inevitable pictures or merely trailing their fingers through the water of their dreams.

All of them liked my father very much and, after he'd brought them back from their circles in the harbour, they invited him to their rented cabins which were located high on a hill overlooking the village to which they were so alien. He proceeded to get very drunk up there with the beautiful view and the strange company and the abundant liquor, and late in the afternoon he began to sing.

I was just approaching the wharf to deliver my mother's summons when he began, and the familiar yet unfamiliar voice that rolled down from the cabins made me feel as I had never felt before in my young life, or perhaps as I had always felt without really knowing it, and I was ashamed yet proud, younger yet old and saved yet forever lost, and there was nothing I could do to control my legs which trembled nor my eyes which wept, for what they could not tell.

The tourists were equipped with tape recorders and my father sang for more than three hours. His voice boomed down the hill and bounced off the surface of the harbour, which was an unearthly blue on that hot August day, and was then reflected to the wharf and the fishing shanties, where it was absorbed amidst the men who were baiting lines for the next day's haul.

He sang all the old sea chanteys that had come across from the old world and by which men like him had pulled ropes for generations, and he sang the East Coast sea songs that celebrated the sealing vessels of Northumberland Strait and the long liners of the Grand Banks, and of Anticosti, Sable Island, Grand Manan, Boston Harbor, Nantucket, and Block Island. Gradually he shifted to the seemingly unending Gaelic drinking songs with their twenty or more verses and inevitable refrains, and the men in the shanties smiled at the coarseness of some of the verses and at the thought that the singer's immediate audience did not know what they were applauding nor recording to take back to staid old Boston. Later as the sun was setting he switched to the laments and the wild and haunting Gaelic war songs of those spattered Highland ancestors he had never seen, and when his voice ceased, the savage melancholy of three hundred years seemed to hang over the peaceful harbour and the quiet boats and the men leaning in the doorways of their shanties with their cigarettes glowing in the dusk and the women looking to the sea from their open windows with their children in their arms.

When he came home he threw the money he had earned on the kitchen table as he did with all his earnings but my mother refused to touch it, and the next day he went with the rest of the men to bait his trawl in the shanties. The tourists came to the door that evening and my mother met them there and told them that her husband was not in, although he was lying on the bed only a few feet away, with the radio playing and the cigarette upon his lips. She stood in the doorway until they reluctantly went away.

In the winter they sent him a picture which had been taken on the day of the singing. On the back it said, 'To Our Ernest Hemingway' and the 'Our' was underlined. There was also an accompanying letter telling how much they had enjoyed themselves, how popular the tape was proving, and explaining who Ernest Hemingway was. In a way it almost did look like one of those unshaven, taken-in-Cuba pictures of Hemingway. My father looked both massive and incongruous in the setting. His bulky fisherman's clothes were too big for the green and white lawn chair in which he sat, and his rubber boots seemed to take up all of the well-clipped grass square. The beach umbrella jarred with his sunburned face and because he had already been singing for some time, his lips, which chapped in the winds of spring and burned in the water glare of summer, had already cracked in several places, producing tiny flecks of blood at their corners and on the whiteness of his teeth. The bracelets of brass chain which he wore to protect his wrists from chafing seemed abnormally large and his broad leather belt had been slackened and his heavy shirt and underwear were open at the throat, revealing an uncultivated wilderness of white chest hair bordering on the semi-controlled stubble of his neck and chin. His blue eyes had looked directly into the camera and his hair was whiter than the two tiny clouds that hung over his left shoulder. The sea was behind him and its immense blue flatness stretched out to touch the arching blueness of the sky. It seemed very far away from him or else he was so much in the foreground that he seemed too big for it.

Each year another of my sisters would read the books and work in the restaurant. Sometimes they would stay out quite late on the hot summer nights and when they came up the stairs my mother would ask them many long and involved questions which they resented and tried to avoid. Before ascending the stairs they would go into my father's room, and those of us who waited above could hear them throwing his clothes off the chair before sitting on it, or the squeak of the bed as they sat on its edge. Sometimes they would talk to him a long time, the murmur of their voices blending with the music of the radio into a mysterious vapour-like sound which floated softly up the stairs.

I say this again as if it all happened at once and as if all of my sisters were of identical ages and like so many lemmings going into another sea and, again, it was of course not that way at all. Yet go they did, to Boston, to Montreal, to New York with the young men they met during the summers and later married in those far-away cities. The young men were very articulate and handsome and wore fine clothes and drove expensive cars and my sisters, as I said, were very tall and beautiful with their copper-coloured hair, and were tired of darning socks and baking bread.

One by one they went. My mother had each of her daughters for fifteen years, then lost them for two and finally forever. None married a fisherman. My mother never accepted any of the young men, for in her eyes they seemed always a combination of the lazy, the effeminate, the dishonest, and the unknown. They never seemed to do any physical work and she could not comprehend their luxurious vacations and she did not know whence they came nor who they were. And in the end she did not really care, for they were not of her people and they were not of her sea.

I say this now with a sense of wonder at my own stupidity in thinking I was somehow free and would go on doing well in school and playing and helping in the boat and passing into my early teens while streaks of grey began to appear in my mother's dark hair and my father's rubber boots dragged sometimes on the pebbles of the beach as he trudged home from the wharf. And there were but three of us in the house that had at one time been so loud.

Then during the winter that I was fifteen he seemed to grow old and ill all at once. Most of January he lay upon the bed, smoking and reading and listening to the radio while the wind howled about the house and the needle-like snow blistered off the ice-covered harbour and the doors flew out of people's hands if they did not cling to them like death.

In February, when the men began overhauling their lobster traps, he still did not move, and my mother and I began to knit lobster trap headings in the evenings. The twine was as always very sharp and harsh, and blisters formed upon our thumbs and little paths of blood snaked quietly down between our fingers while the seals that had drifted down from distant Labrador wept and moaned like human children on the ice-floes of the Gulf.

In the daytime my mother's brother, who had been my father's partner as long as I could remember, also came to work upon the gear. He was a year older than my mother and was tall and dark and the father of twelve children.

By March we were very far behind and although I began to work very hard in the evenings I knew it was not hard enough and that there were but eight weeks left before the opening of the season on May first. And I knew that my mother worried and my uncle was uneasy and that all of our very lives depended on the boat being ready with her gear and two men, by the date of May the first. And I knew then that *David Copperfield* and *The Tempest* and all of those friends I had dearly come to love must really go forever. So I bade them all good-bye.

The night after my first full day at home and after my mother had gone upstairs he called me into his room, where I sat upon the chair beside his bed. 'You will go back tomorrow,' he said simply.

I refused then, saying I had made my decision and was satisfied.

'That is no way to make a decision,' he said, 'and if you are satisfied I am not. It is best that you go back.' I was almost angry then and told him as all children do that I wished he would leave me alone and stop telling me what to do.

He looked at me a long time then, lying there on the same bed on which he had fathered me those sixteen years before, fathered me his only son, out of who knew what emotions when he was already fifty-six and his hair had turned to snow. Then he swung his legs over the edge of the squeaking bed and sat facing me and looked into my own dark eyes with his of crystal blue and placed his hand upon my knee. 'I am not telling you to do anything,' he said softly, 'only asking you.'

The next morning I returned to school. As I left, my mother followed me to the porch and said, 'I never thought a son of mine would choose useless books over the parents that gave him life.'

In the weeks that followed he got up rather miraculously, and the gear was ready and the *Jenny Lynn* was freshly painted by the last two weeks of April when the ice began to break up and the lonely screaming gulls returned to haunt the silver herring as they flashed within the sea.

On the first day of May the boats raced out as they had always done, laden down almost to the gunwales with their heavy cargoes of traps. They were almost like living things as they plunged through the waters of the spring and manoeuvred between the still floating icebergs of crystal-white and emerald green on their way to the traditional grounds that they sought out every May. And those of us who sat that day in the high school on the hill, discussing the watery imagery of Tennyson, watched them as they passed back and forth beneath us until by afternoon the piles of traps which had been stacked upon the wharf were no longer visible but were spread about the bottoms of the sea. And the *Jenny Lynn* went too, all day, with my uncle tall and dark, like a lat-ter-day Tashtego standing at the tiller with his legs wide apart and guiding her deftly between the floating pans of ice and my father in the stern standing in the same way with his hands upon the ropes that lashed the cargo to the deck. And at night my mother asked, 'Well, how did things go in the boat today?'

And the spring wore on and the summer came and school ended in the third week of June and the lobster season on July first and I wished that the two things I loved so dearly did not exclude each other in a manner that was so blunt and too clear.

At the conclusion of the lobster season my uncle said he had been offered a berth on a deep-sea dragger and had decided to accept. We all knew that he was leaving the *Jenny Lynn* forever and that before the next lobster season he would buy a boat of his own. He was expecting another child and would be supporting fifteen people by the next spring and could not chance my father against the family that he loved.

I joined my father then for the trawling season, and he made no protest and my mother was quite happy. Through the summer we baited the tubs of trawl in the afternoon and set them at sunset and revisited them in the darkness of the early morning. The men would come tramping by our house at four a.m. and we would join them and walk with them to the wharf and be on our way before the sun rose out of the ocean where it seemed to spend the night. If I was not up they would toss pebbles to my window and I would be very embarrassed and tumble downstairs to where my father lay fully clothed atop his bed, reading his book and listening to his radio and smoking his cigarette. When I appeared he would swing off his bed and put on his boots and be instantly ready and then we would take the lunches my mother had prepared the night before and walk off toward the sea. He would make no attempt to wake me himself.

It was in many ways a good summer. There were few storms and we went out almost every day and we lost a minimum of gear and seemed to land a maximum of fish and I tanned dark and brown after the manner of my uncles.

My father did not tan—he never tanned—because of his reddish complexion, and the salt water irritated his skin as it had for sixty years. He burned and reburned over and over again and his lips still cracked so that they bled when he smiled, and his arms, especially the left, still broke out into the oozing salt-water boils as they had ever since as a child I had first watched him soaking and bathing them in a variety of ineffectual solutions. The chafe-preventing bracelets of brass linked chain that all the men wore about their wrists in early spring were his the full season and he shaved but painfully and only once a week.

And I saw then, that summer, many things that I had seen all my life as if for the first time and I thought that perhaps my father had never been intended for a fisherman either physically or mentally. At least not in the manner of my uncles; he had never really loved it. And I remembered that, one evening in his room when we were talking about *David Copperfield*, he had said that he had always wanted to go to the university and I had dismissed it then in the way one dismisses one's father's saying he would like to be a tight-rope walker, and we had gone on to talk about the Peggottys and how they loved the sea.

And I thought then to myself that there were many things wrong with all of us and all our lives and I wondered why my father, who was himself an only son, had not married before he was forty and then I wondered why he had. I even thought that perhaps he had had to marry my mother and checked the dates on the flyleaf of the Bible where I learned that my oldest sister had been born a prosaic eleven months after the marriage, and I felt myself then very dirty and debased for my lack of faith and for what I had thought and done.

And then there came into my heart a very great love for my father and I thought it was very much braver to spend a life doing what you really do not want rather than self-ishly following forever your own dreams and inclinations. And I knew then that I could never leave him alone to suffer the iron-tipped harpoons which my mother would forever hurl into his soul because he was a failure as a husband and a father who had retained none of his own. And I felt that I had been very small in a secret place within me and that even the completion of high school was for me a silly shallow selfish dream.

So I told him one night very resolutely and very powerfully that I would remain with him as long as he lived and we would fish the sea together. And he made no protest but only smiled through the cigarette smoke that wreathed his bed and replied, 'I hope you will remember what you've said.'

The room was now so filled with books as to be almost Dickensian, but he would not allow my mother to move or change them and he continued to read them, sometimes two or three a night. They came with great regularity now, and there were more hardcovers, sent by my sisters who had gone so long ago and now seemed so distant and so prosperous, and sent also pictures of small red-haired grandchildren with baseball bats and dolls, which he placed upon his bureau and which my mother gazed at wistfully when she thought no one would see. Red-haired grandchildren with baseball bats and dolls who would never know the sea in hatred or in love.

And so we fished through the heat of August and into the cooler days of September when the water was so clear we could almost see the bottom and the white mists rose like delicate ghosts in the early morning dawn. And one day my mother said to me, 'You have given added years to his life.'

And we fished on into October when it began to roughen and we could no longer risk night sets but took our gear out each morning and returned at the first sign of the squalls; and on into November when we lost three tubs of trawl and the clear blue water turned to a sullen grey and the trochoidal waves rolled rough and high and washed across our bows and decks as we ran within their troughs. We wore heavy sweaters now and the awkward rubber slickers and the heavy woollen mitts which soaked and froze into masses of ice that hung from our wrists like the limbs of gigantic monsters until we thawed them against the exhaust pipe's heat. And almost every day we would leave for home before noon, driven by the blasts of the northwest wind coating our eyebrows with ice and freezing our eyelids closed as we leaned into a visibility that was hardly there, charting our course from the compass and the sea, running the waves and between them but never confronting their towering might.

And I stood at the tiller now, on these homeward lunges, stood in the place and in the manner of my uncle, turning to look at my father and to shout over the roar of the engine and the slop of the sea to where he stood in the stern, drenched and dripping with the snow and the salt and the spray and his bushy eyebrows caked in ice. But on November twenty-first, when it seemed we might be making the final run of the season, I turned and he was not there and I knew even in that instant that he would never be again.

On November twenty-first the waves of the grey Atlantic are very high and the waters are very cold and there are no signposts on the surface of the sea. You cannot tell where you have been five minutes before and in the squalls of snow you cannot see. And it takes longer than you would believe to check a boat that has been running before a gale and turn her ever so carefully in a wide and stupid circle, with timbers creaking and straining, back into the face of storm. And you know that it is useless and that your voice does not carry the length of the boat and that even if you knew the original spot, the relentless waves would carry such burden perhaps a mile or so by the time you could return. And you know also, the final irony, that your father, like your uncles and all the men that form your past, cannot swim a stroke.

The lobster beds off the Cape Breton coast are still very rich and now, from May to July, their offerings are packed in crates of ice, and thundered by the gigantic transport trucks, day and night, through New Glasgow, Amherst, Saint John, and Bangor and Portland and into Boston where they are tossed still living into boiling pots of water, their final home.

And though the prices are higher and the competition tighter, the grounds to which the *Jenny Lynn* once went remain untouched and unfished as they have for the last ten years. For if there are no signposts on the sea in storm, there are certain ones in calm, and the lobster bottoms were disturbed in calm before any of us can remember, and the grounds my father fished were those his father fished before him and there were others before and before and before. Twice the big boats have come from forty and fifty miles, lured by the promise of the grounds, and strewn the bottom with their traps, and twice they have returned to find their buoys cut adrift and their gear lost and destroyed. Twice the Fisheries Officer and the Mounted Police have come and asked many long and involved questions, and twice they have received no answers from the men leaning in the doors of their shanties and the women standing at their windows with their children in their arms. Twice they have gone away saying: 'There are no legal boundaries in the Marine area'; 'No one can own the sea'; 'Those grounds don't wait for anyone.'

But the men and the women, with my mother dark among them, do not care for what they say, for to them the grounds are sacred and they think they wait for me.

It is not an easy thing to know that your mother lives alone on an inadequate insurance policy and that she is too proud to accept any other aid. And that she looks through her lonely window onto the ice of winter and the hot flat calm of summer and the rolling waves of fall. And that she lies awake in the early morning's darkness when the rubber boots of the men scrunch upon the gravel as they pass beside her house on their way down to the wharf. And she knows that the footsteps never stop, because no man goes from her house, and she alone of all the Lynns has neither son nor son-in-law who walks toward the boat that will take him to the sea. And it is not an easy thing to know that your mother looks upon the sea with love and on you with bitterness because the one has been so constant and the other so untrue.

But neither is it easy to know that your father was found on November twenty-eighth, ten miles to the north and wedged between two boulders at the base of the rock-strewn cliffs where he had been hurled and slammed so many many times. His hands were shredded ribbons, as were his feet which had lost their boots to the suction of the sea, and his shoulders came apart in our hands when we tried to move him from the rocks. And the fish had eaten his testicles and the gulls had pecked out his eyes and the white-green stubble of his whiskers had continued to grow in death, like the grass on graves, upon the purple, bloated mass that was his face. There was not much left of my father, physically, as he lay there with the brass chains on his wrists and the seaweed in his hair.

1968

Bharati Mukherjee
b. 1940

Indian-born Bharati Mukherjee received her BA (1959) from the University of Calcutta, her MA (1961) from the University of Baroda, and her MFA (1963) and PhD (1979) from the University of Iowa. She emigrated from the United States to Canada in 1966, and, after living in Montreal and Toronto, returned in 1980 to the United States, where she currently teaches English at the University of California, Berkeley. Her fiction, like her life, is an exploration of cultural displacement, as her East Indian protagonists confront personal and social struggles both in India and in North America. In 'The Lady from Lucknow', Nafeesa Hafeez, a Muslim housewife, is carrying on an extramarital affair in Atlanta, Georgia; when the affair is revealed, her self-examination commences.

The author of several novels and collections of short stories, she also co-wrote, with her husband, the writer Clark Blaise, *Days and Nights in Calcutta* (1977), an autobiographical account of her return (with her husband) for a year to India. Her most recent book is *The Tree Bride* (2004).

The Lady from Lucknow

When I was four, one of the girls next door fell in love with a Hindu. Her father intercepted a love note from the boy, and beat her with his leather sandals. She died soon after. I was in the room when my mother said to our neighbour, 'The Nawab-*sahib* had no choice, but Husseina's heart just broke, poor dear.' I was an army doctor's daughter, and I pictured the dead girl's heart—a rubbery squeezable organ with auricles and ventricles—first swelling, then bursting and coating the floor with thick, slippery blood.

We lived in Lucknow at the time, where the Muslim community was large. This was just before the British took the fat, diamond-shaped subcontinent and created two nations, a big one for the Hindus and a littler one for us. My father moved us to Rawalpindi in Pakistan two months after Husseina died. We were a family of soft, voluptuous children, and my father wanted to protect us from the Hindus' shameful lust.

I have fancied myself in love many times since, but never enough for the emotions to break through tissue and muscle. Husseina's torn heart remains the standard of perfect love.

At seventeen I married a good man, the fourth son of a famous poet-cum-lawyer in Islamabad. We have a daughter, seven, and a son, four. In the Muslim communities we have lived in, we are admired. Iqbal works for IBM, and because of his work we have made homes in Lebanon, Brazil, Zambia, and France. Now we live in Atlanta, Georgia, in a wide, new house with a deck and a backyard that runs into a golf course. IBM has been generous to us. We expect to pass on this good, decent life to our children. Our children are ashamed of the dingy cities where we got our start.

Some Sunday afternoons when Iqbal isn't at a conference halfway across the world, we sit together on the deck and drink gin and tonics as we have done on Sunday afternoons in a dozen exotic cities. But here, the light is different somehow. A gold haze comes off the golf course and settles on our bodies, our new house. When the light shines right in my eyes, I pull myself out of the canvas deck chair and lean against the railing that still smells of forests. Everything in Atlanta is so new!

'Sit,' Iqbal tells me. 'You'll distract the golfers. Americans are crazy for sex, you know that.'

He half rises out of his deck chair. He lunges for my breasts in mock passion. I slip out of his reach.

At the bottom of the backyard, the golfers, caddies, and carts are too minute to be bloated with lust.

But, who knows? One false thwock! of their golfing irons, and my little heart, like a golf ball, could slice through the warm air and vanish into the jonquil-yellow beyond.

It isn't trouble that I want, though I do have a lover. He's an older man, an immunologist with the Centers for Disease Control right here in town. He comes to see me when Iqbal is away at high-tech conferences in sunny, remote resorts. Just think, Beirut was once such a resort! Lately my lover comes to me on Wednesdays even if Iqbal's in town.

'I don't expect to live till ninety-five,' James teases on the phone. His father died at ninety-three in Savannah. 'But I don't want a bullet in the brain from a jealous husband right now.'

Iqbal owns no firearms. Jealously would inflame him.

Besides, Iqbal would never come home in the middle of the day. Not even for his blood-pressure pills. The two times he forgot them last month, I had to take the bottle downtown. One does not rise through the multinational hierarchy coming home in midday, arriving late, or leaving early. Especially, he says, if you're a 'not-quite' as we are. It is up to us to set the standards.

Wives who want to be found out will be found out. Indiscretions are deliberate. The woman caught in mid-shame is a woman who wants to get out. The rest of us carry on.

James flatters me indefatigably; he makes me feel beautiful, exotic, responsive. I am a creature he has immunized of contamination. When he is with me, the world seems a happy enough place.

Then he leaves. He slips back into his tweed suit and backs out of my driveway.

I met James Beamish at a reception for foreign students on the Emory University campus. Iqbal avoids these international receptions because he thinks of them as excuses for looking back when we should be looking forward. These evenings are almost always tedious, but I like to go; just in case there's someone new and fascinating. The last two years, I've volunteered as host in the 'hospitality program'. At Thanksgiving and Christmas, two lonely foreign students are sent to our table.

That first evening at Emory we stood with name tags on lapels, white ones for students and blue ones for hosts. James was by a long table, pouring Chablis into a plastic glass. I noticed him right off. He was dressed much like the other resolute, decent men in the room. But whereas the other men wore white or blue shirts under their dark wool suits, James's shirt was bright red.

His wife was with him that evening, a stoutish woman with slender ankles and expensive shoes.

'Darling,' she said to James. 'See if you can locate our Palestinian.' Then she turned to me, and smiling, peered into my name tag.

'I'm Nafeesa Hafeez,' I helped out.

'Na-fee-sa,' she read out. 'Did I get that right?'

'Yes, perfect,' I said.

'What a musical name,' she said. 'I hope you'll be very happy here. Is this your first time abroad?'

James came over with a glass of Chablis in each hand. 'Did we draw this lovely lady? Oops, I'm sorry, you're a *host*, of course.' A mocking blue light was in his eyes. 'Just when I thought we were getting lucky, dear.'

'Darling, ours is a Palestinian. I told you that in the car. This one is obviously not Palestinian, are you dear?' She took a bright orange notebook out of her purse and showed me the name.

I had to read it upside-down. Something Waheed. School of Dentistry.

'What are you drinking?' James asked. He kept a glass for himself and gave me the other one.

Maybe James Beamish said nothing fascinating that night, but he was attentive, even after the Beamishes' Palestinian joined us. Mrs Beamish was brave, she asked the dentist about his family and hometown. The dentist described West Beirut in detail. The shortage of bread and vegetables, the mortar poundings, the babies bleeding. I wonder when aphasia sets in. When does a dentist, even a Palestinian dentist, decide it's time to cut losses.

Then my own foreign student arrived. She was an Indian Muslim from Lucknow, a large, bold woman who this far from our common hometown claimed me as a countrywoman. India, Pakistan, she said, not letting go of my hand, what does it matter?

I'd rather have listened to James Beamish but I couldn't shut out the woman's voice. She gave us her opinions on Thanksgiving rituals. She said, 'It is very odd that the pumpkin vegetable should be used for dessert, no? We are using it as vegetable only. Chhi! Pumpkin as a sweet. The very idea is horrid.'

I promised that when she came to our house for Thanksgiving, I'd make sweetmeats out of ricotta cheese and syrup. When you live in as many countries as Iqbal had made me, you can't tell if you pity, or if you envy, the women who stayed back.

I didn't hear from James Beamish for two weeks. I thought about him. In fact I couldn't get him out of my mind. I went over the phrases and gestures, the mocking light in the eyes, but they didn't add up to much. After the first week, I called Amina and asked her to lunch. I didn't know her well but her husband worked at the Centers for Disease Control. Just talking to someone connected with the Centers made me feel good. I slipped his name into the small talk with Amina and her eyes popped open, 'Oh, he's famous!' she exclaimed, and I shrugged modestly. I stayed home in case he should call. I sat on the deck and in spite of the cold, pretended to read Barbara Pym novels. Lines from Donne and Urdu verses about love floated in my skull.

I wasn't sure Dr Beamish would call me. Not directly, that is. Perhaps he would play a subtler game, get his wife to invite Iqbal and me for drinks. Maybe she'd even include their Palestinian and my Indian and make an international evening out of it. It sounded plausible.

Finally James Beamish called me on a Tuesday afternoon, around four. The children were in the kitchen, and a batch of my special chocolate sludge cookies was in the oven.

'Hi,' he said, then nothing for a bit. Then he said, 'This is James Beamish from the CDC. I've been thinking of you.'

He was between meetings, he explained. Wednesday was the only flexible day in his week, his day for paperwork. Could we have lunch on Wednesday?

The cookies smelled gooey hot, not burned. My daughter had taken the cookie sheet out and put in a new one. She'd turned the cold water faucet on so she could let the water drip on a tiny rosebud burn on her arm.

I felt all the warm, familiar signs of lust and remorse. I dabbed the burn with an ice cube wrapped in paper towel and wondered if I'd have time to buy a new front-closing bra after Iqbal got home.

James I had lunch in a Dekalb County motel lounge.

He would be sixty-five in July, but not retire till sixty-eight. Then he would live in Tonga, in Fiji, see the world, travel across Europe and North America in a Winnebago. He wouldn't be tied down. He had five daughters and two grandsons, the younger one aged four, a month older than my son. He had been in the navy during the war (*his* war), and he had liked that.

I said, ' "Goodbye, Mama, I'm off to Yokohama." ' It was silly, but it was the only war footage I could come up with, and it made him laugh.

'You're special,' he said. He touched my knee under the table. 'You've already been everywhere.'

'Not because I've wanted to.'

He squeezed my knee again, then paid with his Mastercharge card.

As we were walking through the parking lot to his car (it was a Cougar or a Buick, and not German or British as I'd expected), James put his arm around my shoulders. I may have seen the world but I haven't gone through the American teenage rites of making out in parked cars and picnic grounds, so I walked briskly out of his embrace. He let his hand slide off my shoulder. The hand slid down my back. I counted three deft little pats to my bottom before he let his hand fall away.

Iqbal and I are sensual people, but secretive. The openness of James Beamish's advance surprised me.

I got in his car, wary, expectant.

'Do up the seatbelt,' he said.

He leaned into his seatbelt and kissed me lightly on the lips. I kissed him back, hard. 'You don't panic easily, do you?' he said. The mocking blue light was in his eyes again. His tongue made darting little thrusts and probes past my lips.

Yes, I do, I would have said if he'd let me.

We held hands on the drive to my house. In the driveway he parked behind my Honda. 'Shall I come in?'

I said nothing. Love and freedom drop into our lives. When we have to beg or even agree, it's already too late.

'Let's go in.' He said softly.

I didn't worry about the neighbours. In his grey wool slacks and tweed jacket, he looked too old, too respectable, for any sordid dalliance with a not-quite's wife.

Our house is not that different in size and shape from the ones on either side. Only the inside smells of heavy incense, and the walls are hung with rows of miniature paintings from the reign of Emperor Akbar. I took James's big wrinkled hand in mine. Adultery in my house is probably no different, no quieter, than in other houses in this neighbourhood.

Afterwards it wasn't guilt I felt (guilt comes with desire not acted), but wonder that while I'd dashed out Tuesday night and bought myself silky new underwear, James had worn an old T-shirt and lemon-pale boxer shorts. Perhaps he hadn't planned on seducing a Lucknow lady that afternoon. Adventure and freedom had come to him out of the blue, too. Or perhaps only younger men like Iqbal make a fetish of doing sit-ups and dieting and renewing their membership at the racquet club when they're on the prowl.

October through February our passion held. When we were together, I felt cherished. I only played at being helpless, hysterical, cruel. When James left, I'd spend the rest of the afternoon with a Barbara Pym novel. I kept the novels open at pages in which excellent British women recite lines from Marvell to themselves. I didn't read. I watched the golfers trudging over brown fairways instead. I let the tiny golfers—clumsy mummers—tell me stories of ambitions unfulfilled. Golf carts lurched into the golden vista. I felt safe.

In the first week of March we met in James's house for a change. His wife was in Madison to babysit a grandson while his parents flew to China for a three-week tour. It was a thrill to be in his house. I fingered the book spines, checked the colour of sheets and towels, the brand names of cereals and detergents. Jane Fonda's Workout record was on the VCR. He was a man who took exceptional care of himself, this immunologist. Real intimacy, at last. The lust of the winter months had been merely foreplay. I felt at home in his house, in spite of the albums of family photographs on the coffee table and the brutish metal vulvas sculpted by a daughter in art school and stashed in the den. James was more talkative in his own house. He showed me the photos he wanted me to see, named real lakes and mountains. His family was real, and not quite real. The daughters were hardy, outdoor types. I saw them hiking in Zermatt and bicycling through Europe. They had red cheeks and backpacks. Their faces were honest and marvellously ordinary. What would they say if they knew their father, at sixty-five, was in bed with a married woman from Lucknow? I feared and envied their jealousy more than any violence in my husband's heart.

Love on the decline is hard to tell from love on the rise. I have lived a life perched on the edge of ripeness and decay. The traveller feels at home everywhere, because she is never at home anywhere. I felt the hot red glow of blood rushing through capillaries.

His wife came back early, didn't call, caught a ride from Hartsfield International with a friend. She had been raised in Saskatchewan, and she'd remained thrifty.

We heard the car pull into the driveway, the loud 'thank yous' and 'no, I couldn'ts' and then her surprised shout, 'James? Are you ill? What're you doing home?' as she shut the front door.

We were in bed, sluggish cozy and still moist under the goosedown quilt that the daughter in Madison had sent them as a fortieth anniversary gift some years before. His clothes were on top of a long dresser; mine were on the floor, the stockings wrinkled and looking legless.

James didn't go to pieces. I had to admire that. He said. 'Get in the bathroom. Get dressed. I'll take care of this.'

I am submissive by training. To survive, the Asian wife will usually do as she is told. But this time I stayed in bed.

'How are you going to explain me away, James? Tell her I'm the new cleaning woman?' I laughed, and my laugh tinkled flirtatiously, at least to me.

'Get in the bathroom.' This was the fiercest I'd ever heard him.

'I don't think so,' I said. I jerked the quilt off my body but didn't move my legs.

So I was in bed with the quilt at my feet, and James was by the dresser buttoning his shirt when Kate Beamish stood at the door.

She didn't scream. She didn't leap for James's throat—or mine. I'd wanted passion, but Kate didn't come through. I pulled the quilt over me.

I tried insolence. 'Is your wife not the jealous kind?' I asked.

'Let's just get over this as quietly and quickly as we can, shall we?' she said. She walked to the window in her brown Wallabies. 'I don't see any unfamiliar cars, so I suppose you'll expect James to drive you home.'

'She's the jealous type,' James said. He moved towards his wife and tried to guide her out of the bedroom.

'I'm definitely the jealous kind,' Kate Beamish said. 'I might have stabbed you if I could take you seriously. But you are quite ludicrous lounging like a Goya nude on my bed.' She gave a funny little snort. I noticed straggly hairs in her nostrils and looked away.

James was running water in the bathroom sink. Only the panicky ones falls apart and call their lawyers from the bedroom.

She sat on my side of the bed. She stared at me. If that stare had made me feel secretive and loathsome, I might not have wept, later. She plucked the quilt from my breasts as an internist might, and snorted again. 'Yes,' she said, 'I don't deny a certain interest he might have had,' but she looked through my face to the pillow behind, and dropped the quilt as she stood. I was shadow without depth or colour, a shadow-temptress who would float back to a city of teeming millions when the affair with James had ended.

I had thought myself provocative and fascinating. What had begun as an adventure had become shabby and complex. I was just another involvement of a white man in a pokey little outpost, something that 'men do' and then come to their senses while the *memsahibs* drink gin and tonic and fan their faces. I didn't merit a stab wound through the heart.

It wasn't the end of the world. It was humorous, really. Still. I let James call me a cab. That half-hour wait for the cab, as Kate related tales of the grandson to her distracted husband was the most painful. It came closest to what Husseina must have felt. At least her father, the Nawab-*sahib*, had beaten her.

I have known all along that perfect love has to be fatal. I have survived on four of the five continents. I get by because I am at least moderately charming and open-minded. From time to time, James Beamish calls me. 'She's promised to file for divorce.' Or 'Let's go away for a weekend. Let's go to Bermuda. Have lunch with me this Wednesday.' Why do I hear a second voice? She has laughed at me. She has mocked my passion.

I want to say yes. I want to beg him to take me away to Hilton Head in his new, retirement Winnebago. The golden light from the vista is too yellow. Yes, *please*, let's run away, keep this new and simple.

I can hear the golfballs being thwocked home by clumsy mummers far away where my land dips. My arms are numb, my breathing loud and ugly from pressing hard against the cedar railing. The pain in my chest will not go away. I should be tasting blood in my throat by now.

1985

Thomas King

b. 1943

Born in Roseville, California, of Cherokee and Greek descent, Thomas King left university after one year to travel to Australia and New Zealand, where he worked as a photojournalist. In 1967 he returned to university in the US, obtaining his BA (1970) and his MA (1972) from Chico State University. He subsequently taught at the University of Minnesota, the University of Lethbridge, and the University of Guelph, interrupting his teaching to obtain his PhD (1986) from the University of Utah. An important voice in Aboriginal studies and an outspoken advocate for Native rights, he ran as a candidate for the New Democratic Party in the 2008 Canadian federal election.

King has written for film, television, and radio, in addition to writing short stories and novels and, most recently, under the pseudonym Hartley GoodWeather, detective fiction. In his writings, he rejects the post-colonial approach to Aboriginal works as inappropriate, Aboriginal literature being a response not to colonialism but to Aboriginal traditions. 'Borders', from his short-story collection *One Good Story, That One* (1993), suggests that Canadians are more like Americans than they like to believe.

Borders

When I was twelve, maybe thirteen, my mother announced that we were going to go to Salt Lake City to visit my sister who had left the reserve, moved across the line, and found a job. Laetitia had not left home with my mother's blessing, but over time my mother had come to be proud of the fact that Laetitia had done all of this on her own.

'She did real good,' my mother would say.

Then there were the fine points to Laetitia's going. She had not, as my mother liked to tell Mrs Manyfingers, gone floating after some man like a balloon on a string. She hadn't snuck out of the house, either, and gone to Vancouver or Edmonton or Toronto to chase rainbows down alleys. And she hadn't been pregnant.

'She did real good.'

I was seven or eight when Laetitia left home. She was seventeen. Our father was from Rocky Boy on the American side.

'Dad's American,' Laetitia told my mother, 'so I can go and come as I please.'

'Send us a postcard.'

Laetitia packed her things, and we headed for the border. Just outside of Milk River, Laetitia told us to watch for the water tower.

'Over the next rise. It's the first thing you see.'

'We got a water tower on the reserve,' my mother said. 'There's a big one in Lethbridge, too.'

'You'll be able to see the tops of the flagpole, too. That's where the border is.'

When we got to Coutts, my mother stopped at the convenience store and bought her and Laetitia a cup of coffee. I got an Orange Crush.

'This is real lousy coffee.'

'You're just angry because I want to see the world.'

'It's the water. From here on down, they got lousy water.'

'I can catch the bus from Sweetgrass. You don't have to lift a finger.'

'You're going to have to buy your water in bottles if you want good coffee.'

There was an old wooden building about a block away, with a tall sign in the yard that said 'Museum'. Most of the roof had been blown away. Mom told me to go and see when the place was open. There were boards over the windows and doors. You could tell that the place was closed, and I told Mom so, but she said to go and check anyway. Mom and Laetitia stayed by the car. Neither of them moved. I sat down on the steps of the museum and watched them, and I don't know that they ever said anything to each other. Finally, Laetitia got her bag out of the trunk and gave Mom a hug.

I wandered back to the car. The wind had come up, and it blew Laetitia's hair across her face. Mom reached out and pulled the strands out of Laetitia's eyes, and Laetitia let her.

'You can still see the mountain from here,' my mother told Laetitia in Blackfoot.

'Lots of mountains in Salt Lake,' Laetitia told her in English.

'The place is closed,' I said. 'Just like I told you.'

Laetitia tucked her hair into her jacket and dragged her bag down the road to the brick building with the American flag flapping on a pole. When she got to where the guards were waiting, she turned, put the bag down, and waved to us. We waved back. Then my mother turned the car around, and we came home.

We got postcards from Laetitia regular, and, if she wasn't spreading jelly on the truth, she was happy. She found a good job and rented an apartment with a pool.

'And she can't even swim,' my mother told Mrs Manyfingers.

Most of the postcards said we should come down and see the city, but whenever I mentioned this, my mother would stiffen up.

So I was surprised when she bought two new tires for the car and put on her blue dress with the green and yellow flowers. I had to dress up, too, for my mother did not want us crossing the border looking like Americans. We made sandwiches and put them in a big box with pop and potato chips and some apples and bananas and a big jar of water.

'But we can stop at one of those restaurants, too, right?'

'We maybe should take some blankets in case you get sleepy.'

'But we can stop at one of those restaurants, too, right?'

The border was actually two towns, though neither one was big enough to amount to anything. Coutts was on the Canadian side and consisted of the convenience store and gas station, the museum that was closed and boarded up, and a motel. Sweetgrass was on the American side, but all you could see was an overpass that arched across the highway and disappeared into the prairies. Just hearing the names of these towns, you would expect that Sweetgrass, which is a nice name and sounds like it is related to other places such as Medicine Hat and Moose Jaw and Kicking Horse Pass, would be on the Canadian side, and that Coutts, which sounds abrupt and rude, would be on the American side. But this was not the case.

Between the two borders was a duty-free shop where you could buy cigarettes and liquor and flags. Stuff like that.

We left the reserve in the morning and drove until we got to Coutts.

'Last time we stopped here', my mother said, 'you had an Orange Crush. You remember that?'

'Sure,' I said. 'That was when Laetitia took off.'

'You want another Orange Crush?'

'That means we're not going to stop at a restaurant, right?'

My mother got a coffee at the convenience store, and we stood around and watched the prairies move in the sunlight. Then we climbed back in the car. My mother straightened the dress across her thighs, leaned against the wheel, and drove all the way to the border in first gear, slowly, as if she were trying to see through a bad storm or riding high on black ice.

The border guard was an old guy. As he walked to the car, he swayed from side to side, his feet set wide apart, the holster on his hip pitching up and down. He leaned into the window, looked into the back seat, and looked at my mother and me.

'Morning, ma'am.'

'Good morning.'

'Where you heading?'

'Salt Lake City.'

'Purpose of your visit?'

'Visit my daughter.'

'Citizenship?'

'Blackfoot,' my mother told him.

'Ma'am?'

'Blackfoot,' my mother repeated.

'Canadian?'

'Blackfoot.'

It would have been easier if my mother had just said 'Canadian' and been done with it, but I could see she wasn't going to do that. The guard wasn't angry or anything. He smiled and looked towards the building. Then he turned back and nodded.

'Morning, ma'am.'

'Good morning.'

'Any firearms or tobacco?'

'No.'

'Citizenship?'

'Blackfoot.'

He told us to sit in the car and wait, and we did. In about five minutes, another guard came out with the first man. They were talking as they came, both men swaying back and forth like two cowboys headed for a bar or a gunfight.

'Morning, ma'am.'

'Good morning.'

'Cecil tells me you and the boy are Blackfoot.'

'That's right.'

'Now, I know that we got Blackfeet on the American side and the Canadians got Blackfeet on their side. Just so we can keep our records straight, what side do you come from?'

I knew exactly what my mother was going to say and I could have told them if they had asked me.

'Canadian side or American side?' asked the guard.

'Blackfoot side,' she said.

It didn't take them long to lose their sense of humour, I can tell you that. The one guard stopped smiling altogether and told us to park our car at the side of the building and come in.

We sat on a wood bench for about an hour before anyone came over to talk to us. This time it was a woman. She had a gun, too.

'Hi,' she said. 'I'm Inspector Pratt. I understand there is a little misunderstanding.'

'I'm going to visit my daughter in Salt Lake City,' my mother told her. 'We don't have any guns or beer.'

'It's a legal technicality, that's all.'

'My daughter's Blackfoot, too.'

The woman opened a briefcase and took out a couple of forms and began to write on one of them. 'Everyone who crosses our border has to declare their citizenship. Even Americans. It helps us keep track of the visitors we get from the various countries.'

She went on like that for maybe fifteen minutes, and a lot of the stuff she told us was interesting.

'I can understand how you feel about having to tell us your citizenship, and here's what I'll do. You tell me, and I won't put it down on the form. No-one will know but you and me.'

Her gun was silver. There were several chips in the wood handle and the name 'Stella' was scratched into the metal butt.

We were in the border office for about four hours, and we talked to almost everyone there. One of the men bought me a Coke. My mother brought a couple of sandwiches in from the car. I offered part of mine to Stella, but she said she wasn't hungry.

I told Stella that we were Blackfoot and Canadians, but she said that that didn't count because I was a minor. In the end, she told us that if my mother didn't declare her citizenship, we would have to go back to where we came from. My mother stood up and thanked Stella for her time. Then we got back in the car and drove to the Canadian border, which was only about a hundred yards away.

I was disappointed. I hadn't seen Laetitia for a long time, and I had never been to Salt Lake City. When she was still at home, Laetitia would go on and on about Salt Lake City. She had never been there, but her boyfriend Lester Tallbull had spent a year in Salt Lake at a technical school.

'It's a great place,' Lester would say. 'Nothing but blondes in the whole state.'

Whenever he said that, Laetitia would slug him on his shoulder hard enough to make him flinch. He had some brochures on Salt Lake and some maps, and every so often the two of them would spread them out on the table.

'That's the temple. It's right downtown. You got to have a pass to get in.'

'Charlotte says anyone can go in and look around.'

'When was Charlotte in Salt Lake? Just when the hell was Charlotte in Salt Lake?'

'Last year.'

'This is Liberty Park. It's got a zoo. There's good skiing in the mountains.'

'Got all the skiing we can use,' my mother would say. 'People come from all over the world to ski at Banff. Cardston's got a temple, if you like those kinds of things.'

'Oh, this one is real big,' Lester would say. 'They got armed guards and everything.'

'Not what Charlotte says.'

'What does she know?'

Lester and Laetitia broke up, but I guess the idea of Salt Lake stuck in her mind.

The Canadian border guard was a young woman, and she seemed happy to see us. 'Hi,' she said. 'You folks sure have a great day for a trip. Where are you coming from?'

'Standoff.'

'Is that in Montana?'

'No.'

'Where are you going?'

'Standoff.'

The woman's name was Carol and I don't guess she was any older than Laetitia. 'Wow, you both Canadians?'

'Blackfoot.'

'Really? I have a friend I went to school with who is Blackfoot. Do you know Mike Harley?'

'No.'

'He went to school in Lethbridge, but he's really from Browning.'

It was a nice conversation and there were no cars behind us, so there was no rush.

'You're not bringing any liquor back, are you?'

'No.'

'Any cigarettes or plants or stuff like that?'

'No.'

'Citizenship?'

'Blackfoot.'

'I know,' said the woman, 'and I'd be proud of being Blackfoot if I were Blackfoot. But you have to be American or Canadian.'

When Laetitia and Lester broke up, Lester took his brochures and maps with him, so Laetitia wrote to someone in Salt Lake City, and, about a month later, she got a big envelope of stuff. We sat at the table and opened up all the brochures, and Laetitia read each one out loud.

'Salt Lake City is the gateway to some of the world's most magnificent skiing.

'Salt Lake City is the home of one of the newest professional basketball franchises, the Utah Jazz.

'The Great Salt Lake is one of the natural wonders of the world.'

It was kind of exciting seeing all those colour brochures on the table and listening to Laetitia read all about how Salt Lake City was one of the best places in the entire world.

'That Salt Lake City place sounds too good to be true,' my mother told her.

'It has everything.'

'We got everything right here.'

'It's boring here.'

'People in Salt Lake City are probably sending away for brochures of Calgary and Lethbridge and Pincher Creek right now.'

In the end, my mother would say that maybe Laetitia should go to Salt Lake City, and Laetitia would say that maybe she would.

We parked the car to the side of the building and Carol led us into a small room on the second floor. I found a comfortable spot on the couch and flipped through some back issues of *Saturday Night* and *Alberta Report*.

When I woke up, my mother was just coming out of another office. She didn't say a word to me. I followed her down the stairs and out to the car. I thought we were going home, but she turned the car around and drove back towards the American border, which made me think we were going to visit Laetitia in Salt Lake City after all. Instead she pulled into the parking lot of the duty-free store and stopped.

'We going to see Laetitia?'

'No.'

'We going home?'

Pride is a good thing to have, you know. Laetitia had a lot of pride, and so did my mother. I figured that someday, I'd have it, too.

'So where are we going?'

Most of that day, we wandered around the duty-free store, which wasn't very large. The manager had a name tag with a tiny American flag on one side and a tiny Canadian flag on the other. His name was Mel. Towards evening, he began suggesting that we should be on our way. I told him we had nowhere to go, that neither the Americans nor the Canadians would let us in. He laughed at that and told us that we should buy something or leave.

The car was not very comfortable, but we did have all that food and it was April, so even if it did snow as it sometimes does on the prairies, we wouldn't freeze. The next morning my mother drove to the American border.

It was a different guard this time, but the questions were the same. We didn't spend as much time in the office as we had the day before. By noon, we were back at the Canadian border. By two we were back in the duty-free shop parking lot.

The second night in the car was not as much fun as the first, but my mother seemed in good spirits, and, all in all, it was as much an adventure as an inconvenience. There wasn't much food left and that was a problem, but we had lots of water as there was a faucet at the side of the duty-free shop.

One Sunday, Laetitia and I were watching television. Mom was over at Mrs Many-fingers's. Right in the middle of the program, Laetitia turned off the set and said she was going to Salt Lake City, that life around here was too boring. I had wanted to see the rest of the program and really didn't care if Laetitia went to Salt Lake City or not. When Mom got home, I told her what Laetitia had said.

What surprised me was how angry Laetitia got when she found out that I had told Mom.

'You got a big mouth.'

'That's what you said.'

'What I said is none of your business.'

'I didn't say anything.'

'Well, I'm going for sure, now.'

That weekend, Laetitia packed her bags, and we drove her to the border.

Mel turned out to be friendly. When he closed up for the night and found us still parked in the lot, he came over and asked us if our car was broken down or something. My mother thanked him for his concern and told him that we were fine, that things would get straightened out in the morning.

'You're kidding,' said Mel. 'You'd think they could handle the simplest things.'

'We got some apples and a banana,' I said, 'but we're all out of ham sandwiches.'

'You know, you read about these things, but you just don't believe it. You just don't believe it.'

'Hamburgers would be even better because they got more stuff for energy.'

My mother slept in the back seat. I slept in the front because I was smaller and could lie under the steering wheel. Late that night, I heard my mother open the car door. I found her sitting on her blanket leaning against the bumper of the car.

'You see all those stars,' she said. 'When I was a little girl, my grandmother used to take me and my sisters out on the prairies and tell us stories about all the stars.'

'Do you think Mel is going to bring us any hamburgers?'

'Every one of those stars has a story. You see that bunch of stars over there that look like a fish?'

'He didn't say no.'

'Coyote went fishing, one day. That's how it all started.' We sat out under the stars that night, and my mother told me all sorts of stories. She was serious about it, too. She'd tell them slow, repeating parts as she went, as if she expected me to remember each one.

Early the next morning, the television vans began to arrive, and guys in suits and women in dresses came trotting over to us, dragging microphones and cameras and lights behind them. One of the vans had a table set up with orange juice and sandwiches and fruit. It was for the crew, but when I told them we hadn't eaten for a while, a really skinny blonde woman told us we could eat as much as we wanted.

They mostly talked to my mother. Every so often one of the reporters would come over and ask me questions about how it felt to be an Indian without a country. I told them we had a nice house on the reserve and that my cousins had a couple of horses we rode when we went fishing. Some of the television people went over to the American border, and then they went to the Canadian border.

Around noon, a good-looking guy in a dark blue suit and an orange tie with little ducks on it drove up in a fancy car. He talked to my mother for a while, and, after they were done talking, my mother called me over, and we got into our car. Just as my mother started the engine, Mel came over and gave us a bag of peanut brittle and told us that justice was a damn hard thing to get, but that we shouldn't give up.

I would have preferred lemon drops, but it was nice of Mel anyway.

'Where are we going now?'

'Going to visit Laetitia.'

The guard who came out to our car was all smiles. The television lights were so bright they hurt my eyes, and, if you tried to look through the windshield in certain directions, you couldn't see a thing.

'Morning, ma'am.'

'Good morning.'

'Where you heading?'

'Salt Lake City.'

'Purpose of your visit?'

'Visit my daughter.'

'Any tobacco, liquor, or firearms?'

'Don't smoke.'

'Any plants or fruit?'

'Not any more.'

'Citizenship?'

'Blackfoot.'

The guard rocked back on his heels and jammed his thumbs into his gun belt. 'Thank you,' he said, his fingers patting the butt of the revolver. 'Have a pleasant trip.'

My mother rolled the car forward, and the television people had to scramble out of the way. They ran alongside the car as we pulled away from the border, and, when they couldn't run any farther, they stood in the middle of the highway and waved and waved and waved.

We got to Salt Lake City the next day. Laetitia was happy to see us, and, that first night, she took us out to a restaurant that made really good soups. The list of pies took up a whole page. I had cherry. Mom had chocolate. Laetitia said that she saw us on television the night before and, during the meal, she had us tell her the story over and over again.

Laetitia took us everywhere. We went to a fancy ski resort. We went to the temple. We got to go shopping in a couple of large malls, but they weren't as large as the one in Edmonton, and Mom said so.

After a week or so, I got bored and wasn't at all sad when my mother said we should be heading back home. Laetitia wanted us to stay longer, but Mom said no, that she had things to do back home and that, next time, Laetitia should come up and visit. Laetitia said she was thinking about moving back, and Mom told her to do as she pleased, and Laetitia said that she would.

On the way home, we stopped at the duty-free shop, and my mother gave Mel a green hat that said 'Salt Lake' across the front. Mel was a funny guy. He took the hat and blew his nose and told my mother that she was an inspiration to us all. He gave us some more peanut brittle and came out into the parking lot and waved at us all the way to the Canadian border.

It was almost evening when we left Coutts. I watched the border through the rear window until all you could see were the tops of the flagpoles and the blue water tower, and then they rolled over a hill and disappeared.

1991

◆

Rohinton Mistry

b. 1952

◆

Born in Bombay, India, Rohinton Mistry obtained his BA (1974) in mathematics and economics from the University of Bombay before immigrating in 1975 to Toronto, where he found employment as a clerk in the accounting department of a bank. He enrolled on a part-time basis at the University of Toronto, graduating with a second BA (1983) in English and history.

His first book, a collection of linked short stories titled *Tales from Firozsha Baag* (1987),

from which 'The Collectors' is taken, examines the immediacy of daily life in a Bombay apartment building. Throughout the stories the worlds of the Parsi community evoke memories of Joyce's *Dubliners*. In his three novels, *Such a Long Journey* (1991), *A Fine Balance* (1995), and *Family Matters* (2002), the most vulnerable members of society follow the unending struggle, always through suffering, to affirm human dignity.

The Collectors

I

When Dr Burjor Mody was transferred from Mysore to assume the principalship of the Bombay Veterinary College, he moved into Firozsha Baag with his wife and son Pesi. They occupied the vacant flat on the third floor of C Block, next to the Bulsara family.

Dr Mody did not know it then, but he would be seeing a lot of Jehangir, the Bulsara boy; the boy who sat silent and brooding, every evening, watching the others play, and called *chaarikhao* by them—quite unfairly, since he never tattled or told tales—(Dr Mody would call him, affectionately, the observer of C Block). And Dr Mody did not know this, either, at the time of moving, that Jehangir Bulsara's visits at ten a.m. every Sunday would become a source of profound joy for himself. Or that just when he would think he had found someone to share his hobby with, someone to mitigate the perpetual disappointment about his son Pesi, he would lose his precious Spanish dancing-lady stamp and renounce Jehangir's friendship, both in quick succession. And then two years later, he himself would—but *that* is never knowable.

Soon after moving in, Dr Burjor Mody became the pride of the Parsis in C Block. C Block, like the rest of Firozsha Baag, had a surfeit of low-paid bank clerks and book-keepers, and the arrival of Dr Mody permitted them to feel a little better about them-selves. More importantly, in A Block lived a prominent priest, and B Block boasted a chartered accountant. Now C Block had a voice in Baag matters as important as the others did.

While C Block went about its routine business, confirming and authenticating the sturdiness of the object of their pride, the doctor's big-boned son Pesi established him-self as leader of the rowdier elements among the Baag's ten-to-sixteen population. For Pesi, too, it was routine business; he was following a course he had mapped out for himself ever since the family began moving from city to city on the whims and megrims of his father's employer, the government.

To account for Pesi's success was the fact of his brutish strength. But he was also the practitioner of a number of minor talents which appealed to the crowd where he would be leader. The one no doubt complemented the other, the talents serving to dis-semble the brutish qualifier of strength, and the brutish strength encouraging the crowd to perceive the appeal of his talents.

Hawking, for instance, was one of them. Pesi could summon up prodigious quan-tities of phlegm at will, accompanied by sounds such as the boys had seldom heard except in accomplished adults: deep, throaty, rasping, resonating rolls which culmi-nated in a pthoo, with the impressive trophy landing in the dust at their feet, its size leaving them all slightly envious. Pesi could also break wind that sounded like ques-tions, exclamations, fragments of the chromatic scale, and clarion calls, while the oth-ers sniffed and discussed the merits of pungency versus tonality. This ability earned him the appellation of Pesi *paadmaroo*, and he wore the sobriquet with pride.

Perhaps his single most important talent was his ability to improvise. The peculi-arities of a locale were the raw material for his inventions. In Firozsha Baag, behind the three buildings, or blocks, as they were called, were spacious yards shared by all three blocks. These yards planted in Pesi's fecund mind the seed from which grew a new game: stoning-the-cats.

Till the arrival of the Mody family the yards were home for stray and happy felines, well fed on scraps and leftovers disgorged regularly as clockwork, after meal-times, by the three blocks. The ground floors were the only ones who refrained. They voiced their protests in a periodic cycle of reasoning, pleading, and screaming of obscenities, because the garbage collected outside their windows where the cats took up permanent residency, miaowing, feasting, and caterwauling day and night. If the cascade of food was more than the cats could devour, the remainder fell to the fortune of the rats. Finally, flies and insects buzzed and hovered over the dregs, little pools of pulses and curries fermenting and frothing, till the *kuchrawalli* came next morning and swept it all away.

The backyards of Firozsha Baag constituted its squalid underbelly. And this would be the scenario for stoning-the-cats, Pesi decided. But there was one hitch: the back-yards were off limits to the boys. The only way in was through the *kuchrawalli's* little shack standing beyond A Block, where her huge ferocious dog, tied to the gate, kept the boys at bay. So Pesi decreed that the boys gather at the rear windows of their homes, preferably at a time of day when the adults were scarce, with the fathers away at work and the mothers not yet finished with their afternoon naps. Each boy brought a pile of small stones and took turns, chucking three stones each. The game could just as easily have been stoning-the-rats; but stoned rats quietly walked away to safety, whereas the yowls of cats provided primal satisfaction and verified direct hits: no yowl, no point.

The game added to Pesi's popularity—he called it a howling success. But the parents (except the ground floor) complained to Dr Mody about his son instigating their children to torment poor dumb and helpless creatures. For a veterinarian's son to harass animals was shameful, they said.

As might be supposed, Pesi was the despair of his parents. Over the years Dr Mody had become inured to the initial embarrassment in each new place they moved to. The routine was familiar: first, a spate of complaints from indignant parents claiming their sons *bugree nay dhoor thai gaya*—were corrupted to become useless as dust; next, the protestations giving way to sympathy when the neighbours saw that Pesi was the worm in the Modys' mango.

And so it was in Firozsha Baag. After the furor about stoning-the-cats had died down, the people of the Baag liked Dr Mody more than ever. He earned their respect for the initiative he took in Baag matters, dealing with the management for things like broken lifts, leaking water tanks, crumbling plaster, and faulty wiring. It was at his urging that the massive iron gate, set in the stone wall which ran all around the buildings, compound and backyards, was repaired, and a watchman installed to stop beggars and riff-raff. (And although Dr Mody would be dead by the time of the *Shiv Sena* riots, the tenants would remember him for the gate which would keep out the rampaging mobs.) When the Bombay Municipality tried to appropriate a section of Baag property for its road-widening scheme, Dr Mody was in the forefront of the battle, winning a compromise whereby the Baag only lost half the proposed area. But the Baag's esteem did nothing to lighten the despair for Pesi that hung around the doctor.

At the birth of his son, Dr Mody had deliberated long and hard about the naming. Peshotan, in the Persian epic *Shah-Nameh*, was the brother of the great Asfandyar, and a noble general, lover of art and learning, and man of wise counsel. Dr Mody had decided his son would play the violin, acquire the best from the cultures of East and West, thrill to the words of Tagore and Shakespeare, appreciate Mozart and Indian ragas; and one day, at the proper moment, he would introduce him to his dearest activity, stamp-collecting.

But the years passed in their own way. Fate denied fruition to all of Dr Mody's plans; and when he talked about stamps, Pesi laughed and mocked his beloved hobby. This was the point at which, hurt and confused, he surrendered his son to whatever destiny was in store. A perpetual grief entered to occupy the void left behind after the aspirations for his son were evicted.

The weight of grief was heaviest around Dr Mody when he returned from work in the evenings. As the car turned into the compound he usually saw Pesi before Pesi saw him, in scenes which made him despair, scenes in which his son was abusing someone, fighting, or making lewd gestures.

But Dr Mody was careful not to make a public spectacle of his despair. While the car made its way sluggishly over the uneven flagstones of the compound, the boys would stand back and wave him through. With his droll comments and jovial countenance he was welcome to disrupt their play, unlike two other car-owners of Firozsha Baag: the priest in A Block and the chartered accountant in B who habitually berated, from inside their vehicles, the sons of bank clerks and bookkeepers for blocking the driveway with their games. Their well-worn curses had become so predictable and ineffective that sometimes the boys chanted gleefully, in unison with their nemeses: 'Worse than *saala* animals!' or '*junglee* dogs-cats have more sense!' or 'you *sataans* ever have any lesson-*paani* to do or not!'

There was one boy who always stayed apart from his peers—the Bulsara boy, from the family next door to the Modys. Jehangir sat on the stone steps every evening while the gentle land breezes, drying and cooling the sweaty skins of the boys at play, blew out to sea. He sat alone through the long dusk, a source of discomfiture to the others. They resented his melancholy, watching presence.

Dr Mody noticed Jehangir, too, on the stone steps of C Block, the delicate boy with the build much too slight for his age. Next to a hulk like Pesi he was diminutive, but things other than size underlined his frail looks: he had slender hands, and forearms with fine downy hair. And while facial fuzz was incipient in most boys of his age (and Pesi was positively hirsute), Jehangir's chin and upper lip were smooth as a young woman's. But it pleased Dr Mody to see him evening after evening. The quiet contemplation of the boy on the steps and the noise and activity of the others at play came together in the kind of balance that Dr Mody was always looking for and was quick to appreciate.

Jehangir, in his turn, observed the burly Dr Mody closely as he walked past him each evening. When he approached the steps after parking his car, Jehangir would say '*Sahibji*' in greeting, and smile wanly. He saw that despite Dr Mody's constant jocularity there was something painfully empty about his eyes. He noticed the peculiar way he scratched the greyish-red patches of psoriasis on his elbows, both elbows simultaneously, by folding his arms across his chest. Sometimes Jehangir would arise from the stone steps and the two would go up together to the third floor. Dr Mody asked him once, 'You don't like playing with the other boys? You just sit and watch them?' The boy shook his head and blushed, and Dr Mody did not bring up the matter after that.

Gradually, a friendship of sorts grew between the two. Jehangir touched a chord inside the doctor which had lain silent for much too long. Now affection for the boy developed and started to linger around the region hitherto occupied by grief bearing Pesi's name.

II

One evening, while Jehangir sat on the stone steps waiting for Dr Mody's car to arrive, Pesi was organizing a game of *naargolio*. He divided the boys into two teams, then discovered he was one short. He beckoned to Jehangir, who said he did not want to play. Scowling, Pesi handed the ball to one of the others and walked over to him.

He grabbed his collar with both hands, jerking him to his feet. '*Arré choosya*!' he yelled, 'want a pasting?' and began dragging him by the collar to where the boys had piled up the seven flat stones for *naargolio*.

At that instant, Dr Mody's car turned into the compound, and he spied his son in one of those scenes which could provoke despair. But today the despair was swept aside by rage when he saw that Pesi's victim was the gentle and quiet Jehangir Bulsara. He left the car in the middle of the compound with the motor running. Anger glinted in his eyes. He kicked over the pile of seven flat stones as he walked blindly towards Pesi who, having seen his father, had released Jehangir. He had been caught by his father often enough to know that it was best to stand and wait. Jehangir, meanwhile, tried to keep back the tears.

Dr Mody stopped before his son and slapped him hard, once on each cheek, with the front and back of his right hand. He waited, as if debating whether that was enough, then put his arm around Jehangir and led him to the car.

He drove to his parking spot. By now, Jehangir had control of his tears, and they walked to the steps of C Block. The lift was out of order. They climbed the stairs to the third floor and knocked. He waited with Jehangir.

Jehangir's mother came to the door. '*Sahibji*, Dr Mody,' she said, a short, middle-aged woman, very prim, whose hair was always in a bun. Never without a *mathoobanoo*, she could do wonderful things with that square of fine white cloth which was tied and knotted to sit like a cap on her head, snugly packeting the bun. In the evenings, after the household chores were done, she removed the *mathoobanoo* and wore it in a more conventional manner, like a scarf.

'*Sahibji*,' she said, then noticed her son's tear-stained face. '*Arré*, Jehangoo, what happened, who made you cry?' Her hand flew automatically to the *mathoobanoo*, tugging and adjusting it as she did whenever she was concerned or agitated.

To save the boy embarrassment, Dr Mody intervened: 'Go, wash your face while I talk to your mother.' Jehangir went inside, and Dr Mody told her briefly about what had happened. 'Why does he not play with the other boys?' he asked finally.

'Dr Mody, what to say. The boy never wants even to go out. *Khoedai salaamat raakhé*, wants to sit at home all the time and read story books. Even this little time in the evening he goes because I force him and tell him he will not grow tall without fresh air. Every week he brings new-new story books from school. First, school library would allow only one book per week. But he went to Father Gonzalves who is in charge of library and got special permission for two books. God knows why he gave it.'

'But reading is good, Mrs Bulsara.'

'I know, I know, but a mania like this, all the time?'

'Some boys are outdoor types, some are indoor types. You shouldn't worry about Jehangir, he is a very good boy. Look at my Pesi, now there is a case for worry,' he said, meaning to reassure her.

'No, no. You mustn't say that. Be patient, *Khoedai* is great,' said Mrs Bulsara, consoling him instead. Jehangir returned, his eyes slightly red but dry. While washing his face he had wet a lock of his hair which hung down over his forehead.

'Ah, here comes my indoor champion,' smiled Dr Mody, and patted Jehangir's shoulder, brushing back the lock of hair. Jehangir did not understand, but grinned anyway; the doctor's joviality was infectious. Dr Mody turned again to the mother. 'Send him to my house on Sunday at ten o'clock. We will have a little talk.'

After Dr Mody left, Jehangir's mother told him how lucky he was that someone as important and learned as Burjor Uncle was taking an interest in him. Privately, she hoped he would encourage the boy towards a more all-round approach to life and to the things other boys did. And when Sunday came she sent Jehangir off to Dr Mody's promptly at ten.

Dr Mody was taking his bath, and Mrs Mody opened the door. She was a dour-faced woman, spare and lean—the opposite of her husband in appearance and disposition, yet retaining some quality from long ago which suggested that it had not always been so. Jehangir had never crossed her path save when she was exchanging civilities with his mother, while making purchases out by the stairs from the vegetablewalla or fruitwalla.

Not expecting Jehangir's visit, Mrs Mody stood blocking the doorway and said: 'Yes?' Meaning, what nuisance now?

'Burjor Uncle asked me to come at ten o'clock.'

'Asked you to come at ten o'clock? What for?'

'He just said to come at ten o'clock.'

Grudgingly, Mrs Mody stepped aside. 'Come in then. Sit down there.' And she indicated the specific chair she wanted him to occupy, muttering something about a *baap* who had time for strangers' children but not for his own son.

Jehangir sat in what must have been the most uncomfortable chair in the room. This was his first time inside the Modys' flat, and he looked around with curiosity. But his gaze was quickly restricted to the area of the floor directly in front of him when he realized that he was the object of Mrs Mody's watchfulness.

Minutes ticked by under her vigilant eye. Jehangir was grateful when Dr Mody emerged from the bedroom. Being Sunday, he had eschewed his usual khaki half-pants for loose and comfortable white pyjamas. His *sudra* hung out over it, and he strode vigorously, feet encased in a huge pair of *sapaat*. He smiled at Jehangir, who happily noted the crow's-feet appearing at the corners of his eyes. He was ushered into Dr Mody's room, and man and boy both seemed glad to escape the surveillance of the woman.

The chairs were more comfortable in Dr Mody's room. They sat at his desk and Dr Mody opened a drawer to take out a large book.

'This was the first stamp album I ever had,' said Dr Mody. 'It was given to me by my Nusserwanji Uncle when I was your age. All the pages were empty.' He began turning them. They were covered with stamps, each a feast of colour and design. He talked as he turned the pages, and Jehangir watched and listened, glancing at the stamps flying past, at Dr Mody's face, then at the stamps again.

Dr Mody spoke not in his usual booming, jovial tones but softly, in a low voice charged with inspiration. The stamps whizzed by, and his speech was gently underscored by the rustle of the heavily laden pages that seemed to turn of their own volition in the quiet room. (Jehangir would remember this peculiar rustle when one day, older, he'd stand alone in this very room, silent now forever, and turn the pages of Nusserwanji Uncle's album.) Jehangir watched and listened. It was as though a mask had descended over Dr Mody, a faraway look upon his face, and a shining in the eyes which heretofore Jehangir had only seen sad with despair or glinting with anger or just plain and empty, belying his constant drollery. Jehangir watched, and listened to the euphonious voice hinting at wondrous things and promises and dreams.

The album on the desk, able to produce such changes in Dr Mody, now worked its magic through him upon the boy. Jehangir, watching and listening, fascinated, tried to read the names of the countries at the top of the pages as they sped by: Antigua . . . Australia . . . Belgium . . . Bhutan . . . Bulgaria . . . and on through to Malta and Mauritius . . . Romania and Russia . . . Togo and Tonga . . . and a final blur through which he caught Yugoslavia and Zanzibar.

'Can I see it again?' he asked, and Dr Mody handed the album to him.

'So what do you think? Do you want to be a collector?'

Jehangir nodded eagerly and Dr Mody laughed. 'When Nusserwanji Uncle showed me his collection I felt just like that. I'll tell your mother what to buy for you to get you started. Bring it here next Sunday, same time!'

And next Sunday Jehangir was ready at nine. But he waited by his door with a Stamp Album For Beginners and a packet of 100 Assorted Stamps—All Countries. Going too early would mean sitting under the baleful eyes of Mrs Mody.

Ten o'clock struck and the clock's tenth bong was echoed by the Modys' doorchimes. Mrs Mody was expecting him this time and did not block the doorway. Wordlessly, she beckoned him in. Burjor Uncle was ready, too, and came out almost immediately to rescue him from her arena.

'Let's see what you've got there,' he said when they were in his room. They removed the cellophane wrapper, and while they worked Dr Mody enjoyed himself as much as the boy. His deepest wish appeared to be coming true: he had at last found someone to share his hobby with. He could not have hoped for a finer neophyte than Jehangir. His young recruit was so quick to learn how to identify and sort stamps by countries, learn the different currencies, spot watermarks. Already he was skilfully folding and moistening the little hinges and mounting the stamps as neatly as the teacher.

When it was almost time to leave, Jehangir asked if he could examine again Nusserwanji Uncle's album, the one he had seen last Sunday. But Burjor Uncle led him instead to a cupboard in the corner of the room. 'Since you enjoy looking at my stamps, let me show you what I have here.' He unlocked its doors.

Each of the cupboard's four shelves was piled with biscuit tins and sweet tins: round, oval, rectangular, square. It puzzled Jehangir: all this bore the unmistakable stamp of the worthless hoardings of senility, and did not seem at all like Burjor Uncle. But Burjor Uncle reached out for a box at random and showed him inside. It was chock-full of stamps! Jehangir's mouth fell open. Then he gaped at the shelves, and Burjor Uncle laughed. 'Yes, all these tins are full of stamps. And that big cardboard box at the bottom contains six new albums, all empty.'

Jehangir quickly tried to assign a number in his mind to the stamps in the containers of Maghanlal Bisuitwalla and Lokmanji Mithaiwalla, to all of the stamps in the round tins and the oval tins, the square ones and the oblong ones. He failed.

Once again Dr Mody laughed at the boy's wonderment. 'A lot of stamps. And they took me a lot of years to collect. Of course, I am lucky I have many contacts in foreign countries. Because of my job. I meet the experts from abroad who are invited by the Indian Government. When I tell them about my hobby they send me stamps from their countries. But no time to sort them, so I pack them in boxes. One day, after I retire, I will spend all my time with my stamps.' He paused, and shut the cupboard doors. 'So what you have to do now is start making lots of friends, tell them about your hobby. If they also collect, you can exchange duplicates with them. If they don't, you can still ask them for all the envelopes they may be throwing away with stamps on them. You do something for them, they will do something for you. Your collection will grow depending on how smart you are!'

He hesitated, and opened the cupboard again. Then he changed his mind and shut it—it wasn't yet time for the Spanish dancing-lady stamp.

III

On the pavement outside St Xavier's Boys School, not far from the ornate iron gates, stood two variety stalls. They were the stalls of *Patla Babu* and *Jhaaria Babu*. Their real names were never known. Nor was known the exact source of the schoolboy inspiration that named them thus, many years ago, after their respective thinness and fatness.

Before the schoolboys arrived in the morning the two would unpack their cases and set up the displays, beating the beggars to the choice positions. Occasionally, there were disputes if someone's space was violated. The beggars did not harbour great hopes for alms from schoolboys but they stood there, nonetheless, like mute lessons in realism and the harshness of life. Their patience was rewarded when they raided the dustbins after breaks and lunches.

At the end of the school day the pavement community packed up. The beggars shuffled off into the approaching dark, *Patla Babu* went home with his cases, and *Jhaaria Babu* slept near the school gate under a large tree to whose trunk he chained his boxes during the night.

The two sold a variety of nondescript objects and comestibles, uninteresting to any save the eyes and stomachs of schoolboys: *supari*, A-1 chewing gum (which, in a most ungumlike manner, would, after a while, dissolve in one's mouth), *jeeragoli*, marbles, tops, *aampapud* during the mango season, pens, Camel Ink, pencils, rulers, and stamps in little cellophane packets.

Patla Babu and *Jhaaria Babu* lost some of their goods regularly due to theft. This was inevitable when doing business outside a large school like St Xavier's, with a population as varied as its was. The loss was an operating expense stoically accepted, like the success or failure of the monsoons, and they never complained to the school authorities or held it against the boys. Besides, business was good despite the losses: insignificant items like a packet of *jeeragoli* worth ten paise, or a marble of the kind that sold three for five paise. More often than not, the stealing went on for the excitement of it, out of bravado or on a dare. It was called 'flicking' and was done without any malice towards *Patla* and *Jhaaria*.

Foremost among the flickers was a boy in Jehangir's class called Eric D'Souza. A tall, lanky fellow who had been suspended a couple of times, he had had to repeat the year on two occasions, and held out the promise of more repetitions. Eric also had the reputation of doing things inside his half-pants under cover of his desk. In a class of fifty boys it was easy to go unobserved by the teacher, and only his immediate neighbours could see the ecstasy on his face and the vigorous back and forth movement of his hand. When he grinned at them they looked away, pretending not to have noticed anything.

Jehangir sat far from Eric and knew of his habits only by hearsay. He was oblivious to Eric's eye which had been on him for quite a while. In fact, Eric found Jehangir's delicate hands and fingers, his smooth legs and thighs very desirable. In class he gazed for hours, longingly, at the girlish face, curly hair, long eyelashes.

Jehangir and Eric finally got acquainted one day when the class filed out for games period. Eric had been made to kneel down by the door for coming in late and disturbing the class, and Jehangir found himself next to him as he stood in line. From his kneeling position Eric observed the smooth thighs emerging from the half-pants (half-pants was the school uniform requirement), winked at him, and unhindered by his underwear, inserted a pencil up the pant leg. He tickled Jehangir's genitals seductively with the eraser end, expertly, then withdrew it. Jehangir feigned a giggle, too shocked to say anything. The line started to move for the playground.

Shortly after this incident, Eric approached Jehangir during breaktime. He had heard that Jehangir was desperate to acquire stamps.

'*Arré* man, I can get you stamps, whatever kind you want,' he said.

Jehangir stopped. He had been slightly confused ever since the pass with the pencil; Eric frightened him a little with his curious habits and forbidden knowledge. But it had not been easy to accumulate stamps. Sundays with Burjor Uncle continued to be as fascinating as the first. He wished he had new stamps to show—the stasis of his collection might be misinterpreted as lack of interest. He asked Eric: 'Ya? You want to exchange?'

'No *yaar*, I don't collect. But I'll get them for you. As a favour, man.'

'Ya? What kind do you have?'

'I don't have, man. Come on with me to *Patla* and *Jhaaria*, just show me which ones you want. I'll flick them for you.'

Jehangir hesitated. Eric put his arm around him: 'C'mon man, what you scared for, I'll flick. You just show me and go away.' Jehangir pictured the stamps on display in cellophane wrappers: how well they would add to his collection. He imagined album pages bare no more but covered with exquisite stamps, each one mounted carefully and correctly, with a hinge, as Burjor Uncle had showed him to.

They went outside, Eric's arm still around him. Crowds of schoolboys were gathered around the two stalls. A multitude of groping, exploring hands handled the merchandise and browsed absorbedly, a multitude that was a prerequisite for flicking to begin. Jehangir showed Eric the individually wrapped stamps he wanted and moved away. In a few minutes Eric joined him triumphantly.

'Got them?'

'Ya ya. But come inside. He could be watching, man.'

Jehangir was thrilled. Eric asked, 'You want more or what?'

'Sure,' said Jehangir.

'But not today. On Friday. If you do me a favour in visual period on Thursday.'

Jehangir's pulse speeded slightly—visual period, with its darkened hall and projector, and the intimacy created by the teacher's policing abilities temporarily suspended. He remembered Eric's pencil. The cellophane-wrapped stamp packets rustled and crackled in his hand. And there was the promise of more. There had been nothing unpleasant about the pencil. In fact it had felt quite, well, exciting. He agreed to Eric's proposal.

On Thursday, the class lined up to go to the Visual Hall. Eric stood behind Jehangir to ensure their seats would be together.

When the room was dark he put his hand on Jehangir's thigh and began caressing it. He took Jehangir's hand and placed it on his crotch. It lay there inert. Impatient, he whispered, 'Do it, man, c'mon!' But Jehangir's lacklustre stroking was highly unsatisfactory. Eric arrested the hand, reached inside his pants and said, 'OK, hold it tight and rub it like this.' He encircled Jehangir's hand with his to show him how. When Jehangir had attained the right pressure and speed he released his own hand to lean back and sigh contentedly. Shortly Jehangir felt a warm stickiness fill his palm and fingers, and the hardness he held in his hand grew flaccid.

Eric shook off the hand. Jehangir wiped his palm with his hanky. Eric borrowed the hanky to wipe himself. 'Want me to do it for you?' he asked. But Jehangir declined. He was thinking of his hanky. The odour was interesting, not unpleasant at all, but he would have to find some way of cleaning it before his mother found it.

The following day, Eric presented him with more stamps. Next Thursday's assignation was also fixed.

And on Sunday Jehangir went to see Dr Mody at ten o'clock. The wife let him in, muttering something under her breath about being bothered by inconsiderate people on the one day that the family could be together.

Dr Mody's delight at the new stamps fulfilled Jehangir's every expectation: 'Wonderful, wonderful! Where did you get them all? No, no, forget it, don't tell me. You will think I'm trying to learn your tricks. I already have enough stamps to keep me busy in my retirement. Ha! ha!'

After the new stamps had been examined and sorted Dr Mody said, 'Today, as a reward for your enterprise, I'm going to show you a stamp you've never seen before.' From the cupboard of biscuit and sweet tins he took a small satin-covered box of the type in which rings or bracelets are kept. He opened it and, without removing the stamp from inside, placed it on the desk.

The stamp said España Correos at the bottom and its denomination was noted in the top left corner: 3 PTAS. The face of the stamp featured a flamenco dancer in the most exquisite detail and colour. But it was something in the woman's countenance, a look, an ineffable sparkle he saw in her eyes, which so captivated Jehangir.

Wordlessly, he studied the stamp. Dr Mody waited restlessly as the seconds ticked by. He kept fidgeting till the little satin-covered box was shut and back in his hands, then said, 'So you like the Spanish dancing-lady. Everyone who sees it likes it. Even my wife who is not interested in stamp-collecting thought it was beautiful. When I retire I can spend more time with the Spanish dancing-lady. And all my other stamps.' He relaxed once the stamp was locked again in the cupboard.

Jehangir left, carrying that vision of the Spanish dancer in his head. He tried to imagine the stamp inhabiting the pages of his album, to greet him every time he opened it, with the wonderful sparkle in her eyes. He shut the door behind him and immediately, as though to obliterate his covetous fantasy, loud voices rose inside the flat.

He heard Mrs Mody's, shrill in argument, and the doctor's, beseeching her not to yell lest the neighbours would hear. Pesi's name was mentioned several times in the quarrel that ensued, and accusations of neglect, and something about the terrible affliction on a son of an unloving father. The voices followed Jehangir as he hurried past the inquiring eyes of his mother, till he reached the bedroom at the other end of the flat and shut the door.

When the school week started, Jehangir found himself looking forward to Thursday. His pulse was racing with excitement when visual period came. To save his hanky this time he kept some paper at hand.

Eric did not have to provide much guidance. Jehangir discovered he could control Eric's reactions with variations in speed, pressure, and grip. When it was over and Eric offered to do it to him, he did not refuse.

The weeks sped by and Jehangir's collection continued to grow, visual period by visual period. Eric's and his masturbatory partnership was whispered about in class, earning the pair the title of *moothya-maroo*. He accompanied Eric on the flicking forays, helping to swell the milling crowd and add to the browsing hands. Then he grew bolder, studied Eric's methods, and flicked a few stamps himself.

But this smooth course of stamp-collecting was about to end. *Patla Babu* and *Jhaaria Babu* broke their long tradition of silence and complained to the school. Unlike marbles and *supari*, it was not a question of a few paise a day. When Eric and Jehangir struck, their haul could be totalled in rupees reaching double digits; the loss was serious enough to make the *Babus* worry about their survival.

The school assigned the case to the head prefect to investigate. He was an ambitious boy, always snooping around, and was also a member of the school debating team and the Road Safety Patrol. Shortly after the complaint was made he marched into Jehangir's class one afternoon just after lunch break, before the teacher returned, and made what sounded very much like one of his debating speeches: 'Two boys in this class have been stealing stamps from *Patla Babu* and *Jhaaria Babu* for the past several weeks. You may ask: who are those boys? No need for names. They know who they are and I know who they are, and I am asking them to return the stamps to me tomorrow. There will be no punishment if this is done. The *Babus* just want their stamps back. But if the missing stamps are not returned, the names will be reported to the principal and to the police. It is up to the two boys.'

Jehangir tried hard to appear normal. He was racked with trepidation, and looked to the unperturbed Eric for guidance. But Eric ignored him. The head prefect left amidst mock applause from the class.

After school, Eric turned surly. Gone was the tender, cajoling manner he reserved for Jehangir, and he said nastily: 'You better bring back all those fucking stamps tomorrow.' Jehangir, of course, agreed. There was no trouble with the prefect or the school after the stamps were returned.

But Jehangir's collection shrunk pitiably overnight. He slept badly the entire week, worried about explaining to Burjor Uncle the sudden disappearance of the bulk of his collection. His mother assumed the dark rings around his eyes were due to too much reading and not enough fresh air. The thought of stamps or of *Patla Babu* or *Jhaaria Babu* brought an emptiness to his stomach and a bitter taste to his mouth. A general sense of ill-being took possession of him.

He went to see Burjor Uncle on Sunday, leaving behind his stamp album. Mrs Mody opened the door and turned away silently. She appeared to be in a black rage, which exacerbated Jehangir's own feelings of guilt and shame.

He explained to Burjor Uncle that he had not bothered to bring his album because he had acquired no new stamps since last Sunday, and also, he was not well and would not stay for long.

Dr Mody was concerned about the boy, so nervous and uneasy; he put it down to his feeling unwell. They looked at some stamps Dr Mody had received last week from his colleagues abroad. Then Jehangir said he'd better leave.

'But you *must* see the Spanish dancing-lady before you go. Maybe she will help you feel better. Ha! ha!' and Dr Mody rose to go to the cupboard for the stamp. Its viewing at the end of each Sunday's session had acquired the significance of an esoteric ritual.

From the next room Mrs Mody screeched: 'Burjorji! Come here at once!' He made a wry face at Jehangir and hurried out.

In the next room, all the vehemence of Mrs Mody's black rage of that morning poured out upon Dr Mody: 'It has reached the limit now! No time for your own son and Sunday after Sunday sitting with some stranger! What does he have that your own son does not? Are you a *baap* or what? No wonder Pesi has become this way! How can I blame the boy when his own *baap* takes no interest . . .'

'Shh! The boy is in the next room! What do you want, that all the neighbours hear your screaming?'

'I don't care! Let them hear! You think they don't know already? You think you are . . .'

Mrs Bulsara next door listened intently. Suddenly, she realized that Jehangir was in there. Listening from one's own house was one thing—hearing a quarrel from inside the quarrellers' house was another. It made feigning ignorance very difficult.

She rang the Modys' doorbell and waited, adjusting her *mathoobanoo*. Dr Mody came to the door.

'Burjorji, forgive me for disturbing your stamping and collecting work with Jehangir. But I must take him away. Guests have arrived unexpectedly. Jehangir must go to the Irani, we need cold drinks.'

'That's okay, he can come next Sunday.' Then added, 'He *must* come next Sunday,' and noted with satisfaction the frustrated turning away of Mrs Mody who waited out of sight of the doorway. 'Jehangir! Your mother is calling.'

Jehangir was relieved at being rescued from the turbulent waters of the Mody household. They left without further conversation, his mother tugging in embarrassment at the knots of her *mathoobanoo*.

As a result of this unfortunate outburst, a period of awkwardness between the women was unavoidable. Mrs Mody, though far from garrulous, had never let her domestic sorrows and disappointments interfere with the civilities of neighbourly relations, which she respected and observed at all times. Now for the first time since the arrival of the Modys in Firozsha Baag these civilities experienced a hiatus.

When the *muchhiwalla* arrived next morning, instead of striking a joint deal with him as they usually did, Mrs Mody waited till Mrs Bulsara had finished. She stationed an eye at her peephole as he emphasized the freshness of his catch. 'Look *bai*, it is *saféd paani*,' he said, holding out the pomfret and squeezing it near the gills till white fluid oozed out. After Mrs Bulsara had paid and gone, Mrs Mody emerged, while the former took her turn at the peephole. And so it went for a few days till the awkwardness had run its course and things returned to normal.

But not so for Jehangir; on Sunday, he once again had to leave behind his sadly depleted album. To add to his uneasiness, Mrs Mody invited him in with a greeting of 'Come *bawa* come,' and there was something malignant about her smile.

Dr Mody sat at his desk, shoulders sagging, his hands dangling over the arms of the chair. The desk was bare—not a single stamp anywhere in sight, and the cupboard in the corner locked. The absence of his habitual, comfortable clutter made the room cold and cheerless. He was in low spirits; instead of the crow's-feet at the corners of his eyes were lines of distress and dejection.

'No album again?'

'No. Haven't got any new stamps yet,' Jehangir smiled nervously.

Dr Mody scratched the psoriasis on his elbows. He watched Jehangir carefully as he spoke. 'Something very bad has happened to the Spanish dancing-lady stamp. Look,' and he displayed the satin-covered box minus its treasure. 'It is missing.' Half-fearfully, he looked at Jehangir, afraid he would see what he did not want to. But it was inevitable. His last sentence evoked the head prefect's thundering debating-style speech of a few days ago, and the ugliness of the entire episode revisited Jehangir's features—a final ignominious postscript to Dr Mody's loss and disillusion.

Dr Mody shut the box. The boy's reaction, his silence, the absence of his album, confirmed his worst suspicions. More humiliatingly, it seemed his wife was right. With great sadness he rose from his chair. 'I have to leave now, something urgent at the College.' They parted without a word about next Sunday.

Jehangir never went back. He thought for a few days about the missing stamp and wondered what could have happened to it. Burjor Uncle was too careful to have misplaced it; besides, he never removed it from its special box. And the box was still there. But he did not resent him for concluding he had stolen it. His guilt about *Patla Babu* and *Jhaaria Babu*, about Eric and the stamps was so intense, and the punishment deriving from it so inconsequential, almost non-existent, that he did not mind this undeserved blame. In fact, it served to equilibrate his scales of justice.

His mother questioned him the first few Sundays he stayed home. Feeble excuses about homework, and Burjor Uncle not having new stamps, and it being boring to look at the same stuff every Sunday did not satisfy her. She finally attributed his abnegation of stamps to sensitivity and a regard for the unfortunate state of the Modys' domestic affairs. It pleased her that her son was capable of such concern. She did not press him after that.

IV

Pesi was no longer to be seen in Firozsha Baag. His absence brought relief to most of the parents at first, and then curiosity. Gradually, it became known that he had been sent away to a boarding-school in Poona.

The boys of the Baag continued to play their games in the compound. For better or worse, the spark was lacking that lent unpredictability to those languid coastal evenings of Bombay; evenings which could so easily trap the unwary, adult or child, within a circle of lassitude and depression in which time hung heavy and suffocating.

Jehangir no longer sat on the stone steps of C Block in the evenings. He found it difficult to confront Dr Mody day after day. Besides, the boys he used to watch at play suspected some kind of connection between Pesi's being sent away to boarding-school, Jehangir's former friendship with Dr Mody, and the emerging of Dr Mody's constant sorrow and despair (which he had tried so hard to keep private all along, and had succeeded, but was now visible for all to see). And the boys resented Jehangir for whatever his part was in it—they bore him open antagonism.

Dr Mody was no more the jovial figure the boys had grown to love. When his car turned into the compound in the evenings, he still waved, but no crow's-feet appeared at his eyes, no smile, no jokes.

Two years passed since the Mody family's arrival in Firozsha Baag.

In school, Jehangir was as isolated as in the Baag. Most of his effeminateness had, of late, transformed into vigorous signs of impending manhood. Eric D'Souza had been expelled for attempting to sodomize a junior boy. Jehangir had not been involved in this affair, but most of his classmates related it to the furtive activities of their callow days and the stamp-flicking. *Patla Babu* and *Jhaaria Babu* had disappeared from the pavement outside St Xavier's. The Bombay police, in a misinterpretation of the nation's mandate: *garibi hatao*—eradicate poverty, conducted periodic round-ups of pavement dwellers, sweeping into their vans beggars and street-vendors, cripples and alcoholics, the homeless and the hungry, and dumped them somewhere outside the city limits; when the human detritus made its way back into the city, another clean-up was scheduled. *Patla* and *Jhaaria* were snared in one of these raids, and never found their way back. Eyewitnesses said their stalls were smashed up and *Patla Babu* received a *lathi* across his forehead for trying to salvage some of his inventory. They were not seen again.

Two years passed since Jehangir's visits to Dr Mody had ceased.

It was getting close to the time for another transfer for Dr Mody. When the inevitable orders were received, he went to Ahmedabad to make arrangements. Mrs Mody was to join her husband after a few days. Pesi was still in boarding-school, and would stay there.

So when the news arrived from Ahmedabad of Dr Mody's death of heart failure, Mrs Mody was alone in the flat. She went next door with the telegram and broke down.

The Bulsaras helped with all the arrangements. The body was brought to Bombay by car for a proper Parsi funeral. Pesi came from Poona for the funeral, then went back to boarding-school.

The events were talked about for days afterwards, the stories spreading first in C Block, then through A and B. Commiseration for Mrs Mody was general. The ordeal of the body during the two-day car journey from Ahmedabad was particularly horrifying, and was discussed endlessly. Embalming was not allowed according to Parsi rituals, and the body in the trunk, although packed with ice, had started to smell horribly in the heat of the Deccan Plateau which the car had had to traverse. Some hinted that this torment suffered by Dr Mody's earthly remains was the Almighty's punishment for neglecting his duties as a father and making Mrs Mody so unhappy. Poor Dr Mody, they said, who never went a day without a bath and talcum powder in life, to undergo this in death. Someone even had, on good authority, a count of the number of eau de cologne bottles used by Mrs Mody and the three occupants of the car over the course of the journey—it was the only way they could draw breath, through cologne-watered handkerchiefs. And it was also said that ever after, these four could never tolerate eau de cologne—opening a bottle was like opening the car trunk with Dr Mody's decomposing corpse.

A year after the funeral, Mrs Mody was still living in Firozsha Baag. Time and grief had softened her looks, and she was no longer the harsh and dour-faced woman Jehangir had seen during his first Sunday visit. She had decided to make the flat her permanent home now, and the trustees of the Baag granted her request 'in view of the unfortunate circumstances'.

There were some protests about this, particularly from those whose sons or daughters had been postponing marriages and families till flats became available. But the majority, out of respect for Dr Mody's memory, agreed with the trustee's decision. Pesi continued to attend boarding-school.

One day, shortly after her application had been approved by the trustees, Mrs Mody visited Mrs Bulsara. They sat and talked of old times, when they had first moved in, and about how pleased Dr Mody had been to live in a Parsi colony like Firozsha Baag after years of travelling, and then the disagreements she had had with her husband over Pesi and Pesi's future; tears came to her eyes, and also to Mrs Bulsara's, who tugged at the corner of her *mathoobanoo* to reach it to her eyes and dry them. Mrs Mody confessed how she had hated Jehangir's Sunday visits although he was such a fine boy, because she was worried about the way poor Burjorji was neglecting Pesi: 'But he could not help it. That was the way he was. Sometimes he would wish *Khoedai* had given him a daughter instead of a son. Pesi disappointed him in everything, in all his plans, and . . .' and here she burst into uncontrollable sobs.

Finally, after her tears subsided she asked, 'Is Jehangir home?' He wasn't. 'Would you ask him to come and see me this Sunday? At ten? Tell him I won't keep him long.'

Jehangir was a bit apprehensive when his mother gave him the message. He couldn't imagine why Mrs Mody would want to see him.

On Sunday, as he prepared to go next door, he was reminded of the Sundays with Dr Mody, the kindly man who had befriended him, opened up a new world for him, and then repudiated him for something he had not done. He remembered the way he would scratch the greyish-red patches of psoriasis on his elbows. He could still picture the sorrow on his face as, with the utmost reluctance, he had made his decision to end the friendship. Jehangir had not blamed Dr Mody then, and he still did not; he knew how overwhelmingly the evidence had been against him, and how much that stamp had meant to Dr Mody.

Mrs Mody led him in by his arm: 'Will you drink something?'

'No, thank you.'

'Not feeling shy, are you? You always were shy.' She asked him about his studies and what subjects he was taking in high school. She told him a little about Pesi, who was still in boarding-school and had twice repeated the same standard. She sighed. 'I asked you to come today because there is something I wanted to give you. Something of Burjor Uncle's. I thought about it for many days. Pesi is not interested, and I don't know anything about it. Will you take his collection?'

'The album in his drawer?' asked Jehangir, a little surprised.

'Everything. The album, all the boxes, everything in the cupboard. I know you will use it well. Burjor would have done the same.'

Jehangir was speechless. He had stopped collecting stamps, and they no longer held the fascination they once did. Nonetheless, he was familiar with the size of the collection, and the sheer magnitude of what he was now being offered had its effect. He remembered the awe with which he had looked inside the cupboard the first time its doors had been opened before him. So many sweet tins, cardboard boxes, biscuit tins . . .

'You will take it? As a favour to me, yes?' she asked a second time, and Jehangir nodded. 'You have some time today? Whenever you like, just take it.' He said he would ask his mother and come back.

There was a huge, old iron trunk which lay under Jehangir's bed. It was dented in several places and the lid would not shut properly. Undisturbed for years, it had rusted peacefully beneath the bed. His mother agreed that the rags it held could be thrown away and the stamps temporarily stored in it till Jehangir organized them into albums. He emptied the trunk, wiped it out, lined it with brown paper and went next door to bring back the stamps.

Several trips later, Dr Mody's cupboard stood empty. Jehangir looked around the room in which he had once spent so many happy hours. The desk was in exactly the same position, and the two chairs. He turned to go, almost forgetting, and went back to the desk. Yes, there it was in the drawer, Dr Mody's first album, given him by his Nusserwanji Uncle.

He started to turn the heavily laden pages. They rustled in a peculiar way—what was it about that sound? Then he remembered: that first Sunday, and he could almost hear Dr Mody again, the soft inspired tones speaking of promises and dreams, quite different from his usual booming jovial voice, and that faraway look in his eyes which had once glinted with rage when Pesi had tried to bully him . . .

Mrs Mody came into the room. He shut the album, startled: 'This is the last lot.' He stopped to thank her but she interrupted: 'No, no. What is the thank-you for? You are doing a favour to me by taking it, you are helping me to do what Burjor would like.' She took his arm. 'I wanted to tell you. From the collection one stamp is missing. With the picture of the dancing-lady.'

'I know!' said Jehangir. 'That's the one Burjor Uncle lost and thought that I . . .'

Mrs Mody squeezed his arm which she was still holding and he fell silent. She spoke softly, but without guilt: 'He did not lose it. I destroyed it.' Then her eyes went moist as she watched the disbelief on his face. She wanted to say more, to explain, but could not, and clung to his arm. Finally, her voice quavering pitiably, she managed to say, 'Forgive an old lady,' and patted his cheek. Jehangir left in silence, suddenly feeling very ashamed.

Over the next few days, he tried to impose some order on that greatly chaotic mass of stamps. He was hoping that sooner or later his interest in philately would be rekindled. But that did not happen; the task remained futile and dry and boring. The meaningless squares of paper refused to come to life as they used to for Dr Mody in his room every Sunday at ten o'clock. Jehangir shut the trunk and pushed it back under his bed where it had lain untroubled for so many years.

From time to time his mother reminded him about the stamps: 'Do something Jehangoo, do something with them.' He said he would when he felt like it and had the time; he wasn't interested for now.

Then, after several months, he pulled out the trunk again from under his bed. Mrs Bulsara watched eagerly from a distance, not daring to interrupt with any kind of advice or encouragement: her Jehangoo was at that difficult age, she knew, when boys automatically did the exact reverse of what their parents said.

But the night before Jehangir's sleep had been disturbed by a faint and peculiar rustling sound seeming to come from inside the trunk. His reasons for dragging it out into daylight soon became apparent to Mrs Bulsara.

The lid was thrown back to reveal clusters of cockroaches. They tried to scuttle to safety, and he killed a few with his slipper. His mother ran up now, adding a few blows of her own *chappal,* as the creatures began quickly to disperse. Some ran under the bed into hard-to-reach corners; others sought out the trunk's deeper recesses.

A cursory examination showed that besides cockroaches, the trunk was also infested with white ants. All the albums had been ravaged. Most of the stamps which had not been destroyed outright were damaged in one way or another. They bore haphazard perforations and brown stains of the type associated with insects and household pests.

Jehangir picked up an album at random and opened it. Almost immediately, the pages started to fall to pieces in his hands. He remembered what Dr Mody used to say: 'This is my retirement hobby. I will spend my retirement with my stamps.' He allowed the tattered remains of Burjor Uncle's beloved pastime to drop back slowly into the trunk.

He crouched beside the dented, rusted metal, curious that he felt no loss or pain. Why, he wondered. If anything, there was a slight sense of relief. He let his hands stray through the contents, through worthless paper scraps, through shreds of the work of so many Sunday mornings, stopping now and then to regard with detachment the bizarre patterns created by the mandibles of the insects who had feasted night after night under his bed, while he slept.

With an almost imperceptible shrug, he arose and closed the lid. It was doubtful if anything of value remained in the trunk.

1987

◆

Louise Erdrich
b. 1954

◆

Born in Little Falls, Minnesota, of a Chippewa mother and a German-American father, Louise Erdrich obtained her BA from Dartmouth College (1976) and her MA from Johns Hopkins University (1979) and has taught creative writing at both places. A prolific and diverse author, she has written two volumes of poetry, *Jacklight* (1984) and *Baptism of Desire* (1989); collaborated with her now-deceased husband, anthropologist Michael Dorris, on *The Crown of Columbus* (1991), a novel based on their experience and understanding of contemporary Aboriginal life; authored Aboriginal novels for children; and written a series of adult novels that focus on her Chippewa ancestors in the fictional community of Argus, North Dakota, from 1912 to contemporary times. In her fiction she explores universal family life cycles while showing the losses suffered by Aboriginal communities and how these and other changes have affected contemporary Native experience. 'Fleur', which became a chapter in the novel *Tracks* (1988), examines the title character's youth and inexperience, though most honest people are compelled to admit 'that they don't know anything,' a homage to the enduring power of stories.

Fleur

The first time she drowned in the cold and glassy waters of Lake Turcot, Fleur Pillager was only a girl. Two men saw the boat tip, saw her struggle in the waves. They rowed over to the place she went down, and jumped in. When they dragged her over the gunwales, she was cold to the touch and stiff, so they slapped her face, shook her by the heels, worked her arms back and forth, and pounded her back until she coughed up lake water. She shivered all over like a dog, then took a breath. But it wasn't long afterward that those two men disappeared. The first wandered off, and the other, Jean Hat, got himself run over by a cart.

It went to show, my grandma said. It figured to her, all right. By saving Fleur Pillager, those two men had lost themselves.

The next time she fell in the lake, Fleur Pillager was twenty years old and no one touched her. She washed onshore, her skin a dull dead grey, but when George Many Women bent to look closer, he saw her chest move. Then her eyes spun open, sharp black riprock, and she looked at him. 'You'll take my place,' she hissed. Everybody scattered and left her there, so no one knows how she dragged herself home. Soon after that we noticed Many Women changed, grew afraid, wouldn't leave his house, and would not be forced to go near water. For his caution, he lived until the day that his sons brought him a new tin bathtub. Then the first time he used the tub he slipped, got knocked out, and breathed water while his wife stood in the other room frying breakfast.

Men stayed clear of Fleur Pillager after the second drowning. Even though she was good-looking, nobody dared to court her because it was clear that Misshepeshu, the waterman, the monster, wanted her for himself. He's a devil, that one, love-hungry with desire and maddened for the touch of young girls, the strong and daring especially, the ones like Fleur.

Our mothers warn us that we'll think he's handsome, for he appears with green eyes, copper skin, a mouth tender as a child's. But if you fall into his arms, he sprouts horns, fangs, claws, fins. His feet are joined as one and his skin, brass scales, rings to the touch. You're fascinated, cannot move. He casts a shell necklace at your feet, weeps gleaming chips that harden into mica on your breasts. He holds you under. Then he takes the body of a lion or a fat brown worm. He's made of gold. He's made of beach moss. He's a thing of dry foam, a thing of death by drowning, the death a Chippewa cannot survive.

Unless you are Fleur Pillager. We all knew she couldn't swim. After the first time, we thought she'd never go back to Lake Turcot. We thought she'd keep to herself, live quiet, stop killing men off by drowning in the lake. After the first time, we thought she'd keep the good ways. But then, after the second drowning, we knew that we were dealing with something much more serious. She was haywire, out of control. She messed with evil, laughed at the old women's advice, and dressed like a man. She got herself into some half-forgotten medicine, studied ways we shouldn't talk about. Some say she kept the finger of a child in her pocket and a powder of unborn rabbits in a leather thong around her neck. She laid the heart of an owl on her tongue so she could see at night, and went out, hunting, not even in her own body. We know for sure because the next morning, in the snow or dust, we followed the tracks of her bare feet and saw where they changed, where the claws sprang out, the pad broadened and pressed into the dirt. By night we heard her chuffing cough, the bear cough. By day her silence and the wide grin she threw to bring down our guard made us frightened. Some thought that Fleur Pillager should be driven off the reservation, but not a single person who spoke like this had the nerve. And finally, when people were just about to get together and throw her out, she left on her own and didn't come back all summer. That's what this story is about.

During that summer, when she lived a few miles south in Argus, things happened. She almost destroyed that town.

When she got down to Argus in the year of 1920, it was just a small grid of six streets on either side of the railroad depot. There were two elevators, one central, the other a few miles west. Two stores competed for the trade of the three hundred citizens, and three churches quarrelled with one another for their souls. There was a frame building for Lutherans, a heavy brick one for Episcopalians, and a long narrow shingled Catholic church. This last had a tall slender steeple, twice as high as any building or tree.

No doubt, across the low, flat wheat, watching from the road as she came near Argus on foot, Fleur saw that steeple rise, a shadow thin as a needle. Maybe in that raw space it drew her the way a lone tree draws lightning. Maybe, in the end, the Catholics are to blame. For if she hadn't seen that sign of pride, that slim prayer, that marker, maybe she would have kept walking.

But Fleur Pillager turned, and the first place she went once she came into town was to the back door of the priest's residence attached to the landmark church. She didn't go there for a handout, although she got that, but to ask for work. She got that too, or the town got her. It's hard to tell which came out worse, her or the men or the town, although the upshot of it all was that Fleur lived.

The four men who worked at the butcher's had carved up about a thousand carcasses between them, maybe half of that steers and the other half pigs, sheep, and game animals like deer, elk, and bear. That's not even mentioning the chickens, which were beyond counting. Pete Kozka owned the place, and employed Lily Veddar, Tor Grunewald, and my stepfather, Dutch James, who had brought my mother down from the reservation the year before she disappointed him by dying. Dutch took me out of school to take her place. I kept house half the time and worked the other in the butcher shop, sweeping floors, putting sawdust down, running a hambone across the street to a customer's bean pot or a package of sausage to the corner. I was a good one to have around because until they needed me, I was invisible. I blended into the stained brown wall, a skinny, big-nosed girl with staring eyes. Because I could fade into a corner or squeeze beneath a shelf, I knew everything, what the men said when no one was around, and what they did to Fleur.

Kozka's Meats served farmers for a fifty-mile area, both to slaughter, for it had a stock pen and chute, and to cure the meat by smoking it or spicing it in sausage. The storage locker was a marvel, made of many thicknesses of brick, earth insulation, and Minnesota timber, lined inside with sawdust and vast blocks of ice cut from Lake Turcot, hauled down from home each winter by horse and sledge.

A ramshackle board building, part slaughterhouse, part store, was fixed to the low, thick square of the lockers. That's where Fleur worked. Kozka hired her for her strength. She could lift a haunch or carry a pole of sausages without stumbling, and she soon learned cutting from Pete's wife, a string-thin blonde who chain-smoked and handled the razor-sharp knives with nerveless precision, slicing close to her stained fingers. Fleur and Fritzie Kozka worked afternoons, wrapping their cuts in paper, and

Fleur hauled the packages to the lockers. The meat was left outside the heavy oak doors that were only opened at 5:00 each afternoon, before the men ate supper.

Sometimes Dutch, Tor, and Lily ate at the lockers, and when they did I stayed too, cleaned floors, restoked the fires in the front smokehouse, while the men sat around the squat cast-iron stove spearing slats of herring onto hardtack bread. They played long games of poker or cribbage on a board made from the planed end of a salt crate. They talked and I listened, although there wasn't much to hear since almost nothing ever happened in Argus. Tor was married, Dutch had lost my mother, and Lily read circulars. They mainly discussed about the auctions to come, equipment, or women.

Every so often, Pete Kozka came out front to make a whist, leaving Fritzie to smoke cigarettes and fry raised doughnuts in the back room. He sat and played a few rounds but kept his thoughts to himself. Fritzie did not tolerate him talking behind her back, and the one book he read was the New Testament. If he said something, it concerned weather or a surplus of sheep stomachs, a ham that smoked green or the markets for corn and wheat. He had a good-luck talisman, the opal-white lens of a cow's eye. Playing cards, he rubbed it between his fingers. That soft sound and the slap of cards was about the only conversation.

Fleur finally gave them a subject.

Her cheeks were wide and flat, her hands large, chapped, muscular. Fleur's shoulders were broad as beams, her hips fishlike, slippery, narrow. An old green dress clung to her waist, worn thin where she sat. Her braids were thick like the tails of animals, and swung against her when she moved, deliberately, slowly in her work, held in and half-tamed, but only half. I could tell, but the others never saw. They never looked into her sly brown eyes or noticed her teeth, strong and curved and very white. Her legs were bare, and since she padded around in beadwork moccasins they never saw that her fifth toes were missing. They never knew she'd drowned. They were blinded, they were stupid, they only saw her in the flesh.

And yet it wasn't just that she was a Chippewa, or even that she was a woman, it wasn't that she was good-looking or even that she was alone that made their brains hum. It was how she played cards.

Women didn't usually play with men, so the evening that Fleur drew a chair up to the men's table without being so much as asked, there was a shock of surprise.

'What's this,' said Lily. He was fat with a snake's cold pale eyes and precious skin, smooth and lily-white, which is how he got his name. Lily had a dog, a stumpy mean little bull of a thing with a belly drum-tight from eating pork rinds. The dog liked to play cards just like Lily, and straddled his barrel thighs through games of stud, rum poker, vingt-un. The dog snapped at Fleur's arm that first night, but cringed back, its snarl frozen, when she took her place.

'I thought', she said, her voice was soft and stroking, 'you might deal me in.'

There was a space between the heavy bin of spiced flour and the wall where I just fit. I hunkered down there, kept my eyes open, saw her black hair swing over the chair, her feet solid on the wood floor. I couldn't see up on the table where the cards slapped down, so after they were deep in their game I raised myself up in the shadows, and crouched on a sill of wood.

I watched Fleur's hands stack and ruffle, divide the cards, spill them to each player in a blur, rake them up and shuffle again. Tor, short and scrappy, shut one eye and squinted the other at Fleur. Dutch screwed his lips around a wet cigar.

'Gotta see a man,' he mumbled, getting up to go out back to the privy. The others broke, put their cards down, and Fleur sat alone in the lamplight that glowed in a sheen across the push of her breasts. I watched her closely, then she paid me a beam of notice for the first time. She turned, looked straight at me, and grinned the white wolf grin a Pillager turns on its victims, except that she wasn't after me.

'Pauline there,' she said, 'how much money you got?'

We'd all been paid for the week that day. Eight cents was in my pocket.

'Stake me,' she said, holding out her long fingers. I put the coins in her palm and then I melted back to nothing, part of the walls and tables. It was a long time before I understood that the men would not have seen me no matter what I did, how I moved. I wasn't anything like Fleur. My dress hung loose and my back was already curved, an old woman's. Work had roughened me, reading made my eyes sore, caring for my mother before she died had hardened my face. I was not much to look at, so they never saw me.

When the men came back and sat around the table, they had drawn together. They shot each other small glances, stuck their tongues in their cheeks, burst out laughing at odd moments, to rattle Fleur. But she never minded. They played their vingt-un, staying even as Fleur slowly gained. Those pennies I had given her drew nickels and attracted dimes until there was a small pile in front of her.

Then she hooked them with five-card draw, nothing wild. She dealt, discarded, drew, and then she sighed and her cards gave a little shiver. Tor's eye gleamed, and Dutch straightened in his seat.

'I'll pay to see that hand,' said Lily Veddar.

Fleur showed, and she had nothing there, nothing at all.

Tor's thin smile cracked open, and he threw his hand in too.

'Well, we know one thing,' he said, leaning back in his chair, 'the squaw can't bluff.'

With that I lowered myself into a mound of swept sawdust and slept. I woke up during the night, but none of them had moved yet, so I couldn't either. Still later, the men must have gone out again, or Fritzie come out to break the game, because I was lifted, soothed, cradled in a woman's arms and rocked so quiet that I kept my eyes shut while Fleur rolled me into a closet of grimy ledgers, oiled paper, balls of string, and thick files that fit beneath me like a mattress.

The game went on after work the next evening. I got my eight cents back five times over, and Fleur kept the rest of the dollar she'd won for a stake. This time they didn't play so late, but they played regular, and then kept going at it night after night. They played poker now, or variations, for one week straight, and each time Fleur won exactly one dollar, no more and no less, too consistent for luck.

By this time, Lily and the other men were so lit with suspense that they got Pete to join the game with them. They concentrated, the fat dog sitting tense in Lily Veddar's lap, Tor suspicious, Dutch stroking his huge square brow, Pete steady. It wasn't that Fleur won that hooked them in so, because she lost hands too. It was rather that she never had a freak hand or even anything above a straight. She only took on her low cards, which didn't sit right. By chance, Fleur should have gotten a full or flush by now. The irritating thing was she beat with pairs and never bluffed, because she couldn't, and still she ended up each night with exactly one dollar. Lily couldn't believe, first of all, that a woman could be smart enough to play cards, but even if she was, that she would then be stupid enough to cheat for a dollar at night. By day I watched him turn the problem over, his hard white face dull, small fingers probing at his knuckles, until he finally thought he had Fleur figured out as a bit-time player, caution her game. Raising the stakes would throw her.

More than anything now, he wanted Fleur to come away with something but a dollar. Two bits less or ten more, the sum didn't matter, just so he broke her streak.

Night after night she played, won her dollar, and left to stay in a place that just Fritzie and I knew about. Fleur bathed in the slaughtering tub, then slept in the unused brick smokehouse behind the lockers, a windowless place tarred on the inside with scorched fats. When I brushed against her skin I noticed that she smelled of the walls, rich and woody, slightly burnt. Since that night she put me in the closet I was no longer afraid of her, but followed her close, stayed with her, became her moving shadow that the men never noticed, the shadow that could have saved her.

August, the month that bears fruit, closed around the shop, and Pete and Fritzie left for Minnesota to escape the heat. Night by night, running, Fleur had won thirty dollars, and only Pete's presence had kept Lily at bay. But Pete was gone now, and one payday, with the heat so bad no one could move but Fleur, the men sat and played and waited while she finished work. The cards sweat, limp in their fingers, the table was slick with grease, and even the walls were warm to the touch. The air was motionless. Fleur was in the next room boiling heads.

Her green dress, drenched, wrapped her like a transparent sheet. A skin of lakeweed. Black snarls of veining clung to her arms. Her braids were loose, half-unravelled, tied behind her neck in a thick loop. She stood in steam, turning skulls through a vat with a wooden paddle. When scraps boiled to the surface, she bent with a round tin sieve and scooped them out. She'd filled two dishpans.

'Ain't that enough now?' called Lily. 'We're waiting.' The stump of a dog trembled in his lap, alive with rage. It never smelled me or noticed me above Fleur's smoky skin. The air was heavy in my corner, and pressed me down. Fleur sat with them.

'Now what do you say?' Lily asked the dog. It barked. That was the signal for the real game to start.

'Let's up the ante,' said Lily, who had been stalking this night all month. He had a roll of money in his pocket. Fleur had five bills in her dress. The men had each saved their full pay.

'Ante a dollar then,' said Fleur, and pitched hers in. She lost, but they let her scrape along, cent by cent. And then she won some. She played unevenly, as if chance was all she had. She reeled them in. The game went on. The dog was stiff now, poised on Lily's knees, a ball of vicious muscle with its yellow eyes slit in concentration. It gave advice, seemed to sniff the lay of Fleur's cards, twitched and nudged. Fleur was up, then down, saved by a scratch. Tor dealt seven cards, three down. The pot grew, round by round, until it held all the money. Nobody folded. Then it all rode on one last card and they went silent. Fleur picked hers up and blew a long breath. The heat lowered like a bell. Her card shook, but she stayed in.

Lily smiled and took the dog's head tenderly between his palms.

'Say, Fatso,' he said, crooning the words, 'you reckon that girl's bluffing?'

The dog whined and Lily laughed. 'Me too,' he said, 'let's show.' He swept his bills and coins into the pot and then they turned their cards over.

Lily looked once, looked again, then he squeezed the dog up like a fist of dough and slammed it on the table.

Fleur threw her arms out and drew the money over, grinning that same wolf grin that she'd used on me, the grin that had them. She jammed the bills in her dress, scooped the coins up in a waxed white paper that she tied with string.

'Let's go another round,' said Lily, his voice choked with burrs. But Fleur opened her mouth and yawned, then walked out back to gather slops for the one big hog that was waiting in the stock pen to be killed.

The men sat still as rocks, their hands spread on the oiled wood table. Dutch had chewed his cigar to damp shreds, Tor's eye was dull. Lily's gaze was the only one to follow Fleur. I didn't move. I felt them gathering, saw my stepfather's veins, the ones in his forehead that stood out in anger. The dog had rolled off the table and curled in a knot below the counter, where none of the men could touch it.

Lily rose and stepped out back to the closet of ledgers where Pete kept his private stock. He brought back a bottle, uncorked and tipped it between his fingers. The lump in his throat moved, then he passed it on. They drank, quickly felt the whisky's fire, and planned with their eyes things they couldn't say out loud.

When they left, I followed. I hid out back in the clutter of broken boards and chicken crates beside the stock pen, where they waited. Fleur could not be seen at first, and then the moon broke and showed her, slipping cautiously along the rough board chute with a bucket in her hand. Her hair fell, wild and coarse, to her waist, and her dress was a floating patch in the dark. She made a pig-calling sound, rang the tin pail lightly against the wood, froze suspiciously. But too late. In the sound of the ring Lily moved, fat and nimble, stepped right behind Fleur and put out his creamy hands. At his first touch, she whirled and doused him with the bucket of sour slops. He pushed her against the big fence and the package of coins split, went clinking and jumping, winked against the wood. Fleur rolled over once and vanished in the yard.

The moon fell behind a curtain of ragged clouds, and Lily followed into the dark muck. But he tripped, pitched over the huge flank of the pig, who lay mired to the snout, heavily snoring. I sprang out of the weeds and climbed the side of the pen, stuck like glue. I saw the sow rise to her neat, knobby knees, gain her balance, and sway, curious, as Lily stumbled forward. Fleur had backed into the angle of rough wood just beyond, and when Lily tried to jostle past, the sow tipped up on her hind legs and struck, quick and hard as a snake. She plunged her head into Lily's thick side and snatched a mouthful of his shirt. She lunged again, caught him lower, so that he grunted in pained surprise. He seemed to ponder, breathing deep. Then he launched his huge body in a swimmer's dive.

The sow screamed as his body smacked over hers. She rolled, striking out with her knife-sharp hooves, and Lily gathered himself upon her, took her foot-long face by the ears and scraped her snout and cheeks against the trestle of the pen. He hurled the sow's tight skull against an iron post, but instead of knocking her dead, he merely woke her from her dream.

She reared, shrieked, drew him with her so that they posed standing upright. They bowed jerkily to each other, as if to begin. Then his arms swung and flailed. She sank her black fangs into his shoulder, clasping him, dancing him forward and backward through the pen. Their steps picked up pace, went wild. The two dipped as one, box-stepped, tripped each other. She ran her split foot through his hair. He grabbed her kinked tail. They went down and came up, the same shape and then the same colour, until the men couldn't tell one from the other in that light and Fleur was able to launch herself over the gates, swing down, hit gravel.

The men saw, yelled, and chased her at a dead run to the smokehouse. And Lily too, once the sow gave up in disgust and freed him. That is where I should have gone to Fleur, saved her, thrown myself on Dutch. But I went stiff with fear and couldn't unlatch myself from the trestles or move at all. I closed my eyes and put my head in my arms, tried to hide, so there is nothing to describe but what I couldn't block out, Fleur's hoarse breath, so loud it filled me, her cry in the old language, and my name repeated over and over among the words.

The heat was still dense the next morning when I came back to work. Fleur was gone but the men were there, slack-faced, hungover. Lily was paler and softer than ever, as if his flesh had steamed on his bones. They smoked, took pulls off a bottle. It wasn't noon yet. I worked a while, waiting shop and sharpening steel. But I was sick, I was smothered, I was sweating so hard that my hands slipped on the knives, and I wiped my fingers clean of the greasy touch of the customers' coins. Lily opened his mouth and roared once, not in anger. There was no meaning to the sound. His boxer dog, sprawled limp beside his foot, never lifted its head. Nor did the other men.

They didn't notice when I stepped outside, hoping for a clear breath. And then I forgot them because I knew that we were all balanced, ready to tip, to fly, to be crushed as soon as the weather broke. The sky was so low that I felt the weight of it like a yoke. Clouds hung down, witch teats, a tornado's green-brown cones, and as I watched one flicked out and became a delicate probing thumb. Even as I picked up my heels and ran back inside, the wind blew suddenly, cold, and then came rain.

Inside, the men had disappeared already and the whole place was trembling as if a huge hand was pinched at the rafters, shaking it. I ran straight through, screaming for Dutch or for any of them, and then I stopped at the heavy doors of the lockers, where they had surely taken shelter. I stood there a moment. Everything went still. Then I heard a cry building in the wind, faint at first, a whistle and then a shrill scream that tore through the walls and gathered around me, spoke plain so I understood that

I should move, put my arms out, and slam down the great iron bar that fit across the hasp and lock.

Outside, the wind was stronger, like a hand held against me. I struggled forward. The bushes tossed, the awnings flapped off storefronts, the rails of porches rattled. The odd cloud became a fat snout that nosed along the earth and sniffled, jabbed, picked at things, sucked them up, blew them apart, rooted around as if it was following a certain scent, then stopped behind me at the butcher shop and bored down like a drill.

I went flying, landed somewhere in a ball. When I opened my eyes and looked, stranger things were happening.

A herd of cattle flew through the air like giant birds, dropping their dung, their mouths open in stunned bellows. A candle, still lighted, blew past, and tables, napkins, garden tools, a whole school of drifting eyeglasses, jackets on hangers, hams, a checkerboard, a lampshade, and at last the sow from behind the lockers, on the run, her hooves a blur, set free, swooping, diving, screaming as everything in Argus fell apart and got turned upside down, smashed, and thoroughly wrecked.

Days passed before the town went looking for the men. They were bachelors, after all, except for Tor, whose wife had suffered a blow to the head that made her forgetful. Everyone was occupied with digging out, in high relief because even though the Catholic steeple had been torn off like a peaked cap and sent across five fields, those huddled in the cellar were unhurt. Walls had fallen, windows were demolished, but the stores were intact and so were the bankers and shop owners who had taken refuge in their safes or beneath their cash registers. It was a fair-minded disaster, no one could be said to have suffered much more than the next, at least not until Fritzie and Pete came home.

Of all the businesses in Argus, Kozka's Meats had suffered worst. The boards of the front building had been split to kindling, piled in a huge pyramid, and the shop equipment was blasted far and wide. Pete paced off the distance the iron bathtub had been flung—a hundred feet. The glass candy case went fifty, and landed without so much as a cracked pane. There were other surprises as well, for the back rooms where Fritzie and Peter lived were undisturbed. Fritzie said the dust still coated her china figures, and upon her kitchen table, in the ashtray, perched the last cigarette she'd put out in haste. She lit it up and finished it, looking through the window. From there, she could see that the old smokehouse Fleur had slept in was crushed to a reddish sand and the stockpens were completely torn apart, the rails stacked helter-skelter. Fritzie asked for Fleur. People shrugged. Then she asked about the others and, suddenly, the town understood that three men were missing.

There was a rally of help, a gathering of shovels and volunteers. We passed boards from hand to hand, stacked them, uncovered what lay beneath the pile of jagged splinters. The lockers, full of the meat that was Pete and Fritzie's investment, slowly came into sight, still intact. When enough room was made for a man to stand on the roof, there were calls, a general urge to hack through and see what lay below. But Fritzie shouted that she wouldn't allow it because the meat would spoil. And so the work continued, board by board, until at last the heavy oak doors of the freezer were revealed and people pressed to the entry. Everyone wanted to be the first, but since it was my step-father lost, I was let go in when Pete and Fritzie wedged through into the sudden icy air.

Pete scraped a match to his boot, lit the lamp Fritzie held, and then the three of us stood still in its circle. Light glared off the skinned and hanging carcasses, the crates of wrapped sausages, the bright and cloudy blocks of lake ice, pure as winter. The cold bit into us, pleasant at first, then numbing. We must have stood there a couple of minutes before we saw the men, or more rightly, the humps of fur, the iced and shaggy hides they wore, the bearskins they had taken down and wrapped around themselves. We stepped closer and tilted the lantern beneath the flaps of fur into their faces. The dog was there, perched among them, heavy as a doorstop. The three had hunched around a barrel where the game was still laid out, and a dead lantern and an empty bottle, too. But they had thrown down their last hands and hunkered tight, clutching one another, knuckles raw from beating at the door they had also attacked with hooks. Frost stars gleamed off their eyelashes and the stubble of their beards. Their faces were set in concentration, mouths open as if to speak some careful thought, some agreement they'd come to in each other's arms.

Power travels in the bloodlines, handed out before birth. It comes down through the hands, which in the Pillagers were strong and knotted, big, spidery, and rough, with sensitive fingertips good at dealing cards. It comes through the eyes, too, belligerent, darkest brown, the eyes of those in the bear clan, impolite as they gaze directly at a person.

In my dreams, I look straight back at Fleur, at the men. I am no longer the watcher on the dark sill, the skinny girl.

The blood draws us back, as if it runs through a vein of earth. I've come home and, except for talking to my cousins, live a quiet life. Fleur lives quiet too, down on Lake Turcot with her boat. Some say she's married to the waterman, Misshepeshu, or that she's living in shame with white men or windigos, or that she's killed them all. I'm about the only one here who ever goes to visit her. Last winter, I went to help out in her cabin when she bore a child, whose green eyes and skin the colour of an old penny made more talk, as no one could decide if the child was mixed blood or what, fathered in a smokehouse, or by a man with brass scales, or by the lake. The girl is bold, smiling in her sleep, as if she knows what people wonder, as if she hears the old men talk, turning the story over. It comes up different every time and has no ending, no beginning. They get the middle wrong too. They only know that they don't know anything.

1986

POETRY

POETRY

The Elements of Poetry

INTRODUCTION

What Good Is Poetry?

If you ask a poet, 'What good is poetry?' you may get an answer like Marianne Moore's 'I, too, dislike it,' or A.M. Klein's 'The poet does not count.' The modern poet is not likely to make grandiose claims for his or her craft, and we will try not to betray that honest and tough-minded attitude.

Poetry, with all its artificial rules, is essentially a game for two—a writer and a reader. The reader must be willing to play, or else the game will not work. Physical games have practical benefits. They promote physical fitness that is necessary to good health. A language game like poetry also has its uses, but they are by-products rather than its proper ends. Poetry exercises a valuable part of the mind: the imagination. Poetry can also help us learn to control and respond to language. But it is a game first of all, where, as Robert Frost said, 'the work is play for mortal stakes.'

A game can require great exertion, but it must reward that exertion with pleasure or there is no point playing it. Anyone who has ever responded to a nursery rhyme or to a well-crafted song lyric has experienced the fundamental pleasure of poetry. More complicated and sophisticated poems offer essentially the same kind of pleasure. We labour to understand the rules of the game so that we do not need to think about them when we are playing. We master technique to make our execution easier. When we are really proficient the work becomes play.

The Qualities of Poetry

Part of the pleasure of poetry lies in its relation to music. It awakens in us a fundamental response to rhythmic repetitions of various kinds. Learning to read poetry is partly a matter of learning to respond to subtle and delicate rhythmic patterns as well as to the most obvious and persistent ones. But poetry is not just a kind of music. It is a special combination of musical and linguistic qualities—of sounds regarded both as pure sound and as meaningful speech. In particular, poetry is expressive language. It does for us what Samuel Beckett's character Watt wanted done for him:

> Not that Watt desired information, for he did not. But he desired words to be applied to his situation, to Mr Knott, to the house, to the grounds, to his duties, to the stairs, to his bedroom, to the kitchen, and in a general way to the conditions of being in which he found himself.

Poetry performs this function of applying words to our situations, to the conditions of being in which we find ourselves. By doing so, it gives us pleasure because it helps us articulate our states of mind. The poets we value are those who speak for us and help us learn to speak for ourselves. A revealing instance of a poet's learning to apply words to his own situation, and finding in their order and symmetry a soothing pleasure, is captured by James Joyce. Here we see a nine-year-old child making an important discovery about the nature and uses of poetry:

[*Bray: in the parlour of the house in Martello Terrace*]

MR MANCE (*comes in with a stick*) . . . O, you know, he'll have to apologise, Mr Joyce.

MRS JOYCE O yes . . . Do you hear that, Jim?

MR VANCE Or else—if he doesn't—the eagles'll come and pull out his eyes.

MRS JOYCE O, but I'm sure he will apologise.

JOYCE (*under the table, to himself*)
—Pull out his eyes,
Apologise,
Apologise,
Pull out his eyes.
Apologise,
Pull out his eyes,
Pull out his eyes,
Apologise.

The coincidence of sound that links the four-word phrase 'Pull out his eyes' with the four-syllable word 'Apologise' offers the child a refuge from Mr Vance that is far more secure than the table under which he is hiding. In his novel *A Portrait of the Artist as a Young Man*, Joyce uses this moment from his own life to illustrate his protagonist's vocation for verbal art.

As a poem, the child's effort here is a simple one, but it achieves a real effect because of the contrast between the meaning of its two basic lines that sound so much alike. Gentle, conciliatory 'apologise' and fiercely vindictive 'pull out his eyes' should not fit together so neatly, the poem implies, and in doing so, it makes an ethical criticism of Mr Vance, who, after all, coupled them in the first place. Young Joyce's deliberate wit has made a poem from the old man's witless tirade.

Marianne Moore qualifies her dislike of poetry this way:

I, too, dislike it: there are things that are important beyond all this fiddle.
    Reading it, however, with a perfect contempt for it, one discovers in
        it after all, a place for the genuine.
            Hands that can grasp, eyes
        that can dilate, hair that can rise
            if it must, these things are important not because a

high-sounding interpretation can be put upon them but because they are
    useful. . . .

And Klein completes his evaluation of the poet thus:

> Therefore he seeds illusions. Look, he is
> the nth Adam taking a green inventory
> in world but scarcely uttered, naming, praising,
> the flowering fiats in the meadow, the
> syllabled fur, stars aspirate, the pollen
> whose sweet collusion sounds eternally.
> For to praise
>
> the world—he, solitary man—is breath
> to him. Until it has been praised, that part
> has not been. Item by exciting item—
> air to his lungs, and pressured blood to his heart—
> they are pulsated, and breathed, until they map,
> not the world's, but his own body's chart!
>
> And now in imagination he has climbed
> another planet, the better to look
> with single camera view upon this earth—
> its total scope, and each afflated tick,
> its talk, its trick, its tracklessness—and this,
> this, he would like to write down in a book!
>
> To find a new function for the *déclassé* craft
> archaic like the fletcher's; to make a new thing;
> to say the word that will become sixth sense;
> perhaps by necessity and indirection bring
> new forms to life, anonymously, new creeds—
> O, somehow pay back the daily larcenies of the lung!

Poetry, then, is a kind of musical word game that we value because of its expressive qualities. Not all poems are equally musical, or equally playful, or equally expressive. Nor are they necessarily musical, playful, or expressive in the same way. But we may consider these three qualities the basic constituents of poetry so that we may examine some of the various ways in which poets combine and modify them in making different kinds of poems. Recognizing various poetic possibilities is important to the study of poetry because the greatest single problem for the reader of a poem is the problem of tact.

Tact

Tact acknowledges the diversity of poetry. A tactful approach to a poem is one that is appropriate to the special nature of the poem under consideration. Reading a poem for the first time ought to be a little like meeting a person for the first time. An initial conversation may lead to friendship, dislike, indifference, or any of dozens of other shades of attitude from love to hate. If the relationship progresses, it will gain in intimacy as surface politeness is replaced by exchange of ideas and feelings at a deeper level.

Of course, we need to speak the same language if we are to communicate in any meaningful way. So we generally make friends with people who speak the same language or languages we do, and we read poems written in those languages. But speaking the same language means more than just inheriting or acquiring the same linguistic patterns. Some poems, like some people, seem to talk to us not merely in our native language but in our own idiom as well. We understand them easily and naturally. Others speak to us in ways that seem strange and puzzling. With poems, as with people, our first response to the puzzling should be a polite effort to eliminate misunderstanding. We need not adopt any false reverence before a poem of an earlier age, but we should treat it with respect, paying attention to its words, trying to adjust to its idiom. This may turn out to be rewarding, or it may not. But only after we have made an honest attempt to understand a poem are we entitled to reject or accept it.

Since the English language has changed considerably over the centuries and continues to change, a greater effort is often required to understand an older poem than a modern one. Notions of what poetry is and should be have also changed over time and continue to change. The poetry game has not always been played by the same rules. The difference between a love lyric by an Elizabethan sonneteer and a contemporary poem of love may be as great as the difference between Elizabethan tennis and modern tennis. The Elizabethans played tennis indoors in an intricately walled court that required great finesse to master all its angles. The modern game is flat and open, all power serves and rushes to the net. Which ought to remind us that Robert Frost likened free verse (verse with unrhymed, irregular lines) to playing tennis with the net down. Such a game would make points easy to score but would not be much fun to play. Poetry, like tennis, depends on artificial rules and hindrances. These arbitrary restrictions are what give it its game-like quality.

Unlike the rules of tennis, the rules of poetry have never been written down. Although many critics over the years have tried to produce a 'poetics' that would operate like a code of rules, they have always failed because poetry is always changing. In fact poetic 'rules' are not really rules but conventions, which are always changing and which must change to prevent poems from being turned out on a mass scale according to formulas. All poets learn from their predecessors, but any poet who merely imitates them produces flat, stale poems. A poet is above all one who finds a unique idiom, a special voice for his or her own poetry. The tactful reader quickly picks up on the conventions operating in any particular poem and pays careful attention to the idiom of every poet, in order to understand and appreciate or criticize each separate poetic performance.

The following parts of this discussion are designed to help the reader of poetry acquire tact. They are arranged to present certain basic elements drawn from the whole system of poetic conventions. Tact itself cannot be 'learned' because it is of the spirit. But if the instinct for it is there, tact can be developed and refined through conscious effort.

EXPRESSION

Drama and Narration

Drama usually implies actors on a stage speaking to one another in a sequence of situations or scenes. A short poem with a single speaker is dramatic only in a limited sense. Yet *some* poems are very dramatic; the element of drama in them must be grasped if we are to understand them at all. And *all* poems are dramatic to some extent, however slight.

We can approach the dramatic element in poetry by assuming that every poem shares some qualities with a speech in a play: that it is spoken aloud by a 'speaker' who is a character in a situation that implies a certain relationship with other characters; and we assume that this speech is 'overheard' by an audience. We may have to modify these assumptions. For instance, the poem may be more like a soliloquy or unspoken thought than like a part of a dialogue. Or it may seem more like a letter or a song than a speech. Still, in approaching our poem we must make a tentative decision about who the speaker is, what the situation is, and whom the speaker seems to be addressing. In poems that are especially dramatic, the interest of the poem will depend on the interest of the character and situation presented. But because dramatic poems are short and compressed in comparison with plays, the reader must usually do a good deal of guessing or inferring in order to grasp the elements of character and situation. How well people read a poem will depend on how plausible their inferences are.

Consider the following lines from the beginning of a dramatic poem by Robert Bringhurst. This imaginary speech is attributed to Francesco Petrarca, the fourteenth-century Italian poet, scholar, and humanist, better known as Petrarch.

> I, Francesco, this April day . . .
> death stirs like a bud in the sunlight, and Urban
> has got off his French duff and re-entered Rome
> and for three years running has invited me to Rome . . .
> 5 over the bright hills and down the Cassia,
> back through Arezzo one more time . . .
> my age sixty-five and my birthday approaching,
> the muggers on the streets in broad daylight in Rome,
> the hawks and the buzzards. . . .
>   Take this down.
> 10 No one has thought too deeply of death.
> So few have left anything toward or against it.
> Peculiar, since thinking of death can never be
> wasted thinking, nor can it be come to
> too quickly. A man carries his death with him
> 15 everywhere, waiting, but seldom thinking
> of waiting. Death is uncommonly like the soul.

What I own other than that ought to fall
of its own weight and settle. But beggars and tycoons
and I are concerned with our possessions,
20   and a man with a reputation for truth
must have one also for precision.
                I leave
my soul to my saviour, my corpse to the earth.
And let it be done without any parades.
I don't care very much where I'm buried,
25   so it please God and whoever is digging.
Still, you will ask. You will badger me.
If I am dead you will badger each other.
But don't lug my bones through the public streets
in a box to be gabbled at and gawked at and followed.
30   Let it be done without any parades.

If I die here in Padova, bury me here
near the friend who is dead who invited me here.
If I die on my farm, you can use the chapel
I mean to build there, if I ever build it.
35   If not, try the village down the road.

If in Venezia, near the doorway.
If in Milano, next to the wall.
In Pavia, anywhere. Or if in Rome—
if in Rome, in the centre, of course, if there's room.
40   These are the places I think I might die in,
in Italy.
      Or if I happen to be in Parma,
there is the cathedral, of which for some reason
I am the archdeacon. But I will avoid
going to Parma. It would scarcely be possible,
45   I suppose, in Parma, not to have a parade.

At any rate, put what flesh I have left
in a church. A Franciscan church if there is one.
I don't want it feeding a tree from which
rich people's children swipe apples.

50   Two hundred ducats go to the church in which
I am buried, with another hundred to be given
out in that parish to the poor, in small doses.
The money to the church, let it buy a piece of land
and the land be rented and the rental from the land

55   pay for an annual mass in my name.
      I will be fitter company in that sanctuary
      then, present in spirit and name only,
      than this way, muttering to the blessed virgin
      through my hemorrhoids and bad teeth. I should be glad
60   to be rid of this sagging carcass.
                           Don't write that.

Now consider, in order, each of these questions:

1. What can we infer about the situation and its development?

2. To whom is Petrarch speaking in the opening lines?

3. What inferences could we make about Petrarch's attitude towards death?

4. In lines 26–7 the speaker addresses a different person. Whom is he addressing?

5. What kind of man do the details in these lines suggest is speaking?

6. How would you describe the progress of the situation? How might the events presented in these sixty lines be retold in the form of a story narrated by an observer of the action?

This series of questions—and their answers—should suggest the kind of inferential activity that many dramatic poems require of their readers. The words are points of departure, and the real poem is the one we create with our own imaginative but logical response to the poet's words. The poet offers us the pleasure of helping to create his poem, and also the pleasure of entering a world remote from our own in time and space. Dramatic poems like Bringhurst's do not so much apply words to our situations as take us out of ourselves into situations beyond our experience. When we speak Petrarch's words aloud or read them imaginatively, we are refreshed by this assumption of a strange role and this expression of a personality other than our own. Our minds are expanded, and we return to ourselves enriched by the experience. Yet even the strangest characters will often express ideas and attitudes we recognize as related to our own, related to certain moods or conditions of being in which we have found ourselves. Everyone who has ever considered his or her own death has something in common with Francesco Petrarca as he begins to speak.

The line between the dramatic and narrative elements in a poem is not always clear. But a narrative poem gives us a story as told by a narrator from a perspective outside the action, while a dramatic poem presents a fragment of an action (or story) through the voice, or point of view, of a character involved in that action. The principal speaker in a narrative poem addresses the audience directly, telling us about the situation and perhaps offering us introductions to characters who function as dramatic elements in the poem. In the days when long stories were recited aloud by bardic poets, verse was the natural form for narration, because it provided easily memorizable units of composition and a regular, flowing rhythm into which these units might be fitted. But now that printing has converted most of the audience for fiction from listeners to readers, stories today are typically told in prose. The only narrative verse form that is alive today is the ballad, which justifies its use of rhyme and rhythm by being set to music and sung. Verse meant to be sung has its own rules and conventions, which will be discussed later on. But here we can talk about the narrative element in ballads and other forms of fiction in verse, and how versified fiction differs from the kind of story we expect to find in prose.

If we think of a dramatic poem as something like a self-contained fragment torn from a play, which through its compression encourages us to fill out its dramatic frame by acts of inference and imagination, then we may think of a narrative poem as related to prose fiction in a similar way. In comparison to stories, narrative poems are compressed and elliptical, shifting their focus, concentrating on striking details, and leaving us to make appropriate connections and draw appropriate conclusions. In fact, there is a strong tendency toward the dramatic in short verse narratives—a tendency to present more dialogue or action in relation to description than we would expect to find in prose fiction dealing with the same subject matter.

We find poetic elements in much prose fiction and fictional elements in many poems. Here we are concerned mainly with the special problems posed by the compressed and elliptical form taken by fiction in short poems, where the compactness and brevity often move narration in the direction of drama. Consider the combination of drama and narration in the following poem by D.H. Lawrence:

The Piano

Softly, in the dusk, a woman is singing to me;
Taking me back down the vista of years, till I see
A child sitting under the piano, in the boom of the tingling strings
And pressing the small, poised feet of a mother who smiles as she sings.

5   In spite of myself, the insidious mastery of song
Betrays me back, till the heart of me weeps to belong
To the old Sunday evenings at home, with winter outside
And hymns in the cosy parlour, the tinkling piano our guide.

So now it is vain for the singer to burst into clamour
10 With the great black piano appassionato. The glamour
Of childish days is upon me, my manhood is cast
Down in the flood of remembrance, I weep like a child for the past.

Here the speaker seems to be addressing us directly as a narrator. But he is describing a scene in which he is the central character, and describing it in the present tense as something in progress. Drama is always now; narrative is always then. But this scene mingles now and then, bringing two pianos, and two pianists, linking the speaker's childish self with his present manhood. In a sense, the poem depends for its effect on its combination of now and then, drama and narration, uniting man and child in its last clause: 'I weep like a child for the past.'

Because this is a poem, tightly compressed, it is possible for us to miss an essential aspect of the dramatic situation it presents. Why is it 'vain' for the singer to play the piano 'appassionato'? Why does it mean when the speaker says that his 'manhood' is cast down? These elliptical references seem intended to suggest that the woman at the piano is in some sense wooing the man who listens, attempting to arouse his passion through her performance. But ironically, she only reminds him of his mother, casting down his manhood, reducing him from a lover to a son, from a man to a child.

It is interesting to compare this version of Lawrence's poem to an early version. Looking at the early draft, we might consider Lawrence's revisions as an attempt to achieve a more satisfactory combination of narrative and drama, and a more intense poem. The early version tells a different story from the later one—almost the opposite story. And it contains much that Lawrence eliminated. Examine the revisions in detail. In doing so, consider what each change accomplishes. Which changes are most important, most effective?

The Piano
(Early version)

Somewhere beneath that piano's superb sleek black
Must hide my mother's piano, little and brown, with the back
That stood close to the wall, and the front's faded silk both torn,
And the keys with little hollows, that my mother's fingers had worn.

5   Softly, in the shadows, a woman is singing to me
Quietly, through the years I have crept back to see
A child sitting under the piano, in the boom of the shaking strings
Pressing the little poised feet of the mother who smiles as she sings.

The full throated woman has chosen a winning, living song
10 And surely the heart that is in me must belong
To the old Sunday evenings, when darkness wandered outside
And hymns gleamed on our warm lips, as we watched mother's fingers glide.

Or this is my sister at home in the old front room
Singing love's first surprised gladness, alone in the gloom.
15 She will start when she sees me, and blushing, spread out her hands
To cover my mouth's raillery, till I'm bound in her shame's heartspun bands.

A woman is singing me a wild Hungarian air
And her arms, and her bosom, and the whole of her soul is bare,
And the great black piano is clamouring as my mother's never could clamour
20 And my mother's tunes are devoured of this music's ravaging glamour.

Description and Meditation

Description is the element in poetry closest to painting and sculpture. Poets like Edmund Spenser, John Keats, and Alfred, Lord Tennyson have been sensitive to this relationship: Spenser maintained that the poet's wit 'passeth Painter farre', while Keats admitted that a painted piece of Greek pottery could 'express a flowery tale more sweetly than our rhyme'. In fact, portraying something with words has both advantages and disadvantages in comparison to plastic representation. Words are rich in meaning and suggestions but weak for rendering precise spatial relations and shades of colour. What descriptive words do best is convey an attitude or feeling through the objects that they describe.

Take a simple description from a short poem by William Carlos Williams:

> A red wheel
> barrow
>
> glazed with rain
> water
>
> beside the white
> chickens.

We sense a word game here in the arbitrary arrangement of the words in lines, as they lead us to consider a visual image dominated by contrasting colours and textures—feathery white and glazed red, living and inanimate things. But it is hard to sense distinctly any attitude conveyed by the description, which seems like a poor substitute for a painting.

Here is the entire poem:

> so much depends
> upon
>
> a red wheel
> barrow
>
> glazed with rain
> water
>
> beside the white
> chickens.

Now we can see how the description itself depends upon the assertion 'so much depends' for its animation. The assertion directs our search for meaning and conveys the speaker's attitude toward the objects described. We may wonder how anything can 'depend' on such insignificant objects, and yet this response is a response not just to a description but to a poem as well. The poem is created by the distance between this sweeping statement and the apparent insignificance of the objects it refers to. We understand, finally, that the poet is using this distance to make us feel his concern for trivial things, his sense that there is beauty in humble objects. Beyond that, he is encouraging us to share his alertness to the beautiful in things that are neither artful nor conventionally pretty. He is advising us to keep our eyes open, and he does it not with a direct admonition but with a description charged with the vigour of his own response to the visible world.

It is of the essence of poetic description that it comes to us charged with the poet's feelings and attitudes. Sometimes these will be made explicit by statement or commentary in the poem. Sometimes they will remain implicit, matters of tone, rhythm, and metaphor. Consider the opening four lines of a poem by Tennyson. What attitudes or emotions are conveyed by them, and how are they conveyed?

> The woods decay, the woods decay and fall,
> The vapours weep their burthen to the ground,
> Man comes and tills the field and lies beneath,
> And after many a summer dies the swan.

The topic is decay and death, presented in terms of generalized natural description. In the opening line the ongoing process of decay is emphasized by the exact repetition of a whole clause. In line 2 the vapours are presented as sentient creatures who weep. In line 3 the whole human adult life is compressed into just nine words, a few seconds, a patch of earth. In the climatic position, reserved by an inversion of normal syntax for the last place in the sentence, comes the death of the swan. Human life and death are thus surrounded by decay and death in other natural things, and in this way reduced, distanced. Death is not horrible but natural, and characterized by a melancholy beauty.

These lines of description serve in the poem as the beginning of a dramatic monologue. The nature of the speaker and that of his situation (as we come to understand them) help us to refine our grasp of the tone and the attitude these lines convey toward the objects they describe. Here is the opening verse-paragraph of the poem:

Tithonus

> The woods decay, the woods decay and fall,
> The vapours weep their burthen to the ground,
> Man comes and tills the field and lies beneath,
> And after many a summer dies the swan.
> 5 Me only cruel immortality
> Consumes: I wither slowly in thine arms,
> Here at the quiet limit of the world,
> A white-haired shadow roaming like a dream
> The ever-silent spaces of the East,
> 10 Far-folded mists, and gleaming halls of morn.

The speaker is Tithonus, a mythological prince who became the lover of the dawn goddess; she made him immortal but could not prevent him from growing older throughout eternity. In the light of lines 5 and 6, the first four lines are enriched with the wistful envy of one who is unable to die. At the close of the poem (some seventy lines later) the speaker returns to the images of line 3 in speaking of 'happy men that have the power to die' and of 'the grassy barrows of the happier dead'. He asks for release so that he may become 'earth in earth' and forget his unhappy existence.

The melancholy beauty of the opening lines becomes more lovely and less sad as we move toward the conclusion of the poem with its powerful projection of one's return to earth as the most desirable of consummations. Behind the dramatic speaker in the poem—the mythological Tithonus—stands the poet, reminding us that death is natural and the appropriate end of life. In this poem, description and drama collaborate to suggest rather than state a meaning.

Serious English poetry has often embodied in particular poems a movement from description to overt meditation. This movement is frequently found in religious poetry, in which poets move from contemplation of created things to an awareness of their divine creator. William Wordsworth was a master—perhaps *the* master—of this kind of poetic movement in English. Thus, a selection from Wordsworth makes a fitting conclusion to this discussion of description and meditation. The poem is a sonnet, in which the first eight lines (the *octet*) are devoted to description of nature, and the last six (the *sestet*) take the form of a meditation on Wordsworth's daughter Caroline. 'Abraham's bosom' is a reference to the passage in the New Testament (Luke 16: 22) that proclaims that the righteous will join the patriarch Abraham in heaven after death. It is a reference to heaven.

> It is a beauteous evening, calm and free,
> The holy time is quiet as a Nun
> Breathless with adoration; the broad sun
> Is sinking down in its tranquility;
> 5 The gentleness of heaven broods o'er the Sea:
> Listen! the mighty Being is awake,
> And doth with his eternal motion make
> A sound like thunder—everlastingly.
> Dear Child! dear Girl! that walkest with me here,
> 10 If thou appear untouched by solemn thought,
> Thy nature is not therefore less divine:
> Thou liest in Abraham's bosom all the year;
> And worshipp'st at the Temple's inner shrine,
> God being with thee when we know it not.

Word Games

Language can help us perceive connections between disparate things, or it can help us make discriminations that separate similar things. In poetry these two aspects of language take the form of metaphorical comparison and ironic contrast. Metaphor and irony are the twin bases of poetical language, and the reader of poetry must be espe-cially alert and tactful in responding to metaphorical and ironic language. It is because poetry places such stress on these crucial aspects of language that it is of such great use in developing linguistic skills in its readers.

In the following sections on metaphoric and ironic language we have not tried to present an exhaustive list of poetical devices to be carefully noted and memorized. We have tried instead to examine some of the main varieties of metaphoric and ironic lan-guage, with a view to introducing these two crucial varieties of poetical wordplay.

Some Varieties of Metaphorical Language

Simile

Simile is the easiest form of metaphor to perceive because in it the images or ideas being joined are stated and explicitly linked by the word *as* or *like* or a similar linking word. Similes are often quite simple:

> O my Love's like a red, red rose

But even a statement of resemblance as simple and direct as this one of Robert Burns's asks us to consider the ways in which his beloved is like a rose—and not a white or yellow rose, but a red rose. And not just a red rose but a 'red, red' rose. What the redness of the rose has to do with the qualities of the speaker's beloved is the first question this simile poses for us. In the poem, the simile is further complicated by a second line:

> O my Love's like a red, red rose,
> That's newly sprung in June;

Here we are asked to associate the freshness of the flower and its early blooming with the qualities of the speaker's beloved. The next two lines add a second image, com-pounding the simile:

> O my Love's like the melodie
> That's sweetly played in tune.

The first image emphasizes the spontaneous naturalness of the beloved, the sec-ond her harmonious composure. Both roses and sweet melodies are pleasing, so that, in a sense, the poet is using his similes to make the simple statement that the woman he loves is pleasing to behold. But the simile is also saying that she has a complicated kind of appeal: like the rose, to sight and smell; like the melody, to the sense of sound; like the rose, a natural, fresh quality; like the melody, a deliberate artfulness intended to please. The simile also conveys the strength of the poet's feeling; his choice of images tells us something about the qualities of his feeling for her because it is *he* who has found these words—which themselves have some of the qualities of spontaneous freshness and tuneful order.

A single simile can also be elaborated, as in the traditional epic simile, in which the image is often extensive enough to require the construction *as . . . so*, or *like . . . thus*. An extended simile, by multiplying possible points of contact between the thing presented and the illustrative image it is likened to, can often become very complicated, with the illustrative image itself becoming a thing to be illustrated or developed with other images still. Consider, for example, this epic simile from Book IV, Canto III of Edmund Spenser's *Faerie Queene*:

27

> Like as the tide that comes from th' Ocean main,
> Flows up the Shanon with contrary force,
> And overruling him in his own reign,
> Drives back the current of his kindly course,
> And makes it seem to have some other source:
> But when the flood is spent, then back again
> His borrowed waters forced to redisbourse,
> He sends the sea his own with double gain,
> And tribute eke withal, as to his Soveraine.

28

> Thus did the battle vary to and fro . . .

Metaphor

The word *metaphor* is used both as a general term for all kinds of poetic linking of images and ideas, and also as a specific term for such linking when the thing and image are not presented as a direct analogy (A *is like* B) but by discussing one in terms of the other (A *is* B-ish, or A B's: Albert *is* a dog or Albert *barked* at me). For example, within Spenser's epic simile we can find metaphor at work. Part of the simile describes hand-to-hand combat in terms of the ebb and flow of tides where the River Shannon meets the Atlantic Ocean. The ebb and flow of the waters illustrate the shifting tide of battle. But this basic simile in Spenser is enriched by the idea of Shannon and the Atlantic as hostile powers engaged in a struggle, with the ocean tide invading the river and 'overruling him in his own reign'.

The power struggle is itself further complicated by a financial metaphor. The phrase 'when the flood is spent' means literally when the incoming tide has expended its force and lost its momentum. But Spenser chooses to use the financial overtones in the word 'spent' to enrich his metaphor. From 'spent' he moves to 'borrowed' and 'redisburse', and to the concept of repayment with 100 per cent interest in the expression 'double gain'. This transaction between ocean and river can be seen as a combat or a loan. Finally, Spenser merges these two metaphors in the last line of the stanza by calling this double payment the 'tribute' of a lesser feudal power to a higher. And here Spenser turns his metaphor into a simile within the basic simile, with the expression 'as to his Soveraine'.

This interweaving of similes and metaphors is both playful and decorative. The metaphors seem to emerge naturally and blend easily with one another. But in fact they tell us nothing much about the course of the combat beyond suggesting that the fight ebbs and flows. The struggle is not so much described as dignified by this heroic comparison to two sovereign forces of nature.

In poems that depend heavily on metaphoric processes for their interest, the subtle interaction of images and ideas almost defies analysis, yet such poems may depend on our attempts to follow their metaphoric threads. For us to understand such a poem, to feel it, we must start our thoughts along the lines indicated by the metaphors. Consider Shakespeare's Sonnet 73 as an example of this kind of poem:

> That time of year thou may'st in me behold
> When yellow leaves, or none, or few, do hang
> Upon those boughs which shake against the cold,
> Bare ruin'd choirs where late the sweet birds sang.
> 5 In me thou see'st the twilight of such day
> As after sunset fadeth in the West,
> Which by and by black night doth take away,
> Death's second self, that seals up all in rest.
> In me thou see'st the glowing of such fire
> 10 That on the ashes of his youth doth lie,
> As the death-bed whereon it must expire,
> Consumed with that which it was nourished by.
> This thou perceiv'st, which makes thy love more strong,
> To love all that well which thou must leave ere long.

The images of the first twelve lines are all elaborations of the simple notion that the speaker is getting old. The last two lines are a dramatic assertion, also rather simple. The speaker tells his listener that the listener will love him all the more precisely because old age and death threaten their relationship. We can infer that the speaker is older than the listener, and in terms of the dramatic situation we are entitled to wonder whether these self-assured words are merely wishful thinking or an honest appraisal of the listener's attitude. How, then, does the imagery of the first twelve lines contribute to our understanding of the situation? We have in these lines three separate but related metaphors, each developed for four lines. The speaker says, in effect, 'You see in me—autumn; you see in me—twilight; you see in me—embers.'

These three metaphors for aging have in common certain qualities: a growing coldness and darkness, suggestions of finality and impending extinction. But each image generates its own attitude and emphasizes a different aspect of the aging process. The first four lines suggest an analogy between an aging person and trees whose leaves have fallen, leaving them exposed to cold winds. And the bare trees suggest, by a further reach of metaphor, a ruined and desolate church. Above all, this complex metaphor generates sympathy for the speaker, a sympathy based on our concern for lost beauty, for destruction of spiritual things, and for victims of the forces of nature.

The next four lines, focusing on the twilight after sunset, threaten coming darkness. By another extension of metaphor, 'black night' is called 'Death's second self'. The brevity of the time between sunset and night increases our sense of sympathetic urgency, and the introduction of 'Death' takes us full circle through the metaphors back to their object, an aging man. The next four lines also introduce a complex metaphor. The speaker compares himself to the glowing embers of a dying fire that lies upon 'the ashes of his youth'. The fire becomes human here and returns us again to the life of the speaker.

This final image is the most intense of the three because it likens the arrival of old age not merely to a seasonal change, worked by the passage of time, but to the consumption or destruction of matter that can never be restored to its original state. The ashes of the fire lying upon its deathbed are forcible reminders that the speaker's body will soon lie upon a deathbed, and will become ashes, to be returned to the ashes and dust of the grave. It is the emotional force of all 'This' that the speaker maintains, in the next-to-last line, the listener must perceive. And the confidence of the assertion is partly the confidence of a poet who still has his poetical power. He can still sing like a sweet bird and move his hearer with his poetry. The imagery justifies the dramatic situation, and the situation intensifies the significance of the imagery.

The Conceit

It is useful to think of the conceit as an extension of the simile in which aspects of the basic analogy are developed with a kind of relentless ingenuity. The 'metaphysical' poets of the late sixteenth and the seventeenth centuries specialized in witty conceits. Here, for example, John Donne combines a dramatic situation with development of a conceit so that the images become an argument persuading his listener to give in to his romantic overtures.

The Flea

Mark but this flea, and mark this,
How little that which thou deny'st me is;
Me it sucked first, and now sucks thee,
And in this flea, our two bloods mingled be;
5 Confess it, this cannot be said
A sin, or shame, or loss of maidenhead,
Yet this enjoys before it woo,
And pampered swells with one blood made of two,
And this, alas, is more than we would do.

10 Oh stay, three lives in one flea spare,
Where we almost, nay more than married are.

This flea is you and I, and this
Our marriage bed, and marriage temple is;
Though parents grudge, and you, we are met,
15 And cloistered in these living walls of jet.
    Though use make you apt to kill me,
    Let not to this, self murder added be,
    And sacrilege, three sins in killing three.

Cruel and sudden, hast thou since
20 Purpled thy nail, in blood of innocence?
In what could this flea guilty be,
Except in that drop which it sucked from thee?
Yet thou triumph'st, and say'st that thou
Find'st not thyself, nor me the weaker now;
25   'Tis true, then learn how false, fears be;
    Just so much honour, when thou yield'st to me,
    Will waste, as this flea's death took life from thee.

In the opening lines the speaker makes the basic analogy between the flea's having bitten both himself and the lady and the sexual dalliance he is attempting to initiate. In the rest of the poem he develops the analogy as an argument in a changing dramatic context. At the start of the second stanza the lady has threatened to kill the flea; by the third stanza she has done so. The speaker has imaginatively transformed the flea into a marriage bed, a temple, a cloister, and a figure of the Holy Trinity (Father, Son, and Holy Ghost), so that the flea's destruction can be hyperbolically described as murder, suicide, and sacrilege. All of this is in preparation for the turn of the argument in the last three lines of the poem. Donne's conceit is both ingenious and playful.

The Symbol

The symbol can be seen as an extension of the metaphor. In it, instead of saying that A is B-ish, or calling an A a B, the poet presents us with one half of the analogy only and requires us to supply the missing part. This invites the reader to be creative and imaginative in a situation controlled by the poet. The following is a symbolic poem by W.B. Yeats:

The Dolls

A doll in the doll-maker's house
Looks at the cradle and bawls:
'That is an insult to us.'
But the oldest of all the dolls,
5 Who had seen, being kept for show,
Generations of his sort,

> Out-screams the whole shelf: 'Although
> There's not a man can report
> Evil of this place,
> 10 The man and the woman bring
> Hither, to our disgrace,
> A noisy and filthy thing.'
> Hearing him groan and stretch
> The doll-maker's wife is aware
> 15 Her husband has heard the wretch,
> And crouched by the arm of his chair,
> She murmurs into his ear,
> Head upon shoulder leant:
> 'My dear, my dear, O dear,
> 20 It was an accident.'

This whole incident stands in a metaphoric relation to something else. In other words, the poem is only apparently about dolls and doll-makers. It is really about something symbolized by the incident narrated. Identifying the true subject of the poem requires us to work carefully from the situation toward possible analogies in the world of ideas and experience, first by exploring the situation and images in the poem. The situation derives from the doll-maker's two kinds of creation: his dolls and his child. The dolls in their lifeless perfection resent the noise and filth produced by the human child. The human baby is, in fact, as the doll-maker's wife apologetically points out, not 'made' in the same sense as dolls are made. Birth is an 'accident'; dolls are deliberately constructed. The situation leads us outward until we see it as an illustration of the opposition between art and life, between the ideal and the real. The doll-maker himself thus symbolizes any artist who is obliged to live in the real world but create idealized objects, or any person who faces the impossible problem of realizing his ideas—or idealizing reality.

Having got this far from the concrete situation of the poem, the reader is in a position to return and consider the ways in which Yeats has used language to control his tone and charge the scene with emotion. How should we react to the various characters in this drama? What, finally, should our attitude be toward the real/ideal conflict that the drama illustrates?

The Pun

Often disdained as a 'low' form of wit, the pun is essentially a kind of metaphor that can be used lightly and facetiously or for more serious purposes. Consider some verses by Thomas Hood (selected by William Empson to exemplify punning techniques):

> How frail is our uncertain breath!
> The laundress seems full hale, but death
> Shall her 'last linen' bring;

> The groom will die, like all his kind;
> And even the stable boy will find
> This life no stable thing. . . .
>
> Cook, butler, Susan, Jonathan,
> The girl that scours the pot and pan
> And those that tend the steeds,
> All, all shall have another sort
> Of service after this—in short
> The one the parson reads.

These puns on 'stable' and 'service' are playful but not funny. They use the basic device of the pun—dissimilar meanings for the same 'word', or rather the same sound—to convey an attitude toward an idea. That both the life of a servant and the servant's funeral are somehow included in that one piece of language—'service'—brings home to us the interconnection of life and death, which is the point of the poem.

Shakespeare was a master of the pun as of other metaphorical devices. Hamlet's bitter, punning responses to his uncle's smooth speeches are deadly serious and powerfully dramatic in their witty compression of his resentment.

> KING   . . . But now, my cousin Hamlet, and my son—
> HAMLET [*Aside*] A little more than kin and less than kind!
> KING   How is it that the clouds still hang on you?
> HAMLET   Not so, my lord. I am too much i' the sun.

Hamlet and the King are more than *kin* (twice related: uncle/nephew and step-father/son) but Hamlet feels they are not kindred spirits, not the same *kind*. And being called *son* by his father's murderer rouses all Hamlet's bitterness, causing him to return the King's metaphorical question about Hamlet's overcast mood with a pun that brings the metaphor back to the literal with a sarcastic bite: I am too much in the *son*.

The Language of Animation and Personification
In addition to their playful or ingenious aspects, metaphorical devices help to generate the qualities of compression and intensity that we value in poetry. Similar qualities are often achieved by other means, such as animation and personification.

Animation
Animation is a means of portraying objects or animals with a greater degree of awareness or purposefulness than we normally credit them with. When Tennyson writes, 'The vapours weep their burden to the ground,' he gives life to the vapours, animating them with an emotion, sadness, that only living creatures experience. Less lovely scenes can also be intensified by animation. Consider these lines from Samuel Johnson's 'Vanity of Human Wishes', which describe the treatment given the portraits of a statesman

whose power has waned. Those who were once honoured to gaze upon his features, now that no more is to be gained from the man, suddenly find the likeness ugly:

> From every room descends the painted face,
> That hung the bright palladium of the place;
> And, smoked in kitchens, or in auctions sold,
> To better features yields the frame of gold;
> For now no more we trace in every line
> Heroic worth, benevolence divine;
> The form distorted justifies the fall,
> And detestation rids th' indignant wall.

In the last line Johnson intensifies his satire by animating the wall on which the picture hangs—even it is indignant and wishes to be rid of these odious features. The job of removing the portraits has been carried out by a person who has been transformed into an attitude—'detestation'.

Personification

In the example from Dr Johnson, we have a kind of reverse personification, in which a human being becomes an abstract idea. Personification usually works the other way, clothing abstractions with the attributes of personality. Love is the most common of all the ideas presented as sentient beings. In mythology, Love operates as the god Cupid or Eros, offering poets a ready-made personification that they have often used. The mechanical use of traditional personification can be dull and dreary. But observe Sir Philip Sidney as he personifies Love in this sonnet, and finds ways to make concrete a whole range of other abstractions such as reverence, fear, hope, will, memory, and desire. If Love is *personified* here, these other notions are *objectified*—turned into material objects.

> I on my horse, and Love on me doth try
> Our horsemanships, while by strange work I prove
> A horseman to my horse, a horse to Love;
> And now man's wrongs in me, poor beast, descry.
> 5 The reins wherewith my rider doth me tie,
> Are humbled thoughts, which bit of reverence move,
> Curb'd in with fear, but with gilt boss above
> Of hope, which makes it seem fair to the eye.
> The wand is will; thou, fancy, saddle art,
> 10 Girt fast by memory, and while I spur
> My horse, he spurs with sharp desire my heart:
> He sits me fast, however I do stir:
> And now hath made me to his hand so right,
> That in the manage my self takes delight.

The dominant image of Love as horseman provides the subordinate imagery for making concrete the other abstractions that serve to amplify this picture of a love-ridden man. The effectiveness of the poem depends on the ingenuity with which the poet has matched the objects and ideas to one another, relating all to the dominant personification of Love. Like Spenser's epic simile, Sidney's personification seems to breed subordinate metaphors easily, gracefully, and naturally.

The Anti-Metaphorical Language of Irony

Verbal irony may be said to start with simple negation of resemblance in situations where resemblance is customarily insisted upon or expected, as in Shakespeare's sonnet 130, which begins,

> My mistress' eyes are nothing like the sun;
> Coral is far more red than her lips red:
> If snow be white, why then her breasts are dun;
> If hairs be wires, black wires grow on her head.

The 'anti-similes' of the first three lines serve the same function as the ugly metaphor in line 4. All four lines present attacks on what the speaker will name in the last line of the poem as 'false compare'—the misuse of metaphor in the language of poetry.

Usually irony is not so straightforward. We normally think of it as involving some deliberate misleading of the reader—some gap between what the words *seem* to be saying and what they *are* saying. In the same sonnet, after eight more lines of plain speaking about an ordinary human female, Shakespeare's speaker concludes:

> And yet, by heaven, I think my love as rare
> As any she belied by false compare.

What we might have taken as criticism of the speaker's mistress turns out to be praise after all. She is not uglier than the others; she just has a lover who will not exaggerate her beauty with the usual clichés. The irony lies in the disparity between the apparent disparagement of the woman in the first part of the poem and the praise of her at the end. We can see, then, in those opening lines, a kind of understatement, which works in the end to convince us of the woman's beauty more effectively than a conventionally exaggerated simile of 'false compare' would have done.

Understatement and overstatement are two of the most frequently used kinds of verbal irony. When Jonathan Swift causes a character to observe (in prose), 'Last Week I saw a Woman *flay'd*, and you will hardly believe, how much it altered her Person for the worse'—the main thing that strikes us is the awful inadequacy of the sentiment for the event. Disparity, contrast, incongruity—these elements are at the heart of verbal irony.

Successful irony implicitly argues that all words are inadequate for the representation of things. The poet as maker of metaphors may be seen as a genuine magician, bringing new things into the world, or as a charlatan pretending with feeble words to unite things that are essentially separate. Metaphor celebrates the creative dimension of language, while irony exposes language's inadequacies. For example, in Marvell's 'To His Coy Mistress' the exaggerated declarations of the extent that the speaker's love would require 'Had we but world enough and time' are all based on the view that of course we do *not* have world enough and time. Even before we get there, we sense the presence of the 'But' on which the poem will make its turn:

> But at my back I always hear
> Time's winged chariot hurrying near;

The contrast between what the speaker *would* do:

> Two hundred years should go to praise
> Thine eyes, and on thy forehead gaze:
> Two hundred to adore each breast:
> And thirty thousand to the rest;

and what he does urge:

> Now let us sport us while we may,

is an ironic one, enhanced by the extreme distance in time between hundreds or thousands of years and 'Now'.

Irony can also take the form of metaphorical overstatement, as it does in Alexander Pope's description of coffee being poured into a China cup:

> From silver spouts the grateful liquors glide,
> While China's earth receives the smoking tide.

These lines are metaphorical in that they present one thing (pouring a cup of coffee) in terms of another image (a kind of burning flood pouring over the mainland of China), but they are ironic in that the equation is made mainly so that we will perceive the disparity between the two images and enjoy their incongruity. Something of this reverse, anti-metaphorical wit is present in many metaphors.

John Donne's 'The Flea' has a witty, ironic dimension derived from the inappropriateness of his basic image. To call a flea a temple is to establish a far-fetched metaphor. The conceits used by Donne and other 'metaphysical' poets of his time often have an ironic dimension. Samuel Johnson characterized the metaphysical poets precisely in terms of this dimension—a special and extreme form of 'wit' based on the 'discovery of occult resemblances in things apparently unlike', and resulting in poems in which 'the most heterogeneous ideas are yoked by violence together.' Johnson's description emphasizes ('yoked by violence') the tension between metaphoric comparison and ironic contrast in many metaphysical conceits. Conceits tend to be witty, cerebral, unnatural, while metaphors are serious, imaginative, and natural. The metaphors of Romantic poetry are perceptions of relationships felt to exist. Metaphysical conceits often establish powerful but artificial relationships where one would least expect to find them.

Linking incongruous things is a feature of most kinds of witty poetry. A simple list with one incongruous element can serve to indict a whole way of life, as when Alexander Pope surveys the debris on a young woman's dressing table:

> Puffs, Powders, Patches, Bibles, Billet-doux

The inclusion of Bibles among love letters and cosmetics suggests a confusion between worldly and spiritual values—a failure to distinguish between true and false worth. The list is funny, but in an ironic and satiric way—as is this list of possible calamities from the same poem:

> Whether the nymph shall break Diana's law,
> Or some frail China jar receive a flaw;
> Or stain her honour or her new brocade;
> Forget her prayers or miss a masquerade;
> Or lose her heart or necklace at a ball; . . .

Here Pope mixes several serious matters of the spirit with trivial and worldly items. The breaking of 'Diana's law' of chastity is equated with damage to a jar. A single verb, 'stain', governs two objects—'honour' and 'brocade'—of different qualities and intensities. By this manipulation of grammar Pope makes us forcibly aware of the frivolousness of an attitude toward life that equates things that should have different values. He brings those two objects under that one verb so that we will feel a powerful urge to part them in our minds, resolving the incongruity by separating the elements he has brought together.

Beyond Metaphor and Irony

Much of the best modern poetry presents combinations of images and ideas so stretched and disconnected that they go beyond metaphor and yet so serious and appropriate they transcend irony also. The difficulty in understanding many modern poems stems from a profusion of images that seem ironically disconnected but nevertheless suggest genuine metaphorical connection. We can find a relatively simple illustration in a few lines from a ballad by W.H. Auden, 'As I Walked Out One Evening':

> The glacier knocks in the cupboard,
> The desert sighs in the bed
> And the crack in the tea-cup opens
> A lane to the land of the dead.

Here Auden seems to be operating with ironic incongruities—the glacier in the cupboard and so on—but the sum of these incongruities is a coherent statement about the absurd and empty horror that threatens much of modern life. Such a collection of images seems to combine qualities of conceit and symbol with ironic incongruity, leaving us to resolve the problems of whether these assertions are ironic overstatements or powerful metaphors for our condition.

A poem composed of a number of these high-tension ironic metaphors can be immediately intelligible in a general way and still difficult to reduce to prose sense at every point. But we should make the effort to establish prose sense—or possible prose senses—for each image and situation, because even if we do not succeed entirely, we will be testing the ultimate intelligibility of the poem, the durability of its interest. As with certain kinds of modern art, it is sometimes hard to separate the fraudulent from the real in contemporary poetry. If we cannot discover intelligibility and coherence in a poem, if its images and situations do not enhance one another, we are confronted by either a flawed poem or a poem that is beyond us—one that we have not yet learned how to read. Differences in poetic quality cannot be demonstrated conclusively, yet they exist.

MUSIC

The musical element in poetry is the hardest to talk about because it is non-verbal. Our responses to rhythm and pleasing combinations of sounds are in a sense too immediate, too fundamental to be understood in words. Yet music is important in all poetry, and for most poetry written before the last half-century it is crucial. It is important, then, to find words to grasp this poetical element, in order to do justice to most poetic achievement.

Students generally prefer discussing one aspect of poetry to another in an order something like this:

1. ideas
2. situations
3. language
4. metrics.

But if we are concerned about what makes poetry *poetry* rather than another kind of composition, we should probably reverse this order. If a piece of writing is neither especially rhythmical nor especially ironic nor metaphorical in its language, it is not poetry, regardless of its dramatic situations or the ideas it presents. The following sections introduce some of the fundamental aspects of versification.

Metrics

Metrics has to do with all rhythmical effects in poetry. In English versification this means that it is largely a matter of accents and pauses. The pauses are determined by the usual grammatical principles that govern our speech and writing, and are indicated by the usual grammatical symbols—periods, commas, and so on—but one new factor is added. The end of a line of verse is itself a mark of punctuation. If a line ends with a regular mark of punctuation we call it *end-stopped*. If the last word of a line is

followed by no punctuation and is part of a continuing grammatical unit like a preposi-
tional phrase, we call the line *run-on* or *enjambed*. In end-stopped lines, the line-end
works *with* punctuation and reinforces it, making each line a tight unit of thought. In
enjambed lines the line-end works *against* the punctuation, throwing certain words into
a prominence that they would not ordinarily have. The enjambed line adds a special
kind of poetical punctuation to the language: something at once more and less than a
comma. Poets who use free-verse forms with no regular rhythm are dependent on
enjambment to give their words a special poetical quality.

Consider again the poem by Williams:

> so much depends
> upon
>
> a red wheel
> barrow
>
> glazed with rain
> water
>
> beside the white
> chickens.

If we write this out as prose we get, 'So much depends upon a red wheelbarrow, glazed
with rainwater, beside the white chickens.' This is a simple, declarative prose sentence,
with a couple of adjectival phrases tacked on, set off with commas. Has anything been
lost by this rearrangement of the poem on the page? Decidedly so. The assertion being
made is much less convincing in plain prose. The free-verse form of the sentence uses
its line-endings to work against the prose movement, slowing it up, and providing a metrical equivalent for the visual highlighting of the images. Just where we would bring the
words closest together in prose—making single words out of 'wheel' and 'barrow',
'rain' and 'water'—Williams has pulled them apart by breaking the line in mid-word.

The poem may or may not carry us to final agreement with its assertion, but in the
free-verse form it certainly convinces us of the speaker's earnestness. We get a sense
of how much he cares about what he is saying from the care with which he has spaced
out his words. And when we read the poem aloud, with little pauses at line-ends, it carries us farther toward conviction than the same sentence in its prosaic form.

Williams's poem is a simple illustration of how poetry's special line-end punctuation can group words in a rhythm different from the natural rhythm of normal speech or
prose. Here is a further illustration of how a poet can use the line-end to achieve an
ironic effect that would be almost impossible to duplicate in prose. e.e. cummings
begins a poem this way:

> pity this busy monster, manunkind,
> not.

The first word of the second line absolutely reverses the meaning of the first line. We pause, with a comma, at the end of line 1. We stop entirely, with a period, after the first word of line 2. We hover, thus, with the wrong meaning until we are given the word that changes it, whereupon we stop to contemplate the admonition offered us in the whole opening sentence. Consider it rearranged as plain prose:

> Pity this monster, manunkind, not.

or, more prosaically:

> Do not pity this busy monster, manunkind.

By unravelling the poetical arrangement and combination of the words, we have destroyed the force of the admonition, taking away its suspense and eliminating the recoil in the original last word.

In verse that is not markedly rhythmical, unusual pauses and arrangements of words are the principal metrical device. In verse that is regularly rhythmical, however, the rhythm or metre itself is the crucial metrical element. Poetical arrangement does something to prosaic language, but not so much as does rhythm, which lifts an utterance and moves it in the direction of music. Just as the line-end pauses in a poem can work with or against the normal grammatical pauses of speech and prose, poetic rhythm can work both with and against our normal patterns of pronunciation.

In speech we begin with standard grammatical pronunciations for words. Take the word 'defence'. Normally we pronounce this word by accenting the first syllable lightly and the second syllable heavily. Indicating light accent by ∪ and heavy accent by ⎯, we pronounce the word this way:

$$\overset{\cup}{}\ \overset{\text{⎯}}{}$$
$$\text{defence.}$$

That is grammatical accent or grammatical stress. But in certain situations we might change this pronunciation for purposes of emphasis, as in, 'Today's coaches preach *de*-fence first, *off*-ence second.' Here we pronounce the word

$$\overset{\text{⎯}}{}\ \overset{\cup}{}$$
$$\text{defence.}$$

This is not grammatical stress but rhetorical stress. We have altered the usual pattern of light and heavy accent in order to make a point. (Grammar, of course, keeps changing, and the repeated use of one particular rhetorical pattern can eventually alter standard pronunciation. Broadcasts of hockey and basketball games, for instance, are helping to make *de*-fence the standard way to accent this word.)

Both grammatical and rhetorical stress operate in poetry, where they are complicated by a third kind of accent, which we call poetical stress. Poetical stress is a regular system of accents that establishes the basic rhythm of a poem. There are only two

fundamental systems of poetic stress in English verse, though they have many variations. Most frequently, English verse alternates light and heavy accents, giving every
other syllable the same stress, like this:

U — U— U — U— U —
The woods decay, the woods decay and fall

Less frequently, English verse uses two light syllables between each heavy stress, like
this:

U U—U U — U U — U U —
The Assyrian came down like the wolf on the fold

U U —U U — U U —U U —
And his cohorts were gleaming in purple and gold

The rhythm of this second metrical pattern is more insistent than that of the first. The
simple da-*dum*, da-*dum* of 'The woods decay' is more like the spoken language than
the da-da-*dum*, da-da-*dum* of 'like the wolf on the fold'.

When discussing metrics, we use the term *feet* for the units that are repeated to
make a pattern. In the first example above, we have five repeated units in the line, five
feet divided this way:

U — | U— | U — | U— | U —
The woods I decay, I the woods I decay I and fall

In the second example each line has four feet, divided like this:

U U —| U U — | U U —| U U —
And his co I horts were gleam I ing in pur I ple and gold

In describing metrical patterns we usually state the number of feet in the basic line
and name the standard foot in each line. The traditional name for the foot used in the
first example (da-*dum*) is the *iamb*. The traditional name for the foot used in the second example (da-da-*dum*) is the *anapest*. In referring to the number of feet in the basic
line of a poem, it is customary to use numerical prefixes derived from the Greek. Thus,

one-foot line	=	*mono*	+	*meter*	=	monometer
two-foot line	=	*di*	+	*meter*	=	dimeter
three-foot line	=	*tri*	+	*meter*	=	trimeter
four-foot line	=	*tetra*	+	*meter*	=	tetrameter
five-foot line	=	*penta*	+	*meter*	=	pentameter
six-foot line	=	*hexa*	+	*meter*	=	hexameter

The iamb and the anapest have a variant foot that is made by placing the accented syllable at the beginning of each foot rather than at the end. These are called the *trochee*
(*dum*-da) and the *dactyl* (*dum*-da-da). They are not used consistently for one good

reason. Rhyme in poetry tends to be pleasing only if it includes the last accented syllable in a line and *all the unaccented syllables that follow it.* Thus, if you write:

U — |U — | U   — |U —
Upon I a mid I night drear I y once

you need to find only a one-syllable rhyme for your rhyming line, such as:

Upon a midnight dreary once
I tried my hand at kicking punts

But if you use the trochee, and write

— U|— U|—   U | — U
Once u I pon a I midnight I dreary

then you must rhyme

Once upon a midnight dreary
Of kicking punts my foot was weary.

The trochaic foot can, in fact, grow wearisome if carried through to the rhyme word
consistently, so we often get a variation that looks like this:

— U — U —   U —
Tiger, Tiger, burning bright

— U — U — U —
In the forests of the night

These lines first appear trochaic (*dum*-da) and end by looking iambic (da-*dum*). The two
lines could be made fully iambic by a slight change in each:

U — U — U — U —
O, Tiger, Tiger burning bright

U — U — U — U —
Within the forests of the night

or we could make them fully trochaic by this kind of alteration:

— U — U — U — U
Tiger, Tiger burning brightly,

— U — U — U — U
Roaming through the forest nightly

In order to name the metrical pattern of 'Tiger, Tiger' we must supply an imaginary unaccented syllable at the start or end of the line, like this:

U —| U —| U — | U —
× Ti | ger, Ti | ger, burn | ing bright

or this:

— U | — U | — U | — U
Tiger, | Tiger, | burning | bright ×

These manoeuvrings strongly suggest that the special terminology of metrical analysis is not important in itself, and that beyond the major distinction between the two-syllable foot and the three-syllable foot, we do not need to be too fussy in terms of how we classify them.

What, then, is the use of all these special terms? The art of metrics involves a poet's ability to generate and maintain a consistent metre without destroying normal patterns of grammar and syntax. To succeed metrically, a poet must make language dance without making it unnatural. A crucial aspect of this art is perceptible only when we have the terminology to recognize it. Any unvaryingly regular metre quickly becomes boring through repetition. But a totally irregular poem is wholly without the kind of interest and pleasure that rhythm provides.

All good poets who work in regular metres introduce metrical variations into their poems. The simplest way to understand this is to see the variations as substitutions of a different sort of foot for the one called for by the established metre of the poem. As an example of metrical variation, consider this stanza from 'The Railway Station', a sonnet by Archibald Lampman:

U — U — U — U — U —
1   The darkness brings no quiet here, the light

— — U — U — U — U —
2   No waking: ever on my blinded brain

U — U — U — U — U —
3   The flare of lights, the rush, the cry, and strain,

U — U — U — U — U —
4   The engines' scream, the hiss and thunder smite:

The metre is basically iambic, but there is variation. Both grammar and rhetoric urge us to accent and elongate the sound of the word 'No' at the beginning of the second line, giving this foot two accented syllables and no unaccented one. This is a kind of foot that is often used as a substitute but never as the metrical basis for a whole poem. Its technical name is a *spondee*. Lampman has used the spondee here for a slight variation of his rhythm.

Having noticed that substitution, we might notice also the word 'no' in the poem's opening line. Because of its position in the line we are not tempted to give it the emphasis we give to 'No' at the start of line 2, yet it can take a heavy accent. The basic terminology of metrical analysis establishes only the simple distinction between heavy and light, so it cannot take us too far into any metrical subtleties. In scansion, however, we need to consider subtleties and should probably be ready to use at least one more symbol to indicate a stress between heavy and light. Using a combination of the two stress marks we already have in operation to indicate an intermediate stress, we might re-scan the first line of the stanza this way:

1   The darkness brings no quiet here, the light

Then we could point out that the intermediate accent on 'no' makes the middle foot of line 1 partly spondaic. Line 2 opens with a spondee, and lines 3 and 4 are strictly iambic.

Having established the fairly regular metre of the opening stanza, let us consider the second stanza of the poem:

5   I see the hurrying crowds, the clasp, the flight,

6   Faces that touch, eyes that are dim with pain:

7   I see the hoarse wheels turn, and the great train

8   Move labouring out into the bourneless night.

This stanza introduces quite a bit of variation to the iambic metre established in the opening four lines. The middle foot of line 5 has an extra unaccented syllable, making it an anapest rather than an iamb. This extra syllable quickens the tempo of the line. A similar effect occurs in line 6, where the substitution of trochees for iambs in the first and third feet results in consecutive unaccented syllables. The pace in lines 7 and 8 slows significantly with three spondees, two of which combine, in the final foot of line 7 and the first foot of line 8, to create four consecutive accented syllables.

The metre of the poem's closing stanza—a sestet—is once again fairly regular:

9   So many souls within its dim recesses,

10   So many bright, so many mournful eyes:

11   Mine eyes that watch grow fixed with dreams and guesses;

12   What threads of life, what hidden histories,

13   What sweet or passionate dreams and dark distresses,

14   What unknown thoughts, what various agonies.

The iambic metre is complicated by the extra syllable of feminine rhyme in lines 9, 11, and 13 ('re*cesses*', '*guesses*', 'dis*tresses*'—two-syllable rhymes are called *feminine*) and by the paired unaccented syllables that close lines 12 and 14 (each of these lines ends with a *pyrrhic* foot, consisting of two unaccented syllables). The second foot of line 14 is partly spondaic, for although the iambic metre calls for a stress on the second syllable ('un-'), the word 'unknown' is naturally stressed on its second syllable. These long syllables slow the first part of the final line, while the short ones in the second part speed it up.

Thus far we have considered the metrics of this poem only in terms of its pleasing variation within a firmly established pattern. We can see how the pattern is established in the first stanza and varied in the second stanza before it is reasserted in the closing six lines. Now we are in a position to deal with the question of the relation of the metrics to the meaning of the poem.

The railway station is the site of the speaker's contemplation about the diversity of human experience. His role as a passive observer is contrasted with the real joys and suffering of the people he watches in lines 10–11, where his eyes watch the 'bright' and 'mournful eyes' of others, trying to guess at their individual histories. The opening stanza is visual and aural. The speaker sets the scene of the railway station, describing the atmosphere with a series of sights and sounds in lines 3–4. These are frozen images, caught in the regular iambic metre of the opening stanza.

In the second stanza the speaker describes the activity of the railway station. As we read lines 5–6 we feel the tempo of the poem quickening, and this helps us imagine the hurrying crowds the speaker describes. In lines 7–8 the focus shifts to the train as it pulls out of the station. The longer accented syllables slow the pace of the poem, aptly reflecting the train as it labours to gather speed. By the end of the stanza the train has departed, and the poem has resumed its iambic metre.

The final stanza focuses on the speaker as he speculates on what he has been observing. His thoughts are carried along in fairly regular iambic lines, a pattern that contrasts with the variable metre that is used to describe the action in the second stanza. Metrics help reinforce the distinction between the speaker and the activity of the railway station. The speaker is not a participant in the events: he is an observer.

Before considering rhyme and other sound effects further, we need to look at one last important dimension of metrics. The standard line of English verse that is meant to be spoken rather than sung is a line of five iambic feet—iambic pentameter. This is the basic line of Chaucer's *Canterbury Tales*, of Spenser's *Faerie Queene*, of Shakespeare's plays, of Milton's *Paradise Lost*, of the satires of Dryden and Pope, of Byron's *Don Juan*, of Wordsworth's *The Prelude*, of Browning's *The Ring and the Book*. This line often appears unrhymed, as in Shakespeare's plays (for the most part), *Paradise Lost*, and *The Prelude*, or in pairs of rhymed lines. Technically, the unrhymed iambic pentameter line is called *blank verse*; the paired rhymes are called *couplets*. In both of these iambic pentameter forms, an important element is the mid-line pause, or *caesura*. Varying the location of the caesura is an important way of preventing monotony in blank verse and pentameter couplets. Consider, for example, these opening lines of Book II of *Paradise Lost*:

> High on a Throne of Royal State, which far
> Outshone the wealth of *Ormus* and of *Ind,*
> Or where the gorgeous East with riches hand
> Show'rs on her King's *Barbaric* Pearl and Gold,
> 5 Satan exalted sat, by merit rais'd
> To that bad eminence; and from despair
> Thus high uplifted beyond hope, aspires
> Beyond thus high, insatiate to pursue
> Vain was with Heav'n, and by success untaught
> 10 His proud imaginations thus display'd.

If we locate the obvious caesuras—those indicated by internal punctuation marks—we find this situation:

line 1 – end of 4th foot
line 2 – none
line 3 – none
line 4 – none
line 5 – end of 3rd foot
line 6 – end of 3rd foot
line 7 – end of 4th foot
line 8 – end of 2nd foot
line 9 – end of 2nd foot
line 10 – none

In reading a poem aloud, we will find ourselves pausing slightly at some point in nearly every line, whether a pause is indicated by punctuation or not. Thus, we can mark the whole passage this way, using a single slash for a slight pause, two for a noticeable one, and three for a full stop:

> High on a throne of Royal State, // which far
> Outshone / the wealth of Ormus / and of Ind,

> Or where the gorgeous East / with riches hand
> Show'rs on her kings / Barbaric Peal and Gold,
> 5 Satan exalted sat, // by merit rais'd
> To that bad eminence; /// and from despair
> Thus high uplifted beyond hope, // aspires
> Beyond thus high, // insatiate to pursue
> Vain war with Heav'n, // and by success untaught
> 10 His proud imaginations / thus display'd.

By varying end-stopped lines with enjambed, and deploying caesuras of varying strengths at different points in his line, Milton continually shifts his pauses to prevent the march of his lines from growing wearisome. He also uses substitute feet frequently—especially a trochee or spondee in the first foot of a line. There are three trochees and one spondee in the first feet of these ten lines.

Now consider Alexander Pope's use of enjambment, caesura, and substitution of feet in the following lines. Pope uses a tight form, with punctuation coming nearly always at the end of each couplet. These closed couplets (as opposed to enjambed, or open, couplets) in iambic pentameter are called *heroic couplets* because they were the standard verse form of Restoration heroic drama (but they might better be called satiric, because they have been most successful in the satiric poems of John Dryden, Pope, and Samuel Johnson).

Using such a tight form as the heroic couplet requires great skill to avoid monotony. When we read only the real masters of such a form, we tend to take such skills for granted, but it is far from easy. In the following two passages, from his 'Essay on Criticism', we find Pope discussing poetic blunders and poetic skill, modulating his own verse deftly to illustrate the points he is making. (The *Alexandrine* referred to is an iambic hexameter line, occasionally used for variety in English iambic pentameter forms.)

> These equal syllables alone require,
> Though oft the ear the open vowels tire;
> While expletives their feeble aid do join;
> And ten low words oft creep in one dull line:
> While they ring round the same unvaried chimes,
> With sure returns of still expected rhymes;
> Where'er you find 'the cooling western breeze',
> In the next line, it 'whispers through the trees':
> If crystal streams 'with pleasing murmurs creep',
> The reader's threatened (not in vain) with 'sleep':
> Then, at the last and only couplet fraught
> With some unmeaning thing they call a thought,
> A needless Alexandrine ends the song
> That, like a wounded snake, drags its slow length along.

True ease in writing comes from art, not chance,
As those move easiest who have learned to dance.
'Tis not enough no harshness gives offence,
The sound must seem an Echo to the sense:
Soft is the strain when Zephyr gently blows,
And the smooth stream in smoother numbers flows;
But when loud surges lash the sounding shore,
The hoarse, rough verse should like the torrent roar:
When Ajax strives some rock's vast weight to throw,
The line too labours, and the words move slow;
Not so, when swift Camilla scours the plain,
Flies o'er th' unbending corn, and skims along the main.

Rhyme is an important element in musical poetry, but much less so in dramatic poetry—where it can be too artificial—or in meditative poetry. Associated with rhyme as elements designed to generate a pleasure in sound that is almost purely aesthetic are such devices as *alliteration* and *assonance*. Alliteration is the repetition of the same sound at the beginning of words in the same line or adjacent lines. Assonance is the repetition of vowel sounds in the same or adjacent lines. For full rhyme we require the same vowel sounds that end in the same consonantal sounds. 'Fight' and 'foot' are alliterative. 'Fight' and 'bike' are assonant, 'Fight' and 'fire' are both assonant and alliterative but do not make a rhyme. 'Fight' and 'bite' make a rhyme. Consider the metrical and sonic effects in this stanza of a poem by Swinburne:

Till the slow sea rise and the sheer cliff crumble,
Till terrace and meadow the deep gulfs drink,
Till the strength of the waves of the high tides humble
The fields that lessen, the rocks that shrink,
Here now in his triumph where all things falter,
Stretched out on the spoils that his own hand spread,
As a god self-slain on his own strange altar,
Death lies dead.

The metre is mainly a mixture of anapests and spondees—an exotic combination of rapid and slow feet. When reading it, try to discern a pattern in the way the feet are combined. Is there variation in the pattern? Consider also what rhyme, assonance, and alliteration contribute to the pattern.

In addition to its purely aesthetic or decorative effect, designed to charm the reader out of a critical posture and into a receptive one, rhyme can be used for the opposite effect. In satiric or comic verse, strained rhymes are often used to awaken the reader's wits and give a comic kind of pleasure. In the following stanza from Byron's *Don Juan*, the poet uses feminine and even triple rhyme with deliberate clumsiness:

> 'Tis pity learnèd virgins ever wed
>   With persons of no sort of education,
>   Or gentlemen, who, though well born and bred,
>   Grow tired of scientific conversation:
>   I don't choose to say much upon this head,
>   I'm a plain man, and in a single station,
>   But—Oh! ye lords of ladies intellectual,
>   Inform us truly, have they not hen-peck'd you all?

The last rhyme in particular is surprising, audacious, and deliberately strained—echoing in this way the sense of the stanza. Like imagery and metrics, rhyme can be used harmoniously or ironically to establish or to break a mood.

Before closing, we should note that it is customary to indicate the rhyme scheme of any given poetic selection by assigning letters of the alphabet to each rhyming sound, repeating each letter as the sound is repeated. The rhyme scheme of the Byron stanza we just considered would be designated this way: *abababcc*, with *a* standing for the sounds in *wed*, *bred*, and *head*; *b*, for . . . *ation*; and *c*, for . . . *ectual* and . . . *eck'd you all*.

APPROACHING A POEM

Earlier we suggested that an initial reading of a poem is like meeting a person for the first time. We do not, if we are honest, keep in readiness a number of different approaches to poems or to people. We try to keep our integrity. But at the same time we must recognize and accept the otherness that we face. In getting to know a person or a poem we make the kind of accommodation that we have called tact. But we do not pretend, and we try not to let our prejudices govern the way we respond to superficial qualities. We do not judge people by the clothes they are wearing, and we do not judge a poem by words or ideas taken out of their full poetic context. We do not consider a statement in a poem without attention to its dramatic context, the overtones generated by its metaphors and ironies, the mood established by its metrics. And we try to give each element of every poem its proper weight.

Of course, there can be no single method for treating every poem with tact. What is required is a flexible procedure through which we can begin to understand the nature of any poem. The suggestions below are intended to facilitate such a procedure. Like everything else in this book they should serve as scaffolding only—a temporary structure inside of which the real building takes shape. Like any scaffolding, this one must be discarded as soon as it becomes constricting or loses its usefulness. This procedure is not designed to be memorized and applied mechanically. Like good manners learned by rote, it will have served its purpose once it has been replaced by naturally tactful behaviour.

1. Try to grasp the expressive dimension of the poem first. This means getting a clear sense of the nature and situation of the speaker. What are the circumstances under which he or she says, writes, or thinks these words? Who hears them? Are they part of an ongoing action that is implied by them?

2. Consider the relative importance of the narrative–dramatic dimension and the descriptive–meditative dimension in the poem. Is the main interest psychological or philosophical—in character or in idea? Or is the poem's verbal playfulness or music its main reason for being? How do the nature of the speaker and the situation in which the speaker talks colour the ideas and attitudes presented?

3. After you have a sense of the poem's larger, expressive dimension, re-read it with particular attention to the play of language. Consider the way that metaphor and irony colour the ideas and situations. How does the language work to characterize the speaker or to colour the ideas presented with shadings of attitude? How important is sheer wordplay or verbal wit in the poem? How well do the images and ideas fit together and reinforce one another in a metaphoric or ironic way?

4. Re-read the poem yet again, this time with special attention to its musical dimension. To the extent that it seems important, analyze the relation of rhythm and rhyme to the expressive dimension of the poem.

5. Throughout this process, reading the poem aloud can help you detect emphases and locate problems. Parts of a poem you haven't fully understood will prove troublesome in the reading. Questions of tone and attitude will become more insistent in oral performance. Thus, it is advisable to work toward a reading performance as a final check on the degree to which you have mastered situation, ideas, images, attitudes, and music. An expert may be able to read through a piece of piano music and hear in her mind a perfect performance of it. Most of us need to tap out the notes before we can grasp melodies, harmonies, and rhythms with any sureness. Reading poetry aloud helps us establish our grasp of it—especially if a patient and knowledgeable instructor is there to correct our performance and encourage us to try again.

One last piece of advice, in the form of some lines by the Spanish poet Antonio Machado, translated by Robert Bly:

> People possess four things
> that are no good at sea
> anchor, rudder, oars
> And the fear of going down.

Geoffrey Chaucer

1342–1400

Geoffrey Chaucer was born in the early 1340s, the son of a prosperous merchant family. A member of diplomatic missions, a controller of customs, a justice of the peace, and a member of parliament, he moved in royal circles throughout his life. In his longest work—and an unfinished one—*The Canterbury Tales*, a group of pilgrims travelling together to Canterbury to worship at the shrine of Thomas à Becket decide to recount two tales each along the way. The 'General Prologue'

introduces the pilgrims, and 'The Miller's Tale', the second tale in the series, is a fabliau, a comic account of the lower classes.

Chaucer is buried in Westminster Abbey because he was a member of the parish and a tenant of the Abbey. No one in England in 1400, the year of his death, could have imagined that Chaucer's tomb would be the beginning of Poets' Corner, nor that Chaucer himself would come to be acknowledged as the father of poetry in English.

From *The Canterbury Tales*

The Miller's Prologue and Tale

FROM THE GENERAL PROLOGUE

The MILLERE was a stout carl[1] for the nones;[2]
Ful byg[3] he was of brawn, and eek of bones.
That proved wel, for over al[4] ther he cam,
At wrastlynge he wolde have alwey the ram.[5]
5   He was short-sholdred,[6] brood, a thikke knarre;[7]
Ther was no dore that he nolde[8] heve of harre,[9]
Or breke it at a rennyng[10] with his heed.
His berd as any sowe or foxe was reed,
And therto brood, as though it were a spade.
10   Upon the cop[11] right of his nose he hade

1 fellow
2 indeed
3 strong
4 wherever
5 *have . . . ram*: always win the ram (given as a prize)
6 stoutly built (with a thick neck)
7 stout fellow
8 would not
9 lift off its hinges
10 by running up against it
11 top

A werte,[12] and theron stood a toft of herys,[13]
Reed as the brustles[14] of a sowes erys;[15]
His nosethirles[16] blake were and wyde.
A swerd and a bokeler bar he by his side.

15 His mouth as greet was as a greet forneys.[17]
He was a janglere[18] and a goliardeys,[19]
And that was moost of synne and harlotries.
Wel koude he stelen corn[20] and tollen thries;[21]
And yet he hadde a thombe of gold,[22] pardee.[23]

20 A whit cote and a blew hood wered he.
A baggepipe wel koude he blowe and sowne,[24]
And therwithal he broghte us out of towne.

The Miller's Prologue

Heere folwen the wordes bitwene the Hoost and the Millere.

Whan that the knight had thus his tale ytoold,
In al the route nas ther yong ne oold
That he ne seyde it was a noble storie
And worthy for to drawen to memorie,[25]

5 And namely the gentils[26] everichon.
Oure Hooste lough and swoor, 'So moot I gon,
This gooth aright; unbokeled is the male.[27]
Lat se now who shal telle another tale;
For trewely the game is wel bigonne.

10 Now telleth ye, sir Monk, if that ye konne,[28]
Somwhat to quite with[29] the Knyghtes tale.'
The Millere, that for dronken[30] was al pale,

12 wart
13 tuft of hairs
14 bristles
15 sow's ears
16 nostrils
17 large cauldron
18 a teller of dirty stories
19 buffoon
20 steal grain
21 take toll (payment) three times
22 golden thumb; an ironic reference to a proverb, with the implication that there are no honest millers
23 indeed
24 play
25 *drawen . . . memorie*: remember
26 gentlefolk
27 *unbokeled . . . male*: the pouch is opened, i.e. the game is well begun
28 know
29 with which to repay, or match
30 because of being drunk

So that unnethe[31] upon his hors he sat,
He nolde avalen[32] neither hood ne hat,
15 Ne abyde no man for his curteisie,
But in Pilates voys[33] he gan to crie,
And swoor, 'By armes, and by blood and bones,
I kan a noble tale for the nones,
With which I wol now quite[34] the Knyghtes tale.'
20 Oure Hooste saugh that he was dronke of ale,
And seyde, 'Abyd,[35] Robyn, my leeve[36] brother;
Som better man shal telle us first another.
Abyd, and lat us werken thriftily.'[37]
     'By Goddes soule,' Quod he, 'that wol nat I;
25 For I wol speke or elles go my wey.'
Oure Hoost answerde, 'Tel on, a devel wey![38]
Thou art a fool; thy wit is overcome.'
     'Now herkneth', quod the Millere, 'alle and some![39]
But first I make a protestacioun
30 That I am dronke; I knowe it by my soun.
And therefore if that I mysspeke or seye,
Wyte it[40] the ale of Southwerk, I you preye.
For I wol telle a lengende and a lyf
Bothe of a carpenter and of his wyf,
35 How that a clerk hath set the wrightes cappe.'[41]
     The Reve answerde and seyde, 'Stynt thy clappe![42]
Lat be thy lewed dronken harlotrye.
It is a synne and eek a greet folye
To apeyren[43] any man, or hym defame,
40 And eek to bryngen wyves in swich fame.
Thou mayst ynogh of othere thynges seyn.'
     This dronke Millere spak ful soone ageyn[44]
And seyde, 'Leve brother Osewold,
Who hath no wyf, he is no cokewold.[45]

31 hardly
32 take off
33 a loud, ranting voice
34 pay back, requite
35 wait
36 dear
37 properly
38 in the Devil's name
39 one and all
40 blame it on
41 *set . . . cappe*: deceived, made a fool of the carpenter
42 stop your noisy talk, hold your tongue
43 injure
44 in reply
45 cuckold

45 But I sey nat therfore that thou art oon;
Ther been ful goode wyves many oon,
And evere a thousand goode ayeyns[46] oon badde.
That knowestow wel thyself, but if thou madde.[47]
Why artow angry with my tale now?

50 I have a wyf, pardee, as wel as thow;
Yet nolde I, for the oxen in my plogh,
Take upon me moore than ynogh,
As demen of[48] myself that I were oon;[49]
I wol bileve[50] wel that I am noon.

55 An housbonde shal nat been inquisityf
Of Goddes pryvetee,[51] nor of his wyf.
So he may fynde Goddes foyson[52] there,
Of the remenant nedeth nat enquere.'
            What sholde I moore seyn, but this Millere

60 He nolde his wordes for no man forbere,
But tolde his cherles[53] tale in his manere.
M'athynketh[54] that I shal reherce[55] it here.
And therefore every gentil wight I preye,
For Goddes love, demeth nat that I seye

65 Of yvel entente, but for I moot reherce
Hir tales alle, be they bettre or werse,
Or elles falsen som of my mateere.
And therefore, whoso list it nat yheere,
Turne over the leef and chese[56] another tale;

70 For he shal fynde ynowe, grete and smale,[57]
Of storial[58] thyng that toucheth[59] gentillesse,
And eek moralitee and hoolynesse.
Blameth nat me if that ye chese amys.
The Millere is a cherl; ye knowe wel this.

75 So was the Reve eek and othere mo,
And harlotrie they tolden bothe two.

46 as opposed to
47 go mad
48 to judge, believe of
49 i.e. a cuckold
50 want to believe
51 secrets
52 God's plenty
53 low-born fellows'
54 it displeases me, I regret
55 repeat, narrate
56 choose
57 of every sort
58 historical, true
59 concerns

Avyseth yow,[60] and put me out of blame;
And eek men shal nat maken ernest of game.[61]

The Miller's Tale

Heere bigynneth the Millere his tale.

Whilom ther was dwellynge at Oxenford
A riche gnof,[62] that gestes[63] heeld to bord,[64]
And of his craft he was a carpenter.
With hym ther was dwellynge a poure scoler,[65]
5   Hadde lerned art,[66] but al his fantasye[67]
Was turned for to lerne astrologye,
And koude[68] a certeyn of conclusiouns,[69]
To demen by interrograciouns,[70]
If that men asked hym, in certain houres
10   Whan that men sholde have droghte or elles shoures,
Or if men asked hym what sholde bifalle
Of every thyng; I may nat rekene hem alle.
    This clerk was cleped[71] hende[72] Nicholas.
Of deerne[73] love he koude and of solas;[74]
15   And therto he was sleigh[75] and ful privee,[76]
And lyk a mayden meke for to see.
A chamber hadde he in that hostelrye
Allone, withouten any compaignye,
Ful fetisly ydight with herbes swoote;[77]
20   And he hymself as sweete as is the roote
Of lycorys or any cetewale.[78]
His Almageste,[79] and bookes grete and smale,

60 consider, think about (this)
61 *make . . . game*: take a joke seriously
62 churl
63 lodgers
64 as boarders
65 impoverished student
66 the arts curriculum at university, esp. logic
67 fancy, desire
68 knew
69 *a . . . conclusions*: a certain number of astrological operations
70 *To . . . interrograciouns*: to determine by scientific calculations
71 named
72 courteous
73 secret
74 pleasure, satisfaction (of sexual desires)
75 sly
76 discreet, secretive
77 *Ful . . . swoote*: very elegantly adorned with sweet-smelling herbs
78 zedoary (a spice resembling ginger, used as a condiment and stimulant)
79 ptolemy's treatise on astrology

His astrelabie,[80] longynge for[81] his art,
His augrym stones[82] layen faire apart,
25 On shelves couched[83] at his beddes heed;
His presse[84] ycovered with a faldyng reed;[85]
And al above ther lay a gay sautrie,[86]
On which he made a-nyghtes[87] melodie
So sweetly that all the chambre rong;
30 And *Angelus ad virginem*[88] he song;
And after that he song the Kynges Noote.[89]
Ful often blessed was his myrie throte.
And thus this sweete clerk his ryme spente
After his freendes fyndyng and his rente.[90]
35   This carpenter hadde wedded newe a wyf,
Which that he lovede moore than his lyf;
Of eighteteene yeer she was of age.
Jalous he was, and heeld hire narwe[91] in cage,
For she was wylde and yong, and he was old
40 And demed hymself been lik a cokewold.
He knew nat Catoun,[92] for his wit was rude,[93]
That bad man sholde wedde his simylitude.[94]
Men sholde wedden after hire estaat,
For youthe and elde[95] is often at debaat.
45 But sith that he was fallen in the snare,
He moste endure, as oother folk, his care.
    Fair was this yonge wyf, and therwithal
As any wezel hir body gent[96] and smal.
A ceynt[97] she werede, barred[98] al of silk,
50 A barmclooth[99] as whit as morne milk

---

80 astrolabe
81 belonging to, necessary for (his art, astronomy)
82 counters, for use on an abacus
83 arranged
84 cupboard, linen press
85 coarse red woollen cloth
86 psaltry
87 at night
88 'The angel to the virgin [Mary]'
89 The King's Tune
90 *After . . . rente*: according to what his friends provided and his income
91 closely
92 cato, author of an elementary school text
93 ignorant, unlearned
94 equal, counterpart
95 old age
96 delicate
97 belt
98 with decorative strips
99 apron

Upon hir lendes,[1] ful of many a goore.[2]
Whit was hir smok,[3] and broyden[4] al bifoore
And eek bihynde, on hir coler[5] aboute,
Of col-blak silk, withinne and eek withoute.
55   The tapes[6] of hir white voluper[7]
Were of the same suyte of[8] hir coler;
Hir filet[9] brood of silk, and set ful hye.
And sikerly[10] she hadde a likerous[11] ye;
Ful smale ypulled[12] were hire browes two,
60   And tho were bent and blake as any sloo.[13]
She was ful moore blisful on to see
Than is the newe pere-jonette[14] tree,
And softer than the wolle[15] is of a wether.[16]
And by hir girdle[17] heeng a purs of lether,
65   Tasseled with silk and perled[18] with latoun.[19]
In al this world, to seken up and doun,
There nys no man so wys that koude thenche[20]
So gay a popelote[21] or swich a wenche.
Ful brighter was the shynyng of hir hewe
70   Than in the Tour[22] the noble[23] yforged newe.
But of hir song, it was as loude and yerne[24]
As any swalwe[25] sittynge on a berne.[26]
Therto she koude skippe and make game,
As any kyde or calf folwynge his dame.[27]

1 loins
2 flounce
3 shift, undergarment (over which aprons and more elaborate items of clothing are worn)
4 embroidered
5 collar
6 ribbons
7 cap
8 same colour as
9 headband
10 truly
11 flirtatious
12 plucked
13 sloe (a plum-like fruit)
14 early-ripe pear
15 wool
16 sheep (ram)
17 belt
18 adorned
19 a brass-like alloy
20 imagine
21 little doll
22 Tower of London (the mint)
23 a gold coin
24 eager, lively
25 swallow
26 barn
27 mother (dam)

75 Hir mouth was sweete as bragot[28] or the meeth,[29]
Or hoord of apples leyd in hey or heeth.
Wynsynge[30] she was, as is a joly[31] colt,
Long as a mast, and upright as a bolt.[32]
A brooch she baar upon hir lowe coler,
80 As brood as is the boos of a bokeler.[33]
Hir shoes were laced on hir legges hye.
She was a prymerole, a piggesnye,[34]
For any lord to leggen[35] in his bedde,
Or yet for any good yeman to wedde.

85 　　Now, sire, and eft,[36] sire, so bifel the cas
That on a day this hende Nicholas
Fil with this yonge wyf to rage[37] and pleye,
Whil that hir housbonde was at Oseneye,
As clerkes ben ful subtile and ful queynte;[38]
90 And prively he caughte hire by the queynte,[39]
And seyde, 'Ywis,[40] but if ich have my wille,
For deerne[41] love of thee, lemman,[42] I spille.'[43]
And heeld hire harde by the haunchebones,[44]
And seyde, 'Lemman, love me al atones,[45]
95 Or I wol dyen, also[46] God me save!'
And she sproong[47] as a colt dooth in the trave,[48]
And with hir heed she wryed faste[49] awey,
And seyde, 'I wol nat kisse thee, by my fey!
Why, lat be!' quod she. 'Lat be, Nicholas,
100 Or I wol crie "out, harrow" and "allas"!
Do wey youre handes, for youre curteisye!'

28 country drink
29 mead
30 skittish
31 spirited
32 crossbow bolt
33 *boos . . . bokeler*: raised centre of a shield
34 primrose, 'pig's eye', names of flowers
35 lay
36 again
37 sport (sexually)
38 ingenious, clever
39 elegant, pleasing (thing), i.e. pudendum
40 truly, indeed
41 secret
42 my love, sweetheart
43 die
44 thighs
45 at once, immediately
46 as
47 sprang
48 frame for holding a horse to be shod
49 turned rapidly, twisted

This Nicholas gan mercy for to crye,
And spak so faire, and profred him[50] so faste,
That she hir love hym graunted atte laste,
105 And swoor hir ooth, by Seint Thomas of Kent,[51]
That she wol been at his comandement,
Whan that she may hir leyser[52] wel espie.
'Myn housbonde is so ful of jalousie
That but ye wayte[53] wel and been privee,[54]
110 I woot right wel I nam but deed,' quod she.
'Ye moste been ful deerne,[55] as in this cas.'
    'Nay, therof care thee noght,' quod Nicholas.
'A clerk hadde litherly biset his whyle,[56]
But if he koude a carpenter bigyle.'
115 And thus they been accorded and ysworn
To wayte a tyme, as I have told biforn.
    Whan Nicholas had doon thus everideel
And thakked[57] hire aboute the lendes[58] weel,
He kiste hire sweete and taketh his sawtrie,
120 And pleyeth faste, and maketh melodie.
    Thanne fil it thus, that to the paryssh chirche,
Cristes owene wekes for to wirche,
This goode wyf went on an haliday.[59]
Hir forheed shoon as bright as any day,
125 So was it wasshen whan she leet[60] hir werk.
Now was ther of that chirche a parissh clerk,
The which that was ycleped Absolon.
Crul[61] was his heer, and as the gold it shoon,
And strouted as a fanne[62] large and brode;
130 Ful streight and evene lay his joly shode.[63]
His rode[64] was reed, his eyen greye as goos.
With Poules window[65] corven[66] on his shoos,

50 pressed his suit
51 Thomas Becket
52 opportunity
53 await, watch for (an opportunity)
54 discreet, secretive
55 secretive
56 *litherly . . . whyle*: wasted his time
57 patted
58 loins
59 holy day
60 left
61 curled
62 stretched out like a fan
63 parted hair
64 complexion
65 window of St Paul's
66 carved

In hoses rede he wente fetisly.[67]
Yclad he was ful smal[68] and properly

135 Al in a kirtel[69] of a light waget;[70]
Ful faire and thikke been the poyntes[71] set.
And thereupon he hadde a gay surplys[72]
As whit as is the blosme upon the rys.[73]
A myrie child[74] he was, so God me save.

140 Wel koude he laten blood,[75] and clippe[76] and shave,
And maken a chartre[77] of lond or acquitaunce.[78]
In twenty manere[79] koude he trippe and daunce
After the scole[80] of Oxenforde tho,
And with his legges casten[81] to and fro,

145 And pleyen songes on a smal rubible;[82]
Therto he song som tyme a loud quynyble;[83]
And as wel koude he pleye on a giterne.[84]
In al the toun nas brewhous ne taverne
That he ne visited with his solas,[85]

150 Ther any gaylard tappestere[86] was.
But sooth so seyn, he was somdeel squaymous[87]
Of fartyng, and of speche daungerous.[88]
This Absolon, that jolif[89] was and gay,
Gooth with a sencer[90] on the haliday,

155 Sensynge[91] the wyves of the parisshe faste;
And many a lovely look on hem he caste,
And namely on this carpenteris wyf.

67 elegantly
68 tightly, in close-fitting clothes
69 tunic
70 light blue
71 laces
72 surplice (ecclesiastical gown)
73 twig
74 young man
75 let blood (as a medical treatment)
76 cut hair
77 deed
78 quittance (legal release of property)
79 twenty ways
80 in the style, fashion
81 move quickly
82 rebeck, a kind of fiddle
83 high treble
84 cithern, a stringed instrument
85 entertainment
86 merry barmaid
87 somewhat squeamish
88 fastidious
89 pretty, lively
90 censer
91 censing

To looke on hire hym thoughte a myrie lyf,
She was so proper and sweete and likerous.
160 I dar wel seyn, if she hadde been a mous,
And he a cat, he wolde hire hente anon.
This parissh clerk, this joly Absolon,
Hath in his herte swich a love-longynge
That of no wyf took he noon offrynge;
165 For curteisie, he seyde, he wolde noon.

    The moone, whan it was nyght, ful brighte shoon,
And Absolon his gyterne hath ytake;
For paramours[92] he thoghte for to wake.
And forth he gooth, jolif and amorous,
170 Til he cam to the carpenteres hous
A litel after cokkes hadde ycrowe,
And dressed hym[93] up by a shot-wyndowe[94]
That was upon the carpenteris wal.
He syngeth in his voys gentil and smal,[95]
175 'Now, deere lady, if thy wille be,
I praye yow that ye wole rewe[96] on me,'
Ful wel acordaunt to[97] his gyternynge.[98]
This carpenter awook, and herde him synge,
And spak unto his wyf, and seyde anon,
180 'What! Alison! Herestow nat Absolon,
That chaunteth[99] thus under oure boures[1] wal?'
And she answerde hir housbonde therwithal,
'Yis, God woot, John, I here it every deel.'[2]

    This passeth forth; what wol ye bet than weel?[3]
185 Fro day to day this joly Absolon
So woweth hire that hym is wo bigon.
He waketh al the nyght and al the day;
He kembeth[4] his lokkes brode, and made hym gay;
He woweth hire by meenes[5] and brocage,[6]
190 And swoor he wolde been hir owene page;

---

92 for the sake of love
93 took his place
94 hinged window (one that opens and closes)
95 high
96 have mercy
97 in harmony with
98 playing on the cithern
99 sings
 1 next to our bedchamber's
 2 every bit
 3 better than well (i.e. what more would you have?)
 4 combs
 5 go-betweens, intermediaries
 6 use of an agent

He syngeth, brokkynge[7] as a nyghtyngale;
He sente hire pyment,[8] meeth, and spiced ale,
And wafres,[9] pipyng hoot out of the gleede;[10]
And, for she was of town, he profred meede;[11]

195   For som folk wol ben wonnen for richesse,
And somme for strokes,[12] and somme for gentillesse.
     Somtyme, to shewe his lightnesse[13] and maistrye,[14]
He pleyeth Herodes[15] upon a scaffold hye.[16]
But what availleth hym as in this cas?

200   She loveth so this hende Nicholas
That Absolon may blowe the bukkes horn;[17]
He ne hadde for his labour but a scorn.
And thus she maketh Absolon hire ape,
And al his ernest turneth til a jape.[18]

205   Ful sooth is this proverbe, it is no lye,
Men seyn right thus: 'Alwey the nye slye[19]
Maketh the ferre leeve to be looth.'[20]
For though that Absolon be wood or wrooth,
By cause that he fer was from hire sight,

210   This nye Nicholas stood in his light.[21]
     Now ber thee wel, thou hende Nicholas,
For Absolon may waille and synge 'allas'.
And so bifel it on a Saterday,
This carpenter was goon til Osenay;

215   And hende Nicholas and Alisoun
Acorded been to this conclusioun,
That Nicholas shal shapen hym a wyle[22]
This sely[23] jalous housbonde to bigyle;
And if so be the game wente aright,

220   She sholde slepen in his arm al nyght.
For this was his desir and hire also.

---

7 trilling
8 spiced, sweetened wine
9 cakes
10 fire
11 offered money
12 i.e. by force
13 agility
14 skill
15 the part of Herod
16 stage
17 *blowe . . . horn*: go whistle
18 joke
19 nigh (at hand) sly one
20 *ferre . . . looth*: distant loved one to be disliked
21 in his way (i.e. prevented his being seen)
22 trick
23 innocent, simple, hapless

And right anon, witouten wordes mo,
This Nicholas no lenger wolde tarie,
But dooth ful softe unto his chamber carie
225 Bothe mete and drynke for a day or tweye,
And to hire housbonde bad hire for to seye,
If that he axed after Nicholas,
She sholde seye she nyste where he was;
Of al that day she saugh hym nat with ye;
230 She trowed[24] that he was in maladye,[25]
For, for no cry hir mayde koude hum calle,
He nolde answere for thyng that myghte falle.[26]
  This passeth forth al thilke Saterday,
That Nicholas stille in his chamber lay,
235 And eet and sleep, or dide what hym leste,
Til Sonday, that the sonne gooth to reste.
This sely carpenter hath greet merveyle
Of[27] Nicholas, or what thyng myghte hym eyle,[28]
And seyde, 'I am adrad, by Seint Thomas,
240 It stondeth nat aright with Nicholas.
God shilde[29] that he deyed sodeynly!
This world is now ful tikel,[30] sikerly.
I saugh today a cors[31] yborn to chirche
That now, on Monday last, I saugh hym[32] wirche.[33]
245 'Go up,' quod he unto his knave[34] anoon,
'Clepe[35] at his dore, or knokke with a stoon.
Looke how it is, and tel me boldely.'
  This knave gooth hym up ful sturdily,[36]
And at the chambre dore whil that he stood,
250 He cride and knocked as that he were wood,
'What, how! What do ye, maister Nicholay?
How may ye slepen al the longe day?'
  But al for noght; he herde nat a word.
An hole he foond, ful lowe upon a bord,
255 Ther as the cat was wont in for to crepe,

24 believed
25 ill
26 befall, happen
27 *hath . . . Of*: wondered about
28 ail
29 God forbid
30 unstable, ticklish
31 corpse
32 *That . . . him*: whom
33 work
34 servant
35 call out
36 boldly

And at that hole he looked in ful depe,
And at the laste he hadde of hym a sight.
This Nicholas sat evere capyng upright,[37]
As he had kiked[38] on the newe moone.

260   Adoun he gooth, and tolde his maister soone[39]
In what array[40] he saugh this ilke man.
     This carpenter to blessen hym bigan,
And seyde, 'Help us, Seinte Frydeswyde![41]
A man woot litel what hym shal bityde.

265   This an is falle, with his astromye,[42]
In som woodnesse or in som agonye.[43]
I thoghte ay wel how that it sholde be!
Men sholde nat knowe of Goddes pryvetee.[44]
Ye, blessed be alwey a lewed man

270   That noght but oonly his bileve kan![45]
So ferde[46] another clerk with astromye;
He walked in the feeldes for to prye[47]
Upon the sterres, what ther sholde bifalle,
Til he was in a marle-pit[48] yfalle;

275   He saugh nat that. But yet, by Seint Thomas,
Me reweth soore of[49] hende Nicholas.
He shal be rated of[50] his studiyng,
If that I may, by Jhesus, hevene kyng!
Get me a staf, that I may underspore,[51]

280   Whil that thou, Robyn, hevest up the dore.
He shal[52] out of his studiyng, as I gesse.'
And to the chambre dore he gan hym dresse.
His knave was a strong carl for the nones,
And by the haspe he haaf it of[53] atones;[54]

285   Into the floor the dore fil anon.

37 gaping straight up
38 gazed
39 immediately
40 condition
41 St Frideswide, noted for her healing powers
42 astonomy
43 fit
44 God's secrets
45 *That . . . kan!*: who knows nothing but his creed
46 fared
47 gaze
48 clay pit
49 *Me . . . of*: I feel sorry for
50 scolded for
51 pry up from under
52 shall come (verb of motion is understood)
53 heaved it off
54 at once

This Nicholas sat ay as stille as stoon,
And evere caped[55] upward into the eir.
This carpenter wende he were[56] in despeir,
And hente hym by the sholdres myghtily,
290 And shook hym harde, and cride spitously,[57]
'What! Nicholay! What, how! What, looke adoun!
Awak, and thenk on Cristes passioun!
I crouche[58] thee from elves[59] and fro wightes.'[60]
Therwith the nyght-spel[61] seyde he anon-rightes[62]
295 On foure halves of the hous aboute,
And on the threshfold of the dore withoute:
'Jhesu Crist and Seinte Benedight,
Blesse this hous from every wikked wight,[63]
For nyghtes verye,[64] the white *pater-noster*![65]
300 Where wentestow, Seinte Petres soster?'[66]
    And atte laste this hende Nicholas
Gan for to sik[67] soore, and seyde, 'Allas!
Shal al the world be lost eftsoones now?'[68]
    This carpenter answerde, 'What seystow?
305 What! Thynk on God, as we doon, men that swynke.'[69]
    This Nicholas answerde, 'Fecche me drynke,
And after wol I speke in pryvetee
Of certeyn thyng that toucheth[70] me and thee.
I wol telle it noon oother man, certeyn.'
310   This carpenter goth doun, and comth ageyn,
And broghte of myghty ale a large quart;
And whan that ech of hem had dronke his part,
This Nicholas his dore faste shette,
And doun the carpenter by hym he sette.
315   He sayde, 'John, myn hooste, lief[71] and deere,
Thou shalt upon thy trouthe swere me heere

55 gaped
56 supposed he was
57 vigorously, loudly
58 make the sign of the cross as a blessing over
59 evil spirits
60 (evil) creatures
61 a charm
62 straightaway
63 creature
64 *For . . . verye*: against evil spirits of the night (?)
65 a charm
66 *Where . . . soster?*: Where did you go, St Peter's sister?
67 sigh
68 right now
69 work
70 concerns
71 beloved

That to no wight thou shalt this conseil wreye[72]
For it is Cristes conseil that I seye,
And if thou telle it man, thou art forlore;[73]

320 For this vengeaunce thou shalt han therfore,
That if thou wreye[74] me, thou shalt be wood.'
'Nay, Crist forbade it, for his hooly blood!'
Quod tho this sely[75] man, 'I nam no labbe,[76]
Ne, though I seye, I nam nat lief to gabbe.[77]

325 Sey what thou wolt, I shal it nevere telle
To child ne wyf, by hym that harwed helle!'[78]
    'Now John,' quod Nicholas, 'I wol nat lye;
I have yfounde in my astrologye,
As I have looked in the moone bright,

330 That now a Monday next, at quarter nyght,[79]
Shal falle a reyn, and that so wilde and wood
That half so greet was nevere Noes[80] flood.
This world', he seyde, 'in lasse than an hour
Shal al be dreynt,[81] so hidous is the shour.

335 Thus shal mankynde drenche,[82] and lese hir lyf.'[83]
    This carpenter answerde, 'Allas, my wyf!
And shal she drenche? Allas, myn Alisoun!'
For sorwe of this he fil almoost adoun,
And seyde, 'Is ther no remedie in this cas?'

340 'Why, yis, for Gode,' quod hende Nicholas,
'If thou wolt werken after loore[84] and reed.[85]
Thou mayst nat werken after thyn owene heed;[86]
For thus seith Salomon, that was ful trewe:
"Werk al by conseil, and thou shalt nat rewe."[87]

345 And if thou werken wolt by good conseil,
I undertake,[88] withouten mast and seyl,
Yet shal I saven hire and thee and me.

72 reveal
73 lost
74 betray
75 innocent, ignorant, hapless
76 blabbermouth
77 *I nam . . . gabbe*: I do not like to gab
78 *hym . . . helle*: Christ, who despoiled Hell of its captives
79 a quarter way through the night; in April, after midnight
80 Noah's
81 drowned
82 drown
83 their lives
84 learning
85 (good) advice
86 head (i.e. ideas)
87 be sorry
88 affirm, declare

Hastow nat herd hou saved was Noe,
Whan that oure Lord hadde warned hym biforn
350   That al the world with water sholde be lorn?'[89]
      'Yis,' quod this Carpenter, 'ful yoore ago.'[90]
      'Hastou nat herd', quod Nicholas, 'also
The sorwe of Noe[91] with his felaweshipe,
Er that he myghte gete his wyf to shipe?
355   Hym hadde be levere, I dar wel undertake,
At thilke tyme, than alle his wetheres blake
That she hadde had a ship hirself allone.[92]
And therfore, woostou what is best to doone?
This asketh haste, and of an hastif thyng
360   Men may nat preche or maken tariyng.
      'Anon go gete us faste into this in[93]
A knedyng trogh,[94] or ellis a kymelyn,[95]
For ech of us, but looke that they be large,
In which we mowe swymme[96] as in a barge,
365   And han therinne vitaille suffisant[97]
But for a day—fy on the remenant!
The water shal aslake[98] and goon away
Aboute pryme[99] upon the nexte day.
But Robyn may nat wite of this, thy knave,
370   Ne eek thy mayde Gille I may nat save;
Axe nat why, for though thou aske me,
I wol nat tellen Goddes pryvetee.
Suffiseth thee, but if thy wittes madde,[1]
To han as greet a grace as Noe hadde.
375   Thy wyf shal I wel saven, out of doute.
Go now thy wey, and speed thee heer-aboute.[2]
      'But whan thou hast, for hire and thee and me,
Ygeten us thise knedyng tubbes thre,
Thanne shaltow hange hem in the roof ful hye,

---

89 lost
90 long ago
91 Noah, here as a character in the popular mystery plays
92 *Hym hadde be levere . . . allone*: He would have preferred, I dare affirm, that she had a ship all to herself, than have all his black sheep; i.e. he would have given all his sheep for this.
93 house
94 a large trough for kneading dough
95 a large tub for brewing beer
96 float
97 enough food
98 subside
99 around 9 a.m.
1 go mad
2 about this matter

380   That no man of oure purveiaunce³ espye.
     And whan thou thus hast doon as I have seyd,
     And hast oure vitaille faire in hem yleyd,
     And eek an ax to smyte the corde atwo,⁴
     Whan that the water comth, that we may go
385   And breke an hole an heigh, upon the gable,
     Unto the gardyn-ward,⁵ over the stable,
     That we may frely passen forth oure way,
     Whan that the grete shour is goon away.
     Thanne shaltou swymme as myrie, I undertake,
390   As dooth the white doke after hire drake.
     Thanne wol I clepe, "How, Alison! How, John!
     Be myrie, for the flood wol passe anon."
     And thou wolt seyn, "Hayl, maister Nicholay!
     Good morwe, I se thee wel, for it is day."
395   And thanne shul we be lordes al oure lyf
     Of al the world, as Noe and his wyf.
       'But of o thyng I warne thee ful right:
     Be wel avysed⁶ on that ilke nyght
     That we ben entred into shippes bord,
400   That noon of us ne speke nat a word,
     Ne clepe, ne crie, but be in his preyere;
     For it is Goddes owene heeste⁷ deere.
       'Thy wyf and thou moote hange fer atwynne;⁸
     For that bitwixe yow shal be no synne,
405   Namoore in lookyng than ther shal in deede.
     This ordinance is seyd. Go, God thee speede!
     Tomorwe at nyght, whan men ben alle aslepe,
     Into oure knedyng-tubbes wol we crepe,
     And sitten there, abidyng Goddes grace.
410   Go now thy wey; I have no lenger space⁹
     To make of this no lenger sermonyng.¹⁰
     Men seyn thus, "sende the wise, and sey no thyng."
     Thou art so wys, it needeth thee nat teche.
     Go, save oure lyf, and that I the biseche.'
415   This sely carpenter goth forth his wey.
     Ful ofte he seide, 'Allas and weylawey,'

---

3 preparations
4 in two
5 toward the garden
6 well warned
7 commandment
8 apart
9 time
10 talk

And to his wyf he tolde his pryvetee,

And she was war, and knew it bet[11] than he,

What al this queynte cast[12] was for to seye.[13]

420 But nathelees she ferde as she wolde deye,

And seyde, 'Allas! go forth thy wey anon,

Help us to scape, or we been dede echon![14]

I am thy trewe, verray wedded wyf;

Go, deere spouse, and help to save oure lyf.'

425   Lo, which a[15] greet thyng is affeccioun![16]

Men may dyen of ymaginacioun,[17]

So depe may impressioun be take.

This sely carpenter bigynneth quake;

Hym thynketh verraily that he may see

430 Noees flood come walwynge[18] as the see

To drenchen Alisoun, his hony deere.

He wepeth, weyleth, maketh sory cheere;[19]

He siketh with ful many a sory swogh;[20]

He gooth and geteth hym a knedyng trogh,

435 And after that a tubbe and a kymelyn,

And pryvely he sente hem to his in,

And heng him in the roof in pryvetee.

His owene hand[21] he made laddres thre,

To clymben by the ronges and the stalkes[22]

440 Unto the tubbes hangynge in the balkes,[23]

And hem vitailled,[24] bothe trogh and tubbe,

With breed, and chese, and good ale in a jubbe,[25]

Suffisynge right ynogh as for a day.

But er that he hadde maad al this array,[26]

445 He sente his knave and eek his wenche[27] also,

Upon his nede[28] to London for to go.

11 better
12 ingenious plot
13 mean
14 each one
15 what a
16 emotion
17 fantasy
18 surging
19 *maketh sory cheere*: looks sad, wretched
20 groan
21 *His owene hand*: by himself
22 uprights (of the ladder)
23 beams
24 stocked with provisions
25 large container, jug
26 preparation
27 servant girl
28 business

And on the Monday, whan it drow to nyght,
He shette his dore withoute candel-lyght,
And dressed[29] alle thynge as it sholde be.
450   And shortly, up they clomben alle thre;
They seten stille wel a furlong way.[30]
      'Now, *Pater-noster*, clom!'[31] seyde Nicholay,
And 'Clom!' quod John, and 'Clom!' seyde Alisoun.
This carpenter seyde his devocioun,
455   And stille he sit, and biddeth[32] his preyere,
Awaitynge on the reyn, if he it heere.
      The dede sleep, for wery bisynesse,[33]
Fil on this carpenter right, as I gesse,
Aboute corfew-tyme,[34] or litel moore;
460   For travaille of his goost[35] he groneth soore,
And eft[36] he routeth,[37] for his heed myslay.[38]
Doun of the laddre stalketh Nicholay,
And Alisoun ful softe adoun she spedde;
Withouten wordes mo they goon to bedde,
465   Ther as the carpenter is wont[39] to lye.
There was the revel and the melodye;
And thus lith Alison and Nicholas,
In bisyness of myrthe and of solas,
Til that the belle laudes[40] gan to rynge,
470   And frere in the cauncel gonne synge.
      This parissh clerk, this amorous Absolon,
That is for love alwey so wo bigon,
Upon the Monday was at Oseneye
With compaignye, hym to disporte and pley,
475   And axed upon cas[41] a cloisterer
Ful prively after John the carpenter;
And he drough[42] hym apart out of the chirche,
And seyde, 'I noot; I saugh hym heere nat wirche
Syn Saterday; I trowe that he be went

29 arranged
30 a couple of minutes
31 *Now . . . clom!*: now say a Paternoster (Lord's Prayer) and then hush!
32 prays
33 wearied by this work
34 dusk
35 suffering of his spirit, mental anguish
36 likewise
37 snores
38 lay wrong
39 accustomed
40 an early morning service, before daybreak
41 by chance
42 drew

480   For tymber, ther oure abbot hath hym sent;
       For he is wont for tymber for to go
       And dwellen at the grange[43] a day or two;
       Or elles he is at his hous, certeyn.
       Where that he be, I kan nat soothly seyn.'

485   This Absolon fuly joly was and light,[44]
       And thoghte, 'Now is tyme to wake al nyght,
       For sikirly I saugh hym nat stirynge
       Aboute his dore, syn day bigan to sprynge.
         'So moot I thryve,[45] I shal, at cokkes crow,

490   Ful pryvely knokken at his wyndowe
       That stant[46] ful lowe upon his boures wal.
       To Alison now wol I tellen al
       My love-longynge, for yet I shal nat mysse[47]
       That at the leeste wey[48] I shal hire kisse.

495   Som maner confort shal I have, parfay.[49]
       My mouth hath icched[50] al this longe day;
       That is a signe of kissyng atte leeste.
       Al nyght me mette[51] eek I was at a feeste.
       Therfore I wol go slepe an houre or tweye,

500   And al the nyght thanne wol I wake and pleye.'
         Whan that the first cok hath crowe, anon
       Up rist[52] this joly lovere Absolon,
       And hym arraieth gay,[53] at poynt-devys.[54]
       But first he cheweth greyn[55] and lycorys,

505   To smellen sweete, er he hadde kembd his heer.
       Under his tonge a trewe-love[56] he beer,
       For therby wende he to ben gracious.[57]
       He rometh to the carpenteres hous,
       And stille he stant under[58] the shot-wyndowe[59]—

---

43 outlying farm
44 happy
45 *So . . . thryve*: as I may prosper
46 stands
47 fail
48 at least
49 indeed, by my faith
50 itched
51 I dreamed
52 rises
53 *hym arraieth gay*: dresses himself handsomely
54 in every detail, completely
55 grain of Paradise, cardamom seed, a breath freshener
56 a four-leafed sprig of herb paris (Paris quadrifolia) in the shape of a fourfold true-love knot
57 attractive
58 next to
59 hinged window

510 Unto his brest it raughte,[60] it was so lowe—
And softe he cougheth with a semy soun:[61]
'What do ye, hony-comb, sweete Alisoun,
My faire bryd,[62] my sweete cynamome?[63]
Awaketh, lemman[64] myn, and speketh to me!

515 Wel litel thynken ye upon my wo,
That for youre love I swete ther I go.
No wonder is thogh that I swelte[65] and swete;[66]
I moorne[67] as dooth a lamb after the tete.
Ywis,[68] lemman, I have swich love-longynge

520 That lik a turtel[69] trewe is my moornynge.
I may nat ete na moore than a mayde.'
        'Go fro the wyndow, Jakke fool,'[70] she sayde;
'As help me God, it wol nat be "com pa me".[71]
I love another—and elles I were to blame—

525 Wel bet than thee, by Jhesu, Absolon.
Go forth thy wey, or I wol caste a ston,
And lat me slepe, a twenty devel wey!'[72]
        'Allas,' quod Absolon, 'and weylawey,
That trewe love was evere so yvel biset![73]

530 Thanne kysse me, syn it may be no bet,
For Jhesus love, and for the love of me.'
        'Wiltow thanne go thy wey therwith?' quod she.
        'Ye, certes, lemman,' quod this Absolon.
        'Thanne make thee redy,' quod she, 'I come anon.'

535 And unto Nicholas she seyde stille,
'Now hust,[74] and thou shalt laughen al thy fille.'
        This Absolon doun sette hym on his knees
And seyde, 'I am a lord at alle degrees;[75]
For after this I hope ther cometh moore.

540 Lemman, thy grace, and sweete bryd, thyn oore!'[76]

60 reached
61 small, gentle sound
62 bird (i.e. sweetheart)
63 cinnamon
64 sweetheart
65 grow faint
66 sweat
67 yearn
68 truly, indeed
69 turtledove
70 you idiot
71 come kiss me
72 in the name of twenty devils
73 *so yvel biset*: in such miserable circumstances
74 be quiet
75 in every way
76 mercy, grace

    The wyndow she undoth,[77] and that in haste
'Have do,'[78] quod she, 'com of,[79] and speed the faste,[80]
Lest that oure neighebores thee espie.'
    This Absolon gan wype his mouth ful drie.
545 Derk was the nyght as pich, or as the cole,
And at the wyndow out she putte hir hole,
And Absolon, hym fil no bet ne wers,
But with his mouth he kiste hir naked ers
Ful savourly, er he were war of this.
550 Abak he stirte, and thoughte it was amys,
For wel he wiste a womman hath no berd.
He felte a thyng al rough and long yherd,[81]
And seyde, 'Fy! allas! what have I do?'
    'Tehee!' quod she, and clapte the wyndow to,
555 And Absolon gooth forth a sory pas.[82]
    'A berd! A berd!'[83] quod hende Nicholas,
'By Goddes corpus,[84] this goth faire and weel.'
    This sely Absolon herde every deel,[85]
And on his lippe he gan for anger byte,
560 And to hymself he seyde, 'I shal thee quyte.'[86]
    Who rubbeth now, who froteth[87] now his lippes
With dust, with sond, with straw, with clooth, with chippes,
But Absolon, that seith ful ofte, 'Allas!'
'My soule bitake[88] I unto Sathanas,
565 But me were levere than al this toun,'[89] quod he,
'Of this despit[90] awroken[91] for to be.
Allas,' quod he, 'allas, I ne hadde ybleynt!'[92]
His hoote love was coold and al yqueynt;[93]
For fro that tyme that he hadde kist hir ers,
570 Of paramours he sette nat a kers,[94]
For he was heeled of his maladie.

77 opens
78 finish up
79 hurry up
80 be quick
81 long-haired
82 *a sory pas*: sadly
83 beard
84 body
85 every bit
86 pay back (revenge)
87 rubs
88 give
89 *But . . . toun*: if I would not rather than (own) all this town
90 insult
91 avenged
92 turned away
93 quenched
94 cress (i.e. something of no value)

Ful ofte paramours he gan deffie,[95]
And weep as dooth a child that is ybete.
A softe paas he wente over the strete

575 Until[96] a smyth men cleped daun[97] Gerveys,
That in his forge smythed plough harneys;[98]
He sharpeth[99] shaar[1] and kultour[2] bisily.
This Absolon knokketh al esily,[3]
And seyde, 'Undo,[4] Gerveys, and that anon.'

580 'What, who artow?' 'It am I, Absolon.'
'What, Absolon! for Cristes sweete tree,[5]
Why rise ye so rathe?[6] Ey, benedicitee!
What eyleth yow? Som gay gerl,[7] God it woot,
Hath broght yow thus upon the viritoot.[8]

585 By Seinte Note,[9] ye woot wel what I mene.'
This Absolon ne roghte nat a bene[10]
Of al his pley; no word agayn he yaf;
He hadde moore tow on his distaf[11]
Than Gerveys knew, and seyde, 'Freend so deere,

590 That hoote kultour in the chymenee[12] heere,
As lene[13] it me; I have therwith to doone,
And I wol brynge it thee agayn ful soone.'
Gerveys answerde, 'Certes, were it gold,
Or in a poke nobles alle untold,[14]

595 Thou sholdes have, as I am trewe smyth.
Ey, Cristes foo![15] What wol ye do therwith?'
'Therof', quod Absolon, 'be as be may.
I shal wel telle it thee to-morwe day'—
And caughte the kultour by the colde stele.[16]

95 repudiate
96 to
97 sir
98 ploughing equipment
99 sharpens
 1 ploughshare
 2 vertical blade at the front of the plough
 3 gently
 4 open up
 5 dear cross
 6 early
 7 good-looking girl
 8 *upon the virtroot*: astir (?)
 9 St Neot
10 *roghte . . . bene*: cared not a bean
11 flax on his distaff (i.e. more business on hand)
12 hearth
13 lend
14 bag of countless gold coins
15 ah, by Christ's foe (i.e. the Devil)
16 handle

600 Ful softe out at the dore he gan to stele,
   And wente unto the carpenteris wal.
   He cogheth first, and knokketh therwithal
   Upon the wyndowe, right as he dide er.
    This Alison answerde, 'Who is ther
605 That knokketh so? I warante[17] it a theef.'
    'Why, nay,' quod he, 'God woot, my sweete leef,[18]
   I am thyn Absolon, my deerelyng.[19]
   Of gold', quod he, 'I have thee broght a ryng.
   My mooder yaf it me, so God me save;
610 Ful fyn it is, and therto wel ygrave.[20]
   This wol I yeve thee, if thou me kisse.'
    This Nicholas was risen for to pisse,
   And thoughte he wolde amenden al the jape;[21]
   He sholde kisse his ers er that he scape.
615 And up the wyndowe dide he hastily,
   And out his ers he putteth pryvely
   Over the buttok, to the haunche-bon;[22]
   And therwith spak this clerk, this Absolon,
   'Spek, sweete bryd, I noot nat where thou art.'
620 This Nicholas anon leet fle a fart
   As greet as it had been a thonder-dent,[23]
   That with the strook he was almoost yblent;[24]
   And he was redy with his iren hoot,
   And Nicholas amydde the ers he smoot.
625 Of[25] gooth the skyn an hande-brede aboute,[26]
   The hoote kultour brende so his toute,[27]
   And for the smert[28] he wende for to dye.[29]
   As he were wood, for wo he gan to crye,
   'Help! Water! Water! Help, for Goddes herte!'[30]
630 This carpenter out of his slomber sterte,
   And herde oon crien 'Water!' as he were wood,

17 swear
18 beloved
19 darling
20 engraved
21 make the joke even better
22 thigh
23 thunder clap
24 blinded
25 off
26 a hand's width all around
27 rump
28 pain
29 thought he would die
30 heart

And thoughte, 'Allas, now comth Nowelis[31] flood!'
He sit hym up withouten wordes mo,
And with his ax he smoot the corde atwo,

635 And doun gooth al; he foond neither to selle,
Ne breed ne ale,[32] til he cam to the celle[33]
Upon the floor, and ther aswowne[34] he lay.

Up stirte hire Alison and Nicholay,
And criden 'Out' and 'Harrow' in the strete.

640 The neighebores, bothe smale and grete,[35]
In ronnen[36] for to gauren on[37] this man,
That yet aswowne lay, bothe pale and wan,
For with the fal he brosten[38] hadde his arm.
But stonde he moste unto his owene harm;[39]

645 For whan he spak, he was anon bore doun
With[40] hende Nicholas and Alisoun.
They tolden every man that he was wood;
He was agast[41] so of Nowelis flood
Thurgh fantasie that of his vanytee[42]

650 He hadde yboght hym knedyng tubbes thre,
And hadde hem hanged in the roof above;
And that he preyed hem, for Goddes love,
To sitten in the roof, *par compaignye*.[43]

The folk gan laughen at his fantasye;

655 Into the roof they kiken[44] and they cape,[45]
And turned al his harm unto a jape.
For what so that this carpenter answerde,
It was for noght; no man his reson herde.
With othes grete he was so sworn adoun[46]

660 That he was holde wood in al the toun;
For every clerk anonright[47] heeld[48] with oother.

31 Noah's
32 *he foond . . . ne ale*: he did not stop to sell bread or ale on the way (i.e. he wasted no time)
33 floor
34 in a faint
35 i.e. everyone
36 ran
37 stare at
38 broken
39 *But stonde . . . harm*: but he had to stand up, though it turned out badly for him
40 by
41 frightened
42 foolishness
43 for fellowship's sake, to keep him company
44 stare
45 gape
46 overcome by oaths
47 immediately
48 held, agreed

They seyde, 'The man is wood, my leeve brother';
And every wight gan laughen at this stryf.
Thus swyved[49] was this carpenteris wyf,
665 For al his kepyng[50] and his jalousye,
And Absolon hath kist hir nether ye,[51]
And Nicholas is scalded in the towte.
This tale is doon, and God save al the rowte!
Heere endeth the Millere his tale.

49 copulated with
50 guarding
51 lower eye

◆

William Shakespeare
1564–1616

◆

William Shakespeare was born into a middle-class family in the Warwickshire market town of Stratford-on-Avon. His father, a glover by trade, was a leading citizen who held the office of bailiff, a position equivalent to mayor. As a boy, Shakespeare attended the very strict Stratford Grammar School, where the curriculum consisted of grammar, reading, writing, and recitation, done almost entirely in Latin. In 1582, when he was eighteen, Shakespeare married Anne Hathaway. Little else is known of him until 1592, by which time he had established himself as an author and playwright in the London theatre world. He turned to writing poetry when an outbreak of the plague closed the London theatres from the summer of 1592 until June 1594. Most of

Shakespeare's 154 sonnets were written between 1593 and 1599, and about ten were written between then and 1609, the year they were published. The sonnets were dedicated 'To the Onlie Begetter of these ensuing Sonnets Mr W.H.', who was probably Shakespeare's patron but whose identity is not known. Nor have scholars been able to establish identities for the characters found in the sonnets: the poet's young friend of high social position who is addressed in sonnets 1–126; the 'dark lady' of sonnets 127–54, who causes joy and pain for the poet; and a rival poet. Though the autobiographical mystery is tantalizing, it is probably wiser to read and enjoy the sonnets for the mastery of language and form that was to inspire so many other poets.

Sonnets

18

Shall I compare thee to a summer's day?
Thou art more lovely and more temperate.
Rough winds do shake the darling buds of May,
And summer's lease hath all too short a date.
5 Sometime too hot the eye of heaven shines,

And often is his gold complexion dimmed,
And every fair from fair sometime declines,
By chance or nature's changing course untrimmed;
But thy eternal summer shall not fade

10 Nor lose possession of that fair thou ow'st,
Nor shall death brag thou wander'st in his shade
When in eternal lines to time thou grow'st.
  So long as men can breathe or eyes can see,
  So long lives this, and this gives life to thee.

29

When, in disgrace with fortune and men's eyes,
I all alone beweep my outcast state,
And trouble deaf heaven with my bootless cries,
And look upon myself and curse my fate,

5 Wishing me like to one more rich in hope,
Featured like him, like him with friends possessed,
Desiring this man's art and that man's scope,
With what I most enjoy contented least:
Yet in these thoughts myself almost despising,

10 Haply I think on thee, and then my state,
Like to the lark at break of day arising
From sullen earth, sings hymns at heaven's gate;
  For thy sweet love remembered such wealth brings
  That then I scorn to change my state with kings'.

35

No more be grieved at that which thou hast done:
Roses have thorns, and silver fountains mud.
Clouds and eclipses stain both moon and sun,
And loathsome canker lives in sweetest bud.

5 All men make faults, and even I in this,
Authorizing thy trespass with compare,
Myself corrupting salving thy amiss,
Excusing thy sins more than thy sins are;
For to thy sensual fault I bring in sense—

10 Thy adverse party is thy advocate—
And 'gainst myself a lawful plea commence.
Such civil war is in my love and hate
  That I an accessory needs must be
  To that sweet thief which sourly robs from me.

55

Not marble nor the gilded monuments
Of princes shall outlive this powerful rime,
But you shall shine more bright in these contents
Than unswept stone besmeared with sluttish time.
5 When wasteful war shall statues overturn,
And broils root out the work of masonry,
Nor Mars his sword nor war's quick fire shall burn
The living record of your memory.
'Gainst death and all oblivious enmity
10 Shall you pace forth; your praise shall still find room
Even in the eyes of all posterity
That wear this world out to the ending doom.
So, till the judgement that yourself arise,
You live in this, and dwell in lovers' eyes.

65

Since brass, nor stone, nor earth, nor boundless sea,
But sad mortality o'ersways their power,
How with this rage shall beauty hold a plea,
Whose action is no stronger than a flower?
5 O how shall summer's honey breath hold out
Against the wrackful siege of battering days
When rocks impregnable are not so stout,
Nor gates of steel so strong, but time decays?
O fearful meditation! Where, alack,
10 Shall time's best jewel from time's chest lie hid,
Or what strong hand can hold his swift foot back,
Or who his spoil of beauty can forbid?
O none, unless this miracle have might:
That in black ink my love may still shine bright.

73

That time of year thou mayst in me behold
When yellow leaves, or none, or few, do hang
Upon those boughs which shake against the cold,
Bare ruined choirs where late the sweet birds sang.
5 In me thou seest the twilight of such day
As after sunset fadeth in the west,
Which by and by black night doth take away,
Death's second self, that seals up all in rest.

In me thou seest the glowing of such fire
10 That on the ashes of his youth doth lie
As the death-bed whereon it must expire,
Consumed with that which it was nourished by.
  This thou perceiv'st, which makes thy love more strong,
  To love that well which thou must leave ere long.

130

My mistress' eyes are nothing like the sun;
Coral is far more red than her lips' red.
If snow be white, why then her breasts are dun;
If hairs be wires, black wires grow on her head.
5 I have seen roses damasked, red and white,
But no such roses see I in her cheeks;
And in some perfumes is there more delight
Than in the breath that from my mistress reeks.
I love to hear her speak, yet well I know
10 That music hath a far more pleasing sound.
I grant I never saw a goddess go:
My mistress when she walks treads on the ground.
  And yet, by heaven, I think my love as rare
  As any she belied with false compare.

1609

John Donne
1572–1631

As a young man, John Donne appears to have pursued knowledge and women with equal passion — or so his earlier lyrics would lead us to believe. He may well have been more interested in flouting Elizabethan poetic conventions than in recounting his romantic adventures. Certainly he had his share of the latter, when as a young law student he was using his personal charm, wit, and learning to gain preferment in Elizabethan court circles. But his career in state affairs ended abruptly in 1601 when, working as a secretary to Sir Thomas Egerton, he eloped with Egerton's sixteen-year-old niece. Elopement was unlawful, and Donne had not the means to support a wife and family. Until 1615, when his fine sermons had made him well known, Donne lived on the edge of poverty. At the urging of King James he became an Anglican priest and was one of the greatest preachers of his time. But though he achieved material security, he was not a happy man. His poetry and devotional writing reveal a constant spiritual struggle that was worsened by frequent illness. During his lifetime, his eloquent devotional writing was widely read, but the genius of his love poetry, published after his death in 1633, with its stunningly unconventional metaphors and the strong, irregular rhythms of ordinary speech, was considered 'rough', and was not fully appreciated until Herbert Grierson's edition of his poems appeared in 1912.

The Good Morrow

I wonder, by my troth, what thou and I
Did, till we loved? Were we not weaned till then,
But sucked on country pleasures, childishly?
Or snorted we in the seven sleepers' den?
5 'Twas so; but this, all pleasures fancies be.
If ever any beauty I did see,
Which I desired, and got, 'twas but a dream of thee.

And now good morrow to our waking souls,
Which watch not one another out of fear;
10 For love all love of other sights controls,
And makes one little room an everywhere.
Let sea-discoverers to new worlds have gone,
Let maps to other, worlds on worlds have shown,
Let us possess one world; each hath one, and is one.

15 My face in thine eye, thine in mine appears,
And true plain hearts do in the faces rest;
Where can we find two better hemispheres
Without sharp North, without declining West?
Whatever dies was not mixed equally;
20 If our two loves be one, or thou and I
Love so alike that none do slacken, none can die.

1633

The Sun Rising

Busy old fool, unruly sun,
   Why doest thou thus
Through windows and through curtains call on us?
Must to thy motions lovers' seasons run?
5   Saucy pedantic wretch, go chide
     Late schoolboys and sour prentices,
Go tell court-huntsmen that the king will ride,

       Call country ants to harvest offices;
       Love, all alike, no season knows, nor clime,
10   Nor hours, days, months, which are the rags of time.

          Thy beams, so reverend, and strong
             Why shouldst thou think?
       I could eclipse and cloud them with a wink,
       But that I would not lose her sight so long;
15   If her eyes have not blinded thine,
           Look, and tomorrow late tell me
       Whether both the Indias of spice and mine
       Be where thou left'st them, or lie here with me.
       Ask for those kings whom thou saw'st yesterday,
20   And thou shalt hear, all here in one bed lay.

          She is all states, and all princes I;
             Nothing else is.
       Princes do but play us; compared to this,
       All honour's mimic, all wealth alchemy.
25   Thou, sun, art half as happy as we,
           In that the world's contracted thus;
       Thine age asks ease, and since thy duties be
       To warm the world, that's done in warming us.
       Shine here to us, and thou art everywhere;
30   This bed thy centre is, these walls thy sphere.

                              1633

The Canonization

For God's sake hold your tongue and let me love;
       Or chide my palsy or my gout,
My five grey hairs or ruined fortune flout,
        With wealth your state, your mind with arts improve,
5   Take you a course, get you a place,
         Observe His Honour, or His Grace,
Or the King's real, or his stamped face
        Contemplate; what you will, approve,
        So you will let me love.

10   Alas, alas, who's injured by my love?
        What merchant's ships have my sighs drown'd?
       Who says my tears have overflowed his ground?

When did my colds a forward spring remove?
  When did the heats which my veins fill
15   Add one more to the plaguey bill?[1]
Soldiers find wars, and Lawyers find out still
  Litigious men, which quarrels move,
  Though she and I do love.

Call us what you will, we are made such by love;
20   Call her one, me another fly,
We are tapers too, and at our own cost die,
  And we in us find the Eagle and the Dove.
    The Phoenix[2] riddle hath more wit
    By us: we two being one, are it.
25 So to one neutral thing both sexes fit;
  We die and rise the same, and prove
  Mysterious by this love.

We can die by it, if not live by love,
  And if unfit for tombs and hearse
30 Our legend be, it will be fit for verse;
  And if no piece of chronicle we prove,
    We'll build in sonnets pretty rooms;
    As well a well-wrought urn becomes
The greatest ashes, as half-acre tombs,
35   And by these hymns, all shall approve
  Us *canonized* for Love;

And thus invoke us: You whom reverend love
  Made one another's hermitage;
You, to whom love was peace, that now is rage;
40   Who did the whole world's soul contract, and drove
    Into the glasses of your eyes
    (So made such mirrors, and such spies,
That they did all to you epitomize);
  Countries, towns, courts: Beg from above
45   A pattern of your love!

1633

---

1 a list of those who have died of the plague
2 a mythical bird of no sex that lived a thousand years, then burned itself and was reborn from the ashes

The Flea

Mark but this flea, and mark in this,
How little that which thou deny'st me is;
Me it sucked first, and now sucks thee,
And in this flea, our two bloods mingled be;
5   Confess it, this cannot be said
A sin, or shame, or loss of maidenhead,
    Yet this enjoys before it woo,
      And pampered swells with one blood made of two,
      And this, alas, is more than we would do.

10   Oh stay, three lives in one flea spare,
Where we almost, nay more than married are.
This flea is you and I, and this
Our marriage bed, and marriage temple is;
Though parents grudge, and you, we are met,
15   And cloistered in these living walls of jet.
    Though use make you apt to kill me,
      Let not to this, self-murder added be,
      And sacrilege, three sins in killing three.

    Cruel and sudden, hast thou since
20   Purpled thy nail, in blood of innocence?
In what could this flea guilty be,
Except in that drop which it sucked from thee?
Yet thou triumph'st, and say'st that thou
Find'st not thyself, nor me the weaker now;
25   'Tis true, then learn how false, fears be;
    Just so much honour, when thou yield'st to me,
    Will waste, as this flea's death took life from thee.

1633

The Relic

When my grave is broke up again
Some second guest to entertain
(For graves have learned that womanhead
To be to more than one a bed)
5   And he that digs it spies
A bracelet of bright hair about the bone,
        Will he not let us alone,
And think that there a loving couple lies,
Who thought that this device might be some way
10   To make their souls, at the last busy day,
Meet at this grave, and make a little stay?

If this fall in a time, or land,
Where mis-devotion doth command,
Then he that digs us up, will bring
15   Us to the Bishop and the King
        To make us relics; then
Thou shalt be a Mary Magdalen,[1] and I
        A something else thereby;
All women shall adore us, and some men;
20   And since at such time, miracles are sought,
I would have that age by this paper taught
What miracles we harmless lovers wrought.

First, we loved well and faithfully,
Yet knew not what we loved, nor why;
25   Difference of sex no more we knew
        Than our guardian angels do;
        Coming and going, we
Perchance might kiss, but not between those meals;
        Our hands ne'er touched the seals
30   Which nature, injured by late law, sets free:
These miracles we did; but now, alas,
All measure and all language I should pass,
Should I tell what a miracle she was.

1633

1 In Christian tradition Mary Magdalene was a prostitute who reformed to follow Jesus—which suggests that the 'something else' in the next line refers to Christ.

Holy Sonnets

10

Death, be not proud, though some have callèd thee
Mighty and dreadful, for thou are not so;
For those whom thou think'st thou dost overthrow
Die not, poor Death, nor yet canst thou kill me.
5   From rest and sleep, which but thy pictures be,
Much pleasure; then from thee much more must flow,
And soonest our best men with thee do go,
Rest of their bones, and soul's delivery.
Thou art slave to fate, chance, kings, and desperate men,
10   And dost with poison, war, and sickness dwell,
And poppy or charms can make us sleep as well
And better than thy stroke; why swell'st thou then?
One short sleep past, we wake eternally
And death shall be no more; Death, thou shalt die.

14

Batter my heart, three-personed God; for you
As yet but knock, breathe, shine, and seek to mend;
That I may rise and stand, o'erthrow me, and bend
Your force to break, blow, burn, and make me new.
5   I, like an usurped town, to another due,
Labour to admit you, but oh, to no end.
Reason, your viceroy in me, me should defend,
But is captived, and proves weak or untrue.
Yet dearly I love you, and would be loved fain,
10   But am betrothed unto your enemy:
Divorce me, untie or break that knot again,
Take me to you, imprison me, for I,
Except you enthrall me, never shall be free,
Nor ever chaste, except you ravish me.

1633

Robert Herrick
1591–1674

The son of a prosperous London goldsmith, Robert Herrick was apprenticed to this trade at the age of twelve, but gave it up ten years later to attend Cambridge. After receiving his BA in 1617, he returned to London with the aim of pursuing a literary life. Herrick was an admirer and pupil of the popular playwright Ben Jonson, with whom he enjoyed 'lyric Feasts' (drinking and talking) in such taverns as The Sun and The Dog. In 1627 he entered the priesthood of the Church of England, a common career for younger sons of prosperous families. Two years later, he was named vicar of Dean Priory in Devonshire, a locale noted for its brutish peasantry, who provided unpleasant subject matter for Herrick's satirical poetry. Pleasanter subjects were such inhabitants of the vicarage as Herrick's maid Prudence, his pet sparrow Phill, and his beloved spaniel Tracie. But out of this bachelor's imagination emerged the best subjects: the bewitching and beribboned Julia and Corinna, who grace his most lyrical poetry. They dance through a pastoral world of happy pagan ritual, gathering rosebuds and strewing them through the dewy grass in celebration of the joys of this life, a life made the more poignant by an awareness of the next life fast approaching.

Delight in Disorder

A sweet disorder in the dress
Kindles in clothes a wantonness.
A lawn[1] about the shoulders thrown
Into a fine distraction;
5   An erring lace, which here and there
Enthralls the crimson stomacher;[2]
A cuff neglectful, and thereby
Ribbons to flow confusedly;
A winning wave, deserving note,
10 In the tempestuous petticoat;
A careless shoestring, in whose tie
I see a wild civility:
Do more bewitch me than when art
Is too precise in every part.

1648

1 fine linen (as a scarf)
2 a separate piece for the centre front of a bodice

Upon Julia's Clothes

Whenas in silks my Julia goes,
Then, then (methinks) how sweetly flows
That liquefaction of her clothes.

Next, when I cast mine eyes and see
5   That brave vibration each way free;
O how that glittering taketh me!

1648

To the Virgins, to Make Much of Time

Gather ye rosebuds while ye may,
    Old time is still a-flying;
And this same flower that smiles today,
    To-morrow will be dying.

5   The glorious lamp of heaven, the sun,
        The higher he's a-getting,
    The sooner will his race be run,
        And nearer he's to setting.

    That age is best which is the first,
10   When youth and blood are warmer;
    But being spent, the worse, and worst
        Times still succeed the former.

    Then be not coy, but use your time,
        And while ye may, go marry;
15   For having lost but once your prime,
        You may forever tarry.

1648

John Milton
1608–1674

One of the most educated and learned of the major English poets, John Milton was born in Cheapside, London, and attended Saint Paul's School, where he studied Latin and Greek and mastered many modern European languages as well as Hebrew. In 1625 he entered Christ's College, Cambridge, where he received his BA (1629) and MA (1632). Rather than study with an aim to joining the ministry, he retired to his father's country home to read and to embark on a writing career. He wrote his elegy *Lycidas* in 1637 as a memorial to Edward King, his Cambridge classmate for six years, who had drowned that summer. He then travelled for two years on the continent. On his return to England, he became an apologist for Oliver Cromwell, defending the decision of Parliament to execute Charles I in 1649. Although he went blind in 1651, Milton continued to work as Latin secretary to Cromwell's Council of State. With the Restoration of the monarchy under Charles II in 1660, Milton found himself in political disfavour and was imprisoned. Through the intervention of friends his life was spared. During his last years he completed his epic *Paradise Lost* (1667), his shorter epic *Paradise Regained* (1671), and his tragedy *Samson Agonistes* (1671).

On Shakespeare

What needs my Shakespeare for his honoured bones
The labour of an age in pilèd stones,
Or that his hallowed relics should be hid
Under a star-ypointing pyramid?
5   Dear son of memory, great heir of fame,
What need'st thou such weak witness of thy name?
Thou in our wonder and astonishment
Hast built thyself a live-long monument.
For whilst to th' shame of slow-endeavouring art,
10   Thy easy numbers flow, and that each heart
Hath from the leaves of thy unvalued book
Those Delphic lines with deep impression took;
Then thou, our fancy of itself bereaving,
Dost make us marble with too much conceiving;
15   And so sepùlchered in such pomp dost lie,
That kings for such a tomb would wish to die.

How Soon Hath Time

How soon hath Time, the subtle thief of youth,
    Stolen on his wing my three-and-twentieth year!
    My hasting days fly on with full career,
    But my late spring no bud or blossom show'th.
5   Perhaps my semblance might deceive the truth
    That I to manhood am arrived so near;
    And inward ripeness doth much less appear,
    That some more timely-happy spirits indu'th.
    Yet, be it less or more, or soon or slow,
10 It shall be still in strictest measure even
    To that same lot, however mean or high,
Toward which Time leads me, and the will of Heaven,
    All is, if I have grace to use it so,
    As ever in my great Task-Master's eye.

1645

Lycidas

In this Monody[1] the Author bewails a learned Friend, unfortunately drowned in his passage from Chester on the Irish Sea, 1637; and, by occasion, foretells the ruin of our corrupted Clergy, then in their height.

    Yet once more, O ye laurels, and once more,
    Ye myrtles brown, with ivy never sere,
    I come to pluck your berries harsh and crude,
    And with forced fingers rude
5   Shatter your leaves before the mellowing year.
    Bitter constraint and sad occasion dear
    Compels me to disturb your season due;
    For Lycidas is dead, dead ere his prime,
    Young Lycidas, and hath not left his peer.
10   Who would not sing for Lycidas? He knew
    Himself to sing, and build the lofty rhyme.
    He must not float upon his watery bier
    Unwept, and welter to the parching wind,
    Without the meed of some melodious tear.
15   Begin, then, Sisters of the sacred well[2]

---

1 a dirge or elegy sung by a single voice. 'Lycidas' was first published in a volume of commemorative verse for Edward King, a friend of Milton's from his student days at Cambridge University.
2 *Sisters . . . well*: the muses, who dance at the altar of Jove at their sacred well, Aganippe, on Mt Helicon

That from beneath the seat of Jove doth spring;
Begin, and somewhat loudly sweep the string.
Hence with denial vain and coy excuse:
So may some gentle Muse
20 With lucky words favour my destined urn,
And as he passes turn,
And bid fair peace be to my sable shroud!
For we were nursed upon the self-same hill,
Fed the same flock, by fountain, shade, and rill;
25 Together both, ere the high lawns appeared
Under the opening eyelids of the Morn,
We drove afield, and both together heard
What time the grey-fly winds her sultry horn,
Batt'ning our flocks with the fresh dews of night,
30 Oft till the star that rose at evening bright
Toward heaven's descent had sloped his westering wheel.
Meanwhile the rural ditties were not mute,
Tempered to th' oaten flute;
Rough Satyrs danced, and Fauns with cloven heel
35 From the glad sound would not be absent long;
And old Damaetas[3] loved to hear our song.
　　But, oh! the heavy change, now thou art gone,
Now thou art gone, and never must return!
Thee, Shepherd, thee the woods, and desert caves,
40 With wild thyme and the gadding vine o'ergrown,
And all their echoes, mourn.
The willows, and the hazel copses green,
Shall now no more be seen,
Fanning their joyous leaves to thy soft lays.
45 As killing as the canker to the rose,
Or taint-worm to the weanling herds that graze,
Or frost to flowers, that their gay wardrobe wear,
When first the white-thorn blows;
Such, Lycidas, thy loss to shepherd's ear.
50 　　Where were ye, Nymphs, when the remorseless deep
Closed o'er the head of your loved Lycidas?
For neither were ye playing on the steep,
Where your old bards, the famous Druids, lie,
Nor on the shaggy top on Mona[4] high,
55 Nor yet where Deva spreads her wizard stream.
Ay me! I fondly dream

---

3 a conventional pastoral name, referring probably to a Cambridge tutor
4 also known as Anglesey, an island off the northwest coast of Wales. King's ship apparently went down nearby.

Had ye been there, . . . for what could that have done?
What could the Muse[5] herself that Orpheus bore,
The Muse herself, for her enchanting son,
60 Whom universal nature did lament,
When, by the rout that made the hideous roar,
His gory visage down the stream was sent,
Down the swift Hebrus to the Lesbian shore?
    Alas! what boots it with incessant care
65 To tend the homely, slighted, shepherd's trade,
And strictly meditate the thankless Muse?
Were it not better done, as others use,
To sport with Amaryllis[6] in the shade,
Or with the tangles of Neaera's hair?
70 Fame is the spur that the clear spirit doth raise
(That last infirmity of noble mind)
To scorn delights, and live laborious days;
But the fair guerdon when we hope to find,
And think to burst out into sudden blaze,
75 Comes the blind Fury[7] with th' abhorred shears,
And slits the thin-spun life. 'But not the praise,'
Phoebus[8] replied, and touched my trembling ears:
'Fame is no plant that grows on mortal soil,
Nor in the glistering foil
80 Set off to the world, nor in broad rumour lies,
But lives and spreads aloft by those pure eyes
And perfect witness of all-judging Jove;
As he pronounces lastly on each deed,
Of so much fame in heaven expect thy meed.'
85   O fountain Arethuse,[9] and thou honoured flood,
Smooth-sliding Mincius,[10] crowned with vocal reeds,
That strain I heard was of a higher mood.
But now my oat proceeds,
And listens to the Herald of the Sea
90 That came in Neptune's plea.
He asked the waves, and asked the felon winds,
What hard mishap hath doomed this gentle swain?
And questioned every gust of rugged wings
That blows from off each beaked promontory.

5 Calliope the Muse of epic poetry and mother of Orpheus. Angry female votaries of Dionysus tore him to pieces and flung his head into the river Hebrus.
6 conventional female pastoral name
7 Atropos, third of the Fates, cuts the thread of life that is spun and measured by the other two.
8 Apollo, god of poetry
9 a fountain in Sicily, emblematic of early pastoral of Theocritus
10 the river on which Virgil was born

95   They knew not of his story;
      And sage Hippotades[11] their answer brings,
      That not a blast was from his dungeon strayed;
      The air was calm, and on the level brine
      Sleek Panope[12] with all her sisters played,
100   It was that fatal and perfidious bark,
      Built in th' eclipse, and rigged with curses dark,
      That sunk so low that sacred head of thine.

        Next, Camus,[13] reverend sire, went footing slow,
      His mantle hairy, and his bonnet sedge,
105   Inwrought with figures dim, and on the edge
      Like to that sanguine flower inscribed with woe.
      'Ah! who hath reft', quoth he, 'my dearest pledge?'
      Last came, and last did go,
      The Pilot of the Galilean Lake;[14]
110   Two massy keys he bore of metals twain
      (The golden opes, the iron shuts amain).
      He shook his mitred locks, and stern bespake:—
      'How well could I have spared for thee, young swain,
      Enow of such as, for their bellies' sake,
115   Creep, and intrude, and climb into the fold!
      Of other care they little reck'ning make
      Than how to scramble at the shearers' feast,
      And shove away the worthy bidden guest.
      Blind mouths! that scarce themselves know how to hold
120   A sheep-hook, or have learned aught else the least
      That to the faithful herdman's art belongs!
      What recks it them? What need they? They are sped;
      And, when they list, their lean and flashy songs
      Grate on their scrannel pipes of wretched straw;
125   The hungry sheep look up, and are not fed,
      But, swoln with wind and the rank mist they draw,
      Rot inwardly, and foul contagion spread:
      Besides what the grim wolf with privy paw
      Daily devours apace, and nothing said.
130   But that two-handed engine at the door
      Stands ready to smite once, and smite no more.'
        Return, Alpheus,[15] the dread voice is past
      That shrunk thy streams; return, Sicilian Muse,[16]

11 the god of winds
12 one of the Nereids or sea-nymphs
13 the god of the river Cam, representing Cambridge
14 St Peter
15 a Greek river god
16 relates to Theocritan pastoral poetry

And call the vales, and bid them hither cast
135   Their bells and flowers of a thousand hues.
Ye valleys low, where the mild whispers use
Of shades, and wanton winds, and gushing brooks,
On whose fresh lap the swart star[17] sparely looks,
Throw hither all your quaint enamelled eyes,
140   That on the green turf suck the honied showers,
And purple all the ground with vernal flowers.
Bring the rathe primrose that forsaken dies,
The tufted crow-toe, and pale jessamine,
The white pink, and the pansy freaked with jet,
145   The glowing violet,
The musk-rose, and the well-attired woodbine,
With cowslips wan that hang the pensive head,
And every flower that sad embroidery wears:
Bid amaranthus all his beauty shed,
150   And daffadillies fill their cups with tears,
To strew the laureate hearse where Lycid lies.
For so, to interpose a little ease,
Let our frail thoughts dally with false surmise.
Ay me! whilst thee the shores and sounding seas
155   Wash far away, where'er thy bones are hurled;
Whether beyond the stormy Hebrides,
Where thou perhaps under the whelming tide
Visit'st the bottom of the monstrous world;
Or whether thou, to our moist vows denied,
160   Sleep'st by the fable of Bellerus old,
Where the great Vision of the guarded mount
Looks toward Namancos, and Bayona's hold;
Look homeward, Angel, now, and melt with ruth:
And, O ye dolphins, waft the hapless youth.
165   Weep no more, woeful shepherds, weep no more,
For Lycidas, your sorrow, is not dead,
Sunk though he be beneath the wat'ry floor.
So sinks the day-star in the ocean bed,
And yet anon repairs his drooping head,
170   And tricks his beams, and with new-spangled ore
Flames in the forehead of the morning sky:
So Lycidas sunk low, but mounted high,
Through the dear might of Him that walked the waves;
Where, other groves and other streams along,
175   With nectar pure his oozy locks he laves,

---

17 Sirius, the Dog Star

And hears the unexpressive nuptial song,
In the blest kingdoms meek of joy and love.
There entertain him all the Saints above,
In solemn troops, and sweet societies,
180   That sing, and singing in their glory move,
And wipe the tears forever from his eyes.
Now, Lycidas, the shepherds weep no more;
Henceforth thou art the Genius of the shore,
In thy large recompense, and shalt be good
185   To all that wander in that perilous flood.
     Thus sang the uncouth swain to th' oaks and rills,
While the still morn went out with sandals grey:
He touched the tender stops of various quills,
With eager thought warbling his Doric[18] lay:
And now the sun had stretched out all the hills,
190   And now was dropped into the western bay;
At last he rose, and twitched his mantle blue:
Tomorrow to fresh woods, and pastures new.

1638

18 Greek dialect of the pastoral poets such as Theocritus

When I Consider How My Light Is Spent

When I consider how my light is spent,
   Ere half my days in this dark world and wide,
   And that one talent which is death to hide
   Lodged with me useless, though my soul more bent
5 To serve therewith my Maker, and present
   My true account, lest he returning chide;
   'Doth God exact day-labour, light denied?'
   I fondly ask; but Patience, to prevent
That murmur, soon replies, 'God doth not need
10   Either man's work or his own gifts. Who best
   Bear his mild yoke, they serve him best: his state
Is kingly: thousands at his bidding speed,
   And post o'er land and ocean without rest;
   They also serve who only stand and wait.'

1673

Andrew Marvell

1621–1678

Andrew Marvell is an elusive figure whose life presents as <u>many paradoxes</u> as his poetry does. During his lifetime he was known as a <u>public servant</u> and a <u>politician</u>, and not as a poet. But during this public career he was writing a private kind of poetry, extolling pastoral solitude and the inner life of the mind. He was a Puritan, yet he wrote one of the <u>most erotic</u> proposals of all time, 'To His Coy Mistress'.

Marvell was born in Winestead, England, near Hull, where his father was rector of the parish church. He went to Trinity College, Cambridge, at the age of twelve and <u>mastered six ancient languages</u>. After his father died in 1641, he worked as <u>a clerk</u> in a Hull business house. He later travelled to Europe for four years before becoming a tutor to the twelve-year-old daughter of Lord Fairfax, whose garden at Nun Appleton House probably inspired the 'green thoughts' of Marvell's lyrics, for he wrote prolifically during this period. In 1657, Marvell was an <u>assistant</u> to the blind poet John Milton, then Cromwell's Latin <u>secretary</u>, and in 1659 he was <u>elected to Parliament</u>, where he represented Hull for the rest of his life. When his poems were published in 1681— three years after his death — they were considered out of date and were ignored. Though his work was appreciated by later poets such as Blake, Wordsworth, and Tennyson, Marvell did not receive full critical attention until the twentieth century.

To His Coy Mistress

[handwritten margin note: I would spend all my age in admiring you]

Had we but world enough, and time,
This coyness, lady, were no crime.
We would sit down, and think which way
To walk, and pass our long love's day.
5 Thou by the Indian Ganges' side
Should'st rubies find: I by the tide
Of Humber would complain. I would
Love you ten years before the Flood,
And you should, if you please, refuse
10 Till the conversion of the Jews.
My vegetable love should grow
Vaster than empires, and more slow;
An hundred years should go to praise
Thine eyes, and on thy forehead gaze;
15 Two hundred to adore each breast,
But thirty thousand to the rest;
An age at least to every part,
And the last age should show your heart.
For, lady, you deserve this state,
20 Nor would I love at lower rate.

But at my back I always hear
Time's wingèd chariot hurrying near: *[handwritten: Time is short]*
And yonder all before us lie
Deserts of vast eternity.
25 Thy beauty shall no more be found;
Nor, in thy marble vault, shall sound
My echoing song: then worms shall try
That long-preserved virginity.
And your quaint honour turn to dust,
30 And into ashes all my lust.
The grave's a fine and private place,
But none, I think, do there embrace.
    Now, therefore, while the youthful hue
Sits on thy skin like morning dew,
35 And while thy willing soul transpires *[handwritten: desire]*
At every pore with instant fires,
Now let us sport us while we may;
And now, like amorous birds of prey,
Rather at once our Time devour, *[handwritten: Let's go for it — cease time — devour time]*
40 Than languish in his slow-chapt power. *[handwritten: slow-jaws]*
Let us roll all our strength and all *[handwritten: entwined in a vigorous way]*
Our sweetness up into one ball,
And tear our pleasures with rough strife
Thorough the iron gates of life.
45 Thus, though we cannot make our sun *[handwritten: we can't stop time]*
Stand still, yet we will make him run.

1681

The Garden

How vainly men themselves amaze
To win the palm, the oak, or bays;
And their incessant labours see
Crowned from some single herb, or tree,
5 Whose short and narrow-vergèd shade
Does prudently their toils upbraid;
While all flowers and all trees do close
To weave the garlands of repose!

Fair Quiet, have I found thee here,
10 And Innocence, thy sister dear!
Mistaken long, I sought you then
In busy companies of men.

Your sacred plants, if here below,
Only among the plants will grow;
15 Society is all but rude
To this delicious solitude.

No white nor red was ever seen
So amorous as this lovely green.
Fond lovers, cruel as their flame,
20 Cut in these trees their mistress' name:
Little, alas! they know or heed
How far these beauties hers exceed!
Fair trees! wheres'e'er your barks I wound
No name shall but your own be found.

25 When we have run our passion's heat,
Love hither makes his best retreat.
The gods, that mortal beauty chase,
Still in a tree did end their race;
Apollo hunted Daphne so,
30 Only that she might laurel grow;
And Pan did after Syrinx speed,
Not as a nymph, but for a reed.

What wondrous life is this I lead!
Ripe apples drop about my head;
35 The luscious clusters of the vine
Upon my mouth do crush their wine;
The nectarine, and curious peach,
Into my hands themselves do reach;
Stumbling on melons, as I pass,
40 Ensnared with flowers, I fall on grass.

Meanwhile, the mind, from pleasure less,
Withdraws into its happiness:
The mind, that ocean where each kind
Does straight its own resemblance find;
45 Yet it creates, transcending these,
Far other worlds, and other seas;
Annihilating all that's made
To a green thought in a green shade.

Here at the fountain's sliding foot,
50 Or at some fruit-tree's mossy root,
Casting the body's vest aside,

My soul into the boughs does glide:
There like a bird it sits, and sings,
Then whets and combs its silver wings;
55 And, till prepared for longer flight,
Waves in its plumes the various light.

Such was that happy garden-state,
While man there walked without a mate:
After a place so pure and sweet,
60 What other help could yet be meet?
But 'twas beyond a mortal's share
To wander solitary there:
Two paradises 'twere in one,
To live in paradise alone.

65 How well the skilful gardener drew
Of flowers, and herbs, this dial new;
Where, from above, the milder sun
Does through a fragrant zodiac run;
And, as it works, the industrious bee
70 Computes its time as well as we.
How could such sweet and wholesome hours
Be reckoned but with herbs and flowers!

1681

The Fair Singer

To make a final conquest of all me,
Love did compose so sweet an enemy,
In whom both beauties to my death agree,
Joining themselves in fatal harmony;
5 That while she with her eyes my heart does bind,
She with her voice might captivate my mind.

I could have fled from one but singly fair:
My disentangled soul itself might save,
Breaking the curlèd trammels of her hair;
10 But how should I avoid to be her slave,
Whose subtle art invisibly can wreath
My fetters of the very air I breathe?

It had been easy fighting in some plain,
Where victory might hang in equal choice.
15 But all resistance against her is vain,
Who has th' advantage both of eyes and voice.
And all my forces needs must be undone,
She having gainèd both the wind and sun.

1681

The Coronet

When for the thorns with which I long, too long,
　　With many a piercing wound,
　　My Saviour's head have crown'd
I seek with garlands to redress that wrong:
5　　Through every garden, every mead,
I gather flow'rs (my fruits are only flow'rs)
　　Dismantling all the fragrant tow'rs
That once adorn'd my shepherdess's head.
And now when I have summed up all my store,
10　　Thinking (so I myself deceive)
　　So rich a chaplet thence to weave
As never yet the King of glory wore:
　　Alas I find the serpent old
　　That, twining in his speckled breast,
15　　About the flow'rs disguised does fold,
　　With wreaths of fame and interest.
Ah, foolish man, that would'st debase with them,
And mortal glory, heaven's diadem!
But Thou who only could'st the serpent tame
20 Either his slippery knots at once untie,
And disentangle all his winding snare:
Or shatter too with him my curious frame:
And let these wither, so that he may die,
　　Though set with skill and chosen out with care.
25 That they, while Thou on both their spoils dost tread,
May crown Thy feet, that could not crown Thy head.

1681

Alexander Pope
1688–1744

Alexander Pope was born in London, the son of a linen merchant, and was privately educated. As a Roman Catholic, he could not attend university, hold public office, or vote. Deformed by tuberculosis of the spine, he was left with a hunched, crooked frame and was just four-and-a-half feet tall. He taught himself Greek, learned French and Italian, and read extensively in English and Latin poetry. In his verse *Essay on Criticism* (1711), he outlined the ideals of the neoclassical tradition in criticism. With some of his friends and fellow writers, including Jonathan Swift and John Gay — both Tories like himself — he formed the Scriblerus Club to satirize all forms of false learning and pedantry.

Pope established his reputation as a poet with his translation of Homer's *Iliad* (1715–20) and attacked his literary and personal enemies — those who had maligned him for his religion or his deformity — with his mock epic *The Dunciad* (1728). He often used the epistles of Horace as models for his own verse epistles on the cultural, moral, and political malaise of his time. Translator, editor, and critic, he was a superb poet whose mastery of the heroic couplet confirmed the form as the standard for the time.

The Rape of the Lock

AN HEROI-COMICAL POEM

CANTO I

What dire offence from am'rous causes springs,
What mighty contests rise from trivial things,
I sing — This verse to *Caryll*, Muse! is due;
This, ev'n Belinda may vouchsafe to view:
5 Slight is the subject, but not so the praise,
If she inspire, and he approve my lays.
    Say what strange motive, Goddess! could compel
A well-bred Lord t'assault a gentle Belle?
Oh say what stranger cause, yet unexplored,
10 Could make a gentle Belle reject a Lord?
In tasks so bold, can little men engage,
And in soft bosoms dwells such mighty rage?
Sol through white curtains shot a tim'rous ray,
And op'd those eyes that must eclipse the day;
15 Now lapdogs give themselves the rousing shake,
And sleepless lovers, just at twelve, awake:

Thrice rung the bell, the slipper knocked the ground,
And the pressed watch returned a silver sound.
Belinda still her downy pillow pressed,
20 Her guardian Sylph prolonged the balmy rest.
'Twas he had summoned to her silent bed
The morning dream that hovered o'er her head.
A youth more glitt'ring than a birth-night Beau,
(That ev'n in slumber caused her cheek to glow)
25 Seemed to her ear his winning lips to lay,
And thus in whispers said, or seemed to say:
'Fairest of mortals, thou distinguished care
Of thousand bright inhabitants of air!
If e'er one vision touched thy infant thought,
30 Of all the nurse and all the priest have taught,
Of airy elves by moonlight shadows seen,
The silver token, and the circled green,
Or virgins visited by angel-pow'rs,
With golden crowns and wreaths of heav'nly flow'rs,
35 Hear and believe! thy own importance know,
Nor bound thy narrow views to things below.
Some secret truths from learned pride concealed,
To maids alone and children are revealed:
What though no credit doubting wits may give?
40 The fair and innocent shall still believe.
Know, then, unnumbered spirits round thee fly,
The light militia of the lower sky;
These, though unseen, are ever on the wing,
Hang o'er the box, and hover round the ring.
45 Think what an equipage thou hast in air,
And view with scorn two pages and a chair.
As now your own, our beings were of old,
And once enclosed in woman's beauteous mould;
Thence, by a soft transition, we repair
50 From earthly vehicles to these of air.
Think not, when woman's transient breath is fled,
That all her vanities at once are dead:
Succeeding vanities she still regards,
And though she plays no more, o'erlooks the cards.
55 Her joy in gilded chariots, when alive,
And love of ombre, after death survive.
For when the fair in all their pride expire,
To their first elements their souls retire:
The sprites of fiery termagants in flame

60   Mount up, and take a salamander's name.
     Soft yielding minds to water glide away,
     And sip, with nymphs, their elemental tea.
     The graver prude sinks downward to a gnome,
     In search of mischief still on earth to roam.
65   The light coquettes in sylphs aloft repair,
     And sport and flutter in the fields of air.
       'Know farther yet; Whoever fair and chaste
     Rejects mankind, is by some sylph embraced:
     For spirits, freed from mortal laws, with ease
70   Assume what sexes and what shapes they please.
     What guards the purity of melting maids,
     In courtly balls, and midnight masquerades,
     Safe from the treach'rous friend, and daring spark,
     The glance by day, the whisper in the dark;
75   When kind occasion prompts their warm desires,
     When music softens, and when dancing fires?
     'Tis but their sylph, the wise celestials know,
     Though honour is the word with men below.
       'Some nymphs there are, too conscious of their face,
80   For life predestined to the gnomes' embrace.
     These swell their prospects and exalt their pride,
     When offers are disdained, and love denied.
     Then gay ideas crowd the vacant brain;
     While peers and dukes, and all their sweeping train,
85   And garters, stars, and coronets appear,
     And in soft sounds, Your Grace salutes their ear.
     'Tis these that early taint the female soul,
     Instruct the eyes of young coquettes to roll,
     Teach infant cheeks a bidden blush to know,
90   And little hearts to flutter at a beau.
       'Oft when the world imagine women stray,
     The sylphs through mystic mazes guide their way,
     Through all the giddy circle they pursue,
     And old impertinence expel by new.
95   What tender maid but must a victim fall
     To one man's treat, but for another's ball?
     When Florio speaks, what virgin could withstand,
     If gentle Damon did not squeeze her hand?
     With varying vanities, from ev'ry part,
100   They shift the moving toyshop of their heart;
     Where wigs with wigs, with sword-knots sword-knots
       strive,

Beaus banish beaus, and coaches coaches drive.
This erring mortals levity may call,
Oh blind to truth! The sylphs contrive it all.
105   'Of these am I, who thy protection claim,
A watchful sprite, and Ariel is my name.
Late, as I ranged the crystal wilds of air,
In the clear mirror of thy ruling star
I saw, alas! some dread event impend,
110 Ere to the main this morning sun descend.
But Heav'n reveals not what, or how, or where:
Warned by thy sylph, oh pious maid, beware!
This to disclose is all thy guardian can.
Beware of all, but most beware of man!'
115   He said; when Shock, who thought she slept too long,
Leapt up, and waked his mistress with his tongue.
'Twas then Belinda! if report say true,
Thy eyes first opened on a billet-doux;
Wounds, charms, and ardours, were no sooner read,
120 But all the vision vanished from thy head.
  And now, unveiled, the toilet stands displayed,
Each silver vase in mystic order laid.
First, robed in white, the nymph intent adores
With head uncovered, the cosmetic pow'rs.
125 A heav'nly image in the glass appears,
To that she bends, to that her eyes she rears;
Th' inferior priestess, at her altar's side,
Trembling, begins the sacred rites of pride.
Unnumbered treasures ope at once, and here
130 The various off'rings of the world appear;
From each she nicely culls with curious toil,
And decks the goddess with the glitt'ring spoil.
This casket India's glowing gems unlocks,
And all Arabia breathes from yonder box.
135 The tortoise here and elephant unite,
Transformed to combs, the speckled and the white.
Here files of pins extend their shining rows,
Puffs, powders, patches, bibles, billet-doux.
Now awful beauty puts on all its arms;
140 The fair each moment rises in her charms,
Repairs her smiles, awakens ev'ry grace,
And calls forth all the wonders of her face;
Sees by degrees a purer blush arise,
And keener lightnings quicken in her eyes.

145 The busy sylphs surround their darling care;
These set the head, and those divide the hair,
Some fold the sleeve, while others plait the gown;
And Betty's praised for labours not her own.

CANTO II

Not with more glories, in th' Ethereal Plain,
The sun first rises o'er the purpled main,
Than issuing forth, the rival of his beams
Launched on the bosom of the silver Thames.
5 Fair nymphs, and well-dressed youths around her shone,
But ev'ry eye was fixed on her alone.
On her white breast a sparkling cross she wore,
Which Jews might kiss, and infidels adore.
Her lively looks a sprightly mind disclose,
10 Quick as her eyes, and as unfixed as those:
Favours to none, to all she smiles extends,
Oft she rejects, but never once offends.
Bright as the sun, her eyes the gazers strike,
And, like the sun, they shine on all alike.
15 Yet graceful ease, and sweetness void of pride,
Might hide her faults, if Belles had faults to hide:
If to her share some female errors fall,
Look on her face, and you'll forget 'em all.
This nymph, to the destruction of mankind,
20 Nourished two locks, which graceful hung behind
In equal curls, and well conspired to deck
With shining ringlets her smooth ivory neck.
Love in these labyrinths his slaves detains,
And mighty hearts are held in slender chains.
25 With hairy sprindges we the birds betray,
Slight lines of hair surprise the finny prey,
Fair tresses man's imperial race ensnare,
And beauty draws us with a single hair.
Th' adventurous Baron the bright locks admired,
30 He saw, he wished, and to the prize aspired:
Resolved to win, he meditates the way,
By force to ravish, or by fraud betray;
For when success a lover's toil attends,
Few ask, if fraud or force attained his ends.
35 For this, ere Phoebus rose, he had implored
Propitious Heav'n, and ev'ry pow'r adored,

But chiefly Love — to Love an altar built,
Of twelve vast French romances, neatly gilt.
There lay three garters, half a pair of gloves;
40 And all the trophies of his former loves.
With tender billet-doux he lights the pyre,
And breathes three am'rous sighs to raise the fire.
Then prostrate falls, and begs with ardent eyes
Soon to obtain, and long possess the prize:
45 The pow'rs gave ear, and granted half his prayer,
The rest, the winds dispersed in empty air.
    But now secure the painted vessel glides,
The sunbeams trembling on the floating tides,
While melting music steals upon the sky,
50 And softened sounds along the waters die.
Smooth flow the waves, the zephyrs gently play,
Belinda smiled, and all the world was gay.
All but the sylph — With careful thoughts oppressed,
Th' impending woe sat heavy on his breast.
55 He summons strait his denizens of air;
The lucid squadrons round the sails repair:
Soft o'er the shrouds Aerial whispers breathe,
That seemed but zephyrs to the train beneath.
Some to the sun their insect-wings unfold,
60 Waft on the breeze, or sink in clouds of gold.
Transparent forms, too fine for mortal sight,
Their fluid bodies half dissolved in light.
Loose to the wind their airy garments flew,
Thin glitt'ring textures of the filmy dew;
65 Dipped in the richest tincture of the skies,
Where light disports in ever-mingling dyes,
While ev'ry beam new transient colours flings,
Colours that change whene'er they wave their wings.
Amid the circle, on the gilded mast,
70 Superior by the head, was Ariel placed;
His purple pinions opening to the sun,
He raised his azure wand, and thus begun.
    'Ye Sylphs and Sylphids, to your chief give ear,
Fays, Fairies, Genii, Elves, and Daemons hear!
75 Ye know the spheres and various tasks assigned,
By laws eternal to th' aerial kind.
Some in the fields of purest aether play,
And bask and whiten in the blaze of day.
Some guide the course of wand'ring orbs on high,

80   Or roll the planets through the boundless sky.
     Some less refined, beneath the moon's pale light
     Pursue the stars that shoot athwart the night,
     Or suck the mists in grosser air below,
     Or dip their pinions in the painted bow,
85   Or brew fierce tempests on the wintry main,
     Or o'er the glebe distill the kindly rain.
     Others on earth o'er human race preside,
     Watch all their ways, and all their actions guide:
     Of these the chief the care of nations own,
90   And guard with arms divine the British Throne.
       'Our humbler province is to tend the fair,
     Not a less pleasing, though less glorious care.
     To save the powder from too rude a gale,
     Nor let th' imprisoned essences exhale,
95   To draw fresh colours from the vernal flow'rs,
     To steal from rainbows e'er they drop in show'rs
     A brighter wash; to curl their waving hairs,
     Assist their blushes, and inspire their airs;
     Nay oft, in dreams, invention we bestow,
100   To change a flounce, or add a furbelow.
       'This day, black omens threat the brightest fair
     That e'er deserved a watchful spirit's care;
     Some dire disaster, or by force, or sleight,
     But what, or where, the fates have wrapped in night.
105   Whether the nymph shall break Diana's law,
     Or some frail china jar receive a flaw,
     Or stain her honour, or her new brocade,
     Forget her prayers, or miss a masquerade,
     Or lose her heart, or necklace, at a ball;
110   Or whether Heav'n has doomed that Shock must fall.
     Haste then, ye spirits! to your charge repair:
     The flutt'ring fan be Zephyretta's care;
     The drops to thee, Brillante, we consign;
     And, Momentilla, let the watch be thine;
115   Do thou, Crispissa, tend her fav'rite lock;
     Ariel himself shall be the guard of Shock.
       'To fifty chosen sylphs, of special note,
     We trust th' important charge, the petticoat:
     Oft have we known that sev'nfold fence to fail,
120   Though stiff with hoops, and armed with ribs of whale.
     Form a strong line about the silver bound,
     And guard the wide circumference around.

'Whatever spirit, careless of his charge,
His post neglects, or leaves the fair at large,
125 Shall feel sharp vengeance soon o'ertake his sins,
Be stopped in vials, or transfixed with pins;
Or plunged in lakes of bitter washes lie,
Or wedged whole ages in a bodkin's eye:
Gums and pomatums shall his flight restrain,
130 While clogged he beats his silken wings in vain;
Or alum styptics with contracting power
Shrink his thin essence like a rivelled flower.
Or as Ixion fixed, the wretch shall feel
The giddy motion of the whirling mill,
135 In fumes of burning chocolate shall glow,
And tremble at the sea that froths below!'
    He spoke; the spirits from the sails descend;
Some, orb in orb, around the nymph extend,
Some thrid the mazy ringlets of her hair,
140 Some hang upon the pendants of her ear;
With beating hearts the dire event they wait,
Anxious, and trembling for the birth of fate.

CANTO III

Close by those meads forever crowned with flow'rs,
Where Thames with pride surveys his rising tow'rs,
There stands a structure of majestic frame,
Which from the neighb'ring Hampton takes its name.
5 Here Britain's statesmen oft the fall foredoom
Of foreign tyrants, and of nymphs at home;
Here thou, great Anna! whom three realms obey,
Dost sometimes counsel take — and sometimes tea.
    Hither the heroes and the nymphs resort,
10 To taste awhile the pleasures of a court;
In various talk th' instructive hours they past,
Who gave the ball, or paid the visit last:
One speaks the glory of the British Queen,
And one describes a charming Indian screen;
15 A third interprets motions, looks, and eyes;
At ev'ry word a reputation dies.
Snuff, or the fan, supply each pause of chat,
With singing, laughing, ogling, and all that.
    Mean while declining from the noon of day,
20 The sun obliquely shoots his burning ray;

The hungry judges soon the sentence sign,
And wretches hang that jurymen may dine;
The merchant from th' Exchange returns in peace,
And the long labours of the toilette cease —

25   Belinda now, whom thirst of fame invites,
Burns to encounter two adventurous knights,
At ombre singly to decide their doom;
And swells her breast with conquests yet to come.
Strait the three bands prepare in arms to join,

30   Each band the number of the Sacred Nine.
Soon as she spreads her hand, th' aerial guard
Descend, and sit on each important card:
First Ariel perched upon a Matadore,
Then each, according to the rank they bore;

35   For sylphs, yet mindful of their ancient race,
Are, as when women, wondrous fond of place.
     Behold, four Kings in majesty revered,
With hoary whiskers and a forky beard;
And four fair Queens whose hands sustain a flow'r,

40   Th' expressive emblem of their softer pow'r;
Four Knaves in garbs succinct, a trusty band,
Caps on their heads, and halberds in their hand;
And particoloured troops, a shining train,
Draw forth to combat on the velvet plain.

45   The skilful nymph reviews her force with care;
'Let spades be trumps!' she said, and trumps they were.
    Now move to war her sable Matadores,
In show like leaders of the swarthy Moors.
Spadillio first, unconquerable lord!

50   Let off two captive trumps, and swept the board.
As many more Manillio forced to yield,
And marched a victor from the verdant field.
Him Basto followed, but his fate more hard
Gained but one trump and one plebeian card.

55   With his broad sabre next, a chief in years,
The hoary Majesty of Spades appears,
Puts forth one manly leg, to sight revealed;
The rest, his many-coloured robe concealed.
The rebel-Knave, who dares his prince engage,

60   Proves the just victim of his royal rage.
Ev'n mighty Pam, that kings and queens o'erthrew,
And mowed down armies in the fights of Lu,
Sad chance of war! now, destitute of aid,

Falls undistinguished by the victor spade!
65   Thus far both armies to Belinda yield;
Now to the Baron Fate inclines the field.
His warlike Amazon her host invades,
Th' imperial consort of the crown of spades.
The club's black tyrant first her victim died,
70 Spite of his haughty mien, and barb'rous pride:
What boots the regal circle on his head,
His giant limbs in state unwieldy spread?
That long behind he trails his pompous robe,
And of all monarchs only grasps the globe?
75   The Baron now his diamonds pours apace;
Th' embroidered King who shows but half his face,
And his refulgent Queen, with pow'rs combined,
Of broken troops an easy conquest find.
Clubs, diamonds, hearts, in wild disorder seen,
80 With throngs promiscuous strew the level green.
Thus when dispersed a routed army runs,
Of Asia's troops, and Afric's sable sons,
With like confusion different nations fly,
Of various habit and of various dye,
85 The pierced battalions disunited fall,
In heaps on heaps; one fate o'erwhelms them all.
     The Knave of diamonds tries his wily arts,
And wins (oh shameful Chance!) the Queen of hearts.
At this, the blood the virgin's cheek forsook,
90 A livid paleness spreads o'er all her look;
She sees, and trembles at th' approaching ill,
Just in the jaws of ruin, and Codille.
And now, (as oft in some distempered state)
On one nice trick depends the gen'ral fate.
95 An Ace of hearts steps forth: the King unseen
Lurked in her hand, and mourned his captive Queen.
He springs to vengeance with an eager pace,
And falls like thunder on the prostrate Ace.
The nymph exulting fills with shouts the sky,
100 The walls, the woods, and long canals reply.
     Oh thoughtless mortals! ever blind to Fate,
Too soon dejected, and too soon elate!
Sudden these honours shall be snatched away,
And cursed for ever this victorious day.
105   For lo! the board with cups and spoons is crowned,
The berries crackle, and the mill turns round.

On shining altars of Japan they raise
The silver lamp; the fiery spirits blaze.
From silver spouts the grateful liquors glide,
110   While China's earth receives the smoking tide.
At once they gratify their scent and taste,
And frequent cups prolong the rich repast.
Strait hover round the fair her airy band;
Some, as she sipped, the fuming liquor fanned,
115   Some o'er her lap their careful plumes displayed,
Trembling, and conscious of the rich brocade.
Coffee, (which makes the politician wise,
And see through all things with his half-shut eyes)
Sent up in vapours to the Baron's brain
120   New stratagems, the radiant lock to gain.
Ah cease, rash youth! desist ere 'tis too late,
Fear the just gods, and think of Scylla's fate!
Changed to a bird, and sent to flit in air,
She dearly pays for Nisus' injured hair!
125   But when to mischief mortals bend their will,
How soon they find fit instruments of ill!
Just then, Clarissa drew with tempting grace
A two-edged weapon from her shining case;
So ladies in romance assist their knight,
130   Present the spear, and arm him for the fight.
He takes the gift with rev'rence, and extends
The little engine on his fingers' ends,
This just behind Belinda's neck he spread,
As o'er the fragrant steams she bends her head:
135   Swift to the lock a thousand sprites repair,
A thousand wings, by turns, blow back the hair,
And thrice they twitched the diamond in her ear,
Thrice she looked back, and thrice the foe drew near.
Just in that instant, anxious Ariel sought
140   The close recesses of the virgin's thought;
As on the nosegay in her breast reclined,
He watched th' ideas rising in her mind,
Sudden he viewed, in spite of all her art,
An earthly lover lurking at her heart.
145   Amazed, confused, he found his pow'r expired,
Resigned to Fate, and with a sigh retired.
     The peer now spreads the glittering forfex wide,
T' enclose the lock; now joins it, to divide.
Ev'n then, before the fatal engine closed,

150 A wretched sylph too fondly interposed;
Fate urged the shears, and cut the sylph in twain,
(But airy substance soon unites again),
The meeting points the sacred hair dissever
From the fair head, forever and forever!

155 Then flashed the living lightning from her eyes,
And screams of horror rend th' affrighted skies.
Not louder shrieks to pitying Heav'n are cast,
When husbands or when lapdogs breathe their last,
Or when rich China vessels, fallen from high,

160 In glitt'ring dust and painted fragments lie!
'Let wreaths of triumph now my temples twine,'
(The victor cried) 'the glorious prize is mine!
While fish in streams, or birds delight in air,
Or in a coach and six the British fair,

165 As long as Atalantis shall be read,
Or the small pillow grace a lady's bed,
While visits shall be paid on solemn days,
When numerous wax-lights in bright order blaze,
While nymphs take treats, or assignations give,

170 So long my honour, name, and praise shall live!'
What time would spare, from steel receives its date,
And monuments, like men, submit to Fate!
Steel could the labour of the gods destroy,
And strike to dust th' imperial tow'rs of Troy;

175 Steel could the works of mortal pride confound,
And hew triumphal arches to the ground.
What wonder then, fair nymph! thy hairs should feel
The conqu'ring force of unresisted steel?

CANTO IV

But anxious cares the pensive nymph oppressed,
And secret passions laboured in her breast.
Not youthful kings in battle seized alive,
Not scornful virgins who their charms survive,

5 Not ardent lovers robbed of all their bliss,
Not ancient ladies when refused a kiss,
Not tyrants fierce that unrepenting die,
Not Cynthia when her manteau's pinned awry,
E'er felt such rage, resentment and despair,

10 As thou, sad virgin! for thy ravished hair.
For, that sad moment, when the sylphs withdrew,

And Ariel weeping from Belinda flew,
Umbriel, a dusky melancholy sprite,
As ever sullied the fair face of light,
15   Down to the central earth, his proper scene,
Repaired to search the gloomy Cave of Spleen.
    Swift on his sooty pinions flits the Gnome,
And in a vapour reached the dismal dome.
No cheerful breeze this sullen region knows,
20   The dreaded East is all the wind that blows.
Here, in a grotto, sheltered close from air,
And screened in shades from day's detested glare,
She sighs for ever on her pensive bed,
Pain at her side, and megrim at her head.
25   Two handmaids wait the throne: alike in place,
But diff'ring far in figure and in face.
Here stood Ill Nature like an ancient maid,
Her wrinkled form in black and white arrayed;
With store of prayers, for mornings, nights, and noons,
30   Her hand is filled; her bosom with lampoons.
    There Affectation with a sickly mien
Shows in her cheek the roses of eighteen,
Practised to lisp, and hang the head aside,
Faints into airs, and languishes with pride;
35   On the rich quilt sinks with becoming woe,
Wrapped in a gown, for sickness, and for show.
The Fair Ones feel such maladies as these,
When each new nightdress gives a new disease.
    A constant vapour o'er the palace flies;
40   Strange phantoms rising as the mists arise;
Dreadful, as hermit's dreams in haunted shades,
Or bright as visions of expiring maids.
Now glaring fiends, and snakes on rolling spires,
Pale spectres, gaping tombs, and purple fires:
45   Now lakes of liquid gold, Elysian scenes,
And crystal domes, and angels in machines.
    Unnumbered throngs on ev'ry side are seen
Of bodies changed to various forms by spleen.
Here living teapots stand, one arm held out,
50   One bent; the handle this, and that the spout:
A pipkin there like Homer's tripod walks;
Here sighs a jar, and there a goose pie talks;
Men prove with child, as pow'rful fancy works,
And maids turned bottles, call aloud for corks.

55   Safe past the gnome through this fantastic band,
A branch of healing spleenwort in his hand.
Then thus addressed the power — 'Hail wayward Queen!
Who rule the sex to fifty from fifteen,
Parent of vapors and of female wit,
60   Who give th' hysteric, or poetic fit,
On various tempers act by various ways,
Make some take physic, others scribble plays;
Who cause the proud their visits to delay,
And send the godly in a pet to pray.
65   A nymph there is, that all thy pow'r disdains,
And thousands more in equal mirth maintains.
But oh! if e'er thy Gnome could spoil a grace,
Or raise a pimple on a beauteous face,
Like citron-waters matrons' cheeks inflame,
70   Or change complexions at a losing game;
If e'er with airy horns I planted heads,
Or rumpled petticoats, or tumbled beds,
Or caused suspicion when no soul was rude,
Or discomposed the headdress of a prude,
75   Or e'er to costive lapdog gave disease,
Which not the tears of brightest eyes could ease:
Hear me, and touch Belinda with chagrin;
That single act gives half the world the spleen.'
     The goddess with a discontented air
80   Seems to reject him, though she grants his prayer.
A wondrous bag with both her hands she binds,
Like that where once Ulysses held the winds;
There she collects the force of female lungs,
Sighs, sobs, and passions, and the war of tongues.
85   A vial next she fills with fainting fears,
Soft sorrows, melting griefs, and flowing tears.
The gnome rejoicing bears her gift away,
Spreads his black wings, and slowly mounts to day.
     Sunk in Thalestris' arms the nymph he found,
90   Her eyes dejected and her hair unbound.
Full o'er their heads the swelling bag he rent,
And all the Furies issued at the vent.
Belinda burns with more than mortal ire,
And fierce Thalestris fans the rising fire.
95   'O wretched maid!' she spread her hands, and cried,
(While Hampton's echoes, 'Wretched maid!' replied)
'Was it for this you took such constant care

The bodkin, comb, and essence to prepare;
For this your locks in paper-durance bound,
100 For this with torturing irons wreathed around?
For this with fillets strained your tender head,
And bravely bore the double loads of lead?
Gods! shall the ravisher display your hair,
While the fops envy, and the ladies stare!
105 Honour forbid! at whose unrivalled shrine
Ease, pleasure, virtue, all, our sex resign.
Methinks already I your tears survey,
Already hear the horrid things they say,
Already see you a degraded toast,
110 And all your honour in a whisper lost!
How shall I, then, your helpless fame defend?
'Twill then be infamy to seem your friend!
And shall this prize, th' inestimable prize,
Exposed thro' crystal to the gazing eyes,
115 And heightened by the diamond's circling rays,
On that rapacious hand for ever blaze?
Sooner shall grass in Hyde Park Circus grow,
And wits take lodgings in the sound of Bow;
Sooner let Earth, Air, Sea, to Chaos fall,
120 Men, monkeys, lapdogs, parrots, perish all!'
    She said; then raging to Sir Plume repairs,
And bids her beau demand the precious hairs:
(Sir Plume, of amber snuffbox justly vain,
And the nice conduct of a clouded cane)
125 With earnest eyes, and round unthinking face,
He first the snuffbox opened, then the case,
And thus broke out —'My lord, why, what the devil?
Z——ds! damn the lock! 'fore Gad, you must be civil!
Plague on't! 'tis past a jest— nay prithee, pox!
130 Give her the hair'— he spoke, and rapped his box.
    'It grieves me much' (replied the peer again)
'Who speaks so well should ever speak in vain.
But by this lock, this sacred lock I swear,
(Which never more shall join its parted hair,
135 Which never more its honours shall renew,
Clipped from the lovely head where late it grew)
That while my nostrils draw the vital air,
This hand, which won it, shall for ever wear.'
He spoke, and speaking, in proud triumph spread
140 The long-contended honours of her head.

But Umbriel, hateful gnome! forbears not so;
He breaks the vial whence the sorrows flow.
Then see! the nymph in beauteous grief appears,
Her eyes half languishing, half drowned in tears;
145 On her heaved bosom hung her drooping head,
Which, with a sigh, she raised; and thus she said:
    'Forever cursed be this detested day,
Which snatched my best, my fav'rite curl away!
Happy! ah ten times happy, had I been,
150 If Hampton Court these eyes had never seen!
Yet am not I the first mistaken maid,
By love of courts to num'rous ills betrayed.
Oh had I rather un-admired remained
In some lone isle, or distant northern land;
155 Where the gilt chariot never marks the way,
Where none learn ombre, none e'er taste bohea!
There kept my charms concealed from mortal eye,
Like roses that in deserts bloom and die.
What moved my mind with youthful lords to roam?
160 O had I stayed, and said my prayers at home!
'Twas this, the morning omens seemed to tell;
Thrice from my trembling hand the patch-box fell;
The tott'ring china shook without a wind,
Nay, Poll sat mute, and Shock was most unkind!
165 A sylph too warned me of the threats of fate,
In mystic visions, now believed too late!
See the poor remnants of these slighted hairs!
My hands shall rend what ev'n thy rapine spares:
These, in two sable ringlets taught to break,
170 Once gave new beauties to the snowy neck.
The sister-lock now sits uncouth, alone,
And in its fellow's fate foresees its own;
Uncurled it hangs, the fatal sheers demands;
And tempts once more thy sacrilegious hands.
175 Oh hadst thou, cruel! been content to seize
Hairs less in sight, or any hairs but these!'

CANTO V

She said: the pitying audience melt in tears,
But Fate and Jove had stopped the Baron's ears.
In vain Thalestris with reproach assails,
For who can move when fair Belinda fails?

5   Not half so fixed the Trojan could remain,
While Anna begged and Dido raged in vain.
Then grave Clarissa graceful waved her fan;
Silence ensued, and thus the nymph began.
   'Say, why are beauties praised and honoured most,
10   The wise man's passion, and the vain man's toast?
Why decked with all that land and sea afford,
Why angels called, and angel-like adored?
Why round our coaches crowd the white-gloved beaus,
Why bows the side-box from its inmost rows?
15   How vain are all these glories, all our pains,
Unless good sense preserve what beauty gains:
That men may say, when we the front-box grace,
"Behold the first in virtue, as in face!"
Oh! if to dance all night, and dress all day,
20   Charmed the smallpox, or chased old age away,
Who would not scorn what housewife's cares produce,
Or who would learn one earthly thing of use?
To patch, nay ogle, might become a saint,
Nor could it sure be such a sin to paint.
25   But since, alas! frail beauty must decay,
Curled or uncurled, since locks will turn to grey,
Since painted or not painted, all shall fade,
And she who scorns a man, must die a maid;
What then remains, but well our pow'r to use,
30   And keep good humour still whate'er we lose?
And trust me, Dear! good humour can prevail,
When airs, and flights, and screams, and scolding fail.
Beauties in vain their pretty eyes may roll;
Charms strike the sight, but merit wins the soul.'
35   So spoke the dame, but no applause ensued;
Belinda frowned, Thalestris called her prude.
'To arms, to arms!' the fierce virago cries,
And swift as lightning to the combat flies.
All side in parties, and begin th' attack;
40   Fans clap, silks rustle, and tough whalebones crack;
Heroes' and heroines' shouts confus'dly rise,
And bass, and treble voices strike the skies.
No common weapons in their hands are found;
Like gods they fight, nor dread a mortal wound.
45   So when bold Homer makes the gods engage,
And heav'nly breasts with human passions rage;
'Gainst Pallas, Mars; Latona, Hermes arms;
And all Olympus rings with loud alarms.

Jove's thunder roars, Heav'n trembles all around;
50 Blue Neptune storms, the bellowing deeps resound;
Earth shakes her nodding tow'rs, the ground gives way;
And the pale ghosts start at the flash of day!
    Triumphant Umbriel on a sconce's height
Clapped his glad wings, and sat to view the fight:
55 Propped on their bodkin spears, the sprites survey
The growing combat, or assist the fray.
    While through the press enraged Thalestris flies,
And scatters death around from both her eyes,
A beau and witling perished in the throng;
60 One died in metaphor, and one in song.
'O cruel nymph! a living death I bear,'
Cried Dapperwit, and sunk beside his chair.
A mournful glance Sir Fopling upwards cast,
'Those eyes are made so killing'— was his last:
65 Thus on Maeander's flow'ry margin lies
Th' expiring swan, and as he sings he dies.
    When bold Sir Plume had drawn Clarissa down,
Chloe stepped in, and killed him with a frown;
She smiled to see the doughty hero slain,
70 But at her smile, the beau revived again.
    Now Jove suspends his golden scales in air,
Weighs the men's wits against the lady's hair;
The doubtful beam long nods from side to side;
At length the wits mount up, the hairs subside.
75   See fierce Belinda on the Baron flies,
With more than usual lightning in her eyes;
Nor feared the Chief th' unequal fight to try,
Who sought no more than on his foe to die.
But this bold lord, with manly strength endued,
80 She with one finger and a thumb subdued:
Just where the breath of life his nostrils drew,
A charge of snuff the wily virgin threw;
The gnomes direct, to ev'ry atom just,
The pungent grains of titillating dust.
85 Sudden, with starting tears each eye o'erflows,
And the high dome re-echoes to his nose.
'Now meet thy fate,' incensed Belinda cried,
And drew a deadly bodkin from her side.
(The same, his ancient personage to deck,
90 Her great great grandsire wore about his neck
In three seal rings; which after, melted down,
Formed a vast buckle for his widow's gown:

Her infant grandame's whistle next it grew,
The bells she jingled, and the whistle blew;
95   Then in a bodkin graced her mother's hairs,
Which long she wore, and now Belinda wears.)
    'Boast not my fall' (he cried) 'insulting foe!
Thou by some other shalt be laid as low.
Nor think, to die dejects my lofty mind;
100   All that I dread is leaving you behind!
Rather than so, ah let me still survive,
And burn in Cupid's flames — but burn alive.'
    'Restore the lock!' she cries; and all around
'Restore the lock!' the vaulted roofs rebound.
105   Not fierce Othello in so loud a strain
Roared for the handkerchief that caused his pain.
But see how oft ambitious aims are crossed,
And chiefs contend till all the prize is lost!
The lock, obtained with guilt, and kept with pain,
110   In ev'ry place is sought, but sought in vain:
With such a prize no mortal must be blest,
So Heav'n decrees! with Heav'n who can contest?
    Some thought it mounted to the lunar sphere,
Since all things lost on earth, are treasured there.
115   There heroes' wits are kept in pond'rous vases,
And beaus' in snuffboxes and tweezer cases.
There broken vows, and deathbed alms are found,
And lovers' hearts with ends of riband bound;
The courtier's promises, and sick man's prayers,
120   The smiles of harlots, and the tears of heirs,
Cages for gnats, and chains to yoke a flea,
Dried butterflies, and tomes of casuistry.
    But trust the Muse — she saw it upward rise,
Though marked by none but quick poetic eyes:
125   (So Rome's great founder to the Heav'ns withdrew,
To Proculus alone confessed in view.)
A sudden star, it shot through liquid air,
And drew behind a radiant trail of hair.
Not Berenice's locks first rose so bright,
130   The heavens bespangling with dishevelled light.
The sylphs behold it kindling as it flies,
And pleased pursue its progress through the skies.
    This the beau monde shall from the Mall survey,
And hail with music its propitious ray.
135   This, the blest lover shall for Venus take,
And send up vows from Rosamonda's lake.

This Partridge soon shall view in cloudless skies,
When next he looks through Galileo's eyes;
And hence th' egregious wizard shall foredoom
140 The fate of Louis, and the fall of Rome.
Then cease, bright nymph! to mourn the ravished hair
Which adds new glory to the shining sphere!
Not all the tresses that fair head can boast
Shall draw such envy as the lock you lost.
145 For, after all the murders of your eye,
When, after millions slain, yourself shall die;
When those fair suns shall set, as set they must,
And all those tresses shall be laid in dust;
This lock, the Muse shall consecrate to fame,
150 And midst the stars inscribe Belinda's Name!

1712–14

Epistle IV
To Richard Boyle, Earl of Burlington

The Argument:
Of the Use of Riches
The Vanity of Expence in People of Wealth and Quality. The abuse of the word Taste, v. 13.
That the first principle and foundation, in this as in everything else, is Good Sense, v. 40.
The chief proof of it is to follow Nature, *even in works of mere Luxury and Elegance.*
Instanced in Architecture *and* Gardening, *where all must be adapted to the* Genius *and*
Use *of the Place, and the Beauties not forced into it, but resulting from it, v. 50. How men*
are disappointed in their most expensive undertakings, for want of this true Foundation,
without which nothing can please long, if at all; and the best Examples *and* Rules *will but*
be perverted into something burdensome *or ridiculous, v. 65, &c. to 92. A description of*
the false Taste *of* Magnificence; *the first grand Error of which is to imagine that Greatness*
consists in the Size *and* Dimension, *instead of the* Proportion *and* Harmony *of the whole,*
v. 97, *and the second, either in joining together* Parts incoherent, *or too* minutely *resem-*
bling, or in the Repetition *of the same too frequently, v. 105, &c. A word or two of false*
Taste in Books, *in* Music, *in* Painting, *even in* Preaching *and* Prayer, *and lastly in*
Entertainments, v. 133, &c. Yet PROVIDENCE *is justified in giving Wealth to be squandered*
in this manner, since it is dispersed to the Poor and Laborious part of mankind, v. 169.
[*Recurring to what is laid down in the first book, Ep. ii. and in the Epistle preceding this, v.*
159, &c.] *What are the* proper Objects *of Magnificence, and a proper field for the Expence*
of Great Men, v. 177, &c. *and finally, the Great and Public Works which become a* Prince,
v. 191, *to the end.*

My Lord,

The Clamour raised about this Epistle could not give me so much pain, as I received pleasure in seeing the general Zeal of the World in the cause of a Great Man who is Beneficent, and the particular Warmth of your Lordship in that of a private Man who is innocent.

It was not the Poem *that deserved this from you; for as I had the Honour to be your friend, I cou'd not treat you quite like a Poet: but sure the* Writer *deserved more Candor even from those who knew him not, that to promote a Report which in regard to that Noble Person, was* Impertinent; *in regard to me,* Villainous. *Yet I had no great Cause to wonder, that a Character belonging to* twenty *shou'd be applied to* one; *since, by that means,* nineteen *wou'd escape the Ridicule.*

I was too well content with my Knowledge of that Noble Person's Opinion in this Affair, to trouble the publick about it. But since Malice and Mistake are so long a dying, I take the opportunity of this third Edition to declare His Belief, *not only of* My Innocence, *but of* Their Malignity, *of the former of which my own Heart is as conscious, as I fear of theirs must be of the latter. His Humanity feels a Concern for the Injury done to* Me, *while His Greatness of Mind can bear with Indifference the Insult offered to* Himself.

However, my Lord, I own, that Critics of this Sort can intimidate me, nay half incline me to write no more: It wou'd be making the Town a Compliment which I think it deserves, and which some, I am sure, wou'd take very kindly. This way of Satire is dangerous, as long as Slander raised by Fools of the lowest Rank, can find any Countenance from those of a Higher. Even from the Conduct shewn on this occasion, I have learnt there are some who wou'd rather be wicked *than* ridiculous; *and therefore it may be safer to attack* Vices *than* Follies. *I will leave my Betters in the quiet Possession of their* Idols, *their* Groves, *and their* High-Places; *and change my Subject from their* Pride *to their* Meanness, *from their* Vanities *to their* Miseries: *And as the only certain way to avoid Misconstruction, to lessen Offence, and not to multiply ill-natured Applications, I may probably in my next make use of* Real *Names and not of* Fictitious *Ones.*

I am,

My Lord,

Your Faithful,

Affectionate Servant,

A. POPE.

'Tis strange, the Miser should his Cares employ,
To gain those Riches he can ne'er enjoy:
Is it less strange, the Prodigal should waste
His wealth, to purchase what he ne'er can taste?
5 Not for himself he sees, or hears, or eats;
Artists must chuse his Pictures, Music, Meats:
He buys for Topham,[1] Drawings and Designs,

---

1 'A Gentleman famous for judicious collection of Drawings' [Pope's note]: Richard Topham (d. 1735), Keeper of the Records in the Tower of London

For Pembroke[2] Statues, dirty Gods, and Coins;
Rare monkish Manuscripts for Hearne[3] alone,
10   And Books for Mead, and Butterflies for Sloane.[4]
Think we all these are for himself? no more
Than his fine Wife, alas! or finer Whore.
    For what has Virro painted, built, and planted?
Only to show, how many Tastes he wanted.
15   What brought Sir Visto's ill got wealth to waste?
Some Daemon whispered, 'Visto! have a Taste.'
Heav'n visits with a Taste the wealthy fool,
And needs no Rod but Ripley[5] with a Rule.
See! sportive fate, to punish aukward pride,
20   Bids Bubo[6] build, and sends him such a Guide:
A standing sermon, at each year's expence,
That never Coxcomb reached Magnificence!
    You show us, Rome was glorious, not profuse,[7]
And pompous buildings once were things of Use.
25   Yet shall (my Lord) your just, your noble rules
Fill half the land with Imitating-Fools;
Who random drawings from your sheets shall take,
And of one beauty many blunders make;
Load some vain Church with old Theatric state,
30   Turn Arcs of triumph to a Garden-gate;
Reverse your Ornaments, and hang them all
On some patched dog-hole eked with ends of wall,
Then clap four slices of Pilaster on't,
That, laced with bits of rustic, makes a Front:
35   Or call the winds thro' long arcades to roar,
Proud to catch cold at a Venetian[8] door;
Conscious they act a true Palladian part,
And if they starve, they starve by rules of art.
    Oft have you hinted to your brother Peer,
40   A certain truth, which many buy too dear:
Something there is, more needful than Expence,

2 Thomas Herbert (*c.* 1656–1733), eighth Earl of Pembroke and a Whig politician
3 Thomas Hearne (1678–1735), a famous medievalist and medical scholar
4 'Two eminent Physicians: the one [Richard Mead 1673–1754] had an excellent Library, the other [Sir Hans Sloane 1660–1753] the finest collection in Europe of natural curiosities; both men of great learning and humanity' [Pope's note].
5 'This man was a carpenter, employed by a first Minister [Sir Robert Walpole], who raised him to an Architect, without any genius in the art; and after some wretched proofs of his insufficiency in public Buildings, made him Comptroller of the Board of works' [Pope's note].
6 George Bubb (1691–1762), a Whig politician and literary patron
7 'The Earl of Burlington was then publishing the Designs of Inigo Jones, and the Antiquities of Rome by Palladio' [Pope's note].
8 'A Door or Window, so called, from being much practised at Venice, by Palladio and others' [Pope's note].

And something previous ev'n to Taste—'tis Sense:
Good Sense, which only is the gift of Heav'n,
And tho' no Science, fairly worth the seven:

45 A Light, which in yourself you must perceive;
Jones and Le Nôtre have it not to give.[9]

To build, to plant, whatever you intend,
To rear the Column, or the Arch to bend,
To swell the Terras, or to sink the Grot;

50 In all, let Nature never be forgot.
But treat the Goddess like a modest fair,
Nor over-dress, nor leave her wholly bare;
Let not each beauty ev'ry where be spy'd,
Where half the skill is decently to hide.

55 He gains all points, who pleasingly confounds,
Surprizes, varies, and conceals the Bounds.

Consult the Genius of the Place in all;
That tells the Waters or to rise, or fall,
Or helps th'ambitious Hill the heav'ns to scale,

60 Or scoops in circling theatres the Vale;
Calls in the Country, catches op'ning glades,
Joins willing woods, and varies shades from shades;
Now breaks, or now directs, th'intending Lines,
Paints as you plant, and as you work, designs.

65 Still follow Sense, of ev'ry Art the Soul,
Parts answ'ring parts shall slide into a whole,
Spontaneous beauties all around advance,
Start ev'n from Difficulty, strike from Chance;
Nature shall join you; Time shall make it grow

70 A Work to wonder at—perhaps a STOW.[10]

Without it, proud Versailles! thy glory falls,
And Nero's Terraces desert their walls:
The vast Parterres a thousand hands shall make,
Lo! COBHAM comes, and floats them with a Lake:

75 Or cut wide views thro' Mountains to the Plain,
You'll wish your hill or sheltered seat again.
Ev'n in an ornament its place remark,
Nor in an Hermitage set Dr Clarke.[11]

Behold Villario's ten-years toil compleat;

80 His Arbours darken, his Espaliers meet;

9 '*Inigo Jones* the celebrated Architect, and M. Le Nôtre [1613–1700], the designer of the best Gardens of France' [Pope's note].
10 'The seat and gardens of the Lord Viscount Cobham in Buckinghamshire' [Pope's note].
11 'Dr S. Clarke's busto placed by the Queen in the Hermitage, while the Dr duely frequented the Court' [Pope's note]; Samuel Clarke (1675–1729), a philosopher and divine.

The Wood supports the Plain, the parts unite,
And strength of Shade contends with strength of light:
A waving Glow the bloomy beds display,
Blushing in bright diversities of day,
85   With silver-quiv'ring rills maeandered o'er—
Enjoy them, you! Villario can no more;
Tired of the scene Parterres and Fountains yield,
He finds at last he better likes a Field.
     Thro' his young Woods how pleased Sabinus strayed
90   Or sat delighted in the thick'ning shade,
With annual joy the red'ning shoots to greet,
Or see the stretching branches long to meet.
His Son's fine Taste an op'ner Vista loves,
Foe to the Dryads of his Father's groves,
95   One boundless Green, or flourished Carpet views,[12]
With all the mournful family of Yews;[13]
The thriving plants ignoble broomsticks made,
Now sweep those Alleys they were born to shade.
     At Timon's Villa[14] let us pass a day,
100   Where all cry out, 'What sums are thrown away!'
So proud, so grand, of that stupendous air,
Soft and Agreeable come never there.
Greatness, with Timon, dwells in such a draught
As brings all Brobdignag before your thought.
105   To compass this, his building is a Town,
His pond an Ocean, his parterre a Down:
Who but must laugh, the Master when he sees?
A puny insect, shiv'ring at a breeze.
Lo! What huge heaps of littleness around!
110   The whole, a laboured Quarry above ground.
Two Cupids squirt before: a Lake behind
Improves the keenness of the Northern wind.
His Gardens next your admiration call,
On ev'ry side you look, behold the Wall!
115   No pleasing Intricacies intervene,
No artful wildness to perplex the scene;
Grove nods at grove, each Alley has a brother,

12 'The two extremes in parterres, which are equally faulty; a *boundless Green*, large and naked as a field, or a *flourished Carpet*, where the greatness and nobleness of the piece is lessened by being divided into too many parts, with scrolled works and beds, of which the examples are frequent' [Pope's note].
13 'Touches upon the ill taste of those who are so fond of Ever-greens (particularly Yews, which are the most tonsile) as to destroy the nobler Forest-trees, to make way for such little ornaments as Pyramids of dark-green, continually repeated, not unlike a Funeral procession' [Pope's note].
14 'This description is intended to comprize the principles of a false Taste of Magnificence, and to exemplify what was said before, that nothing but Good Sense can obtain it' [Pope's note].

And half the platform just reflects the other.
The suff'ring eye inverted Nature sees,
120 Trees cut to Statues, Statues thick as trees,
With here a Fountain, never to be played,
And there a Summer-house, that knows no shade.
Here Amphitrite sails thro' myrtle bow'rs;
There Gladiators fight, or die, in flow'rs;[15]
125 Un-watered see the drooping sea-horse mourn,
And swallows roost in Nilus' dusty Urn.
　　My Lord advances with majestic mien,
Smit with the mighty pleasure, to be seen:
But soft—by regular approach—not yet—
130 First thro' the length of yon hot Terrace sweat,[16]
And when up ten steep slopes you've dragged your thighs,
Just at his Study-door he'll bless your eyes.
　　His Study! with what Authors is it stored?[17]
In Books, not Authors, curious is my Lord;
135 To all their dated Backs he turns you round:
These Aldus[18] printed, those Du Suëil[19] has bound.
Lo some are Vellom, and the rest as good
For all his Lordship knows, but they are Wood.
For Locke or Milton 'tis in vain to look,
140 These shelves admit not any modern book.
　　And now the Chapel's silver bell you hear,
That summons you to all the Pride of Pray'r:
Light quirks of Music, broken and uneven,[20]
Make the soul dance upon a Jig to Heav'n.
145 On painted Cielings you devoutly stare,[21]
Where sprawl the Saints of Verrio or Laguerre,
On gilded clouds in fair expansion lie,
And bring all Paradise before your eye.
To rest, the Cushion and soft Dean invite,

---

15 'The two statues of the *Gladiator pugnans* and *Gladiator moriens*' [Pope's note].
16 'The *Approaches and Communications* of house with garden, or of one part with another, ill judged and inconvenient' [Pope's note].
17 'The false Taste in Books; a satyr on the vanity in collecting them, more frequent in men of Fortune than the study to understand them. Many delight chiefly in the elegance of the print, or of the binding; some have carried it so far, as to cause the upper shelves to be filled with painted books of wood; others pique themselves so much upon books in a language they do not understand as to exclude the most useful in one they do' [Pope's note].
18 Aldus Manutio (1450–1515), the Venetian printer who introduced italic type
19 Abbé Du Suëil (1673–1746), a well-known Paris bookbinder
20 'The false Taste in Music, improper to the subjects, as of light airs in Churches, often practised by the organists, &c.' [Pope's note].
21 'Verrio [1639–1707] painted many cielings, &c. at Windsor, Hamptoncourt, &c., and Laguerre [1663–1721] at Blenheim-castle, and other Places' [Pope's note].

150   Who never mentions Hell to ears polite.[22]
       But hark! the chiming Clocks to dinner call;
    A hundred footsteps scrape the marble Hall:
    The rich Buffet well-coloured Serpents grace,[23]
    And gaping Tritons spew to wash your face.

155   Is this a dinner? this a Genial room?[24]
    No, 'tis a Temple, and a Hecatomb,
    A solemn Sacrifice, performed in state,
    You drink by measure, and to minutes eat.
    So quick retires each flying course, you'd swear

160   Sancho's dread Doctor and his Wand were there.[25]
    Between each Act the trembling salvers ring,
    From soup to sweet-wine, and God bless the King.
    In plenty starving, tantalized in state,
    And complaisantly helped to all I hate,

165   Treated, caressed, and tired, I take my leave,
    Sick of his civil Pride from Morn to Eve;
    I curse such lavish cost, and little skill,
    And swear no Day was ever past so ill.
       Yet[26] hence the Poor are cloathed, the Hungry fed;

170   Health to himself, and to his Infants bread
    The Lab'rer bears: What his hard Heart denies,
    His charitable Vanity supplies.
       Another age shall see the golden Ear
    Imbrown the Slope, and nod on the Parterre,

175   Deep Harvests bury all his pride has planned,
    And laughing Ceres re-assume the land.
       Who then shall grace, or who improve the Soil?
    Who plants like BATHURST,[27] or who builds like BOYLE.[28]
    'Tis Use alone that sanctifies Expence,

180   And Splendor borrows all her rays from Sense.
       His Father's Acres who enjoys in peace,
    Or makes his Neighbours glad, if he encrease;

---

22 'This is a fact; a reverend Dean [Knightly Chetwood (1650–1720), Dean of Gloucester] preaching at Court, threatened the sinner with punishment in "a place which he thought it not decent to name in so polite assembly"' [Pope's note].

23 'Taxes the incongruity of *Ornaments* (tho' sometimes practised by the ancients) where an open mouth ejects the water into a fountain, or where the shocking images of serpents, &c. are introduced in Grottos or Buffets' [Pope's note].

24 'The proud Festivals of some men are here set forth to ridicule, where pride destroys the ease, and formal regularity all the pleasurable enjoyment of the entertainment' [Pope's note].

25 'See Don Quixote, chap. xlvii' [Pope's note].

26 'The *Moral* of the whole, where PROVIDENCE is justified in giving Wealth to those who squander it in this manner. A bad Taste employs more hands, and diffuses Expence more than a good one' [Pope's note].

27 Allan, Lord Bathurst (1684–1775), a landscape architect, to whom Pope addressed a later essay on the use of riches

28 Boyle is the family name of the Earl of Burlington, to whom this poem is dedicated.

Whose chearful Tenants bless their yearly toil,
Yet to their Lord owe more than to the soil;
185 Whose ample Lawns are not ashamed to feed
The milky heifer and deserving steed;
Whose rising Forests, not for pride or show,
But future Buildings, future Navies grow:
Let his plantation stretch from down to down,
190 First shade a Country, and then raise a Town.
 You too proceed! make falling Arts your care,
Erect new wonders, and the old repair;
Jones and Palladio to themselves restore,
And be whate'er Vitruvius[29] was before:
195 Till Kings call forth th' Ideas of your mind,
(Proud to accomplish what such hands designed,)
Bid Harbours open, public Ways extend,
Bid Temples, worthier of the God, ascend,
Bid the broad Arch the dang'rous Flood contain,
200 The Mole projected break the roaring Main;
Back to his bounds their subject Sea command,
And roll obedient Rivers thro' the Land:
These Honours, Peace to happy Britain brings,
These are Imperial Works, and worthy Kings.

1731

29 M. Vitruvius Pollio (b. 88 BC), a Roman architect and engineer

William Blake
1757–1827

William Blake's wife once said, 'I have very little of Mr Blake's company. He is always in Paradise.' Living with a visionary and literary genius was probably not easy, especially for a woman who had been illiterate until her marriage, when her husband taught her to read and write. Blake, the son of a tradesman and interested in the mystical ideas of Swedenborg and Jacob Boehme, was mostly self-taught, and formally schooled only in drawing. At the age of fourteen he was apprenticed for seven years to an engraver, and he later supported himself with engraving and printing work. He lived most of his life in London, whose dull and ugly streets infused him with the sense of social injustice so poignantly expressed in such poems as 'The Chimney-Sweeper' and 'London'. For Blake, the world of senses was full of symbols and a source of the metaphors in his poetry. In his earlier poems he turned to forms such as the ballad as inspiration for new forms and techniques. Utterly unorthodox in his religious and moral beliefs, he developed a complete mythology of his own, a radically spiritual interpretation of the Bible. He sought a vision that would transfigure the natural, or fallen, world, revealing its correspondence with an eternal form (see 'Auguries of Innocence', below). Much of his poetry was printed with his engravings, for he made little distinction between these two expressive forms. In his art, he refused to cater to popular taste, and his work was largely ignored by the public. Like many geniuses, he seemed not to belong to his time or place, and though he battled with poverty for much of his life, he died serene and full of joy.

From *Songs of Innocence*

The Lamb

Little lamb who made thee
Dost thou know who made thee
Gave thee life & bid thee feed
By the stream & o'er the mead;
5   Gave thee clothing of delight,
Softest clothing wooly bright;
Gave thee such a tender voice,
Making all the vales rejoice!
Little Lamb who made thee
10   Dost thou know who made thee

Little Lamb I'll tell thee,
Little Lamb I'll tell thee!
He is callèd by thy name,
For he calls himself a Lamb:
15   He is meek & he is mild,
He became a little child:
I a child & thou a lamb,
We are callèd by his name.
Little Lamb God bless thee.
20   Little Lamb God bless thee.

1789

From *Songs of Experience*

The Clod and the Pebble

'Love seeketh not itself to please,
Nor for itself hath any care,
But for another gives its ease,
And builds a heaven in hell's despair.'

5   So sung a little clod of clay,
       Trodden with the cattle's feet,
       But a pebble of the brook
       Warblèd out these metres meet:

       'Love seeketh only self to please,
10   To bind another to its delight,
       Joys in another's loss of ease,
       And builds a hell in heaven's despite.'

The Chimney-Sweeper

       A little black thing among the snow,
       Crying "weep, 'weep' in notes of woe!
       'Where are thy father and mother, say?'—
       'They are both gone up to church to pray.

5   'Because I was happy upon the heath,
       And smiled among the winter's snow,
       They clothed me in the clothes of death,
       And taught me to sing the notes of woe.

       'And because I am happy, and dance and sing,
10   They think they have done me no injury,
       And are gone to praise God and his Priest and King,
       Who make up a heaven of our misery.'

The Sick Rose

       O Rose, thou art sick:
       The invisible worm,
       That flies in the night,
       In the howling storm,

5   Has found out thy bed
       Of crimson joy;
       And his dark secret love
       Does thy life destroy.

The Tyger

Tyger! Tyger! burning bright
In the forests of the night,
What immortal hand or eye
Could frame thy fearful symmetry?

5   In what distant deeps or skies
Burnt the fire of thine eyes?
On what wings dare he aspire?
What the hand dare seize the fire?

And what shoulder, and what art,
10 Could twist the sinews of thy heart?
And when thy heart began to beat,
What dread hand? and what dread feet?

What the hammer? what the chain?
In what furnace was thy brain?
15 What the anvil? what dread grasp
Dare its deadly terrors clasp?

When the stars threw down their spears,
And water'd heaven with their tears,
Did he smile his work to see?
20 Did he who made the Lamb make thee?

Tyger! Tyger! burning bright
In the forests of the night,
What immortal hand or eye,
Dare frame thy fearful symmetry?

London

I wander through each charter'd[1] street,
Near where the charter'd Thames does flow,
And mark in every face I meet
Marks of weakness, marks of woe.

1 pre-empted and rented out

5   In every cry of every man,
In every infant's cry of fear,
In every voice in every ban,
The mind-forg'd manacles I hear.

How the chimney-sweeper's cry
10   Every blackening church appalls;
And the hapless soldier's sigh
Runs in blood down palace walls.

But most through midnight streets I hear
How the youthful harlot's curse
15   Blasts the new born infant's tear,
And blights with plagues the marriage hearse.

1794

Auguries of Innocence

To see a world in a grain of sand
And a heaven in a wild flower,
Hold infinity in the palm of your hand,
And eternity in an hour.

5   A robin redbreast in a cage
Puts all heaven in a rage.
A dove-house filled with doves and pigeons
Shudders hell through all its regions.
A dog starved at his master's gate
10   Predicts the ruin of the state.
A horse misused upon the road
Calls to heaven for human blood.
Each outcry of the hunted hare
A fibre from the brain does tear.
15   A skylark wounded in the wing,
A cherubim does cease to sing;
The game cock clipped and armed for fight
Does the rising sun affright.
Every wolf's and lion's howl
20   Raises from hell a human soul.
The wild deer wandering here and there,

Keeps the human soul from care.
The lamb misused breeds public strife
And yet forgives the butcher's knife.
25   The bat that flits at close of eve
Has left the brain that won't believe.
The owl that calls upon the night
Speaks the unbeliever's fright.
He who shall hurt the little wren
30   Shall never be beloved by men.
He who the ox to wrath has moved
Shall never be by woman loved.
The wanton boy that kills the fly
Shall feel the spider's enmity.
35   He who torments the chafer's sprite
Weaves a bower in endless night.
The caterpillar on the leaf
Repeats to thee thy mother's grief.
Kill not the moth nor butterfly,
40   For the last judgment draweth nigh.
He who shall train the horse to war
Shall never pass the polar bar.
The beggar's dog and widow's cat,
Feed them and thou wilt grow fat.
45   The gnat that sings his summer's song
Poison gets from slander's tongue.
The poison of the snake and newt
Is the sweat of envy's foot.
The poison of the honey bee
50   Is the artist's jealousy.
The prince's robes and beggar's rags
Are toadstools on the miser's bags.
A truth that's told with bad intent
Beats all the lies you can invent.
55   It is right it should be so;
Man was made for joy and woe;
And when this we rightly know,
Through the world we safely go.
Joy and woe are woven fine,
60   A clothing for the soul divine;
Under every grief and pine
Runs a joy with silken twine.
The babe is more than swadling bands,
Throughout all these human lands;
65   Tools were made, and born were hands,

Every farmer understands.
Every tear from every eye
Becomes a babe in eternity;
This is caught by females bright,
70   And returned to its own delight.
The bleat, the bark, bellow, and roar
Are waves that beat on heaven's shore.
The babe that weeps the rod beneath
Writes revenge in realms of death.
75   The beggar's rags, fluttering in air,
Does to rags the heavens tear.
The soldier, armed with sword and gun,
Palsied strikes the summer's sun.
The poor man's farthing is worth more
80   Than all the gold on Afric's shore.
One mite wrung from the lab'rer's hands
Shall buy and sell the miser's lands;
Or, if protected from on high,
Does that whole nation sell and buy.
85   He who mocks the infant's faith
Shall be mocked in age and death.
He who shall teach the child to doubt
The rotting grave shall never get out.
He who respects the infant's faith
90   Triumphs over hell and death.
The child's toys and the old man's reasons
Are the fruits of the two seasons.
The questioner, who sits so sly
Shall never know how to reply.
95   He who replies to words of doubt
Doth put the light of knowledge out.
The strongest poison ever known
Came from Caesar's laurel crown.
Naught can deform the human race
100 Like to the armour's iron brace.
When gold and gems adorn the plow
To peaceful arts shall envy bow.
A riddle, or the cricket's cry,
Is to doubt a fit reply.
105 The emmet's inch and eagle's mile
Make lame philosophy to smile.
He who doubts from what he sees
Will ne'er believe, do what you please.
If the sun and moon should doubt,

110 They'd immediately go out.
To be in a passion you good may do,
But no good if a passion is in you.
The whore and gambler, by the state
Licensed, build that nation's fate.
115 The harlot's cry from street to street
Shall weave Old England's winding sheet.
The winner's shout, the loser's curse,
Dance before dead England's hearse.
Every night and every morn
120 Some to misery are born.
Every morn and every night
Some are born to sweet delight.
Some are born to sweet delight,
Some are born to endless night.
125 We are led to believe a lie
When we see not through the eye,
Which is born in a night to perish in a night,
When the soul slept in beams of light.
God appears, and God is light,
130 To those poor souls who dwell in night,
But does a human form display
To those who dwell in realms of day.

1863

William Wordsworth
1770–1850

William Wordsworth was born and educated at the edge of the Lake District in Cumberland, England, where he spent his youth roaming the countryside, absorbing the sights and sounds that would inspire his greatest poems. The headmaster of his boarding school encouraged Wordsworth's early interest in poetry, an interest that deepened when he attended St John's College, Cambridge. In 1791, after graduation, he travelled to the continent, excited by the possibilities of the French Revolution. In France he met Annette Vallon, with whom he had a child. But after financial problems forced him to return to England, the outbreak of war prevented Wordsworth from getting back to France. His ardour for Vallon eventually cooled, and they never married. Wordsworth settled with his sister Dorothy in a cottage at Racedown, and then moved to Alfoxden, Somerset, to be near Samuel Taylor Coleridge, with whom he wrote the *Lyrical Ballads*. The *Ballads* signalled a new trend in poetry, and a break with the neoclassical tradition. Subjects for poetry, according to Wordsworth, should be 'incidents and situations from common life', and they should be written in language 'really used by men', rather than in the elevated diction typical of eighteenth-century poetry.

Wordsworth and Dorothy eventually moved back to the Lake District, settling in Grasmere in a little house called Dove Cottage. Wordsworth married a woman he had known since childhood and steadily acquired a reputation as an outstanding poet, as well as financial security. For the young Wordsworth, nature was invested with an almost divine radiance, but such vision was lost as he grew older, and in the *Immortality Ode*, Wordsworth mourns this loss and tries to take comfort 'In years that bring the philosophic mind'. It is generally agreed that Wordsworth's best poetry was written before 1807 when his youthful experience was the source of his poetry. Much of his later poetry is prosaic, reflecting an orthodoxy that replaced his earlier revolutionary fervour. He was named poet laureate of England in 1843.

I Wandered Lonely as a Cloud

I wandered lonely as a cloud
That floats on high o'er vales and hills,
When all at once I saw a crowd,
A host, of golden daffodils;
5 Beside the lake, beneath the trees,
Fluttering and dancing in the breeze.

Continuous as the stars that shine
And twinkle on the milky way,
They stretched in never-ending line
10 Along the margin of a bay:
Ten thousand saw I at a glance,
Tossing their heads in sprightly dance.

The waves beside them danced; but they
Outdid the sparkling waves in glee:
15 A poet could not but be gay,
In such a jocund company:
I gazed — and gazed — but little thought
What wealth the show to me had brought:

For oft, when on my couch I lie
20 In vacant or in pensive mood,
They flash upon that inward eye
Which is the bliss of solitude;
And then my heart with pleasure fills,
And dances with the daffodils.

1807

Ode

Intimations of Immortality
from Recollections of Early Childhood

The Child is father of the Man;
And I could wish my days to be
Bound each to each by natural piety.

I

There was a time when meadow, grove, and stream,
The earth, and every common sight,
      To me did seem
      Apparelled in celestial light,
5 The glory and the freshness of a dream.
It is not now as it hath been of yore;—
      Turn whereso'er I may,
      By night or day,
The things which I have seen I now can see no more.

II

10   The Rainbow comes and goes
      And lovely is the Rose,
      The Moon doth with delight
Look round her when the heavens are bare,
      Waters on a starry night
15   Are beautiful and fair;
    The sunshine is a glorious birth;
    But yet I know, where'er I go,
That there hath past away a glory from the earth.

III

Now, while the birds thus sing a joyous song,
20   And while the young lambs bound
      As to the tabor's sound,
To me alone there came a thought of grief:
A timely utterance gave that thought relief,
      And I again am strong:

25 The cataracts blow their trumpets from the steep;
No more shall grief of mine the season wrong;
I hear the Echoes through the mountains throng,
The Winds come to me from the fields of sleep,
      And all the earth is gay;
30   Land and sea
        Give themselves up to jollity.
        And with the heart of May
      Doth every Beast keep holiday;—
        Thou Child of Joy,
35 Shout round me, let me hear thy shouts, thou happy Shepherd-boy!

IV

Ye blessèd Creatures, I have heard the call
    Ye to each other make; I see
The heavens laugh with you in your jubilee;
    My heart is at your festival,
40   My head hath its coronal,
The fulness of your bliss, I feel—I feel it all.
      Oh evil day! if I were sullen
      While Earth herself is adorning,
        This sweet May-morning,
45   And the Children are culling
        On every side,
    In a thousand valleys far and wide,
    Fresh flowers; while the sun shines warm,
And the Babe leaps up on his Mother's arm:—
50   I hear, I hear, with joy I hear!
    —But there's a Tree, of many, one,
A single Field which I have looked upon,
Both of them speak of something that is gone:
      The Pansy at my feet
55   Doth the same repeat:
Whither is fled the visionary gleam?
Where is it now, the glory and the dream?

V

Our birth is but a sleep and a forgetting:
The Soul that rises with us, our life's Star,
60   Hath had elsewhere its setting,

And cometh from afar:
Not in entire forgetfulness,
And not in utter nakedness,
But trailing clouds of glory do we come
65   From God, who is our home:
Heaven lies about us in our infancy!
Shades of the prison-house begin to close
Upon the growing Boy,
But He beholds the light, and whence it flows,
70   He sees it in his joy;
The Youth, who daily farther from the east
Must travel, still is Nature's Priest,
And by the vision splendid
Is on his way attended;
75 At length the Man perceives it die away,
And fade into the light of common day.

VI

Earth fills her lap with pleasures of her own;
Yearnings she hath in her own natural kind,
And, even with something of a Mother's mind,
80   And no unworthy aim,
The homely Nurse doth all she can
To make her Foster-child, her Inmate Man,
Forget the glories he hath known,
And that imperial palace whence he came.

VII

85 Behold the Child among his new-born blisses,
A six years' Darling of a pigmy size!
See, where 'mid work of his own hand he lies,
Fretted by sallies of his mother's kisses,
With light upon him from his father's eyes!
90 See, at his feet, some little plan or chart,
Some fragment from his dream of human life,
Shaped by himself with newly-learned art;
A wedding or a festival,
A mourning or a funeral;
95   And this hath now his heart,
And unto this he frames his song.

Then will he fit his tongue
To dialogues of business, love, or strife;
But it will not be long
100   Ere this be thrown aside,
And with new joy and pride
The little Actor cons another part;
Filling from time to time his 'humorous stage'
With all the Persons, down to palsied Age,
105 That Life brings with her in her equipage;
As if his whole vocation
Were endless imitation.

VIII

Thou, whose exterior semblance doth belie
Thy Soul's immensity;
110 Thou best Philosopher, who yet dost keep
Thy heritage, thou Eye among the blind,
That, deaf and silent, read'st the eternal deep,
Haunted for ever by the eternal mind,—
Mighty Prophet! Seer blest!
115   On whom those truths do rest,
Which we are toiling all our lives to find,
In darkness lost, the darkness of the grave,
Thou, over whom thy Immortality
Broods like the Day, a Master o'er a Slave,
120 A Presence which is not to be put by;
Thou little Child, yet glorious in the might
Of heaven-born freedom on thy being's height,
Why with such earnest pains dost thou provoke
The years to bring the inevitable yoke,
125 Thus blindly with thy blessedness at strife?
Full soon thy Soul shall have her earthly freight,
And custom lie upon thee with a weight,
Heavy as frost, and deep almost as life!

IX

O joy! that in our embers
130   Is something that doth live
That nature yet remembers
What was so fugitive!

The thought of our past years in me doth breed
Perpetual benediction: not indeed
135   For that which is most worthy to be blest;
Delight and liberty, the simple creed
Of Childhood, whether busy or at rest,
With new-fledged hope still fluttering in his breast:—
     Not for these I raise
140   The song of thanks and praise:
     But for those obstinate questionings
     Of sense and outward things,
     Fallings from us, vanishings;
     Blank misgivings of a Creature
145   Moving about in worlds not realised,
High instincts before which our mortal Nature
Did tremble like a guilty Thing surprised:
     But for those first affections,
     Those shadowy recollections,
150   Which, be they what they may,
Are yet the fountain-light of all our day,
Are yet a master-light of all our seeing;
     Uphold us, cherish, and have power to make
Our noisy years seem moments in the being
155   Of the eternal Silence: truths that wake,
     To perish never:
Which neither listlessness, nor mad endeavour,
     Nor Man nor Boy,
Nor all that is at enmity with joy,
160   Can utterly abolish or destroy!
     Hence in a season of calm weather
     Though inland far we be,
Our Souls have sight of that immortal sea
     Which brought us hither,
165   Can in a moment travel thither,
And see the Children sport upon the shore,
And hear the mighty waters rolling evermore.

X

Then sing, ye Birds, sing, sing a joyous song!
     And let the young Lambs bound
170   As to the tabor's sound!
We in thought will join your throng,
     Ye that pipe and ye that play,

Ye that through your hearts today
Feel the gladness of the May!
175 What though the radiance which was once so bright
Be now for ever taken from my sight,
    Though nothing can bring back the hour
Of splendour in the grass, of glory in the flower;
    We will grieve not, rather find
180   Strength in what remains behind;
    In the primal sympathy
    Which having been must ever be;
    In the soothing thoughts that spring
    Out of human suffering;
185   In the faith that looks through death,
In years that bring the philosophic mind.

XI

And O, ye Fountains, Meadows, Hills, and Groves,
Forebode not any severing of our loves!
Yet in my heart of hearts I feel your might;
190 I only have relinquished one delight
To live beneath your more habitual sway.
I love the Brooks which down their channels fret,
Even more than when I tripped lightly as they;
The innocent brightness of a new-born Day
195   Is lovely yet;
The Clouds that gather round the setting sun
Do take a sober colouring from an eye
That hath kept watch o'er man's mortality;
Another race hath been, and other palms are won.
200 Thanks to the human heart by which we live,
Thanks to its tenderness, its joys, and fears,
To me the meanest flower that blows can give
Thoughts that do often lie too deep for tears.

1807

Sonnets

4

Composed upon Westminster Bridge,
September 3, 1802

Earth has not anything to show more fair:
Dull would he be of soul who could pass by
A sight so touching in its majesty:
This City now doth, like a garment, wear
5   The beauty of the morning; silent, bare,
Ships, towers, domes, theatres, and temples lie
Open unto the fields, and to the sky;
All bright and glittering in the smokeless air.
Never did sun more beautifully steep
10   In his first splendour, valley, rock, or hill;
Ne'er saw I, never felt, a calm so deep!
The river glideth at his own sweet will:
Dear God! the very houses seem asleep;
And all that mighty heart is lying still!

14

The world is too much with us; late and soon,
Getting and spending, we lay waste our powers:
Little we see in Nature that is ours;
We have given our hearts away, a sordid boon!
5   This Sea that bares her bosom to the moon;
The winds that will be howling at all hours,
And are up-gathered now like sleeping flowers;
For this, for everything, we are out of tune;
It moves us not.—Great God! I'd rather be
10   A Pagan suckled in a creed outworn;
So might I, standing on this pleasant lea,
Have glimpses that would make me less forlorn;
Have sight of Proteus rising from the sea;
Or hear old Triton blow his wreathèd horn.

1807

Lines

Composed a few miles above Tintern Abbey
on revisiting the Banks of the Wye during a tour.
July 13, 1798

Five years have passed; five summers, with the length
Of five long winters! and again I hear
These waters, rolling from their mountain-springs
With a soft inland murmur. Once again
5   Do I behold these steep and lofty cliffs,
That on a wild secluded scene impress
Thoughts of more deep seclusion; and connect
The landscape with the quiet of the sky.
The day is come when I again repose
10   Here, under this dark sycamore, and view
These plots of cottage ground, these orchard tufts,
Which at this season, with their unripe fruits,
Are clad in one green hue, and lose themselves
'Mid groves and copses. Once again I see
15   These hedgerows, hardly hedgerows, little lines
Of sportive wood run wild; these pastoral farms,
Green to the very door; and wreaths of smoke
Sent up, in silence, from among the trees!
With some uncertain notice, as might seem
20   Of vagrant dwellers in the houseless woods,
Or of some Hermit's cave, where by his fire
The Hermit sits alone.

             These beauteous forms,
Through a long absence, have not been to me
As is a landscape to a blind man's eye;
25   But oft, in lonely rooms, and 'mid the din
Of towns and cities, I have owed to them,
In hours of weariness, sensations sweet,
Felt in the blood, and felt along the heart;
And passing even into my purer mind,
30   With tranquil restoration—feelings too
Of unremembered pleasures; such, perhaps,
As have no slight or trivial influence
On that best portion of a good man's life,
His little, nameless, unremembered, acts
35   Of kindness and of love. Nor less, I trust,

To them I may have owed another gift,
Of aspect more sublime; that blessed mood,
In which the burthen of the mystery,
In which the heavy and the weary weight
40 Of all this unintelligble world,
Is lightened—that serene and blessed mood,
In which the affections greatly lead us on—
Until, the breath of this corporeal frame
And even the motion of our human blood
45 Almost suspended, we are laid asleep
In body, and become a living soul;
While with an eye made quiet by the power
Of harmony, and the deep power of joy,
We see into the life of things.

                                                      If this
50 Be but a vain belief, yet, oh! how oft—
In darkness and amid the many shapes
Of joyless daylight; when the fretful stir
Unprofitable, and the fever of the world,
Have hung upon the beatings of my heart—
55 How oft, in spirit, have I turned to thee,
O sylvan Wye! thou wanderer through the woods,
How often has my spirit turned to thee!

    And now, with gleams of half-extinguished thought,
With many recognitions dim and faint,
60 And somewhat of a sad perplexity,
The picture of the mind revives again;
While here I stand, not only with the sense
Of present pleasure, but with pleasing thoughts
That in this moment there is life and food
65 For future years. And so I dare to hope,
Though changed, no doubt, from what I was when first
I came among these hills; when like a roe
I bounded o'er the mountains, by the sides
Of the deep rivers, and the lonely streams,
70 Wherever nature led—more like a man
Flying from something that he dreads than one
Who sought the thing he loved. For nature then
(The coarser pleasures of my boyish days,
And their glad animal movements all gone by)
75 To me was all in all.—I cannot paint
What then I was. The sounding cataract

Haunted me like a passion; the tall rock,
The mountain, and the deep and gloomy wood,
Their colours and their forms, were then to me
80 An appetite; a feeling and a love,
That had no need of a remoter charm,
By thought supplied, nor any interest
Unborrowed from the eye.—That time is past,
And all its aching joys are now no more,
85 And all its dizzy raptures. Not for this
Faint I, nor mourn nor murmur; other gifts
Have followed; for such loss, I would believe,
Abundant recompense. For I have learned
To look on nature, not as in the hour
90 Of thoughtless youth; but hearing oftentimes
The still, sad music of humanity,
Nor harsh nor grating, though of ample power
To chasten and subdue. And I have felt
A presence that disturbs me with the joy
95 Of elevated thoughts; a sense sublime
Of something far more deeply interfused,
Whose dwelling is the light of setting suns,
And the round ocean and the living air,
And the blue sky, and in the mind of man:
100 A motion and a spirit, that impels
All thinking things, all objects of all thought,
And rolls through all things. Therefore am I still
A lover of the meadows and the woods,
And mountains; and of all that we behold
105 From this green earth; of all the mighty world
Of eye, and ear—both what they half create,
And what perceive; well pleased to recognize
In nature and the language of the sense
The anchor of my purest thoughts, the nurse,
110 The guide, the guardian of my heart, and soul
Of all my moral being.

       Nor perchance,
If I were not thus taught, should I the more
Suffer my genial spirits to decay:
For thou art with me here upon the banks
115 Of this fair river; thou my dearest Friend,
My dear, dear Friend; and in thy voice I catch
The language of my former heart, and read
My former pleasures in the shooting lights

Of thy wild eyes. Oh! yet a little while
120 May I behold in thee what I was once,
My dear, dear Sister! and this prayer I make,
Knowing that Nature never did betray
The heart that loved her; 'tis her privilege,
Through all the years of this our life, to lead
125 From joy to joy: for she can so inform
The mind that is within us, so impress
With quietness and beauty, and so feed
With lofty thoughts, that neither evil tongues,
Rash judgments, nor the sneers of selfish men,
130 Nor greetings where no kindness is, nor all
The dreary intercourse of daily life,
Shall e'er prevail against us, or disturb
Our cheerful faith, that all which we behold
Is full of blessings. Therefore let the moon
135 Shine on thee in thy solitary walk;
And let the misty mountain winds be free
To blow against thee: and, in after years,
When these wild ecstasies shall be matured
Into a sober pleasure; when thy mind
140 Shall be a mansion for all lovely forms,
Thy memory be as a dwelling place
For all sweet sounds and harmonies; oh! then,
If solitude, or fear, or pain, or grief
Should be thy portion, with what healing thoughts
145 Of tender joy wilt thou remember me,
And these my exhortations! Nor, perchance—
If I should be where I no more can hear
Thy voice, nor catch from thy wild eyes these gleams
Of past existence—wilt thou then forget
150 That on the banks of this delightful stream
We stood together; and that I, so long
A worshiper of Nature, hither came
Unwearied in that service; rather say
With warmer love—oh! with far deeper zeal
155 Of holier love. Nor wilt thou then forget,
That after many wanderings, many years
Of absence, these steep woods and lofty cliffs,
And this green pastoral landscape, were to me
More dear, both for themselves and for thy sake!

1798

John Keats
1795–1821

'Here lies one whose name was writ in water.' This is the epitaph John Keats chose for his gravestone. Though his life was pitifully brief, his name survives as one of the greatest of English poets. Perhaps his creative fire burned the more intensely because he knew he would be doomed by the tuberculosis that had killed other members of his family. His father had died when Keats was nine, his mother when he was fifteen, and at that time his formal schooling came to an end. At his school in Enfield, the handsome, small but tough boy was well liked by his classmates, and it was during this period that he became fascinated with the classical mythology that was to structure much of his poetry. He was apprenticed to an apothecary-surgeon and then continued his medical studies and was licensed to practise. But his love for literature made him give up medicine for poetry and what was to be a difficult life. Yet during the most difficult period of his life — when he was deeply in love with Fanny Brawne but too poor to marry her, when his brother Tom had just died of tuberculosis, and when the symptoms of that awful disease appeared in him — he produced some of his finest poetry: the Odes and his verse romances. He died at the age of twenty-five in Rome, where he had gone in a desperate search for health in a warmer climate.

Ode to a Nightingale

1

My heart aches, and a drowsy numbness pains
   My sense, as though of hemlock I had drunk,
Or emptied some dull opiate to the drains
   One minute past, and Lethe-wards[1] had sunk:
5 'Tis not through envy of thy happy lot,
   But being too happy in thine happiness,—
     That thou, light-wingèd Dryad[2] of the trees,
     In some melodious plot
Of beechen green, and shadows numberless,
10   Singest of summer in full-throated ease.

2

O, for a draught of vintage! that hath been
   Cool'd a long age in the deep-delved earth,
Tasting of Flora[3] and the country green,

1 toward Lethe, the river of Hades whose waters cause forgetfulness
2 a wood nymph
3 a goddess of flowers, here personifying flowers

Dance, and Provençal song, and sunburnt mirth!
15   O for a beaker full of the warm South,
Full of the true, the blushful Hippocrene,[4]
With beaded bubbles winking at the brim,
And purple-stained mouth;
That I might drink, and leave the world unseen,
20   And with thee fade away into the forest dim:

3

Fade far away, dissolve, and quite forget
What thou among the leaves hast never known,
The weariness, the fever, and the fret
Here, where men sit and hear each other groan;
25   Where palsy shakes a few, sad, last grey hairs,
Where youth grows pale, and spectre-thin, and dies;
Where but to think is to be full of sorrow
And leaden-eyed despairs,
Where Beauty cannot keep her lustrous eyes,
30   Or new Love pine at them beyond tomorrow.

4

Away! away! for I will fly to thee,
Not charioted by Bacchus[5] and his pards,
But on the viewless wings of Poesy,
Though the dull brain perplexes and retards:
35   Already with thee! tender is the night,
And haply the Queen-Moon is on her throne,
Cluster'd around by all her starry fays;
But here there is no light,
Save what from heaven is with the breezes blown
40   Through verdurous glooms and winding mossy ways.

5

I cannot see what flowers are at my feet,
Nor what soft incense hangs upon the boughs,
But, in embalmèd darkness, guess each sweet

4 fountain of the Muses on Mt Helicon
5 god of wine, whose chariot is drawn by leopards

Wherewith the seasonable month endows
45 The grass, the thicket, and the fruit-tree wild;
   White hawthorn, and the pastoral eglantine;
     Fast fading violets cover'd up in leaves;
       And mid-May's eldest child.
The coming musk-rose, full of dewy wine,
50   The murmurous haunt of flies on summer eves.

6

Darkling I listen; and, for many a time
   I have been half in love with easeful Death,
Call'd him soft names in many a musèd rhyme,
   To take into the air my quiet breath;
55 Now more than ever seems it rich to die,
   To cease upon the midnight with no pain,
     While thou art pouring forth thy soul abroad
       In such an ecstasy!
Still wouldst thou sing, and I have ears in vain—
60   To thy high requiem become a sod.

7

Thou wast not born for death, immortal Bird!
   No hungry generations tread thee down;
The voice I hear this passing night was heard
   In ancient days by emperor and clown:
65 Perhaps the self-same song that found a path
   Through the sad heart of Ruth,[6] when, sick for home,
     She stood in tears amid the alien corn;
       The same that oft-times hath
Charm'd magic casements, opening on the foam
70   Of perilous seas, in faery lands forlorn.

8

Forlorn! the very word is like a bell
   To toll me back from thee to my sole self!
Adieu! the fancy cannot cheat so well

6 In the Bible, Ruth forsook her native land to live in Israel with Naomi, her mother-in-law.

As she is fam'd to do, deceiving elf.
75 Adieu! adieu! thy plaintive anthem fades
Past the near meadows, over the still stream,
Up the hill-side; and now 'tis buried deep
In the next valley-glades:
Was it a vision, or a waking dream?
80 Fled is that music:——Do I wake or sleep?

1819

Ode on a Grecian Urn

1

Thou still unravish'd bride of quietness,
Thou foster-child of silence and slow time,
Sylvan historian, who canst thus express
A flowery tale more sweetly than our rhyme:
5 What leaf-fring'd legend haunts about thy shape
Of deities or mortals, or of both,
In Tempe or the dales of Arcady?[1]
What men or gods are these? What maidens loth?
What mad pursuit? What struggle to escape?
10 What pipes and timbrels?[2] What wild ecstasy?

2

Heard melodies are sweet, but those unheard
Are sweeter; therefore, ye soft pipes, play on;
Not to the sensual ear, but, more endear'd,
Pipe to the spirit ditties of no tone;
15 Fair youth, beneath the trees, thou canst not leave
Thy song, nor ever can those trees be bare;
Bold lover, never, never canst thou kiss,
Though winning near the goal — yet, do not grieve;
She cannot fade, though thou hast not thy bliss,
20 For ever wilt thou love, and she be fair!

1 In Greek poetry, Tempe and Arcady are symbols of pastoral beauty.
2 tambourines

3

Ah, happy, happy boughs! that cannot shed
   Your leaves, nor ever bid the Spring adieu;
And, happy melodist, unwearièd,
   For ever piping songs for ever new;
25 More happy love! more happy, happy love!
   For ever warm and still to be enjoy'd,
     For ever panting, and for ever young;
All breathing human passion far above,
   That leaves a heart high-sorrowed and cloy'd,
30   A burning forehead, and a parching tongue.

4

Who are these coming to the sacrifice?
   To what green altar, O mysterious priest,
Lead'st thou that heifer lowing at the skies,
   And all her silken flanks with garlands drest?
35 What little town by river or sea shore,
   Or mountain-built with peaceful citadel,
     Is emptied of this folk, this pious morn?
And, little town, thy streets for evermore
   Will silent be; and not a soul to tell
40   Why thou art desolate, can e'er return.

5

O Attic shape! Fair attitude! with brede
   Of marble men and maidens overwrought,
With forest branches and the trodden weed;
   Thou, silent form, dost tease us out of thought
45 As doth eternity: Cold Pastoral!
   When old age shall this generation waste,
     Thou shalt remain, in midst of other woe
Than ours, a friend to man, to whom thou say'st,
   'Beauty is truth, truth beauty,'— that is all
50   Ye know on earth, and all ye need to know.

1820

Ode to Autumn

1

Season of mists and mellow fruitfulness!
  Close bosom-friend of the maturing sun;
Conspiring with him how to load and bless
  With fruit the vines that round the thatch-eaves run;
5   To bend with apples the moss'd cottage-trees,
    And fill all fruit with ripeness to the core;
      To swell the gourd, and plump the hazel shells
    With a sweet kernel; to set budding more
And still more, later flowers for the bees,
10 Until they think warm days will never cease;
    For summer has o'er-brimm'd their clammy cells.

2

Who hath not seen thee oft amid thy store?
  Sometimes whoever seeks abroad may find
Thee sitting careless on a granary floor,
15   Thy hair soft-lifted by the winnowing wind;
Or on a half-reap'd furrow sound asleep,
  Drowsed with the fume of poppies, while thy hook
    Spares the next swath and all its twinèd flowers;
And sometimes like a gleaner thou dost keep
20 Steady thy laden head across a brook;
  Or by a cider-press, with patient look,
    Thou watchest the last oozings, hours by hours.

3

Where are the songs of Spring? Aye, where are they?
  Think not of them,— thou hast thy music too,
25 While barred clouds bloom the soft-dying day
    And touch the stubble-plains with rosy hue;
Then in a wailful choir the small gnats mourn
  Among the river-sallows, borne aloft
    Or sinking as the light wind lives or dies;
30   And full-grown lambs loud bleat from hilly bourn;
Hedge-crickets sing, and now with treble soft
The redbreast whistles from a garden-croft:
    And gathering swallows twitter in the skies.

1820

La Belle Dame sans Merci: A Ballad

I

O what can ail thee, knight at arms,
    Alone and palely loitering?
The sedge has wither'd from the lake,
    And no birds sing.

II

5   O what can ail thee, knight at arms,
    So haggard and so woe-begone?
The squirrel's granary is full,
    And the harvest's done.

III

I see a lily on thy brow
10   With anguish moist and fever dew,
And on thy cheeks a fading rose
    Fast withereth too.

IV

I met a lady in the meads,
    Full beautiful, a faery's child;
15 Her hair was long, her foot was light,
    And her eyes were wild.

V

I made a garland for her head
    And bracelets too, and fragrant zone;
She look'd at me as she did love,
20   And made sweet moan.

VI

I set her on my pacing steed,
    And nothing else saw all day long,
For sidelong would she bend, and sing
    A faery's song.

VII

25 She found me roots of relish sweet,
        And honey wild, and manna dew,
    And sure in language strange she said —
        I love thee true.

VIII

    She took me to her elfin grot,
30   And there she wept, and sigh'd full sore,
    And there I shut her wild wild eyes
        With kisses four.

IX

    And there she lulled me asleep,
        And there I dream'd — Ah! woe betide!
35 The latest dream I ever dream'd
        On the cold hill's side.

X

    I saw pale kings, and princes too,
        Pale warriors, death pale were they all;
    They cried — 'La belle dame sans merci
40   Hath thee in thrall!'

XI

I saw their starv'd lips in the gloam
    With horrid warning gaped wide,
And I awoke and found me here
    On the cold hill's side.

XII

45 And this is why I sojourn here,
        Alone and palely loitering,
    Though the sedge is wither'd from the lake,
        And no birds sing.

1820

Bright Star

Bright Star! would I were steadfast as thou art —
    Not in lone splendour hung aloft the night
And watching, with eternal lids apart
    Like Nature's patient sleepless Eremite,[1]
5 The moving waters at their priestlike task
    Of pure ablution round earth's human shores,
Or gazing on the new soft fallen mask
    Of snow upon the mountains and the moors —
No — yet still steadfast, still unchangeable,
10   Pillowed upon my fair love's ripening breast,
To feel forever its soft fall and swell,
    Awake forever in a sweet unrest,
Still, still to hear her tender-taken breath,
And so live ever — or else swoon to death.

1838

1 religious hermit

On the Sonnet

If by dull rhymes our English must be chained,
　　And, like Andromeda,[1] the Sonnet sweet
Fettered, in spite of pained loveliness;
Let us find out, if we must be constrained,
　　Sandals more interwoven and complete
To fit the naked foot of poesy;
Let us inspect the lyre, and weigh the stress
Of every chord, and see what may be gained
　　By ear industrious, and attention meet;
Misers of sound and syllable, no less
Than Midas of his coinage, let us be
　　Jealous of dead leaves in the bay-wreath crown;
So, if we may not let the Muse be free,
　　She will be bound with garlands of her own.

1848

1 Ethiopian princess chained as prey for a monster and rescued by Perseus, who then married her

---

Alfred, Lord Tennyson

1809–1892

Alfred Tennyson was the fourth son born into an eccentric but loving family in Lincolnshire, England. Eleven children and many pets, including an owl and a monkey, filled Somersby Rectory, which was presided over by George Clayton Tennyson, a clergyman of erratic moods, and his wife Elizabeth, a gentle and beautiful woman who was so casual a housekeeper that she often forgot to order food for family meals. The house was full of books; both parents loved poetry and often read it to their children, who at very early ages started composing their own.

Tennyson spent four miserable years at Louth Grammar School, an institution that featured thrashing as an incentive to learning. At the age of eleven he returned home to be tutored by his father. Because George Tennyson was frequently ill, Alfred often escaped to roam the countryside, composing and reciting his poetry aloud, a habit he kept for the rest of his life. He went to Trinity College, Cambridge, where he became close friends with Arthur Henry Hallam, whose lively wit complemented Tennyson's shyness and melancholy humour. Hallam's sudden death at the age of twenty-two was a shock from which Tennyson never fully recovered. Some of his greatest poetry, including 'Ulysses' and *In Memoriam*, resulted from his struggle with grief, faith, and doubt.

After leaving Cambridge, Tennyson, who never wanted to be anything but a poet, assumed a sort of nomadic existence, inviting himself to the homes of friends in London and in the countryside. He would stay for weeks or months at a time, filling the rooms with pungent pipesmoke, composing aloud, and consuming large amounts of port. By 1850, when *In Memoriam* was published to great acclaim and when he became poet laureate, he finally felt himself financially secure enough to marry Emily Sellwood after a fourteen-year courtship. When he died he was the most popular poet in Victorian England and North America, and he was buried with his head crowned with laurel from Virgil's tomb, and a copy of Shakespeare's *Cymbeline*, the last thing he read, in his hand.

The Lady of Shalott

PART I

On either side the river lie
Long fields of barley and of rye,
That clothe the wold and meet the sky;
And through the field the road runs by
5   To many-towered Camelot;
And up and down the people go,
Gazing where the lilies blow
Round an island there below,
    The island of Shalott.

10 Willows whiten, aspens quiver
Little breezes dusk and shiver
Through the wave that runs for ever
By the island in the river
    Flowing down to Camelot.
15 Four grey walls, and four grey towers,
Overlook a space of flowers
And the silent isle imbowers
    The Lady of Shalott.

By the margin, willow-veiled,
20 Slide the heavy barges trailed
By slow horses; and unhailed
The shallop flitteth silken-sailed
    Skimming down to Camelot;
But who hath seen her wave her hand?
25 Or at the casement seen her stand?
Or is she known in all the land,
    The Lady of Shalott?

Only reapers, reaping early
In among the bearded barley,
30   Hear a song that echoes cheerly
From the river winding clearly,
      Down to towered Camelot:
And by the moon the reaper weary,
Piling sheaves in uplands airy,
35   Listening, whispers ''Tis the fairy
      Lady of Shalott.'

PART II

There she weaves by night and day
A magic web with colours gay.
She has heard a whisper say,
40   A curse is on her if she stay
      To look down to Camelot.
She knows not what the curse may be,
And so she weaveth steadily,
And little other care hath she,
45   The Lady of Shalott.

And moving through a mirror clear
That hangs before her all the year,
Shadows of the world appear.
There she sees the highway near
50   Winding down to Camelot;
There the river eddy whirls,
And there the surly village-churls,
And the red cloaks of market girls,
      Pass onward from Shalott.

55   Sometimes a troop of damsels glad,
An abbot on an ambling pad,
Sometimes a curly shepherd-lad,
Or long-haired page in crimson clad,
      Goes by to towered Camelot;
60   And sometimes through the mirror blue
The knights come riding two and two:
She hath no loyal knight and true,
      The Lady of Shalott.

But in her web she still delights
65   To weave the mirror's magic sights,
For often through the silent nights
A funeral, with plumes and lights
      And music, went to Camelot;
Or when the moon was overhead,
70   Came two young lovers lately wed:
'I am half sick of shadows,' said
      The Lady of Shalott.

PART III

A bow-shot from her bower-eaves,
He rode between the barley-sheaves,
75   The sun came dazzling through the leaves,
And flamed upon the brazen greaves
      Of bold Sir Lancelot.
A red-cross knight for ever kneeled
To a lady in his shield,
80   That sparkled on the yellow field,
      Beside remote Shalott.

The gemmy bridle glittered free,
Like to some branch of stars we see
Hung in the golden Galaxy.
85   The bridle bells rang merrily
      As he rode down to Camelot;
And from his blazoned baldric slung
A mighty silver bugle hung,
And as he rode his armour rung,
90   Beside remote Shalott.

All in the blue unclouded weather
Thick-jewelled shone the saddle-leather,
The helmet and the helmet-feather
Burned like one burning flame together,
95   As he rode down to Camelot.
As often through the purple night,
Below the starry clusters bright,
Some bearded meteor, trailing light,
      Moves over still Shalott.

100   His broad clear brow in sunlight glowed;
        On burnished hooves his war-horse trode;
        From underneath his helmet flowed
        His coal-black curls as on he rode,
            As he rode down to Camelot.
105   From the bank and from the river
        He flashed into the crystal mirror,
        'Tirra lirra,' by the river
            Sang Sir Lancelot.

        She left the web, she left the loom,
110   She made three paces through the room,
        She saw the water-lily bloom,
        She saw the helmet and the plume,
            She looked down to Camelot.
        Out flew the web and floated wide;
115   The mirror cracked from side to side;
        'The curse is come upon me,' cried
            The Lady of Shalott.

PART IV

        In the stormy east-wind straining,
        The pale yellow woods were waning,
120   The broad stream in his banks complaining.
        Heavily the low sky raining
            Over towered Camelot;
        Down she came and found a boat
        Beneath a willow left afloat,
125   And round about the prow she wrote
            The Lady of Shalott.

        And down the river's dim expanse
        Like some bold seer in a trance,
        Seeing all his own mischance—
130   With a glassy countenance
            Did she look to Camelot.
        And at the closing of the day
        She loosened the chain, and down she lay;
        The broad stream bore her far away,
135   The Lady of Shalott.

Lying, robed in snowy white
That loosely flew to left and right—
The leaves upon her falling light—
Through the noises of the night
140   She floated down to Camelot;
And as the boat-head wound along
The willowy hills and fields among,
They heard her singing her last song,
    The Lady of Shalott.

145 Heard a carol, mournful, holy,
Chanted loudly, chanted lowly,
Till her blood was frozen slowly,
And her eyes were darkened wholly,
    Turned to towered Camelot.
150 For ere she reached upon the tide
The first house by the water-side,
Singing in her song she died,
    The Lady of Shalott.

Under tower and balcony,
155 By garden-wall and gallery,
A gleaming shape she floated by,
Dead-pale between the houses high,
    Silent into Camelot.
Out upon the wharfs they came,
160 Knight and burgher, lord and dame,
And round the prow they read her name,
    The Lady of Shalott.

Who is this? and what is here?
And in the lightened palace near
165 Died the sound of royal cheer;
And they crossed themselves for fear,
    All the knights at Camelot;
But Lancelot mused a little space;
He said, 'She has a lovely face;
170 God in his mercy lend her grace,
    The Lady of Shalott.'

1832

Ulysses

It little profits that an idle king,
By this still hearth, among these barren crags,
Matched with an aged wife, I mete and dole
Unequal laws unto a savage race,
5 That hoard, and sleep, and feed, and know not me.

I cannot rest from travel: I will drink
Life to the lees: all times I have enjoyed
Greatly, have suffered greatly, both with those
That loved me, and alone; on shore, and when
10 Thro' scudding drifts the rainy Hyades
Vext the dim sea: I am become a name;
For always roaming with a hungry heart
Much have I seen and known: cities of men,
And manners, climates, councils, governments,
15 Myself not least, but honoured of them all;
And drunk delight of battle with my peers,
Far on the ringing plains of windy Troy.
I am a part of all that I have met;
Yet all experience is an arch wherethro'
20 Gleams that untravelled world, whose margin fades
For ever and for ever when I move.
How dull it is to pause, to make an end,
To rust unburnished, not to shine in use!
As tho' to breathe were life. Life piled on life
25 Were all too little, and of one to me
Little remains: but every hour is saved
From that eternal silence, something more,
A bringer of new things; and vile it were
For some three suns to store and hoard myself,
30 And this grey spirit yearning in desire
To follow knowledge like a sinking star,
Beyond the utmost bound of human thought.

This is my son, mine own Telemachus,
To whom I leave the sceptre and the isle—
35 Well-loved of me, discerning to fulfill
This labour, by slow prudence to make mild
A rugged people, and thro' soft degrees
Subdue them to the useful and the good.
Most blameless is he, centred in the sphere

40   Of common duties, decent not to fail
      In offices of tenderness, and pay
      Meet adoration to my household gods
      When I am gone. He works his work, I mine.

        There lies the port; the vessel puffs her sail:
45   There gloom the dark broad seas. My mariners,
      Souls that have toiled, and wrought, and thought with me—
      That ever with a frolic welcome took
      The thunder and the sunshine, and opposed
      Free hearts, free foreheads—you and I are old;
50   Old age hath yet his honour and his toil;
      Death closes all: but something ere the end,
      Some work of noble note, may yet be done,
      Not unbecoming men that strove with Gods.
      The lights begin to twinkle from the rocks:
55   The long day wanes: the slow moon climbs: the deep
      Moans round with many voices. Come, my friends,
      'Tis not too late to seek a newer world.
      Push off, and sitting well in order smite
      The sounding furrows; for my purpose holds
60   To sail beyond the sunset, and the baths
      Of all the western stars, until I die.
      It may be that the gulfs will wash us down:
      It may be we shall touch the Happy Isles,
      And see the great Achilles, whom we knew.
65   Tho' much is taken, much abides; and tho'
      We are not now that strength which in old days
      Moved earth and heaven; that which we are, we are;
      One equal temper of heroic hearts,
      Made weak by time and fate, but strong in will
70   To strive, to seek, to find, and not to yield.

1842

Tears, Idle Tears

      Tears, idle tears, I know not what they mean,
      Tears from the depth of some divine despair
      Rise in the heart, and gather to the eyes,
      In looking on the happy Autumn-fields,
5   And thinking of the days that are no more.

Fresh as the first beam glittering on a sail,
That brings our friends up from the underworld,
Sad as the last which reddens over one
That sinks with all we love below the verge;
10   So sad, so fresh, the days that are no more.

Ah, sad and strange as in dark summer dawns
The earliest pipe of half-awakened birds
To dying ears, when unto dying eyes
The casement slowly grows a glimmering square;
15   So sad, so strange, the days that are no more.

Dear as remembered kisses after death,
And sweet as those by hopeless fancy feigned
On lips that are for others; deep as love,
Deep as first love, and wild with all regret;
20   O Death in Life, the days that are no more.

1847

From *In Memoriam*

7

Dark house, by which once more I stand
    Here in the long unlovely street,
    Doors, where my heart was used to beat
So quickly, waiting for a hand,

5   A hand that can be clasped no more—
    Behold me, for I cannot sleep,
    And like a guilty thing I creep
At earliest morning to the door.

He[1] is not here; but far away
10   The noise of life begins again,
    And ghastly thro' the drizzling rain
On the bald street breaks the blank day.

---

1 Arthur Henry Hallam, Tennyson's friend, whose death inspired the sequence of poems entitled *In Memoriam A.H.H.*

8

A happy lover who has come
  To look on her that loves him well,
  Who 'lights and rings the gateway bell,
And learns her gone and far from home;

5 He saddens, all the magic light
  Dies off at once from bower and hall,
  And all the place is dark, and all
The chambers emptied of delight:

So find I every pleasant spot
10 In which we two were wont to meet,
  The field, the chamber and the street,
For all is dark where thou are not.

Yet as that other, wandering there
  In those deserted walks, may find
15 A flower beat with rain and wind,
Which once she fostered up with care;

So seems it in my deep regret,
  O my forsaken heart, with thee
  And this poor flower of poesy
20 Which little cared for fades not yet.

But since it pleased a vanished eye,
  I go to plant it on his tomb,
  That if it can it there may bloom,
Or dying, there at least may die.

115

Now fades the last long streak of snow,
  Now burgeons every maze of quick
  About the flowering squares, and thick
By ashen roots the violets blow.

5 Now rings the woodland loud and long,
  The distance takes a lovelier hue,
  And drowned in yonder living blue
The lark becomes a sightless song.

Now dance the lights on lawn and lea,
10   The flocks are whiter down the vale,
     And milkier every milky sail
On winding stream or distant sea;

Where now the seamew pipes, or dives
     In yonder greening gleam, and fly
15   The happy birds, that change their sky
To build and brood; that live their lives

From land to land; and in my breast
     Spring wakens too; and my regret
     Becomes an April violet,
20 And buds and blossoms like the rest.

1850

Robert Browning
1812–1889

Robert Browning is a poet of masks. While we know a lot about his life, we seldom feel that we really know him. He hides behind the faces of the rogues' gallery in his dramatic monologues, allowing his characters to present psychological portraits of themselves, but not of him. His greatest work, *The Ring and the Book*, is a seventeenth-century Roman murder mystery featuring the despicable Count Guido Franceschini. It is recounted through dramatic monologues in which each character presents a contrasting point of view. Browning's interest in things Italian started when he was a boy living in the London suburb of Camberwell. Largely educated at home by tutors, he all but devoured his father's 6,000-volume library, from which he acquired much of his wide knowledge of Italian history, art, and literature. He lived happily with his parents until the age of thirty-four, when he eloped to Italy with the poet Elizabeth Barrett, rescuing her from her jealous, tyrannical father. This love affair was the great romance of its time, and continued for fifteen idyllic years mostly in Italy, until Elizabeth's death in 1861.

Like Tennyson, Browning was enormously productive, and also like Tennyson, he was an extremely popular poet. Shortly before his death, the first Browning Society was formed. These literary groups blossomed throughout the English-speaking world, revering Browning as the great affirmative voice of the age, a voice that, they sincerely believed, would refute Tennysonian doubt.

Soliloquy of the Spanish Cloister

Gr-r-r—there go, my heart's abhorrence!
    Water your damned flower-pots, do!
If hate killed men, Brother Lawrence,
    God's blood, would not mine kill you!
5 What? your myrtle-bush wants trimming?
    Oh, that rose has prior claims—
Needs its leaden vase filled brimming?
    Hell dry you up with its flames!

At the meal we sit together;
10   *Salve tibi!*[1] I must hear
Wise talk of the kind weather,
    Sort of season, time of year:
Not a plenteous cork-crop: scarcely
    Dare we hope oak-galls, I doubt;
15 *What's the Latin name for 'parsley'?*
    What's the Greek name for Swine's Snout?

Whew! We'll have our platter burnished,
    Laid with care on our own shelf!
With a fire-new spoon we're furnished,
20   And a goblet for ourself,
Rinsed like something sacrificial
    Ere 'tis fit to touch our chaps—
Marked with L. for our initial!
    (He-he! There his lily snaps!)

25 *Saint*, forsooth! while brown Dolores
    Squats outside the Convent bank
With Sanchicha, telling stories,
    Steeping tresses in the tank,
Blue-black, lustrous, thick like horsehairs,
30   —Can't I see his dead eye glow,
Bright as 'twere a Barbary corsair's?
    (That is, if he'd let it show!)

When he finishes refection,
    Knife and fork he never lays
35 Cross-wise, to my recollection,
    As do I, in Jesu's praise.
I, the Trinity illustrate,

---

1 Greeting to you!

Drinking watered orange-pulp—
In three sips the Arian² frustrate;
40   While he drains his at one gulp!

Oh, those melons! if he's able
    We're to have a feast; so nice!
One goes to the Abbot's table,
    All of us get each a slice.
45   How go on your flowers? None double?
    Not one fruit-sort can you spy?
Strange!—And I, too, at such trouble,
    Keep them close-nipped on the sly!

There's a great text in Galatians,³
50   Once you trip on it, entails
Twenty-nine distinct damnations,
    One sure, if another fails;
If I trip him just a-dying,
    Sure of heaven as sure can be,
55   Spin him round and send him flying
    Off to hell, a Manichee?⁴

Or, my scrofulous French novel
    On grey paper with blunt type!
Simply glance at it, you grovel
60   Hand and foot in Belial's⁵ gripe;
If I double down its pages
    At the woeful sixteenth print,
When he gathers his greengages,
    Ope a sieve and slip it in't?

65   Or, there's Satan!—one might venture
    Pledge one's soul to him, yet leave
Such a flaw in the indenture
    As he'd miss till, past retrieve,
Blasted lay that rose-acacia
70   We're so proud of! *Hy, Zy, Hine.* . . .
    'St, there's Vespers!⁶ *Plena Gratia*
    Ave, Virgo! Gr-r-r—you swine!

2 a follower of the heretic Arius, who denied the Trinity
3 one of St Paul's Epistles
4 a follower of the heretic Mani
5 a devil
6 evening prayers. The speaker intones 'Hail Virgin, full of grace.'

My Last Duchess

Ferrara

That's my last Duchess painted on the wall,
Looking as if she were alive. I call
That piece a wonder, now: Frà Pandolf's hands
Worked busily a day, and there she stands.
5 Will't please you sit and look at her? I said
'Frà Pandolf' by design, for never read
Strangers like you that pictured countenance,
The depth and passion of its earnest glance,
But to myself they turned (since none puts by
10 The curtain I have drawn for you, but I)
And seemed as they would ask me, if they durst,
How such a glance came there; so, not the first
Are you to turn and ask thus. Sir, 'twas not
Her husband's presence only, called that spot
15 Of joy into the Duchess' cheek; perhaps
Frà Pandolf chanced to say, 'Her mantle laps
Over my lady's wrist too much,' or 'Paint
Must never hope to reproduce the faint
Half-flush that dies along her throat': such stuff
20 Was courtesy, she thought, and cause enough
For calling up that spot of joy. She had
At heart—how shall I say?—too soon made glad,
Too easily impressed: she liked whate'er
She looked on, and her looks went everywhere.
25 Sir, 'twas all one! My favour at her breast,
The dropping of the daylight in the West,
The bough of cherries some officious fool
Broke in the orchard for her, the white mule
She rode with around the terrace—all and each
30 Would draw from her alike the approving speech.
Or blush, at least. She thanked men,—good! but thanked
Somehow—I know not how—as if she ranked
My gift of a nine-hundred-years-old name
With anybody's gift. Who'd stoop to blame
35 This sort of trifling? Even had you skill
In speech—(which I have not)—to make your will
Quite clear to such an one, and say, 'Just this
Or that in you disgusts me; here you miss,
Or there exceed the mark'—and if she let
40 Herself be lessoned so, nor plainly set

Her wits to yours, forsooth, and made excuse,
—E'en then would be some stooping; and I choose
Never to stoop. Oh sir, she smiled, no doubt,
Whene'er I passed her; but who passed without

45 Much the same smile? This grew; I gave commands;
Then all smiles stopped together. There she stands
As if alive. Will't please you rise? We'll meet
The company below, then. I repeat,
The Count your master's known munificence

50 Is ample warrant that no just pretence
Of mine for dowry will be disallowed;
Though his fair daughter's self, as I avowed
At starting, is my object. Nay, we'll go
Together down, sir. Notice Neptune, though,

55 Taming a sea-horse, thought a rarity,
Which Claus of Innsbruck cast in bronze for me!

1842

The Bishop Orders His Tomb at Saint Praxed's Church

Rome, 15—

Vanity, saith the preacher, vanity!
Draw round my bed: is Anselm keeping back?
Nephews—sons mine . . . ah God, I know not! Well—
She, men would have to be your mother once,

5 Old Gandolf envied me, so fair she was!
What's done is done, and she is dead beside,
Dead long ago, and I am Bishop since,
And as she died so must we die ourselves,
And thence ye may perceive the world's a dream.

10 Life, how and what is it? As here I lie
In this state-chamber, dying by degrees,
Hours and long hours in the dead night, I ask,
'Do I live, am I dead?' Peace, peace seems all.
Saint Praxed's ever was the church for peace;

15 And so, about this tomb of mine. I fought
With tooth and nail to save my niche, ye know:
—Old Gandolf cozened me, despite my care;
Shrewd was that snatch from out the corner South
He graced his carrion with, God curse the same!

20 Yet still my niche is not so cramped but thence

One sees the pulpit o' the epistle-side,
And somewhat of the choir, those silent seats,
And up into the aery dome where live
The angels, and a sunbeam's sure to lurk:
25 And I shall fill my slab of basalt there,
And 'neath my tabernacle take my rest,
With those nine columns round me, two and two,
The odd one at my feet where Anselm stands:
Peach-blossom marble all, the rare, the ripe
30 As fresh-poured red wine of a mighty pulse.
—Old Gandolf with his paltry onion-stone,
Put me where I may look at him! True peach,
Rosy and flawless: how I earned the prize!
Draw close: that conflagration of my church
35 —What then? So much was saved if aught were missed!
My sons, ye would not be my death? Go dig
The white-grape vineyard where the oil-press stood,
Drop water gently till the surface sink,
And if ye find . . . Ah God, I know not, I! . . .
40 Bedded in store of rotten fig-leaves soft,
And corded up in a tight olive-frail,
Some lump, ah God, of *lapis lazuli*,
Big as a Jew's head cut off at the nape,
Blue as a vein o'er the Madonna's breast . . .
45 Sons, all have I bequeathed you, villas, all,
That brave Frascati villa with its bath,
So, let the blue lump poise between my knees,
Like God the Father's globe on both his hands
Ye worship in the Jesus Church so gay,
50 For Gandolf shall not choose but see and burst!
Swift as a weaver's shuttle fleet our years:
Man goeth to the grave, and where is he?
Did I say basalt for my slab, sons? Black—
'Twas ever antique-black I meant! How else
55 Shall ye contrast my frieze to come beneath?
The bas-relief in bronze ye promised me,
Those Pans and Nymphs ye wot of, and perchance
Some tripod, thyrsus, with a vase or so,
The Saviour at his sermon on the mount,
60 Saint Praxed in a glory, and one Pan
Ready to twitch the Nymph's last garment off,
And Moses with the tables . . . but I know
Ye mark me not! What do they whisper thee,
Child of my bowels, Anselm? Ah, ye hope

65 To revel down my villas while I gasp
  Bricked o'er with beggar's mouldy travertine
  Which Gandolf from his tomb-top chuckles at!
  Nay, boys, ye love me—all of jasper, then!
  'Tis jasper ye stand pledged to, lest I grieve.
70 My bath must needs be left behind, alas!
  One block, pure green as a pistachio-nut,
  There's plenty jasper somewhere in the world—
  And have I not Saint Praxed's ear to pray
  Horses for ye, and brown Greek manuscripts,
75 And mistresses with great smooth marbly limbs?
  —That's if ye carve my epitaph aright,
  Choice Latin, picked phrase, Tully's every word,
  No gaudy ware like Gandolf's second line—
  Tully, my masters? Ulpian serves his need!
80 And then how I shall lie through centuries,
  And hear the blessed mutter of the mass,
  And see God made and eaten all day long,
  And feel the steady candle-flame, and taste
  Good, strong, thick, stupefying incense-smoke!
85 For as I lie here, hours of the dead night,
  Dying in state and by such slow degrees,
  I fold my arms as if they clasped a crook,
  And stretch my feet forth straight as stone can point,
  And let the bedclothes, for a mortcloth, drop
90 Into great laps and folds of sculptor's-work:
  And as yon tapers dwindle, and strange thoughts
  Grow, with a certain humming in my ears,
  About the life before I lived this life,
  And this life too, popes, cardinals and priests,
95 Saint Praxed at his sermon on the mount,
  Your tall pale mother with her talking eyes,
  And new-found agate urns as fresh as day,
  And marble's language, Latin pure, discreet,
  —Aha, ELUCESCEBAT[1] quoth our friend?
100 No Tully, said I, Ulpian at the best!
  Evil and brief hath been my pilgrimage.
  All *lapis*, all, sons! Else I give the Pope
  My villas! Will ye ever eat my heart?
  Ever your eyes were as a lizard's quick,
105 They glitter like your mother's for my soul,
  Or ye would heighten my impoverished frieze,

1 He was famous: not in the pure Latin of Cicero (Tully) but in the debased style of Ulpian.

Piece out its starved design, and fill my vase
With grapes, and add a visor and a Term,
And to the tripod ye would tie a lynx
110 That in his struggle throws the thyrsus down,
To comfort me on my entablature
Whereon I am to lie till I must ask,
'Do I live, am I dead?' There, leave me, there!
For ye have stabbed me with ingratitude
115 To death—ye wish it—God, ye wish it! Stone—
Gritstone, a-crumble! Clammy squares which sweat
As if the corpse they keep were oozing through—
And no more *lapis* to delight the world!
Well, go! I bless ye. Fewer tapers there,
120 But in a row: and, going, turn your backs
—Aye, like departing altar-ministrants,
And leave me in my church, the church for peace,
That I may watch at leisure if he leers—
Old Gandolf—at me, from his onion-stone,
125 As still he envied me, so fair she was!

1845

Porphyria's Lover

The rain set early in tonight
The sullen wind was soon awake,
It tore the elm-tops down for spite,
 And did its worst to vex the lake:
5 I listen'd with heart fit to break.
When glided in Porphyria; straight
 She shut the cold out and the storm,
And kneel'd and made the cheerless grate
 Blaze up, and all the cottage warm;
10 Which done, she rose, and from her form
Withdrew the dripping cloak and shawl,
 And laid her soil'd gloves by, untied
Her hat and let the damp hair fall,
 And, last, she sat down by my side
15 And call'd me. When no voice replied,
She put my arm about her waist,
 And made her smooth white shoulder bare,
And all her yellow hair displaced,

And, stooping, made my cheek lie there,
20   And spread, o'er all, her yellow hair,
Murmuring how she loved me—she
        Too weak, for all her heart's endeavour,
To set its struggling passion free
        From pride, and vainer ties dissever,
25   And give herself to me for ever.
But passion sometimes would prevail,
        Nor could tonight's gay feast restrain
A sudden thought of one so pale
        For love of her, and all in vain:
30   So, she was come through wind and rain.
Be sure I look'd up at her eyes
        Happy and proud; at last I knew
Porphyria worshipp'd me; surprise
        Made my heart swell, and still it grew
35   While I debated what to do.
That moment she was mine, mine, fair,
        Perfectly pure and good: I found
A thing to do, and all her hair
        In one long yellow string I wound
40   Three times her little throat around,
And strangled her. No pain felt she;
        I am quite sure she felt no pain.
As a shut bud that holds a bee,
        I warily oped her lids: again
45   Laugh'd the blue eyes without a stain.
And I untighten'd next the tress,
        About her neck; her cheek once more
Blush'd bright beneath my burning kiss:
        I propp'd her head up as before,
50   Only, this time my shoulder bore
Her head, which droops upon it still:
        The smiling rosy little head,
So glad it has its utmost will,
        That all it scorn'd at once is fled,
55   And I, its love, am gain'd instead!
Porphyria's love: she guess'd not how
        Her darling one wish would be heard.
And thus we sit together now,
        And all night long we have not stirr'd,
60   And yet God has not said a word!

1836

Walt Whitman
1819–1892

In 1844 Ralph Waldo Emerson called for a truly American poet who would see that 'America is a poem in our eyes.' Eleven years later Walt Whitman's 'barbaric yawp', as he himself called it, gave answer to Emerson's request. The voice was distinctly American, and the form broke away from conventional metrical regularity, its line swelling and undulating with oceanic rhythm, echoing the biblical psalmists, or declaiming oratorically in the best American political tradition. It was an expansive voice for an expanding nation, and Whitman saw himself as prophet and seer celebrating individualism and democratic idealism as it manifested itself in all experience. Though Emerson was impressed with the first edition of *Leaves of Grass*, he was shocked at some of Whitman's subject matter. The book initially was not considered respectable, and each new edition was inevitably pronounced 'obscene'.

Whitman was born on Long Island, New York, and grew up in Brooklyn, though he returned frequently to Long Island and his beloved ocean. Mostly self-educated, he attended school for only six years and then worked variously as an office boy, schoolteacher, newspaper editor, and carpenter. During the Civil War he was a wound dresser in a Washington army hospital, and after the war he lost his job in the Office of Indian Affairs when it was discovered he had written an 'indecent' book. Never financially secure, Whitman supported himself as he could, continuing to expand and rearrange the poetry of *Leaves of Grass*, which began to gain acceptance and recognition only toward the end of his life.

Crossing Brooklyn Ferry

I

Flood-tide below me! I see you face to face!
Clouds of the west—sun there half an hour high—I see you also face to face.

Crowds of men and women attired in the usual costumes, how curious you are to me!
On the ferry-boats the hundreds and hundreds that cross, returning home, are more curious to me than you suppose,
5   And you that shall cross from shore to shore years hence are more to me, and more in my meditations, than you might suppose.

2

The impalpable sustenance of me from all things at all hours of the day,
The simple, compact, well-join'd scheme, myself disintegrated, every one disintegrated yet part of the scheme,

The similitudes of the past and those of the future,
The glories strung like beads on my smallest sights and hearings, on the walk
   in the street and the passage over the river,
10   The current rushing so swiftly and swimming with me far away,
The others that are to follow me, the ties between me and them,
The certainty of others, the life, love, sight, hearing of others.
Others will enter the gates of the ferry and cross from shore to shore,
Others will watch the run of the flood-tide,
15   Others will see the shipping of Manhattan north and west, and the heights of
   Brooklyn to the south and east,
Others will see the islands large and small;
Fifty years hence, others will see them as they cross, the sun half an hour high,
A hundred years hence, or ever so many hundred years hence, others will see
   them,
Will enjoy the sunset, the pouring-in of the flood-tide, the falling-back to the
   sea of the ebb-tide.

3

20   It avails not, time nor place—distance avails not,
I am with you, you men and women of a generation, or ever so many generations hence,
Just as you feel when you look on the river and sky, so I felt,
Just as any of you is one of a living crowd, I was one of a crowd,
Just as you are refresh'd by the gladness of the river and the bright flow, I was
   refresh'd,
25   Just as you stand and lean on the rail, yet hurry with the swift current, I stood
   yet was hurried,
Just as you look on the numberless masts of ships and the thick-stemm'd pipes
   of steamboats, I look'd.

I too many and many a time cross'd the river of old,
Watched the Twelfth-month sea-gulls, saw them high in the air floating with
   motionless wings, oscillating their bodies,
Saw how the glistening yellow lit up parts of their bodies and left the rest in
   strong shadow,
30   Saw the slow-wheeling circles and the gradual edging toward the south,
Saw the reflection of the summer sky in the water,
Had my eyes dazzled by the shimmering track of beams,
Look'd at the fine centrifugal spokes of light round the shape of my head in
   the sunlit water,
Look'd on the haze on the hills southward and south-westward,
35   Look'd on the vapour as it flew in fleeces tinged with violet,

Look'd toward the lower bay to notice the vessels arriving,

Saw their approach, saw aboard those that were near me,

Saw the white sails of schooners and sloops, saw the ships at anchor,

The sailors at work in the rigging or out astride the spars,

40 The round masts, the swinging motion of the hulls, the slender serpentine pennants,

The large and small steamers in motion, the pilots in their pilot-houses,

The white wake left by the passage, the quick tremulous whirl of the wheels,

The flags of all nations, the falling of them at sunset,

The scallop-edged waves in the twilight, the ladled cups, the frolicsome crests and glistening,

45 The stretch afar growing dimmer and dimmer, the grey walls of the granite storehouses by the docks,

On the river the shadowy group, the big steam-tug closely flank'd on each side by the barges, the hay-boat, the belated lighter,

On the neighbouring shore the fires from the foundry chimneys burning high and glaringly into the night,

Casting their flicker of black contrasted with wild red and yellow light over the tops of houses and down into the clefts of streets.

4

These and all else were to me the same as they are to you,

50 I loved well those cities, loved well the stately and rapid river,

The men and women I saw were all near to me,

Others the same—others who look back on me because I look'd forward to them,

(The time will come, though I stop here to-day and to-night.)

5

What is it then between us?

55 What is the count of the scores or hundreds of years between us?

Whatever it is, it avails not—distance avails not, and place avails not,

I too lived, Brooklyn of ample hills was mine,

I too walk'd the streets of Manhattan island, and bathed in the waters around it,

I too felt the curious abrupt questionings stir within me,

60 In the day among crowds of people sometimes they came upon me,

In my walks home late at night or as I lay in my bed they came upon me,

I too had been struck from the float forever held in solution,

I too had receiv'd identity by my body,
That I was I knew was of my body, and what I should be I knew I should be
    of my body.

6

65   It is not upon you alone the dark patches fall,
    The dark threw its patches down upon me also,
    The best I had done seem'd to me blank and suspicious,
    My great thoughts as I supposed them, were they not in reality meagre?
    Nor is it you alone who knows what it is to be evil,
70   I am he who knew what it was to be evil,
    I too knitted the old knot of contrariety,
    Blabb'd, blush'd, resented, lied, stole, grudg'd,
    Had guile, anger, lust, hot wishes I dared not speak,
    Was wayward, vain, greedy, shallow, sly, cowardly, malignant,
75   The wolf, the snake, the hog, not wanting in me,
    The cheating look, the frivolous word, the adulterous wish, not wanting,
    Refusals, hates, postponements, meanness, laziness, none of these wanting,
    Was one with the rest, the days and haps of the rest,
    Was call'd by my nighest name by clear loud voices of young men as they saw
        me approaching or passing,
80   Felt their arms on my neck as I stood, or the negligent leaning of their flesh
        against me as I sat,
    Saw many I loved in the street or ferry-boat or public assembly, yet never told
        them a word,
    Lived the same life with the rest, the same old laughing, gnawing, sleeping,
    Play'd the part that still looks back on the actor or actress,
    The same old role, the role that is what we make it, as great as we like,
85   Or as small as we like, or both great and small.

7

    Closer yet I approach you,
    What thought you have of me now, I had as much of you—I laid in my stores
        in advance,
    I consider'd long and seriously of you before you were born.

    Who was to know what should come home to me?
90   Who knows but I am enjoying this?
    Who knows, for all the distance, but I am as good as looking at you now, for
        all you cannot see me?

8

Ah, what can ever be more stately and admirable to me than mast-hemm'd
    Manhattan?
River and sunset and scallop-edg'd waves of flood-tide?
The sea-gulls oscillating their bodies, the hay-boat in the twilight, and the
    belated lighter?
95   What gods can exceed these that clasp me by the hand, and with voices I love
    call me promptly and loudly by my nighest name as I approach?
What is more subtle than this which ties me to the woman or man that looks
    in my face?
Which fuses me into you now, and pours my meaning into you?
We understand then do we not?
What I promis'd without mentioning it, have you not accepted?
100 What the study could not teach—what the preaching could not accomplish is
    accomplish'd, is it not?

9

Flow on, river! flow with the flood-tide, and ebb with the ebb-tide!
Frolic on, crested and scallop-edg'd waves!
Gorgeous clouds of the sunset! drench with your splendour me, or the men
    and women generations after me!
Cross from shore to shore, countless crowds of passengers!
105 Stand up, tall masts of Mannahatta! stand up, beautiful hills of Brooklyn!
Throb, baffled and curious brain! throw out questions and answers!
Suspend here and everywhere, eternal float of solution!
Gaze, loving and thirsty eyes, in the house or street or public assembly!
Sound out, voices of young men! loudly and musically call me by my nighest
    name!
110 Live, old life! play the part that looks back on the actor or actress!
Play the old role, the role that is great or small according as one makes it!
Consider, you who peruse me, whether I may not in unknown ways be looking
    upon you;
Be firm, rail over the river, to support those who lean idly, yet haste with the
    hasting current;
Fly on, sea-birds! fly sideways, or wheel in large circles high in the air;
115 Receive the summer sky, you water, and faithfully hold it till all downcast eyes
    have time to take it from you!
Diverge, fine spokes of light, from the shape of my head, or any one's head, in
    the sunlit water!
Come on, ships from the lower bay! pass up or down, white-sail'd schooners,
    sloops, lighters!

Flaunt away, flags of all nations! be duly lower'd at sunset!
Burn high your fires, foundry chimneys! cast black shadows at nightfall! cast
    red and yellow light over the tops of the houses!
120 Appearances, now or henceforth, indicate what you are,
You necessary film, continue to envelop the soul,
About my body for me, and your body for you, be hung out divinest aromas,
Thrive, cities—bring your freight, bring your shows, ample and sufficient
    rivers,
Expand, being than which none else is perhaps more spiritual,
125 Keep your places, objects than which none else is more lasting.

You have waited, you always wait, you dumb, beautiful ministers,
We receive you with free sense at last, and are insatiate henceforward,
Not you any more shall be able to foil us, or withhold yourselves from us,
We use you, and do not cast you aside—we plant you permanently within us,
130 We fathom you not—we love you—there is perfection in you also,
You furnish your parts toward eternity,
Great or small, you furnish your parts toward the soul.

1856

I Hear America Singing

I hear America singing, the varied carols I hear,
Those of mechanics, each one singing his as it should be blithe and strong,
The carpenter singing his as he measures his plank or beam,
The mason singing his as he makes ready for work, or leaves off work.
5 The boatman singing what belongs to him in his boat, the deckhand singing
    on the steamboat deck,
The shoemaker singing as he sits on his bench, the hatter singing as he stands,
The wood-cutter's song, the ploughboy's on his way in the morning, or at noon
    intermission or at sundown,
The delicious singing of the mother, or of the young wife at work, or of the
    girl sewing or washing,
Each singing what belongs to him or her and to none else,
10 The day what belongs to the day—at night the party of young fellows, robust,
    friendly,
Singing with open mouths their strong melodious songs.

1860

A Sight in Camp in the Daybreak Grey and Dim

A sight in camp in the daybreak grey and dim,
As from my tent I emerge so early sleepless,
As slow I walk in the cool fresh air the path near by the hospital tent,
Three forms I see on stretchers lying, brought out there untended lying,
5   Over each the blanket spread, ample brownish woolen blanket,
Grey and heavy blanket, folding, covering all.

Curious I halt and silent stand,
Then with light fingers I from the face of the nearest the first just lift the blanket;
Who are you elderly man so gaunt and grim, with well-grey'd hair, and flesh
    all sunken about the eyes?
10 Who are you my dear comrade?
Then to the second I step—and who are you my child and darling?
Who are you sweet boy with cheeks yet blooming?

Then to the third—a face nor child nor old, very calm, as of beautiful yellow-
    white ivory;
Young man I think I know you—I think this face is the face of the Christ
    himself,
15 Dead and divine and brother of all, and here again he lies.

1865

The Ox-Tamer

In a far-away northern county in the placid pastoral region,
Lives my farmer friend, the theme of my recitative, a famous tamer of oxen,
There they bring him the three-year-olds and the four-year-olds to break them,
He will take the wildest steer in the world and break him and tame him,
5   He will go fearless without any whip where the young bullock chafes up and
    down the yard,
The bullock's head tosses restless high in the air with raging eyes,
Yet see you! how soon his rage subsides—how soon this tamer tames him;
See you! on the farms hereabout a hundred oxen young and old, and he is the
    man who has tamed them,
They all know him, all are affectionate to him;
10 See you! some are such beautiful animals, so lofty looking;
Some are buff-colour'd, some mottled, one has a white line running along his
    back, some are brindled,
Some have wide flaring horns (a good sign)—see you! the bright hides,

See, the two with stars on their foreheads—see, the round bodies and broad
    backs,
How straight and square they stand on their legs—what fine sagacious eyes!
15 How they watch their tamer—they wish him near them—how they turn to
    look after him!
What yearning expression! how uneasy they are when he moves away from
    them;
Now I marvel what it can be he appears to them, (books, politics, poems,
    depart—all else departs,)
I confess I envy only his fascination—my silent, illiterate friend,
Whom a hundred oxen love there in his life on farms,
20 In the northern county far, in the placid pastoral region.

                                                        1874

The Dalliance of the Eagles

Skirting the river road, (my forenoon walk, my rest,)
Skyward in air a sudden muffled sound, the dalliance of the eagles,
The rushing amorous contact high in space together,
The clinching interlocking claws, a living, fierce, gyrating wheel,
5 Four beating wings, two beaks, a swirling mass tight grappling,
In tumbling turning clustering loops, straight downward falling,
Till o'er the river pois'd, the twain yet one, a moment's lull,
A motionless still balance in the air, then parting, talons loosing,
Upward again on slow-firm pinions slanting, their separate diverse flight,
10 She hers, he his, pursuing.

                                                         1880

Emily Dickinson
1830–1886

Emily Dickinson provided another new voice for American poetry, but one quite the opposite of that of her contemporary Walt Whitman. She is as coiled and condensed as he is loose and expansive; as private as he is public. She was born and raised in Amherst, Massachusetts, studying at Amherst Academy before entering nearby Mount Holyoke Female Seminary. But less than a year later she returned home because she could not accept the

Seminary's rigid brand of Christianity, and because she was homesick. She lived the rest of her life in her father's house, rarely leaving Amherst, and eventually becoming a recluse, seeing only a few visitors a year. Though some biographers have characterized Dickinson as a frail, highly eccentric spinster, hiding from the world and frustrated in life and in love, the power of her poetry and the sheer amount of her literary output belie such a picture. Instead, we might consider her withdrawal from society a choice for the freedom to pursue the career of a poet. She produced over 1,700 poems, of which only 7 were published during her lifetime. Though the form of her poetry looks simple, with its patterns of metre and rhyme suggesting her use of nineteenth-century hymnals as models of prosody, there is nothing simplistic in what she says, and her unconventional punctuation forces us to pause with her thoughts as she examines faith and doubt, death, nature, and varieties of love.

[Success Is Counted Sweetest]

Success is counted sweetest
By those who ne'er succeed.
To comprehend a nectar
Requires sorest need.

5   Not one of all the purple Host
Who took the Flag today
Can tell the definition
So clear of Victory

As he defeated—dying—
10 On whose forbidden ear
The distant strains of triumph
Burst agonized and clear!

1878

[I'm 'Wife'—I've Finished That]

I'm 'wife'—I've finished that—
That other state—
I'm Czar—I'm 'Woman' now—
It's safer so—

5   How odd the Girl's life looks
Behind this soft Eclipse—
I think that Earth feels so
To folks in Heaven—now—

This being comfort—then
10   That other kind—was pain—
But why compare?
I'm 'Wife'! Stop there!

1890

[The Heart Asks Pleasure—First]

The Heart asks Pleasure—first—
And then—Excuse from Pain—
And then—those little Anodynes
That deaden suffering—
5   And then—to go to sleep—
And then—if it should be
The will of its Inquisitor
The privilege to die—

1890

[Because I Could Not Stop for Death]

Because I could not stop for Death—
He kindly stopped for me—
The Carriage held but just Ourselves—
And Immortality.

5   We slowly drove—He knew no haste
And I had put away
My labour and my leisure too,
For His Civility—

We passed the School, where Children strove
10   At Recess—in the Ring—
We passed the Fields of Gazing Grain—
We passed the Setting Sun—

Or rather—He passed Us—
The Dews drew quivering and chill—
15   For only Gossamer, my Gown—
My Tippet—only Tulle—

We paused before a House that seemed
A Swelling of the Ground—
The Roof was scarcely visible—
20 The Cornice—in the Ground—

Since then—'tis Centuries—and yet
Feels shorter than the Day
I first surmised the Horses' Heads
Were toward Eternity—

1890

[What Is—'Paradise']

What is—'Paradise'—
Who live there—
Are they 'Farmers'—
Do they 'hoe'—
5 Do they know that this is 'Amherst'—
And that I—am coming—too—
Do they wear 'new shoes'—in 'Eden'—
Is it always pleasant—there—
Won't they scold us—when we're hungry—
10 Or tell God—how cross we are—
You are sure there's such a person
As 'a Father'—in the sky—
So if I get lost—there—ever—
Or do what the nurse calls 'die'—
15 I shan't walk the 'Jasper'—barefoot—
Ransomed folks—won't laugh at me—
Maybe—'Eden' a'nt so lonesome
As New England used to be!

1891

[I Never Hear the Word]

I never hear the word 'escape'
Without a quicker blood,
A sudden expectation,
A flying attitude!

5   I never hear of prisons broad
     By soldiers battered down,
     But I tug childish at my bars
     Only to fail again!

1891

[I Heard a Fly Buzz]

     I heard a Fly buzz—when I died—
     The Stillness in the Room
     Was like the Stillness in the Air—
     Between the Heaves of Storm—

5   The Eyes around—had wrung them dry—
     And Breaths were gathering firm
     For that last Onset—when the King
     Be witnessed—in the Room—

     I willed my Keepsakes—Signed away
10 What portion of me be
     Assignable—and then it was
     There interposed a Fly—

     With Blue—uncertain stumbling Buzz—
     Between the light—and me—
15 And then the Windows failed—and then
     I could not see to see—

1896

Thomas Hardy
1840–1928

One of the great novelists of English litera-ture, Thomas Hardy pursued a writing career in fiction, poetry, and drama that spanned more than six decades. Born near Dorchester in southwestern England, the area that would become Wessex in his writings, he was apprenticed to an architect at the age of fif-teen. In 1861 he moved to London to continue his architectural work. At the same time he began to write poetry and fiction; his first novel, *Desperate Remedies*, appeared in 1871. His commitment to fiction led him to abandon a career in architecture, freeing him to publish fifteen novels, including *The Mayor of Casterbridge* (1885) and *Tess of the D'Urbervilles* (1891), as well as several collections of short fic-tion. Hardy's poetry, like his fiction, explores in naturalistic terms the hapless condition of humankind, caught in a world without design, providence, or God. Unable to return to the religious faith of his Victorian upbringing, he shares with many modern poets a belief in the futility and waste of human existence.

Hap

If but some vengeful god would call to me
From up the sky, and laugh: 'Thou suffering thing,
Know that thy sorrow is my ecstasy,
That thy love's loss is my hate's profiting!'

5   Then would I bear it, clench myself, and die,
Steeled by the sense of ire unmerited;
Half-eased in that a Powerfuller than I
Had willed and meted me the tears I shed.

But not so. How arrives it joy lies slain,
10   And why unblooms the best hope ever sown!
—Crass Casualty obstructs the sun and rain,
And dicing Time for gladness casts a moan. . . .
These purblind Doomsters had as readily strown
Blisses about my pilgrimage as pain.

1898

The Darkling Thrush

I leant upon a coppice gate
    When Frost was spectre-grey
And Winter's dregs made desolate
    The weakening eye of day.
5   The tangled bine-stems scored the sky
    Like strings of broken lyres,
And all mankind that haunted nigh
    Had sought their household fires.

The land's sharp features seemed to be
10   The Century's corpse outleant,
His crypt the cloudy canopy,
    The wind his death-lament.
The ancient pulse of germ and birth
    Was shrunken hard and dry,
15 And every spirit upon earth
    Seemed fervourless as I.

At once a voice arose among
    The bleak twigs overhead
In a full-hearted evensong
20   Of joy illimited;
An aged thrush, frail, gaunt, and small,
    In blast-beruffled plume,
Had chosen thus to fling his soul
    Upon the growing gloom.

25 So little cause for carolings
    Of such ecstatic sound
Was written on terrestrial things
    Afar or nigh around,
That I could think there trembled through
30   His happy good-night air
Some blessed Hope, whereof he knew
    And I was unaware.

1901

The Convergence of the Twain

(Lines on the loss of the *Titanic*)

I

In a solitude of the sea
Deep from human vanity,
And the Pride of Life that planned her, stilly couches she.

II

Steel chambers, late the pyres
5   Of her salamandrine fires,
Cold currents thrid, and turn to rhythmic tidal lyres.

III

Over the mirrors meant
To glass the opulent
The sea-worm crawls—grotesque, slimed, dumb, indifferent.

IV

10   Jewels in joy designed
To ravish the sensuous mind
Lie lightless, all their sparkles bleared and black and blind.

V

Dim moon-eyed fishes near
Gaze at the gilded gear
15 And query: 'What does this vaingloriousness down here?' . . .

VI

Well: while was fashioning
This creature of cleaving wing,
The Immanent Will that stirs and urges everything

Prepared a sinister mate
20 For her—so gaily great—
A Shape of Ice, for the time far and dissociate.

VIII

And as the smart ship grew
In stature, grace, and hue,
In shadowy silent distance grew the Iceberg too.

IX

25 Alien they seemed to be:
No mortal eye could see
The intimate welding of their later history.

X

Or sign that they were bent
By paths coincident
30 On being anon twin halves of one august event,

XI

Till the Spinner of the Years
Said 'Now!' And each one hears,
And consummation comes, and jars two hemispheres.

1912

The Oxen

Christmas Eve, and twelve of the clock.
   'Now they are all on their knees.'
An elder said as we sat in a flock
   By the embers in hearthside ease.

5   We pictured the meek mild creatures where
      They dwelt in their strawy pen,
Nor did it occur to one of us there
      To doubt they were kneeling then.

So fair a fancy few would weave
10   In these years! Yet, I feel,
If someone said on Christmas Eve,
      'Come; see the oxen kneel,

In the lonely barton by yonder coomb
      Our childhood used to know,'
15   I should go with him in the gloom,
      Hoping it might be so.

1917

During Wind and Rain

     They sing their dearest songs—
     He, she, all of them—yea,
     Treble and tenor and bass,
        And one to play;
5   With the candles mooning each face. . . .
        Ah, no; the years O!
How the sick leaves reel down in throngs!

     They clear the creeping moss—
     Elders and juniors—aye,
10   Making the pathways neat
        And the garden gay;
     And they build a shady seat. . . .
        Ah, no; the years, the years;
See, the white storm-birds wing across!

15   They are blithely breakfasting all—
       Men and maidens—yea,
       Under the summer tree,
           With a glimpse of the bay,
       While pet fowl come to the knee. . . .
20   Ah, no; the years O!
       And the rotten rose is ript from the wall.

       They change to a high new house,
       He, she, all of them—aye,
       Clocks and carpets and chairs
25   On the lawn all day,
       And brightest things that are theirs. . . .
           Ah, no; the years, the years;
       Down their carved names the rain-drop ploughs.

                                                    1917

In Time of 'The Breaking of Nations'

I

       Only a man harrowing clods
           In a slow silent walk
       With an old horse that stumbles and nods
           Half asleep as they stalk.

II

5   Only thin smoke without flame
           From the heaps of couch-grass;
       Yet this will go onward the same
           Though Dynasties pass.

III

       Yonder a maid and her wight
10   Come whispering by:
       War's annals will fade into night
           Ere their story die.

                                                    1916

Gerard Manley Hopkins
1844–1889

Born in Stratford, Essex, Gerard Manley Hopkins showed an early interest in poetry, winning a prize for his work at Highgate School in London. As he entered Balliol College in Oxford, he aspired to become a painter. Caught up in the Oxford Movement, a revival of ritualistic Christianity, he converted to Catholicism in 1866. Two years later he joined the Jesuits; he was ordained as a priest in 1877, and served as a missionary in the squalid slums of Liverpool. Hopkins later took a church at Oxford, and near the end of his life was a professor of Greek at University College, Dublin.

While studying for the priesthood, Hopkins had burned all his poetry, but in 1875, still struggling with the demands of his faith and with his aesthetic interests, he began writing again, exploring this struggle in his poetry.

An intense observer of the natural world, Hopkins saw patterns, which he called 'inscapes', in natural phenomena, and his poetry attempts to convey the complex unity of his sensual observation. Yet his is primarily a poetry for the ear. Experimenting in prosody, he drew on rhythms of early English poetry, modelling his 'sprung rhythm' on ordinary speech. Wrenching and straining syntax into original and startling forms, he presents us with an inspired vision of the beauty of nature infused with the glory of God. During his lifetime Hopkins's poems were little known outside his small circle of friends. The first volume of his work was not published until 1918, thirty years after his death, when it was widely read and admired by many of the younger modern poets.

God's Grandeur

The world is charged with the grandeur of God.
    It will flame out, like shining from shook foil;
    It gathers to a greatness, like the ooze of oil
Crushed. Why do men then now not reck his rod?
5 Generations have trod, have trod, have trod;
    And all is seared with trade; bleared, smeared with toil;
    And wears man's smudge and shares man's small: the soil
Is bare now, nor can foot feel, being shod.

And for all this, nature is never spent;
10   There lives the dearest freshness deep down things;
And though the last lights off the black West went
    Oh, morning, at the brown brink eastward, springs—
Because the Holy Ghost over the bent
    World broods with warm breast and with ah! bright wings.

The Windhover

To Christ Our Lord

I caught this morning morning's minion, king-
    dom of daylight's dauphin, dapple-dawn-drawn Falcon, in his riding
    Of the rolling level underneath him steady air, and striding
High there, how he rung upon the rein of a wimpling wing
5 In his ecstasy! then off, off forth on swing,
    As a skate's heel sweeps smooth on a bow-bend: the hurl and gliding
    Rebuffed the big wind. My heart in hiding
Stirred for a bird,—the achieve of, the mastery of the thing!

Brute beauty and valour and act, oh, air, pride, plume, here
10   Buckle! AND the fire that breaks from thee then, a billion
Times told lovelier, more dangerous, O my chevalier!

    No wonder of it: shéer plód makes plough down sillion
Shine, and blue-bleak embers, ah my dear,
    Fall, gall themselves, and gash gold-vermilion.

1918

Pied Beauty

Glory be to God for dappled things—
    For skies of couple-colour as a brinded cow;
        For rose-moles all in stipple upon trout that swim;
Fresh-firecoal chestnut-falls; finches' wings;
5   Landscape plotted and pieced—fold, fallow, and plough;
        And áll trádes, their gear and tackle and trim.
All things counter, original, spare, strange;
    Whatever is fickle, freckled (who knows how?)
        With swift, slow; sweet, sour; adazzle, dim;
10 He fathers-forth whose beauty is past change:
                        Praise him.

1918

Spring and Fall: To a Young Child

Márgarét, are you gríeving
Over Goldengrove unleaving?
Leáves, líke the things of man, you
With your fresh thoughts care for, can you?
5 Áh! ás the heart grows older
It will come to such sights colder
By and by, nor spare a sigh
Though worlds of wanwood leafmeal lie;
And yet you *will* weep and know why.
10 Now no matter, child, the name:
Sórrow's spríngs áre the same.
Nor mouth had, no nor mind, expressed
What heart heard of, ghost guessed:
It ís the blight man was born for,
15 It is Margaret you mourn for.

1918

[Though Art Indeed Just, Lord]

Justus quidem tu es, Domine, si disputem tecum: verumtamen
Justa loquar ad te: Quare via impiorum prosperatur? &c.[1]

Thou art indeed just, Lord, if I contend
With thee; but, sir, so what I plead is just.
Why do sinners' ways prosper? and why must
Disappointment all I endeavour end?

5 Wert thou my enemy, O thou my friend,
How wouldst thou worse, I wonder, than thou dost
Defeat, thwart me? Oh, the sots and thralls of lust
Do in spare hours more thrive than I that spend,

Sir, life upon thy cause. See, banks and brakes
10 Now, leavèd how thick! lacèd they are again
With fretty chervil, look, and fresh wind shakes

Them; birds build—but not I build; no, but strain,
Time's eunuch, and not breed one work that wakes.
Mine, O thou lord of life, send my roots rain.

1918

1 quoted from the biblical prophet Jeremiah, and translated in the first three lines of the poem

Archibald Lampman
1861–1899

Archibald Lampman was born in Morpeth, Ontario, of United Empire Loyalist stock. A case of rheumatic fever when he was seven left him lame for four years and probably weakened his health permanently. His early education had to take place at home, although by the age of nine he was able to attend a private school. He graduated from the University of Toronto in 1882. After teaching high school for four months, he resigned and joined the Post Office Department in Ottawa, where he worked until his death from pneumonia.

A nature poet, Lampman took comfort and poetic delight in the changing seasons and their dramatic effect on natural life. Yet his verse, unlike that of many of his Canadian contemporaries, also ventures into social commentary. 'The City of the End of Things', published in 1899, is a startling apocalyptic vision, a denunciation of commercial society. In 1942 the critic E.K. Brown discovered among Lampman's scribblers and notebooks 'At the Long Sault: May 1660', a stirring lyrical evocation of a great moment in Canadian history and an indication of new directions that his poetry might have followed had death not cut short his career.

The Railway Station

The darkness brings no quiet here, the light
    No waking: ever on my blinded brain
    The flare of lights, the rush, and cry, and strain,
The engines' scream, the hiss and thunder smite:

5 I see the hurrying crowds, the clasp, the flight,
    Faces that touch, eyes that are dim with pain:
    I see the hoarse wheels turn, and the great train
Move labouring out into the bourneless night.

So many souls within its dim recesses,
10   So many bright, so many mournful eyes:
Mine eyes that watch grow fixed with dreams and guesses;
    What threads of life, what hidden histories,
What sweet or passionate dreams and dark distresses,
What unknown thoughts, what various agonies!

The Death of Tennyson

They tell that when his final hour drew near,
He whose fair praise the ages shall rehearse,
Whom now the living and the dead hold dear;
Our grey-haired master of immortal verse,
5 Called for his Shakespeare, and with touch of rue
Turned to that page in stormy Cymbeline
That bears the dirge. Whether he read none knew,
But on the book he laid his hand serene,
And kept it there unshaken, till there fell
10 The last grey change, and from before his eyes,
This glorious world that Shakespeare loved so well,
Slowly, as at a beck, without surprise —
Its woe, its pride, its passion, and its play —
Like mists and melting shadows passed away.

1892

The City of the End of Things

Beside the pounding cataracts
Of midnight streams unknown to us
'Tis builded in the leafless tracts
And valleys huge of Tartarus.[1]
5 Lurid and lofty and vast it seems;
It hath no rounded name that rings,
But I have heard it called in dreams
The City of the End of Things.

Its roofs and iron towers have grown
10 None knoweth how high within the night,
But in its murky streets far down
A flaming terrible and bright
Shakes all the stalking shadows there,
Across the walls, across the floors,
15 And shifts upon the upper air
From out a thousand furnace doors;
And all the while an awful sound
Keeps roaring on continually,

---

1 the infernal abyss below Hades: true hell where Zeus threw rebel Titans

And crashes in the ceaseless round
20   Of a gigantic harmony.

Through its grim depths re-echoing
And all its weary height of walls,
With measured roar and iron ring,
The inhuman music lifts and falls.
25   Where no thing rests and no man is,
And only fire and night hold sway;
The beat, the thunder and the hiss
Cease not, and change not, night nor day.

And moving at unheard commands,
30   The abysses and vast fires between,
Flit figures that with clanking hands
Obey a hideous routine;
They are not flesh, they are not bone,
They see not with the human eye,
35   And from their iron lips is blown
A dreadful and monotonous cry;
And whoso of our mortal race
Should find that city unaware,
Lean Death would smite him face to face,
40   And blanch him with its venomed air:
Or caught by the terrific spell,
Each thread of memory snapt and cut,
His soul would shrivel and its shell
Go rattling like an empty nut.

45   It was not always so, but once,
In days that no man thinks upon,
Fair voices echoed from its stones,
The light above it leaped and shone:
Once there were multitudes of men,
50   That built that city in their pride,
Until its might was made, and then
They withered age by age and died.
But now of that prodigious race,
Three only in an iron tower,
55   Set like carved idols face to face,
Remain the masters of its power;
And at the city gate a fourth,
Gigantic and with dreadful eyes,
Sits looking toward the lightless north,

60   Beyond the reach of memories;
     Fast rooted to the lurid floor,
     A bulk that never moves a jot,
     In his pale body dwells no more,
     Or mind or soul,— an idiot!

65   But sometimes in the end those three
     Shall perish and their hands be still,
     And with the master's touch shall flee
     Their incommunicable skill.
     A stillness absolute as death

70   Along the slacking wheels shall lie,
     And, flagging at a single breath,
     The fires shall moulder out and die.
     The roar shall vanish at its height,
     And over that tremendous town

75   The silence of eternal night
     Shall gather close and settle down.
     All its grim grandeur, tower and hall,
     Shall be abandoned utterly,
     And into rust and dust shall fall

80   From century to century;
     Nor ever living thing shall grow,
     Nor trunk of tree, nor blade of grass;
     No drop shall fall, no wind shall blow,
     Nor sound of any foot shall pass:

85   Alone of its accursèd state,
     One thing the hand of Time shall spare,
     For the grim Idiot at the gate
     Is deathless and eternal there.

                               1895

Winter-Solitude

I saw the city's towers on a luminous pale-grey sky;
Beyond them a hill of the softest mistiest green,
With naught but frost and the coming of night between,
And a long thin cloud above it the colour of August rye.

5 I sat in the midst of a plain on my snowshoes with bended knee
Where the thin wind stung my cheeks,
And the hard snow ran in little ripples and peaks,
Like the fretted floor of a white and petrified sea.

And a strange peace gathered about my soul and shone,
10   As I sat reflecting there,
   In a world so mystically fair,
So deathly silent — I so utterly alone.

February, 1893

1943

At the Long Sault: May 1660[1]

Under the day-long sun there is life and mirth
   In the working earth,
And the wonderful moon shines bright
   Through the soft spring night,
5   The innocent flowers in the limitless woods are springing
   Far and away
   With the sound and the perfume of May,
And ever up from the south the happy birds are winging,
   The waters glitter and leap and play
10   While the grey hawk soars.

But far in an open glade of the forest set
   Where the rapid plunges and roars,
Is a ruined fort with a name that men forget,—
   A shelterless pen
15   With its broken palisade,
   Behind it, musket in hand,
   Beyond message or aid
   In this savage heart of the wild,
   Mere youngsters, grown in a moment to men,
20   Grim and alert arrayed,
   The comrades of Daulac stand.
   Ever before them, night and day,
   The rush and skulk and cry
   Of foes, not men but devils, panting for prey;
25   Behind them the sleepless dream
Or the little frail-walled town,[2] far away by the plunging stream.
   Of maiden and matron and child,
With ruin and murder impending, and none but they
   To beat back the gathering horror

---

1 On 1 May 1660 Adam Dollard des Ormeaux (sometimes called Daulac), with sixteen companions and forty-four Hurons and Algonkins, laid an ambush for some Iroquois at an abandoned fort on the Ottawa River. The Iroquois were joined by a reinforcement of 500, but it took them ten days to vanquish the French and their allies. Until fairly recently this event was considered to have saved the colony of Montreal from Iroquois attack, and the French were considered martyrs for the faith.
2 Montreal

30 Deal death while they may,
        And then die.

Day and night they have watched while the little plain
Grew dark with the rush of the foe, but their host
Broke ever and melted away, with no boast
35 But to number their slain;
And now as the days renew
Hunger and thirst and care
Were they never so stout, so true,
Press at their hearts; but none
40 Falters or shrinks or utters a coward word,
Though each setting sun
Brings from the pitiless wild new hands to the Iroquois horde,
And only to them despair.

Silent, white-faced, again and again
45 Charged and hemmed round by furious hands,
Each for a moment faces them all and stands
In his little desperate ring; like a tired bull moose
Whom scores of sleepless wolves, a ravening pack,
Have chased all night, all day
50 Through the snow-laden woods, like famine let loose;
And he turns at last in his track
Against a wall of rock and stands at bay;
Round him with terrible sinews and teeth of steel
They charge and recharge; but with many a furious plunge and wheel,
55 Hither and thither over the trampled snow,
He tosses them bleeding and torn;
Till, driven, and ever to and fro
Harried, wounded, and weary grown,
His mighty strength gives way
60 And all together they fasten upon him and drag him down.

So Daulac turned him anew
With a ringing cry to his men
In the little raging forest glen,
And his terrible sword in the twilight whistled and slew.
65 And all his comrades stood
With their backs to the pales,[3] and fought
Till their strength was done;

---

3 a row of spiked wooden poles, here the walls of the fort

The thews that were only mortal flagged and broke
Each struck his last wild stroke,
70 And they fell one by one,
And the world that had seemed so good
Passed like a dream and was naught.

And then the great night came
With the triumph-songs of the foe and the flame
75 Of the camp-fires.
Out of the dark the soft wind woke,
The song of the rapid rose alway
And came to the spot where the comrades lay,
Beyond help or care,
80 With none but the red men round them
To gnash their teeth and stare.

All night by the foot of the mountain
     The little town lieth at rest,
The sentries are peacefully pacing;
85   And neither from East nor from West
Is there rumour of death and danger;
     None dreameth tonight in his bed
That ruin was near and the heroes
     That met it and stemmed it are dead.

90 But afar in the ring of the forest,
     Where the air is so tender with May
And the waters are wild in the moonlight
     They lie in their silence of clay.

The numberless stars out of heaven
95   Look down with a pitiful glance;
And the lilies asleep in the forest
     Are closed like the lilies of France.[4]

1943

___

4 that is, the fleur-de-lis, the emblematic flower of France, often appearing as a heraldic emblem on the shields
   of warriors

William Butler Yeats
1865–1939

William Butler Yeats was born at Sandymount, near Dublin, Ireland. His father, John Butler Yeats, was a well-known artist. Educated at schools in London and Dublin, Yeats was never an outstanding scholar, and after attending art school for two years, he left to devote himself to poetry. As a boy, he had loved to roam the countryside of County Sligo, listening to folk tales told around peat fires and absorbing the 'symbols, popular beliefs, and old scraps of verse that made Ireland romantic to herself'. His early poems are full of Irish mythology, with the poet striking a romantic pose and musically intoning in archaic diction.

Yeats grew out of this phase, influenced by the movement for Irish nationalism, and he turned to actual events and real people to speak for 'the new Ireland, overwhelmed by responsibility, [which] begins to long for psychological truth.' In 1899, with the help of Lady Gregory, herself a writer and promoter of Irish literature, he founded the Irish National Theater. He went on to become a public figure, serving from 1922 until 1928 as a senator of the Irish Free State, at the same time as he was achieving worldwide recognition as a great poet. In 1917 he married Georgie Hyde-Lees, who claimed to have powers as a spiritualist medium. She would fall into trances, and through automatic writing she produced many of the symbols Yeats used in *A Vision*, a work that presents his theories of the cyclical patterns of history, human psychology, and the soul's migrations after death. After his death, he was buried as he requested in County Sligo, near the mountain that had figured so much both in Irish legend and in Yeats's poetry: 'Under bare Ben bulben's head / In Drumcliff churchyard Yeats is laid.'

The Lake Isle of Innisfree

I will arise and go now, and go to Innisfree,
And a small cabin build there, of clay and wattles made:
Nine bean-rows will I have there, a hive for the honeybee,
And live alone in the bee-loud glade.

5   And I shall have some peace there, for peace comes dropping slow,
Dropping from the veils of the morning to where the cricket sings;
There midnight's all a glimmer, and noon a purple glow,
And evening full of the linnet's wings.

I will arise and go now, for always night and day
10   I hear lake water lapping with low sounds by the shore;
While I stand on the roadway, or on the pavements grey,
I hear it in the deep heart's core.

The Dolls

A DOLL in the doll-maker's house
Looks at the cradle and balls:
'That is an insult to us.'
But the oldest of all the dolls
5   Who had seen, being kept for show,
Generations of his sort,
Out-screams the whole shelf: 'Although
There's not a man can report
Evil of this place,
10   The man and the woman bring
Hither to our disgrace,
A noisy and filthy thing.'
Hearing him groan and stretch
The doll-maker's wife is aware
15   Her husband has heard the wretch,
And crouched by the arm of his chair,
She murmurs into his ear,
Head upon shoulder leant:
'My dear, my dear, oh dear,
20   It was an accident.'

1916

The Wild Swans at Coole

The trees are in their autumn beauty,
The woodland paths are dry,
Under the October twilight the water
Mirrors a still sky;
5   Upon the brimming water among the stones
Are nine-and-fifty swans.

The nineteenth autumn has come upon me
Since I first made my count;
I saw, before I had well finished,
10   All suddenly mount
And scatter wheeling in great broken rings
Upon their clamorous wings.

I have looked upon those brilliant creatures,
And now my heart is sore.
15 All's changed since I, hearing at twilight,
The first time on this shore,
The bell-beat of their wings above my head,
Trod with a lighter tread.

Unwearied still, lover by lover,
20 They paddle in the cold
Companionable streams or climb the air;
Their hearts have not grown old;
Passion or conquest, wander where they will,
Attend upon them still.

25 But now they drift on the still water,
Mysterious, beautiful;
Among what rushes will they build,
By what lake's edge or pool
Delight men's eyes when I awake some day
30 To find they have flown away?

1917

The Second Coming

Turning and turning in the widening gyre
The falcon cannot hear the falconer;
Things fall apart; the centre cannot hold;
Mere anarchy is loosed upon the world
5 The blood-dimmed tide is loosed, and everywhere
The ceremony of innocence is drowned;
The best lack all conviction, while the worst
Are full of passionate intensity.

Surely some revelation is at hand;
10 Surely the Second Coming is at hand.
The Second Coming! Hardly are those words out
When a vast image out of *Spiritus Mundi*
Troubles my sight: somewhere in sands of the desert
A shape with lion body and the head of a man,
15 A gaze blank and pitiless as the sun,
Is moving its slow thighs, while all about it

Reel shadows of the indignant desert birds.
The darkness drops again; but now I know
That twenty centuries of stony sleep
20 Were vexed to nightmare by a rocking cradle,
And what rough beast, its hour come round at last,
Slouches towards Bethlehem to be born?

1920

Leda and the Swan [1]

A sudden blow: the great wings beating still
Above the staggering girl, her thighs caressed
By the dark webs, her nape caught in his bill
He holds her helpless breast upon his breast.

5   How can those terrified vague fingers push
The feathered glory from her loosening thighs?
And how can body, laid in that white rush,
But feel the strange heart beating where it lies?

A shudder in the loins engenders there
10 The broken wall, the burning roof and tower
And Agamemnon dead.
                                    Being so caught up,
So mastered by the brute blood of the air,
Did she put on his knowledge with his power
Before the indifferent beak could let her drop?

1924

1 Zeus, in the form of a swan, ravished Leda, who gave birth to Helen, whose desertion of her husband, King Menelaus, caused the Trojan War. Another of Leda's daughters, Clytemnestra, murdered her husband Agamemnon.

Among School Children

I

I walk through the long schoolroom questioning;
A kind old nun in a white hood replies;
The children learn to cipher and to sing,
To study reading-books and history,

5   To cut and sew, be neat in everything
In the best modern way—the children's eyes
In momentary wonder stare upon
A sixty-year-old smiling public man.

II

I dream of a Ledaean body, bent
10   Above a sinking fire, a tale that she
Told of a harsh reproof, or trivial event
That changed some childish day to tragedy—
Told, and it seemed that our two natures blent
Into a sphere from youthful sympathy,
15   Or else, to alter Plato's parable,
Into the yolk and white of the one shell.

III

And thinking of that fit of grief or rage
I look upon one child or t'other there
And wonder if she stood so at that age—
20   For even daughters of the swan can share
Something of every paddler's heritage—
And had that colour upon cheek or hair,
And thereupon my heart is driven wild:
She stands before me as a living child.

IV

25   Her present image floats into the mind—
Did Quattrocento finger fashion it
Hollow of cheek as though it drank the wind
And took a mess of shadows for its meat?
And I though never of Ledaean kind
30   Had pretty plumage once—enough of that,
Better to smile on all that smile, and show
There is a comfortable kind of old scarecrow.

V

What youthful mother, a shape upon her lap
Honey of generation had betrayed,
35   And that must sleep, shriek, struggle to escape
As recollection or the drug decide,
Would think her son, did she but see that shape
With sixty or more winters on its head,
A compensation for the pang of his birth,
40   Or the uncertainty of his setting forth?

VI

Plato thought nature but a spume that plays
Upon a ghostly paradigm of things;
Solider Aristotle played the taws
Upon the bottom of the king of kings;
45   World-famous golden-thighed Pythagoras
Fingered upon a fiddle-stick or strings
What a star sang and careless Muses heard:
Old clothes upon old sticks to scare a bird.

VII

Both nuns and mothers worship images,
50   But those the candles light are not as those
That animate a mother's reveries,
But keep a marble or a bronze repose.
And yet they too break hearts—O Presences
That passion, piety or affection knows,
55   And that all heavenly glory symbolise—
O self-born mockers of man's enterprise;

VIII

Labour is blossoming or dancing where
The body is not bruised to pleasure soul,
Nor beauty born out of its own despair,
60   Nor blear-eyed wisdom out of midnight oil.
O chestnut tree, great rooted blossomer,
Are you the leaf, the blossom or the bole?

O body swayed to music, O brightening glance,
How can we know the dancer from the dance?

1927

Sailing to Byzantium[1]

That is no country for old men. The young
In one another's arms, birds in the trees
—Those dying generations—at their song,
The salmon-falls, the mackerel-crowded seas,
5 Fish, flesh, or fowl, commend all summer long
Whatever is begotten, born, and dies.
Caught in that sensual music all neglect
Monuments of unaging intellect.

An aged man is but a paltry thing,
10 A tattered coat upon a stick, unless
Soul clap its hands and sing, and louder sing
For every tatter in its mortal dress,
Nor is there singing school but studying
Monuments of its own magnificence;
15 And therefore I have sailed the seas and come
To the holy city of Byzantium.

O sages standing in God's holy fire
As in the gold mosaic of a wall,
Come from the holy fire, perne in a gyre,[2]
20 And be the singing-masters of my soul.
Consume my heart away; sick with desire
And fastened to a dying animal
It knows not what it is; and gather me
Into the artifice of eternity.

25 Once out of nature I shall never take
My bodily form from any natural thing,
But such a form as Grecian goldsmiths make
Of hammered gold and gold enamelling
To keep a drowsy emperor awake;
30 Or set upon a golden bough to sing
To lords and ladies of Byzantium
Of what is past, or passing, or to come.

1927

1 now Istanbul
2 revolve in a spiral

After Long Silence

> Speech after long silence; it is right,
> All other lovers being estranged or dead,
> Unfriendly lamplight hid under its shade,
> The curtains drawn upon unfriendly night,
> 5   That we descant and yet again descant
> Upon the supreme theme of Art and Song:
> Bodily decrepitude is wisdom; young
> We loved each other and were ignorant.

1932

The Circus Animals' Desertion

I

> I sought a theme and sought for it in vain,
> I sought it daily for six weeks or so.
> Maybe at last, being but a broken man,
> I must be satisfied with my heart, although
> 5   Winter and summer till old age began
> My circus animals[1] were all on show,
> Those stilted boys, that burnished chariot,
> Lion and woman and the Lord knows what.

II

> What can I but enumerate old themes?
> 10   First that sea-rider Oisin led by the nose
> Through three enchanted islands, allegorical dreams,
> Vain gaiety, vain battle, vain repose,
> Themes of the embittered heart, or so it seems,
> That might adorn old songs or courtly shows;
> 15   But what cared I that set him on to ride,
> I, starved for the bosom of his faery bride?

---

1 In the course of the poem, Yeats alludes to much of his previous work, especially his mythological and symbolic figures.

And then a counter-truth filled out its play,
The Countess Cathleen was the name I gave it;
She, pity-crazed, had given her soul away,
20 But masterful Heaven had intervened to save it.
I thought my dear must her own soul destroy,
So did fanaticism and hate enslave it,
And this brought forth a dream and soon enough
This dream itself had all my thought and love.

25 And when the Fool and Blind Man stole the bread
Cuchulain fought the ungovernable sea;
Heart-mysteries there, and yet when all is said
It was the dream itself enchanted me:
Character isolated by a deed
30 To engross the present and dominate memory.
Players and painted stage took all my love,
And not those things that they were emblems of.

III

Those masterful images because complete
Grew in pure mind, but out of what began?
35 A mound of refuse or the sweeping of a street,
Old kettles, old bottles, and a broken can,
Old iron, old bones, old rags, that raving slut
Who keeps the till. Now that my ladder's gone,
I must lie down where all the ladders start,
40 In the foul rag-and-bone shop of the heart.

1939

Robert Frost
1874–1963

Robert Frost was born in San Francisco, where his father was a journalist and an aspiring politician. Frost's mother wrote poetry and introduced her son to Scottish poetry and to such poets as Wordsworth, Bryant, and Emerson, whose use of nature in their work undoubtedly influenced Frost. After his father died, Frost's family moved to New England, where his mother taught school. After graduating from high school in Lawrence, Massachusetts, where he was class poet and where he shared the post of valedictorian with Elinor White, whom he later married, Frost attended Dartmouth and Harvard. He did not graduate, but returned home to marry Elinor. They moved to a farm in Derry, New Hampshire, where Frost taught school, wrote poetry, and tried to run a farm. These were years of hardship for the growing family, and discouraged by his inability to interest American publishers in his poetry, Frost sold the farm, and the family moved to England. Shortly after his arrival, his first collection of poetry, *A Boy's Will*, was accepted for publication; *North of Boston* followed soon after. Frost met Ezra Pound, who introduced Frost's poetry to American publishers, and three years later, when the family returned to the United States at the outbreak of the First World War, Frost had achieved recognition as a major poetic talent.

Frost has always had a wide audience of readers; there are those who read him as a New England nature poet who extols the values of rural America and its work ethic, and those who read him as one who sees nature as other, as a sometimes barren landscape against which human dramas are played out, as they so effectively are in Frost's dramatic narratives. Frost described poetry as 'a momentary stay against confusion', but he also said: 'The figure a poem makes. It begins in delight and ends in wisdom. The figure is the same as for love.'

Mending Wall

Something there is that doesn't love a wall,
That sends the frozen-ground-swell under it
And spills the upper boulders in the sun,
And makes gaps even two can pass abreast.
5   The work of hunters is another thing:
I have come after them and made repair
Where they have left not one stone on a stone,
But they would have the rabbit out of hiding,
To please the yelping dogs. The gaps I mean,
10   No one has seen them made or heard them made,
But at spring mending-time we find them there.
I let my neighbour know beyond the hill;
And on a day we meet to walk the line
And set the wall between us once again.
15   We keep the wall between us as we go.
To each the boulders that have fallen to each.

And some are loaves and some so nearly balls
We have to use a spell to make them balance:
'Stay where you are until our backs are turned!'
20 We wear our fingers rough with handling them.
Oh, just another kind of outdoor game,
One on a side. It comes to little more:
There where it is we do not need the wall:
He is all pine and I am apple orchard.
25 My apple trees will never get across
And eat the cones under his pines, I tell him.
He only says, 'Good fences make good neighbours.'
Spring is the mischief in me, and I wonder
If I could put a notion in his head:
30 '*Why* do they make good neighbours? Isn't it
Where there are cows? But here there are no cows.
Before I built a wall I'd ask to know
What I was walling in or walling out,
And to whom I was like to give offence.
35 Something there is that doesn't love a wall,
That wants it down.' I could say 'Elves' to him,
But it's not elves exactly, and I'd rather
He said it for himself. I see him there
Bringing a stone grasped firmly by the top
40 In each hand, like an old-stone savage armed.
He moves in darkness as it seems to me,
Not of woods only and the shade of trees.
He will not go behind his father's saying,
And he likes having thought of it so well
45 He says again, 'Good fences make good neighbours.'

1914

After Apple-Picking

My long two-pointed ladder's sticking through a tree
Toward heaven still,
And there's a barrel that I didn't fill
Beside it, and there may be two or three
5 Apples I didn't pick upon some bough.
But I am done with apple-picking now.
Essence of winter sleep is on the night,
The scent of apples: I am drowsing off.
I cannot rub the strangeness from my sight
10 I got from looking through a pane of glass

I skimmed this morning from the drinking trough
And held against the world of hoary grass.
It melted, and I let it fall and break.
But I was well
15 Upon my way to sleep before it fell,
And I could tell
What form my dreaming was about to take.
Magnified apples appear and disappear,
Stem end and blossom end,
20 And every fleck of russet showing clear.
My instep arch not only keeps the ache,
It keeps the pressure of a ladder-round.
I feel the ladder sway as the boughs bend.
And I keep hearing from the cellar bin
25 The rumbling sound
Of load on load of apples coming in.
For I have had too much
Of apple-picking: I am overtired
Of the great harvest I myself desired.
30 There were ten thousand thousand fruit to touch,
Cherish in hand, lift down, and not let fall.
For all
That struck the earth,
No matter if not bruised or spiked with stubble,
35 Went surely to the cider-apple heap
As of no worth.
One can see what will trouble
This sleep of mine, whatever sleep it is.
Were he not gone,
40 The woodchuck could say whether it's like his
Long sleep, as I describe its coming on,
Or just some human sleep.

1916

Birches

When I see birches bend to left and right
Across the lines of straighter darker trees,
I like to think some boy's been swinging them.
But swinging doesn't bend them down to stay
5 As ice-storms do. Often you must have seen them
Loaded with ice a sunny winter morning

After a rain. They click upon themselves
As the breeze rises, and turn many-coloured
As the stir cracks and crazes their enamel.
10 Soon the sun's warmth makes them shed crystal shells
Shattering and avalanching on the snow-crust—
Such heaps of broken glass to sweep away
You'd think the inner dome of heaven had fallen.
They are dragged to the withered bracken by the load,
15 And they seem not to break; though once they are bowed
So low for long, they never right themselves:
You may see their trunks arching in the woods
Years afterwards, trailing their leaves on the ground
Like girls on hands and knees that throw their hair
20 Before them over their heads to dry in the sun.
But I was going to say when Truth broke in
With all her matter-of-fact about the ice-storm
I should prefer to have some boy bend them
As he went out and in to fetch the cows—
25 Some boy too far from town to learn baseball,
Whose only play was what he found himself,
Summer or winter, and could play alone.
One by one he subdued his father's trees
By riding them down over and over again
30 Until he took the stiffness out of them,
And not one but hung limp, not one was left
For him to conquer. He learned all there was
To learn about not launching out too soon
And so not carrying the tree away
35 Clear to the ground. He always kept his poise
To the top branches, climbing carefully
With the same pains you use to fill a cup
Up to the brim, and even above the brim.
Then he flung outward, feet first, with a swish,
40 Kicking his way down through the air to the ground.
So was I once myself a swinger of birches.
And so I dream of going back to be.
It's when I'm weary of considerations,
And life is too much like a pathless wood
45 Where your face burns and tickles with the cobwebs
Broken across it, and one eye is weeping
From a twig's having lashed across it open.
I'd like to get away from earth awhile
And then come back to it and begin over.
50 May no fate wilfully misunderstand me

And half grant what I wish and snatch me away
Not to return. Earth's the right place for love:
I don't know where it's likely to go better.
I'd like to go by climbing a birch tree,
55 And climb black branches up a snow-white trunk
Toward heaven, till the tree could bear no more,
But dipped its top and set me down again.
That would be good both going and coming back.
One could do worse than be a swinger of birches.

1916

Design

I found a dimpled spider, fat and white,
On a white heal-all, holding up a moth
Like a white piece of rigid satin cloth—
Assorted characters of death and blight
5 Mixed ready to begin the morning right,
Like the ingredients of a witches' broth—
A snow-drop spider, a flower like a froth,
And dead wings carried like a paper kite.

What had that flower to do with being white,
10 The wayside blue and innocent heal-all?
What brought the kindred spider to that height,
Then steered the white moth thither in the night?
What but design of darkness to appall?—
If design govern in a thing so small.

1922

Stopping by Woods on a Snowy Evening

Whose woods these are I think I know.
His house is in the village, though;
He will not see me stopping here
To watch his woods fill up with snow.

5 My little horse must think it queer
To stop without a farmhouse near
Between the woods and frozen lake
The darkest evening of the year.

He gives his harness bells a shake
10   To ask if there is some mistake.
The only other sound's the sweep
Of easy wind and downy flake.

The woods are lovely, dark, and deep,
But I have promises to keep,
15   And miles to go before I sleep,
And miles to go before I sleep.

1923

Provide, Provide

The witch that came (the withered hag)
To wash the steps with pail and rag,
Was once the beauty Abishag,[1]

The picture pride of Hollywood
5   Too many fall from great and good
For you to doubt the likelihood.

Die early and avoid the fate.
Or if predestined to die late,
Make up your mind to die in state.

10   Make the whole stock exchange your own!
If need be occupy a throne,
Where nobody can call you crone.

Some have relied on what they knew;
Others on simply being true.
15   What worked for them might work for you.

No memory of having starred
Atones for later disregard,
Or keeps the end from being hard.

Better to go down dignified
20   With boughten friendship at your side
Than none at all. Provide, provide!

1934

1 a biblical beauty brought in to warm dying King David

Wallace Stevens

1879–1955

Wallace Stevens was born in Reading, Pennsylvania, where his father was an attorney and a schoolteacher with an interest in poetry. After graduating from high school, Stevens attended Harvard for three years. He was writing poetry at this time, some of which was published in the Harvard *Advocate*, and when he left Harvard, he intended to pursue a literary career in New York City. He became a reporter for the *Herald Tribune*, but did not like the job. He entered law school and was admitted to the bar, but was unsuccessful in private practice. He then joined the legal staff of a bonding company, and feeling himself sufficiently settled, he married Elsie Moll, a young woman from his home town. Seven years later, he joined the Hartford Accident and Insurance Company and, in 1916, moved to Connecticut, where he lived the rest of his life.

Stevens wrote his poetry during his spare time, and though he had some literary friends such as William Carlos Williams and Marianne Moore, his business activities kept him at some remove from literary circles. *Harmonium*, his first volume of poems, appeared in 1923, and though Stevens began to acquire a reputation as one of the outstanding poets of the twentieth century, his co-workers at the insurance company were not aware of this until he won the Bollingen Prize in 1950. This was partly because of Stevens's natural reticence about himself, and partly because he doubtless felt they would not understand. Certainly, it is difficult to reconcile the pragmatics of Stevens's business activities with the gaiety of language and the celebration of the imagination in his poetry.

Sunday Morning

I

Complacencies of the peignoir, and late
Coffee and oranges in a sunny chair,
And the green freedom of a cockatoo
Upon a rug mingle to dissipate
5 The holy hush of ancient sacrifice.
She dreams a little, and she feels the dark
Encroachment of that old catastrophe,
As a calm darkens among water-lights.
The pungent oranges and bright, green wings
10 Seem things in some procession of the dead,
Winding across wide water, without sound.
The day is like wide water, without sound,
Stilled for the passing of her dreaming feet
Over the seas, to silent Palestine,
15 Dominion of the blood and sepulchre.

II

Why should she give her bounty to the dead?
What is divinity if it can come
Only in silent shadows and in dreams?
Shall she not find in comforts of the sun,
20 In pungent fruit and bright, green wings, or else
In any balm or beauty of the earth,
Things to be cherished like the thought of heaven?
Divinity must live within herself:
Passions of rain, or moods in falling snow;
25 Grievings in loneliness, or unsubdued
Elations when the forest blooms; gusty
Emotions on wet roads on autumn nights;
All pleasures and all pains, remembering
The bough of summer and the winter branch.
30 These are the measures destined for her soul.

III

Jove in the clouds had his inhuman birth.
No mother suckled him, no sweet land gave
Large-mannered motions to his mythy mind.
He moved among us, as a muttering king,
35 Magnificent, would move among his hinds,
Until our blood, commingling, virginal,
With heaven, brought such requital to desire
The very hinds discerned it, in a star.
Shall our blood fail? Or shall it come to be
40 The blood of paradise? And shall the earth
Seem all paradise that we shall know?
The sky will be much friendlier then than now,
A part of labour and a part of pain,
And next in glory to enduring love,
45 Not this dividing and indifferent blue.

IV

She says, 'I am content when wakened birds,
Before they fly, test the reality
Of misty fields, by their sweet questionings;
But when the birds are gone, and their warm fields

50   Return no more, where, then, is paradise?'
      There is not any haunt of prophecy,
      Nor any old chimera of the grave,
      Neither the golden underground, nor isle
      Melodious, where spirits gat them home,
55   Nor visionary south, nor cloudy palm
      Remote on heaven's hill, that has endured
      As April's green endures; or will endure
      Like her remembrance of awakened birds,
      Or her desire for June and evening, tipped
60   By the consummation of the swallow's wings.

V

      She says, 'But in contentment I still feel
      The need of some imperishable bliss.'
      Death is the mother of beauty; hence from her,
      Alone, shall come fulfillment to our dreams
65   And our desires. Although she strews the leaves
      Of sure obliteration on our paths,
      The path sick sorrow took, the many paths
      Where triumph rang its brassy phrase, or love
      Whispered a little out of tenderness,
70   She makes the willow shiver in the sun
      For maidens who were wont to sit and gaze
      Upon the grass, relinquished to their feet.
      She causes boys to pile new plums and pears
      On disregarded plate. The maidens taste
75   And stray impassioned in the littering leaves.

VI

      Is there no change of death in paradise?
      Does ripe fruit never fall? Or do the boughs
      Hang always heavy in that perfect sky,
      Unchanging, yet so like our perishing earth,
80   With rivers like our own that seek for seas
      They never find, the same receding shores
      That never touch with inarticulate pang?
      Why set the pear upon those river banks
      Or spice the shores with odours of the plum?
85   Alas, that they should wear our colours there,

The silken weavings of our afternoons,
And pick the strings of our insipid lutes!
Death is the mother of beauty, mystical,
Within whose burning bosom we devise
90 Our earthly mothers waiting, sleeplessly.

VII

Supple and turbulent, a ring of men
Shall chant in orgy on a summer morn
Their boisterous devotion to the sun,
Not as a god, but as a god might be,
95 Naked among them, like a savage source.
Their chant shall be a chant of paradise,
Out of their blood, returning to the sky;
And in their chant shall enter, voice by voice,
The windy lake wherein their lord delights,
100 The trees, like serafin, and echoing hills,
That choir among themselves long afterward.
They shall know well the heavenly fellowship
Of men that perish and of summer morn.
And whence they came and whither they shall go
105 The dew upon their feet shall manifest.

VIII

She hears, upon that water without sound,
A voice that cries, 'The tomb in Palestine
Is not the porch of spirits lingering.
It is the grave of Jesus, where he lay.'
110 We live in an old chaos of the sun,
Or old dependency of day and night,
Or island solitude, unsponsored, free,
Of that wide water, inescapable.
Deer walk upon our mountains, and the quail
115 Whistle about us their spontaneous cries;
Sweet berries ripen in the wilderness;
And, in the isolation of the sky,
At evening, casual flocks of pigeons make
Ambiguous undulations as they sink,
120 Downward to darkness, on extended wings.

1915

Anecdote of the Jar

I placed a jar in Tennessee,
And round it was, upon a hill.
It made the slovenly wilderness
Surround that hill.

5 The wilderness rose up to it,
And sprawled around, no longer wild.
The jar was round upon the ground
And tall and of a port in air.

It took dominion everywhere.
10 The jar was grey and bare.
It did not give of bird or bush,
Like nothing else in Tennessee.

1923

Thirteen Ways of Looking at a Blackbird

I

Among twenty snowy mountains,
The only moving thing
Was the eye of the blackbird.

II

I was of three minds,
5 Like a tree
In which there are three blackbirds.

III

The blackbird whirled in the autumn winds.
It was a small part of the pantomime.

IV

A man and a woman
10   Are one.
A man and a woman and a blackbird
Are one.

V

I do not know which to prefer,
The beauty of inflections
15   Or the beauty of innuendoes,
The blackbird whistling
Or just after.

VI

Icicles filled the long window
With barbaric glass.
20   The shadow of the blackbird
Crossed it, to and fro.
The mood
Traced in the shadow
An indecipherable cause.

VII

25   O thin men of Haddam,
Why do you imagine golden birds?
Do you not see how the blackbird
Walks around the feet
Of the women about you?

VIII

30   I know noble accents
And lucid, inescapable rhythms;
But I know, too,
That the blackbird is involved
In what I know.

IX

35   When the blackbird flew out of sight,
It marked the edge
Of one of many circles.

X

At the sight of blackbirds
Flying in a green light,
40   Even the bawds of euphony
Would cry out sharply.

XI

He rode over Connecticut
In a glass coach.
Once, a fear pierced him,
45   In that he mistook
The shadow of his equipage
For blackbirds.

XII

The river is moving.
The blackbird must be flying.

XIII

50   It was evening all afternoon.
It was snowing
And it was going to snow.
The blackbird sat
In the cedar-limbs.

1931

The Snow Man

One must have a mind of winter
To regard the frost and the boughs
Of the pine-trees crusted with snow;

And have been cold a long time
5   To behold the junipers shagged with ice,
The spruces rough in the distant glitter

Of the January sun; and not to think
Of any misery in the sound of the wind,
In the sound of a few leaves,

10 Which is the sound of the land
Full of the same wind
That is blowing in the same bare place

For the listener, who listens in the snow,
And, nothing himself, beholds
15 Nothing that is not there and the nothing that is.

1931

A High-Toned Old Christian Woman

Poetry is the supreme fiction, madame.
Take the moral law and make a nave of it
And from the nave build haunted heaven. Thus,
The conscience is converted into palms,
5 Like windy citherns hankering for hymns.
We agree in principle. That's clear. But take
The opposing law and make a peristyle,
And from the peristyle project a masque
Beyond the planets. Thus, our bawdiness,
10 Unpurged by epitaph, indulged at last,
Is equally converted into palms,
Squiggling like saxophones. And palm for palm,
Madame, we are where we began. Allow,
Therefore, that in the planetary scene
15 Your disaffected flagellants, well-stuffed,
Smacking their muzzy bellies in parade,

Proud of such novelties of the sublime,
Such tink and tank and tunk-a-tunk-tunk,
May, merely may, madame, whip from themselves
20   A jovial hullabaloo among the spheres.
This will make widows wince. But fictive things
Wink as they will. Wink most when widows wince.

1923

Of Modern Poetry

The poem of the mind in the act of finding
What will suffice. It has not always had
To find: the scene was set; it repeated what
Was in the script.
                            Then the theatre was changed
5   To something else. Its past was a souvenir.
It has to be living, to learn the speech of the place.
It has to face the men of the time and to meet
The women of the time. It has to think about war
And it has to find what will suffice. It has
10   To construct a new stage. It has to be on that stage
And, like an insatiable actor, slowly and
With meditation, speak words that in the ear,
In the delicatest ear of the mind, repeat,
Exactly, that which it wants to hear, at the sound
15   Of which, an invisible audience listens,
Not to the play, but to itself, expressed
In an emotion as of two people, as of two
Emotions becoming one. The actor is
A metaphysician in the dark, twanging
20   An instrument, twanging a wiry string that gives
Sounds passing through sudden rightness, wholly
Containing the mind, below which it cannot descend,
Beyond which it has no will to rise.
                                                    It must
Be the finding of a satisfaction, and may
25   Be of a man skating, a woman dancing, a woman
Combing. The poem of the act of the mind.

1942

E.J. Pratt
1882–1964

Edwin John Pratt was born in Western Bay, Newfoundland, and grew up in the fishing outports of the British colony. Upon graduation from St John's Methodist College, he served as preacher and teacher in several island communities. In 1907 he entered Victoria College, University of Toronto, to study philosophy, and earned his BA (1911), MA (1912), and PhD (1917). In 1913 he received a Bachelor of Divinity and was ordained into the Methodist ministry. In 1920 he accepted an appointment in Victoria College's English department, where he taught until his retirement in 1953.

Pratt's first collection of poetry, *Newfoundland Verse* (1923), began his careful evocations of seascapes and humankind's relentless confrontation with maritime life in its many shapes and moods. During the 1930s he turned to more socially oriented poetic narratives. In such national epics as *Brébeuf and His Brethren* (1940) and *Towards the Last Spike* (1952) he revealed his detailed research in Canadian history and served as his country's poetic mythmaker.

The Shark

He seemed to know the harbour,
So leisurely he swam;
His fin,
Like a piece of sheet-iron,
5 Three-cornered,
And with knife-edge,
Stirred not a bubble
As it moved
With its base-line on the water.

10 His body was tubular
And tapered
And smoke-blue,
And as he passed the wharf
He turned,
15 And snapped at a flat-fish
That was dead and floating.
And I saw the flash of a white throat,
And a double row of white teeth,
And eyes of metallic grey,
20 Hard and narrow and slit.

Then out of the harbour,

With that three-cornered fin
Shearing without a bubble the water
Lithely,
25   Leisurely,
He swam—
That strange fish,
Tubular, tapered, smoke-blue,
Part vulture, part wolf,
30   Part neither—for his blood was cold.

1923

One Hour of Life

This little face will never know
Cut of wind or bite of snow:
The sea will never wind its sheet
Around those pallid hands and feet.

5   Nor shall its sleeping heart, grown cold
After a pulse of life, unfold
That futile challenge on the face
Of one who with a last embrace

Could only cheat the earth to save
10   The plunder for another grave:
But in that hour of battle she
Forgot the patience of the sea.

1924

Erosion

It took the sea a thousand years,
A thousand years to trace
The granite features of this cliff,
In crag and scarp and base.

5   It took the sea an hour one night,
An hour of storm to place
The sculpture of these granite seams
Upon a woman's face.

1931

Silences

There is no silence upon earth or under the earth like the silence under the sea;
No cries announcing birth,
No sounds declaring death.
There is silence when the milt is laid on the spawn in the weeds and fungus of
    the rock-clefts;
5   And silence in the growth and struggle for life.
The bonitoes pounce upon the mackerel,
And are themselves caught by the barracudas,
The sharks kill the barracudas
And the great molluscs rend the sharks,
10 And all noiselessly—
Though swift be the action and final the conflict,
The drama is silent.

There is no fury upon the earth like the fury under the sea.
For growl and cough and snarl are the tokens of spendthrifts who know not
    the ultimate economy of rage.
15 Moreover, the pace of the blood is too fast.
But under the waves the blood is sluggard and has the same temperature as
    that of the sea.

There is something pre-reptilian about a silent kill.

Two men may end their hostilities just with their battle-cries.
'The devil take you,' says one.
20 'I'll see you in hell first,' says the other.
And these introductory salutes followed by a hail of gutturals and sibilants are
    often the beginning of friendship, for who would not prefer to be lustily
    damned than to be half-heartedly blessed?
No one need fear oaths that are properly enunciated, for they belong to the
    inheritance of just men made perfect, and, for all we know, of such may be
    the Kingdom of Heaven.
But let silent hate be put away for it feeds upon the heart of the hater.
Today I watched two pairs of eyes. One pair was black and the other grey. And
    while the owners thereof, for the space of five seconds, walked past each
    other, the grey snapped at the black and the black riddled the grey.
25 One looked to say—'The cat,'
And the other—'The cur.'
But no words were spoken;
Not so much as a hiss or a murmur came through the perfect enamel of the
    teeth; not so much as a gesture of enmity.

If the right upper lip curled over the canine, it went unnoticed.
30 The lashes veiled the eyes not for an instant in the passing.
And as between the two in respect to candour of intention or eternity of wish,
    there was no choice, for the stare was mutual and absolute.
A word would have dulled the exquisite edge of the feeling,
An oath would have flawed the crystallization of the hate.
For only such culture could grow in a climate of silence,—
35 Away back before the emergence of fur or feather, back to the unvocal sea and
    down deep where the darkness spills its wash on the threshold of light,
    where the lids never close upon the eyes, where the inhabitants slay in
    silence and are silently slain.

                                                     1936

The Deed

Where are the roadside minstrels gone who strung
Their fiddles to the stirrup cavalcades?
What happened to the roses oversung
By orchard lovers in their serenades?

5 A feudal dust that draggle-tailed the plumes
Blinded the minstrels chasing cavaliers:
Moonlight that sucked the colour from the blooms
Had soaked the lyrists and the sonneteers.

Where is the beauty still inspired by rhyme,
10 Competing with those garden miracles,
When the first ray conspires with wind to chime
The matins of the Canterbury bells?

Not in the fruit or flower nor in the whir
Of linnet's wings or plaint of nightingales,
15 Nor in the moonstruck latticed face of her
Who cracked the tenor sliding up his scales.

We saw that beauty once—an instant run
Along a ledge of rock, a curve, a dive;
Nor did he count the odds of ten to one
20 Against his bringing up that boy alive.

This was an arch beyond the salmon's lunge,
There was a rainbow in the rising mists:
Sea-lapidaries started at the plunge
To cut the facets of their amethysts.

25   But this we scarcely noticed, since the deed
Had power to cleanse a grapnel's rust, transfigure
The blueness of the lips, unmat the weed
And sanctify the unambiguous rigour.

For that embrace had trapped the evening's light,
30   Racing to glean the red foam's harvestings:
Even the seagulls vanished from our sight,
Though settling with their pentecostal wings.

1952

William Carlos Williams
1883–1963

Born in Rutherford, New Jersey, to an English father and a Puerto Rican mother, William Carlos Williams attended preparatory schools in Switzerland and Paris, and after graduating from Horace Mann High School in New York went to medical school at the University of Pennsylvania. There he was friendly with poets Ezra Pound and Hilda Doolittle, and over a dish of prunes in a Philadelphia boarding house, he met painter Charles Demuth, with whom he shared a keen interest in modernist painting. Williams did further pediatric study in Leipzig, Germany, and in 1912 he began his medical practice in Rutherford, a practice in which he was fully active until he suffered a stroke in 1952.

Williams wrote his poetry at night and between professional appointments, for while he was 'determined to be a poet', he was convinced that 'only medicine, a job I enjoyed, would make it possible for me to live and write as I wanted to.' And write he did: in addition to numerous volumes of poetry, he published short stories, essays, novels, and an autobiography. Energetic and feisty, he railed against T.S. Eliot's poetry of literary allusion, stressing that American poets should break with traditional conventions and use the diction and rhythms of American speech. Like Whitman, he celebrated the 'vitality of the body' as he saw and felt it in his everyday life as a physician. His most ambitious work, *Paterson*, is an epic that gives metaphoric expression to an American city and its people, past and present, while presenting new poetic forms that greatly influenced other American poets.

The Widow's Lament in Springtime

Sorrow is my own yard
where the new grass
flames as it has flamed
often before but not
5   with the cold fire
that closes round me this year.
Thirtyfive years
I lived with my husband.
The plumtree is white today
10   with masses of flowers.
Masses of flowers
load the cherry branches
and colour some bushes
yellow and some red
15   but the grief in my heart
is stronger than they
for though they were my joy
formerly, today I notice them
and turn away forgetting.
20   Today my son told me
that in the meadows
at the edge of the heavy woods
in the distance, he saw
trees of white flowers.
25   I feel that I would like
to go there
and fall into those flowers
and sink into the marsh near them.

1921

Spring and All

By the road to the contagious hospital
under the surge of the blue
mottled clouds driven from the
northeast—a cold wind. Beyond, the
5   waste of broad, muddy fields
brown with dried weeds, standing and fallen

patches of standing water
the scattering of tall trees

All along the road the reddish
10   purplish, forked, upstanding, twiggy
stuff of bushes and small trees
with dead, brown leaves under them
leafless vines—

Lifeless in appearance, sluggish
15   dazed spring approaches—

They enter the new world naked,
cold, uncertain of all
save that they enter. All about them
the cold, familiar wind—

20   Now the grass, tomorrow
the stiff curl of wildcarrot leaf
One by one objects are defined—
It quickens: clarity, outline of leaf

But now the stark dignity of
25   entrance—Still, the profound change
has come upon them: rooted, they
grip down and begin to awaken

1923

The Red Wheelbarrow

so much depends
upon

a red wheel
barrow

5   glazed with rain
water

beside the white
chickens.

1923

Flowers by the Sea

When over the flowery, sharp pasture's
edge, unseen, the salt ocean

lifts its form—chicory and daisies
tied, released, seem hardly flowers alone

5   but colour and the movement—or the shape
perhaps—of restlessness, whereas

the sea is circled and sways
peacefully upon its plantlike stem

1923

The Last Words of My English Grandmother

There were some dirty plates
and a glass of milk
beside her on a small table
near the rank, dishevelled bed—

5   Wrinkled and nearly blind
she lay and snored
rousing with anger in her tones
to cry for food,

Gimme something to eat—
10   They're starving me—
I'm all right I won't go
to the hospital. No, no, no

Give me something to eat
Let me take you
15   to the hospital, I said
and after you are well

you can do as you please.
She smiled, Yes
you do what you please first
20   then I can do what I please—

Oh, oh, oh! she cried
as the ambulance men lifted
her to the stretcher—
Is this what you call

25   making me comfortable?
By now her mind was clear—
Oh you think you're smart
you young people,

she said, but I'll tell you
30   you don't know anything.
Then we started.
On the way

we passed a long row
of elms. She looked at them
35   awhile out of
the ambulance window and said,

What are all those
fuzzy-looking things out there?
Trees? Well, I'm tired
40   of them and rolled her head away.

1924

The Yachts

contend in a sea which the land partly encloses
shielding them from the too-heavy blows
of an ungoverned ocean which when it chooses

tortures the biggest hulls, the best man knows
5   to pit against its beatings, and sinks them pitilessly.
Mothlike in mists, scintillant in the minute

brilliance of cloudless days, with broad bellying sails
they glide to the wind tossing green water
from their sharp prows while over them the crew crawls

10   ant-like, solicitously grooming them, releasing,
    making fast as they turn, lean far over and having
    caught the wind again, side by side, head for the mark.

    In a well guarded arena of open water surrounded by
    lesser and greater craft which, sycophant, lumbering
15   and flittering follow them, they appear youthful, rare

    as the light of a happy eye, live with the grace
    of all that in the mind is fleckless, free and
    naturally to be desired. Now the sea which holds them

    is moody, lapping their glossy sides, as if feeling
20   for some slightest flaw but fails completely.
    Today no race. Then the wind comes again. The yachts

    move, jockeying for a start, the signal is set and they
    are off. Now the waves strike at them but they are too
    well made, they slip through, though they take in canvas.

25   Arms with hands grasping seek to clutch at the prows.
    Bodies thrown recklessly in the way are cut aside.
    It is a sea of faces about them in agony, in despair

    until the horror of the race dawns staggering the mind,
    the whole sea become an entanglement of watery bodies
30   lost to the world bearing what they cannot hold. Broken,

    beaten, desolate, reaching from the dead to be taken up
    they cry out, failing, failing! their cries rising
    in waves still as the skillful yachts pass over.

1935

Landscape with the Fall of Icarus [1]

    According to Brueghel
    when Icarus fell
    it was spring

---

1 This is the second poem of a series based on the paintings of the Flemish artist Pieter Brueghel. This painting
  shows the mythical youth Icarus, son of Daedalus, falling into the sea after the wings made for him by his father
  had melted. W.H. Auden also based a poem on this painting (see p. 610).

a farmer was ploughing
5 his field
the whole pageantry

of the year was
awake tingling
near

10 the edge of the sea
concerned
with itself

sweating in the sun
that melted
15 the wings' wax

unsignificantly
off the coast
there was

a splash quite unnoticed
20 this was
Icarus drowning

1962

Marianne Moore
1887–1972

Marianne Moore was born in Kirkwood, Missouri, to a very devout Presbyterian family. After her father abandoned the family following a mental breakdown and the collapse of his business, Moore and her mother moved to Carlisle, Pennsylvania. Moore attended Metzger Institute, where her mother taught, and went on to Bryn Mawr College. Though she was getting better grades in biology than in literature, she aspired to write poetry. After her graduation in 1909, she taught at the United States Indian School in Carlisle, and starting in 1915, her poetry began to be accepted by literary journals.

The Moores were a close family, and when her brother, a Presbyterian minister, took a position in Brooklyn, she and her mother joined him. Moore worked as a tutor and secretary in a girls' school, and as an assistant in a branch library. She was at this time enjoying the company of artists and writers, as well as writing and publishing her poetry. For three years she edited *The Dial*, a literary magazine. After that, she concentrated solely on her writing. In later years Moore was renowned as probably the most literate baseball fan the Brooklyn Dodgers ever had.

Poetry

I, too, dislike it: there are things that are important beyond all this fiddle.
    Reading it, however, with a perfect contempt of it, one discovers in
    it after all, a place for the genuine.
        Hands that can grasp, eyes
5   that can dilate, hair that can rise
            if it must, these things are important not because a

high-sounding interpretation can be put upon them but because they are
    useful. When they become so derivative as to become unintelligible,
    the same thing may be said for all of us, that we
10   do not admire what
        we cannot understand: the bat
            holding on upside down or in quest of something to

eat, elephants pushing, a wild horse taking a roll, a tireless wolf under
    a tree, the immovable critic twitching his skin like a horse that feels a flea,
    the base-
15 ball fan, the statistician—
        nor is it valid
            to discriminate against 'business documents and

school-books';[1] all these phenomena are important. One must make a distinction
    however: when dragged into prominence by half poets, the result is not poetry,
20   nor till the poets among us can be
        'literalists of
        the imagination'[2]—above
            insolence and triviality and can present

for inspection, imaginary gardens with real toads in them, shall we have
25   it. In the meantime, if you demand on the one hand,
        the raw material of poetry in
        all its rawness and
        that which is on the other hand
            genuine, then you are interested in poetry.

1921

---

1 Tolstoy in his *Diary* writes: 'Where the boundary between prose and poetry lies, I shall never be able to understand. . . . Poetry is verse; prose is not verse. Or else poetry is everything with the exception of business documents and school books' [Marianne Moore's note].

2 W.B. Yeats in his essay 'William Blake and the Imagination' speaks of Blake as a 'too literal realist of the imagination, as others are of nature' [Marianne Moore's note].

The Fish

wade
through black jade.
   Of the crow-blue mussel-shells, one keeps
   adjusting the ash-heaps;
5   Opening and shutting itself like

an
injured fan.
   The barnacles which encrust the side
   of the wave, cannot hide
10   there for the submerged shafts of the

sun,
split like spun
   glass, move themselves with spotlight swiftness
   into crevices—
15   in and out, illuminating

the
turquoise sea
   of bodies. The water drives a wedge
   of iron through the iron edge
20   of the cliff; whereupon the stars,

pink
rice-grains, ink-
   bespattered jelly-fish, crabs like green
   lilies, and submarine
25   toadstools, slide each on the other.

All
external
   marks of abuse are present on this
   defiant edifice—
30   all the physical features of

ac-
cident—lack
   of cornice, dynamite grooves, burns, and
   hatchet strokes, these things stand
35   out on it; the chasm-side is

dead.
Repeated
    evidence has proved that it can live
    on what can not revive
40   its youth. The sea grows old in it.

1921

Nevertheless

you've seen a strawberry
        that's had a struggle; yet
        was, where the fragments met

a hedgehog or a star-
5   fish for the multitude
        of seeds. What better food

than apple-seeds—the fruit
        within the fruit—locked in
        like counter-curved twin

10   hazel-nuts? Frost that kills
        the little rubber-plant-
        leaves of *kok-saghyz* stalks, can't

harm the roots; they still grow
        in frozen ground. Once where
15   there was a prickly-pear-

leaf clinging to barbed wire,
        a root shot down to grow
        in earth two feet below;

as carrots form mandrakes
20   or a ram's-horn root some-
        times. Victory won't come

to me unless I go
        to it; a grape-tendril
        ties a knot in knots till

25   knotted thirty times,—so
        the bound twig that's under-
        gone and over-gone, can't stir.

> The weak overcomes its
>   menace, the strong over-
> 30   Comes itself. What is there
>
> like fortitude! What sap
>   went through that little thread
>   to make the cherry red!

1944

A Jellyfish

> Visible, invisible,
>   a fluctuating charm
> an amber-tinctured amethyst
>   inhabits it, your arm
> 5   approaches and it opens
>   and it closes; you had meant
> to catch it and it quivers;
>   you abandon your intent.

1959

T.S. Eliot
1888–1965

Thomas Stearns Eliot was born in St Louis, Missouri, the youngest of seven children of a well-to-do family with deep roots in New England. Both parents were cultured and well read, and Eliot showed an early interest in literature; his first published poem, an imitation of Ben Jonson, appeared in Smith Academy's literary journal when Eliot was fifteen. Eliot went on to Harvard for his undergraduate and graduate work, absorbing Dante and Donne and discovering the French symbolist poets who would have a strong influence on his early work. He went on to Oxford to do further studies in Greek and philosophy, finally completing his dissertation on philosopher F.H. Bradley in 1916. But by then he wished to pursue a literary rather than an academic career, and he was already achieving a reputation in literary circles with the publication of his 'Preludes' and 'J. Alfred Prufrock'.

In 1915, Eliot had entered into what was to prove a disastrous marriage, and was supporting himself and his wife by working in Lloyd's Bank, writing book reviews, and editing journals. Somehow he found time to write, and in 1922, after a struggle with a mental breakdown, and with the editorial help of Ezra Pound, *The Waste Land* was published. This was the most influential poem of its time, partly because of its innovative fragmented structure, and partly because to many it symbolized the enervation and spiritual emptiness of the post–World War I period. The poetry Eliot wrote after *The Waste Land* is generated from a spiritual struggle that

culminated in his joining the Anglican Church. He considered the meditative poetry of *Four Quartets* his finest work, though some critics feel that his Christian orthodoxy dulled his poetic edge. Nevertheless, he was considered the major poet of his generation, and won the Nobel Prize for Literature in 1948.

The Love Song of J. Alfred Prufrock

S'io credessi che mia risposta fosse
A persona che mai tornasse al mondo,
Questa fiamma staria senza più scosse.
Ma per ciò che giammai de questo fondo
Non tornò vivo alcun, s'i'odo il vero
Senza tema d'infamia ti rispondo.[1]

  Let us go then, you and I,
When the evening is spread out against the sky
Like a patient etherized upon a table;
Let us go, through certain half-deserted streets,
5 The muttering retreats
Of restless nights in one-night cheap hotels
And sawdust restaurants with oyster-shells:
Streets that follow like a tedious argument
Of insidious intent
10 To lead you to an overwhelming question. . . .
Oh, do not ask, 'What is it?'
Let us go and make our visit.

  In the room the women come and go
Talking of Michelangelo.

15 The yellow fog that rubs its back upon the window-panes,
The yellow smoke that rubs its muzzle on the window-panes,
Licked its tongue into the corners of the evening,
Lingered upon the pools that stand in drains,
Let fall upon its back the soot that falls from chimneys,

---

1 'If I believed that my answer were to a person who should ever return to the world, this flame would stand with-out further movement; but since never one returns alive from this deep, if I hear true, I answer you without fear of infamy' (*Inferno*, xxvii, 61–6). These words are the response a damned soul in Hell makes when a question is put to him.

20   Slipped by the terrace, made a sudden leap,
      And seeing that it was a soft October night,
      Curled once about the house, and fell asleep.

        And indeed there will be time
      For the yellow smoke that slides along the street
25   Rubbing its back upon the window-panes;
      There will be time, there will be time
      To prepare a face to meet the faces that you meet;
      There will be time to murder and create,
      And time for all the works and days of hands
30   That lift and drop a question on your plate;
      Time for you and time for me,
      And time yet for a hundred indecisions,
      And for a hundred visions and revisions,
      Before the taking of a toast and tea.

35   In the room the women come and go
      Talking of Michelangelo.

        And indeed there will be time
      To wonder, 'Do I dare?' and, 'Do I dare?'
      Time to turn back and descend the stair,
40   With a bald spot in the middle of my hair—
      (They will say: 'How his hair is growing thin!')
      My morning coat, my collar mounting firmly to the chin,
      My necktie rich and modest, but asserted by a simple pin—
      (They will say: 'But how his arms and legs are thin!')
45   Do I dare
      Disturb the universe?
      In a minute there is time
      For decisions and revisions which a minute will reverse.

      For I have known them all already, known them all—
50   Have known the evenings, mornings, afternoons,
      I have measured out my life with coffee spoons;
      I know the voices dying with a dying fall
      Beneath the music from a farther room.
        So how should I presume?

55   And I have known the eyes already, known them all—
      The eyes that fix you in a formulated phrase,
      And when I am formulated, sprawling on a pin,
      When I am pinned and wriggling on the wall,

Then how should I begin

60 To spit out all the butt-ends of my days and ways?
    And how should I presume?

And I have known the arms already, known them all—
Arms that are braceleted and white and bare
(But in the lamplight, downed with light brown hair!)
65 Is it perfume from a dress
That makes me so digress?
Arms that lie along a table, or wrap about a shawl.
    And should I then presume?
    And how should I begin?

70 Shall I say, I have gone at dusk through narrow streets
And watched the smoke that rises from the pipes
Of lonely men in shirt-sleeves, leaning out of windows? . . .

    I should have been a pair of ragged claws
    Scuttling across the floors of silent seas.

75 And the afternoon, the evening, sleeps so peacefully!
Smoothed by long fingers,
Asleep . . . tired . . . or it malingers,
Stretched on the floor, here beside you and me.
Should I, after tea and cakes and ices,
80 Have the strength to force the moment to its crisis?
But though I have wept and fasted, wept and prayed,
Though I have seen my head (grown slightly bald) brought in upon
    a platter,[2]
I am no prophet—and here's no great matter;
I have seen the moment of my greatness flicker,
85 And I have seen the eternal Footman hold my coat, and
    snicker,
And in short, I was afraid.

And would it have been worth it, after all,
After the cups, the marmalade, the tea,
Among the porcelain, among some talk of you and me,

2 The head of John the Baptist was 'brought in upon a platter' at the request of Salome as a reward for her dancing before Herod.

90   Would it have been worth while,
    To have bitten off the matter with a smile,
    To have squeezed the universe into a ball
    To roll it toward some overwhelming question,
    To say: 'I am Lazarus, come from the dead,
95   Come back to tell you all, I shall tell you all'—
    If one, settling a pillow by her head,
       Should say: 'That is not what I meant at all.
       That is not it, at all.'

      And would it have been worth it, after all,
100 Would it have been worth while,
    After the sunsets and the dooryards and the sprinkled streets,
    After the novels, after the teacups, after the skirts that trail along
       the floor—
    And this, and so much more?—
    It is impossible to say just what I mean!
105 But as if a magic lantern threw the nerves in patterns on a screen:
    Would it have been worth while
    If one, settling a pillow or throwing off a shawl,
    And turning toward the window, should say:
       'That is not it at all,
110   That is not what I meant, at all.'

          *   *   *

    No! I am not Prince Hamlet, nor was meant to be;
    Am an attendant lord, one that will do
    To swell a progress,[3] start a scene or two,
    Advise the prince; no doubt, an easy tool,
115 Deferential, glad to be of use,
    Politic, cautious, and meticulous;
    Full of high sentence, but a bit obtuse;
    At times, indeed, almost ridiculous—
    Almost, at times, the Fool.

120   I grow old. . . . I grow old. . . . .
    I shall wear the bottoms of my trousers rolled.

      Shall I part my hair behind? Do I dare to eat a peach?
    I shall wear white flannel trousers, and walk upon the beach.
    I have heard the mermaids singing, each to each.

---

3 a ceremonial procession at a royal court

125   I do not think that they will sing to me.

I have seen them riding seaward on the waves
Combing the white hair of the waves blown back
When the wind blows the water white and black.

We have lingered in the chambers of the sea
130   By sea-girls wreathed with seaweed red and brown
Till human voices wake us, and we drown.

1915

The Hollow Men

Mistah Kurtz—he dead.
A penny for the Old Guy

I

We are the hollow men
We are the stuffed men
Leaning together
Headpiece filled with straw. Alas!
5   Our dried voices, when
We whisper together
Are quiet and meaningless
As wind in dry grass
Or rats' feet over broken glass
10   In our dry cellar

Shape without form, shade without colour,
Paralyzed force, gesture without motion;

Those who have crossed
With direct eyes, to death's other Kingdom
15   Remember us—if at all—not as lost
Violent souls, but only
As the hollow men
The stuffed men.

II

      Eyes I dare not meet in dreams
20   In death's dream kingdom
      These do not appear:
      There, the eyes are
      Sunlight on a broken column
      There, is a tree swinging
25   And voices are
      In the wind's singing
      More distant and more solemn
      Than a fading star.

        Let me be no nearer
30   In death's dream kingdom
        Such deliberate disguises
      Let me also wear
      Rat's coat, crowskin, crossed staves
      In a field
35   Behaving as the wind behaves
      No nearer—

        Not that final meeting
      In the twilight kingdom

III

      This is the dead land
40   This is cactus land
      Here the stone images
      Are raised, here they receive
      The supplication of a dead man's hand
      Under the twinkle of a fading star.

45   Is it like this
      In death's other kingdom
      Waking alone
      At the hour when we are
      Trembling with tenderness
50   Lips that would kiss
      Form prayers to broken stone.

IV

The eyes are not here
There are no eyes here
In this valley of dying stars
55 In this hollow valley
This broken jaw of our lost kingdoms

In this last of meeting places
We grope together
And avoid speech
60 Gathered on this beach of the tumid river

Sightless, unless
The eyes reappear
As the perpetual star
Multifoliate rose
65 Of death's twilight kingdom
The hope only
Of empty men.

V

Here we go round the prickly pear
Prickly pear prickly pear
70 *Here we go round the prickly pear*
At five o'clock in the morning.

Between the idea
And the reality
Between the motion
75 And the act
Falls the Shadow
For Thine is the Kingdom

Between the conception
And the creation
Between the emotion
80 And the response
Falls the Shadow
Life is very long

Between the desire
And the spasm
Between the potency
85   And the existence
Between the essence
And the descent
Falls the Shadow
                        For Thine is the Kingdom

For Thine is
90   Life is
For Thine is the

        This is the way the world ends
        This is the way the world ends
        This is the way the world ends
95   *Not with a bang but a whimper.*

                                                                    1925

Journey of the Magi

'A cold coming we had of it,
Just the worst time of the year
For a journey, and such a long journey:
The ways deep and the weather sharp,
5   The very dead of winter.'
And the camels galled, sore-footed, refractory,
Lying down in the melting snow.
There were times we regretted
The summer palaces on slopes, the terraces,
10   And the silken girls bringing sherbet.
Then the camel men cursing and grumbling
And running away, and wanting their liquor and women,
And the night-fires going out, and the lack of shelters,
And the cities hostile and the towns unfriendly
15   And the villages dirty and charging high prices:
A hard time we had of it.
At the end we preferred to travel all night,
Sleeping in snatches,
With the voices singing in our ears, saying
20   That this was all folly.

Then at dawn we came down to temperate valley,
Wet, below the snow line, smelling of vegetation;
With a running stream and a water-mill beating the darkness,
And three trees on the low sky,
25 And an old white horse galloped away in the meadow.
Then we came to a tavern with vine-leaves over the lintel,
Six hands at an open door dicing for pieces of silver,
And feet kicking the empty wine-skins.
But there was no information, and so we continued
30 And arrived at evening, not a moment too soon
Finding the place; it was (you may say) satisfactory.

All this was a long time ago, I remember,
And I would do it again, but set down
This set down
35 This: were we led all that way for
Birth or Death? There was a Birth, certainly,
We had evidence and no doubt. I had seen birth and death,
But had thought they were different; this Birth was
Hard and bitter agony for us, like Death, our death.
40 We returned to our places, these Kingdoms,
But no longer at ease here, in the old dispensation,
With an alien people clutching their gods.
I should be glad of another death.

1927

Marina

Quis hic locus, quae
regio, quae mundi plaga?[1]

What seas what shores what grey rocks and what islands
What water lapping the bow
And scent of pine and the woodthrush singing through the fog
What images return
5 O my daughter.

Those who sharpen the tooth of the dog, meaning
Death
Those who glitter with the glory of the hummingbird, meaning
Death

---

1 'What place is this, what kingdom, what part of the world?' (Seneca, *Hercules Furens*)

10   Those who sit in the sty of contentment, meaning
Death
Those who suffer the ecstasy of the animals, meaning
Death

Are become unsubstantial, reduced by a wind,
15   A breath of pine, and the woodsong fog
By this grace dissolved in place

What is this face, less clear and clearer
The pulse in the arm, less strong and stronger—
Given or lent? more distant than stars and nearer than the eye

20   Whispers and small laughter between leaves and hurrying feet
Under sleep, where all the waters meet.

Bowsprit cracked with ice and paint cracked with heat.
I made this, I have forgotten
And remember.
25   The rigging weak and the canvas rotten
Between one June and another September.
Made this unknowing, half conscious, unknown, my own.
The garboard strake leaks, the seams need caulking.
This form, this face, this life
30   Living to live in a world of time beyond me; let me
Resign my life for this life, my speech for that unspoken,
The awakened, lips parted, the hope, the new ships.

What seas what shores what granite islands towards my timbers
And woodthrush calling through the fog
35   My daughter.

1930

e.e. cummings
1894–1962

He was born Edward Estlin Cummings, the son of a Harvard English professor who was later pastor of the Old South Church in Boston. cummings took his BA and MA at Harvard, and then joined the Norton Harjes Ambulance Corps in France during World War I. Because of the wrong-headed suspicions of a censor regarding 'unpatriotic' letters, cummings was imprisoned in a French concentration camp for three months, a period that is memorably evoked in his novel *The Enormous Room*, which made him famous. After the war he lived in Paris and studied painting before settling in

New York's Greenwich Village with other writers and artists, where he continued to paint and to write poetry. He developed an innovative, playful poetic style, flaunting the rules of syntax, grammar, and punctuation in order to make the reader see words and their relationships in a new way. In the form of his poetry and in his themes, he strikes out against conformity and celebrates the vitality of human love. He was not a poet of ideas but was one of the most joyful singers of the traditional themes of love and spring, as well as one of the sharpest satirists in modern poetry.

Buffalo Bill 's

Buffalo Bill 's
defunct
    who used to
        ride a watersmooth-silver
                stallion
5   and break onetwothreefourfive pigeonsjustlikethat
                                Jesus

he was a handsome man
                      and what i want to know is
10   how do you like your blueeyed boy
Mister Death

1920

Spring is like a perhaps hand

Spring is like a perhaps hand
(which comes carefully
out of Nowhere)arranging
a window,into which people look(while

5   people stare
      arranging and changing placing
      carefully there a strange
      thing and a known thing here)and

      changing everything carefully

10   spring is like a perhaps
      Hand in a window
      (carefully to
      and fro moving New and
      Old things,while
15   people stare carefully
      moving perhaps
      fraction of flower here placing
      an inch of air there)and

      without breaking anything.

1925

somewhere i have never travelled

somewhere i have never travelled,gladly beyond
any experience,your eyes have their silence:
in your most frail gesture are things which enclose me,
or which i cannot touch because they are too near

5   your slightest look easily will unclose me
    though i have closed myself as fingers,
    you open always petal by petal myself as Spring opens
    (touching skilfully,mysteriously)her first rose

    or if your wish be to close me,i and
10   my life will shut very beautifully,suddenly,
    as when the heart of this flower imagines
    the snow carefully everywhere descending;

    nothing which we are to perceive in this world equals
    the power of your intense fragility:whose texture
15   compels me with the colour of its countries,
    rendering death and forever with each breathing

(i do not know what it is about you that closes
and opens;only something in me understands
the voice of your eyes is deeper than all roses)
20 nobody,not even the rain,has such small hands

1931

my father moved through dooms of love

my father moved through dooms of love
through sames of am through haves of give,
singing each morning out of each night
my father moved through depths of height

5   this motionless forgetful where
turned at his glance to shining here;
that if(so timid air is firm)
under his eyes would stir and squirm

newly as from unburied which
10 floats the first who,his april touch
drove sleeping selves to swarm their fates
woke dreamers to their ghostly roots

and should some why completely weep
my father's fingers brought her sleep:
15 vainly no smallest voice might cry
for he could feel the mountains grow.

Lifting the valleys of the sea
my father moved through griefs of joy;
praising a forehead called the moon
20 singing desire into begin

joy was his song and joy so pure
a heart of star by him could steer
and pure so now and now so yes
the wrists of twilight would rejoice

25 keen as midsummer's keen beyond
conceiving mind of sun will stand,
so strictly(over utmost him
so hugely)stood my father's dream

his flesh was flesh his blood was blood:
30 no hungry man but wished him food;
no cripple wouldn't creep one mile
uphill to only see him smile.

Scorning the pomp of must and shall
my father moved through dooms of feel;
35 his anger was as right as rain
his pity was as green as grain

septembering arms of year extend
less humbly wealth to foe and friend
than he to foolish and to wise
40 offered immeasurable is

proudly and(by octobering flame
beckoned)as earth will downward climb,
so naked for immortal work
his shoulders marched against the dark

45 his sorrow was as true as bread:
no liar looked him in the head;
if every friend became his foe
he'd laugh and build a world with snow.

My father moved through theys of we,
50 singing each new leaf out of each tree
(and every child was sure that spring
danced when she heard my father sing)

then let men kill which cannot share,
let blood and flesh be mud and mire,
55 scheming imagine,passion willed,
freedom a drug that's bought and sold

giving to steal and cruel kind,
a heart to fear,to doubt a mind,
to differ a disease of same,
60 conform the pinnacle of am

though dull were all we taste as bright,
bitter all utterly things sweet,
maggoty minus and dumb death
all we inherit,all bequeath

65 and nothing quite so least as truth
—i say though hate were why men breathe—
because my father lived his soul
love is the whole and more than all

1940

pity this busy monster

pity this busy monster,manunkind,

not. Progress is a comfortable disease:
your victim(death and life safely beyond)

plays with the bigness of his littleness
5 —electrons deify one razorblade
into a mountainrange;lenses extend

unwish through curving wherewhen till unwish
returns on its unself.
                                A world of made
10 is not a world of born—pity poor flesh

and trees,poor stars and stones,but never this
fine specimen of hypermagical

ultraomnipotence. We doctors know

a hopeless case if—listen:there's a hell
15 of a good universe next door;let's go

1944

W.H. Auden

1907–1973

Wystan Hugh Auden was born in York, England, and developed an early interest in geology during family outings on the limestone moors of Yorkshire; evocations of those barren, simple landscapes can be found in much of his poetry. These outings took him also to Hadrian's wall, and to investigations of pre-Norman churches and crosses. It seems natural that when he was at Oxford he should study Anglo-Saxon poetry, whose rhythms and alliteration he later emulated. He experimented with many other forms, including the folk ballad, and was an extremely talented versifier. His first book of poetry appeared in 1928; this was followed by *September Poems*, and in 1932, *The Orators*.

Auden became well known as one of the major voices of the 1930s, an 'age of anxiety' resulting from worldwide depression and growing threat of another war. Influenced by Freud, Auden wrote of the guilt and fears of the human heart, but he wrote just as strongly of the power of love as the only force that could overcome anxiety. He came to the United States in 1939 and taught at a number of colleges and universities, becoming an American citizen in 1946. A prolific writer, he produced a large number of reviews and essays in addition to his poetry. He also wrote plays with Christopher Isherwood and opera librettos with Chester Kallmann. In 1957 he bought a farmhouse in Kirchstetten, Austria, where he spent springs and summers until his death there in 1973.

Who's Who

A shilling life will give you all the facts:
How Father beat him, how he ran away,
What were the struggles of his youth, what acts
Made him the greatest figure of his day:

5   Of how he fought, fished, hunted, worked all night,
Though giddy, climbed new mountains; named a sea:
Some of the last researchers even write
Love made him weep his pints like you and me.

With all his honours on, he sighed for one
10   Who, say astonished critics, lived at home;
Did little jobs about the house with skill
And nothing else; could whistle; would sit still
Or potter round the garden; answered some
Of his long marvellous letters but kept none.

As I Walked Out One Evening

As I walked out one evening,
  Walking down Bristol Street,
The crowds upon the pavement
  Were fields of harvest wheat.

5 And down by the brimming river
  I heard a lover sing
Under an arch of the railway:
  'Love has no ending.

'I'll love you, dear, I'll love you
10   Till China and Africa meet,
And the river jumps over the mountain
  And the salmon sing in the street,

'I'll love you till the ocean
  Is folded and hung up to dry
15 And the seven stars go squawking
  Like geese about the sky.

'The years shall run like rabbits,
  For in my arms I hold
The Flower of the Ages,
20   And the first love of the world.'

But all the clocks in the city
  Began to whirr and chime:
'O let not Time deceive you,
  You cannot conquer Time.

25 'In the burrows of the Nightmare
  Where Justice naked is,
Time watches from the shadow
  And coughs when you would kiss.

'In headaches and in worry
30   Vaguely life leaks away,
And Time will have his fancy
  Tomorrow or today.

'Into many a green valley
  Drifts the appalling snow;
35 Time breaks the threaded dances
  And the diver's brilliant bow.

'O plunge your hands in water,
    Plunge them in up to the wrist;
Stare, stare in the basin
40   And wonder what you've missed.

'The glacier knocks in the cupboard,
    The desert sighs in the bed,
And the crack in the tea-cup opens
    A lane to the land of the dead.

45 'Where the beggars raffle the banknotes
    And the Giant is enchanting to Jack,
And the Lily-white Boy is a Roarer,
    And Jill goes down on her back.

'O look, look in the mirror,
50   O look in your distress;
Life remains a blessing
    Although you cannot bless.

'O stand, stand at the window
    As the tears scald and start;
55 You shall love your crooked neighbour
    With your crooked heart.'

It was late, late in the evening,
    The lovers they were gone;
The clocks had ceased their chiming,
60   And the deep river ran on.

1940

Lullaby

Lay your sleeping head, my love,
Human on my faithless arm;
Time and fevers burn away
Individual beauty from
5   Thoughtful children, and the grave
Proves the child ephemeral:
But in my arms till break of day
Let the living creature lie,
Mortal, guilty, but to me
10   The entirely beautiful.

Soul and body have no bounds:
To lovers as they lie upon
Her tolerant enchanted slope
In their ordinary swoon,
15 Grave the vision Venus sends
Of supernatural sympathy,
Universal love and hope;
While an abstract insight wakes
Among the glaciers and the rocks
20 The hermit's carnal ecstasy.

Certainty, fidelity
On the stroke of midnight pass
Like vibrations of a bell
And fashionable madmen raise
25 Their pedantic boring cry:
Every farthing of the cost,
All the dreaded cards foretell,
Shall be paid, but from this night
Not a whisper, not a thought,
30 Not a kiss nor look be lost.

Beauty, midnight, vision dies:
Let the winds of dawn that blow
Softly round your dreaming head
Such a day of welcome show
35 Eye and knocking heart may bless,
Find our mortal world enough;
Noons of dryness find you fed
By the involuntary powers,
Nights of insult let you pass
40 Watched by every human love.

1940

Musée des Beaux Arts[1]

About suffering they were never wrong,
The Old Masters: how well they understood
Its human position; how it takes place
While someone else is eating or opening a window or just walking dully along;

1 Museum of Fine Arts. See the note to William Carlos Williams's 'Landscape with the Fall of Icarus', p. 586.

5   How, when the aged are reverently, passionately waiting
For the miraculous birth, there always must be
Children who did not specially want it to happen, skating
On a pond at the edge of the wood:
They never forgot
10 That even the dreadful martyrdom must run its course
Anyhow in a corner, some untidy spot
Where the dogs go on with their doggy life and the torturer's horse
Scratches its innocent behind on a tree.

In Brueghel's *Icarus*, for instance: how everything turns away
15 Quite leisurely from the disaster; the ploughman may
Have heard the splash, the forsaken cry,
But for him it was not an important failure; the sun shone
As it had to on the white legs disappearing into the green
Water; and the expensive delicate ship that must have seen
20 Something amazing, a boy falling out of the sky,
Had somewhere to get to and sailed calmly on.

1940

In Memory of W.B. Yeats

(d. Jan. 1939)

I

He disappeared in the dead of winter:
The brooks were frozen, the airports almost deserted,
And snow disfigured the public statues;
The mercury sank in the mouth of the dying day.
5 What instruments we have agree
The day of his death was a dark cold day.

Far from his illness
The wolves ran on through the evergreen forests,
The pleasant river was untempted by the fashionable quays;
10 By mourning tongues
The death of the poet was kept from his poems.

But for him it was his last afternoon as himself,
An afternoon of nurses and rumours;
The provinces of his body revolted,

15 The squares of his mind were empty,
Silence invaded the suburbs,
The current of his feeling failed; he became his admirers.

Now he is scattered among a hundred cities
And wholly given over to unfamiliar affections,
20 To find his happiness in another kind of wood
And be punished under a foreign code of conscience.
The words of a dead man
Are modified in the guts of the living.

But in the importance and noise of to-morrow
25 When the brokers are roaring like beasts on the floor of the Bourse,
And the poor have the sufferings to which they are fairly accustomed,
And each in the cell of himself is almost convinced of his freedom,
A few thousand will think of this day
As one thinks of a day when one did something slightly unusual.
30 What instruments we have agree
The day of his death was a dark cold day.

II

You were silly like us; your gifts survived it all:
The parish of rich women, physical decay,
Yourself. Mad Ireland hurt you into poetry.
35 Now Ireland has her madness and her weather still,
For poetry makes nothing happen: it survives
In the valley of its making where executives
Would never want to tamper, flows on south
From ranches of isolation and the busy griefs,
40 Raw towns that we believe and die in; it survives,
A way of happening, a mouth.

III

Earth, receive an honoured guest:
William Yeats is laid to rest.
Let the Irish vessel lie
45   Emptied of its poetry.

In the nightmare of the dark
All the dogs of Europe bark,

And the living nations wait,
Each sequestered in its hate;

50   Intellectual disgrace
Stares from every human face,
And the seas of pity lie
Locked and frozen in each eye.

Follow, poet, follow right
55   To the bottom of the night,
With your unconstraining voice
Still persuade us to rejoice;

With the farming of a verse
Make a vineyard of the curse,
60   Sing of human unsuccess
In a rapture of distress;

In the deserts of the heart
Let the healing fountain start,
In the prison of his days
65   Teach the free man how to praise.

1940

The Unknown Citizen

To JS/07/M/378
This Marble Monument
Is Erected by the State

He was found by the Bureau of Statistics to be
One against whom there was no official complaint,
And all the reports on his conduct agree
That, in the modern sense of an old-fashioned word, he was a saint,
5   For in everything he did he served the Greater Community.
Except for the War till the day he retired
He worked in a factory and never got fired,
But satisfied his employers, Fudge Motors Inc.
Yet he wasn't a scab or odd in his views,
10   For his Union reports that he paid his dues,
(Our report on his Union shows it was sound)

And our Social Psychology workers found
That he was popular with his mates and liked a drink.
The Press are convinced that he bought a paper every day

15 And that his reactions to advertisements were normal in every way.
Policies taken out in his name prove that he was fully insured,
And his Health-card shows he was once in hospital but left it cured.
Both Producers Research and High-Grade Living declare
He was fully sensible to the advantages of the Instalment Plan

20 And had everything necessary to the Modern Man,
A phonograph, a radio, a car and a frigidaire.
Our researchers into Public Opinion are content
That he held the proper opinions for the time of year;
When there was peace, he was for peace; when there was war, he went.

25 He was married and added five children to the population,
Which our Eugenist says was the right number for a parent of his generation,
And our teachers report that he never interfered with their education.
Was he free? Was he happy? The question is absurd:
Had anything been wrong, we should certainly have heard.

1940

A.M. Klein

1909–1972

Abraham Moses Klein was born in Ratno, Ukraine. His family emigrated in 1910 to Montreal, where he spent the rest of his life. Though he was raised in an orthodox Jewish family, he abandoned his strict orthodoxy during his high-school years and embarked on a passionate and lifelong dedication to Zionism. He graduated from McGill University in 1930 and from the law school of the University of Montreal in 1933. But the practice of law never satisfied him, for writing consumed his attention. He published five volumes of poetry, the novel *The Second Scroll* (1951), several short stories, and numerous literary essays and reviews.

Klein's early poetry explores the humour, pathos, and richness of his Jewish heritage. The influence of T.S. Eliot and the symbolist poets is evident in his later colloquial and ironic poems of social commentary, where he decries the absence of human dignity in a commercial world. His final volume of poetry, *The Rocking Chair and Other Poems* (1948), a beautiful evocation of Canada and its traditions, concludes with 'Portrait of the Poet as Landscape', which examines the poet's tragic isolation in the secular world. He was deeply distressed by the events of the Second World War and its aftermath, and as a result he suffered prolonged psychological anxiety in the early 1950s. For the last two decades of his life, he lived in virtual seclusion, relinquishing any commitment to his writing.

Soirée of Velvel Kleinburger

In back-room dens of delicatessen stores,
In curtained parlours of garrulous barber shops,
While the rest of the world most comfortably snores
On mattresses, or on more fleshly props,
5   My brother Velvel vigils in the night,
Not as he did last night with two French whores,
But with a deck of cards that once were white.

He sees three wan ghosts, as the thick smoke fades,
Dealing him clubs, and diamonds, hearts and spades.

10   His fingers, pricked with a tailor's needle, draw
The well-thumbed cards; while Hope weighs down his jaw.

    O for the ten spade in its proper place,
      Followed by knave in linen lace,
        The queen with her gaunt face,
15   The king and mace,
          The ace!

Then Velvel adds a footnote to his hoax:
I will not have your wherefores and your buts;
For I am for the Joker and his jokes;
20   I laugh at your alases and tut-tuts,
My days, they vanish into circular smokes,
My life lies on a tray of cigarette butts.

For it is easy to send pulpit wind
From bellies sumptuously lined;
25   Easy to praise the sleep of the righteous, when
The righteous sleep on cushions ten,
And having risen from a well-fed wife
Easy it is to give advice on life.

But you who upon sated palates clack a moral,
30   And pick a sermon from between your teeth,
Tell me with what bay, tell me with what laurel
Shall I entwine the heaven-praising wreath,
I, with whom Deity sets out to quarrel?

But, prithee, wherefore these thumbed cards?

35 O do not make a pack of cards your thesis
And frame no lesson on a house of cards
Where diamonds go lustreless, and hearts go broken
And clubs do batter the skull to little shards,
And where, because the spade is trump
40 One must perforce kiss Satan's rump.

For I have heard these things from teachers
With dirty beards and hungry features.

Now, after days in dusty factories,
Among machines that manufacture madness
45 I have no stomach for these subtleties
About rewards and everlasting gladness;
And having met your over-rated dawns,
Together with milkmen watering their milk,
And having trickled sweat, according to a scale of wages,
50 Sewing buttons to warm the navels of your business sages,
I have brought home at dusk,
My several bones, my much-flailed husk.

My meals are grand,
When supper comes
55 I feed on canned
Aquariums.

The salmon dies.
The evening waits
As I catch flies
60 From unwashed plates.

And my true love,
She combs and combs,
The lice from off
My children's domes.

65 Such is the idyll of my life.
But I will yet achieve
An easier living and less scrawny wife
And not forever will the foreman have
The aces up his sleeve,
70 But some day I will place the lucky bet.
(Ho! Ho! the social revolutions on a table of roulette!)

Alas, that Velvel's sigh makes eddies in the smoke.
For what's the use?
While the pale faces grin, his brow is hot;
75 He grasps a deuce . . . .

A nicotined hand beyond the smoke sweeps off the pot.

O good my brother, should one come to you
And knock upon the door at mid of night
And show you, writ in scripture, black on white,
80 That this is no way for a man to do?—
What a pale laughter from these ghosts, and 'Who
Are you, my saint, to show us what is right?
Make a fifth hand, and we will be contrite;
Shuffle the cards, be sociable, Reb. Jew.'

85 My brother's gesture snaps; *I spoke.*
His cheeks seek refuge in his mouth.
His nostrils puff superior smoke.
His lips are brown with drouth.

              Hum a hymn of sixpence,
90   A tableful of cards
              Fingers slowly shuffling
              Ambiguous rewards.
              When the deck is opened
              The pauper once more gave
95   His foes the kings and aces
              And took himself the knave.

Once more he cuts the cards, and dreams his dream;
A rolls-Royce hums within his brain;
Before it stands a chauffeur, tipping his hat,
100 'You say that it will rain, Sir; it will rain!'
Upon his fingers diamonds gleam,
His wife wears gowns of ultra-Paris fashion,
And she boasts jewels as large as wondrous eyes
The eyes of Og, the giant-king of Bashan.

105 So Velvel dreams; dreaming, he rises, and
Buttons his coat, coughs in his raised lapel,
Gropes his way home; he rings a raucous bell.

1932

The Rocking Chair

It seconds the crickets of the province. Heard
in the clean lamplit farmhouses of Quebec,—
wooden,—it is no less a national bird;
and rivals, in its cage, the mere stuttering clock.
5   To its time, the evenings are rolled away;
and in its peace the pensive mother knits
contentment to be worn by her family,
grown-up, but still cradled by the chair in which she sits.

It is also the old man's pet, pair to his pipe,
10   the two aids of his arithmetic and plans,
plans rocking and puffing into market-shape;
and it is the toddler's game and dangerous dance.
Moved to the verandah, on summer Sundays, it is,
among the hanging plants, the girls, the boyfriends,
15   sabbatical and clumsy, like the white haloes
dangling above the blue serge suits of the young men.

It has a personality of its own;
is a character (like that old drunk Lacoste,
exhaling amber,[1] and toppling on his pins);
20   it is alive; individual; and no less
an identity than those about it. And
it is tradition. Centuries have been flicked
from its arcs, alternately flicked and pinned.
It rolls with the gait of St Malo.[2] It is act

25   and symbol, symbol of this static folk
which moves in segments, and returns to base,—
a sunken pendulum: *invoke, revoke*;
loosed yon, leashed hither, motion on no space.
O, like some Anjou ballad, all refrain,[3]
30   which turns about its longing, and seems to move
to make a pleasure out of repeated pain,
its music moves, as if always back to a first love.

1948

1 perfume (perhaps from having drunk bay rum or cologne)
2 with the walk of sailors (St Malo is a town on the coast of France.)
3 Anjou is a former province of western France. What Klein seems to have in mind is the repetitive quality of those French-Canadian songs that had their root in medieval France. About these, Edith Fowke quotes an early traveller in Canada: '[the song] seems endless. After each short line comes the refrain, and the story twines itself along like a slender creeping plant' (*The Penguin Book of Canadian Folk Songs*, 1973).

Portrait of the Poet as Landscape

I

Not an editorial-writer, bereaved with bartlett,[1]
mourns him, the shelved Lycidas.[2]
No actress squeezes a glycerine tear for him.
The radio broadcast lets his passing pass.
5   And with the police, no record. Nobody, it appears,
either under his real name or his alias,
missed him enough to report.

It is possible that he is dead, and not discovered.
It is possible that he can be found some place
10   in a narrow closet, like the corpse in a detective story,
standing, his eyes staring, and ready to fall on his face.
It is also possible that he is alive
and amnesiac, or mad, or in retired disgrace,
or beyond recognition lost in love.

15   We are sure only that from our real society
he has disappeared; he simply does not count,
except in the pullulation[3] of vital statistics—
somebody's vote, perhaps, an anonymous taunt
of the Gallup poll, a dot in a government table—
20   but not felt, and certainly far from eminent—
in a shouting mob, somebody's sigh.

O, he who unrolled our culture from his scroll—
the prince's quote, the rostrum-rounding roar—
who under one name made articulate
25   heaven, and under another the seven-circled air,[4]
is, if he is at all, a number, an x,
a Mr Smith in a hotel register,—
incognito, lost, lacunal.[5]

---

1 Bartlett's *Familiar Quotations*
2 Klein is referring here to Milton's pastoral elegy mourning the death by drowning of the young poet Edward King (see p. 440).
3 rapid breeding; teeming
4 According to the pre-Copernican versions of the universe, the earth was surrounded by seven concentric spheres (the sun, the moon, and the five known planets).
5 i.e. of a lacuna or empty space

II

The truth is he's not dead, but only ignored—
30 like the mirroring lenses forgotten on a brow
that shine with the guilt of their unnoticed world.
The truth is he lives among neighbours, who, though they will allow
him a passable fellow, think him eccentric, not solid,
a type that one can forgive, and for that matter, forgo.

35 Himself he has his moods, just like a poet.
Sometimes, depressed to nadir, he will think all lost,
will see himself as throwback, relict,[6] freak,
his mother's miscarriage, his great-grandfather's ghost,
and he will curse his quintuplet senses, and their tutors
40 in whom he put, as he should not have put, his trust.

Then he will remember his travels over that body—
the torso verb, the beautiful face of the noun,
and all those shaped and warm auxiliaries!
A first love it was, the recognition of his own.
45 Dear limbs adverbial, complexion of adjective,
dimple and dip of conjugation!

And then remember how this made a change in him
affecting for always the glow and growth of his being;
how suddenly was aware of the air, like shaken tinfoil,[7]
50 of the patents of nature, the shock of belated seeing,
the loneliness peering from the eyes of crowds;
the integers of thought; the cube-roots of feeling.

Thus, zoomed to zenith, sometimes he hopes again,
and sees himself as a character, with a rehearsed role:
55 the Count of Monte Cristo,[8] come for his revenges;
the unsuspecting heir, with papers; the risen soul;
or the chloroformed prince awakening from his flowers;
or—deflated again—the convict on parole.

---

6 an organism from a previous age surviving in a changed environment
7 This is an echo of the opening lines of Hopkins' 'God's Grandeur' (see p. 543).
8 In the novel *The Count of Monte Cristo* (1844–5), by Alexandre Dumas père, an innocent man, imprisoned on
trumped-up charges, escapes to the Island of Monte Cristo, where he finds fabulous riches. He returns to Paris
a powerful man, and under various guises, takes revenge on those responsible for his ill treatment.

III

He is alone; yet not completely alone.
60 Pins on a map of a colour similar to his,
each city has one, sometimes more than one;
here, caretakers of art, in colleges;
in offices, there, with arm-bands, and green-shaded;
and there, pounding their catalogued beats in libraries,—

65 everywhere menial, a shadow's shadow.
And always for their egos—their outmoded art.
Thus, having lost the bevel[9] in the ear,
they know neither up nor down, mistake the part
for the whole, curl themselves in a comma,
70 talk technics, make a colon their eyes. They distort—

such is the pain of their frustration—truth
to something convolute and cerebral.
How they do fear the slap of the flat of the platitude!
Now Pavlov's victims, their mouths water at bell,
75 the platter empty.
           See they set twenty-one jewels
into their watches; the time they do not tell!

Some, patagonian[10] in their own esteem,
and longing for the multiplying word,
join party and wear pins, now have a message,
80 and ear, and the convention-hall's regard.
Upon the knees of ventriloquists, they own,
of their dandled[11] brightness, only the paint and board.

And some go mystical, and some go mad.
One stares at a mirror all day long, as if
85 to recognize himself; another courts
angels,—for here he does not fear rebuff;
and a third, alone, and sick with sex, and rapt,
doodles him symbols convex and concave.

O schizoid solitudes! O purities
90 curdling upon themselves! Who live for themselves,
or for each other, but for nobody else;

9 a tool for ascertaining angles
10 gigantic (because the Patagonian Indians of South America are said to be the tallest human beings)
11 moved lightly up and down on the knee

desire affection, private and public loves;
are friendly, and then quarrel and surmise
the secret perversions of each other's lives.

IV

95   He suspects that something has happened, a law
been passed, a nightmare ordered. Set apart,
he finds himself, with special haircut and dress,
as on a reservation. Introvert.
He does not understand this; sad conjecture
100   muscles and palls thrombotic on his heart.

He thinks an impostor, having studied his personal biography,
his gestures, his moods, now has come forward to pose
in the shivering vacuums his absence leaves.
Wigged with his laurel, that other, and faked with his face,
105   he pats the heads of his children, pecks his wife,
and is at home, and slippered, in his house.

So he guesses at the impertinent silhouette
that talks to his phone-piece and slits open his mail.
Is it the local tycoon who for a hobby
110   plays poet, he so epical in steel?
The orator, making a pause? Or is that man
he who blows his flash of brass in the jittering hall?

Or is he cuckolded by the troubadour
rich and successful out of celluloid?
115   Or by the don who unrhymes atoms? Or
the chemist death built up? Pride, lost impostor'd pride,
it is another, another, whoever he is,
who rides where he should ride.

V

Fame, the adrenalin: to be talked about;
120   to be a verb; to be introduced as *The*:
to smile with endorsement from slick paper; make
caprices anecdotal; to nod to the world; to see
one's name like a song upon the marquees played;
to be forgotten with embarrassment; to be—
125   to be.

It has its attractions, but is not the thing;
nor is it the ape mimesis[12] who speaks from the tree
ancestral; nor the merkin joy[13] . . . .
Rather it is stark infelicity
130   which stirs him from his sleep, undressed, asleep
to walk upon roofs and window-sills and defy
the gape of gravity.

VI

Therefore he seeds illusions. Look, he is
the nth Adam taking a green inventory
135   in world but scarcely uttered, naming, praising,
the flowering fiats in the meadow, the
syllabled fur, stars aspirate, the pollen
whose sweet collusion sounds eternally.
For to praise

140   the world—he, solitary man—is breath
to him. Until it has been praised, that part
has not been. Item by exciting item—
air to his lungs, and pressured blood to his heart—
they are pulsated, and breathed, until they map,
145   not the world's, but his own body's chart!

And now in imagination he has climbed
another planet, the better to look
with single camera view upon this earth—
its total scope, and each afflated[14] tick,
150   its talk, its trick, its tracklessness—and this,
this, he would like to write down in a book!

To find a new function for the *déclassé* craft
archaic like the fletcher's;[15] to make a new thing;
to say the word that will become sixth sense;
155   perhaps by necessity and indirection bring
new forms to life, anonymously, new creeds—
O, somehow pay back the daily larcenies of the lung!

---

12 imitation (perhaps in reference to the Aristotelian concept of poetry as an imitation of an action)
13 a deceptive joy; 'merkin': a wig for the female pubic area
14 breathed upon, inspired
15 arrow-maker

These are not mean ambitions. It is already something
merely to entertain them. Meanwhile, he
160 makes of his status as zero a rich garland,
a halo of his anonymity,
and lives alone, and in his secret shines
like phosphorus. At the bottom of the sea.

1948

Elizabeth Bishop
1911–1979

Though born in Worcester, Massachusetts, Elizabeth Bishop considered herself a Canadian by upbringing, if not by birth. She spent her early years in Great Village, Nova Scotia, and many later summers in the Maritimes. In 1930 she entered Vassar College, where, as a senior, she was introduced to Marianne Moore, destined to become a close friend and a formative influence on her career. Their friendship may well have been the cause of her decision to pursue writing rather than medicine. Throughout her life Bishop was passionately fond of travelling. After graduating from Vassar in 1934 she moved to New York City and, the following year, to Europe. France and Florida, Mexico and Brazil — these were her homes for extended periods. In 1970 she settled in Boston, where she taught at Harvard University and later at the Massachusetts Institute of Technology. One of the finest lyric poets of the twentieth century, she does not reveal in her writings any exhaustive philosophy or approach to life. Rather, she shows the rich texture and variety of the world with its joys and pains, injustices and confusions.

The Map

Land lies in water; it is shadowed green.
Shadows, or are they shallows, at its edges
showing the line of long sea-weeded ledges
where weeds hang to the simple blue from green.
5 Or does the land lean down to lift the sea from under,
drawing it unperturbed around itself?
Along the fine tan sandy shelf
is the land tugging at the sea from under?

The shadow of Newfoundland lies flat and still.
10 Labrador's yellow, where the moony Eskimo
has oiled it. We can stroke these lovely bays,

under a glass as if they were expected to blossom,
or as if to provide a clean cage for invisible fish.
The names of seashore towns run out to sea,
15   the names of cities cross the neighbouring mountains
—the printer here experiencing the same excitement
as when emotion too far exceeds its cause.
These peninsulas take the water between thumb and finger
like women feeling for the smoothness of yard-goods.

20   Mapped waters are more quiet than the land is,
lending the land their waves' own conformation:
and Norway's hare runs south in agitation,
profiles investigate the sea, where land is.
Are they assigned, or can the countries pick their colours?
25   —What suits the character or the native waters best.
Topography displays no favourites; North's as near as West.
More delicate than the historians' are the map-makers' colours.

1955

First Death in Nova Scotia

In the cold, cold parlour
my mother laid out Arthur
beneath the chromographs:
Edward, Prince of Wales,
5   with Princess Alexandra,
and King George with Queen Mary.
Below them on the table
stood a stuffed loon
shot and stuffed by Uncle
10   Arthur, Arthur's father.

Since Uncle Arthur fired
a bullet into him,
he hadn't said a word.
He kept his own counsel
15   on his white, frozen lake,
the marble-topped table.
His breast was deep and white,
cold and caressable;
his eyes were red glass,
20   much to be desired.

'Come,' said my mother,
'Come and say goodbye
to your little cousin Arthur.'
I was lifted up and given
25   one lily of the valley
to put in Arthur's hand.
Arthur's coffin was
a little frosted cake,
and the red-eyed loon eyed it
30   from his white, frozen lake.

Arthur was very small.
He was all white, like a doll
that hadn't been painted yet.
Jack Frost had started to paint him
35   the way he always painted
the Maple Leaf (Forever).
He had just begun on his hair,
a few red strokes, and then
Jack Frost had dropped the brush
40   and left him white, forever.

The gracious royal couples
were warm in red and ermine;
their feet were well wrapped up
in the ladies' ermine trains.
45   They invited Arthur to be
the smallest page at court.
But how could Arthur go,
clutching his tiny lily,
with his eyes shut up so tight
50   and the roads deep in snow?

1965

In the Waiting Room

In Worcester, Massachusetts,
I went with Aunt Consuelo
to keep her dentist's appointment
and sat and waited for her
5   in the dentist's waiting room.
It was winter. It got dark

early. The waiting room
was full of grown-up people,
arctics and overcoats,
10   lamps and magazines.
My aunt was inside
what seemed like a long time
and while I waited I read
the *National Geographic*
15   (I could read) and carefully
studied the photographs:
The inside of a volcano,
black, and full of ashes;
then it was spilling over
20   in rivulets of fire.
Osa and Martin Johnson
dressed in riding breeches,
laced boots, and pith helmets.
A dead man slung on a pole
25   —'Long Pig,' the caption said.
Babies with pointed heads
wound round and round with string;
black, naked women with necks
wound round and round with wire
30   like the necks of light bulbs.
Their breasts were horrifying.
I read it right straight through.
I was too shy to stop.
And then I looked at the cover:
35   the yellow margins, the date.

Suddenly, from inside,
came an *oh!* of pain
—Aunt Consuelo's voice—
not very loud or long.
40   I wasn't at all surprised;
even then I knew she was
a foolish, timid woman.
I might have been embarrassed,
but wasn't. What took me
45   completely by surprise
was that it was me:
my voice, in my mouth.
Without thinking at all
I was my foolish aunt,

50 I—we—were falling, falling,
  our eyes glued to the cover
  of the *National Geographic*,
  February, 1918.

  I said to myself: three days
55 and you'll be seven years old.
  I was saying it to stop
  the sensation of falling off
  the round, turning world
  into cold, blue-black space.
60 But I felt: you are an *I*,
  you are an *Elizabeth*,
  you are one of *them*.
  Why should you be one, too?
  I scarcely dared to look
65 to see what it was I was.
  I gave a sidelong glance
  —I couldn't look any higher—
  at shadowy grey knees,
  trousers and skirts and boots
70 and different pairs of hands
  lying under the lamps.
  I knew that nothing stranger
  had ever happened, that nothing
  stranger could ever happen.
75 Why should I be my aunt,
  or me, or anyone?
  What similarities—
  boots, hands, the family voice
  I felt in my throat, or even
80 the *National Geographic*
  and those awful hanging breasts—
  held us all together
  or made us all just one?
  How—I didn't know any
85 word for it—how 'unlikely'. . . .
  How had I come to be here,
  like them, and overhear
  a cry of pain that could have
  got loud and worse but hadn't?

90 The waiting room was bright
  and too hot. It was sliding

beneath a big black wave,
another, and another.

Then I was back in it.
95 The War was on. Outside
in Worcester, Massachusetts,
were night and slush and cold,
and it was still the fifth
of February, 1918.

1976

One Art

The art of losing isn't hard to master;
so many things seem filled with the intent
to be lost that their loss is no disaster.

Lose something every day. Accept the fluster
5   of lost door keys, the hour badly spent.
The art of losing isn't hard to master.

Then practice losing farther, losing faster:
places, and names, and where it was you meant
to travel. None of these will bring disaster.

10 I lost my mother's watch. And look! my last, or
next-to-last, of three loved houses went.
The art of losing isn't hard to master.

I lost two cities, lovely ones. And, vaster,
some realms I owned, two rivers, a continent.
15 I miss them, but it wasn't a disaster.

—Even losing you (the joking voice, a gesture
I love) I shan't have lied. It's evident
the art of losing's not too hard to master
though it may look like (*Write* it!) like disaster.

1976

Irving Layton
1912–2006

Irving Layton was born in Romania to Jewish parents and emigrated with his family to Montreal as an infant. He graduated from Macdonald College in 1939 and, after military service during the Second World War, obtained his MA in political science and economics from McGill University. He taught for a while in a Montreal secondary school, and later taught literature at many universities in Canada and abroad. Along with Louis Dudek and John Sutherland he edited *First Statement*, a magazine promoting poetry in plain language, ostensibly opposing the cosmopolitan writers — including P.K. Page —

associated with the rival publication *Preview*.

Following the publication of his first volume of poetry, *Here and Now*, in 1945, Layton established himself as the most prolific poet in Canada, publishing, on average, a book of poems every year over the next forty years. His poetry is sometimes relentlessly personal in its subject matter, challenging the reader to shed shackles of domestic, sexual, and cultural complacency. At other times his poetic voice is that of an Old Testament prophet in his own Jewish tradition, decrying man's inhumanity to man. At still other times his voice has the refined cadences of a delicate and sensitive lyric poet.

The Cold Green Element

At the end of the garden walk
the wind and its satellite wait for me;
their meaning I will not know
    until I go there,
5 but the black-hatted undertaker

who, passing, saw my heart beating in the grass,
is also going there. Hi, I tell him,
a great squall in the Pacific blew a dead poet
    out of the water,
10 who now hangs from the city's gates.

Crowds depart daily to see it, and return
with grimaces and incomprehension;
if its limbs twitched in the air
    they would sit at its feet
15 peeling their oranges.

And turning over I embrace like a lover
the trunk of a tree, one of those
for whom the lightning was too much
    and grew a brilliant
20   hunchback with a crown of leaves.

The ailments escaped from the labels
of medicine bottles are all fled to the wind;
I've seen myself lately in the eyes
    of old women,
25   spent streams mourning my manhood,

in whose old pupils the sun became
a bloodsmear on broad catalpa[1] leaves
and hanging from ancient twigs,
    my murdered selves
30   sparked the air like the muted collisions

of fruit. A black dog howls down my blood,
a black dog with yellow eyes;
he too by someone's inadvertence
    saw the bloodsmear
35   on the broad catalpa leaves.

But the furies clear a path for me to the worm
who sang for an hour in the throat of a robin,
and misled by the cries of young boys
    I am again
40   a breathless swimmer in that cold green element.

1955

1 a kind of tree with large heart-shaped leaves

Berry Picking

Silently my wife walks on the still wet furze
Now darkgreen the leaves are full of metaphors
Now lit up is each tiny lamp of blueberry.
The white nails of rain have dropped and the sun is free.

5   And whether she bends or straightens to each bush
To find the children's laughter among the leaves
Her quiet hands seem to make the quiet summer hush—
Berries or children, patient she is with these.

I only vex and perplex her; madness, rage
10 Are endearing perhaps put down upon the page;
Even silence daylong and sullen can then
Enamour as restraint or classic discipline.

So I envy the berries she puts in her mouth,
The red and succulent juice that stains her lips;
15 I shall never taste that good to her, nor will they
Displease her with a thousand barbarous jests.

How they lie easily for her hand to take,
Part of the unoffending world that is hers;
Here beyond complexity she stands and stares
20 And leans her marvellous head as if for answers.

No more the easy soul my childish craft deceives
Nor the simpler one for whom yes is always yes;
No, now her voice comes to me from a far way off
Though her lips are redder than the raspberries.

1958

Whatever Else Poetry Is Freedom

Whatever else poetry is freedom.
Forget the rhetoric, the trick of lying
All poets pick up sooner or later. From the river,
Rising like the thin voice of grey castratos[1]—the mist;
5 Poplars and pines grow straight but oaks are gnarled;
Old codgers must speak of death, boys break windows;
Women lie honestly by their men at last.

And I who gave my Kate a blackened eye
Did to its vivid changing colours
10 Make up an incredible musical scale;
And now I balance on wooden stilts and dance
And thereby sing to the loftiest casements.
See how with polish I bow from the waist.
Space for these stilts! More space or I fail!

---

1 historically: males castrated before puberty to retain a soprano or alto singing voice into adulthood

15   And a crown I say for my buffoon's head.
Yet no more fool am I than King Canute,[2]
Lord of our tribe, who scanned and scorned;
Who half-deceived, believed; and, poet, missed
The first white waves come nuzzling at his feet;
20   Then damned the courtiers and the foolish trial
With a most bewildering and unkingly jest.

It was the mist. It lies inside one like a destiny.
A real Johah it lies rotting like a lung.
And I know myself undone who am a clown
25   And wear a wreath of mist for a crown;
Mist with the scent of dead apples,
Mist swirling from black oily waters at evening,
Mist from the fraternal graves of cemeteries.

It shall drive me to beg my food and at last
30   Hurl me broken I know and prostrate on the road;
Like a huge toad I saw, entire but dead,
That Time mordantly had blackened; O pressed
To the moist earth it pled for entry.
I shall be I say that stiff toad for sick with mist
35   And crazed I smell the odour of mortality.

And Time flames like a paraffin stove
And what it burns are the minutes I live.

At certain middays, I have watched the cars
Bring me from afar their windshield suns;
40   What lay to my hand were blue fenders,
The suns extinguished, the drivers wearing sunglasses.
And it made me think I had touched a hearse.

So whatever else poetry is freedom. Let
Far off the impatient cadences reveal
45   A padding for my breathless stilts. Swivel,
O hero, in the fleshy groves, skin and glycerine,
And sing of lust, the sun's accompanying shadow
Like a vampire's wing, the stillness in dead feet—
Your stave[3] brings resurrection, O aggrievèd king.

1958

---

2 Eleventh-century king of England who is said to have placed his throne on the shore and commanded the tide not to rise. When the tide rolled over him anyway, he explained that he had done this to rebuke his courtiers, who thought or acted as if he had God-like powers.

3 rod, lance: but also with the punning meaning of 'stanza'

Keine Lazarovitch
1870–1959

When I saw my mother's head on the cold pillow,
Her white waterfalling hair in the cheeks' hollows,
I thought, quietly circling my grief, of how
She had loved God but cursed extravagantly his creatures.

5   For her final mouth was not water but a curse,
A small black hole, a black rent in the universe,
Which damned the green earth, stars and trees in its stillness
And the inescapable lousiness of growing old.

And I record she was comfortless, vituperative,
10   Ignorant, glad, and much else besides; I believe
She endlessly praised her black eyebrows, their thick weave,
Till plagiarizing Death leaned down and took them for his mould.

And spoiled a dignity I shall not again find,
And the fury of her stubborn limited mind;
15   Now none will shake her amber beads and call God blind,
Or wear them upon a breast so radiantly.

O fierce she was, mean and unaccommodating;
But I think now of the toss of her gold earrings,
Their proud carnal assertion, and her youngest sings
20   While all the rivers of her red veins move into the sea.

1961

Dylan Thomas
1914–1953

Born in Swansea, Wales, Dylan Thomas attended the Swansea Grammar School where his father was Senior English Master. Never much of a scholar, Thomas did well only in English, and loved to act in school plays and small theatre productions. When he left school in 1931, he worked for two newspapers, writing on books and theatre, and his explorations of the pubs and streets of his seaport town provided him with material for the short stories he was writing at the time. He was also writing poems in penny exercise books, composing much of his carefully crafted syllabic verse in pubs, with a glass of beer by his notebook. Much of his finest poetry was written before he was twenty, and from 1933 on he was published regularly. Thomas enjoyed playing the role of poet and became known as an extraordinarily fine reader of poetry, doing regular poetry readings for BBC radio. Though he was popular and making a good income, he was always in debt and incapable of managing money. On his tours to the United States, he was renowned not just for his readings but for his wild drinking bouts. He died suddenly and prematurely in New York after downing eighteen straight whiskies.

The Force That through the Green Fuse Drives the Flower

The force that through the green fuse drives the flower
Drives my green age; that blasts the roots of trees
Is my destroyer.
And I am dumb to tell the crooked rose
5 My youth is bent by the same wintry fever.

The force that drives the water through the rocks
Drives my red blood; that dries the mouthing streams
Turns mine to wax.
And I am dumb to mouth unto my veins
10 How at the mountain spring the same mouth sucks.

The hand that whirls the water in the pool
Stirs the quicksand; that ropes the blowing wind
Hauls my shroud sail.
And I am dumb to tell the hanging man
15 How of my clay is made the hangman's lime.

The lips of time leech to the fountain head;
Love drips and gathers, but the fallen blood
Shall calm her sores.

And I am dumb to tell a weather's wind
20   How time has ticked a heaven round the stars.

And I am dumb to tell the lover's tomb
How at my sheet goes the same crooked worm.

1933

A Refusal to Mourn the Death, by Fire,
of a Child in London

Never until the mankind making
Bird beast and flower
Fathering and all humbling darkness
Tells with silence the last light breaking
5   And the still hour
Is come of the sea tumbling in harness

And I must enter again the round
Zion of the water bead
And the synagogue of the ear of corn
10   Shall I let pray the shadow of a sound
Or sow my salt seed
In the least valley of sackcloth to mourn

The majesty and burning of the child's death.
I shall not murder
15   The mankind of her going with a grave truth
Nor blaspheme down the stations of the breath
With any further
Elegy of innocence and youth.

Deep with the first dead lies London's daughter,
20   Robed in the long friends,
The grains beyond age, the dark veins of her mother,
Secret by the unmourning water
Of the riding Thames.
After the first death, there is no other.

1946

Do Not Go Gentle into That Good Night

Do not go gentle into that good night,
Old age should burn and rave at close of day;
Rage, rage against the dying of the light.

Though wise men at their end know dark is right,
5   Because their words had forked no lightning they
Do not go gentle into that good night.

Good men, the last wave by, crying how bright
Their frail deeds might have danced in a green bay,
Rage, rage against the dying of the light.

10   Wild men who caught and sang the sun in flight,
And learn, too late, they grieved it on its way,
Do not go gentle into that good night.

Grave men, near death, who see with blinding sight
Blind eyes could blaze like meteors and be gay,
15   Rage, rage against the dying of the light.

And you, my father, there on the sad height,
Curse, bless, me now with your fierce tears, I pray.
Do not go gentle into that good night.
Rage, rage against the dying of the light.

1951

Fern Hill

Now as I was young and easy under the apple boughs
About the lilting house and happy as the grass was green,
      The night above the dingle starry,
        Time let me hail and climb
5   Golden in the heydays of his eyes,
And honoured among wagons I was prince of the apple towns
And once below a time I lordly had the trees and leaves
      Trail with daisies and barley
      Down the rivers of the windfall light.

10   And as I was green and carefree, famous among the barns
     About the happy yard and singing as the farm was home,
         In the sun that is young once only,
             Time let me play and be
             Golden in the mercy of his means,
15   And green and golden I was huntsman and herdsman, the calves
     Sang to my horn, the foxes on the hills barked clear and cold,
             And the sabbath rang slowly
             In the pebbles of the holy streams.

     All the sun long it was running, it was lovely, the hay
20   Fields high as the house, the tunes from the chimneys, it was air
             And playing, lovely and watery
                 And fire green as grass.
             And nightly under the simple stars
     As I rode to sleep the owls were bearing the farm away,
25   All the moon long I heard, blessed among stables, the night-jars
             Flying with the ricks, and the horses
                 Flashing into the dark

     And then to awake, and the farm, like a wanderer white
     With the dew, come back, the cock on his shoulder: it was all
30   Shining, it was Adam and maiden,
                 The sky gathered again
             And the sun grew round that very day.
     So it must have been after the birth of the simple light
     In the first, spinning place, the spellbound horses walking warm
35   Out of the whinnying green stable
                 On to the fields of praise.

     And honoured among foxes and pheasants by the gay house
     Under the new made clouds and happy as the heart was long,
             In the sun born over and over,
40   I ran my heedless ways,
                 My wishes raced through the house high hay
     And nothing I cared, at my sky blue trades, that time allows
     In all his tuneful turning so few and such morning songs
             Before the children green and golden
45   Follow him out of grace,

     Nothing I cared, in the lamb white days, that time would take me
     Up to the swallow thronged loft by the shadow of my hand,
             In the moon that is always rising,
                 Nor that riding to sleep

50   I should hear him fly with the high fields
        And wake to the farm forever fled from the childless land.
        Oh as I was young and easy in the mercy of his means,
              Time held me green and dying
          Though I sang in my chains like the sea.

                                             1946

P.K. Page
b. 1916

Born in Swanage, Dorset, England, Patricia Kathleen Page emigrated with her family to Alberta in 1919. She lived in many areas of Canada before settling in 1941 in Montreal, where she edited, along with Patrick Anderson and F.R. Scott, *Preview* magazine, a literary journal designed to 'preview', or try out, new poetry written in a cosmopolitan mode. She engaged in many occupations, including radio actor, research assistant, and scriptwriter for the National Film Board. In 1950 she married W.A. Irwin, commissioner for the film board, who later became Canadian high commissioner to Australia and then ambassador to Brazil and to Mexico.

Page published her first poems as well as a novel, *The Sun and the Moon*, in 1944. In addition to several short stories, she has published numerous collections of poetry, including *Planet Earth: Poems Selected and New* (2002). Under her married name, P.K. Irwin, she has also achieved eminence as a painter. 'In all essential particulars writing and painting are interchangeable,' she has observed. Like the painter that she is, she explores in her poetry an image or a scene by gathering together precise details and impressions in a rich tapestry. Since 1964 she has lived in Victoria, British Columbia.

The Stenographers

    After the brief bivouac of Sunday,
    their eyes, in the forced march of Monday to Saturday,
    hoist the white flag, flutter in the snow-storm of paper,
    haul it down and crack in the mid-sun of temper.

5   In the pause between the first draft and the carbon
    they glimpse the smooth hours when they were children—
    the ride in the ice-cart, the ice-man's name,
    the end of the route and the long walk home;

remember the sea where floats at high tide
10 were sea marrows growing on the scatter-green vine
or spools of grey toffee, or wasps' nests on water;
remember the sand and the leaves of the country.

Bell rings and they go and the voice draws their pencil
like a sled across snow; when its runners are frozen
15 rope snaps and the voice then is pulling no burden
but runs like a dog on the winter of paper.

Their climates are winter and summer—no wind
for the kites of their hearts—no wind for a flight;
a breeze at the most, to tumble them over
20 and leave them like rubbish—the boy-friends of blood.

In the inch of the noon as they move they are stagnant.
The terrible calm of the noon is their anguish;
the lip of the counter, the shapes of the straws
like icicles breaking their tongues, are invaders.

25 Their beds are their oceans—salt water of weeping
the waves that they know—the tide before sleep;
and fighting to drown they assemble their sheep
in columns and watch them leap desks for their fences
and stare at them with their own mirror-worn faces.

30 In the felt of the morning the calico-minded,
sufficiently starched, insert papers, hit keys,
efficient and sure as their adding machines;
yet they weep in the vault, they are taut as net curtains
stretched upon frames. In their eyes I have seen
35 the pin men[1] of madness in marathon trim
race round the track of the stadium pupil.

1946

1 'stick figures, such as children draw' [Page's note]

Photos of a Salt Mine

How innocent their lives look,
how like a child's
dream of caves and winter, both combined;
the steep descent to whiteness
5   and the stope[1]
with its striated walls
their folds all leaning as if pointing to
the greater whiteness still,
that great white bank

10   with its decisive front,
that seam upon a slope,
salt's lovely ice.

And wonderful underfoot the snow of salt
the fine
15   particles a broom could sweep,
one thinks
muckers might make angels in its drifts
as children do in snow,
lovers in sheets,
20   lie down and leave imprinted where they lay
a feathered creature holier than they.

And in the outworked stopes
with lamps and ropes
up miniature matterhorns
25   the miners climb
probe with their lights
the ancient folds of rock—
syncline[2] and anticline—
and scoop from darkness an Aladdin's cave:
30   rubies and opals glitter from its walls.

But hoses douse the brilliance of these jewels,
melt fire to brine.
Salt's bitter water trickles thin and forms,
slow fathoms down,

---

1 an excavation in the form of steps made as ore is mined from vertical or steeply inclined veins
2 a low, troughlike fold in stratified rock, the opposite of 'anticline': a fold with strata sloping downwards on both
sides away from a common crest

35 a lake within a cave,
lacquered with jet—
white's opposite.
There grey on black the boating miners float
to mend the stays and struts of that old stope
40 and deeply underground
their words resound,
are multiplied by echo, swell and grow
and make a climate of a miner's voice.

So all the photographs like children's wishes
45 are filled with caves or winter,
innocence
has acted as a filter,
selected only beauty from the mine.
Except in the last picture,
50 it is shot
from an acute high angle. In a pit
figures the size of pins are strangely lit
and might be dancing but you know they're not.
Like Dante's vision of the nether hell[3]
55 men struggle with the bright cold fires of salt,
locked in the black inferno of the rock:
the filter here, not innocence but guilt.

1954

3 In *The Inferno*, which forms the first part of Dante's fourteenth-century poem *The Divine Comedy*, hell is divided into three parts. The lowest part contains both fire and ice.

Arras[1]

Consider a new habit—classical,
and trees espaliered on the wall like candelabra.
How still upon that lawn our sandalled feet.

But a peacock rattling his rattan tail and screaming
5 has found a point of entry. Through whose eye
did it insinuate in furled disguise
to shake its jewels and silk upon that grass?

1 a wall hanging, particularly a tapestry

The peaches hang like lanterns. No one joins
those figures on the arras.

Who am I

10   or who am I become that walking here
I am observer, other, Gemini,
starred for a green garden of cinema?

I ask, what did they deal me in this pack?
The cards, all suits, are royal when I look.

15   My fingers slipping on a monarch's face
twitch and grow slack.
I want a hand to clutch, a heart to crack.

No one is moving now, the stillness is
infinite. If I should make a break. . . .

20   take to my springy heels. . . . ? But nothing moves.
The spinning world is stuck upon its poles,
the stillness points a bone² at me. I fear
the future on this arras.

I confess:

It was my eye.

25   Voluptuous it came.
Its head the ferrule³ and its lovely tail
folded so sweetly; it was strangely slim
to fit the retina. And then it shook
and was a peacock—living patina,

30   eye-bright, maculate!
Does no one care?

I thought their hands might hold me if I spoke.
I dreamed the bite of fingers in my flesh,
their poke smashed by an image, but they stand

35   as if with a treacle,⁴ motionless,
folding slow eyes on nothing. While they stare
another line has trolled the encircling air,
another bird assumes its furled disguise.

1967

---

2 'Aboriginal projective magic. A prepared human or kangaroo bone is pointed by a sorcerer at an intended victim (who may be miles away) to bring about his death' [from Page's glossary of Australian terms in *Cry Ararat!*].
3 a metal cap used to reinforce or secure the end of a pole or handle—here belonging to an umbrella
4 molasses or sweet syrup, used here as the kind that entraps the insects it attracts

The New Bicycle

All the molecules in the house
re-adjust on its arrival,
make way for its shining presence
its bright dials,
5   and after it has settled
and the light
has explored its surfaces
—and the night—
they compose themselves again
10 in another order.

One senses the change at once
without knowing what one senses.
Has somebody cleaned the windows
used different soap
15 or is there a bowl of flowers
on the mantelpiece?—
for the air makes another shape
it is thinner or denser,
a new design
20 is invisibly stamped upon it.

How we all adapt ourselves
to the bicycle
aglow in the furnace room,
turquoise where turquoise
25 has never before been seen,
its chrome gleaming
on gears and pedals,
its spokes glistening.
Lightly resting on the incised
30 rubber of its airy tires
it has changed us all.

1985

Deaf-Mute in the Pear Tree

His clumsy body is a golden fruit
pendulous in the pear tree

Blunt fingers among the multitudinous buds

Adriatic blue the sky above and through
5   the forking twigs

Sun ruddying tree's trunk, his trunk
his massive head thick-nobbed with burnished curls
tight-clenched in bud

(Painting by Generalić. Primitive.)

10   I watch him prune with silent secateurs

Boots in the crotch of branches shift their weight
heavily as oxen in a stall

Hear small inarticulate mews from his locked mouth
a kitten in a box

15   Pear clippings fall
                soundlessly on the ground
Spring finches sing
            soundlessly in the leaves

A stone. A stone in ears and on his tongue

Through palm and fingertip he knows the tree's
quick springtime pulse

20   Smells in its sap the sweet incipient pears

Pale sunlight's choppy water glistens on
his mutely snipping blades

and flags and scraps of blue
above him make regatta of the day

25   But when he sees his wife's foreshortened shape
sudden and silent in the grass below
uptilt its face to him

then air is kisses, kisses

stone dissolves

30 his locked throat finds a little door

and through it feathered joy
flies screaming like a jay

1985

Robert Lowell
1917–1977

Robert Lowell's poetry is primarily autobio-graphical, revealing his deep interest in his family's New England history, as well as his reactions to his lineage. He was born in Boston and attended St Mark's School (founded by his grandfather). Then, as was proper for young men of good family in Boston, he went on to Harvard. But after two years he left and went to study with poet and critic John Crowe Ransom at Kenyon College. He converted to Catholicism in 1940, and during World War II he tried unsuccessfully to enlist in the navy. He refused to be drafted into the army, and as a conscientious objector, was jailed for six months.

Lowell's first book of poetry was published in 1944, and in 1947 he won the Pulitzer Prize for *Lord Weary's Castle* and became consultant in poetry at the Library of Congress. *Life Studies* (1959) reveals some influence of the self-revelatory mode of the Beat poets, and of William Carlos Williams's colloquial American diction. Lowell's form is highly controlled as he strives for a tone of 'heightened conversation' in these complex and personal portraits that many consider his finest poetry. During his career, Lowell taught at several universities, including Harvard, wrote for the theatre, and translated European poetry. In his last book, *Day by Day*, he returned to an exploration of his childhood.

'To Speak of Woe That Is in Marriage'

'It is the future generation that presses into being by means of these exuberant feelings and supersensible soap bubbles of ours.'

—Schopenhauer

'The hot night makes us keep our bedroom windows open.
Our magnolia blossoms. Life begins to happen.
My hopped up husband drops his home disputes,

and hits the streets to cruise for prostitutes,
5   free-lancing out along the razor's edge.
This screwball might kill his wife, then take the pledge.
Oh the monotonous meanness of his lust. . . .
It's the injustice . . . he is so unjust—
whiskey-blind, swaggering home at five.
10   My only thought is how to keep alive.
What makes him tick? Each night now I tie
ten dollars and his car key to my thigh. . . .
Gored by the climacteric of his want,
he stalls above me like an elephant.'

1959

Skunk Hour

for Elizabeth Bishop

Nautilus Island's hermit
heiress still lives through winter in her Spartan cottage;
her sheep still graze above the sea.
Her son's a bishop. Her farmer
5   is first selectman in our village;
she's in her dotage.

Thirsting for
the hierarchic privacy
of Queen Victoria's century,
10   she buys up all
the eyesores facing her shore,
and lets them fall.

The season's ill—
we've lost our summer millionaire,
15   who seemed to leap from an L.L. Bean
catalogue. His nine-knot yawl
was auctioned off to lobstermen.
A red fox stain covers Blue Hill.

And now our fairy
20   decorator brightens his shop for fall;
his fishnet's filled with orange cork,

orange, his cobbler's bench and awl;
there is no money in his work,
he'd rather marry.

25 One dark night,
my Tudor Ford climbed the hill's skull;
I watched for love-cars. Lights turned down,
they lay together, hull to hull,
where the graveyard shelves on the town. . . .
30 My mind's not right.

A car radio bleats,
'Love, O careless Love. . . .' I hear
my ill-spirit sob in each blood cell,
as if my hand were at its throat. . . .
35 I myself am hell;
nobody's here—

only skunks, that search
in the moonlight for a bite to eat.
They march on their soles up Main Street:
40 white stripes, moonstruck eyes' red fire
under the chalk-dry and spar spire
of the Trinitarian Church.

I stand on top
of our back steps and breathe the rich air—
45 a mother skunk with her column of kittens swills the garbage pail.
She jabs her wedge-head in a cup
of sour cream, drops her ostrich tail,
and will not scare.

1959

Water

It was a Maine lobster town—
each morning boatloads of hands
pushed off for granite
quarries on the islands,

5   and left dozens of bleak
white frame houses stuck
like oyster shells
on a hill of rock,

and below us, the sea lapped
10 the raw little match-stick
mazes of a weir,
where the fish for bait were trapped.

Remember? We sat on a slab of rock.
From this distance in time,
15 it seems the colour
of iris, rotting and turning purpler,

but it was only
the usual grey rock
turning the usual green
20 when drenched by the sea.

The sea drenched the rock
at our feet all day,
and kept tearing away
flake after flake.

25 One night you dreamed
you were a mermaid clinging to a wharf-pile,
and trying to pull
off the barnacles with your hands.

We wished our two souls
30 might return like gulls
to the rock. In the end,
the water was too cold for us.

1959

For the Union Dead

'Relinquunt Omnia Servare Rem Publicam.'[1]

The old South Boston Aquarium stands
in a Sahara of snow now. Its broken windows are boarded.
The bronze weathervane cod has lost half its scales.
The airy tanks are dry.

5   Once my nose crawled like a snail on the glass;
my hand tingled
to burst the bubbles
drifting from the noses of the cowed, compliant fish.

My hand draws back. I often sigh still
10   for the dark downward and vegetating kingdom
of the fish and reptile. One morning last March,
I pressed against the new barbed and galvanized

fence on the Boston Common. Behind their cage,
yellow dinosaur steamshovels were grunting
15   as they cropped up tons of mush and grass
to gouge their underworld garage.

Parking spaces luxuriate like civic
sandpiles in the heart of Boston.
A girdle of orange, Puritan-pumpkin coloured girders
20   braces the tingling Statehouse,

shaking over the excavations, as it faces Colonel Shaw[2]
and his bell-cheeked Negro infantry
on St Gaudens' shaking Civil War relief,
propped by a plank splint against the garage's earthquake.

25   Two months after marching through Boston,
half the regiment was dead;
at the dedication,
William James could almost hear the bronze Negroes breathe.

Their monument sticks like a fishbone
30   in the city's throat.
Its Colonel is as lean
as a compass-needle.

---

1 'They give up everything to serve the republic.'
2 Robert Gould Shaw led the first northern black regiment, the Massachusetts 54th. He and many of his men
   were killed leading an attack on Fort Wagner, South Carolina.

He has an angry wrenlike vigilance,
a greyhound's gentle tautness;
35   he seems to wince at pleasure,
and suffocate for privacy.

He is out of bounds now. He rejoices in man's lovely,
peculiar power to choose life and die—
when he leads his black soldiers to death,
40   he cannot bend his back.

On a thousand small town New England greens,
the old white churches hold their air
of sparse, sincere rebellion; frayed flags
quilt the graveyards of the Grand Army of the Republic.

45   The stone statues of the abstract Union Soldier
grow slimmer and younger each year—
wasp-waisted, they doze over muskets
and muse through their sideburns . . .

Shaw's father wanted no monument
50   except the ditch,
where his son's body was thrown
and lost with his 'niggers'.

The ditch is nearer.
There are no statues for the last war here;
55   on Boylston Street, a commercial photograph
shows Hiroshima boiling

over a Mosler Safe, the 'Rock of Ages'
that survived the blast. Space is nearer.
When I crouch to my television set,
60   the drained faces of Negro school-children rise like balloons.

Colonel Shaw
is riding on his bubble,
he waits
for the blessèd break.

65   The Aquarium is gone. Everywhere,
giant finned cars nose forward like fish;
a savage servility
slides by on grease.

1959

Margaret Avison

1918–2007

Born in Galt (now Cambridge), Ontario, Margaret Avison graduated in English from Victoria College, University of Toronto, in 1940. She also studied at Indiana University (1955) and, on a Guggenheim Fellowship, at the University of Chicago (1956–7). Her first collection of poetry, *Winter Sun* (1960), won the Governor General's Award, as did her later collection *No Time* (1989). During the 1960s she returned to the University of Toronto to pursue graduate studies. She was a librarian, a lecturer at Scarborough College, University of Toronto, and a social worker for the Presbyterian Church Mission in Toronto. Her poems are often careful and close observations of physical landscapes, and, like Gerard Manley Hopkins, she delights in the natural world's ability to shadow forth spiritual realities. In 2003 *Concrete and Wild Carrot* won the Griffin Poetry Prize.

Snow

Nobody stuffs the world in at your eyes.
The optic heart must venture: a jail-break
And re-creation. Sedges and wild rice
Chase rivery pewter. The astonished cinders quake
5 With rhizomes. All ways through the electric air
Trundle candy-bright disks; they are desolate
Toys if the soul's gates seal, and cannot bear,
Must shudder under, creation's unseen freight.
But soft, there is snow's legend: colour of mourning
10 Along the yellow Yangtze where the wheel
Spins an indifferent stasis that's death's warning.
Asters of tumbled quietness reveal
Their petals. Suffering this starry blur
The rest may ring your change, sad listener.

1960

New Year's Poem

The Christmas twigs crispen and needles rattle
Along the windowledge.
　　　　A solitary pearl
Shed from the necklace spilled at last week's party
5 Lies in the suety, snow-luminous plainness

Of morning, on the windowledge beside them.
And all the furniture that circled stately
And hospitable when these rooms were brimmed
With perfumes, furs, and black-and-silver
10   Crisscross of seasonal conversation, lapses
Into its previous largeness.
             I remember
Anne's rose-sweet gravity, and the stiff grave
Where cold so little can contain;
15   I mark the queer delightful skull and crossbones
Starlings and sparrows left, taking the crust,
And the long loop of winter wind
Smoothing its arc from dark Arcturus down
To the bricked corner of the drifted courtyard,
20   And the still windowledge.
                Gentle and just pleasure
It is, being human, to have won from space
This unchill, habitable interior
Which mirrors quietly the light
25   Of the snow, and the new year.

1960

The Swimmer's Moment

For everyone
The swimmer's moment at the whirlpool comes,
But many at that moment will not say
'This is the whirlpool, then.'
5   By their refusal they are saved
From the black pit, and also from contesting
The deadly rapids, and emerging in
The mysterious, and more ample, further waters.
And so their bland-blank faces turn and turn
10   Pale and forever on the rim of suction
They will not recognize.
Of those who dare the knowledge
Many are whirled into the ominous centre
That, gaping vertical, seals up
15   For them an eternal boon of privacy,
So that we turn away from their defeat
With a despair, not for their deaths, but for
Ourselves, who cannot penetrate their secret

Nor even guess at the anonymous breadth
20 Where one or two have won:
(The silver reaches of the estuary).

1960

Butterfly Bones;
or Sonnet against Sonnets

The cyanide jar seals life, as sonnets move
towards final stiffness. Cased in a white glare
these specimens stare for peering boys, to prove
strange certainties. Plane dogsled and safari
5 assure continuing range. The sweep-net skill,
the patience, learning, leave all living stranger.
Insect—or poem—waits for the fix, the frill
precision can effect, brilliant with danger.
What law and wonder the museum spectres
10 bespeak is cryptic for the shivery wings,
the world cut-diamond-eyed, those eyes' reflectors,
or herbal grass, sunned motes, fierce listening.
Might sheened and rigid trophies strike men blind
like Adam's lexicon locked in the mind?

1960

In a Season of Unemployment

These green painted park benches are
all new. The Park Commissioner had them
planted.
Sparrows go on
5 having dust baths at the edge of
the park maple's shadow, just where
the bench is cemented down, planted
and then cemented.

Not a breath moves
10 this newspaper.
I'd rather read it by the Lapland sun at midnight. Here we're
bricked in early by a
stifling dark.

On that bench a man in a
15 pencil-striped white shirt
keeps his head up and steady.

The newspaper-astronaut says
'I feel excellent under the condition of weightlessness.'
And from his bench a
20 scatter of black bands in the hollow air
ray out—too quick for the eye—
and cease.

'Ground observers watching him on a TV circuit said
At the time of this report he
25 was smiling,' Moscow radio reported.
I glance across at him, and mark that
he is feeling
excellent too, I guess, and
30 weightless and
'smiling'.

1966

We the Poor Who Are Always with Us

The cumbering hungry
and the uncaring ill
become too many
try as we will.

5 Try on and on, still?
In fury, fly
out, smash shards (and quail
at tomorrow's new supply,
and fail anew to find and smash the why?)

10 It is not hopeless.
One can crawling move
in useless recognition
there, still free to love
past use, where none survive.

15   And there is reason in
     the hope that then can shine
     when other hope is none.

1978

◆

Robert Kroetsch
b. 1927

◆

Born in Heisler, Alberta, Robert Kroetsch obtained his BA (1948) from the University of Alberta, his MA (1955) from Middlebury College, and his PhD (1961) from the University of Iowa. He taught in the Department of English of the State University of New York in Binghamton before returning to Canada to teach at the University of Manitoba. He turned to poetry in the midst of a distinguished career as a novelist and critic. In his short lyrics, which he began to write in the early 1970s, he fashions a complex archaeological metaphor out of auto-biography, gathering up the fragments of his many stories to dig up his own being as a poet. His poetry becomes an ongoing set of field notes, signposts of where the poet has been. In marking out the landscapes that are filled with past stories waiting to be unearthed, he creates poetry in the state of becoming, always aware of what can be and still is not. His *Hornbooks of Rita K* (2001) watches an 'archivist' working his way through the writings of a prairie poet whose initials are the same as the book's real author.

The Poet's Mother

I

In the death of my mother
I read the empty sky.

In the death of my mother
I learn to bite the wind.

5   In the death of my mother
I hear the clarinet.

In the death of my mother
I say goodbye to myself.

In the death of my mother
10   I speak to the grass.

In the death of my mother
I enter the cave.

In the death of my mother
I recite my name.

2

15   I have sought my mother
on the shores of a dozen islands.

I have sought my mother
inside the covers
of ten thousand books.

20   I have sought my mother
in the bars of a hundred cities.

I have sought my mother
on the head of a pin.

I have sought my mother
25   in the arms of younger women.

I have sought my mother
in the spaces between
the clouds.

I have sought my mother
30   under the typewriter keys.

3

In the fall of snow
I hear my mother.
I know she is there.
In the weight of the snow
35   I hear her silence.

I count white stones
in October moonlight.

I break dry bread
with a flock of gulls.

40 I tear sheep's wool
from barbed wire fences

The visible,
the visible—

where are you?

4

45 These are the scars
that make us whole.

These are the scars
that empty us
into our lives.

50 Hold your horses.
It was a nice trip
to heaven. Let us
now visit the

earth.
55 The scarred earth
is our only
home.

Mother, where are you?

1989

From *The Hornbooks of Rita K*

[HORNBOOK #43]

Rita thought of calling her book *Chance of Flurries*. That
she elected not to is fortunate, since I would surely
propose other titles for her unfinished magnum opus.

We write as a way of inviting love. Each text is a request
5   that says, please, love me a little.

Rita Kleinhart was an admirer of snow. Snow, she remarks,
is the caress of impossible meanings. Snow is closure
without ending. Snow is the veil that lets us see the shape
of the dream.

10   Rita left two solitary lines that seem to belong nowhere:

> A skiff of snow, this morning, rides the stubble sun.
> The gosling, holding madly still, accounts the gun.

I, too, have walked in the ribald dark, asking forgiveness. In
the absence of the gun, snow suffices.

[HORNBOOK #45]

What is the heart but the muscular, thick skin of an
abiding secret?

She referred to me as the intrigued lover.

Broken, she said, and wrote these lines after that solitary
5   word, as if she had put down a title:

> He is the intrigued lover who loves first
> his own hands. His hands betray my nipples.
> His hands are scissors that break rocks.
> And yet he is the intrigued lover who asks,
10   Where do you go when you close your eyes?

There is a break on the page. Then she continues:

> You of the stalled orgasm, fearing an end—
> I give you nothing. Die by your own hand.
> Love is a pleasure of the mouth. Eat your words.

15 Surely she intends these final lines for me. She is nothing
    if not direct. I see in these lines intimations of her
    disappearance; what is love but a disappearing act that
    leaves the beholder staggering in blind pursuit? I find Rita
    nowhere, and yet I am in her arms when I awaken. She ties
20 me to her bed.

Her restless words begin, like the lick of snow, their
incisions.

                                                    2001

Phyllis Webb
b. 1927

Born in Victoria, British Columbia, Phyllis Webb graduated from the University of British Columbia in 1949. After running unsuccessfully as a CCF candidate for the provincial legislature in 1949 she moved to Montreal, where she pursued graduate studies at McGill University and came into contact with many of the city's writers, including F.R. Scott. During the 1960s she lived in Toronto, where she conceived the CBC radio program 'Ideas'; from 1966 until 1969 she served as its executive producer. At the end of the decade she returned to the West Coast and settled on Saltspring Island, which remains her home.

Webb's seamless verses are intense lyrical examinations, often of human loneliness and despair, and the perfect shape of her poems brings an order to the seeming shapelessness of the human condition. Just as love offers some meaning to the chaos of life, so, too, poetry offers some order to the chaos. Webb has taught at the University of British Columbia and the University of Victoria.

Marvell's Garden[1]

    Marvell's garden, that place of solitude,
    is where I'd choose to live
    yet is the fixed sundial
    that turns me round
5   unwillingly
    in a hot glade
    as closer, closer I come to contradiction
    to the shade green within the green shade.

---

1 This is a reply to Andrew Marvell's poem 'The Garden' (see p. 447).

The garden where Marvell scorned love's solicitude—
10 that dream—and played instead an arcane solitaire,
shuffling his thoughts like shadowy chance
across the shrubs of ecstasy,
and cast the myths away to flowering hours
as yes, his mind, that sea, caught at green
15 thoughts shadowing a green infinity.

And yet Marvell's garden was not Plato's
garden—and yet—he did care more for the form
of things than for the thing itself—
ideas and visions,
20 resemblances and echoes,
things seeming and being
not quite what they were.

That was his garden, a kind of attitude
struck out of an earth too carefully attended,
25 wanting to be left alone.
And I don't blame him for that.
God knows, too many fences fence us out
and his garden closed in on Paradise.

On Paradise! When I think of his hymning
30 Puritans in the Bermudas, the bright oranges
lighting up that night! When I recall
his rustling tinsel hopes
beneath the cold decree of steel.
Oh, I have wept for some new convulsion
35 to tear together this world and his.

But then I saw his luminous plumèd Wings
prepared for flight,
and then I heard him singing glory
in a green tree,
40 and then I caught the vest he'd laid aside
all blest with fire.

And I have gone walking slowly in
his garden of necessity
leaving brothers, lovers, Christ
45 outside my walls
where they have wept without
and I within.

1956

Lament

Knowing that everything was wrong,
how can we go on giving birth
either to poems or the troublesome lie,
to children, most of all, who sense
5   the stress in our distracted wonder
the instant of their entry with their cry?

For every building in this world
receives our benediction of disease.
Knowing that everything is wrong
10   means only that we all know where we're going.

But I, how can I, I
craving the resolution of my earth,
take up my little gang of sweet pretence
and saunter day-dreary down the alleys, or pursue
15   the half-disastrous night? Where is that virtue
I would claim with tense impersonal unworth,
where does it dwell, that virtuous land
where one can die without a second birth?

It is not here, neither in the petulance
20   of my cries, nor in the tracers of my active fear,
not in my suicide of love, my dear.
That place of perfect animals and men
is simply the circle we would charm our children in
and why we frame our lonely poems in
25   the shape of a frugal sadness.

1962

To Friends Who Have Also Considered Suicide

It's still a good idea.
Its exercise is discipline;
to remember to cross the street without looking,
to remember not to jump when the cars side-swipe,
5   to remember not to bother to have clothes cleaned,
to remember not to eat or want to eat,
to consider the numerous methods of killing oneself,

that is surely the finest exercise of the imagination:
death by drowning, sleeping pills, slashed wrists,
10 kitchen fumes, bullets through the brain or through
the stomach, hanging by the neck in attic or basement,
a clean frozen death—the ways are endless.
And consider the drama! It's better than a whole season
at Stratford when you think of the emotion of your
15 family on hearing the news and when you imagine
how embarrassed some will be when the body is found.
One could furnish a whole chorus in a Greek play
with expletives and feel sneaky and omniscient
at the same time. But there's no shame
20 in this concept of suicide.
It has concerned our best philosophers
and inspired some of the most popular
of our politicians and financiers.
Some people swim lakes, others climb flagpoles,
25 some join monasteries, but we, my friends,
who have considered suicide take our daily walk
with death and are not lonely.
In the end it brings more honesty and care
than all the democratic parliaments of tricks.
30 It is the 'sickness unto death'[1]; it is death;
it is not death; it is the sand from the beaches
of a hundred civilizations, the sand in the teeth
of death and barnacles our singing tongue:
and this is 'life' and we owe at least this much
35 contemplation to our western fact: to Rise,
Decline, Fall, to futility and larks,
to the bright crustaceans of the oversky.

1962

1 The phrase is taken from *The Sickness Unto Death* (1849) by Danish philosopher and theologian Sören Kierkegaard (1813–55); for Kierkegaard, the 'sickness unto death' is despair.

The Days of the Unicorns

I remember when the unicorns
roved in herds through the meadow
behind the cabin, and how they would
lately pause, tilting their jewelled

5   horns to the falling sun as we shared
the tensions of private property
and the need to be alone.

Or as we walked along the beach
a solitary delicate beast
10 might follow on his soft paws
until we turned and spoke the words
to console him.

It seemed they were always near
ready to show their eyes and stare
15 us down, standing in their creamy
skins, pink tongues out
for our benevolence.

As if they knew that always beyond
and beyond the ladies were weaving them
20 into their spider looms.

I knew where they slept
and how the grass was bent
by their own wilderness
and I pitied them.

25 It was only yesterday, or seems
like only yesterday when we could
touch and turn and they came
perfectly real into our fictions.
But they moved on with the courtly sun
30 grazing peacefully beyond the story
horns lowering and lifting and
lowering.

I know this is scarcely credible now
as we cabin ourselves in cold
35 and the motions of panic
and our cells destroy each other
performing music and extinction
and the great dreams pass on
to the common good.

1984

Adrienne Rich
b. 1929

A drienne Rich was born in Baltimore, Maryland, and completed her first book of poetry, *A Change of World* (1952), while still an undergraduate at Radcliffe College in Cambridge, Massachusetts. W.H. Auden, who had chosen her book for publication in the Yale Series of Younger Poets, described her poems as 'neatly and modestly dressed', as poems that 'respect their elders but are not cowed by them.' Rich's work quickly evolved from closed forms to a poetics of change, rooted in a radical imagination and politics. Apparent in her poetry is her maturation from 'the girl who wrote poems, who defined herself in writing poems, and the girl who was to define herself by her relationship with men', to the poet who was 'able to write for the first time, directly about experiencing myself as a woman'. Much of her poetry deals with the separation between men and women, between self and others, though her more recent poetry emphasizes the possibility of a 'common language' that will transcend such separation.

Rich has taught at a number of colleges and universities, including Stanford University. Her most recent books of poetry are *The School Among the Ruins* and *Telephone Ringing in the Labyrinth*. Her prose works include *Of Woman Born: Motherhood as Experience and Institution*, and a selection of her essays, *A Human Eye: Essays on Art in Society*, was published in 2009. She has been the recipient of the Dorothea Tanning Prize of the Academy of American Poets 'for mastery in the art of poetry', the Lannan Foundation Lifetime Achievement Award, and the National Book Foundation's award for Distinguished Contribution to American Letters. She has lived, since 1984, in California.

The Afterwake

Nursing your nerves
to rest, I've roused my own; well,
now for a few bad hours!
Sleep sees you behind closed doors.
5   Alone, I slump in his front parlour.
You're safe inside. Good. But I'm
like a midwife who at dawn
has all in order: bloodstains
washed up, teapot on the stove,
10   and starts her five miles home
walking, the birthyell still
exploding in her head.

Yes, I'm with her now: here's
the streaked, livid road
15   edged with shut houses
breathing night out and in.
Legs tight with fatigue,

we move under morning's coal-blue star,
colossal as this load
20 of unexpired purpose, which drains
slowly, till scissors of cockcrow snip the air.

1963

Moving in Winter

Their life, collapsed like unplayed cards,
is carried piecemeal through the snow:
Headboard and footboard now, the bed
where she has lain desiring him
5   where overhead his sleep will build
its canopy to smother her once more;
their table, by four elbows worn
evening after evening while the wax runs down;
mirrors grey with reflecting them,
10 bureaus coffining from the cold
things that can shuffle in a drawer,
carpets rolled up around those echoes
which, shaken out, take wing and breed
new altercations, the old silences.

1957

Novella

Two people in a room, speaking harshly.
One gets up, goes out to walk.
(That is the man.)
The other goes into the next room
5   and washes the dishes, cracking one.
(That is the woman.)
It gets dark outside.
The children quarrel in the attic.
She has no blood left in her heart.
10 The man comes back to a dark house.
The only light is in the attic.
He has forgotten his key.
He rings at his own door
and hears sobbing on the stairs.
15 The lights go on in the house.
The door closes behind him.
Outside, separate as minds,
the stars too come alight.

1963

Night-Pieces: For a Child

1. The Crib

You sleeping I bend to cover.
Your eyelids work. I see
your dream, cloudy as a negative,
swimming underneath.
5   You blurt a cry. Your eyes
spring open, still filmed in dream.
Wider, they fix me—
—death's head, sphinx, medusa?
You scream.
10   Tears lick my cheeks, my knees
droop at your fear.
Mother I no more am,
but woman, and nightmare.

2. Her Waking

Tonight I jerk astart in a dark
hourless as Hiroshima,
almost hearing you breathe
in a cot three doors away.

5   You still breathe, yes—
and my dream with its gift of knives,
its murderous hider and seeker,
ebbs away, recoils

back into the egg of dreams,
10   the vanishing point of mind.
All gone.

But you and I—
swaddled in a dumb dark
old as sickheartedness,
15   modern as pure annihilation—

we drift in ignorance.
If I could hear you now
mutter some gentle animal sound!
If milk flowed from my breast again. . . .

1966

Rape

There is a cop who is both prowler and father:
he comes from your block, grew up with your brothers,
had certain ideals.
You hardly know him in his boots and silver badge,
5   on horseback, one hand touching his gun.

You hardly know him but you have to get to know him:
he has access to machinery that could kill you.
He and his stallion clop like warlords among the trash,
his ideals stand in the air, a frozen cloud
10   from between his unsmiling lips.

And so, when the time comes, you have to turn to him,
the maniac's sperm still greasing your thighs,
your mind whirling like crazy. You have to confess
to him, you are guilty of the crime
15   of having been forced.

And you see his blue eyes, the blue eyes of all the family
whom you used to know, grow narrow and glisten,
his hand types out the details
and he wants them all
20   but the hysteria in your voice pleases him best.

You hardly know him but now he thinks he knows you:
he has taken down your worst moment
on a machine and filed it in a file.
He knows, or thinks he knows, how much you imagined;
25   he knows, or thinks he knows, what you secretly wanted.

He has access to machinery that could get you put away;
and if, in the sickening light of the precinct,
and if, in the sickening light of the precinct,
your details sound like a portrait of your confessor,
30   will you swallow, will you deny them, will you lie your way home?

1973

Sylvia Plath
1932–1963

Sylvia Plath was the daughter of a high-school teacher of Austrian parentage, and a professor of biology at Boston University, who had emigrated to the United States from Prussia at the age of sixteen and who was an authority on bees. After her father's death in 1940, Plath and her family moved to Wellesley, where her mother taught high school and encouraged her children in their literary pursuits. By the time Plath entered Smith College, she was beginning to have her poems and short stories published. She graduated from Smith in 1955 and won a Fulbright Scholarship to Newnham College, Cambridge. There she met, and in 1956 married, British poet Ted Hughes. Except for a year during which Plath taught freshman English at Smith College, the couple lived in England. In 1960, Plath published her first book of poems, *Colossus*, and her first child was born. After the birth of a second child in 1962, Plath and Hughes separated. Plath was frequently ill, working to support herself and her children, and waking before daybreak to write her poetry, turning out two to three poems a day. The strain proved too great, and she took her life in February 1963.

Sheep in Fog

The hills step off into whiteness.
People or stars
Regard me sadly, I disappoint them.

The train leaves a line of breath.
5   O slow
Horse the colour of rust,

Hooves, dolorous bells—
All morning the
Morning has been blackening,

10   A flower left out.
My bones hold a stillness, the far
Fields melt my heart.

They threaten
To let me through to a heaven
15   Starless and fatherless, a dark water.

1966

Daddy

You do not do, you do not do
Any more, black shoe
In which I have lived like a foot
For thirty years, poor and white,
5   Barely daring to breathe or Achoo.

Daddy, I have had to kill you.
You died before I had time—
Marble-heavy, a bag full of God,
Ghastly statue with one grey toe
10   Big as a Frisco seal

And a head in the freakish Atlantic
Where it pours bean green over blue
In the waters off beautiful Nauset.
I used to pray to recover you.
15   Ach, du.

In the German tongue, in the Polish town
Scraped flat by the roller
Of wars, wars, wars.
But the name of the town is common.
20   My Polack friend

Says there are a dozen or two.
So I never could tell where you
Put your foot, your root,
I never could talk to you.
25   The tongue stuck in my jaw.

It stuck in a barb wire snare.
Ich, ich, ich, ich,
I could hardly speak.
I thought every German was you.
30   And the language obscene

An engine, an engine
Chuffing me off like a Jew.
A Jew to Dachau, Auschwitz, Belsen.
I began to talk like a Jew.
35   I think I may well be a Jew.

The snows of the Tyrol, the clear beer of Vienna
Are not very pure or true.
With my gypsy ancestress and my weird luck
And my Taroc pack and my Taroc pack
40   I may be a bit of a Jew.

I have always been scared of *you*.
With your Luftwaffe, your gobbledygoo.
And your neat mustache
And your Aryan eye, bright blue.
45   Panzer-man, panzer-man, O You—

Not God but a swastika
So black no sky could squeak through.
Every woman adores a Fascist,
The boot in the face, the brute
50   Brute heart of a brute like you.

You stand at the blackboard, daddy,
In the picture I have of you,
A cleft in your chin instead of your foot
But no less a devil for that, no not
55   Any less the black man who

Bit my pretty red heart in two.
I was ten when they buried you.
At twenty I tried to die
And get back, back, back to you.
60   I thought even the bones would do.

But they pulled me out of the sack,
And they stuck me together with glue.
And then I knew what to do.
I made a model of you,
65   A man black with a Meinkampf look

And a love of the rack and the screw.
And I said I do, I do.
So daddy, I'm finally through.
The black telephone's off at the root,
70   The voices just can't worm through.

If I've killed one man, I've killed two—
The vampire who said he was you
And drank my blood for a year,
Seven years, if you want to know.
75   Daddy, you can lie back now.

There's a stake in your fat black heart
And the villagers never liked you.
They are dancing and stamping on you.
They always *knew* it was you.
80   Daddy, daddy, you bastard, I'm through.

1966

Kindness

Kindness glides about my house.
Dame Kindness, she is so nice!
The blue and red jewels of her rings smoke
In the windows, the mirrors
5   Are filling with smiles.

What is so real as the cry of a child?
A rabbit's cry may be wilder
But it has no soul.
Sugar can cure everything, so Kindness says.
10   Sugar is a necessary fluid,

Its crystals a little poultice.
O kindness, kindness
Sweetly picking up pieces!
My Japanese silks, desperate butterflies,
15   May be pinned any minute, anaesthetized.

And here you come, with a cup of tea
Wreathed in steam.
The blood jet is poetry,
There is no stopping it.
20   You hand me two children, two roses.

1966

Edge

The woman is perfected.
Her dead

Body wears the smile of accomplishment,
The illusion of a Greek necessity

5   Flows in the scrolls of her toga,
Her bare

Feet seem to be saying:
We have come so far, it is over.

Each dead child coiled, a white serpent,
10   One at each little

Pitcher of milk, now empty.
She has folded

Them back into her body as petals
Of a rose close when the garden

15   Stiffens and odours bleed
From the sweet, deep throats of the night flower.

The moon has nothing to be sad about,
Staring from her hood of bone.

She is used to this sort of thing.
20   Her blacks crackle and drag.

1966

Words

Axes
After whose stroke the wood rings,
And the echoes!
Echoes travelling
5   Off from the centre like horses.

The sap
Wells like tears, like the
Water striving
To re-establish its mirror
10 Over the rock

That drops and turns,
A white skull,
Eaten by weedy greens.
Years later I
15 Encounter them on the road—

Words dry and riderless,
The indefatigable hooftaps.
While
From the bottom of the pool, fixed stars
20 Govern a life.

1966

Margaret Atwood
b. 1939

◆

The most prolific writer of her generation in Canada, Margaret Atwood is the author and editor of more than thirty books of poetry, short fiction, and literary criticism, as well as novels. Born in Ottawa, she spent her early years in the bush country of Quebec and northern Ontario; when she was seven years old, her family settled in Toronto. Atwood graduated from the University of Toronto in 1961, obtained her MA from Radcliffe College, and pursued doctoral studies in Victorian literature at Harvard University. Her first volume of poetry, *Double Persephone*, appeared in 1961; her first novel, *The Edible Woman*, appeared in 1967. She sees her work, poetry and fiction, as an artistic lens focused carefully and caringly on contemporary society. Her poetry, which may seem almost prosaic in its stark verse patterns, captures with clinical precision the subjects of her sensitive explorations. An ardent nationalist, she is a frequent and articulate speaker for Canada on both the national and international stages.

At the Tourist Centre in Boston

There is my country under glass,
a white relief-
map with red dots for the cities,
reduced to the size of a wall

5   and beside it 10 blownup snapshots
one for each province,
in purple-browns and odd reds,
the green of the trees dulled;
all blues however
10   of an assertive purity.

Mountains and lakes and more lakes
(though Quebec is a restaurant and Ontario the empty
interior of the parliament buildings),
with nobody climbing the trails and hauling out
15   the fish and splashing in the water

but arrangements of grinning tourists —
look here, Saskatchewan
is a flat lake, some convenient rocks
where two children pose with a father
20   and the mother is cooking something
in immaculate slacks by a smokeless fire,
her teeth white as detergent.

Whose dream is this, I would like to know:
is this a manufactured
25   hallucination, a cynical fiction, a lure
for export only?

I seem to remember people,
at least in the cities, also slush,
machines and assorted garbage. Perhaps
30   that was my private mirage
which will just evaporate
when I go back. Or the citizens will be gone,
run off to the peculiarly-
green forests
35   to wait among the brownish mountains
for the platoons of tourists
and plan their old red massacres.

1968

Death of a Young Son by Drowning

He, who navigated with success
the dangerous river of his own birth
once more set forth

on a voyage of discovery
5   into the land I floated on
but could not touch to claim.

His feet slid on the bank,
the currents took him;
he swirled with ice and trees in the swollen water

10   and plunged into distant regions,
his head a bathysphere;
through his eyes' thin glass bubbles

he looked out, reckless adventurer
on a landscape stranger than Uranus
15   we have all been to and some remember.

There was an accident; the air locked,
he was hung in the river like a heart.
They retrieved the swamped body,

cairn of my plans and future charts,
20   with poles and hooks
from among the nudging logs.

It was spring, the sun kept shining, the new grass
lept to solidity;
my hands glistened with details.

25   After the long trip I was tired of waves.
My foot hit rock. The dreamed sails
collapsed, ragged.

I planted him in this country
like a flag.

1970

Variations on the Word *Love*

This is a word we use to plug
holes with. It's the right size for those warm
blanks in speech, for those red heart-
shaped vacancies on the page that look nothing
5   like real hearts. Add lace
and you can sell
it. We insert it also in the one empty
space on the printed form
that comes with no instructions. There are whole
10   magazines with not much in them
but the word *love*, you can
rub it all over your body and you
can cook with it too. How do we know
it isn't what goes on at the cool
15   debaucheries of slugs under damp
pieces of cardboard? As for the weed-
seedlings nosing their tough snouts up
among the lettuces, they shout it.
Love! Love! sing the soldiers, raising
20   their glittering knives in salute.

Then there's the two
of us. This word
is far too short for us, it has only
four letters, too sparse
25   to fill those deep bare
vacuums between the stars
that press on us with their deafness.
It's not love we don't wish
to fall into, but that fear.
30   This word is not enough but it will
have to do. It's a single
vowel in this metallic
silence, a mouth that says
O again and again in wonder
35   and pain, a breath, a finger-
grip on a cliffside. You can
hold on or let go.

1981

Variation on the Word *Sleep*

I would like to watch you sleeping,
which may not happen.
I would like to watch you,
sleeping. I would like to sleep
5   with you, to enter
your sleep as its smooth dark wave
slides over my head

and walk with you through that lucent
wavering forest of bluegreen leaves
10 with its watery sun & three moons
towards the cave where you must descend,
towards your worst fear
I would like to give you the silver
branch, the small white flower, the one
15 word that will protect you
from the grief at the centre
of your dream, from the grief
at the centre. I would like to follow
you up the long stairway
20 again & become
the boat that would row you back
carefully, a flame
in two cupped hands
to where your body lies
25 beside me, and you enter
it as easily as breathing in

I would like to be the air
that inhabits you for a moment
only. I would like to be that unnoticed
30 & that necessary.

1981

Interlunar

Darkness waits apart from any occasion for it;
like sorrow it is always available.
This is only one kind,

the kind in which there are stars
5   above the leaves, brilliant as steel nails
and countless and without regard.

We are walking together
on dead wet leaves in the intermoon
among the looming nocturnal rocks
10 which would be pinkish grey
in daylight, gnawed and softened
by moss and ferns, which would be green,
in the musty fresh yeast smell
of trees rotting, each returning
15 itself to itself

and I take your hand, which is the shape a hand
would be if you existed truly.
I wish to show you the darkness
you are so afraid of.

20 Trust me. This darkness
is a place you can enter and be
as safe in as you are anywhere;
you can put one foot in front of the other
and believe the sides of your eyes.
25 Memorize it. You will know it
again in your own time.
When the appearances of things have left you,
you will still have this darkness.
Something of your own you can carry with you.

30 We have come to the edge:
the lake gives off its hush;
in the outer night there is a barred owl
calling, like a moth
against the ear, from the far shore
35 which is invisible.
The lake, vast and dimensionless,
doubles everything, the stars,
the boulders, itself, even the darkness
that you can walk so long in
40 it becomes light.

1984

The Door

The door swings open,
you look in.
It's dark in there,
most likely spiders:
5   nothing you want.
You feel scared.
The door swings closed.

The full moon shines,
it's full of delicious juice;
10   you buy a purse,
the dance is nice.
The door opens
and swings closed so quickly
you don't notice.

15   The sun comes out,
you have swift breakfasts
with your husband, who is still thin;
you wash the dishes,
you love your children,
20   you read a book,
you go to the movies.
It rains moderately.

The door swings open,
you look in:
25   why does this keep happening now?
Is there a secret?
The door swings closed.

The snow falls,
you clear the walk while breathing heavily;
30   it's not as easy as once.
Your children telephone sometimes.
The roof needs fixing.
You keep yourself busy.
The spring arrives.

35   The door swings open:
it's dark in there,
with many steps going down.
But what is that shining?
Is it water?

40   The door swings closed.

The dog has died.
This happened before.
You got another;
not this time though.
45   Where is your husband?
You gave up the garden.
It became too much.
At night there are blankets;
nonetheless you are wakeful.

50   The door swings open:
O god of hinges,
god of long voyages,
you have kept faith.
It's dark in there.
55   You confide yourself to the darkness.
You step in.
The door swings closed.

2007

Roy Miki
b. 1942

◆

Born in Winnipeg, Roy Miki obtained his BA (1964) from the University of Manitoba, his MA (1969) from Simon Fraser University, and his PhD (1980) from the University of British Columbia. A poet and professor in the Department of English at Simon Fraser University, he is also the editor of *West Coast Line: A Journal of Contemporary Writing and Criticism*. As an editor, he has also published collections by George Bowering and Roy Kiyooka, and he has written a book on Wallace Stevens. His personal and language-centred poetry has won many prizes, including the Governor General's Award for *Surrender* (2002). He has also written political books on the Japanese-Canadian experience and the question of redress for Canadian behaviour during the Second World War.

make it new

i have altered my tactics to reflect the new era

already the magnolia broken by high winds
heals itself

the truncated branches already
5   speak to me.

the hallucinated cartoons spread their wings
no less eagles than the amber destination
of wanton discourses—
                discards

      say what you will
10   the mountain ranges
once so populated with fleeting images
      look more attractive

      histoires statistics documents
daily polls headlines make the blood rush

15   the earth is not heavy
with the weight of centuries
                nor do bodies
of multitudes tread muted on fleet denizens

in the declension of plumed echoes
    or is it contractual fumes
20   the sunset clause expires

2001

attractive

the distaste for turmoil
embroiled oceanic slips

like wandering on tarmac
looking for insularity
5   finding dry grass

the promise of unbridled
recompense—risen dough
in the non-chalence forms

bleached by similitude
10   the probate will runs on
neutral—gravity's weal

it's the sonic boom of
a lingual disequilibrium

the disinherited tracts of
15   murmur's master stroke

two syllables making out
in the compact rumble seat

tease of would you take
a turn if you had a choice

20   rather the brain child of
sea wagers than intervals

raucous vibes in the sunder
down of lyric i am ambushed

let's get serious a poetic
25   *text has to resonate*

                      has
to transport emotion to an
island called identity

what you want is the death
of continuity the death of
30   *narration*

                    death itself

you're a cancer

               on the
body of real literature

you're a wart

               on the
backside of texts erotique

35   *you're the clad maw*

       of iron hick crescendo

babble brain

         yeah like self
reliance is a liberal habit

the lame leap freight cars
40   the careen of nomadic lobes
the lubricants rescue the wheels

2001

subversion in tokyo

      1

offset on the page
the follow up seduction
equal to

rivulets of end
5   *rime give way*

sat on the premise
in the place marked
by footfalls

primed for the takeover
10   *of unnamed agents*
of chorded echoes

stood out in the crowd
waving angles a brush
the rail

15   *let breath out of*
rectangular vehicles
rib the retinue

on the periphery
the alliance whets
20   the forecast

he (the young boy)
climbs the stairs
drops a coin chants

the decoding is no
25   warning and offers
no consolation

the crow's hah startles
the voice nearly audible
why these letters bind

30   barred from the mirror
the docile chagrin
takes an effort

wonder what the dime sighs
the wishbone always last
35   *to record effects*

the timing offered no
respite out of time
all as out takes

bear with me lateral
40   *inculcations embossage*
an aberrant calling

2

found inside the
shrine's elsewhere
crowded in

45   *the need to write*
to fall on letters
is not a right

bowing the ease
the interest from
50   nestling toward

> *i circle the densha*
> *sitting with my elbows*
> *tucked in oddities of optics*

escape zones untranslated
55   rant against the lines
dipped into

> *geta bare feet*
> *figure in newsprint*
> *who could be my brother*

60   all the while
a transition to
camouflage the scene

2001

on the sublime

a poem does not beg for forgiveness. it's not like real life.
not a case of relationships gone awry. its social
innuendoes are not a matter of secrets told in privacy.

once the consideration of intent is or was misplaced.
5   once it was a misdemeanour to forego the forlorn.

memory is a stranger. a maverick sound that crowds out
noise. the ease of its deployment is dependent on the size
of the ache.

when it drops into a sullied lap.

10   i hesitate to use the first person in this instance. a binge
of bebop is no ticket to oblivion. the causal routes are
dogged with yelping signatures with nowhere to sign.

the sojourner notwithstanding.

'we' listened at the fork in the road. 'i've heard that
15   before.' the clause was held in perpetuity.

cacophonous airwaves are all the rage. the rollycoaster
on overdrive dallies then engages in tumult. fear is driven
deeper into the social debt of syntax controls and
formations that giggle on freeway billboards.

20   if its hem is showing.

'i wander by the corner store, gazing at the figures
winking back.' the encounter has ripple effects that
accumulate and announce the dispatch. the few who are
deaf to tonal variations listen to the heat waves instead.

25   the transportation wins approval.

when logic fails, logic hails a cab. 'we' cruise the early
morning city streets. the headlines as headlights. a
concept dying on the dashboard.

2001

Michael Ondaatje
b. 1943

Born in Sri Lanka (then Ceylon), Michael Ondaatje moved to England in 1954 before settling in Canada in 1963. He obtained his BA from the University of Toronto and his MA from Queen's University. He taught English at the University of Western Ontario before joining the Department of English at Glendon College, York University, in 1971. Poet and novelist, critic and editor, he constantly questions the dimension between poetry and prose and between fact and fiction in writing that challenges his readers' perception and understanding of reality. *The Collected Works of Billy the Kid* (1970), a collage of poetry, prose, and photographs, is a discontinuous narrative of Billy the Kid and Pat Garrett that explores the traditional interpretation of this duo as insane outlaw-renegade and sane representative of law and order. *Running in the Family* (1982), also a collage, is the story of Ondaatje's own family, transformed into fiction. Always intensely visual, his poetry eschews formal structures in order to capture with vivid immediacy the dramatic dimensions of a particular character or moment. He has won international acclaim for both his poetry and his novels, including *The English Patient*, which was awarded the prestigious Booker Prize and made into a successful Hollywood film.

Bearhug

Griffin calls to come and kiss him goodnight
I yell ok. Finish something I'm doing,
then something else, walk slowly round
the corner to my son's room.
5 He is standing arms outstretched
waiting for a bearhug. Grinning.

Why do I give my emotion an animal's name,
give it that dark squeeze of death?
This is the hug which collects
10 all his small bones and his warm neck against me.
The thin tough body under the pyjamas
locks to me like a magnet of blood.

How long was he standing there
like that, before I came?

1979

Letters & Other Worlds

*'for there was no more darkness for him and, no doubt like
Adam before the fall, he could see in the dark'* [1]

My father's body was a globe of fear
His body was a town we never knew
He hid that he had been where we were going
His letters were a room he seldom lived in
5 In them the logic of his love could grow

My father's body was a town of fear
He was the only witness to its fear dance
He hid where he had been that we might lose him
His letters were a room his body scared

10 He came to death with his mind drowning.
On the last day he enclosed himself
in a room with two bottles of gin, later
fell the length of his body
so that brain blood moved
15 to new compartments

---

1 translation from Alfred Jarry's *La Dragonne* (1943), cited in *The Banquet Years* by Roger Shattuck (1955)

that never knew the wash of fluid
and he died in minutes of a new equilibrium.

His early life was a terrifying comedy
and my mother divorced him again and again.
20   He would rush into tunnels magnetized
by the white eye of trains
and once, gaining instant fame,
managed to stop a Perahara[2] in Ceylon
—the whole procession of elephants dancers
25   local dignitaries—by falling
dead drunk into the street.

As a semi-official, and semi-white at that,
the act was seen as a crucial
turning point in the Home Rule Movement
30   and led to Ceylon's independence in 1948.
(My mother had done her share too—
her driving so bad
she was stoned by villagers
whenever her car was recognized)

35   For 14 years of marriage
each of them claimed he or she
was the injured party.
Once on the Colombo docks
saying goodbye to a recently married couple
40   my father, jealous
at my mother's articulate emotion,
dove into the waters of the harbour
and swam after the ship waving farewell.
My mother pretending no affiliation
45   mingled with the crowd back to the hotel.

Once again he made the papers
though this time my mother
with a note to the editor
corrected the report—saying he was drunk
50   rather than broken hearted at the parting of friends.
The married couple received both editions
of *The Ceylon Times* when their ship reached Aden.[3]

2 religious ceremony celebrated by a parade
3 capital of the British colony of the same name (Aden is now the capital of Southern Yemen)

And then in his last years
he was a silent drinker,
55 the man who once a week
disappeared into his room with bottles
and stayed there until he was drunk
and until he was sober.

There speeches, head dreams, apologies,
60 the gentle letters, were composed.
With the clarity of architects
he would write of the row of blue flowers
his new wife had planted,
the plans for electricity in the house,
65 how my half-sister fell near a snake
and it had awakened and not touched her.
Letters in a clear hand of the most complete empathy
his heart widening and widening and widening
to all manner of change in his children and friends
70 while he himself edged
into the terrible acute hatred
of his own privacy
till he balanced and fell
the length of his body
75 the blood screaming in
the empty reservoir of bones
the blood searching in his head without metaphor

1973

Elizabeth

Catch, my Uncle Jack said
and oh I caught this huge apple
red as Mrs Kelly's bum.

It's red as Mrs Kelly's bum, I said
5 and Daddy roared
and swung me on his stomach with a heave.
Then I hid the apple in my room
till it shrunk like a face
growing eyes and teeth ribs.

10   Then Daddy took me to the zoo
he knew a man there
they put a snake around my neck
and it crawled down the front of my dress.
I felt its flicking tongue
15   dripping onto me like a shower.
Daddy laughed and said Smart Snake
and Mrs Kelly with us scowled.

In the pond where they kept the goldfish
Philip and I broke the ice with spades
20   and tried to spear the fishes;

we killed one and Phillip ate it,
then he kissed me
with raw saltless fish in his mouth.

My sister Mary's got bad teeth
25   and said I was lucky, then she said
I had big teeth, but Philip said I was pretty.
He had big hands that smelled.

I would speak of Tom, soft laughing,
who danced in the mornings round the sundial
30   teaching me the steps from France, turning
with the rhythm of the sun on the warped branches,
who'd hold my breast and watch it move like a snail
leaving his quick urgent love in my palm.
And I kept his love in my palm till it blistered.

35   When they axed his shoulders and neck
the blood moved like a branch into the crowd.
And he staggered with his hanging shoulder
cursing their thrilled cry, wheeling,
waltzing in the French style to his knees
40   holding his head with the ground,
blood settling on his clothes like a blush;
this way
when they aimed the thud into his back.

And I find cool entertainment now
45   with white young Essex, and my nimble rhymes.[1]

1979

1 The 'Elizabeth' of this poem is Elizabeth I (1533–1603), who assumed the throne of England in 1558 following the reigns of her father, Henry VIII (1491–1547), her brother Edward VI (1537–53), and her sister Mary Tudor (1515–58). 'Philip' is Philip II of Spain (1527–98), who married Mary Tudor in 1554; 'Tom' is Lord Thomas Seymour of Sudeley (1508?–49), whose repeated attempts to compromise and marry the adolescent Elizabeth, as well as to overthrow his brother Edward Seymour, the protector of Edward VI, led to his execution; 'Essex' is the second Earl of Essex, Robert Devereux (1566–1601), soldier and favourite of Elizabeth, who was executed for attempting to incite an uprising against the court. 'Uncle Jack' and 'Mrs Kelly' are characters invented by Ondaatje.

The Cinnamon Peeler

If I were a cinnamon peeler[1]
I would ride your bed
and leave the yellow bark dust
on your pillow.

5   Your breasts and shoulders would reek
you could never walk through markets
without the profession of my fingers
floating over you. The blind would
stumble certain of whom they approached
10 though you might bathe
under rain gutters, monsoon.

Here on the upper thigh
at this smooth pasture
neighbour to your hair
15 or the crease
that cuts your back. This ankle.
You will be known among strangers
as the cinnamon peeler's wife.

I could hardly glance at you
20 before marriage
never touch you
—your keen nosed mother, your rough brothers.
I buried my hands
in saffron, disguised them
25 over smoking tar,
helped the honey gatherers . . .

1 one who peels the cinnamon bark, the source of the spice, from the trees

When we swam once
I touched you in water
and our bodies remained free,
30   you could hold me and be blind of smell.
You climbed on the bank and said
        this is how you touch other women
the grass cutter's wife, the lime burner's daughter.
And you searched your arms
35   for the missing perfume
                and knew

        what good is it
to be the lime burner's daughter
left with no trace
40   as if not spoken to in the act of love
as if wounded without the pleasure of a scar.

You touched
your belly to my hands
in the dry air and said
45   I am the cinnamon
peeler's wife. Smell me.

1982

Robert Bringhurst
b. 1946

Born in Los Angeles, California, of Canadian parents, Robert Bringhurst studied at the Massachusetts Institute of Technology and the University of Utah before taking his BA in comparative literature from Indiana University (1973) and his MFA in creative writing from the University of British Columbia (1975). A restlessly intellectual poet who is never sentimental or confessional, he broke away from the modernist techniques of Pound and Eliot to create his own unique way of regarding the world around him. Showing little support for the crass materialism of the present age, he captures the beauty of the past and the wisdom of the ages in austere poetry that is often rich with allusions. 'I wanted — no matter how preposterous and impossible it might be — to learn all the words and grammars in the world,' he affirms. 'Poetry nevertheless precedes them all and can make its way, if it must, with the help of none.' It is the importance Bringhurst places on the past that makes him a tireless researcher into North American cultural history, seeking an understanding of the diverse cultures and their oral literatures.

Essay on Adam

There are five possibilities. One: Adam fell.
Two: he was pushed. Three: he jumped. Four:
he only looked over the edge, and one look silenced him.
Five: nothing worth mentioning happened to Adam.

5   The first, that he fell, is too simple. The fourth,
fear, we have tried. It is useless. The fifth,
nothing happened, is dull. The choices are these:
he jumped or was pushed. And the difference between them

is only an issue of whether the demons
10   work from the inside out or from the outside
in: the one
theological question.

1975

The Stonecutter's Horses

Sepe de eo mecum cogitans de quo nemo nimis pauci satis cogitant. . . .[1]

§ Pavia, 4 April 1370:

Francesco Petrarca (1304–1374)[2]

[Francesca], *his illegitimate daughter*

Franceschino da Brossano, *in law Petrarca's
adopted son, but in actuality his son-in-law*

I, Francesco, this April day . . .
death stirs like a bud in the sunlight, and Urban
has got off his French duff and re-entered Rome[3]
and for three years running has invited me to Rome . . .
5   over the bright hills and down the Cassia,
back through Arezzo one more time . . .

---

1 'Thinking often about what no one considers very much and few enough. . . .'
2 the Italian poet, scholar, and humanist best known as Petrarch (the Latinized form of his name)
3 With the appointment of a French pope, Clement V, in 1305, the seat of the papacy was moved to Avignon and
    fell under the control of the French monarchy until 1378. Pope Urban V made an unsuccessful attempt to bring
    the papacy from Avignon to Rome (1367–70), a move Petrarch had long supported.

my age sixty-five and my birthday approaching,
the muggers on the streets in broad daylight in Rome,
the hawks and the buzzards. . . .
                                        Take this down.

10   No one has thought too deeply of death.
      So few have left anything toward or against it.
      Peculiar, since thinking of death can never be
      wasted thinking, nor can it be come to
      too quickly. A man carries his death with him
15   everywhere, waiting, but seldom thinking
      of waiting. Death is uncommonly like the soul.

      What I own other than that ought to fall
      of its own weight and settle. But beggars and tycoons
      and I are concerned with our possessions,
20   and a man with a reputation for truth
      must have one also for precision.
                                        I leave
      my soul to my saviour, my corpse to the earth.
      And let it be done without any parades.
      I don't care very much where I'm buried,
25   so it please God and whoever is digging.
      Still, you will ask. You will badger me.
      If I am dead you will badger each other.
      But don't lug my bones through the public streets
      in a box to be gabbled at and gawked at and followed.
30   Let it be done without any parades.

      If I die here in Padova, bury me here
      near the friend who is dead who invited me here.
      If I die on my farm, you can use the chapel
      I mean to build there, if I ever build it.
35   If not, try the village down the road.

      If in Venezia, near the doorway.
      If in Milano, next to the wall.
      In Pavia, anywhere. Or if in Rome—
      if in Rome, in the centre, of course, if there's room.
40   These are the places I think I might die in
      in Italy.
                  Or if I happen to be in Parma,
      there is the cathedral, of which for some reason

I am the archdeacon. But I will avoid
going to Parma. It would scarcely be possible,
45 I suppose, in Parma, not to have a parade.

At any rate, put what flesh I have left
in a church. A Franciscan church if there is one.
I don't want it feeding a tree from which
rich people's children swipe apples.

50 Two hundred ducats go to the church in which
I am buried, with another hundred to be given
out in that parish to the poor, in small doses.
The money to the church, let it buy a piece of land
and the land be rented and the rental from the land
55 pay for an annual mass in my name.
I will be fitter company in that sanctuary
then, present in spirit and name only,
than this way, muttering to the blessed virgin
through my hemorrhoids and bad teeth. I should be glad
60 to be rid of this sagging carcass.
                              Don't write that.

I have cleared no fields of their stones. I have built
no barns and no castles. I have built a name
out of other men's voices by banging my own
like a kitchen pan. My name to the Church
65 with the money it takes to have it embalmed.

Very few other things. My Giotto[4] to the Duke.
Most men cannot fathom its beauty. Those
who know painting are stunned by it. The Duke
does not need another Giotto, but the Duke knows painting.

70 To Dondi,[5] money for a plain ring to remind him
to read me.
              To Donato—what? I forgive him
the loan of whatever he owes me. And I
myself am in debt to della Seta. Pay

---

4 that is, a work by innovative Florentine painter Giotto di Bondone (c. 1267–1337)
5 Giovanni Dondi (c. 1318–1389), a noted humanist and friend of Petrarch's, a professor of medicine, mathematics, and philosophy. 'Donato' is Donato degli Albanzani da Pratovecchio, who translated Petrarch's *De viris illus-tribus*—a series of biographies of figures from Antiquity (begun c. 1338)—into Italian. Lombardo della Seta assisted Petrarch in the writing of this work.

that, if I haven't paid it. And give him
75   my silver cup. Della Seta drinks
water. Damned metal ruins the wine.

To Boccaccio,[6] I am unworthy to leave
anything, and have nothing worthy to leave.
Money then, for a coat to keep himself warm
80   when he works after dark, as he frequently does,
while the river wind stutters and bleats at his window,
and his hand-me-down cordwood fizzles and steams.

My lute to Tommaso.[7] I hope he will play it
for God and himself and not to gain fame
85   for his playing.
                            These are such trivial legacies.

Money to Pancaldo,[8] but not for the card table.
Money to Zilio—at least his back salary.
Money to the other servants. Money to the cook.
Money to their heirs if they die before I do.
90   Give my Bible back to the Church.
                                        And my horses . . .
my horses.
                    Let a few of my friends, if they wish to,
draw lots for my horses. Horses
are horses. They cannot be given away.

The rest to my heir and executor, Brossano,
95   who knows he is to split it, and how he is to split it,
and the names I prefer not to put into this
instrument. Names of no other importance.
Care for them. Care for them here in this house
if you can. And don't sell off the land to get money
100   in any case. Selling the earth without cause
from the soul is simony, Brossano. Real-estate
hucksters are worse than funeral parades.
I have lived long enough in quite enough
cities, notwithstanding the gifts

---

6 Giovanni Boccaccio (1313–74), the famous Italian poet and storyteller best known for *The Decameron* (1351–3);
   his work was influenced by Petrarch, and they were lifelong friends from the time of their initial meeting in
   1350. His old age was troubled by poverty and ill health.
7 The poet Tommaso Caloiro, also known as Tomasso da Messina, was a friend and correspondent of Petrarch's.
8 'Pancaldo': Like Zilio, one of Petrarch's servants.

105   of free lodging in some of them, long enough, Brossano,
to know the breath moves underfoot in the clay.
The stone quarried and cut and reset
in the earth is a lover's embrace, not an overlay.

The heart splits like a chinquapin pod,
110   spilling its angular seed on the ground.

Though we ride to Rome and back aboard animals,
nothing ever takes root on the move.
I have seen houses and fields bartered
like cargo on shipboard. But nothing takes root
115   without light in the eye and earth in the hand.

The land is our solitude and our silence.
A man should hoard what little silence
he is given and what little solitude he can get.

Just the one piece over the mountains
120   ought, I think, to be given away. Everything
I have ever done that has lasted began there.
And I think my heir will have no need to go there.

If Brossano die before I do,
look to della Seta. And for his part, let him
125   look into that cup. He will know my mind.

A man who can write as I can ought not
to talk of such things at such length. Keep this
back if you can. Let the gifts speak
for themselves if you can, small though they are.
130   But I don't like the thought of what little there is
spilling into the hands of lawyers through lawsuits.
The law is no ritual meant to be practised
in private by scavengers. Law is the celebration
of duty and the ceremony of vengeance. The Duke's
135   law has nothing to do with my death
or with horses.
            Done.
               Ask the notary to come over
precisely at noon. I will rewrite it
and have it to sign by the time he arrives.

1979

Leda and the Swan[1]

for George Faludy

Before the black beak reappeared
like a grin from in back of a drained cup,
letting her drop,
she fed at the sideboard of his thighs,
5   the lank air tightening in the sunrise,
yes. But no, she put on no knowledge
with his power. And it was his power alone
that she saved of him for her daughter.
Not his knowledge.
10 No.
He was the one who put on knowledge.
He was the one who looked down out of heaven
with a dark croak, knowing more
than he had ever known before,
15 and knowing he knew it:

knowing the xylophone of her bones,
the lute of her back and the harp of her belly,
the flute of her throat,
woodwinds and drums of her muscles,
20 knowing the organ pipes of her veins;

knowing her as a man knows mountains he has hunted
naked and alone in—
knowing the fruits, the roots and the grasses,
the tastes of the streams
25 and the depths of the mosses,
knowing as he moves in the darkness he is also
resting at noon in the shade of her blood—
leaving behind him in the sheltered places
glyphs meaning mineral and moonlight and mind
30 and possession and memory,
leaving on the outcrops signs meaning mountain
and sunlight and lust and rest and forgetting.

Yes. And the beak that opened to croak
of his knowing that morning creaked like a rehung
35 door and said nothing, felt nothing. The past
is past. What is known is as lean

1 Compare with Yeats's poem, p. 556

as the day's edge and runs
one direction. The truth floats
down, out of fuel,
40 indigestible, like a feather. The lady
herself, though—whether
or not she was truth or untruth, or both, or was neither—
she dropped through the air like a looped rope,
a necklace of meaning, remembering
45 everything forward and backward—
the middle, the end, the beginning—
and lit like a fishing skiff gliding aground.

That evening, of course, while her husband, to whom
she told nothing, strode like the king
50 of Lakonia through the orchestra
pit of her body, touching
this key and that string in his passing,
she lay like so much
green kindling,
55 fouled tackle and horse harness under his hands
and said nothing, felt
nothing, but only
lay thinking
not flutes, lutes and xylophones,
60 no: thinking soldiers
and soldiers and soldiers and soldiers
and daughters,
the rustle of knives in his motionless wings.

1982

Dionne Brand

b. 1953

Dionne Brand was born in Guayaguayare, Trinidad, and emigrated in 1970 to Canada, where she 'joined the civil rights, feminist and socialist movements. I was only seventeen but I already knew that to live freely in the world as a Black woman I would have to involve myself in political action as well as writing.' She obtained her BA (1975) in English and philosophy from the University of Toronto, later completing her MA (1988) in educational studies. As an editor and essayist as well as a poet and fiction writer, she concerns herself with the damage and tragedy brought about by sexism and racism, especially with the repres-

sion that continues to exist in Canada. From her own experiences as an immigrant in a supposedly tolerant new land, as someone from a racial minority, and as a lesbian, she writes cogently of dislocation. In *Land to Light On* (1997), which won the Governor General's Award for Poetry and the Trillium Award for Literature, she studies immigrant exile, voicing despair in a world brutalized by global politics and oppressed by its failure to achieve equality for women and racialized people. The immigrant condition is central also to *Thirsty* (2002), a long poem that presents the modern city of Toronto with a murky, indeed tragic underside.

Islands Vanish

XIII

In this country where islands vanish, bodies submerge,
the heart of darkness is these white roads, snow
at our throats, and at the windshield a thick white cop
in a blue steel windbreaker peering into our car, suspiciously,
5   even in the blow and freeze of a snowstorm, or perhaps
not suspicious but as a man looking at aliens.
Three Blacks in a car on a road blowing eighty miles an hour
in the wind between a gas station and Chatham. We stumble
on our antiquity. The snow-blue laser of a cop's eyes fixes us
10   in this unbearable archaeology.

How quickly the planet can take itself back. I saw this
once in the summer in daylight, corn dangling bronze, flat
farm land growing flatter, eaten up in highways, tonight,
big and rolling it is storming in its sleep. A cop is standing at its
15   lip.

Coca-Cola can light, the car shakes, trembles along as in a
gutter, a bellow of wind rushes into my face breathless

checking the snowbank, I might have seen something
out there, every two minutes the imagination conjures
20   an exact bridge, the mind insists on solidity, we lose
the light of the car ahead, in the jagged beam of the cop's
blistering eye we lose the names of things, the three of us,
two women who love women, one man with so many demons
already his left foot is cold, still, making our way to Chatham,
25   Buxton, waiting as they once waited for Black travellers like us,
blanketed, tracked in this cold shimmering.

Out there I see nothing . . . not one thing out there
just the indifference of a cop. It takes us six hours
to travel three. I coil myself up into a nerve and quarrel
30   with the woman, lover, and the man for landing me in
this white hell.

We have been in this icy science only a short time. What
we are doing here is not immediately understandable
and no one is more aware of it than we, she from Uganda
35   via Kenya running from arranged marriages, he from Sri
Lanka via Colombo English-style boarding school to make him
the minister of the interior, me hunting for slave castles with a
pencil for explosives, what did we know that our pan-colonial
flights would end up among people who ask stupid questions
40   like, where are you from . . . and now here we are on their road,
in their snow, faced with their childishness.

How are we to say that these paths are involuntary and
the line of trees we are looking for will exist when we
find it, that this snow is just a cipher for our feverishness.

45   Only Sarah Vaughan thank god sings in this snow, Sarah
and her big band . . . gotta right to sing the blues . . .
I desert the others to her voice, fanning fire, then, even Sarah
cannot take me away but she moves the car and we live
on whatever she's given to this song, each dive of her voice,
50   each swoop, her vibrato holds us to the road, the outcome
of this white depends on Sarah's entries and exits from a
note. We cannot turn back, ahead Buxton must hear this so we
can arrive, up ahead Sarah singing she can see the midnight sun.

Only this much sound, only this much breath, only this much
55   grace, only how long, only how much road can take us away.

That cop's face has it. 'They had been in this vast and dark
country only a short time.'[1] Something there, written as
wilderness, wood, nickel, water, coal, rock, prairie, erased
as Athabasca, Algonquin, Salish, Inuit . . . hooded in Buxton
60   fugitive, Preston Black Loyalist, railroaded to gold mountain,
swimming in *Komagata Maru* . . . Are we still moving?
Each body submerged in its awful history. When will we arrive?
In a motel room later, we laugh, lie that we are not harmed,
play poker and fall asleep, he on the floor with his demons,
65   she, legs wrapped around me.

How can we say that when we sign our names in letters
home no one can read them, when we send photographs
they vanish. Black heart, blackheart . . . can't take it tonight
across this old road . . . take me home some other way.

        1997

1   from Joseph Conrad's 'An Outpost of Progress'

From *thirsty*

I

This city is beauty
unbreakable and amorous as eyelids,
in the streets, pressed with fierce departures,
submerged landings,
5   I am innocent as thresholds
and smashed night birds, lovesick,
as empty elevators

let me declare doorways,
corners, pursuit, let me say
10   standing here in eyelashes, in
invisible breasts, in the shrinking lake

in the tiny shops of untrue recollections,
the brittle, gnawed life we live,
I am held, and held

15 the touch of everything blushes me,
pigeons and wrecked boys,
half-dead hours, blind musicians,
inconclusive women in bruised dresses
even the habitual grey-suited men with terrible
20 briefcases, how come, how come
I anticipate nothing as intimate as history

would I have had a different life
failing this embrace with broken things,
iridescent veins, ecstatic bullets, small cracks
25 in the brain, would I know these particular facts,
how a phrase scars a cheek, how water
dries love out, this, a thought as casual
as any second eviscerates a breath
and this, we meet in careless intervals,
30 in coffee bars, gas stations, in prosthetic
conversations, lotteries, untranslatable
mouths, in versions of what we may be,
a tremor of the hand in the realization
of endings, a glancing blow of tears
35 on skin, the keen dismissal in speed

II

There was a Sunday morning scent,
an early morning air, then the unarranged light
that hovers on a street before a city wakes
unrelieved to the war fumes of fuel exhaust

40 The city was empty, except for the three,
they seemed therefore poised, as when you are alone
anywhere all movement is arrested, light, dun,
except, their hearts, scintillant as darkness

clothy blooms of magnolia, bedraggled shrubs,
45 wept over a past winter, a car sped by,
scattering from sleep, their mirage disquiets,
the subway, tumescent, expectant like a grave

They had hoped without salvation for a trolley,
they arrived at the corner impious, then,
50 wracked on the psalmody of the crossroad,
they felt, the absences of a morning

They circled sovereign thoughts, taking
for granted the morning, the solidity of things,
the bank to one corner, the driving school on another,
55 the milk store and the church

each her own separate weight,
each carried it in some drenched region of flesh,
the calculus of silence, its chaos,
the wraith and rate of absence pierced them

60 Chloe bathed in black, then the youngest,
leather bag strapped to a still school
girlish back, the last a precise look to her yet,
a violet lace, a hackle from forehead to neck

captured in individual doubt, a hesitation,
65 and what they could not put into words,
indevotion, on this eighteenth Sunday
every cool black-dressed year since 1980

This slender lacuna beguiles them,
a man frothing a biblical lexis at Christie
70 Pits, the small barren incline where his mad sermons
cursed bewildered subway riders, his faith unstrained

then nothing of him but his parched body's declension
a curved caesura, mangled with clippers, and
clematis cirrhosa and a budding grape vine he was still
75 to plant when he could, saying when he had fallen, '. . . thirsty . . .'

III

That north burnt country ran me down
to the city, mordant as it is, the whole
terror of nights with yourself and what
will happen, animus, loose like that, sweeps
80 you to embrace its urban meter,
the caustic piss of streets,

you surrender your heart to a numb symmetry
of procedures, you study the metaphysics of
corporate instructions and not just,
85   besieged by now, the ragged, serrated theories
of dreams walking by, banked in sleep

that wild waiting at traffic lights off
the end of the world, where nothing is simple,
nothing, in the city there is no simple love
90   or simple fidelity, the heart is slippery,
the body convulsive with disguises
abandonments, everything is emptied,
wrappers, coffee cups, discarded shoes,
trucks, street corners, shop windows, cigarette
95   ends, lungs, ribs, eyes, love,
the exquisite rush of nothing,
the damaged horizon of skyscraping walls,
nights insomniac with pinholes of light

2002

George Elliott Clarke
b. 1960

Born in Windsor Plains, Nova Scotia, George Elliott Clarke obtained his BA (1984) from the University of Waterloo, his MA (1986) from Dalhousie University, and his PhD (1993) from Queen's University. Activist, poet, playwright, and professor of literature at the University of Toronto, he hails from 'Africadia', a word he coined to suggest that he was formed by the combined inheritances of Africa and Acadia, regarding himself as a fusion of Black and Canadian. He is committed to the expansion of the traditions of Nova Scotia to include the contributions of the Black community. In his powerful verse novel *Whylah Falls* (1990) he recounts as fiction the true story of the 1985 death in Weymouth Falls of Graham Jarvis, whose killer was ultimately acquitted by an all-white jury; the poems celebrate both the enduring vitality and the tragedy of this small community. His most recent collection of poetry is *I & I* (2009).

From *Whylah Falls*

Look Homeward, Exile

I can still see that soil crimsoned by butchered
Hog and imbrued with rye, lye, and homely
Spirituals everybody must know,
Still dream of folks who broke or cracked like shale:
5 Pushkin, who twisted his hands in boxing,
Marrocco, who ran girls like dogs and got stabbed,
Lavinia, her teeth decayed to black stumps,
Her lovemaking still in demand, spitting
Black phlegm—her pension after twenty towns,
10 And Toof, suckled on anger that no Baptist
Church could contain, who let wrinkled Eely
Seed her moist womb when she was just thirteen.
    And the tyrant sun that reared from barbed-wire
Spewed flame that charred the idiot crops
15 To Depression, and hurt my granddaddy
To bottle after bottle of sweet death,
His dreams beaten to one, tremendous pulp,
Until his heart seized, choked; his love gave out.
    But Beauty survived, secreted
20 In freight trains snorting in their pens, in babes
Whose faces were coal-black mirrors, in strange
Strummers who plucked Ghanaian banjos, hummed
Blind blues—precise, ornate, rich needlepoint,
In sermons scorched with sulphur and brimstone,
25 And in my love's dark, orient skin that smelled
Like orange peels and tasted like rum, good God!
    I remember my Creator in the old ways:
I sit in taverns and stare at my fists;
I knead earth into bread, spell water into wine.
30 Still, nothing warms my wintry exile—neither
Prayers nor fine love, neither votes nor hard drink:
For nothing heals those saints felled in green beds,
Whose loves are smashed by just one word or glance
Or pain—a screw jammed in thick, straining wood.

Bees' Wings

This washed-out morning, April rain descants,
Weeps over gravity, the broken bones
Of gravel and graveyards, and Cora puts
Away gold dandelions to sugar
5   And skew into gold wine, then discloses
That Pablo gutted his engine last night
Speeding to Beulah Beach under a moon
As pocked and yellowed as aged newsprint.
Now, Othello, famed guitarist, heated
10   By rain-clear rum, voices transparent notes
Of sad, anonymous heroes who hooked
Mackerel and slept in love-pried-open thighs
And gave out booze in vain crusades to end
Twenty centuries of Christianity.
15   His voice is simple, sung air; without notes,
There's nothing. His unknown, imminent death
(The feel of iambs ending as trochees
In a slow, decasyllabic death-waltz;
His vertebrae trellised on his stripped spine
20   Like a xylophone or keyboard of nerves)
Will also be nothing: the sun pours gold
Upon Shelley, his sis', light as bees' wings,
Who roams a garden sprung from rotten wood
And words, picking green nouns and fresh, bright verbs,
25   For there's nothing I will not force language
To do to make us one—whether water
Hurts like whisky or the sun burns like oil
Or love declines to weathered names on stone.

Blank Sonnet

The air smells of rhubarb, occasional
Roses, or first birth of blossoms, a fresh,
Undulant hurt, so body snaps and curls
Like flower. I step through snow as thin as script,
5   Watch white stars spin dizzy as drunks, and yearn
To sleep beneath a patchwork quilt of rum,
I want the slow, sure collapse of language

Washed out by alcohol. Lovely Shelley,
I have no use for measured, cadenced verse
10 If you won't read. Icarus-like, I'll fall
Against this page of snow, tumble blackly
Across vision to drown in the white sea
That closes every poem—the white reverse
That cancels the blackness of each image.

1990

Le Tombeau de Bishop

for Sandra Barry

Cruel scrutiny is your furious power:
It orders light—orcharded, hoarded fast
In your dark poems: miniature Bibles
Monstrous with agonies of pneumonia
5   Or cranky Bedlams, shelving sick mothers
Like just-hooked fish, their eyes jumpy with shock.
    To dredge your poems is to grapple nightmares—
Offal of Presbyterian-depressed
Nouvelle-Écosse (its poverty of love,
10   Its raw, tubercular winters)—and snag
Images smelling of hookrust and flesh,
Death-randy.
                    Photographic, spiky, rank,
Your gospels dramatize the malicious,
Narrow cold that cankers our compassion
15   And blisters our dreams, freezing us into
This penal colony peninsula.
    Peeling back our pitched ensembles of blossoms,
You expose a snow-riled landscape, our warped
Shacks, our nicest incests, our plums slumped in dirt.
20   Your metaphors pierce us like frigid spears
Or hot, Botticellian syphilis.
Accurate as aches, you chill and scald us.
    Dread Elizabeth Bishop, seize our lives,
Anatomize them—like a liar's diary.
25   Your lyrics still inflict wounds choice eyes brave—
Their lines slash icy, incendiary.

2001

Paris Annapolis

There is a light in Paris—Baudelaire's
Or Rimbaud's—that cuts like grey *Pernod*
Drizzling misery in the brain. You pick
It up in smeared glasses, blurry with tears—
5   The glycerine light of memory, pale,
Unstable, unholy water, panicked
As paeans and elegies to how *Love*
Perishes in a thousand sins, famous
And rehearsed, the way it always must die.
10   Once I floated along the Seine, my brain
Pickled wicked on Belgian beer that's ten
Per cent alcohol, and I wrote of her,
And the river cried out to me to drown.
    All my years have been mere dodges of death.
15   I came here to this valley, to forget—
To lush pastures, to forget a parched love.
But that spectacular, parrhesian light—
The Parisian light of the Annapolis
Valley, that frosty brightness lilting
20   Over Gothic orchards, gargoyle apple trees
Reaped by apocalyptic autumn,
A thousand white, clapboard Notre Dames
Pastelling the Annapolis as the Seine,
That river, queasy like the Quai d'Orsay—
25   Shines her image upon my welling heart
That brims at Heaven like a word-swamped page,
Brooking a delirium that banks clouds
(Their liquid palimpsests), and asks that soul
Steep under unadulterate Beauty.
30   And I sink, eyeing Gallic moonlight sculpt
An Arc de Triomphe from frank, conjuncting trees,
From this flaming stream, a Champs Elysées—
Or an ash-white Napoleonic tomb.

2001

Burning Poems

A pen burns paper. A black *Blitzkrieg*
Blazes, leaving the glinting odour of charred
Diction, a vocabulary in ashes: Detritus.
The word-scorched paper smells darkly.

5   How oblivion buckles. Or suffers arrest.
The chancy arson that parades as poetry
Smells of paper yellowed and time-seared,
Mottled, reeking of always-flaming news.

Walcott's holocaust. Pound's inferno.
10 Layton's *Fornalutx*. My own slavish suttee.
Every poem is its own pyre, flamboyant,
The smoking words laying waste to *Time*.

2001

DRAMA

DRAMA

The Elements of Drama

CONTEXTS OF DRAMA

Drama, Literature, and Representational Art

The essence of drama is imitative action. When actors appear on stage, they make believe they are people other than themselves, much as children do, and in doing so create a world apart—a world modelled on ours, resembling ours, yet separate.

Drama, of course, is not child's play, but it does share with it the essential quality of *enactment*. This quality should remind us that drama is not solely a form of literature. It is at once literary art *and* representational art. As literary art a play is a fiction, made of words. It has a plot, characters, and dialogue. But it is a special kind of fiction—a fiction *acted out* rather than narrated. In a novel or short story, we learn about characters and events through the words of a narrator who stands between us and them. But in a play nothing stands between us and the total makeup of its world. Characters appear and events happen without any intermediate comment or explanation. Drama, then, offers us a *direct* presentation of its imaginative reality. In this sense it is representational art.

In studying drama we are faced with a paradox. Because it is literature, a play can be read. But because it is representational art, a play is meant to be witnessed. Viewed another way, the text of a play is something like the score of a symphony—a finished work, yet only a potentiality until it is performed. Most plays, after all, are written to be performed. (Those that are written only to be read are usually referred to as *closet dramas*.) For most of us, however, the experience of drama is usually confined to plays in print, and this means that we have to be unusually resourceful in our study of drama. Careful reading is not enough. We have to be creative in order to imagine drama on the stage. This means that we must not only attend to the meanings and implications of words but also envision those words in performance. By doing so, we can begin to experience the understanding and pleasure that spectators gain when they attend a play in a theatre. This is where our study begins.

Drama and Theatrical Performance

The magic of theatre, its ability to conjure up such incredible characters as the Ghost in *Hamlet* or the Witches in *Macbeth*, depends on the power of spectacle. By spectacle we mean all the sights and sounds of performance—the slightest twitch or the boldest thrust of a sword, the faintest whisper or the loudest cry. Spectacle, in short, is the means by which the fictional world of a play is brought to life in the theatre. When we witness a play, our thoughts and feelings may be stirred as much by the spectacle as by the words themselves. Thus in reading the text of a play, we should continually try to imagine its spectacle. This requires us to adopt a special approach to reading.

The text of a play is a script for performance, and we should read it as if we were directors and actors involved in staging the play. Once we begin to interpret it as a script, we can see that the text contains innumerable cues from which we can construct the spectacle in our mind's eye. These cues, if we are attentive to them, will tell us about the various elements that make up the total spectacle: *setting, costuming, props, blocking* (the arrangement of characters on the stage), *movement, gestures, intonation,* and *pacing* (the tempo and coordination of performance). By keeping those elements continuously in mind, we can imagine what the play looks and sounds like on stage. We can enter the world of the play, and by doing so not only understand, but also experience, its meaning.

Some dramatists, such as Ibsen, Shaw, and Beckett, provide extensive and explicit directions for performance in parenthetical remarks preceding the dialogue and interspersed with it. But no matter how extensive their remarks may be, they are never complete guides to production. They still require us to infer elements of the spectacle from the dialogue itself. Other dramatists such as Sophocles and Shakespeare provide little, if any, explicit guidance about staging. When we read their plays, we must gather our cues almost entirely from the dialogue, just as directors staging their plays must do.

It is important to bear in mind that the *King Lear* we see in a modern theatre is not the spectacle Shakespeare's seventeenth-century audiences would have seen when they witnessed the play. The Globe Theatre, where Shakespeare's plays were originally produced, was an open-air structure without sets or lights of any kind. The spectators of Shakespeare's time could not have witnessed the 'realistic' illusion of a storm such as the one in Act III of *King Lear*. They would have seen the action take place in broad daylight on a bare stage without a backdrop. Thus they would have depended wholly upon the language and the actors to evoke the setting. Even so, they would have had a more intimate involvement with the characters and the action, for the Globe stage, rather than being set behind an arch, extended out into the audience itself. Their experience of the scene would thus have been quite different from the experience offered by a modern stage version. In light of that difference, we might ask which version is valid. Both, in fact, are valid, but for different reasons. The modern version is valid because it is true to the theatrical conditions of our own time. Most modern theatres, after all, are not designed like the Globe, and if we attend a performance of *King Lear* we should not expect it to duplicate the scene as produced in Shakespeare's day. But when we are reading the play, we can imagine how it would have been produced in the Globe and thus be true to the theatrical conditions for which Shakespeare created it.

Imagining a play in the context of the theatre for which it was written will give us an understanding that we may bring to any production of the play we may happen to witness. We can compare our imagined production with the production on stage, and in this way we can recognize how the director and actors have adapted the original context of the play to their own theatrical circumstances. If, for example, we were to attend a production of *King Lear*, we might see the storm scene performed on a bare stage, without sets or props of any kind. Having imagined the play in its original theatrical context, we would then not be surprised or puzzled by that bare stage, but would recognize that the director was attempting to incorporate an important element of seventeenth-century theatre in a contemporary production. Thus, by being historically informed play-readers, we can also become critically enlightened play-goers.

Drama and Other Literary Forms

When we consider drama as a representational art—a theatrical event to be performed and witnessed—we are concerned with the uniquely dramatic experience created by a play in performance. But any performance is an *interpretation* of how the lines should be acted and delivered. Thus every production of a play stresses some words and minimizes others, includes some meanings and excludes others. No single production can convey all the implications in the language of a play. This should remind us that drama is also a form of literary art and should be understood in relation not just to the theatre but also to other forms of literature—story, poem, and essay.

Each literary form has a unique way of using words and communicating them to the reader. Drama in its pure form uses words to create action through the dialogue of characters talking to one another rather than to the reader: its essential quality is interaction. But different forms, though they may be unique, also share similarities. Drama resembles a story in its concern with plot and character. Like a poem, it is overheard by, rather than addressed to, the reader. Like an essay, it is capable of being used to explore issues and propose ideas. Using these relationships as points of departure, we can examine some of the ways in which drama takes on the characteristics and devices of the other literary forms.

Drama and Narration

A play is at its most dramatic when it uses dialogue to create interaction. But the interaction always takes place within a specific context—a background in time and place without which it cannot be properly understood. To bring about this understanding, drama turns to the narrative techniques of the story. This is not to say we should expect to find storytellers addressing us directly in plays, though occasionally they do turn up. More often the characters become storytellers in their dialogue with one another. This kind of storytelling typically occurs at the beginning of a play, and it is called the *exposition* because it sets forth and explains in a manner typical of narrative.

Exposition is important not only because it establishes the mood of a play but also because it conveys information about the world of that play. Through expository dialogue the dramatist may reveal information about the public state of affairs, as Sophocles does in the opening lines of *Oedipus Rex*, or disclose information about the past deeds and private relations of the characters. This information often comes in snatches of dialogue that, as in life itself, we must piece together on our own. Once we have done so, we have a framework for understanding the action that takes place during the play.

Related to exposition is another narrative device called *retrospection.* Characters, during the action, often look back on significant events that have taken place before the time of the play. This 'looking back' is retrospection, and it is an important element of narration. Sometimes retrospection may lead to major revelations about the characters and the motivations for their behaviour. In some cases, it may be the principal activity of the play, as in *Oedipus Rex*, where the chief character becomes preoccupied with piecing together elements from the past, and the climax occurs when his retrospection leads him to discoveries about the past that totally reverse his view of himself and his world.

Exposition and retrospection are narrative elements that refer to pre-play action, but there are occasions when narration is used to convey the action of the play itself—when narration replaces character interaction to advance the plot. Narration is used when offstage action is reported rather than represented—for even when characters are offstage they are still doing things that we must know about in order to have a full understanding of the action. When offstage action is reported, a play takes on elements of a story. Words are being used to develop a view of character and situation rather than to create action through dialogue. This process can be seen operating in *Oedipus Rex* when the Second Messenger tells the Choragus about the death of Iocastê and the self-blinding of Oedipus. The interaction on stage ceases entirely for the length of almost fifty lines, and what we get instead has all the features of a miniature story. The Messenger first establishes his narrative authority and then moves into his tale, supplying detailed information, offering explanations for facts he cannot provide, reporting dialogue, and concluding with a general reflection on the fate of Oedipus and Iocastê, whose experience he sees as epitomizing the 'misery of mankind'. One reason that Sophocles has these events reported instead of presented on stage is that they are too gruesome to be displayed. But it is true also that through the Messenger's report, Sophocles is able to provide a comment on the meaning of the events.

The Messenger's commentary brings us to the last important element of narration in drama: *choric commentary*. When the narrator of a story wishes to comment on characters and events, he or she can do so at will. But the dramatist, of course, cannot suddenly appear in the play—or on stage—to provide a point of view on the action. The dramatist's alternative is the *chorus*, or *choric characters*—that is, characters who are relatively detached from the action and can thus stand off from it, somewhat like a narrator, to reflect on the significance of events. In Greek drama the chorus performed this function.

The existence of a chorus, however, is no guarantee that its opinions are always to be trusted. Sometimes the chorus can be as wrongheaded as any of the more involved characters. Sometimes it is completely reliable, as it is in *Oedipus Rex*, where it comments, in its concluding remarks, about the frailty of the human condition. Choric commentary, then, provides a point of view, but not necessarily an authoritative one, or one to be associated necessarily with the dramatist. In each case it has to be judged in the context of the entire play. But whether it is valid, or partially reliable, or completely invalid, the chorus does provoke us to reflect on the meaning of events by providing commentary for us to assess.

After the classical Greek period, the formal chorus disappeared almost entirely from drama, though remnants of the chorus can be found in later plays—even in mod-

ern drama. It is important to recognize that despite the absence of a formally designated chorus, choric characters persist in drama. Minor characters such as messengers, servants, clowns, whether or not they are directly involved in the action, can carry
out the functions of a chorus, as the Fool does in *King Lear*. Ultimately, any character
is capable of becoming a commentator of a sort, simply by standing off from the action
and viewing it as a spectator rather than as a participant. The reflections of these characters should be taken no less seriously than those of a chorus.

Drama and Meditation
When we recall that interaction through dialogue is the basis of drama, we can readily
see that a play is committed by its nature to showing us the public side of its characters. Realizing this, we can see as well the artistic problem a dramatist faces when trying to reveal the private side of the same characters. The narrator of a story can
manage this problem by telling us the innermost thoughts of the characters. But a
dramatist must turn to the conventions of the poem, using words addressed by a
speaker talking or thinking to himself or herself.

When we read a purely lyric poem, we tend to assume that the situation is private
rather than public and that we can overhear the words even though they might never
be spoken aloud. When we read or watch a play, we must make a similar effort of the
imagination. To assist our efforts, dramatists have traditionally organized their plays in
order to make sure that characters thinking to themselves are seen in private. That
special situation is captured by the term *soliloquy*, which means, literally, 'to speak
alone'. But it is true also that we have private thoughts even in the presence of others, and this has been recognized by dramatists such as Richard Brinsley Sheridan,
whose characters may often be seen thinking to themselves in the most public situations. Whatever the circumstances, private or public, the soliloquy makes unusual
demands on both actors and audience.

As readers, we should be aware that the soliloquy can perform a variety of functions, and, since it is so unusual an element in drama, it achieves its purposes with
great effectiveness. Customarily, the soliloquy is a means of giving expression to a
complex state of mind and feeling, and in most cases the speaker is seen struggling
with problems of the utmost consequence. This accounts for the intensity we often find
in the soliloquy. We are all familiar, for example, with Hamlet's predicaments—to be or
not to be, to kill or not to kill the king—and these are typical of the weighty issues that
usually burden the speaker of a soliloquy. In soliloquy, then, the interaction among characters is replaced by the interaction of a mind with itself.

When a play shifts from dramatic interaction to meditation, its process of events
is temporarily suspended, and the soliloquizing character necessarily becomes a
spectator of his or her world. In this way the soliloquy, like choric commentary,
offers the dramatist a means of providing a point of view on the action of the play.
In reading a soliloquy, then, we should examine it not only as the private revelation of
a character but also as a significant form of commentary on other characters and
events.

In considering the soliloquy, we have been examining only one element of meditation in drama. It is possible for plays to become primarily or even exclusively meditative, though this may sound like a contradiction of dramatic form. If drama depends on the interaction of characters through dialogue, how is it possible for internalized thought and feeling to be the principal subject of a play? This can happen in a number of ways. One way—a traditional way—is to create a cast of characters who represent not persons but abstractions—who embody aspects, or qualities, or thoughts, or feelings of a single mind. This is a common device in morality plays, which were popular in the fifteenth and early sixteenth centuries. These religious dramas portrayed personified virtues in an attempt to instill Christian values. So, in *Everyman* (c. 1515), one of the best known of the morality plays, the title character is shown in conversation with characters named Beauty, Strength, Discretion, and Five Wits. Interaction among characters of this sort is meant to represent the interaction of a mind with itself, and so it constitutes the dramatization of a meditative experience achieved through what we might call an allegory of the mind.

We can also recognize plays dramatizing mental processes through methods other than allegory. Many modern plays, such as Sharon Pollock's *Doc* or Michel Tremblay's *For the Pleasure of Seeing Her Again*, include not only soliloquies and other kinds of monologue but also imaginary sequences depicting dreams and fantasies. And some modern plays, such as *Krapp's Last Tape*, consist exclusively of a single character talking to himself. Plays such as these reflect the influence of modern psychological theories about the behaviour of the mind. Writing in 1932, the playwright Eugene O'Neill defined the 'modern dramatist's problem' as discovering how to 'express those profound hidden conflicts of the mind which the probings of psychology continue to disclose to us'. Almost fifty years earlier, in 1888, the Swedish dramatist Johan Strindberg anticipated the same idea, writing, 'I have noticed that what interests people most nowadays is the psychological action.' Looking at their statements side by side, we can see that they share the same concern: O'Neill speaks of 'hidden conflicts of the mind', and Strindberg of 'psychological action'. We might also call it *meditative drama*.

Whatever form a meditative drama may take, we as readers must be alert to the 'hidden conflicts' it aims to dramatize. To recognize such conflicts we must be attentive to not just the external but also the 'internal' action. We should examine both plot and dialogue for what they can tell us about the mental life of the characters. And rather than looking for a clearly defined sequence of events, we should expect to find a kind of movement as irregular and hazy as the workings of the mind itself.

Drama and Persuasion

A play could be exclusively a piece of persuasion only if it consisted of a single character—the dramatist—presenting ideas directly to the audience. Of course, such a performance would be difficult to distinguish from a lecture. This extreme case should remind us that drama is rarely, if ever, simply an exposition or assertion of ideas. Ideas can be found throughout the dialogue of almost any play, but as we have seen in the preceding sections, it is best to assume that those ideas are sentiments of the characters rather than the opinions of the dramatist. A character is a character, the drama-tist is the dramatist, and dramatists are never present to speak for themselves, except in prefaces, prologues, epilogues, stage directions—and other statements outside the framework of the play.

Although dramatists cannot speak for themselves, their plays can. The essential quality of drama—interaction—may be made to serve the purposes of an essay. Dialogue, plot, and character may be used to expound ideas and sway the opinions of an audience. The desire to persuade usually implies the existence of conflicting ideas, and plays with a persuasive intention are customarily designed to demonstrate the superiority of one idea, or a set of attitudes, over another. Thus, characters may become spokespersons for ideas, dialogue a way of debating ideas, and action a means of testing ideas. Plays of this kind inevitably force audiences and readers to examine the merits of each position and align themselves with one side or the other. In reading such plays, we must be attentive not only to the motives and personalities of characters but also to the ideas they espouse. Similarly, we must be interested not only in the fate of the characters but also in the success or failure of their ideas. Ultimately, then, these plays do not allow us the pleasure of simply witnessing the inter-action of characters. Like essays, they are intended to challenge our ideas and change our minds.

Because they focus on conflicting beliefs and ideas, plays with a persuasive pur-pose often embody elements similar to a formal argument or debate. Like *Pygmalion*, they usually set up opposing values in their opening scenes. Thus Shaw establishes a conflict between the 'Professor of Phonetics' Henry Higgins and the Cockney flower-seller Eliza Doolittle, whose speech qualifies her for the group Shaw describes in his preface as 'people with troubled accents that cut them off from all high employment'. In defending their ideas, these characters behave so much like contestants in a debate that their dialogue sounds like disputation rather than conversation. And in the process of reading or witnessing the debate, we are clearly invited to take a stand ourselves, to side with one view or the other. The choice, of course, is not an easy one, and the play is designed to keep us from making a simple choice.

MODES OF DRAMA

Drama, The World, and Imitation

Drama, as we said at the start, creates a world modelled on our own: its essence is imitative action. But drama is not imitative in the ordinary sense of the word. It does not offer us a literal copy of reality, for the truth of drama does not depend on repro-ducing the world exactly as it is. Drama is true to life by being false to our conventional notions of reality.

The coincidences discovered at the end of *The Importance of Being Earnest* are unimaginable. The scheming and contrivance of the characters in *The School for Scandal* are outrageous. The Bingo scene in *The Rez Sisters* is surreal. And yet each of these plays creates a world that we recognize as being in some sense like our own.

Our problem, then, is to define the special sense in which drama is imitative. We can begin by recognizing that its mode of imitation must be selective rather than all-inclusive, intensive rather than extensive. It has to be, since time is short and space is limited in the theatre. Faced with limitations in stage size and performance time, the dramatist obviously cannot hope to reproduce the world exactly as it is. By selecting and intensifying things, however, the dramatist can emphasize the dominant patterns and essential qualities of human experience. Thus, our understanding of any play requires that we define the principles of emphasis that determine the makeup of its world and the experience of its characters.

In defining the emphasis of a play, we can ask ourselves whether the dramatist has focused on the beautiful or the ugly, on the orderly or the chaotic, on what is best or what is worst in the world. A play that emphasizes the beautiful and the orderly tends toward an idealized vision of the world, which is the mode we call *romance*. A play focusing on the ugly and chaotic tends toward a debased view of the world; we call this mode *satire*. Both of these emphases depend for their effect on extreme views of human nature and existence.

In contrast to the extreme conditions of romance and satire, another pair of dramatic processes takes place in a world neither as beautiful as that of romance nor as ugly as that of satire—in a world more nearly like our own. Rather than focusing on essential qualities in the world, these processes—*comedy* and *tragedy*—emphasize the dominant patterns of experience that characters undergo in the world. In comedy the principal characters typically begin in a state of opposition either to one another or to their world—often to both. By the end of the play, their opposition is replaced by harmony. In this way the characters are integrated with one another and with their world. In tragedy, however, the hero and the hero's world begin in a condition of harmony that subsequently disintegrates, leaving the character by the end of the play completely isolated or destroyed.

With these four possibilities in mind, we might draw a simple diagram such as this:

ROMANCE
(beauty)

COMEDY   TRAGEDY
(integrative)   (disintegrative)

SATIRE
(ugliness)

The vertical axis emphasizes the essential qualities in the world; the horizontal axis emphasizes the dominant patterns of human experience; the point of intersection—

which represents the absence of any emphasis—represents the world as it is. In this way we can immediately visualize each of the four points of emphasis, its distinguishing characteristics, and its relation to each of the others. Once we have recognized these possibilities, we might be tempted to categorize plays in terms of the characteristics we have identified with each emphasis. Yet it is important to recognize that each emphasis is at best an abstraction—a definition formulated in order to generalize about a number of plays, not an explanation of any one play in particular. Thus, when we turn to individual plays we should not necessarily expect that they can be accurately described and understood simply by labelling them comedy or tragedy, satire or romance.

As a way of anticipating some of the complexities, we can see in the diagram that each emphasis borders on two others. Comedy, for example, tends toward romance on the one hand, and satire on the other. The same is true of tragedy, and the others. Even the antithetical possibilities, as we see, can interact. This should hardly surprise us, for if the world can incorporate both the beautiful and the ugly, then so can a play. These categories will serve us best if we use them tactfully as guides to understanding rather than as a rigid system of classification. But before they can serve us as guides, we must familiarize ourselves with their characteristics in greater detail.

Tragedy and Comedy

Tragedies typically end in death and mourning, comedies in marriage and dancing. That difference accounts for the two familiar masks of drama, one expressing sorrow, the other joy, one provoking tears, the other laughter. That difference also accounts for the commonly held notion that tragedy is serious and comedy frivolous. But when we consider that both modes are probably descended from primitive fertility rites—tragedy from ritual sacrifice, comedy from ritual feasting—we can recognize that they dramatize equally important dimensions of human experience. Tragedy embodies the inevitability of individual death, comedy the irrepressibility of social rebirth. So, like autumn and spring, tragedy and comedy are equally significant phases in a natural cycle of dramatic possibilities. Indeed, like the seasons of the year and the nature of human experience, they are inextricably bound up with one another.

Every comedy contains a potential tragedy—the faint possibility that harmony may not be achieved, that the lovers may not come together to form a new society. And every tragedy contains a potential comedy—the faint possibility that disaster may be averted, that the hero or heroine may survive. This in turn should remind us that we must be concerned not only with the distinctive endings of tragedy and of comedy, but also with the means by which each of those ends is reached. Catastrophe in and of itself does not constitute tragedy, nor does marriage alone (or any other favourable outcome) make for comedy. The unique experience of each mode is produced by the design of its plot and the nature of the characters who take part in it. We can see this most clearly by looking first at the elements of tragedy, then at the elements of comedy.

Tragedy was first defined by the Greek philosopher Aristotle (384–322 BCE), who inferred its essential elements from witnessing the plays of his own time. His observations, which he set down in his *Poetics*, cannot be expected to explain all the tragedies that have ever been written; no single theory could do so. But Aristotle's theory has influenced more dramatists—and critics—than any other propounded since his time, and thus it remains the best guide we have to the nature of tragedy.

Aristotle considered plot to be the most important element of tragedy, because he believed that 'all human happiness or misery takes the form of action,' that 'it is in our actions—what we do—that we are happy or the reverse.' In discussing tragedy, he emphasized the design of the plot and set out several important qualities that contribute to its effect. First, he stressed the *unity* of a tragic plot. By unity he meant that the plot represents a single action, or story, with a definite beginning, middle, and end, and further that all its incidents are 'so closely connected that the transposal or withdrawal of any one of them will disjoin or dislocate the whole.' By close connection he meant that the incidents are causally related to one another so that their sequence is probable and necessary. Ultimately, then, we can see that, in emphasizing the unity of a tragic plot, Aristotle was calling attention to the quality of the inevitable that we associate with tragedy. Thus in reading a tragedy we should try to define the chain of cause and effect that links each incident in the plot. In this way we will understand the process that makes its catastrophe inevitable, and in this way we will gain insight into the meaning of the catastrophe.

In examining the plot of a tragedy such as *Oedipus Rex*, we may be tempted to look at its catastrophe as not only inevitable but also inescapable. Aristotle, however, did not see the inevitable change in the fortunes of the tragic hero as being the result of chance, of coincidence, of fate, or even of some profound flaw in the character of the hero. Rather, he saw the change of fortune as being caused by 'some error of judgment', a 'great error' on the part of the hero. In defining this element of tragedy, Aristotle clearly regarded the hero, and not some condition beyond human control, as responsible for initiating the chain of events leading to his or her change in fortune. Even a profound flaw in character is, after all, beyond human control. Accordingly, Aristotle described the tragic hero as an 'intermediate kind of personage' in moral character, neither 'preeminently virtuous and just' nor afflicted 'by vice and depravity'. Simply put, the tragic hero is someone morally 'like ourselves', in whom we can engage our emotional concern. Thus, according to Aristotle's theory, we should not regard tragic protagonists such as Oedipus or King Lear as victims of absurd circumstances, but should try to identify the sense in which they are agents of their own undoing.

Even as we attempt to understand the nature of their errors, we should not forget that most tragic heroes are admirable characters—people, as Aristotle tells us, who deservedly enjoy 'great reputation and prosperity'. The reputation of a tragic hero is a function not simply of social rank but also of his or her commitment to noble purposes. Oedipus is not just a king but also a man committed to discovering the truth and ridding his city of the plague. King Lear is not only a king but a father who loves and trusts his children. Our response to these characters should therefore combine judgment with sympathy and admiration.

Once we make the effort to discover their error, we should find that we undergo an experience that parallels that of the protagonists themselves. We should find that we are compelled by the process of events—by the turn of the plot—to recognize how they have undone themselves. The protagonist's act of recognition is defined by Aristotle as the *discovery* because it entails 'a change from ignorance to knowledge'. And the discovery, as Aristotle recognized, is caused inevitably by a *reversal*, an incident or sequence of incidents that goes contrary to the protagonist's expectations. Reversal and discovery are crucial elements of the tragic experience because they crystallize its meaning for the protagonist—and for us. When events go contrary to their expectations, when the irony of their situation becomes evident, they—and we—have no choice but to recognize exactly how the noblest intentions can bring about the direst consequences. Thus, in its discovery, as in its entire plot, tragedy affirms both the dignity and the frailty of human existence.

Discovery scenes take place in comedy as well, but rather than accounting for an inevitable disaster, comic discoveries reveal information that enables characters to avoid a probable catastrophe. Lost wills may be found, or mistaken identities corrected, or some other fortuitous circumstance may be revealed. Somehow comedy always manages to bring about a happy turn of events for its heroes—and those heroes are rarely the sole or primary agents of their success. Usually, in fact, they get a large helping hand from chance, or coincidence, or some other lucky state of affairs. Comedy thrives on improbability. And in doing so it defies the mortal imperatives of tragedy.

In this sense comedy embodies the spirit of spring, with its eternal promise of rebirth and renewal; it embodies, too, the festive air and festive activities we associate with spring. The term *comedy*, in fact, is derived from a Greek word, *komoidia*, that means 'revel-song', and revelry always finds its way into comedy, whether in the form of feasts and dancing, tricks and joking, sex and loving—or all of them combined. The perils that develop in the world of comedy rarely seem perilous to us. Although the characters themselves may feel temporarily threatened, the festive air makes us sense that ultimately no permanent damage will be done.

Though comedy avoids the experience of death, it does not ignore the significance of life. Comic plots usually arise out of conflicts that embody opposing values and beliefs. These conflicts inevitably pit one set of attitudes against another, one kind of social vision against another. In reading comedies, therefore, we should try to identify the attitudes that bring characters into conflict. In *The School for Scandal*, for example, the malicious hypocrite Joseph Surface is committed to securing wealth and the good opinion of others, while his brother, the affable libertine Charles, is committed to the pursuit of pleasure at great expense and regardless of the opinion of others. In *Pygmalion*, Henry Higgins is committed to social structure and etiquette, Eliza Doolittle to social freedom. Once we have identified those conflicting values, we will discover that they can help us to understand the meaning of a comic plot.

Comedy usually begins with a state of affairs dominated by one kind of social idea, and so the resolution of a comic plot—achieved through its scenes of discovery—

embodies the triumph of a new social order. Whoever wins out in comedy is invariably on the right side, no matter how improbable the victory may seem. Thus it is that the characters who oppose the new order of things—the 'blocking figures'—are usually subjected to comic ridicule throughout the play. Comedy, after all, expresses an irreverent attitude toward old and inflexible ideas, toward any idea that stifles natural and reasonable impulses in the human spirit. But comedy, as we said earlier, also embodies the generous and abundant spirit of spring. Its heroes and heroines—the proponents of the new society—always seek to include their opponents in the final comic festivities. Comedy seeks not to destroy the old, but rather to reclaim it. And in this may be seen the ultimate expression of its exuberant faith in life.

Tragicomedy, Naturalism, and Absurdist Drama

Tragedy, comedy, satire, and romance—each of these primary modes embodies its own unique pattern of dramatic experience. Each incorporates distinctly different kinds of plots and characters, distinctly different kinds of conflicts and discovery scenes, and each achieves a distinctly different view of human existence. Thus, when we read or witness a tragedy or comedy, a satire or romance, we undergo an experience that is more or less clear-cut. We feel sorrow or joy, scorn or admiration. We know, in short, exactly how we feel, exactly what we think.

But some plays—many modern ones, especially—do not arouse such clear-cut responses. As we read or watch them, our feelings and judgments may be confused, or ambiguous, or mixed in one way or another. When we read a play such as *The Rez Sisters* we may feel torn between sorrow and joy, scorn and admiration. Indeed, we may not know exactly how we feel, or exactly what we think. When we find ourselves experiencing such mixed feelings, we will probably discover that the play has been designed to leave us in an unresolved state of mind—that it does not embody a clear-cut pattern of catastrophe or rebirth (as in tragedy or comedy) or present clear-cut images of good or evil (as in romance or satire). Many plays, rather than being dominated by a single mode, combine differing or opposing modes of dramatic experience. In characterizing such works we use the term *tragicomedy*, as a means of defining the ambiguous experience that we witness in the play and feel within ourselves. Tragicomedy leaves us with a complex reaction, similar to the uncertainty we often feel in response to life itself.

Uncertainty about the nature of human existence is a fundamental source of the tragicomic quality we find in many modern and contemporary plays. In some, that quality is produced by a *naturalistic* view of human nature and experience—a view of men and women as influenced by psychological, social, and economic forces so complex that the behaviour of individuals cannot be easily judged or explained. That view of human nature led Johan Strindberg, for example, to create characters whom he describes as being 'somewhat "characterless"'—characters, that is, who are influenced by 'a whole series of motives', rather than by any single, or simple, purpose. Like other naturalistic dramatists, Strindberg is unwilling to offer us simple explanations to account for human behaviour:

A suicide is committed. Business troubles, says the man of affairs. Unrequited love, say the women. Sickness, says the invalid. Despair, says the down-and-out. But it is possible that the motive lay in all or none of these directions, or that the dead man concealed his actual motive by revealing quite another, likely to reflect more to his glory.

Just as we cannot definitely account for their actions, the characters in a realistic drama cannot themselves perceive, much less control, all the forces influencing their behaviour. Typically, then, the protagonists of naturalistic drama, such as the central characters in *The Rez Sisters* or Victor Franz in *The Price*, are placed in dramatic situations portraying them as being in some sense victims of their environment. They may attempt to alter their circumstances, or they may wilfully deceive themselves about the nature of them, or they may acquiesce in them, or they may sit in judgment upon them; but whatever action they take, it does not lead to a clear-cut resolution of the kind we associate with tragedy and comedy. Nor does their situation allow us to make the clear-cut moral judgment that we do of characters in satire and romance. For this reason naturalistic drama leaves us with a problematic view of human experience, and the most we can hope for is to understand, to the degree that we humanly can, the psychological, social, and economic circumstances that are contributing to the problematic situations of its characters.

In some modern plays the problematic situation is produced by conditions that transcend even naturalistic explanations. In these plays we sense the presence of some profound situation that afflicts the characters but is in the end indefinable. In *Krapp's Last Tape*, we are faced with a single character whose existence is defined almost exclusively by an insatiable appetite for bananas, an unquenchable thirst for soda water, and an obsessive fixation on his tape-recorded diary. These mysterious, even ridiculous, circumstances lead us to wonder whether there is any ultimate source of meaning *at all* in the world of such plays, or for that matter whether there is *any* rational source of explanation *at all* for the experience of the characters. For this reason, such plays are known as *absurdist* drama.

The 'absurdity' of absurdist drama is usually evident not only in its plot but in its dialogue. Often, for example, the conversation of characters does not make perfect sense, either because they are talking at cross purposes or because their language has no clear point of reference to anything in their world. Yet even as we read the dialogue we will find it to be at once laughably out of joint and terrifyingly uncommunicative. In much the same way we may be puzzled by the resolution of these plays. We may be left wondering whether the characters' situation at the end is in any significant respect different from what it was at the beginning, wondering whether the play is tragic or comic, wondering even whether there is any single word or concept—like 'tragicomedy'—that can adequately express the possibility that human existence may be meaningless. Ultimately, then, absurdist drama, like the other modes, does embody a view of human existence, but rather than perceiving existence as dominated by one pattern or another, one quality or another, that view implies that existence may have no pattern or meaning at all.

ELEMENTS OF DRAMA

Contexts, Modes, and the Elements of Drama

Characters, dialogue, plot—these are the indispensable elements of drama. Together they make possible the imitative world of every play, for characters are like people, dialogue and plot like the things people say and do. But *likeness* does not mean *identicalness*. As we indicated in our discussion of dramatic modes, the 'truth' of drama does not depend on reproducing the world exactly as it is. For this reason, we should not expect to find characters who talk and act in just the same way that we do, nor should we expect to find plots that develop in just the same way that ordinary events do. The characters who populate the worlds of romance and satire, for example, are modelled less on specific people than on human potentialities. Similarly, the plots elaborated in comedy and tragedy are based less on real occurrences than on basic patterns of human experience. The elements of drama, then, are highly specialized versions of the elements that make up the world as it is. The particular version we encounter in any single play will be determined by a variety of circumstances—by the mode of the play, the purpose of the play, the literary form of the play, and the design of the theatre for which it was written. We should always keep these circumstances in mind when we study the elements of drama.

Dialogue

The dialogue of a play is a specialized form of conversation. Designed as it is to serve the needs created by the various contexts and modes of drama, it can hardly be expected to sound exactly like our customary patterns of speech. In ordinary conversation, for example, we adjust our style to meet the needs of the people we are talking with, and we reinforce our words with a wide range of facial expressions, bodily gestures, and vocal inflections, many of which we use unconsciously. If we recognize that we are not being understood, we may stammer momentarily while trying to rephrase our feelings and ideas. Before we have managed to get the words out, someone may have interrupted us and completely changed the topic of conversation. Whatever the case, we find ourselves continuously adjusting to circumstances that are as random as our thoughts and the thoughts of those we are speaking with. If we were to transcribe and then listen to the tape of an ordinary conversation, even one that we considered coherent and orderly, we would probably find it far more erratic and incoherent than we had imagined.

Drama cannot afford to reproduce conversation as faithfully as though it were recorded. To begin with, the limitations of performance time require that characters express their ideas and feelings much more economically than we do in the leisurely course of ordinary conversation. The conditions of theatrical performance demand also that dialogue be formulated so that it can not only be heard by characters talking to one another but also be overheard and understood by the audience in the theatre. Thus, the continuity of dialogue must be clearly marked out at every point. On the basis of what is overheard, the audience—or the reader—must be able to develop a full understanding of the characters and the plot.

Dialogue, then, is an extraordinarily significant form of conversation, for it is the means by which every play conveys the total makeup of its imaginative world. And this is not all. Dialogue must convey clues about this imaginative world that will help the director, the set designer, and the actors perform their roles. This means that the dialogue must serve as a script for all the elements of production and performance—in short, for the entire theatrical realization of a play.

Because it has to serve so many purposes all at once, dialogue is necessarily a more artificial form of discourse than ordinary conversation. Thus, in reading any segment of dialogue, we should always keep in mind its special purposes. It is a script for theatrical production, and that means that we should see what it can tell us about the total spectacle: the setting, the arrangement of characters on the stage, their physical movements, gestures, facial expressions, and inflections. It is also a text for conveying the imaginative world of the play, which means that we should see what it can tell us about the character speaking, the character listening, and the other characters not present; about the public and private relations among the characters, and the quality of the world they inhabit; about the events that have taken place prior to the play, the events that have taken place offstage during the play, the events that have caused the interaction of the characters during the dialogue itself, and the events that are likely to follow from their interaction. If we read the dialogue with all these concerns in mind, we will find in the end that it takes us out of ourselves and leads us into the imaginative experience of the play.

Plot

Plot is a specialized form of experience. We can see just how specialized it is if we consider for a moment what happens to us in the course of our everyday lives. Between waking and sleeping we perform a variety of actions and probably converse with a number of people. But most of these events have little to do with one another, and they are usually not part of any single purpose. In general, the events that take place in our daily existence do not embody a significant pattern or process. If they have any pattern at all, it is merely the product of habit and routine.

On the other hand, in drama every event is part of a carefully designed pattern and process. This process is what we call plot. Plot, then, is not at all like the routine, and often random, course of our daily existence. Rather, it is a wholly interconnected system of events, deliberately selected and arranged for the purpose of fulfilling a complex set of imaginative and theatrical purposes. Plot is really an extremely artificial element, and it has to be so. Within the limits of a few hours the interest of spectators—and readers—has to be deeply engaged and continuously sustained. That requires a system of events that quickly develops complications and suspense, and leads in turn to a climax and resolution. Interest must also be aroused by events that make up a process capable of being represented on stage. And the totality of events must create a coherent imitation of the world.

In order to understand how plot fulfills these multiple purposes, we should first recognize that plot comprises *everything* that takes place in the imaginative world of a play. In other words, it is not confined to what takes place on stage (the *scenario*): it includes off-stage action as well. Thus, if we wish to identify the plot of a play, we have to distinguish it from the scenario. The scenario embodies the plot and presents it to us, but it is not itself the plot. Here is another way to understand this distinction: in a plot all the events are necessarily arranged *chronologically*, whereas in a scenario events are arranged *dramatically*—that is, in an order that will create the greatest impact on the audience. In some cases that order may be non-chronological. We may reach the end of a scenario before we learn about events that took place years before. For this reason, in studying the plot of a play, we must consider not only the events of which it consists but also the order in which those events are presented by the scenario.

The ordering of events can best be understood if we think of the scenario as being constructed of a series of dramatic units: each time a character enters or leaves the stage, a new dramatic unit begins. The appearance or departure of a character or group of characters is almost like a form of punctuation that we should note carefully whenever we are reading or witnessing a play. As one grouping of characters gives way to another, the dramatic situation necessarily changes—sometimes slightly, sometimes very perceptibly—to carry the play forward in the evolution of its process and the fulfillment of its plot. It is important to examine each unit individually in order to discover not only what on-stage action takes place within it but also what off-stage action is revealed within it. Then we should determine how the off-stage action that is reported affects the on-stage action, as well as how it shapes our own understanding of the characters and the plot.

Consider, for example, the opening dramatic unit of *Oedipus Rex*. Here we witness a conversation between Oedipus and a priest, in which the priest pleads with Oedipus to rid Thebes of the plague, while Oedipus assures him that he is eager to cure the city of its sickness. During that conversation we also learn from the priest that, in years past, Oedipus had through his wisdom and knowledge liberated the city from the domination of the Sphinx, and we learn from Oedipus that he has recently sent his brother-in-law, Kreon, to seek advice from the oracle at Delphi. These two reports of off-stage action establish the heroic stature of Oedipus, revealing him to be an exceptionally effective and responsible leader. The dramatic unit leads the priest and Oedipus—and us as spectators—to expect that he will be equally successful in this crisis. In this way we see that the unit not only identifies the motivating problem of the plot but also establishes Oedipus as the hero of the play, and that, moreover, it creates a set of positive expectations about his ability to overcome the problem. (He does, of course, overcome the problem but not without undoing himself in the process.) The unit, then, is crucial in creating a complicated mixture of true and false expectations within both the characters and us.

In addition to examining dramatic units individually, we should examine them in relation to one another—in other words, in context. Context is one of the dramatist's most useful techniques for influencing our perception and understanding of characters and plot. Dramatists usually arrange events so as to produce significant parallels or contrasts between them. Thus, if we look at the units in context, we will be able to perceive those relationships and their implications.

Finally, of course, we must move beyond pairs and series of units to an overview of all the units together. By doing this we will be able to recognize the dominant process of the play. That is, we will be able to perceive how it sets up the complications and works toward the discoveries and resolution of tragedy, comedy, satire, romance, or tragicomedy. By examining the overall design of the plot, we can recognize the dominant view of experience represented in the play.

It should be apparent that plot is an extremely complicated element, one that can best be understood through a detailed analysis of dramatic units. Here, then, are some reminders and suggestions to follow in analyzing the plot of any play. Identify all the events that take place within the plot and the chronological order in which they occur. In order to do this, examine the scenario closely, paying attention to instances of implied and reported action. Once you have established the details and makeup of the plot, examine how the plot is presented by the scenario. In order to do this, examine each dramatic unit in detail, beginning with the first and proceeding consecutively through the play. Remember that a single dramatic unit can serve a variety of purposes. Remember, too, that every unit exists within a context of units—within the context of units that immediately precede and follow it, and within the context of all the units of the play.

Character

Although characters in a play are like real people in some respects, they are by no means identical to people in real life. Real people, after all, exist in the world as it is, whereas characters exist in an imaginative world shaped by the theatrical contexts and imitative purposes of drama. In the classical Greek theatre, for example, a character was defined visually by the fixed expression of his or her mask. Clearly, it would have been impossible for spectators to regard such characters as identical to complex human personalities. And if we look at Oedipus, we can see that he is conceived in terms of a few dominant traits that could be projected through the bold acting required by the enormous size of the ancient Greek theatre.

Because of its sustained interest in psychological behaviour, modern drama tends to put a great deal of emphasis on character. Yet even plays—such as *Hedda Gabler* or *For the Pleasure of Seeing Her Again*—that are concerned specifically with the workings of the human mind do not embody characters who can be taken as identical to real people. It would be misleading to think of Ibsen's Hedda, for example, or Michel Tremblay's Nana as a fully developed personality. Although each represents a complex study in human psychology, they are conceived to dramatize specific ideas about the impact of the family and society upon the individual. In other words, they exhibit patterns of behaviour that are *typical* rather than *actual*.

Although dramatic characters are not real people, they are endowed with human capacities. They talk and act and interact with one another. They experience pleasure and endure pain. They feel, and they act on their feelings. They believe, and they behave according to their beliefs. It would be inhuman of us not to respond to their humanity. But we can respond appropriately only if we know what we are responding to: we have to consider all of the ways in which characters are revealed and defined by dialogue and plot.

The most immediate way to understand a character is to examine in detail everything the character says in order to identify the important attitudes, beliefs, and feelings of that character. It is important to examine not only the content but also the style of such utterances. Look, for example, at the kinds of words and images and sentence structures that mark the character's dialogue, for often these elements of style provide insight into subtle aspects of character. A further source of information is what others in the play say about the character. Since characters, like real people, are repeatedly talking about one another—to their faces and behind their backs—what they have to say will often provide valuable insights into the character.

The things a character does may reveal as much as what the character says and what others have to say. In examining actions, pay careful attention to context, for characters are likely to behave differently in different situations. The challenge in such a case is to determine whether the character has actually changed, for what appears to be a change in character may simply be the result of our knowing the character more fully. Another important key to understanding is to compare and contrast a character with others in the play. A study of this kind often sharpens the perceptions we have gained from examining the character in isolation.

Character analysis can be a source of pleasure and understanding in its own right, but it should ultimately lead us more deeply into the play as a whole. For that reason, when we analyze characters, we should always keep in mind the theatrical contexts and imaginative purposes that shape their being. In this way we shall be able to appreciate the dramatic imitation of a world created by the wedding of literary and of representational art.

A GUIDE TO OUR PLAYS

Theatre, as we have come to understand it, originates in the Greek tragedies of the fifth century BCE. Tragedy was an important part of annual spring festivals honouring Dionysus, the god of agriculture and fertility. During the proceedings, an actor would come on stage to carry on a conversation with the chorus. Together, they would recite the triumphs and failures of the major character. It became customary at the festivals to have each competing poet write three tragedies and a satyr play of a burlesque nature.

Aeschylus, the creator of tragedy, introduced a second actor/character. Although his plays still centred on the chorus, they began to take on a new life. Of approximately seventy plays that he wrote, only seven have survived, and we know that he made a dramatic whole of the three tragedies he wrote for the festivals by using the three dramas to treat a single story over an extended period of time. His plays present human actions in relation to the overriding will of the gods.

Sophocles, Aeschylus's successor, put aside the practice of composing his tragedies in groups of three. He also introduced a third actor/character to the stage, reducing considerably the significance of the chorus, and he showed a vital interest in character. Of more than 110 plays that he wrote, only seven have survived.

No longer focusing on the gods themselves, Sophocles shifts his focus to the human beings who populate our world, and his plays reveal a strong sense of tragic moments in the lives of men and women who are both heroic and deeply human. Though he wrote his plays well over two thousand years ago, many of his insights into human experience are enduring and timeless. He wrote, for example, of Antigone and her sister Ismene, an account that Sheila Watson reworked in a contemporary setting in her story 'Antigone'. *Oedipus Rex*, the most renowned of all Greek tragedies, has influenced literatures from its time to the present. However, in the festival in which it was first performed, held around the year 425 BCE, it gained only second prize; first prize in that year's contest went to Philocles, a nephew of Aeschylus of whom little else—including his work—is known.

At the start of the play, Oedipus's kingdom, the city of Thebes, is suffering from a plague, and in the opening scene a crowd of suppliants appeal to the great king to find them some relief from their woe. Sixteen years have passed since Oedipus freed Thebes from the tyranny of King Laïos by solving a riddle posed by the Sphinx; his act of heroism earned him the hand of the queen and the crown of the king. An intelligent and determined ruler, he is also a man of strong temper, too sure of himself. The chain of events that leads to his downfall has already begun in the early scenes when the strengths and weaknesses of his character are evident. What befalls him is part of the complex web of human life.

In *King Lear*, which was first performed in 1605, Shakespeare, who had already written histories, comedies, and some tragedies, reached the zenith of his art with the retelling of the story of a fabled king and his three daughters. Going back to native English sources, he fashioned the tale into a play that Alfred, Lord Tennyson considered 'too titanic'. It presents a state of society where people's passions are, as Tennyson commented, 'savage and uncurbed. No play like this anywhere—not even the *Agamemnon* [by Aeschylus]—is so terrifically human.'

The Lear tale goes back as far as Geoffrey of Monmouth's *History of the Kings of Britain* (1137), which tells of how the monarch divides his kingdom in half, forsaking his fair-speaking daughter Cordelia. Shakespeare may have read this in the original Latin (no Elizabethan translation exists), or he may have taken details from more recent writers who were directly or indirectly influenced by Geoffrey—writers such as Holinshed, Sir Philip Sidney, or even Edmund Spenser. Whatever his sources were, Shakespeare chose to dramatize his story in pre-Roman, pre-Christian Britain, making *King Lear* his first and earliest English history play.

To the basic plot of the Lear story Shakespeare added the subplot of Gloucester and his two sons, which parallels that of Lear and his three daughters. Thus, the play's opening scene shows Cordelia's rebellion against her father's wishes, just as the second scene reveals the duplicity of Edmund's rebellion against his father. Lear, in the opening scene, wishes to divide his kingdom among his three daughters, exacting as his price their declarations of love for him: 'Which of you shall we say doth love us most?' At this moment, he wishes to abdicate his kingly responsibilities, though not necessarily his kingly position. The play traces his abdication and the subsequent assaults to his human dignity. At the end of the play, we can only agree with the last speaker: 'The oldest hath borne most: we that are young / Shall never see so much, nor live so long.'

In magnificent poetry *King Lear* explores both one man's folly in abdicating his position and the dire consequences of his decision. People are blinded; people are murdered; people die. The tragedy ends with Edgar, Lear's godson, whom Lear himself named, inheriting the throne of England.

Like tragedy, comedy arose, though fifty years later than tragedy, in the same festivals honouring Dionysus. The Greek comedies were originally filled with abuse and obscenity, and they were intended primarily to ward off evil spirits. Later, Aristophanes wrote strikingly original plays that were ripe with moral invective and political criticism. Comedies, as we have noted, always bring their characters together at the end, unlike tragedies, which lead to the outcast condition or death of one or more people in the play.

Our two classic comedies come respectively from the late eighteenth and nineteenth centuries. In 1888 the *Dramatic Review* polled all the English drama critics of the day, asking them to name the English comedy—excluding those by Shakespeare and those translated from other languages—that they considered to be the best. Richard Brinsley Sheridan's *The School for Scandal* won by an overwhelming vote.

First produced at London's Drury Lane Theatre on 8 May 1777, *The School for Scandal* presents a satirical portrait of the world of backbiting and vindictiveness. Lady Teazle, a young countrywoman married to the much older Sir Peter, comes to London aspiring to be fashionable in society's eyes. In the famous screen scene (Act IV, Scene 3), she learns of her husband's abiding affection for her, which gives her the self-assurance to reject Lady Sneerwell and the alternative world of gossip and deceit.

More than a century later, on 14 February 1895, Oscar Wilde premiered *The Importance of being Earnest* at London's St James's Theatre. Subtitled 'A Trivial Comedy for Serious People', Wilde's masterpiece revolves around the dalliances, scheming, and social commentary of Algernon 'Algy' Moncrieff and John 'Jack' Worthing. The result is a perfect comedy filled with mistaken identities, would-be lovers, and a happy revelation and reunion at the conclusion.

Across the sea from Wilde and his theatrical escapades, the Norwegian playwright Henrik Ibsen was creating plays that mark the beginning of modern naturalistic drama. His work typically reveals a conflict between the world of human imagination and its personal aspirations and an oppressive society that restricts or destroys such flights of fancy. The death of an individual may be tragic, but it is also liberating, because it frees the isolated individual from the constrictions of society.

Hedda Gabler centres around one woman's battle with her social environment. Positioned in her claustrophobic reception room, Hedda seeks some higher form of life than her society offers. Men often have outlets for their aspirations; women have almost none. Hedda looks longingly for some kind of perspective on her world, remaining finally isolated and alone in her thoughts.

The setting of Arthur Miller's *The Price*, the attic of a Manhattan brownstone soon to be torn down, follows the path of modern naturalistic drama and continues Ibsen's careful exploration of people trapped in their own lives. Miller presents two brothers meeting again after a long period of estrangement and failing to find their bond of loyalty. 'The production must therefore withhold judgment in favor of presenting both men in all their humanity and from their own viewpoints,' Miller states in his closing production note. 'Actually, each has merely proved to the other what the other has known but dared not face.'

George Bernard Shaw proposed ways of improving society, often by amalgamating the stage and the lectern. He wrote lengthy prefaces and sequels to his plays to make certain that the issues raised were being fully and properly treated. Through another reworking of a Greek myth, *Pygmalion*, his romance, as he calls the play, casts the mythical Greek sculptor as a professor of phonetics and the Galatea figure—his creation brought to life—as a young Cockney girl. 'His relation to her is too godlike to be altogether agreeable,' Shaw states in his sequel, and, as a consequence, she marries not the professor but a young, infatuated lover. Delightful as *Pygmalion* is, we often wonder about the propriety of the ending. Is it satisfactory to readers and playgoers? Consider the musical adaptation, *My Fair Lady*, and notice how Alan Jay Lerner altered the play's conclusion to give his work a romantic ending.

The 'Theatre of the Absurd', a category encompassing dramatists of the 1950s and 1960s who view the world as essentially mysterious and unknowable, often presents actions and events filled with purposelessness and loss. The leading figure of absurdist drama, Samuel Beckett, places his characters in situations that are frequently meaningless. Krapp switches on his tape, switches it off, switches it on again, then off, then on, all the time listening intently to the personal relationship he knew thirty years ago. Edward Albee's *The Zoo Story* portrays strangers in New York City prattling aimlessly in rambling, and frequently puzzling, conversation; then one of them meets his death. *The Zoo Story* had its American début on a double bill with *Krapp's Last Tape*.

Three plays in this collection showcase the variety and depth of contemporary Canadian theatre.

Sharon Pollock's *Doc*, which premiered in 1984 at Theatre Calgary, is a semi-autobiographical work that explores a woman's relationship with her successful father, a Maritime doctor, whose wife, like Pollock's own mother, has died tragically. The detailed time sequences underscore and emphasize the theme of female identity.

In *The Rez Sisters* (1986), Tomson Highway brings his Aboriginal roots to the surface in this celebratory, award-winning play that reflects the dramatist's deep commitment to preserving his First Nations heritage. Electrifying in its initial and subsequent successes on stages throughout Canada, the play marked the arrival on the Canadian scene of Aboriginal theatre.

The dean of Canadian playwrights, Michel Tremblay, wrote the hauntingly beautiful *For the Pleasure of Seeing Her Again* (1998) to dramatize the loving relationship he shared with his mother, who has died. It is joyous and fantastical, funny and touching.

All of the plays in our anthology repay reading and re-reading. Each one highlights specific features of the drama of its time. Whether you are reading the plays, or seeing them, or even acting in them, you will be startled by their undeniable lustre.

Sophocles
496–406 BCE

B orn in Greece, where his father was a wealthy and influential businessman, Sophocles became a very influential and admired public figure in Athens during the remarkable century of its rise and fall as a great city-state. During his lifetime he served his country as an ambassador, general, and treasurer; he served its religion as a priest of the god of healing; and he served its culture as a preeminent tragic dramatist. His plays, like those of his Greek contemporaries, were written and produced for an extraordinary drama competition that was held in Athens each spring as the major event in a festival celebrating Dionysus, the Greek god who embodied the power and fertility of nature. Each tragic dramatist who chose to compete submitted a set of either three or four plays (*trilogies* or *tetralogies*), and Sophocles won the contest twenty-four times. He reportedly wrote more than 120 plays, but only 7 of them have survived, all of them showing him to have been a master in the conception and elaboration of tragically compelling plots and characters. His best known plays — *Antigone* (c. 440), *Oedipus Rex* (c. 425), and *Oedipus at Colonus* (406) — though written more than thirty years apart, all deal with related characters and themes from the haunting myth of Oedipus and Thebes.

Oedipus Rex[1]

CHARACTERS

OEDIPUS	MESSENGER
A PRIEST	SHEPHERD OF LAÏOS
KREON	SECOND MESSENGER
TEIRESIAS	CHORUS OF THEBAN ELDERS
IOKASTÊ	

The scene: Before the palace of Oedipus, King of Thebes. A central door and two lateral doors open onto a platform which runs the length of the façade. On the platform, right and left, are altars; and three steps lead down into the 'orchêstra', or chorus-ground. At the beginning of the action these steps are crowded by suppliants who have bought branches and chaplets of olive leaves and who sit in various attitudes of despair.

Oedipus enters.

1 an English version by Dudley Fitts and Robert Fitzgerald

PROLOGUE

OEDIPUS: My children, generations of the living
    In the line of Kadmos, nursed at his ancient hearth:
    Why have you strewn yourselves before these altars
    In supplication, with your boughs and garlands?

5   The breath of incense rises from the city
    With a sound of prayer and lamentation.
                         Children,
    I would not have you speak through messengers,
    And therefore I have come myself to hear you—
    I, Oedipus, who bear the famous name.

To a Priest

10   You, there, since you are eldest in the company,
    Speak for them all, tell me what preys upon you,
    Whether you come in dread, or crave some blessing:
    Tell me, and never doubt that I will help you
    In every way I can; I should be heartless
15   Were I not moved to find you suppliant here.
PRIEST: Great Oedipus, O powerful King of Thebes!
    You see how all the ages of our people
    Cling to your altar steps: here are boys
    Who can barely stand alone, and here are priests
20   By weight of age, as I am a priest of God,
    And young men chosen from those yet unmarried;
    As for the others, all that multitude,
    They wait with olive chaplets in the squares,
    At the two shrines of Pallas, and where Apollo
25   Speaks in the glowing embers.
                    Your own eyes
    Must tell you: Thebes is tossed on a murdering sea
    And can not lift her head from the death surge.
    A rust consumes the buds and fruits of the earth;
    The herds are sick; children die unborn,
30   And labour is vain. The god of plague and pyre
    Raids like detestable lightning through the city,
    And all the house of Kadmos is laid waste,
    All emptied, and all darkened: Death alone
    Battens upon the misery of Thebes.

35   You are not one of the immortal gods, we know;
    Yet we have come to you to make our prayer

As to the man surest in mortal ways
And wisest in the ways of God. You saved us
From the Sphinx, that flinty singer, and the tribute
40 We paid to her so long; yet you were never
Better informed than we, nor could we teach you:
A god's touch, it seems, enabled you to help us.

Therefore, O mighty power, we turn to you:
Find us our safety, find us a remedy,
45 Whether by counsel of the gods or of men.
A king of wisdom tested in the past
Can act in a time of troubles, and act well.
Noblest of men, restore
Life to your city! Think how all men call you
50 Liberator for your boldness long ago;
Ah, when your years of kingship are remembered,
Let them not say *We rose, but later fell—*
Keep the State from going down in the storm!
Once, years ago, with happy augury,
55 You brought us fortune; be the same again!
No man questions your power to rule the land:
But rule over men, not over a dead city!
Ships are only hulls, high walls are nothing,
When no life moves in the empty passageways.

60 OEDIPUS: Poor children! You may be sure I know
All that you longed for in your coming here.
I know that you are deathly sick; and yet,
Sick as you are, not one is as sick as I.
Each of you suffers in himself alone
65 His anguish, not another's; but my spirit
Groans for the city, for myself, for you.

I was not sleeping, you are not waking me.
No, I have been in tears for a long while
And in my restless thought walked many ways.
70 In all my search I found one remedy,
And I have adopted it: I have sent Kreon,
Son of Menoikeus, brother of the Queen,
To Delphi, Apollo's place of revelation,
To learn there, if he can,
75 What act or pledge of mine may save the city.
I have counted the days, and now, this very day,
I am troubled, for he has overstayed his time.
What is he doing? He has been gone too long.

80

Yet whenever he comes back, I should do ill
Not to take any action the god orders.

PRIEST: It is a timely promise. At this instant
They tell me Kreon is here.

OEDIPUS: O Lord Apollo!
May his news be fair as his face is radiant!

PRIEST: Good news, I gather: he is crowned with bay,

85

The chaplet is thick with berries.

OEDIPUS: We shall soon know;
He is near enough to hear us now.

Enter Kreon.

                                    O Prince:

Brother: son of Menoikeus:
What answer do you bring us from the God?

KREON: A strong one. I can tell you, great afflictions

90

Will turn out well, if they are taken well.

OEDIPUS: What was the oracle? These vague words
Leave me still hanging between hope and fear.

KREON: Is it your pleasure to hear me with all these
Gathered around us? I am prepared to speak,

95

But should we not go in?

OEDIPUS: Speak to them all.
It is for them I suffer, more than for myself.

KREON: Then I will tell you what I heard at Delphi.
In plain words
The god commands us to expel from the land of Thebes

100

An old defilement we are sheltering.
It is a deadly thing, beyond cure;
We must not let it feed upon us longer.

OEDIPUS: What defilement? How shall we rid ourselves of it?

KREON: By exile or death, blood for blood. It was

105

Murder that brought the plague-wind on the city.

OEDIPUS: Murder of whom? Surely the god has named him?

KREON: My lord: Laïos once ruled this land,
Before you came to govern us.

OEDIPUS: I know:
I learned of him from others; I never saw him.

110

KREON: He was murdered; and Apollo commands us now
To take revenge upon whoever killed him.

OEDIPUS: Upon whom? Where are they? Where shall we find a clue
To solve that crime, after so many years?

KREON: Here in this land, he said. Search reveals

115   Things that escape an inattentive man.

     OEDIPUS: Tell me: Was Laïos murdered in his house,

      Or in the fields, or in some foreign country?

     KREON: He said he planned to make a pilgrimage.

      He did not come home again.

     OEDIPUS: And was there no one,

120   No witness, no companion, to tell what happened?

     KREON: They were all killed but one, and he got away

      So frightened that he could remember one thing only.

     OEDIPUS: What was that one thing? One may be the key

      To everything, if we resolve to use it.

125   KREON: He said that a band of highwaymen attacked them,

      Outnumbered them, and overwhelmed the King.

     OEDIPUS: Strange, that a highwayman should be so daring—

      Unless some faction here bribed him to do it.

     KREON: We though of that. But after Laïos' death

130   New troubles arose and we had no avenger.

     OEDIPUS: What troubles could prevent your hunting down the killers?

     KREON: The riddling Sphinx's song

      Made us deaf to all mysteries but her own.

     OEDIPUS: Then once more I must bring what is dark to light.

135   It is most fitting that Apollo shows,

      As you do, this compunction for the dead.

      You shall see how I stand by you, as I should,

      Avenging this country and the god as well,

      And not as though it were for some distant friend,

140   But for my own sake, to be rid of evil.

      Whoever killed King Laïos might—who knows?—

      Lay violent hands even on me—and soon.

      I act for the murdered king in my own interest.

      Come, then, my children: leave the altar steps,

145   Lift up your olive boughs!

                  One of you go

      And summon the people of Kadmos to gather here.

      I will do all that I can; you may tell them that.

Exit a Page.

      So, with the help of God.

      We shall be saved—or else indeed we are lost.

150 PRIEST: Let us rise, children. It was for this we came,
And now the King has promised it.
Phoibos has sent us an oracle; may he descend
Himself to save us and drive out the plague.

*Exeunt Oedipus and Kreon into the palace by the central door. The Priest
and the Suppliants disperse right and left. After a short pause the Chorus
enters the* orchêstra.

PÁRODOS

CHORUS: What is God singing in his profound **Strophe 1**
Delphi of gold and shadow?
What oracle for Thebes, the sunwhipped city?

Fear unjoints me, the roots of my heart tremble.

5 Now I remember, O Healer, your power and wonder:
Will you send doom like a sudden cloud, or weave it
Like nightfall of the past?

Speak, speak to us, issue of holy sound;
Dearest to our Expectancy: be tender!

10 Let me pray to Athenê, the immortal daughter of Zeus, **Antistrophe 1**
And to Artemis her sister
Who keeps her famous throne in the market ring,
And to Apollo, archer from distant heaven—

O gods, descend! Like three streams leap against
15 The fires of our grief, the fires of darkness;
Be swift to bring us rest!

As in the old time from the brilliant house
Of air you stepped to save us, come again!

Now our afflictions have no end **Strophe 2**
20 Now all our stricken host lies down
And no man fights off death with his mind;

The noble plowland bears no grain,
And groaning mothers can not bear—

See, how our lives like birds take wing,
25   Like sparks that fly when a fire soars,
To the shore of the god of evening.

The plague burns on, it is pitiless,   **Antistrophe 2**
Though pallid children laden with death
Lie unwept in the stony ways,

30   And old grey women by every path
Flock to the strand about the altars

There to strike their breasts and cry
Worship of Phoibos in wailing prayers:
Be kind, God's golden child!

35   There are no swords in this attack by fire,   **Strophe 3**
No shields, but we are ringed with cries.

Send the besieger plunging from our homes
Into the vast sea-room of the Atlantic
Or into the waves that foam eastward of Thrace—
40   For the day ravages what the night spares—

Destroy our enemy, lord of the thunder!
Let him be riven by lightning from heaven!
Phoibos Apollo, stretch the sun's bowstring,   **Antistrophe 3**
That golden cord, until it sing for us,
45   Flashing arrows in heaven!
                    Artemis, Huntress,
Race with flaring lights upon our mountains!

O scarlet god, O golden-banded brow,
O Theban Bacchos in a storm of Maenads,

    Enter Oedipus, centre.

Whirl upon Death, that all the Undying hate!
50   Come with blinding torches, come in joy!

SCENE I

OEDIPUS: Is this your prayer? It may be answered. Come,
    Listen to me, act as the crisis demands,
    And you shall have relief from all these evils.

    Until now I was a stranger to this tale,
5   As I had been a stranger to the crime.
    Could I track down the murderer without a clue?
    But how, friends,
    As one who became a citizen after the murder,
    I make this proclamation to all Thebans:

10   If any man knows by whose hand Laïos, son of Labdakos,
    Met his death, I direct that man to tell me everything,
    No matter what he fears for having so long withheld it.
    Let it stand as promised that no further trouble
    Will come to him, but he may leave the land in safety.

15   Moreover: If anyone knows the murderer to be foreign,
    Let him not keep silent: he shall have his reward from me.
    However, if he does conceal it; if any man
    Fearing for his friend or for himself disobeys this edict,
    Hear what I propose to do:

20   I solemnly forbid the people of this country,
    Where power and throne are mine, ever to receive that man
    Or speak to him, no matter who he is, or let him
    Join in sacrifice, lustration, or in prayer.
    I decree that he be driven from every house,
25   Being, as he is, corruption itself to us: the Delphic
    Voice of Apollo has pronounced this revelation.
    Thus I associate myself with the oracle
    And take the side of the murdered king.

    As for the criminal, I pray to God—
30   Whether it be a lurking thief, or one of a number—
    I pray that the man's life be consumed in evil and wretchedness.
    And as for me, this curse applies no less
    If it should turn out that the culprit is my guest here,
    Sharing my hearth.
                    You have heard the penalty.

35   I lay it on you now to attend to this
For my sake, for Apollo's, for the sick
Sterile city that heaven has abandoned.
Suppose the oracle had given you no command:
Should this defilement go uncleansed for ever?

40   You should have found the murderer: your king,
A noble king, had been destroyed!
                          Now I,
Having the power that he held before me,
Having this bed, begetting children there
Upon his wife, as he would have, had he lived—

45   Their son would have been my children's brother,
If Laïos had had luck in fatherhood!
(And now his bad fortune has struck him down)—
I say I take the son's part, just as though
I were his son, to press the fight for him

50   And see it won! I'll find the hand that brought
Death to Labdakos' and Polydoros' child,
Heir of Kadmos' and Agenor's line.
And as for those who fail me,
May the gods deny them the fruit of the earth,

55   Fruit of the womb, and may they rot utterly!
Let them be wretched as we are wretched, and worse!
For you, for loyal Thebans, and for all
Who find my actions right, I pray the favour
Of justice, and of all the immortal gods.

60 CHORAGOS: Since I am under oath, my lord, I swear
I did not do this murder, I can not name
The murderer. Phoibos ordained the search;
Why did he not say who the culprit was?
    OEDIPUS: An honest question. But no man in the world

65   Can make the gods do more than the gods will.
    CHORAGOS: There is an alternative, I think—
    OEDIPUS: Tell me.
Any or all, you must not fail to tell me.
    CHORAGOS: A lord clairvoyant to the lord Apollo,
As we all know, is the skilled Teiresias.

70   One might learn much about this from him, Oedipus.
    OEDIPUS: I am not wasting time:
Kreon spoke of this, and I have sent for him—
Twice, in fact; it is strange that he is not here.
    CHORAGOS: The other matter—that old report—seems useless.

75 OEDIPUS: What was that? I am interested in all reports.

CHORAGOS: The King was said to have been killed by highwaymen.

OEDIPUS: I know. But we have no witnesses to that.

CHORAGOS: If the killer can feel a particle of dread,
    Your curse will bring him out of hiding!

OEDIPUS: No.

80   The man who dared that act will fear no curse.

Enter the blind seer Teiresias, led by a Page.

CHORAGOS: But there is one man who may detect the criminal.
    This is Teiresias, this is the holy prophet
    In whom, alone of all men, truth was born.

OEDIPUS: Teiresias: seer: student of mysteries,

85   Of all that's taught and all that no man tells,
    Secrets of Heaven and secrets of the earth:
    Blind though you are, you know the city lies
    Sick with plague; and from this plague, my lord,
    We find that you alone can guard or save us.

90   Possibly you did not hear the messengers?
    Apollo, when we sent to him,
    Sent us back word that this great pestilence
    Would lift, but only if we established clearly
    The identity of those who murdered Laïos.

95   They must be killed or exiled.
                         Can you use
    Birdflight or any art of divination
    To purify yourself, and Thebes, and me
    From this contagion? We are in your hands.
    There is no fairer duty

100   Than that of helping others in distress.

TEIRESIAS: How dreadful knowledge of the truth can be
    When there's no help in truth! I knew this well
    But did not act on it: else I should not have come.

OEDIPUS: What is troubling you? Why are you eyes so cold?

105 TEIRESIAS: Let me go home. Bear your own fate, and I'll
    Bear mine. It is better so: trust what I say.

OEDIPUS: What you say is ungracious and unhelpful
    To your native country. Do not refuse to speak.

TEIRESIAS: When it comes to speech, your own is neither temperate

110   Nor opportune. I wish to be more prudent.

OEDIPUS: In God's name, we all beg you—

TEIRESIAS: You are all ignorant.
    No; I will never tell you what I know.
    Now it is my mystery; then, it would be yours.

OEDIPUS: What! You do know something, and will not tell us?
115   You would betray us all and wreck the State?
TEIRESIAS: I do not intend to torture myself, or you.
    Why persist in asking? You will not persuade me.
OEDIPUS: What a wicked old man you are! You'd try a stone's
    Patience! Out with it! Have you no feeling at all?
120 TEIRESIAS: You call me unfeeling. If you could only see
    The nature of your own feelings . . . .
OEDIPUS: Why,
    Who would not feel as I do? Who could endure
    Your arrogance toward the city?
TEIRESIAS: What does it matter?
    Whether I speak or not, it is bound to come.
125 OEDIPUS: Then, if 'it' is bound to come, you are bound to tell me.
TEIRESIAS: No, I will not go on. Rage as you please.
OEDIPUS: Rage? Why not!
                                    And I'll tell you what I think:
    You planned it, you had it done, you all but
    Killed him with your own hands: if you had eyes,
130   I'd say the crime was yours, and yours alone.
TEIRESIAS: So? I charge you, then,
    Abide by the proclamation you have made:
    From this day forth
    Never speak again to these men or to me;
135   You yourself are the pollution of this country.
OEDIPUS: You dare say that! Can you possibly think you have
    Some way of going free, after such insolence?
TEIRESIAS: I have gone free. It is the truth sustains me.
OEDIPUS: Who taught you shamelessness? It was not your craft.
140 TEIRESIAS: You did. You made me speak. I did not want to.
OEDIPUS: Speak what? Let me hear it again more clearly.
TEIRESIAS: Was it not clear before? Are you tempting me?
OEDIPUS: I did not understand it. Say it again.
TEIRESIAS: I say that you are the murderer whom you seek.
145 OEDIPUS: Now twice you have spat out infamy. You'll pay for it!
TEIRESIAS: Would you care for more? Do you wish to be really angry?
OEDIPUS: Say what you will. Whatever you say is worthless.
TEIRESIAS: I say you live in hideous shame with those
    Most dear to you. You can not see the evil.
150 OEDIPUS: Can you go on babbling like this for ever?
TEIRESIAS: I can, if there is power in truth.
OEDIPUS: There is:
    But not for you, not for you,
    You sightless, witless, senseless, mad old man!

TEIRESIAS: You are the madman. There is no one here
155 Who will not curse you soon, as you curse me.
OEDIPUS: You child of total night! I would not touch you;
 Neither would any man who sees the sun.
TEIRESIAS: True: it is not from you my fate will come.
 That lies within Apollo's competence,
160 As it is his concern.
OEDIPUS: Tell me, who made
 These fine discoveries? Kreon? or someone else?
TEIRESIAS: Kreon is no threat. You weave your own doom.
OEDIPUS: Wealth, power, craft of statesmanship!
 Kingly position, everywhere admired!
165 What savage envy is stored up against these,
 If Kreon, whom I trusted, Kreon my friend,
 For this great office which the city once
 Put in my hands unsought—if for this power
 Kreon desires in secret to destroy me!

170 He has bought this decrepit fortune-teller, this
 Collector of dirty pennies, this prophet fraud—
 Why, he is no more clairvoyant than I am!
            Tell us:
 Has your mystic mummery ever approached the truth?
 When that hellcat the Sphinx was performing here,
175 What help were you to these people?
 Her magic was not for the first man who came along:
 It demanded a real exorcist. Your birds—
 What good were they? or the gods, for the matter of that?
 But I came by,
180 Oedipus, the simple man, who knows nothing—
 I thought it out for myself, no birds helped me!
 And this is the man you think you can destroy.
 That you may be close to Kreon when he's king!
 Well, you and your friend Kreon, it seems to me,
185 Will suffer most. If you were not an old man,
 You would have paid already for your plot.
CHORAGOS: We can not see that his words or yours
 Have been spoken except in anger, Oedipus,
 And of anger we have no need. How to accomplish
190 The god's will best: that is what most concerns us.
TEIRESIAS: You are a king. But where argument's concerned
 I am your man, as much a king as you.
 I am not your servant, but Apollo's;
 I have no need of Kreon's name.

195   Listen to me. You mock my blindness, do you?
        But I say that you, with both your eyes, are blind:
        You can not see the wretchedness of your life,
        Nor in whose house you live, no, nor with whom.
        Who are your father and mother? Can you tell me?
200   You do not even know the blind wrongs
        That you have done them, on earth and in the world below.
        But the double lash of your parents' curse will whip you
        Out of this land some day, with only night
        Upon your precious eyes.
205   Your cries then—where will they not be heard?
        What fastness of Kithairon will not echo them?
        And that bridal-descant of yours—you'll know it then,
        The song they sang when you came here to Thebes
        And found your misguided berthing.
210   All this, and more, that you can not guess at now,
        Will bring you to yourself among your children.

        Be angry, then. Curse Kreon. Curse my words.
        I tell you, no man that walks upon the earth
        Shall be rooted out more horribly than you.
215 OEDIPUS: Am I to bear this from him?—Damnation
        Take you! Out of this place! Out of my sight!
    TEIRESIAS: I would not have come at all if you had not asked me.
    OEDIPUS: Could I have told that you'd talk nonsense, that
        You'd come here to make a fool of yourself, and of me?
220 TEIRESIAS: A fool? Your parents thought me sane enough.
    OEDIPUS: My parents again!—Wait: who were my parents?
    TEIRESIAS: This day will give you a father, and break your heart.
    OEDIPUS: Your infantile riddles! Your damned abracadabra!
    TEIRESIAS: You were a great man once at solving riddles.
225 OEDIPUS: Mock me with that if you like; you will find it true.
    TEIRESIAS: It was true enough. It brought about your ruin.
    OEDIPUS: But if it saved this town?
    TEIRESIAS: [*To the Page*]   Boy, give me your hand.
    OEDIPUS: Yes, boy; lead him away.
                  —While you are here
        We can do nothing. Go; leave us in peace.
230 TEIRESIAS: I will go when I have said what I have to say.
        How can you hurt me? And I tell you again:
        The man you have been looking for all this time,
        The damned man, the murderer of Laïos,
        That man is in Thebes. To your mind he is foreign-born,
235   But it will soon be shown that he is a Theban,

A revelation that will fail to please. A blind man,
Who has his eyes now; a penniless man, who is rich now;
And he will go tapping the strange earth with his staff.
To the children with whom he lives now he will be
240 Brother and father—the very same; to her
Who bore him, son and husband—the very same
Who came to his father's bed, wet with his father's blood.

Enough. Go think that over.
If later you find error in what I have said,
245 You may say that I have no skill in prophecy.

Exit Teiresias, led by his Page. Oedipus goes into the palace.

ODE I

CHORUS: The Delphic stone of prophecies   **Strophe 1**
         Remembers ancient regicide
         And a still bloody hand.

         That killer's hour of flight has come.
5   He must be stronger than riderless
         Coursers of untiring wind,
         For the son of Zeus armed with his father's thunder
         Leaps in lightning after him;
         And the Furies hold his track, the sad Furies.

10   Holy Parnassos' peak of snow   **Antistrophe 1**
         Flashes and blinds that secret man,
         That all shall hunt him down:
         Though he may roam the forest shade
         Like a bull gone wild from pasture
15   To rage through glooms of stone.
         Doom comes down on him; flight will not avail him;
         For the world's heart calls him desolate,
         And the immortal voices follow, for ever follow.

         But now a wilder thing is heard   **Strophe 2**
20   From the old man skilled at hearing Fate in the wing-beat of a bird.
         Bewildered as a blown bird, my soul hovers and can not find
         Foothold in this debate, or any reason or rest of mind.
         But no man ever brought—none can bring

Proof of strife between Thebes' royal house,
25 Labdakos' line, and the son of Polybos;
And never until now has any brought word
Of Laïos' dark death staining Oedipus the King.

Divine Zeus and Apollo hold **Antistrophe 2**
Perfect intelligence alone of all tales ever told;
30 And well though this diviner works, he works in his own night;
No man can judge that rough unknown or trust in second sight,
For wisdom changes hands among the wise.
Shall I believe my great lord criminal
At a raging word that a blind old man let fall?
35 I saw him, when the carrion woman faced him of old,
Prove his heroic mind. These evil words are lies.

SCENE II

KREON: Men of Thebes:
I am told that heavy accusations
Have been brought against me by King Oedipus.
I am not the kind of man to bear this tamely.

5 If in these present difficulties
He holds me accountable for any harm to him
Through anything I have said or done — why, then,
I do not value life in this dishonour.

It is not as though this rumour touched upon
10 Some private indiscretion. The matter is grave.
The fact is that I am being called disloyal
To the State, to my fellow citizens, to my friends.
CHORAGOS: He may have spoken in anger, not from his mind.
KREON: But did you not hear him say I was the one
15 Who seduced the old prophet into lying?
CHORAGOS: The thing was said; I do not know how seriously.
KREON: But you were watching him! Were his eyes steady?
Did he look like a man in his right mind?
CHORAGOS: I do not know.
I can not judge the behaviour of great men.
20 But here is the King himself.

Enter Oedipus.

OEDIPUS: So you dared come back.
Why? How brazen of you to come to my house,
You murderer!
Do you think I do not know
That you plotted to kill me, plotted to steal my throne?
Tell me, in God's name: am I coward, a fool,

25 That you should dream you could accomplish this?
A fool who could not see your slippery game?
A coward, not to fight back when I saw it?
You are the fool, Kreon, are you not? hoping
With support or friends to get a throne?

30 Thrones may be won or bought: you could do neither.
KREON: Now listen to me. You have talked; let me talk, too.
You can not judge unless you know the facts.
OEDIPUS: You speak well: there is one fact; but I find it hard
To learn from the deadliest enemy I have.

35 KREON: That above all I must dispute with you.
OEDIPUS: That above all I will not hear you deny.
KREON: If you think there is anything good in being stubborn
Against all reason, then I say you are wrong.
OEDIPUS: If you think a man can sin against his own kind

40 And not be punished for it, I say you are mad.
KREON: I agree. But tell me: what have I done to you?
OEDIPUS: You advised me to send for that wizard, did you not?
KREON: I did. I should do it again.
OEDIPUS: Very well. Now tell me:
How long has it been since Laïos—
KREON: What of Laïos?

45 OEDIPUS: Since he vanished in that onset by the road?
KREON: It was long ago, a long time.
OEDIPUS: And this prophet,
Was he practicing here then?
KREON: He was; and with honour, as now.
OEDIPUS: Did he speak of me at that time?
KREON: He never did;
At least, not when I was present.
OEDIPUS: But . . . the inquiry?

50 I suppose you held one?
KREON: We did, but we learned nothing.
OEDIPUS: Why did the prophet not speak against me then?
KREON: I do not know; and I am the kind of man
Who holds his tongue when he has no facts to go on.
OEDIPUS: There's one fact that you know, and you could tell it.

55 KREON: What fact is that? If I know it, you shall have it.

OEDIPUS: If he were not involved with you, he could not say
 That it was I who murdered Laïos.

KREON: If he says that, you are the one that knows it!—
 But now it is my turn to question you.

60 OEDIPUS: Put your questions. I am no murderer.

KREON: First, then: You married my sister?

OEDIPUS: I married your sister.

KREON: And you rule the kingdom equally with her?

OEDIPUS: Everything that she wants she has from me.

KREON: And I am the third, equal to both of you?

65 OEDIPUS: That is why I call you a bad friend.

KREON: No. Reason it out, as I have done.
 Think of this first: Would any sane man prefer
 Power, with all a king's anxieties,
 To that same power and the grace of sleep?

70 Certainly not I.
 I have never longed for the king's power—only his rights.
 Would any wise man differ from me in this?
 As matters stand, I have my way in everything
 With your consent, and no responsibilities.

75 If I were king, I should be a slave to policy.
 How could I desire a sceptre more
 Than what is now mine—untroubled influence?
 No, I have not gone mad; I need no honours,
 Except those with the perquisites I have now.

80 I am welcome everywhere; every man salutes me,
 And those who want your favour seek my ear,
 Since I know how to manage what they ask.
 Should I exchange this ease for that anxiety?
 Besides, no sober mind is treasonable.

85 I hate anarchy
 And never would deal with any man who likes it.

 Test what I have said. Go to the priestess
 At Delphi, ask if I quoted her correctly.
 And as for this other thing: if I am found

90 Guilty of treason with Teiresias,
 Then sentence me to death. You have my word
 It is a sentence I should cast my vote for—
 But not without evidence!
        You do wrong
 When you take good men for bad, bad men for good.

95   A true friend thrown aside—why, life itself
      Is not more precious!
                        In time you will know this well:
      For time, and time alone, will show the just man,
      Though scoundrels are discovered in a day.
      CHORAGOS: This is well said, and a prudent man would ponder it.
100   Judgments too quickly formed are dangerous.
      OEDIPUS: But is he not quick in his duplicity?
      And shall I not be quick to parry him?
      Would you have me stand still, holding my peace, and let
      This man win everything, through my inaction?
105   KREON: And you want—what is it, then? To banish me?
      OEDIPUS: No, not exile. It is your death I want,
          So that all the world may see what treason means.
      KREON: You will persist, then? You will not believe me?
      OEDIPUS: How can I believe you?
      KREON: Then you are a fool.
110   OEDIPUS: To save myself?
      KREON: In justice, think of me.
      OEDIPUS: You are evil incarnate.
      KREON: But suppose that you are wrong?
      OEDIPUS: Still I must rule.
      KREON: But not if you rule badly.
      OEDIPUS: O city, city!
      KREON: It is my city, too!
      CHORAGOS: Now, my lords, be still. I see the Queen,
115   Iokastê, coming from her palace chambers;
      And it is time she came, for the sake of you both.
      This dreadful quarrel can be resolved through her.

          Enter Iokastê.

      IOKASTÊ: Poor foolish men, what wicked din is this?
      With Thebes sick to death, is it not shameful
120   That you should rake some private quarrel up?
          [*To Oedipus*]
      Come into the house
                          —And you, Kreon, go now:
      Let us have no more of this tumult over nothing.
      KREON: Nothing? No, sister: what your husband plans for me
      Is one of two great evils: exile or death.
125   OEDIPUS: He is right.
                      Why, woman I have caught him squarely
      Plotting against my life.

KREON: No! Let me die
    Accurst if ever I have wished you harm!

IOKASTÊ: Ah, believe it, Oedipus!
    In the name of the gods, respect this oath of his
130 For my sake, for the sake of these people here!

CHORAGOS: **Strophe 1**
    Open your mind to her, my lord. Be ruled by her, I beg you!

OEDIPUS: What would you have me do?

CHORAGOS: Respect Kreon's word. He has never spoken like a fool,
    And now he has sworn an oath.

135 OEDIPUS: You know what you ask?

CHORAGOS: I do.

OEDIPUS: Speak on, then.

CHORAGOS: A friend so sworn should not be baited so,
    In blind malice, and without final proof.

OEDIPUS: You are aware, I hope, that what you say
    Means death for me, or exile at the least.

140 CHORAGOS: **Strophe 2**
    No, I swear by Helios, first in Heaven!
    May I die friendless and accurst,
    The worst of deaths, if ever I meant that!
    It is the withering fields
    That hurt my sick heart:
145   Must we bear all these ills,
    and now you bad blood as well?

OEDIPUS: Then let him go. And let me die, if I must,
    Or be driven by him in shame from the land of Thebes.
    It is your unhappiness, and not his talk,
150 That touches me.
              As for him—
    Wherever he goes, hatred will follow him.

KREON: Ugly in yielding, as you were ugly in rage!
    Natures like yours chiefly torment themselves.

OEDIPUS: Can you not go? Can you not leave me?

KREON: I can.
155 You do not know me; but the city knows me,
    And in its eyes I am just, if not in yours.

                                  Exit Kreon.

CHORAGOS: **Antistrophe 1**
    Lady Iokastê, did you not ask the King to go to his chambers?

IOKASTÊ: First tell me what has happened.

CHORAGOS: There was suspicion without evidence; yet it rankled
160 As even false charges will.

IOKASTÊ: On both sides?

CHORAGOS:　　　　　　　On both.

IOKASTÊ:　　　　　　　　　But what was said?

CHORAGOS: Oh let it rest, let it be done with!

　　　　Have we not suffered enough?

OEDIPUS: You see to what your decency has brought you:

165　　　　You have made difficulties where my heart saw none.

CHORAGOS:　　　　　　　　　　　　　　　　**Antistrophe 2**

　　　　　Oedipus, it is not once only I have told you—

　　　　　　You must know I should count myself unwise

　　　　　To the point of madness, should I now forsake you—

　　　　　　You, under whose hand,

170　　　　　　In the storm of another time,

　　　　　　　Our dear land sailed out free.

　　　　　　　But now stand fast at the helm!

IOKASTÊ: In God's name, Oedipus, inform your wife as well:

　　　　Why are you so set in this hard anger?

175　OEDIPUS: I will tell you, for none of these men deserves

　　　　My confidence as you do. It is Kreon's work,

　　　　His treachery, his plotting against me.

IOKASTÊ: Go on, if you can make this clear to me.

OEDIPUS: He charges me with the murder of Laïos.

180　IOKASTÊ: Has he some knowledge? Or does he speak from hearsay?

OEDIPUS: He would not commit himself to such a charge,

　　　　But he has brought in that damnable soothsayer

　　　　To tell his story.

IOKASTÊ:　　　　　　Set your mind at rest.

　　　　If it is a question of soothsayers, I tell you

185　　　　That you will find no man whose craft gives knowledge

　　　　Of the unknowable.

　　　　　　　　　　Here is my proof:

　　　　An oracle was reported to Laïos once

　　　　(I will not say from Phoibos himself, but from

　　　　His appointed ministers, at any rate)

190　　　　That his doom would be death at the hands of his own son—

　　　　His son, born of his flesh and of mine!

　　　　Now, you remember the story: Laïos was killed

　　　　By marauding strangers where three highways meet;

　　　　But his child had not been three days in this world

195　　　　Before the King had pierced the baby's ankles

　　　　And left him to die on a lonely mountainside.

Thus, Apollo never caused that child
To kill his father, and it was not Laïos' fate
To die at the hands of his son, as he had feared.
200   This is what prophets and prophecies are worth!
Have no dread of them.
                    It is God himself
Who can show us what he wills, in his own way.

OEDIPUS: How strange a shadowy memory crossed my mind,
Just now while you were speaking; it chilled my heart.

205 IOKASTÊ: What do you mean? What memory do you speak of?

OEDIPUS: If I understand you, Laïos was killed
At a place where three roads meet.

IOKASTÊ: So it was said:
We have no later story.

OEDIPUS: Where did it happen?

IOKASTÊ: Phokis, it is called: at a place where the Theban Way
210   Divides into the roads toward Delphi and Daulia.

OEDIPUS: When?

IOKASTÊ: We had the news not long before you came
And proved the right to your succession here.

OEDIPUS: Ah, what net has God been weaving for me?

IOKASTÊ: Oedipus! Why does this trouble you?

OEDIPUS: Do not ask me yet.
215   First, tell me how Laïos looked, and tell me
How old he was.

IOKASTÊ: He was tall, his hair just touched
With white; his form was not unlike your own.

OEDIPUS: I think that I myself may be accurst
By my own ignorant edict.

IOKASTÊ: You speak strangely.
220   It makes me tremble to look at you, my King.

OEDIPUS: I am not sure that the blind man can not see.
But I should know better if you were to tell me—

IOKASTÊ: Anything—though I dread to hear you ask it.

OEDIPUS: Was the King lightly escorted, or did he ride
225   With a large company, as a ruler should?

IOKASTÊ: There were five men with him in all: one was a herald;
And a single chariot, which he was driving.

OEDIPUS: Alas, that makes it plain enough!
                        But who—
Who told you how it happened?

IOKASTÊ: A household servant,
230   The only one to escape.

OEDIPUS: And is he still
    A servant of ours?

IOKASTÊ: No; for when he came back at last
    And found you enthroned in the place of the dead king,
    He came to me, touched my hand with his, and begged
    That I would send him away to the frontier district

235   Where only the shepherds go—
    As far away from the city as I could send him.
    I granted his prayer; for although the man was a slave,
    He had earned more than this favour at my hands.

OEDIPUS: Can he be called back quickly?

IOKASTÊ: Easily.

240   But why?

OEDIPUS: I have taken too much upon myself
    Without enquiry; therefore I wish to consult him.

IOKASTÊ: Then he shall come.
                         But am I not one also
    To whom you might confide these fears of yours?

OEDIPUS: That is your right; it will not be denied you,
245   Now least of all; for I have reached a pitch
    Of wild foreboding. Is there anyone
    To whom I should sooner speak?

    Polybos of Corinth is my father.
    My mother is a Dorian: Meropê.
250   I grew up chief among the men of Corinth
    Until a strange thing happened—
    Not worth my passion, it may be, but strange.

    At a feast, a drunken man maundering in his cups
    Cries out that I am not my father's son!
255   I contained myself that night, though I felt anger
    And a sinking heart. The next day I visited
    My father and mother, and questioned them. They stormed,
    Calling it all the slanderous rant of a fool;
    And this relieved me. Yet the suspicion
260   Remained always aching in my mind;
    I knew there was talk; I could not rest;
    And finally, saying nothing to my parents,
    I went to the shrine at Delphi.

    The god dismissed my question without reply;
265   He spoke of other things.
                     Some were clear,

Full of wretchedness, dreadful, unbearable:
As that I should lie with my own mother, breed
Children from whom all men would turn their eyes;
And that I should be my father's murderer.

270   I heard all this, and fled. And from that day
Corinth to me was only in the stars
Descending in that quarter of the sky,
As I wandered farther and farther on my way
To a land where I should never see the evil

275   Sung by the oracle. And I came to this country
Where, so you say, King Laïos was killed.
I will tell you all that happened there, my lady.

There were three highways
Coming together at a place I passed;

280   And there a herald came towards me, and a chariot
Drawn by horses, with a man such as you describe
Seated in it. The groom leading the horses
Forced me off the road at his lord's command;
But as this charioteer lurched over towards me

285   I struck him in my rage. The old man saw me
And brought his double goad down upon my head
As I came abreast.
                He was paid back, and more!
Swinging my club in this right hand I knocked him
Out of his car, and he rolled on the ground.
                      I killed him.

290   I killed them all.
Now if that stranger and Laïos were—kin,
Where is a man more miserable than I?
More hated by the gods? Citizen and alien alike
Must never shelter me or speak to me—

295   I must be shunned by all.
                    And I myself
Pronounced this malediction upon myself!

Think of it: I have touched you with these hands,
These hands that killed your husband. What defilement!

Am I all evil, then? It must be so,

300   Since I must flee from Thebes, yet never again
See my own countrymen, my own country,
For fear of joining my mother in marriage

And killing Polybos, my father.

                                    Ah,

If I was created so, born to this fate,
305   Who could deny the savagery of God?

O holy majesty of heavenly powers!
May I never see that day! Never!
Rather let me vanish from the race of men
Than know the abomination destined me!

310   CHORAGOS: We too, my lord, have felt dismay at this.
      But there is hope: you have yet to hear the shepherd.
      OEDIPUS: Indeed, I fear no other hope is left me.
      IOKASTÊ: What do you hope from him when he comes?
      OEDIPUS: This much:
      If his account of the murder tallies with yours,
315   Then I am cleared.
      IOKASTÊ: What was it that I said
      Of such importance?
      OEDIPUS: Why, 'marauders', you said,
      Killed the King, according to this man's story.
      If he maintains that still, if there were several,
      Clearly the guilt is not mine: I was alone.
320   But if he says one man, singlehanded, did it,
      Then the evidence all points to me.
      IOKASTÊ: You may be sure that he said there were several;
      And can he call back that story now? He can not.
      The whole city heard it as plainly as I.
325   But suppose he alters some detail of it:
      He can not ever show that Laïos' death
      Fulfilled the oracle: for Apollo said
      My child was doomed to kill him; and my child—
      Poor baby!—it was my child that died first.

330   No. From now on, where oracles are concerned,
      I would not waste a second thought on any.
      OEDIPUS: You may be right.
                              But come: let someone go
      For the shepherd at once. This matter must be settled.
      IOKASTÊ: I will send for him.
335   I would not wish to cross you in anything.
      And surely not in this.—Let us go in.

                                    Exeunt into the palace.

ODE II

CHORUS: Let me be reverent in the ways of right,   **Strophe 1**
  Lowly the paths I journey on;
  Let all my words and actions keep
  The laws of the pure universe
5 From highest Heaven handed down.
  For Heaven is their bright nurse,
  Those generations of the realms of light;
  Ah, never of mortal kind were they begot,
  Nor are they slaves of memory, lost in sleep:
10 Their Father is greater than Time, and ages not.

  The tyrant is a child of Pride   **Antistrophe 1**
  Who drinks from his great sickening cup
  Recklessness and vanity,
  Until from his high crest headlong
15 He plummets to the dust of hope.
  That strong man is not strong.
  But let no fair ambition be denied;
  May God protect the wrestler for the State
  In government, in comely policy,
20 Who will fear God, and on His ordinance wait.

  Haughtiness and the high hand of disdain   **Strophe 2**
  Tempt and outrage God's holy law;
  And any mortal who dares hold
  No immortal Power in awe
25 Will be caught up in a net of pain:
  The price for which his levity is sold.
  Let each man take due earnings, then,
  And keep his hands from holy things,
  And from blasphemy stand apart—
30 Else the crackling blast of heaven
  Blows on his head, and on his desperate heart.
  Though fools will honour impious men,
  In their cities no tragic poet sings.

  Shall we lose faith in Delphi's obscurities,   **Antistrophe 2**
35 We have heard the world's core
  Discredited, and the sacred wood
  Of Zeus at Elis praised no more?
  The deeds and the strange prophecies
  Must make a pattern yet to be understood.

40   Zeus, if indeed you are lord of all,
        Throned in light over night and day,
        Mirror this in your endless mind:
        Our masters call the oracle
        Words on the wind, and the Delphic vision blind!
45   Their hearts no longer know Apollo,
        And reverence for the gods has died away.

SCENE III

Enter Iokastê.

IOKASTÊ: Princess of Thebes, it has occurred to me
        To visit the altars of the gods, bearing
        These branches as a suppliant, and this incense.
        Our King is not himself: his noble soul
5   Is overwrought with fantasies of dread,
        Else he would consider
        The new prophecies in the light of the old.
        He will listen to any voice that speaks disaster,
        And my advice goes for nothing.

        She approaches the altar, right.

                                To you, then, Apollo,
10   Lycéan lord, since you are nearest, I turn in prayer.

        Receive these offerings, and grant us deliverance
        From defilement. Our hearts are heavy with fear
        When we see our leader distracted, as helpless sailors
        Are terrified by the confusion of their helmsman.

        Enter Messenger.

15   MESSENGER: Friends, no doubt you can direct me:
        Where shall I find the house of Oedipus,
        Or, better still, where is the King himself?
        CHORAGOS: It is this very place, stranger; he is inside.
        This is his wife and mother of his children.
20   MESSENGER: I wish her happiness in a happy house,
        Blest in all the fulfillment of her marriage.
        IOKASTÊ: I wish as much for you: your courtesy
        Deserves a like good fortune. But now, tell me:
        Why have you come? What have you to say to us?
25   MESSENGER: Good news, my lady, for your house and your husband.

IOKASTÊ: What news? Who sent you here?

MESSENGER: I am from Corinth.
  The news I bring ought to mean joy for you,
  Though it may be you will find some grief in it.

IOKASTÊ: What is it? How can it touch us in both ways?

30 MESSENGER: The word is that the people of the Isthmus
  Intend to call Oedipus to be their king.

IOKASTÊ: But old King Polybos—is he not reigning still?

MESSENGER: No. Death holds him in his sepulchre.

IOKASTÊ: What are you saying? Polybos is dead?

35 MESSENGER: If I am not telling the truth, may I die myself.

IOKASTÊ: [*To a Maidservant*]
  Go in, go quickly; tell this to your master.

  O riddlers of God's will, where are you now!
  This was the man whom Oedipus, long ago,
  Feared so, fled so, in dread of destroying him—

40 But it was another fate by which he died.

   Enter Oedipus, centre.

OEDIPUS: Dearest Iokastê, why have you sent for me?

IOKASTÊ: Listen to what this man says, and then tell me
  What has become of the solemn prophecies.

OEDIPUS: Who is this man? What is his news for me?

45 IOKASTÊ: He has come from Corinth to announce your father's death!

OEDIPUS: Is it true, stranger? Tell me in your own words.

MESSENGER: I can not say it more clearly: the King is dead.

OEDIPUS: Was it by treason? Or by an attack of illness?

MESSENGER: A little thing brings old men to their rest.

50 OEDIPUS: It was sickness, then?

MESSENGER: Yes, and his many years.

OEDIPUS: Ah!
  Why should a man respect the Pythian hearth, or
  Give heed to the birds that jangle above his head?
  They prophesied that I should kill Polybos,
  Kill my own father; but he is dead and buried,

55 And I am here—I never touched him, never,
  Unless he died of grief for my departure,
  And thus, in a sense, through me. No. Polybos
  Has packed the oracles off with him underground.
  They are empty words.

IOKASTÊ: Had I not told you so?

60 OEDIPUS: You had; it was my faint heart that betrayed me.

IOKASTÊ: From now on never think of those things again.

OEDIPUS: And yet—must I not fear my mother's bed?

IOKASTÊ: Why should anyone in this world be afraid,
     Since Fate rules us and nothing can be foreseen?
65   A man should live only for the present day.
     Have no more fear of sleeping with your mother:
     How many men, in dreams, have lain with their mothers!
     No reasonable man is troubled by such things.

OEDIPUS: That is true; only—
70   If only my mother were not still alive!
     But she is alive. I can not help my dread.

IOKASTÊ: Yet this news of your father's death is wonderful.

OEDIPUS: Wonderful. But I fear the living woman.

MESSENGER: Tell me, who is this woman that you fear?

75   OEDIPUS: It is Meropê, man; the wife of King Polybos.

MESSENGER: Meropê? Why should you be afraid of her?

OEDIPUS: An oracle of the gods, a dreadful saying.

MESSENGER: Can you tell me about it or are you sworn to silence?

OEDIPUS: I can tell you, and I will.
80   Apollo said through his prophet that I was the man
     Who should marry his own mother, shed his father's blood
     With his own hands. And so, for all these years
     I have kept clear of Corinth, and no harm has come—
     Though it would have been sweet to see my parents again.

85   MESSENGER: And is this the fear that drove you out of Corinth?

OEDIPUS: Would you have me kill my father?

MESSENGER: As for that
     You must be reassured by the news I gave you.

OEDIPUS: If you could reassure me, I would reward you.

MESSENGER: I had that in mind, I will confess: I thought
90   I could count on you when you returned to Corinth.

OEDIPUS: No: I will never go near my parents again.

MESSENGER: Ah, son, you still do not know what you are doing—

OEDIPUS: What do you mean? In the name of God tell me!

MESSENGER: —If these are your reasons for not going home.

95   OEDIPUS: I tell you, I fear the oracle may come true.

MESSENGER: And guilt may come upon you through your parents?

OEDIPUS: That is the dread that is always in my heart.

MESSENGER: Can you not see that all your fears are groundless?

OEDIPUS: Groundless? Am I not my parents' son?

100 MESSENGER: Polybos was not your father.

OEDIPUS: Not my father?

MESSENGER: No more your father than the man speaking to you.

OEDIPUS: But you are nothing to me!

MESSENGER: Neither was he.

OEDIPUS: Then why did he call me son?

MESSENGER: I will tell you:

    Long ago he had you from my hands, as a gift.

105 OEDIPUS: Then how could he love me so, if I was not his?

MESSENGER: He had no children, and his heart turned to you.

OEDIPUS: What of you? Did you buy me? Did you find me by chance?

MESSENGER: I came upon you in the woody vales of Kithairon.

OEDIPUS: And what were you doing there?

MESSENGER: Tending my flocks.

110 OEDIPUS: A wandering shepherd?

MESSENGER: But your saviour, son, that day.

OEDIPUS: From what did you save me?

MESSENGER: Your ankles should tell you that.

OEDIPUS: Ah, stranger, why do you speak of that childhood pain?

MESSENGER: I pulled the skewer that pinned your feet together.

OEDIPUS: I have had the mark as long as I can remember.

115 MESSENGER: That was why you were given the name you bear.

OEDIPUS: God! Was it my father or my mother who did it? Tell me!

MESSENGER: I do not know. The man who gave you to me

    Can tell you better than I.

OEDIPUS: It was not you that found me, but another?

120 MESSENGER: It was another shepherd gave you to me.

OEDIPUS: Who was he? Can you tell me who he was?

MESSENGER: I think he was said to be one of Laïos' people.

OEDIPUS: You mean the Laïos who was king here years ago?

MESSENGER: Yes; King Laïos; and the man was one of his herdsmen.

125 OEDIPUS: Is he still alive? Can I see him?

MESSENGER: These men here

    Know best about such things.

OEDIPUS: Does anyone here

    Know this shepherd that he is talking about?

    Have you seen him in the fields, or in the town?

    If you have, tell me. It is time things were made plain.

130 CHORAGOS: I think the man he means is that same shepherd

    You have already asked to see. Iokastê perhaps

    Could tell you something.

OEDIPUS: Do you know anything

    About him, Lady? Is he the man we have summoned?

    Is that the man this shepherd means?

IOKASTÊ: Why think of him?

135   Forget this herdsman. Forget it all.

    This talk is a waste of time.

OEDIPUS: How can you say that,

When the clues to my true birth are in my hands?

IOKASTÊ: For God's love, let us have no more questioning!
Is your life nothing to you?
140   My own is pain enough for me to bear.

OEDIPUS: You need not worry. Suppose my mother a slave,
And born of slaves: no baseness can touch you.

IOKASTÊ: Listen to me, I beg you: do not do this thing!

OEDIPUS: I will not listen; the truth must be made known.

145 IOKASTÊ: Everything that I say is for your own good!

OEDIPUS: My own good
Snaps my patience, then; I want none of it.

IOKASTÊ: You are fatally wrong! May you never learn who you are!

OEDIPUS: Go, one of you, and bring the shepherd here.
Let us leave this woman to brag of her royal name.

150 IOKASTÊ: Ah, miserable!
That is the only word I have for you now.
That is the only word I can ever have.

                                     Exit into the Palace.

CHORAGOS: Why has she left us, Oedipus? Why has she gone
In such a passion of sorrow? I fear this silence:
155   Something dreadful may come of it.

OEDIPUS: Let it come!
However base my birth, I must know about it.
The Queen, like a woman, is perhaps ashamed
To think of my low origin. But I
Am a child of Luck; I can not be dishonoured.
160   Luck is my mother; the passing months, my brothers,
Have seen me rich and poor.
                       If this is so,
How could I wish that I were someone else?
How could I not be glad to know my birth?

ODE III

CHORUS: If ever the coming time were known   **Strophe**
    To my heart's pondering,
    Kithairon, now by Heaven I see the torches
    At the festival of the next full moon,
5   And see the dance, and hear the choir sing
    A grace to your gentle shade:

Mountain where Oedipus was found,
O mountain guard of a noble race!
May the god who heals us lend his aid,

10   And let that glory come to pass
For our king's cradling-ground.

Of the nymphs that flower beyond the years,   **Antistrophe**
Who bore you, royal child,
To Pan of the hills or the timberline Apollo,

15   Cold in delight where the upland clears,
Or Hermês for whom Kyllenê's heights are piled?
Or flushed as evening cloud,
Great Dionysos, roamer of mountains,
He—was it he who found you there,

20   And caught you up in his own proud
Arms from the sweet god-ravisher
Who laughed by the Muses' fountains?

SCENE IV

OEDIPUS: Sirs: though I do not know the man,
I think I see him coming, this shepherd we want:
He is old, like our friend here, and the men
Bringing him seem to be servants of my house.

5   But you can tell, if you have ever seen him.

Enter Shepherd escorted by servants.

CHORAGOS: I know him, he was Laïos' man. You can trust him.
OEDIPUS: Tell me first, you from Corinth: is this the shepherd
We were discussing?
MESSENGER: This is the very man.
OEDIPUS: [*To Shepherd*]
Come here. No, look at me. You must answer

10   Everything I ask.—You belonged to Laïos?
SHEPHERD: Yes: born his slave, brought up in his house.
OEDIPUS: Tell me: what kind of work did you do for him?
SHEPHERD: I was a shepherd of his, most of my life.
OEDIPUS: Where mainly did you go for pasturage?

15   SHEPHERD: Sometimes Kithairon, sometimes the hills nearby.
OEDIPUS: Do you remember ever seeing this man out there?
SHEPHERD: What would he be doing there? This man?
OEDIPUS: This man standing here. Have you ever seen him before?
SHEPHERD: No. At least, not to my recollection.

20 MESSENGER: And that is not strange, my lord. But I'll refresh
       His memory: he must remember when we two
       Spent three whole seasons together, March to September,
       On Kithairon or thereabouts. He had two flocks;
       I had one. Each autumn I'd drive mine home

25 And he would go back with his to Laïos' sheepfold.——
       Is this not true, just as I have described it?

SHEPHERD: True, yes; but it was all so long ago.

MESSENGER: Well, then: do you remember, back in those days,
       That you gave me a baby boy to bring up as my own?

30 SHEPHERD: What if I did? What are you trying to say?

MESSENGER: King Oedipus was once that little child.

SHEPHERD: Damn you, hold your tongue!

OEDIPUS: No more of that!
       It is your tongue needs watching, not this man's.

SHEPHERD: My King, my Master, what is it I have done wrong?

35 OEDIPUS: You have not answered his question about the boy.

SHEPHERD: He does not know . . . He is only making trouble . . .

OEDIPUS: Come, speak plainly, or it will go hard with you.

SHEPHERD: In God's name, do not torture an old man!

OEDIPUS: Come here, one of you; bind his arms behind him.

40 SHEPHERD: Unhappy king! What more do you wish to learn?

OEDIPUS: Did you give this man the child he speaks of?

SHEPHERD: I did.
       And I would to God I had died that very day.

OEDIPUS: You will die now unless you speak the truth.

SHEPHERD: Yet if I speak the truth, I am worse than dead.

OEDIPUS: [To Attendant]

45   He intends to draw it out, apparently——

SHEPHERD: No! I have told you already that I gave him the boy.

OEDIPUS: Where did you get him? From your house? From somewhere else?

SHEPHERD: Not from mine, no. A man gave him to me.

OEDIPUS: Is that man here? Whose house did he belong to?

50 SHEPHERD: For God's love, my King, do not ask me any more!

OEDIPUS: You are a dead man if I have to ask you again.

SHEPHERD: Then . . . Then the child was from the palace of Laïos.

OEDIPUS: A slave child? or a child of his own line?

SHEPHERD: Ah, I am on the brink of dreadful speech!

55 OEDIPUS: And I of dreadful hearing. Yet I must hear.

SHEPHERD: If you must be told, then . . .
                                            They said it was Laïos' child:
       But it is your wife who can tell you about that.

OEDIPUS: My wife!—Did she give it to you?

SHEPHERD: My Lord, she did.

OEDIPUS: Do you know why?

SHEPHERD: I was told to get rid of it.

60 OEDIPUS: Oh heartless mother!

SHEPHERD: But in dread of prophecies . . .

OEDIPUS: Tell me.

SHEPHERD: It was said that the boy would kill his own father.

OEDIPUS: Then why did you give him over to this old man?

SHEPHERD: I pitied the baby, my King,

65   And I thought that this man would take him far away
         To his own country.
                              He saved him—but for what a fate!
         For if you are what this man says you are,
         No man living is more wretched than Oedipus.

OEDIPUS: Ah God!
         It was true!
                    All the prophecies!
                                        —Now,

70   O Light, may I look on you for the last time!
         I, Oedipus,
         Oedipus, damned in his birth, in his marriage damned,
         Damned in the blood he shed with his own hand!

         He rushes into the palace.

ODE IV

CHORUS: Alas for the seed of men.   **Strophe 1**
         What measure shall I give these generations
         That breathe on the void and are void
         And exist and do not exist?

5   Who bears more weight of joy
         Than mass of sunlight shifting in images,
         Or who shall make his thought stay on
         That down time drifts away?

         Your splendour is all fallen.

10   O naked brow of wrath and tears,
         O change of Oedipus!
         I who saw your days call no man blest—
         Your great days like ghósts góne.

That mind was a strong bow.   **Antistrophe 1**

15 Deep, how deep you drew it then, hard archer,
At a dim fearful range,
And brought dear glory down!

You overcame the stranger—
The virgin with her hooking lion claws—
20 And though death sang, stood like a tower
To make pale Thebes take heart.
Fortress against our sorrow!

True king, giver of laws,
Majestic Oedipus!
25 No prince in Thebes had ever such renown,
No prince won such grace of power.

And now of all men ever known   **Strophe 2**
Most pitiful is this man's story:
His fortunes are most changed, his state
30 Fallen to a low slave's
Ground under bitter fate.

O Oedipus, most royal one!
The great door that expelled you to the light
Gave at night—ah, gave night to your glory:
35 As to the father, to the fathering son.

All understood too late.

How could that queen whom Laïos won,
The garden that he harrowed at his height,
Be silent when the act was done?

40 But all eyes fail before time's eye,   **Antistrophe 2**
All actions come to justice there.
Though never willed, though far down the deep past,
Your bed, your dread sirings,
Are brought to book at last.

45 Child by Laïos doomed to die,
Then doomed to lose that fortunate little death,
Would God you never took breath in this air
That with my wailing lips I take to cry:

For I weep the world's outcast.

50   I was blind, and now I can tell why:
      Asleep, for you had given ease of breath
      To Thebes, while the false years went by.

ÉXODOS

Enter, from the palace, Second Messenger.

SECOND MESSENGER: Elders of Thebes, most honoured in this land,
      What horrors are yours to see and hear, what weight
      Of sorrows to be endured, if, true to your birth,
      You venerate the line of Labdakos!
5   I think neither Istros nor Phasis, those great rivers,
      Could purify this place of all the evil
      It shelters now, or soon must bring to light—
      Evil not done unconsciously, but willed.

      The greatest griefs are those we cause ourselves.
10   CHORAGOS: Surely, friend, we have grief enough already;
      What new sorrow do you mean?
SECOND MESSENGER: The Queen is dead.
CHORAGOS: O miserable Queen! But at whose hand?
SECOND MESSENGER: Her own.
      The full horror of what happened you can not know,
      For you did not see it; but I, who did, will tell you
15   As clearly as I can how she met her death.

      When she had left us,
      In passionate silence, passing through the court,
      She ran to her apartment in the house,
      Her hair clutched by the fingers of both hands.
20   She closed the doors behind her; then, by that bed
      Where long ago the fatal son was conceived—
      That son who should bring about his father's death—
      We heard her call upon Laïos, dead so many years,
      And heard her wail for the double fruit of her marriage,
25   A husband by her husband, children by her child.
      Exactly how she died I do not know:
      For Oedipus burst in moaning and would not let us
      Keep vigil to the end: it was by him
      As he stormed about the room that our eyes were caught.

30 From one to another of us he went, begging a sword,
Hunting the wife who was not his wife, the mother
Whose womb had carried his own children and himself.
I do not know: it was none of us aided him,
But surely one of the gods was in control!

35 For with a dreadful cry
He hurled his weight, as though wrenched out of himself,
At the twin doors: the bolts gave, and he rushed in.
And there we saw her hanging, her body swaying
From the cruel cord she had noosed about her neck.

40 A great sob broke from him, heartbreaking to hear,
As he loosed the rope and lowered her to the ground.

I would blot out from my mind what happened next!
For the King ripped from her gown the golden brooches
That were her ornament, and raised them, and plunged them down

45 Straight into his own eyeballs, crying, 'No more,
No more shall you look on the misery about me,
The horrors of my own doing! Too long you have known
The faces of those whom I should never have seen,
Too long been blind to those for whom I was searching!

50 From this hour, go in darkness!' And as he spoke,
He struck at his eyes—not once, but many times;
And the blood spattered his beard,
Bursting from his ruined sockets like red hail.

So from the unhappiness of two this evil has sprung,

55 A curse on the man and woman alike. The old
Happiness of the house of Labdakos
Was happiness enough: where is it today?
It is all wailing and ruin, disgrace, death—all
The misery of mankind that has a name—

60 And it is wholly and for ever theirs.

CHORAGOS: Is he in agony still? Is there no rest for him?

SECOND MESSENGER: He is calling for someone to open the doors wide
So that all the children of Kadmos may look upon
His father's murderer, his mother's—no,

65 I can not say it!
         And then he will leave Thebes,
Self-exiled, in order that the curse
Which he himself pronounced may depart from the house.
He is weak, and there is none to lead him,
So terrible is his suffering.
         But you will see:

70 Look, the doors are opening; in a moment
You will see a thing that would crush a heart of stone.

The central door is opened; Oedipus, blinded, is led in.

CHORAGOS: Dreadful indeed for men to see.
Never have my own eyes
Looked on a sight so full of fear.

75 Oedipus!
What madness came upon you, what daemon
Leaped on your life with heavier
Punishment than a mortal man can bear?
No: I can not even

80 Look at you, poor ruined one.
And I would speak, question, ponder,
If I were able. No.
You make me shudder.

OEDIPUS: God. God.

85 Is there a sorrow greater?
Where shall I find harbour in this world?
My voice is hurled far on a dark wind.
What has God done to me?

CHORAGOS: Too terrible to think of, or to see.

90 OEDIPUS: O cloud of night,   **Strophe 1**
Never to be turned away: night coming on,
I can not tell how: night like a shroud!
My fair winds brought me here.

                                   O God. Again
The pain of the spikes where I had sight,

95 The flooding pain
Of memory, never to be gouged out.

CHORAGOS: This is not strange.
You suffer it all twice over, remorse in pain,
Pain in remorse.

100 OEDIPUS: Ah dear friend   **Antistrophe 1**
Are you faithful even yet, you alone?
Are you still standing near me, will you stay here,
Patient, to care for the blind?
                                   The blind man!
Yet even blind I know who it is attends me,

105 By the voice's tone—
Though my new darkness hide the comforter.

CHORAGOS: Oh fearful act!
    What god was it drove you to rake black
    Night across your eyes?

110 OEDIPUS: Apollo. Apollo. Dear   **Strophe 2**
    Children, the god was Apollo.
    He brought my sick, sick fate upon me.
    But the blinding hand was my own!
    How could I bear to see
115   When all my sight was horror everywhere?

CHORAGOS: Everywhere; that is true.
OEDIPUS: And now what is left?
    Images? Love? A greeting even,
    Sweet to the senses? Is there anything?
120   Ah, no, friends: lead me away.
    Lead me away from Thebes.
                        Lead the great wreck
    And hell of Oedipus, whom the gods hate.

CHORAGOS: Your misery, you are not blind to that.
    Would God you had never found it out!

125 OEDIPUS: Death take the man who unbound   **Antistrophe 2**
    My feet on that hillside
    And delivered me from death to life! What life?
    If only I had died,
    This weight of monstrous doom
130   Could not have dragged me and my darlings down.

CHORAGOS: I would have wished the same.
OEDIPUS: Oh never to have come here
    With my father's blood upon me! Never
    To have been the man they call his mother's husband!
135   Oh accurst! Oh child of evil,
    To have entered that wretched bed—
                       the selfsame one!
    More primal than sin itself, this fell to me.

CHORAGOS: I do not know what words to offer you.
    You were better dead than alive and blind.

140 OEDIPUS: Do not counsel me any more. This punishment
    That I have laid upon myself is just.
    If I had eyes,

I do not know how I could bear the sight
Of my father, when I came to the house of Death,
145 Or my mother; for I have sinned against them both
So vilely that I could not make my peace
By strangling my own life.
                              Or do you think my children,
Born as they were born, would be sweet to my eyes?
Ah never, never! Nor this town with its high walls,
150 Nor the holy images of the gods.
                              For I,
Thrice miserable!—Oedipus, noblest of all the line
Of Kadmos, have condemned myself to enjoy
These things no more, by my own malediction
Expelling that man whom the gods declared
155 To be a defilement in the house of Laïos.
After exposing the rankness of my own guilt,
How could I look men frankly in the eyes?
No, I swear it,
If I could have stifled my hearing at its source,
160 I would have done it and made all this body
A tight cell of misery, blank to light and sound:
So I should have been safe in my dark mind
Beyond external evil.
                              Ah Kithairon!
Why did you shelter me? When I was cast upon you,
165 Why did I not die? Then I should never
Have shown the world my execrable birth.

Ah Polybos! Corinth, city that I believed
The ancient seat of my ancestors: how fair
I seemed, your child! And all the while this evil
170 Was cancerous within me!
                              For I am sick
In my own being, sick in my origin.

O three roads, dark ravine, woodland and way
Where three roads met: you, drinking my father's blood,
My own blood, spilled by my own hand: can you remember
175 The unspeakable things I did there, and the things
I went on from there to do?
                              O marriage, marriage!
The act that engendered me, and again the act
Performed by the son in the same bed—
                                          Ah, the net

Of incest, mingling fathers, brothers, sons,
180   With brides, wives, mothers: the last evil
That can be known by men: no tongue can say
How evil!

        No. For the love of God, conceal me.
Somewhere far from Thebes; or kill me; or hurl me
Into the sea, away from men's eyes for ever.
185   Come, lead me. You need not fear to touch me.
Of all men, I alone can bear this guilt.

    Enter Kreon.

CHORAGOS: Kreon is here now. As to what you ask,
He may decide the course to take. He only
Is left to protect the city in your place.
190 OEDIPUS: Alas, how can I speak to him? What right have I
To beg his courtesy whom I have deeply wronged?
KREON: I have not come to mock you, Oedipus,
Or to reproach you, either.
    [*To Attendants*]   —You standing there:
If you have lost all respect for man's dignity,
195 At least respect the flame of Lord Helios:
Do not allow this pollution to show itself
Openly here, an affront to the earth
And Heaven's rain and the light of day. No, take him
Into the house as quickly as you can.
200 For it is proper
That only the close kindred see his grief.
OEDIPUS: I pray you in God's name, since your courtesy
Ignores my dark expectation, visiting
With mercy this man of all men most execrable:
205 Give me what I ask—for your good, not for mine.
KREON: And what is it that you turn to me begging for?
OEDIPUS: Drive me out of this country as quickly as may be
To a place where no human voice can ever greet me.
KREON: I should have done that before now—only,
210 God's will had not been wholly revealed to me.
OEDIPUS: But his command is plain: the parricide
Must be destroyed. I am that evil man.
KREON: That is the sense of it, yes; but as things are,
We had best discover clearly what is to be done.
215 OEDIPUS: You would learn more about a man like me?
KREON: You are ready now to listen to the god.
OEDIPUS: I will listen. But it is to you
That I must turn for help. I beg you, hear me.

The woman in there—
220   Give her whatever funeral you think proper:
She is your sister.
                    —But let me go, Kreon!
Let me purge my father's Thebes of the pollution
Of my living here, and go out to the wild hills,
To Kithairon, that has won such fame with me,
225   The tomb my mother and father appointed for me,
And let me die there, as they willed I should.
And yet I know
Death will not ever come to me through sickness
Or in any natural way: I have been preserved
230   For some unthinkable fate. But let that be.

As for my sons, you need not care for them.
They are men, they will find some way to live.
But my poor daughters, who have shared my table,
Who never before have been parted from their father—
235   Take care of them, Kreon; do this for me.
And will you let me touch them with my hands
A last time, and let us weep together?
Be kind, my lord,
Great prince, be kind!
                    Could I but touch them,
240   They would be mine again, as when I had my eyes.

      Enter Antigone and Ismene, attended.

Ah, God!
Is it my dearest children I hear weeping?
Has Kreon pitied me and sent my daughters?
KREON: Yes, Oedipus: I knew that they were dear to you
245   In the old days, and know you must love them still.
OEDIPUS: May God bless you for this—and be friendlier
Guardian to you than he has been to me!

Children, where are you?
Come quickly to my hands: they are your brother's—
250   Hands that have brought your father's once clear eyes
To this way of seeing—
                    Ah dearest ones,
I had neither sight nor knowledge then, your father
By the woman who was the source of his own life!
And I weep for you—having no strength to see you—
255   I weep for you when I think of the bitterness

That men will visit upon you all your lives.
What homes, what festivals can you attend
Without being forced to depart again in tears?
And when you come to marriageable age,
260 Where is the man, my daughters, who would dare
Risk the bane that lies on all my children?
Is there any evil wanting? Your father killed
His father; sowed the womb of her who bore him;
Engendered you at the fount of his own existence!
265 That is what they will say of you.

                                    Then, whom
Can you ever marry? There are no bridegrooms for you,
And your lives must wither away in sterile dreaming.

O Kreon, son of Menoikeus!
You are the only father my daughters have,
270 Since we, their parents, are both of us gone for ever.
They are your own blood: you will not let them
Fall into beggary and loneliness;
You will keep them from the miseries that are mine!
Take pity on them; see, they are only children,
275 Friendless except for you. Promise me this,
Great Prince, and give me your hand in token of it.

    Kreon clasps his right hand.

Children:
I could say much, if you could understand me,
But as it is, I have only this prayer for you:
280 Live where you can, be as happy as you can—
Happier, please God, than God has made your father.
KREON: Enough. You have wept enough. Now go within.
OEDIPUS: I must; but it is hard.
KREON: Time eases all things.
OEDIPUS: You know my mind, then?
KREON: Say what you desire.
285 OEDIPUS: Send me from Thebes!
KREON: God grant that I may!
OEDIPUS: But since God hates me . . .
KREON: No, he will grant your wish.
OEDIPUS: You promise?
KREON: I can not speak beyond my knowledge.
OEDIPUS: Then lead me in.
KREON: Come now, and leave your children.

OEDIPUS: No! Do not take them from me!

KREON: Think no longer

290   That you are in command here, but rather think

How, when you were, you served your own destruction.

Exeunt into the house all but the Chorus; the Choragos chants directly to
the audience.

CHORAGOS: Men of Thebes: look upon Oedipus.

This is the king who solved the famous riddle
And towered up, most powerful of men.
295   No mortal eyes but looked on him with envy.
Yet in the end ruin swept over him.

Let every man in mankind's frailty
Consider his last day; and let none
Presume on his good fortune until he find
300   Life, at his death, a memory without pain.

c. 425 BC

William Shakespeare
1564–1616

William Shakespeare was born and raised in Stratford-upon-Avon, where his father was a glover, tanner, and dealer in hides. He was educated locally at the King's New School, where he acquired some familiarity with the classics, particularly Latin grammar and literature. He did not go on to attend one of the universities, however. Instead, he went off to London, probably attracted by the touring theatrical companies of the period, to make a career for himself as an actor and dramatist. He made his way to London sometime in the late 1580s, when public theatre was just beginning to become a popular enterprise in the city, and he likely started out as an actor with one of the local companies. By 1590 his earliest plays were being produced, and during his remaining twenty-three years of involvement with the theatre he wrote thirty-seven plays, while becoming a leading actor and shareholder in one of the major theatrical companies of the period. His plays cover a broad range of dramatic modes, extending from the comedies and history plays that figured largely in his early career, through the problem plays, tragedies, and romances that predominated in his later career. His plays reflect an equally broad range of experience, extending from the English battle scenes and tavern life of *1 Henry IV*, to the Roman and Egyptian court scenes of *Antony and Cleopatra*, and to the fantastic island world of *The Tempest*. Like most of his contemporaries he borrowed ideas for many of his works from classical, continental, or — as in the case of *King Lear* — native sources.

A Note on this Version

No single authoritative edition of *King Lear* exists. The play comes to modern readers through two early printed versions of the text: the First Quarto, published in 1608 during Shakespeare's life, and the First Folio, published in 1623 after his death. Although the two initial versions of Shakespeare's play are verbally iden-

tical at many points, several differences exist between them. Each contains words, lines, and even entire passages not found in the other version. The play printed here is based on the version included in the *Oxford Shakespeare* (edited by J.W. Craig). It generally follows the text of the Folio edition, but also includes several of the lines and passages found only in the Quarto.

King Lear

CHARACTERS

LEAR, King of Britain
KING OF FRANCE
DUKE OF BURGUNDY
DUKE OF CORNWALL
DUKE OF ALBANY
EARL OF KENT
EARL OF GLOUCESTER
EDGAR, Son to Gloucester
EDMUND, Bastard Son to Gloucester
CURAN, a Courtier
OSWALD, Steward to Goneril
OLD MAN, Tenant to Gloucester

DOCTOR
FOOL
AN OFFICER, Employed by Edmund
A GENTLEMAN, Attendant on Cordelia
A HERALD
SERVANTS, to Cornwall
GONERIL,
REGAN, } Daughters to Lear
CORDELIA,
KNIGHTS OF LEAR'S TRAIN,
OFFICERS, MESSENGERS, SOLDIERS,
ATTENDANTS

The scene: Britain

ACT I

SCENE 1

A Room of State in King Lear's Palace.

    Enter Kent, Gloucester, and Edmund.

KENT: I thought the king had more affected[1] the Duke of Albany than Cornwall.

GLOUCESTER: It did always seem so to us; but now, in the division of the kingdom, it appears not which of the dukes he values most; for equalities are so weighed[2] that curiosity[3] in neither can make choice of either's

5   moiety.[4]

KENT: Is not this your son, my lord?

---

1 *had . . . affected*: was more partial to, preferred
2 *equalities . . . weighed*: shares are so carefully equalized. ll. 3–5 i.e. neither duke can find ground for preferring the other's share to his own
3 careful examination
4 part, share (not necessarily half)

GLOUCESTER: His breeding,[5] sir, hath been at my charge: I have so often blushed to acknowledge him, that now I am brazed[6] to it.

KENT: I cannot conceive[7] you.

10 GLOUCESTER: Sir, this young fellow's mother could; whereupon she grew round-wombed, and had, indeed, sir, a son for her cradle ere she had a husband for her bed. Do you smell a fault?

KENT: I cannot wish the fault undone, the issue[8] of it being so proper.[9]

GLOUCESTER: But I have a son, sir, by order of law,[10] some year[11] elder than
15 this, who yet is no dearer in my account:[12] though this knave came something[13] saucily into the world before he was sent for, yet was his mother fair; there was good sport at his making, and the whoreson[14] must be acknowledged. Do you know this noble gentleman, Edmund?

EDMUND: No, my lord.

20 GLOUCESTER: My Lord of Kent: remember him hereafter as my honourable friend.

EDMUND: My services to your lordship.

KENT: I must love you, and sue[15] to know you better.

EDMUND: Sir, I shall study deserving.[16]

25 GLOUCESTER: He hath been out[17] nine years, and away he shall again. The king is coming.

Sennet.[18] Enter Lear, Cornwall, Albany, Goneril, Regan, Cordelia, and Attendants.

LEAR: Attend[19] the Lords of France and Burgundy, Gloucester.

GLOUCESTER: I shall, my leige.   [*Exeunt Gloucester and Edmund.*]

LEAR: Meantime we shall express[20] our darker[21] purpose.
30   Give me the map there. Know that we have divided
    In three our kingdom; and 'tis our fast[22] intent
    To shake all cares and business from our age,
    Conferring them on younger strengths, while we
    Unburden'd crawl toward death. Our son[23] of Cornwall,

5 upbringing
6 hardened (as in one slang sense of 'brass')
7 understand
8 *both* (1) result *and* (2) offspring
9 handsome
10 *son . . . law*: legitimate, born in wedlock
11 about a year
12 reckoning
13 somewhat
14 rascal (literally 'son of a whore' but often used playfully, like 'knave' above)
15 beg
16 try to be worth (the effort you make)
17 away from home, abroad
18 a set of notes on a trumpet heralding a procession
19 wait upon (and bring in)
20 expound, show
21 hitherto unrevealed (i.e. the details of the division)
22 firm, fixed
23 (-in-law), Duke of Cornwall

35   And you, our no less loving son of Albany,
       We have this hour a constant[24] will to publish
       Our daughters' several dowers,[25] that future strife
       May be prevented now. The princes, France and Burgundy,
       Great rivals in our youngest daughter's love,
40   Long in our court have made their amorous sojourn,[26]
       And here are to be answer'd.[27] Tell me, my daughters,—
       Since now we will divest us both of rule,
       Interest[28] of territory, cares of state,—
       Which of you shall we say doth love us most?
45   That we our largest bounty may extend
       Where nature[29] doth with merit challenge.[30] Goneril,
       Our eldest-born, speak first.
    GONERIL: Sir, I love you more than words can wield the matter;
       Dearer than eye-sight, space,[31] and liberty;
50   Beyond what can be valu'd, rich or rare;
       No less than life, with[32] grace, health, beauty, honour;
       As much as child e'er lov'd, or father found;[33]
       A love that makes breath poor and speech unable;[34]
       Beyond all manner of so much[35] I love you.
55   CORDELIA [*Aside*]: What shall Cordelia do? Love, and be silent.
    LEAR: Of all these bounds, even from this line to this,
       With shadowy[36] forests and with champains[37] rich'd,
       With plenteous rivers and wide-skirted meads,
       We make thee lady: to thine and Albany's issue
60   Be this perpetual. What says our second daughter,
       Our dearest Regan, wife to Cornwall? Speak.
    REGAN: I am made of that self[38] metal[39] as my sister,
       And prize me at her worth.[40] In my true heart[41]
       I find she names my very deed of love;[42]

24 firm
25 respective dowries
26 stay for purposes of love (to woo Cordelia)
27 *are . . . answer'd*: await a decision
28 right, title to (and so possession of)
29 affection
30 claim (it)
31 the world (unless the word simply expands the notion of 'liberty')
32 combined with
33 experienced (love)
34 unequal to expressing it
35 *all . . . much*: all degree of such comparisons
36 shady
37 meadows, open country
38 same
39 (1) material, (2) temperament (in this sense now spelt *mettle*)
40 *prize . . . worth*: I count myself equal to her (in my affection for you)
41 *In . . . heart*: in all sincerity
42 *names . . . love*: exactly describes my love

65   Only she comes too short: that[43] I profess
          Myself an enemy to all other joys
          Which the most precious square of sense[44] possesses
          And find I am alone felicitate[45]
          In your dear highness' love.
       CORDELIA   [*Aside*]: Then, poor Cordelia!
70   And yet not so; since, I am sure, my love's
          More richer than my tongue.
       LEAR: To thee and thine, hereditary ever,[46]
          Remain this ample third of our fair kingdom,
          No less in space, validity,[47] and pleasure,
75   Than that conferr'd on Goneril. Now, our joy,
          Although our last, not least; to whose young love
          The vines of France and milk of Burgundy[48]
          Strive to be interess'd;[49] what can you say to draw
          A third more opulent than your sisters? Speak.
80   CORDELIA: Nothing, my lord.
       LEAR: Nothing?
       CORDELIA: Nothing.
       LEAR: Nothing will come of nothing: speak again.
       CORDELIA: Unhappy that I am, I cannot heave
85   My heart into my mouth: I love your majesty
          According to my bond;[50] nor more nor less.
       LEAR: How, how, Cordelia! mend your speech a little,
          Lest you may mar your fortunes.
       CORDELIA: Good my lord,
          You have begot me, bred me, lov'd me: I
90   Return those duties back as are right fit,[51]
          Obey you, love you, and most honour you.
          Why have my sisters husbands, if they say
          They love you all?[52] Haply, when I shall wed,
          That lord whose hand must take my plight[53] shall carry
95   Half my love with him, half my care and duty:
          Sure I shall never marry like my sisters,
          To love my father all.
       LEAR: But goes thy heart with this?

43 in that
44 *most . . . sense*: most delicate sense
45 made happy
46 and to your heirs for ever
47 value
48 i.e. the King of F., rich in vineyards, and the Duke of B., rich in pastures
49 concerned, bound up with (interess is an old form of interest, Lat. *interesse*)
50 obligation (cf. 'bounden duty and service' of *Prayer Book*)
51 duties right and fit to be returned
52 entirely
53 plighted troth, vows

CORDELIA: Ay, good my lord.

LEAR: So young, and so untender?

100 CORDELIA: So young, my lord, and true.

LEAR: Let it be so; thy truth then be thy dower:[54]
For, by the sacred radiance of the sun,
The mysteries of Hecate[55] and the night,
By all the operation[56] of the orbs[57]
105 From whom we do exist and cease to be,
Here I disclaim all my paternal care,
Propinquity[58] and property of blood,[59]
And as a stranger to my heart and me
Hold thee from this for ever. The barbarous Scythian,
110 Or he that makes his generation[60] messes[61]
To gorge his appetite, shall to my bosom
Be as well neighbour'd,[62] pitied, and reliev'd,
As thou my sometime daughter.

KENT: Good my liege,—

LEAR: Peace, Kent!
115 Come not between the dragon and his wrath[63]
I lov'd her most, and thought to set my rest[64]
On her kind nursery.[65] Hence, and avoid my sight!
So be my grave my peace, as here I give
Her father's heart from[66] her! Call France. Who stirs?[67]
120 Call Burgundy. Cornwall and Albany,
With my two daughters' dowers digest the third;
Let pride, which she calls plainness, marry her.[68]
I do invest you jointly with my power,
Pre-eminence, and all the large effects[69]
125 That troop with[70] majesty. Ourself by monthly course,[71]
With reservation of[72] a hundred knights,

54 dowry
55 Hécate (here two syllables)
56 work, influence
57 heavenly bodies
58 *lit.* nearness, so kinship
59 ownership of your blood
60 children
61 dishes
62 *as . . . neighbour'd*: held as near
63 *Come . . . wrath*: i.e. don't try to stop my (natural) wrath (cf. l. 165 below)
64 *set . . . rest*: stake my all (a gaming metaphor, but also involving the ordinary sense of 'rest')
65 nursing
66 away from
67 *Who stirs?*: make haste
68 *Let . . . her*: let her pride find her a husband, i.e. let her find one for herself without a dowry
69 manifestations of splendour
70 *troop with*: accompany
71 *by . . . course*: for a month in turn
72 *With . . . of*: i.e. reserving to ourselves (properly a legal word for an exception)

By you to be sustain'd, shall our abode
Make with you by due turn. Only we shall retain
The name and all th' addition[73] to a king;
130 The sway, revenue, execution of the rest,
Beloved sons, be yours: which to confirm,
This coronet part between you.

KENT: Royal Lear,
Whom I have ever honour'd as my king,
Lov'd as my father, as my master follow'd,
135 As my great patron thought on in my prayers,—

LEAR: The bow is bent and drawn; make from[74] the shaft.

KENT: Let it fall rather, though the fork[75] invade
The region of my heart: be Kent unmannerly
When Lear is mad. What wouldst thou do, old man?
140 Think'st thou that duty shall have dread to speak
When power to flattery bows? To plainness[76] honour's bound
When majesty falls to folly. Reserve thy state;[77]
And, in thy best consideration,[78] check
This hideous rashness: answer my life my judgment,[79]
145 Thy youngest daughter does not love thee least;
Nor are those empty-hearted whose low sound
Reverbs[80] no hollowness.

LEAR: Kent, on thy life,[81] no more.

KENT: My life I never held[82] but as a pawn
To wage[83] against thine enemies; nor fear to lose it,
150 Thy safety being the motive.

LEAR: Out of my sight!

KENT: See better, Lear; and let me still remain
The true blank of thine eye.[84]

LEAR: Now, by Apollo,—

KENT: Now, by Apollo, king,
Thou swear'st thy gods in vain.

LEAR: O vassal! miscreant![85]

[Laying his hand on his sword.]

73 title
74 *make from*: avoid
75 head, barb
76 plain-speaking
77 regal power
78 *best consideration*: considering the matter more carefully
79 *answer . . . judgment*: let my life answer for (the correctness of) my judgment
80 echoes back
81 *on . . . life*: as you value your life
82 accounted
83 *pawn to wage*: stake to wager, risk
84 *let . . . eye*: keep me always in view, always with you (*blank* = *white* centre of a target)
85 *vassal! miscreant!* and *recreant!* (160): all used loosely as terms of abuse, 'villain'

155   ALBANY: ⎫
       CORNWALL: ⎬ Dear sir, forbear.

     KENT: Do;[86]

         Kill thy physician, and the fee bestow
         Upon the foul disease.[87] Revoke thy gift;[88]
         Or, whilst I can vent clamour from my throat,
160   I'll tell thee thou dost evil.

     LEAR: Hear me, recreant!
         On thine allegiance, hear me!
         Since thou hast sought to make us break our vow,—
         Which we durst never yet,—and, with strain'd[89] pride
         To come betwixt our sentence and our power,—[90]
165   Which nor our nature nor our place can bear,—
         Our potency made good,[91] take thy reward,
         Five days we do allot thee for provision
         To shield thee from diseases[92] of the world;
         And, on the sixth, to turn[93] thy hated back
170   Upon our kingdom: if, on the tenth day following
         Thy banish'd trunk[94] be found in our dominions,
         The moment is thy death. Away! By Jupiter,
         This shall not be revok'd.

     KENT: Fare thee well, king; sith[95] thus thou wilt appear,[96]
175   Freedom lives hence, and banishment is here.
         [*To Cordelia.*] The gods to their dear shelter take thee, maid,
         That justly think'st and hast most rightly said!
         [*To Regan and Goneril.*] And your large[97] speeches may your deeds approve,[98]
         That good effects may spring from words of love.
180   Thus Kent, O princes! bids you all adieu;
         He'll shape his old course[99] in a country new.   [*Exit.*]

      Flourish.[100] *Re-enter Gloucester, with France, Burgundy, and Attendants.*

---

86   execute your will
87   *the fee . . . disease*: i.e. make things worse for yourself
88   i.e. of Cordelia's share
89   exaggerated
90   *our power*: the execution of it
91   *potency . . . good*: power shown to be (still) valid
92   discomforts (consequent on lack of preparation for exile)
93   we sentence thee to turn
94   body
95   since
96   show thyself
97   grand
98   make good
99   *shape . . . course*: make his way, old as he is, *or* continues his old habits (of plain-speaking etc.)
100   a blast of trumpets or horns

GLOUCESTER: Here's France and Burgundy, my noble lord.

LEAR: My Lord of Burgundy,
    We first address toward[101] you, who with this king
185   Hath rivall'd for[102] our daughter. What, in the least,
    Will you require in present dower with her,
    Or cease your quest of love?

BURGUNDY: Most royal majesty,
    I crave no more than hath your highness offer'd,
    Nor will you tender[103] less.

LEAR: Right noble Burgundy,
190   When she was dear to us we did hold her so.[104]
    But now her price is fall'n. Sir, there she stands:
    If aught within that little-seeming substance,[105]
    Or all of it, with our displeasure piec'd,[106]
    And nothing more, may fitly like[107] your Grace,
195   She's there, and she is yours.

BURGUNDY: I know no answer.

LEAR: Will you, with those infirmities she owes,[108]
    Unfriended, new-adopted to our hate,
    Dower'd with our curse, and stranger'd with[109] our oath,
    Take her, or leave her?

BURGUNDY: Pardon me, royal sir;
200   Election makes not up[110] on such conditions.

LEAR: Then leave her, sir; for, by the power that made me,
    I tell you all her wealth.—[*To France.*] For you,[111] great king,
    I would not from your love make such a stray[112]
    To[113] match you where I hate; therefore, beseech you
205   To avert[114] your liking a more worthier way[115]
    Than on a wretch whom nature is asham'd
    Almost to acknowledge hers.

FRANCE: This is most strange,
    That she, who even but now was your best[116] object,

101 *address* (ourselves) *toward*: speak to
102 entered into rivalry for
103 offer
104 dear (in value), worth a good dowry
105 *little-seeming substance*: person of few pretensions (sarcastic)
106 pieced out (with), added (to it)
107 please
108 owns
109 made a stranger (to us) by (cf. l. 108)
110 *Election . . . up*: choice does not decide, will not choose
111 as for you
112 *make . . . stray*: depart from, i.e. offend against
113 as to
114 turn aside
115 *a . . . way*: in a worthier direction
116 favourite

The argument[117] of your praise, balm of your age,[118]
210 The best, the dearest, should in this trice[119] of time
Commit a thing so monstrous, to dismantle[120]
So many folds of favour. Sure, her offence
Must be of such unnatural degree
That monsters[121] it, or your fore-vouch'd affection
215 Fall into taint;[122] which to believe of her,
Must be a faith that reason without miracle
Could never plant in me.

CORDELIA: I yet beseech your majesty—
If for[123] I want that glib and oily art
To speak and purpose not;[124] since what I well intend,
220 I'll do't before I speak—that you make known
It is no vicious blot nor other foulness,[125]
No unchaste action, or dishonour'd[126] step,
That hath depriv'd me of your grace and favour,
But even for want of[127] that for which I am richer,
225 A still-soliciting[128] eye, and such a tongue
That I am glad I have not, though not to have it
Hath lost me in your liking.

LEAR: Better thou
Hadst not been born than not to have pleas'd me better.

FRANCE: Is it but this? A tardiness in nature[129]
230 Which often leaves the history[130] unspoke
That it intends to do? My Lord of Burgundy,
What say you to the lady?[131] Love is not love
When it is mingled with regards[132] that stand
Aloof from the entire[133] point. Will you have her?
235 She is herself a dowry.

BURGUNDY: Royal Lear,
Give but that portion which yourself propos'd,

117 subject
118 *balm . . . age*: see ll. 116–17
119 moment (Spanish)
120 shed off
121 makes it monstrous
122 *your . . . taint*: your previously affirmed affection must be discredited
123 If (you are disowning me) because
124 *purpose not*: not intend to carry out
125 i.e. no wickedness, such as murder or fornication
126 dishonourable
127 *even . . . of*: it is just because I lack
128 always begging (for something)
129 *tardiness in nature*: natural slowness (to speak)
130 verbal record
131 *What . . . lady?*: How do you like the lady?
132 considerations (so *respects*, l. 242)
133 whole

And here I take Cordelia by the hand,
Duchess of Burgundy.

LEAR: Nothing: I have sworn; I am firm.

240 BURGUNDY: I am sorry, then, you have so lost a father
That you must lose a husband.

CORDELIA: Peace be with[134] Burgundy!
Since that respects of fortune are his love,
I shall not be his wife.

FRANCE: Fairest Cordelia, that art most rich, being poor;

245 Most choice, forsaken; and most lov'd, despis'd!
Thee and thy virtues here I seize upon:
Be it lawful I take up what's cast away.
Gods, gods! 'tis strange that from their cold'st neglect
My love should kindle to inflam'd respect.[135]

250 Thy dowerless daughter, king, thrown to my chance,[136]
Is queen of us, of ours, and our fair France:
Not all the dukes of waterish[137] Burgundy
Shall buy this unpriz'd[138] precious maid of me.
Bid them farewell, Cordelia, though unkind:[139]

255 Thou losest here, a better where[140] to find.

LEAR: Thou hast her, France; let her be thine, for we
Have no such daughter, nor shall ever see
That face of hers again, therefore be gone
Without our grace, our love, our benison.[141]

260 Come, noble Burgundy.

*Flourish. Exeunt Lear, Burgundy, Cornwall, Albany, Gloucester,
and Attendants.*

FRANCE: Bid farewell to your sisters.

CORDELIA: The jewels[142] of our father, with wash'd eyes
Cordelia leaves you: I know you what you are;
And like a sister am most loath to call

265 Your faults as they are nam'd.[143] Use well our father:
To your professed bosoms[144] I commit him:

134 *Peace be with*: good-bye to
135 *inflam'd respect*: ardent esteem
136 lot
137 perhaps literally 'well-watered', but certainly implying that the man is as thin-blooded as his country is
inferior in wines to France (cf. l. 77)
138 *either* not (properly) valued *or* priceless
139 see III. iv. 58
140 place (to parallel 'here')
141 blessing
142 *The jewels*: vocative case
143 *as . . . nam'd*: by their true names
144 love

But yet, alas! stood I within his grace,
I would prefer[145] him to a better place.
So farewell to you both.

270 REGAN: Prescribe not us our duties.

GONERIL: Let your study
Be to content your lord, who hath receiv'd you
At fortune's alms;[146] you have obedience scanted,
And well are worth the want that you have wanted.[147]

CORDELIA: Time shall unfold what plighted[148] cunning hides;
275 Who[149] covers faults, at last shame them derides.
Well may you prosper!

FRANCE: Come, my fair Cordelia.

[Exeunt France and Cordelia.]

GONERIL: Sister, it is not little I have to say of what most nearly appertains to
us both. I think our father will hence[150] to-night.

REGAN: That's most certain, and with you; next month with us.

280 GONERIL: You see how full of changes his age is;[151] the observation we have
made of it hath not been little: he always loved our sister most; and with
what poor judgment he hath now cast her off appears too grossly.[152]

REGAN: 'Tis the infirmity of his age; yet he hath ever but slenderly known
himself.

285 GONERIL: The best and soundest of his time hath been but rash;[153] then, must
we look to receive from his age, not alone the imperfections of long-
engraffed condition,[154] but, therewithal the unruly waywardness that
infirm and choleric years[155] bring with them.

REGAN: Such unconstant starts[156] are we like[157] to have from him as this of
290 Kent's banishment.

GONERIL: There is further compliment[158] of leave-taking between France and
him. Pray you, let us hit together:[159] if our father carry[160] authority with

---

145 advance, recommend
146 *At . . . alms*: as a humble gift of fortune; cf. l. 251
147 *are . . . wanted*: deserve the destitution that has befallen you
148 folded
149 those who (antecedent to *them*)
150 *will* go *hence*
151 *full . . . is*: changeable he is now he is old
152 obviously
153 hot-headed
154 *long-engraffed condition*: a temperament that has become firmly fixed (ingrafted) by habit
155 *infirm . . . years*: years of physical weakness and proneness to anger
156 *unconstant starts*: fits of waywardness
157 likely
158 formal civility
159 *hit together*: strike a bargain, i.e. make joint plans
160 i.e. still wields

such dispositions[161] as he bears, this last surrender[162] of his will but offend[163] us.

295   REGAN: We shall further think on 't.

GONERIL: We must do something, and i' the heat.[164]   [*Exeunt.*]

161 moods
162 harm (stronger than nowadays)
163 i.e. of the crown
164 *i'...heat*: at once (cf. 'strike while the iron is hot')

SCENE 2

A Hall in the Earl of Gloucester's Castle.

Enter Edmund, with a letter.

EDMUND: Thou, Nature, art my goddess; to thy law
    My services are bound. Wherefore should I
    Stand in the plague of custom,[1] and permit
    The curiosity[2] of nations to deprive me,[3]
5   For that I am some twelve or fourteen moonshines
    Lag of[4] a brother? Why bastard? wherefore base?
    When my dimensions[5] are as well compact,[6]
    My mind as generous,[7] and my shape as true,
    As honest madam's[8] issue? Why brand they us
10 With base? with baseness? bastardy? base, base?
    Who in the lusty stealth[9] of nature[10] take
    More composition and fierce quality
    Than doth, within a dull, stale, tired bed,
    Go to the creating a whole tribe of fops,[11]
15 Got[12] 'tween asleep and wake? Well then,
    Legitimate Edgar, I must have your land:
    Our fathers' love is to the bastard Edmund

1 *stand...custom*: suffer from the inferior position custom assigns to bastards
2 scrupulousness, squeamishness
3 keep me out of my rights
4 *lag of*: behind (in coming into the world)
5 *my dimensions*: the proportions of my body
6 made
7 high-spirited
8 *honest madam's*: the true wife
9 secret act
10 (sexual) desire
11 fools
12 begotten

As[13] to the legitimate. Fine word, 'legitimate!'
Well, my legitimate, if this letter speed,
20 And my invention thrive, Edmund the base
Shall top[14] the legitimate:—I grow, I prosper;
Now, gods, stand up for bastards!

Enter Gloucester.

GLOUCESTER: Kent banished thus! And France in choler[15] parted![16]
And the king gone to-night![17] subscrib'd[18] his power!
25 Confin'd to exhibition![19] All this done
Upon the gad![20] Edmund, how now! what news?
EDMUND: So please you lordship, none.   [*Putting up the letter.*]
GLOUCESTER: Why so earnestly seek you to put up[21] that letter?
EDMUND: I know no news, my lord.
30 GLOUCESTER: What paper were you reading?
EDMUND: Nothing, my lord.
GLOUCESTER: No? What needed then that terrible[22] dispatch[23] of it into your
pocket? the quality of nothing hath not such need to hide itself. Let's see;
come; if it be nothing, I shall not need spectacles.
35 EDMUND: I beseech you, sir, pardon me;[24] it is a letter from my brother that
I have not all o'er-read, and for[25] so much as I have perused, I find it not fit
for your o'er-looking.[26]
GLOUCESTER: Give me the letter, sir.
EDMUND: I shall offend, either to detain or give it. The contents, as in part
40 I understand them, are to blame.
GLOUCESTER: Let's see, let's see.
EDMUND: I hope, for my brother's justification, he wrote this but as an essay[27]
or taste of my virtue.
GLOUCESTER: 'This policy and reverence of age[28] makes the world bitter to
45 the best of our times;[29] keeps our fortunes from us till our oldness cannot

13 as much as
14 get the better of
15 anger
16 departed
17 last night
18 surrendered
19 an allowance (cf. university use)
20 *upon the gad*: suddenly (as if pricked by a gad, = goad)
21 put away
22 frightened (*not* our slang use)
23 haste in putting away
24 excuse me from showing it you
25 as for
26 examination
27 trial
28 *policy . . . age*: policy of reverence for old age
29 *the best . . . times*: our best days, i.e. men in their prime

relish them. I begin to find an idle and fond [30] bondage in the oppression of aged tyranny,[31] who sways,[32] not as it hath power, but as it is suffered. Come to me, that of this I may speak more. If our father would sleep till I waked him, you should enjoy half his revenue for ever, and live the beloved of your

50 brother, EDGAR.'—Hum! Conspiracy! 'Sleep till I waked him, you should enjoy half his revenue.'—My son Edgar! Had he a hand to write this? a heart and brain to breed it in? When came this to you? Who brought it?

EDMUND: It was not brought me, my lord; there's the cunning of it; I found it thrown in at the casement[33] of my closet.

55 GLOUCESTER: You know the character[34] to be your brother's?

EDMUND: If the matter were good, my lord, I durst swear it were his; but, in respect of that,[35] I would fain think it were not.

GLOUCESTER: It is his.

EDMUND: It is his hand, my lord; but I hope his heart is not in the contents.

60 GLOUCESTER: Hath he never heretofore sounded you in this business?

EDMUND: Never, my lord: but I have often heard him maintain it to be fit that, sons at perfect age,[36] and fathers declined,[37] the father should be as ward to the son, and the son manage his revenue.

GLOUCESTER: O villain, villain! His very opinion in the letter! Abhorred villain!

65 Unnatural, detested, brutish villain! worse than brutish! Go, sirrah, seek him; I'll apprehend him. Abominable villain! Where is he?

EDMUND: I do not well know, my lord. If it shall please you to suspend your indignation against my brother till you can derive from him better testimony of his intent, you shall run a certain course;[38] where,[39] if you

70 violently proceed against him, mistaking his purpose, it would make a great gap[40] in your own honour, and shake in pieces the heart of his obedience. I dare pawn[41] down my life for him, that he hath writ this to feel[42] my affection to your honour, and to no other pretence of danger.[43]

GLOUCESTER: Think you so?

---

30 foolish
31 *aged tyranny*: my aged father (abstract for concrete, as often)
32 rules
33 (open) window
34 handwriting
35 its goodness or lack of it, i.e. (in this case) its badness
36 *perfect age*: the prime of life
37 in years
38 *run ... course*: act safely
39 whereas
40 breach
41 see I. i. 148
42 try
43 *to no ... danger*: not with a view to any (other) dangerous design

75 EDMUND: If your honour judge it meet, I will place you where you shall hear us confer on this, and by an auricular[44] assurance have your satisfaction; and that without any further delay than this very evening.

GLOUCESTER: He cannot be such a monster—

EDMUND: Nor is not, sure.

80 GLOUCESTER: —to his father, that so tenderly and entirely loves him. Heaven and earth! Edmund, seek him out; wind me into him,[45] I pray you; frame the business after your own wisdom. I would unstate myself[46] to be in a due resolution.[47]

EDMUND: I will seek him, sir, presently;[48] convey[49] the business as I shall find
85 means, and acquaint you withal.[50]

GLOUCESTER: These late eclipses in the sun and moon portend no good to us: though the wisdom of nature can reason it thus and thus,[51] yet nature finds itself scourged by the sequent effects.[52] Love cools, friendship falls off, brothers divide: in cities, mutinies;[53] in countries, discord; in palaces,
90 treason; and the bond cracked between son and father. This villain of mine comes under the prediction; there's son against father: the king falls from bias of nature;[54] there's father against child. We have seen the best of our time: machinations,[55] hollowness,[56] treachery, and all ruinous disorders, follow us disquietly to our graves. Find out this villain, Edmund; it shall
95 lose thee nothing: do it carefully. And the noble and true-hearted Kent banished! his offence, honesty! 'Tis strange! [*Exit.*]

EDMUND: This is the excellent foppery[57] of the world, that, when we are sick in fortune,—often the surfeit[58] of our own behaviour,—we make guilty of our disasters the sun, the moon, and the stars; as if we were villains by
100 necessity, fools by heavenly compulsion, knaves, thieves, and treachers[59] by spherical predominance,[60] drunkards, liars, and adulterers by an enforced obedience of planetary influence; and all that we are evil in, by a divine thrusting on: an admirable evasion[61] of whoremaster[62] man, to lay his

44 through the ear
45 *wind . . . him*: insinuate yourself, get into familiar talk with him, please (*me* is not the object of 'wind' but the so-called ethic dative)
46 *unstate myself*: give up my position
47 *to be . . . resolution*: to have my doubts resolved
48 immediately
49 carry out
50 *acquaint you withal*: inform you of it
51 *the wisdom . . . and thus*: natural philosophy can give good explanations
52 *sequent effects*: effects that follow (eclipses)
53 disturbances
54 *from . . . nature*: away from natural inclination (i.e. of affection towards Cordelia)
55 plots
56 insincerity
57 folly
58 evil result
59 traitors
60 *spherical predominance*: dominance of some special star
61 of responsibility
62 lecherous

goatish[63] disposition to the charge of a star! My father compounded with
105 my mother under the dragon's tail,[64] and my nativity was under *Ursa
Major*;[65] so that it follows I am rough and lecherous. 'Sfoot! I should have
been that I am had the maidenliest star in the firmament twinkled on
my bastardizing.[66] Edgar—

Enter Edgar.

and pat[67] he comes, like the catastrophe of the old[68] comedy: my cue[69] is
110 villanous melancholy, with a sigh like Tom o' Bedlam.[70] O, these eclipses
do portend these divisions! *Fa, sol, la, mi.*[71]

EDGAR: How now, brother Edmund! What serious contemplation are you in?

EDMUND: I am thinking, brother, of a prediction I read this other day, what[72]
should follow these eclipses.

115 EDGAR: Do you busy yourself with that?

EDMUND: I promise you the effects he writes of succeed[73] unhappily; as of
unnaturalness between the child and the parent; death, dearth, dissolutions
of ancient amities; divisions in state; menaces and maledictions against king
and nobles; needless diffidences,[74] banishment of friends, dissipation of
120 cohorts,[75] nuptial breaches, and I know not what.

EDGAR: How long have you been a sectary astronomical?[76]

EDMUND: Come, come; when saw you my father last?

EDGAR: The night gone by.

EDMUND: Spake you with him?

125 EDGAR: Ay, two hours together.

EDMUND: Parted you in good terms? Found you no displeasure in him by word
or countenance?

EDGAR: None at all.

EDMUND: Bethink yourself wherein you may have offended him; and at my
130 entreaty forbear[77] his presence till some little time hath qualified[78] the heat
of his displeasure, which at this instant so rageth in him that with the
mischief of your person it would scarcely allay.[79]

63 lascivious
64 *dragon's tail*: in astronomy, 'the descending node of the moon's orbit with the ecliptic' (*Shorter OED*)
65 *Ursa Major*: the Great Bear
66 unlawful begetting
67 just at the right moment
68 any old
69 part
70 *Tom o' Bedlam*: beggar feigning madness
71 *Fa . . . mi*: Edmund sings or hums a series of musical notes
72 (as to) *what*
73 turn out
74 distrust (of others)
75 *dissipation of cohorts*: just possibly 'troops deserting'
76 *sectary astronomical*: follower of, believer in astrology
77 avoid
78 reduced
79 subside

EDGAR: Some villain hath done me wrong.

EDMUND: That's my fear. I pray you have a continent forbearance[80] till the
135   speed of his rage goes slower, and, as I say, retire with me to my lodging,
from whence I will fitly[81] bring you to hear my lord speak. Pray you, go;
there's my key. If you do stir abroad, go armed.

EDGAR: Armed, brother!

EDMUND: Brother, I advise you to the best; go armed; I am no honest man if there
140   be any good meaning[82] toward you; I have told you what I have seen and
heard; but faintly, nothing like the image and horror[83] of it; pray you, away.

EDGAR: Shall I hear from you anon?

EDMUND: I do serve you in this business.   [Exit Edgar.]

    A credulous father, and a brother noble,
145   Whose nature is so far from doing harms
    That he suspects none; on whose foolish honesty
    My practices[84] ride easy! I see the business.
    Let me, if not by birth, have lands by wit:
    All with me's meet that I can fashion fit.[85]   [Exit.]

80 *a . . . forbearance*: the restraint to keep away
81 at a suitable time
82 intentions
83 *image . . . horror*: horrible reality
84 plots
85 to my purpose

SCENE 3

A Room in the Duke of Albany's Palace.

    Enter Goneril and Oswald her Steward.

GONERIL: Did my father strike my gentleman for chiding of his fool?

OSWALD: Ay, madam.

GONERIL: By day and night[1] he wrongs me; every hour
    He flashes into[2] one gross crime[3] or other,
5   That sets us all at odds:[4] I'll not endure it:
    His knights grow riotous, and himself upbraids us
    On every trifle. When he returns from hunting
    I will not speak with him; say I am sick:
    If you come slack of former services,
10   You shall do well; the fault of it I'll answer.[5]

1 *By . . . night*: probably 'continually', rather than an oath
2 *flashes into*: breaks out into
3 offence
4 *sets . . . odds*: upsets
5 (for), be responsible for

OSWALD: He's coming, madam; I hear him.   [*Horns within.*]

GONERIL: Put on what weary negligence you please,

    You and your fellows; I'd have it come to question:[6]

    If he distaste[7] it, let him to my sister,

15   Whose mind and mine, I know, in that are one,

    Not to be over-rul'd. Idle[8] old man,

    That still would manage those authorities[9]

    That he hath given away! Now, by my life,

    Old fools are babes again, and must be us'd

20   With checks as flatteries, when they are seen abus'd.[10]

    Remember what I have said.

OSWALD: Well, madam.

GONERIL: And let his knights have colder looks among you;

    What grows of it,[11] no matter; advise your fellows so:

    I would breed from hence occasions,[12] and I shall,

25   That I may speak: I'll write straight to my sister

    To hold my very course.[13] Prepare for dinner.   [*Exeunt.*]

6 *I'd . . . question*: I want it discussed
7 dislike (as Q reads)
8 foolish
9 *manage . . . authorities*: exercise the powers
10 *us'd . . . abus'd*: rebuked as well as flattered when they are seen to be misled (by their followers) *or* deluded
11 *grows of it*: results from it
12 opportunities
13 *my . . . course*: exactly my course

SCENE 4

A Hall in the Same.

    Enter Kent, disguised.

KENT: If but as well I other accents borrow,

    That can my speech defuse,[1] my good intent

    May carry through itself to that full issue[2]

    For which I raz'd[3] my likeness. Now, banish'd Kent

5   If thou canst serve where thou dost stand condemn'd,

    So may it come, thy master, whom thou lov'st,

    Shall find thee full of labours.

    Horns within. Enter Lear, Knights, and Attendants.

1 confuse, disguise
2 *my . . . issue*: I may be able to bring off the purpose
3 erased

LEAR: Let me not stay a jot[4] for dinner: go, get it ready.   [*Exit an Attendant.*]
How now! what art thou?

10   KENT: A man, sir.

LEAR: What dost thou profess?[5] What wouldst thou with us?

KENT: I do profess to be no less than I seem; to serve him truly that will put me
in trust; to love him that is honest; to converse[6] with him that is wise, and
says a little; to fear judgment;[7] to fight when I cannot choose; and to eat

15   no fish.[8]

LEAR: What art thou?

KENT: A very honest-hearted fellow, and as poor as the king.

LEAR: If thou be as poor for a subject as he is for a king, thou art poor enough.
What wouldst thou?

20   KENT: Service.

LEAR: Whom wouldst thou serve?

KENT: You.

LEAR: Dost thou know me, fellow?

KENT: No, sir; but you have that in your countenance[9] which I would fain

25   call master.

LEAR: What's that?

KENT: Authority.

LEAR: What services canst thou do?

KENT: I can keep honest counsel,[10] ride, run, mar a curious[11] tale in telling it,

30   and deliver a plain message bluntly; that which ordinary men are fit for,
I am qualified in, and the best of me is diligence.

LEAR: How old art thou?

KENT: Not so young, sir, to love[12] a woman for singing, nor so old to dote on
her for any thing; I have years on my back forty-eight.

35   LEAR: Follow me; thou shalt serve me: if I like thee no worse after dinner I will
not part from thee yet. Dinner, ho! dinner! Where's my knave?[13] my fool?
Go you and call my fool hither.   [*Exit an Attendant.*]

Enter Oswald.

You, you, sirrah, where's my daughter?

OSWALD: So please you,[14]—   [*Exit.*]

4 *stay a jot*: wait a moment
5 *What . . . profess?*: what is your business, job? (But Kent takes the word in the sense of 'claim'.)
6 have to do with (Lat. *conversari*)
7 here *or* hereafter
8 *eat no fish*: be a loyal subject (not fast like a Papist)
9 bearing
10 *honest counsel*: an honourable secret
11 elaborate, difficult (Kent is only a plain man.)
12 (as) *to love*
13 boy (as in a pack of cards)
14 *So . . . you*: excuse me (as he goes out)

40   LEAR: What says the fellow there? Call the clotpoll[15] back.   [*Exit a Knight.*]
        Where's my fool, ho? I think the world's asleep. How now! where's
        that mongrel?[16]

        Re-enter Knight.

    KNIGHT: He says, my lord, your daughter is not well.

    LEAR: Why came not the slave back to me when I called him?

45   KNIGHT: Sir, he answered me in the roundest[17] manner, he would not.

    LEAR: He would not!

    KNIGHT: My lord, I know not what the matter is; but, to my judgment,
        your highness is not entertained with that ceremonious affection as you
        were wont; there's a great abatement of kindness as well in the general
50   dependants as in the duke also and your daughter.

    LEAR: Ha! sayest thou so?

    KNIGHT: I beseech you, pardon me, my lord, if I be mistaken; for my duty
        cannot be[18] silent when I think your highness wronged.

    LEAR: Thou but rememberest me of mine own conception: I have perceived a
55   most faint[19] neglect of late; which I have rather blamed as mine own
        jealous curiosity[20] than as a very pretence[21] and purpose of unkindness:
        I will look further into 't. But where's my fool? I have not seen him this
        two days.

    KNIGHT: Since my young lady's going into France, sir, the fool hath much
60   pined him away.

    LEAR: No more of that; I have noted it well. Go you and tell my daughter
        I would speak with her.   [*Exit an Attendant.*]
        Go you, call hither my fool.   [*Exit an Attendant.*]

        Re-enter Oswald.

        O! you sir, come you hither, sir. Who am I, sir?

65   OSWALD: My lady's father.

    LEAR: 'My lady's father!' my lord's knave: you whoreson dog! you slave! you cur!

    OSWALD: I am none of these, my lord; I beseech your pardon.

    LEAR: Do you bandy[22] looks with me, you rascal?   [*Striking him.*]

    OSWALD: I'll not be struck, my lord.

---

15 clodpate, blockhead
16 i.e. Oswald
17 plainest
18 *my . . . be*: my sense of duty forbids me to be
19 slight *or* (possibly) cold
20 watchfulness, suspicion
21 *very pretence*: real intention
22 exchange (originally in tennis)

70 KENT: Nor tripped neither, you base football player.   [*Tripping up his heels.*]

LEAR: I thank thee, fellow; thou servest me, and I'll love thee.

KENT: Come, sir, arise, away! I'll teach you differences:²³ away, away! If you will measure your lubber's length again, tarry; but away! Go to;²⁴ have you wisdom?²⁵ So.²⁶   [*Pushes Oswald out.*]

75 LEAR: Now, my friendly knave, I thank thee: there's earnest²⁷ of thy service.
   [*Gives Kent money.*]

     Enter Fool.

FOOL: Let me hire him too: here's my coxcomb.²⁸   [*Offers Kent his cap.*]

LEAR: How now, my pretty knave! how dost thou?

FOOL: Sirrah, you were best²⁹ take my coxcomb.

KENT: Why, fool?

80 FOOL: Why? for taking one's part that's out of favour. Nay, an³⁰ thou canst not smile as the wind sits,³¹ thou'lt catch cold shortly: there, take my coxcomb. Why, this fellow has banished two on 's³² daughters, and did the third a blessing against his will: if thou follow him thou must needs wear my coxcomb. How now, nuncle!³³ Would I had two coxcombs and two
85 daughters!

LEAR: Why, my boy?

FOOL: If I gave them all my living, I'd keep my coxcombs myself. There's mine; beg another of thy daughters.

LEAR: Take heed, sirrah; the whip.

90 FOOL: Truth's a dog must to kennel; he must be whipped out when Lady the brach³⁴ may stand by the fire and stink.

LEAR: A pestilent gall³⁵ to me!

FOOL [*To Kent.*]: Sirrah, I'll teach thee a speech.

LEAR: Do.

95 FOOL: Mark it nuncle:—

     Have more than thou showest,

     Speak less than thou knowest,

     Lend less than thou owest,³⁶

23 i.e. of rank (between you and a king)
24 *Go to*: Pshaw! (expression of impatience)
25 *have . . . wisdom?*: are you in your senses?
26 good (as Oswald goes out)
27 a pledge (of further reward)
28 fool's cap
29 *you . . . best*: you had better (*literally* it were, i.e. would be, best for you)
30 if
31 *smile . . . sits*: see which way things are going, trim your sail to the breeze
32 of his
33 contracted for 'mine uncle', a regular address of fools to their master
34 bitch
35 irritant *or* bitterness
36 ownest

Ride more than thou goest,[37]
100   Learn more than thou trowest,[38]
Set less than thou throwest;[39]
Leave thy drink and thy whore,
And keep in-a-door,[40]
And thou shalt have more
105   Than two tens to a score.[41]

KENT: This is nothing, fool.

FOOL: Then 'tis like the breath of an unfree'd lawyer, you gave me nothing for't. Can you make no use of nothing, nuncle?

LEAR: Why, no, boy; nothing can be made out of nothing.

110 FOOL [*To Kent*.]: Prithee, tell him, so much the rent of his land comes to: he will not believe a fool.

LEAR: A bitter fool!

FOOL: Dost thou know the difference, my boy, between a bitter fool and a sweet fool?

115 LEAR: No, lad; teach me.

FOOL: That lord that counsell'd thee
                  To give away thy land,
                  Come place him here by me,
                  Do thou for him stand:
120   The sweet and bitter fool
                  Will presently appear;
                  The one in motley[42] here,
                  The other found out there.

LEAR: Dost thou call me fool, boy?

125 FOOL: All thy other titles thou hast given away; that thou wast born with.

KENT: This is not altogether fool, my lord.

FOOL: No, faith, lords and great men will not let me;[43] if I had a monopoly out,[44] they would have part on 't, and ladies too: they will not let me have all fool to myself; they'll be snatching. Nuncle, give me an egg, and I'll give
130 thee two crowns.

LEAR: What two crowns shall they be?

FOOL: Why, after I have cut the egg i' the middle and eat up the meat, the two crowns[45] of the egg. When you clovest thy crown i' the middle, and gavest away both parts, thou borest thine ass on thy back o'er the dirt:[46] thou hadst

37 walkest
38 i.e. (probably) don't believe all you hear
39 i.e. stake less than you win (at a throw)
40 indoors
41 *And . . . score*: i.e. you'll do well
42 fool's dress (as I am)
43 *let me*: (be the complete fool)
44 taken out, granted (as often by Stuart kings)
45 i.e. half shells
46 *borest . . . dirt*: reversed the proper order of things (from a fable of Aesop)

135   little wit in thy bald crown when thou gavest thy golden one away. If I speak
           like myself[47] in this, let him be whipped that first finds it so.

> Fools had ne'er less grace[48] in a year;
> For wise men are grown foppish,[49]
> And know not how their wits to wear,[50]
140   Their manners are so apish.

LEAR: When were you wont to be so full of songs, sirrah?

FOOL: I have used it,[51] nuncle, ever since thou madest thy daughters thy
mothers; for when thou gavest them the rod and puttest down thine
own breeches,

> Then they for sudden joy did weep,
145   And I for sorrow sung,
> That such a king should play bo-peep,[52]
> And go the fools among.

Prithee, nuncle, keep a schoolmaster that can teach thy fool to lie: I would
150   fain learn to lie.

LEAR: An you lie, sirrah, we'll have you whipped.

FOOL: I marvel what kin thou and thy daughters are: they'll have me whipped
for speaking true, thou'lt have me whipped for lying; and sometimes I am
whipped for holding my peace. I had rather be any kind o' thing than a
155   fool; and yet I would not be thee, nuncle; thou hast pared thy wit o' both
sides, and left nothing i' the middle:[53] here comes one o' the parings.

Enter Goneril.

LEAR: How now, daughter! what makes[54] that frontlet[55] on? Methinks you are
too much of late i' the frown.

FOOL: Thou wast a pretty fellow when thou hadst no need to care for her
160   frowning; now thou art an O without a figure.[56] I am better than thou art
now; I am a fool, thou art nothing. [*To Goneril.*] Yes, forsooth, I will hold
my tongue; so your face bids me, though you say nothing.

47 *like myself*: foolishly
48 *had . . . grace*: were never less in favour
49 foolish
50 *their . . . wear*: show their wisdom
51 *used it*: made it my habit
52 *play bo-peep*: behave like a child
53 *pared . . . middle*: i.e. by giving away both halves of thy kingdom
54 means
55 i.e. frown (*lit.* cloth worn on forehead)
56 *an . . . figure*: a mere cipher, thing of nought

Mum, mum;
He that keeps nor crust nor crumb,
165   Weary of all, shall want some.

That's a shealed peascod.[57]   [*Pointing to Lear.*]

GONERIL: Not only, sir, this your all-licens'd fool,
But other of your insolent retinue
Do hourly carp and quarrel, breaking forth
170   In rank[58] and not-to-be-endured riots. Sir,
I had thought, by making this well known unto you,
To have found a safe redress;[59] but now grow fearful,
By what yourself too late have spoke and done,
That you protect this course, and put it on[60]
175   By your allowance; which if you should, the fault
Would not 'scape censure, nor the redresses sleep,
Which, in the tender of a wholesome weal,[61]
Might in their working do you that offence,
Which else was shame,[62] that then necessity
180   Will call discreet proceeding.[63]

FOOL: For you trow, nuncle.
    The hedge-sparrow fed the cuckoo so long,
    That it had its head bit off by its young.[64]
So out went the candle, and we were left darkling.[65]

185   LEAR: Are you our daughter?

GONERIL: I would you would make use of your good wisdom,
Whereof I know you are fraught;[66] and put away
These dispositions[67] which of late transform you
From what you rightly are.

190   FOOL: May not an ass know when the cart draws the horse?[68] Whoop, Jug!
I love thee.

LEAR: Does any here know me? This is not Lear:
Does Lear walk thus? speak thus? Where are his eyes?
Either his notion[69] weakens, his discernings[70]

57 *shealed peascod*: pod without peas (provincial form of 'shelled')
58 *gross*
59 *safe redress*: sure remedy
60 *put it on*: encourage it
61 *in . . . weal*: in their regard for a healthy state of affairs
62 *Which . . . shame*: which would be disgraceful if the motive (behind my remedial action) were not good
63 *that . . . proceeding*: i.e. although, considering the need, people would approve my conduct ('that' = 'which' again—an awkward construction)
64 *its* (as often) apparent young, i.e. the young cuckoo (corresponding to Goneril)
65 in the dark
66 stored
67 moods
68 cf. l. 134

195   Are lethargied.[71] Ha! waking?[72] 'tis not so.

             Who is it that can tell me who I am?

      FOOL: Lear's shadow.

      LEAR: I would[73] learn that; for, by the marks of sovereignty, knowledge and

            reason, I should be false[74] persuaded I had daughters.

200   FOOL: Which[75] they will make an obedient father.

      LEAR: Your name, fair gentlewoman?

      GONERIL: This admiration,[76] sir, is much o' the favour[77]

            Of other your[78] new pranks. I do beseech you

            To understand my purposes aright:

205   As you are old and reverend, should[79] be wise.

            Here do you keep a hundred knights and squires;

            Men so disorder'd,[80] so debosh'd,[81] and bold,

            That this our court, infected with their manners,

            Shows like a riotous inn: epicurism[82] and lust

210   Make it more like a tavern or a brothel

            Than a grac'd[83] palace. The shame itself doth speak

            For[84] instant remedy; be then desir'd[85]

            By her that else will take the thing she begs,

            A little to disquantity[86] your train;

215   And the remainder, that shall still depend,[87]

            To be[88] such men as may besort[89] your age,

            Which know themselves and you.

      LEAR: Darkness and devils!

            Saddle my horses; call my train together.

            Degenerate bastard! I'll not trouble thee:

220   Yet have I left a daughter.

69 understanding
70 powers of discernment
71 dulled
72 am I awake?
73 I must
74 falsely
75 whom (Lear's shadow)
76 (feigned) surprise
77 nature
78 *other* (of) *your*
79 (you) *should*
80 disorderly
81 debauched
82 epicureanism, luxury
83 honourable
84 *speak for:* demand
85 *be . . . desir'd:* let yourself be requested
86 reduce the number of
87 serve you
88 *the remainder . . . be:* allow the remainder to be
89 suit

GONERIL: You strike my people, and your disorder'd rabble
Make servants of their betters.

Enter Albany.

LEAR: Woe, that[90] too late repents;
[*To Albany.*]   O! sir, are you come?
Is it your will? Speak, sir. Prepare my horses.
225   Ingratitude, thou marble-hearted fiend,
More hideous, when thou show'st thee in a child
Than the[91] sea-monster.

ALBANY: Pray, sir, be patient.

LEAR [*To Goneril.*]: Detested kite! thou liest:
My train are men of choice and rarest parts,
230   That all particulars of duty know,
And in the most exact regard[92] support
The worships[93] of their name. O most small fault,[94]
How ugly didst thou in Cordelia show!
Which, like an engine,[95] wrench'd my frame of nature[96]
235   From the fix'd place, drew from my heart all love,
And added to the gall. O Lear, Lear, Lear!
Beat at this gate, that let thy folly in,   [*Striking his head.*]
And thy dear[97] judgment out! Go, go, my people.

ALBANY: My lord, I am guiltless, as I am ignorant
240   Of what hath mov'd you.

LEAR: It may be so, my lord.
Hear, Nature, hear! dear goddess, hear!
Suspend thy purpose, if thou didst intend
To make this creature fruitful!
Into her womb convey sterility!
245   Dry up in her the organs of increase,
And from her derogate[98] body never spring
A babe to honour her! If she must teem,[99]
Create her child of spleen, that it may live
And be a thwart[100] disnatur'd[101] torment to her!

90 *Woe, that*: Woe to him who
91 a (generic use, cf. I. ii. 109)
92 *in . . . regard*: with scrupulous care
93 honour (plural sometimes used when a plurality of persons is concerned)
94 *O . . . fault*: i.e. Cordelia's obstinacy
95 the rack (a torture, wrenching the body apart)
96 *frame of nature*: system of natural affection
97 precious
98 debased
99 bear children
100 cross, perverse
101 unnatural

250   Let it stamp wrinkles in her brow of youth,
       With cadent[102] tears fret[103] channels in her cheeks,
       Turn all her mother's pains and benefits[104]
       To laughter and contempt, that she may feel
       How sharper than a serpent's tooth it is
255   To have a thankless child! Away, away!   [*Exit.*]
    ALBANY: Now, gods that we adore, whereof comes this?
    GONERIL: Never afflict yourself to know the cause;
       But let his disposition have that scope[105]
       That dotage gives it.

           Re-enter Lear.

260   LEAR: What! fifty of my followers at a clap,[106]
       Within a fortnight?
    ALBANY: What's the matter, sir?
    LEAR: I'll tell thee. [*To Goneril.*] Life and death! I am asham'd
       That thou hast power to shake my manhood thus,
265   That these hot tears, which break from me perforce,
       Should make thee worth them. Blasts and fogs upon thee!
       Th' untented[107] woundings of a father's curse
       Pierce every sense about thee! Old fond[108] eyes,
       Beweep[109] this cause again, I'll pluck ye out,
270   And cast you, with the waters that you lose,[110]
       To temper[111] clay. Yea, is it come to this?
       Let it be so: I have another daughter,
       Who, I am sure, is kind and comfortable:[112]
       When she shall hear this of thee, with her nails
275   She'll flay thy wolvish visage. Thou shalt find
       That I'll resume the shape which thou dost think
       I have cast off for ever; thou shalt, I warrant thee.

                              [*Exeunt Lear, Kent, and Attendants.*]

    GONERIL: Do you mark that?
    ALBANY: I cannot be so partial, Goneril,
280   To the great love I bear you.[113]—

102 falling
103 wear away
104 kindness done to the child
105 disposition: cf. l. 188
106 *at a clap:* at a stroke, all at once
107 unexplored, deep, and so incurable (a surgeon probed a wound with a 'tent' or roll of lint)
108 foolish
109 if you weep for
110 waste
111 moisten
112 comforting
113 *I cannot . . . you:* i.e. so prejudiced by my love for you (as to approve your conduct now)

GONERIL: Pray you, content.[114] What, Oswald, ho! [*To the Fool*.]: You, sir,
more knave than fool, after your master.

FOOL: Nuncle Lear, nuncle Lear! tarry, and take the fool with thee.

285   A fox, when one has caught her,
                     And such a daughter,
                     Should sure[115] to the slaughter,
                     If my cap would buy a halter;
                     So the fool follows after.   [*Exit.*]

GONERIL: This man[116] hath had good counsel. A hundred knights!

290   'Tis politic and safe to let him keep
       At point[117] a hundred knights; yes, that on every dream,
       Each buzz,[118] each fancy, each complaint, dislike,
       He may enguard[119] his dotage with their powers,
       And hold our lives in mercy.[120] Oswald, I say!

295 ALBANY: Well, you may fear too far.

GONERIL: Safer than trust too far.
       Let me still[121] take away the harms I fear,
       Not fear still to be taken:[122] I know his heart.[123]
       What he hath utter'd I have writ my sister;
       If she sustain him and his hundred knights,

300   When I have show'd the unfitness,—

        Re-enter Oswald.

                             How now, Oswald!
       What![124] have you writ that letter to my sister?

OSWALD: Ay, madam.

GONERIL: Take you some company, and away to horse:
       Inform her full[125] of my particular[126] fear;

305   And thereto add such reasons of your own
       As may compact[127] it more. Get you gone,
       And hasten your return.   [*Exit Oswald.*]
               No, no, my lord,
       This milky gentleness and course[128] of yours

---

114 (be) *content*: calm, almost 'shut up!'
115 should surely go
116 *This man*: Lear (the whole speech is ironical)
117 *At point*: armed and ready
118 rumour
119 guard
120 *in mercy*: at his mercy
121 always
122 overtaken by harm
123 *his heart*: i.e. (perhaps) that he is plotting to recover his throne
124 Well!
125 fully
126 personal
127 strengthen
128 *gentleness . . . course*: gentleness of your course (hendiadys)

Though I condemn not, yet, under pardon,

310 You are much more attask'd[129] for want of wisdom
Than prais'd for harmful mildness.[130]

ALBANY: How far your eyes may pierce I cannot tell:
Striving to better, oft we mar what's well.

GONERIL: Nay, then—

315 ALBANY: Well, well; the event.[131]   [*Exeunt.*]

129 blamed, held to account
130 *harmful mildness*: a mildness which can only prove harmful to us
131 *the event*: (let us see) what turns out

SCENE 5

Court before the Same.

Enter Lear, Kent, and Fool.

LEAR: Go you before to Gloucester[1] with these letters.[2] Acquaint my daughter
no further with any thing you know than comes from her demand out of[3]
the letter. If your diligence be not speedy I shall be there before you.

KENT: I will not sleep, my lord, till I have delivered your letter.   [*Exit.*]

5 FOOL: If a man's brains were in 's heels, were 't[4] not in danger of kibes?[5]

LEAR: Ay, boy.

FOOL: Then, I prithee, be merry; thy wit shall not go slip-shod.[6]

LEAR: Ha, ha, ha!

FOOL: Shalt see thy other daughter will use thee kindly;[7] for though she's as
10 like this[8] as a crab[9] is like an apple, yet I can tell what I can tell.

LEAR: What canst tell, boy?

FOOL: She will taste as like this as a crab does to a crab. Thou canst tell why
one's nose stands i' the middle on 's face?

LEAR: No.

15 FOOL: Why, to keep one's eyes of either side 's[10] nose, that what a man cannot
smell out, he may spy into.

LEAR: I did her wrong,—

FOOL: Canst tell how an oyster makes his shell?

LEAR: No.

1 the town, not the Earl
2 this letter (Latin *litterae*)
3 *demand out of*: questions arising out of
4 it, his brain(s)
5 chaps or chilblains
6 in slippers (to ease chilblains on the heel)
7 (1) affectionately, (2) after her kind, or nature (the Fool foresees the second)
8 Goneril
9 (apple)
10 *'s nose*: of one's nose

20 FOOL: Nor I neither; but I can tell why a snail has a house.

LEAR: Why?

FOOL: Why, to put his head in; not to give it away to his daughters, and leave his horns without a case.

LEAR: I will forget my nature.[11] So kind a father! Be my horses ready?

25 FOOL: Thy asses[12] are gone about 'em. The reason why the seven stars[13] are no more than seven is a pretty reason.

LEAR: Because they are not eight?

FOOL: Yes, indeed: thou wouldst make a good fool.

LEAR: To take it again perforce! Monster ingratitude![14]

30 FOOL: If thou wert my fool, nuncle, I'd have thee beaten for being old before thy time.

LEAR: How's that?

FOOL: Thou shouldst not have been old before thou hadst been wise.

LEAR: O! let me not be mad, not mad, sweet heaven;

35   Keep me in temper; I would not be mad!

> *Enter Gentleman.*

How now! Are those horses ready!

GENTLEMAN: Ready, my lord.

LEAR: Come, boy.

FOOL: She that's a maid now, and laughs at my departure,

40   Shall not be a maid long, unless things be cut shorter.[15]   [*Exeunt.*]

11 *my nature*: my natural affection (for my daughters)
12 *Thy asses*: those who are fools enough to serve you still
13 *the . . . stars*: the Pleiades
14 *Either* Lear contemplates trying to resume his royal power by force, *or* he is thinking of Goneril's withdrawing the privileges he had been allowed
15 *She . . . shorter*: i.e. 'The maid who sees only the funny side of the Fool's gibes and does not realize that Lear is going on a tragic journey is such a simpleton that she won't know how to preserve her virginity' (K. Muir)

ACT II

SCENE 1

A Court within the Castle of the Earl of Gloucester.

> *Enter Edmund and Curan, meeting.*

EDMUND: Save thee,[1] Curan.

CURAN: And you, sir. I have been with your father, and given him notice that the Duke of Cornwall and Regan his duchess will be here with him to-night.

5 EDMUND: How comes that?

1 (God) *save thee*

CURAN: Nay, I know not. You have heard of the news abroad?[2] I mean the
whispered ones,[2] for they are yet but ear-kissing arguments?[3]

EDMUND: Not I: pray you, what are they?

CURAN: Have you heard of no likely wars toward,[4] 'twixt the Dukes of
10   Cornwall and Albany?

EDMUND: Not a word.

CURAN: You may do then, in time. Fare you well, sir.   [*Exit.*]

EDMUND: The duke be here tonight! The better![5] best!
This weaves itself perforce into my business.
15   My father hath set guard to take my brother;
And I have one thing, of a queasy question,[6]
Which I must act. Briefness[7] and fortune, work!
Brother, a word; descend:[8] brother, I say!

     Enter Edgar.

My father watches: O sir! fly this place;
20   Intelligence is given where you are hid;
You have now the good advantage of the night.
Have you not spoken 'gainst the Duke of Cornwall?
He's coming hither, now, i' the night, i' the haste,[9]
And Regan with him; have you nothing said
25   Upon his party 'gainst[10] the Duke of Albany?
Advise yourself.

EDGAR: I am sure on 't, not a word.

EDMUND: I hear my father coming; pardon me;
In cunning[11] I must draw my sword upon you;
Draw; seem to defend yourself; now 'quit you well.
30   Yield;[12]—come before my father. Light, ho! here!
Fly, brother. Torches! torches! So, farewell.   [*Exit Edgar.*]
Some blood drawn on me would beget opinion   [*Wounds his arm.*]
Of my more fierce endeavour:[13] I have seen drunkards
Do more than this in sport. Father! father!
35   Stop, stop! No help?

2 news
3 *ear-kissing arguments*: subjects of secret conversation (as with the mouth close to the hearer's ear)
4 in view
5 (all) *the better*
6 *of . . . question*: awkward, ticklish to handle
7 swift action
8 Edgar would have entered on the upper stage
9 *i' the haste*: in haste
10 *Upon . . . 'gainst*: about the party formed by him against
11 in pretence (as if we were enemies)
12 said louder, for Gloucester to hear
13 *beget . . . endeavour*: make men think that I have really been fighting seriously

Enter Gloucester, and Servants with torches.

GLOUCESTER: Now, Edmund, where's the villain?

EDMUND: Here stood he in the dark, his sharp sword out,
    Mumbling of wicked charms, conjuring the moon
    To stand auspicious mistress.[14]

GLOUCESTER: But where is he?

40   EDMUND: Look, sir, I bleed.

GLOUCESTER: Where is the villain, Edmund?

EDMUND: Fled this way, sir. When by no means he could—

GLOUCESTER: Pursue him, ho! Go after. [*Exeunt some Servants.*] 'By no
    means' what?

EDMUND: Persuade me to the murder of your lordship;

45   But that I told him,[15] the revenging gods
    'Gainst parricides did all their thunders bend;
    Spoke with how manifold and strong a bond
    The child was bound to the father; sir, in fine,
    Seeing how loathly opposite[16] I stood

50   To his unnatural purpose, in fell motion,[17]
    With his prepared sword he charges home[18]
    My unprovided[19] body, lanc'd mine arm:
    But when he saw my best alarum'd spirits[20]
    Bold in quarrel's right, rous'd to the encounter,

55   Or whether gasted[21] by the noise I made,
    Full suddenly he fled.

GLOUCESTER: Let him fly far:
    Not in this land shall he remain uncaught;
    And found—dispatch.[22] The noble duke my master,
    My worthy arch[23] and patron, comes to-night:

60   By his authority I will proclaim it,
    That he which finds him shall deserve our thanks,
    Bringing the murderous coward to the stake;
    He that conceals him, death.

---

14 *stand . . . mistress*: favour him as if she were his mistress (as she was of Endymion in classical mythology)
15 *But . . . him*: without my telling him (in reply) that
16 *loathly opposite*: opposed, with loathing, to
17 *fell motion*: fierce thrust
18 *charges home*: makes a home (effective) thrust at
19 unprotected
20 *best . . . spirits*: my best spirits stirred up
21 frightened
22 when he is found, the order will be 'dispatch him!'
23 chief

EDMUND: When I dissuaded him from his intent,
65   And found him pight[24] to do it, with curst speech
     I threaten'd to discover him: he replied,
     'Thou unpossessing[25] bastard! dost thou think,
     If I would[26] stand against thee, would the reposal
     Of any trust, virtue, or worth, in thee
70   Make the words faith'd? No: what I should deny,—
     As this I would; ay, though thou didst produce
     My very character,[27]—I'd turn it all
     To thy suggestion,[28] plot, and damned practice:[29]
     And thou must make a dullard of the world,[30]
75   If they not thought[31] the profits of my death
     Were very pregnant[32] and potential spurs[33]
     To make thee seek it.'
GLOUCESTER: Strong and fasten'd[34] villain!
     Would he deny his letter? I never got[35] him.   [*Tucket within.*]
     Hark! the duke's trumpets. I know not why he comes.
80   All ports I'll bar; the villain shall not 'scape;
     The duke must grant me that: besides, his picture
     I will send far and near, that all the kingdom
     May have due note of him; and of my land,
     Loyal and natural[36] boy, I'll work the means
85   To make thee capable.[37]

Enter Cornwall, Regan, and Attendants.

CORNWALL: How now, my noble friend! since I came hither,—
     Which I can call but now,—I have heard strange news.
REGAN: If it be true, all vengeance comes too short
     Which can pursue the offender. How dost, my lord?
90 GLOUCESTER: O! madam, my old heart is crack'd, it's crack'd.
REGAN: What! did my father's godson seek your life?
     He whom my father name'd?[38] your Edgar!

24 determined
25 *as unable to inherit*
26 should
27 handwriting
28 temptation
29 treachery
30 *make . . . world*: suppose people very stupid
31 *not thought*: should not think
32 clear, obvious (of different derivation from the word meaning 'with child')
33 *potential spurs*: powerful inducements
34 confirmed
35 begot
36 true, affectionate (with a glance at the meaning of 'born out of wedlock')
37 legally able to inherit (cf. l. 67)
38 in baptism

GLOUCESTER: O! lady, lady, shame would have it hid.

REGAN: Was he not companion with the riotous knights

95   That tend upon my father?

GLOUCESTER: I know not, madam; 'tis too bad, too bad.

EDMUND: Yes, madam, he was of that consort.[39]

REGAN: No marvel then though he were ill affected;

      'Tis they have put him on[40] the old man's death,

100   To have the expense and waste of[41] his revenues.

      I have this present evening from my sister

      Been well-inform'd of them, and with such cautions

      That if they come to sojourn at my house,

      I'll not be there.

CORNWALL: Nor I, assure thee, Regan.

105   Edmund, I hear that you have shown your father

      A child-like[42] office.

EDMUND: 'Twas my duty, sir.

GLOUCESTER: He did bewray[43] his practice;[44] and receiv'd

      This hurt you see, striving to apprehend him.

CORNWALL: Is he pursu'd?

GLOUCESTER: Ay, my good lord.

110 CORNWALL: If he be taken he shall never more

      Be fear'd of doing[45] harm; make your own purpose,

      How in my strength you please.[46] For you, Edmund,

      Whose virtue and obedience[47] doth this instant

      So much commend itself, you shall be ours:

115   Natures of such deep trust we shall much need;

      You we first seize on.

EDMUND: I shall serve you, sir,

      Truly, however else.[48]

GLOUCESTER: For him I thank your Grace.

CORNWALL: You know now why we came to visit you,—

REGAN: Thus out of season, threading dark-ey'd[49] night:

120   Occasions, noble Gloucester, of some prize,[50]

      Wherein we must have use of your advice.

      Our father he hath writ, so hath our sister,

39 (accent consórt) company
40 *put him on*: egged him on to (attempt)
41 *To . . . of*: that he might be able to spend wastefully
42 truly filial
43 reveal
44 plot
45 *of doing*: lest he should do
46 *make . . . please*: use my authority and resources as you like in carrying out your purpose
47 *virtue and obedience*: virtuous obedience (hence verb in singular)
48 successfully or not
49 *threading dark-ey'd*: (with a pun on the eye of a needle)
50 *Occasions . . . prize*: incidents of some importance have occurred

Of differences, which I best thought it fit
To answer from[51] our home; the several messengers
125 From hence attend dispatch.[52] Our good old friend,
Lay comforts to your bosom, and bestow
Your needful counsel to our businesses,
Which craves the instant use.[53]

GLOUCESTER: I serve you, madam.
Your Graces are right welcome. [*Exeunt.*]

51 away from
52 *attend dispatch*: wait to be sent out
53 *craves . . . use*: demands immediate execution

SCENE 2

Before Gloucester's Castle.

Enter Kent and Oswald, severally.

OSWALD: Good dawning to thee, friend: art of this house?[1]
KENT: Ay.
OSWALD: Where may we set our horses?
KENT: I' the mire.
5 OSWALD: Prithee, if thou lovest me, tell me.
KENT: I love thee not.
OSWALD: Why, then I care not for thee.
KENT: If I had thee in Lipsbury pinfold,[2] I would make thee care for me.
OSWALD: Why dost thou use me thus? I know thee not.
10 KENT: Fellow, I know thee.
OSWALD: What dost thou know me for?
KENT: A knave, a rascal, an eater of broken meats;[3] a base, proud, shallow, beggarly, three suited,[4] hundred-pound,[5] filthy, worsted-stocking[6] knave; a lily-liver'd,[7] action-taking[8] knave; a whoreson, glass-gazing,[9] super-service-
15 able,[10] finical[11] rogue; one-trunk-inheriting[12] slave; one that wouldst be a

1 *of this house*: a dependant, servant
2 *in Lipsbury pinfold*: possibly 'in my jaws'
3 *eater . . . meats*: finisher up of scraps
4 the allowance of some servants
5 owning only a hundred pounds (the qualification for a jury then)
6 woollen (as opposed to silk)
7 see IV. ii. 50
8 resorting to legal protection (instead of defending himself)
9 vain
10 *either* above his work, *or* over officious
11 affected
12 whose possessions would all go in one chest

bawd, in way of[13] good service, and art nothing but the composition[14] of a
knave, beggar, coward, pandar, and the son and heir of a mongrel bitch: one
whom I will beat into clamorous whining if thou deniest the least syllable
of thy addition.[15]

20 OSWALD: Why, what a monstrous fellow art thou, thus to rail on one that is
neither known of thee nor knows thee!

KENT: What a brazen-faced varlet art thou, to deny thou knowest me! Is it two
days since I tripped up thy heels and beat thee before the king? Draw, you
rogue; for, though it be night, yet the moon shines: I'll make a sop o' the

25 moonshine of you. [*Drawing his sword.*] Draw, you whoreson, cullionly,[16]
barber-monger,[17] draw.

OSWALD: Away! I have nothing to do with thee.

KENT: Draw, you rascal; you come with letters against the king, and take vanity
the puppet's[18] part against the royalty of her father. Draw, you rogue, or I'll

30 so carbonado[19] your shanks: draw, you rascal; come your ways.[20]

OSWALD: Help, ho! murder! help!

KENT: Strike, you slave; stand, rogue, stand; you neat[21] slave, strike.

[*Beating him.*]

OSWALD: Help, oh! murder! murder!

Enter Edmund with his rapier drawn.

EDMUND: How now! What's the matter? [*Parting them.*]

35 KENT: With you,[22] goodman boy, if you please: come, I'll flesh[23] ye; come on,
young master.

Enter Cornwall, Regan, Gloucester, and Servants.

GLOUCESTER: Weapons! arms! What's the matter here?

CORNWALL: Keep peace, upon your lives:
He dies that strikes again. What is the matter?

40 REGAN: The messengers from our sister and the king.

CORNWALL: What is your difference?[24] speak.

OSWALD: I am scarce in breath, my lord.

---

13 *in way of*: in order to perform
14 mixture
15 *thy addition*: these titles
16 rascally
17 frequenter of barbers, fop
18 *vanity the puppet's*: i.e. Goneril's
19 slice, slash
20 *come . . . ways*: come on
21 dandified *or* utter
22 *With you*: my matter, quarrel is with you *or* I'm your man (for a fight)
23 initiate (into bloodshed)
24 (ground of) quarrel

KENT: No marvel, you have so bestirred your valour. You cowardly rascal, nature disclaims[25] in thee: a tailor made thee.

45 CORNWALL: Thou art a strange fellow; a tailor make a man?

KENT: Ay, a tailor, sir: a stone-cutter[26] or a painter could not have made him so ill, though they had been but two hours o' the trade.

CORNWALL: Speak yet, how grew your quarrel?

OSWALD: This ancient ruffian, sir, whose life I have spar'd at suit of his grey
50 beard,—

KENT: Thou whoreson zed! thou unnecessary letter! My lord, if you will give me leave, I will tread this unbolted[27] villain into mortar, and daub the wall of a jakes[28] with him. Spare my grey beard, you wagtail?[29]

CORNWALL: Peace, sirrah!

55 You beastly knave, know you no reverence?

KENT: Yes, sir; but anger hath a privilege.

CORNWALL: Why art thou angry?

KENT: That such a slave as this should wear a sword,
Who wears no honesty. Such smiling rogues as these,
60 Like rats, oft bite the holy cords[30] a-twain
Which are too intrinse[31] t' unloose; smooth[32] every passion
That in the natures of their lords rebel;
Bring oil to fire, snow to their colder moods;
Renege,[33] affirm, and turn their halcyon beaks
65 With every gale and vary[34] of their masters,
Knowing nought, like dogs, but following.
A plague upon your epileptic[35] visage!
Smile you[36] my speeches, as I were a fool?
Goose, if I had you upon Sarum[37] plain,
70 I'd drive ye cackling home to Camelot.[38]

CORNWALL: What! art thou mad, old fellow?

GLOUCESTER: How fell you out? say that.

KENT: No contraries hold more antipathy
Than I and such a knave.

25 disown (any share)
26 sculptor
27 perhaps 'unmitigated' (bolt = sift flour)
28 privy
29 probably 'obsequious', from its bouncing or bobbing
30 *the holy cords*: of intimate relationship
31 intricate, tight
32 flatter, fall in with
33 deny
34 *gale and vary*: varying breeze
35 distorted and pale, as in an epileptic fit
36 *Smile you*: do you smile at?
37 Salisbury
38 supposed to be near Winchester

75 CORNWALL: Why dost thou call him knave? What is his fault?

KENT: His countenance likes[39] me not.

CORNWALL: No more, perchance, does mine, nor his, nor hers.

KENT: Sir, 'tis my occupation[40] to be plain:

I have seen better faces in my time

80 Than stands on any shoulder that I see

Before me at this instant.

CORNWALL: This is some fellow,

Who, having been prais'd for bluntness, doth affect

A saucy roughness, and constrains the garb

Quite from his nature:[41] he cannot flatter, he

85 An honest mind and plain, he must speak truth:

An they will take it, so;[42] if not, he's plain.

These kind of knaves I know, which in this plainness

Harbour more craft and more corrupter[43] ends

Than twenty silly-ducking observants,[44]

90 That stretch their duties nicely.[45]

KENT: Sir, in good sooth, in sincere verity,

Under the allowance of your grand aspect,[46]

Whose influence, like the wreath of radiant fire

On flickering Phoebus' front,—

CORNWALL: What mean'st by this?

95 KENT: To go out of my dialect, which you discommend so much. I know, sir,

I am no flatterer: he that[47] beguiled you in a plain accent was a plain knave;[48]

which for my part I will not be, though I should win your displeasure[49] to

entreat me to 't.[50]

CORNWALL: What was the offence you gave him?

100 OSWALD: I never gave him any:

It pleas'd the king his master very late

To strike at me, upon his misconstruction;[51]

When he, conjunct,[52] and flattering his displeasure,

39 pleases

40 business, habit

41 *constrains . . . nature*: is behaving in a manner quite unnatural to him (garb = fashion, manner, but not of *dress* in Shakespeare)

42 well and good

43 *more corrupter*: double comparative, not uncommon in Shakespeare

44 *silly-ducking observants*: obsequious attendants foolishly bowing and scraping (observe = pay court to)

45 *stretch . . . nicely*: are over-particular in the performance of

46 power, influence (astrological)

47 *he that*: i.e. the 'kind of knaves' referred to in l. 87

48 *a plain knave*: a real knave (which I am not)

49 you, in your displeasure

50 *to 't*: to flatter you

51 *upon his misconstruction*: misunderstanding me; see I. iv. 68

52 joining in with (Lear)

Tripp'd me behind; being down, insulted, rail'd,
105   And put upon him such a deal of man,
       That worthied him,[53] got praises of the king
       For him attempting[54] who was self-subdu'd;
       And, in the fleshment[55] of this dread exploit,
       Drew on me here again.

KENT: None of these rogues and cowards
110   But Ajax is their fool.[56]

CORNWALL: Fetch forth the stocks!
       You stubborn ancient knave, you reverend[57] braggart,
       We'll teach you.

KENT: Sir, I am too old to learn,
       Call not your stocks for me; I serve the king,
       On whose employment I was sent to you;
115   You shall do small respect, show too bold malice
       Against the grace and person of my master,
       Stocking[58] his messenger.

CORNWALL: Fetch forth the stocks! As I have life and honour,
       There shall he sit till noon.

120   REGAN: Till noon! Till night, my lord; and all night too.

KENT: Why, madam, if I were your father's dog,
       You should not use me so.

REGAN: Sir, being his knave, I will.

CORNWALL: This is a fellow of the same colour[59]
       Our sister speaks of. Come, bring away[60] the stocks.   [*Stocks brought out.*]

125   GLOUCESTER: Let me beseech your Grace not to do so.
       His fault is much, and the good king his master
       Will check him for't: your purpos'd low correction
       Is such as basest and contemned'st[61] wretches
       For pilferings and most common trespasses
130   Are punish'd with: the king must take it ill,
       That he, so slightly valu'd in his messenger,
       Should have him thus restrain'd.

CORNWALL: I'll answer[62] that.

---

53 *put . . . worthied him*: made such a show of valour as to win the reputation of honour
54 *him attempting*: attacking a man
55 excitement resulting from first success, see l. 35
56 *their fool*: a fool compared to them
57 grey-headed, old enough to know better
58 putting in stocks
59 complexion, kind
60 bring in
61 most despicable
62 take responsibility for

REGAN: My sister may receive it much more worse
   To have her gentleman abus'd, assaulted,
135 For following her affairs. Put in his legs.   [*Kent is put in the stocks.*]
   Come, my good lord, away.   [*Exeunt all but Gloucester and Kent.*]
GLOUCESTER: I am sorry for thee, friend; 'tis the duke's pleasure,
   Whose disposition, all the world well knows,
   Will not be rubb'd[63] nor stopp'd: I'll entreat for thee.
140 KENT: Pray, do not, sir. I have watch'd[64] and travell'd hard;
   Some time I shall sleep out, the rest I'll whistle.
   A good man's fortune may grow out at heels:[65]
   Give you good morrow!
GLOUCESTER: The duke's to blame in this; 'twill be ill taken.   [*Exit.*]
145 KENT: Good king, that must approve[66] the common saw,[67]
   Thou out of heaven's benediction comest
   To the warm sun.[68]
   Approach, thou beacon[69] to this under globe,[70]
   That by thy comfortable beams I may
150 Peruse this letter. Nothing almost sees miracles
   But misery:[71] I know 'tis from Cordelia,
   Who hath most fortunately been inform'd
   Of my obscured course;[72] and shall find time
   From this enormous state, seeking to give
155 Losses their remedies.[73] All weary and o'er-watch'd,
   Take vantage,[74] heavy eyes, not to behold
   This shameful lodging.
   Fortune, good night, smile once more; turn thy wheel!   [*He sleeps.*]

63 hindered (a 'rub' is an obstacle in bowls)
64 lain awake at night
65 *out at heels*: a metaphor for 'in a bad way', like 'out at elbow' or 'down at heel'
66 prove (the truth of)
67 proverb
68 *Thou . . . sun*: i.e. from better to worse (a surprising sense, but proved by other examples)
69 *thou beacon*: the sun
70 *this . . . globe*: our world, as opposed to heaven (l. 147)
71 the wretched
72 *my . . . course*: what has happened to me who appears to have disappeared
73 *and shall . . . remedies*: and who will find the opportunity to deliver us from this unnatural state of affairs, putting right what is wrong
74 advantage (of the opportunity)

SCENE 3

A Part of the Heath.

     Enter Edgar.

EDGAR: I heard myself proclaim'd;[1]
      And by the happy[2] hollow of a tree
      Escap'd the hunt. No port is free; no place,
      That[3] guard, and most unusual vigilance,
5   Does not attend my taking.[4] While I may 'scape
      I will preserve myself; and am bethought
      To take[5] the basest and most poorest shape
      That ever penury, in contempt of man,
      Brought near to beast; my face I'll grime with filth,
10   Blanket my loins, elf[6] all my hair in knots,
      And with presented[7] nakedness outface
      The winds and persecutions of the sky.
      The country gives me proof and precedent
      Of Bedlam[8] beggars, who with roaring voices,
15   Strike[9] in their numb'd and mortified bare arms
      Pins, wooden pricks,[10] nails, sprigs of rosemary;
      And with this horrible object,[11] from low farms,
      Poor pelting[12] villages, sheep-cotes, and mills,
      Sometime with lunatic bans,[13] sometime with prayers,
20   Enforce their charity. Poor Turlygood![14] poor Tom!
      That's something yet: Edgar I nothing am.[15]   *[Exit.]*

1 see II. i. 60 ff.
2 luckily found
3 i.e. where
4 *attend my taking*: wait to arrest me
5 *am . . . take*: have bethought myself of taking
6 tangle (as an elf might)
7 *either* assumed *or* exposed to view
8 cf. I. ii. 110
9 drive
10 skewers
11 appearance
12 petty
13 curses
14 no certain explanation
15 *Edgar . . . am*: either I am Edgar no more, *or* As Edgar I no longer exist

SCENE 4

Before Gloucester's Castle.

Kent in the stocks.

        Enter Lear, Fool, and Gentleman.

LEAR: 'Tis strange that they[1] should so depart from home,
    And not send back my messenger.
GENTLEMAN: As I learn'd,
    The night before there was no purpose in them
    Of this remove.[2]
KENT: Hail to thee, noble master!
5 LEAR: Ha!
    Mak'st thou this shame thy pastime?
KENT: No, my lord.
FOOL: Ha, ha! he wears cruel[3] garters. Horses are tied by the head, dogs and
    bears by the neck, monkeys by the loins, and men by the legs: when a man
    is over-lusty at legs, then he wears wooden nether-stocks.[4]
10 LEAR: What's he that hath so much thy place[5] mistook
    To set thee here?
KENT: It is both he and she,
    Your son and daughter.
LEAR: No.
KENT: Yes.
15 LEAR: No, I say.
KENT: I say, yea.
LEAR: No, no; they would not.
KENT: Yes, they have.
LEAR: By Jupiter, I swear, no.
20 KENT: By Juno, I swear, ay.
LEAR: They durst not do 't;
    They could not, would not do 't; 'tis worse than murder,
    To do upon respect[6] such violent outrage.
    Resolve me,[7] with all modest[8] haste, which way
    Thou mightst deserve, or they impose, this usage,
25   Coming from us.[9]

---

1 Cornwall and Regan
2 change of residence
3 with a pun on 'crewel' = worsted yarn
4 stockings (as opposed to 'upper stocks' = breeches)
5 rank, status as my envoy
6 *upon respect*: deliberately
7 *Resolve me*: explain to me
8 becoming
9 *Coming . . . us*: seeing that you came from me

KENT: My lord, when at their home
 I did commend your highness' letters to them,
 Ere I was risen from the place that show'd
 My duty kneeling, there came a reeking post,[10]
 Stew'd[11] in his haste, half breathless, panting forth
30 From Goneril his mistress salutations;
 Deliver'd letters, spite of intermission,[12]
 Which presently[13] they read: on whose contents
 They summon'd up their meiny,[14] straight took horse;
 Commanded me to follow, and attend
35 The leisure of their answer; gave me cold looks:
 And meeting[15] here the other messenger,
 Whose welcome, I perceiv'd, had poison'd mine,—
 Being the very fellow which of late
 Display'd[16] so saucily against your highness,—
40 Having more man[17] than wit about me,—drew:
 He rais'd the house with loud and coward cries.
 You son and daughter found this trespass worth
 The shame which here it suffers.
FOOL: Winter's not gone yet,[18] if the wild geese fly that way.
45   Fathers that wear rags
     Do make their children blind,[19]
    But fathers that bear bags[20]
     Shall see their children kind.
    Fortune, that arrant whore,
50   Ne'er turns the key[21] to the poor.
 But for all this thou shalt have as many dolours[22] for[23] thy daughters as
 thou canst tell[24] in a year.
LEAR: O! how this mother[25] swells up toward my heart;
 Hysterica passio![26] down, thou climbing sorrow!
55 Thy element's below. Where is this daughter?

10 messenger
11 sweating
12 *spite of intermission*: in spite of the fact he was interrupting me
13 immediately
14 household, company
15 And I, meeting
16 showed off
17 courage (cf. II. ii. 105)
18 i.e. We are not out of trouble
19 to filial duty
20 of money
21 *turns the key*: to admit
22 griefs (with pun on 'dollars' = money)
23 from, because of
24 (1) recount griefs, (2) count money
25 hysteria
26 *Hysterica passio!*: suffering in the 'mother' (archaic for womb, Gk *hystera*), so-called as commoner in women

KENT: With the earl, sir: here within.

LEAR: Follow me not; stay here. [*Exit.*]

GENTLEMAN: Made you no more offence than what you speak of?

KENT: None.

60   How chance the king comes with so small a number?

FOOL: An thou hadst been set i' the stocks for that question, thou hadst well
        deserved it.[27]

KENT: Why fool?

FOOL: We'll set thee to school to an ant, to teach thee there's no labouring i'
65   the winter. All that follow their noses are led by their eyes but blind men;
        and there's not a nose among twenty but can smell him that's stinking.[28] Let
        go thy hold when a great wheel runs down a hill, lest it break thy neck with
        following it; but the great one that goes up the hill, let him draw thee after.
        When a wise man gives thee better counsel, give me mine again: I would
70   have none but knaves follow it, since a fool gives it.

> That sir[29] which serves and seeks for gain,
>   And follows but for form,
> Will pack[30] when it begins to rain,
>   And leave thee in the storm.
75
> But I will tarry; the fool will stay,
>   And let the wise[31] man fly:
> The knave turns fool[32] that runs away;
>   The fool[33] no knave, perdy.[34]

KENT: Where learn'd you this, fool?

80   FOOL: Not i' the stocks, fool.

Re-enter Lear, with Gloucester.

LEAR: Deny[35] to speak with me! They are sick! they are weary!
        They have travell'd hard to-night! Mere fetches,[36]
        The images[37] of revolt and flying off.[38]
        Fetch me a better answer.

---

27 *And thou . . . it:* i.e. you should know that people desert a losing cause
28 *there's . . . stinking:* i.e. it does not take the keen smell of a blind man to smell out the poor state of Lear's
   fortunes
29 gentleman
30 clear off
31 i.e. worldly wise
32 *turns fool:* i.e. judged from a higher, less self-interested point of view
33 *The fool:* the Fool, I
34 par Dieu
35 refuse
36 tricks, excuses (with pun in l. 84)
37 tokens *or* embodiment (cf. IV. vi. 149)
38 *flying off:* desertion

GLOUCESTER: My dear lord,

85   You know the fiery quality[39] of the duke;
      How unremovable and fix'd he is
      In his own course.

LEAR: Vengeance! plague! death! confusion!
      Fiery! what quality? Why, Gloucester, Gloucester,

90   I'd speak with the Duke of Cornwall and his wife.

GLOUCESTER: Well, my good lord, I have inform'd them so.

LEAR: Inform'd them! Dost thou understand me, man?

GLOUCESTER: Ay, my good lord.

LEAR: The king would speak with Cornwall; the dear father

95   Would with his daughter speak, commands her service:
      Are they inform'd of this? My breath and blood!
      Fiery! the fiery duke! Tell the hot[40] duke that—
      No, but not yet; may be he is not well:
      Infirmity[41] doth still neglect all office[42]

100   Whereto our health is bound;[43] we are not ourselves
      When nature, being oppress'd, commands the mind
      To suffer with the body. I'll forbear;
      And am fall'n out with my more headier will,[44]
      To take the indispos'd and sickly fit

105   For the sound man. Death on my state! [*Looking on Kent.*] Wherefore
      Should he sit here? This act persuades me
      That this remotion[45] of the duke and her
      Is practice[46] only. Give me my servant forth.
      Go, tell the duke and 's wife I'd speak with them

110   Now, presently: bid them come forth and hear me,
      Or at their chamber-door I'll beat the drum
      Till it cry sleep to death.[47]

GLOUCESTER: I would have all well betwixt you.   [*Exit.*]

LEAR: O, me! my heart, my rising heart! but, down!

115   FOOL: Cry to it, nuncle, as the cockney[48] did to the eels when she put 'em i'
      the paste alive; she knapped[49] 'em o' the coxcombs[50] with a stick, and cried,

39 nature
40 hot-tempered
41 a sick man
42 duty
43 *Whereto . . . bound*: which, if well, we should feel bound to perform
44 *And . . . will*: i.e. I turn back from my overhasty determination
45 removal (from their home)
46 a trick
47 *cry . . . death*: drown sleep with its noise (as Macbeth heard a voice 'murder' sleep, Macbeth II. ii. 36–7)
48 (probably) an affected woman
49 rapped, struck
50 heads

'Down, wantons,[51] down!' 'Twas her brother that, in pure kindness to his
horse, buttered his hay.[52]

Enter Cornwall, Regan, Gloucester, and Servants.

LEAR: Good morrow to you both.

CORNWALL: Hail to your Grace!   [*Kent is set at liberty.*]

120 REGAN: I am glad to see your highness.

LEAR: Regan, I think you are; I know what reason
I have to think so: if thou shouldst not be glad,
I would divorce me from thy mother's tomb,
Sepulchring[53] and adultress.—[*To Kent.*] O! are you free?

125 Some other time for that. Beloved Regan,
Thy sister's naught: O Regan! she hath tied
Sharp-tooth'd unkindness, like a vulture, here: [*Points to his heart.*]
I can scarce speak to thee; thou'lt not believe
With how deprav'd a quality[54]—O Regan!

130 REGAN: I pray you, sir, take patience. I have hope
You less know how to value her desert[55]
Than she to scant[56] her duty.

LEAR: Say, how is that?

REGAN: I cannot think my sister in the least
Would fail her obligation: if, sir, perchance

135 She have restrain'd the riots of your followers,
'Tis on such ground, and to such wholesome end,
As clears her from all blame.

LEAR: My curses on her.

REGAN: O, sir! you are old;
Nature in you stands on the very verge

140 Of her confine:[57] you should be rul'd and led
By some discretion[58] that discerns your state
Better than you yourself. Therefore I pray you
That to our sister you do make return;[59]
Say, you have wrong'd her, sir.

LEAR: Ask her forgiveness?

145 Do you but mark how this becomes the house:[60]

---

51 pert, cheeky creatures
52 *buttered his hay*: i.e. did something equally silly
53 (as it would then be) the tomb of
54 manner (she treated me)
55 merits
56 *Than she* (know how) *to scant*: is capable of falling short of
57 boundary, utmost limit
58 discreet people
59 *make return*: return
60 *the house*: our family relationship *or* the royal house

       'Dear daughter, I confess that I am old;
       Age is unnecessary:[61] on my knees I beg   [*Kneeling.*]
       That you'll vouchsafe me raiment, bed, and food.'

REGAN: Good sir, no more; these are unsightly tricks:

150   Return you to my sister.

LEAR: [*Rising.*] Never, Regan.
       She hath abated[62] me of half my train;
       Look'd black upon me; struck me with her tongue,
       Most serpent-like, upon the very heart.
       All the stor'd vengeances of heaven fall

155   On her ingrateful top![63] Strike her young bones,
       You taking[64] airs, with lameness!

CORNWALL: Fie, sir, fie!

LEAR: You nimble lightnings, dart your blinding flames
       Into her scornful eyes! Infect her beauty,
       You fen-suck'd fogs, drawn by the powerful sun,

160   To fall and blast her pride!

REGAN: O the blest gods! So will you wish on me,
       When the rash mood[65] is on.

LEAR: No, Regan, thou shalt never have my curse:
       Thy tender-hefted[66] nature shall not give

165   Thee o'er to harshness: her eyes are fierce, but thine
       Do comfort and not burn. 'Tis not in thee
       To grudge my pleasures, to cut off my train,
       To bandy hasty words, to scant my sizes,[67]
       And, in conclusion, to oppose the bolt[68]

170   Against my coming in: thou better know'st
       The offices of nature, bond of childhood,
       Effects[69] of courtesy, dues of gratitude;
       Thy half o' the kingdom hast thou not forgot,
       Wherein I thee endow'd.

REGAN: Good sir, to the purpose.[70]

175 LEAR: Who put my man i' the stocks?   [*Tucket within.*]

CORNWALL: What trumpet's that?

---

61 useless, has no right to exist
62 curtailed
63 head
64 infecting, infectious
65 *the . . . mood*: cf. I. i. 285
66 (probably) set in a delicate bodily frame (heft = haft = handle), womanly
67 allowances (cf. sizar = exhibitioner, sometimes at Cambridge)
68 *oppose the bolt*: bar the door
69 manifestations
70 *to the purpose*: come to the point

REGAN: I know 't, my sister's; this approves[71] her letter,
    That she would soon be here. Is your lady come?

    Enter Oswald.

LEAR: This is a slave, whose easy-borrow'd[72] pride
    Dwells in the fickle[73] grace of her he follows.
180   Out, varlet, from my sight!

CORNWALL: What means your Grace?

    Enter Goneril.

LEAR: Who stock'd my servant? Regan, I have good hope
    Thou didst not know on 't. Who comes here? O heavens,
    If you do love old men, if your sweet sway
    Allow[74] obedience, if yourselves are old,
185   Make it your cause;[75] send down and take my part!
    [*To Goneril.*] Art not asham'd to look upon this beard?
    O Regan, wilt thou take her by the hand?

GONERIL: Why not by the hand, sir? How have I offended?
    All's not offence that indiscretion[76] finds[77]
190   And dotage terms so.

LEAR: O sides! you are too tough;
    Will you yet hold? How came my man i' the stocks?

CORNWALL: I set him there, sir: but his own disorders
    Deserv'd much less advancement.[78]

LEAR: You! did you?

REGAN: I pray you, father, being weak, seem so.[79]
195   If, till the expiration of your month,
    You will return and sojourn with my sister,
    Dismissing half your train, come then to me:
    I am now from[80] home, and out of that provision
    Which shall be needful for your entertainment.
200 LEAR: Return to her? and fifty men dismiss'd!
    No, rather I abjure all roofs, and choose
    To wage against[81] the enmity o' the air;

71 confirms
72 assumed without justification
73 unreliable (as not given for merit)
74 approve
75 *Make . . . cause*: identify yourselves with my side
76 cf. l. 141
77 holds
78 *much . . . advancement*: greater disgrace
79 *seem so*: admit it, behave accordingly
80 away from
81 *wage* (war) *against*: contend with

To be a comrade with the wolf and owl,
Necessity's sharp pinch![82] Return with her!

205   Why, the hot-blooded France, that dowerless took
Our youngest born, I could as well be brought
To knee[83] his throne, and squire-like, pension beg
To keep base life afoot. Return with her!
Persuade me rather to be slave and sumpter[84]

210   To this detested groom.   [*Pointing to Oswald.*]

GONERIL: At your choice, sir.

LEAR: I prithee, daughter, do not make me mad:
I will not trouble thee, my child; farewell.
We'll no more meet, no more see one another;
But yet thou art my flesh, my blood, my daughter;

215   Or rather a disease that's in my flesh,
Which I must needs call mine: thou art a boil,
A plague-sore, an embossed[85] carbuncle,
In my corrupted blood. But I'll not chide thee;
Let shame come when it will, I do not call it:

220   I do not bid the thunder-bearer[86] shoot,[87]
Nor tell tales of thee to high-judging[88] Jove.
Mend when thou canst; be better at thy leisure:
I can be patient; I can stay with Regan,
I and my hundred knights.

REGAN: Not altogether so:

225   I look'd not for you yet, nor am provided
For your fit welcome. Give ear, sir, to my sister;
For those that mingle reason with your passion[89]
Must be content to think you old, and so[90]—
But she knows what she does.

LEAR: Is this well spoken?

230 REGAN: I dare avouch it, sir: what! fifty followers?
Is it not well? What should you need of more?
Yea, or so many, sith[91] that both charge[92] and danger[93]

82 *Necessity's . . . pinch*: straits to which need will reduce me (cf. 'Necessitie must first pinch you by the throat' in Florio's *Montaigne*)
83 kneel before
84 beast of burden
85 swollen
86 *the thunder-bearer*: the god Jupiter
87 strike with lightning
88 supreme judge *or* judge in heaven
89 *mingle . . . passion*: examine your passionate utterances in the light of reason (but the figure is probably from mixing drinks)
90 *and so—*: sc. not take you seriously (or something similar)
91 since
92 the expense
93 i.e. of disturbance

Speak 'gainst so great a number? How, in one house,
Should many people, under two commands,
235   Hold amity?[94] 'Tis hard; almost impossible.
GONERIL: Why might not you, my lord, receive attendance
    From those that she calls servants, or from mine?
REGAN: Why not, my lord? If then they chanc'd to slack you[95]
    We could control them. If you will come to me,
240   For now I spy a danger, I entreat you
    To bring but five-and-twenty; to no more
    Will I give place or notice.[96]
LEAR: I gave you all—
REGAN: And in good time you gave it.
LEAR: Made you my guardians, my depositaries,[97]
245   But kept a reservation[98] to be follow'd
    With such a number. What! must I come to you
    With five-and-twenty? Regan, said you so?
REGAN: And speak 't again, my lord; no more with me.
LEAR: Those wicked creatures[99] yet do look well-favour'd,
250   When others are more wicked; not being the worst
    Stands in some rank of praise. [*To Goneril.*] I'll go with thee:
    Thy fifty yet doth double five-and-twenty,
    And thou art twice her love.[100]
GONERIL: Hear me, my lord.
    What need you five-and-twenty, ten, or five,
255   To follow in a house, where twice so many
    Have a command to tend you?
REGAN: What need one?
LEAR: O! reason not[101] the need; our basest beggars
    Are in the poorest thing superfluous:[102]
    Allow not nature[103] more than nature needs,
260   Man's life is cheap as[104] beast's. Thou art a lady;
    If only to go warm were gorgeous,
    Why, nature needs not what thou gorgeous wear'st,

94 friendship
95 *slack you*: be negligent in serving you
96 recognition
97 trustees
98 *kept a reservation*: made a saving clause or exception (see I. i. 126)
99 *Those . . . creatures*: i.e. Goneril
100 *art . . . love*: show me twice as much love
101 *reason not*: don't argue about
102 possessing more than they actually need
103 *Allow not nature*: if you don't allow men to possess
104 *cheap as*: of as little value as

Which scarcely keeps thee warm.[105] But, for true need,[106]—
You heavens, give me that[107] patience, patience I need!

265   You see me here, you gods, a poor old man,
As full of grief as age; wretched in both!
If it be you that stir these daughters' hearts
Against their father, fool me not so much
To[108] bear it tamely; touch me with noble anger,

270   And let not women's weapons, water-drops,
Stain my man's cheeks! No, you unnatural hags,
I will have such revenges on you both
That all the world shall—I will do such things,—
What they are yet I know not,—but they shall be

275   The terrors of the earth. You think I'll weep;
No, I'll not weep:
I have full cause of weeping, but this heart
Shall break into a hundred thousand flaws[109]
Or ere[110] I'll weep. O fool! I shall go mad.

                      [Exeunt Lear, Gloucester, Kent, and Fool.]

280 CORNWALL: Let us withdraw; 'twill be a storm.   *[Storm heard at a distance.]*
REGAN: This house is little: the old man and his people
    Cannot be well bestow'd.[111]
GONERIL: 'Tis his own blame; hath[112] put himself from[113] rest,
    And must needs taste his folly.

285 REGAN: For his particular,[114] I'll receive him gladly,
    But not one follower.
GONERIL: So am I purpos'd.
    Where is my Lord of Gloucester?
CORNWALL: Follow'd the old man forth. He is return'd.

    Re-enter Gloucester.

GLOUCESTER: The king is in high rage.
CORNWALL: Whither is he going?
290 GLOUCESTER: He calls to horse; but will I know not whither.

---

105 *if only . . . need*: i.e. If the need for warmth were the only purpose of wearing (fine) clothes, well, your body does not need the fine clothes you wear—which incidentally hardly do keep you warm. (The first 'gorgeous' is not the logical word but is effective.)
106 *for . . . need*: as for what I really need most
107 the omission of this word would improve sense and metre
108 *fool . . . To*: do not make me such a fool as to (perhaps with reference to a Fool who has to endure what his master does to him)
109 cracks *and/or* fragments
110 *Or ere*: before (which each word means)
111 accommodated
112 he hath
113 out of
114 *his particular*: himself alone

CORNWALL: 'Tis best to give him way;[115] he leads himself.[116]

GONERIL: My lord, entreat him by no means to stay.

GLOUCESTER: Alack! the night comes on, and the bleak winds
Do sorely ruffle;[117] for many miles about
There's scarce a bush.

REGAN:　　　　　　　　O! sir, to wilful men,
The injuries that they themselves procure
Must be their schoolmasters. Shut up your doors;
He is attended with[118] a desperate train,
And what they may incense him to, being apt
to have his ear abus'd,[119] wisdom bids fear.

CORNWALL: Shut up your doors, my lord; 'tis a wild night:
My Regan counsels well: come out o' the storm. 　　　[*Exeunt.*]

295

300

115 *give him way*: let him be
116 *leads himself*: insists on his own way
117 bluster
118 by
119 misled

ACT III

SCENE 1

A Heath.

> *A storm, with thunder and lightning. Enter Kent and a Gentleman, meeting.*

KENT: Who's here, beside foul weather?

GENTLEMAN: One minded like the weather, most unquietly.

KENT: I know you. Where's the king?

GENTLEMAN: Contending with the fretful elements;
Bids the wind blow the earth into the sea,
Or swell the curled waters 'bove the main,[1]
That things[2] might change or cease; tears his white hair,
Which the impetuous blasts, with eyeless[3] rage,
Catch in their fury, and make nothing of;[4]
Strives in his little world of man to out-scorn
The to-and-fro-conflicting wind and rain.
This night, wherein the cub-drawn[5] bear would couch,[6]

5

10

1 mainland (as in 'Spanish main')
2 the order of the world *natura rerum*
3 blind
4 *make ... of*: show no respect for
5 drained by her cubs (and so ravenous)
6 lie down

The lion and the belly-pinched wolf
Keep their fur dry, unbonneted[7] he runs,
15   And bids what will take all.[8]

KENT: But who is with him?

GENTLEMAN: None but the fool, who labours to out-jest[9]
His heart-struck[10] injuries.

KENT: Sir, I do know you;
And dare, upon the warrant of my note,[11]
Commend a dear[12] thing to you. There is division,
20   Although as yet the face of it be cover'd
With mutual cunning, 'twixt Albany and Cornwall;
Who have—as who have not, that their great stars
Thron'd and set high—servants, who seem no less,[13]
Which are to France the spies and speculations[14]
25   Intelligent of[15] our state; what hath been seen,
Either in snuffs[16] and packings[17] of the dukes,
Or the hard rein[18] which both of them have borne
Against the old kind king; or something deeper,
Whereof perchance these are but furnishings;[19]
30   But, true it is, from France there comes a power[20]
Into this scatter'd[21] kingdom; who already,
Wise in our negligence, have secret feet[22]
In some of our best ports, and are at point[23]
To show their open banner. Now to you:[24]
35   If on my credit you dare build[25] so far
To make your speed to Dover, you shall find
Some that will thank you, making[26] just report
Of how unnatural and bemadding sorrow

---

7 bare-headed (reminding us also of the *crown* he has given up)
8 *what . . . all*: everything go hang (a gesture of despair)
9 jest him out of
10 which have struck him to the heart (cf. II. iv. 152–3)
11 *upon . . . note*: on the strength of my knowledge
12 important
13 *seem no less*: at any rate appear to be servants
14 observers, spies (abstract for concrete, as often)
15 *Intelligent of*: giving information about
16 resentments, quarrels
17 plots
18 *hard rein*: metaphor from curbing a horse severely
19 the trimmings
20 army
21 divided
22 *secret feet*: landed secretly
23 *at point*: ready
24 *Now to you*: to come to your part
25 *on . . . build*: trust me
26 when you make

The king hath cause to plain.[27]
40 I am a gentleman of blood and breeding,
And from some knowledge and assurance[28] offer
This office to you.

GENTLEMAN: I will talk further with you.

KENT: No, do not.
For confirmation that I am much more
45 Than my out-wall,[29] open this purse, and take
What it contains. If you shall see Cordelia,—
As doubt not but you shall,—show her this ring,
And she will tell you who your fellow[30] is
That yet you do not know. Fie on this storm!
50 I will go seek the king.

GENTLEMAN: Give me your hand. Have you no more to say?

KENT: Few words, but, to effect,[31] more than all yet;
That, when we have found the king,—in which your pain
That way, I'll this,[32]—he that first lights on him
55 Holla the other. [*Exeunt severally.*]

27 complain of
28 *knowledge and assurance*: sure knowledge
29 exterior (suggests)
30 (present) companion
31 *to effect*: in importance
32 *your . . . this*: let it be your task to go that way while I go this way

SCENE 2

Another Part of the Heath. Storm still.

Enter Lear and Fool.

LEAR: Blow winds, and crack your cheeks! rage! blow!
You cataracts[1] and hurricanoes,[2] spout
Till you have drench'd our steeples, drown'd the cocks![3]
You sulphurous and thought-executing[4] fires,
5 Vaunt-couriers[5] to oak-cleaving thunderbolts,
Singe my white head! And thou, all-shaking thunder,
Strike flat the thick rotundity o' the world!

1 waterspouts (from heaven)
2 emphatic form of 'hurricanes'
3 weathercocks
4 *either* swift as thought *or* executing Jove's wishes
5 precursors

Crack nature's moulds,[6] all germens[7] spill[8] at once
That make ingrateful man!

10 FOOL: O nuncle, court holy-water[9] in a dry house is better than this rain-water
out o' door. Good nuncle, in, and ask thy daughters' blessing;[10] here's a
night pities neither wise man nor fool.

LEAR: Rumble thy bellyful! Spit, fire! spout, rain!
Nor rain, wind, thunder, fire, are my daughters:
15 I tax[11] not you, you elements, with unkindness;
I never gave you kingdom, call'd you children,
You owe me no subscription:[12] then, let fall
Your horrible pleasure; here I stand, your slave,
A poor, infirm, weak, and despis'd old man.
20 But yet I call you servile ministers,[13]
That have with two pernicious daughters join'd
Your high-engender'd battles[14] 'gainst a head
So old and white as this. O! O! 'tis foul.

FOOL: He that has a house to put his head in has a good head-piece.[15]

25 The cod-piece[16] that will house
Before the head has any.[17]
The head and he shall louse;[18]
So beggars marry many.[19]
The man that makes his toe
30 What he his heart should make,
Shall of a corn cry woe,
And turn his sleep to wake.[20]

For there was never yet fair woman but she made mouths[21] in a glass.

Enter Kent.

LEAR: No, I will be the pattern of all patience;
35 I will say nothing.

6 *nature's moulds*: the moulds in which things are made
7 seeds
8 destroy
9 *court holy-water*: flattery (a common phrase at the time)
10 *ask . . . blessing*: apologize to and make peace with
11 charge (cf. I. iv. 310)
12 submission
13 agents
14 *high-engender'd battles*: battalions bred in the sky
15 *both* headcovering *and* brain
16 covering worn by men between legs under close-fitting hose
17 house
18 be lousy, infected with lice
19 *So . . . many*: (perhaps) in that condition many beggars marry
20 *The cod-piece . . . wake*: i.e. the man who prefers a meaner part of his body to the more honourable will get himself into trouble
21 *made mouths*: made faces, preened herself

KENT: Who's there?

FOOL: Marry, here's grace[22] and a cod-piece;[23] that's a wise man and a fool.

KENT: Alas! sir, are you here? things that love night
Love not such sights as these; the wrathful skies
40   Gallow[24] the very wanderers of the dark,
And make them keep their caves.[25] Since I was man
Such sheets of fire, such bursts of horrid thunder,
Such groans of roaring wind and rain, I never
Remember to have heard; man's nature cannot carry[26]
45   The affliction nor the fear.

LEAR: Let the great gods,
That keep this dreadful pother[27] o'er our heads,
Find out their enemies now. Tremble, thou wretch,
That hast within thee undivulged crimes,
Unwhipp'd of[28] justice; hide thee, thou bloody hand;
50   Thou perjur'd,[29] and thou simular of[30] virtue
That art incestuous; caitiff,[31] to pieces shake,[32]
That under covert[33] and convenient seeming[34]
Hast practis'd on[35] man's life; close[36] pent-up guilts,[37]
Rive your concealing continents,[38] and cry
55   These dreadful summoners[39] grace.[40] I am a man
More sinn'd against than sinning.

KENT: Alack! bare-headed!
Gracious my lord, hard by here is a hovel;
Some friendship will it lend[41] you 'gainst the tempest;
Repose you there while I to this hard[42] house,—
60   More harder than the stone whereof 'tis rais'd,[43]—

22 the king's grace
23 *a cod-piece*: something comparatively worthless
24 frighten (now only in dialect)
25 *keep . . . caves*: cf. III. i. 12–14
26 bear
27 disturbance, commotion
28 by
29 *perjur'd* (man)
30 *simular of*: pretender to
31 wretch
32 *to . . . shake*: i.e. with fear and trembling
33 secret
34 pretence, hypocrisy
35 *practis'd on*: plotted against
36 (adjective)
37 crimes (for criminals)
38 *Rive . . . continents*: burst open the receptacles that hide you
39 officers who summon to justice
40 *cry . . . grace*: beg mercy from
41 afford
42 cruel
43 built

Which even but now, demanding after you,
Denied me to come in,[44] return and force
Their scanted courtesy.

LEAR: My wits begin to turn
65   Come on, my boy. How dost, my boy? Art cold?
I am cold myself. Where is this straw, my fellow?
The art of our necessities[45] is strange,
That can make vile[46] things precious. Come, your hovel.
Poor fool and knave, I have one part in my heart
That's sorry yet for thee.

70   FOOL: He that has a little tiny wit,
With hey, ho, the wind and the rain,
Must make content with his fortunes fit,[47]
Though the rain it raineth every day.

LEAR: True, my good boy. Come, bring us to this hovel.

[Exeunt Lear and Kent.]

75   FOOL: This is a brave[48] night to cool a courtezan.
I'll speak a prophecy ere I go:

When priests are more in word than matter;[49]
When brewers mar their malt with water;
When nobles are their tailors' tutors;[50]
80   No heretics burn'd, but wenches' suitors;[51]
When every case in law is right;
No squire in debt, nor no poor knight;[52]
When slanders do not live in tongues;
Nor cutpurses come not to throngs;
85   When usurers tell[53] their gold i' the field;
And bawds and whores do churches build;
Then shall the realm of Albion[54]
Come to great confusion:
Then comes the time, who lives[55] to see't,
90   That going shall be us'd with feet.[56]

This prophecy Merlin shall make; for I live before his time.   *[Exit.]*

44 *Denied . . . in*: refused me admittance
45 *The art . . . necessities*: necessity is an art, like alchemy, which can change the nature of things
46 worthless
47 *make . . . fit*: make content fit his fortunes, make the best of what he has
48 fine
49 *more . . . matter*: preach more than they practise
50 *are . . . tutors*: teach their tailors the latest fashions
51 *wenches' suitors*: i.e. lovers burn with lust and its results
52 *no . . . knight*: no knight poor
53 count out
54 England
55 *who lives*: for whoever lives
56 *going . . . feet*: feet shall be used to walk on (the lame conclusion is intentional)

SCENE 3

A room in Gloucester's Castle.

Enter Gloucester and Edmund.

GLOUCESTER: Alack, alack! Edmund, I like not this unnatural dealing. When I
desired their leave that I might pity[1] him, they took from me the use of
mine own house; charged me, on pain of their perpetual displeasure,
neither to speak of him, entreat for him, nor any way sustain him.

5   EDMUND: Most savage, and unnatural!

GLOUCESTER: Go to;[2] say you nothing. There is division between the dukes,
and a worse matter[3] than that. I have received a letter this night; 'tis
dangerous to be spoken; I have locked the letter in my closet. These injuries
the king now bears will be revenged home;[4] there's part of a power[5] already

10   footed;[6] we must incline to[7] the king. I will seek him and privily relieve
him; go you and maintain talk with the duke, that my charity be not of
him perceived. If he ask for me, I am ill and gone to bed. If I die for it, as
no less is threatened me, the king, my old master, must be relieved. There
is some strange thing toward,[8] Edmund; pray you, be careful.   [*Exit.*]

15   EDMUND: This courtesy, forbid thee,[9] shall the duke
Instantly know; and of that letter too:
This seems a fair deserving,[10] and must draw me
That which my father loses; no less than all:
The younger rises when the old doth fall.   [*Exit.*]

---

1 show pity, i.e. relieve (cf. l. 4 'sustain')
2 *Go to*: come!
3 *a worse matter*: the French landing
4 fully (cf. II. i. 51)
5 force
6 see III. i. 32
7 *incline to*: side with
8 imminent
9 *courtesy . . . thee*: (bit of) kindness which was forbidden you
10 that for which one deserves well, service

SCENE 4

The Heath. Before a Hovel.

Enter Lear, Kent, and Fool.

KENT: Here[1] is the place, my lord; good my lord, enter:
    The tyranny of the open night's[2] too rough
    For nature[3] to endure.   *[Storm still.]*

LEAR: Let me alone.

KENT: Good my lord, enter here.

LEAR: Wilt break my heart?[4]

5 KENT: I'd rather break mine own. Good my lord, enter.

    LEAR: Thou think'st 'tis much that this contentious[5] storm
        Invades us to the skin: so 'tis to thee;
        But where the greater malady is fix'd,
        The lesser is scarce felt. Thou'dst shun a bear;
10   But if thy flight lay toward the roaring sea,
        Thou'dst meet the bear i' the mouth. When the mind's free[6]
        The body's delicate;[7] the tempest in my mind
        Doth from my senses take all feeling else
        Save what beats there.[8] Filial ingratitude!
15   Is it not as[9] this mouth should tear his hand
        For lifting food to 't? But I will punish home:
        No, I will weep no more. In such a night
        To shut me out! Pour on; I will endure.
        In such a night as this! O Regan, Goneril!
20   Your old kind father, whose frank heart gave all,
        O! that way madness lies; let me shun that;
        No more of that.

KENT: Good, my lord, enter here.

    LEAR: Prithee, go in thyself; seek thine own ease:
        This tempest will not give me leave[10] to ponder
25   On things would hurt me more. But I'll go in.
        [To the Fool.] In, boy; go first. You houseless poverty,[11]—
        Nay, get thee in. I'll pray, and then I'll sleep.   *[Fool goes in.]*

---

1 see III. ii. 57
2 *The open night*: night in the open
3 human nature, man
4 *Wilt . . . heart*: explained by 23–5
5 quarrelsome, contending with us
6 at ease
7 fastidious (about its comfort)
8 i.e. in the mind (when the thought that throbs is 'Filial ingratitude')
9 as if
10 *will . . . leave*: does not leave me free
11 (abstract for concrete)

Poor naked wretches, whereso'er you are,
That bide[12] the pelting of this pitiless storm,
30 How shall your houseless heads and unfed sides,
Your loop'd and window'd raggedness,[13] defend you
From seasons such as these? O! I have ta'en
Too little care of this. Take physic, pomp;
Expose thyself to feel what wretches feel,
35 That thou mayst shake the superflux[14] to them,
And show the heavens more just.
EDGAR [*Within.*]: Fathom and half,[15] fathom and half! Poor Tom![16]

[The Fool runs out from the hovel.]

FOOL: Come not in here, nuncle; here's a spirit.
Help me! help me!
40 KENT: Give me thy hand. Who's there?
FOOL: A spirit, a spirit: he says his name's poor Tom.
KENT: What art thou that dost grumble here i' the straw?
Come forth.

Enter Edgar disguised as a madman.

EDGAR: Away! the foul fiend follows me!
45 Through the sharp hawthorn blow the winds.
Hum! go to thy cold bed and warm thee.
LEAR: Didst thou give all to thy two daughters?
And art thou come to this?
EDGAR: Who gives anything to poor Tom? whom the foul fiend hath led
50 through fire and through flame, through ford and whirlpool, o'er bog and
quagmire; that hath laid knives under his pillow, and halters in his pew: set
ratsbane by his porridge; made him proud of heart, to ride on a bay
trotting-horse over four-inched[17] bridges, to course[18] his own shadow for a
traitor. Bless thy five wits! Tom's a-cold. O! do de, do de, do de.[19] Bless
55 thee from whirlwinds, star-blasting,[20] and taking![21] Do poor Tom some
charity, whom the foul fiend vexes. There[22] could I have him now, and
there, and there again, and there. *[Storm still.]*

12 endure
13 *loop'd . . . raggedness*: clothes full of holes (loop = hole)
14 *the superflux*: your superfluity (metaphor from an overladen tree)
15 *Fathom and half*: suggested by the heavy rain
16 *Poor Tom*: cf. II. iii. 20
17 four inches wide
18 pursue
19 *do . . . de*: represents chattering teeth and shivering
20 being struck by the evil influence of stars
21 infection (cf. II. iv. 156)
22 as he pretends to feel the devil biting some part of his body, perhaps in the form of vermin (see 137)

LEAR: What! have his daughters brought him to this pass?
Couldst thou save nothing? Didst thou give them all?

60 FOOL: Nay, he reserved a blanket, else we had been all shamed.

LEAR: Now all the plagues that in the pendulous[23] air
Hang fated[24] o'er men's faults light on thy daughters!

KENT: He hath no daughters, sir.

LEAR: Death, traitor! nothing could have subdu'd nature
65 To such a lowness, but his unkind[25] daughters.
Is it the fashion that discarded fathers
Should have thus little mercy on their flesh?
Judicious punishment! 'twas this flesh begot
Those pelican daughters.[26]

70 EDGAR: Pillicock[27] sat on Pillicock-hill:
Halloo, halloo, loo, loo![28]

FOOL: This cold night will turn us all to fools and madmen.

EDGAR: Take heed o' the foul fiend. Obey thy parents; keep thy word justly;
swear not; commit[29] not with man's sworn spouse; set not thy sweet heart
75 on proud array. Tom's a-cold.

LEAR: What hast thou been?

EDGAR: A servingman,[30] proud in heart and mind; that curled my hair, wore
gloves[31] in my cap, served the lust of my mistress's heart, and did the act of
darkness with her; swore as many oaths as I spake words, and broke them
80 in the sweet face of heaven; one that slept in the contriving of lust, and
waked to do it. Wine loved I deeply, dice dearly, and in woman out-
paramoured the Turk:[32] false of heart, light of ear,[33] bloody of hand; hog in
sloth, fox in stealth, wolf in greediness, dog in madness, lion in prey. Let not
the creaking of shoes nor the rustling of silks betray thy poor heart to
85 woman: keep thy foot out of brothels, thy hand out of plackets,[34] thy pen
from lenders'[35] books, and defy the foul fiend. Still through the hawthorn
blows the cold wind; says suum, mun ha no nonny.[36] Dolphin[37] my boy,
my boy; sessa![38] let him trot by. [*Storm still.*]

23 hanging over us
24 full of fate
25 unnatural (also suggesting 'cruel')
26 pelicans were supposed to feed their young on their life-blood
27 darling, pretty knave (the line, adapted from an old one, was suggested by the word 'pelican')
28 properly a cry to encourage hounds
29 sin
30 *either* lover *or* servant
31 as a favour
32 *the Turk*: the Sultan with his many wives
33 *light of ear*: quick to believe evil
34 openings in petticoats or skirts
35 money lenders
36 *suum . . . nonny*: the refrain of a song
37 perhaps addressing an imaginary horse (but Dolphin = Dauphin of France)
38 an interjection of uncertain meaning (perhaps = *cessez*, stop!, perhaps 'off with you')

LEAR: Why, thou wert better in thy grave than to answer[39] with thy uncovered
90   body this extremity of the skies. Is man no more than this? Consider him
well. Thou[40] owest the worm no silk, the beast no hide, the sheep no
wool, the cat no perfume. Ha! here's three on 's are sophisticated;[41] thou art
the thing itself; unaccommodated[42] man is no more but such a poor, bare,
forked animal as thou art. Off, off, you lendings![43] Come; unbutton here.

[Tearing off his clothes.]

95   FOOL: Prithee, nuncle, be contented; 'tis a naughty[44] night to swim in. Now a
little fire in a wide field were like an old lecher's heart; a small spark, all the
rest on 's body cold. Look! here comes a walking fire.

Enter Gloucester with a torch.

EDGAR: This is the foul fiend Flibbertigibbet: he begins at curfew, and walks
till the first cock;[45] he gives the web and the pin,[46] squinies[47] the eye, and
100   makes the harelip; mildews the white[48] wheat, and hurts the poor creature
of earth.[49]

Swithold[50] footed thrice the old;[51]
He met the night-mare,[52] and her nine-fold;[53]
        Bid her alight,
105   And her troth plight,[54]
And aroint thee, witch, aroint[55] thee!

KENT: How fares your Grace?
LEAR: What's he?[56]
KENT: Who's there? What is't you seek?
110   GLOUCESTER: What are you there? Your names?

39 expose yourself to
40 man (in Edgar's state)
41 adulterated, unnatural
42 without the advantages (*Lat.* commoda) of civilization
43 borrowed articles, things not man's own
44 bad
45 *first cock*: cockcrow.
46 *the web . . . pin*: cataract, an eye disease
47 makes it squint
48 ripening
49 *the . . . earth*: mankind
50 St Withold
51 wold
52 incubus, demon (*not* female horse)
53 brood
54 *her . . . plight*: give her pledge (not to vex men)
55 begone
56 i.e. Gloucester

EDGAR: Poor Tom; that eats the swimming frog; the toad, the tadpole, the wall-newt,[57] and the water;[58] that in the fury of his heart, when the foul rages, eats cow-dung for sallets;[59] swallows the old rat and the fiend ditch-dog; drinks the green mantle[60] of the standing pool; who is whipped from
115   tithing[61] to tithing, and stock-punished,[62] and imprisoned; who hath had three suits to his back, six shirts to his body, horse to ride, and weapon to wear;

> But mice and rats and such small deer[63]
> Have been Tom's food for seven long year.

120   Beware my follower.[64] Peace, Smulkin! peace, thou fiend.
GLOUCESTER: What! hath your Grace no better company?
EDGAR: The prince of darkness is a gentleman; Modo he's call'd, and Mahu.
GLOUCESTER: Our flesh and blood,[65] my lord, is grown so vile,
     That it doth hate what gets[66] it.
125 EDGAR: Poor Tom's a-cold.
GLOUCESTER: Go in with me. My duty cannot suffer[67]
     To obey in all[68] your daughters' hard commands:
     Though their injunction be to bar my doors,
     And let this tyrannous night take hold upon you,
130   Yet have I ventur'd to come seek you out
     And bring you where both fire and food is ready.
LEAR: First let me talk with this philosopher.
     What is the cause of thunder?
KENT: Good my lord, take his offer; go into the house.
135 LEAR: I'll take a word with this same learned Theban.
     What is your study?[69]
EDGAR: How to prevent[70] the fiend, and to kill vermin.
LEAR: Let me ask you one word in private.
KENT: Importune him once more to go, my lord;
140   His wits begin to unsettle.
GLOUCESTER: Canst thou blame him?   [*Storm still.*]

---

57 lizard
58 newt
59 salads
60 covering, screen
61 hamlet (originally holding *ten* families)
62 punished by being put in the stocks
63 beasts
64 familiar spirit
65 *Our . . . blood*: our children
66 begets
67 submit, agree
68 *in all*: in everything
69 pursuit, brand of learning
70 anticipate, so defeat

His daughters seek his death. Ah! that good Kent;
He said it would be thus, poor banish'd man!
Thou sayst the king grows mad; I'll tell thee, friend,
I am almost mad myself. I had a son,

145 Now outlaw'd from my blood;[71] he sought my life,
But lately, very late; I lov'd him, friend,
No father his son dearer; true to tell thee,   [*Storm continues.*]
The grief hath craz'd my wits. What a night's this!
I beseech your Grace,—

LEAR: O! cry you mercy,[72] sir.

150 Noble philosopher, your company.

EDGAR: Tom's a-cold.

GLOUCESTER: In, fellow, there, into the hovel: keep thee warm.

LEAR: Come, let's in all.

KENT: This way, my lord.

LEAR: With him;
I will keep still with my philosopher.

155 KENT: Good my lord, soothe[73] him; let him take the fellow.

GLOUCESTER: Take him you on.

KENT: Sirrah, come on; go along with us.

LEAR: Come, good Athenian.

GLOUCESTER: No words, no words: hush.

EDGAR: Child[74] Rowland[75] to the dark tower came,

160 His[76] word was still, Fie, foh, and fum,
I smell the blood of a British man.   [*Exeunt.*]

---

71 *outlaw'd . . . blood*: disinherited
72 *cry you mercy*: (I) beg your pardon
73 humour
74 Sir (title of a young knight)
75 Roland (Charlemagne's hero)
76 the giant's

SCENE 5

A Room in Gloucester's Castle.

Enter Cornwall and Edmund.

CORNWALL: I will have my revenge ere I depart his house.

EDMUND: How, my lord, I may be censured, that nature thus gives way to loyalty, something fears me to think of.[1]

CORNWALL: I now perceive it was not altogether your brother's evil disposition
5   made him seek his[2] death; but a provoking merit, set a-work by a reprove-able badness in himself.[3]

EDMUND: How malicious is my fortune, that I must repent to be just![4] This is the letter[5] he spoke of, which approves[6] him an intelligent party[7] to the advantages of France. O heavens! that this treason were not, or not I the
10   detector!

CORNWALL: Go with me to the duchess.

EDMUND: If the matter of this paper be certain, you have mighty business in hand.

CORNWALL: True, or false, it hath made thee Earl of Gloucester. Seek out where
15   thy father is, that he may be ready for our apprehension.[8]

EDMUND [*Aside*]: If I find him comforting[9] the king, it will stuff his suspicion more fully.[10] I will persever[11] in my course of loyalty, though the conflict be sore between that and my blood.[12]

CORNWALL: I will lay trust upon thee; and thou shalt find a dearer father in
20   my love.   [*Exeunt.*]

1 *How . . . of*: i.e. I am rather afraid what people will think of me for allowing my natural affection to give way to my sense of duty
2 Gloucester's
3 *a provoking . . . himself*: i.e. (probably) Gloucester's deserts inviting punishment, which, however, was only brought into action by Edgar's own wickedness
4 *to be just*: of being loyal
5 *the letter*: see III. iii. 7
6 proves
7 *intelligent party*: person giving intelligence, informer
8 arrest
9 supporting, strengthening
10 *stuff . . . fully*: make our suspicion of him more justified
11 persevere
12 natural temperament

SCENE 6

A Chamber in a Farmhouse adjoining the Castle.

Enter Gloucester, Lear, Kent, Fool, and Edgar.

GLOUCESTER: Here is better than the open air; take it thankfully. I will piece
out[1] the comfort with what addition I can: I will not be long from you.

KENT: All the power of his wits has given way to his impatience. The gods
reward your kindness! [*Exit Gloucester.*]

5 EDGAR: Frateretto[2] calls me, and tells me Nero is an angler in the lake of darkness. Pray, innocent,[3] and beware the foul fiend.

FOOL: Prithee, nuncle, tell me whether a madman be a gentleman or a yeoman!

LEAR: A king, a king!

FOOL: No; he's a yeoman that has a gentleman to his son;[4] for he's a mad
10 yeoman that sees his son a gentleman before him.

LEAR: To have a thousand with red burning spits[5]
Come hizzing[6] in upon 'em,—

EDGAR: The foul fiend bites my back.

FOOL: He's mad that trusts in the tameness of a wolf, a horse's health,[7] a boy's
15 love, or a whore's oath.

LEAR: It shall be done; I will arraign them straight.
[*To Edgar.*] Come, sit thou here, most learned justicer;[8]
[*To the Fool.*] Thou, sapient sir, sit here. Now, you she foxes!

EDGAR: Look, where he[9] stands and glares! wantest thou eyes[10] at trial,
20 madam?[11] Come o'er the bourn,[12] Bessy, to me,—

FOOL: Her boat hath a leak,
And she must not speak
Why she dares not come over to thee.

EDGAR: The foul fiend haunts poor Tom in the voice of a nightingale. Hop-
25 dance cries in Tom's belly for two white[13] herring. Croak[14] not, black angel;
I have no food for thee.

KENT: How do you, sir? Stand you not so amaz'd:[15]
Will you lie down and rest upon the cushions?

1 *piece out*: increase
2 an imaginary familiar spirit; so Hop-dance (24–5) (both from Harsnett)
3 simple man
4 *has . . . son*: has his son a gentleman (i.e. a reversal of nature, like your daughters' conduct)
5 Lear is brooding over the very course he would like to see the Furies take on his daughters
6 a variant of 'hissing', perhaps in order to sound like 'whizzing'
7 *a . . . health*: perhaps as described by the vendor; or simply as horses are delicate animals
8 judge
9 a fiend *or* (possibly) Lear
10 *wantest . . . eyes*: do you want people to look at you? *or* can't you see him?
11 Goneril or Regan (present on trial in imagination)
12 stream (the line is a fragment of an old song)
13 (probably) fresh
14 in the stomach, from hunger
15 dumbfounded

LEAR: I'll see their trial first. Bring in their evidence.[16]

30   [*To Edgar.*] Thou robed man of justice, take thy place;
     [*To the Fool.*] And thou, his yoke-fellow of equity,
     Bench by his side. [*To Kent.*] You are o' the commission,[17]
     Sit you too.

EDGAR: Let us deal justly.

35   Sleepest or wakest thou, jolly shepherd?
              Thy sheep be in the corn;
         And for one blast of thy minikin[18] mouth,[19]
            Thy sheep shall take no harm.[20]

     Purr! The cat[21] is grey.

40 LEAR: Arraign her first; 'tis Goneril. I here take my oath before this
     honourable assembly, she kicked the poor king her father.

FOOL: Come hither, mistress. Is your name Goneril?

LEAR: She cannot deny it.

FOOL: Cry you mercy, I took you for a joint-stool.[22]

45 LEAR: And here's another,[23] whose warp'd[24] looks proclaim
     What store[25] her heart is made on. Stop her there!
     Arms, arms, sword, fire! Corruption in the place!
     False justicer, why hast thou let her 'scape?

EDGAR: Bless thy five wits!

50 KENT: O pity! Sir, where is the patience now
     That you so oft have boasted to retain?

EDGAR [*Aside*]: My tears begin to take his part so much,
     They'll mar my counterfeiting.

LEAR: The little dogs and all,

55   Tray, Blanch, and Sweet-heart, see, they bark at me.

EDGAR: Tom will throw his head at them. Avaunt, you curs!

     Be thy mouth or black or[26] white,
     Tooth that poisons if it bite;
     Mastiff, greyhound, mongrel grim,
60   Hound or spaniel, brach or lym;[27]

---

16 *their evidence*: the witnesses against them
17 *o' the commission*: commissioned, appointed a justice of the peace
18 dainty
19 i.e. while you turn aside to play us a tune
20 perhaps ironical, as the sheep would harm the corn more than the corn them
21 *the cat*: a 'familiar' again, called 'Purr' (in Harsnett), or Purr may be only the sound
22 stool made carefully by a 'joiner' or carpenter (in fact Lear took the stool for Goneril)
23 i.e. Regan
24 crooked, perverse
25 material (but probably a corruption, perhaps for 'stone', since 'store' can hardly mean stuff)
26 *or . . . or*: either . . . or
27 a kind of bloodhound

Or bobtail tike or trundle-tail;[28]
Tom will make them weep and wail:
For, with throwing thus my head,
Dogs leap the hatch,[29] and all are fled.

65 Do de, de, de. Sessa![30] Come, march to wakes and fairs and market-towns.
Poor Tom, thy horn[31] is dry.

LEAR: Then let them anatomize[32] Regan, see what breeds about her heart.
Is there any cause in nature that makes these hard hearts?
[*To Edgar.*] You, sir, I entertain[33] you for one of my hundred; only I do not
70 like the fashion of your garments: you will say, they are Persian[34] attire; but
let them be changed.

KENT: Now, good my lord, lie here and rest awhile.

LEAR: Make no noise, make no noise; draw the curtains:[35] so, so, so. We'll go
to supper i' the morning: so, so, so.

75 FOOL: And I'll go to bed at noon.

Re-enter Gloucester.

GLOUCESTER: Come hither, friend: where is the king thy master?

KENT: Here, sir; but trouble him not, his wits are gone.

GLOUCESTER: Good friend, I prithee, take him in thy arms;
I have o'erheard a plot of death upon[36] him.
80 There is a litter ready; lay him in 't,
And drive toward Dover, friend, where thou shalt meet
Both welcome and protection. Take up thy master:
If thou shouldst dally half an hour, his life,
With thine, and all that offer[37] to defend him,
85 Stand in assured loss.[38] Take up, take up;
And follow me, that will to some provision[39]
Give thee quick conduct.[40]

28 long-tailed
29 *leap the hatch*: make a hurried exit
30 *Do de . . . Sessa*: see III. iv. 54 and 88
31 the Bedlam beggar's drinking flask
32 dissect
33 take on
34 proverbial for 'luxurious' (here ironical)
35 of old-fashioned beds
36 against
37 presume, dare
38 *Stand . . . loss*: are certain to be lost
39 *some provision*: something provided (l. 80)
40 guidance

KENT: Oppress'd nature sleeps:
    This rest might yet have balm'd[41] thy broken sinews,[42]
    Which, if convenience will not allow,[43]
90 Stand in hard cure.[44]—[*To the Fool.*] Come, help to bear thy master;
    Thou must not stay behind.
GLOUCESTER: Come, come, away.

        [*Exeunt Kent, Gloucester, and the Fool, bearing away Lear.*]

EDGAR: When we our betters see bearing our woes,[45]
    We scarcely think our miseries our foes.
    Who alone[46] suffers suffers most i' the mind,
95 Leaving free[47] things and happy shows[48] behind;
    But then the mind much sufferance doth o'erskip,
    When grief hath mates, and bearing[49] fellowship.
    How light and portable[50] my pain seems now,
    When that which makes me bend makes the king bow;
100 He childed as I father'd:[51] Tom, away!
    Mark the high noises,[52] and thyself bewray[53]
    When false opinion,[54] whose wrong thought defiles thee,
    In thy just proof[55] repeals[56] and reconciles[57] thee.
    What will hap[58] more to-night, safe 'scape the king!
105 Lurk, lurk.[59]   [*Exit.*]

---

41 healed like a balm
42 *broken sinews*: racked nerves
43 *if . . . allow*: unless circumstances are favourable
44 *Stand . . . cure*: are hardly likely to be cured
45 *our woes*: the same trouble as we have
46 emphasize *alone*
47 carefree, free from distress
48 sights
49 when suffering (has)
50 easy to bear
51 *childed . . . father'd*: treated by his children as I by my father
52 *high noises*: disturbances in the state, in high quarters
53 *thyself bewray*: only reveal who you really are
54 *false opinion*: wrong suspicions (felt about you)
55 *In . . . proof*: when your character is vindicated
56 recalls you (from banishment)
57 restores you to your position and reconciles you to your father
58 *What . . . hap*: whatever happens
59 hide yourself, lie low

SCENE 7

A Room in Gloucester's Castle.

Enter Cornwall, Regan, Goneril, Edmund, and Servants.

CORNWALL: Post speedily to my lord your husband; show him this letter: the
army of France is landed. Seek out the traitor Gloucester.

[*Exeunt some of the Servants.*]

REGAN: Hang him instantly.

GONERIL: Pluck out his eyes.

5 CORNWALL: Leave him to my displeasure. Edmund, keep you our sister
company: the revenges we are bound to take upon your traitorous father
are not fit for your beholding. Advise the duke, where you are going, to a
most festinate[1] preparation: we are bound to[2] the like. Our posts[3] shall be
swift and intelligent[4] betwixt us. Farewell, dear sister: farewell, my Lord
10 of Gloucester.[5]

Enter Oswald.

How now? Where's the king?

OSWALD: My Lord of Gloucester hath convey'd him hence:
Some five or six and thirty of his knights,
Hot questrists[6] after him, met him at gate;
15 Who, with some other of the lord's dependants,
Are gone with him toward Dover, where they boast
To have well-armed friends.

CORNWALL: Get horses for your mistress.

GONERIL: Farewell, sweet lord, and sister.

CORNWALL: Edmund, farewell.   [*Exeunt Goneril, Edmund, and Oswald.*]
                                   Go seek the traitor Gloucester,
20 Pinion him like a thief, bring him before us.   [*Exeunt other Servants.*]
Though well we may not pass upon[7] his life
Without the form of justice, yet our power
Shall do a courtesy to[8] our wrath, which men
May blame but not control. Who's there? The traitor?

Re-enter Servants, with Gloucester.

1 speedy
2 *bound to*: purposed to, proposing (so also, probably in 6)
3 messengers
4 bringing good information
5 see III. v. 14–15
6 seekers (*Lat.* quaero)
7 *pass* (sentence) *upon*
8 *do . . . to*: bow before, give way to

25 REGAN: Ingrateful fox! 'tis he.

CORNWALL: Bind fast his corky[9] arms.

GLOUCESTER: What mean your Graces? Good my friends, consider
You are my guests: do me no foul play, friends.

CORNWALL: Bind him, I say.   [Servants bind him.]

REGAN: Hard, hard. O filthy[10] traitor!

30 GLOUCESTER: Unmerciful lady as you are, I'm none.

CORNWALL: To this chair bind him. Villain, thou shalt find—

                             [Regan plucks his beard.]

GLOUCESTER: By the kind gods, 'tis most ignobly done
To pluck me by the beard.

REGAN: So white, and such a traitor!

GLOUCESTER: Naughty[11] lady,

35 These hairs, which thou dost ravish from my chin,
Will quicken,[12] and accuse thee: I am your host:
With robbers' hands my hospitable favours[13]
You should not ruffle[14] thus. What will you do?

CORNWALL: Come, sir, what letters had you late[15] from France?

40 REGAN: Be simple-answer'd,[16] for we know the truth.

CORNWALL: And what confederacy have you with the traitors
Late footed[17] in the kingdom?

REGAN: To whose hands have you sent the lunatic king?
Speak.

45 GLOUCESTER: I have a letter guessingly set down,[18]
Which came from one that's of a neutral heart,
And not from one oppos'd.

CORNWALL: Cunning.

REGAN: And false.

CORNWALL: Where hast thou sent the king?

GLOUCESTER: To Dover.

REGAN: Wherefore to Dover? Wast thou not charg'd at peril—

50 CORNWALL: Wherefore to Dover? Let him answer that.

GLOUCESTER: I am tied to the stake, and I must stand the course.[19]

REGAN: Wherefore to Dover?

---

9 dry (as he is old)

10 beastly, disgraceful

11 wicked (not then a childish word)

12 come to life

13 *my . . . favours*: the features of me, your host

14 disturb, violate (cf. II. iv. 294, where, however, it was intransitive)

15 lately

16 *Be simple-answer'd*: answer straightforwardly

17 see III. i. 32

18 *guessingly set down*: written from conjecture, not knowledge

19 attack of the dogs in bear-baiting

GLOUCESTER: Because I would not see thy cruel nails
Pluck out his poor old eyes; nor thy fierce sister
In his anointed[20] flesh stick boarish fangs.
The sea, with such a storm as his bare head
In hell-black night endur'd, would have bouy'd up,[21]
And quench'd the stelled[22] fires;
Yet, poor old heart, he holp[23] the heavens to rain.
If wolves had at thy gate howl'd that dern[24] time,
Thou shouldst have said, 'Good porter, turn the key,'[25]
All cruels else[26] subscrib'd:[27] but I shall see
The winged vengeance[28] overtake such children.
CORNWALL: See 't shalt thou never. Fellows, hold the chair.
Upon these eyes of thine I'll set my foot.
GLOUCESTER: He that will think to live till he be old,
Give me some help! O cruel! O ye gods!　　　　　　[*Gloucester's eye put out.*]
REGAN: One side will mock another; the other too.[29]
CORNWALL: If you see vengeance—
FIRST SERVANT:　　　　　　　　　　Hold your hand, my lord:
I have serv'd you ever since I was a child,
But better service have I never done you
Than now to bid you hold.
REGAN:　　　　　　　　　　How now, you dog!
FIRST SERVANT: If you did wear a beard upon your chin,
I'd shake it[30] on this quarrel.
REGAN:　　　　　　　　　　What do you mean?
CORNWALL: My villain![31]　　　　　　　　　　　　　　[*Draws.*]
FIRST SERVANT: Nay then, come on, and take the chance of anger.[32]

　　　　　　　　　　　[*Draws. They fight. Cornwall is wounded.*]

REGAN: Give me thy sword. A peasant stand up thus!

　　　　　　　　　　　[*Takes a sword and runs at him behind.*]

FIRST SERVANT: O! I am slain. My lord, you have one eye left
To see some mischief on him.[33] O!　　　　　　　　[*Dies.*]

55
60
65
70
75

20 royal
21 risen up, like a buoy
22 *either* starry *or* (more probably) fixed (Middle Eng. stellen = fix), or part of both
23 encouraged (lit. helped)
24 dreary, dread
25 *turn the key*: i.e. admit them
26 *All . . . else*: all other cruel things (except the storm)
27 being admitted
28 *winged vengeance*: vengeance of heaven (as in Jove's arrows)
29 *the other* (eye) *too*
30 *shake it*: i.e. challenge you to fight
31 serf (perhaps also in modern sense as in l. 93)
32 *take . . . anger*: take the chance result where anger, not skill, directs the weapons
33 Cornwall

80 CORNWALL: Lest it see more, prevent it.[34] Out, vile jelly!
        Where is thy lustre now?

    GLOUCESTER: All dark and comfortless. Where's my son Edmund?
        Edmund, enkindle all the sparks of nature
        To quit[35] this horrid act.

    REGAN: Out, treacherous villain!
85   Thou call'st on him that hates thee; it was he
        That made the overture[36] of thy treasons to us,
        Who is too good to pity thee.

    GLOUCESTER: O my follies! Then Edgar was abus'd.[37]
        Kind gods, forgive me that, and prosper him!

90 REGAN: Go thrust him out at gates, and let him smell
        His way to Dover.   [*Exit one with Gloucester.*]
                        How is't, my lord? How look you?[38]

    CORNWALL: I have receiv'd a hurt. Follow me, lady.
        Turn out that eyeless villain; throw this slave
        Upon the dunghill. Regan, I bleed apace:
95   Untimely comes this hurt. Give me your arm.

                                        [*Exit Cornwall led by Regan.*]

    SECOND SERVANT: I'll never care what wickedness I do
        If this man come to good.

    THIRD SERVANT: If she live long,
        And, in the end, meet the old[39] course of death,
        Women will all turn monsters.

100 SECOND SERVANT: Let's follow the old earl, and get the Bedlam
        To lead him where he would:[40] his roguish madness
        Allows itself to any thing.[41]

    THIRD SERVANT: Go thou; I'll fetch some flax, and whites of eggs,
        To apply to his bleeding face. Now, heaven help him!   [*Exeunt severally.*]

---

34 *Lest . . . prevent it*: prevent it from seeing more
35 requite, avenge
36 disclosure
37 deceived
38 *How look you?*: What do you appear like (almost) How do you feel?
39 usual, ordinary
40 like to be led
41 *his . . . any thing*: as he (the Bedlamite, Edgar) is a mad vagrant he will lend himself to anything, go anywhere he is asked, *or* his madness affords him licence to do what he likes

ACT IV

SCENE 1

The Heath.

> *Enter Edgar.*

EDGAR: Yet better thus,[1] and known to be contemn'd,[2]
  Than still[3] contemn'd and flatter'd. To be worst,
  The lowest and most dejected thing of fortune,[4]
  Stands still in esperance,[5] lives not in fear:
5 The lamentable change is from the best;
  The worst returns to laughter.[6] Welcome, then,
  Thou unsubstantial air that I embrace:
  The wretch that thou hast blown unto the worst
  Owes nothing to[7] thy blasts. But who comes here?

> *Enter Gloucester, led by an Old Man.*

10 My father, poorly led?[8] World, world, O world!
  But that[9] thy strange mutations make us hate thee,
  Life would not yield to age.[10]

OLD MAN: O my good lord!
  I have been your tenant, and your father's tenant,
  These fourscore years.

15 GLOUCESTER: Away, get thee away; good friend, be gone;
  Thy comforts can do me no good at all;
  Thee they may hurt.

OLD MAN: You cannot see your way.

GLOUCESTER: I have no way, and therefore want no eyes;
  I stumbled when I saw. Full oft 'tis seen,
20 Our means secure us[11] and our mere defects
  Prove our commodities.[12] Ah! dear son Edgar,
  The food[13] of thy abused[14] father's wrath;

1 *Yet* (it is better to be) *thus*
2 *known . . . contemn'd*: known to yourself to be, conscious of being despised
3 all the same
4 *most . . . fortune*: the thing (i.e. creature) cast down lowest by fortune
5 *stands . . . esperance*: puts you in a situation of permanent hopefulness
6 *returns to laughter*: may yet see you happy again
7 *Owes . . . to*: has paid his full debt to, and has therefore nothing more to fear from
8 *poorly led*: led by a poor man
9 *But that*: if it were not that
10 *Life . . . age*: we should not be reconciled to old age and death
11 *Our . . . us*: our resources make us careless (*Lat.* securus)
12 *our mere . . . commodities*: it is precisely our weaknesses that turn out to our advantage
13 object
14 misled

Might I but live to see thee in my touch,
I'd say I had eyes again.[15]

OLD MAN: How now! Who's there?

25   EDGAR [*Aside*]: O gods! Who is't can say, 'I am at the worst?'
      I am worse than e'er I was.

OLD MAN: 'Tis poor mad Tom.

EDGAR [*Aside*]: And worse I may be yet; the worst is not,
      So long as we can say, 'This is the worst.'

OLD MAN: Fellow, where goest?

GLOUCESTER: Is it a beggar-man?

30   OLD MAN: Madman and beggar too.

GLOUCESTER: He has some reason,[16] else he could not beg.
      I' the last night's storm I such a fellow saw,
      Which made me think a man a worm: my son[17]
      Came then into my mind; and yet my mind

35   Was then scarce friends with him: I have heard more[18] since.
      As flies to wanton[19] boys, are we to the gods;
      They kill us for their sport.

EDGAR [*Aside*]:   How should this be?[20]
      Bad is the trade that must play fool to sorrow,[21]
      Angering itself and others.—[*To Gloucester.*] Bless thee, master!

40   GLOUCESTER: Is that the naked fellow?

OLD MAN: Ay, my lord.

GLOUCESTER: Then, prithee, get thee gone. If, for my sake,
      Thou wilt o'ertake us, hence a mile or twain,
      I' the way toward Dover, do it for ancient love;
      And bring some covering for this naked soul

45   Who I'll entreat to lead me.

OLD MAN: Alack, sir! he is mad.

GLOUCESTER: 'Tis the times' plague,[22] when madmen lead the blind.
      Do as I bid thee, or rather do thy pleasure;
      Above the rest,[23] be gone.

OLD MAN: I'll bring him the best 'parel[24] that I have,

50   Come on 't[25] what will.   [*Exit.*]

---

15 *I'd . . . again*: i.e. it would be as good as recovering my sight
16 *He . . . reason*: he's not quite mad
17 *my son*: see III. iv. 144
18 viz. III. vii. 85–7
19 playful
20 *How . . . be?*: probably refers to second half of 35
21 i.e. it's a bad job when we have to pretend to folly in the presence of sorrow (as I am now doing)
22 *'Tis . . . plague*: the world's in a bad way
23 *Above the rest*: above all things
24 apparel
25 *on 't*: of it

GLOUCESTER: Sirrah, naked fellow,—

EDGAR: Poor Tom's a-cold. [*Aside*] I cannot daub it[26] further.

GLOUCESTER: Come hither, fellow.

EDGAR [*Aside*]: And yet I must. Bless thy sweet eyes, they bleed.

55 GLOUCESTER: Know'st thou the way to Dover?

EDGAR: Both stile and gate, horse-way and footpath. Poor Tom hath been scared
out of his good wits: bless thee, good man's son, from[27] the foul fiend! Five
fiends have been in poor Tom at once; of lust, as Obidicut; Hobbididance,
prince of dumbness; Mahu, of stealing; Modo, of murder; and Flibber-

60 tigibbet, of mopping and mowing;[28] who since possesses chambermaids and
waiting-women. So, bless thee, master!

GLOUCESTER: Here, take this purse, thou whom the heavens' plagues
Have humbled to[29] all strokes: that I am wretched
Makes thee the happier: heavens, deal so still!

65 Let the superfluous[30] and lust-dieted[31] man,
That slaves your ordinance,[32] that will not see
Because he doth not feel,[33] feel your power quickly;
So distribution should undo excess,
And each man have enough. Dost thou know Dover?

70 EDGAR: Ay, master.

GLOUCESTER: There is a cliff, whose high and bending[34] head
Looks fearfully[35] in[36] the confined[37] deep;
Bring me but to the very brim of it,
And I'll repair the misery thou dost bear

75 With something rich about me; from that place
I shall no leading need.

EDGAR: Give me thy arm:
Poor Tom shall lead thee.   [*Exeunt.*]

---

26 *daub it*: dissemble, pretend (lit. cover up with plaster)
27 *bless . . . from*: God preserve thee from
28 *mopping and mowing*: grimacing, making faces (Fr. *moue*)
29 *humbled to*: humbled into bearing
30 having more than he needs (cf. II. iv. 258), spoilt
31 gluttonous or (perhaps) indulgent to his sexual appetite (cf. III. iv. 81–3)
32 *slaves . . . ordinance*: makes your commands his slaves, enslaves them (esp. the command to charity)
33 (sympathy for others)
34 overhanging
35 frighteningly
36 into
37 bounded by it

SCENE 2

Before the Duke of Albany's Palace.

Enter Goneril and Edmund.

GONERIL: Welcome,[1] my lord; I marvel our mild[2] husband
    Not met[3] us on the way. [*Enter Oswald.*] Now, where's your master?

OSWALD: Madam, within; but never man so chang'd.
    I told him of the army that was landed;
5   He smil'd at it: I told him you were coming;
    His answer was, 'The worse': of Gloucester's treachery
    And of the loyal service of his son,
    When I inform'd him, then he call'd me sot,[4]
    And told me I had turn'd the wrong side out:[5]
10   What most he should dislike seems pleasant to him;
    What like, offensive.[6]

GONERIL [*To Edmund.*]: Then, shall you go no further.
    It is the cowish[7] terror of his spirit
    That dares not undertake;[8] he'll not feel wrongs
    Which tie him to[9] an answer. Our wishes on the way
15   May prove effects.[10] Back, Edmund, to my brother;[11]
    Hasten his musters and conduct his powers:[12]
    I must change arms[13] at home, and give the distaff
    Into my husband's hands. This trusty servant
    Shall pass between us; ere long you are like to hear,
20   If you dare venture in your own behalf,
    A mistress's command. Wear this; spare speech;   [*Giving a favour.*]
    Decline[14] your head: this kiss, if it durst speak,
    Would stretch thy spirits up into the air.
    Conceive,[15] and fare thee well.

1 to our house (see III. vii. 1–10 for their journey together)
2 sarcastic, cf. l. 12
3 *Not met*: did not meet (so in l. 53)
4 fool (not drunkard)
5 *turn'd . . . out*: got things inside out, inverted right and wrong
6 *What* (he should like, seem) *offensive*
7 cowardly (cf. 50 below and I. iv. 308 'milky gentleness')
8 venture take up enterprises
9 *tie him to*: demand, require
10 *Our . . . effects*: What we wished for may be realized (i.e. that you should replace him)
11 (-in-law) Cornwall
12 *conduct his powers*: lead his forces
13 *change arms*: i.e. take in exchange (for the distaff) his warlike weapons
14 put down (for a kiss)
15 take my meaning

25 EDMUND: Yours in the ranks of death.

GONERIL: My most dear Gloucester!

[Exit Edmund.]

O! the difference of man and man!

To thee a woman's services are due:

My fool[16] usurps my bed.

OSWALD: Madam, here comes my lord.   *[Exit.]*

Enter Albany.

GONERIL: I have been worth the whistle.[17]

ALBANY: O Goneril!

30 You are not worth the dust which the rude wind

Blows in your face. I fear[18] your disposition:

That nature, which contemns its origin,

Cannot be border'd certain[19] in itself;

She that herself will sliver[20] and disbranch

35 From her material[21] sap, perforce must wither

And come to deadly use.[22]

GONERIL: No more; the text[23] is foolish.

ALBANY: Wisdom and goodness to the vile seem vile;

Filths savour but themselves.[24] What have you done?

40 Tigers, not daughters, what have you perform'd?

A father, and a gracious aged man,

Whose reverence the head-lugg'd[25] bear would lick,[26]

Most barbarous, most degenerate! have you madded.[27]

Could my good brother suffer you to do it?

45 A man, a prince, by him[28] so benefited!

If that the heavens do not their visible[29] spirits

Send quickly down to tame these vile offences,[30]

It[31] will come,

Humanity must perforce prey on itself,

50 Like monsters of the deep.

16 *My fool*: My husband who is a fool
17 *worth the whistle*: worth something to you (cf. proverb 'It's a poor dog that is not worth the whistling')
18 fear for (what it may lead to)
19 *border'd certain*: contained within fixed bounds, trusted not to break the limits (of right)
20 tear off (as a twig from a branch)
21 forming the substance of a thing, essential
22 *deadly use*: come to a bad end, the only use for dead wood is burning
23 subject of your moral (cf. l. 58) discourse, sermons
24 *Filths . . . themselves*: filthy creatures enjoy only things that are filthy
25 tugged about by the head ('by the nose' in Harsnett!)
26 *Whose . . . lick*: i.e. whose grey hairs even a beast would respect
27 maddened
28 Lear
29 in visible form
30 offenders
31 punishment

GONERIL: Milk-liver'd[32] man!
    That bear'st a cheek for blows, a head for wrongs;[33]
    Who hast not in thy brows an eye discerning
    Thine honour from thy suffering;[34] that not know'st
    Fools do those villains[35] pity who are punish'd
55   Ere they have done their mischief. Where's thy drum?
    France spreads his banners in our noiseless[36] land,
    With plumed helm thy state begins to threat,[37]
    Whilst thou, a moral[38] fool, sitt'st still, and criest
    'Alack! why does he so?'
ALBANY: See thyself, devil!
60   Proper[39] deformity seems not in the fiend
    So horrid as in woman.
GONERIL: O vain fool!
ALBANY: Thou changed and self-cover'd[40] thing, for shame,
    Be-monster not thy feature.[41] Were 't my fitness[42]
    To let these hands obey my blood,[43]
65   They are apt[44] enough to dislocate and tear
    Thy flesh and bones; howe'er[45] thou art a fiend,
    A woman's shape doth shield thee.
GONERIL: Marry, your manhood.—Mew![46]

Enter a Messenger.

ALBANY: What news?
70 MESSENGER: O! my good lord, the Duke of Cornwall's dead;
    Slain by his servant, going to put out
    The other eye of Gloucester.
ALBANY: Gloucester's eyes!

---

32 cowardly (cf. 'the liver white and pale, which is the badge of pusillanimity and cowardice,' 2 *Henry IV*, IV. iii. 103)
33 *That . . . wrongs*: i.e. you are the sort of man to 'turn the other cheek' (Matthew v. 39)
34 *discerning . . . suffering*: able to distinguish between what your honour can let you endure and what it cannot
35 *those villains*: in this case (probably) Lear
36 with no sound of drums or other preparations for war
37 *state . . . threat*: begins to threaten thy power, position
38 moralizing
39 which belongs to him (rightly)
40 veiling thy true (devilish) self
41 appearance
42 *my fitness*: befitting me
43 *my blood*: my instinct
44 ready
45 although
46 pooh! A fig for it

MESSENGER: A servant that he bred, thrill'd[47] with remorse,[48]
Oppos'd against the act, bending[49] his sword
75   To[50] his great master; who, thereat enrag'd,
Flew on him, and amongst them[51] fell'd him dead;
But not without that harmful stroke, which since
Hath pluck'd him after.[52]
ALBANY: This shows you are above,
You justicers,[53] that these our nether[54] crimes
80   So speedily can venge! But, O poor Gloucester!
Lost he his other eye?
MESSENGER: Both, both, my lord.
This letter, madam, craves a speedy answer;
'Tis from your sister.
GONERIL [*Aside*]: One way I like this well;
85   But being widow, and my Gloucester with her,[55]
May all the building in my fancy pluck
Upon my hateful life;[56] another way,[57]
This news is not so tart.[58] [*To Messenger.*] I'll read and answer.   [*Exit.*]
ALBANY: Where was his son when they did take his eyes?
90   MESSENGER: Come with my lady hither.
ALBANY: He is not here.
MESSENGER: No, my good lord; I met him back[59] again.
ALBANY: Knows he the wickedness?
MESSENGER: Ay, my good lord; 'twas he inform'd against him,
And quit the house on purpose that their punishment
95   Might have the freer course.
ALBANY: Gloucester, I live
To thank thee for the love thou show'dst the king,
And to revenge thine eyes. Come hither, friend:
Tell me what more thou knowest.   [*Exeunt.*]

47 excited
48 pity (as often)
49 directing
50 against
51 *amongst them*: between them they (he and Regan)
52 *pluck'd him after*: snatched away him too (to death)
53 judges (as in III. vi. 17, where it was a conjecture)
54 committee on earth (the *lower* world as opposed to heaven)
55 *But . . . her*: i.e. the fact that Regan is a widow and Gloucester, whom I desire, is with her
56 *May . . . life*: i.e. may pull down all my fine schemes and so make my life hateful to me
57 *another way*: the 'one way' cf. l. 84. Goneril sees a chance of the whole kingdom
58 bitter
59 going back (Edmund had only escorted Goneril home)

SCENE 3

The French Camp, near Dover.

    Enter Kent and a Gentleman.

KENT: Why the King of France is so suddenly gone back know you the reason?

GENTLEMAN: Something he left imperfect in the state, which since his coming
forth is thought of; which imports[1] to the kingdom so much fear and
danger, that his personal return was most required and necessary.

5 KENT: Who hath he left behind him general?

GENTLEMAN: The Marshal of France, Monsieur la Far.

KENT: Did your letters pierce[2] the queen to any demonstration of grief?

GENTLEMAN: Ay, sir; she took them, read them in my presence;
And now and then an ample tear trill'd down

10   Her delicate cheek; it seem'd she was a queen
Over her passion;[3] who,[4] most rebel-like,
Sought to be king o'er her.

KENT: O! then it mov'd her.

GENTLEMAN: Not to a rage; patience and sorrow strove
Who should express her goodliest.[5] You have seen

15   Sunshine and rain at once; her smiles and tears
Were like a better way;[6] those happy smilets
That play'd on her ripe lip seem'd not to know
What guests were in her eyes; which[7] parted thence.
As pearls from diamonds[8] dropp'd. In brief,

20   Sorrow would be a rarity most belov'd
If all could so become[9] it.

KENT: Made she no verbal question?[10]

GENTLEMAN: Faith, once or twice she heav'd the name of 'father'
Pantingly forth, as if it press'd her heart;
Cried, 'Sisters! sisters! Shame of ladies! sisters!

25   Kent! father! sisters! What, i' the storm? i' the night?
Let pity not be believed!'[11] There she shook
The holy water from her heavenly eyes,

---

1 involves, carries with it
2 wound, excite
3 motion (*not* anger)
4 which
5 *Who . . . goodliest*: as to which should become her best
6 *like . . . way*: like that (sunshine and rain together), only better (a comma could be inserted after 'like')
7 the guest, i.e. tears
8 her eyes
9 suit
10 *Made . . . question?*: Didn't she say anything?
11 to exist, if people can do such things (but 'not believe it' is a likely reading)

And clamour-moisten'd,[12] then away she started
To deal with grief alone.

KENT: It is the stars,

30   The stars above us, govern our conditions;[13]
Else one self mate and make[14] could not beget
Such different issues. You spoke not with her since?

GENTLEMAN: No.

KENT: Was this before the king[15] return'd?

GENTLEMAN: No, since.

35   KENT: Well, sir, the poor distress'd Lear 's i' the town,
Who sometime,[16] in his better tune,[17] remembers
What we are come about, and by no means
Will yield[18] to see his daughter.

GENTLEMAN: Why, good sir?

KENT: A sovereign[19] shame so elbows him:[20] his own unkindness,

40   That stripp'd her from his benediction, turn'd her
To foreign casualties,[21] gave her dear rights
To his dog-hearted daughters,—these things sting
His mind so venomously that burning shame
Detains him from Cordelia.

GENTLEMAN: Alack! poor gentleman.

45   KENT: Of Albany's and Cornwall's powers[22] you heard not?

GENTLEMAN: 'Tis so,[23] they are afoot.

KENT: Well, sir, I'll bring you to our master Lear,
And leave you to attend him. Some dear cause[24]
Will in concealment wrap me up awhile;

50   When I am known aright, you shall not grieve
Lending me this acquaintance.[25] I pray you, go
Along with me.   [*Exeunt.*]

---

12 having her outburst, emotion, calmed by a flood of tears
13 character
14 *one . . . make*: the same husband and wife ('make' comes from a root meaning 'equal')
15 *the king* (of France)
16 *sometime*(s)
17 *better tune*: saner moments
18 agree
19 (1) all-powerful, *but also* (2) worthy of a king
20 *elbows him*: pushes him away (from her)
21 *foreign casualties*: the chances of life abroad
22 forces
23 *'Tis so*: it is true that
24 *dear cause*: important reason (cf. III. i. 19)
25 *Lending . . . acquaintance*: for having got to know me

SCENE 4

The Same. A Tent.

Enter with drum and colours, Cordelia, Doctor, and Soldiers.

CORDELIA: Alack! 'tis he: why, he was met even now
　　　　As mad as the vex'd[1] sea; singing aloud;
　　　　Crown'd with rank[2] fumiter[3] and furrow weeds,[4]
　　　　With burdocks, hemlock, nettles, cuckoo-flowers,[5]
5　　　Darnel, and all the idle weeds that grow
　　　　In our sustaining[6] corn. A century[7] send forth;
　　　　Search every acre in the high-grown field.
　　　　And bring him to our eye.　　　　　　　　　　　　*[Exit an Officer.]*
　　　　　　　　　　　　What can[8] man's wisdom
　　　　In the restoring his bereaved[9] sense?
10　　He that helps[10] him take all my outward worth.[11]
　　DOCTOR: There is means, madam;
　　　　Our foster-nurse of nature[12] is repose,
　　　　The which he lacks; that to provoke[13] in him,
　　　　Are many simples operative,[14] whose power
15　　Will close the eye of anguish.
　　CORDELIA:　　　　　　　　　　All bless'd secrets,
　　　　All you unpublish'd virtues[15] of the earth,
　　　　Spring with[16] my tears! be aidant and remediate[17]
　　　　In the good man's distress! Seek, seek for him,
　　　　Lest his ungovern'd rage dissolve the life
20　　That wants the means to lead it.[18]

　　　　Enter a Messenger.

1 stirred up (by winds)
2 luxuriant
3 fumitory
4 *furrow weeds*: weeds that grow in ploughed land
5 (uncertain)
6 life-giving
7 a hundred men
8 knows, can do
9 lost
10 heals
11 *outward worth*: possessions
12 *Our . . . nature*: the foster-nurse of our nature
13 induce
14 *simples operative*: effective (medicinal) plants
15 properties, (healing) powers
16 *Spring with*: spring up watered by
17 remedial
18 *That . . . it*: i.e. which lacks the power (sanity) to control it(self)

MESSENGER: News, madam;
    The British powers are marching hitherward.
CORDELIA: 'Tis known before; our preparation stands
    In expectation of them. O dear father!
    It is thy business that I go about;
25   Therefore great France[19]
    My mourning and important[20] tears hath pitied,
    No blown[21] ambition doth our arms incite,
    But love, dear love, and our ag'd father's right,
    Soon may I hear and see him!   [*Exeunt.*]

19 the king of France
20 importunate, urgent
21 proud

SCENE 5

A Room in Gloucester's Castle.

    Enter Regan and Oswald.

REGAN: But are my brother's[1] powers set forth?
OSWALD: Ay, madam.
REGAN: Himself in person there?
OSWALD: Madam, with much ado:[2]
    Your sister is the better soldier.
REGAN: Lord Edmund spake not with your lord at home?
5 OSWALD: No, madam.
REGAN: What might import[3] my sister's letter to him?
OSWALD: I know not, lady.
REGAN: Faith, he is posted hence on serious matter.
    It was great ignorance,[4] Gloucester's eyes being out,
10 To let him live; where he arrives he moves
    All hearts against us. Edmund, I think, is gone,
    In pity of his misery, to dispatch
    His nighted[5] life; moreover, to descry
    The strength o' the enemy.
15 OSWALD: I must needs after him, madam, with my letter.
REGAN: Our troops set forth to-morrow; stay with us,
    The ways are dangerous.

1 *brother*(-in-law)'s
2 *with much ado*: i.e. Goneril had great difficulty in getting Albany to take up arms in a bad cause
3 signify
4 folly
5 darkened, blinded

OSWALD: I may not, madam;
      My lady charg'd my duty[6] in this business.

REGAN: Why should she write to Edmund? Might not you

20   Transport her purposes by word? Belike,[7]
      Something—I know not what. I'll love thee much,
      Let me unseal the letter.

OSWALD: Madam, I had rather—[8]

REGAN: I know your lady does not love her husband;
      I am sure of that: and at her late being here

25   She gave strange oeilliades[9] and most speaking[10] looks
      To noble Edmund. I know you are of her bosom.[11]

OSWALD: I, madam!

REGAN: I speak in understanding; you are, I know't:
      Therefore I do advise you, take this note:[12]

30   My lord is dead; Edmund and I have talk'd,[13]
      And more convenient is he for my hand
      Than for your lady's. You may gather[14] more.
      If you do find him, pray you, give him this,[15]
      And when your mistress hears thus much from you,

35   I pray desire her call her wisdom to her:[16]
      So, fare you well.
      If you do chance to hear of that blind traitor,
      Preferment falls on him that cuts him off.[17]

OSWALD: Would I could meet him, madam: I would show

40   What party I do follow.

REGAN: Fare thee well.   [*Exeunt.*]

---

6 *charg'd my duty*: invoked my sense of duty to her (to deliver this letter at once)
7 probably
8 *I had rather*—: s.d. refusing the letter (Johnson)
9 glad eyes
10 eloquent of her wishes
11 *of her bosom*: trusted by her
12 *take this note*: (probably) take note of this
13 come to an understanding
14 infer
15 a token *or* letter
16 *call her . . . her*: show some sense (remember she has a husband)
17 *Preferment . . . off*: i.e. you will be promoted if you kill him

SCENE 6

The Country near Dover.

Enter Gloucester, and Edgar dressed like a peasant.

GLOUCESTER: When shall I come to the top of that same hill?[1]
EDGAR: You do climb up it now; look how we labour.
GLOUCESTER: Methinks the ground is even.
EDGAR: Horrible steep:
　　Hark! do you hear the sea?
GLOUCESTER: No, truly.
5　EDGAR: Why, then your other senses grow imperfect
　　By your eyes' anguish.
GLOUCESTER: So may it be, indeed.
　　Methinks thy voice is alter'd, and thou speak'st
　　In better phrase and matter than thou didst.
EDGAR: Y'are much deceiv'd; in nothing am I chang'd
10　But in my garments.
GLOUCESTER: Methinks you're better spoken.
EDGAR: Come on, sir; here's the place: stand still.
　　How fearful
　　And dizzy 'tis to cast one's eyes so low!
　　The crows and choughs[2] that wing the midway air
15　Show scarce so gross[3] as beetles; half way down
　　Hangs one that gathers samphire,[4] dreadful trade!
　　Methinks he seems no bigger than his head.
　　The fishermen that walk upon the beach
　　Appear like mice, and yond tall anchoring bark
20　Diminish'd to her cock,[5] her cock a buoy
　　Almost too small for sight. The murmuring surge,
　　That on the unnumber'd[6] idle[7] pebbles[8] chafes,
　　Cannot be heard so high. I'll look no more,
　　Lest my brain turn, and the deficient sight[9]
25　Topple down headlong.
GLOUCESTER: Set me where you stand.

1　*that same hill*: see IV. i. 71
2　still a cliff bird in Cornwall
3　large
4　a herb used for pickles
5　cock-boat, ship's boat
6　innumerable
7　moved to no purpose
8　(used as plural)
9　*the . . . sight*: I, through failing sight

EDGAR: Give me your hand; you are now within a foot
    Of the extreme verge: for all beneath the moon
    Would I not leap upright.[10]

GLOUCESTER: Let go my hand.
    Here, friend, 's another purse;[11] in it a jewel
30   Well worth a poor man's taking: fairies and gods
    Prosper it with thee![12] Go thou further off;
    Bid me farewell, and let me hear thee going.

EDGAR: Now fare you well, good sir.

GLOUCESTER: With all my heart.

EDGAR: Why I do trifle thus with his despair
35   Is done to cure it.[13]

GLOUCESTER: O you mighty gods!
    This world I do renounce, and, in your sights,
    Shake patiently my great affliction off;
    If I could bear it longer, and not fall
    To quarrel with[14] your great opposeless[15] wills,
40   My snuff and loathed part of nature should
    Burn itself out.[16] If Edgar live, O, bless him!
    Now, fellow, fare thee well.

EDGAR: Gone, sir:[17] farewell.   [*Gloucester falls forward.*]
    [*Aside*] And yet I know not how[18] conceit[19] may rob
    The treasury of life when life itself
45   Yields to the theft;[20] had he been where he thought
    By this had thought been past. Alive or dead?
    [*To Gloucester.*] Ho, you sir! friend! Hear you, sir? speak![21]
    Thus might he pass indeed; yet he revives.[22]
    What are you, sir?

GLOUCESTER: Away and let me die.

50 EDGAR: Hadst thou been aught but gossamer, feathers, air,
    So many fathom down precipitating,[23]
    Thou'dst shiver'd like an egg; but thou dost breathe,
    Hast heavy substance, bleed'st not, speak'st, art sound.

10 *leap upright*: he is so near the edge that even such a movement would be fatal
11 *another purse*: see IV. i. 62
12 *Prosper . . . thee.* make the purse lucky for you (perhaps a reference to a belief that fairies multiplied treasure trove)
13 *Why . . . it*: i.e. The object of my trifling . . . is to cure it (a mixture of constructions)
14 *quarrel with*: rebel against
15 irresistible
16 *My . . . out*: i.e. I would let the miserable remnant of my life expire naturally, instead of seeking my own death
    (snuff = the half-burnt wick)
17 *Gone, sir*: answer to l. 31
18 *I . . . how*: I don't know how it is that
19 imagination
20 *when . . . theft*: when there is no longer the will to live
21 is spoken in a different voice as if by a stranger who has found Gloucester at the foot of the cliff
22 (an aside)
23 falling headlong

Ten masts at each[24] make not the altitude
55 Which thou hast perpendicularly fell:
Thy life's a miracle. Speak yet again.
GLOUCESTER: But have I fallen or no?
EDGAR: From the dread summit of this chalky bourn.[25]
Look up a-height;[26] the shrill-gorg'd[27] lark so far
60 Cannot be seen or heard: do but look up.
GLOUCESTER: Alack! I have no eyes.
Is wretchedness depriv'd that benefit
To end itself by death? 'Twas yet some comfort,
When misery could beguile[28] the tyrant's rage,
65 And frustrate his proud will.
EDGAR: Give me your arm:
Up: so. How is't? Feel you your legs? You stand.
GLOUCESTER: Too well, too well.
EDGAR: This is above all strangeness.
Upon the crown o' the cliff, what thing was that
Which parted from you?
GLOUCESTER: A poor unfortunate beggar.
70 EDGAR: As I stood here below methought his eyes
Were two full moons; he had a thousand noses,
Horns whelk'd[29] and wav'd like the enridged[30] sea:
It was some fiend; therefore, thou happy father,[31]
Think that the clearest[32] gods, who make them honours
75 Of men's impossibilities, have preserv'd thee.
GLOUCESTER: I do remember now; henceforth I'll bear
Affliction till it do cry out itself
'Enough, enough,' and die. That thing you speak of
I took it for a man; often 'twould say
80 'The fiend, the fiend': he led me to that place.
EDGAR: Bear free[33] and patient[34] thoughts. But who comes here?

Enter Lear, fantastically dressed with flowers.[35]

The safer sense will ne'er accommodate
His master thus.[36]

24 *at each*: on end
25 the limit of the sea (cf. IV. i. 72)
26 on high
27 shrill-throated, high-voiced
28 cheat (by death)
29 (probably) twisted
30 ridged, furrowed
31 ambiguous, since it could be addressed to any old man
32 purest, open and righteous
33 free from fear, happy (and so not inclined to suicide) *or* generous towards men and (34) patient towards God
35 based on IV. iv. 3–6
36 *The . . . thus*: i.e. a man in his right senses would not get himself up like this ('safer' = saner)

LEAR: No, they cannot touch[37] me for coining;
85   I am the king himself.

EDGAR: O thou side-piercing[38] sight!

LEAR: Nature's above art[39] in that respect. There's your press-money.[40] That fellow handles his bow like a crow-keeper:[41] draw me[42] a clothier's yard.[43]
Look, look! a mouse. Peace, peace! this piece of toasted cheese will do 't.
90   There's my gauntlet;[44] I'll prove it on a giant. Bring up the brown bills.[45] O!
well flown, bird;[46] i' the clout,[47] hewgh![48] Give the word.[49]

EDGAR: Sweet marjoram.[50]

LEAR: Pass.

GLOUCESTER: I know that voice.

95 LEAR: Ha! Goneril, with a white beard! They flatter'd me like a dog,[51] and told
me I had white hairs[52] in my beard ere the black ones were there. To say 'ay'
and 'no' to everything I said! 'Ay' and 'no' too was no good divinity.[53] When
the rain came to wet me once and the wind to make me chatter, when the
thunder would not peace at my bidding, there I found 'em, there I smelt
100   'em out. Go to, they are not men o' their words: they told me I was everything; 'tis a lie, I am not ague-proof.

GLOUCESTER: The trick[54] of that voice I do well remember:
Is 't not the king?

LEAR: Ay, every inch the king:
When I do stare, see how the subject quakes.
105 I pardon that man's life. What was thy cause?[55]
Adultery?
Thou shalt not die: die for adultery! No:
The wren goes to 't, and the small gilded fly
Does lecher in my sight.

37 get at, punish
38 heart-rending
39 *Nature's . . . art*: (probably) a king's above a coiner (issuer of false money)
40 payment given a man forced into the services (cf. press-gang)
41 scarer of birds
42 for me to see
43 *clothier's yard*: long arrow
44 mailed glove as a challenge
45 *brown bills*: halberds painted brown *or* the bearers of them
46 here used for arrow
47 mark, target
48 the whistling sound of the arrow in the air
49 password
50 used as a remedy for madness
51 *like a dog*: as a dog fawns on people
52 *white hairs*: i.e. the wisdom of age
53 *no . . . divinity*: not sound theologically (in view of St Paul's words 'For the Son of God, Jesus Christ . . . was
not yea and nay, but in him was yea,' 2 Cor. i. 19)
54 accent
55 crime, subject of accusation

110   Let copulation thrive; for Gloucester's bastard son
       Was kinder to his father than my daughters
       Got 'tween the lawful sheets.
       To 't luxury,[56] pell-mell![57] for I lack soldiers.
       Behold yond simpering dame,
115   Whose face between her forks presageth snow;[58]
       That minces[59] virtue, and does shake the head
       To hear of pleasure's name;
       The fitchew[60] nor the soiled[61] horse goes to 't
       With a more riotous appetite.
120   Down from the waist they are Centaurs,[62]
       Though women all above:
       But to[63] the girdle do the gods inherit,[64]
       Beneath is all the fiends':
       There's hell, there's darkness, there is the sulphurous pit, burning, scalding,
125   stench, consumption; fie, fie, fie! pah, pah! Give me an ounce of civet,[65]
       good apothecary, to sweeten my imagination: there's money for thee.
       GLOUCESTER: O! let me kiss that hand!
       LEAR: Let me wipe it first; it smells of mortality.[66]
       GLOUCESTER: O ruin'd piece[67] of nature! This great world
130   Shall so[68] wear out to nought. Dost thou know me?
       LEAR: I remember thine eyes well enough. Dost thou squiny[69] at me? No, do
       thy worst, blind Cupid;[70] I'll not love. Read thou this challenge; mark but
       the penning of it.
       GLOUCESTER: Were all the letters suns, I could not see.
135   EDGAR [*Aside*]: I would not take this from report; it is,
       And my heart breaks at it.
       LEAR: Read.
       GLOUCESTER: What! with the case[71] of eyes?

56 lust
57 promiscuously
58 *Whose . . . snow*: i.e. Whose face would make you think she had little sexual desire
59 affects
60 (1) pole-cat, *and* (2) harlot
61 overfed
62 half men, half horses, in Greek mythology
63 *But to*: only as far as
64 own
65 scent
66 (1) humanity, *and perhaps also* (2) death
67 (perhaps) masterpiece
68 as you have done
69 squint
70 *blind Cupid*: the sign over brothels (may recall Gloucester's sin)
71 sockets

LEAR: O, ho! are you there with me?[72] No eyes in your head, nor no money in
140   your purse? Your eyes are in a heavy case,[73] your purse in a light: yet you see
       how this world goes.

GLOUCESTER: I see it feelingly.[74]

LEAR: What! art mad? A man may see how this world goes with no eyes. Look
       with thine ears: see how yond justice rails upon yon simple[75] thief. Hark, in
145   thine ear: change places; and, handy-dandy,[76] which is the justice, which is
       the thief? Thou hast seen a farmer's dog bark at a beggar?

GLOUCESTER: Ay, sir.

LEAR: And the creature[77] run from the cur? There thou mightst behold the great
       image[78] of authority; a dog's[79] obey'd in office.[80]
150   Thou rascal beadle,[81] hold thy bloody hand!
       Why dost thou lash that whore? Strip thine own back;
       Thou hotly lusts to use her in that kind[82]
       For which thou whipp'st her. The usurer hangs the cozener.[83]
       Through tatter'd clothes small vices do appear;
155   Robes and furr'd gowns[84] hide all. Plate sin with gold,[85]
       And the strong lance of justice hurtless[86] breaks;
       Arm it in rags, a pigmy's straw doth pierce it.
       None does offend, none, I say none; I'll able[87] 'em:
       Take that of me, my friend, who have the power
160   To seal the accuser's lips. Get thee glass eyes;
       And, like a scurvy politician,[88] seem[89]
       To see the things thou dost not. Now, now, now, now;
       Pull off my boots; harder, harder; so.

EDGAR [*Aside*]: O! matter[90] and impertinency[91] mix'd;
165   Reason in madness!

---

72 *are . . . me?*: Is that what you mean?
73 *in . . . case*: because in a bad way
74 by my sense of feeling (perhaps also suggests 'I feel it deeply')
75 humble
76 take which you like (from a children's game)
77 human being
78 type, example
79 even a dog
80 *in office*: in a position of authority
81 parish constable
82 *in that kind*: i.e. lustfully
83 *The . . . cozener*: i.e. a magistrate who has a man hanged for a petty theft may himself lend money for interest
    (condemned by medieval church)
84 *furr'd gowns*: worn by judges and aldermen
85 *Plate . . . gold*: give the sinner the armour of riches
86 inflicting no wound
87 vouch for, protect
88 *scurvy politician*: rascally schemer
89 pretend
90 good sense
91 irrelevance, nonsense

LEAR: If thou wilt weep my fortunes, take my eyes;
   I know thee well enough; thy name is Gloucester:[92]
   Thou must be patient; we came crying hither:
   Thou know'st the first time that we smell the air
170   We waul[93] and cry. I will preach to thee: mark.
GLOUCESTER: Alack! alack the day!
LEAR: When we are born, we cry that we are come
   To this great stage of fools. This'[94] a good block![95]
   It were a delicate stratagem to shoe
175   A troop of horse with felt; I'll put it in proof,[96]
   And when I have stol'n upon these sons-in-law,
   Then, kill, kill, kill, kill, kill, kill!

   Enter Gentleman, with Attendants.

GENTLEMAN: O! here he is; lay hand upon him. Sir,
   Your most dear daughter—
180   LEAR: No rescue? What! a prisoner? I am even[97]
   The natural fool of[98] fortune. Use me well;
   You shall have ransom. Let me have surgeons;
   I am cut to the brains.[99]
GENTLEMAN: You shall have any thing.
LEAR: No seconds?[100] All myself?
185   Why this would make a man a man of salt,[101]
   To use his eyes for garden water-pots,
   Ay, and laying autumn's dust.
GENTLEMAN: Good sir,—
LEAR: I will die bravely as a bridegroom.[102] What!
   I will be jovial: come, come; I am a king,
190   My masters, know you that?
GENTLEMAN: You are a royal one, and we obey you.
LEAR: Then there's life in it.[103] Nay, an you get it, you shall get it by running.
   Sa, sa, sa, sa.[104]   *[Exit. Attendants follow.]*

92 see l. 130
93 wail (cf. caterwaul)
94 This is
95 (perhaps) a felt hat
96 *in proof*: on trial
97 Lear has been found by Cordelia's attendants whom he imagines to be enemies
98 *The . . . of*: born to be the sport, victim of (bad) fortune
99 *cut . . . brains*: cf. 'cut to the heart'
100 supporters
101 *a . . . salt*: all tears (but cf. Lot's wife in Genesis xix. 26)
102 *as a bridegroom*: meeting death like a bride
103 *there's . . . it*: there's still hope for me
104 *Sa, sa*: a cry inciting to action, as to hunting dogs

GENTLEMAN: A sight most pitiful in the meanest wretch,
195   Past speaking of in a king! Thou hast one daughter,
        Who redeems nature[105] from the general curse
        Which twain have brought her to.

EDGAR: Hail, gentle sir!

GENTLEMAN: Sir, speed you:[106] what's your will?

EDGAR: Do you hear aught, sir, of a battle toward?[107]

200 GENTLEMAN: Most sure and vulgar;[108] every one hears that,
        Which can distinguish sound.

EDGAR: But, by your favour,
        How near's the other army?

GENTLEMAN: Near, and on speedy foot; the main descry
        Stands on the hourly thought.[109]

EDGAR: I thank you, sir: that's all.

205 GENTLEMAN: Though that the queen on special cause is here,
        Her army is mov'd on.

EDGAR: I thank you, sir.

                                [*Exit Gentleman.*]

GLOUCESTER: You ever-gentle gods, take my breath from me:[110]
        Let not my worser spirit[111] tempt me again
        To die before you please!

EDGAR: Well pray you, father.[112]

210 GLOUCESTER: Now, good sir, what are you?

EDGAR: A most poor man, made tame to fortune's blows;
        Who, by the art of[113] known and feeling[114] sorrows,
        Am pregnant to[115] good pity. Give me your hand,
        I'll lead you to some biding.[116]

GLOUCESTER: Hearty thanks:
215   The bounty and the benison[117] of heaven
        To boot, and boot![118]

        Enter Oswald.

---

105 human nature, disgraced by Goneril and Regan
106 (God) *speed you*
107 imminent
108 commonly known
109 *the main . . . thought:* the sight of the main body is expected every hour
110 i.e. let me die in heaven's good time
111 *my . . . spirit:* the worse part of me, my evil genius (a phrase used in Sonnet 144)
112 see l. 73, and cf. l. 242 &c.
113 *by . . . of:* taught by
114 heart-felt
115 *pregnant to:* disposed to show
116 abode, resting place
117 blessing
118 *To boot, and boot:* in addition, and may it help you (two meanings of 'boot')

OSWALD: A proclaim'd prize![119] Most happy!
That eyeless head of thine was first fram'd[120] flesh
To raise my fortunes. Thou old unhappy traitor,
Briefly thyself remember:[121] the sword is out[122]

220 That must destroy thee.

GLOUCESTER: Now let thy friendly[123] hand
Put strength enough to 't. [*Edgar interposes.*]

OSWALD: Wherefore, bold peasant,
Dar'st thou support a publish'd traitor? Hence;
Lest that infection of his fortune take
Like hold on thee.[124] Let go his arm.

225 EDGAR: Chill[125] not let go, zur, without vurther 'casion.[126]

OSWALD: Let go, slave, or thou diest.

EDGAR: Good gentleman, go your gait,[127] and let poor volk pass. An chud ha'
bin zwaggered[128] out of my life, 'twould not ha' ben zo long as 'tis by a
vortnight. Nay, come not near th' old man; keep out, che vor ye,[129] or

230 ise[130] try whether your costard[131] or my ballow[132] be the harder. Chill be
plain with you.

OSWALD: Out, dunghill!

EDGAR: Chill pick your teeth,[133] zur. Come; no matter vor your foins.[134]

[*They fight and Edgar knocks him down.*]

OSWALD: Slave, thou hast slain me. Villain,[135] take my purse.

235 If ever thou wilt thrive, bury my body;
And give the letters which thou find'st about me
To Edmund Earl of Gloucester; seek him out
Upon[136] the English party:[137] O! untimely death. [*Dies.*]

---

119 *A . . . prize*: a publish'd traitor (l. 222) for whose arrest a reward had been offered
120 made
121 *thyself remember*: remember your sins, prepare for death
122 unsheathed
123 Gloucester desires to die
124 *Lest . . . thee*: lest the same fate overtake you
125 I will
126 reason
127 way
128 *An . . . zwaggered*: If I could have been bullied
129 *che vor ye*: I warrant you
130 I shall
131 head (lit. a kind of apple)
132 cudgel
133 *pick . . . teeth*: i.e. fight you
134 thrusts
135 serf
136 on, among
137 *party*: side

EDGAR: I know thee well: a serviceable villain;[138]
240   As duteous to the vices of thy mistress
As badness would desire.

GLOUCESTER: What! is he dead?

EDGAR: Sit you down, father; rest you.
Let's see his pockets: these letters that he speaks of
May be my friends. He's dead; I am only sorry
245   He hath no other deaths-man. Let us see:
Leave,[139] gentle wax; and, manners, blame us not:
To know our enemies' minds, we'd rip their hearts;
Their papers, is more lawful.

     'Let our reciprocal vows be remembered. You have many opportunities
250   to cut him[140] off; if your will want not,[141] time and place will be fruitfully
offered. There is nothing done if he return the conqueror; then am I the
prisoner, and his bed my gaol; from the loathed warmth whereof deliver
me, and supply the place for[142] your labour.
     'Your — wife, so I would say —
255   'Affectionate servant,
                     'GONERIL.'

O undistinguish'd[143] space[144] of woman's will![145]
A plot upon her virtuous husband's life,
And the exchange my brother! Here, in the sands,
260   Thee I'll rake up,[146] the post[147] unsanctified
Of murderous lechers; and in the mature time[148]
With this ungracious[149] paper strike the sight
Of the death-practis'd[150] duke. For him 'tis well
That of thy death and business I can tell.

265   GLOUCESTER: The king is mad: how stiff[151] is my vile sense,
That I stand up, and have ingenious[152] feeling
Of my huge sorrows! Better I were distract:[153]

138 rascal
139 by your leave
140 Albany
141 *want not*: is not deficient
142 as a reward for
143 indistinguishable, illimitable
144 range
145 desire, lust (cf. IV. ii. 32–3 with this whole line)
146 *rake up*: bury
147 messenger, postman
148 *in . . . time*: at the right moment
149 disgraceful
150 whose death has been plotted
151 unbending, unfeeling
152 intelligent, conscious
153 *distract*(ed): mad

So should my thoughts be sever'd from my griefs,[154]
And woes by wrong imaginations[155] lose
270   The knowledge of themselves.   [*Drums afar off.*]

EDGAR: Give me your hand:
Far off, methinks, I hear the beaten drum.
Come, father, I'll bestow[156] you with a friend.   [*Exeunt.*]

154 *So . . . grief*: i.e. I should not realize my miseries
155 *wrong imaginations*: illusions
156 lodge

SCENE 7

A Tent in the French Camp.

   Enter Cordelia, Kent, Doctor, and Gentleman.

CORDELIA: O thou good Kent! how shall I live and work
To match[1] thy goodness? My life will be too short,
And every measure[2] fail me.
KENT: To be acknowledg'd, madam, is o'erpaid.
5   All my reports[3] go with the modest truth,
Nor more nor clipp'd, but so.[4]
CORDELIA: Be better suited:[5]
These weeds[6] are memories of those worser hours:
I prithee, put them off.
KENT: Pardon me, dear madam;
Yet[7] to be known shortens my made intent;[8]
10   My boon I make it[9] that you know me not
Till time and I think meet.[10]
CORDELIA: Then be 't so, my good lord.—[*To the Doctor.*] How does the king?
DOCTOR: Madam, sleeps still.
CORDELIA: O you kind gods,
15   Cure this great breach in his abused nature!
The untun'd and jarring senses, O! wind up[11]
Of this child-changed[12] father!

1 come up to, in recompensing it
2 degree (of gratitude, compared with Kent's services)
3 *my reports*: the reports I have given you
4 *Nor more . . . so*: neither exaggerated nor understated but accurate
5 *suited*: dressed
6 clothes
7 at present
8 *my . . . intent*: the plan I have made
9 *My . . . it*: the favour I ask is
10 *Till . . . meet*: i.e. Till I think the time ripe
11 *wind up*: tune
12 *child-changed*: (1) changed into a child (in mind), (2) changed by (the cruelty of) his children—very probably *both*

DOCTOR: So please[13] your majesty
    That we may wake the king? he hath slept long.

CORDELIA: Be govern'd by your knowledge, and proceed
20   I' the sway of your own will.[14] Is he array'd?

Enter Lear in his chair, carried by Servants.

GENTLEMAN: Ay, madam; in the heaviness of sleep,
    We put fresh garments on him.

DOCTOR: Be by, good madam, when we do awake him;
    I doubt not of his temperance.[15]

CORDELIA: Very well.   [*Music.*]

25 DOCTOR: Please you, draw near. Louder the music there.

CORDELIA: O my dear father! Restoration,[16] hang
    Thy medicine on my lips, and let this kiss
    Repair those violent harms that my two sisters
    Have in thy reverence made!

KENT: Kind and dear princess!

30 CORDELIA: Had you not been their father, these white flakes[17]
    Had challeng'd pity of[18] them. Was this a face
    To be expos'd against the warring winds?
    To stand against the deep[19] dread-bolted[20] thunder?
    In the most terrible and nimble stroke
35   Of quick cross[21] lightning? to watch[22]—poor perdu!—
    With this thin helm?[23] Mine enemy's dog,
    Though he had bit me, should have stood that night
    Against[24] my fire. And wast thou fain, poor father,
    To hovel thee with swine and rogues forlorn,
40   In short[25] and musty straw? Alack, alack!
    'Tis wonder that thy life and wits at once
    Had not concluded all.[26] He wakes; speak to him.

DOCTOR: Madam, do you; 'tis fittest.

CORDELIA: How does my royal lord? How fares your majesty?

---

13 may it please
14 *I' . . . will:* as you think best
15 sanity
16 the power of restoring the senses (personified)
17 *white flakes:* his snowy hair and beard
18 from
19 deep-voiced
20 armed with the dreaded thunderbolt
21 forked
22 stand exposed
23 *thin helm:* unprotected head
24 in front of
25 cut short (and therefore uncomfortable), and/or scanty
26 *concluded all:* entirely ended

45 LEAR: You do me wrong to take me out o' the grave;
    Thou art a soul in bliss; but I am bound
    Upon a wheel of fire, that[27] mine own tears
    Do scald[28] like molten lead.

CORDELIA: Sir, do you know me?

LEAR: You are a spirit, I know; when did you die?

50 CORDELIA: Still, still, far wide.[29]

DOCTOR: He's scarce awake; let him alone awhile.

LEAR: Where have I been? Where am I? Fair daylight?
    I am mightily abus'd.[30] I should even die with pity
    To see another thus. I know not what to say.

55 I will not swear these are my hands: let's see;
    I feel this pin prick. Would I were assur'd
    Of my condition!

CORDELIA: O! look upon me, sir,
    And hold your hands in benediction o'er me.
    No, sir, you must not kneel.

LEAR: Pray, do not mock me:

60 I am a very foolish fond[31] old man,
    Fourscore and upward, not an hour more or less;
    And, to deal plainly,
    I fear I am not in my perfect mind.
    Methinks I should know you and know this man;

65 Yet I am doubtful: for I am mainly[32] ignorant
    What place this is, and all the skill I have
    Remembers not these garments; nor I know not
    Where I did lodge last night. Do not laugh at me;
    For, as I am a man, I think this lady

70 To be my child Cordelia.

CORDELIA: And so I am, I am.

LEAR: Be your tears wet? Yes, faith. I pray, weep not:
    If you have poison for me, I will drink it.
    I know you do not love me; for your sisters
    Have, as I do remember, done me wrong:

75 You have some cause, they have not.

CORDELIA: No cause, no cause.

LEAR: Am I in France?

KENT: In your own kingdom, sir.

---

27 so that
28 scald me
29 astray (in mind)
30 deceived, deluded (cf. l. 77 below)
31 simple, foolish
32 completely

LEAR: Do not abuse me.

DOCTOR: Be comforted, good madam; the great rage,[33]
　　You see, is kill'd in him; and yet it is danger
80　　To make him even o'er[34] the time he has lost.
　　Desire him to go in; trouble him no more
　　Till further settling.[35]

CORDELIA: Will 't please your highness walk?[36]

LEAR:　　　　　　　　　　　　　You must bear with me.
　　Pray you now, forget and forgive: I am old and foolish.

　　　　　　　　[*Exeunt Lear, Cordelia, Doctor, and Attendants.*]

85　GENTLEMAN: Holds it true, sir, that the Duke of Cornwall was so slain?

KENT: Most certain, sir.

GENTLEMAN: Who is conductor of his people?

KENT: As 'tis said, the bastard son of Gloucester.

GENTLEMAN: They say Edgar, his banished son, is with the Earl of Kent in
90　　Germany.

KENT: Report is changeable. 'Tis time to look about; the powers of the kingdom
　　approach apace.

GENTLEMAN: The arbitrement[37] is like to be bloody. Fare you well, sir.　　[*Exit.*]

KENT: My point and period[38] will be throughly wrought,
95　　Or well or ill, as this day's battle's fought.　　　　　　　　　[*Exit.*]

---

33 frenzy, madness
34 *even o'er*: smooth over, straighten out, make the recollection continuous
35 *Till . . . settling*: till his mind has had more time to settle down again
36 withdraw
37 decision (of the war)
38 *point and period*: object and end

ACT V

SCENE 1

The British Camp near Dover.

> *Enter, with drum and colours, Edmund, Regan, Officers, Soldiers,*
> *and Others.*

EDMUND: Know[1] of the duke if his last purpose hold,[2]
    Or whether since[3] he is advis'd[4] by aught
    To change the course; he's full of alteration
    And self-reproving; bring his constant pleasure.[5]

                            [To an Officer, who goes out.]

5 REGAN: Our sister's man[6] is certainly miscarried.
  EDMUND: 'Tis to be doubted,[7] madam.
  REGAN: Now, sweet lord,
    You know the goodness I intend upon you:[8]
    Tell me, but truly, but then[9] speak the truth,
    Do you not love my sister?
  EDMUND: In honour'd[10] love.
10 REGAN: But have you never found my brother's way
    To the forefended[11] place?
  EDMUND: That thought abuses[12] you.
  REGAN: I am doubtful that you have been conjunct
    And bosom'd with her, as far as we call hers.[13]
  EDMUND: No, by mine honour, madam.
15 REGAN: I never shall endure her:[14] dear my lord,
    Be not familiar with her.
  EDMUND: Fear[15] me not.
    She and the duke her husband!

> *Enter with drums and colours, Albany, Goneril, and Soldiers.*

1 find out
2 still holds good
3 since then
4 induced
5 *constant pleasure*: firm decision
6 *Our . . . man*: Oswald (see IV. vi. 238)
7 feared (so 'doubtful' in l. 12 = afraid)
8 *goodness I intend* (to confer) *upon you*: i.e. my hand
9 even if it is what I fear
10 honourable, not adulterous
11 forbidden
12 deceives
13 i.e. intimate with her to the fullest degree
14 *endure her*: i.e. bear to see her separate us
15 distrust

GONERIL [*Aside*]: I had rather lose the battle than that sister
    Should loosen him and me.

20 ALBANY: Our very loving sister, well be-met.[16]
    Sir, this I heard, the king is come to his daughter,
    With others; whom the rigour of our state[17]
    Forc'd to cry out.[18] Where I could not be honest
    I never yet was valiant: for this business,

25   It toucheth us, as[19] France invades our land,
    Not bolds[20] the king, with others, whom, I fear,
    Most just and heavy causes make oppose.[21]

EDMUND: Sir, you speak nobly.

REGAN: Why is this reason'd?[22]

GONERIL: Combine together 'gainst the enemy;

30   for these domestic and particular[23] broils
    Are not the question here.

ALBANY: Let's then determine
    With the ancient of war[24] on our proceeding.

EDMUND: I shall attend you presently[25] at your tent.

REGAN: Sister, you'll go with us?

35 GONERIL: No.

REGAN: 'Tis most convenient; pray you, go with us.

GONERIL [*Aside*]: O, ho! I know the riddle.[26] [*Aloud.*] I will go.

        Enter Edgar, disguised.

EDGAR: If e'er your Grace had speech with man so poor,
    Hear me one word.

ALBANY: I'll overtake you. Speak.

    [*Exeunt Edmund, Regan, Goneril, Officers, Soldiers, and Attendants.*]

40 EDGAR: Before you fight the battle, ope this letter.
    If you have victory, let the trumpet sound
    For him that brought it: wretched though I seem,
    I can produce a champion that will prove
    What is avouched[27] there. If you miscarry,

16 met
17 *our state*: our rule
18 *cry out*: protest, rebel
19 *toucheth us, as*: concerns me in so far as
20 *Not bolds*: not in so far as the king of France emboldens (supports)
21 *whom . . . oppose*: who, I fear, have good and weighty reasons for taking up arms against us
22 *Why . . . reason'd?*: Why all this argument (about the cause of rebellion)?
23 private
24 *the . . . war*: veteran soldiers
25 at once
26 *the riddle*: i.e. what you are after
27 asserted

45   Your business of the world[28] hath so an end,
         And machination[29] ceases. Fortune love you!
      ALBANY: Stay till I have read the letter.
      EDGAR: I was forbid it.
         When time shall serve, let but the herald cry,
         And I'll appear again.
50   ALBANY: Why, fare thee well: I will o'erlook[30] thy paper.   [*Exit Edgar.*]

         Re-enter Edmund.

      EDMUND: The enemy's in view; draw up your powers.
         Here is the guess[31] of their true strength and forces
         By diligent discovery;[32] but your haste
         Is now urg'd on you.
      ALBANY: We will greet the time.[33]   [*Exit.*]
55   EDMUND: To both sisters have I sworn my love;
         Each jealous[34] of the other, as the stung
         Are of the adder. Which of them shall I take?
         Both? one? or neither? Neither can be enjoy'd
         If both remain alive: to take the widow
60   Exasperates, makes mad her sister Goneril;
         And hardly shall I carry out my side,[35]
         Her husband being alive. Now then, we'll use
         His countenance[36] for the battle; which being done
         Let her who would be rid of him devise
65   His speedy taking off.[37] As for the mercy
         Which he intends to Lear, and to Cordelia,
         The battle done, and they within our power,
         Shall[38] never see his pardon; for my state[39]
         Stands on me[40] to defend, not to debate.   [*Exit.*]

28 *Your . . . world*: your worldly concerns, your life
29 plotting, i.e. Edmund's
30 look over, peruse
31 estimate
32 inquiry, spying
33 *greet the time*: go to meet the occasion, emergency
34 suspicious
35 *carry . . . side*: attain my object, i.e. the throne
36 authority, prestige
37 *taking off*: murder (a euphemism like 'liquidation' today)
38 they shall (grammatical confusion)
39 position
40 *Stands on me*: (it) concerns me, it is up to me

SCENE 2

A Field between the two Camps.

> *Alarum within. Enter, with drum and colours, Lear, Cordelia, and their*
> *Forces; and exeunt. Enter Edgar and Gloucester.*

EDGAR: Here, father, take the shadow of this tree
>   for your good host;[1] pray that the right may thrive.
>   If ever I return to you again,
>   I'll bring you comfort.
GLOUCESTER: Grace go with you, sir!   [*Exit Edgar.*]

Alarum; afterwards a retreat. Re-enter Edgar.

5   EDGAR: Away, old man! give me thy hand: away!
>   King Lear hath lost, he and his daughter ta'en.
>   Give me thy hand; come on.
GLOUCESTER: No further, sir; a man may rot even here.
EDGAR: What! in ill thoughts again? Men must endure[2]
10   Their going hence, even as their coming hither:
>   Ripeness is all.[3] Come on.
GLOUCESTER: And that's true too.   [*Exeunt.*]

1 shelterer, protection
2 wait for, live patiently until
3 *Ripeness is all*: the important thing is to be ready for death when it does come

SCENE 3

The British Camp, near Dover.

> *Enter, in conquest, with drum and colours, Edmund; Lear and Cordelia,*
> *prisoners; Officers, Soldiers, &c.*

EDMUND: Some officers take them away: good guard,[1]
>   Until their greater pleasures first be known
>   That[2] are to censure[3] them.
CORDELIA: We are not the first
>   Who, with best meaning,[4] have incurr'd the worst.
5   For thee, oppress'd king, am I cast down;

1 *good guard*: keep good guard over them
2 *their . . . That*: the pleasure (decision as to their fate) of those higher authorities (Albany &c.) who
3 judge
4 *with . . . meaning*: trying to act for the best

Myself could else out-frown false Fortune's frown.[5]
Shall we not see these daughters and these sisters?

LEAR: No, no, no, no! Come, let's away to prison;
We two alone will sing like birds i' the cage:[6]

10 When thou dost ask me blessing, I'll kneel down,
And ask of thee forgiveness: so we'll live,
And pray, and sing, and tell old tales, and laugh
At gilded butterflies,[7] and hear poor rogues
Talk of court news; and we'll talk with them too,

15 Who loses and who wins; who's in, who's out;
And take upon 's the mystery of things
As if we were God's spies:[8] and we'll wear out,[9]
In a wall'd prison, packs and sets of great ones
That ebb and flow by the moon.[10]

EDMUND: Take them away.

20 LEAR: Upon such sacrifices,[11] my Cordelia,
The gods themselves throw incense. Have I caught thee?
He that parts us shall bring a brand from heaven,[12]
And fire us hence like foxes.[13] Wipe thine eyes;
The good years[14] shall devour them, flesh and fell,[15]

25 Ere they shall make us weep: we'll see 'em starve first.
Come.   [*Exeunt Lear and Cordelia, guarded.*]

EDMUND: Come hither, captain; hark,
Take thou this note; [*Giving a paper.*] go follow them to prison:
One step I have advan'd thee; if thou dost

30 As this instructs thee, thou dost make the way
To noble fortunes; know thou this, that men
Are as the time is; to be tender-minded
Does not become a sword;[16] thy great employment
Will not bear question;[17] either say thou'lt do't,

35 Or thrive by other means.

OFFICER: I'll do't, my lord.

---

5 *out-frown . . . frown*: defy misfortune
6 *also* meant a prison
7 *gilded butterflies*: court gallants (cf. l. 85)
8 *And . . . spies*: i.e. imagine we understand the ways of God in the world as if we were His agents or saw with His eyes
9 *wear out*: outlast
10 *packs . . . moon*: sets and parties at court who go in and out of favour like the changes of the moon
11 *such sacrifices*: as our imprisonment
12 *He . . . heaven*: i.e. no power on earth shall separate us
13 *like foxes*: as foxes are smoked out of their holes
14 *The good years*: the Devil
15 skin
16 *a sword*: i.e. a soldier
17 investigation, discussion

EDMUND: About it; and write happy[18] when thou hast done.
　　Mark,—I say, instantly, and carry it[19] so
　　As I have set it down.

OFFICER: I cannot draw a cart nor eat dried oats;

40　　If it be man's work I will do it.　　　　　　　　　　　[*Exit.*]

　　　Flourish. Enter Albany, Goneril, Regan, Officers, and Attendants.

ALBANY: Sir, you have show'd to-day your valiant strain,[20]
　　And fortune led you well; you have the captives
　　Who were the opposites of[21] this day's strife;
　　We do require them of you, so to use them

45　　As we[22] shall find their merits[23] and our safety
　　May equally determine.

EDMUND:　　　　　　　　　Sir, I thought it fit
　　To send the old and miserable king
　　To some retention, and appointed guard;
　　Whose[24] age has charms in it, whose title more,

50　　To pluck the common bosom[25] on his side,
　　And turn our impress'd lances[26] in our eyes[27]
　　Which do command them. With him I sent the queen;
　　My reason all the same; and they are ready
　　To-morrow, or at further space, to appear

55　　Where you shall hold your session. At this time
　　We sweat and bleed; the friend hath lost his friend,
　　And the best quarrels,[28] in the heat,[29] are curs'd
　　By those that feel their sharpness;
　　The question of Cordelia and her father

60　　Requires a fitter place.

ALBANY:　　　　　　　　Sir, by your patience,[30]
　　I hold you but a subject of this war,
　　Not as a brother.

REGAN:　　　　　　That's as we list[31] to grace him:
　　Methinks our pleasure might have been demanded,

18 *write happy*: count yourself happy
19 *carry it* (out)
20 lineage
21 *the opposites of*: our opponents in
22 I and my counsellors
23 deserts, deeds
24 refers back to 'king'
25 *the . . . bosom*: the affections of the common people
26 *our . . . lances*: the soldiers we had conscripted
27 *in our eyes*: against ourselves
28 *the . . . quarrels*: battles in the best causes
29 *in the heat (of the moment)*: before passions have cooled
30 *by . . . patience*: if you will excuse me saying so
31 choose

Ere you had spoke so far. He led our powers,
65   Bore the commission of my place[32] and person;
The which immediacy[33] may well stand up,[34]
And call itself your brother.

GONERIL: Not so hot;[35]
In his own grace he doth exalt himself
More than in your addition.[36]

REGAN: In my rights,
70   By me invested, he compeers the best.

GONERIL: That were the most, if[37] he should husband you.

REGAN: Jesters do oft prove prophets.

GONERIL: Holla, holla!
That eye that told you so look'd but a-squint.

REGAN: Lady, I am not well; else I should answer
75   From a full-flowing stomach.[38] General,
Take thou my soldiers, prisoners, patrimony;
Dispose of them, of me; the walls[39] are thine;
Witness the world, that I create thee here
My lord and master.

GONERIL: Mean you to enjoy him?
80   ALBANY: The let-alone[40] lies not in your good will.

EDMUND: Nor in thine, lord.

ALBANY: Half-blooded[41] fellow, yes.

REGAN [*To Edmund*.]: Let the drum strike, and prove my title thine.

ALBANY: Stay yet; hear reason. Edmund, I arrest thee
On capital treason; and, in thy attaint,[42]
85   This gilded[43] serpent. [*Pointing to Goneril.*] For your claim, fair sister,
I bar it in the interest of my wife;
'Tis she is sub-contracted[44] to this lord,
And I, her husband, contradict your bans.
If you will marry, make your love to me,
90   My lady is bespoke.

GONERIL: An interlude![45]

---

32 rank
33 closeness to me
34 *well . . . up*: i.e. justify him in standing up, &c.
35 *Not so hot*: Don't be in such a hurry
36 *your addition*: the position you have claimed for him
37 *the most* (he could do, even) *if*
38 *full-flowing stomach*: the eloquence of passion
39 *the walls*: of my fortress (metaphorically), i.e. I myself
40 power to forbid it
41 bastard
42 impeachment
43 gilded-over, fair-seeming
44 betrothed for the second time
45 *An interlude*: (This is as good as) a play

ALBANY: Thou art arm'd, Gloucester; let the trumpet sound:
    If none appear to prove upon thy person
    Thy heinous, manifest, and many treasons,
    There is my pledge; [*Throws down a glove.*] I'll prove it on thy heart,
95   Ere I taste bread, thou art in nothing less
    Than I have here proclaim'd thee.

REGAN: Sick! O sick!

GONERIL [*Aside*]: If not, I'll ne'er trust medicine.[46]

EDMUND: There's my exchange: [*Throws down a glove.*] what in the world he is
    That names me traitor, villain-like he lies.
100   Call by thy trumpet: he that dares approach,
    On him, on you, who not? I will maintain
    My truth and honour firmly.

ALBANY: A herald, ho!

EDMUND: A herald, ho! a herald!

ALBANY: Trust to thy single virtue;[47] for thy soldiers,
105   All levied in my name, have in my name
    Took their discharge.

REGAN: My sickness grows upon me.

ALBANY: She is not well; convey her to my tent.   [*Exit Regan, led.*]
    Come hither, herald,—

        Enter a Herald.

                    Let the trumpet sound,—
    And read out this.

110   OFFICER: Sound, trumpet!   [*A trumpet sounds.*]

HERALD: 'If any man of quality or degree within the lists[48] of the army will main-
    tain upon Edmund, supposed Earl of Gloucester, that he is a manifold traitor,
    let him appear at the third sound of the trumpet. He is bold in his defence.'

EDMUND: Sound!   [*First Trumpet.*]

115   HERALD: Again!   [*Second Trumpet.*]

HERALD: Again!   [*Third Trumpet.*]

                                            [*Trumpet answers within.*]

        Enter Edgar, armed, with a Trumpet before him.[49]

ALBANY: Ask him his purposes, why he appears
    Upon this call o' the trumpet.

HERALD: What are you?
    Your name? your quality?[50] and why you answer
120   This present summons?

46 euphemism for 'poison'
47 valour (*virtus*)
48 role, muster
49 *with . . . him*: preceded by a trumpeter
50 rank

EDGAR: Know, my name is lost;
　　　By treason's tooth bare-gnawn[51] and canker-bit:[52]
　　　Yet am I noble as the adversary
　　　I come to cope.[53]
ALBANY: Which is that adversary?
EDGAR: What's he that speaks for Edmund Earl of Gloucester?
125　EDMUND: Himself: what sayst thou to him?
EDGAR: Draw thy sword,
　　　That, if my speech offend a noble heart,
　　　Thy arm may do thee justice; here is mine:
　　　Behold, it[54] is the privilege of mine honours,
　　　My oath, and my profession:[55] I protest,
130　Maugre[56] thy strength, youth, place, and eminence,
　　　Despite thy victor[57] sword and fire-new[58] fortune,
　　　Thy valour and thy heart,[59] thou art a traitor,
　　　False to thy gods, thy brother, and thy father,
　　　Conspirant[60] 'gainst this high illustrious prince,
135　And, from the extremest upward[61] of thy head
　　　To the descent[62] and dust below thy foot,
　　　A most toad-spotted[63] traitor. Say thou 'No',
　　　This sword, this arm, and my best spirits are bent
　　　To prove upon thy heart, whereto I speak,
140　Thou liest.
EDMUND: In wisdom I should ask thy name;
　　　But since thy outside looks so fair and war-like,
　　　And that thy tongue some say[64] of breeding breathes,
　　　What[65] safe[66] and nicely[67] I might well delay
　　　By rule of knighthood, I disdain and spurn;[68]
145　Back do I toss these treasons to thy head,[69]

---

51 gnawed bare
52 devoured, as by the canker worm
53 engage
54 to fight, to maintain the truth of my assertion
55 *my profession*: of knighthood
56 in spite of
57 (lately) victorious
58 fresh like coins from the mint. Edmund is a *novus homo*, a *parvenu*
59 courage
60 conspiring *or* a conspirer
61 top
62 lowest part, sole of the feet
63 covered with shame as a toad with spots
64 suggestion, trace
65 i.e. the combat
66 safely (from the point of view of honour)
67 by insisting on the exact code of honour (which only requires me to answer an equal; see l. 152 below)
68 *I . . . spurn*: viz. to insist on my rights (change of construction)
69 *to thy head*: in thy teeth

With the hell-hated[70] lie o'erwhelm thy heart,
Which,[71] for[72] they yet glance by and scarcely bruise,
This sword of mine shall give them instant way,[73]
Where they shall rest for ever. Trumpets, speak!

[Alarums. They fight. Edmund falls.]

150 ALBANY: Save him, save him!

GONERIL: This is practice,[74] Gloucester:
By the law of arms thou wast not bound to answer
An unknown opposite; thou art not vanquish'd,
But cozen'd[75] and beguil'd.

ALBANY: Shut your mouth, dame,
Or with this paper[76] shall I stop it. Hold, sir;[77]
155 Thou[78] worse than any name, read thine own evil:
No tearing, lady; I perceive you know it.   *[Gives the letter to Edmund.]*

GONERIL: Say, if I do, the laws are mine, not thine:
Who can arraign me for 't.   *[Exit.]*

ALBANY: Most monstrous!
Know'st thou this paper?

EDMUND: Ask me not what I know.

160 ALBANY: Go after her: she's desperate; govern her.[79]   *[Exit an Officer.]*

EDMUND: What you have charg'd me with, that have I done,
And more, much more; the time will bring it out:
'Tis past, and so am I. But what art thou
That hast this fortune on me?[80] If thou'rt noble,
165 I do forgive thee.

EDGAR: Let's exchange charity.[81]
I am no less in blood than thou art, Edmund;
If more, the more thou hast wrong'd me.
My name is Edgar, and thy father's son.
The gods are just, and of our pleasant vices
170 Make instruments to plague us:
The dark and vicious place where thee he got[82]
Cost him his eyes.

70 hated like hell
71 treasons
72 because
73 *give . . . way*: press them urgently back (upon you)
74 treachery
75 tricked
76 *this paper*: the love-letter of Goneril to Edmund (see IV. vi. 262)
77 *Hold, sir*: wait a moment (to Edmund)
78 Goneril
79 *govern her*: control her, e.g. prevent her suicide
80 *fortune on me*: advantage given thee by fortune over me
81 including forgiveness
82 *The . . . got*: i.e. the act of adultery which led to your birth

EDMUND: Thou hast spoken right, 'tis true;
  The wheel is come full circle; I am here.

ALBANY: Methought thy very gait did prophesy

175 A royal nobleness; I must embrace thee:
  Let sorrow split my heart, if ever I
  Did hate thee or thy father.

EDGAR: Worthy prince, I know 't.

ALBANY: Where have you hid yourself?
  How have you known the miseries of your father?

180 EDGAR: By nursing them, my lord. List a brief tale;
  And, when 'tis told, O that my heart would burst!
  The bloody proclamation to escape[83]
  That follow'd me so near,—O! our lives' sweetness,[84]
  That we the pain of death would hourly die

185 Rather than die at once!—taught me to shift[85]
  Into a madman's rags, to assume a semblance
  That very dogs disdain'd: and in this habit
  Met I my father with his bleeding rings,[86]
  Their precious stones new lost; became his guide,

190 Led him, begg'd for him, sav'd him from despair;
  Never,—O fault!—reveal'd myself unto him,
  Until some half hour past, when I was arm'd;
  Not sure, though hoping, of this good success,
  I ask'd his blessing, and from first to last

195 Told him my pilgrimage: but his flaw'd[87] heart,—
  Alack! too weak the conflict to support;
  'Twixt two extremes of passion, joy and grief,
  Burst smilingly.

EDMUND: This speech of yours hath mov'd me,
  And shall perchance do good; but speak you on;

200 You look as you had something more to say.

ALBANY: If there be more, more woeful, hold it in;
  For I am almost ready to dissolve,[88]
  Hearing of this.

EDGAR: This would have seem'd a period[89]
  To such as love not sorrow; but another,[90]

---

83 *to escape*: governs 'the bloody proclamation'
84 *our . . . sweetness*: how highly we value our lives!
85 change
86 eye-sockets
87 cracked, worn out
88 in tears, melt away
89 limit, ending
90 sorrow *or* tale

205   To amplify too much,[91] would make much more,
     And top extremity.[92]
     Whilst I was big[93] in clamour came there a man,
     Who, having seen me in my worst estate,[94]
     Shunn'd my abhorr'd society; but then, finding
210   Who 'twas that so endur'd, with his strong arms
     He fasten'd on my neck, and bellow'd out
     As[95] he'd burst heaven; threw him on my father;
     Told the most piteous tale of Lear and him
     That ever ear receiv'd; which in recounting
215   His grief grew puissant,[96] and the strings of life
     Began to crack: twice then the trumpet sounded,
     And there I left him tranc'd.[97]

ALBANY: But who was this?

EDGAR: Kent, sir, the banish'd Kent; who in disguise
     Follow'd his enemy[98] king, and did him service
220   Improper for[99] a slave.

Enter a Gentleman, with a bloody knife.

GENTLEMAN: Help, help! O help!

EDGAR: What kind of help?

ALBANY: Speak, man.

EDGAR: What means that bloody knife?

GENTLEMAN: 'Tis hot, it smokes;
     It came even from the heart of—O! she's dead.

ALBANY: Who dead? speak, man.

225 GENTLEMAN: Your lady, sir, your lady: and her sister
     By her is poison'd; she confesses it.

EDMUND: I was contracted[100] to them both: all three
     Now marry in an instant.

EDGAR: Here comes Kent.

ALBANY: Produce the bodies, be they alive or dead:
230   This judgment of the heavens, that makes us tremble,
     Touches us not with pity.   [*Exit Gentleman.*]

     Enter Kent.

---

91 *To . . . much*: (probably) by increasing what is already excessive
92 *top extremity*: pass the (due) limit
93 loud
94 state
95 as if
96 (too) powerful
97 insensible
98 (turned) hostile
99 *Improper for*: too humble even for
100 engaged, promised

                              O! is this he?
            The time will not allow the compliment[101]
            Which very manners urges.
      KENT: I am come
            To bid my king and master aye good-night;
235   Is he not here?
      ALBANY: Great thing of us forgot!
            Speak, Edmund, where's the king? and where's Cordelia?
            Seest thou this object,[102] Kent?

                        [*The bodies of Goneril and Regan are brought in.*]

      KENT: Alack! why thus?
      EDMUND: Yet Edmund was belov'd:
            The one the other poison'd for my sake,
240   And after[103] slew herself.
      ALBANY: Even so. Cover their faces.
      EDMUND: I pant for life:[104] some good I mean to do
            Despite of mine own nature. Quickly send,
            Be brief in it, to the castle; for my writ[105]
245   Is on the life of Lear and on Cordelia.
            Nay, send in time.
      ALBANY: Run, run! O run!
      EDGAR: To whom, my lord? who has the office? send
            Thy token of reprieve.
      EDMUND: Well thought on: take my sword,
250   Give it the captain.
      ALBANY: Haste thee, for thy life.   [*Exit Edgar.*]
      EDMUND: He hath commission from thy wife and me
            To hang Cordelia in the prison, and
            To lay the blame upon her own despair,
            That she fordid[106] herself.
255   ALBANY: The gods defend her! Bear him hence awhile.   [*Edmund is borne off.*]

      Enter Lear, with Cordelia dead in his arms; Edgar, Officer, and Others.

      LEAR: Howl, howl, howl, howl! O! you are men of stones:[107]
            Had I your tongues and eyes, I'd use them so
            That heaven's vaults should crack. She's gone for ever.

---

101 formal courtesy (as in I. i. 291)
102 sight, something thrown in the way (Lat. *obicio*)
103 *after*(wards)
104 *pant for life*: struggle to live a little longer
105 writing, the order given (ll. 28 above)
106 destroyed
107 *men of stones*: unfeeling

I know when one is dead, and when one lives;
260   She's dead as earth. Lend me a looking-glass;
        If that her breath will mist or stain the stone,[108]
        Why, then she lives.

KENT: Is this the promis'd end?[109]

EDGAR: Or image[110] of that horror?

ALBANY: Fall and cease![111]

LEAR: This feather stirs; she lives! if it be so,
265   It is a chance which does redeem all sorrows
        That ever I have felt.

KENT [*Kneeling*.]:   O, my good master!

LEAR: Prithee, away.

EDGAR: 'Tis noble Kent, your friend.

LEAR: A plague upon you, murderers, traitors all!
        I might have sav'd her; now, she's gone for ever!
270   Cordelia, Cordelia! stay a little. Ha!
        What is 't thou sayst? Her voice was ever soft,
        Gentle and low, an excellent thing in woman.
        I kill'd the slave[112] that was a-hanging thee.

OFFICER: 'Tis true, my lord, he did.

LEAR: Did I not, fellow?
275   I have seen the day, with my good biting falchion[113]
        I would have made them skip: I am old now,
        And these same crosses[114] spoil me.[115] Who are you?
        Mine eyes are not o' the best: I'll tell you straight.[116]

KENT: If fortune brag of two she lov'd and hated,[117]
280   One of them[118] we behold.

LEAR: This is a dull[119] sight. Are you not Kent?

KENT: The same,
        Your servant Kent. Where is your servant Caius?[120]

LEAR: He's a good fellow, I can tell you that;
        He'll strike,[121] and quickly too. He's dead and rotten.

285 KENT: No, my good lord; I am the very man—

---

108 a mirror of polished stone
109 *the . . . end*: the end of the world foretold (in biblical prophecy)
110 copy, reproduction (cf. 'great doom's image', Macbeth II. iii. 61)
111 *Fall and cease!*: (probably) let the heavens fall and all things come to an end!
112 *the slave*: not literal, but abusive
113 a kind of light sword
114 troubles
115 *spoil me*: destroy me (as a fighter)
116 straightaway, in a moment
117 *two . . . hated*: one whom she raised up (to the highest) and one whom she put down (to the lowest)
118 *One of them*: in Lear
119 melancholy
120 *Where . . . Caius?*: probably Kent is inviting Lear to recognize in him the former Caius
121 as he did Oswald (I. iv. 68)

LEAR: I'll see that straight.[122]

KENT: That, from your first of difference[123] and decay,
 Have followed your sad steps.

LEAR: You are welcome hither.

KENT: Nor no man else;[124] all's cheerless, dark, and deadly:

290 Your eldest daughters have fordone themselves,
 And desperately[125] are dead.

LEAR: Ay, so I think.

ALBANY: He knows not what he says, and vain it is
 That we present us[126] to him.

EDGAR: Very bootless.[127]

   Enter an Officer.

OFFICER: Edmund is dead, my lord.

ALBANY: That's but a trifle here.

295 Your lords and noble friends, know our[128] intent;
 What comfort to this great decay[129] may come
 Shall be applied: for us, we will resign,
 During the life of this old majesty,
 To him our absolute power:—[*To Edgar and Kent.*] You, to your rights;[130]

300 With boot and such addition[131] as your honours[132]
 Have more than merited. All friends shall taste
 The wages[133] of their virtue, and all foes
 The cup of their deservings. O! see, see!

LEAR: And my poor fool[134] is hang'd! No, no, no life!

305 Why should a dog, a horse, a rat, have life,
 And thou no breath at all? Thou'lt come no more,
 Never, never, never, never, never!
 Pray you, undo this button: thank you, sir.
 Do you see this? Look on her, look, her lips,

310 Look there, look there!   [*Dies.*]

EDGAR: He faints!—my lord, my lord!

---

122 cf. l. 278. But Lear is only half conscious of what is going on
123 *your . . . difference*: the commencement of your change of fortunes
124 *Nor . . . else*: *either* neither I nor anyone else can be very welcome (well come?) to this scene (which suits what follows), *or* a continuation of his words at l. 285
125 in despair
126 ourselves
127 useless
128 the royal plural, since Albany represents those to whom Lear surrendered power
129 *great decay*: ruin of greatness (Lear)
130 *to . . . rights*: betake you to, enjoy your rights
131 *boot . . . addition*: the profit of such additions
132 honourable deeds
133 rewards
134 *poor fool*: (term of endearment) Cordelia

KENT: Break, heart;[135] I prithee, break.

EDGAR: Look up, my lord.

KENT: Vex not his ghost:[136] O! let him pass; he hates him
    That would upon the rack[137] of this tough world
    Stretch him out longer.

EDGAR: He is gone, indeed.

315 KENT: The wonder is he hath endur'd so long:
    He but usurp'd[138] his life.

ALBANY: Bear them from hence. Our present business
    Is general woe. [*To Kent and Edgar.*] Friends of my soul, you twain
    Rule in this realm,[139] and the gor'd[140] state sustain.

320 KENT: I have a journey, sir, shortly to go;
    My master calls me, I must not say no.

ALBANY: The weight of this sad time we must obey;
    Speak what we feel, not what we ought to say.[141]
    The oldest[142] hath borne most: we that are young,

325 Shall never see so much, nor live so long.[143] [*Exeunt, with a dead march.*]

135 *Break, heart: either* to his own heart *or* of Lear's
136 spirit
137 metaphor from an instrument of torture ('racking' the limbs)
138 kept what was due to death
139 *this realm*: (probably) that half of Britain which had been Regan's share
140 maimed, injured
141 *Speak . . . say*: i.e. (probably) at present we can only speak from the heart, not prudently as after reflection
142 *The oldest*: especially Lear
143 In the quarto text of *Lear* the final speech is attributed to Albany; in the folio text this speech is attributed to Edgar.

Richard Brinsley Sheridan
1751–1816

Born in Dublin, Anglo-Irish playwright and politician Richard Brinsley Sheridan was raised in a show-business family: his father was an actor and theatre manager, his mother a playwright. Educated first by tutors, he was sent to Harrow, a West London independent school, from 1762 until 1769. *The Rivals*, his first play, opened at London's Covent Garden Theatre in 1775. The following year he became manager of the Drury Lane Theatre. His major plays belong to the period from 1775 to 1779, for in 1780 he entered politics as a Whig member of parliament. He spent more than three decades in the House of Commons, holding several high offices including treasurer of the navy. *The School for Scandal*, universally acknowledged as his comic masterpiece, had its premiere at the Drury Lane Theatre on 8 May 1777.

The School for Scandal

A PORTRAIT

ADDRESSED TO A LADY WITH THE COMEDY OF THE SCHOOL FOR SCANDAL
BY R.B. SHERIDAN, ESQ.

Tell me, ye prim adepts in Scandal's school
Who rail by precept, and detract by rule,
Lives there no character, so tried, so known,
So decked with grace—and so unlike your own—
5   That even *you* assist her fame to raise,
Approve by envy, and by silence praise?
Attend!—a model shall attract your view—
Daughters of calumny, I summon YOU:—
You shall decide if this a *portrait* prove,
10   Or fond creation of the Muse and Love.
Attend!—ye virgin critics shrewd and sage,
Ye matron censors of this childish age,
Whose peering eye and wrinkled front declare
A fixed antipathy to *young* and *fair*:
15   By cunning, cautious; or by nature cold,
In maiden malice virulently bold!
Attend!—ye skilled to coin the precious tale,
Creating proof, where innuendos fail!
Whose practised mem'ries, cruelly exact,
20   Omit no circumstance, except the fact!—
Attend!—all ye who boast,—or old or young—
The living libel of a sland'rous tongue!
So shall my theme as far contrasted be
As saints by fiends—or hymns by calumny.
25   Come, gentle *Amoret* (for 'neath that name
In worthier verse is sung thy beauty's fame),
      Come—for but thee who seeks the Muse?—and while
Celestial blushes check thy conscious smile,
With timid grace, and hesitating eye,
30   The perfect model which I boast—supply!
Vain Muse!—couldst thou the humblest sketch create
Of *her*, or slightest charm couldst imitate—
Could thy blest strain, in kindred colours, trace
The faintest wonder of her form, or face—
35   Poets would study the immortal line,
And *Reynolds* own his *art* subdued by *thine*!
That art, which well might added lustre give
To nature's best!—and heaven's superlative!—

On *Granby*'s cheek might bid new glories rise,
40 Or point a purer beam from *Devon*'s eyes!—
　　Hard is the task to shape that beauty's praise,
Whose judgment scorns the homage—flatt'ry pays?
But praising *Amoret*—we cannot err:—
No tongue o'ervalues heav'n—nor flatters her!
45 Yet *she* by fate's perverseness!—she alone
Would doubt out truth, nor deem such praise her own!
　　Adorning fashion, unadorned by dress,
Simple from taste, and not from carelessness;
Discreet in gesture, in deportment mild,
50 Not stiff with prudence, nor uncouthly wild—
No state has *Amoret*—no studied mien;
She frowns no *goddess*—and she moves no *queen*!
The softer charm that in her manner lies
Is fram'd to captivate, yet not surprise;
55 It justly suits th' expression of her face,—
'Tis less than dignity, and more than grace!
　　On her pure cheek the native hue is such,
That form'd by heav'n to be admir'd so much,
The hand that made her with such partial care
60 Might well have fix'd a fainter crimson there,
And bade the gentle inmate of her breast—
Inshrined Modesty—supply the rest.
　　But who the peril of her lips shall paint?
Strip them of smiles—still, still all words were faint!
65 But moving—Love himself appears to teach
Their *action*, tho' denied to rule her *speech*!
And thou who *seest* her speak, and dost not *hear*,
Mourn not her distant accents 'scape thine ear,
Viewing those lips—thou still may'st make pretence
70 To judge of what she says—and swear 'tis sense;
Cloth'd with such grace, with such expression fraught,
They move in meaning, and they pause in thought!
But dost thou further watch, with charm'd surprise,
The mild irresolution of her eyes?
75 Curious to mark—how frequent they repose,
In brief eclipse, and momentary close?
Ah! seest thou not!—an ambushed Cupid there—
Too tim'rous of his charge!—with jealous care
Veils, and unveils those beams of heav'nly light,
80 Too full—too fatal else for mortal sight?
Nor yet, such pleasing vengeance fond to meet—
In pard'ning dimples hope a safe retreat,

What tho' her peaceful breast should ne'er allow
Subduing frowns to arm her alter'd brow,
85   By Love! I swear—and by his gentle wiles!—
More fatal still—the mercy of her smiles!
    Thus lovely!—thus adorn'd!—possessing all
Of bright, or fair that can to woman fall,
The height of vanity might well be thought
90   Prerogative in her,—and Nature's fault.
Yet gentle *Amoret*—in mind supreme
As well as charms—rejects the vainer theme;
And half mistrustful of her beauty's store
She barbs with wit—those darts too keen before.
95   Read in all knowledge that her sex should reach,
Tho' *Grenville* or the Muse should deign to teach,
Fond to improve—nor tim'rous to discern
How far it is a woman's grace to learn;
In *Millar*'s catalogue she would not prove
100 Apollo's *priestess*, but Apollo's *love*,
    Grac'd by those signs—which truth delights to own,
The timid blush, and mild submitted tone:
Whate'er she says—tho' sense appear throughout—
Bears the unartful hue of female doubt.
105 Deck'd with that charm, how lovely *wit* appears,
How graceful *science* when that robe she wears!
Such too her talents, and her bent of mind
As speak a sprightly heart—by thought refin'd:
A taste for mirth—by contemplation school'd,
110 A turn for ridicule—by candour rul'd,
A scorn of folly—which she tries to hide;
An awe of talent—which she owns with pride.
    Peace, idle Muse!—no more thy strain prolong,
But yield a theme, thy warmest praises wrong,
115 Just to her merit, tho' thou canst not raise
Thy feeble verse—behold th' acknowledged praise
Has spread conviction thro' the envious train,
And cast a fatal gloom o'er Scandal's reign!
And lo! each pallid hag, with blister's tongue,
120 Mutters assent to all thy zeal has sung,
Owns all the colours just—the outline true,
Thee my inspirer—and my model—CREWE!

PROLOGUE

Spoken by Mr King   Written by D. Garrick, Esq.

A School for Scandal! tell me, I beseech you,
Needs there a school this modish art to teach you?
No need of lessons now, the knowing think—
We might as well be taught to eat and drink.

5   Caus'd by a dearth of scandal, should the vapours
Distress our fair ones—let 'em read the papers;
Their pow'rful mixtures such disorders hit;
Crave what they will, there's *quantum sufficit*.
     'Lord!' cries my Lady Wormwood (who loves tattle,

10 And puts much salt and pepper in her prattle),
Just ris'n at noon, all night at cards when threshing
Strong tea and scandal—'Bless me, how refreshing!
Give me the papers, Lisp—how bold and free! [*sips*]
*Last night Lord L—— [*sips*] was caught with Lady D*—

15 For aching heads what charming sal volatile! [*sips*]
If Mrs B—— will still continue flirting,
We hope she'll DRAW, *or we'll* UNDRAW *the curtain.*
Fine satire, poz—in public all abuse it,
But, by ourselves [*sips*], our praise we can't refuse it.

20 Now, Lisp, read *you*—there, at that dash and star.'
'Yes, ma'am.—*A certain Lord has best beware,*
Who lives not twenty miles from Grosv'nor Square;
For should he Lady W—— find willing,
WORMWOOD *is bitter*'—'Oh! that's me! the villain!

25 Throw it behind the fire, and never more
Let that vile paper come within my door.'—
     Thus at our friends we laugh, who feel the dart;
To reach our feelings, we ourselves must smart.
Is our young bard so young, to think that he

30 Can stop the full spring-tide of calumny?
Knows he the world so little and its trade?
Alas! the Dev'l is sooner *rais'd* than *laid.*
So strong, so swift, the monster there's no gagging:
Cut Scandal's head off—still the tongue is wagging.

35 Proud of your smiles, once lavishly bestow'd,
Again your young Don Quixote take the road:
To show his gratitude, he draws his pen,
And seeks this hydra, Scandal, in his den.
For your applause, all perils he would through—

40 He'll fight—that's *write*—a cavalliero true,
Till ev'ry drop of blood—that's *ink*—is spilt for you.

CHARACTERS

Men	**Women**
SIR PETER TEAZLE	LADY TEAZLE
SIR OLIVER SURFACE	MARIA
JOSEPH SURFACE	LADY SNEERWELL
CHARLES SURFACE	MRS CANDOUR
CRABTREE	
SIR BENJAMIN BACKBITE	
ROWLEY	
TRIP	
MOSES	
SNAKE	
CARELESS	

and other Companions to CHARLES [SURFACE], *Servants, etc.*

The Scene: London

ACT I

SCENE 1

Lady Sneerwell's house

Lady Sneerwell at the dressing-table—

Snake drinking chocolate

LADY SNEERWELL: The paragraphs, you say, Mr Snake, were all inserted?

SNAKE: They were, Madam, and as I copied them myself in a feigned hand, there can be no suspicion whence they came.—

LADY SNEERWELL: Did you circulate the report of Lady *Brittle*'s intrigue with Captain *Boastall*?

SNAKE: That is in as fine a train as your ladyship could wish.—In the common course of things, I think it must reach Mrs *Clackit*'s ears within four-and-twenty hours and then you know the business is as good as done.

LADY SNEERWELL: Why, truly, Mrs *Clackit* has a very pretty talent—and a great deal of industry.

SNAKE: True, Madame, and has been tolerably successful in her day.—To my knowledge, she has been the cause of six matches being broken off, and three sons being disinherited, of four forced elopements, as many close confinements, nine separate maintenances, and two divorces.—Nay, I have more than once traced her causing a *Tête-à-Tête* in the *Town and Country Magazine*—when the parties perhaps had never seen each other's faces before in the course of their lives.

LADY SNEERWELL: She certainly has talents, but her manner is gross.

SNAKE: 'Tis very true,—she generally designs well, has a free tongue, and a bold invention—but her colouring is too dark and her outline often extravagant. She wants that *delicacy* of *hint*, and *mellowness* of *sneer*, which distinguish your lady-ship's scandal.

LADY SNEERWELL: Ah! you are partial Snake.

SNAKE: Not in the least—everybody allows that Lady *Sneerwell* can do more with a *word* or a *look* than many can with the most laboured detail, even when they happen to have a little truth on their side to support it.

LADY SNEERWELL: Yes, my dear Snake, and I am no hypocrite to deny the satisfaction I reap from the success of my efforts. Wounded myself, in the early part of my life by the envenomed tongue of slander, I confess I have since known no pleasure equal to the reducing of others to the level of my own injured reputation.

SNAKE: Nothing can be more natural. But, Lady Sneerwell, there is one affair in which you have lately employed me wherein I confess I am at a loss to guess your motives.

LADY SNEERWELL: I conceive you mean with respect to my neighbour, Sir Peter Teazle, and his family.

SNAKE: I do; here are two young men, to whom Sir Peter has acted as a kind of guardian since their father's death; the elder possessing the most amiable character and universally well spoken of; the other, the most dissipated and extravagant young fellow in the kingdom, without friends or character,—the former an avowed admirer of your ladyship and apparently your favourite; the latter attached to Maria, Sir Peter's ward, and confessedly beloved by her. Now on the face of these circumstances it is utterly unaccountable to me why you, the widow of a city knight, with a good jointure, should not close with the passion of a man of such character and expectations as Mr *Surface*—and more so why you should be so uncommonly earnest to destroy the mutual attachment subsisting between his brother *Charles* and *Maria*.

LADY SNEERWELL: Then at once to unravel this mystery I must inform you that love has no share whatever in the intercourse between Mr *Surface* and me.

SNAKE: No!

LADY SNEERWELL: His real attachment is to *Maria* or her fortune—but finding in his brother a favoured rival, he has been obliged to mask his pretensions, and profit by my assistance.

SNAKE: Yet still—I am more puzzled why you should interest yourself in his success.

LADY SNEERWELL: Heav'ns! how dull you are!—Cannot you surmise the weakness which I hitherto through shame have concealed even from you? Must I confess that *Charles*—that libertine, that extravagant, that bankrupt in fortune and reputation—that he it is for whom I am thus anxious and malicious, and to gain whom I would sacrifice everything?

SNAKE: Now indeed your conduct appears consistent—but how came you and Mr *Surface* so confidential?

LADY SNEERWELL: For our mutual interest. I have found him out a long time since—I know him to be artful, selfish, and malicious—in short, a sentimental knave.

SNAKE: Yet, Sir Peter vows he has not his equal in England—and above all, he praises him as a man of sentiment.

LADY SNEERWELL: True and with the assistance of his sentiments and hypocrisy he has bought him entirely into his interest with regard to Maria.

Enter Servant

SERVANT: Mr Surface.

LADY SNEERWELL: Show him up.

[*Exit Servant*]

He generally calls about this time—I don't wonder at people's giving him to me for a lover.—

Enter Joseph Surface

JOSEPH SURFACE: My dear Lady Sneerwell—how do you do to-day?—Mr Snake, your most obedient.

LADY SNEERWELL: Snake has just been arraigning me on our mutual attachment, but I have informed him of our real views—you know how useful he has been to us, and believe me the confidence is not ill placed.

JOSEPH SURFACE: Madam, it is impossible for me to suspect a man of Mr *Snake's* sensibility and discernment.

LADY SNEERWELL: Well, well, no compliments now;—but tell me when you saw your mistress, *Maria*, or what is more material to me, your brother?

JOSEPH SURFACE: I have not seen either since I left you—but I can inform you that they never meet. Some of your stories have taken a good effect on Maria.

LADY SNEERWELL: Ah! my dear Snake the merit of this belongs to you. But do your brother's distresses increase?

JOSEPH SURFACE: Every hour—I am told he has had another execution in the house yesterday; in short his dissipation and extravagance exceed any thing I ever heard of.

LADY SNEERWELL: Poor Charles!

JOSEPH SURFACE: True, Madam;—notwithstanding his vices, one can't help feeling for him.—Aye, poor Charles! I'm sure I wish it was in *my* power to be of any essential service to him.—For the man who does not share in the distresses of a brother, even tho' merited by his own misconduct, deserves—

LADY SNEERWELL: O lud! you are going to be moral, and forget that you are among friends.

JOSEPH SURFACE: Egad, that's true!—I'll keep that sentiment till I see Sir Peter. However it is certainly a charity to rescue Maria from such a libertine, who if he is to be reclaimed, can be so only by a person of your ladyship's superior accomplishments and understanding.

SNAKE: I believe, Lady Sneerwell, here's company coming,—I'll go and copy the letter I mentioned to you.—Mr Surface, your most obedient. [*Exit Snake*]

JOSEPH SURFACE: Sir, your very devoted.—Lady Sneerwell, I am sorry you have put any further confidence in that fellow.

LADY SNEERWELL: Why so?

JOSEPH SURFACE: I have lately detected him in frequent conference with old *Rowley*, who was formerly my father's steward and has never, you know, been a friend of mine.

LADY SNEERWELL: And do you think he would betray us?

JOSEPH SURFACE: Nothing more likely: take my word for't Lady Sneerwell, that fellow hasn't virtue enough to be faithful even to his own villainy.—Hah! Maria!

Enter Maria

LADY SNEERWELL: Maria, my dear, how do you do?—what's the matter?

MARIA: There is that disagreeable lover of mine, Sir *Benjamin Backbite*, has just called at my guardian's with his odious uncle, *Crabtree*—so I slipped out and run hither to avoid them.

LADY SNEERWELL: Is that all?

JOSEPH SURFACE: If my brother *Charles* had been of the party, Ma'am, perhaps you would not have been so much alarmed.

LADY SNEERWELL: Nay now—you are severe, for I dare swear the truth of the matter is, Maria heard *you* were here—but, my dear, what has Sir Benjamin done that you should avoid him so?

MARIA: Oh he has done nothing—but 'tis for what he has said—his conversation is a perpetual libel on all his acquaintance.

JOSEPH SURFACE: Aye and the worst of it is, there is no advantage in not knowing him; for he'll abuse a stranger just as soon as his best friend—and his uncle's as bad.

LADY SNEERWELL: Nay but we should make allowance, Sir Benjamin is a wit and a poet.

MARIA: For my part, I own, Madam, wit loses its respect with me when I see it in company with malice.—What do you think Mr Surface?

JOSEPH SURFACE: Certainly, Madam, to smile at the jest which plants a thorn in another's breast is to become a principal in the mischief.

LADY SNEERWELL: Pshaw! there's no possibility of being witty—without a little ill nature: the malice of a good thing is the barb that makes it stick.—What's your opinion Mr Surface?

JOSEPH SURFACE: To be sure Madam, that conversation where the spirit of raillery is suppressed will ever appear tedious and insipid.

MARIA: Well, I'll not debate how far scandal may be allowable; but in a man, I am sure, it is always contemptible.—We have pride, envy, rivalship, and a thousand motives to depreciate each other; but the male—slanderer—must have the cowardice of woman before he can traduce one.

Enter Servant

SERVANT: Madam, Mrs Candour is below and if your ladyship's at leisure, will leave her carriage.—

LADY SNEERWELL: Beg her to walk in.

[*Exit Servant*]

Now, Maria, however, here is a character to your taste for tho' Mrs Candour is a little talkative, everybody allows her to be the best-natured and best sort of woman.

MARIA: Yes, with a very gross affectation of good nature and benevolence, she does more mischief than the direct malice of old Crabtree.—

JOSEPH SURFACE: 'Efaith 'tis very true, Lady Sneerwell. Whenever I hear the current running against the characters of my friends, I never think them in such danger as when Candour undertakes their defence.

LADY SNEERWELL: Hush, here she is!

Enter Mrs Candour

MRS CANDOUR: My dear Lady Sneerwell, how have you been this century?—Mr Surface, what news do you hear?—tho' indeed it is no matter, for I think one hears nothing else but scandal.

JOSEPH SURFACE: Just so, indeed Madam.

MRS CANDOUR: Ah, Maria, child!—what, is the whole affair off between you and Charles? His extravagance, I presume—the town talks of nothing else.

MARIA: I am very sorry Ma'am, the town has so little to do.

MRS CANDOUR: True, true, child, but there is no stopping people's tongues. I own I was hurt to hear it, as indeed I was to learn, from the same quarter, that your guardian, Sir Peter, and Lady Teazle have not agreed lately so well as could be wished.

MARIA: 'Tis strangely impertinent for people to busy themselves so.

MRS CANDOUR: Very true child, but what's to be done? People will talk—there's no preventing it.—Why it was but yesterday I was told that Miss Gadabout had eloped with Sir Filigree Flirt—but, Lord! there's no minding what one hears—tho' to be sure, I had this from very good authority.—

MARIA: Such reports are highly scandalous.

MRS CANDOUR: So they are child—shameful, shameful! But the world is so censorious, no character escapes. Lord now!—who would have suspected your friend, Miss Prim, of an indiscretion? Yet such is the ill nature of people, that they say her uncle stopped her last week just as she was stepping into the York Diligence with her dancing-master.

MARIA: I'll answer for't there are no grounds for the report.

MRS CANDOUR: Oh no foundation in the world I dare swear; no more probably, than for the story circulated last month of Mrs Festino's affair with Colonel Cassino;—though to be sure that matter was never rightly cleared up.

JOSEPH SURFACE: The licence of invention some people take is monstrous indeed.

MARIA: 'Tis so.—But in my opinion, those who report such things are equally culpable.

MRS CANDOUR: To be sure they are; tale-bearers are as bad as the tale-makers.—'Tis an old observation and a very true one—but what's to be done, as I said before? how will you prevent people from talking?—Today Mrs Clackit assured me Mr and Mrs Honeymoon were at last become mere man and wife like the rest of their acquaintances.—She likewise hinted that a certain widow in the next street had got rid of her dropsy and recovered her shape in a most surprising manner—and at the same time Miss Tattle, who was by, affirmed that Lord Buffalo had discovered his lady at a house of no extraordinary fame—and that Sir Harry Bouquet and Tom Saunter were to measure swords on a similar provocation. But lord, do you think I would report these things? No, no, tale-bearers as I said before are just as bad as tale-makers.

JOSEPH SURFACE: Ah! Mrs Candour—if everybody had your forbearance and good nature!

MRS CANDOUR: I confess, Mr Surface, I cannot bear to hear people attacked behind their backs, and when ugly circumstances come out against one's acquaintance I own I always love to think the best.——By the by I hope it is not true that your brother is absolutely ruined?

JOSEPH SURFACE: I am afraid his circumstances are very bad indeed, Ma'am.

MRS CANDOUR: Ah!—I heard so—but you must tell him to keep up his spirits—everybody almost is in the same way! Lord Spindle, Sir Thomas Splint, Captain Quinze, and Mr Nickit—all up, I hear, within this week! so if Charles is undone he'll find half his acquaintances ruined too—and that you know is a consolation.

JOSEPH SURFACE: Doubtless Ma'am—a very great one.

Enter Servant

SERVANT: Mr Crabtree and Sir Benjamin Backbite.   [*Exit Servant*]

LADY SNEERWELL: So Maria, you see your lover pursues you—positively you shan't escape.

Enter Crabtree and Sir Benjamin Backbite

CRABTREE: Lady Sneerwell, I kiss your hands. Mrs Candour, I don't believe you are acquainted with my nephew, Sir Benjamin Backbite. Egad, Ma'am, he has a pretty wit, and is a pretty poet too; isn't he, Lady Sneerwell?

SIR BENJAMIN: O fie, uncle!

CRABTREE: Nay, egad it's true—I'll back him at a rebus or a charade against the best rhymer in the kingdom. Has your ladyship heard the epigram he wrote last week on Lady Frizzle's feather catching fire?—Do, Benjamin, repeat it—or the charade you made last night extempore at Mrs Drowzie's conversazione.——Come now; your *first* is the name of a fish, your *second* a great naval commander, and—

SIR BENJAMIN: Uncle, now—prithee—

CRABTREE: 'Efaith, Ma'am, 'twould surprise you to hear how ready he is at these things.

LADY SNEERWELL: I wonder Sir Benjamin, you never publish anything.

SIR BENJAMIN: To say truth, Ma'am 'tis very vulgar to print and as my little productions are mostly satires and lampoons on particular people, I find they circulate more by giving copies in confidence to the friends of the parties—however, I have some love elegies, which when favoured with this lady's smiles, I mean to give to the public.

CRABTREE: 'Fore heav'n, Ma'am, they'll immortalize you—you'll be handed down to posterity like Petrarch's Laura, or Waller's Sacharissa.

SIR BENJAMIN: Yes, Madam, I think you will like them when you shall see them on a beautiful quarto page, where a neat rivulet of text shall murmur through a meadow of margin.—'Fore gad they will be the most elegant things of their kind.

CRABTREE: But ladies, that's true—have you heard the news?

MRS CANDOUR: What, sir, do you mean the report of—

CRABTREE: No, Ma'am, that's not it.—Miss Nicely is going to be married to her own footman.

MRS CANDOUR: Impossible!

CRABTREE: Ask Sir Benjamin.

SIR BENJAMIN: 'Tis very true Ma'am—everything is fixed, and the wedding livery bespoke.

CRABTREE: Yes—and they *do* say there were pressing reasons for't.

LADY SNEERWELL: Why I have heard something of this before.

MRS CANDOUR: It can't be—and I wonder any one should believe such a story of so prudent a lady as Miss Nicely.

SIR BENJAMIN: O lud, ma'am! that's the very reason 'twas believed at once. She has always been so *cautious* and so *reserved* that everybody was sure there was some reason for it at bottom.

MRS CANDOUR: Why to be sure, a tale of scandal is as fatal to the credit of a prudent lady of her stamp as a fever is generally to those of the strongest constitutions; but there is a sort of puny, sickly reputation that is always ailing, yet will outlive the robuster characters of a hundred prudes.

SIR BENJAMIN: True Madam, there are valetudinarians in reputation as well as constitution, who being conscious of their weak part, avoid the least breath of air and supply their want to stamina by care and circumspection.

MRS CANDOUR: Well but this may be all a mistake. You know Sir Benjamin very trifling circumstances often give rise to the most injurious tales.

CRABTREE: That they do I'll be sworn Ma'am. Did you ever hear how Miss Piper came to lose her lover and her character last summer at Tunbridge?—Sir Benjamin, you remember it.

SIR BENJAMIN: O to be sure!—the most whimsical circumstance—

LADY SNEERWELL: How was it, pray?

CRABTREE: Why one evening at Mrs Ponto's assembly, the conversation happened to turn on the difficulty of breeding Nova-Scotia sheep in this country. Says a young lady in company, 'I have known instances of it for Miss Letitia Piper, a first cousin of mine, had a Nova-Scotia sheep that produced her twins.' 'What!' cries the old Dowager Lady Dundizzy (who you know is as deaf as a post), 'has Miss Piper had twins?'—this mistake, as you may imagine, threw the whole company into a fit of laughing—however, 'twas the next morning everywhere reported and in a few days believed by the whole town, that Miss Letitia Piper had actually been brought to bed of a fine boy and a girl—and in less than a week there were people who could name the father and the farm-house where the babies were put out to nurse!

LADY SNEERWELL: Strange, indeed!

CRABTREE: Matter of fact I assure you.—O lud! Mr Surface, pray is it true that your uncle, Sir Oliver, is coming home?

JOSEPH SURFACE: Not that I know of, indeed, sir.

CRABTREE: He has been in the East Indies a long time, you can scarcely remember him, I believe.—Sad comfort whenever he returns to hear how your brother has gone on!

JOSEPH SURFACE: Charles has been imprudent sir, to be sure, but I hope no busy people have already prejudiced Sir Oliver against him—he may reform.

SIR BENJAMIN: To be sure he may—for my part I never believed him to be so utterly void of principle as people say—and tho' he has lost all his friends, I am told nobody is better spoken of by the Jews.

CRABTREE: That's true, egad, nephew—if the Old Jewry were a ward I believe Charles would be an alderman, no man more popular there; 'fore gad, I hear he pays as many annuities as the Irish tontine, and that whenever he's sick, they have prayers for the recovery of his health in the Synagogue.

SIR BENJAMIN: Yet no man lives in greater splendour:—they tell me when he entertains his friends, he can sit down to dinner with a dozen of his own securities, have a score tradesmen waiting in the antechamber and an officer behind every guest's chair.

JOSEPH SURFACE: This may be entertainment to you gentlemen, but you pay very little regard to the feelings of a brother.

MARIA: Their malice is intolerable—Lady Sneerwell, I must wish you a good morning—I'm not very well. [Exit Maria]

MRS CANDOUR: O dear! she changes colour very much!

LADY SNEERWELL: Do, Mrs Candour, follow her—she may want assistance.

MRS CANDOUR: That I will with all my soul, Ma'am—poor dear girl! who knows what her situation may be! [Exit Mrs Candour]

LADY SNEERWELL: 'Twas nothing but that she could not bear to hear Charles reflected on, notwithstanding their difference.

SIR BENJAMIN: The young lady's *penchant* is obvious.

CRABTREE: But, Benjamin, you mustn't give up the pursuit for that—follow her, and put her into good humour—repeat her some of your own verses. Come, I'll assist you.

SIR BENJAMIN: Mr Surface, I did not mean to hurt you, but depend upon't your brother is utterly undone. [Going]

CRABTREE: O lud! aye—undone as ever man was—can't raise a guinea. [Going]

SIR BENJAMIN: Any everything sold, I'm told, that was movable. [Going]

CRABTREE: I have seen one that was at his house—not a thing left but some empty bottles that were overlooked, and the family pictures, which I believe are framed in the wainscot.— [Going]

SIR BENJAMIN: And I am very sorry to hear also some bad stories against him. [Going]

CRABTREE: O he has done many mean things, that's certain. [Going]

SIR BENJAMIN: But however, as he's your brother— [Going]

CRABTREE: We'll tell you all another opportunity.

[Exeunt Crabtree and Sir Benjamin]

LADY SNEERWELL: Ha! ha! ha! 'tis very hard for them to leave a subject they have not quite run down.

JOSEPH SURFACE: And I believe the abuse was no more acceptable to your ladyship than to Maria.

LADY SNEERWELL: I doubt her affections are farther engaged than we imagined; but the family are to be here this evening, so you may as well dine where you are and we shall have an opportunity of observing farther. In the meantime I'll go and plot mischief and you shall study sentiments. [*Exeunt*]

SCENE 2

Sir Peter Teazle's house

Enter Sir Peter

SIR PETER: When an old bachelor takes a young wife, what is he to expect?—'Tis now six months since Lady Teazle made me the happiest of men—and I have been the miserablest dog ever since that ever committed wedlock!—we tift a little going to church and came to a quarrel before the bells were done ringing. I was more than once nearly choked with gall during the honeymoon, and had lost all comfort in life before my friends had done wishing me joy!—yet I chose with caution—a girl bred wholly in the country, who never knew luxury beyond one silk gown, nor dissipation above the annual gala of a race-ball. Yet now she plays her part in all the extravagant fopperies of the fashion and the town with as ready a grace as if she had never seen a bush nor a grass-plot out of Grosvenor Square! I am sneered at by my old acquaintance—paragraphed in the newspapers. She dissipates my fortune, and contradicts all my humours—yet the worst of it is, I doubt I love her, or I should never bear all this. However, I'll never be weak enough to own it.

Enter Rowley

ROWLEY: Oh, Sir Peter, your servant,—how is it with you, sir?

SIR PETER: Very bad, Master Rowley, very bad—I meet with nothing but crosses and vexations.

ROWLEY: What can have happened to trouble you since yesterday?

SIR PETER: A good question to a married man!

ROWLEY: Nay I'm sure your lady, Sir Peter, can't be the cause of your uneasiness.

SIR PETER: Why, has anyone told you she was dead?

ROWLEY: Come, come, Sir Peter, you love her notwithstanding your tempers don't exactly agree.

SIR PETER: But the fault is entirely hers, Master Rowley—I am myself the sweetest-tempered man alive and hate a teasing temper—so I tell her a hundred times a day.

ROWLEY: Indeed!

SIR PETER: Aye and what is very extraordinary in all our disputes she is always in the wrong! but Lady Sneerwell and the set she meets at her house encourage the perverseness of her disposition. Then, to complete my vexations, Maria, my ward, whom I ought to have the power of a father over, is determined to turn rebel too, and absolutely refuses the man whom I have long resolved on for her husband—meaning I suppose to bestow herself on his profligate brother.

ROWLEY: You know, Sir Peter, I have always taken the liberty to differ with you on the subject of these two young gentlemen.—I only wish you may not be deceived in your opinion of the elder—for Charles, my life on't! he will retrieve his errors yet. Their worthy father, once my honoured master, was at his years nearly as wild a spark—yet when he died, he did not leave a more benevolent heart to lament his loss.

SIR PETER: You are wrong Master Rowley—on their father's death, you know, I acted as a kind of guardian to them both, till their uncle Sir Oliver's Eastern liberality gave them an early independence. Of course, no person could have more opportunities of judging of their hearts, and I was never mistaken in my life. Joseph is indeed a model for the young men of the age. He is a man of sentiment—and acts up to the sentiments he professes, but for the other, take my word for't, if he had any grains of virtue by descent, he has dissipated them with the rest of his inheritance. Ah! my old friend Sir Oliver will be deeply mortified when he finds how part of his bounty has been misapplied.

ROWLEY: I am sorry to find you so violent against the young man, because this may be the most critical period of his fortune.—I came hither with news that will surprise you.

SIR PETER: What! let me hear.

ROWLEY: Sir Oliver *is* arrived and at this moment in town.

SIR PETER: How!—you astonish me—I thought you did not expect him this month.—

ROWLEY: I did not: but his passage has been remarkably quick.

SIR PETER: Egad I shall rejoice to see my old friend—'tis sixteen years since we met—we have had many a day together; but does he still enjoin us not to inform his nephews of his arrival?

ROWLEY: Most strictly—he means before it is known to make some trial of their dispositions.

SIR PETER: Ah, there needs no art to discover their merits!—however, he shall have his way—but pray does he know I am married?

ROWLEY: Yes, and will soon wish you joy.

SIR PETER: What, as we drink health to a friend in a consumption! Ah! Oliver will laugh at me—we used to rail at matrimony together—but he has been steady to his text.—Well he must be at my house, tho'—I'll instantly give orders for his reception. But, Master Rowley, don't drop a word that Lady Teazle and I ever disagree.

ROWLEY: By no means.

SIR PETER: For I should never be able to stand Noll's jokes—so I'll have him think, Lord forgive me! that we are a very happy couple.

ROWLEY: I understand you—but then you must be very careful not to differ while he's in the house with you.

SIR PETER: Egad, and so we must—and that's impossible. Ah! Master Rowley, when an old bachelor marries a young wife, he deserves—no—the crime carries the punishment along with it. [*Exeunt*]

End of Act 1st.

ACT II

SCENE I

Sir Peter Teazle's house

> *Enter Sir Peter and Lady Teazle*

SIR PETER: Lady Teazle, Lady Teazle, I'll not bear it!

LADY TEAZLE: Sir Peter, Sir Peter, you may bear it or not, as you please, but I ought to have my own way in everything, and what's more, I *will* too—what! tho' I was educated in the country, I know very well that women of fashion in London are accountable to nobody after they are married.

SIR PETER: Very well, Ma'am, very well!—so a husband is to have no influence, no authority?

LADY TEAZLE: Authority! no, to be sure—if you wanted authority over me, you should have adopted me and not married me; I am sure you were old enough.

SIR PETER: Old enough!—aye there it is—well, well, Lady Teazle, tho' my life may be made unhappy by your temper, I'll not be ruined by your extravagance.

LADY TEAZLE: My extravagance—I'm sure I'm not more extravagant than a woman of fashion ought to be.

SIR PETER: No, no, Madam, you shall throw away no more sums on such unmeaning luxury. 'Slife! to spend as much to furnish your dressing-room with flowers in winter as would suffice to turn the Pantheon into a greenhouse and give a *fête champêtre* at Christmas!

LADY TEAZLE: Lord Sir Peter, am I to blame because flowers are dear in cold weather? You should find fault with the climate, and not with me. For my part, I am sure I wish it was spring all the year round, and that roses grew under one's feet!

SIR PETER: Oons! Madam—if you had been born to this, I shouldn't wonder at your talking thus.—But you forget what your situation was when I married you.

LADY TEAZLE: No, no, I don't—'twas a very disagreeable one, or I should never have married *you*.

SIR PETER: Yes, yes, Madam, you were then in somewhat an humbler style—the daughter of a plain country squire. Recollect, Lady Teazle, when I saw you first, sitting at your tambour in a pretty figured linen gown, with a bunch of keys by your side, your hair combed smooth over a roll, and your apartment hung with fruits in worsted, of your own working.

LADY TEAZLE: O yes, I remember it very well, and a curious life I led!——my daily occupation to inspect the dairy, superintend the poultry, make extracts from the family receipt-book, and comb my aunt Deborah's lap-dog.

SIR PETER: Yes, yes, Ma'am, 'twas so indeed.

LADY TEAZLE: And then, you know, my evening amusements——to draw patterns for ruffles which I had not the materials to make——to play Pope Joan with the curate——to read a novel to my aunt——or to be stuck down to an old spinet to strum my father to sleep after a fox-chase.

SIR PETER: I am glad you have a good memory. Yes, Madam, these were the recreations I took you from. But now you must have your coach, *vis-à-vis* and three powdered footmen before your chair——and in summer a pair of white cats to draw you to Kensington Gardens.——No recollection I suppose when you were content to ride double behind the butler on a docked coach-horse?

LADY TEAZLE: No——I swear I never did that——I deny the butler, and the coach-horse.

SIR PETER: This, Madam, was your situation——and what have I not done for you?——I have made you a woman of fashion, of fortune, of rank——in short I have made you my wife.

LADY TEAZLE: Well then, and there is but one thing more you can make me to add to the obligation——and that is——

SIR PETER: My widow I suppose?

LADY TEAZLE: Hem! hem!

SIR PETER: Thank you, Madam——but don't flatter yourself, for, tho' your ill-conduct may disturb my peace, it shall never break my heart I promise you: however, I am equally obliged to you for the hint.

LADY TEAZLE: Then why will you endeavour to make yourself so disagreeable to me, and thwart me in every little elegant expense?

SIR PETER: 'Slife Madame, I say, had you any of these elegant expenses when you married me?

LADY TEAZLE: Lud, Sir Peter! would you have me be out of fashion?

SIR PETER: The fashion, indeed——what had you to do with fashion before you married me?

LADY TEAZLE: For my part, I should think you would like to have your wife thought a woman of taste.

SIR PETER: Aye——there again——taste! Zounds! Madam, you had no taste when you married me!

LADY TEAZLE: That's very true, indeed, Sir Peter! and, *after* having married you, I am sure I should never pretend to taste again!——But now, Sir Peter, if we have finished our daily jangle, I presume I may go to my engagement at Lady Sneerwell's?

SIR PETER: Aye——there's another precious circumstance!——a charming set of acquaintance you have made there.

LADY TEAZLE: Nay, Sir Peter, they are people of rank and fortune, and remarkably tenacious of reputation.

SIR PETER: Yes, egad, they are tenacious of reputation with a vengeance for they don't choose anybody should have a character——but themselves! such a crew! ah! many a wretch had rid on a hurdle who has done less mischief than those utterers of forged tales, coiners of scandal,—and clippers of reputation.

LADY TEAZLE: What! would you restrain the freedom of speech?

SIR PETER: O! they have made you just as bad as any one of the society.

LADY TEAZLE: Why, I believe I do bear a part with a tolerable grace. But I vow I have no malice against the people I abuse; when I say an ill-natured thing 'tis out of pure humour—and I take it for granted they deal exactly in the same manner with me. But Sir Peter, you know you promised to come to Lady Sneerwell's too.

SIR PETER: Well, well, I'll call in just to look after my own character.

LADY TEAZLE: Then indeed, you must make haste after me or you'll be too late—so good-bye to ye.   [*Exit Lady Teazle*]

SIR PETER: So, I have gained much by my intended expostulations—yet with what a charming air she contradicts everything I say, and how pleasingly she shows her contempt of my authority! Well, tho' I can't make her love me, there is a great satisfaction in quarrelling with her, and I think she never appears to such advantage as when she's doing everything in her power to plague me.   [*Exit*]

SCENE 2

Lady Sneerwell's

Lady Sneerwell, Mrs Candour, Crabtree, Sir Benjamin Backbite, and Joseph Surface

LADY SNEERWELL: Nay, positively we will hear it.

JOSEPH SURFACE: Yes, yes the epigram by all means.

SIR BENJAMIN: Plague on't, uncle—'tis mere nonsense.

CRABTREE: No, no, 'fore gad, very clever for an extempore!

SIR BENJAMIN: But ladies, you should be acquainted with the circumstances.—You must know that one day last week, as Lady Betty Curricle was taking the dust in Hyde Park, in a sort of duodecimo phaëton she desired me to write some verses on her ponies, upon which I took out my pocket-book and in one moment produced the following:

> 'Sure never were seen two such beautiful ponies!
> Other horses are clowns—and these—macaronies!
> Nay, to give 'em this title I'm sure isn't wrong—
> —Their legs are so slim, and their tails are so long.'

CRABTREE: There ladies—done in the smack of a whip, and on horseback too!

JOSEPH SURFACE: A very Phoebus, mounted—indeed, Sir Benjamin.

SIR BENJAMIN: O dear sir—trifles—trifles.

Enter Lady Teazle and Maria

MRS CANDOUR: I must have a copy.

LADY SNEERWELL: Lady Teazle, I hope we shall see Sir Peter.

LADY TEAZLE: I believe he'll wait on your ladyship—presently.

LADY SNEERWELL: Maria my love, you look grave. Come, you shall sit down to cards with Mr Surface.

MARIA: I take very little pleasure in cards—however I'll do as your ladyship pleases.

LADY TEAZLE [*aside*]: I am surprised Mr Surface should sit down with *her*.—I thought he would have embraced this opportunity of speaking to me before Sir Peter came.

MRS CANDOUR [*coming forward*]: Now I'll die but you are so scandalous I'll forswear your society.

LADY TEAZLE: What's the matter, Mrs Candour?

MRS CANDOUR: They'll not allow our friend Miss Vermilion to be handsome.

LADY SNEERWELL: O surely she's a pretty woman.

CRABTREE: I am very glad you think so, Ma'am.

MRS CANDOUR: She has a charming fresh colour.

LADY TEAZLE: Yes, when it is fresh put on.

MRS CANDOUR: O fie! I'll swear her colour is natural—I have seen it come and go.

LADY TEAZLE: I dare swear you have, Ma'am—it goes of a night and comes again in the morning.

MRS CANDOUR: Ha! ha! ha! how I hate to hear you talk so! but surely now her sister is, or was, very handsome.

CRABTREE: Who? Mrs Evergreen?—O Lord, she's six-and-fifty if she's an hour!

MRS CANDOUR: Now positively you wrong her; fifty-two or fifty-three is the utmost—and I don't think she looks more.

SIR BENJAMIN: Ah! there is no judging by her looks unless one could see her face.

LADY SNEERWELL: Well, well, if Mrs Evergreen *does* take some pains to repair the ravages of time, you must allow she effects it with great ingenuity—and surely that's better than the careless manner in which the widow Ochre caulks her wrinkles.

SIR BENJAMIN: Nay, now Lady Sneerwell, you are severe upon the widow. Come, come, it is not that she paints so ill—but when she has finished her face, she joins it on so badly to her neck that she looks like a mended statue, in which the connoisseur sees at once that the head's modern tho' the trunk's antique.

CRABTREE: Ha! ha! ha! well, you make me laugh but I vow I hate you for't.—What do you think of Miss Simper?

SIR BENJAMIN: Why she has very pretty teeth.

LADY TEAZLE: Yes and on that account, when she is neither speaking nor laughing (which very seldom happens), she never absolutely shuts her mouth but leaves it always on a jar as it were.

MRS CANDOUR: How can you be so ill-natured?

LADY TEAZLE: Nay I allow even that's better than the pains Mrs Prim takes to conceal her losses in front. She draws her mouth till it positively resembles the aperture of a poor's-box, and all her words appear to slide out edgeways.

LADY SNEERWELL: Very well Lady Teazle I see you can be a little severe.

LADY TEAZLE: In defence of a friend it is but justice;—but here comes Sir Peter to spoil our pleasantry.

Enter Sir Peter Teazle

SIR PETER: Ladies your most obedient. [*aside*]—Mercy on me, here is the whole set! a character dead at every word I suppose.

MRS CANDOUR: I am rejoiced you are come, Sir Peter—They have been so censorious. They will allow good qualities to nobody—not even good nature to our friend Mrs Pursy.

LADY TEAZLE: What, the fat dowager, who was at Mrs Codille's last night?

MRS CANDOUR: Nay, her bulk is her misfortune and, when she takes such pains to get rid of it, you ought to reflect on her.

LADY SNEERWELL: That's very true indeed.

LADY TEAZLE: Yes, I know she almost lives on acids and small whey; laces herself by pulleys; and often, in the noon of summer, you may see her on a little squat pony with her hair plaited up behind like a drummer's, and puffing round the Ring on a full trot.

MRS CANDOUR: I thank you Lady Teazle for defending her.

SIR PETER: Yes, a good defence truly.

MRS CANDOUR: But Sir Benjamin is as censorious as Miss Sallow.

CRABTREE: Yes, and she is a curious being to pretend to be censorious!—an awkward gawky, without any one good point under heaven!

MRS CANDOUR: Positively you shall not be so very severe—Miss Sallow is a relation of mine by marriage and, as for her person, great allowance is to be made, for let me tell you a woman labours under many disadvantages who tries to pass for a girl at six-and-thirty.—

LADY SNEERWELL: Tho' surely she is handsome still—and for the weakness in her eyes, considering how much she reads by candle-light, it is not to be wondered at.

MRS CANDOUR: True, and then as to her manner, upon my word I think it is particularly graceful, considering she never had the least education;—for you know her mother was a Welsh milliner and her father a sugar-baker at Bristol.—

SIR BENJAMIN: Ah! you are both of you too good-natured!

SIR PETER [*aside*]: Yes, damned good-natured! this their own relation! mercy on me!

SIR BENJAMIN: And Mrs Candour is of so moral a turn, she can sit for an hour to hear Lady Stucco talk sentiment.

LADY TEAZLE: Nay, I vow Lady Stucco is very well with the dessert after dinner; for she's just like the French fruit one cracks for mottoes—made up of paint and proverb.—

MRS CANDOUR: Well, I never will join in ridiculing a friend and so I constantly tell my cousin Ogle, and you all know what pretensions she has to be critical in beauty.

CRABTREE: O to be sure! she has herself the oddest countenance that ever was seen; 'tis a collection of features from all the different countries of the globe.

SIR BENJAMIN: So she has indeed—an Irish front!

CRABTREE: Caledonian locks!

SIR BENJAMIN: Dutch nose!

CRABTREE: Austrian lip!

SIR BENJAMIN: Complexion of a Spaniard!

CRABTREE: And teeth *á la Chinoise*!

SIR BENJAMIN: In short her face resembles *a table d'hôte* at Spa, where no two guests are of a nation—

CRABTREE: Or a congress at the close of a general war—wherein all the members, even to her eyes, appear to have a different interest, and her nose and chin are the only parties likely to join issue.

MRS CANDOUR: Ha! ha! ha!

SIR PETER [*aside*]: Mercy on my life!—a person they dine with twice a week!

MRS CANDOUR: Nay but I vow you shall not carry the laugh off so—for give me leave to say that Mrs Ogle—

SIR PETER: Madam, madam, I beg your pardon. There's no stopping these gentlemen's tongues—but when I tell *you*, Mrs Candour, that the lady they are abusing is a particular friend of mine—I hope you'll not take her part.

LADY SNEERWELL: Well said, Sir Peter! but you are a cruel creature—too phlegmatic yourself for jest and too peevish to allow wit on others.

SIR PETER: Ah, Madam, true wit is more nearly allied to good nature than your ladyship is aware of.

LADY TEAZLE: True Sir Peter, I believe they are so near akin that they can never be united.

SIR BENJAMIN: Or rather, Madam, suppose them man and wife because one so seldom sees them together.

LADY TEAZLE: But Sir Peter is such an enemy to scandal, I believe he would have it put down by parliament.

SIR PETER: 'Fore heaven! Madam, if they were to consider the sporting with reputation of as much importance as poaching on manors, and pass *An Act for the Preservation of Fame*, I believe there are many would thank them for the bill.

LADY SNEERWELL: O lud! Sir Peter, would you deprive us of our privileges?

SIR PETER: Aye Madam, and then no person should be permitted to kill characters or run down reputations but qualified old maids, and disappointed widows.

LADY SNEERWELL: Go, you monster!

MRS CANDOUR: But sure you would not be quite so severe on those who only report what they hear.

SIR PETER: Yes Madam, I would have the law-merchant for them too, and in all cases of slander currency, whenever the drawer of the lie was not to be found, the injured party should have a right to come on any of the indorsers.

CRABTREE: Well, for my part I believe there never was a scandalous tale without some foundation.

LADY SNEERWELL: Come ladies, shall we sit down to cards in the next room?

Enter Servant and whispers Sir Peter

SIR PETER: I'll be with them directly.—[*Exit Servant*] [*aside*] I'll get away unperceived.

LADY SNEERWELL: Sir Peter, you are not leaving us?

SIR PETER: Your ladyship must excuse me—I'm called away by particular business— but I leave my character behind me.   [*Exit Sir Peter*]

SIR BENJAMIN: Well certainly, Lady Teazle, that lord of yours is a strange being— I could tell you some stories of him would make you laugh heartily, if he wasn't your husband.

LADY TEAZLE: O pray don't mind that—come, do let's hear them.

[*They join the rest of the company all taking as they are going into the next room*]

JOSEPH SURFACE [*rising with Maria*]: Maria, I see you have no satisfaction in this society.

MARIA: How is it possible that I should?—if to raise malicious smiles at the infirmities and misfortunes of those who have never injured us be the province of wit and humour, heaven grant me a double portion of dulness!

JOSEPH SURFACE: Yet they appear more ill-natured than they are. They have no malice at heart.

MARIA: Then is their conduct still more contemptible; for in my opinion, nothing could—excuse the intemperance of their tongues but a natural and ungovernable bitterness of mind.

JOSEPH SURFACE: But can you Maria, feel thus for others, and be unkind to me alone? Is hope to be denied the tenderest passion?

MARIA: Why will you distress me by renewing this subject?

JOSEPH SURFACE: Ah! Maria you would not treat me thus and oppose your guardian Sir Peter's wishes but that I see that profligate *Charles* is still a favoured rival.

MARIA: Ungenerously urged! but whatever my sentiments of that unfortunate young man are, be assured I shall not feel more bound to give him up because his distresses have lost him the regard even of a brother.

Lady Teazle returns

JOSEPH SURFACE: Nay but Maria, do not leave me with a frown—by all that's honest I swear—gad's life here's Lady Teazle. [*aside*]—You must not—no, you shall not— for tho' I have the greatest regard for Lady Teazle—

MARIA: Lady Teazle!

JOSEPH SURFACE: Yet were Sir Peter to suspect—

LADY TEAZLE [*coming forward*]: What's this pray? do you take her for me?—Child, you are wanted in the next room.—

[*Exit Maria*]

What is all this, pray?

JOSEPH SURFACE: O the most unlucky of circumstances in nature! Maria has somehow suspected the tender concern I have for your happiness, and threatened to acquaint Sir Peter with her suspicions, and I was just endeavouring to reason with her when you came.

LADY TEAZLE: Indeed!—but you seemed to adopt a very tender method of reasoning—do you *usually* argue on your knees?

JOSEPH SURFACE: O she's a child—and I thought a little bombast—but Lady Teazle, when are you to give me your judgment on my library as you promised?

LADY TEAZLE: No, no—I begin to think it would be imprudent, and you know I admit you as a lover no further than *fashion* requires.

JOSEPH SURFACE: True—a mere Platonic cicisbeo, what every London wife is *entitled* to.

LADY TEAZLE: Certainly one must not be out of fashion, however I have so much of my country prejudices left—that tho' Sir Peter's ill humour may vex me ever so, it never shall provoke me to—

JOSEPH SURFACE: The only revenge in your power—well I applaud your moderation.

LADY TEAZLE: Go—you are an insinuating wretch!—but we shall be missed—let us join the company.

JOSEPH SURFACE: But we had best not return together.

LADY TEAZLE: Well, don't stay—for Maria shan't come to hear any more of your reasoning I promise you. [*Exit Lady Teazle*]

JOSEPH SURFACE: A curious dilemma truly my politics have run me into.—I wanted at first only to ingratiate myself with Lady Teazle that she might not be my enemy with Maria—and I have I don't know how, become her serious lover. Sincerely I begin to wish I had never made such a point of gaining so *very good* character, for it has led me into so many cursed rogueries that I doubt I shall be exposed at last. [*Exit*]

SCENE 3

Sir Peter's

Enter Sir Oliver Surface and Rowley

SIR OLIVER: Ha! ha! ha! and so my old friend is married hey?—a young wife out of the country!—Ha! ha! ha! that he should have stood bluff to old bachelor so long and sink into a husband at last!

ROWLEY: But you must not rally him on the subject, Sir Oliver—'tis a tender point I assure you, tho' he has been married only seven months.

SIR OLIVER: Then he has been just half a year on the stool of repentance—poor Peter! but you say he has entirely given up Charles—never sees him, hey?

ROWLEY: His prejudice against him is astonishing—and I am sure greatly increased, by a jealousy of him with Lady Teazle, which he has been industriously led into, by a scandalous society—in the neighbourhood, who have contributed not a little to Charles's ill name; whereas the truth is I believe, if the lady is partial to either of them, his brother is the favourite.

SIR OLIVER: Aye—I know there are a set of malicious, prating, prudent gossips, both male and female, who murder characters to kill time and will rob a young fellow of his good name before he has years to know the value of it.—But I am not to be prejudiced against my nephew by such I promise you! No, no—if Charles has done nothing false or mean, I shall compound for his extravagance.

ROWLEY: Then my life on't, you will reclaim him. Ah sir, it gives me new life to find that *your* heart is not turned against him, and that the son of my good old master has one friend, however, left.

SIR OLIVER: What! shall I forget Master Rowley, when I was at his years myself—egad, my brother and I were neither of us very *prudent* youths—and yet I believe you have not seen many better men than your old master was.

ROWLEY: Sir, 'tis this reflection gives me assurance that Charles may yet be a credit to his family—but here comes Sir Peter.

SIR OLIVER: Egad, so he does.—Mercy on me! He's greatly altered, and seems to have a settled married look—one may read husband in his face at a distance!

Enter Sir Peter Teazle

SIR PETER: Hah! Sir Oliver—my old friend! Welcome to England a thousand times!

SIR OLIVER: Thank you, thank you, Sir Peter—and 'efaith I am glad as glad to find you well, believe me.

SIR PETER: Ah! 'tis a long time since we met—sixteen years I doubt, Sir Oliver, and many a cross accident in the time.

SIR OLIVER: Aye I have had my share—but what! I find you are married, hey, my old boy!—well, well, it can't be helped—and so I wish you joy with all my heart.

SIR PETER: Thank you, thank you, Sir Oliver—yes, I have entered the happy state—but we'll not talk of that now.

SIR OLIVER: True, true, Sir Peter—old friends should not begin on grievances at first meeting—no, no, no.

ROWLEY [*to Sir Oliver*]: Take care pray, sir.

SIR OLIVER: Well, so one of my nephews I find is a wild rogue, hey?

SIR PETER: Wild! ah! my old friend, I grieve for your disappointment there. He's a lost young man indeed—however his brother will make you amends; *Joseph* is indeed what a youth should be—everybody in the world speaks well of him.

SIR OLIVER: I am sorry to hear it—he has too good a character to be an honest fellow.—Everybody speaks well of him! Pshaw! then he has bowed as low to knaves and fools, as to the honest dignity of genius or virtue.

SIR PETER: What, Sir Oliver, do you blame him for not making enemies?

SIR OLIVER: Yes, if he has merit enough to deserve them.

SIR PETER: Well, well, you'll be convinced when you know him. 'Tis edification to hear him converse—he professes the noblest sentiments.

SIR OLIVER: Ah, plague on his sentiments!—if he salutes me with a scrap of morality in his mouth, I shall be sick directly.—But, however, don't mistake me Sir Peter, I don't mean to defend Charles's errors—but before I form my judgment of either of them, I intend to make a trial of their hearts—and my friend Rowley and I have planned something for the purpose.

ROWLEY: And Sir Peter shall own, he has been for once mistaken.

SIR PETER: O my life on Joseph's honour!

SIR OLIVER: Well, come, give us a bottle of good wine, and we'll drink the lads' healths and tell you our scheme.

SIR PETER: *Allons* then!

SIR OLIVER: And don't, Sir Peter, be so severe against your old friend's son. Odds my
life! I am not sorry that he has run out of the course a little—for my part I hate
to see prudence clinging to the green suckers of youth—'tis like ivy round a
sapling, and spoils the growth of the tree.   [*Exeunt*]

End of Act the Second.

ACT III

SCENE I

Sir Peter's

Sir Peter Teazle, Sir Oliver Surface, and Rowley

SIR PETER: Well then—we will see this fellow first and have our wine afterwards. But
how is this, Master Rowley? I don't see the jest of your scheme.

ROWLEY: Why sir, this Mr Stanley whom I was speaking of, is nearly related to them,
by their mother; he was once a merchant in Dublin, but has been ruined by a
series of undeserved misfortunes. He has applied by letter since his confinement
both to Mr *Surface* and *Charles*—from the former he has received nothing but evasive promises of future service, while Charles has done all that his extravagance has
left him power to do—and he is at this time endeavouring to raise a sum of money,
part of which, in the midst of his own distresses, I know he intends for the service of poor Stanley.

SIR OLIVER: Ah! he is my brother's son.

SIR PETER: Well, but how is Sir Oliver personally to—

ROWLEY: Why sir, I will inform Charles and his brother that Stanley has obtained permission to apply in person to his friends, and as they have neither of them ever
seen him let Sir Oliver assume his character, and he will have a fair opportunity of
judging at least of the benevolence of their dispositions, and believe me, sir, you
will find in the youngest brother one who, in the midst of folly and dissipation,
has still, as our immortal bard expresses it—

> 'a tear or pity, and a hand
> Opens as day, for melting charity.'

SIR PETER: Pshaw! what signifies his having an open hand or purse either when he has
nothing left to give!—well—well—make the trial if you please; but where is the
fellow whom you brought for Sir Oliver to examine relative to Charles's affairs?

ROWLEY: Below, waiting his commands, and no one can give him better intelligence.—This, Sir Oliver, is a friendly Jew who to do him justice, has done everything in his power to bring your nephew to a proper sense of his extravagance.

SIR PETER: Pray let us have him in.

ROWLEY: Desire Mr Moses to walk upstairs.

SIR PETER: But why should you suppose he will speak the truth?

ROWLEY: O, I have convinced him that he has no chance of recovering certain sums advanced to Charles, but thro' the bounty of Sir Oliver, who he knows is arrived; so that you may depend on his fidelity to his interest. I have also another evidence in my power, one Snake, whom I have detected in a matter little short of forgery, and shall shortly produce to remove some of your prejudices Sir Peter, relative to Charles and Lady Teazle.

SIR PETER: I have heard too much on that subject.

ROWLEY: Here comes the honest Israelite.

Enter Moses

—This is Sir Oliver.

SIR OLIVER: Sir, I—understand you have lately had great dealings with my nephew Charles.

MOSES: Yes Sir Oliver—I have done all I could for him, but he was ruined before he came to me for assistance.

SIR OLIVER: That was unlucky, truly—for you have had no opportunity of showing your talents.

MOSES: None at all—I hadn't the pleasure of knowing his distresses—till he was some thousands worse than nothing.

SIR OLIVER: Unfortunate indeed! but I suppose you have done all in your power for him, honest Moses?

MOSES: Yes, he knows that. This very evening I was to have brought him a gentleman from the city, who doesn't know him, and will I believe advance him some money.

SIR PETER: What, one Charles has never had money from before?

MOSES: Yes; Mr Premium, of Crutched Friars—formerly a broker.

SIR PETER: Egad Sir Oliver, a thought strikes me!—Charles, you say, doesn't know Mr Premium?

MOSES: Not at all.

SIR PETER: Now then Sir Oliver, you may have a better opportunity of satisfying your-self than by an old romancing tale of a poor relation;—go with my friend Moses and represent Mr *Premium*, and then I'll answer for't, you will see your nephew in all his glory.

SIR OLIVER: Egad, I like this idea better than the other, and I may visit Joseph after-wards, as old *Stanley.*

SIR PETER: True—so you may.

ROWLEY: Well, this is taking Charles rather at a disadvantage to be sure. However, Moses—you understand Sir Peter, and will be faithful.

MOSES: You may depend upon me—this is near the time I was to have gone.

SIR OLIVER: I'll accompany you as soon as you please, Moses; but hold! I have forgot one thing—how the plague shall I be able to pass for a Jew?

MOSES: There's no need—the principal is Christian.

SIR OLIVER: Is he?—I'm sorry to hear it—but then again, an't I rather too smartly dressed to look like a money-lender?

SIR PETER: Not at all; 'twould not be out of character, if you went in your own carriage—would it, Moses?

MOSES: Not in the least.

SIR OLIVER: Well but—how must I talk? there's certainly some cant of usury, and mode of treating, that I ought to know.

SIR PETER: Oh there's not much to learn—the great point as I take it, is to be exorbitant enough in your demands, hey, Moses?

MOSES: Yes, that's a very great point.

SIR OLIVER: I'll answer for't I'll not be wanting in that. I'll ask him eight or ten per cent on the loan at least.

MOSES: If you ask him no more than that, you'll be discovered immediately.

SIR OLIVER: Hey! what the plague! how much then?

MOSES: That depends upon the circumstances. If he appears not very anxious for the supply, you should require only forty or fifty per cent, but if you find him in great distress and want the moneys very bad—you may ask double.

SIR PETER: A good honest trade you're learning, Sir Oliver.

SIR OLIVER: Truly I think so—and not unprofitable.

MOSES: Then you know—you haven't the moneys yourself, but are forced to borrow them for him of a friend.

SIR OLIVER: O I borrow it of a friend, do I?

MOSES: Yes, and your friend is an unconscionable dog, but you can't help it.

SIR OLIVER: My friend is an unconscionable dog, is he?

MOSES: Yes, and he himself hasn't the moneys by him—but is forced to sell stock—at a great loss.

SIR OLIVER: He is forced to sell stock, is he, at a great loss, is he? Well, that's very kind of him.

SIR PETER: 'Efaith, Sir Oliver—Mr Premium, I mean—you'll soon be master of the trade. But Moses, wouldn't you have him run out a little against the Annuity Bill? that would be in character I should think.

MOSES: Very much.

ROWLEY: And lament that a young man now must be at years to discretion before he is suffered to ruin himself?

MOSES: Aye, great pity!

SIR PETER: And abuse—the public—for allowing merit to an act whose only object is to snatch misfortune and imprudence from the rapacious relief of usury! and give the minor a chance of inheriting his estate, without being undone by coming into possession.

SIR OLIVER: So, so—Moses shall give me further instructions as we go together.

SIR PETER: You will not have much time for your nephew lives hard by.

SIR OLIVER: O never fear! my tutor appears so able that tho' Charles lived in the next street, it must be my own fault if I am not a complete rogue before I turn the corner.

[*Exeunt Sir Oliver and Moses*]

SIR PETER: So—now I think Sir Oliver will be convinced;—you are partial Rowley, and would have prepared Charles for the other plot.

ROWLEY: No, upon my word, Sir Peter.

SIR PETER: Well, go bring me this Snake, and I'll hear what he has to say presently.— I see Maria, and want to speak with her.—

[*Exit Rowley*]

I should be glad to be convinced, my suspicions of Lady Teazle and Charles were unjust. I have never yet opened my mind on this subject to my friend *Joseph*—I'm determined I will do it—he will give me his opinion sincerely.

Enter Maria

So, child, has Mr Surface returned with you?

MARIA: No, sir—he was engaged.

SIR PETER: Well, Maria, do you not reflect the more you converse with that amiable young man, what return his partiality for you deserves?

MARIA: Indeed Sir Peter, your frequent importunity on this subject distresses me extremely—you compel me to declare that I know no man who has ever paid me a particular attention whom I would not prefer to Mr Surface.

SIR PETER: So!—here's perverseness! no, no, Maria, 'tis Charles only whom you would prefer—'tis evident his vices and follies have won your heart.

MARIA: This is unkind sir—you know I have obeyed you in neither seeing nor corresponding with him. I have heard enough to convince me that he is unworthy my regard—yet I cannot think it culpable, if while my understanding severely condemns his vices, my heart suggests some pity for his distresses.

SIR PETER: Well, well, pity him as much as you please but give your heart and hand— to a worthier object.

MARIA: Never to his brother!

SIR PETER: Go, perverse and obstinate! but take care Madam, you have never yet known what the authority of a guardian is—don't compel me to inform you of it.—

MARIA: I can only say you shall not have *just* reason. 'Tis true by my father's will I am for a short period bound to regard you as his substitute, but must cease to think you so when you would compel me to be miserable.   [*Exit Maria*]

SIR PETER: Was ever man so crossed as I am! everything conspiring to fret me!—I had not been involved in matrimony a fortnight before her father—hale and hearty man—died—on purpose I believe, for the pleasure of plaguing me with the care of his daughter. But here comes my helpmate!—She appears in great good humour.— How happy I should be if I could tease her into loving me tho' but a little.

Enter Lady Teazle

LADY TEAZLE: Lud! Sir Peter, I hope you haven't been quarrelling with Maria—it isn't using me well to be ill humoured when I am not by!

SIR PETER: Ah! Lady Teazle, you might have the power to make me good humoured at all times.

LADY TEAZLE: I am sure I wish I had—for I want you to be in charming sweet temper at this moment. Do be good humoured now, and let me have two hundred pounds, will you?

SIR PETER: Two hundred pounds! what, an't I to be in a good humour without paying for it!—but speak to me thus, and 'efaith there's nothing I could refuse you. You shall have it—but seal me a bond for the repayment.

LADY TEAZLE: O no—there—my note of hand will do as well.

SIR PETER [*kissing her hand*]: And you shall no longer reproach me with not giving you an independent settlement—I mean shortly to surprise you—but shall we always live thus, hey?

LADY TEAZLE: If you please I'm sure I don't care how soon we leave off quarrelling, provided you'll own you were tired first.

SIR PETER: Well—then let our future contest be, who shall be most obliging.

LADY TEAZLE: I assure you, Sir Peter, good nature becomes you. You look now as you did before we were married!—when you used to walk with me under the elms and tell me stories of what a gallant you were in your youth and chuck me under the chin—you would—and ask me if I thought I could love an old fellow who would deny me nothing—didn't you?

SIR PETER: Yes, yes, and you were as kind and attentive.

LADY TEAZLE: Aye so I was, and would always take your part when my acquaintance used to abuse you and turn you into ridicule.

SIR PETER: Indeed!

LADY TEAZLE: Aye, and when my cousin Sophy has called you a stiff, peevish old bachelor, and laughed at me for thinking of marrying one who might be my father, I have always defended you—and said I didn't think you so ugly by any means and that I dared say you'd make a very good sort of a husband.

SIR PETER: And you prophesied right—and we shall certainly now be the happiest couple—

LADY TEAZLE: And never differ again!

SIR PETER: No, never!—tho' at the same time indeed, my dear Lady Teazle, you must watch your temper very narrowly, for in all our little quarrels—my dear—if you recollect, my love, you always began first.

LADY TEAZLE: I beg your pardon sir, my dear Sir Peter, indeed you always gave the provocation.

SIR PETER: Now, see my—angel! take care—*contradicting* isn't the way to keep friends.

LADY TEAZLE: Then, don't *you* begin it, my love!

SIR PETER: There now—you—you are going on—you don't perceive, my life, that you are just doing the very thing which you know always makes me angry.

LADY TEAZLE: Nay, you know if you will be angry without any reason—

SIR PETER: There—now you want to quarrel again.

LADY TEAZLE: No, I am sure I don't—but if you will be so peevish—

SIR PETER: There—now who begins first?

LADY TEAZLE: Why you to be sure, I said nothing—but there's no bearing your temper.

SIR PETER: No, no, Madam, the fault's in your own temper.

LADY TEAZLE: Aye, you are just what my cousin Sophy said you would be.

SIR PETER: Your cousin Sophy is a forward, impertinent gipsy.

LADY TEAZLE: You are a great bear, I'm sure, to abuse my relations.

SIR PETER: Now may all the plagues of marriage be doubled on me if ever I try to be friends with you any more!

LADY TEAZLE: So much the better.

SIR PETER: No, no, Madam; 'tis evident you never cared a pin for me, and I was a madman to marry you—a pert rural coquette that had refused half the honest squires in the neighbourhood.

LADY TEAZLE: And I am sure I was a fool to marry you—and old dangling bachelor, who was single at fifty only because he never could meet with any one who would have him.

SIR PETER: Aye, aye, Madam, but you were pleased enough to listen to me—*you* never had such an offer before.

LADY TEAZLE: No! didn't I refuse Sir Twivy Tarrier, who everybody said would have been a better match—for his estate is just as good as yours—and he has broke his neck since we have been married!

SIR PETER: I have done with you Madam—you are an unfeeling ungrateful—but there's an end of everything. I believe you capable of anything that's bad—yes Madam I now believe the reports relative to you and Charles—Madam—yes madam, you and Charles—are not without grounds—

LADY TEAZLE: Take care Sir Peter—you had better not insinuate any such thing! I'll not be suspected *without cause* I promise you.

SIR PETER: Very—well Madam—very well—a separate maintenance as soon as you please. Yes, Madam, or a divorce—I'll make an example of myself for the benefit of all old bachelors. Let us separate, Madam.

LADY TEAZLE: Agreed—agreed—and now, my dear Sir Peter, we are of a mind once more, we may be the *happiest couple*, and *never differ* again you know; ha! ha!—well you are going to be in a passion I see, and I shall only interrupt you—so, bye! bye! [*Exit*]

SIR PETER: Plagues and tortures! can't I make her angry neither? O I am the miserablest fellow!—But I'll not bear her presuming to keep her temper—no, she may break my heart but she shan't keep her temper. [*Exit*]

SCENE 2

Charles's house

> *Enter Trip, Moses, and Sir Oliver Surface*

TRIP: Here, Master Moses! if you'll stay a moment, I'll try whether—what's the gentleman's name?

SIR OLIVER: Mr—. [*aside*] Moses, what *is* my name?

MOSES: Mr Premium.—

TRIP: Premium—very well. [*Exit Trip, taking snuff*]

SIR OLIVER: To judge by the servants, one wouldn't believe the master was ruined. But what!—sure, this was my brother's house?

MOSES: Yes sir; Mr Charles bought it of Mr Joseph with the furniture, pictures, &c., just as the old gentleman left it—Sir Peter thought it a great piece of extravagance in him.

SIR OLIVER: In my mind, the other's economy in *selling* it to him, was more reprehensible by half.

TRIP: My master says you must wait, gentlemen; he has company, and can't speak with you yet.

SIR OLIVER: If he knew *who* it was wanted to see him, perhaps he wouldn't have sent such a message?

TRIP: Yes, yes, sir, he knows you are here, I didn't forget little Premium—no, no, no.

SIR OLIVER: Very well—and pray sir, what may be your name?

TRIP: Trip, sir—my name is Trip, at your service.

SIR OLIVER: Well then, Mr Trip, you have a pleasant sort of place here I guess.

TRIP: Why yes—here are three or four of us pass our time agreeably enough—but when our wages are sometimes a little in arrear—and not very great either—but fifty pounds a year and find our own bags and bouquets.

SIR OLIVER [*aside*]: Bags and bouquets! halters and bastinadoes!

TRIP: But *à propos*, Moses, have you been able to get me that little bill discounted?

SIR OLIVER [*aside*]: Wants to raise money too!—mercy on me! has his distresses I warrant, like a lord—and affects creditors and duns!

MOSES: 'Twas not to be done indeed, Mr Trip. [*gives the note*]

TRIP: Good lack, you surprise me! My friend *Brush* has indorsed it and I thought when he put his mark on the back of a bill 'twas as good as cash.

MOSES: No, 'twouldn't do.

TRIP: A small sum—but twenty pounds. Hark'ee Moses, do you think you couldn't get it me by way of annuity?

SIR OLIVER [*aside*]: An annuity! ha! ha! ha! a footman raise money by way of annuity! Well done luxury, egad!

MOSES: But you must insure your place.

TRIP: Oh, with all my heart—I'll insure my place and my life too, if you please.

SIR OLIVER [*aside*]: It's more than I would your neck.

TRIP: But then, Moses, it must be done before this d——d register takes place—one wouldn't like to have one's name made public you know.

MOSES: No certainly, but is there nothing you could deposit?

TRIP: Why, nothing capital of my master's wardrobe has dropped lately—but I could give you a mortgage on some of his winter clothes with equity of redemption before November—or—you shall have the reversion—of the French velvet—or a post-obit on the blue and silver—these, I should think Moses, with a few pair of point ruffles as a collateral security—hey, my little fellow?

MOSES: Well, well. [*bell rings*]

TRIP: Gad, I heard the bell—I believe, gentlemen, I can now introduce you. Don't forget the annuity, little Moses; this way, gentlemen, insure my place! you know—

SIR OLIVER [*aside*]: If the man be a shadow of his master, this is the temple of dissipation indeed! [*Exeunt*]

SCENE 3

Charles [Surface], Careless, &c., &c. at a table with wine, &c.

CHARLES SURFACE: 'Fore heaven, 'tis true—there's the great degeneracy of the age. Many of our acquaintance have taste, spirit, and politeness—but plague on't, they won't drink.

CARELESS: It is so indeed, Charles—they give in to all the substantial luxuries of the table and abstain from nothing but wine and wit.

CHARLES SURFACE: Oh, certainly society suffers by it intolerably—for now, instead of the social spirit of raillery that used to mantle over a glass of bright Burgundy, their conversation is becoming just like the Spa-water they drink, which has all the pertness and flatulence of champagne without its spirit or flavour.

1 GENTLEMAN: But what are *they* to do who love play better than wine?

CARELESS: True—there's Harry diets himself for gaming and is now under a hazard regimen.

CHARLES SURFACE: Then he'll have the worst of it—what, you wouldn't train a horse for the course by keeping him from corn! For my part, egad, I am now never so successful as when I am a little—merry—let me throw on a bottle of champagne and I never lose—at least I never feel my losses which is exactly the same thing.

2 GENTLEMAN: Aye, that I believe.

CHARLES SURFACE: And then, what man can pretend to be a believer in love who is an abjurer of wine?—'Tis the test by which the lover knows his own heart—fill a dozen bumpers to a dozen beauties, and she that floats at top is the maid that has bewitched you.

CARELESS: Now then Charles, be honest and give us your real favourite.

CHARLES SURFACE: Why, I have withheld her only in compassion to you—if I toast her, you must give a round of her peers—which is impossible on earth!

CARELESS: Oh then we'll find some canonized vestals or heathen goddesses that will do, I warrant!

CHARLES SURFACE: Here then, bumpers, you rogues—bumpers! Maria—Maria— [*drink*]

1 GENTLEMAN: Maria who?

CHARLES SURFACE: O damn the surname! 'tis too formal to be registered in Love's calendar. But now Sir Toby Bumper, beware—we must have beauty superlative.

CARELESS: Nay, never study Sir Toby—we'll stand to toast, tho' your mistress should want an eye—and you know you have a song will excuse you.

SIR TOBY: Egad, so I have—and I'll give him the song instead of the lady.— [*sings*]

SONG AND CHORUS

Here's to the maiden of bashful fifteen,
Here's to the widow of fifty,
Here's to the flaunting extravagant quean,
And here's to the housewife that's thrifty.
Chorus. Let the toast pass—
Drink to the lass—
I'll warrant she'll prove an excuse for the glass!
Here's to the charmer whose dimples we prize!
Now to the maid who has none, sir,
Here's to the girl with a pair of blue eyes,
—And here's to the nymph with but one, sir!
Chorus. Let the toast pass, &c.
Here's to the maid with a bosom of snow,
Now to her that's as brown as a berry,
Here's to the wife with a face full of woe,
And now for the damsel that's merry.
Chorus. Let the toast pass, &c.
For let 'em be clumsy or let 'em be slim,
Young or ancient, I care not a feather,
—So fill a pint bumper quite up to the brim
—And let us e'en toast 'em together
Chorus. Let the toast pass, &c.

ALL: Bravo! Bravo!

Enter Trip, and whispers Charles Surface

CHARLES SURFACE: Gentlemen, you must excuse me a little. Careless, take the chair, will you?

CARELESS: Nay prithee, Charles, what now?—this is one of your peerless beauties, I suppose, has dropped in by chance.

CHARLES SURFACE: No—faith—to tell you the truth, 'tis a Jew, and a broker, who are come by appointment.

CARELESS: Oh damn it, let's have the Jew in—

1 GENTLEMAN: Aye, and the broker too by all means.

2 GENTLEMAN: Yes, yes, the Jew and the broker.

CHARLES SURFACE: Egad, with all my heart—Trip, bid the gentlemen walk in.—

[Exit Trip]

Tho' there's one of them a stranger I can tell you.

CARELESS: Charles, let us give them some generous Burgundy—and perhaps they'll grow conscientious.

CHARLES SURFACE: O hang 'em, no—wine does but draw forth a man's *natural* qualities; and to make *them* drink, would only be to whet their knavery.

Enter Trip, Sir Oliver Surface, and Moses

CHARLES SURFACE: So, honest Moses; walk in—walk in, pray, Mr Premium—that's the gentleman's name, isn't it, Moses?

MOSES: Yes, sir.

CHARLES SURFACE: Set chairs, Trip—sit down, Mr Premium. Glasses, Trip. Sit down, Moses.—Come Mr Premium, I'll give you a sentiment—here's 'Success to usury!'—Moses, fill the gentleman a bumper.

MOSES: Success to usury!

CARELESS: Right, Moses—usury is prudence and industry and deserves to succeed.

SIR OLIVER: Then here's—all the success it deserves!

CARELESS: No, no—that won't do, Mr Premium. You have demurred to the toast, and must drink it in a pint bumper.

1 GENTLEMAN: A pint bumper, at least.

MOSES: O pray, sir, consider—Mr Premium's a gentleman.

CARELESS: And therefore loves good wine.

2 GENTLEMAN: Give Moses a quart glass—this is mutiny, and a high contempt of the chair.

CARELESS: Here—now for't—I'll see justice done to the last drop of my bottle.

SIR OLIVER: Nay, pray, gentlemen—I did not expect this usage.

CHARLES SURFACE: No, hang it, Careless, you shan't: Mr Premium's a stranger.

SIR OLIVER [*aside*]: Odd! I wish I was well out of this company.

CARELESS: Plague on 'em then—if they won't drink, we'll not sit down with 'em; come, Harry, the dice are in the next room; Charles, you'll join us—when you have finished your business with these gentlemen—

CHARLES SURFACE: I will. I will.—   [*Exeunt*]
Careless!

CARELESS [*returning*]: Well—

CHARLES SURFACE: Perhaps I may want you.

CARELESS: O you know I am always ready—word, note, or bond, 'tis all the same to me.   [*Exit*]

MOSES: Sir, this is Mr Premium, a gentleman of the strictest honour and secrecy—and always performs what he undertakes. Mr Premium, this is—

CHARLES SURFACE: Pshaw! have done!—Sir, my friend Moses is a very honest fellow, but a little slow at expression; he'll be an hour giving us our titles. Mr Premium, the plain state of the matter is this—I am an extravagant fellow who wants money to borrow. You I take to be a prudent old fellow, who has got money to lend. I am blockhead enough to give you fifty per cent sooner than not have it, and you I presume are rogue enough to take a hundred if you could get it. Now, sir, you see we are acquainted at once, and may proceed to business without farther ceremony.

SIR OLIVER: Exceeding frank upon my word. I see, sir, you are not a man of many compliments.

CHARLES SURFACE: Oh no, sir—plain dealing in business I always think best.

SIR OLIVER: Sir, I like you the better for't. However you are mistaken in one thing—
I have no money to lend. But I believe I could procure some of a friend; but then
he's an unconscionable dog—isn't he, Moses? and must sell stock to accommodate
you—mustn't he, Moses?

MOSES: Yes, indeed!—you know I always speak the truth, and scorn to tell a lie!

CHARLES SURFACE: Right! People that expect truth generally do—but these are trifles,
Mr Premium.—What! I know money isn't to be bought without paying for't!

SIR OLIVER: Well, but what security could you give—you have no land I suppose?

CHARLES SURFACE: Not a mole-hill, nor a twig, but what's in beau-pots out at
the window.

SIR OLIVER: Nor any stock, I presume?

CHARLES SURFACE: Nothing but live stock—and that's only a few pointers and ponies.
But pray Mr Premium, are you acquainted at all with any of my connections?

SIR OLIVER: Why, to say truth I am.

CHARLES SURFACE: Then you must know that I have a devilish rich uncle in the East
Indies, Sir *Oliver Surface*, from whom I have the greatest expectations.

SIR OLIVER: That you have a wealthy uncle I have heard—but how your expectations
will turn out is more I believe than you can tell.

CHARLES SURFACE: O no—there can be no doubt of it—they tell me I'm a prodigious
favourite—and that he talks of leaving me everything.

SIR OLIVER: Indeed! this is the first I've heard on't.

CHARLES SURFACE: Yes, yes, 'tis just so. Moses knows 'tis true; don't you, Moses?

MOSES: Oh yes—I'll swear to't—

SIR OLIVER [*aside*]: Egad, they'll persuade me presently I'm at Bengal.

CHARLES SURFACE: Now I propose Mr Premium, if it's agreeable to you, to grant you
a post-obit on Sir Oliver's life, tho' at the same time the old fellow has been so liberal to me that I give you my word I should be very sorry to hear anything had
happened to him.

SIR OLIVER: Not more than *I* should I assure you. But the bond you mention happens
to be just the worst security you could offer me—for I might live to a hundred
and never recover the principal.

CHARLES SURFACE: O yes, you would—the moment Sir Oliver dies you know you'd
come on me for the money.

SIR OLIVER: Then I believe I should be the most unwelcome dun you ever had in
your life.

CHARLES SURFACE: What, I suppose you are afraid now that Sir Oliver is too good
a life.

SIR OLIVER: No, indeed I am not—tho' I have heard he is as hale and healthy as any
man of his years in Christendom.

CHARLES SURFACE: There again you are misinformed. No, no, the climate has hurt
him considerably—poor uncle Oliver—yes, he breaks apace, I'm told—and so
much altered lately that his nearest relations don't know him.

SIR OLIVER: No!—ha! ha! ha! so much altered lately that his relations don't know him!
Ha! ha! ha! that's droll, egad—ha! ha! ha!

CHARLES SURFACE: Ha! ha! you're glad to hear that, little Premium.

SIR OLIVER: No, no, I'm not.

CHARLES SURFACE: Yes, yes, you are—ha! ha! ha!—you know that mends your chance.

SIR OLIVER: But I'm told Sir Oliver is coming over—nay, some say he is actually arrived.

CHARLES SURFACE: Pshaw! sure I must know better than you whether he's come or not. No, no, rely on't, he is at this moment at Calcutta, isn't he Moses?

MOSES: Oh, yes, certainly.

SIR OLIVER: Very true, as you say, you must know better than I, tho' I have it from pretty good authority—haven't I, Moses?

MOSES: Yes, most undoubted!

SIR OLIVER: But, sir, as I understand you want a few hundreds immediately, is there nothing you would dispose of?

CHARLES SURFACE: How do you mean?

SIR OLIVER: For instance now—I have heard—that your father left behind him a great quantity of massy old plate.

CHARLES SURFACE: O lud, that's gone, long ago—Moses can tell you better than I can.

SIR OLIVER [*aside*]: Good lack! all the family race-cups and corporation-bowls!—[*aloud*]: then it was also supposed that his library was one of the most valuable and complete—

CHARLES SURFACE: Yes, yes, so it was—vastly too much so for a private gentleman—for my part I was always of a communicative disposition, so I thought it a shame to keep so much knowledge to myself.

SIR OLIVER [*aside*]: Mercy on me! learning that had run in the family like an heir-loom!—[*aloud*]: Pray, what are become of the books?

CHARLES SURFACE: You must inquire of the auctioneer, Master Premium, for I don't believe even Moses can direct you there.

MOSES: I never meddle with books.

SIR OLIVER: So, so, nothing of the family property left, I suppose?

CHARLES SURFACE: Not much indeed, unless you have a mind to the family pictures—I have got a room full of ancestors above—and if you have a taste for old paintings, egad, you shall have 'em a bargain.

SIR OLIVER: Hey! and the devil! sure, you wouldn't sell your forefathers, would you?

CHARLES SURFACE: Every man of 'em, to the best bidder.

SIR OLIVER: What! your great-uncles and aunts?

CHARLES SURFACE: Aye, and my great-grandfathers and grandmothers too.

SIR OLIVER [*aside*]: Now I give him up! [*aloud*]:—What the plague, have you no bowels for your own kindred?—Odds life—do you take me for Shylock in the play, that you would raise money of me, on your own flesh and blood?

CHARLES SURFACE: Nay, my little broker, don't be angry—what need you care, if you have your money's worth?

SIR OLIVER: Well, I'll be the purchaser—I think I can dispose of the family.—[*aside*]: Oh, I'll never forgive him—this—never!

Enter Careless

CARELESS: Come Charles, what keeps you?

CHARLES SURFACE: I can't come yet, 'efaith! we are going to have a sale above—here's little Premium will buy all my ancestors—

CARELESS: Oh, burn your ancestors!

CHARLES SURFACE: No, he may do that afterwards if he pleases. Stay, Careless, we want you; egad, you shall be auctioneer. So come along with us.

CARELESS: Oh, have with you, if that's the case.—I can handle a hammer as well as a dice box!

SIR OLIVER [*aside*]: Oh, the profligates!

CHARLES SURFACE: Come Moses, you shall be appraiser if we want one.—Gad's life, little Premium, you don't seem to like the business.

SIR OLIVER: Oh yes, I do vastly—ha! ha! yes, yes, I think it a rare joke to sell one's family by auction—ha! ha!—[*aside*]: Oh, the prodigal!

CHARLES SURFACE: To be sure! when a man wants money, where the plague should he get assistance, if he can't make free with his own relations? [*Exeunt*]

End of the third Act.

ACT IV

SCENE I

Picture-room at Charles's

Enter Charles Surface, Sir Oliver, Moses, and Careless

CHARLES SURFACE: Walk in, gentlemen, pray walk in!—here they are, the family of the Surfaces up to the Conquest.

SIR OLIVER: And, in my opinion a goodly collection.

CHARLES SURFACE: Aye, aye, these are done in true spirit of portrait-painting—no volunteer grace, or expression—not like the works of your modern Raphael, who gives you the strongest resemblance yet contrives to make your own portrait independent of you; so that you may sink the original and not hurt the picture. No, no the merit of these is the inveterate likeness—all stiff and awkward as the originals, and like nothing in human nature beside!

SIR OLIVER: Ah! we shall never see such figures of men again.

CHARLES SURFACE: No, I hope not. You see, Master Premium, what a domestic character I am—here I sit of an evening surrounded by my family. But come, get to your pulpit, Mr Auctioneer—here's an old gouty chair of my grandfather's—will answer the purpose.

CARELESS: Aye, aye, this will do—but, Charles, I have ne'er a hammer, and what's an auctioneer without his hammer?

CHARLES SURFACE: Egad, that's true. What parchment have we here? [*takes down a roll*] 'Richard heir to Thomas'—our genealogy in full! Here Careless, you shall have no common bit of mahogany—here's the family tree for you, you rogue—this shall be your hammer, and now you may knock down my ancestors with their own pedigree.

SIR OLIVER [*aside*]: What an unnatural rogue!—an *ex post facto* parricide!

CARELESS: Yes, yes, here's a list of your generation indeed.—Faith Charles, this is the most convenient thing you could have found for the business, for 'twill serve not only as a hammer, but a catalogue into the bargain.—But come, begin—a-going, a-going, a-going!—

CHARLES SURFACE: Bravo, Careless!—well, here's my great uncle Sir Richard Raviline, a marvellous good general in his day I assure you. He served in all the Duke of Marlborough's wars, and got that cut over his eye at the battle of Malplaquet. What say you, Mr Premium? look at him—there's a hero for you! not cut out of his feathers, as your modern clipped captains are—but enveloped in wig and regimentals—as a general should be. What do you bid?

MOSES: Mr Premium would have you speak.

CHARLES SURFACE: Why then, he shall have him for ten pounds and I am sure that's not dear for a staff-officer.

SIR OLIVER [*aside*]: Heaven deliver me! his famous uncle Richard for ten pounds!— [*aloud*] Very well, sir, I take him at that.

CHARLES SURFACE: Careless, knock down my uncle Richard.—Here now is a maiden sister of his, my great-aunt Deborah, done by Kneller, thought to be in his best manner, and a very formidable likeness. There she is, you see, a shepherdess feeding her flock. You shall have her for five pounds ten—the sheep are worth the money.

SIR OLIVER [*aside*]: Ah! poor Deborah! a woman who set such a value on herself?— [*aloud*] Five pound ten!—She's mine.

CHARLES SURFACE: Knock down my aunt Deborah! Here now are two that were a sort of cousins of theirs—you see, Moses, these pictures were done some time ago, when beaux wore wigs, and the ladies wore their own hair.

SIR OLIVER: Yes, truly, head-dresses appear to have been a little lower in those days.

CHARLES SURFACE: Well, take that couple for the same.

MOSES: 'Tis good bargain.

CHARLES SURFACE: Careless!—This now is a grandfather of my mother's, a learned judge, well known on the western circuit. What do you rate him at, Moses?

MOSES: Four guineas.

CHARLES SURFACE: Four guineas! Gad's life, you don't bid me the price of his wig! Mr Premium, *you* have more respect for the woolsack; do let us knock his lordship down at fifteen.

SIR OLIVER: By all means.

CARELESS: Gone.—

CHARLES SURFACE: And there are two brothers of his, William and Walter Blunt, Esquires, both members of Parliament and noted speakers, and what's very extraordinary, I believe this is the first time they were ever bought and sold.

SIR OLIVER: That's very extraordinary, indeed! I'll take them at your own price for the honour of Parliament.

CARELESS: Well said, little Premium—I'll knock 'em down at forty.

CHARLES SURFACE: Here's a jolly fellow—I don't know what relation, but he was mayor of Manchester; take him at eight pounds.

SIR OLIVER: No, no—six will do for the mayor.

CHARLES SURFACE: Come, make it guineas and I'll throw you the two aldermen there into the bargain.

SIR OLIVER: They're mine.

CHARLES SURFACE: Careless, knock down the mayor and aldermen. But, plague on't! we shall be all day—retailing in this manner. Do let us deal wholesale—what say you, little Premium? Give me three hundred pounds for the rest of the family in the lump.

CARELESS: Aye, aye, that will be the best way.—

SIR OLIVER: Well, well, anything to accommodate you; they are mine. But there is one portrait, which you have always passed over.

CARELESS: What, that ill-looking fellow over the settee?

SIR OLIVER: Yes sir, I mean that, tho' I don't think him so ill-looking a little fellow by any means.

CHARLES SURFACE: What, that? Oh that's my uncle Oliver, 'twas done before he went to India.

CARELESS: Your uncle Oliver! Gad! then you'll never be friends, Charles. That now, to me, is as stern a looking rogue as ever I saw—an unforgiving eye, and a damned disinheriting countenance! an inveterate knave, depend on't. Don't you think so, little Premium?

SIR OLIVER: Upon my soul sir, I do not; I think it is as honest a looking face as any in the room, dead or alive. But I suppose your uncle Oliver goes with the rest of the lumber?

CHARLES SURFACE: No, hang it, I'll not part with poor Noll. The old fellow has been very good to me, and egad, I'll keep his picture while I've a room to put it in.

SIR OLIVER [aside]: The rogue's my nephew after all!—[aloud]: But sir, I have somehow taken a fancy to that picture.

CHARLES SURFACE: I'm sorry for't, for you certainly will not have it. Oons! haven't you got enough of 'em?

SIR OLIVER [aside]: I forgive him everything!—[aloud]: But, sir, when I take a whim in my head I don't value money—I'll give you as much for that as for all the rest.

CHARLES SURFACE: Don't tease me, master broker; I tell you I'll not part with it, and there's an end on't.

SIR OLIVER [aside]: How like his father the dog is!—[aloud]: Well, well, I have done. [aside]—I did not perceive it before, but I think I never saw such a resemblance.— [aloud]: Well, sir—here is a draught for your sum.

CHARLES SURFACE: Why, 'tis for eight hundred pounds!

SIR OLIVER: You will not let Oliver go?

CHARLES SURFACE: Zounds! no! I tell you once more.

SIR OLIVER: Then never mind the difference; we'll balance another time, but give me your hand on the bargain—you are an honest fellow Charles—I beg pardon, sir, for being so free.—Come, Moses.

CHARLES SURFACE: Egad, this is a whimsical old fellow—but hark'ee, Premium, you'll prepare lodgings for these gentlemen.

SIR OLIVER: Yes, yes, I'll send for them in a day or two.

CHARLES SURFACE: But hold—do now—send a genteel conveyance for them, for I assure you they were most of them used to ride in their own carriages.

SIR OLIVER: I will, I will, for all but—Oliver.

CHARLES SURFACE: Aye all, but the little honest nabob.

SIR OLIVER: You're fixed on that—

CHARLES SURFACE: Peremptorily.

SIR OLIVER: A dear extravagant rogue!—Good day!—Come, Moses—let me hear now who dare call him profligate!

[*Exeunt Sir Oliver and Moses*]

CARELESS: Why, this is the oddest genius of the sort I ever saw!

CHARLES SURFACE: Egad, he's the prince of brokers I think. I wonder how the devil Moses got acquainted with so honest a fellow.—Ha! here's Rowley. Do, Careless, say I'll join the company in a moment.

CARELESS: I will—but don't now let that old blockhead persuade you to squander any of that money on old musty debts, or any such nonsense, for tradesmen, Charles, are the most exorbitant fellows!—

CHARLES SURFACE: Very true, and paying them is only encouraging them.

CARELESS: Nothing else.

CHARLES SURFACE: Aye, aye, never fear.—

[*Exit Careless*]

So—this was an odd old fellow indeed! Let me see, two-thirds of this is mine by right—five hundred and thirty pounds. 'Fore heaven! I find one's ancestors are more valuable relations than I took 'em for!—Ladies and gentlemen, your most obedient and very grateful humble servant.

Enter Rowley

Ha! Old Rowley, egad, you are just come in time to take leave of your old acquaintance.

ROWLEY: Yes, I heard they were going—but I wonder you can have such spirits under so many distresses.

CHARLES SURFACE: Why there's the point—my distresses are so many that I can't afford to part with my spirits, but I shall be rich and splenetic all in good time. However I suppose you are surprised that I am not more sorrowful at parting with so many near relations; to be sure, 'tis very affecting—but rot 'em, you see they never move a muscle, so why should I?

ROWLEY: There's no making you serious a moment.

CHARLES SURFACE: Yes faith: I am so now—here, my honest Rowley, here, get me this changed and take a hundred pounds of it immediately to old Stanley.

ROWLEY: A hundred pounds! Consider only——

CHARLES SURFACE: Gad's life, don't talk about it! poor Stanley's wants are pressing—and if you don't make haste, we shall have someone call that has a better right to the money.

ROWLEY: Ah! there's the point—I never will cease dunning you with the old proverb—

CHARLES SURFACE: 'Be *just* before you're *generous*,' hey!—why, so I would if I could—but Justice is an old lame hobbling beldame and I can't get her to keep pace with Generosity, for the soul of me.

ROWLEY: Yet, Charles, believe me, one hour's reflection—

CHARLES SURFACE: Aye, aye, it's all very true—but hark'ee, Rowley, while I have, by heaven I'll give—so damn your economy and now for hazard.

SCENE 2

The Parlour

Enter Sir Oliver Surface and Moses

MOSES: Well sir, I think as Sir Peter said, you have seen Mr Charles in high glory.—'Tis great pity he's so extravagant.

SIR OLIVER: True, but he wouldn't sell my picture.

MOSES: And loves wine and women so much.

SIR OLIVER: But he wouldn't sell my picture.

MOSES: And game[s] so deep.

SIR OLIVER: But he wouldn't sell my picture, O, here's Rowley.

Enter Rowley

ROWLEY: So, Sir Oliver, I find you have made a purchase.

SIR OLIVER: Yes, yes, our young rake has parted with his ancestors like old tapestry.

ROWLEY: And here has he commissioned me to redeliver you part of the purchase-money—I mean, tho', in your necessitous character of old *Stanley*.

MOSES: Ah! there is the pity of all! he is so damned charitable.

ROWLEY: And I left a hosier and two tailors in the hall, who I'm sure won't be paid, and this hundred—would satisfy 'em.

SIR OLIVER: Well, well, I'll pay his debts—and his benevolence too; but now I am no more a broker and you shall introduce me to the elder brother as old Stanley.—

ROWLEY: Not yet awhile; Sir Peter I know means to call there about this time.

Enter Trip

TRIP: O gentlemen I beg pardon for not showing you out—this way—Moses, a word.

[*Exeunt Trip and Moses*]

SIR OLIVER: There's a fellow for you!—would you believe it, that puppy intercepted the Jew on our coming and wanted to raise money before he got to his master!

ROWLEY: Indeed!

SIR OLIVER: Yes, they are now planning an annuity business. Ah! Master Rowley, in my day, servants were content with the follies of their masters when they were worn a little threadbare—but now they have their vices like their birthday clothes with the gloss on. [*Exeunt*]

SCENE 3

A library

Joseph Surface and Servant

JOSEPH SURFACE: No letter from Lady Teazle?

SERVANT: No, sir.

JOSEPH SURFACE [*aside*]: I am surprised she hasn't sent if she is prevented from coming! Sir Peter certainly does not suspect me—yet I wish I may not lose the heiress thro' the scrape I have drawn myself in with the wife. However, Charles's imprudence and bad character are great points in my favour. [*knocking*]

SERVANT: Sir, I believe that must be Lady Teazle.

JOSEPH SURFACE: Hold! see—whether it is or not before you go to the door—I have a particular message for you if it should be my brother.

SERVANT: 'Tis her ladyship, sir. She always leaves her chair at the milliner's in the next street.

JOSEPH SURFACE: Stay, stay—draw that screen before the window—that will do—my opposite neighbour is a maiden lady of so curious a temper—[*Servant draws the screen and exit*] I have a difficult hand to play in this affair. Lady Teazle has lately suspected my views on Maria—but she must by no means be let into that secret, at least not till I have her more in my power.

Enter Lady Teazle

LADY TEAZLE: What sentiment in soliloquy! have you been very impatient now?— O lud! don't pretend to look grave. I vow I couldn't come before.

JOSEPH SURFACE: O madam, punctuality is a species of constancy, a very unfashionable quality in a lady.

LADY TEAZLE: Upon my word you ought to pity me. Do you know that Sir Peter is grown so ill-tempered to me of late! and so jealous of *Charles* too—that's the best of the story, isn't it?

JOSEPH SURFACE [*aside*]: I am glad my scandalous friends keep that up.

LADY TEAZLE: I am sure I wish he would let Maria marry him, and then perhaps he would be convinced, don't you Mr Surface?

JOSEPH SURFACE [*aside*]: Indeed I do not. [*aloud*]:—Oh, certainly I do—for then my dear Lady Teazle would also be convinced how wrong her suspicions were of my having any designs on the silly girl.

LADY TEAZLE: Well, well, I'm inclined to believe you. But isn't it provoking to have the most ill-natured things said to one? And there's my friend lady Sneerwell has circulated I don't know how many scandalous tales of me! and all without any foundation too—that's what vexes me.

JOSEPH SURFACE: Aye madam, to be sure that *is* the provoking circumstance—without foundation! yes, yes, there's the mortification, indeed—for when a scandalous story is believed against one, there certainly is no comfort like the consciousness of having deserved it.

LADY TEAZLE: No, to be sure—then I'd forgive their malice—but to attack me, who am really so innocent, and who never say an ill-natured thing of anybody—that is, of any friend—and then Sir Peter too—to have him so peevish, and so suspicious, when I know the integrity of my own heart—indeed 'tis monstrous!

JOSEPH SURFACE: But my dear Lady Teazle, 'tis your own fault if you suffer it—when a husband entertains a groundless suspicion of his wife and withdraws his confidence from her, the original compact is broke and she owes it to the honour of her sex to endeavour to outwit him.

LADY TEAZLE: Indeed! so that if he suspects me without cause, it follows that the best way of curing his jealousy is to give him reason for't.

JOSEPH SURFACE: Undoubtedly—for your husband should never be deceived in you, and in that case it becomes you to be frail in compliment to *his* discernment.

LADY TEAZLE: To be sure what you say is very reasonable, and when the consciousness of my own innocence—

JOSEPH SURFACE: Ah, my dear madam, there is the great mistake—'tis this very conscious innocence that is of the greatest prejudice to you. What is it makes you negligent of forms and careless of the world's opinion? why, the *consciousness* of your innocence. What makes you thoughtless in your conduct and apt to run into a thousand little imprudences? why, the *consciousness* of your innocence. What makes you impatient of Sir Peter's temper and outrageous at his suspicions? why, the *consciousness* of your own innocence.

LADY TEAZLE: 'Tis very true.

JOSEPH SURFACE: Now my dear Lady Teazle, if you would but once make a trifling *faux pas*, you can't conceive how cautious you would grow—and how ready to humour and agree with your husband.

LADY TEAZLE: Do you think so?

JOSEPH SURFACE: Oh, I'm sure on't—and then you would find all scandal would cease at once, for in short, your character at present is like a person in a plethora, absolutely dying of too much health.

LADY TEAZLE: So, so—then I perceive your prescription is that I must sin in my own defence—and part with my virtue to preserve my reputation.

JOSEPH SURFACE: Exactly so upon my credit, ma'am.

LADY TEAZLE: Well, certainly this is the oddest doctrine, and the newest receipt for avoiding calumny.

JOSEPH SURFACE: An infallible one, believe me. *Prudence*, like *experience*, must be paid for.

LADY TEAZLE: Why, if my understanding were once convinced—

JOSEPH SURFACE: Oh certainly, Madam, your understanding *should* be convinced— yes, yes—heaven forbid I should persuade you to do anything you *thought* wrong. No, no, I have too much honour to desire it.

LADY TEAZLE: Don't you think we may as well leave honour out of the argument?

JOSEPH SURFACE: Ah, the ill effects of your country education I see, still remain with you.

LADY TEAZLE: I doubt they do, indeed—and I will fairly own to you, that if I could be persuaded to do wrong, it would be by Sir Peter's ill-usage sooner than your honourable logic, after all.

JOSEPH SURFACE: Then by this hand which he is unworthy of—

Enter Servant

'Sdeath, you blockhead—what do you want?

SERVANT: I beg pardon, sir, but I thought you wouldn't choose Sir Peter to come up without announcing him.

JOSEPH SURFACE: Sir Peter!—Oons and the devil!

LADY TEAZLE: Sir Peter! O lud! I'm ruined! I'm ruined!

SERVANT: Sir, 'twasn't I let him in.

LADY TEAZLE: O I'm undone—what will become of me now Mr Logic?—O mercy, he's on the stairs—I'll get behind here—and if ever I'm so imprudent again—

[goes behind the screen]

JOSEPH SURFACE: Give me that book. *[sits down. Servant pretends to adjust his hair]*

Enter Sir Peter Teazle

SIR PETER: Aye, ever improving himself!—Mr Surface, Mr Surface!—

JOSEPH SURFACE: Oh my dear Sir Peter, I beg your pardon. *[gaping and throws away the book]* I have been dozing over a stupid book! well, I am much obliged to you for this call—you haven't been here I believe since I fitted up this room. Books you know are the only things I am a coxcomb in.

SIR PETER: 'Tis very neat indeed. Well, well, that's proper—and you make even your screen a source of knowledge—hung, I perceive, with maps.

JOSEPH SURFACE: Oh yes, I find great use in that screen.

SIR PETER: I dare say you must—certainly—when you want to find anything in a hurry.

JOSEPH SURFACE *[aside]*: Aye, or to hide anything in a hurry either.

SIR PETER: Well, I have a little private business—

JOSEPH SURFACE *[to Servant]*: You needn't stay.

SERVANT: No, Sir. *[Exit]*

JOSEPH SURFACE: Here's a chair, Sir Peter—I beg—

SIR PETER: Well, now we are alone, there is a subject, my dear friend, on which I wish to unburden my mind to you—a point of the greatest moment to my peace; in short, my good friend, Lady Teazle's conduct of late has made me extremely unhappy.

JOSEPH SURFACE: Indeed! I am very sorry to hear it.

SIR PETER: Yes, 'tis but too plain she has not the least regard for me—but what's worse, I have pretty good authority to suspect she must have formed an attachment to another.

JOSEPH SURFACE: You astonish me!

SIR PETER: Yes—and, between ourselves—I think I have discovered the person.

JOSEPH SURFACE: How, you alarm me exceedingly!

SIR PETER: Ah! my dear friend, I knew you would sympathize with me.

JOSEPH SURFACE: Yes, believe me, Sir Peter, such a discovery would hurt me just as much as it would you.

SIR PETER: I am convinced of it—ah! it is a happiness to have a friend whom one can trust even with one's family secrets. But have you no guess who I mean?

JOSEPH SURFACE: I haven't the most distant idea—it can't be Sir Benjamin Backbite!

SIR PETER: O no! What say you to Charles?

JOSEPH SURFACE: My brother! impossible!—

SIR PETER: Ah! my dear friend—the goodness of your own heart misleads you—you judge of others by yourself.

JOSEPH SURFACE: Certainly Sir Peter, the heart that is conscious of its own integrity is ever slow to credit another's treachery.

SIR PETER: True—but your brother has no sentiment—you never hear him talk so.

JOSEPH SURFACE: Yet I can't but think Lady Teazle herself has too much principle—

SIR PETER: Aye, but what's her principle—against the flattery of a handsome, lively young fellow?

JOSEPH SURFACE: That's very true.

SIR PETER: And then you know the difference of our ages makes it very improbable that she should have a great affection for me—and if she were to be frail and I were to make it public, why the town would only laugh at me, the foolish old bachelor who had married a girl.

JOSEPH SURFACE: That's true, to be sure—they *would* laugh.

SIR PETER: Laugh! aye—and make ballads—and paragraphs—and the devil knows what of me.

JOSEPH SURFACE: No, you must never make it public.

SIR PETER: But then again—that the nephew of my old friend, Sir Oliver, should be the person to attempt such a wrong, hurts me more nearly.

JOSEPH SURFACE: Aye there's the point; when ingratitude barbs the dart of injury, the wound has double danger in it.

SIR PETER: Aye, I that was in a manner left his guardian—in whose house he had been so often entertained—who never in my life denied him my advice.

JOSEPH SURFACE: O 'tis not to be credited! There *may* be a man capable of such baseness to be sure, but for my part, till you can give me positive proofs, I cannot but doubt it.—However, if this should be proved on him, he is no longer a brother of mine! I disclaim kindred with him—for the man who can break thro' the laws of hospitality—and attempt the wife—of his friend, deserves to be branded as the pest of society.

SIR PETER: What a difference there is between you! What noble sentiments!

JOSEPH SURFACE: Yet I cannot suspect Lady Teazle's honour.

SIR PETER: I am sure I wish to think well of her—and to remove all ground of quarrel between us. She has lately reproached me more than once, with having made no settlement on her—and in our last quarrel she almost hinted that she should not break her heart if I was dead. Now as we seem to differ in our ideas of expense, I have resolved she shall be her own mistress in that respect for the future—and if I *were* to die, she shall find that I have not been inattentive to her interest while living. Here my friend, are the drafts of two deeds, which I wish to have your opinion on. By one, she will enjoy eight hundred a year independent while I live and by the other, the bulk of my fortune after my death.

JOSEPH SURFACE: This conduct, Sir Peter, is indeed truly generous.—[*aside*]: I wish it may not corrupt my pupil.

SIR PETER: Yes, I am determined she shall have no cause to complain, tho' I would not have her acquainted with the latter instance of my affection yet awhile.

JOSEPH SURFACE [*aside*]: Nor I, if I could help it.

SIR PETER: And now my dear friend, if you please we will talk over the situation of your hopes with *Maria*.

JOSEPH SURFACE [*softly*]: No, no, Sir Peter; another time if you please.

SIR PETER: I am sensibly chagrined at the little progress you seem to make in her affection.

JOSEPH SURFACE: I beg you will not mention it—[*softly*]: what are my disappointments when your happiness is in debate!—'[*aside*]: Sdeath, I should be ruined every way!

SIR PETER: And tho' you are so averse to my acquainting Lady Teazle with your passion, I am sure she's not your enemy in the affair.

JOSEPH SURFACE: Pray Sir Peter, now oblige me.—I am really too much affected by the subject we have been speaking on to bestow a thought on my own concerns. The man who is entrusted with his friend's distresses can never—

> *Enter Servant*

Well, Sir?

SERVANT: Your brother, sir, is speaking to a gentleman in the street, and says he knows you are within.

JOSEPH SURFACE: 'Sdeath, blockhead—I'm not within—I'm out for the day.

SIR PETER: Stay—hold—a thought has struck me—you shall be at home.

JOSEPH SURFACE: Well, well, let him up.—   [*Exit Servant*]
He'll interrupt Sir Peter—however—

SIR PETER: Now my good friend, oblige me I entreat you. Before Charles comes, let me conceal myself somewhere. Then do you tax him on the point we have been talking on, and his answers may satisfy me at once.

JOSEPH SURFACE: O fie, Sir Peter—would you have me join in so mean a trick—to trepan my brother to—!

SIR PETER: Nay, you tell me you are *sure* he is innocent—if so, you do him the greatest service by giving him an opportunity to clear himself, and, you will set my heart at rest. Come, you shall not refuse me—here behind this screen will be [*goes to the screen*]—hey! what the devil! there seems to be *one* listener here already—I'll swear I saw a petticoat.

JOSEPH SURFACE: Ha! ha! ha!—well, this is ridiculous enough. I'll tell you, Sir Peter, tho' I hold a man of intrigue to be a most despicable character, yet you know it doesn't follow that one is to be an absolute Joseph either! Hark'ee! 'tis a little French milliner, a silly rogue that plagues me—and having some character—on your coming she ran behind the screen.

SIR PETER: Ah, you rogue!—but egad, she has overheard all I have been saying of my wife.

JOSEPH SURFACE: O 'twill never go any further, you may depend on't!

SIR PETER: No!—then 'efaith, let her hear it out.—Here's a closet will do as well.

JOSEPH SURFACE: Well, go in then.

SIR PETER: Sly rogue! sly rogue! *[goes into the closet]*

JOSEPH SURFACE: A very narrow escape, indeed! and a curious situation I'm in, to part a man and wife in this manner.

LADY TEAZLE [*peeping from the screen*]: Couldn't I steal off?

JOSEPH SURFACE: Keep close, my angel—

SIR PETER [*peeping out*]: Joseph, tax him home!—

JOSEPH SURFACE: Back, my dear friend!

LADY TEAZLE [*peeping*]: Couldn't you lock Sir Peter in?

JOSEPH SURFACE: Be still, my life—

SIR PETER [*peeping*]: You're sure the little milliner won't blab?

JOSEPH SURFACE: In! in!—my good Sir Peter—'fore gad, I wish I had a key to the door.

Enter Charles Surface

CHARLES SURFACE: Hallo! brother, what has been the matter? Your fellow would not let me up at first. What, have you had a Jew or a wench with you?

JOSEPH SURFACE: Neither brother, I assure you.

CHARLES SURFACE: But—what has made Sir Peter steal off? I thought he had been with you.

JOSEPH SURFACE: He was, brother—but, hearing *you* were coming he did not choose to stay.

CHARLES SURFACE: What, was the old gentleman afraid I wanted to borrow money of him!

JOSEPH SURFACE: No, sir—but I am sorry to find Charles that you have lately given that worthy man grounds for great uneasiness.

CHARLES SURFACE: Yes, they tell me I do that to a great many worthy men. But how so, pray?

JOSEPH SURFACE: To be plain with you, brother, he thinks you are endeavouring to gain Lady Teazle's affections from him.

CHARLES SURFACE: Who, I! O lud! not I, upon my word.—Ha! ha! ha! so the old fellow has found out that he has got a young wife, has he?—or what's worse, has her ladyship discovered that she has an old husband?

JOSEPH SURFACE: This is no subject to jest on, brother.—He who can laugh—

CHARLES SURFACE: True, true, brother, as you were going to say—then seriously, I never had the least idea of what you—charge me with, upon my honour.

JOSEPH SURFACE [*aloud*]: Well, it will give Sir Peter great satisfaction to hear this.

CHARLES SURFACE: To be sure I once thought the lady seemed to have taken a fancy to me—but upon my soul, I never gave her the least encouragement.—Besides, you know my attachment to Maria.

JOSEPH SURFACE: But sure, brother, even if Lady Teazle had betrayed the fondest partiality for you—

CHARLES SURFACE: Why, look'ee, Joseph, I hope I shall never deliberately do a dishonourable action—but if a pretty woman were purposely to throw herself in my way—and that pretty woman married to a man old enough to be her father—

JOSEPH SURFACE: Well!—

CHARLES SURFACE: Why, I believe I should be obliged to borrow a little of your morality, that's all.—But brother, do you know now that you surprise me exceedingly, by naming *me* with Lady Teazle—for faith, I alway[s] understood you were her favourite.

JOSEPH SURFACE: O, for shame, Charles—this retort is foolish.

CHARLES SURFACE: Nay, I swear I have seen you exchange such significant glances—

JOSEPH SURFACE: Nay, nay, sir this is no jest—

CHARLES SURFACE: Egad, I'm serious! don't you remember—one day when I called here—

JOSEPH SURFACE: Nay, prithee, Charles—

CHARLES SURFACE: And found you together—

JOSEPH SURFACE: Zounds, sir, I insist—

CHARLES SURFACE: And another time when your servant—

JOSEPH SURFACE: Brother, brother, a world with you!—[*aside*]: Gad, I must stop him.

CHARLES SURFACE: Informed me, I say, that—

JOSEPH SURFACE: Hush!—I beg your pardon, but Sir Peter has overheard all we have been saying—I knew you would clear yourself or I should not have consented.

CHARLES SURFACE: How, Sir Peter!—where is he?

JOSEPH SURFACE: Softly, there! [*points to the closet*]

CHARLES SURFACE: Oh, 'fore heaven, I'll have him out.—Sir Peter, come forth—

JOSEPH SURFACE: No, no—

CHARLES SURFACE: I say, Sir Peter, come into court.—[*pulls in Sir Peter*] What, my old guardian!—What—turn inquisitor and take evidence incog.?

SIR PETER: Give me your hand, Charles—I believe I have suspected you wrongfully—but you mustn't be angry with Joseph—'twas my plan.

CHARLES SURFACE: Indeed!—

SIR PETER: But I acquit you.—I promise you I don't think near so ill of you as I did. What I have heard has given me great satisfaction.

CHARLES SURFACE [*half aside*]: Egad then, 'twas lucky you didn't hear any more—wasn't it, Joseph?

SIR PETER: Ah! you would have retorted on him.

CHARLES SURFACE: Aye, aye, that was a joke.

SIR PETER: Yes, yes, I know his honour too well.

CHARLES SURFACE [*half aside*]: But you might as well have suspected him as me in this matter, for all that. Mightn't he, Joseph?

SIR PETER: Well, well, I believe you.

JOSEPH SURFACE [*aside*]: Would they were both out of the room!

Enter Servant who whispers Joseph Surface

JOSEPH SURFACE: Lady Sneerwell!—stop her by all means—[*Exit Servant*] Gentlemen—I beg your pardon—I must wait on you downstairs—here's a person come on particular business.

CHARLES SURFACE: Well, you can see him in another room. Sir Peter and I haven't met a long time, and I have something to say to him.

JOSEPH SURFACE: They must not be left together.—I'll send Lady Sneerwell away, and return directly. [*aside*]—Sir Peter, not a word of the French milliner.

[*Exit Joseph Surface*]

SIR PETER: O not for the world!—Ah, Charles, if you associated more with your brother, one might indeed hope for your reformation. He is a man of sentiment—well! there is nothing in the world so noble as a man of sentiment!

CHARLES SURFACE: Pshaw! He is too moral by half, and so apprehensive of his good name, as he calls it, that I suppose he would as soon let a priest into his house as a girl.

SIR PETER: No, no,—come, come,—you wrong him. No, no Joseph is no rake, but he is not such a saint in that respect either,—[*aside*]: I have a great mind to tell him—we should have a laugh!

CHARLES SURFACE: Oh, hang him! He's a very anchorite, a young hermit.

SIR PETER: Hark'ee, you must not abuse him. He may chance to hear of it again, I promise you.

CHARLES SURFACE: Why, you won't tell him?

SIR PETER: No—but—this way.—[*aside*]: Egad, I'll tell him! [*aloud*]:—Hark'ee! have you a mind to have a good laugh at Joseph?

CHARLES SURFACE: I should like it of all things.

SIR PETER: Then, 'efaith we will—[*aside*] I'll be quit with him for discovering me.—He had a girl with him when I called.

CHARLES SURFACE: What, Joseph! you jest.

SIR PETER: Hush! [*whispers*]—a little—French milliner—and the best of the jest is—she's in the room now.

CHARLES SURFACE: The devil she is!

SIR PETER: Hush—I tell you— [*points*]

CHARLES SURFACE: Behind the screen—'slife, let's unveil her!

SIR PETER: No, no! He's coming—you shan't, indeed!

CHARLES SURFACE: O egad! we'll have a peep at the little milliner.

SIR PETER: Not for the world!—Joseph will never forgive me.

CHARLES SURFACE: I'll stand by you—

SIR PETER [*struggling with Charles*]: Odds, here he is—

Joseph Surface enters just as Charles throws down the screen

CHARLES SURFACE: Lady Teazle! by all that's wonderful!

SIR PETER: Lady Teazle! by all that's horrible!

CHARLES SURFACE: Sir Peter, this is one the smartest French milliners I ever saw—
egad, you seem all to have been diverting yourselves here at hide and seek—and
I don't see who is out of the secret!—Shall I beg your ladyship to inform me!—not
a word! Brother, will you please explain this matter?—what! Morality dumb
too?—Sir Peter, tho' I *found* you in the dark, perhaps you are not so now. All mute!
Well tho' *I* can make nothing of the affair I suppose you perfectly understand one
another—so I'll leave you to yourselves.—[*going*] Brother, I'm sorry to find you
have given that worthy man so much uneasiness!—Sir Peter, there's nothing *in the
world so noble as a man of sentiment*!

> [*(They) stand for some time looking at each other*]

JOSEPH SURFACE: Sir Peter—notwithstanding I confess that appearances are against
me—if you will afford me your patience—I make no doubt but I shall explain
everything to your satisfaction.

SIR PETER: If you please—

JOSEPH SURFACE: The fact is, sir—that Lady Teazle, knowing my pretensions to your
ward Maria—I say sir, Lady Teazle being apprehensive of the jealousy of your temper—and knowing my friendship to the family—she, sir, I say—called here—in
order that I might explain those pretensions—but on your coming—being apprehensive—as I said of your jealousy—she withdrew—and this, you may depend
on't is the whole truth of the matter.

SIR PETER: A very clear account upon my word, and I dare swear the lady will vouch
for every article of it.

LADY TEAZLE [*coming forward*]: For not one word of it, Sir Peter.

SIR PETER: How! don't you even think it worth while to agree in the lie?

LADY TEAZLE: There is not one syllable of truth in what that gentleman has told you.

SIR PETER: I believe you, upon my soul, Ma'am!

JOSEPH SURFACE [*aside*]: 'Sdeath Madam, will you betray me?

LADY TEAZLE: Good Mr Hypocrite, by your leave I will speak for myself.

SIR PETER: Aye, let her alone, sir—you'll find she'll make out a better story than *you*
without prompting.

LADY TEAZLE: Hear me, Sir Peter—I came hither, on no matter relating to your ward,
and even ignorant of this gentleman's pretensions to her—but I came, seduced by
his insidious arguments, at least to listen to his pretended passion, if not to sacrifice *your* honour to his baseness.

SIR PETER: Now I believe, the truth *is* coming indeed—

JOSEPH SURFACE: The woman's mad!

LADY TEAZLE: No, sir—she has recovered her senses, and your own arts have furnished
her with the means.—Sir Peter, I do not expect you to credit me—but the tenderness you expressed for me when I am sure could not think I was a witness
to it, has penetrated to my heart and had I left the place without the shame of this

discovery, my future life should have spoke the sincerity of my gratitude.—As for that smooth-tongue hypocrite, who would have seduced the wife of his too credulous friend while he affected honourable addresses to his ward—I behold him now in a light so truly despicable, that I shall never again respect myself for having listened to him.   [*Exit*]

JOSEPH SURFACE: Notwithstanding all this, Sir Peter, heaven knows—

SIR PETER: That you are a villain!—and so I leave you to your conscience.

JOSEPH SURFACE: You are too rash, Sir Peter—you shall hear me! the man who shuts out conviction by refusing to—

SIR PETER: Oh!

[*Exeunt, Joseph Surface following and speaking*]

End of Act 4th.

ACT V

SCENE I

The library

Enter Joseph Surface and Servant

JOSEPH SURFACE: Mr Stanley! why should you think I would see him?—you *must* know he comes to ask something!

SERVANT: Sir, I should not have let him in, but that Mr Rowley came to the door with him.

JOSEPH SURFACE: Pshaw! Blockhead! to suppose that I should *now* be in a temper to receive visits from poor relations!—well, why don't you show the fellow up?

SERVANT: I will, sir.—Why, sir, it was not my fault that Sir Peter discovered my lady—

JOSEPH SURFACE: Go, fool!

[*Exit Servant*]

Sure, Fortune never played a man of my policy such a trick, before—my character with Sir Peter! my hopes with Maria!—destroyed in a moment!—I'm in a rare humour to listen to other people's distresses!—I shan't be able to bestow even a benevolent sentiment on Stanley.—So! here he comes and Rowley with him. I must try to recover myself—and put a little charity into my face, however.   [*Exit*]

Enter Sir Oliver Surface and Rowley

SIR OLIVER: What! does he avoid us?—that was he, was it not?

ROWLEY: It was, sir—but I doubt you are come a little too abruptly—his nerves are so weak that the sight of a poor relation may be too much for him.—I should have gone first to break you to him.

SIR OLIVER: A plague to his nerves!—Yet this is he whom Sir Peter extols as a man of the most benevolent way of thinking!—

ROWLEY: As to his way of thinking, I cannot pretend to decide; for to do him justice, he appears to have as much speculative benevolence as any private gentleman in the kingdom, tho' he is seldom so sensual as to indulge himself in the exercise of it.

SIR OLIVER: Yet has a string of charitable sentiments, I suppose, at his fingers' ends!

ROWLEY: Or rather at his tongue's end, Sir Oliver, for I believe there is no sentiment he has more faith in than that 'Charity begins at home.'

SIR OLIVER: And his, I presume, is of that domestic sort which never stirs abroad at all.

ROWLEY: I doubt you'll find it so—but he's coming—I mustn't seem to interrupt you and you know, immediately as you leave him, I come in to announce your arrival in your real character.

SIR OLIVER: True—and afterwards you'll meet me at Sir Peter's.

ROWLEY: Without losing a moment. [*Exit Rowley*]

SIR OLIVER: So! I don't like the complaisance of his features.

Re-enter Joseph Surface

JOSEPH SURFACE: Sir, I beg you ten thousand pardons, for keeping you a moment waiting. Mr Stanley, I presume.

SIR OLIVER: At your service.

JOSEPH SURFACE: Sir, I beg you will do me the honour to sit down—I entreat you, sir.

SIR OLIVER: Dear sir—there's no occasion.—[*aside*]; Too civil by half!

JOSEPH SURFACE: I have not the pleasure of knowing you, Mr Stanley—but I am extremely happy to see you look so well. You were nearly related to my mother, I think, Mr Stanley.

SIR OLIVER: I was, sir—so nearly that my present poverty, I fear, may do discredit to her wealthy children—else I should not have presumed to trouble you.

JOSEPH SURFACE: Dear sir, there needs no apology—he that is in distress, tho' a stranger, has a right to claim kindred with the wealthy.—I am sure I wish I was of that class, and had it in my power to offer you even a small relief.

SIR OLIVER: If your uncle, Sir Oliver, were here, I should have a friend.

JOSEPH SURFACE: I wish he were, sir, with all my heart—you should not want an advocate with him, believe me, sir.

SIR OLIVER: I should not *need* one—my distresses would recommend me;—but I imagined his bounty had enabled *you* to become the agent of his charity.

JOSEPH SURFACE: My dear sir, you were strangely misinformed. Sir Oliver is a worthy man—a very worthy sort of man—but—avarice, Mr Stanley, is the vice of age. I will tell you, my good sir, in confidence, what he has done for me has been a mere nothing, tho' people I know have thought otherwise, and for my part, I never chose to contradict the report.

SIR OLIVER: What! has he never transmitted you bullion! rupees! pagodas!

JOSEPH SURFACE: O dear sir, nothing of the kind—no, no, a few presents now and then—china—shawls—Congou tea—avadavats, and Indian crackers—little more, believe me.

SIR OLIVER [*aside*]: Here's gratitude for twelve thousand pounds—avadavats and Indian crackers!

JOSEPH SURFACE: Then, my dear sir, you have heard I doubt not of the extravagance of my brother. There are very few would credit what I have done for that unfortunate young man.

SIR OLIVER [*aside*]: Not I, for one!

JOSEPH SURFACE: The sums I have lent him—indeed I have been exceedingly to blame—it was an amiable weakness! However, I don't pretend to defend it—and now I feel it doubly culpable, since it has deprived me of the power of serving *you*, Mr Stanley, as my heart directs.

SIR OLIVER [*aside*]: Dissembler!—[*aloud*]: Then, sir, you cannot assist me?

JOSEPH SURFACE: At present it grieves me to say I cannot, but whenever I have the ability, you may depend upon hearing from me.

SIR OLIVER: I am extremely sorry—

JOSEPH SURFACE: Not more than I am, believe me—to pity without the power to relieve, is still more painful than to ask and be denied.

SIR OLIVER: Kind sir, your most obedient humble servant.

JOSEPH SURFACE: You leave me deeply affected, Mr Stanley.—William, be ready to open the door.

SIR OLIVER: O dear sir, no ceremony.

JOSEPH SURFACE: Your very obedient.

SIR OLIVER: Sir, your most obsequious.

JOSEPH SURFACE: You may depend upon hearing from me—whenever I can be of service.

SIR OLIVER: Sweet sir, you are too good.

JOSEPH SURFACE: In the meantime, I wish you health and spirits.

SIR OLIVER: Your ever grateful—and perpetual humble servant.

JOSEPH SURFACE: Sir, yours as sincerely.

SIR OLIVER: Now I am satisfied! [*Exit*]

JOSEPH SURFACE [*solus*]: This is one bad effect of a good character; it invites applications from the unfortunate, and there needs no small degree of address to gain the reputation of benevolence without incurring the expense. The silver ore of pure charity is an expensive article in the catalogue of a man's good qualities—whereas the sentimental French plate I use instead of it, makes just as good a show, and pays no tax.—

Enter Rowley

ROWLEY: Mr Surface, your servant—I was apprehensive of interrupting you—tho' my business demands immediate attention—as this note will inform you.

JOSEPH SURFACE: Always happy to see Mr Rowley.—[*reads*] How! *'Oliver—Surface!'*— My uncle arrived!

ROWLEY: He is indeed—we have just parted—quit well, after a speedy voyage, and impatient to embrace his worthy nephew.

JOSEPH SURFACE: I am astonished!—William! stop Mr Stanley, if he's not gone.

ROWLEY: O—he's out of reach, I believe.

JOSEPH SURFACE: Why didn't you let me know this when you came in together?

ROWLEY: I thought you had particular—business—but I must be gone to inform your brother, and appoint him here to meet his uncle. He will be with you in a quarter of an hour.

JOSEPH SURFACE: So he says. Well, I am strangely overjoyed at his coming.—[*aside*]: Just at this time!

ROWLEY: You will be delighted to see how well he looks.

JOSEPH SURFACE: O—I'm rejoiced to hear it.—[*aside*]: Just at this time!

ROWLEY: I'll tell him how impatiently you expect him.

JOSEPH SURFACE: Do, do; pray give my best duty and affection. Indeed, I cannot express the sensations I feel at the thought of seeing him.—

[*Exit Rowley*]

Certainly his coming just at this time is the cruellest piece of ill fortune. [*Exit*]

SCENE 2

At Sir Peter's

> *Enter Mrs Candour and Maid*

MAID: Indeed, Ma'am, my lady will see nobody at present.

MRS CANDOUR: Did you tell her it was her friend Mrs Candour?

MAID: Yes, Madam, but she begs you will excuse her.

MRS CANDOUR: Do go again—I shall be glad to see her if it be only for a moment, for I am sure she must be in great distress.—

[*Exit Maid*]

Dear heart, how provoking!—I'm not mistress of half the circumstances!—We shall have the whole affair in the newspapers with the names of the parties at length, before I have dropped the story at a dozen houses.

> *Enter Sir Benjamin Backbite*

O dear Sir Benjamin, you heard I suppose—

SIR BENJAMIN: Of Lady Teazle and Mr Surface—

MRS CANDOUR: And Sir Peter's discovery—

SIR BENJAMIN: O, the strangest piece of business, to be sure!

MRS CANDOUR: Well, I never was so surprised in my life! I am sorry for all parties, indeed I am.

SIR BENJAMIN: Now I don't pity Sir Peter at all—he was so extravagantly partial to Mr Surface.

MRS CANDOUR: Mr Surface!—why, 'twas with Charles Lady Teazle was detected.

SIR BENJAMIN: No such thing—Mr Surface is the gallant.

MRS CANDOUR: No, no—Charles is the man. 'Twas Mr Surface brought Sir Peter on purpose to discover them.

SIR BENJAMIN: I tell you I have it from one—

MRS CANDOUR: And I have it from one—

SIR BENJAMIN: Who had it from one, who had it——

MRS CANDOUR: From one immediately—but here's Lady Sneerwell—perhaps she knows the whole affair.

Enter Lady Sneerwell

LADY SNEERWELL: So, my dear Mrs Candour! Here's a sad affair of our friend Lady Teazle.

MRS CANDOUR: Aye!—my dear friend, who could have thought it.

LADY SNEERWELL: Well, there's no trusting appearances, tho' indeed, she was always too lively for me.

MRS CANDOUR: To be sure her manners were a little too free—but she was very young.

LADY SNEERWELL: And *had*, indeed, some good qualities.

MRS CANDOUR: So she had indeed!—but have you heard the particulars?

LADY SNEERWELL: No—but everybody says that Mr Surface—

SIR BENJAMIN: Aye there, I told you—Mr Surface was the man.

MRS CANDOUR: No, no, indeed—the assignation was with Charles.

LADY SNEERWELL: With Charles!—you alarm me, Mrs Candour.

MRS CANDOUR: Yes, yes, he was the lover. Mr Surface—do him justice—was only the informer.

SIR BENJAMIN: Well, I'll not dispute with you, Mrs Candour, but be it which it may, I hope that Sir Peter's wound will not——

MRS CANDOUR: Sir Peter's wound!—O mercy! I didn't hear word of their fighting.

LADY SNEERWELL: Nor I, a syllable.

SIR BENJAMIN: No! what, no mention of the duel?

MRS CANDOUR: Not a word.

SIR BENJAMIN: O lord—yes, yes—they fought before they left the room.

LADY SNEERWELL: Pray let us hear.

MRS CANDOUR: Aye, do oblige us with the duel.

SIR BENJAMIN: 'Sir' says Sir Peter—immediately after the discovery—'you are a most ungrateful fellow.'

MRS CANDOUR: Aye to Charles—

SIR BENJAMIN: No, no—to Mr Surface—'a most ungrateful fellow and old as I am, sir,' says he, 'I insist on immediate satisfaction.'

MRS CANDOUR: Aye, that must have been to Charles for 'tis very unlikely Mr Surface should go to fight in his house.

SIR BENJAMIN: 'Gad's life, Ma'am, not at all—'giving me immediate satisfaction.'— On this, madam, Lady Teazle, seeing Sir Peter in such danger, ran out of the room in strong hysterics, and Charles after her, calling out for hartshorn and water! Then, madam, they began to fight with swords—

Enter Crabtree

CRABTREE: With pistols, nephew—I have it from undoubted authority.

MRS CANDOUR: O Mr Crabtree, then it is all true!

CRABTREE: Too true, indeed, ma'am, and Sir Peter's dangerously wounded—

SIR BENJAMIN: By a thrust in *seconde* quite through his left side—

CRABTREE: By a bullet lodged in the thorax.

MRS CANDOUR: Mercy on me! Poor Sir Peter!

CRABTREE: Yes, Ma'am—tho' Charles would have avoided the matter if he could.

MRS CANDOUR: I knew Charles was the person.

SIR BENJAMIN: Oh, my uncle I see, knows nothing of the matter.

CRABTREE: But Sir Peter taxed him with the basest ingratitude—

SIR BENJAMIN: That I told you, you know.

CRABTREE: Do nephew, let me speak!—and insisted on an immediate—

SIR BENJAMIN: Just as I said.

CRABTREE: Odds life! Nephew, allow others to know something too—a pair of pistols lay on the bureau—for Mr Surface, it seems, had come the night before late from Salt-Hill, where he had been to see the Montem with a friend, who has a son at Eton—so unluckily, the pistols were left charged.

SIR BENJAMIN: I heard nothing of this.

CRABTREE: Sir Peter forced Charles to take one and they fired, it seems pretty nearly together. Charles's shot took place as I told you, and Sir Peter's missed—but what is very extraordinary, the ball struck against a little bronze Pliny that stood over the chimney-piece, grazed out of the window at a right angle, and wounded the postman, who was just coming in the door with a double letter from North-hamptonshire.

SIR BENJAMIN: My uncle's account is more circumstantial I must confess—but I believe mine is the true one for all that.

LADY SNEERWELL [*aside*]: I am more interested in this affair than they imagine and must have better information.   [*Exit Lady Sneerwell*]

SIR BENJAMIN [*after a pause looking at each other*]: Ah!—Lady Sneerwell's alarm is very easily accounted for.

CRABTREE: Yes, yes, they certainly *do* say—but that's neither here nor there.

MRS CANDOUR: But, pray, where is Sir Peter at present?

CRABTREE: Oh! they brought him home and he is now in the house, tho' the servants are ordered to deny it.

MRS CANDOUR: I believe so, and Lady Teazle, I suppose attending him.

CRABTREE: Yes, yes—I saw one of the Faculty enter just before me.

SIR BENJAMIN: Hey! who comes here?

CRABTREE: Oh, this is he—the physician, depend on't.

MRS CANDOUR: Oh, certainly, it must be the physician and now we shall know.

Enter Sir Oliver Surface

CRABTREE: Well doctor, what hopes?

MRS CANDOUR: Aye doctor, how's your patient?

SIR BENJAMIN: Now doctor, isn't it a wound with a small-sword?

CRABTREE: A bullet lodged in the thorax, for a hundred!

SIR OLIVER: Doctor!—a wound with a small-sword! and a bullet in the thorax? Oons! are you mad, good people?

SIR BENJAMIN: Perhaps, sir you are not a doctor?

SIR OLIVER: Truly, I am to thank you for my degree, if I am.

CRABTREE: Only a friend of Sir Peter's then, I presume; but, sir, you must have heard
of this accident—

SIR OLIVER: Not a word!

CRABTREE: Not of his being dangerously wounded?

SIR OLIVER: The devil he is!

SIR BENJAMIN: Run thro' the body—

CRABTREE: Shot in the breast—

SIR BENJAMIN: By one Mr Surface—

CRABTREE: Aye, the younger.

SIR OLIVER: Hey! what the plague! you seem to differ strangely in your accounts—
however, you agree that Sir Peter is dangerously wounded.

SIR BENJAMIN: Oh, yes, we agree there.

CRABTREE: Yes, yes, I believe there can be no doubt of that.

SIR OLIVER: Then, upon my word, for a person in that situation he is the most imprudent man alive—for here he comes, walking as if nothing at all were the matter.

Enter Sir Peter Teazle

Odds heart, Sir Peter—you are come in good time, I promise you, for we had just
given you over.

SIR BENJAMIN: Egad, uncle, this is the most sudden recovery!

SIR OLIVER: Why, man, what do you do out of bed with a small-sword through your
body, and bullet lodged in your thorax!

SIR PETER: A small-sword and a bullet—

SIR OLIVER: Aye, these gentlemen would have killed you, without law or physic, and
wanted to dub me a doctor—to make me an accomplice.

SIR PETER: Why, what is all this?

SIR BENJAMIN: We rejoice, Sir Peter, that the story of the duel is not true—and are sincerely sorry for your other misfortunes.

SIR PETER [*aside*]: So, so—all over the town already.

CRABTREE: Tho' Sir Peter, you were certainly vastly to blame to marry at all, at
your years.

SIR PETER: Sir, what business is that of yours?

MRS CANDOUR: Tho' indeed, as Sir Peter made so good a husband, he's very much to
be pitied!

SIR PETER: Plague on your pity, Ma'am, I desire none of it.

SIR BENJAMIN: However, Sir Peter, you must not mind the laughing and jests you will
meet with on this occasion.

SIR PETER: Sir, I desire to be master in my own house.

CRABTREE: 'Tis no uncommon case, that's one comfort.

SIR PETER: I insist on being left to myself; without ceremony, I insist on your leaving
my house directly!

MRS CANDOUR: Well, well, we are going and depend on't we'll make the best report of you we can.

SIR PETER: Leave my house!

CRABTREE: And tell how hardly you have been treated.

SIR PETER: Leave my house!

SIR BENJAMIN: And how patiently you bear it.

SIR PETER: Fiends! vipers! furies!—Oh that their own venom would choke them!

[*Exeunt Mrs Candour, Sir Benjamin Backbite, Crabtree, &c.*]

SIR OLIVER: They are very provoking indeed, Sir Peter.

Enter Rowley

ROWLEY: I heard high words—what has ruffled you, Sir Peter?

SIR PETER: Pshaw, what signifies asking! Do I ever pass a day without my vexations?

SIR OLIVER: Well, I'm not inquisitive—I come only to tell you that I have seen both my nephews in the manner we proposed.

SIR PETER: A precious couple they are!

ROWLEY: Yes, and Sir Oliver is convinced that your judgment was right, Sir Peter.

SIR OLIVER: Yes, I find *Joseph* is indeed the man after all.

ROWLEY: Yes, as Sir Peter says, he's a man of sentiment.

SIR OLIVER: And acts up to the sentiments he professes.

ROWLEY: It certainly is edification to hear him talk.

SIR OLIVER: Oh, he's a model for the young men of the age!—but how's this, Sir Peter!—you don't join in your friend Joseph's praise as I expected.

SIR PETER: Sir Oliver, we live in a damned wicked world, and the fewer we praise the better.

ROWLEY: What, do *you* say so, Sir Peter—who were never mistaken in your life?

SIR PETER: Pshaw! Plague on you both! I see by your sneering you have heard the whole affair. I shall go mad among you!

ROWLEY: Then to fret you no longer, Sir Peter, we are indeed acquainted with it all. I met Lady Teazle coming from Mr Surface's, so humbled that she deigned to request me, to be her advocate with you.

SIR PETER: And does Sir Oliver know all too?

SIR OLIVER: Every circumstance!

SIR PETER: What, of the closet—and the screen, hey?

SIR OLIVER: Yes, yes, and the little French milliner. O I have been vastly diverted with the story! ha! ha!

SIR PETER: 'Twas very pleasant.

SIR OLIVER: I never laughed more in my life I assure you, ha! ha!

SIR PETER: O vastly diverting! ha! ha!

ROWLEY: To be sure, Joseph with his sentiments—ha! ha!

SIR PETER: Yes, yes, his sentiments—ha! ha! A hypocritical villain!

SIR OLIVER: Aye, and that rogue Charles—to pull Sir Peter out of the closet—ha! ha!

SIR PETER: Ha! ha! 'twas devilish entertaining to be sure!

SIR OLIVER: Ha! ha! egad, Sir Peter, I should like to have seen your face when the screen was thrown down, ha! ha!

SIR PETER: Yes, yes, my face when the screen was thrown down, ha! ha! O I must never show my head again!

SIR OLIVER: But come, come, it isn't fair to laugh at you neither, my old friend—tho' upon my soul, I can't help it.

SIR PETER: O pray don't restrain your mirth on my account.—It does not hurt me at all—I laugh at the whole affair myself—yes, yes. I think being a standing jest for all one's acquaintances a very happy situation. O yes, and then of a morning to read the paragraphs about Mr S——, Lady T——, and Sir P——, will be so entertaining!—

ROWLEY: Without affectation, Sir Peter, you may despise the ridicule of fools. But I see Lady Teazle—going towards the next room. I am sure you must desire a reconciliation as earnestly as she does.

SIR OLIVER: Perhaps my being here, prevents her coming to you. Well, I'll leave honest Rowley to mediate between you—but he must bring you all presently to Mr Surface's, where I am now returning, if not to reclaim a libertine, at least to expose hypocrisy.

SIR PETER: Ah!—I'll be present at your discovering yourself there with all my heart—tho' 'tis a vile unlucky place for discoveries!

ROWLEY: We'll follow.

[Exit Sir Oliver Surface]

SIR PETER: She is not coming here, you see, Rowley.

ROWLEY: No, but she has left the door of that room open you perceive. See, she is in tears!

SIR PETER: Certainly a little mortification appears very becoming in a wife! don't you think it will do her good to let her pine a little?

ROWLEY: O, this is ungenerous in you!

SIR PETER: Well, I know not what to think. You remember, Rowley, the letter I found of hers, evidently intended for Charles?

ROWLEY: A mere forgery, Sir Peter—laid in your way on purpose. This is one of the points which I intend *Snake* shall give you conviction on.

SIR PETER: I wish I were once satisfied of that. She looks this way—what a remarkably elegant turn of the head she has! Rowley, I'll go to her.

ROWLEY: Certainly.

SIR PETER: Tho' when it is known that we are reconciled, people will laugh at me ten times more!

ROWLEY: Let them laugh and retort their malice only by showing them you are happy in spite of it.

SIR PETER: 'Efaith, so I will—and if I'm not mistaken, we may yet be the happiest couple in the country.

ROWLEY: Nay, Sir Peter—he who once lays aside suspicion—

SIR PETER: Hold, my dear Rowley—if you have any regard for me, never let me hear you utter anything like a sentiment—I have had enough of *them* to serve me the rest of my life! [*Exeunt*]

SCENE 3

The library

Joseph Surface and Lady Sneerwell

LADY SNEERWELL: Impossible! Will not Sir Peter immediately be reconciled to Charles, and of consequence no longer oppose his union with *Maria*? The thought is distraction to me!

JOSEPH SURFACE: Can passion furnish a remedy?

LADY SNEERWELL: No, nor cunning either—O I was a fool! an idiot! to league with such a blunderer!

JOSEPH SURFACE: Sure, Lady Sneerwell, *I* am the greatest sufferer—yet you see I bear the accident with calmness.

LADY SNEERWELL: Because the disappointment doesn't reach your *heart*; your *interest* only attached you to Maria. Had you felt for *her*, what *I* have for that *ungrateful* libertine, neither your temper nor hypocrisy could prevent your showing the sharpness of your vexation.

JOSEPH SURFACE: But why should your reproaches fall on *me* for this disappointment?

LADY SNEERWELL: Are you not the cause of it?—what had you to do to bate in your pursuit of Maria to pervert Lady Teazle by the way? Had you not a sufficient field for your roguery in blinding Sir Peter and supplanting your brother? I hate such avarice of crimes—'tis an unfair monopoly, and never prospers.

JOSEPH SURFACE: Well, I admit I have been to blame. I confess I deviated from the direct road of wrong, but I don't think we're so totally defeated neither.

LADY SNEERWELL: No!

JOSEPH SURFACE: You tell me you have made a trial of Snake since we met, and that you still believe him faithful to us.

LADY SNEERWELL: I do believe so.

JOSEPH SURFACE: And that he has undertaken, should it be necessary, to swear and prove that Charles is at this time contracted by vows and honour to your ladyship—which some of his former letters to you will serve to support?

LADY SNEERWELL: This, indeed, might have assisted.

JOSEPH SURFACE: Come, come; it is not too late yet.—[*knocking*] But hark! this is probably my uncle, Sir Oliver—retire to that room. We'll consult farther when he's gone.

LADY SNEERWELL: Well!—but if *he* should find you out too—

JOSEPH SURFACE: O, I have no fear of that. Sir Peter will hold his tongue for his own credit['s] sake—and you may depend on't I shall soon discover Sir Oliver's weak side!

LADY SNEERWELL: I have no diffidence of your abilities—only be constant to one roguery at a time. [*Exit*]

JOSEPH SURFACE: I will—I will—So! 'tis confounded hard—after such bad fortune, to be baited by one's confederate in evil. Well at all events, my character is so better than Charles's that I certainly—hey! what!—this is not *Sir Oliver*, but *old Stanley* again!—Plague on't that he should return to tease me just now—we shall have Sir Oliver come and find him—here—and—

Enter Sir Oliver Surface

Gad's life, Mr Stanley, why have you come back to plague me just at this time?—you must not stay now, upon my word!

SIR OLIVER: Sir, I hear your uncle Oliver is expected here, and tho' he has been so penurious to *you*, I'll try what he'll do for *me*.

JOSEPH SURFACE: Sir, 'tis impossible for you to stay now, so I must beg—Come any other time and I promise you, you shall be assisted.

SIR OLIVER: No—Sir Oliver and I must be acquainted.

JOSEPH SURFACE: Zounds, sir! then I insist on your quitting the room directly.

SIR OLIVER: Nay, sir!

JOSEPH SURFACE: Sir, I insist on't—here, William show this gentleman out. Since you compel me, sir—not one moment—this is such insolence!

[*going to push him out*]

Enter Charles Surface

CHARLES SURFACE: Hey-day! what's the matter now?—what the devil, have you got hold of my little broker here? Zounds, brother—don't hurt little Premium. What's the matter, my little fellow?

JOSEPH SURFACE: So! He has been with you too, has he?

CHARLES SURFACE: To be sure he has!—why, 'tis as honest a little—But sure, Joseph, you have not been borrowing money too, have you?

JOSEPH SURFACE: Borrowing—no!—but brother, you know here we expect Sir Oliver every—

CHARLES SURFACE: O gad! that's true—Noll musn't find the little broker here, to be sure.

JOSEPH SURFACE: Yet Mr *Stanley* insists—

CHARLES SURFACE: Stanley! why his name is *Premium*.

JOSEPH SURFACE: No, no, Stanley.

CHARLES SURFACE: No, no, Premium.

JOSEPH SURFACE: Well, no matter which—but—

CHARLES SURFACE: Aye, aye, Stanley or Premium, 'tis the same thing, as you say, for I suppose he goes by half a hundred names besides A.B.'s at the coffee-houses. [*knock*]

JOSEPH SURFACE: Death! here's Sir Oliver at the door. [*knocking again*] Now I beg, Mr Stanley—

CHARLES SURFACE: Aye, and I beg, Mr Premium—

SIR OLIVER: Gentlemen—

JOSEPH SURFACE: Sir, by heaven you shall go!

CHARLES SURFACE: Aye, out with him certainly.

SIR OLIVER: This violence—

JOSEPH SURFACE: 'Tis your own fault.

CHARLES SURFACE: Out with him, to be sure! [*both forcing Sir Oliver out*]

    Enter Sir Peter and Lady Teazle, Maria, and Rowley

SIR PETER: My old friend, Sir Oliver!—hey—what in the name of wonder!—Here are dutiful nephews!—assault their uncle at the first visit—

LADY TEAZLE: Indeed Sir Oliver, 'twas well we came in to rescue you.

ROWLEY: Truly it was—for I perceive, Sir Oliver, the character of old Stanley was no protection to you.

SIR OLIVER: Nor of Premium, either—the necessities of the *former* couldn't extort a shilling from *that* benevolent gentleman and now, egad, I stood a chance of faring worse than my ancestors, and being knocked down without being bid for.

        [*after a pause, Joseph and Charles turning to each other*]

JOSEPH SURFACE: Charles!

CHARLES SURFACE: Joseph!

JOSEPH SURFACE: 'Tis now complete!

CHARLES SURFACE: Very.

SIR OLIVER: Sir Peter, my friend, and Rowley too—look on that elder nephew of mine. You know what he has already received from my bounty, and you know also, how gladly I would have regarded half my fortune as held in trust for him—judge then my disappointment in discovering him to be destitute of truth—charity—and gratitude.

SIR PETER: Sir Oliver, I would be more surprised at this declaration if I had not myself found him selfish, treacherous, and hypocritical!

LADY TEAZLE: And if the gentleman pleads not guilty to these, pray let him call me to his character.

SIR PETER: Then I believe we need add no more—if he knows himself, he will consider it as the most perfect punishment, that he is known by the world.

CHARLES SURFACE [*aside*]: If they talk this way to *Honesty*, what will they say to *me* by and by?

SIR OLIVER: As for that prodigal, his brother there—

CHARLES SURFACE [*aside*]: Aye, now comes my turn—the damned family pictures will ruin me.

JOSEPH SURFACE: Sir Oliver!—uncle!—will you honour me with a hearing?

CHARLES SURFACE [*aside*]: Now if Joseph would make one of his long speeches, I might recollect myself a little.

SIR OLIVER: I suppose you would undertake to justify yourself entirely?

JOSEPH SURFACE: I trust I could.

SIR OLIVER: Pshaw!—well, sir—and *you* [*to Charles*] could justify yourself too I suppose?

CHARLES SURFACE: Not that I know of, Sir Oliver.

SIR OLIVER: What!—little Premium has been let too much into the secret I presume.

CHARLES SURFACE: True, sir—but they were family secrets and should never be mentioned again you know.

ROWLEY: Come, Sir Oliver, I know you cannot speak of Charles's follies with anger.

SIR OLIVER: Odd's heart, no more I can—nor with gravity either. Sir Peter, do you know the rogue bargained with me for all his ancestors—sold me judges and generals by the foot and maiden aunts as cheap as broken china!

CHARLES SURFACE: To be sure Sir Oliver, I did make a little free with the family canvas, that's the truth on't. My ancestors may certainly rise in evidence against me, there's no denying it. But believe me sincere when I tell you—and upon my soul I would not say it if I was not—that if I do not appear mortified at the exposure of my follies, it is because I feel at this moment the warmest satisfaction in seeing you, my liberal benefactor.

SIR OLIVER: Charles—I believe you—give me your hand again. The ill-looking little fellow over the settee has made our peace, sirrah.

CHARLES SURFACE: Then sir, my gratitude to the original is still increased.

LADY TEAZLE [*pointing to Maria*]: Yet I believe, Sir Oliver, here is one whom Charles is still more anxious to be reconciled to.

SIR OLIVER: O I have heard of his attachment there and with the young lady's pardon, if I construe right that blush—

SIR PETER: Well, child, speak your sentiments.

MARIA: Sir, I have little to say, but that I shall rejoice to hear that he is happy. For me, whatever claim I had to his affection, I willingly resign it to one who has a better title.

CHARLES SURFACE: How, Maria!

SIR PETER: Hey-day! what's the mystery now?—while he appeared an incorrigible rake, you would give your hand to no one else, and now that he is likely to reform, I warrant you won't have him!

MARIA: His own heart—and Lady Sneerwell know the cause.

CHARLES SURFACE: Lady Sneerwell!

JOSEPH SURFACE: Brother, it is with great concern I am obliged to speak on this point, but my regard to justice compels me—and Lady Sneerwell's injuries can no longer be concealed. [*goes to the door*]

Enter Lady Sneerwell

SIR PETER: So! another French milliner, egad!—He has one in every room in the house, I suppose!

LADY SNEERWELL: Ungrateful Charles!—well may you be surprised and feel for the indelicate situation which your perfidy has forced me into.

CHARLES SURFACE: Pray, uncle, is this another plot of yours? for as I have life, I don't understand it.

JOSEPH SURFACE: I believe, sir, there is but the evidence of one person more necessary to make it extremely clear.

SIR PETER: And that person, I imagine, is Mr Snake.—Rowley, you were perfectly right to bring him with us, and pray let him appear.

ROWLEY: Walk in, Mr Snake.

Enter Snake

I thought his testimony might be wanted, however, it happens unluckily that he comes to confront Lady Sneerwell and not to support her.

LADY SNEERWELL [*aside*]: Villain!—treacherous to me at last! [*aloud*]:—Speak, fellow, have you too conspired against me?

SNAKE: I beg your ladyship ten thousand pardons—you paid me extremely liberally for the lie in question—but I have unfortunately been offered double to speak the truth.

SIR PETER: Plot and counterplot, egad—I wish your ladyship joy of the success of your negotiation.

LADY SNEERWELL: The torments of shame and disappointment on you all!—

LADY TEAZLE: Hold, Lady Sneerwell—before you go, let me thank you for the trouble you and that gentleman have taken in writing letters to me from Charles, and answering them yourself—and let me also request you to make my respects to the Scandalous College, of which you are president—and inform them, that Lady Teazle, licentiate, begs leave to return the diploma they granted her—as she leaves off practice, and kills characters no longer.

LADY SNEERWELL: You too, Madam!—provoking—insolent!—may your husband live these fifty years! [*Exit*]

SIR PETER: Oons! what a fury—

LADY TEAZLE: A malicious creature, indeed!

SIR PETER: Hey—not for her last wish?

LADY TEAZLE: O no—

SIR OLIVER: Well, sir, and what have you to say now?

JOSEPH SURFACE: Sir, I am so confounded to find that Lady *Sneerwell* could be guilty of suborning Mr *Snake* in this manner to impose on us all, that I know not what to say—however, lest her revengeful spirit should prompt her to injure my brother, I had certainly better follow her directly. [*Exit*]

SIR PETER: Moral to the last drop!

SIR OLIVER: Aye, and marry her, Joseph, if you can.—Oil and vinegar, egad:—you'll do very well together.

ROWLEY: I believe we have no more occasion for Mr Snake at present.

SNAKE: Before I go, I beg pardon once and for all for whatever uneasiness I have been the humble instrument of causing to the parties present.

SIR PETER: Well, well, you have made atonement by a good deed at last.

SNAKE: But I must request of the company that it shall never be known.

SIR PETER: Hey!—what the plague!—are you ashamed of having done a right thing once in your life?

SNAKE: Ah! Sir—consider I live by the badness of my character!—I have nothing but my infamy to depend on! and if it were once known that I had been betrayed into an honest action, I should lose every friend I have in the world.

SIR OLIVER: Well, well, we'll not traduce you by saying anything in your praise, never fear.

[Exit Snake]

SIR PETER: There's a precious rogue—yet that fellow is a writer and a critic!

LADY TEAZLE: See, Sir Oliver, there needs no persuasion now to reconcile your nephew and Maria.

[Charles and Maria apart]

SIR OLIVER: Aye, aye, that's as it should be and egad, we'll have the wedding to-morrow morning.

CHARLES SURFACE: Thank you, my dear uncle!

SIR PETER: What! you rogue, don't you ask the girl's consent first?

CHARLES SURFACE: O I have done that a long time—above a minute ago—and she has looked yes.

MARIA: For shame, Charles—I protest, Sir Peter, there has not been a word—

SIR OLIVER: Well then, the fewer the better—may your love for each other never know abatement.

SIR PETER: And may you live as happily together as Lady Teazle and I intend to do.

CHARLES SURFACE: Rowley, my old friend, I am sure you congratulate me and I suspect that I owe you much.

SIR OLIVER: You do, indeed, Charles.

ROWLEY: If my efforts to serve you had not succeeded you would have been in my debt for the attempt—but deserve to be happy—and you overpay me.

SIR PETER: Aye, honest Rowley always said you would reform.

CHARLES SURFACE: Why as to reforming, Sir Peter, I'll make no promises, and that I take to be a proof that I intend to set about it. But here shall be my monitor—my gentle guide.—Ah! can I leave the virtuous path those eyes illumine?

> Tho' thou, dear maid, shouldst waive thy beauty's sway,
> —Thou still must rule, because I *will* obey;
> An humbled fugitive from Folly view,
> No sanctuary near but *Love* and—YOU;
>   *[to the audience]*
> *You* can, indeed, each anxious fear remove,
> For even *Scandal* dies, if *you* approve.

Finis

EPILOGUE

WRITTEN BY G. COLMAN, ESQ.   SPOKEN BY MRS ABINGTON

    I, who was late so volatile and gay,
    Like a trade-wind, must now blow all one way;
    Bend all my cares, my studies, and my vows,
    To one old rusty weather cock—my spouse;—
5   So wills our virtuous bard!—the motley Bayes
    Of crying epilogues and laughing plays.
        Old bachelors, who marry smart young wives,
    Learn from our play, to regulate your lives;
    Each bring his dear to town—all faults upon her—
10 London will prove the very source of honour:
    Plunged fairly in, like a cold bath it serves,
    When principles relax—to brace the nerves.
        Such is my case;—and yet I might deplore
    That the gay dream of dissipation's o'er,
15 And say, ye fair, was ever lively wife,
    Born with a genius for the highest life,
    Like my untimely blasted in her bloom,
    Like me condemned to such a dismal doom?
    Save money—when I just knew how to waste it!
20 Leave London—just as I began to taste it!
    Must I then watch the early crowing cock,
    The melancholy ticking of a clock?
    In the lone rustic hall forever pounded,
    With dogs, cats, rats, and squalling brats surrounded?
25 With humble curates can I now retire,
    (While good Sir Peter boozes with the squire,)
    And at backgammon mortify my soul,
    That pants for loo, or flutters at a vole?
    Seven's the main? Dear sound!—that must expire,
30 Lost at hot cockles, round a Christmas fire!
    The transient hour of fashion, too soon spent,
    Farewell the tranquil mind, farewell content!
    Farewell the plumèd head, the cushioned tête,
    That takes the cushion from its proper seat!
35 That sprit-stirring drum!—card drums I mean,
    Spadille—odd trick—pam—basto—king and queen!
    And you, ye knockers, that with brazen throat,
    The welcome visitor's approach denote;
    Farewell! all quality of high renown,
40 Pride, pomp, and circumstance of glorious town!

Farewell! your revels I partake no more
And Lady Teazle's occupation's o'er—
All this I told our bard—he smiled, and said 'twas clear,
I ought to play deep tragedy next year.
45 Meanwhile he drew wise morals from his play,
And in these solemn periods stalked away:
'Blest were the fair like you; her faults who stopped,
And closed her follies when the curtain dropped!
No more in vice or error to engage,
50 Or play the fool at large, on life's great stage.'

1777

Henrik Ibsen
1828–1906

Born in Skien, Norway, a small town where his father was then a successful merchant, Henrik Ibsen grew up amid the painful circumstances that were brought about by the decline of his father's business, which ended in bankruptcy when Henrik was eight years old. His family was then forced to move from their large and comfortable home to a small attic apartment, and by the time Ibsen was sixteen he had been sent off to another town to make his own way as a druggist's apprentice. When he was twenty-two he moved to Christiana (now Oslo), hoping to study medicine at the city's university, but his failure to gain admission led him to make a career out of the playwriting that he had begun several years earlier. During the next sixteen years, he was influenced largely by the nationalistic and romantic movement in Norwegian theatre, and thus gave himself over mostly to writing blank verse plays on subjects drawn from Norwegian myth and history. But in 1869, with *The League of Youth*, a play exposing the corruption of provincial politics and politicians, Ibsen began to write realistic prose plays about the social problems of his time. His best-known problem plays—*A Doll's House* (1879) and *Ghosts* (1881)—were highly controversial in his own time, especially among his Norwegian compatriots, who regarded them as attacking such traditional values as marriage and the family. Social reformers then and now have hailed them as eloquent pleas in defence of women's rights. These plays may also be seen as foreshadowing his late dramatic studies of psychologically troubled men and women in *Rosmersholm* (1886) and *Hedda Gabler* (1890).

Hedda Gabler[1]

CHARACTERS

JÖRGEN TESMAN, the holder of a
   University Fellowship in cultural history
MRS HEDDA TESMAN, his wife
MISS JULIANE TESMAN, his aunt

MRS ELVSTED
MR BRACK, a judge
EJLERT LÖVBORG
BERTE, the Tesmans' maid

The action takes place in Tesman's villa on the west side of the town

ACT I

A spacious, handsome, and tastefully appointed reception room, decorated in dark colours. In the back wall there is a wide doorway with the hangings pulled back. This opening leads to a smaller room in the same style as the reception room. In the wall to the right of the outer room is a folding door leading to the hall. In the opposite wall, to the left, is a glass door, also with the curtains drawn aside. Through the windows we see part of a covered verandah outside, and trees in autumn colours. In the foreground stands an oval table, covered with a heavy cloth, and with chairs around it. Downstage by the right wall are a large, dark, porcelain stove, a high-backed armchair, an upholstered footrest, and two stools. Up in the right-hand corner, a corner sofa and a small round table. Downstage on the left, a little away from the wall, a sofa. Above the glass door, a piano. On either side of the doorway at the back is a whatnot with objects in terra-cotta and majolica.——By the back wall of the inner room are a sofa, a table, and a couple of chairs. Over this sofa hangs the portrait of a handsome, elderly man in the uniform of a general. Over the table, a hanging lamp with a matte, milky-white glass shade.——All around the reception room there are numerous bunches of flowers arranged in vases and glasses. More lie on the tables. The floors of both rooms are covered with thick carpets.——Morning light. The sun is shining in at the glass door.

Miss Juliane Tesman, with hat and parasol, comes in from the hall, followed by Berte, who carries a bunch of flowers wrapped in paper. Miss Tesman is a good-looking lady of benevolent aspect, some 65 years old, neatly but simply dressed in a grey costume. Berte is a serving-maid getting on in years, with a plain and somewhat countrified exterior.

MISS TESMAN [*stops just inside the room, listens and speaks softly*]: Well, I declare! I don't
   believe they are up yet.
BERTE [*similarly subdued*]: Why, that's what I said, Miss. So late the steamer was last
   night. And then afterwards! Gracious . . . all the things the young mistress wanted
   unpacked before she could get off to bed.

1 translated by Jens Arup

MISS TESMAN: Well, well . . . let them have a good rest and welcome. But we'll give them a breath of the fresh morning air when they do come down.

She crosses to the glass door and throws it wide open.

BERTE [*by the table, not knowing what to do with the flowers in her hand*]: I'm sure there isn't a decent place left for them. Maybe I'd better put them here, Miss.

She places the flowers on the front of the piano.

MISS TESMAN: And so now you've got yourself a new mistress, Berte my dear. The Lord knows, I found it more than hard to let you go.

BERTE [*close to tears*]: And what about me then, Miss? What am I to say! For so many years now I've been with you and Miss Rina.

MISS TESMAN: We must make the best of it, Berte. There's really no other way. Jörgen must have you in the house with him, you see. He simply must. You've always looked after him, ever since he was a little boy.

BERTE: Yes but, Miss, I get so worried about her, too, lying at home. The poor dear, she's quite helpless. And then with that new girl, now! She'll never learn to make things right for the poor lady, she won't.

MISS TESMAN: Oh, I'll soon get her into the way of it. And I'll see to most things myself, you may be sure. You needn't be so anxious for my poor sister's sake, my dear Berte.

BERTE: Yes, but then there's another thing too, Miss. I'm really so scared I'll never give satisfaction to the young mistress.

MISS TESMAN: Oh, Heavens . . . just to begin with of course there might be this and that. . . .

BERTE: Because she's ever so particular.

MISS TESMAN: Why, of course she is. General Gabler's daughter. The way she was used to having things in the General's time. Do you remember her riding along the road with her father? In that long black habit? And with a feather in her hat?

BERTE: I should think I would remember! . . . But I declare, I never once dreamed they'd make a match of it, her and Mr Jörgen, not in those days I didn't.

MISS TESMAN: Nor I. . . . But now here's a point, Berte, while I remember it: you mustn't say mister about Jörgen from now on. He's a doctor.

BERTE: Yes, the lady did say about that too . . . last night . . . soon as they came in at the door. Is it really true then, Miss?

MISS TESMAN: Why certainly it's true. Just fancy, Berte . . . they made him a doctor abroad. Now, on the journey, you know. And I never knew the first thing about it . . . till he told me down there on the quay.

BERTE: Well, I should think he could get to be anything at all, he could. He's that clever. But I'd never have thought he'd have taken to doctoring people, too.

MISS TESMAN: Oh no, he's not that sort of doctor. . . . [*She nods significantly.*] And by the way, you'll probably have to call him something even finer pretty soon.

BERTE: Well I never! What sort of thing, Miss?

MISS TESMAN [*smiles*]: Hm . . . wouldn't you like to know! . . . [*emotionally*] Ah, dear God . . . if my sainted brother could look up from the grave and see what's become of his little boy! [*She looks around.*] But what's this, Berte . . . why on earth have you done that? Taken all the loose covers off?

BERTE: The lady told me to do it. She doesn't like loose covers on the chairs, she said.

MISS TESMAN: But will they be coming in here . . . I mean for every day?

BERTE: That's what it sounded like. The lady, that is. As for himself . . . the doctor . . . he didn't say anything.

Jörgen Tesman enters from the right of the inner room, humming a tune and carrying an open, empty suitcase. He is a man of 33, of middle height and youthful appearance; slightly plump, his face round, open, and cheerful. Fair hair and beard. He wears glasses, and is dressed in comfortable, slightly slovenly, indoor clothes.

MISS TESMAN: Good morning, good morning, Jörgen!

TESMAN [*in the doorway*]: Aunt Julle! Dear Aunt Julle! [*goes over and pumps her hand*] Come all this way . . . so early in the morning! Eh?

MISS TESMAN: Well, of course I had to come and see how you've all settled in.

TESMAN: And you never even had a proper night's rest!

MISS TESMAN: Oh, that won't do me any harm.

TESMAN: Well, well, and you managed all right getting home from the quay, I hope? Eh?

MISS TESMAN: Oh yes, I did very well . . . thank Heavens. Mr Brack was so very kind as to take me right to the door.

TESMAN: We were so dreadfully sorry we couldn't take you in the cab. But you could see for yourself. . . . Hedda had so many cases that had to come.

MISS TESMAN: Yes, she really did have a great many cases.

BERTE [*to Tesman*]: Should I maybe go in and ask the mistress whether she wants me for anything?

TESMAN: No thank you, Berte . . . I don't think you'd better. If there is anything she'll ring, she said.

BERTE [*crossing to the right*]: All right, then.

TESMAN: Hey, wait a moment . . . take this along, will you.

BERTE [*taking the suitcase*]: I'll put it up in the loft. [*She goes out at the hall door.*]

TESMAN: Just think, Auntie . . . the whole of that case was crammed full of nothing but notes. It's quite incredible, really, all the things I managed to dig up round about in those old archives. Fantastic old things that no one knew anything about. . . .

MISS TESMAN: Well to be sure, I don't expect you wasted your time on your honeymoon, did you, Jörgen?

TESMAN: I can assure you I didn't. But do take your hat off, Auntie. There now! Let me undo that ribbon. Eh?

MISS TESMAN [*as he does so*]: Oh, my dear . . . it's just as though you were home with us still.

TESMAN [*turning the hat around in his hand*]: My, my . . . that's a fine and fancy hat you've given yourself!

MISS TESMAN: I bought it because of Hedda.

TESMAN: Because of Hedda? Eh?

MISS TESMAN: Yes, so Hedda won't be ashamed of me, if we should happen to walk together in the street.

TESMAN [*patting her cheek*]: You always think of everything, don't you, Auntie Julle. [*He puts the hat on a chair by the table.*] And now . . . there we are . . . now we'll sit down on the sofa here. And we'll have a little chat until Hedda turns up.

They sit down. She puts her parasol in the corner by the sofa.

MISS TESMAN [*takes both his hands and looks at him*]: How wonderfully good it is to see you here again, as well as ever, and full of life, Jörgen! Ah . . . sainted Joachim's little boy!

TESMAN: For me too! To be with you again, Auntie Julle! You've always been both father and mother to me.

MISS TESMAN: Yes, I know you'll always have a soft spot in your heart for your old aunts.

TESMAN: But there's absolutely no improvement in Auntie Rina. Eh?

MISS TESMAN: Oh no, dear . . . we don't expect any, poor thing. She just lies there as she has done all these years. But God grant that I may keep her a little while yet! I don't know what I'd do without her, Jörgen. Especially now, you know, when I haven't got you to cope with any more.

TESMAN [*patting her back*]: There now, Auntie! . . .

MISS TESMAN [*suddenly switching to another tone*]: Well just think of it, so now you're a married man, Jörgen! . . . And to think that you'd be the one to walk off with Hedda Gabler! The lovely Hedda Gabler! Imagine it! So many admirers she always had around her!

TESMAN [*hums a bit and smirks*]: Yes I dare say there are one or two of my good friends who wouldn't mind being in my shoes. Eh?

MISS TESMAN: And then that you were able to take such a honeymoon, too! Five months . . . almost six. . . .

TESMAN: Oh well . . . for me it was a sort of academic trip too, you know. I had to look through all those old records. And the books I had to plough through!

MISS TESMAN: Yes, I suppose you did. [*lowers her voice confidentially*] But tell me, no, Jörgen . . . isn't there anything . . . any other news you can tell me?

TESMAN: From the trip, you mean?

MISS TESMAN: Yes.

TESMAN: Well, I don't think there's much I didn't get into my letters. I was given a doctorate . . . but I told you about that last night.

MISS TESMAN: Oh, all those things, yes. But I mean to say . . . haven't you any . . . as it were . . . any prospects of . . . ?

TESMAN: Prospects?

MISS TESMAN: Oh, good Heavens, Jörgen . . . after all I am your old aunt!

TESMAN: Why certainly I can talk of prospects.

MISS TESMAN: Oh!

TESMAN: I have the best prospect in the world of becoming a professor, one of these days.

MISS TESMAN: Oh yes, professor. . . .

TESMAN: Or . . . I may as well say I'm certain to get it. But dear Auntie Julle . . . you know all this yourself!

MISS TESMAN [*suppressing a smile*]: Why, to be sure I do. You're quite right. [*changing the subject*] . . . But you were telling me about the journey. . . . It must have cost a pretty penny, Jörgen?

TESMAN: Oh well, the cost . . . that big fellowship helped quite a bit, you know.

MISS TESMAN: But I just can't imagine how you could make it do for both of you.

TESMAN: No, I suppose that would need a bit of imagination. Eh?

MISS TESMAN: And then when you're travelling with a lady. That makes everything so very much more expensive, I'm told.

TESMAN: Oh of course . . . it's bound to make a bit of difference. But Hedda had to have that trip, Aunt! She really had to. I couldn't do less.

MISS TESMAN: No, I suppose not. A honeymoon trip, that seems to be part of the trimmings, these days. . . . But tell me now . . . have you had a good look round the house?

TESMAN: Indeed I have. I've been up and about since dawn.

MISS TESMAN: Well, and how do you like it all?

TESMAN: Very much! Oh, very much indeed! There's just one thing, I don't quite know what we're going to do about those two empty rooms, you know, between the back room there and Hedda's bedroom.

MISS TESMAN [*with a smile*]: Ah, my dear Jörgen, you might find a use for them . . . when the time comes.

TESMAN: Why yes, Auntie Julle, you've got something there! As I gradually add to my collection of books, then. . . . Eh?

MISS TESMAN: Precisely, my dear boy. I was thinking of your books.

TESMAN: Most of all I'm pleased for Hedda, though. Before we got engaged she always said that old Lady Falk's villa was the only house she'd really like to live in.

MISS TESMAN: Yes, think of it . . . and then just after you'd gone away it came up for sale.

TESMAN: Yes, Aunt Julle, we really were lucky. Eh?

MISS TESMAN: But expensive, my dear Jörgen! It'll be a terrible expense for you . . . all this.

TESMAN [*looks at her rather crestfallen*]: Why yes, I suppose it will, Auntie?

MISS TESMAN: Oh my dear!

TESMAN: How much, do you think? Approximately? Eh?

MISS TESMAN: I simply can't tell you, before all the bills have come in.

TESMAN: Oh well, luckily Brack was able to get very favourable terms for me. He said as much when he wrote to Hedda.

MISS TESMAN: Yes, don't you worry about that, my boy. . . . Anyway, I've given security for the furniture and all the carpets.

TESMAN: Security? You have? But Auntie Julle . . . what sort of security could you offer?

MISS TESMAN: I made out a mortgage on the annuity.

TESMAN [*leaps up*]: What! On your . . . and Aunt Rina's annuity!

MISS TESMAN: Well, there didn't seem to be any other way of doing it, you know.

TESMAN [*places himself in front of her*]: But have you gone out of your mind, Auntie! That annuity . . . you and Aunt Rina, it's the only thing you've got to live on.

MISS TESMAN: There now . . . don't get so excited about it. It's just a formality, you know. Mr Brack said so too, and he's a judge. He was the one who helped me to arrange the whole thing. Just a formality, he said.

TESMAN: Yes, that's all very well. But all the same . . .

MISS TESMAN: And now you're getting your own salary to draw on. And good gracious, if we did have to spend a little . . . ? A helping hand, just to begin with . . .? Why, we'd be only too happy.

TESMAN: Oh, Auntie . . . you'll never stop sacrificing yourself for me!

MISS TESMAN [*rises and puts her hands on his shoulders*]: Isn't it the only joy I have in this world, to help you along your road, my darling boy? You, who have neither father nor mother to look to? And now we're very nearly there, my boy! There were some black days among the rest. But, thanks be to God, you've made good, Jörgen!

TESMAN: Yes, it's queer, really, the way it all turned out.

MISS TESMAN: Yes . . . and the people who stood in your way . . . and wanted to keep you back . . . you outran them all. They've fallen by the wayside, Jörgen! And your most dangerous adversary, he fell lower than any of them, he did . . . And now he must lie on the bed he's made for himself . . . the poor depraved creature.

TESMAN: Have you heard anything of Ejlert? Since I went off, I mean.

MISS TESMAN: Only that he's supposed to have published a new book.

TESMAN: What's that! Ejlert Lövborg? Just recently, you mean? Eh?

MISS TESMAN: Yes, so they say. Do you think it's likely to amount to anything much? Now when your new book arrives . . . that'll be another matter, Jörgen! What's it going to be about?

TESMAN: It will be an account of the domestic crafts of mediaeval Brabant.

MISS TESMAN: Just think . . . and you can write about things like that!

TESMAN: Incidentally, it may be quite a while before I get it finished. There are all these extensive collections of material, you know, they all have to be sorted out first.

MISS TESMAN: Yes, collecting things and sorting them out . . . you've always been good at that. You're not Joachim's son for nothing!

TESMAN: I'm ever so keen to get going on it. Especially now, with my own comfortable and charming house to sit and work in.

MISS TESMAN: Ah, and most of all, now that you've won the wife of your heart, dear Jörgen.

TESMAN [*embracing her*]: Oh yes, Auntie Julle! Hedda . . . that's the most wonderful thing of all! [*looks towards the doorway*] But here she is, isn't she? Eh?

Hedda comes in from the left of the back room. She is a lady of 29. Her face and her figure are aristocratic and elegant in their proportions. He complexion is of an even pallor. Her eyes are steel grey, and cold, clear, and dispassionate. Her hair is an attractive medium brown in colour, but not particularly ample. She is dressed in a tasteful, somewhat loose-fitting morning gown.

MISS TESMAN [*goes to meet her*]: Good morning, dear Hedda! A very good morning to you!

HEDDA [*offers her hand*]: Good morning, dear Miss Tesman! Such an early visit. So very kind.

MISS TESMAN [*appearing somewhat put out*]: Well, and did the young mistress sleep well in her new home?

HEDDA: Thank you, I slept tolerably well.

TESMAN [*laughs*]: Tolerably! That's a good one, Hedda! You were sleeping like a log, you were, when I got up.

HEDDA: How fortunate. But then, Miss Tesman, one always has to get used to new things. Bit by bit. [*looks towards the window*] Ugh . . . the maid's been and opened the verandah door. The place is flooded with sunlight.

MISS TESMAN [*moving towards the door*]: Well, let's shut it.

HEDDA: Oh no, don't do that! Dear Tesman, go and draw the curtains. That gives a softer light.

TESMAN [*at the door*]: So be it . . . so be it. . . . There you are, Hedda . . . now you've got both shade and fresh air.

HEDDA: Yes, we can do with a bit of fresh air. All these blessed flowers. . . . But dear Miss Tesman . . . won't you take a seat?

MISS TESMAN: No, thank you very much. Now I know everything's all right . . . thanks be to God! And I'd better be thinking of getting home again. To her, lying and waiting so patiently, poor dear.

TESMAN: You'll give her my love, won't you. And say I'll pop in to see her later in the day.

MISS TESMAN: Yes, yes, I'll tell her. Oh, here's another thing, Jörgen . . . [*She feels in her skirt pocket.*] I almost went and forgot it. I've got a little something for you.

TESMAN: What can it be, Aunt? Eh?

MISS TESMAN [*extracts a flat object wrapped in newspaper and hands it to him*]: There you are, my boy.

TESMAN [*opens it*]: Oh my goodness! . . . So you kept them for me, Auntie Julle! Hedda! Now isn't that nice of her, Hedda! Eh?

HEDDA [*by the right-hand whatnot*]: Of course, dear. What is it?

TESMAN: My old house shoes! My slippers, Hedda!

HEDDA: Ah yes. You mentioned them quite frequently on the trip, I remember.

TESMAN: Yes, I did miss them so. [*He goes to her.*] Here, just take a look at them, Hedda!

HEDDA [*crossing to the stove*]: Thank you, they wouldn't appeal to me.

TESMAN [*following her*]: Think of it . . . Aunt Rina lay there and embroidered them for me. Weak as she was. Oh, you can't imagine how many memories they have for me.

HEDDA [*by the table*]: But not for me, particularly.

MISS TESMAN: Why, Hedda's quite right about that, Jörgen.

TESMAN: Yes, but I do think, now that she's one of the family . . .

HEDDA [*interrupts*]: We'll never be able to manage with that maid, Tesman.

MISS TESMAN: Not manage with Berte?

TESMAN: My dear . . . why on earth should you say that? Eh?

HEDDA [*points*]: Look at that! She's left her old hat lying on the chair there.

TESMAN [*appalled, drops the slippers on the floor*]: But . . . but Hedda . . . !

HEDDA: Just think . . . somebody might come in and see it.

TESMAN: No but Hedda . . . that . . . that's Auntie Julle's hat!

HEDDA: Is it?

MISS TESMAN [*takes the hat*]: Yes indeed it's mine. And as it happens it isn't so very old either, my dear young lady.

HEDDA: I really didn't look at it so very closely, Miss Tesman.

MISS TESMAN [*ties on the hat*]: As a matter of fact I'm wearing it for the very first time. And that's the God's truth.

TESMAN: And an awfully fine hat it is too. Really smart!

MISS TESMAN: Oh, that's as it may be, my dear Jörgen. [*looks around*] And my parasol . . . ? Here it is. [*She takes it.*] Because that happens to be mine too. [*under her breath*] Not Berte's.

TESMAN: A new hat and a new parasol! Think of that, Hedda!

HEDDA: Yes, really charming.

TESMAN: Yes, aren't they just? Eh? But Aunt, take a good look at Hedda before you go! Charming's the word for her, eh?

MISS TESMAN: Oh my dear, that's nothing new. Hedda's been lovely all her life.

[*She nods and starts across to the right.*]

TESMAN [*following her*]: Yes, but have you noticed how well and bonny she looks? I declare she's filled out beautifully on the trip.

HEDDA [*moves irritably*]: Oh, do you have to . . . !

MISS TESMAN [*has stopped and turned*]: Filled out?

TESMAN: Yes, Aunt Julle, you don't notice it so much when she's wearing that dress, But I . . . well, I have occasion to . . .

HEDDA [*at the verandah door, impatiently*]: Oh, you don't have occasion for anything!

TESMAN: It must be the mountain air in the Tyrol. . . .

HEDDA [*curtly interrupting*]: I'm exactly the same as I was when we left.

TESMAN: Yes, that's what you say. But you aren't, you know. Can't you see it too, Auntie?

MISS TESMAN [*She has folded her hands and gazes at Hedda.*]: Lovely . . . lovely . . . lovely Hedda. [*She goes to Hedda, takes her head and inclines it towards her with both hands, and kisses her hair.*] God bless you and keep you, Hedda Tesman. For Jörgen's sake.

HEDDA [*frees herself*]: Oh . . . ! Leave me be!

MISS TESMAN [*in quiet rapture*]: Every single day I'll come and visit you both.

TESMAN: Yes, Auntie, that'll be wonderful! Eh?

MISS TESMAN: Goodbye . . . goodbye!

She goes out at the hall door. Tesman follows her out. The door stays half open, and we hear Tesman repeating his message of love to Aunt Rina, and thanking again for the slippers.

While this is going on Hedda walks about the room, raises her arms and clenches her fists as though in a frenzy. Then she draws the curtains back from the verandah door, stands there, and looks out.

After a while Tesman comes back and shuts the door behind him.

TESMAN [*picking up the slippers from the floor*]: What are you looking at, Hedda?

HEDDA [*calm and collected once more*]: I'm just looking at the leaves on the trees. They're so yellow. And so withered.

TESMAN [*rewraps the slippers and lays them on the table*]: Yes, well, it's September now, you know.

HEDDA [*ill at ease again*]: Why yes . . . already it's . . . it's September.

TESMAN: Don't you think Aunt Julle was odd, dear? Almost affected? What can have got into her, do you think? Eh?

HEDDA: Well, I hardly know her. Isn't she usually like that?

TESMAN: Why, no, not like she was just now.

HEDDA [*leaving the window*]: Do you think she was very put out about that hat business?

TESMAN: Oh, not so particularly. Perhaps a little just for a moment. . . .

HEDDA: Well, what manner of behaviour is that, anyway, flinging her hat just anywhere in the drawing room! It's not done.

TESMAN: Well, you may be quite sure that Aunt Julle won't do it again.

HEDDA: Oh, never mind. I'll propitiate her.

TESMAN: Oh my dear, sweet Hedda, if only you would!

HEDDA: When you go down there later you can invite her over for this evening.

TESMAN: Yes, certainly I will. And there's another thing, Hedda, that would make her so very happy.

HEDDA: Well?

TESMAN: Couldn't you bring yourself to give her a kiss when you meet? For my sake, Hedda? Eh?

HEDDA: Oh, don't ask me, Tesman, for God's sake. I've told you before, I just couldn't. I'll try to call her Aunt. And she'll have to be content with that.

TESMAN: Oh well . . . I just thought, now that you belong to the family, you . . .

HEDDA: Hm . . . I'm not at all sure . . .   [*She goes upstage towards the doorway.*]

TESMAN [*after a pause*]: Is there anything the matter with you, Hedda? Eh?

HEDDA: I was just looking at my old piano. It doesn't go with the rest of the things.

TESMAN: As soon as I get my first cheque, we'll see about getting it changed.

HEDDA: Oh no . . . not changed. I don't want to part with it. We'd better put it in the back room, there. And then we can get another one for this room. At a suitable moment, I mean.

TESMAN [*rather put out*]: Yes . . . I suppose that would be an alternative.

HEDDA [*takes the bunch of flowers from the piano*]: These flowers weren't here last night when we arrived.

TESMAN: Aunt Julle probably brought them.

HEDDA [*looks into the bouquet*]: A card. [*takes it out and reads*] 'Will come again later today.' Can you guess who it's from.

TESMAN: No. Who is it from? Eh?

HEDDA: It says 'Mrs Carl Elvsted'.

TESMAN: Really! Mrs Elvsted! Miss Rysing, as she used to be.

HEDDA: Exactly. That woman with the provoking hair that everyone made such a fuss of. An old flame of yours, too, I'm told.

TESMAN [*laughs*]: Oh, it didn't last long. And besides, that was before I met you, Hedda. But just think . . . that she should be back in town.

HEDDA: It's odd that she should come here. I hardly know her, apart from school.

TESMAN: No, and I haven't seen her for . . . oh good Lord, it must be years. I don't know how she can bear to be stuck right up there, so many miles away. Eh?

HEDDA [*thinks a moment, then suddenly speaks*]: I say, Tesman . . . wasn't it up there somewhere that he went . . . that . . . Ejlert Lövborg?

TESMAN: Yes, it must be just about there.

Berte appears at the hall door.

BERTE: She's here again, ma'am, the lady who looked in with the flowers earlier on. [*She points.*] The ones you're holding, ma'am.

HEDDA: She is, is she. Well, be so good as to let her in.

Berte opens the door to Mrs Elvsted and goes out herself.—Mrs Elvsted is a slight woman with soft, attractive features. Her eyes are light blue, large, round, and somewhat protruding, with a scared, questioning expression. Her hair is strikingly fair, almost whitish-yellow, and unusually rich and wavy. She is a couple of years younger than Hedda. She wears a dark going-out dress, tastefully styled but not quite in the latest fashion.

HEDDA [*goes to meet her in a friendly manner*]: Good morning, my dear Mrs Elvsted. How nice to see you once again.

MRS ELVSTED [*nervous, trying to control herself*]: Yes, it's a long time now since we met.

TESMAN [*offering his hand*]: And since we met, too. Eh?

HEDDA: Thank you for your lovely flowers. . . .

MRS ELVSTED: Oh, thank you. . . . I would have come here at once, yesterday afternoon. But then I heard you were abroad. . . .

TESMAN: You've just arrived in town? Eh?

MRS ELVSTED: Yes. I got in about lunch time yesterday. Oh, I was quite in despair when I heard you were away.

HEDDA: In despair! But why?

TESMAN: But my dear Mrs Rysing—Mrs Elvsted I mean to say . . .

HEDDA: I hope there isn't anything wrong?

MRS ELVSTED: Yes, there is. And I don't know another soul here, not anyone I could turn to, apart from you.

HEDDA [*puts the flowers on the table*]: Come . . . we'll sit here on the sofa. . . .

MRS ELVSTED: Oh, I can hardly keep still, let alone sit down!

HEDDA: Of course you can. Come along.

She persuades Mrs Elvsted onto the sofa, and sits beside her.

TESMAN: Well? What is it then . . . ?

HEDDA: Is it something that's happened up at your place?

MRS ELVSTED: Well . . . it both is and yet isn't. Oh, I do so hope you won't misunderstand me.

HEDDA: Well, in that case you'd better tell us all about it, from the beginning, Mrs Elvsted.

TESMAN: After all, that's the reason why you came. Eh?

MRS ELVSTED: Yes . . . yes of course it is. And so I'd better tell you . . . if you don't already know it . . . that Ejlert Lövborg is also in town.

HEDDA: Lövborg is . . . !

TESMAN: What, Ejlert Lövborg back again! Think of that, Hedda!

HEDDA: Yes, yes, I heard!

MRS ELVSTED: He's been here now for about a week. Think of it . . . a whole week! In this dangerous place. Alone! And all the bad influences there are here.

HEDDA: But . . . excuse me, Mrs Elvsted, but how can this possibly concern you?

MRS ELVSTED [*gives her a scared look, then speaks quickly*]: He used to come and teach the children.

HEDDA: Your children?

MRS ELVSTED: My husband's. I haven't got any.

HEDDA: Stepchildren, then.

MRS ELVSTED: Yes.

TESMAN [*slightly incoherent*]: But was he sufficiently . . . I don't quite know how to put it . . . sort of . . . well, regular in his life and habits, so that he could be trusted with . . . ? Eh?

MRS ELVSTED: For the last two years, there's been nothing that anyone could hold against him.

TESMAN: Hasn't there really? Think of that, Hedda!

HEDDA: Yes, I'm listening.

MRS ELVSTED: Nothing at all, I assure you. Not in any way. But all the same . . . Now that I know he's down here . . . in the big city . . . I'm so dreadfully worried about him.

TESMAN: Well, why didn't he stay where he was, then? With you and your husband? Eh?

MRS ELVSTED: When the book came out, you see, he just couldn't contain himself any more, up there.

TESMAN: Why yes of course . . . Aunt Julle said he'd published a new book.

MRS ELVSTED: Yes, a big new book, dealing with cultural development . . . sort of altogether. It's a fortnight ago, now. And then when it sold so many copies . . . and caused such an enormous stir . . .

TESMAN: Did it! Did it indeed? I suppose it was something he had tucked away from his good period, then.

MRS ELVSTED: From before, you mean?

TESMAN: Yes.

MRS ELVSTED: No, he wrote the whole thing while he was with us. Just now . . . during the last year.

TESMAN: Well, that really is good news, Hedda! Think of that!

MRS ELVSTED: Oh yes, if only everything's all right!

HEDDA: Have you seen him here in town?

MRS ELVSTED: No, not yet. It was so difficult, trying to discover his address. But this morning I got it at last.

HEDDA [*gives her a searching glance*]: You know, it seems a little odd that your husband . . . hm . . .

MRS ELVSTED [*with a nervous start*]: That my husband? What?

HEDDA: That he should send you down to town on this errand. That he didn't come in himself to look after his friend.

MRS ELVSTED: Oh no, no . . . my husband doesn't have the time. And then there was . . . some shopping I had to do.

HEDDA [*with a little smile*]: Oh, well, that's different, then.

MRS ELVSTED [*gets up quickly, ill at ease*]: And now I beg of you, Mr Tesman, please . . . receive Ejlert Lövborg well, if he comes here! And he's sure to. I know . . . you were such good friends before. And then you're both interested in the same subject. The same field of studies . . . so far as I understand it.

TESMAN: Well, it used to be before, anyway.

MRS ELVSTED: Yes, and that's why I ask you so particularly, . . . please do . . . please would you keep an eye on him as well. You will, won't you Mr Tesman . . . you promise you will.

TESMAN: Yes of course, I'll be only too happy, Mrs Rysing . . .

HEDDA: Elvsted.

TESMAN: I'll certainly do absolutely everything I can for Ejlert. You may be sure of that.

MRS ELVSTED: Oh, how very kind you are! [*She presses his hands.*] Thank you, Mr Tesman, thank you! [*alarmed*] Yes, because my husband is so particularly fond of him!

HEDDA [*rising*]: You ought to write to him, Tesman. Perhaps he won't come on his own initiative.

TESMAN: Yes, wouldn't that be the best idea, Hedda? Eh?

HEDDA: And the sooner the better. You'd better do it now, at once.

MRS ELVSTED [*beseechingly*]: Yes, if only you would!

TESMAN: I'll do it right away. Do you have his address, Mrs . . . Mrs Elvsted?

MRS ELVSTED: Yes. [*She takes a piece of paper from her pocket and hands it to him.*] I wrote it there.

TESMAN: Good, good. I'll go in, then . . . [*He looks around.*] Oh yes, what happened to . . . ? Oh, there they are.

He picks up the packet with the slippers and is about to go.

HEDDA: Now be sure to write something really warm and friendly. A good long letter.

TESMAN: Yes, I'll do that.

MRS ELVSTED: But for goodness sake don't say that I asked you to invite him!

TESMAN: No, of course not . . . that goes without saying. Eh?

He goes out to the right through the back room.

HEDDA [*goes over to Mrs Elvsted, smiles, and speaks in a low voice*]: There! Two birds with one stone.

MRS ELVSTED: What do you mean by that?

HEDDA: Couldn't you see that I wanted him to leave us?

MRS ELVSTED: Yes, to write the letter . . .

HEDDA: And so that I could speak to you alone.

MRS ELVSTED [*flustered*]: What, about all this?

HEDDA: Exactly.

MRS ELVSTED [*scared*]: But there isn't anything else, Mrs Tesman! Really, nothing more to say!

HEDDA: Oh there is indeed. There's a great deal more. That's perfectly obvious. Come here . . . we'll sit down and have a nice talk about it.

She forces Mrs Elvsted into the armchair by the stove, and sits down herself on one of the stools.

MRS ELVSTED [*anxious, looking at her watch*]: But Mrs Tesman, please . . . I should have left long ago.

HEDDA: Oh, you can't be in such an enormous hurry. . . . Well, then. Now you tell me a bit about your life at home.

MRS ELVSTED: Oh, that's just the one thing I really didn't want to talk about.

HEDDA: But you can tell me, my dear . . . ? After all, we were at school together.

MRS ELVSTED: Yes, but you were in the class above. Oh, I was dreadfully frightened of you in those days!

HEDDA: Frightened? Of me?

MRS ELVSTED: Oh, dreadfully frightened. When we met on the steps you always used to pull my hair.

HEDDA: No, did I really?

MRS ELVSTED: Yes, and you once said you were going to burn it off.

HEDDA: Oh, that was just something I said, you know.

MRS ELVSTED: Yes, but I was such a fool in those days. . . . And anyway, since then . . . we've grown such miles apart. We don't meet the same sort of people at all.

HEDDA: Well, we must try to bridge the gap again. We spoke freely to each other at school, at least, and we always called each other by our Christian names. . . .

MRS ELVSTED: Oh, I'm sure you're wrong about that.

HEDDA: Oh no I'm not! I remember it perfectly. And so we'll be good friends again, like we were in the old days. [*She moves her chair closer.*] There! [*She kisses her cheek.*] From now on you're to call me Hedda.

MRS ELVSTED [*presses and pats her hand*]: Oh, you're so kind and good to me! I'm just not used to such kind treatment.

HEDDA: There, now! And I'm going to call you my darling Thora.

MRS ELVSTED: I'm called Thea.

HEDDA: Quite right. Of course. Thea, I meant. [*looks at her sympathetically*] And so you're not accustomed to kind treatment, my poor Thea? Not even in your own home!

MRS ELVSTED: Oh, if only I had a home! But I haven't got one. Never had one.

HEDDA [*looks at her a little*]: I rather thought it must be something like that.

MRS ELVSTED [*stares helplessly in front of her*]: Yes . . . yes . . . yes.

HEDDA: I don't quite remember how it was, now. But didn't you go up there in the first place as Mr Elvsted's housekeeper?

MRS ELVSTED: Oh, actually I was meant to be a governess. But his wife . . . in those days . . . she was an invalid . . . and usually stayed in bed. So I had to look after the house as well.

HEDDA: But then . . . after that . . . you became the mistress of the house.

MRS ELVSTED [*heavily*]: Yes, I became his wife.

HEDDA: Let me see . . . About how long ago would that be, now?

MRS ELVSTED: That I got married?

HEDDA: Yes.

MRS ELVSTED: That was five years ago.

HEDDA: That's right, five years it must be.

MRS ELVSTED: Oh, those five years . . . ! Well, the last two or three at least. Oh, if only you knew, Mrs Tesman . . .

HEDDA [*hits her lightly on the hand*]: Mrs Tesman? Now that's naughty, Thea.

MRS ELVSTED: Oh no, I'm sorry . . . Hedda. I'll try. But if only you could imagine what it was like . . .

HEDDA [*casually*]: Ejlert Lövborg's been up there about three years, hasn't he?

MRS ELVSTED [*looks at her uncertainly*]: Ejlert Lövborg? Yes . . . so he has.

HEDDA: Did you know him before that? From town?

MRS ELVSTED: Hardly at all. Well, that is . . . I'd heard of him, of course.

HEDDA: But then up there . . . he used to come to your house quite often?

MRS ELVSTED: Yes, he came over every day. He had to come and read with the children. Because in the long run I couldn't manage it all by myself.

HEDDA: No indeed, I can imagine. . . . And your husband . . . ? I suppose he travels quite a bit in his position?

MRS ELVSTED: Well, of course . . . he's in charge of the whole administration of the district, so he has to keep an eye on things.

HEDDA [*leaning against the arm of the chair*]: Thea . . . poor, sweet Thea . . . now you must tell me all about it . . . as it really is.

MRS ELVSTED: Well, what do you want to know?

HEDDA: Tell me, what's your husband really like, Thea? I mean, well . . . to be with? Does he treat you well?

MRS ELVSTED [*evasively*]: He thinks he does everything for the best.

HEDDA: It just seems to me that he must be a little old for you. Over twenty years older, isn't he?

MRS ELVSTED [*roused*]: Oh, that as well. Just everything about him! There's simply nothing . . . we just haven't a thought in common. We don't share a thing, he and I.

HEDDA: But isn't he fond of you all the same? In his own way?

MRS ELVSTED: Oh, I don't know what he is. I think he just finds me useful. And then it doesn't cost much to keep me. I'm cheap.

HEDDA: That's foolish of you.

MRS ELVSTED [*shakes her head*]: Can't be anything else. Not with him. I don't believe he thinks of anyone except himself. And then perhaps a bit the children.

HEDDA: And then he's fond of Ejlert Lövborg, Thea.

MRS ELVSTED [*looks at her*]: Of Ejlert Lövborg! What gives you that idea?

HEDDA: But my dear . . . it seems to me that when he sends you all this way to town to look for him . . . [*smiles almost imperceptibly*] And besides, you told Tesman so yourself.

MRS ELVSTED [*with a nervous laugh*]: Did I? Well, I suppose I did. [*a subdued outburst*] No . . . I may as well make a clean breast of it at once! It's bound to come out anyway, in the end.

HEDDA: But Thea, my dear . . . ?

MRS ELVSTED: Brief and to the point, then! I never told my husband I was leaving.

HEDDA: What are you saying! Didn't he know you were leaving!

MRS ELVSTED: Of course not. Anyway he wasn't at home. He'd gone on a tour of inspection. Oh, I just couldn't bear it any longer, Hedda! Not another minute! So terribly alone I'd have been, up there, from now on.

HEDDA: Well! And then?

MRS ELVSTED: I just packed up a few of my belongings. The essentials. Without letting anyone see. And then I left.

HEDDA: Just like that?

MRS ELVSTED: Yes. And took the train to town.

HEDDA: But my dear, sweet Thea . . . I don't know how you dared!

MRS ELVSTED [*gets up from the chair and walks across the floor*]: Well what on earth else would you have me do?

HEDDA: But what do you think your husband will say when you go back?

MRS ELVSTED: Back up there?

HEDDA: Yes, yes.

MRS ELVSTED: I'll never go back up there.

HEDDA [*gets up, and goes closer to her*]: Then you've really . . . in all seriousness . . . run away from it all?

MRS ELVSTED: Yes. I didn't think there was anything else I could do.

HEDDA: And then . . . that you left so openly.

MRS ELVSTED: Oh, there's no hiding that sort of thing, anyway.

HEDDA: But what do you think people will say about you, Thea?

MRS ELVSTED: Oh, they'll just have to say what they please. [*She sits depressed and exhausted on the sofa.*] I simply had to do what I did.

HEDDA [*after a short pause*]: And what's going to happen to you now? What are you going to do with yourself?

MRS ELVSTED: I don't know yet. I just know that I must live here, where Ejlert Lövborg's living. . . . If I have to live at all.

HEDDA [*moves a chair across from the table, sits by her, and strokes her hands*]: Tell me, Thea . . . how did it come about, this . . . this familiarity between you and Ejlert Lövborg?

MRS ELVSTED: Oh, it just happened, bit by bit. I got a sort of control over him.

HEDDA: Really?

MRS ELVSTED: He left off his old ways. Not because I asked him to. I never dared to do that. But he knew all right that I didn't like that sort of thing. And then he gave it up.

HEDDA [*concealing an involuntary sneer*]: And so you've reclaimed the prodigal . . . as they say . . . little Thea.

MRS ELVSTED: Well, that's what he says, anyway. And he . . . for his part . . . he's made me into a sort of real person. Taught me to think . . . and to understand quite a lot of things.

HEDDA: Did he give you lessons too, then?

MRS ELVSTED: No, not lessons, like that. But he talked to me. Talked of so fantastically many things. And then came that beautiful, happy time, when I shared his work! Was allowed to help him!

HEDDA: He let you help him?

MRS ELVSTED: Yes! When he wrote anything, we always had to do it together.

HEDDA: Like two good companions, then.

MRS ELVSTED [*animated*]: Companions! Yes, imagine, Hedda . . . that's what he used to say! . . . Oh, I ought to be so wonderfully happy. But I can't be, quite. For I can't be sure that it will really last.

HEDDA: Are you still so uncertain of him, then?

MRS ELVSTED [*heavily*]: There's the shadow of a woman who stands between us.

HEDDA [*looks at her with keen interest*]: Who might that be?

MRS ELVSTED: Don't know. Someone or other from . . . from his past. Someone he can't really forget.

HEDDA: What has he told you . . . about this?

MRS ELVSTED: He's only ever once . . . sort of indirectly . . . touched on it.

HEDDA: Well! And what did he say?

MRS ELVSTED: He said that when they parted, she threatened to shoot him with a pistol.

HEDDA [*cold and collected*]: Oh rubbish! People don't have such things here.

MRS ELVSTED: No. And that's why I think it must be that red-haired singer, whom he once . . .

HEDDA: Yes, I suppose that's possible.

MRS ELVSTED: Because I can remember someone telling me that she carried a loaded pistol.

HEDDA: Oh well . . . then it must be her, then.

MRS ELVSTED [*wrings her hands*]: Yes but just think, Hedda . . . now I hear that the woman . . . she's in town again! Oh . . . I'm quite distracted. . . .

HEDDA [*glancing towards the back room*]: Sh! Here's Tesman coming. [*gets up, and whispers*] Thea . . . all this must be just between you and me.

MRS ELVSTED [*jumping up*]: Oh yes . . . yes! For God's sake . . . !

    Jörgen Tesman, with a letter in his hand, comes from the right of the inner room.

TESMAN: There now . . . the epistle is signed and sealed.

HEDDA: That's splendid. But I think Mrs Elvsted wants to go now. I won't be a moment. I'm just going as far as the garden gate.

TESMAN: Oh Hedda . . . do you think Berte could see to this?

HEDDA [*takes the letter*]: I'll tell her.

    Berte comes in from the hall.

BERTE: Mr Brack is here and says please may he come in.

HEDDA: Yes, ask Mr Brack to step inside. And then . . . I say, . . . then put this letter in the post box.

BERTE [*takes the letter*]: Yes, ma'am.

    She opens the door for Mr Brack, and goes out herself. Brack is a gentleman of 45. Stocky, but well built and elastic in his movements. His face roundish, with a good profile. Hair short, still almost black, and carefully dressed. Eyes lively and playful. Thick eyebrows, thick moustache cut short at the ends. He is dressed in a stylish walking suit, perhaps a little too youthful in cut for a man of his age. He uses an eyeglass, which he now and again allows to fall.

BRACK [*bowing, his hat in his hand*]: Is it permissible to call so early in the day?

HEDDA: Of course it is.

TESMAN [*takes his hand*]: We're always glad to see you. [*He introduces.*] Mr Brack . . . Miss Rysing . . .

HEDDA: Oh . . . !

BRACK [*bows*]: Ah . . . delighted to make your acquaintance. . . .

HEDDA [*looks at him and laughs*]: How charming to view you by daylight, Mr Brack!

BRACK: You find me . . . perhaps a little changed?

HEDDA: Yes, you look rather younger, I think.

BRACK: Accept my humble gratitude.

TESMAN: But what do you say to Hedda, then! Eh? Isn't she blossoming? She's positively . . .

HEDDA: Oh, pray leave me out of this. You'd do better to thank Mr Brack for all the trouble he's taken . . . .

BRACK: Oh, not at all . . . I do assure you it was a pleasure. . . .

HEDDA: Yes, you're a loyal soul. But my friend's standing here and dying to get away. Au revoir, Mr Brack. I'll be back in a moment.

Mutual leave-taking. Mrs Elvsted and Hedda leave by the hall door.

BRACK: Well, now . . . and does everything come up to the lady's expectations?

TESMAN: Oh yes, and we can't thank you enough. That is . . . a little shifting back and forth may be necessary, I gather. And there are one or two things missing. We'll doubtless have to acquire a few trifles yet.

BRACK: Oh, will you? Really?

TESMAN: But we won't be putting you to any further trouble. Hedda said she'd take care of the necessary purchases herself. . . . But I say, shan't we sit down? Eh?

BRACK: Thank you, just for a moment. [*sits by the table*] There's a little matter I'd like to talk to you about, my dear Tesman.

TESMAN: Oh? Ah, I'm with you! [*He sits down.*] The entertainment has its serious side, no doubt. Eh?

BRACK: Oh, as yet there's no tearing hurry about the financial side. Though incidentally, I should be happier if we'd arranged things a little more modestly.

TESMAN: But that would have been quite out of the question! Think of Hedda, man! You, who know her so well. . . . I couldn't possibly have expected her to put up with a genteel suburb!

BRACK: Ah, no . . . there's the rub.

TESMAN: And then . . . fortunately . . . it can't be long before I get that appointment.

BRACK: Well, you know . . . these things have a habit of taking their time.

TESMAN: Perhaps you've heard some more about it? Eh?

BRACK: Nothing in any way definite, but . . . [*He breaks off.*] Oh, by the way, I do have one piece of news for you.

TESMAN: Oh?

BRACK: Your old friend Ejlert Lövborg is back in town.

TESMAN: I know that already.

BRACK: Oh? How did you come to know it?

TESMAN: She told us, the lady who just went out with Hedda.

BRACK: She did. What was her name again? I didn't quite catch . . .

TESMAN: Mrs Elvsted.

BRACK: Aha . . . so that's who it was, then. Yes . . . I believe he stayed with them up there.

TESMAN: And just think . . . I was so delighted to hear that he's become quite a sober citizen again!

BRACK: Yes, that's what they say.

TESMAN: And he's supposed to have published a new book. Eh?

BRACK: Yes, by God he has!

TESMAN: And what's more, it's been very well received!

BRACK: It's been quite exceptionally well received.

TESMAN: Just think . . . isn't that wonderfully good news? That fellow, with all his extraordinary talents. . . . I was terribly convinced that he'd gone to the dogs for good.

BRACK: Yes, pretty nearly everyone thought the same.

TESMAN: But I just can't imagine what he's going to do with himself now! What on earth can he possibly find to live on? Eh?

During the last speech, Hedda has come in from the hall.

HEDDA [*to Brack, laughing a little scornfully*]: Tesman's forever worrying about what people are going to find to live on.

TESMAN: Oh Heavens . . . we're sitting here talking about poor Ejlert Lövborg, my dear.

HEDDA [*looks at him quickly*]: Oh yes? [*sits down in the armchair by the stove and asks indifferently*] What's the matter with him?

TESMAN: Well . . . he must have spent all the money he inherited ages ago. And I don't suppose he can write a new book every year. Eh? Well, then . . . I really can't for the life of me see how he's going to exist at all.

BRACK: Perhaps I could tell you a little about that.

TESMAN: Oh?

BRACK: You must remember that he's got relations with quite a lot of influence.

TESMAN: Oh well, his relations . . . I'm afraid they've disowned him entirely.

BRACK: They used to regard him as the white hope of the family.

TESMAN: Yes, they used to, yes! But he's been and dished all that himself.

HEDDA: Who knows? [*She smiles faintly.*] Up at the Elvsteds' they've been busy reclaiming him. . . .

BRACK: And then there's this new book he's written. . . .

TESMAN: Oh well, I hope to goodness they will help him to get something. I've just written to him. Oh, Hedda, I asked him to come round this evening.

BRACK: But my dear Tesman, you're coming to my bachelor party this evening. You promised last night on the quay.

HEDDA: Had you forgotten, Tesman?

TESMAN: Yes, by all that's holy.

BRACK: In any case, I think you may rely on him to find an excuse.

TESMAN: Why should you think that? Eh?

BRACK [*a little hesitantly, rising and leaning his hands on the back of the chair*]: My dear Tesman . . . And you too, madam. . . . I can no longer allow you to remain in ignorance of something that . . . that . . .

TESMAN: Something to do with Ejlert . . . ?

BRACK: Both him and yourself.

TESMAN: But come on then, Mr Brack!

BRACK: You ought to prepare yourself for the discovery that your appointment may not come quite as soon as you hope and expect.

TESMAN [*jumps up in alarm*]: Has something happened to delay it? Eh?

BRACK: The appointment to the professorship might conceivably be contested by another candidate. . . .

TESMAN: Another candidate! Think of that, Hedda!

HEDDA [*leans further back in her chair*]: Ah, yes . . . yes!

TESMAN: But who on earth! Surely not . . . ?

BRACK: Quite correct. Ejlert Lövborg.

TESMAN [*clasps his hands together*]: No, no . . . this is quite unthinkable! Quite impossible! Eh?

BRACK: Hm . . . we may very well find it happening, all the same.

TESMAN: Oh but my dear sir . . . but that would be quite incredibly inconsiderate of him! [*He flings his arms about.*] Yes, because . . . just think . . . I'm a married man! We got married on our expectations, Hedda and I. Been and borrowed vast sums. We're in debt to Auntie Julle, too! Because, good God . . . the post was as good as promised to me. Eh?

BRACK: Come, come, come . . . you'll most probably get it, too. But only after a bit of competition.

HEDDA [*immobile in her chair*]: Just think, Tesman . . . it'll be quite a sporting event.

TESMAN: But my dearest Hedda, how can you take it all so calmly!

HEDDA [*as before*]: Oh, I don't at all. I await the result with breathless expectation.

BRACK: Well, anyway, Mrs Tesman, it's as well that you should know how matters stand. I mean . . . before you embark on those little purchases you apparently threaten to make.

HEDDA: This can't change anything so far as that's concerned.

BRACK: No? Well, that's all right, then. I'll say goodbye! [*to Tesman*] When I take my constitutional this afternoon I'll step in and fetch you, shall I?

TESMAN: Oh yes, yes . . . I hardly know where I am.

HEDDA [*reclining, stretching out her hand*]: Goodbye, Mr Brack! We look forward to your return.

BRACK: Many thanks. Goodbye, goodbye.

TESMAN [*escorting him to the door*]: Goodbye, my dear Mr Brack! You really must excuse all this. . . .

> *Brack goes out at the hall door.*

TESMAN [*trails across the floor*]: Ah, Hedda . . . one should never go building castles in the air. Eh?

HEDDA [*looks at him and smiles*]: And do you?

TESMAN: Yes . . . it can't be denied . . . it was idiotically romantic to go and get married, and buy a house, just on expectations alone.

HEDDA: You may be right about that.

TESMAN: Well . . . at least we have got our lovely house, Hedda! Just think . . . the house we'd both set out hearts on. Our dream house, I might almost call it. Eh?

HEDDA [*rises slowly and tiredly*]: The agreement was that we were to live a social life. Entertain.

TESMAN: Yes, oh Heavens . . . I was so looking forward to it! Just think, to see you as the hostess . . . presiding over a select group of friends! Eh? . . . Well, well, well . . . for the time being we'll just have to be the two of us, Hedda. Just see Aunt Julle once in a while. . . . Oh, for you everything should have been so very . . . very different . . . !

HEDDA: And I suppose I won't get my footman just yet awhile.

TESMAN: Oh no . . . a manservant, you must see that that's quite out of the question.

HEDDA: And the saddle-horse I was to have had . . .

TESMAN [*appalled*]: The saddle-horse!

HEDDA: . . . I suppose I daren't even think of that, now.

TESMAN: No, God preserve us . . . that goes without saying!

HEDDA [*moving across*]: Oh, well . . . I've got one thing at least that I can pass the time with.

TESMAN [*ecstatic*]: Oh, thank the good Lord for that! And what might that be, Hedda? Eh?

HEDDA [*at the centre doorway, looking at him with concealed contempt*]: My pistols . . . Jörgen.

TESMAN [*alarmed*]: Pistols!

HEDDA [*with cold eyes*]: General Gabler's pistols.

> *She goes out to the left through the back room.*

TESMAN [*runs to the doorway and shouts after her*]: No, for the love of God, my darling Hedda . . . don't touch those dangerous contraptions! For my sake, Hedda! Eh?

ACT II

> *The room at the Tesmans' as in the first Act, except that the piano has been removed and an elegant little writing-desk with a bookshelf put in its place. A small table has been placed by the sofa on the left. Most of the flowers have been removed. Mrs Elvsted's bunch of flowers stands on the large table in the foreground. . . . It is afternoon.*
>
> *Hedda, now dressed to receive visitors, is alone in the room. She is standing by the open glass door, loading a revolver-type pistol. Its companion lies in an open case on the writing-desk.*

HEDDA [*looks down into the garden and shouts*]: Hullo again, Mr Brack!

BRACK [*down in the garden some distance away*]: Good afternoon to you, Mrs Tesman!

HEDDA [*raises the pistol and takes aim*]: I'm going to shoot you, sir!

BRACK [*shouting down below*]: No-no-no! Don't stand there aiming right at me!

HEDDA: That's what comes of sneaking round the back!

> *She fires.*

BRACK [*closer*]: Are you quite mad . . . !

HEDDA: Oh good Lord . . . did I hit you perhaps?

BRACK [*still outside*]: Stop fooling about, I tell you!

HEDDA: Come inside then, Mr Brack.

> *Mr Brack, already dressed for the evening's occasion, comes in through the glass door. He carries a light overcoat on his arm.*

BRACK: What the devil . . . do you still play at that game? What are you shooting at?

HEDDA: Oh, I just stand here and shoot into the blue.

BRACK [*eases the pistol out of her hand*]: By your leave, my lady. [*looks at it*] Ah yes . . . I seem to recognize this fellow. [*looks around*] Now then, where's the case? Ah, here. [*He replaces the pistol and shuts the case.*] And now we won't play with those toys any more today.

HEDDA: Well, what in God's name do you want me to do with myself?

BRACK: Haven't you had any visitors?

HEDDA [*shuts the verandah door*]: Not a soul. I suppose the crowds are all in the country still.

BRACK: And Tesman's not in either, perhaps?

HEDDA [*at the writing-desk, puts the pistol in the drawer*]: No. As soon as he'd eaten he ran off to his aunts. He didn't expect you so soon.

BRACK: Hm . . . and I didn't think of that. Stupid of me.

HEDDA [*turns her head and looks at him*]: Why stupid?

BRACK: Because then I could have come out here . . . even a little earlier.

HEDDA [*crosses the floor*]: And then you'd have found no one at all, I've been in my room, changing after lunch.

BRACK: And isn't there the minutest chink in the door that would have permitted communication?

HEDDA: Why, you forgot to arrange one of those.

BRACK: That was also stupid of me.

HEDDA: Well, we'd better sit down here then. And wait. Because Tesman won't be home in a hurry.

BRACK: Well, well, good Heavens, I shall be patient.

> *Hedda sits in the corner of the sofa. Brack lays his coat over the nearest chair and seats himself, but keeps his hat in his hand. A short pause. They look at one another.*

HEDDA: Well?

BRACK [*in the same tone*]: Well?

HEDDA: I asked first.

BRACK [*leans forward slightly*]: Well, my lady, what do you say to a comfortable little gossip.

HEDDA [*leans further back in the sofa*]: Doesn't it seem to you that it's an eternity since we talked together? Oh . . . I don't count those few words last night and this morning.

BRACK: But . . . between ourselves? Just the two of us, you mean?

HEDDA: Well, yes. More or less.

BRACK: I've gone around here day after day longing for you to come back again.

HEDDA: And for the matter of that, I've been longing for the same thing.

BRACK: You have? Really, my lady? And I was convinced you were having a wonderful time on the trip!

HEDDA: Oh, magnificent!

BRACK: But Tesman was always saying so in his letters.

HEDDA: Yes, he was! He's absolutely in his element if he's given leave to grub around in libraries. And sit copying out ancient parchments . . . or whatever they are.

BRACK [*a little maliciously*]: After all, that is his particular *raison d'être*. Part of it, anyway.

HEDDA: Yes, that's it. So it was all very fine for him. . . . But for me! Oh no, my dear Brack . . . for me it was horribly tedious.

BRACK [*sympathizing*]: Was it really as bad as all that?

HEDDA: Oh yes, use your imagination . . . ! For six months on end, never meeting anyone who knew anybody in our circle. Who could talk about our own affairs.

BRACK: Well, no . . . I'd have felt the want of that myself.

HEDDA: And then the most unbearable thing of all . . .

BRACK: Well?

HEDDA: . . . . everlastingly having to be together with . . . with the selfsame person. . . .

BRACK [*nods assentingly*]: Day in and day out . . . yes. Think of it . . . at all possible times of the . . .

HEDDA: I said everlastingly.

BRACK: So be it. But I should have thought that in the case of our estimable Tesman, it would have been possible to . . .

HEDDA: Tesman is . . . an academic, my dear sir.

BRACK: Undeniably.

HEDDA: And academics aren't a bit amusing as travelling companions. Not in the long run, anyway.

BRACK: Not even . . . the academic with whom one happens to be . . . in love?

HEDDA: Ugh . . . don't use that glutinous word!

BRACK [*pulled up*]: What's this, my lady!

HEDDA [*half laughingly, half bitterly*]: Well, you ought to have a try at it! Hearing about the history of civilization day in and day out. . . .

BRACK: Everlastingly.

HEDDA: Yes-yes-yes! and then this stuff about mediaeval domestic crafts . . . ! That's the most sickening of the lot!

BRACK [*looks at her inquiringly*]: But, tell me . . . how am I then to account for the fact that . . . ? Hm. . . .

HEDDA: That Jörgen Tesman and I made a match of it, you mean?

BRACK: Well, let's put it that way.

HEDDA: Oh, Heavens, does it seem to you so strange, then?

BRACK: Both yes and no . . . my lady.

HEDDA: I'd really danced myself tired, my dear sir. I had had my day. . . . [*She gives a little shudder.*] Oh, no . . . I'm not going to say that. Nor think it, either.

BRACK: With respect, madam, you've no reason to.

HEDDA: Oh . . . reason. . . . [*She sums him up with her look.*] And Jörgen Tesman . . . you must allow that he's a most worthy person in every way.

BRACK: Oh, solid worth. Heaven preserve us.

HEDDA: And I can't see that there's anything specifically ridiculous about him. . . . Or what do you say?

BRACK: Ridiculous? No-o . . . I wouldn't say that exactly. . . .

HEDDA: Well. But then he's a most diligent research worker, at any rate! . . . And after all, he might get somewhere with it in time, in spite of everything.

BRACK [*looks at her a little uncertainly*]: But I thought you believed, like everybody else, that he'd make a really outstanding man.

HEDDA [*with a tired expression*]: Yes, so I did. . . . And then when he came along and was so pathetically eager to be allowed to support me. . . . I don't really see why I shouldn't let him?

BRACK: Well of course, if you put it like that. . . .

HEDDA: It was more than any of my other gallant friends were prepared to do, dear Mr Brack.

BRACK [*laughs*]: Ah, I regret I can't answer for all the others. But as for myself, as you know I've always observed a . . . a certain respect for the bonds of holy matrimony. In a general sort of way, my lady.

HEDDA [*banteringly*]: Well no, I never really had any very high hopes of you.

BRACK: I demand no more than a nice intimate circle of acquaintances, where I can rally round with advice and assistance, and where I'm allowed to come and go as . . . as a trusted friend. . . .

HEDDA: Of the master of the house, you mean?

BRACK [*inclines his head*]: Candidly . . . of the lady, for choice. But naturally of the man as well. D'you know . . . this sort of . . . let me put it, this sort of triangular relationship . . . it's really highly convenient for all concerned.

HEDDA: Yes, I'd have been glad of a third on the trip, often enough. Ugh . . . sitting there, just two people alone in the compartment . . . !

BRACK: Fortunately, the nuptial journey is at an end. . . .

HEDDA [*shakes her head*]: The journey'll be a long one . . . a long one yet. I've just come to a stopping-place on the line.

BRACK: Well, then you jump out. And move around a little, my lady.

HEDDA: I'll never jump out.

BRACK: Are you quite sure?

HEDDA: Yes. Because there's always someone there who'll . . .

BRACK [*laughing*]: . . . who'll look at your legs, you mean?

HEDDA: Exactly.

BRACK: Oh well, good Lord. . . .

HEDDA [*with a gesture of dismissal*]: Don't like it. . . . Then I'd sooner stay where I am . . . in the compartment. Two people alone together.

BRACK: Well then, if somebody else climbs into the compartment.

HEDDA: Ah yes . . . that's quite another thing!

BRACK: A trusted and sympathetic friend . . .

HEDDA: . . . who can converse on all manner of lively topics . . .

BRACK: . . . and who's not in the least academic!

HEDDA [*with an audible sigh*]: Yes, that really is a relief.

BRACK [*hears the front door opening and listens*]: The triangle is completed.

HEDDA [*half aloud*]: And the train drives on.

Jörgen Tesman, in a grey walking suit and with a soft hat, comes in from the hall. He has quite a number of unbound books under his arm and in his pockets.

TESMAN [*goes up to the table by the corner sofa*]: Poof . . . hot work dragging all these around. [*He puts down the books.*] To put it elegantly, I'm sweating, Hedda. Why, what's this . . . you're here already, Mr Brack? Eh? Berte didn't tell me anything about that.

BRACK [*gets up*]: I came up through the garden.

HEDDA: What are those books you've got there?

TESMAN [*turns a few pages*]: Oh, new academic publications that I simply had to have.

HEDDA: Academic publications?

BRACK: Aha, they're academic publications, Mrs Tesman.

Brack and Hedda exchange a knowing smile.

HEDDA: Do you need still more academic publications?

TESMAN: Oh yes, my dear Hedda . . . can't get too many of those. One must keep up with everything that's written.

HEDDA: Yes, I suppose one must.

TESMAN [*searching among the books*]: And look here . . . here we are, I've got hold of Ejlert Lövborg's new book, too. [*He holds it out.*] Perhaps you'd like to have a look at it, Hedda? Eh?

HEDDA: No thank you. Or . . . yes, perhaps I will, later on.

TESMAN: I glanced at a few pages on my way up.

BRACK: Well, and what did you think of it, then? . . . From the academic point of view?

TESMAN: I think it's remarkable how soberly he's argued it. He never used to write like this before. [*gathers up the books*] But now I'm going to go in with all this. It'll be a joy to cut the pages . . . ! And then I'll have to get into some other clothes. [*to Brack*] I take it we don't have to leave straight away, do we? Eh?

BRACK: No indeed . . . there's no hurry for a long while yet.

TESMAN: Ah well, I'll take my time then. [*goes with the books, but stops in the doorway and turns*] Oh, while I think of it, Hedda . . . Aunt Julle won't be able to come this evening.

HEDDA: Won't she? Is it because of that affair with the hat, perhaps?

TESMAN: Oh, good gracious! How can you think that of Auntie Julle? Just think . . . ! But the thing is Aunt Rina's so very ill, you see.

HEDDA: She always is.

TESMAN: Yes, but today she was quite exceptionally bad, poor thing.

HEDDA: Well, then it's only reasonable that the other one should stay with her. I'll have to make the best of it.

TESMAN: And you can't imagine, Hedda, how overjoyed Aunt Julle was in spite of everything . . . because you looked so well from the trip!

HEDDA [*half under her breath, getting up*]: Oh, these everlasting aunts!

TESMAN: Eh?

HEDDA [*crossing to the glass door*]: Nothing.

TESMAN: Oh, all right then. [*He goes out through the back room to the right.*]

BRACK: What was that about a hat?

HEDDA: Oh, it was to do with Miss Tesman this morning. She'd put her hat down there on the chair. [*looks at him and smiles*] And I pretended I thought it was the maid's.

BRACK [*shakes his head*]: But my dearest lady, how could you do such a thing! To that harmless old soul!

HEDDA [*nervously, walking across*]: Oh, you know how it is . . . these things just suddenly come over me. And then I can't resist them. [*flings herself down in the armchair by the stove*] Oh, I don't know myself how to explain it.

BRACK [*behind the armchair*]: You're not really happy . . . that's probably what it is.

HEDDA [*looking straight ahead*]: And I don't really know why I should be . . . happy. Or perhaps you might be able to tell me?

BRACK: Yes . . . among other things, because you've got just the home you wanted.

HEDDA [*looks up at him and laughs*]: Do you also believe that fairy story?

BRACK: Why, isn't there anything in it?

HEDDA: Oh yes . . . there's something in it.

BRACK: Well?

HEDDA: There's this much in it, that I used Tesman as an escort to take me home from evening parties last summer. . . .

BRACK: Ah, regrettably . . . I had to go quite a different way.

HEDDA: True enough, you were going a rather different way, last summer.

BRACK [*laughs*]: Touché, my lady! Well . . . but you and Tesman, then . . . ?

HEDDA: Yes, well then we came past this house one evening. And Tesman, poor fellow, was floundering and dithering. Because he couldn't think of anything to talk about. So I felt sorry for the poor erudite man. . . .

BRACK [*smiles skeptically*]: Did you? Hm. . . .

HEDDA: Yes, by your leave sir, I did. And then . . . to help him along a bit . . . I happened to say, just on the impulse, that I'd like to live here in this villa.

BRACK: No more than that?

HEDDA: Not that particular evening.

BRACK: But afterwards, then?

HEDDA: Ah yes. My impulsiveness had its consequences, my dear Mr Brack.

BRACK: Unfortunately . . . impulsiveness does that only too frequently, my lady.

HEDDA: Thank you! But in this ardour for Lady Falk's villa Jörgen Tesman and I met in mutual understanding, you see! It brought on engagement and marriage and honeymoon and the whole lot. Ah well, Mr Brack . . . as one makes one's bed one must lie on it . . . I almost said.

BRACK: But this is delicious! And perhaps you didn't really care about the place at all?

HEDDA: No, God knows I did not.

BRACK: Well, but now, then? Now that we've arranged everything a bit comfortably for you!

HEDDA: Ugh . . . I think it smells of lavender and pot-pourri in all the rooms. . . . But perhaps Auntie Julle brought that smell in with her.

BRACK [*laughs*]: No, I think it's more probably a relic of the late lamented Lady Falk.

HEDDA: Yes, it has a sort of odour of death. Like a bouquet the day after a ball. [*clasps her hands at the back of her neck, leans back in the chair and looks at him*] Ah, dear Mr Brack . . . you just can't imagine how excruciatingly bored I'll be, out here.

BRACK: Don't you think that for you too, my lady, life might have something or other up its sleeve?

HEDDA: Anything . . . in any way inviting?

BRACK: Well of course that would be best.

HEDDA: Lord knows what sort of thing that would be. I often wonder whether . . . [*She breaks off.*] But that wouldn't be any good either.

BRACK: Who knows? Let me hear about it.

HEDDA: Whether I could get Tesman to go in for politics, I mean.

BRACK [*laughs*]: Tesman! Oh now seriously . . . anything like politics, he wouldn't be any . . . manner of use at that.

HEDDA: No, I don't suppose he would. . . . But don't you think I might get him to do it, all the same?

BRACK: Well . . . what possible satisfaction could that give you? When he's no good? Why should you want him to?

HEDDA: Because I'm bored, d'you hear! [*after a pause*] So you think it would be quite out of the question for Tesman to end up as Prime Minister?

BRACK: Hm . . . you know, my lady . . . to do that he'd have to be quite a rich man, for a start.

HEDDA [*rises impatiently*]: Yes, there we have it! It's these paltry circumstances I've landed up in . . . ! [*She moves across.*] That's what makes life so pitiful! So positively ludicrous! . . . Because that's what it is.

BRACK: I think it's something else that's the trouble.

HEDDA: What, then?

BRACK: You've never had to go through any really stirring experience.

HEDDA: Anything serious, you mean?

BRACK: Yes, I suppose one could put it that way too. But now . . . it might come.

HEDDA [*tosses her head*]: Oh, you're thinking of all the commotion about this wretched professorship! But that'll be Tesman's own affair. I'm not going to give it a thought.

BRACK: No-no, well we won't talk about that. But then when you're faced with . . . what I may . . . perhaps a little pompously . . . refer to as a sacred and . . . and exacting responsibility? [*smiles*] A new responsibility, my little lady.

HEDDA [*angry*]: Be quiet! You'll never see anything of the sort!

BRACK [*carefully*]: We'll talk about it in a year's time . . . at the very latest.

HEDDA [*shortly*]: I've no aptitude for any such thing, Mr Brack. No responsibilities for me, thank you!

BRACK: Why shouldn't you, like most other women, have a natural aptitude for a vocation that . . . ?

HEDDA [*at the glass door*]: Oh, be quiet, I say! . . . I've often thought there's only one thing in the world I'm any good at.

BRACK [*moves closer*]: And what might that be, may I venture to ask?

HEDDA [*standing and looking out*]: Boring myself to death. So now you know. [*turns, looks towards the inner room, and laughs*] Ah yes, right enough! Here comes the professor.

BRACK [*cautioning her in a low voice*]: Now, now, now, my lady!

> *Jörgen Tesman, dressed for the party, holding his gloves and his hat, comes in from the right of the back room.*

TESMAN: Hedda . . . did Ejlert Lövborg send to say he wasn't coming? Eh?

HEDDA: No.

TESMAN: Well then, you'll see, he'll be here in a moment.

BRACK: Do you really think he'll come?

TESMAN: Yes, I'm almost sure of it. Because I don't think you can have been right about what you said this morning.

BRACK: Oh?

TESMAN: Well at any rate Auntie Julle said she couldn't see how he could possibly think of putting himself up against me, as things are. Think of that!

BRACK: Well, then everything's perfectly all right.

TESMAN [*puts his hat, with the gloves inside, on a chair to the right*]: Yes, but you won't mind if we give him as long as possible.

BRACK: Oh, we've got any amount of time. Nobody'll be coming to my place until seven or half past.

TESMAN: Well, we can keep Hedda company until then. And see what happens. Eh?

HEDDA [*carrying Brack's overcoat and hat over to the corner sofa*]: And if the worst comes to the worst Mr Lövborg can always stay here with me.

BRACK [*wants to carry his things himself*]: Allow me, Mrs Tesman! . . . What do you mean by the worst?

HEDDA: If he won't go with you and Tesman.

TESMAN [*looks at her uncertainly*]: But, dearest Hedda . . . do you think it would be quite the thing for him to stay with you? Eh? Remember Aunt Julle can't come.

HEDDA: No, but Mrs Elvsted's coming. And we'll all three have a nice cup of tea together.

TESMAN: Oh well, then, that's quite all right!

BRACK [*smiles*]: And perhaps that arrangement would be the most wholesome thing for him.

HEDDA: How so?

BRACK: Oh, come, Mrs Tesman, you've twitted me often enough about my little bachelor parties. Only to be recommended, wasn't it, to men of the most steadfast principles?

HEDDA: But surely Mr Lövborg is steadfast enough now. A prodigal reformed. . . .

> *Berte appears at the hall door.*

BERTE: Ma'am, there's a gentleman who wants to come in. . . .

HEDDA: Let him come.

TESMAN [*quietly*]: I'm sure it's him! Think of it!

Ejlert Lövborg comes in from the hall. He is slim and lean; the same age as Tesman, but looks older and a little haggard. Hair and beard dark brown, face longish and pale, patches of colour on either cheekbone. He is dressed in an elegant, black, and quite new suit. Dark gloves and a top hat in his hands. He remains standing close to the door and bows hurriedly. He seems a little embarrassed.

TESMAN [*goes to him and pumps his hand*]: My dear Ejlert . . . . so we meet again in spite of everything!

EJLERT LÖVBORG [*speaks in a low voice*]: Thanks for the letter, Tesman. [*approaches Hedda*] May I take your hand as well, Mrs Tesman?

HEDDA [*taking the hand he offers*]: So pleased you came, Mr Lövborg. [*with a gesture*] I wonder if you two gentlemen . . . . ?

LÖVBORG [*with a slight inclination*]: Mr Brack, I believe.

BRACK [*following suit*]: How do you do. Some years ago now. . . .

TESMAN [*to Lövborg, his hands on Lövborg's shoulders*]: And now you must behave just as if you were at home, Ejlert! Isn't that right, Hedda? . . . And I hear you're going to settle here in town again? Eh?

LÖVBORG: That is so.

TESMAN: Well, and why not indeed? Hey listen . . . I've got hold of your new book. But I just haven't had a moment to read it yet.

LÖVBORG: You might as well save yourself the bother.

TESMAN: Why do you say that?

LÖVBORG: Because there's nothing much to it.

TESMAN: Oh but . . . what a thing for you to say!

BRACK: But it's been enormously praised, they tell me.

LÖVBORG: That was just what I wanted. So I wrote a book that nobody could disagree with.

BRACK: Very sensible.

TESMAN: Yes but, my dear Ejlert . . . !

LÖVBORG: Because I'm trying now to build up a position for myself. Starting over again.

TESMAN [*a bit embarrassed*]: Why yes, I suppose you are? Eh?

LÖVBORG [*smiles, puts down his hat and pulls a packet wrapped in paper from his coat pocket*]: But when this one comes out . . . Jörgen Tesman . . . then you're to read it. Because this is the real thing. I put some of myself into this one.

TESMAN: Really? And what's that about?

LÖVBORG: It's the continuation.

TESMAN: The continuation? Of what?

LÖVBORG: Of the book.

TESMAN: The new one?

LÖVBORG: Of course.

TESMAN: Yes but, my dear Ejlert . . . it carries on right to the present day!

LÖVBORG: That is so. And this one deals with the future.

TESMAN: With the future! But ye gods, we don't know anything about that!

LÖVBORG: No. But there are one or two things to be said about it, all the same. [*opens the packet*] Here, look at this. . . .

TESMAN: But that isn't your writing.

LÖVBORG: I dictated it. [*turns the leaves*] It's in two sections. The first is about the social forces involved, and this other bit . . . [*he ruffles the pages further on*] . . . that's about the future course of civilization.

TESMAN: Amazing! It just wouldn't enter my head to write about anything like that.

HEDDA [*at the glass door, drumming her fingers on the pane*]: Hm. . . . No-no.

LÖVBORG [*wraps up the papers again, and puts the packet on the table*]: I brought it along so that I could read you a bit this evening.

TESMAN: Well yes, that was frightfully decent of you, old man. But this evening . . . ? [*looks at Brack*] I don't really know if we can manage it. . . .

LÖVBORG: Well, some other time then. There's no hurry.

BRACK: I ought to tell you, Mr Lövborg . . . there's going to be a little entertainment at my place this evening. More or less in honour of Tesman, you understand. . . .

LÖVBORG [*looks for his hat*]: Ah . . . in that case I won't . . .

BRACK: No, just a moment. Wouldn't you do me the very great honour of joining us?

LÖVBORG [*shortly and firmly*]: No, I'm afraid I can't. Thank you very much indeed.

BRACK: Oh, come along! Do be persuaded. We'll be quite a small and select gathering. And I guarantee that it'll be 'lively', as my la— . . . as Mrs Tesman expresses it.

LÖVBORG: I don't doubt it. But all the same . . .

BRACK: Then you could bring along your manuscript and read to Tesman over at my place. There are plenty of rooms.

TESMAN: Yes, just think, Ejlert . . . what about that! Eh?

HEDDA [*intervenes*]: But my dear, when Mr Lövborg doesn't want to! I'm sure that Mr Lövborg would far sooner stay where he is and take a bit of supper with me.

LÖVBORG [*looks at her*]: With you, Mrs Tesman?

HEDDA: And then with Mrs Elvsted.

LÖVBORG: Oh. . . . [*casually*] I met her for a moment this afternoon.

HEDDA: Did you? Well, she's coming out here. And so you'll almost have to stay, Mr Lövborg. Because otherwise there'll be no one to see her home.

LÖVBORG: That's true. Well, thank you very much, Mrs Tesman . . . I'll stay here then.

HEDDA: Then I'll just have a word with the maid. . . .

> *She goes to the hall door and rings. Berte comes in. Hedda speaks to her quietly and points towards the inner room. Berte nods and goes out again.*

TESMAN [*while this is going on, to Lövborg*]: Tell me, Ejlert . . . is it this new subject . . . this business about the future . . . that you'll be lecturing about?

LÖVBORG: Yes.

TESMAN: Because I heard at the bookseller's that you're giving a series of lectures here this autumn.

LÖVBORG: I am. You mustn't hold it against me, Tesman.

TESMAN: No, no, of course I wouldn't dream of it. But . . . ?

LÖVBORG: I can see that for you this must be rather an embarrassment.

TESMAN [*dejected*]: Oh well, I can't possibly expect you to . . .

LÖVBORG: But I shall wait till you've received your appointment.

TESMAN: You'll wait till . . . ! Yes but . . . yes but . . . aren't you going to compete for it? Eh?

LÖVBORG: No. I only intend to outshine you. In reputation.

TESMAN: But, good heavens . . . so Auntie Julle was right after all! There . . . I said she would be! Hedda! Just think, Hedda . . . Ejlert Lövborg isn't going to stand in our way at all!

HEDDA [*shortly*]: Our way? Leave me out of it.

She goes upstage towards the back room, where Berte is placing a tray with decanters and glasses on the table. Hedda nods her approval and comes forward again. Berte goes out.

TESMAN [*while this is going on*]: Well, Mr Brack, what about that! . . . What do you say? Eh?

BRACK: Well, I say that honour and reputation . . . hm . . . these things certainly have their appeal. . . .

TESMAN: Yes of course they do. But all the same . . .

HEDDA [*looks at Tesman with a cold smile*]: You stand there looking as if you'd been struck by lightning.

BRACK: And it was quite a thunderstorm that passed over us, Mrs Tesman.

HEDDA [*points to the back room*]: Now, would all you gentlemen like to go inside and take a glass of cold punch?

BRACK [*looks at his watch*]: By way of an hors d'oeuvre? That wouldn't be a bad idea.

TESMAN: Excellent, Hedda! Just what we need! I really feel in the mood for something now.

HEDDA: You'll have some too, Mr Lövborg.

LÖVBORG [*dismissing the subject*]: No thank you. Not for me.

BRACK: But good Lord . . . there's nothing lethal about cold punch, let me tell you.

LÖVBORG: Not perhaps for everyone.

HEDDA: Well then, I'll entertain Mr Lövborg in the meanwhile.

TESMAN: All right, dear Hedda, you do that.

Tesman and Brack go into the inner room, sit down, drink punch, smoke cigarettes, and carry on an animated conversation during the following scene. Ejlert Lövborg remains standing by the stove. Hedda goes to the desk.

HEDDA [*in a slightly loud voice*]: And now if you like I'll show you some photographs. We took an excursion through the Tyrol . . . Tesman and I . . . on our way home.

She produces an album, and, laying it on the small table, sits down at the upper end of the sofa. Ejlert Lövborg comes closer, stops, and looks at her. Then he takes a chair and sits on her left, with his back to the inner room.

HEDDA [*opens the album*]: Do you see this range of mountains, Mr Lövborg? That is the Ortler Group. Tesman wrote it underneath the picture. There you are: The Ortler Group at Meran.

LÖVBORG [*who has not once taken his eyes off her, says softly and slowly*]: Hedda . . . Gabler!

HEDDA [*with a quick sidelong glance at him*]: Now! Sh!

LÖVBORG [*softly repeats*]: Hedda Gabler!

HEDDA [*looks in the album*]: That was once my name. When . . . when we two used to know each other.

LÖVBORG: And from now on . . . and for the rest of my life . . . I must stop saying Hedda Gabler.

HEDDA [*still turning the pages*]: Yes, you must. And I think you'd better start practising at once. The sooner the better, I should say.

LÖVBORG [*with bitterness in his voice*]: Hedda Gabler married. And married to . . . Jörgen Tesman!

HEDDA: Yes . . . that's the way of it.

LÖVBORG: Oh Hedda . . . darling Hedda, how could you throw yourself away like that?

HEDDA [*with a sharp look*]: Now. None of that!

LÖVBORG: None of what?

Tesman comes in and goes towards the sofa.

HEDDA [*hears him coming and says indifferently*]: And this, Mr Lövborg, was taken in the Ampezzo Valley. Just look at those rock formations. [*looks amiably up at Tesman*] What were those peculiar mountains called, dear?

TESMAN: Let me look. Ah, those are the Dolomites.

HEDDA: That's right! . . . those are the Dolomites, Mr Lövborg.

TESMAN: Oh, Hedda . . . I just wanted to ask you if you wouldn't like a little punch in here all the same? For yourself at least. Eh?

HEDDA: Yes, thank you very much. And maybe a few cakes.

TESMAN: No cigarettes?

HEDDA: No.

TESMAN: Very good.

He goes into the back room and away to the right. Brack sits within, occasionally keeping an eye on Hedda and Lövborg.

LÖVBORG [*quietly, as before*]: Answer me then, dearest Hedda, how could you go and do such a thing?

HEDDA [*apparently immersed in the album*]: If you continue to address me like that I shan't speak to you at all.

LÖVBORG: Even when we're alone, won't you let me?

HEDDA: I can't dictate your thoughts, Mr Lövborg. But you will speak to me with respect.

LÖVBORG: Ah, I see. Because of your love . . . for Jörgen Tesman.

HEDDA [*glances sideways at him and smiles*]: Love? That's good!

LÖVBORG: Not love, then!

HEDDA: But no kind of unfaithfulness! I'll have none of that.

LÖVBORG: Hedda . . . answer one single question. . . .

HEDDA: Sh!

Tesman, with a tray, comes in from the back room.

TESMAN: Here we are! This is what you've been waiting for!

[*He puts the tray on the table.*]

HEDDA: Why don't you leave that to the maid?

TESMAN [*fills the glasses*]: Because I think it's such fun to wait on you, Hedda.

HEDDA: But now you've filled them both. And Mr Lövborg doesn't want . . .

TESMAN: No, but Mrs Elvsted must be here soon.

HEDDA: Oh yes, that's true . . . Mrs Elvsted. . . .

TESMAN: Had you forgotten her? Eh?

HEDDA: We're so taken up with this. [*shows him a picture*] Do you remember that little village?

TESMAN: Ah, that's the one below the Brenner Pass! That was where we stayed the night . . .

HEDDA: . . . and met all those lively summer visitors.

TESMAN: Yes, that's the place. Just think . . . if only you could have been with us, Ejlert! Well then! [*He goes in again and sits down by Brack.*]

LÖVBORG: Answer me just this one question, Hedda . . .

HEDDA: Well?

LÖVBORG: Was there no love in your relationship to me either? Not a trace . . . not a suspicion of love in that either?

HEDDA: Can there have been, I wonder? My memory is that we were two good companions. Really sincere friends. [*smiles*] You were especially candid.

LÖVBORG: You were the one who wanted it like that.

HEDDA: When I think back to that time, wasn't there something beautiful, something attractive . . . something courageous too, it seems to me . . . about this . . . this secret intimacy, this companionship that no one even dreamed of.

LÖVBORG: There was, Hedda, wasn't there! . . . When I came up to your father's in the afternoons. . . . And the General used to sit by the window, reading papers . . . his back towards us . . . .

HEDDA: And we sat in the corner sofa . . .

LÖVBORG: Always with the same magazine in front of us . . .

HEDDA: Yes . . . for want of an album.

LÖVBORG: Yes, Hedda . . . and then when I used to confess to you . . . ! Told you things about myself that none of the others knew at that time. Sat there and admitted that I'd been out on the razzle for whole days and nights. For days on end. Oh, Hedda . . . what power was it in you that forced me to reveal all those things?

HEDDA: Do you think it was a power in me?

LÖVBORG: Well, how else can I explain it? And all those . . . those roundabout questions you used to put to me . . .

HEDDA: And which you were so quick to understand. . . .

LÖVBORG: That you could sit and ask like that! Quite confidently!

HEDDA: Roundabout questions, if you please.

LÖVBORG: Yes, but confidently all the same, Cross-examine me about . . . about all those things!

HEDDA: And that you could answer, Mr Lövborg.

LÖVBORG: Yes, that's just what I find so incredible . . . now afterwards. But tell me then, Hedda . . . wasn't it love at the back of it all? Wasn't it on your part a desire to absolve me . . . when I came to you and confessed? Wasn't that a part of it?

HEDDA: No, not exactly.

LÖVBORG: Why did you do it, then?

HEDDA: Do you find it so hard to understand that a young girl . . . when it can happen like that . . . in secret . . .

LÖVBORG: Well?

HEDDA: That she should want to find out about a world that . . .

LÖVBORG: That . . . ?

HEDDA: . . . that she isn't supposed to know anything about?

LÖVBORG: So that was it?

HEDDA: That as well . . . I rather think it was that as well.

LÖVBORG: Our common lust for life. But then why couldn't that at least have gone on?

HEDDA: That was your own fault.

LÖVBORG: It was you who broke it off.

HEDDA: Yes, because there was an imminent danger that the game would become a reality. Shame on you, Ejlert Lövborg, how could you offer such violences to . . . to your confidential companion!

LÖVBORG [*presses his fists together*]: Oh, why didn't you play it out! Why didn't you shoot me down, as you threatened!

HEDDA: I'm too much afraid of a scandal.

LÖVBORG: Yes, Hedda, at bottom you're a coward.

HEDDA: An awful coward. [*in a different tone*] Which was lucky for you. And now you've consoled yourself so beautifully up at the Elvsteds'.

LÖVBORG: I know what Thea's told you.

HEDDA: And perhaps you told her something about us?

LÖVBORG: Not a word. She's too stupid to understand anything like that.

HEDDA: Stupid?

LÖVBORG: She's stupid about things like that.

HEDDA: And I'm a coward. [*leans a little closer to him, and without meeting his eyes says softly*] But now I'm going to confess something to you.

LÖVBORG [*in suspense*]: What?

HEDDA: That I didn't dare to shoot you . . .

LÖVBORG: Yes!

HEDDA: . . . that wasn't my worst cowardice . . . that evening.

LÖVBORG [*looks at her for a moment, takes her meaning, and whispers passionately*]: Oh Hedda! Hedda Gabler! Now I think I see what it was that lay behind our companionship! You and I . . . ! So it was your lust for life . . .

HEDDA [*quietly with a sharp glance at him*]: Have a care! Don't assume any such thing!

It has started to get dark. The hall door is opened by Berte.

HEDDA [*clasps the album shut and cries out with a smile*]: At last! Thea, my dear . . . come in then!

Mrs Elvsted comes in from the hall. She is dressed for a social occasion. The door shuts behind her.

HEDDA [*on the sofa, stretching out her arms towards Mrs Elvsted*]: Dearest Thea . . . you can't imagine how I've been longing for you to come!

Mrs Elvsted, in passing, exchanges a greeting with the gentlemen in the inner room; then crosses to the table and gives Hedda her hand. Ejlert Lövborg has stood up. He and Mrs Elvsted exchange a nod of greeting without speaking.

MRS ELVSTED: Shouldn't I go in and have a word with your husband?

HEDDA: Oh, don't worry. Let them stay where they are. They'll be gone soon.

MRS ELVSTED: Are they going?

HEDDA: Yes, they're going out on the spree.

MRS ELVSTED [*quickly, to Lövborg*]: But not you?

LÖVBORG: No.

HEDDA: Mr Lövborg . . . he'll stay here with us.

MRS ELVSTED [*takes a chair and makes to sit down beside Lövborg*]: Oh, it's good to be here!

HEDDA: No you don't, Thea my pet! Not there! You come over here like a good girl. I want to be in the middle.

MRS ELVSTED: All right, just as you please.

She goes round the table and sits on the sofa on Hedda's right. Lövborg resumes his chair.

LÖVBORG [*after a little pause, to Hedda*]: Isn't she lovely to sit and look at?

HEDDA [*passes a hand lightly over Mrs Elvsted's hair*]: Just to look at?

LÖVBORG: Yes. Because we two . . . she and I . . . we're really good companions. We trust each other completely. And so we can sit and talk together in full confidence.

HEDDA: Nothing roundabout, Mr Lövborg?

LÖVBORG: Oh, well . . .

MRS ELVSTED [*quietly, clinging to Hedda*]: Oh, how happy I am, Hedda! Because, do you know what he also says . . . . he says I've inspired him, too.

HEDDA [*looking at her with a smile*]: Does he really say that, Thea?

LÖVBORG: And then she has the courage to act, Mrs Tesman!

MRS ELVSTED: Oh Heavens . . . me, courage!

LÖVBORG: Infinite courage . . . for her companion.

HEDDA: Oh courage . . . . oh yes! If only one had that.

LÖVBORG: What, then, do you mean?

HEDDA: Then life might be liveable, in spite of everything. [*switches to another tone*] But now, Thea my dear . . . now you must let me give you a glass of cold punch.

MRS ELVSTED: No thank you . . . I never drink anything like that.

HEDDA: Well, then you must, Mr Lövborg.

LÖVBORG: Thank you, not for me either.

MRS ELVSTED: No, he doesn't either!

HEDDA [*looks at him steadily*]: But when I want you to?

LÖVBORG: Makes no difference.

HEDDA [*laughs*]: And so I've got no power over you at all? Is that it?

LÖVBORG: Not where that's concerned.

HEDDA: But quite seriously, I do think you should have some all the same. For your own sake.

MRS ELVSTED: Oh, but Hedda . . . !

LÖVBORG: How do you mean?

HEDDA: Or rather, because of other people.

LÖVBORG: Oh?

HEDDA: Otherwise people might so easily get the idea that you're not . . . not really confident, really sure of yourself.

MRS ELVSTED [*quietly*]: Oh, no Hedda, no . . . !

LÖVBORG: People can think whatever they like . . . for the time being.

MRS ELVSTED [*happy*]: Yes, that's right!

HEDDA: It was so obvious with Mr Brack just now.

LÖVBORG: What do you mean?

HEDDA: He smiled so contemptuously when you didn't dare to join them in there at the table.

LÖVBORG: Didn't I dare! I quite naturally preferred to stay here and talk to you.

MRS ELVSTED: Of course he did, Hedda!

HEDDA: Well, Mr Brack wasn't to know that. And I also saw the way he smiled and glanced at Tesman when you didn't dare to go along to this wretched little party, either.

LÖVBORG: Dare! Do you say I didn't dare!

HEDDA: I don't. But that's the way Mr Brack understood it.

LÖVBORG: Let him.

HEDDA: So you're not going?

LÖVBORG: I'll stay with you and Thea.

MRS ELVSTED: Yes, Hedda . . . of course he's going to stay!

HEDDA [*nods and smiles approvingly at Lövborg*]: Firm as a rock, then. A man who is steadfast in his principles. Well, that's how a man should be! [*turns to Mrs Elvsted and pats her*] There, wasn't that what I said this morning when you came in here in such a state of desperation. . . .

LÖVBORG [*pulled up*]: Desperation?

MRS ELVSTED [*in a panic*]: Hedda . . . oh but Hedda . . . !

HEDDA: Just look at him! There isn't the slightest need for you to go about in mortal terror . . . [*She breaks off.*] There! Now we can all be lively!

LÖVBORG [*shocked*]: But . . . what is all this, Mrs Tesman?

MRS ELVSTED: Oh God, oh God, Hedda! What are you saying? What are you trying to do?

HEDDA: Hush, now! That odious Mr Brack has got his eye on you.

LÖVBORG: So you were in mortal terror. On my account.

MRS ELVSTED [*quietly wailing*]: Oh, Hedda . . . now you've really made me unhappy!

LÖVBORG [*looks at her steadily for a moment. His face is tense.*]: So that was my companion's confident belief in me.

MRS ELVSTED [*piteously*]: Oh, my dear, you must let me explain . . . !

LÖVBORG [*takes one of the full punch glasses, raises it, and says quietly, in a hoarse voice*]: Your health, Thea! [*He empties the glass, puts it down, and picks up the other.*]

MRS ELVSTED [*quietly*]: Oh Hedda, Hedda . . . how could you have wanted this to happen?

HEDDA: I wanted it? Don't be absurd!

LÖVBORG: And yours too, Mrs Tesman! Thanks for the truth. Here's to it!

[*He drinks and makes to refill the glass.*]

HEDDA [*putting her hand on his arm*]: Now, now . . . no more for the moment. Remember you're going to a party.

MRS ELVSTED: No, no, no!

HEDDA: Quiet! They're sitting looking at you.

LÖVBORG [*puts down the glass*]: Thea . . . be honest with me.

MRS ELVSTED: Yes!

LÖVBORG: Did your husband know you were coming down to look for me?

MRS ELVSTED [*wrings her hands*]: Oh Hedda . . . did you hear what he asked me?

LÖVBORG: Did you arrange it between you that you should come to town to keep an eye on me? Or maybe it was the old man himself who suggested it? Aha, now I've got it . . . he wanted me back in the office again! Or was he short of a fourth at cards?

MRS ELVSTED [*quietly, painfully*]: Oh Lövborg . . . !

LÖVBORG [*grabs a glass and starts to fill it*]: And here's one to old Elvsted, too!

HEDDA [*firmly*]: No more now. Remember you're going out to read to Tesman.

LÖVBORG [*quietly, putting down the glass*]: I'm sorry, Thea. I've made a fool of myself. Taking it like that, I mean. Don't be angry with me, my dear . . . dear companion. I'll show you . . . both you and the others . . . that however worthless I may have been in the past, I . . . I've found my feet again! With your help, Thea.

MRS ELVSTED [*ecstatically happy again*]: Oh, thank God . . . !

In the meanwhile Brack has been looking at his watch. He and Tesman get up and come into the drawing room.

BRACK [*taking his hat and coat*]: Well, Mrs Tesman, our time is up.

HEDDA: I suppose it is.

LÖVBORG [*getting up*]: Mine too, Mr Brack.

MRS ELVSTED [*quietly and imploringly*]: Oh Lövborg . . . don't do it!

HEDDA [*pinches her arm*]: They can hear you!

MRS ELVSTED [*crying out faintly*]: Ow!

LÖVBORG [*to Brack*]: You were so kind as to invite me.

BRACK: Oh, so you've changed your mind?

LÖVBORG: Yes, if I may.

BRACK: A very great pleasure.

LÖVBORG [*pockets his manuscript and addresses Tesman*]: Because there are one or two things I'd like to show you before I hand it in.

TESMAN: Just think . . . that'll be wonderful! . . . But I say, Hedda, how will you get Mrs Elvsted home then? Eh?

HEDDA: Oh, we'll manage somehow.

LÖVBORG [*looking at the ladies*]: Mrs Elvsted? Why, naturally I'll come back and fetch her. [*goes closer*] Somewhere about ten o'clock, Mrs Tesman. Will that suit you?

HEDDA: Yes, that'll be splendid.

TESMAN: Oh well, then everything's in order. But you mustn't expect me so early, Hedda.

HEDDA: Oh that's all right. Just you stay as long as . . . ever you like.

MRS ELVSTED [*with suppressed anxiety*]: Mr Lövborg . . . I'll stay here then, till you come.

LÖVBORG [*his hat in his hand*]: Why of course.

BRACK: And now, gentlemen, let the revels commence! I trust it will be lively, as a certain lovely lady has it.

HEDDA: Ah, if only that lovely lady could come along as an invisible onlooker . . . !

BRACK: Why invisible?

HEDDA: So as to hear a little of your liveliness . . . unexpurgated, Mr Brack.

BRACK [*laughs*]: Ah, now that's something I wouldn't recommend to the lovely lady!

TESMAN [*also laughing*]: That's a good one, Hedda! Think of that!

BRACK: Well, goodbye, goodbye, ladies!

LÖVBORG [*bowing in departure*]: About ten, then.

> *Brack, Lövborg, and Tesman go out at the hall door. Simultaneously Berte comes in from the back room with a lighted lamp, which she places on the large table, and goes out the way she came.*

MRS ELVSTED [*has got up, and wanders uneasily about the room*]: Hedda . . . Hedda . . . how is all this going to end!

HEDDA: Ten o'clock . . . and back he'll come. I can just see him. With vine leaves in his hair. Flushed and confident . . .

MRS ELVSTED: Yes, oh I do so hope it's like that.

HEDDA: And then, my dear . . . then he'll be master of himself again. He'll be a free man for the rest of his life.

MRS ELVSTED: Oh yes, oh God . . . if only he would come back, just as you see him.

HEDDA: He'll come . . . just exactly like that! [*She gets up and goes closer to her.*] You may doubt him as much as you please. I believe in him. And then we'll be able to see . . .

MRS ELVSTED: You've got some reason for all this, Hedda!

HEDDA: Yes, I have. For once in my life I want to feel that I control a human destiny.

MRS ELVSTED: But surely you do already?

HEDDA: I don't, and I never have done.

MRS ELVSTED: But what about your husband?

HEDDA: Yes, that would really be something, wouldn't it. Oh, if only you knew how destitute I am. And you're allowed to be rich! [*She passionately grips Mrs Elvsted in her arms.*] I think I'll burn your hair off after all.

MRS ELVSTED: Let me go! Let me go! I'm frightened of you, Hedda!

BERTE [*in the doorway*]: Everything's ready, ma'am, in the dining room.

HEDDA: Good. We're coming.

MRS ELVSTED: No, no, no! I'd sooner go home alone! Now, at once!

HEDDA: Nonsense! First you're going to have some tea, you little goose. And then . . . at ten o'clock . . . then Ejlert Lövborg will come . . . with vine leaves in his hair.

[*She pulls Mrs Elvsted towards the doorway almost by main force.*]

ACT III

The room at the Tesmans'. The curtains are drawn across the centre doorway, and also at the glass door. The lamp, with a shade, and half turned down, is alight on the table. The door of the stove stands open; the fire within has almost burnt itself out.

Mrs Elvsted, wrapped in a large shawl and with her feet on a footstool, is reclining in the armchair close to the stove. Hedda, still fully dressed, is lying asleep on the sofa with a rug over her.

MRS ELVSTED [*after a pause, starts up in the chair and listens anxiously. Then she sinks back wearily and wails quietly*]: Still not back! Oh God . . . oh God . . . still not back!

Berte comes tiptoeing carefully in at the hall door. She carries a letter in her hand.

MRS ELVSTED [*turns and whispers urgently*]: Well . . . has anybody come?

BERTE [*quietly*]: Yes, a young woman just came with this letter.

MRS ELVSTED [*quickly, stretching out her hand*]: A letter! Give it to me!

BERTE: No, ma'am, it's for Dr Tesman.

MRS ELVSTED: Oh. . . .

BERTE: It was Miss Tesman's maid who brought it. I'll put it on the table here.

MRS ELVSTED: Yes, do that.

BERTE [*puts down the letter*]: Perhaps I'd best put out the lamp. It's smoking a bit.

MRS ELVSTED: Yes, put it out. It'll soon be light now.

BERTE [*dousing the lamp*]: It's broad daylight.

MRS ELVSTED: Yes, daylight! And still not back . . . !

BERTE: Oh, bless you, ma'am . . . I knew this would happen.

MRS ELVSTED: You knew it?

BERTE: Yes, when I saw that a certain person was back in town. . . . And then when he went off with them. We know what to expect of that gentleman.

MRS ELVSTED: Not so loud. You'll wake Mrs Tesman.

BERTE [*looks at the sofa and sighs*]: Oh the poor dear . . . let her have her sleep. . . . Shan't I put a bit more on the fire?

MRS ELVSTED: Thank you, not on my account.

BERTE: All right, then.   [*She goes out quietly at the hall door.*]

HEDDA [*is woken by the closing of the door and looks up*]: What's that . . . !

MRS ELVSTED: It was just the maid. . . .

HEDDA [*looks around*]: Here . . . ! Oh yes, I remember . . . [*Sits up on the sofa, stretches and rubs her eyes.*] What's the time, Thea?

MRS ELVSTED [*looks at her watch*]: It's gone seven.

HEDDA: When did Tesman come in?

MRS ELVSTED: He isn't back yet.

HEDDA: Not back yet?

MRS ELVSTED [*getting up*]: No one came at all.

HEDDA: And we sat there watching and waiting till four in the morning. . . .

MRS ELVSTED [*wringing her hands*]: Oh, and how I did wait for him!

HEDDA [*yawns, and speaks with her hand over her mouth*]: Ah well . . . we could have saved ourselves the trouble.

MRS ELVSTED: Did you sleep at all?

HEDDA: Oh yes . . . I think I slept quite well. Didn't you?

MRS ELVSTED: Not a wink. I just couldn't, Hedda! It was quite impossible.

HEDDA [*gets up and goes towards her*]: Now, now, now! There's nothing to worry about. It's quite obvious what's happened.

MRS ELVSTED: Well, what has happened, then? Just tell me that!

HEDDA: Well, naturally, they must have carried on till all hours at Mr Brack's . . .

MRS ELVSTED: Yes, oh God . . . I suppose they did. But all the same . . .

HEDDA: And then of course Tesman didn't want to come home and make a din and ring the bell in the middle of the night. [*laughs*] Perhaps he didn't want to show himself either . . . right on top of a night like that.

MRS ELVSTED: But for goodness sake . . . where else could he have gone?

HEDDA: He obviously went along up to the aunts to sleep it off there. They still have his old room.

MRS ELVSTED: No, there at least he can't be. Because just now a letter came for him from Miss Tesman. It's lying there.

HEDDA: Oh? [*looks at the writing on the envelope*] Yes, it's from Auntie Julle all right, in her own fair hand. Well, he must have stopped over at Mr Brack's, then. And Ejlert Lövborg, he's sitting there reading aloud . . . with vine leaves in his hair.

MRS ELVSTED: Oh, Hedda, you're just saying all this, you don't really believe it yourself.

HEDDA: You really are a little ninny, Thea.

MRS ELVSTED: Yes, I suppose I am, really.

HEDDA: And you look tired to death.

MRS ELVSTED: Yes, I am tired to death.

HEDDA: And so you're to do as I tell you. You're to go into my room and lie down on the bed for a little while.

MRS ELVSTED: Oh no, no . . . anyway I wouldn't sleep.

HEDDA: Of course you would.

MRS ELVSTED: Yes, but your husband must be back soon. And then I must hear at once . . .

HEDDA: I'll let you know when he comes.

MRS ELVSTED: Do you promise me, Hedda?

HEDDA: Yes, yes, that's all right. Just you go in and sleep till then.

MRS ELVSTED: Thank you. Well, I'll try, then. [*She goes out through the inner room.*]

> *Hedda goes over to the glass door and draws the curtains aside. Full daylight streams into the room. She then takes a small looking-glass from the desk, inspects herself and arranges her hair. Then she crosses to the hall door and presses the bell.*

> *After a short while Berte comes to the door.*

BERTE: Did you ring, ma'am?

HEDDA: Yes, be so good as to put some more on the stove. I'm cold.

BERTE: Gracious . . . straight away, ma'am . . . I'll have it hot in a moment.

> *She rakes the embers together and puts in a piece of wood.*

BERTE [*stops and listens*]: That was the front door, ma'am.

HEDDA: Then go and attend to it. I'll look after the fire myself.

BERTE: It'll soon burn up. [*She goes out at the hall door.*]

> *Hedda kneels on the footstool and puts more wood into the stove.*

> *After a little while Jörgen Tesman comes in from the hall. He looks tired and rather serious. Creeps on tiptoe towards the doorway, and is about to slip in through the curtains.*

HEDDA [*at the stove, without looking up*]: Good morning.

TESMAN [*turning*]: Hedda! [*comes closer*] But what on earth . . . are you up already! Eh?

HEDDA: Yes, I was up very early this morning.

TESMAN: And I was so sure you'd be sound asleep still! Think of that, Hedda!

HEDDA: Don't talk so loudly. Mrs Elvsted is lying down in my room.

TESMAN: Did Mrs Elvsted stay the night!

HEDDA: Well, nobody came to fetch her.

TESMAN: No, I suppose not.

HEDDA [*shuts the stove door and gets up*]: Well, and did you have a good time at Mr Brack's?

TESMAN: Were you worried about me? Eh?

HEDDA: Good gracious no . . . I wouldn't dream of it. But I asked if you'd had a good time.

TESMAN: Yes, I suppose. For once in a way. . . . But most to begin with, I thought. Then Ejlert read to me. We got there an hour too soon . . . think of that! And Brack had to arrange things. But then Ejlert read to me.

HEDDA [*sits to the right of the table*]: Well? Tell me about it. . . .

TESMAN [*sits on a stool by the stove*]: Oh Hedda, you've no idea, it's going to be ever so good! One of the most remarkable books ever written, I'd almost say. Think of that!

HEDDA: Yes, yes, I don't care so much about that . . .

TESMAN: There's something I'm bound to confess, Hedda. When he'd finished reading . . . something ugly came over me.

HEDDA: Something ugly?

TESMAN: I sat and envied Ejlert that he'd been able to write such a thing. Think of that, Hedda!

HEDDA: Yes, yes, I'm thinking.

TESMAN: And then to know that . . . with all his talents . . . unfortunately he's quite beyond hope of reform, all the same.

HEDDA: I suppose you mean he's got more courage than the rest?

TESMAN: No, good Lord . . . he just can't keep himself under control at all, you know.

HEDDA: Well, and what happened then . . . in the end?

TESMAN: Yes, well, I'd almost have described it as an orgy, Hedda.

HEDDA: Did he have vine leaves in his hair?

TESMAN: Vine leaves? No, I didn't see anything like that. But he made a long and incoherent speech about the woman who had inspired him in his work. Yes, that's how he expressed it.

HEDDA: Did he say who that was?

TESMAN: No, he didn't. But I can only imagine that it must have been Mrs Elvsted. You mark my words!

HEDDA: Well . . . and where did you part company with him?

TESMAN: On the way back to town. We broke up . . . the last of us . . . all together. And Brack came along too to get some fresh air. And then, you see, we agreed that we'd better see Ejlert home. Well, you know, he had quite a few drinks inside him!

HEDDA: I suppose he had.

TESMAN: But now comes the most remarkable thing, Hedda! Or the saddest, I suppose I should say. Oh . . . I'm almost ashamed . . . on Ejlert's behalf . . . to tell you about it. . . .

HEDDA: Well, then . . . ?

TESMAN: Yes, well as we were going along, you see, I happened to fall back a bit behind the others. Just for a minute or two . . . think of it!

HEDDA: Yes, yes, good Lord, but . . . ?

TESMAN: And then as I was hurrying along to catch up . . . well, do you know what I found in the gutter? Eh?

HEDDA: How on earth should I know?

TESMAN: Don't tell anyone, will you, Hedda. Do you hear? Promise me that, for Ejlert's sake! [*He pulls a packet wrapped in paper out of his coat pocket.*] Just think . . . I found this.

HEDDA: Isn't that the packet he had with him here yesterday?

TESMAN: That's it, it's his precious, irreplaceable manuscript! And he's just gone along and dropped it . . . without noticing. Just think of it, Hedda! It's quite pathetic. . . .

HEDDA: But why didn't you give the packet back to him at once?

TESMAN: No, I didn't dare to do that . . . when he was in that condition. . . .

HEDDA: Didn't you tell any of the others that you'd found it either?

TESMAN: Oh no, no. You must see I couldn't have done that, for Ejlert's sake.

HEDDA: So nobody knows at all that you've got Ejlert Lövborg's papers?

TESMAN: No. And no one must get to know it.

HEDDA: What did you talk to him about, afterwards?

TESMAN: I didn't get to talk to him at all. Because as we got into the town we quite lost him . . . him and two or three others. Think of that!

HEDDA: Oh? I suppose they saw him home, then.

TESMAN: Yes, so it seemed. And Brack went off, too.

HEDDA: And what did you get up to then . . . afterwards?

TESMAN: Oh, I went with some of the others, and one of the fellows took us to his place and gave us morning coffee. Or night coffee, I suppose I should say. Eh? But now as soon as I've rested a bit . . . and when poor old Ejlert has had a chance to sleep it off . . . I must go in and give him this.

HEDDA [*stretches out her hand for the packet*]: No . . . don't give it back! Not straight away, I mean. Let me read it first.

TESMAN: No, my dear, sweet Hedda, I swear I just daren't do that.

HEDDA: You daren't?

TESMAN: No . . . because you can just imagine, he'll be quite desperate when he wakes up and finds he's lost his manuscript. Because this is the only copy he's got, you know! He told me so himself.

HEDDA [*looks at him keenly*]: But can't a thing like that be rewritten? Over again, I mean?

TESMAN: No, I don't think that would do at all. Because the inspiration . . . you see . . .

HEDDA: Yes, yes . . . that's it, I suppose . . . [*casually*] Oh, by the way . . . there's a letter for you.

TESMAN: A letter? Just think . . . !

HEDDA [*passes it to him*]: It came early this morning.

TESMAN: From Aunt Julle! What can it be? [*He puts the manuscript down on the other stool, opens the letter, glances through it, and jumps up.*] Oh, Hedda . . . she writes that poor Auntie Rina is at the point of death!

HEDDA: Well, it was to be expected.

TESMAN: And if I want to see her again, I must hurry. I'll rush over at once.

HEDDA [*suppressing a smile*]: You'll rush, will you?

TESMAN: Oh Hedda, my dearest . . . if only I could persuade you to come too! Just think!

HEDDA [*gets up and answers tiredly but firmly*]: No, no, don't ask me. I don't want to look at sickness and death. I must be free of everything that's ugly.

TESMAN: Oh well, for God's sake then . . . ! [*rushes about*] My hat . . . ! My coat . . . ? Oh, in the hall. . . . Oh, I do so hope I'm not going to be too late, Hedda? Eh?

HEDDA: You'd better rush, then. . . .

Berte appears at the hall door.

BERTE: Mr Brack is outside and asks if he can come in.

TESMAN: Now! No, I can't possibly see him now.

HEDDA: But I can. [*to Berte*] Ask Mr Brack to come inside.

> *Berte goes.*

HEDDA [*quickly, whispering*]: The papers, Tesman! [*She whips the packet off the stool.*]

TESMAN: Yes, give them to me!

HEDDA: No, no, I'll look after them till you come back.

> *She goes to the desk and puts the packet in the bookshelf. Tesman stands there in a flap, unable to get his gloves on.*
>
> *Mr Brack comes in from the hall.*

HEDDA [*nods to him*]: Well, you are an early bird.

BRACK: Yes, am I not? [*to Tesman*] Are you going out again?

TESMAN: Yes, I have to go to the aunts. Just think . . . the one who's ill, she's dying, poor thing.

BRACK: Good Lord, is she really? But then you musn't stand here talking to me. At such a serious moment. . . .

TESMAN: Yes, I really must rush. . . . Goodbye! Goodbye!

> [*He hurries out at the hall door.*]

HEDDA [*comes closer*]: It seems it was decidedly lively at your place last night, Mr Brack.

BRACK: I haven't even had time to change my clothes, my lady.

HEDDA: You haven't either?

BRACK: As you see. But what has Tesman told you of the events of the night?

HEDDA: Oh, nothing much. That he went somewhere and drank coffee.

BRACK: Yes, I know about the coffee party. Ejlert Lövborg wasn't there though, I believe?

HEDDA: No, they'd seen him home first.

BRACK: Tesman too?

HEDDA: No, but a few of the others, he said.

BRACK [*smiles*]: Jörgen Tesman really is a credulous soul, my lady.

HEDDA: Yes, God knows he is. But is there something behind all this?

BRACK: Yes, you might say there is.

HEDDA: Well! Let's sit down, dear Mr Brack. Then you'll tell it better.

> *She sits to the left of the table. Brack sits down at the table close to her.*

HEDDA: Well, then?

BRACK: There were particular reasons why I wanted to keep track of my guests . . . or rather, of certain of my guests last night.

HEDDA: And perhaps Ejlert Lövborg was among them?

BRACK: I have to confess . . . he was.

HEDDA: Now you really begin to intrigue me. . . .

BRACK: Do you know where he and a few of the others spent what was left of the night, my lady?

HEDDA: Tell me . . . if it bears telling.

BRACK: Oh yes, it may be told. Well, they adorned a particularly animated soirée.

HEDDA: One of the lively kind?

BRACK: One of the very liveliest.

HEDDA: A bit more about this, Mr Brack . . .

BRACK: Lövborg had also been invited earlier. I happened to know about it. But at that time he declined the invitation. Because now he's put on a new man, as you know.

HEDDA: Up at the Elvsteds', yes. But he went all the same?

BRACK: Well you see, my lady . . . most unfortunately the inspiration took him up at my place last night. . . .

HEDDA: Yes, the spirit did move him, so I'm told.

BRACK: Moved him somewhat vehemently. And, well . . . then he had second thoughts about it, I assume. Because we men, you know, we're not always so firm in our principles as we ought to be.

HEDDA: Oh, I don't doubt that you provide an exception, Mr Brack. But Lövborg . . . ?

BRACK: Well, to cut a long story short . . . he finally adjourned to Mademoiselle Diana's salon.

HEDDA: Mademoiselle Diana's?

BRACK: Mademoiselle Diana was giving the aforesaid soirée. For a select circle of friends and admirers.

HEDDA: Is that a red-haired woman?

BRACK: Most decidedly.

HEDDA: A sort of a . . . singer?

BRACK: Oh yes . . . among other things. And moreover a mighty huntress . . . of men . . . my lady. You must have heard of her. Ejlert Lövborg was one of her most ardent champions . . . in the days of his glory.

HEDDA: And how did it all end, then?

BRACK: Not altogether amicably, it appears. Mademoiselle Diana, I understand, passed from the tenderest possible welcome to actual violence.

HEDDA: Against Lövborg?

BRACK: Yes. He maintained that she, or one of the members of her entourage, had robbed him. He said that he'd lost a pocket-book. And other things as well. In short, he appears to have kicked up the devil of a row.

HEDDA: And what happened then?

BRACK: What happened then was a general mêlée, involving both ladies and gentlemen. Fortunately the police arrived at last.

HEDDA: The police came, too?

BRACK: Yes. But I fear this will have been a costly interlude for that imbecile Lövborg.

HEDDA: Oh!

BRACK: Apparently he put up a spirited resistance. Struck an officer of the law over the head, and tore his tunic. So he had to go along to the police station too.

HEDDA: How do you know all this?

BRACK: The police told me themselves.

HEDDA [*looking away*]: So that was how it was. He didn't have vine leaves in his hair.

BRACK: Vine leaves, my lady?

HEDDA [*in a different voice*]: But tell me now, Mr Brack . . . why should you show such an elaborate interest in Ejlert Lövborg?

BRACK: In the first place, I can't be altogether indifferent if it comes out, when the case is heard, that he came straight from my place.

HEDDA: There'll be a court case, then?

BRACK: Naturally. But it isn't really that so much. No, the fact is I felt it my duty, as a friend of the house, to give you and your husband a full account of his nocturnal escapades.

HEDDA: And why should you feel that, Mr Brack?

BRACK: Well, I have a pretty shrewd suspicion that he intends to use you as a sort of screen.

HEDDA: Why, what gives you that idea?

BRACK: Oh good Heavens . . . we're not blind, my lady. Use your eyes! This Mrs Elvsted person, she won't be leaving town in such a hurry.

HEDDA: Well, and if there is anything between those two, I suppose there are plenty of other places where they can meet.

BRACK: No private household. From now on every decent home will be closed to Ejlert Lövborg once again.

HEDDA: And mine ought to be too, you mean?

BRACK: Yes. I must admit I'd find it extremely awkward if this fellow were to become a constant visitor here. If this superfluous and . . . and unsuitable individual were to insinuate himself into . . .

HEDDA: Into the triangle?

BRACK: Just so. For me it would be like becoming homeless.

HEDDA [*looks at him with a smile*]: So . . . you want to be the only cock in the yard, is that it?

BRACK [*nods slowly and lowers his voice*]: Yes, that's what I want. And I'll fight for that end . . . with every means at my disposal.

HEDDA [*her smile fading*]: You're quite a formidable person . . . when it comes to the point.

BRACK: You think so?

HEDDA: Yes, I'm beginning to think so, now. And I'm content . . . so long as you don't have any sort of hold over me.

BRACK [*laughs equivocally*]: Ah yes, my lady . . . you may be right about that. Who knows, in such a case I might be capable of . . . one thing and another.

HEDDA: Really, Mr Brack! You sound almost as though you mean to threaten me.

BRACK [*rising*]: Oh, far from it! This triangle . . . well, you know, it's best when it's fortified and defended by mutual consent.

HEDDA: I agree with you.

BRACK: Well, now I've said what I wanted to say. And I'd better see about getting back home. Goodbye, my lady!   [*He moves towards the glass door.*]

HEDDA [*getting up*]: Are you going through the garden?

BRACK: Yes, it's a bit nearer for me.

HEDDA: Yes, and then it's round the back way.

BRACK: Very true. I've no objection to going round the back way. At times it can be quite stimulating.

HEDDA: When there's target practice going on, you mean?

BRACK [*at the door, laughing*]: Oh, nobody shoots their tame farmyard cocks!

HEDDA [*also laughing*]: Ah no, when they've only got one of them. . . .

> *Laughing, they nod their farewells. He leaves. She shuts the door behind him.*

> *Hedda stands for a moment with a serious expression, looking out. Then she crosses to the centre doorway and looks in through the curtains. Then moves to the desk, takes Lövborg's packet out of the bookcase, and is about to look at the papers. Berte's voice, raised in altercation, is heard from the hall. Hedda turns and listens. Then she quickly locks the manuscript away in a drawer and puts the key on the writing-pad.*

> *Ejlert Lövborg, wearing his overcoat and holding his hat, flings open the hall door. He looks somewhat confused and excited.*

LÖVBORG [*turned towards the hall*]: And I tell you that I must go in! And that's that!

> *He shuts the door, turns, and sees Hedda. He controls himself at once, and bows.*

HEDDA [*at the desk*]: Well, Mr Lövborg, you're a little late in calling for Thea.

LÖVBORG: Or a little early in calling on you. I apologize.

HEDDA: How do you know she's still here?

LÖVBORG: They told me at her lodgings that she'd been out all night.

HEDDA [*crosses to the table*]: Did you notice anything in particular when they told you that?

LÖVBORG [*looks at her questioningly*]: Notice anything?

HEDDA: I mean, did they seem to be drawing any inference at all?

LÖVBORG [*suddenly understands*]: Oh yes, of course, you're right! I'm dragging her down with me! But as it happened I didn't notice anything. . . . I suppose Tesman isn't up yet?

HEDDA: No . . . I don't think . . .

LÖVBORG: When did he come in?

HEDDA: Very late.

LÖVBORG: Did he tell you anything?

HEDDA: Yes, he said it was a very gay party at Mr Brack's.

LÖVBORG: Nothing else?

HEDDA: No, I don't think so. But I was frightfully sleepy. . . .

> *Mrs Elvsted comes in through the curtains at the back.*

MRS ELVSTED [*comes towards him*]: Oh, Lövborg! At last . . . !

LÖVBORG: Yes, at last. And too late.

MRS ELVSTED [*looks at him anxiously*]: What's too late?

LÖVBORG: Everything's too late now. I'm finished.

MRS ELVSTED: Oh, no, no . . . don't say that!

LÖVBORG: You'll say the same yourself when you hear. . . .

MRS ELVSTED: I don't want to hear anything!

HEDDA: Perhaps you'd prefer to speak to her alone? Because if so I'll go.

LÖVBORG: No, stay . . . I beg you to stay.

MRS ELVSTED: But I don't want to hear about it, I tell you!

LÖVBORG: I'm not going to talk about what happened last night.

MRS ELVSTED: What is it then . . . ?

LÖVBORG: It's just this, that it's all over between us now.

MRS ELVSTED: All over!

HEDDA [*involuntarily*]: I knew it!

LÖVBORG: Because I have no use for you any more, Thea.

MRS ELVSTED: And you can stand there and say that! No use for me any more! Can't I help you now as I did before? Aren't we going to go on working together?

LÖVBORG: I don't intend to do any more work.

MRS ELVSTED [*yielding to despair*]: What am I to do with my life, then?

LÖVBORG: You must try to live your life as though you had never known me.

MRS ELVSTED: Oh, but I can't!

LÖVBORG: See if you can, Thea. You must go back home. . . .

MRS ELVSTED [*in rebellion*]: That I'll never do! Wherever you are, that's where I want to be! I won't be packed off like this! I want to be right here! To be together with you when the book comes out.

HEDDA [*half aloud, tensely*]: Ah yes . . . the book!

LÖVBORG [*looks at her*]: My book and Thea's. Because that's what it is.

MRS ELVSTED: Yes, that's what I feel that it is. And therefore I have a right to be together with you when it comes! I want to see you praised and honoured again. And the joy . . . I want to share the joy of it with you.

LÖVBORG: Thea . . . our book will never be published.

HEDDA: Ah!

MRS ELVSTED: Not published!

LÖVBORG: It's impossible now.

MRS ELVSTED [*in dreadful foreboding*]: Lövborg . . . what have you done to the manuscript!

HEDDA [*looks at him in suspense*]: Yes, the manuscript . . . ?

MRS ELVSTED: Where is it?

LÖVBORG: Oh Thea. . . . Don't ask me to tell you that.

MRS ELVSTED: Yes, yes, I want to know. I've got the right to know. At once.

LÖVBORG: The manuscript. . . . Well, then . . . I've torn the manuscript into a thousand pieces.

MRS ELVSTED [*shrieks*]: Oh no, no . . . !

HEDDA [*involuntarily*]: But that's not . . . !

LÖVBORG [*looks at her*]: Not true, you think?

HEDDA [*collects herself*]: Oh well . . . of course. If you say so yourself. But it sounded so fantastic. . . .

LÖVBORG: True all the same.

MRS ELVSTED [*wrings her hands*]: Oh God . . . oh God, Hedda . . . torn his own work to pieces!

LÖVBORG: I've torn my own life to pieces. So I might as well tear up my life's work as well.

MRS ELVSTED: And you did that last night!

LÖVBORG: Yes, I tell you. Into a thousand pieces. And scattered them out in the fjord. A long way out. At least the water's clean and salt out there. They'll drift with the current and the wind. And after a while they'll sink. Deeper and deeper. Like I will, Thea.

MRS ELVSTED: I want you to know, Lövborg, what you've done to the book. . . . For the rest of my life it'll be for me as though you'd killed a little child.

LÖVBORG: You're right. It was like killing a child.

MRS ELVSTED: But how could you then . . . ! The child was mine, it was also mine.

HEDDA [*almost inaudibly*]: The child . . .

MRS ELVSTED [*sighs deeply*]: So there's an end of it. Well, I'm leaving now, Hedda.

HEDDA: But you're not going back . . . ?

MRS ELVSTED: Oh, I don't know myself what I'll do. There's nothing but darkness ahead of me. [*She goes out at the hall door.*]

HEDDA [*stands for a while and waits*]: So you're not going to take her home, Mr Lövborg?

LÖVBORG: I? Through the streets? And let everybody see her walking with me?

HEDDA: Well, I don't know what else happened last night. But was it so utterly irrevocable?

LÖVBORG: It won't stop at last night. I know that well enough. But then there's another thing, I just can't be bothered with that kind of a life either. Not now again. She's broken my courage, and my defiance.

HEDDA [*looking straight ahead*]: So that silly little fool has had her fingers in a man's destiny. [*looks at him*] But how could you treat her so callously, all the same?

LÖVBORG: Oh, don't say I was callous!

HEDDA: To destroy everything that's filled her mind and her heart for all this long time! Don't you call that callous?

LÖVBORG: I can tell you the truth, Hedda.

HEDDA: The truth?

LÖVBORG: Promise me first . . . give me your word that Thea will never know what I'm going to tell you now.

HEDDA: I give you my word.

LÖVBORG: Well. Then I'll tell you that what I was saying just now wasn't the truth.

HEDDA: About the manuscript?

LÖVBORG: Yes. I didn't tear it up. And I didn't throw it in the fjord, either.

HEDDA: No. . . . But . . . where is it then?

LÖVBORG: I've destroyed it all the same. Destroyed it utterly, Hedda!

HEDDA: I don't understand this.

LÖVBORG: Thea said that for her it was as though I had killed a child.

HEDDA: Yes . . . so she did.

LÖVBORG: But to kill his child . . . that's not the worst thing a father can do.

HEDDA: Not the worst?

LÖVBORG: No. I wanted to spare Thea the worst.

HEDDA: And what is this worst thing, then?

LÖVBORG: Look, Hedda, suppose a man . . . in the early hours of the morning . . . came home to his child's mother after a wild and senseless debauch and said: now listen . . . I've been here and I've been there. To all sorts of places. And I had our child along with me. All over the place. And I've lost him. Just like that. Christ alone knows where he's got to, or who's got hold of him.

HEDDA: Oh but . . . when all's said and done . . . this was only a book. . . .

LÖVBORG: Thea's soul was in that book.

HEDDA: Yes, I can understand that.

LÖVBORG: And so you must understand also that Thea and I . . . that there isn't any future for us any more.

HEDDA: And what are you going to do, then?

LÖVBORG: Nothing. Just put an end to it all. The sooner the better.

HEDDA [*takes a step towards him*]: Ejlert Lövborg . . . listen to me. . . . Couldn't you let it happen . . . beautifully?

LÖVBORG: Beautifully! [*smiles*] Crowned with vine leaves, as you used to imagine?

HEDDA: Oh no. I don't believe in those vine leaves any more. But beautifully all the same! Just for this once! . . . Goodbye. You must go now. And never come here again.

LÖVBORG: Goodbye, Mrs Tesman. And remember me to your husband.

[*He is about to leave.*]

HEDDA: No, wait! I want to give you something to remember me by.

She goes to the desk and opens the drawer, and takes out the pistol case. Then she comes back to Lövborg with one of the pistols.

LÖVBORG [*looks at her*]: That! Is that what you want me to have?

HEDDA [*nods slowly*]: Do you recognize it? It was aimed at you, once.

LÖVBORG: You should have used it then.

HEDDA: Well . . . ! You use it now.

LÖVBORG [*sticking the pistol in his breast pocket*]: Thank you.

HEDDA: And beautifully, Ejlert Lövborg. Promise me that!

LÖVBORG: Goodbye, Hedda Gabler. [*He goes out at the hall door.*]

Hedda listens at the door for a moment. Then she goes to the desk and takes out the packet with the manuscript, peeps inside the wrappers for a moment, takes some of the leaves half way out and looks at them. Then she takes it all over to the armchair by the stove and sits down. After a while she opens the stove door, and unwraps the packet.

HEDDA [*throws one of the folded sheets into the fire and whispers to herself*]: Now I'm burning your child, Thea! With your curly hair! [*throws a few more sheets into the stove*] Your child and Ejlert Lövborg's. [*throws in the rest*] I'm burning . . . burning your child.

ACT IV

The same room at the Tesmans'. It is evening. The outer room is in darkness. The lamp over the table in the inner room is alight. The curtains at the glass door are drawn.

Hedda, dressed in black, is walking aimlessly about the darkened room. Then she goes into the inner room and is lost to view to the left of the doorway. A few chords from the piano are heard. Then she emerges again and goes back into the reception room.

Berte comes in from the right of the inner room, carrying a lighted lamp, which she places on the table by the corner sofa in the reception room. Her eyes show signs of weeping, and she has black bands in her cap. Goes out quietly and carefully to the right. Hedda crosses to the glass door, draws the curtains aside a little, and looks out into the darkness.

After a little while Miss Tesman comes in from the hall, dressed in mourning and wearing a hat and veil. Hedda goes to meet her and gives her her hand.

MISS TESMAN: Yes, Hedda, I come dressed in the colour of mourning. For now my poor sister has passed away at last.

HEDDA: I am already aware of it, as you see. Tesman sent me a note.

MISS TESMAN: Yes, he promised he would. But I felt all the same that here to Hedda . . . in this house of life . . . I must bring the tidings of death myself.

HEDDA: That was extremely kind of you.

MISS TESMAN: Oh, but Rina shouldn't have been taken just now. This is no time for mourning, not in Hedda's house.

HEDDA [*avoiding the subject*]: She died quite peacefully, Miss Tesman?

MISS TESMAN: Oh, she passed over so quietly . . . and so gently. And it was such a blessed joy to her that she could see Jörgen once again. And could say goodbye to him properly. He isn't home yet?

HEDDA: No. He wrote that I wasn't to expect him straight away. But do sit down.

MISS TESMAN: No, thank you, my dear . . . dear Hedda. I should have liked to. But I have so little time. Now I have to attend to her and prepare her as well as I may. She shall go to her grave looking her best.

HEDDA: Is there nothing I can do?

MISS TESMAN: Oh, you mustn't think of it! No, that's not fit work for Hedda Tesman's hands. Nor a fit subject for her thoughts, either. Not at this time.

HEDDA: Oh thoughts . . . they can't be curbed so easily. . . .

MISS TESMAN [*continuing*]: Ah yes, dear God, that's how it goes. We'll be sewing linen for poor Rina; and soon there'll be sewing to be done here too, I fancy. But that'll be of a different kind . . . thanks be to God.

Jörgen Tesman comes in at the hall door.

HEDDA: Well, so you're here at last.

TESMAN: You here, Auntie Julle? With Hedda? Think of that!

MISS TESMAN: I was just going away again, my dear boy. Well, and did you manage to see to it all?

TESMAN: Oh, I'm awfully afraid I'll have forgotten the half of it. I'll have to dash over and see you again tomorrow. I'm all at sixes and sevens today. I just can't think straight.

MISS TESMAN: But Jörgen, my own boy, you mustn't take it like that.

TESMAN: I mustn't? Well, how else, then?

MISS TESMAN: You must be glad, even in your grief. Glad of what has come to pass. As I am.

TESMAN: Oh yes, yes. You're thinking of Auntie Rina.

HEDDA: It will be a little lonely for you now, Miss Tesman.

MISS TESMAN: Why yes, just to begin with. But not for so very long, I sincerely hope. Poor Rina's little room won't be left empty, you may be sure of that!

TESMAN: Oh? Who are you thinking of putting in there, then? Eh?

MISS TESMAN: Oh, there's always some poor invalid or other who needs a bit of care and attention, unfortunately.

HEDDA: Would you really take on another burden of that kind?

MISS TESMAN: Burden! Oh, God forgive you, child . . . this hasn't been a burden to me.

HEDDA: But in the case of a total stranger . . .

MISS TESMAN: Oh, you soon get friendly with people when they're sick. And besides, I also do need to have someone to live for. Ah well, God is good . . . and I fancy there'll soon be a few things for an old aunt to do here in this house, too.

HEDDA: Oh, don't think about us.

TESMAN: Yes, just think how fine it would be if we all three. . . . Yes . . . if only . . .

HEDDA: If only . . . ?

TESMAN [*ill at ease*]: Oh, never mind. It'll all turn out all right, I expect. Let's hope so. Eh?

MISS TESMAN: Well, well. I expect you young people have lots of things you want to talk about. [*smiles*] And perhaps Hedda has something to tell you, too, Jörgen. Goodbye, my dears! I must get back home to Rina. [*She turns at the door.*] Yes, dear God, how strange to think! Now Rina's both here with me, and also with sainted Joachim.

TESMAN: Yes, just think of that, Auntie Julle! Eh?

Miss Tesman goes out at the hall door.

HEDDA [*coldly appraising Tesman*]: I almost think you're more upset about this death than she is.

TESMAN: Oh, it's not just Aunt Rina. I'm so frightfully worried about Ejlert.

HEDDA [*quickly*]: Have you heard anything about him?

TESMAN: I was going to run over to see him this afternoon, to tell him that the manuscript's in good hands.

HEDDA: Well? Didn't you catch him?

TESMAN: No. He wasn't at home. But afterwards I met Mrs Elvsted, and she said he'd been here early this morning.

HEDDA: Yes, just after your left.

TESMAN: And that he said that he'd torn up the manuscript. Eh?

HEDDA: Yes, that's what he said.

TESMAN: But, good Heavens above, the man must have been raving! And then you didn't dare let him have it back, I suppose, Hedda?

HEDDA: No, he didn't get it.

TESMAN: But you did tell him we'd got it?

HEDDA: No. [*quickly*] Did you tell Mrs Elvsted?

TESMAN: No. I didn't like to. But you ought to have said it to him. Just think, he might go and do something desperate! Give me the manuscript, Hedda! I'll rush over with it at once. Where have you got it?

HEDDA [*cold and immobile, supporting herself on the armchair*]: I haven't got it any more.

TESMAN: You haven't got it! But for God's sake . . . what do you mean?

HEDDA: I've burnt it up . . . all of it.

TESMAN [*jumps up in alarm*]: Burnt . . . you've burnt it! Burnt Ejlert Lövborg's manuscript!

HEDDA: Don't shout like that. The maid might hear you.

TESMAN: Burnt! But good God! . . . No, no, no . . . this is quite impossible!

HEDDA: Well, it's true, for all that.

TESMAN: Yes, but . . . do you know what it is that you've done, Hedda? It's a felony . . . it's misappropriation of lost property! Think of that! Yes, you just go and ask Mr Brack, he'll tell you.

HEDDA: I think you'd be well advised not to talk about it . . . either to Mr Brack or anyone else.

TESMAN: But how could you go and do anything so utterly fantastic! How on earth did you come to do such a thing? What got into you? Answer me, Hedda! Eh?

HEDDA [*suppressing an almost imperceptible smile*]: I did it for your sake, Jörgen.

TESMAN: For my sake!

HEDDA: When you came home this morning and told me how he'd read to you . . .

TESMAN: Yes, yes, what about it?

HEDDA: You admitted that you envied him for it.

TESMAN: Oh Heavens above, I didn't mean it so literally.

HEDDA: All the same I couldn't bear the thought that someone else should put you in the shade.

TESMAN [*exclaiming, torn between doubt and happiness*]: Hedda . . . oh gracious . . . is this really true! . . . Yes, but . . . yes, but . . . I never knew you loved me like that, Hedda, not in that way. Think of that!

HEDDA: Well, then I suppose I'd better tell you that . . . that just at this time . . . [*breaks off passionately*] Oh no, no . . . you can go and ask your Auntie Julle. She'll tell you all about it.

TESMAN: Oh, I almost think I know what it is, Hedda! [*claps his hands together*] Oh good Heavens . . . is it really possible! Eh!

HEDDA: Don't shout like that. The maid can hear you.

TESMAN [*laughing in the excess of his joy*]: The maid! Oh, Hedda, you really are price-less! The maid . . . why that's Berte! I'll go out and tell Berte myself!

HEDDA [*clenches her hands as though in desperation*]: Oh, it'll kill me . . . it'll kill me, all this!

TESMAN: All what, Hedda? Eh?

HEDDA [*coldly, in control again*]: All this . . . this farce . . . Jörgen.

TESMAN: Farce? But it's just that I'm so happy. But, perhaps. . . . Well, perhaps I'd bet-ter not tell Berte, then.

HEDDA: Oh yes . . . why not do the thing properly.

TESMAN: No, no, not just yet. But at least I'll have to tell Aunt Julle. And that you've started to call me Jörgen, too! Think of it. Oh, Auntie Julle really will be pleased!

HEDDA: When she hears that I've burnt Ejlert Lövborg's papers . . . for your sake?

TESMAN: Oh, good Lord yes . . . the papers! No, of course, nobody must get to know about that. But your burning zeal on my behalf, Hedda . . . Auntie Julle really must hear about that! I say though, I wonder, is that sort of thing usual with young wives, d'you think? Eh?

HEDDA: I think it would be a good idea if you asked Auntie Julle about that, too.

TESMAN: Yes, yes, I'll do that some time. [*looks uneasy and thoughtful again*] No, but this business with the manuscript! Good Lord, it's . . . it's quite awful, really, to think of poor Ejlert.

    Mrs Elvsted, dressed as for her first visit, with hat and coat, comes in the hall door.

MRS ELVSTED [*greets them hurriedly and speaks in agitation*]: Oh my dear Hedda, do excuse me for coming back again.

HEDDA: What's happened to you, Thea?

TESMAN: Is it something to do with Ejlert Lövborg again? Eh?

MRS ELVSTED: Oh yes . . . I'm so dreadfully afraid that he may have met with an accident.

HEDDA [*grips Mrs Elvsted's arm*]: Oh . . . do you think so!

TESMAN: Oh, but good Heavens . . . why should you think that, Mrs Elvsted?

MRS ELVSTED: Oh, yes, I heard them talking about him at the lodging house . . . just as I came in. There are the most incredible rumours about him going around today.

TESMAN: Yes, just think, I heard something too! And yet I can testify that he went straight off home to bed. Think of that!

HEDDA: Well . . . what were they saying then, at the boarding house?

MRS ELVSTED: Oh, I didn't really discover anything at all. Either because they didn't really know the particulars or else. . . . They all stopped talking when they saw me. And I didn't dare to ask.

TESMAN [*anxiously pacing around*]: We can only hope . . . we can only hope you were mistaken, Mrs Elvsted!

MRS ELVSTED: No, no I'm sure it was him they were talking about. And then I heard one of them say something that sounded like hospital or . . .

TESMAN: Hospital!

HEDDA: Oh no . . . that can't be possible!

MRS ELVSTED: Oh, I was so horribly frightened for him. And then I went to his lodgings and asked after him there.

HEDDA: You could bring yourself to do that, Thea!

MRS ELVSTED: Well, and what else was I to do? Because it seemed to me I just couldn't go on, not knowing.

TESMAN: But I suppose you didn't find him there, either? Eh?

MRS ELVSTED: No. And the people knew nothing whatever about him. He hadn't been home since yesterday afternoon, they said.

TESMAN: Yesterday! Fancy their saying that!

MRS ELVSTED: Oh God, I'm so sure that something must have happened to him!

TESMAN: I say, Hedda . . . what if I go into town, and make a few inquiries round about . . . ?

HEDDA: No, no . . . you'd better not get mixed up in this.

Mr Brack, carrying his hat in his hand, comes in at the hall door, which Berte opens and closes again behind him. He looks serious and bows without speaking.

TESMAN: Oh, Mr Brack, you're here are you? Eh?

BRACK: Yes, I had to come up to see you again this evening.

TESMAN: I can see that you've heard from Aunt Julle.

BRACK: Yes, I also received her message.

TESMAN: Isn't it terribly sad? Eh?

BRACK: Oh, my dear Tesman, that's as you choose to take it.

TESMAN [*looks at him uneasily*]: Is there something else, perhaps?

BRACK: Yes, there is.

HEDDA [*in suspense*]: Bad news, Mr Brack?

BRACK: Also as you choose to take it, Mrs Tesman.

MRS ELVSTED [*in a spontaneous outburst*]: Oh, it's to do with Ejlert Lövborg!

BRACK [*looks at her*]: Why should you think that, madam? Perhaps you know something already . . . ?

MRS ELVSTED [*confused*]: No, no, I know absolutely nothing; but . . .

TESMAN: Well, good gracious man, let's have it then!

BRACK [*shrugs his shoulders*]: Well then . . . I regret to say . . . Ejlert Lövborg has been taken to the hospital. He is not expected to live.

MRS ELVSTED [*crying out*]: Oh my God, my God . . . !

TESMAN: To the hospital! And not expected . . . !

HEDDA [*involuntarily*]: So soon . . . !

MRS ELVSTED [*wailing*]: And we . . . we weren't even reconciled when we parted, Hedda!

HEDDA [*whispers*]: Now Thea . . . Thea!

MRS ELVSTED [*taking no notice of her*]: I must go to him! I must see him alive!

BRACK: It's no use, madam. No one is allowed to see him.

MRS ELVSTED: Oh, but at least tell me what's happened to him! What's the matter with him?

TESMAN: Surely he can't have . . . himself . . . ! Eh?

HEDDA: Yes, I'm certain he did.

MRS ELVSTED: Oh Hedda . . . how can you . . . !

BRACK [*who is watching her all the time*]: Regrettably your guess is correct, Mrs Tesman.

MRS ELVSTED: Oh, but how dreadful!

TESMAN: Did it himself! Think of that!

HEDDA: Shot himself!

BRACK: Correctly guessed again, Mrs Tesman.

MRS ELVSTED [*trying to pull herself together*]: When did this happen, Mr Brack?

BRACK: This afternoon. Between three and four.

TESMAN: Yes, but, good Lord . . . where did he do it, then? Eh?

BRACK [*a little uncertainly*]: Where? Well, I . . . suppose it was at his lodgings.

MRS ELVSTED: No, that can't be right. I was there myself at about half past six.

BRACK: Well, somewhere else then. I don't exactly know about that. I just know that he was found. . . . He had shot himself . . . in the breast.

MRS ELVSTED: Oh, but how dreadful! That he should end like that!

HEDDA [*to Brack*]: He was shot in the breast?

BRACK: Yes . . . as I said.

HEDDA: Not in the temple?

BRACK: In the breast, Mrs Tesman.

HEDDA: Well . . . the breast is good, too.

BRACK: I beg your pardon, Mrs Tesman?

HEDDA [*evasively*]: Oh no . . . nothing.

TESMAN: And the wound may be fatal, you say? Eh?

BRACK: The wound will undoubtedly be fatal. Most probably it's all over already.

MRS ELVSTED: Yes, yes, I feel that it is! It's all over! All over! Oh, Hedda . . . !

TESMAN: Yes but tell me then . . . how did you come to hear of all this?

BRACK [*briefly*]: Through the police, a . . . man there I had to see.

HEDDA [*triumphantly*]: At last . . . a really courageous act!

TESMAN [*alarmed*]: But good Lord . . . what are you saying, Hedda?

HEDDA: I say that there is beauty in this deed.

BRACK: Hm, Mrs Tesman . . .

TESMAN: Beauty! Think of that!

MRS ELVSTED: Oh, Hedda, how can you call a thing like that beautiful?

HEDDA: Ejlert Lövborg has settled accounts with himself. He had the courage to do . . . what had to be done.

MRS ELVSTED: Oh no, it couldn't possibly have been like that! He must have done what he did in a fit of madness.

TESMAN: In desperation, it must have been!

HEDDA: It wasn't like that. I am quite certain of it.

MRS ELVSTED: Yes, it was! A fit of madness! Like when he tore our book to pieces!

BRACK [*pulled up*]: The book? The manuscript, you mean? Did he tear it to pieces?

MRS ELVSTED: Yes, he did that last night.

TESMAN [*whispering softly*]: Oh Hedda, we'll never get clear of this.

BRACK: Hm, how very extraordinary.

TESMAN [*drifting about the stage*]: Think of it! That Ejlert should end his life like that! And not even to leave behind him the work that would have made his name immortal. . . .

MRS ELVSTED: Oh, if only it could be put together again!

TESMAN: Yes, if only it could! I'd give anything on earth . . .

MRS ELVSTED: Perhaps it can, Mr Tesman.

TESMAN: What do you mean?

MRS ELVSTED [*searching in her skirt pocket*]: Look here. I kept the notes, all the notes he used when he dictated.

HEDDA [*a step closer*]: Ah . . . !

TESMAN: You kept them, Mrs Elvsted! Eh?

MRS ELVSTED: Yes, they're all here. I took them with me when I left. And they've just stayed in my pocket. . . .

TESMAN: Oh, let me see them!

MRS ELVSTED [*gives him a handful of small papers*]: But they're in such a muddle. All just anyhow.

TESMAN: Just think, if we could manage it all the same! Perhaps if we two were to have a go at it between us . . .

MRS ELVSTED: Oh, yes, let's try at least . . .

TESMAN: It must be done! It shall be done! I'll devote my life to this work!

HEDDA: You, Jörgen? Your life?

TESMAN: Yes, or at any rate the time I have at my disposal. My own material will just have to wait. Hedda . . . you understand me? Eh? I owe this to Ejlert's memory.

HEDDA: Perhaps you do.

TESMAN: And now, my dear Mrs Elvsted, we must pull ourselves together. God knows, there's no point in crying over spilt milk. Eh? We must try to contemplate the matter calmly. . . .

MRS ELVSTED: Yes, Mr Tesman, I'll do my best.

TESMAN: Well, come along then. We must look at these jottings at once. Now, where shall we sit? Here? No, there, in the back room. You'll excuse us, Mr Brack! You come along with me, Mrs Elvsted.

MRS ELVSTED: Oh God . . . if only it could be done!

Tesman and Mr Elvsted go into the inner room. She removes her hat and coat. They both sit at the table under the hanging lamp, and immerse themselves in an eager examination of the papers. Hedda goes across to the stove and sits in the armchair. After a while Mr Brack joins her.

HEDDA: Ah, Mr Brack . . . what a sense of release it gives, this affair of Ejlert Lövborg.

BRACK: Release, my lady? Well, of course, for him it's a release. . . .

HEDDA: I mean, for me. It's a liberation to know that an act of spontaneous courage is yet possible in this world. An act that has something of unconditional beauty.

BRACK [*smiles*]: Hm . . . my very dear lady . . .

HEDDA: Oh, I know what you're going to say. Because you're something of an academic too, in your own line, like . . . well!

BRACK [*looks at her steadily*]: Ejlert Lövborg was more to you perhaps than you are willing to admit, even to yourself. Or am I mistaken?

HEDDA: I don't answer that kind of question. I just know that Ejlert Lövborg had the courage to live his life in his own fashion. And then now . . . this! This beautiful act. That he had the courage to take his leave of life . . . so early.

BRACK: It pains me, my lady . . . but I am compelled to disabuse you of a beautiful illusion.

HEDDA: Illusion?

BRACK: Which you would in any case have been deprived of fairly soon.

HEDDA: And what might that be?

BRACK: He didn't shoot himself . . . intentionally.

HEDDA: Not intentionally!

BRACK: No. This business with Ejlert Lövborg didn't happen quite as I described it.

HEDDA [*in suspense*]: Did you keep something back? What is it?

BRACK: For the sake of that poor Mrs Elvsted I made use of a few circumlocutions.

HEDDA: What, then?

BRACK: In the first place, he is already dead.

HEDDA: At the hospital?

BRACK: Yes. Without recovering consciousness.

HEDDA: And what else?

BRACK: That the affair did not take place at his lodgings.

HEDDA: Well, that doesn't really make any difference.

BRACK: Does it not? Because as it happens . . . Ejlert Lövborg was found shot in . . . in Mademoiselle Diana's boudoir.

HEDDA [*is about to jump up, but sinks back again*]: No, that's impossible, Mr Brack! He can't have gone there again today!

BRACK: He went there this afternoon. He wanted to recover something that he said they'd taken. He was talking wildly about a child that had been lost. . . .

HEDDA: Oh . . . so that was why . . .

BRACK: I imagined that he might have been referring to his manuscript. But that he apparently destroyed himself. So it must have been his pocket-book, then.

HEDDA: I suppose so. . . . And so . . . he was found there.

BRACK: Yes, there. With a discharged pistol in his breast pocket. The bullet had wounded him fatally.

HEDDA: In the breast.

BRACK: No . . . he was shot in the abdomen.

HEDDA [*looks up with an expression of revulsion*]: That as well! Oh. . . . Everything I touch seems destined to turn into something mean and farcical.

BRACK: There is a further detail, my lady. Another circumstance that might be classified as somewhat distasteful.

HEDDA: And what is that?

BRACK: The pistol that was found on his body . . . .

HEDDA [*holding her breath*]: Well! What about it!

BRACK: It must have been stolen.

HEDDA [*jumps up*]: Stolen! No! That isn't true!

BRACK: There is no possible alternative. He must have stolen it. . . . Sh!

Tesman and Mrs Elvsted have got up from the table in the inner room and come out to the reception room.

TESMAN [*with papers in both hands*]: Oh Hedda . . . it's almost impossible for me to see in there under the lamp. Think of that!

HEDDA: Yes, I'm thinking.

TESMAN: Do you think we might be allowed to sit at your desk for a bit? Eh?

HEDDA: Yes, of course you can. [*quickly*] No, wait a moment! Let me clear away some of these things first.

TESMAN: No, no, let me take all these away. I'll put them on the piano. There you are!

She has pulled an object, covered with sheets of music, out of the bookcase; she adds a few more sheets and carries the whole pile off to the left of the inner room. Tesman puts the papers on the desk, and brings over the lamp from the corner table. He and Mrs Elvsted sit down and proceed with their work. Hedda returns.

HEDDA [*behind Mrs Elvsted's chair, lightly caressing her hair*]: Well, Thea, my sweet . . . and how is the Ejlert Lövborg memorial getting on?

MRS ELVSTED [*looks up at her, discouraged*]: Oh goodness . . . it's going to be dreadfully difficult to sort out.

TESMAN: It must be possible. It simply has to be. And this . . . putting other people's papers in order . . . that's just the sort of thing I'm good at.

Hedda goes across to the stove and sits on one of the stools. Brack stands over her, leaning against the armchair.

HEDDA [*whispers*]: What were you saying about the pistol?

BRACK [*quietly*]: That it must have been stolen.

HEDDA: And why must it have been?

BRACK: Because any other explanation ought to be impossible, my lady.

HEDDA: Indeed.

BRACK [*looks at her*]: Ejlert Lövborg was evidently here this morning. Isn't that so?

HEDDA: Yes.

BRACK: Were you alone with him?

HEDDA: Yes, for a while.

BRACK: And did you not leave the room while he was here?

HEDDA: No.

BRACK: Think carefully. Were you not out of the room even for a moment?

HEDDA: Yes, perhaps just for a moment . . . out in the hall.

BRACK: And where was the case with your pistols during this time?

HEDDA: It was locked in . . .

BRACK: Well, my lady?

HEDDA: The case was standing over there on the writing table.

BRACK: Have you looked at it since then to see whether both pistols are still in place?

HEDDA: No.

BRACK: You don't need to look. I saw the pistol that was found on Lövborg. And I recognized it immediately, from yesterday. And from before that, too.

HEDDA: Have you got the pistol?

BRACK: No, it is in the hands of the police.

HEDDA: And what will the police do with it?

BRACK: Try to discover who owns it.

HEDDA: And do you think they will be successful?

BRACK [*bends over her and whispers*]: No, Hedda Gabler . . . not if I hold my tongue.

HEDDA [*looks at him apprehensively*]: And if you don't . . . what then?

BRACK [*shrugs his shoulders*]: There is always the possibility that the pistol was stolen.

HEDDA [*with determination*]: I'd sooner die!

BRACK [*smiles*] People say such things. But they don't do them.

HEDDA [*without answering*]: And so . . . as the pistol was not stolen. And when the owner is discovered. What happens then?

BRACK: There will be an unpleasant scandal . . . Hedda.

HEDDA: A scandal!

BRACK: Yes, a scandal . . . the thing you are afraid of. You will of course be required to go into the witness box. Both you and Mademoiselle Diana. She will have to explain how the event took place. Whether the wound was inflicted accidentally or deliberately. Was he about to pull the pistol out of his pocket in order to threaten her? And did it then go off? Or did she seize the pistol out of his hand, shoot him down, and then stick the weapon back in his pocket? I wouldn't put it past her. She's a spirited wench, is this Mademoiselle Diana.

HEDDA: But all this revolting business has nothing to do with me.

BRACK: No. But you will be obliged to tell the court why you gave Ejlert Lövborg the pistol. And what inference will be drawn from the fact that you did give it to him?

HEDDA [*lowers her head*]: That's true. I didn't think of that.

BRACK: Well, fortunately there is nothing to fear so long as I keep silence.

HEDDA [*looks up at him*]: And so I am in your power, Mr Brack. From now on I am at your mercy.

BRACK [*whispers more softly*]: Dearest Hedda . . . believe me . . . I shall not abuse the position.

HEDDA: In your power, all the same. Subject to your will and your demands. No longer free! [*She gets up violently.*] No! That's a thought that I'll never endure! Never.

BRACK [*looks at her half tauntingly*]: One generally acquiesces in what is inevitable.

HEDDA [*returns the look*]: Perhaps you're right.

> She crosses to the writing desk.

HEDDA [*suppresses an involuntary smile, and imitates Tesman's intonation*]: Well? Is it going to work out, Jörgen? Eh?

TESMAN: Heaven knows, my love. At any rate it's going to take us months.

HEDDA [*as before*]: Well, think of that! [*She passes her fingers lightly through Mrs Elvsted's hair.*] Isn't this strange for you, Thea? Now you're sitting here together with Tesman . . . as you used to sit with Ejlert Lövborg.

MRS ELVSTED: Oh yes, oh God . . . if only I could inspire your husband in the same way.

HEDDA: Oh, I expect it will come . . . in time.

TESMAN: Yes, d'you know what, Hedda . . . it really does seem to me that I'm beginning to feel something of the sort. But you go and sit down again, now, with Mr Brack.

HEDDA: And is there nothing I can do to help you two?

TESMAN: No, nothing at all. [*turns his head*] We'll just have to rely on you, dear Mr Brack, to keep Hedda company!

BRACK [*with a look to Hedda*]: It will be a pleasure indeed.

HEDDA: Thank you. But tonight I'm tired. I'm going to go in and lie down a bit on the sofa.

TESMAN: Yes, you do that my dear. Eh?

Hedda goes into the inner room and pulls the curtains together behind her. A short pause. Suddenly she is heard to play a wild dance tune on the piano.

MRS ELVSTED [*starts up from her chair*]: Oh . . . what's that!

TESMAN [*runs to the doorway*]: But Hedda, my dear . . . don't play dance music, not tonight! Do think of Aunt Rina! And of Ejlert, too!

HEDDA [*puts her head out between the curtains*]: And of Auntie Julle. And of all the rest of them. . . . I shall be silent in future.   [*She draws the curtains together again.*]

TESMAN [*at the desk*]: I don't think it's good for her to see us at this melancholy task. I'll tell you what, Mrs Elvsted . . . you'll have to move in to Aunt Julle's. Then I'll come up in the evenings. And then we can sit and work there. Eh?

MRS ELVSTED: Yes, perhaps that would be best. . . .

HEDDA [*from the inner room*]: I can hear what you're saying, Tesman. And how am I supposed to survive the evenings out here?

TESMAN [*leafing through the papers*]: Oh, I expect Mr Brack will be kind enough to look in now and again.

BRACK [*in the armchair, shouts cheerfully*]: I'll gladly come every single evening, Mrs Tesman! Don't you worry, we'll have a fine time out here together!

HEDDA [*clearly and distinctly*]: Yes, you're looking forward to that, aren't you, Mr Brack? Yourself as the only cock in the yard. . . .

A shot is heard within. Tesman, Mrs Elvsted, and Brack all start to their feet.

TESMAN: Oh, now she's playing about with those pistols again.

He pulls the curtains aside and runs in. Mrs Elvsted follows. Hedda lies stretched out dead on the sofa. Confusion and shouting. Berte, in alarm, comes in from the right.

TESMAN [*yelling at Brack*]: Shot herself! Shot herself in the temple! Think of that!

BRACK [*half prostrate in the armchair*]: But, good God Almighty . . . people don't do such things!

1890

Oscar Wilde
1854–1900

Playwright and poet, novelist and critic, Oscar Wilde was born in Dublin, Ireland. After majoring in classics at Trinity College, Dublin, he won a scholarship to Oxford University. By the time of his graduation from Oxford in 1878 he was already well known for his commitment to 'art for art's sake' and for his eccentricities in dress and manners. Convinced that 'industry is the root of all ugliness', he sought to raise the taste of his audiences. Between 1892 and 1895 he wrote a series of comedies for the stage—'trivial comedies for serious people', he called them—whose plots were then regarded as scandalous and whose dialogue glistened with his clever wit. In 1895 he was found guilty of homosexual conduct and sentenced to two years in prison with hard labour. His imprisonment led him to write his poem *The Ballad of Reading Gaol* and his prose confession *De Profundis*. After his release from jail he emigrated to France, where he spent his last five years living under an assumed name. *The Importance of Being Earnest* had its premiere at St James's Theatre in London on 14 February 1895.

The Importance of Being Earnest

CHARACTERS

JOHN WORTHING, JP
ALGERNON MONCRIEFF
REV. CANON CHASUBLE, DD
MIRRIMAN, butler
LANE, manservant

LADY BRACKNELL
HON. GWENDOLEN FAIRFAX
CECILY CARDEW
MISS PRISM, governess

ACT I

> *The Scene: Morning room in Algernon's flat in Half-Moon Street. The room is luxuriously and artistically furnished. The sound of a piano is heard in the adjoining room. Lane is arranging the afternoon tea on the table, and after the music has ceased, Algernon enters.*

ALGERNON: Did you hear what I was playing, Lane?

LANE: I didn't think it polite to listen, sir.

ALGERNON: I'm sorry for that, for your sake. I don't play accurately—any one can play accurately—but I play with wonderful expression. As far as the piano is concerned, sentiment is my forte. I keep science for Life.

LANE: Yes, sir.

ALGERNON: And, speaking of the science of Life, have you got the cucumber sandwiches cut for Lady Bracknell?

LANE: Yes, sir. [*Hands them on a salver.*]

ALGERNON [*inspects them, takes two, and sits down on the sofa*]: Oh! . . . by the way, Lane, I see from your book that on Thursday night, when Lord Shoreman and Mr Worthing were dining with me, eight bottles of champagne are entered as having been consumed.

LANE: Yes, sir; eight bottles and a pint.

ALGERNON: Why is it that at a bachelor's establishment the servants invariably drink the champagne? I ask merely for information.

LANE: I attribute it to the superior quality of the wine, sir. I have often observed that in married households the champagne is rarely of a first-rate brand.

ALGERNON: Good Heavens! Is marriage so demoralizing as that?

LANE: I believe it is a very pleasant state, sir. I have had very little experience of it myself up to the present. I have only been married once. That was in consequence of a misunderstanding between myself and a young person.

ALGERNON [*languidly*]: I don't know that I am much interested in your family life, Lane.

LANE: No sir; it is not a very interesting subject. I never think of it myself.

ALGERNON: Very natural, I am sure. That will do, Lane, thank you.

LANE: Thank you, sir.   [*Lane goes out.*]

ALGERNON: Lane's views on marriage seem somewhat lax. Really, if the lower orders don't set us a good example, what on earth is the use of them? They seem, as a class, to have absolutely no sense of moral responsibility.

Enter Lane.

LANE: Mr Ernest Worthing.

Enter Jack. Lane goes out.

ALGERNON: How are you, my dear Ernest? What brings you up to town?

JACK: Oh, pleasure, pleasure! What else should bring one anywhere? Eating as usual, I see, Algy!

ALGERNON [*stiffly*]: I believe it is customary in good society to take some slight refreshment at five o'clock. Where have you been since last Thursday?

JACK [*sitting down on the sofa*]: In the country.

ALGERNON: What on earth do you do there?

JACK [*pulling off his gloves*]: When one is in town one amuses oneself. When one is in the country one amuses other people. It is excessively boring.

ALGERNON: And who are the people you amuse?

JACK [*airily*]: Oh, neighbours, neighbours.

ALGERNON: Got nice neighbours in your part of Shropshire?

JACK: Perfectly horrid! Never speak to one of them.

ALGERNON: How immensely you must amuse them! [*Goes over and takes sandwich.*] By the way, Shropshire is your country, is it not?

JACK: Eh? Shropshire? Yes, of course. Hallo! Why all these cups? Why cucumber sandwiches? Why such reckless extravagance in one so young? Who is coming to tea?

ALGERNON: Oh! merely Aunt Augusta and Gwendolen.

JACK: How perfectly delightful!

ALGERNON: Yes, that is all very well; but I am afraid Aunt Augusta won't quite approve of your being here.

JACK: May I ask why?

ALGERNON: My dear fellow, the way you flirt with Gwendolen is perfectly disgraceful. It is almost as bad as the way Gwendolen flirts with you.

JACK: I am in love with Gwendolen. I have come up to town expressly to propose to her.

ALGERNON: I thought you had come up for pleasure? . . . I call that business.

JACK: How utterly unromantic you are!

ALGERNON: I really don't see anything romantic in proposing. It is very romantic to be in love. But there is nothing romantic about a definite proposal. Why, one may be accepted. One usually is, I believe. Then the excitement is all over. The very essence of romance is uncertainty. If ever I get married, I'll certainly try to forget the fact.

JACK: I have no doubt about that, dear Algy. The Divorce Court was specially invented for people whose memories are so curiously constituted.

ALGERNON: Oh! there is no use speculating on that subject. Divorces are made in Heaven—[*Jack puts out his hand to take a sandwich, Algernon at once interferes.*] Please don't touch the cucumber sandwiches. They are ordered specially for Aunt Augusta. [*Takes one and eats it.*]

JACK: Well, you have been eating them all the time.

ALGERNON: That is quite a different matter. She is my aunt. [*Takes plate from below.*] Have some bread and butter. The bread and butter is for Gwendolen. Gwendolen is devoted to bread and butter.

JACK [*advancing to table and helping himself*]: And very good bread and butter it is too.

ALGERNON: Well, my dear fellow, you need not eat as if you were going to eat it all. You behave as if you were married to her already. You are not married to her already, and I don't think you ever will be.

JACK: Why on earth do you say that?

ALGERNON: Well, in the first place, girls never marry the men they flirt with. Girls don't think it right.

JACK: Oh, that is nonsense!

ALGERNON: It isn't. It is a great truth. It accounts for the extraordinary number of bachelors that one sees all over the place. In the second place, I don't give my consent.

JACK: Your consent!

ALGERNON: My dear fellow, Gwendolen is my first cousin. And before I allow you to marry her, you will have to clear up the whole question of Cecily. [*Rings bell.*]

JACK: Cecily! What on earth do you mean? What do you mean, Algy, by Cecily! I don't know anyone of the name of Cecily.

    Enter Lane.

ALGERNON: Bring me that cigarette case Mr Worthing left in the smoking room the last time he dined here.

LANE: Yes, sir. [*Lane goes out.*]

JACK: Do you mean to say you have had my cigarette case all this time? I wish to goodness you had let me know. I have been writing frantic letters to Scotland Yard about it. I was very nearly offering a large reward.

ALGERNON: Well, I wish you would offer one. I happen to be more than usually hard up.

JACK: There is no good offering a large reward now that the thing is found.

Enter Lane with the cigarette case on a salver. Algernon takes it at once. Lane goes out.

ALGERNON: I think that is rather mean of you, Ernest, I must say. [*Opens case and examines it.*] However, it makes no matter, for, now that I look at the inscription inside, I find that the thing isn't yours after all.

JACK: Of course it's mine. [*Moving to him.*] You have seen me with it a hundred times, and you have no right whatsoever to read what is written inside. It is a very ungentlemanly thing to read a private cigarette case.

ALGERNON: Oh! it is absurd to have a hard and fast rule about what one should read and what one shouldn't. More than half of modern culture depends on what one shouldn't read.

JACK: I am quite aware of the fact, and I don't propose to discuss modern culture. It isn't the sort of thing one should talk of in private. I simply want my cigarette case back.

ALGERNON: Yes; but this isn't your cigarette case. The cigarette case is a present from someone of the name of Cecily, and you said you didn't know anyone of that name.

JACK: Well, if you want to know, Cecily happens to be my aunt.

ALGERNON: Your aunt?

JACK: Charming old lady she is, too. Lives at Tunbridge Wells. Just give it back to me, Algy.

ALGERNON [*retreating to back of sofa*]: But why does she call herself little Cecily if she is your aunt and lives at Tunbridge Wells. [*Reading*] 'From little Cecily with her fondest love.'

JACK [*moving to sofa and kneeling upon it*]: My dear fellow, what on earth is there in that? Some aunts are tall, some aunts are not tall. That is a matter that surely an aunt may be allowed to decide for herself. You seem to think that every aunt should be exactly like your aunt! That is absurd. For Heaven's sake give me back my cigarette case. [*Follows Algernon round the room.*]

ALGERNON: Yes. But why does your aunt call you her uncle? 'From little Cecily, with her fondest love to her dear Uncle Jack.' There is no objection, I admit, to an aunt being a small aunt, but why an aunt, no matter what her size may be, should call her own nephew her uncle, I can't quite make out. Besides, your name isn't Jack at all; it is Ernest.

JACK: It isn't Ernest; it's Jack.

ALGERNON: You have always told me it was Ernest. I have introduced you to everyone as Ernest. You answer to the name Ernest. You look as if your name was Ernest. You are the most earnest-looking person I ever saw in my life. It is perfectly absurd your saying that your name isn't Ernest. It's on your cards. Here is one of them [*taking it from case*]. 'Mr Ernest Worthing, B.4, The Albany.' I'll keep this as a proof that your name is Ernest if ever you attempt to deny it to me, or to Gwendolen, or to anyone else. [*Puts the card in his pocket.*]

JACK: Well, my name is Ernest in town and Jack in the country, and the cigarette case was given to me in the country.

ALGERNON: Yes, but that does not account for the fact that your small Aunt Cecily, who lives at Tunbridge Wells, calls you her dear uncle. Come, old boy, you had much better have the thing out at once.

JACK: My dear Algy, you talk exactly as if you were a dentist. It is very vulgar to talk like a dentist when one isn't a dentist. It produces a false impression.

ALGERNON: Well, that is exactly what dentists always do. Now, go on! Tell me the whole thing. I may mention that I have always suspected you of being a confirmed and secret Bunburyist; and I am quite sure of it now.

JACK: Bunburyist? What on earth do you mean by a Bunburyist?

ALGERNON: I'll reveal to you the meaning of that incomparable expression as soon as you are kind enough to inform me why you are Ernest in town and Jack in the country.

JACK: Well, produce my cigarette case first.

ALGERNON: Here it is. [*Hands cigarette case.*] Now produce your explanation, and pray make it improbable. [*Sits on sofa.*]

JACK: My dear fellow, there is nothing improbable about my explanation at all. In fact it's perfectly ordinary. Old Mr Thomas Cardew, who adopted me when I was a little boy, made me in his will guardian to his granddaughter, Miss Cecily Cardew. Cecily, who addresses me as her uncle from motives of respect that you could not possibly appreciate, lives at my place in the country under the charge of her admirable governess, Miss Prism.

ALGERNON: Where is that place in the country, by the way?

JACK: That is nothing to you, dear boy. You are not going to be invited. . . . I may tell you candidly that the place is not in Shropshire.

ALGERNON: I suspected that, my dear fellow! I have Bunburyed all over Shropshire on two separate occasions. Now, go on. Why are you Ernest in town and Jack in the country?

JACK: My dear Algy, I don't know whether you will be able to understand my real motive. You are hardly serious enough. When one is placed in the position of guardian, one has to adopt a very high moral tone on all subjects. It's one's duty to do so. And as a high moral tone can hardly be said to conduce very much to either one's health or one's happiness, in order to get up to town I have always pretended to have a younger brother of the name of Ernest, who lives in Albany, and gets into the most dreadful scrapes. That, my dear Algy, is the whole truth pure and simple.

ALGERNON: The truth is rarely pure and never simple. Modern life would be very tedious if it were either, and modern literature a complete impossibility!

JACK: That wouldn't be at all a bad thing.

ALGERNON: Literary criticism is not your forte, my dear fellow. Don't try it. You should leave that to the people who haven't been at a University. They do it so well in the daily papers. What you really are is a Bunburyist. I was quite right in saying you are a Bunburyist. You are one of the most advanced Bunburyists I know.

JACK: What on earth do you mean?

ALGERNON: You have invented a very useful younger brother called Ernest, in order that you may be able to come up to town as often as you like. I have invented an invaluable permanent invalid called Bunbury, in order that I may be able to go down into the country whenever I choose. Bunbury is perfectly invaluable. If it wasn't for Bunbury's extraordinary bad health, for instance, I wouldn't be able to dine with you at Willis's tonight, for I have been really engaged to Aunt Augusta for more than a week.

JACK: I haven't asked you to dine with me anywhere tonight.

ALGERNON: I know. You are absurdly careless about sending out invitations. It is very foolish of you. Nothing annoys people so much as not receiving invitations.

JACK: You had better dine with your Aunt Augusta.

ALGERNON: I haven't the smallest intention of doing anything of the kind. To begin with, I dined there on Monday, and once a week is quite enough to dine with one's own relations. In the second place, whenever I do dine there I am always treated as a member of the family, and sent down with either no woman at all, or two. In the third place, I know perfectly well whom she will place me next to, tonight. She will place me next Mary Farquhar, who always flirts with her own husband across the dinner table. That is not very pleasant. Indeed, it is not even decent . . . and that sort of thing is enormously on the increase. The amount of women in London who flirt with their own husbands is perfectly scandalous. It looks so bad. It is simply washing one's clean linen in public. Besides, now that I know you to be a confirmed Bunburyist I naturally want to talk to you about Bunburying. I want to tell you the rules.

JACK: I'm not a Bunburyist at all. If Gwendolen accepts me, I am going to kill my brother, indeed I think I'll kill him in any case. Cecily is a little too interested in him. It is rather a bore. So I am going to get rid of Ernest. And I strongly advise you to do the same with Mr . . . with your invalid friend who has the absurd name.

ALGERNON: Nothing will induce me to part with Bunbury, and if you ever get married, which seems to me extremely problematic, you will be very glad to know Bunbury. A man who marries without knowing Bunbury has a very tedious time of it.

JACK: That is nonsense. If I marry a charming girl like Gwendolen, and she is the only girl I ever saw in life that I would marry, I certainly won't want to know Bunbury.

ALGERNON: Then your wife will. You don't seem to realize, that in married life three is company and two is none.

JACK [*sententiously*]: That, my dear young friend, is the theory that the corrupt French Drama has been propounding for the last fifty years.

ALGERNON: Yes; and that the happy English home has proved in half the time.

JACK: For heaven's sake, don't try to be cynical. It's perfectly easy to be cynical.

ALGERNON: My dear fellow, it isn't easy to be anything nowadays. There's such a lot of beastly competition about. [*The sound of an electric bell is heard.*] Ah! that must be Aunt Augusta. Only relatives, or creditors, ever ring in that Wagnerian manner. Now, if I get her out of the way for ten minutes, so that you can have an opportunity of proposing to Gwendolen, may I dine with you tonight at Willis's?

JACK: I suppose so, if you want to.

ALGERNON: Yes, but you must be serious about it. I hate people who are not serious about meals. It is so shallow of them.

Enter Lane

LANE: Lady Bracknell and Miss Fairfax.

Algernon goes forward to meet them. Enter Lady Bracknell and Gwendolen.

LADY BRACKNELL: Good afternoon, dear Algernon, I hope you are behaving very well.

ALGERNON: I'm feeling very well, Aunt Augusta.

LADY BRACKNELL: That's not quite the same thing. In fact the two things rarely go together. [*Sees Jack and bows to him with icy coldness.*]

ALGERNON [*to Gwendolen*]: Dear me, you are smart!

GWENDOLEN: I am always smart! Am I not, Mr Worthing?

JACK: You're quite perfect, Miss Fairfax.

GWENDOLEN: Oh! I hope I am not that. It would leave no room for developments, and I intend to develop in many directions. [*Gwendolen and Jack sit down together in the corner.*]

LADY BRACKNELL: I'm sorry if we are a little late, Algernon, but I was obliged to call on dear Lady Harbury. I hadn't been there since her poor husband's death. I never saw a woman so altered; she looks quite twenty years younger. And now I'll have a cup of tea and one of those nice cucumber sandwiches you promised me.

ALGERNON: Certainly, Aunt Augusta. [*Goes over to tea table.*]

LADY BRACKNELL: Won't you come and sit here, Gwendolen?

GWENDOLEN: Thanks, mamma, I'm quite comfortable where I am.

ALGERNON [*picking up empty plate in horror*]: Good heavens! Lane! Why are there no cucumber sandwiches? I ordered them specially.

LANE [*gravely*]: There were no cucumbers in the market this morning, sir. I went down twice.

ALGERNON: No cucumbers!

LANE: No, sir. Not even for ready money.

ALGERNON: That will do, Lane, thank you.

LANE: Thank you, sir. [*Goes out.*]

ALGERNON: I am greatly distressed, Aunt Augusta, about there being no cucumbers, not even for ready money.

LADY BRACKNELL: It really makes no matter, Algernon. I had some crumpets with Lady Harbury, who seems to me to be living entirely for pleasure now.

ALGERNON: I hear her hair has turned quite gold from grief.

LADY BRACKNELL: It certainly has changed its colour. From what cause I, of course, cannot say. [*Algernon crosses and hands tea.*] Thank you, I've quite a treat for you tonight, Algernon. I am going to send you down with Mary Farquhar. She is such a nice woman, and so attentive to her husband. It's delightful to watch them.

ALGERNON: I am afraid, Aunt Augusta, I shall have to give up the pleasure of dining with you tonight after all.

LADY BRACKNELL [*frowning*]: I hope not, Algernon. It would put my table completely out. Your uncle would have to dine upstairs. Fortunately he is accustomed to that.

ALGERNON: It is a great bore, and, I need hardly say, a terrible disappointment to me, but the fact is I have just had a telegram to say that my poor friend Bunbury is very ill again. [*Exchanges glances with Jack.*] They seem to think I should be with him.

LADY BRACKNELL: It is very strange. This Mr Bunbury seems to suffer from curiously bad health.

ALGERNON: Yes; poor Bunbury is a dreadful invalid.

LADY BRACKNELL: Well, I must say, Algernon, that I think it is high time that Mr Bunbury made up his mind whether he was going to live or to die. This shilly-shallying with the question is absurd. Nor do I in any way approve of the modern sympathy with invalids. I consider it morbid. Illness of any kind is hardly a thing to be encouraged in others. Health is the primary duty of life. I am always telling that to your poor uncle, but he never seems to take much notice . . . as far as any improvement in his ailments goes. I should be much obliged if you would ask Mr Bunbury, from me, to be kind enough not to have a relapse on Saturday, for I rely on you to arrange my music for me. It is my last reception, and one wants something that will encourage conversation, particularly at the end of the season when everyone has practically said whatever they had to say, which, in most cases, was probably not much.

ALGERNON: I'll speak to Bunbury, Aunt Augusta, if he is still conscious, and I think I can promise you he'll be all right by Saturday. Of course the music is a great difficulty. You see, if one plays good music, people don't listen, and if one plays bad music, people don't talk. But I'll run over the program I've drawn out, if you will kindly come into the next room for a moment.

LADY BRACKNELL: Thank you, Algernon. It is very thoughtful of you. [*Rising, and following Algernon.*] I'm sure the program will be delightful, after a few expurgations. French songs I cannot possibly allow. People always seem to think that they are improper, and either look shocked, which is vulgar, or laugh, which is worse. But German sounds a thoroughly respectable language, and, indeed I believe is so. Gwendolen, you will accompany me.

GWENDOLEN: Certainly, mamma.

Lady Bracknell and Algernon go into the music room; Gwendolen remains behind.

JACK: Charming day it has been, Miss Fairfax.

GWENDOLEN: Pray don't talk to me about the weather, Mr Worthing. Whenever people talk to me about the weather, I always feel quite certain that they mean something else. And that makes me so nervous.

JACK: I do mean something else.

GWENDOLEN: I thought so. In fact, I am never wrong.

JACK: And I would like to be allowed to take advantage of Lady Bracknell's temporary absence. . . .

GWENDOLEN: I would certainly advise you to do so. Mamma has a way of coming back suddenly into a room that I have often had to speak to her about.

JACK [nervously]: Miss Fairfax, ever since I met you I have admired you more than any girl . . . I have ever met since . . . I met you.

GWENDOLEN: Yes, I am quite aware of the fact. And I do often wish that in public, at any rate, you had been more demonstrative. For me you have always had an irresistible fascination. Even before I met you I was far from indifferent to you. [Jack looks at her in amazement.] We live, as I hope you know, Mr Worthing, in an age of ideals. The fact is constantly mentioned in the more expensive monthly magazines, and has reached the provincial pulpits, I am told; and my ideal has always been to love someone of the name of Ernest. There is something in that name that inspires absolute confidence. The moment Algernon first mentioned to me that he had a friend called Ernest, I knew I was destined to love you.

JACK: You really love me, Gwendolen?

GWENDOLEN: Passionately!

JACK: Darling! You don't know how happy you've made me.

GWENDOLEN: My own Ernest!

JACK: But you don't really mean to say that you couldn't love me if my name wasn't Ernest!

GWENDOLEN: But your name is Ernest.

JACK: Yes, I know it is. But supposing it was something else? Do you mean to say you couldn't love me then?

GWENDOLEN [glibly]: Ah! that is clearly a metaphysical speculation, and like most metaphysical speculations has very little reference at all to the actual facts of real life, as we know them.

JACK: Personally, darling, to speak quite candidly, I don't much care about the name of Ernest. . . . I don't think the name suits me at all.

GWENDOLEN: It suits you perfectly. It is a divine name. It has a music of its own. It produces vibrations.

JACK: Well, really, Gwendolen, I must say that I think there are lots of other much nicer names. I think Jack, for instance, a charming name.

GWENDOLEN: Jack? . . . No, there is very little music in the name Jack, if any at all, indeed. It does not thrill. It produces absolutely no vibrations. . . . I have known several Jacks, and they all, without exception, were more than usually plain. Besides, Jack is a notorious domesticity for John! And I pity any woman who is married to a man called John. She would probably never be allowed to know the entrancing pleasure of a single moment's solitude. The only really safe name is Ernest.

JACK: Gwendolen, I must get christened at once—I mean we must get married at once. There is no time to be lost.

GWENDOLEN: Married, Mr Worthing?

JACK [*astounded*]: Well . . . surely. You know that I love you, and you led me to believe, Miss Fairfax, that you were not absolutely indifferent to me.

GWENDOLEN: I adore you. But you haven't proposed to me yet. Nothing has been said at all about marriage. The subject has not even been touched on.

JACK: Well . . . may I propose to you now?

GWENDOLEN: I think it would be an admirable opportunity. And to spare you any possible disappointment, Mr Worthing, I think it only fair to tell you quite frankly beforehand that I am fully determined to accept you.

JACK: Gwendolen!

GWENDOLEN: Yes, Mr Worthing, what have you got to say to me?

JACK: You know what I have got to say to you.

GWENDOLEN: Yes, but you don't say it.

JACK: Gwendolen, will you marry me? [*Goes on his knees.*]

GWENDOLEN: Of course I will, darling. How long you have been about it! I am afraid you have had very little experience in how to propose.

JACK: My own one, I have never loved anyone in the world but you.

GWENDOLEN: Yes, but men often propose for practice. I know my brother Gerald does. All my girl friends tell me so. What wonderfully blue eyes you have, Ernest! They are quite, quite blue. I hope you will always look at me just like that, especially when there are other people present.

   Enter Lady Bracknell.

LADY BRACKNELL: Mr Worthing! Rise, sir, from this semi-recumbent posture. It is most indecorous.

GWENDOLEN: Mamma! [*He tries to rise; she restrains him.*] I must beg you to retire. This is no place for you. Besides, Mr Worthing has not quite finished yet.

LADY BRACKNELL: Finished what, may I ask?

GWENDOLEN: I am engaged to Mr Worthing, Mamma. [*They rise together.*]

LADY BRACKNELL: Pardon me, you are not engaged to anyone. When you do become engaged to someone, I, or your father, should his health permit him, will inform you of the fact. An engagement should come on a young girl as a surprise, pleasant or unpleasant, as the case may be. It is hardly a matter that she could be allowed to arrange for herself. . . . And now I have a few questions to put to you, Mr Worthing. While I am making these inquiries, you, Gwendolen, will wait for me below in the carriage.

GWENDOLEN [*reproachfully*]: Mamma!

LADY BRACKNELL: In the carriage, Gwendolen! [*Gwendolen goes to the door. She and Jack blow kisses to each other behind Lady Bracknell's back. Lady Bracknell looks vaguely about as if she could not understand what the noise was. Finally turns round.*] Gwendolen, the carriage!

GWENDOLEN: Yes, Mamma. [*Goes out, looking back at Jack.*]

LADY BRACKNELL [*sitting down*]: You can take a seat, Mr Worthing. [*Looks in her pocket for notebook and pencil.*]

JACK: Thank you, Lady Bracknell, I prefer standing.

LADY BRACKNELL [*pencil and notebook in hand*]: I feel bound to tell you that you are not down on my list of eligible young men, although I have the same list as the dear Duchess of Bolton has. We work together, in fact. However, I am quite ready to enter your name, should your answers be what a really affectionate mother requires. Do you smoke?

JACK: Well, yes, I must admit I smoke.

LADY BRACKNELL: I am glad to hear it. A man should always have an occupation of some kind. There are far too many idle men in London as it is. How old are you?

JACK: Twenty-nine.

LADY BRACKNELL: A very good age to be married at. I have always been of the opinion that a man who desires to get married should know either everything or nothing. Which do you know?

JACK [*after some hesitation*]: I know nothing, Lady Bracknell.

LADY BRACKNELL: I am pleased to hear it. I do not approve of anything that tampers with natural ignorance. Ignorance is like a delicate exotic fruit; touch it and the bloom is gone. The whole theory of modern education is radically unsound. Fortunately in England, at any rate, education produces no effect whatsoever. If it did, it would prove a serious danger to the upper classes, and probably lead to acts of violence in Grosvenor Square. What is your income?

JACK: Between seven and eight thousand a year.

LADY BRACKNELL [*makes a note in her book*]: In land, or in investments?

JACK: In investments, chiefly.

LADY BRACKNELL: That is satisfactory. What between the duties expected of one during one's lifetime, and the duties exacted from one after one's death, land has ceased to be either a profit or a pleasure. It gives one position, and prevents one from keeping it up. That's all that can be said about land.

JACK: I have a country house with some land, of course, attached to it, about fifteen hundred acres, I believe; but I don't depend on that for my real income. In fact, as far as I can make out, the poachers are the only people who make anything out of it.

LADY BRACKNELL: A country house! How many bedrooms? Well, that point can be cleared up afterwards. You have a town house, I hope? A girl with a simple, unspoiled nature, like Gwendolen, could hardly be expected to reside in the country.

JACK: Well, I own a house in Belgrave Square, but it is let by the year to Lady Bloxham. Of course, I can get it back whenever I like, at six months' notice.

LADY BRACKNELL: Lady Bloxham? I don't know her.

JACK: Oh, she goes out very little. She is a lady considerably advanced in years.

LADY BRACKNELL: Ah, nowadays that is no guarantee of respectability of character. What number in Belgrave Square?

JACK: 149.

LADY BRACKNELL [*shaking her head*]: The unfashionable side. I thought there was something. However, that could easily be altered.

JACK: Do you mean the fashion, or the side?

LADY BRACKNELL [*sternly*]: Both, if necessary, I presume. What are your politics?

JACK: Well, I am afraid I really have none. I am a Liberal Unionist.

LADY BRACKNELL: Oh, they count as Tories. They dine with us. Or come in the evening, at any rate. Now to minor matters. Are your parents living?

JACK: I have lost both my parents.

LADY BRACKNELL: To lose one parent, Mr Worthing, may be regarded as a misfortune; to lose both looks like carelessness. Who was your father? He was evidently a man of some wealth. Was he born in what the Radical papers call the purple of commerce, or did he rise from the ranks of the aristocracy?

JACK: I am afraid I really don't know. The fact is, Lady Bracknell, I said I had lost my parents. It would be nearer the truth to say that my parents seem to have lost me.... I don't actually know who I am by birth. I was . . . well, I was found.

LADY BRACKNELL: Found!

JACK: The late Mr Thomas Cardew, an old gentleman of a very charitable and kindly disposition, found me and gave me the name of Worthing, because he happened to have a first-class ticket for Worthing in his pocket at the time. Worthing is a place in Sussex. It is a seaside resort.

LADY BRACKNELL: Where did the charitable gentleman who had a first-class ticket for this seaside resort find you?

JACK [*gravely*]: In a handbag.

LADY BRACKNELL: A handbag?

JACK [*very seriously*]: Yes, Lady Bracknell. I was in a handbag—a somewhat large, black leather handbag, with handles on it—an ordinary handbag in fact.

LADY BRACKNELL: In what locality did this Mr James, or Thomas, Cardew come across this ordinary handbag?

JACK: In the cloakroom at Victoria Station. It was given to him in mistake for his own.

LADY BRACKNELL: The cloakroom at Victoria Station?

JACK: Yes, the Brighton line.

LADY BRACKNELL: The line is immaterial. Mr Worthing, I confess I feel somewhat bewildered by what you have just told me. To be born, or at any rate bred, in a handbag, whether it had handles or not, seems to me to display a contempt for the ordinary decencies of family life that reminds one of the worst excesses of the French Revolution. And I presume you know what that unfortunate movement led to? As for the particular locality in which the handbag was found, a cloakroom at a railway station might serve to conceal a social indiscretion—has probably, indeed, been used for that purpose before now—but it could hardly be regarded as an assured basis for a recognized position in good society.

JACK: May I ask you then what you would advise me to do? I need hardly say I would do anything in the world to ensure Gwendolen's happiness.

LADY BRACKNELL: I would strongly advise you, Mr Worthing, to try and acquire some relations as soon as possible, and to make a definite effort to produce at any rate one parent, of either sex, before the season is quite over.

JACK: Well, I don't see how I could possibly manage to do that. I can produce the handbag at any moment. It is in my dressing room at home. I really think that should satisfy you, Lady Bracknell.

LADY BRACKNELL: Me, sir! What has it to do with me? You can hardly imagine that I and Lord Bracknell would dream of allowing our only daughter—a girl brought up with the utmost care—to marry into a cloakroom, and form an alliance with a parcel. Good morning, Mr Worthing!

[*Lady Bracknell sweeps out in majestic indignation.*]

JACK: Good morning! [*Algernon, from the other room, strikes up the Wedding March. Jack looks perfectly furious, and goes to the door.*] For goodness' sake don't play that ghastly tune, Algy! How idiotic you are!

The music stops and Algernon enters cheerily.

ALGERNON: Didn't it go off all right, old boy? You don't mean to say Gwendolen refused you? I know it is a way she has. She is always refusing people. I think it is most ill-natured of her.

JACK: Oh, Gwendolen is as right as a trivet. As far as she is concerned, we are engaged. Her mother is perfectly unbearable. Never met such a Gorgon. . . , I don't really know what a Gorgon is like, but I am quite sure that Lady Bracknell is one. In any case, she is a monster, without being a myth, which is rather unfair. . . . I beg your pardon, Algy, I suppose I shouldn't talk about your own aunt in that way before you.

ALGERNON: My dear boy, I love hearing my relations abused. It is the only thing that makes me put up with them at all. Relations are simply a tedious pack of people who haven't got the remotest knowledge of how to live, or the smallest instinct about when to die.

JACK: Oh, that is nonsense!

ALGERNON: It isn't!

JACK: Well, I won't argue about the matter. You always want to argue about things.

ALGERNON: That is exactly what things were originally made for.

JACK: Upon my word, if I thought that, I'd shoot myself. . . . [*A pause.*] You don't think there is any chance of Gwendolen becoming like her mother in about a hundred and fifty years, do you, Algy?

ALGERNON: All women become like their mothers. That is their tragedy. No man does. That's his.

JACK: Is that clever?

ALGERNON: It is perfectly phrased! and quite as true as any observation in civilized life should be.

JACK: I am sick to death of cleverness. Everybody is clever nowadays. You can't go anywhere without meeting clever people. The thing has become an absolute public nuisance. I wish to goodness we had a few fools left.

ALGERNON: We have.

JACK: I should extremely like to meet them. What do they talk about?

ALGERNON: The fools? Oh! about the clever people, of course.

JACK: What fools.

ALGERNON: By the way, did you tell Gwendolen the truth about your being Ernest in town, and Jack in the country?

JACK [*in a very patronizing manner*]: My dear fellow, the truth isn't quite the sort of thing one tells to a nice, sweet, refined girl. What extraordinary ideas you have about the way to behave to a woman!

ALGERNON: The only way to behave to a woman is to make love to her, if she is pretty, and to someone else, if she is plain.

JACK: Oh, that is nonsense.

ALGERNON: What about your brother? What about the profligate Ernest?

JACK: Oh, before the end of the week I shall have got rid of him. I'll say he died in Paris of apoplexy. Lots of people die of apoplexy, quite suddenly, don't they?

ALGERNON: Yes, but it's hereditary, my dear fellow. It's a sort of thing that runs in families. You had much better say a severe chill.

JACK: You are sure a severe chill isn't hereditary, or anything of that kind?

ALGERNON: Of course it isn't!

JACK: Very well, then. My poor brother Ernest is carried off suddenly, in Paris, by a severe chill. That gets rid of him.

ALGERNON: But I thought you said that . . . Miss Cardew was a little too much interested in your poor brother Ernest? Won't she feel his loss a great deal?

JACK: Oh, that is all right. Cecily is not a silly romantic girl, I am glad to say. She has got a capital appetite, goes on long walks, and pays no attention at all to her lessons.

ALGERNON: I would rather like to see Cecily.

JACK: I will take very good care you never do. She is excessively pretty, and she is only just eighteen.

ALGERNON: Have you told Gwendolen yet that you have an excessively pretty ward who is only eighteen?

JACK: Oh! one doesn't blurt these things out to people. Cecily and Gwendolen are perfectly certain to be extremely great friends. I'll bet you anything you like that half an hour after they have met, they will be calling each other sister.

ALGERNON: Women only do that when they have called each other a lot of other things first. Now, my dear boy, if we want to get a good table at Willis's, we really must go and dress. Do you know it is nearly seven?

JACK [*irritably*]: Oh! it always is nearly seven.

ALGERNON: Well, I'm hungry.

JACK: I never knew you when you weren't. . . .

ALGERNON: What shall we do after dinner? Go to a theatre?

JACK: Oh no! I loathe listening.

ALGERNON: Well, let us go to the Club?

JACK: Oh, no! I loathe talking.

ALGERNON: Well, we might trot round to the Empire at ten?

JACK: Oh, no! I can't bear looking at things. It is so silly.

ALGERNON: Well, what shall we do?

JACK: Nothing!

ALGERNON: It is awfully hard work doing nothing. However, I don't mind hard work where there is no definite object of any kind.

Enter Lane.

LANE: Miss Fairfax.

Enter Gwendolen. Lane goes out.

ALGERNON: Gwendolen, upon my word!

GWENDOLEN: Algy, kindly turn your back. I have something very particular to say to Mr Worthing.

ALGERNON: Really, Gwendolen, I don't think I can allow this at all.

GWENDOLEN: Algy, you always adopt a strictly immoral attitude towards life. You are not quite old enough to do that. [*Algernon retires to the fireplace.*]

JACK: My own darling.

GWENDOLEN: Ernest, we may never be married. From the expression on mamma's face I fear we never shall. Few parents nowadays pay any regard to what their children say to them. The old-fashioned respect for the young is fast dying out. Whatever influence I ever had over mamma, I lost at the age of three. But although she may prevent us from becoming man and wife, and I may marry someone else, and marry often, nothing that she can possibly do can alter my eternal devotion to you.

JACK: Dear Gwendolen!

GWENDOLEN: The story of your romantic origin, as related to me by mamma, with unpleasing comments, has naturally stirred the deeper fibres of my nature. Your Christian name has an irresistible fascination. The simplicity of your character makes you exquisitely incomprehensible to me. Your town address at the Albany I have. What is your address in the country?

JACK: The Manor House, Woolton, Hertfordshire.

Algernon, who has been carefully listening, smiles to himself, and writes the address on his shirt cuff. Then picks up the Railway Guide.

GWENDOLEN: There is a good postal service, I suppose? It may be necessary to do something desperate. That of course will require serious consideration. I will communicate with you daily.

JACK: My own one!

GWENDOLEN: How long do you remain in town?

JACK: Till Monday.

GWENDOLEN: Good! Algy, you may turn around now.

ALGERNON: Thanks, I've turned around already.

GWENDOLEN: You may also ring the bell.

JACK: You will let me see you to your carriage, my own darling?

GWENDOLEN: Certainly.

JACK [*to Lane, who now enters*]: I will see Miss Fairfax out.

LANE: Yes, sir. [*Jack and Gwendolen go off.*]

Lane presents several letters on a salver to Algernon. It is to be surmised that they are bills, as Algernon, after looking at the envelopes, tears them up.

ALGERNON: A glass of sherry, Lane.

LANE: Yes, sir.

ALGERNON: Tomorrow, Lane, I'm going Bunburying.

LANE: Yes, sir.

ALGERNON: I shall probably not be back till Monday. You can put up my dress clothes, my smoking jacket, and all the Bunbury suits . . . .

LANE: Yes, sir. [*Handing sherry.*]

ALGERNON: I hope tomorrow will be a fine day, Lane.

LANE: It never is, sir.

ALGERNON: Lane, you're a perfect pessimist.

LANE: I do my best to give satisfaction, sir.

> *Enter Jack, Lane goes off.*

JACK: There's a sensible, intelligent girl! the only girl I ever cared for in my life. [*Algernon is laughing moderately.*] What on earth are you so amused at?

ALGERNON: Oh, I'm a little anxious about poor Bunbury, that is all.

JACK: If you don't take care, your friend Bunbury will get you into a serious scrape some day.

ALGERNON: I love scrapes. They are the only things that are never serious.

JACK: Oh, that's nonsense, Algy. You never talk anything but nonsense.

ALGERNON: Nobody ever does.

> *Jack looks indignantly at him, and leaves the room. Algernon lights a cigarette, reads his shirt-cuff, and smiles.*

ACT II

> *Garden at the Manor House. A flight of grey stone steps leads up to the house. The garden, an old-fashioned one, full of roses. Time of year, July. Basket chairs, and a table covered with books, are set under a large yew tree.*

> *Miss Prism discovered seated at the table. Cecily is at the back, watering flowers.*

MISS PRISM [*calling*]: Cecily, Cecily! Surely such a utilitarian occupation as the watering of flowers is rather Moulton's duty than yours? Especially at a moment when intellectual pleasures await you. Your German grammar is on the table. Pray open it at page fifteen. We will repeat yesterday's lesson.

CECILY [*coming over very slowly*]: But I don't like German. It isn't at all a becoming language. I know perfectly well that I look quite plain after my German lesson.

MISS PRISM: Child, you know how anxious your guardian is that you should improve yourself in every way. He laid particular stress on your German, as he was leaving for town yesterday. Indeed, he always lays stress on your German when he is leaving for town.

CECILY: Dear Uncle Jack is so very serious! Sometimes he is so serious that I think he cannot be quite well.

MISS PRISM [*drawing herself up*]: Your guardian enjoys the best of health, and his gravity of demeanour is especially to be commended in one so comparatively young as he is. I know no one who has a higher sense of duty and responsibility.

CECILY: I suppose that is why he often looks a little bored when we three are together.

MISS PRISM: Cecily! I am surprised at you. Mr Worthing has many troubles in his life. Idle merriment and triviality would be out of place in his conversation. You must remember his constant anxiety about that unfortunate young man his brother.

CECILY: I wish Uncle Jack would allow that unfortunate young man, his brother, to come down here sometimes. We might have a good influence over him, Miss Prism. I am sure you certainly would. You know German, and geology, and things of that kind influence a man very much. [*Cecily begins to write in her diary.*]

MISS PRISM [*shaking her head*]: I do not think that even I could produce any effect on a character that according to his own brother's admission is irretrievably weak and vacillating. Indeed I am not sure that I would desire to reclaim him. I am not in favour of this modern mania for turning bad people into good people at a moment's notice. As a man sows so let him reap. You must put away your diary, Cecily. I really don't see why you should keep a diary at all.

CECILY: I keep a diary in order to enter the wonderful secrets of my life. If I didn't write them down, I should probably forget all about them.

MISS PRISM: Memory, my dear Cecily, is the diary that we all carry about with us.

CECILY: Yes, but it usually chronicles the things that have never happened, and couldn't possibly have happened. I believe that Memory is responsible for nearly all the three-volume novels that Mudie sends us.

MISS PRISM: Do not speak slightingly of the three-volume novel, Cecily. I wrote one myself in earlier days.

CECILY: Did you really, Miss Prism? How wonderfully clever you are! I hope it did not end happily? I don't like novels that end happily. They depress me so much.

MISS PRISM: The good ended happily, and the bad unhappily. That is what Fiction means.

CECILY: I suppose so. But it seems very unfair. And was your novel ever published?

MISS PRISM: Alas, no. The manuscript unfortunately was abandoned. [*Cecily starts.*] I use the word in the sense of lost or mislaid. To your work, child, these speculations are profitless.

CECILY [*smiling*]: But I see dear Dr Chasuble coming up through the garden.

MISS PRISM [*rising and advancing*]: Dr Chasuble! This is indeed a pleasure.

    Enter Canon Chasuble.

CHASUBLE: And how are we this morning? Miss Prism, you are, I trust, well?

CECILY: Miss Prism has just been complaining of a slight headache. I think it would do her so much good to have a short stroll with you in the Park, Dr Chasuble.

MISS PRISM: Cecily, I have not mentioned anything about a headache.

CECILY: No, dear Miss Prism, I know that, but I felt instinctively that you had a headache. Indeed I was thinking about that, and not about my German lesson, when the Rector came in.

CHASUBLE: I hope, Cecily, you are not inattentive.

CECILY: Oh, I am afraid I am.

CHASUBLE: That is strange. Were I fortunate enough to be Miss Prism's pupil, I would hang upon her lips. [*Miss Prism glares.*] I spoke metaphorically.—My metaphor was drawn from bees. Ahem! Mr Worthing, I suppose, has not returned from town yet?

MISS PRISM: We do not expect him till Monday afternoon.

CHASUBLE: Ah yes, he usually likes to spend his Sunday in London. He is not one of those whose sole aim is enjoyment, as, by all accounts, that unfortunate young man his brother seems to be. But I must not disturb Egeria and her pupil any longer.

MISS PRISM: Egeria? My name is Laetitia, Doctor.

CHASUBLE [*bowing*]: A classical allusion merely, drawn from the Pagan authors. I shall see you both no doubt at Evensong?

MISS PRISM: I think, dear Doctor, I will have a stroll with you. I find I have a headache after all, and a walk might do it good.

CHASUBLE: With pleasure, Miss Prism, with pleasure. We might go as far as the schools and back.

MISS PRISM: That would be delightful. Cecily, you will read your Political Economy in my absence. The chapter on the Fall of the Rupee you may omit. It is somewhat too sensational. Even these metallic problems have their melodramatic side.

[*Goes down the garden with Dr Chasuble.*]

CECILY [*picks up books and throws them back on the table*]: Horrid Political Economy! Horrid Geography! Horrid, horrid German!

Enter Merriman with a card on a salver.

MERRIMAN: Mr Ernest Worthington has just driven over from the station. He has brought his luggage with him.

CECILY [*takes the card and reads it*]: 'Mr Ernest Worthing, B.4, The Albany, W.' Uncle Jack's brother! Did you tell him Mr Worthing was in town?

MERRIMAN: Yes, Miss. He seemed very much disappointed. I mentioned that you and Miss Prism were in the garden. He said he was anxious to speak to you privately for a moment.

CECILY: Ask Mr Ernest Worthing to come here. I suppose you had better talk to the housekeeper about a room for him.

MERRIMAN: Yes, Miss. [*Merriman goes off.*]

CECILY: I have never met any really wicked person before. I feel rather frightened. I am so afraid he will look just like everyone else.

Enter Algernon, very gay and debonair.

He does!

ALGERNON [*raising his hat*]: You're my little cousin Cecily, I'm sure.

CECILY: You are under some strange mistake. I am not little. In fact, I believe I am more than usually tall for my age. [*Algernon is rather taken back.*] But I am your cousin Cecily. You, I see from your card, are Uncle Jack's brother, my cousin Ernest, my wicked cousin Ernest.

ALGERNON: Oh! I am not really wicked at all, Cousin Cecily. You mustn't think that I am wicked.

CECILY: If you are not, then you have certainly been deceiving us all in a very inexcusable manner. I hope you have not been leading a double life, pretending to be wicked and being really good all the time. That would be hypocrisy.

ALGERNON [*looks at her in amazement*]: Oh! Of course I have been rather reckless.

CECILY: I am glad to hear it.

ALGERNON: In fact, now you mention the subject, I have been very bad in my own small way.

CECILY: I don't think you should be so proud of that, though I am sure it must have been very pleasant.

ALGERNON: It is much pleasanter being here with you.

CECILY: I can't understand how you are here at all. Uncle Jack won't be back till Monday afternoon.

ALGERNON: That is a great disappointment. I am obliged to go up by the first train on Monday morning. I have a business appointment that I am anxious . . . to miss!

CECILY: Couldn't you miss it anywhere but in London?

ALGERNON: No: the appointment is in London.

CECILY: Well, I know, of course, how important it is not to keep a business engagement, if one wants to retain any sense of the beauty of life, but still I think you had better wait till Uncle Jack arrives. I know he wants to speak to you about your emigrating.

ALGERNON: About my what?

CECILY: Your emigrating. He has gone up to buy your outfit.

ALGERNON: I certainly wouldn't let Jack buy my outfit. He has no taste in neckties at all.

CECILY: I don't think you will require neckties. Uncle Jack is sending you to Australia.

ALGERNON: Australia! I'd sooner die.

CECILY: Well, he said at dinner on Wednesday night, that you would have to choose between this world, the next world, and Australia.

ALGERNON: Oh, well! The accounts I have received of Australia and the next world are not particularly encouraging. This world is good enough for me, Cousin Cecily.

CECILY: Yes, but are you good enough for it?

ALGERNON: I'm afraid I'm not that. That is why I want you to reform me. You might make that your mission, if you don't mind, Cousin Cecily.

CECILY: I'm afraid I've no time, this afternoon.

ALGERNON: Well, would you mind my reforming myself this afternoon?

CECILY: It is rather Quixotic of you. But I think you should try.

ALGERNON: I will. I feel better already.

CECILY: You are looking a little worse.

ALGERNON: That is because I am hungry.

CECILY: How thoughtless of me. I should have remembered that when one is going to lead an entirely new life, one requires regular and wholesome meals. Won't you come in?

ALGERNON: Thank you. Might I have a buttonhole first? I never have any appetite unless I have a buttonhole first.

CECILY: A Maréchal Niel? [*Picks up scissors.*]

ALGERNON: No, I'd sooner have a pink rose.

CECILY: Why? [*Cuts a flower.*]

ALGERNON: Because you are like a pink rose, Cousin Cecily.

CECILY: I don't think it can be right for you to talk to me like that. Miss Prism never says such things to me.

ALGERNON: Then Miss Prism is a shortsighted old lady. [*Cecily puts the rose in his buttonhole.*] You are the prettiest girl I ever saw.

CECILY: Miss Prism says that all good looks are a snare.

ALGERNON: They are the snare that every sensible man would like to be caught in.

CECILY: Oh, I don't think I would care to catch a sensible man. I shouldn't know what to talk to him about.

They pass into the house. Miss Prism and Dr Chasuble return.

MISS PRISM: You are too much alone, dear Dr Chasuble. You should get married. A misanthrope I can understand—a womanthrope, never!

CHASUBLE [*with a scholar's shudder*]: Believe me, I do not deserve so neologistic a phrase. The precept as well as the practice of the Primitive Church was distinctly against matrimony.

MISS PRISM [*sententiously*]: That is obviously the reason why the Primitive Church has not lasted up to the present day. And you do not seem to realize, dear Doctor, that by persistently remaining single, a man converts himself into a permanent public temptation. Men should be more careful; this very celibacy leads weaker vessels astray.

CHASUBLE: But is a man not equally attractive when married?

MISS PRISM: No married man is ever attractive except to his wife.

CHASUBLE: And often, I've been told, not even her.

MISS PRISM: That depends on the intellectual sympathies of the woman. Maturity can always be depended on. Ripeness can be trusted. Young women are green. [*Dr Chasuble starts.*] I spoke horticulturally. My metaphor was drawn from fruits. But where is Cecily?

CHASUBLE: Perhaps she followed us to the schools.

Enter Jack slowly from the back of the garden. He is dressed in the deepest mourning, with crepe hatband and black gloves.

MISS PRISM: Mr Worthing!

CHASUBLE: Mr Worthing?

MISS PRISM: This is indeed a surprise. We did not look for you till Monday afternoon.

JACK [*shakes Miss Prism's hand in a tragic manner*]: I have returned sooner than I expected. Dr Chasuble, I hope you are well?

CHASUBLE: Dear Mr Worthing, I trust this garb of woe does not betoken some terrible calamity?

JACK: My brother.

MISS PRISM: More shameful debts and extravagance?

CHASUBLE: Still leading his life of pleasure?

JACK [*shaking his head*]: Dead!

CHASUBLE: Your brother Ernest dead?

JACK: Quite dead.

MISS PRISM: What a lesson for him! I trust he will profit by it.

CHASUBLE: Mr Worthing, I offer you my sincere condolence. You have at least the consolation of knowing that you were always the most generous and forgiving of brothers.

JACK: Poor Ernest! He had many faults, but it is a sad, sad blow.

CHASUBLE: Very sad indeed. Were you with him at the end?

JACK: No. He died abroad; in Paris, in fact. I had a telegram last night from the manager of the Grand Hotel.

CHASUBLE: Was the cause of death mentioned?

JACK: A severe chill, it seems.

MISS PRISM: As a man sows, so shall he reap.

CHASUBLE [*raising his hand*]: Charity, dear Miss Prism, charity! None of us are perfect. I myself am peculiarly susceptible to draughts. Will the interment take place here?

JACK: No. He seems to have expressed a desire to be buried in Paris.

CHASUBLE: In Paris! [*Shakes his head.*] I fear that hardly points to any very serious state of mind at the last. You would no doubt wish me to make some light allusion to this tragic domestic affliction next Sunday. [*Jack presses his hand convulsively.*] My sermon on the meaning of the manna in the wilderness can be adapted to almost any occasion, joyful, or, as in the present case, distressing. [*All sigh.*] I have preached it at harvest celebrations, christenings, confirmations, on days of humiliation and festal days. The last time I delivered it was in the Cathedral, as a charity sermon on behalf of the Society for the Prevention of Discontent among the Upper Orders. The Bishop, who was present, was much struck by some of the analogies I drew.

JACK: Ah! that reminds me, you mentioned christenings I think, Dr Chasuble? I suppose you know how to christen all right? [*Dr Chasuble looks astounded.*] I mean, of course, you are continually christening, aren't you?

MISS PRISM: It is, I regret to say, one of the Rector's most constant duties in this parish. I have often spoken to the poorer classes on the subject. But they don't seem to know what thrift is.

CHASUBLE: But is there any particular infant in whom you are interested, Mr Worthing? Your brother was, I believe, unmarried, was he not?

JACK: Oh, yes.

MISS PRISM [*bitterly*]: People who live entirely for pleasure usually are.

JACK: But it is not for any child, dear Doctor. I am very fond of children. No! the fact is, I would like to be christened myself, this afternoon, if you have nothing better to do.

CHASUBLE: But surely, Mr Worthing, you have been christened already?

JACK: I don't remember anything about it.

CHASUBLE: But have you any grave doubts on the subject?

JACK: I certainly intend to have. Of course I don't know if the thing would bother you in any way, or if you think I am a little too old now.

CHASUBLE: Not at all. The sprinkling, and, indeed, the immersion of adults is a perfectly canonical practice.

JACK: Immersion!

CHASUBLE: You need have no apprehensions. Sprinkling is all that is necessary, or indeed I think advisable. Our weather is so changeable. At what hour would you wish the ceremony performed?

JACK: Oh, I might trot round above five if that would suit you.

CHASUBLE: Perfectly, perfectly! In fact I have two similar ceremonies to perform at that time. A case of twins that occurred recently in one of the outlying cottages on your own estate. Poor Jenkins the carter, a most hard-working man.

JACK: Oh! I don't see much fun in being christened along with other babies. It would be childish. Would half-past five do?

CHASUBLE: Admirably! Admirably! [*Takes out watch.*] And now, dear Mr Worthing, I will not intrude any longer into a house of sorrow. I would merely beg you not to be too much bowed down by grief. What seem to us bitter trials are often blessings in disguise.

MISS PRISM: This seems to be a blessing of an extremely obvious kind.

Enter Cecily from the house.

CECILY: Uncle Jack! Oh, I am pleased to see you back. But what horrid clothes you have got on. Do go and change them.

MISS PRISM: Cecily!

CHASUBLE: My child! My child! [*Cecily goes toward Jack; he kisses her brow in a melancholy manner.*]

CECILY: What is the matter, Uncle Jack? Do look happy! You look as if you had toothache, and I have got such a surprise for you. Who do you think is in the dining room? Your brother!

JACK: Who?

CECILY: Your brother Ernest. He arrived about half an hour ago.

JACK: What nonsense! I haven't got a brother.

CECILY: Oh, don't say that. However badly he may have behaved to you in the past he is still your brother. You couldn't be so heartless as to disown him. I'll tell him to come out. And you will shake hands with him, won't you, Uncle Jack? [*Runs back into the house.*]

CHASUBLE: These are very joyful tidings.

MISS PRISM: After we had all been resigned to his loss, his sudden return seems to me peculiarly distressing.

JACK: My brother is in the dining room? I don't know what it all means. I think it is perfectly absurd.

Enter Algernon and Cecily hand in hand. They come slowly up to Jack.

JACK: Good heavens! [*Motions Algernon away.*]

ALGERNON: Brother John, I have come down from town to tell you that I am very sorry for all the trouble I have given you, and that I intend to lead a better life in the future. [*Jack glares at him and does not take his hand.*]

CECILY: Uncle Jack, you are not going to refuse your own brother's hand?

JACK: Nothing will induce me to take his hand. I think his coming down here disgraceful. He knows perfectly well why.

CECILY: Uncle Jack, do be nice. There is some good in everyone. Ernest has just been telling me about his poor invalid friend Mr Bunbury whom he goes to visit so often. And surely there must be much good in one who is kind to an invalid and leaves the pleasures of London to sit by a bed of pain.

JACK: Oh! he has been talking about Bunbury, has he?

CECILY: Yes, he has told me about poor Mr Bunbury, and his terrible state of health.

JACK: Bunbury! Well, I won't have him talk to you about Bunbury or about anything else. It is enough to drive one perfectly frantic.

ALGERNON: Of course I admit that the faults were all on my side. But I must say that I think that Brother John's coldness to me is peculiarly painful. I expected a more enthusiastic welcome, especially considering it is the first time I have come here.

CECILY: Uncle Jack, if you don't shake hands with Ernest I will never forgive you.

JACK: Never forgive me?

CECILY: Never, never, never!

JACK: Well, this is the last time I shall ever do it. [*Shakes hand with Algernon and glares.*]

CHASUBLE: It's pleasant, is it not, to see so perfect a reconciliation? I think we might leave the two brothers together.

MISS PRISM: Cecily, you will come with us.

CECILY: Certainly, Miss Prism. My little task of reconciliation is over.

CHASUBLE: You have done a beautiful action today, dear child.

MISS PRISM: We must not be premature in our judgments.

CECILY: I feel very happy.   [*They all go off except Jack and Algernon.*]

JACK: You young scoundrel, Algy, you must get out of this place as soon as possible. I don't allow Bunburying here.

Enter Merriman.

MERRIMAN: I have put Mr Ernest's things in the room next to yours, sir. I suppose that is all right?

JACK: What?

MERRIMAN: Mr Ernest's luggage, sir. I have unpacked it and put in the room next to your own.

JACK: His luggage?

MERRIMAN: Yes, sir. Three portmanteaus, a dressing case, two hat boxes, and a large luncheon basket.

ALGERNON: I am afraid I can't stay more than a week this time.

JACK: Merriman, order the dogcart at once. Mr Ernest has been suddenly called back to town.

MERRIMAN: Yes, sir. [*Goes back into the house.*]

ALGERNON: What a fearful liar you are, Jack. I have not been called back to town at all.

JACK: Yes, you have.

ALGERNON: I haven't heard anyone call me.

JACK: Your duty as a gentleman calls you back.

ALGERNON: My duty as a gentleman has never interfered with my pleasures in the smallest degree.

JACK: I can quite understand that.

ALGERNON: Well, Cecily is a darling.

JACK: You are not to talk of Miss Cardew like that. I don't like it.

ALGERNON: Well, I don't like your clothes. You look perfectly ridiculous in them. Why on earth don't you go up and change? It is perfectly childish to be in deep mourning for a man who is actually staying for a whole week with you in your house as a guest. I call it grotesque.

JACK: You are certainly not staying with me for a whole week as a guest or anything else. You have got to leave . . . by the four-five train.

ALGERNON: I certainly won't leave you so long as you are in mourning. It would be most unfriendly. If I were in mourning you would stay with me, I suppose. I should think it very unkind if you didn't.

JACK: Well, will you go if I change my clothes?

ALGERNON: Yes, if you are not too long. I never saw anybody take so long to dress, and with such little result.

JACK: Well, at any rate, that is better than being overdressed as you are.

ALGERNON: If I am occasionally a little overdressed, I make up for it by being always immensely over-educated.

JACK: Your vanity is ridiculous, your conduct an outrage, and your presence in my garden utterly absurd. However, you have got to catch the four-five, and I hope you will have a pleasant journey back to town. This Bunburying, as you call it, has not been a great success for you. [*Goes into the house.*]

ALGERNON: I think it has been a great success. I'm in love with Cecily, and that is everything.

Enter Cecily at the back of the garden. She picks up the can and begins to water the flowers.

But I must see her before I go, and make arrangements for another Bunbury. Ah, there she is.

CECILY: Oh, I merely came back to water the roses. I thought you were with Uncle Jack.

ALGERNON: He's gone to order the dogcart for me.

CECILY: Oh, is he going to take you for a nice drive?

ALGERNON: He's going to send me away.

CECILY: Then have we got to part?

ALGERNON: I am afraid so. It's a very painful parting.

CECILY: It is always painful to part from people whom one has known for a very brief space of time. The absence of old friends one can endure with equanimity. But even a momentary separation from anyone to whom one has just been introduced is almost unbearable.

ALGERNON: Thank you.

Enter Merriman.

MERRIMAN: The dogcart is at the door, sir. [*Algernon looks appealing at Cecily.*]

CECILY: It can wait, Merriman . . . for . . . five minutes.

MERRIMAN: Yes, miss. [*Exit Merriman.*]

ALGERNON: I hope, Cecily, I shall not offend you if I state quite frankly and openly that you seem to me to be in every way the visible personification of absolute perfection.

CECILY: I think your frankness does you great credit, Ernest. If you will allow me, I will copy your remarks into my diary. [*Goes over to table and begins writing in diary.*]

ALGERNON: Do you really keep a diary? I'd give anything to look at it. May I?

CECILY: Oh no. [*Puts her hand over it.*] You see, it is simply a very young girl's record of her own thoughts and impressions, and consequently meant for publication. When it appears in volume form I hope you will order a copy. But pray, Ernest, don't stop. I delight in taking down from dictation. I have reached 'absolute perfection'. You can go on. I am quite ready for more.

ALGERNON [*somewhat taken aback*]: Ahem! Ahem!

CECILY: Oh, don't cough, Ernest. When one is dictating one should speak fluently and not cough. Besides, I don't know how to spell a cough. [*Writes as Algernon speaks.*]

ALGERNON [*speaking very rapidly*]: Cecily, ever since I first looked upon your wonderful and incomparable beauty, I have dared to love you wildly, passionately, devotedly, hopelessly.

CECILY: I don't think that you should tell me that you love me wildly, passionately, devotedly, hopelessly. Hopelessly doesn't seem to make much sense, does it?

ALGERNON: Cecily.

Enter Merriman.

MERRIMAN: The dogcart is waiting, sir.

ALGERNON: Tell it to come round next week, at the same hour.

MERRIMAN [*looks at Cecily, who makes no sign*]: Yes, sir. [*Merriman retires.*]

CECILY: Uncle Jack would be very much annoyed if he knew you were staying on till next week, at the same hour.

ALGERNON: Oh, I don't care about Jack. I don't care for anybody in the whole world but you. I love you, Cecily. You will marry me, won't you?

CECILY: You silly boy! Of course. Why, we have been engaged for the last three months.

ALGERNON: For the last three months?

CECILY: Yes, it will be exactly three months on Thursday.

ALGERNON: But how did we become engaged?

CECILY: Well, ever since Uncle Jack first confessed to us that he had a younger brother who was very wicked and bad, you of course have formed the chief topic of conversation between myself and Miss Prism. And of course a man who is much talked about is always very attractive. One feels there must be something in him, after all. I daresay it was foolish of me, but I fell in love with you, Ernest.

ALGERNON: Darling. And when was the engagement actually settled?

CECILY: On the 14th of February last. Worn out by your entire ignorance of my existence, I determined to end the matter one way or the other, and after a long struggle with myself I accepted you under this dear old tree here. The next day I bought this little ring in your name, and this is the little bangle with the true lovers' knot I promised you always to wear.

ALGERNON: Did I give you this? It's very pretty, isn't it?

CECILY: Yes, you've wonderfully good taste, Ernest. It's the excuse I've always given for your leading such a bad life. And this is the box in which I keep all your dear letters. [*Kneels at table, opens box, and produces letters tied up with blue ribbon.*]

ALGERNON: My letters! But, my own sweet Cecily, I have never written you any letters.

CECILY: You need hardly remind me of that, Ernest. I remember only too well that I was forced to write your letters for you. I wrote always three times a week, and sometimes oftener.

ALGERNON: Oh, do let me read them, Cecily?

CECILY: Oh, I couldn't possibly. They would make you far too conceited. [*Replaces box.*] The three you wrote me after I had broken off the engagement are so beautiful, and so badly spelled, that even now I can hardly read them without crying a little.

ALGERNON: But was our engagement ever broken off?

CECILY: Of course it was. On the 22nd of last March. You can see the entry if you like. [*Shows diary.*] 'Today I broke off my engagement with Ernest. I feel it is better to do so. The weather still continues charming.'

ALGERNON: But why on earth did you break it off? What had I done? I had done nothing at all. Cecily, I am very much hurt indeed to hear you broke it off. Particularly when the weather was so charming.

CECILY: It would hardly have been a really serious engagement if it hadn't been broken off at least once. But I forgave you before the week was out.

ALGERNON [*crossing to her, and kneeling*]: What a perfect angel you are, Cecily.

CECILY: You dear romantic boy, [*He kisses her, she puts her fingers through his hair.*] I hope your hair curls naturally, does it?

ALGERNON: Yes, darling, with a little help from others.

CECILY: I am so glad.

ALGERNON: You'll never break off our engagement again, Cecily?

CECILY: I don't think I could break it off now that I have actually met you. Besides, of course, there is the question of your name.

ALGERNON: Of course. [*Nervously.*]

CECILY: You must not laugh at me, darling, but it had always been a girlish dream of mine to love someone whose name was Ernest. [*Algernon rises, Cecily also.*] There is something in that name that seems to inspire absolute confidence. I pity any poor married woman whose husband is not called Ernest.

ALGERNON: But, my dear child, do you mean to say you could not love me if I had some other name?

CECILY: But what name?

ALGERNON: Oh, any name you like—Algernon—for instance . . .

CECILY: But I don't like the name of Algernon.

ALGERNON: Well, my own dear, sweet, loving little darling, I really can't see why you should object to the name of Algernon. It is not at all a bad name. In fact, it is rather an aristocratic name. Half of the chaps who get into the Bankruptcy Court are called Algernon. But seriously, Cecily . . . [*moving to her*] if my name was Algy, couldn't you love me?

CECILY [*rising*]: I might respect you, Ernest, I might admire your character, but I fear that I should not be able to give you my undivided attention.

ALGERNON: Ahem! Cecily! [*Picking up hat.*] Your Rector here is, I suppose, thoroughly experienced in the practice of all the rites and ceremonials of the Church?

CECILY: Oh, yes. Dr Chasuble is a most learned man. He has never written a single book, so you can imagine how much he knows.

ALGERNON: I must see him at once on a most important christening—I mean on most important business.

CECILY: Oh!

ALGERNON: I shan't be away more than half an hour.

CECILY: Considering that we have been engaged since February the 14th, and that I only met you today for the first time, I think it is rather hard that you should leave me for so long a period as half an hour. Couldn't you make it twenty minutes?

ALGERNON: I'll be back in no time. [*Kisses her and rushes down the garden.*]

CECILY: What an impetuous boy he is! I like his hair so much. I must enter his proposal in my diary.

 Enter Merriman.

MERRIMAN: A Miss Fairfax just called to see Mr Worthing. On very important business, Miss Fairfax states.

CECILY: Isn't Mr Worthing in his library?

MERRIMAN: Mr Worthing went over in the direction of the Rectory some time ago.

CECILY: Pray ask the lady to come out here; Mr Worthing is sure to be back soon. And you can bring tea.

MERRIMAN: Yes, Miss.   [*Goes out.*]

CECILY: Miss Fairfax! I suppose one of the many good elderly women who are associated with Uncle Jack in some of his philanthropic work in London. I don't quite like women who are interested in philanthropic work. I think it is so forward of them.

 Enter Merriman.

MERRIMAN: Miss Fairfax.

Enter Gwendolen. Exit Merriman.

CECILY [*advancing to meet her*]: Pray let me introduce myself to you. My name is Cecily Cardew.

GWENDOLEN: Cecily Cardew? [*Moving to her and shaking hands.*] What a very sweet name! Something tells me that we are going to be great friends. I like you already more than I can say. My first impressions of people are never wrong.

CECILY: How nice of you to like me so much after we have known each other such a comparatively short time. Pray sit down.

GWENDOLEN [*still standing up*]: I may call you Cecily, may I not?

CECILY: With pleasure!

GWENDOLEN: And you will always call me Gwendolen, won't you?

CECILY: If you wish.

GWENDOLEN: Then that is all quite settled, is it not?

CECILY: I hope so. [*A pause. They both sit down together.*]

GWENDOLEN: Perhaps this might be a favourable opportunity for my mentioning who I am. My father is Lord Bracknell. You have never heard of Papa, I suppose?

CECILY: I don't think so.

GWENDOLEN: Outside the family circle, Papa, I am glad to say, is entirely unknown. I think that is quite as it should be. The home seems to me to be the proper sphere for the man. And certainly once a man begins to neglect his domestic duties he becomes painfully effeminate, does he not? And I don't like that. It makes men so very attractive. Cecily, mamma, whose views on education are remarkably strict, has brought me up to be extremely short-sighted; it is part of her system; so do you mind my looking at you through my glasses?

CECILY: Oh! not at all, Gwendolen, I am very fond of being looked at.

GWENDOLEN [*after examining Cecily carefully through a lorgnette*]: You are here on a short visit, I suppose.

CECILY: Oh no! I live here.

GWENDOLEN [*severely*]: Really? Your mother, no doubt, or some female relative of advanced years, resides here also?

CECILY: Oh no! I have no mother, nor, in fact, any relations.

GWENDOLEN: Indeed?

CECILY: My dear guardian, with the assistance of Miss Prism, has the arduous task of looking after me.

GWENDOLEN: Your guardian?

CECILY: Yes, I am Mr Worthing's ward.

GWENDOLEN: Oh! It is strange he never mentioned to me that he had a ward. How secretive of him! He grows more interesting hourly. I am not sure, however, that the news inspires me with feelings of unmixed delight. [*Rising and going to her.*] I am very fond of you, Cecily; I have liked you ever since I met you! But I am bound to state that now that I know that you are Mr Worthing's ward, I cannot help expressing a wish you were—well, just a little older than you seem to be—and not quite so very alluring in appearance. In fact, if I may speak candidly—

CECILY: Pray do! I think that whenever one has anything unpleasant to say, one should always be quite candid!

GWENDOLEN: Well, to speak with perfect candour, Cecily I wish that you were fully forty-two, and more than usually plain for your age. Ernest has a strong upright nature. He is the very soul of truth and honour. Disloyalty would be as impossible to him as deception. But even men of the noblest possible moral character are extremely susceptible to the influence of the physical charms of others. Modern, no less than Ancient History, supplies us with many most painful examples of what I refer to. If it were not so, indeed, History would be quite unreadable.

CECILY: I beg your pardon, Gwendolen, did you say Ernest?

GWENDOLEN: Yes.

CECILY: Oh, but it is not Mr Ernest Worthing who is my guardian. It is his brother— his elder brother.

GWENDOLEN [*sitting down again*]: Ernest never mentioned to me that he had a brother.

CECILY: I am sorry to say they have not been on good terms for a long time.

GWENDOLEN: Ah! that accounts for it. And now that I think of it I have never heard any man mention his brother. The subject seems distasteful to most men. Cecily, you have lifted a load from my mind. I was growing almost anxious. It would have been terrible if any cloud had come across a friendship like ours, would it not? Of course you are quite, quite sure that it is not Mr Ernest Worthing who is your guardian?

CECILY: Quite sure. [*A pause.*] In fact, I am going to be his.

GWENDOLEN [*inquiringly*]: I beg your pardon?

CECILY [*rather shy and confidingly*]: Dearest Gwendolen, there is no reason why I should make a secret of it to you. Our little country newspaper is sure to chronicle the fact next week. Mr Ernest Worthing and I are engaged to be married.

GWENDOLEN [*quite politely, rising*]: My darling Cecily, I think there must be some slight error. Mr Ernest Worthing is engaged to me. The announcement will appear in the *Morning Post* on Saturday at the latest.

CECILY [*very politely, rising*]: I am afraid you must be under some misconception. Ernest proposed to me exactly ten minutes ago. [*Shows diary.*]

GWENDOLEN [*examines diary through her lorgnette carefully*]: It is very curious, for he asked me to be his wife yesterday afternoon at 5:30. If you would care to verify the incident, pray do so. [*Produces diary of her own.*] I never travel without my diary. One should always have something sensational to read in the train. I am so sorry, dear Cecily, if it is any disappointment to you, but I am afraid I have the prior claim.

CECILY: It would distress me more than I can tell you, dear Gwendolen, if it caused you any mental or physical anguish, but I feel bound to point out that since Ernest proposed to you he clearly has changed his mind.

GWENDOLEN [*meditatively*]: If the poor fellow has been entrapped into any foolish promise I shall consider it my duty to rescue him at once, and with a firm hand.

CECILY [*thoughtfully and sadly*]: Whatever unfortunate entanglement my dear boy may have gotten into, I will never reproach him with it after we are married.

GWENDOLEN: Do you allude to me, Miss Cardew, as an entanglement? You are presumptuous. On an occasion of this kind it becomes more than a moral duty to speak one's mind. It becomes a pleasure.

CECILY: Do you suggest, Miss Fairfax, that I entrapped Ernest into an engagement? How dare you? This is no time for wearing the shallow mask of manners. When I see a spade I call it a spade.

GWENDOLEN [*satirically*]: I am glad to say that I have never seen a spade. It is obvious that our social spheres have been widely different.

Enter Merriman, followed by the footman. He carries a salver, tablecloth, and plate stand. Cecily is about to retort. The presence of the servants exercises a restraining influence, under which both girls chafe.

MERRIMAN: Shall I lay tea here as usual, Miss?

CECILY [*sternly, in a calm voice*]: Yes, as usual.

Merriman begins to clear table and lay cloth. A long pause. Cecily and Gwendolen glare at each other.

GWENDOLEN: Are there many interesting walks in the vicinity, Miss Cardew?

CECILY: Oh! yes! a great many. From the top of one of the hills quite close one can see five counties.

GWENDOLEN: Five counties! I don't think I should like that; I hate crowds.

CECILY [*sweetly*]: I suppose that is why you live in town?

Gwendolen bites her lip, and beats her foot nervously with her parasol.

GWENDOLEN [*looking around*]: Quite a well-kept garden this is, Miss Cardew.

CECILY: So glad you like it, Miss Fairfax.

GWENDOLEN: I had no idea there were any flowers in the country.

CECILY: Oh, flowers are as common here, Miss Fairfax, as people are in London.

GWENDOLEN: Personally I cannot understand how anybody manages to exist in the country, if anybody who is anybody does. The country always bores me to death.

CECILY: Ah! This is what the newspapers call agricultural depression, is it not? I believe the aristocracy are suffering very much from it just at present. It is almost an epidemic amongst them, I have been told. May I offer you some tea, Miss Fairfax?

GWENDOLEN [*with elaborate politeness*]: Thank you. [*Aside.*] Detestable girl! But I require tea!

CECILY [*sweetly*]: Sugar?

GWENDOLEN [*superciliously*]: No, thank you. Sugar is not fashionable any more.

Cecily looks angrily at her, takes up the tongs and puts four lumps of sugar into the cup.

CECILY [*severely*]: Cake or bread and butter?

GWENDOLEN [*in a bored manner*]: Bread and butter, please. Cake is rarely seen at the best houses nowdays.

CECILY [*cuts a very large slice of cake and puts it on the tray*]: Hand that to Miss Fairfax.

Merriman does so, and goes out with the footman. Gwendolen drinks the tea and makes a grimace. Puts down cup at once, reaches out her hand to the bread and butter, looks at it, and finds it is cake. Rises in indignation.

GWENDOLEN: You have filled my tea with lumps of sugar, and though I asked most distinctly for bread and butter, you have given me cake. I am known for the gentleness of my disposition, and the extraordinary sweetness of my nature, but I warn you, Miss Cardew, you may go too far.

CECILY [*rising*]: To save my poor, innocent, trusting boy from the machinations of any other girl there are no lengths to which I would not go.

GWENDOLEN: From the moment I saw you I distrusted you. I felt that you were false and deceitful. I am never deceived in such matters. My first impressions of people are invariably right.

CECILY: It seems to me, Miss Fairfax, that I am trespassing on your valuable time. No doubt you have many other calls of a similar character to make in the neighbourhood.

Enter Jack.

GWENDOLEN [*catches sight of him*]: Ernest! My own Ernest!

JACK: Gwendolen! Darling! [*Offers to kiss her.*]

GWENDOLEN [*drawing back*]: A moment! May I ask if you are engaged to be married to this young lady? [*Points to Cecily.*]

JACK [*laughing*]: To dear little Cecily! Of course not! What could have put such an idea into your pretty little head?

GWENDOLEN: Thank you. You may! [*Offers her cheek.*]

CECILY [*very sweetly*]: I knew there must be some misunderstanding, Miss Fairfax. The gentleman whose arm is at present round your waist is my dear guardian, Mr John Worthing.

GWENDOLEN: I beg your pardon?

CECILY: This is Uncle Jack.

GWENDOLEN [*receding*]: Jack! Oh!

Enter Algernon.

CECILY: Here is Ernest.

ALGERNON [*goes straight over to Cecily without noticing anyone else*]: My own love! [*Offers to kiss her.*]

CECILY [*drawing back*]: A moment, Ernest! May I ask you—are you engaged to be married to this young lady?

ALGERNON [*looking around*]: To what young lady? Good heavens! Gwendolen!

CECILY: Yes: to good heavens, Gwendolen, I mean to Gwendolen.

ALGERNON [*laughing*]: Of course not! What could have put such an idea into your pretty little head?

CECILY: Thank you. [*Presenting her cheek to be kissed.*] You may. [*Algernon kisses her.*]

GWENDOLEN: I felt there was some slight error, Miss Cardew. The gentleman who is now embracing you is my cousin, Mr Algernon Moncrieff.

CECILY [*breaking away from Algernon*]: Algernon Moncrieff! Oh! [*The two girls move towards each other and put their arms round each other's waists as if for protection.*]

CECILY: Are you called Algernon?

ALGERNON: I cannot deny it.

GWENDOLEN: Is your name really John?

JACK [*standing rather proudly*]: I could deny it if I liked. I could deny anything if I liked. But my name certainly is John. It has been John for years.

CECILY [*to Gwendolen*]: A gross deception has been practised on both of us.

GWENDOLEN: My poor wounded Cecily!

CECILY: My sweet wronged Gwendolen!

GWENDOLEN [*slowly and seriously*]: You will call me sister, will you not? [*They embrace. Jack and Algernon groan and walk up and down.*]

CECILY [*rather brightly*]: There is just one question I would like to be allowed to ask my guardian.

GWENDOLEN: An admirable idea! Mr Worthing, there is just one question I would like to be permitted to put to you. Where is your brother Ernest? We are both engaged to be married to your brother Ernest, so it is a matter of some importance to us to know where your brother Ernest is at present.

JACK [*slowly and hesitatingly*]: Gwendolen—Cecily—it is very painful for me to be forced to speak the truth. It is the first time in my life that I have been reduced to such a painful position, and I am really quite inexperienced in doing anything of the kind. However, I will tell you quite frankly that I have no brother Ernest. I have no brother at all. I never had a brother in my life, and I certainly have not the smallest intention of ever having one in the future.

CECILY [*surprised*]: No brother at all?

JACK [*cheerily*]: None!

GWENDOLEN [*severely*]: Had you never a brother of any kind?

JACK [*pleasantly*]: Never. Not even of any kind.

GWENDOLEN: I am afraid it is quite clear, Cecily, that neither of us is engaged to be married to anyone.

CECILY: It is not a very pleasant position for a young girl suddenly to find herself in. Is it?

GWENDOLEN: Let us go into the house. They will hardly venture to come after us there.

CECILY: No, men are so cowardly, aren't they?

[*They return into the house with scornful looks.*]

JACK: This ghastly state of things is what you call Bunburying, I suppose?

ALGERNON: Yes, and a perfectly wonderful Bunbury it is. The most wonderful Bunbury I have ever had in my life.

JACK: Well, you've no right whatsoever to Bunbury here.

ALGERNON: That is absurd. One has a right to Bunbury anywhere one chooses. Every serious Bunburyist knows that.

JACK: Serious Bunburyists? Good heavens!

ALGERNON: Well, one must be serious about something, if one wants to have any amusement in life. I happen to be serious about Bunburying. What on earth you are serious about I haven't got the remotest idea. About everything, I should fancy. You have such an absolutely trivial nature.

JACK: Well, the only small satisfaction I have in the whole of this wretched business is that your friend Bunbury is quite exploded. You won't be able to run down to the country quite so often as you used to do, dear Algy. And a very good thing too.

ALGERNON: Your brother is a little off colour, isn't he, dear Jack? You won't be able to disappear to London quite so frequently as your wicked custom was. And not a bad thing either.

JACK: As for your conduct towards Miss Cardew, I must say that your taking in a sweet, simple, innocent girl like that is quite inexcusable. To say nothing of the fact that she is my ward.

ALGERNON: I can see no possible defence at all for your deceiving a brilliant, clever, thoroughly experienced young lady like Miss Fairfax. To say nothing of the fact that she is my cousin.

JACK: I wanted to be engaged to Gwendolen, that is all. I love her.

ALGERNON: Well, I simply wanted to be engaged to Cecily. I adore her.

JACK: There is certainly no chance of your marrying Miss Cardew.

ALGERNON: I don't think there is much likelihood, Jack, of you and Miss Fairfax being united.

JACK: Well, that is no business of yours.

ALGERNON: If it was my business, I wouldn't talk about it. [*Begins to eat muffins.*] It is very vulgar to talk about one's business. Only people like stockbrokers do that, and then merely at dinner parties.

JACK: How you can sit there calmly eating muffins when we are in this horrible trouble, I can't make out. You seem to me to be perfectly heartless.

ALGERNON: Well, I can't eat muffins in an agitated manner. The butter would probably get on my cuffs. One should always eat muffins quite calmly. It is the only way to eat them.

JACK: I say it's perfectly heartless your eating muffins at all, under the circumstances.

ALGERNON: When I am in trouble, eating is the only thing that consoles me. Indeed, when I am in really great trouble, as any one who knows me intimately will tell you, I refuse everything except food and drink. At the present moment I am eating muffins because I am unhappy. Besides, I am particularly fond of muffins. [*Rising.*]

JACK [*rising*]: Well, there is no reason why you should eat them all in that greedy way. [*Takes muffins from Algernon.*]

ALGERNON [*offering teacake*]: I wish you would have teacake instead. I don't like teacake.

JACK: Good heavens! I suppose a man may eat his own muffins in his own garden.

ALGERNON: But you have just said it is perfectly heartless to eat muffins.

JACK: I said it was perfectly heartless of you, under the circumstances. That is a very different thing.

ALGERNON: That may be. But the muffins are the same. [*He seizes the muffin dish from Jack.*]

JACK: Algy, I wish to goodness you would go.

ALGERNON: You can't possibly ask me to go without having some dinner. It's absurd. I never go without my dinner. No one ever does, except vegetarians and people like that. Besides I have just made arrangements with Dr Chasuble to be christened at a quarter to six under the name of Ernest.

JACK: My dear fellow, the sooner you give up that nonsense the better. I made arrangements this morning with Dr Chasuble to be christened myself at 5:30, and I naturally will take the name of Ernest. Gwendolen would wish it. We can't both be christened Ernest. It's absurd. Besides, I have a perfect right to be christened if I like. There is no evidence that I have ever been christened by anybody. I should think it extremely probable I never was, and so does Dr Chasuble. It is entirely different in your case. You have been christened already.

ALGERNON: Yes, but I have not been christened for years.

JACK: Yes, but you have been christened. That is the important thing.

ALGERNON: Quite so. So I know my constitution can stand it. If you are not quite sure about your ever having been christened, I must say I think it rather dangerous your venturing on it now. It might make you very unwell. You can hardly have forgotten that someone very closely connected with you was very nearly carried off this week in Paris by a severe chill.

JACK: Yes, but you said yourself that a severe chill was not hereditary.

ALGERNON: It usen't to be, I know—but I daresay it is now. Science is always making wonderful improvements in things.

JACK [*picking up the muffin dish*]: Oh, that is nonsense; you are always talking nonsense.

ALGERNON: Jack, you are at the muffins again! I wish you wouldn't. There are only two left. [*Takes them.*] I told you I was particularly fond of muffins.

JACK: But I hate teacake.

ALGERNON: Why on earth then do you allow teacake to be served up for your guests? What ideas you have of hospitality!

JACK: Algernon! I have already told you to go. I don't want you here. Why don't you go!

ALGERNON: I haven't finished my tea yet! and there is still one muffin left.

Jack groans, and sinks into a chair. Algernon still continues eating.

ACT III

Morning room at the Manor House. Gwendolen and Cecily are at the window, looking out into the garden.

GWENDOLEN: The fact that they did not follow us at once into the house, as any one else would have done, seems to me to show that they have some sense of shame left.

CECILY: They have been eating muffins. That looks like repentance.

GWENDOLEN [*after a pause*]: They don't seem to notice us at all. Couldn't you cough?

CECILY: But I haven't got a cough.

GWENDOLEN: They're looking at us. What effrontery!

CECILY: They're approaching. That's very forward of them.

GWENDOLEN: Let us preserve a dignified silence.

CECILY: Certainly. It's the only thing to do now.

Enter Jack followed by Algernon. They whistle some dreadful popular air from a British opera.

GWENDOLEN: This dignified silence seems to produce an unpleasant effect.

CECILY: A most distasteful one.

GWENDOLEN: But we will not be the first to speak.

CECILY: Certainly not.

GWENDOLEN: Mr Worthing, I have something very particular to ask. Much depends on your reply.

CECILY: Gwendolen, your common sense is invaluable. Mr Moncrieff, kindly answer me the following question. Why did you pretend to be my guardian's brother?

ALGERNON: In order that I might have an opportunity of meeting you.

CECILY [*to Gwendolen*]: That certainly seems a satisfactory explanation, does it not?

GWENDOLEN: Yes, dear, if you can believe him.

CECILY: I don't. But that does not affect the wonderful beauty of his answer.

GWENDOLEN: True. In matters of grave importance, style, not sincerity, is the vital thing. Mr Worthing, what explanation can you offer to me for pretending to have a brother? Was it in order that you might have an opportunity of coming up to town to see me as often as possible?

JACK: Can you doubt it, Miss Fairfax?

GWENDOLEN: I have the gravest doubts upon the subject. But I intend to crush them. This is not the moment for German skepticism. [*Moving to Cecily.*] Their explanations appear to be quite satisfactory, especially Mr Worthing's. That seems to me to have the stamp of truth upon it.

CECILY: I am more than content with what Mr Moncrieff said. His voice alone inspires one with absolute credulity.

GWENDOLEN: Then you think we should forgive them?

CECILY: Yes. I mean no.

GWENDOLEN: True! I had forgotten. There are principles at stake that one cannot surrender. Which of us should tell them? The task is not a pleasant one.

CECILY: Could we not speak at the same time?

GWENDOLEN: An excellent idea! I nearly always speak at the same time as other people. Will you take the time from me?

CECILY: Certainly. [*Gwendolen beats time with uplifted finger.*]

GWENDOLEN and CECILY [*speaking together*]: Your Christian names are still an insuperable barrier. That is all!

JACK and ALGERNON [*speaking together*]: Our Christian names! Is that all! But we are going to be christened this afternoon.

GWENDOLEN [*to Jack*]: For my sake you are prepared to do this terrible thing?

JACK: I am.

CECILY [*to Algernon*]: To please me you are ready to face this fearful ordeal?

ALGERNON: I am!

GWENDOLEN: How absurd to talk of the equality of the sexes! Where questions of self-sacrifice are concerned, men are infinitely beyond us.

JACK: We are. [*Clasps hands with Algernon.*]

CECILY: They have moments of physical courage of which we women know absolutely nothing.

GWENDOLEN [*to Jack*]: Darling!

ALGERNON [*to Cecily*]: Darling! [*They fall into each other's arms*]

> *Enter Merriman. When he enters he coughs loudly, seeing the situation.*

MERRIMAN: Ahem! Ahem! Lady Bracknell.

JACK: Good heavens!

> *Enter Lady Bracknell. The couples separate in alarm. Exit Merriman.*

LADY BRACKNELL: Gwendolen! What does this mean?

GWENDOLEN: Merely that I am engaged to be married to Mr Worthing, mamma.

LADY BRACKNELL: Come here. Sit down. Sit down immediately. Hesitation of any kind is a sign of mental decay in the young, of physical weakness in the old. [*Turns to Jack.*] Apprised, sir, of my daughter's sudden flight by her trusty maid, whose confidence I purchased by means of a small coin, I followed her at once by a luggage train. Her unhappy father is, I am glad to say, under the impression that she is attending a more than usually lengthy lecture by the University Extension Scheme on the Influence of a permanent income on Thought. I do not propose to undeceive him. Indeed I have never undeceived him on any question. I would consider it wrong. But of course, you will clearly understand that all communication between yourself and my daughter must cease immediately from this moment. On this point, as indeed on all points, I am firm.

JACK: I am engaged to be married to Gwendolen, Lady Bracknell!

LADY BRACKNELL: You are nothing of the kind, sir. And now as regards Algernon! . . . Algernon!

ALGERNON: Yes, Aunt Augusta.

LADY BRACKNELL: May I ask if it is in this house that your invalid friend Mr Bunbury resides?

ALGERNON [*stammering*]: Oh! No! Bunbury doesn't live here. Bunbury is somewhere else at present. In fact, Bunbury is dead.

LADY BRACKNELL: Dead! When did Mr Bunbury die? His death must have been extremely sudden.

ALGERNON [*airily*]: Oh! I killed Bunbury this afternoon. I mean poor Bunbury died this afternoon.

LADY BRACKNELL: What did he die of?

ALGERNON: Bunbury? Oh, he was quite exploded.

LADY BRACKNELL: Exploded! Was he the victim of a revolutionary outrage? I was not aware that Mr Bunbury was interested in social legislation. If so, he is well punished for his morbidity.

ALGERNON: My dear Aunt Augusta, I mean he was found out! The doctors found out that Bunbury could not live, that is what I mean—so Bunbury died.

LADY BRACKNELL: He seems to have had great confidence in the opinion of his physicians. I am glad, however, that he made up his mind at the last to some definite course of action, and acted under proper medical advice. And now that we have finally got rid of this Bunbury, may I ask, Mr Worthing, who is that young person whose hand my nephew Algernon is now holding in what seems to me a peculiarly unnecessary manner?

JACK: That Lady is Miss Cecily Cardew, my ward. [*Lady Bracknell bows coldly to Cecily.*]

ALGERNON: I am engaged to be married to Cecily, Aunt Augusta.

LADY BRACKNELL: I beg your pardon?

CECILY: Mr Moncrieff and I are engaged to be married, Lady Bracknell.

LADY BRACKNELL [*with a shiver, crossing to the sofa and sitting down.*]: I do not know whether there is anything peculiarly exciting in the air of this particular part of Hertfordshire, but the number of engagements that go on seems to me considerably above the proper average that statistics had laid down for our guidance. I think some preliminary inquiry on my part would not be out of place. Mr Worthing, is Miss Cardew at all connected with any of the larger railway stations in London? I merely desire information. Until yesterday I had no idea that there were any families or persons whose origin was a Terminus. [*Jack looks perfectly furious, but restrains himself.*]

JACK [*in a cold, clear voice*]: Miss Cardew is the granddaughter of the late Mr Thomas Cardew of 149 Belgrave Square, S.W.; Gervase Park, Dorking, Surrey; and the Sporran, Fifeshire, N.B.

LADY BRACKNELL: That sounds not unsatisfactory. Three addresses always inspire confidence, even in tradesmen. But what proof have I of their authenticity?

JACK: I have carefully preserved the Court Guides of the period. They are open to your inspection, Lady Bracknell.

LADY BRACKNELL [*grimly*]: I have known strange errors in that publication.

JACK: Miss Cardew's family solicitors are Messrs Markby, Markby, and Markby.

LADY BRACKNELL: Markby, Markby, and Markby? A firm of the very highest position in their profession. Indeed I am told that one of the Mr Markbys is occasionally to be seen at dinner parties. So far I am satisfied.

JACK [*very irritably*]: How extremely kind of you, Lady Bracknell! I have also in my possession, you will be pleased to hear, certificates of Miss Cardew's birth, baptism, whooping cough, registration, vaccination, confirmation, and the measles; both the German and the English variety.

LADY BRACKNELL: Ah! A life crowded with incident, I see; perhaps somewhat too exciting for a young girl. I am not myself in favour of premature experiences.

[*Rises, looks at her watch.*] Gwendolen! the time approaches for our departure. We have not a moment to lose. As a matter of form, Mr Worthing, I had better ask you if Miss Cardew has any little fortune?

JACK: Oh! about a hundred and thirty thousand pounds in the Funds. That is all. Good-bye, Lady Bracknell. So pleased to have seen you.

LADY BRACKNELL [*sitting down again*]: A moment, Mr Worthing. A hundred and thirty thousand pounds! And in the Funds! Miss Cardew seems to be a most attractive young lady, now that I look at her. Few girls of the present day have any really solid qualities, any of the qualities that last, and improve with time. We live, I regret to say, in an age of surfaces. [*To Cecily*] Come over here, dear. [*Cecily goes across.*] Pretty child! your dress is sadly simple, and your hair seems almost as Nature might have left it. But we can soon alter all that. A thoroughly experienced French maid produces a really marvellous result in a very brief space of time. I remember recommending one to young Lady Lancing, and after three months her own husband did not know her.

JACK: And after six months nobody knew her.

LADY BRACKNELL [*glares at Jack for a few moments. Then bends, with a practiced smile, to Cecily.*]: Kindly turn round, sweet child. [*Cecily turns completely around.*] No, the side view is what I want. [*Cecily presents her profile.*] Yes, quite as I expected. There are distinct social possibilities in your profile. The two weak points in our age are its want of principle and its want of profile. The chin a little higher, dear. Style largely depends on the way the chin is worn. They are worn very high, just at present. Algernon!

ALGERNON: Yes, Aunt Augusta!

LADY BRACKNELL: There are distinct social possibilities in Miss Cardew's profile.

ALGERNON: Cecily is the sweetest, dearest, prettiest girl in the whole world. And I don't care twopence about social possibilities.

LADY BRACKNELL: Never speak disrespectfully of Society, Algernon. Only people who can't get into it do that. [*To Cecily*] Dear child, of course you know that Algernon has nothing but his debts to depend upon. But I do not approve of mercenary marriages. When I married Lord Bracknell I had no fortune of any kind. But I never dreamed for a moment of allowing that to stand in my way. Well, I suppose I must give my consent.

ALGERNON: Thank you, Aunt Augusta.

LADY BRACKNELL: Cecily, you may kiss me!

CECILY [*kisses her*]: Thank you, Lady Bracknell.

LADY BRACKNELL: You may also address me as Aunt Augusta for the future.

CECILY: Thank you, Aunt Augusta.

LADY BRACKNELL: The marriage, I think, had better take place quite soon.

ALGERNON: Thank you, Aunt Augusta.

CECILY: Thank you, Aunt Augusta.

LADY BRACKNELL: To speak frankly, I am not in favour of long engagements. They give people the opportunity of finding out each other's character before marriage, which I think is never advisable.

JACK: I beg your pardon for interrupting you, Lady Bracknell, but this engagement is quite out of the question. I am Miss Cardew's guardian, and she cannot marry without my consent until she comes of age. That consent I absolutely decline to give.

LADY BRACKNELL: Upon what grounds, may I ask? Algernon is an extremely, I may almost say an ostentatiously eligible young man. He has nothing, but he looks everything. What more can one desire?

JACK: It pains me very much to have to speak frankly to you, Lady Bracknell, about your nephew, but the fact is that I do not approve at all of his moral character. I suspect him of being untruthful. [*Algernon and Cecily look at him in indignant amazement.*]

LADY BRACKNELL: Untruthful! My nephew Algernon? Impossible! He is an Oxonian.

JACK: I fear there can be no possible doubt about the matter. This afternoon during my temporary absence in London on an important question of romance, he obtained admissions to my house by means of the false pretense of being my brother. Under an assumed name he drank, I've just been informed by my butler, an entire pint bottle of my Perrier-Jouet, Brut, '89; wine I was specially reserving for myself. Continuing his disgraceful deception, he succeeded in the course of the afternoon in alienating the affections of my only ward. He subsequently stayed to tea, and devoured every single muffin. And what makes his conduct all the more heartless is, that he was perfectly well aware from the first that I have no brother, that I never had a brother, and that I don't intend to have a brother, not even of any kind. I distinctly told him so myself yesterday afternoon.

LADY BRACKNELL: Ahem! Mr Worthing, after careful consideration I have decided entirely to overlook my nephew's conduct to you.

JACK: That is very generous of you, Lady Bracknell. My own decision, however, is unalterable. I decline to give my consent.

LADY BRACKNELL [*to Cecily*]: Come here, sweet child. [*Cecily goes over.*] How old are you, dear?

CECILY: Well, I am really only eighteen, but I always admit to twenty when I go to evening parties.

LADY BRACKNELL: You are perfectly right in making some slight alteration. Indeed, no woman should ever be quite accurate about her age. It looks so calculating. . . . [*In a meditative manner.*] Eighteen, but admitting to twenty at evening parties. Well, it will not be very long before you are of age and free from the restraints of tutelage. So don't think your guardian's consent is, after all, a matter of any importance.

JACK: Pray excuse me, Lady Bracknell, for interrupting you again, but it is only fair to tell you that according to the terms of her grandfather's will Miss Cardew does not come legally of age till she is thirty-five.

LADY BRACKNELL: That does not seem to be a grave objection. Thirty-five is a very attractive age. London society is full of women of the very highest birth who have, of their own free choice, remained thirty-five for years. Lady Dumbleton is an instance in point. To my own knowledge she has been thirty-five ever since she arrived at the age of forty, which was many years ago now. I see no reason why our dear Cecily should not be even still more attractive at the age you mention than she is at present. There will be a large accumulation of property.

CECILY: Algy, could you wait for me till I was thirty-five?

ALGERNON: Of course I could, Cecily. You know I could.

CECILY: Yes, I felt it instinctively, but I couldn't wait all that time. I hate waiting even five minutes for anybody. It always makes me rather cross. I am not punctual myself, I know, but I do like punctuality in others, and waiting, even to be married, is quite out of the question.

ALGERNON: Then what is to be done, Cecily?

CECILY: I don't know, Mr Moncrieff.

LADY BRACKNELL: My dear Mr Worthing, as Miss Cardew states positively that she cannot wait till she is thirty-five—a remark which I am bound to say seems to me to show a somewhat impatient nature—I would beg of you to reconsider your decision.

JACK: But my dear Lady Bracknell, the matter is entirely in your own hands. The moment you consent to my marriage with Gwendolen, I will most gladly allow your nephew to form an alliance with my ward.

LADY BRACKNELL [*rising and drawing herself up*]: You must be quite aware that what you propose is out of the question.

JACK: Then a passionate celibacy is all that any of us can look forward to.

LADY BRACKNELL: That is not the destiny I propose for Gwendolen. Algernon, of course, can choose for himself. [*Pulls out her watch.*] Come, dear [*Gwendolen rises*], we have already missed five, if not six, trains. To miss any more might expose us to comment on the platform.

    Enter Dr Chasuble.

CHASUBLE: Everything is quite ready for the christenings.

LADY BRACKNELL: The christenings, sir! Is not that somewhat premature?

CHASUBLE [*looking rather puzzled, and pointing to Jack and Algernon*]: Both these gentlemen have expressed a desire for immediate baptism.

LADY BRACKNELL: At their age? The idea is grotesque and irreligious! Algernon, I forbid you to be baptized. I will not hear of such excesses. Lord Bracknell would be highly displeased if he learned that that was the way in which you wasted your time and money.

CHASUBLE: Am I to understand then that there are to be no christenings at all this afternoon?

JACK: I don't think that, as things are now, it would be of much practical value to either of us, Dr Chasuble.

CHASUBLE: I am grieved to hear such sentiments from you, Mr Worthing. They savour of the heretical views of the Anabaptists, views that I have completely refuted in four of my unpublished sermons. However, as your present mood seems to be one peculiarly secular, I will return to the church at once. Indeed, I have just been informed by the pew-opener that for the last hour and a half Miss Prism has been waiting for me in the vestry.

LADY BRACKNELL [*starting*]: Miss Prism! Did I hear you mention a Miss Prism?

CHASUBLE: Yes, Lady Bracknell. I am on my way to join her.

LADY BRACKNELL: Pray allow me to detain you for a moment. This matter may prove to be one of vital importance to Lord Bracknell and myself. Is this Miss Prism a female of repellent aspect, remotely connected with education?

CHASUBLE [*somewhat indignantly*]: She is the most cultivated of ladies, and the very picture of respectability.

LADY BRACKNELL: It is obviously the same person. May I ask what position she holds in your household?

CHASUBLE [*severely*]: I am a celibate, madam.

JACK [*interposing*]: Miss Prism, Lady Bracknell, has been for the last three years Miss Cardew's esteemed governess and valued companion.

LADY BRACKNELL: In spite of what I hear of her, I must see her at once. Let her be sent for.

CHASUBLE [*looking off*]: She approaches; she is nigh.

> *Enter Miss Prism hurriedly.*

MISS PRISM: I was told you expected me in the vestry, dear Canon. I have been waiting for you there for an hour and three-quarters. [*Catches sight of Lady Bracknell, who has fixed her with a stony glare. Miss Prism grows pale and quails. She looks anxiously round as if desirous to escape.*]

LADY BRACKNELL [*in a severe, judicial voice*]: Prism! [*Miss Prism bows her head in shame.*] Come here, Prism! [*Miss Prism approaches in a humble manner.*] Prism! Where is that baby? [*General consternation. The Canon starts back in horror. Algernon and Jack pretend to be anxious to shield Cecily and Gwendolen from hearing the details of a terrible public scandal.*] Twenty-eight years ago, Prism, you left Lord Bracknell's house, Number 104, Upper Grosvenor Square, in charge of a perambulator that contained a baby of the male sex. You never returned. A few weeks later, through the elaborate investigations of the Metropolitan police, the perambulator was discovered at midnight standing by itself in a remote corner of Bayswater. It contained the manuscript of a three-volume novel of more than usually revolting sentimentality. [*Miss Prism starts in involuntary indignation.*] But the baby was not there. [*Everyone looks at Miss Prism.*] Prism! Where is that baby? [*A pause.*]

MISS PRISM: Lady Bracknell, I admit with shame that I do not know. I only wish I did. The plain facts of the case are these. On the morning of the day you mentioned, a day that is forever branded on my memory, I prepared as usual to take the baby out in its perambulator. I had also with me a somewhat old, but capacious handbag in which I had intended to place the manuscript of a work of fiction that I had written during my few unoccupied hours. In a moment of mental abstraction, for which I can never forgive myself, I deposited the manuscript in the bassinette and placed the baby in the handbag.

JACK [*who has been listening attentively*]: But where did you deposit the handbag?

MISS PRISM: Do not ask me, Mr Worthing.

JACK: Miss Prism, this is a matter of no small importance to me. I insist on knowing where you deposited the handbag that contained that infant.

MISS PRISM: I left it in the cloakroom of one of the larger railway stations in London.

JACK: What railway station?

MISS PRISM [*quite crushed*]: Victoria. The Brighton line. [*Sinks into a chair.*]

JACK: I must retire to my room for a moment. Gwendolen, wait here for me.

GWENDOLEN: If you are not too long, I will wait here for you all my life. [*Exit Jack in great excitement.*]

CHASUBLE: What do you think this means, Lady Bracknell?

LADY BRACKNELL: I dare not even suspect, Dr Chasuble. I need hardly tell you that in families of high position strange coincidences are not supposed to occur. They are hardly considered the thing. [*Noises heard overhead as if someone was throwing trunks about. Every one looks up.*]

CECILY: Uncle Jack seems strangely agitated.

CHASUBLE: Your guardian has a very emotional nature.

LADY BRACKNELL: This noise is extremely unpleasant. It sounds as if he was having an argument. I dislike arguments of any kind. They are always vulgar, and often convincing.

CHASUBLE [*looking up*]: It has stopped now. [*The noise is redoubled.*]

LADY BRACKNELL: I wish he would arrive at some conclusion.

GWENDOLEN: This suspense is terrible. I hope it will last.

Enter Jack with a handbag of black leather in his hand.

JACK [*rushing over to Miss Prism*]: Is this the handbag, Miss Prism? Examine it carefully before you speak. The happiness of more than one life depends on your answer.

MISS PRISM [*calmly*]: It seems to be mine. Yes, here is the injury it received through the upsetting of a Gower Street omnibus in younger and happier days. Here is the strain on the lining caused by the explosion of a temperance beverage, an incident that occurred at Leamington. And here, on the lock, are my initials. I had forgotten that in an extravagant mood I had them placed there. The bag is undoubtedly mine. I am delighted to have it so unexpectedly restored to me. It has been a great inconvenience being without it all these years.

JACK [*in a pathetic voice*]: Miss Prism, more is restored to you than this handbag. I was the baby you placed in it.

MISS PRISM [*amazed*]: You?

JACK [*embracing her*]: Yes . . . mother!

MISS PRISM [*recoiling in indignant astonishment*]: Mr Worthing. I am unmarried!

JACK: Unmarried! I do not deny that is a serious blow. But after all, who has the right to cast a stone against one who has suffered? Cannot repentance wipe out an act of folly? Why should there be one law for men, and another for women? Mother, I forgive you. [*Tries to embrace her again.*]

MISS PRISM [*still more indignant*]: Mr Worthing, there is some error. [*Pointing the Lady Bracknell.*] There is the lady who can tell you who you really are.

JACK [*after a pause*]: Lady Bracknell, I hate to seem inquisitive, but would you kindly inform me who I am?

LADY BRACKNELL: I am afraid that the news I have to give you will not altogether please you. You are the son of my poor sister, Mrs Moncrieff, and consequently Algernon's elder brother.

JACK: Algy's elder brother! Then I have a brother after all. I knew I had a brother! I always had a brother! Cecily,—how could you have ever doubted that I had a brother. [*Seizes hold of Algernon.*] Dr Chasuble, my unfortunate brother. Miss Prism, my unfortunate brother. Gwendolen, my unfortunate brother. Algy, you young scoundrel, you will have to treat me with more respect in the future. You have never behaved to me like a brother in all your life.

ALGERNON: Well, not till today, old boy, I admit. I did my best, however, though I was out of practice. [*Shakes hands.*]

GWENDOLEN [*to Jack*]: My own! But what own are you? What is your Christian name now that you have become someone else?

JACK: Good heavens! . . . I had quite forgotten that point. Your decision on the subject of my name is irrevocable, I suppose?

GWENDOLEN: I never change except in my affections.

CECILY: What a noble nature you have, Gwendolen!

JACK: Then the question had better be cleared up at once. Aunt Augusta, a moment. At the time when Miss Prism left me in the handbag, had I been christened already?

LADY BRACKNELL: Every luxury that money could buy, including christening, had been lavished on you by your fond and doting parents.

JACK: Then I was christened! That is settled. Now, what name was I given? Let me know the worst.

LADY BRACKNELL: Being the eldest son you were naturally christened after your father.

JACK [*irritably*]: Yes, but what was my father's Christian name?

LADY BRACKNELL [*meditatively*]: I cannot at the present moment recall what the General's Christian name was. But I have no doubt he had one. He was eccentric, I admit. But only in later years. And that was the result of the Indian climate, and marriage, and indigestion, and other things of that kind.

JACK: Algy! Can't you recollect what our father's Christian name was?

ALGERNON: My dear boy, we were never even on speaking terms. He died before I was a year old.

JACK: His name would appear in the Army Lists of the period, I suppose, Aunt Augusta?

LADY BRACKNELL: The General was essentially a man of peace, except in his domestic life. But have no doubt his name would appear in any military directory.

JACK: The Army Lists of the last forty years are here. These delightful records should have been my constant study. [*Rushes to bookcase and tears the books out.*] M. General . . . Mallan, Maxbohm, Magley—what ghastly names they have—Markby, Migsby, Mobbs, Moncrieff! Lieutenant 1840, Captain, Lieutenant-Colonel, Colonel, General 1869, Christian names, Ernest John. [*Puts book very quietly down and speaks quite calmly.*] I have always told you, Gwendolen, my name was Ernest, didn't I? Well it is Ernest after all. I mean it naturally is Ernest.

LADY BRACKNELL: Yes, I remember now that the General was called Ernest. I knew I had some particular reason for disliking the name.

GWENDOLEN: Ernest! My own Ernest! I felt from the first you could have no other name!

JACK: Gwendolen, it is a terrible thing for a man to find out suddenly that all his life he has been speaking nothing but the truth. Can you forgive me?

GWENDOLEN: I can. For I feel that you are sure to change.

JACK: My own one!

CHASUBLE [*to Miss Prism*]: Laetitia! [*Embraces her.*]

MISS PRISM [*enthusiastically*]: Frederick! At last!

ALGERNON: Cecily! [*Embraces her.*] At last!

JACK: Gwendolen! [*Embraces her.*] At last!

LADY BRACKNELL: My nephew, you seem to be displaying signs of triviality.

JACK: On the contrary, Aunt Augusta, I've now realized for the first time in my life the vital Importance of Being Earnest.

Tableau

1899

George Bernard Shaw
1856–1950

Born and raised in Dublin, Ireland, George Bernard Shaw was the youngest child of an unhappy marriage between his drunken, joke-telling father and his artistic, undomestic mother. He dropped out of school when he was fifteen and worked briefly at an office job in Dublin. When he was twenty he moved to London, where he lived with his mother, who helped to support him out of her income as a private music teacher while he tried unsuccessfully to make his way as a novelist. During his late twenties he discovered the economic and political theories of Karl Marx and was so inspired by them that he joined a socialist group known as the Fabians and quickly became one of their leading spokesmen, lecturing and writing pamphlets to reform local government, to revise the poor laws, to promote trade unions, and to support women's rights. By his mid-thirties he had also become a well-known art, literature, and music critic through his reviews for various London newspapers, and he had published his first book, *The Quintessence of Ibsenism* (1891), a manifesto celebrating the socially conscious drama of Ibsen. Having proclaimed the English need for a 'new drama' of social ideas, Shaw took up playwriting in 1892, and from then until his death wrote forty-seven full-length plays promoting his ideas and opinions about economics, politics, society, morality, religion, science, and literature. Most of his plays are comedies, which feature witty men and equally witty women who engage in lively debates that illustrate Shaw's belief in 'free vitality' and the 'life force' as the primary sources of 'creative evolution' within human beings and their social institutions. Among his best-known plays are *Candida* (1895), *Man and Superman* (1903),

Major Barbara (1907), *Pygmalion* (1913), and *Saint Joan* (1924).

Shaw expounded his views not only in his plays but also in prefaces that he wrote for the published versions of his plays. By means of these prefaces, which were sometimes as long as the plays themselves, Shaw used his incisive prose style to explicate his characters, plots, and themes, as well as to gain a wider audience for his ideas than was possible in the theatre alone. Published versions of his plays also allowed him to demonstrate some of the spelling reforms he championed (and insisted upon with his publishers), including contractions without apostrophes and words that are spaced out rather than italicized to convey emphasis. These changes have been retained in the text printed here.

Pygmalion

PREFACE
A Professor of Phonetics

As will be seen later on, Pygmalion needs, not a preface, but a sequel, which I have supplied in its due place.

The English have no respect for their language, and will not teach their children to speak it. They cannot spell it because they have nothing to spell it with but an old foreign alphabet of which only the consonants—and not all of them—have any agreed speech value. Consequently no man can teach himself what it should sound like from reading it; and it is impossible for an Englishman to open his mouth without making some other Englishman despise him. Most European languages are now accessible in black and white to foreigners: English and French are not thus accessible even to Englishmen and Frenchmen. The reformer we need most today is an energetic phonetic enthusiast: that is why I have made such a one the hero of a popular play.

There have been heroes of that kind crying in the wilderness for many years past. When I became interested in the subject towards the end of the eighteen-seventies, the illustrious Alexander Melville Bell, the inventor of Visible Speech, had emigrated to Canada, where his son invented the telephone; but Alexander J. Ellis was still a London patriarch, with an impressive head always covered by a velvet skull cap, for which he would apologize to public meetings in a very courtly manner. He and Tito Pagliardini, another phonetic veteran, were men whom it was impossible to dislike. Henry Sweet, then a young man, lacked the sweetness of character: he was about as conciliatory to conventional mortals as Ibsen or Samuel Butler. His great ability as a phonetician (he was, I think, the best of them all at his job) would have entitled him to high official recognition, and perhaps enabled him to popularize his subject, but for his Satanic contempt for all academic dignitaries and persons in general who thought more of Greek than of phonetics. Once, in the days when the Imperial Institute rose in South Kensington, and Joseph Chamberlain was booming the Empire, I induced the editor of a leading monthly review to commission an article from Sweet on the imperial importance of his subject. When it arrived, it contained nothing but a savagely derisive attack on a professor of language and literature whose chair Sweet regarded as proper to a phonetic expert only. The article, being libellous, had to be returned as impossible; and I had to renounce my dream of dragging its author into the limelight. When I met him afterwards, for the first time in many years, I found to my astonishment that he, who had been a quite tolerably presentable young man, had actually managed by sheer scorn to alter his personal appearance until he had become a sort of walking repudiation of Oxford and all its traditions. It must have been largely in his own despite that he was squeezed into something called a Readership of phonetics there. The future of phonetics rests probably with his pupils, who all swore by him; but nothing could bring the man himself into any sort of compliance with the university to which he nevertheless clung by divine right in an intensely Oxonian way. I daresay his papers, if he has left any, include some satires that may be published without too destructive results fifty years hence. He was, I believe, not in the least an ill-natured man: very much the opposite, I should say; but he would not suffer fools gladly; and to him all scholars who were not rabid phoneticians were fools.

Those who knew him will recognize in my third act the allusion to the Current Shorthand in which he used to write postcards. It may be acquired from a four and six-penny manual published by the Clarendon Press. The postcards which Mrs Higgins describes are such as I have received from Sweet. I would decipher a sound which a cockney would represent by *zerr*, and a Frenchman by *seu*, and then write demanding with some heat what on earth it meant. Sweet, with boundless contempt for my stupidity, would reply that it not only meant but obviously was the word Result, as no other word containing that sound, and capable of making sense with the context, existed in any language spoken on earth. That less expert mortals should require fuller indications was beyond Sweet's patience. Therefore, though the whole point of his current Shorthand is that it can express every sound in the language perfectly, vowels as well as consonants, and that your hand has to make no stroke except the easy and current ones with which you write m, n, and u, l, p, and q, scribbling them at whatever angle comes easiest to you, his unfortunate determination to make this remarkable and quite legible script serve also as a shorthand reduced it in his practice to the most inscrutable of cryptograms. His true objective was the provision of a full, accurate, legible script for our language; but he was led past that by his contempt for the popular Pitman system of shorthand, which he called the Pitfall system. The triumph of Pitman was a triumph of business organization: there was a weekly paper to persuade you to learn Pitman: there were cheap textbooks and exercise books and transcripts of speeches for you to copy, and schools where experienced teachers coached you up to the necessary proficiency. Sweet could not organize his market in that fashion. He might as well have been the Sybil who tore up the leaves of prophecy that nobody would attend to. The four and sixpenny manual, mostly in his lithographed handwriting, that was never vulgarly advertised, may perhaps some day be taken up by a syndicate and pushed upon the public as The Times pushed the Encyclopaedia Britannica; but until then it will certainly not prevail against Pitman. I have bought three copies of it during my lifetime; and I am informed by the publishers that its cloistered existence is still a steady and healthy one. I actually learned the system two several times; and yet the shorthand in which I am writing these lines is Pitman's. And the reason is, that my secretary cannot transcribe Sweet, having been perforce taught in the schools of Pitman. In America I could use the commercially organized Gregg shorthand, which has taken a hint from Sweet by making its letters writable (current, Sweet would have called them) instead of having to be geometrically drawn like Pitman's; but all these systems, including Sweet's, are spoilt by making them available for verbatim reporting, in which complete and exact spelling and word division are impossible. A complete and exact phonetic script is neither practicable nor necessary for ordinary use; but if we enlarge our alphabet to the Russian size, and make our spelling as phonetic as Spanish, the advance will be prodigious.

Pygmalion Higgins is not a portrait of Sweet, to whom the adventure of Eliza Doolittle would have been impossible; still, as will be seen, there are touches of Sweet in the play. With Higgins's physique and temperament Sweet might have set the Thames on fire. As it was, he impressed himself professionally on Europe to an extent that made his comparative personal obscurity, and the failure of Oxford to do justice to his eminence, a puzzle to foreign specialists in his subject. I do not blame Oxford, because I think Oxford is quite right in demanding a certain social amenity from its nurslings (heaven knows it is not exorbitant in its requirements!); for although I well know how hard it is for a man of genius with a seriously underrated subject to maintain serene and kindly relations with the men who underrate it, and who keep all the best places for less important subjects which they profess without originality and sometimes without much capacity for them, still, if he overwhelms them with wrath and disdain, he cannot expect them to heap honours on him.

Of the later generations of phoneticians I know little. Among them towered Robert Bridges, to whom perhaps Higgins may owe his Miltonic sympathies, though here again I must disclaim all portraiture. But if the play makes the public aware that there are such people as phoneticians, and that they are among the most important people in England at present, it will serve its turn.

I wish to boast that Pygmalion has been an extremely successful play, both on stage and screen, all over Europe and North America as well as at home. It is so intensely and deliberately didactic, and its subject is esteemed so dry, that I delight in throwing it at the heads of the wiseacres who repeat the parrot cry that art should never be didactic. It goes to prove my contention that great art can never be anything else.

Finally, and for the encouragement of people troubled with accents that cut them off from all high employment, I may add that the change wrought by Professor Higgins in the flower-girl is neither impossible nor uncommon. The modern concierge's daughter who fulfils her ambition by playing the Queen of Spain in Ruy Blas at the Théâtre Français is one of many thousands of men and women who have sloughed off their native dialects and acquired a new tongue. Our West End shop assistants and domestic servants are bilingual. But the thing has to be done scientifically, or the last state of the aspirant may be worse than the first. An honest slum dialect is more tolerable than the attempts of phonetically untaught persons to imitate the plutocracy. Ambitious flower-girls who read this play must not imagine that they can pass themselves off as fine ladies by untutored imitation. They must learn their alphabet over again, and different, from a phonetic expert. Imitation will only make them ridiculous.

CHARACTERS

CLARA EYNSFORD HILL

MRS EYNSFORD HILL

A BYSTANDER

FREDDY EYNSFORD HILL

ELIZA DOOLITTLE

COLONEL PICKERING

HENRY HIGGINS

A SARCASTIC BYSTANDER

MRS PEARCE

ALFRED DOOLITTLE

MRS HIGGINS

PARLOUR-MAID

ACT I

> *London at 11:15 p.m. Torrents of heavy summer rain. Cab whistles blowing franti-cally in all directions. Pedestrians running for shelter into the portico of St Paul's church (not Wren's cathedral but Inigo Jones's church in Covent Garden vegetable market), among them a lady and her daughter in evening dress. All are peering out gloomily at the rain, except one man with his back turned to the rest, wholly pre-occupied with a notebook in which he is writing.*

> *The church clock strikes the first quarter.*

THE DAUGHTER [*in the space between the central pillars, close to the one on her left*]: I'm getting chilled to the bone. What can Freddy be doing all this time? He's been gone twenty minutes.

THE MOTHER [*on her daughter's right*]: Not so long. But he ought to have got us a cab by this.

A BYSTANDER [*on the lady's right*]: He wont get no cab not until half-past eleven, mis-sus, when they come back after dropping their theatre fares.

THE MOTHER: But we must have a cab. We cant stand here until half-past eleven. It's too bad.

THE BYSTANDER: Well, it aint my fault, missus.

THE DAUGHTER: If Freddy had a bit of gumption, he would have got one at the the-atre door.

THE MOTHER: What could he have done, poor boy?

THE DAUGHTER: Other people got cabs. Why couldnt he?

> *Freddy rushes in out of the rain from the Southampton Street side, and comes between them closing a dripping umbrella. He is a young man of twenty, in evening dress, very wet round the ankles.*

THE DAUGHTER: Well, havnt you got a cab?

FREDDY: Theres not one to be had for love or money.

THE MOTHER: Oh, Freddy, there must be one. You cant have tried.

THE DAUGHTER: It's too tiresome. Do you expect us to go and get one ourselves?

FREDDY: I tell you theyre all engaged. The rain was so sudden: nobody was prepared; and everybody had to take a cab. Ive been to Charing Cross one way and nearly to Ludgate Circus the other; and they were all engaged.

THE MOTHER: Did you try Trafalgar Square?

FREDDY: There wasnt one at Trafalgar Square.

THE DAUGHTER: Did you try?

FREDDY: I tried as far as Charing Cross Station. Did you expect me to walk to Hammersmith?

THE DAUGHTER: You havnt tried at all.

THE MOTHER: You really are very helpless, Freddy. Go again; and dont come back until you have found a cab.

FREDDY: I shall simply get soaked for nothing.

THE DAUGHTER: And what about us? Are we to stay here all night in this draught, with next to nothing on? You selfish pig—

FREDDY: Oh, very well: I'll go, I'll go.

He opens his umbrella and dashes off Strandwards, but comes into collision with a flower girl who is hurrying in for shelter, knocking her basket out of her hands. A blinding flash of lightning, followed instantly by a rattling peal of thunder, orchestrates the incident.

THE FLOWER GIRL: Nah then, Freddy: look wh' y' gowin, deah.

FREDDY: Sorry. [*He rushes off.*]

THE FLOWER GIRL [*picking up her scattered flowers and replacing them in the basket*]: Theres menners f' yer! Tə-oo banches o voylets trod into the mad.

She sits down on the plinth of the column, sorting her flowers, on the lady's right. She is not at all a romantic figure. She is perhaps eighteen, perhaps twenty, hardly older. She wears a little sailor hat of black straw that has long been exposed to the dust and soot of London and has seldom if ever been brushed. Her hair needs washing rather badly: its mousy colour can hardly be natural. She wears a shoddy black coat that reaches nearly to her knees and is shaped to her waist. She has a brown skirt with a coarse apron. Her boots are much the worse for wear. She is no doubt as clean as she can afford to be; but compared to the ladies she is very dirty. Her features are no worse than theirs; but their condition leaves something to be desired; and she needs the services of a dentist.

THE MOTHER: How do you know that my son's name is Freddy, pray?

THE FLOWER GIRL: Ow, eez yə-ooa san, is e? Wal, fewd dan y' də-ooty bawmz a mather should, eed now bettern to spawl a pore gel's flahrzn than ran away athaht pyin. Will ye-oo py me f'them? [*Here, with apologies, this desperate attempt to represent her dialect without a phonetic alphabet must be abandoned as unintelligible outside London.*]

THE DAUGHTER: Do nothing of the sort, mother. The idea!

THE MOTHER: Please allow me, Clara. Have you any pennies?

THE DAUGHTER: No. Ive nothing smaller than sixpence.

THE FLOWER GIRL [*hopefully*]: I can give you change for a tanner, kind lady.

THE MOTHER [*to Clara*]: Give it to me. [*Clara parts reluctantly.*] Now [*to the girl*]: This is for your flowers.

THE FLOWER GIRL: Thank you kindly, lady.

THE DAUGHTER: Make her give you the change. These things are only a penny a bunch.

THE MOTHER: Do hold your tongue, Clara. [*to the girl*]: You can keep the change.

THE FLOWER GIRL: Oh, thank you, lady.

THE MOTHER: Now tell me how you know that young gentleman's name.

THE FLOWER GIRL: I didnt.

THE MOTHER: I heard you call him by it. Dont try to deceive me.

THE FLOWER GIRL [*protesting*]: Who's trying to deceive you? I called him Freddy or Charlie same as you might yourself if you was talking to a stranger and wished to be pleasant.

THE DAUGHTER: Sixpence thrown away! Really, mamma, you might have spared Freddy that. [*She retreats in disgust behind the pillar.*]

> *An elderly gentleman of the amiable military type rushes into the shelter, and closes a dripping umbrella. He is in the same plight as Freddy, very wet about the ankles. He is in evening dress, with a light overcoat. He takes the place left vacant by the daughter.*

THE GENTLEMAN: Phew!

THE MOTHER [*to the gentleman*]: Oh sir, is there any sign of its stopping?

THE GENTLEMAN: I'm afraid not. It started worse than ever about two minutes ago. [*He goes to the plinth beside the flower girl; puts up his foot on it; and stoops to turn down his trouser ends.*]

THE MOTHER: Oh dear! [*She retires sadly and joins her daughter.*]

THE FLOWER GIRL [*taking advantage of the military gentleman's proximity to establish friendly relations with him*]: If it's worse, it's a sign it's nearly over. So cheer up, Captain; and buy a flower off a poor girl.

THE GENTLEMAN: I'm sorry. I havnt any change.

THE FLOWER GIRL: I can give you change, Captain.

THE GENTLEMAN: For a sovereign? Ive nothing less.

THE FLOWER GIRL: Garn! Oh do buy a flower off me, Captain. I can change half-a-crown. Take this for tuppence.

THE GENTLEMAN: Now dont be troublesome: theres a good girl. [*trying his pockets*] I really havnt any change—Stop: heres three hapence, if thats any use to you. [*He retreats to the other pillar.*]

THE FLOWER GIRL [*disappointed, but thinking three halfpence better than nothing*]: Thank you, sir.

THE BYSTANDER [*to the girl*]: You be careful: give him a flower for it. Theres a bloke here behind taking down every blessed word youre saying. [*All turn to the man who is taking notes.*]

THE FLOWER GIRL [*springing up terrified*]: I aint done nothing wrong by speaking to the gentleman. Ive a right to sell flowers if I keep off the kerb. [*hysterically*] I'm a respectable girl: so help me, I never spoke to him except to ask him to buy a flower off me.

General hubbub, mostly sympathetic to the flower girl, but deprecating her excessive sensibility. Cries of Dont start hollerin. Who's hurting you? Nobody's going to touch you. Whats the good of fussing? Steady on. Easy easy, *etc., come from the elderly staid spectators, who pat her comfortingly. Less patient ones bid her shut her head, or ask her roughly what is wrong with her. A remoter group, not knowing what the matter is, crowd in and increase the noise with question and answer:* Whats the row? What—she do? Where is he? A tec taking her down. What! him? Yes: him over there: Took money off the gentleman, *etc.*

THE FLOWER GIRL [*breaking through them to the gentleman, crying wildly*]: Oh, sir, dont let him charge me. You dunno what it means to me. Theyll take away my character and drive me on the streets for speaking to gentlemen. They—

THE NOTE TAKER [*coming forward on her right, the rest crowding after him*]: There! there! there! there! who's hurting you, you silly girl? What do you take me for?

THE BYSTANDER: It's aw rawt: e's a genleman: look at his bə-oots. [*explaining to the note taker*] She thought you was a copper's nark, sir.

THE NOTE TAKER [*with quick interest*]: Whats a copper's nark?

THE BYSTANDER [*inapt at definition*]: It's a—well, it's a copper's nark, as you might say. What else would you call it? A sort of informer.

THE FLOWER GIRL [*still hysterical*]: I take my Bible oath I never said a word—

THE NOTE TAKER [*overbearing but good-humoured*]: Oh, shut up, shut up. Do I look like a policeman?

THE FLOWER GIRL [*far from reassured*]: Then what did you take down my words for? How do I know whether you took me down right? You just shew me what youve wrote about me. [*The note taker opens his book and holds it steadily under her nose, though the pressure of the mob trying to read it over his shoulders would upset a weaker man.*] Whats that? That aint proper writing. I cant read that.

THE NOTE TAKER: I can. [*reads, reproducing her pronunciation exactly*] 'Cheer ap, Keptin; n' baw y flahr orf a pore gel.'

THE FLOWER GIRL [*much distressed*]: It's because I called him Captain. I meant no harm. [*to the gentleman*]: Oh, sir, dont let him lay a charge agen me for a word like that. You—

THE GENTLEMAN: Charge! I make no charge. [*to the note taker*]: Really, sir, if you are a detective, you need not begin protecting me against molestations by young women until I ask you. Anybody could see that the girl meant no harm.

THE BYSTANDERS GENERALLY [*demonstrating against police espionage*]: Course they could. What business is it of yours? You mind your own affairs. He wants promotion, he does. Taking down people's words! Girl never said a word to him. What harm if she did? Nice thing a girl cant shelter from the rain without being insulted, etc., etc., etc. [*She is conducted by the more sympathetic demonstrators back to her plinth, where she resumes her seat and struggles with her emotion.*]

THE BYSTANDER: He aint a tec. He's a blooming busybody: thats what he is. I tell you, look at his bə-oots.

THE NOTE TAKER [*turning on him genially*]: And how are all your people down at Selsey?

THE BYSTANDER [*suspiciously*]: Who told you my people come from Selsey?

THE NOTE TAKER: Never you mind. They did. [*to the girl*] How do you come to be up so far east? You were born in Lisson Grove.

THE FLOWER GIRL [*appalled*]: Oh, what harm is there in my leaving Lisson Grove? It wasnt fit for a pig to live in; and I had to pay four-and-six a week [*in tears*]: Oh, boo—hoo—oo—

THE NOTE TAKER: Live where you like; but stop that noise.

THE GENTLEMAN [*to the girl*]: Come, come! he cant touch you: you have a right to live where you please.

A SARCASTIC BYSTANDER [*thrusting himself between the note taker and the gentleman*]: Park Lane, for instance. I'd like to go into the Housing Question with you, I would.

THE FLOWER GIRL [*subsiding into a brooding melancholy over her basket, and talking very low-spiritedly to herself*]: I'm a good girl, I am.

THE SARCASTIC BYSTANDER [*not attending to her*]: Do you know where I come from?

THE NOTE TAKER [*promptly*]: Hoxton.

Titterings. Popular interest in the note taker's performance increases.

THE SARCASTIC ONE [*amazed*]: Well, who said I didnt? Bly me! you know everything, you do.

THE FLOWER GIRL [*still nursing her sense of injury*]: Aint no call to meddle with me, he aint.

THE BYSTANDER [*to her*]: Of course he aint. Dont you stand it from him. [*to the note taker*]: See here: what call have you to know about people what never offered to meddle with you?

THE FLOWER GIRL: Let him say what he likes. I dont want to have no truck with him.

THE BYSTANDER: You take us for dirt under your feet, dont you? Catch you taking liberties with a gentleman!

THE SARCASTIC BYSTANDER: Yes: tell him where he come from if you want to go fortune-telling.

THE NOTE TAKER: Cheltenham, Harrow, Cambridge, and India.

THE GENTLEMAN: Quite right.

Great laughter. Reaction in the note taker's favour. Exclamations of He knows all about it. Told him proper. Hear him tell the toff where he come from? *etc.*

THE GENTLEMAN: May I ask, sir, do you do this for your living at a music hall?

THE NOTE TAKER: Ive thought of that. Perhaps I shall some day.

The rain has stopped; and the persons on the outside of the crowd begin to drop off.

THE FLOWER GIRL [*resenting the reaction*]: He's no gentleman, he aint, to interfere with a poor girl.

THE DAUGHTER [*out of patience, pushing her way rudely to the front and displacing the gentleman, who politely retires to the other side of the pillar*]: What on earth is Freddy doing? I shall get pneumownia if I stay in this draught any longer.

THE NOTE TAKER [*to himself, hastily making a note of her pronunciation of 'monia'*]: Earlscourt.

THE DAUGHTER [*violently*]: Will you please keep your impertinent remarks to yourself.

THE NOTE TAKER: Did I say that out loud? I didnt mean to. I beg your pardon. Your mother's Epsom, unmistakeably.

THE MOTHER [*advancing between her daughter and the note taker*]: How very curious! I was brought up in Largelady Park, near Epsom.

THE NOTE TAKER [*uproariously amused*]: Ha! Ha! What a devil of a name! Excuse me. [*to the daughter*]: You want a cab, do you?

THE DAUGHTER: Dont dare speak to me.

THE MOTHER: Oh please, please, Clara. [*Her daughter repudiates her with an angry shrug and retires haughtily.*] We should be so grateful to you, sir, if you found us a cab. [*The note taker produces a whistle.*] Oh, thank you. [*She joins her daughter.*]

    The note taker blows a piercing blast.

THE SARCASTIC BYSTANDER: There! I knowed he was a plainclothes copper.

THE BYSTANDER: That aint a police whistle: thats a sporting whistle.

THE FLOWER GIRL [*still preoccupied with her wounded feelings*]: He's no right to take away my character. My character is the same to me as any lady's.

THE NOTE TAKER: I dont know whether youve noticed it; but the rain stopped about two minutes ago.

THE BYSTANDER: So it has. Why didnt you say so before? and us losing our time listening to your silliness! [*He walks off towards the Strand.*]

THE SARCASTIC BYSTANDER: I can tell where you come from. You come from Anwell. Go back there.

THE NOTE TAKER [*helpfully*]: Hanwell.

THE SARCASTIC BYSTANDER [*affecting great distinction of speech*]: Thenk you, teacher. Haw haw! So long. [*He touches his hat with mock respect and strolls off.*]

THE FLOWER GIRL: Frightening people like that! How would he like it himself?

THE MOTHER: It's quite fine now, Clara. We can walk to a motor bus. Come. [*She gathers her skirts above her ankles and hurries off towards the Strand.*]

THE DAUGHTER: But the cab—[*her mother is out of hearing.*] Oh, how tiresome! [*She follows angrily.*]

    All the rest have gone except the note taker, the gentleman, and the flower girl, who sits arranging her basket, and still pitying herself in murmurs.

THE FLOWER GIRL: Poor girl! Hard enough for her to live without being worrited and chivied.

THE GENTLEMAN [*returning to his former place on the note taker's left*]: How do you do it, if I may ask?

THE NOTE TAKER: Simply phonetics. The science of speech. Thats my profession: also my hobby. Happy is the man who can make a living by his hobby! You can spot an Irishman or a Yorkshireman by his brogue. *I* can place any man within six miles. I can place him within two miles in London. Sometimes within two streets.

THE FLOWER GIRL: Ought to be ashamed of himself, unmanly coward!

THE GENTLEMAN: But is there a living in that?

THE NOTE TAKER: Oh yes. Quite a fat one. This is an age of upstarts. Men begin in Kentish Town with £80 a year, and end in Park Lane with a hundred thousand. They want to drop Kentish Town; but they give themselves away every time they open their mouths. Now I can teach them——

THE FLOWER GIRL: Let him mind his own business and leave a poor girl——

THE NOTE TAKER [*explosively*]: Woman: cease this detestable boohooing instantly; or else seek the shelter of some other place of worship.

THE FLOWER GIRL [*with feeble defiance*]: Ive a right to be here if I like, same as you.

THE NOTE TAKER: A woman who utters such depressing and disgusting sounds has no right to be anywhere—no right to live. Remember that you are a human being with a soul and the divine gift of articulate speech: that your native language is the language of Shakespeare and Milton and The Bible; and dont sit there crooning like a bilious pigeon.

THE FLOWER GIRL [*quite overwhelmed, looking up at him in mingled wonder and deprecation without daring to raise her head*]: Ah-ah-ah-ow-ow-ow-oo!

THE NOTE TAKER [*whipping out his book*]: Heavens! what a sound! [*He writes; then holds out the book and reads, reproducing her vowels exactly*]: Ah-ah-ah-ow-ow-ow-oo!

THE FLOWER GIRL [*tickled by the performance, and laughing in spite of herself*]: Garn!

THE NOTE TAKER: You see this creature with her kerbstone English: the English that will keep her in the gutter to the end of her days. Well, sir, in three months I could pass that girl off as a duchess at an ambassador's garden party. I could even get her a place as lady's maid or shop assistant, which requires better English.

THE FLOWER GIRL: Whats that you say?

THE NOTE TAKER: Yes, you squashed cabbage leaf, you disgrace to the noble architecture of these columns, you incarnate insult to the English language: I could pass you off as the Queen of Sheba. [*to the Gentleman*]: Can you believe that?

THE GENTLEMAN: Of course I can. I am myself a student of Indian dialects; and——

THE NOTE TAKER [*eagerly*]: Are you? Do you know Colonel Pickering, the author of Spoken Sanscrit?

THE GENTLEMAN: I am Colonel Pickering. Who are you?

THE NOTE TAKER: Henry Higgins, author of Higgins's Universal Alphabet.

PICKERING [*with enthusiasm*]: I came from India to meet you.

HIGGINS: I was going to India to meet you.

PICKERING: Where do you live?

HIGGINS: 27A Wimpole Street. Come and see me tomorrow.

PICKERING: I'm at the Carlton. Come with me now and lets have a jaw over some supper.

HIGGINS: Right you are.

THE FLOWER GIRL [*to Pickering, as he passes her*]: Buy a flower, kind gentleman. I'm short for my lodging.

PICKERING: I really havnt any change. I'm sorry. [*He goes away.*]

HIGGINS [*shocked at the girl's mendacity*]: Liar. You said you could change half-a-crown.

THE FLOWER GIRL [*rising in desperation*]: You ought to be stuffed with nails, you ought. [*flinging the basket at his feet*] Take the whole blooming basket for sixpence.

> *The church clock strikes the second quarter.*

HIGGINS [*hearing in it the voice of God, rebuking him for his Pharisaic want of charity to the poor girl*]: A reminder. [*He raises his hat solemnly; then throws a handful of money into the basket and follows Pickering.*]

THE FLOWER GIRL [*picking up a half-crown*]: Ah-ow-ooh! [*picking up a couple of florins*] Aaah-ow-ooh! [*picking up several coins*] Aaaaaah-ow-ooh! [*picking up a half-sovereign*] Aaaaaaaaaaaah-ow-ooh!!!

FREDDY [*springing out of a taxicab*]: Got one at last. Hallo! [*to the girl*]: Where are the two ladies that were here?

THE FLOWER GIRL: They walked to the bus when the rain stopped.

FREDDY: And left me with a cab on my hands! Damnation!

THE FLOWER GIRL [*with grandeur*]: Never mind, young man. *I*'m going home in a taxi. [*She sails off to the cab. The driver puts his hand behind him and holds the door firmly shut against her. Quite understanding his mistrust, she shews him her handful of money.*] A taxi fare aint no object to me, Charlie. [*He grins and opens the door.*] Here. What about the basket?

THE TAXIMAN: Give it here. Tuppence extra.

LIZA: No: I dont want nobody to see it. [*She crushes it into the cab and gets in, continuing the conversation through the window.*]: Goodbye, Freddy.

FREDDY [*dazedly raising his hat*]: Goodbye.

TAXIMAN: Where to?

LIZA: Bucknam Pellis [*Buckingham Palace*].

TAXIMAN: What d'ye mean—Bucknam Pellis?

LIZA: Dont you know where it is? In the Green Park, where the King lives. Goodbye, Freddy. Dont let me keep you standing there. Goodbye.

FREDDY: Goodbye. [*He goes.*]

TAXIMAN: Here? Whats this about Bucknam Pellis? What business have you at Bucknam Pellis?

LIZA: Of course I havnt none. But I wasnt going to let him know that. You drive me home.

TAXIMAN: And wheres home?

LIZA: Angel Court, Drury Lane, next Meiklejohn's oil shop.

TAXIMAN: That sounds more like it, Judy. [*He drives off.*]

* * *

Let us follow the taxi to the entrance to Angel Court, a narrow little archway between two shops, one of them Meiklejohn's oil shop. When it stops there, Eliza gets out, dragging her basket with her.

LIZA: How much?

TAXIMAN [*indicating the taximeter*]: Cant you read? A shilling.

LIZA: A shilling for two minutes!!

TAXIMAN: Two minutes or ten: it's all the same.

LIZA: Well. I dont call it right.

TAXIMAN: Ever been in a taxi before?

LIZA [*with dignity*]: Hundreds and thousands of times, young man.

TAXIMAN [*laughing at her*]: Good for you, Judy. Keep the shilling darling, with best love from all at home. Good luck! [*He drives off.*]

LIZA [*humiliated*]: Impidence!

She picks up the basket and trudges up the alley with it to her lodging: a small room with very old wall paper hanging loose in the damp places. A broken pane in the window is mended with paper. A portrait of a popular actor and a fashion plate of ladies' dresses, all wildly beyond poor Eliza's means, both torn from newspapers, are pinned up on the wall. A birdcage hangs in the window; but its tenant died long ago: it remains as a memorial only.

These are the only visible luxuries: the rest is the irreducible minimum of poverty's needs: a wretched bed heaped with all sorts of coverings that have any warmth in them, a draped packing case with a basin and jug on it and a little looking glass over it, a chair and table, the refuse of some suburban kitchen, and an American alarum clock on the shelf above the unused fireplace: the whole lighted with a gas lamp with a penny in the slot meter. Rent: four shillings a week.

Here Eliza, chronically weary, but too excited to go to bed, sits, counting her new riches and dreaming and planning what to do with them, until the gas goes out, when she enjoys for the first time the sensation of being able to put in another penny without grudging it. This prodigal mood does not extinguish her gnawing sense of the need for economy sufficiently to prevent her from calculating that she can dream and plan in bed more cheaply and warmly than sitting up without a fire. So she takes off her shawl and skirt and adds them to the miscellaneous bedclothes. Then she kicks off her shoes and gets into bed without any further change.

ACT II

Next day at 11 a.m. Higgins's laboratory in Wimpole Street. It is a room on the first floor, looking on the street, and was meant for the drawing room. The double doors are in the middle of the back wall; and persons entering find in the corner to their right two tall file cabinets at right angles to one another against the walls. In this corner stands a flat writing-table, on which are a phonograph, a laryngoscope, a row of tiny organ pipes with a bellows, a set of lamp chimneys for singing flames with burners attached to a gas plug in the wall by an indiarubber tube, several tuning-forks of different sizes, a life-size image of half a human head, shewing in section the vocal organs, and a box containing a supply of wax cylinders for the phonograph.

Further down the room, on the same side, is a fireplace, with a comfortable leather-covered easy-chair at the side of the hearth nearest the door, and a coal-scuttle. There is a clock on the mantel-piece. Between the fireplace and the phonograph table is a stand for newspapers.

On the other side of the central door, to the left of the visitor, is a cabinet of shallow drawers. On it is a telephone and the telephone directory. The corner beyond, and most of the side wall, is occupied by a grand piano, with the keyboard at the end furthest from the door, and a bench for the player extending the full length of the keyboard. On the piano is a dessert dish heaped with fruit and sweets, mostly chocolates.

The middle of the room is clear. Besides the easy-chair, the piano bench, and two chairs at the phonograph table, there is one stray chair. It stands near the fireplace. On the walls, engravings: mostly Piranesis and mezzotint portraits. No paintings.

Pickering is seated at the table, putting down some cards and a tuning-fork which he has been using. Higgins is standing up near him, closing two or three file drawers which are hanging out. He appears in the morning light as a robust, vital, appetizing sort of man of forty or thereabouts, dressed in a professional-looking black frock-coat with a white linen collar and black silk tie. He is of the energetic, scientific type, heartily, even violently interested in everything that can be studied as a scientific subject, and careless about himself and other people, including their feelings. He is, in fact, but for his years and size, rather like a very impetuous baby 'taking notice' eagerly and loudly, and requiring almost as much watching to keep him out of unintended mischief. His manner varies from genial bullying when he is in a good humour to stormy petulance when anything goes wrong; but he is so entirely frank and void of malice that he remains likeable even in his least reasonable moments.

HIGGINS [*as he shuts the last drawer*]: Well, I think thats the whole show.

PICKERING: It's really amazing. I havnt taken half of it in, you know.

HIGGINS: Would you like to go over any of it again?

PICKERING [*rising and coming to the fireplace, where he plants himself with his back to the fire*]: No, thank you: not now. I'm quite done up for this morning.

HIGGINS [*following him, and standing beside him on his left*]: Tired of listening to sounds?

PICKERING: Yes. It's a fearful strain. I rather fancied myself because I can pronounce twenty-four distinct vowel sounds: but your hundred and thirty beat me. I cant hear a bit of difference between most of them.

HIGGINS [*chuckling, and going over to the piano to eat sweets*]: Oh, that comes with practice. You hear no difference at first; but you keep on listening, and presently you find theyre all as different as A from B.

Mrs Pearce looks in: she is Higgins's housekeeper.

Whats the matter?

MRS PEARCE [*hesitating, evidently perplexed*]: A young woman asks to see you, sir.

HIGGINS: A young woman! What does she want?

MRS PEARCE: Well, sir, she says youll be glad to see her when you know what she's come about. She's quite a common girl, sir. Very common indeed. I should have sent her away, only I thought perhaps you wanted her to talk into your machines. I hope Ive not done wrong; but really you see such queer people sometimes—youll excuse me, I'm sure, sir—

HIGGINS: Oh, thats all right, Mrs Pearce. Has she an interesting accent?

MRS PEARCE: Oh, something dreadful, sir, really. I dont know how you can take an interest in it.

HIGGINS [*to Pickering*]: Lets have her up. Shew her up, Mrs Pearce. [*He rushes across to his working table and picks out a cylinder to use on the phonograph.*]

MRS PEARCE [*only half resigned to it*]: Very well, sir. It's for you to say. [*She goes downstairs.*]

HIGGINS: This is rather a bit of luck. I'll shew you how I make records. We'll set her talking; and I'll take it down first in Bell's Visible Speech; then in broad Romic; and then we'll get her on the phonograph so that you can turn her on as often as you like with the written transcript before you.

MRS PEARCE [*returning*]: This is the young woman, sir.

> *The flower girl enters in state. She has a hat with three ostrich feathers, orange, sky-blue, and red. She has a nearly clean apron, and the shoddy coat has been tidied a little. The pathos of this deplorable figure, with its innocent vanity and consequential air, touches Pickering, who has already straightened himself in the presence of Mrs Pearce. But as to Higgins, the only distinction he makes between men and women is that when he is neither bullying nor exclaiming to the heavens against some feather-weight cross, he coaxes women as a child coaxes its nurse when it wants to get anything out of her.*

HIGGINS [*brusquely, recognizing her with unconcealed disappointment, and at once, babylike, making an intolerable grievance of it*]: Why, this is the girl I jotted down last night. She's no use: Ive got all the records I want of the Lisson Grove lingo; and I'm not going to waste another cylinder on it. [*to the girl*]: Be off with you: I dont want you.

THE FLOWER GIRL: Dont you be so saucy. You aint heard what I come for yet. [*to Mrs Pearce, who is waiting at the door for further instructions*]: Did you tell him I come in a taxi?

MRS PEARCE: Nonsense, girl! what do you think a gentleman like Mr Higgins cares what you came in?

THE FLOWER GIRL: Oh, we a r e proud! He aint above giving lessons, not him: I heard him say so. Well, I aint come here to ask for any compliment; and if my money's not good enough I can go elsewhere.

HIGGINS: Good enough for what?

THE FLOWER GIRL: Good enough for yə-oo. Now you know, dont you? I'm come to have lessons, I am. And to pay for em tə-oo: make no mistake.

HIGGINS [*stupent*]: Well!!! [*recovering his breath with a gasp*] What do you expect me to say to you?

THE FLOWER GIRL: Well, if you was a gentleman, you might ask me to sit down, I think. Dont I tell you I'm bringing you business?

HIGGINS: Pickering: shall we ask this baggage to sit down, or shall we throw her out the window?

THE FLOWER GIRL [*running away in terror to the piano, where she turns at bay*]: Ah-ah-oh-ow-ow-ow-oo! [*wounded and whimpering*] I wont be called a baggage when Ive offered to pay like any lady.

> *Motionless, the two men stare at her from the other side of the room, amazed.*

PICKERING [*gently*]: But what is it you want?

THE FLOWER GIRL: I want to be a lady in a flower shop stead of sellin at the corner of Tottenham Court Road. But they wont take me unless I can talk more genteel. He said he could teach me. Well, here I am ready to pay him—not asking any favour—and he treats me zif I was dirt.

MRS PEARCE: How can you be such a foolish ignorant girl as to think you could afford to pay Mr Higgins?

THE FLOWER GIRL: Why shouldnt I? I know what lessons cost as well as you do; and I'm ready to pay.

HIGGINS: How much?

THE FLOWER GIRL [*coming back to him, triumphant*]: Now youre taking! I thought youd come off it when you saw a chance of getting back a bit of what you chucked at me last night. [*confidentially*]: Youd had a drop in, hadnt you?

HIGGINS [*peremptorily*]: Sit down.

THE FLOWER GIRL: Oh, if youre going to make a compliment of it—

HIGGINS [*thundering at her*]: Sit down.

MRS PEARCE [*severely*]: Sit down, girl. Do as youre told.

THE FLOWER GIRL: Ah-ah-ah-ow-ow-oo! [*She stands, half rebellious, half bewildered.*]

PICKERING [*very courteous*]: Wont you sit down? [*He places the stray chair near the hearthrug between himself and Higgins.*]

LIZA [*coyly*]: Dont mind if I do. [*She sits down. Pickering returns to the hearthrug.*]

HIGGINS: Whats your name?

THE FLOWER GIRL: Liza Doolittle.

HIGGINS [*declaiming gravely*]: Eliza, Elizabeth, Betsy and Bess,
>> They went to the woods to get a bird's nes':

PICKERING: >> They found a nest with four eggs in it:

HIGGINS: >> They took one apiece, and left three in it.

> *They laugh heartily at their own fun.*

LIZA: Oh, dont be silly.

MRS PEARCE [*placing herself behind Eliza's chair*]: You mustnt speak to the gentleman like that.

LIZA: Well, why wont he speak sensible to me?

HIGGINS: Come back to business. How much do you suppose to pay me for the lessons?

LIZA: Oh, I know whats right. A lady friend of mine gets French lessons for eighteen-pence an hour from a real French gentleman. Well, you wouldnt have the face to ask me the same for teaching me my own language as you would for French; so I wont give more than a shilling. Take it or leave it.

HIGGINS [*walking up and down the room rattling his keys and his cash in his pockets*]: You know, Pickering, if you consider a shilling, not as a simple shilling, but as a percentage of this girl's income, it works out as fully equivalent to sixty or seventy guineas from a millionaire.

PICKERING: How so?

HIGGINS: Figure it out. A millionaire has about £150 a day. She earns about half-a-crown.

LIZA [*haughtily*]: Who told you I only—

HIGGINS [*continuing*]: She offers me two-fifths of her day's income for a lesson. Two-fifths of a millionaire's income for a day would be somewhere about £60. It's hand-some. By George, it's enormous! it's the biggest offer I ever had.

LIZA [*rising, terrified*]: Sixty pounds! What are you talking about? I never offered you sixty pounds. Where would I get—

HIGGINS: Hold your tongue.

LIZA [*weeping*]: But I aint got sixty pounds. Oh—

MRS PEARCE: Dont cry, you silly girl. Sit down. Nobody is going to touch your money.

HIGGINS: Somebody is going to touch you with a broomstick, if you dont stop snivel-ling. Sit down.

LIZA [*obeying slowly*]: Ah-ah-ah-ow-oo-o! One would think you was my father.

HIGGINS: If I decide to teach you, I'll be worse than two fathers to you. Here! [*He offers her his silk handkerchief.*]

LIZA: Whats this for?

HIGGINS: To wipe your eyes. To wipe any part of your face that feels moist. Remember: thats your handkerchief; and thats your sleeve. Dont mistake the one for the other if you wish to become a lady in a shop.

Liza, *utterly bewildered, stares helplessly at him.*

MRS PEARCE: It's no use talking to her like that, Mr Higgins: she doesnt understand you. Besides, youre quite wrong: she doesnt do it that way at all. [*She takes the handkerchief.*]

LIZA [*snatching it*]: Here! You give me that handkerchief. He gev it to me, not you.

PICKERING [*laughing*]: He did. I think it must be regarded as her property, Mrs Pearce.

MRS PEARCE [*resigning herself*]: Serve you right, Mr Higgins.

PICKERING: Higgins: I'm interested. What about the ambassador's garden party? I'll say youre the greatest teacher alive if you make that good. I'll bet you all the expenses of the experiment you cant do it. And I'll pay for the lessons.

LIZA: Oh, you are real good. Thank you, Captain.

HIGGINS [*tempted, looking at her*]: It's almost irresistible. She's so deliciously low—so horribly dirty—

LIZA [*protesting extremely*]: Ah-ah-ah-ah-ow-ow-oo-oo!!! I aint dirty: I washed my face and hands afore I come, I did.

PICKERING: Youre certainly not going to turn her head with flattery, Higgins.

MRS PEARCE [*uneasy*]: Oh, dont say that, sir: theres more ways than one of turning a girl's head; and nobody can do it better than Mr Higgins, though he may not always mean it. I do hope, sir, you wont encourage him to do anything foolish.

HIGGINS [*becoming excited as the idea grows on him*]: What is life but a series of inspired follies? The difficulty is to find them to do. Never lose a chance: it doesnt come every day. I shall make a duchess of this draggletailed guttersnipe.

LIZA [*strongly deprecating this view of her*]: Ah-ah-ah-ow-ow-oo!

HIGGINS [*carried away*]: Yes: in six months—in three if she has a good ear and quick tongue—I'll take her anywhere and pass her off as anything. We'll start today: now! this moment! Take her away and clean her, Mrs Pearce. Monkey Brand, if it wont come off any other way. Is there a good fire in the kitchen?

MRS PEARCE [*protesting*]: Yes; but—

HIGGINS [*storming on*]: Take all her clothes off and burn them. Ring up Whiteley or somebody for new ones. Wrap her up in brown paper til they come.

LIZA: Youre no gentleman, youre not, to talk of such things. I'm a good girl, I am; and I know what the like of you are, I do.

HIGGINS: We want none of your Lisson Grove prudery here, young woman. Youve got to learn to behave like a duchess. Take her away, Mrs Pearce. If she gives you any trouble, wallop her.

LIZA [*springing up and running between Pickering and Mrs Pearce for protection*]: No! I'll call the police, I will.

MRS PEARCE: But Ive no place to put her.

HIGGINS: Put her in the dustbin.

LIZA: Ah-ah-ah-ow-ow-oo!

PICKERING: Oh come, Higgins! be reasonable.

MRS PEARCE [*resolutely*]: You must be reasonable, Mr Higgins: really you must. You cant walk over everybody like this.

> *Higgins, thus scolded, subsides. The hurricane is succeeded by a zephyr of amiable surprise.*

HIGGINS [*with professional exquisiteness of modulation*]: *I* walk over everybody! My dear Mrs Pearce, my dear Pickering, I never had the slightest intention of walking over anyone. All I propose is that we should be kind to this poor girl. We must help her prepare and fit herself for her new station in life. If I did not express myself clearly it was because I did not wish to hurt her delicacy, or yours.

> *Liza, reassured, steals back to her chair.*

MRS PEARCE [*to Pickering*]: Well, did you ever hear anything like that, sir?

PICKERING [*laughing heartily*]: Never, Mrs Pearce: never.

HIGGINS [*patiently*]: Whats the matter?

MRS PEARCE: Well, the matter is, sir, that you cant take a girl up like that as if you were picking up a pebble on the beach.

HIGGINS: Why not?

MRS PEARCE: Why not! But you dont know anything about her. What about her parents? She may be married.

LIZA: Garn!

HIGGINS: There! As the girl very properly says, Garn! Married indeed. Dont you know that a woman of that class looks a worn out drudge of fifty a year after she's married?

LIZA: Whood marry me?

HIGGINS [*suddenly resorting to the most thrillingly beautiful low tones in his best elocutionary style*]: By George, Eliza, the streets will be strewn with the bodies of men shooting themselves for your sake before Ive done with you.

MRS PEARCE: Nonsense, sir. You mustnt talk like that to her.

LIZA [*rising and squaring herself determinedly*]: I'm going away. He's off his chump, he is. I dont want no balmies teaching me.

HIGGINS [*wounded in his tenderest point by her insensibility to his elocution*]: Oh, indeed! I'm mad, am I? Very well, Mrs Pearce: you neednt order the new clothes for her. Throw her out.

LIZA [*whimpering*]: Nah-ow. You got no right to touch me.

MRS PEARCE: You see now what comes of being saucy. [*indicating the door*] This way, please.

LIZA [*almost in tears*]: I didnt want no clothes. I wouldnt have taken them. [*She throws away the handkerchief.*] I can buy my own clothes.

HIGGINS [*deftly retrieving the handkerchief and intercepting her on her reluctant way to the door*]: Youre an ungrateful wicked girl. This is my return for offering to take you out of the gutter and dress you beautifully and make a lady of you.

MRS PEARCE: Stop, Mr Higgins. I wont allow it. It's you that are wicked. Go home to your parents, girl; and tell them to take better care of you.

LIZA: I aint got no parents. They told me I was big enough to earn my own living and turned me out.

MRS PEARCE: Wheres your mother?

LIZA: I aint got no mother. Her that turned me out was my sixth stepmother. But I done without them. And I'm a good girl, I am.

HIGGINS: Very well, then, what on earth is all this fuss about? The girl doesnt belong to anybody—is no use of anybody but me. [*He goes to Mrs Pearce and begins coaxing.*] You can adopt her, Mrs Pearce: I'm sure a daughter would be a great amusement to you. Now dont make any more fuss. Take her downstairs; and—

MRS PEARCE: But whats to become of her? Is she to be paid anything? Do be sensible, sir.

HIGGINS: Oh, pay her whatever is necessary: put it down in the housekeeping book. [*impatiently*] What on earth will she want with money? She'll have her food and her clothes. She'll only drink if you give her money.

LIZA [*turning on him*]: Oh you are a brute. It's a lie: nobody ever saw the sign of liquor on me. [*to Pickering*]: Oh, sir: youre a gentleman: dont let him speak to me like that.

PICKERING [*in good-humoured remonstrance*]: Does it occur to you, Higgins, that the girl has some feelings?

HIGGINS [*looking critically at her*]: Oh no, I dont think so. Not any feelings that we need bother about. [*cheerily*]: Have you, Eliza?

LIZA: I got my feelings same as anyone else.

HIGGINS [*to Pickering, reflectively*]: You see the difficulty?

PICKERING: Eh? What difficulty?

HIGGINS: To get her to talk grammar. The mere pronunciation is easy enough.

LIZA: I dont want to talk grammar. I want to talk like a lady in a flower-shop.

MRS PEARCE: Will you please keep to the point, Mr Higgins. I want to know on what terms the girl is to be here. Is she to have any wages? And what is to become of her when youve finished your teaching? You must look ahead a little.

HIGGINS [*impatiently*]: Whats to become of her if I leave her in the gutter? Tell me that, Mrs Pearce.

MRS PEARCE: Thats her own business, not yours, Mr Higgins.

HIGGINS: Well, when Ive done with her, we can throw her back into the gutter; and then it will be her own business again; so thats all right.

LIZA: Oh, youve no feeling heart in you: you dont care for nothing but yourself. [*She rises and takes the floor resolutely.*] Here! Ive had enough of this. I'm going. [*making for the door*] You ought to be ashamed of yourself, you ought.

HIGGINS [*snatching a chocolate cream from the piano, his eyes suddenly beginning to twinkle with mischief*]: Have some chocolates, Eliza.

LIZA [*halting, tempted*]: How do I know what might be in them? Ive heard of girls being drugged by the likes of you.

> *Higgins whips out his penknife; cuts a chocolate in two; puts one half into his mouth and bolts it; and offers her the other half.*

HIGGINS: Pledge of good faith, Eliza. I eat one half: you eat the other. [*Liza opens her mouth to retort: he pops the half chocolate into it.*] You shall have boxes of them, barrels of them, every day. You shall live on them. Eh?

LIZA [*who has disposed of the chocolate after being nearly choked by it*]: I wouldnt have ate it, only I'm too ladylike to take it out of my mouth.

HIGGINS: Listen, Eliza. I think you said you came in a taxi.

LIZA: Well, what if I did? Ive as good a right to take a taxi as anyone else.

HIGGINS: You have, Eliza; and in future you shall have as many taxis as you want. You shall go up and down and round the town in a taxi every day. Think of that, Eliza.

MRS PEARCE: Mr Higgins: youre tempting the girl. It's not right. She should think of the future.

HIGGINS: At her age! Nonsense! Time enough to think of the future when you havnt any future to think of. No, Eliza: do as this lady does: think of other people's futures; but never think of your own. Think of chocolates, and taxis, and gold, and diamonds.

LIZA: No: I dont want no gold and no diamonds. I'm a good girl, I am. [*She sits down again, with an attempt at dignity.*]

HIGGINS: You shall remain so, Eliza, under the care of Mrs Pearce. And you shall marry an officer in the Guards, with a beautiful moustache: the son of a marquis, who will disinherit him for marrying you, but will relent when he sees your beauty and goodness—

PICKERING: Excuse me, Higgins; but I really must interfere. Mrs Pearce is quite right. If this girl is to put herself in your hands for six months for an experiment in teaching, she must understand thoroughly what she's doing.

HIGGINS: How can she? She's incapable of understanding anything. Besides, do any of us understand what we are doing? If we did, would we ever do it?

PICKERING: Very clever, Higgins; but not to the present point. [*to Eliza*]: Miss Doolittle—

LIZA [*overwhelmed*]: Ah-ah-ow-oo!

HIGGINS: There! Thats all youll get out of Eliza. Ah-ah-ow-oo! No use explaining. As a military man you ought to know that. Give her her orders: thats enough for her. Eliza: you are to live here for the next six months, learning how to speak beautifully, like a lady in a florist's shop. If youre good and do whatever youre told, you shall sleep in a proper bedroom, and have lots to eat, and money to buy chocolates and take rides in taxis. If youre naughty and idle you will sleep in the back kitchen among the black beetles, and be walloped by Mrs Pearce with a broom stick. At the end of six months you shall go to Buckingham Palace in a carriage, beautifully dressed. If the King finds out youre not a lady, you will be taken by the police to the Tower of London, where your head will be cut off as a warning to other presumptuous flower girls. If you are not found out, you shall have a present of seven-and-sixpence to start life with as a lady in a shop. If you refuse this offer you will be a most ungrateful wicked girl; and the angels will weep for you. [*To Pickering*]: Now are you satisfied, Pickering? [*to Mrs Pearce*]: Can I put it more plainly and fairly, Mrs Pearce?

MRS PEARCE [*patiently*]: I think youd better let me speak to the girl properly in private. I dont know that I can take charge of her or consent to the arrangement at all. Of course I know you dont mean her any harm; but when you get what you call interested in people's accents, you never think or care what may happen to them or you. Come with me, Eliza.

HIGGINS: Thats all right. Thank you, Mrs Pearce. Bundle her off to the bathroom.

LIZA [*rising reluctantly and suspiciously*]: Youre a great bully, you are. I wont stay here if I dont like. I wont let nobody wallop me. I never asked to go to Bucknam Palace, I didnt. I was never in trouble with the police, not me. I'm a good girl—

MRS PEARCE: Dont answer back, girl. You dont understand the gentleman. Come with me. [*She leads the way to the door, and holds it open for Eliza.*]

LIZA [*as she goes out*]: Well, what I say is right. I wont go near the King, not if I'm going to have my head cut off. If I'd known what I was letting myself in for, I wouldnt have come here. I always been a good girl; and I never offered to say a word to him; and I dont owe him nothing; and I dont care; and I wont be put upon; and I have my feelings the same as anyone else—

    Mrs Pearce shuts the door; and Eliza's plaints are no longer audible.

*   *   *

    Eliza is taken upstairs to the third floor greatly to her surprise, for she expected to be taken down to the scullery. There Mrs Pearce opens a door and take her into a spare bedroom.

MRS PEARCE: I will have to put you here. This will be your bedroom.

LIZA: O-h, I couldnt sleep here, missus. It's too good for the likes of me. I should be afraid to touch anything. I aint a duchess yet, you know.

MRS PEARCE: You have got to make yourself as clean as the room: then you wont be afraid of it. And you must call me Mrs Pearce, not missus. [*She throws open the door of the dressing-room, now modernized as a bathroom.*]

LIZA: Gawd! whats this? Is this where you wash clothes? Funny sort of copper I call it.

MRS PEARCE: It is not a copper. This is where we wash ourselves, Eliza, and where I am going to wash you.

LIZA: You expect me to get into that and wet myself all over! Not me. I should catch my death. I knew a woman did it every Saturday night; and she died of it.

MRS PEARCE: Mr Higgins has the gentlemen's bathroom downstairs; and he has a bath every morning, in cold water.

LIZA: Ugh! He's made of iron, that man.

MRS PEARCE: If you are to sit with him and the Colonel and be taught you will have to do the same. They wont like the smell of you if you dont. But you can have the water as hot as you like. There are two taps: hot and cold.

LIZA [*weeping*]: I couldnt. I dursnt. Its not natural: it would kill me. Ive never had a bath in my life: not what youd call a proper one.

MRS PEARCE: Well, dont you want to be clean and sweet and decent, like a lady? You know you cant be a nice girl inside if youre a dirty slut outside.

LIZA: Boohoo!!!!

MRS PEARCE: Now stop crying and go back into your room and take off all your clothes. Then wrap yourself in this [*taking down a gown from its peg and handing it to her*] and come back to me. I will get the bath ready.

LIZA [*all tears*]: I cant. I wont. I'm not used to it. Ive never took off all my clothes before. It's not right: it's not decent.

MRS PEARCE: Nonsense, child. Dont you take off all your clothes every night when you go to bed?

LIZA [*amazed*]: No. Why should I? I should catch my death. Of course I take off my skirt.

MRS PEARCE: Do you meant that you sleep in the underclothes you wear in the daytime?

LIZA: What else have I to sleep in?

MRS PEARCE: You will never do that again as long as you live here. I will get you a proper nightdress.

LIZA: Do you mean change into cold things and lie awake shivering half the night? You want to kill me, you do.

MRS PEARCE: I want to change you from a frowzy slut to a clean respectable girl fit to sit with the gentlemen in the study. Are you going to trust me and do what I tell you or be thrown out and sent back to your flower basket?

LIZA: But you dont know what the cold is to me. You dont know how I dread it.

MRS PEARCE: Your bed wont be cold here: I will put a hot water bottle in it. [*pushing her into the bedroom*] Off with you and undress.

LIZA: Oh, if only I'd a known what a dreadful thing it is to be clean I'd never have come. I didnt know when I was well off. I—[*Mrs Pearce pushes her through the door, but leaves it partly open lest her prisoner should take to flight.*]

> Mrs Pearce puts on a pair of white rubber sleeves, and fills the bath mixing hot and cold, and testing the result with the bath thermometer. She perfumes it with a handful of bath salts and adds a palmful of mustard. She then takes a formidable looking long handled scrubbing brush and soaps it profusely with a ball of scented soap.

> Eliza comes back with nothing on but the bath gown huddled tightly around her, a piteous spectacle of abject terror.

MRS PEARCE: Now come along. Take that think off.

LIZA: Oh I couldnt, Mrs Pearce: I reely couldnt. I never done such a thing.

MRS PEARCE: Nonsense. Here: step in and tell me whether it's hot enough for you.

LIZA: Ah-oo! Ah-hoo! It's too hot.

MRS PEARCE [*deftly snatching the gown away and throwing Eliza down on her back*]: It wont hurt you.

> She sets to work with the scrubbing brush.

> Eliza's screams are heartrending.

* * *

> Meanwhile the Colonel has been having it out with Higgins about Eliza. Pickering has come from the hearth to the chair and seated himself astride of it with his arms on the back to cross-examine him.

PICKERING: Excuse the straight question, Higgins. Are you a man of good character where women are concerned?

HIGGINS [*moodily*]: Have you ever met a man of good character where women are concerned?

PICKERING: Yes: very frequently.

HIGGINS [*dogmatically, lifting himself on his hands to the level of the piano, and sitting on it with a bounce*]: Well, I havnt. I find that the moment I let a woman make friends with me, she becomes jealous, exacting, suspicious, and a damned nuisance. I find that the moment I let myself make friends with a woman, I become selfish and tyrannical. Women upset everything. When you let them into your life, you find that the woman is driving at one thing and youre driving at another.

PICKERING: At what, for example?

HIGGINS [*coming off the piano restlessly*]: Oh, Lord knows! I suppose the woman wants to live her own life; and the man wants to live his; and each tries to drag the other on to the wrong track. One wants to go north and the other south; and the result is that both have to go east, though they both hate the east wind. [*He sits down on the bench at the keyboard.*] So here I am, confirmed old bachelor, and likely to remain so.

PICKERING [*rising and standing over him gravely*]: Come, Higgins! You know what I mean. If I'm to be in this business I shall feel responsible for that girl. I hope it's understood that no advantage is to be taken of her position.

HIGGINS: What! That thing! Sacred, I assure you. [*rising to explain*] You see, she'll be a pupil; and teaching would be impossible unless pupils were sacred. Ive taught scores of American millionairesses how to speak English: the best looking women in the world. I'm seasoned. They might as well be blocks of wood. I might as well be a block of wood. It's—

> *Mrs Pearce opens the door. She has Eliza's hat in her hand. Pickering retires to the easy-chair at the hearth and sits down.*

HIGGINS [*eagerly*]: Well, Mrs Pearce: is it all right?

MRS PEARCE [*at the door*]: I just wish to trouble you with a word, if I may, Mr Higgins.

HIGGINS: Yes, certainly. Come in. [*She comes forward.*] Dont burn that, Mrs Pearce. I'll keep it as a curiosity. [*He takes the hat.*]

MRS PEARCE: Handle it carefully, sir, p l e a s e. I had to promise her not to burn it; but I had better put it in the oven for a while.

HIGGINS [*putting it down hastily on the piano*]: Oh! thank you. Well, what have you to say to me?

PICKERING: Am I in the way?

MRS PEARCE: Not at all, sir. Mr Higgins: will you please be very particular what you say before the girl?

HIGGINS [*sternly*]: Of course. I'm always particular about what I say. Why do you say this to me?

MRS PEARCE [*unmoved*]: No, sir: youre not at all particular when youve mislaid anything or when you get a little impatient. Now it doesnt matter before me: I'm used to it. But you really must not swear before the girl.

HIGGINS [*indignantly*]: I swear! [*most emphatically*]: I never swear. I detest the habit. What the devil do you mean?

MRS PEARCE [*stolidly*]: Thats what I mean, sir. You swear a great deal too much. I dont mind your damning and blasting, and w h a t the devil and w h e r e the devil and w h o the devil—

HIGGINS: Mrs Pearce: this language from your lips! Really!

MRS PEARCE [*not to be put off*]—but there is a certain word I must ask you not to use. The girl used it herself when she began to enjoy the bath. It begins with the same letter as bath. She knows no better; she learnt it at her mother's knee. But she must not hear it from your lips.

HIGGINS [*loftily*]: I cannot charge myself with having ever uttered it, Mrs Pearce. [*She looks at him steadfastly. He adds, hiding an uneasy conscience with a judicial air*]: Except perhaps in a moment of extreme and justifiable excitement.

MRS PEARCE: Only this morning, sir, you applied it to your boots, to the butter, and to the brown bread.

HIGGINS: Oh, that! Mere alliteration, Mrs Pearce, natural to a poet.

MRS PEARCE: Well, sir, whatever you choose to call it, I beg you not to let the girl hear you repeat it.

HIGGINS: Oh, very well, very well. Is that all?

MRS PEARCE: No, sir. We shall have to be very particular with this girl as to personal cleanliness.

HIGGINS: Certainly. Quite right. Most important.

MRS PEARCE: I mean not to be slovenly about her dress or untidy in leaving things about.

HIGGINS [*going to her solemnly*]: Just so. I intended to call your attention to that. [*He passes on to Pickering, who is enjoying the conversation immensely.*] It is these little things that matter, Pickering. Take care of the pence and the pounds will take care of themselves is true of personal habits as of money. [*He comes to anchor on the hearthrug, with the air of a man in an unassailable position.*]

MRS PEARCE: Yes, sir. Then might I ask you not to come down to breakfast in your dressing-gown, or at any rate not to use it as a napkin to the extent you do, sir. And if you would be so good as not to eat everything off the same plate, and to remember not to put the porridge saucepan out of your hand on the clean table-cloth, it would be a better example to the girl. You know you nearly choked yourself with a fishbone in the jam only last week.

HIGGINS [*routed from the hearthrug and drifting back to the piano*]: I may do these things sometimes in absence of mind; but surely I dont do them habitually. [*angrily*] By the way: my dressing-gown smells most damnably of benzine.

MRS PEARCE: No doubt it does, Mr Higgins. But if you will wipe your fingers—

HIGGINS [*yelling*]: Oh very well, very well: I'll wipe them in my hair in future.

MRS PEARCE: I hope youre not offended, Mr Higgins.

HIGGINS [*shocked at finding himself thought capable of an unamiable sentiment*]: Not at all, not at all. Youre quite right, Mrs Pearce: I shall be particularly careful before the girl. Is that all?

MRS PEARCE: No, sir. Might she use some of those Japanese dresses you brought from abroad? I really cant put her back into her old things.

HIGGINS: Certainly. Anything you like. Is t h a t all?

MRS PEARCE: Thank you, sir. Thats all. [*She goes out.*]

HIGGINS: You know, Pickering, that woman has the most extraordinary ideas about me. Here I am, a shy, diffident sort of man. Ive never been able to feel really grown-up and tremendous, like other chaps. And yet she's firmly persuaded that I'm an arbitrary overbearing bossing kind of person. I cant account for it.

> *Mrs Pearce returns.*

MRS PEARCE: If you please, sir, the trouble's beginning already. Theres a dustman downstairs, Alfred Doodlittle, wants to see you. He says you have his daughter here.

PICKERING [*rising*]: Phew! I say!

HIGGINS [*promptly*]: Send the blackguard up.

MRS PEARCE: Oh, very well, sir. [*She goes out.*]

PICKERING: He may not be a blackguard, Higgins.

HIGGINS: Nonsense. Of course he's a blackguard.

PICKERING: Whether he is or not, I'm afraid we shall have some trouble with him.

HIGGINS [*confidently*]: Oh no: I think not. If theres any trouble he shall have it with me, not I with him. And we are sure to get something interesting out of him.

PICKERING: About the girl?

HIGGINS: No. I mean his dialect.

PICKERING: Oh!

MRS PEARCE [*at the door*]: Doolittle, sir. [*She admits Doolittle and retires.*]

> *Alfred Doolittle is an elderly but vigorous dustman, clad in the costume of his profession, including a hat with a back brim covering his neck and shoulders. He has well marked and rather interesting features, and seems equally free from fear and conscience. He has a remarkably expressive voice, the result of a habit of giving vent to his feelings without reserve. His present pose is that of wounded honour and stern resolution.*

DOOLITTLE [*at the door, uncertain which of the two gentlemen is his man*]: Professor Iggins?

HIGGINS: Here. Good morning. Sit down.

DOOLITTLE: Morning, Governor. [*He sits down magisterially.*] I come about a very serious matter, Governor.

HIGGINS [*to Pickering*]: Brought up in Hounslow. Mother Welsh. I should think. [*Doolittle opens his mouth, amazed. Higgins continues*]: What do you want, Doolittle?

DOOLITTLE [*menacingly*]: I want my daughter: thats what I want. See?

HIGGINS: Of course you do. Youre her father, arnt you? You dont suppose anyone else wants her, do you? I'm glad to see you have some spark of family feeling left. She's upstairs. Take her away at once.

DOOLITTLE [*rising, fearfully taken aback*]: What!

HIGGINS: Take her away. Do you suppose I'm going to keep your daughter for you?

DOOLITTLE [*remonstrating*]: Now, now, look here, Governor. Is this reasonable? Is it fairity to take advantage of a man like this? The girl belongs to me. You got her. Where do I come in? [*He sits down again.*]

HIGGINS: Your daughter had the audacity to come to my house and ask me to teach her how to speak properly so that she could get a place in a flower-shop. This gentleman and my housekeeper have been here all the time. [*bullying him*] How dare you come here and attempt to blackmail me? You sent her here on purpose.

DOOLITTLE [*protesting*]: No, Governor.

HIGGINS: You must have. How else could you possibly know that she is here?

DOOLITTLE: Dont take a man up like that, Governor.

HIGGINS: The police shall take you up. This is a plant—a plot to extort money by threats. I shall telephone for the police. [*He goes resolutely to the telephone and opens the directory.*]

DOOLITTLE: Have I asked you for a brass farthing? I leave it to the gentleman here: have I said a word about money?

HIGGINS [*throwing the book aside and marching down on Doolittle with a poser*]: What else did you come for?

DOOLITTLE [*sweetly*]: Well, what w o u l d a man come for? Be human, Governor.

HIGGINS [*disarmed*]: Alfred: did you put her up to it?

DOOLITTLE: So help me, Governor, I never did. I take my Bible oath I aint seen the girl these two months past.

HIGGINS: Then how did you know she was here?

DOOLITTLE ['*most musical, most melancholy*']: I'll tell you, Governor, if youll only let me get a word in. I'm willing to tell you. I'm wanting to tell you. I'm waiting to tell you.

HIGGINS: Pickering: this chap has a certain natural gift of rhetoric. Observe the rhythm of his native woodnotes wild. 'I'm willing to tell you: I'm wanting to tell you: I'm waiting to tell you.' Sentimental rhetoric! thats the Welsh strain in him. It also accounts for his mendacity and dishonesty.

PICKERING: Oh, p l e a s e, Higgins: I'm west country myself. [*to Doolittle*] How did you know the girl was here if you didnt send her?

DOOLITTLE: It was like this, Governor. The girl took a boy in the taxi to give him a jaunt. Son of her landlady, he is. He hung about on the chance of her giving him another ride home. Well, she sent him back for her luggage when she heard you was willing for her to stop here. I met the boy at the corner of Long Acre and Endell Street.

HIGGINS: Public house. Yes?

DOOLITTLE: The poor man's club, Governor: why shouldnt I?

PICKERING: Do let him tell his story, Higgins.

DOOLITTLE: He told me what was up. And I ask you, what was my feelings and my duty as a father? I says to the boy, 'You bring me the luggage,' I says—

PICKERING: Why didnt you go for it yourself?

DOOLITTLE: Landlady wouldnt have trusted me with it, Governor. She's that kind of woman: y o u know. I had to give the boy a penny afore he trusted me with it, the little swine. I brought it to her just to oblige you like, and make myself agreeable. Thats all.

HIGGINS: How much luggage?

DOOLITTLE: Musical instrument, Governor. A few pictures, a trifle of jewellery, and a bird-cage. She said she didnt want no clothes. What was I to think from that, Governor? I ask you as a parent what was I to think?

HIGGINS: So you came to rescue her from worse than death, eh?

DOOLITTLE [*appreciatively: relieved at being so well understood*]: Just so, Governor. Thats right.

PICKERING: But why did you bring her luggage if you intended to take her away?

DOOLITTLE: Have I said a word about taking her away? Have I now?

HIGGINS [*determinedly*]: Youre going to take her away, double quick. [*He crosses to the hearth and rings the bell.*]

DOOLITTLE [*rising*]: No, Governor. Dont say that. I'm not the man to stand in my girl's light. Heres a career opening for her, as you might say; and—

Mrs Pearce opens the door and awaits orders.

HIGGINS: Mrs Pearce: this is Eliza's father. He has come to take her away. Give her to him. [*He goes back to the piano, with an air of washing his hands of the whole affair.*]

DOOLITTLE: No. This is a misunderstanding. Listen here—

MRS PEARCE: He cant take her away, Mr Higgins: how can he? You told me to burn her clothes.

DOOLITTLE: Thats right. I cant carry the girl through the streets like a blooming monkey, can I? I put it to you.

HIGGINS: You have put it to me that you want your daughter. Take your daughter. If she has no clothes go out and buy her some.

DOOLITTLE [*desperate*]: Wheres the clothes she come in? Did I burn them or did your missus here?

MRS PEARCE: I am the housekeeper, if you please. I have sent for some clothes for your girl. When they come you can take her away. You can wait in the kitchen. This way, please.

Doolittle, much troubled, accompanies her to the door; then hesitates; finally turns confidentially to Higgins.

DOOLITTLE: Listen here, Governor. You and me is men of the world, aint we?

HIGGINS: Oh! Men of the world, are we? Youd better go, Mrs Pearce.

MRS PEARCE: I think so, indeed, sir. [*She goes, with dignity.*]

PICKERING: The floor is yours, Mr Doolittle.

DOOLITTLE [*to Pickering*]: I thank you, Governor. [*to Higgins, who takes refuge on the piano bench, a little overwhelmed by the proximity of his visitor; for Doolittle has a professional flavour of dust about him.*] Well, the truth is, Ive taken a sort of fancy to you, Governor; and if you want the girl, I'm not so set on having her back home again but what I might be open to an arrangement. Regarded in the light of a young woman, she's a fine handsome girl. As a daughter she's not worth her keep; and so I tell you straight. All I ask is my rights as a father; and youre the last man alive to expect me to let her go for nothing; for I can see youre one of the straight sort, Governor. Well, whats a five-pound note to you? and whats Eliza to me? [*He turns to his chair and sits down judicially.*]

PICKERING: I think you ought to know, Doolittle, that Mr Higgins's intentions are entirely honourable.

DOOLITTLE: Course they are, Governor. If I thought they wasnt, I'd ask fifty.

HIGGINS [*revolted*]: Do you mean to say that you would sell your daughter for £50?

DOOLITTLE: Not in a general way I wouldnt; but to oblige a gentleman like you I'd do a good deal, I do assure you.

PICKERING: Have you no morals, man?

DOOLITTLE [*unabashed*]: Cant afford them, Governor. Neither could you if you was as poor as me. Not that I mean any harm, you know. But if Liza is going to have a bit out of this, why not me too?

HIGGINS [*troubled*]: I dont know what to do, Pickering. There can be no question that as a matter of morals it's a positive crime to give this chap a farthing. And yet I feel a sort of rough justice in his claim.

DOOLITTLE: Thats it, Governor. Thats all I say. A father's heart, as it were.

PICKERING: Well, I know the feeling; but really it seems hardly right—

DOOLITTLE: Dont say that, Governor. Dont look at it that way. What am I, Governors both? I ask you, what a m I? I'm the one of the undeserving poor: thats what I am. Think of what that means to a man. It means that he's up agen middle class moral-ity all the time. If theres anything going, and I put in for a bit of it, it's always the same story: 'Youre undeserving; so you cant have it.' But my needs is as great as the most deserving widow's that ever got money out of six different charities in one week for the death of the same husband. I dont need less than a deserving man: I need more. I dont eat less hearty than him; and I drink a lot more. I want a bit of amusement, cause I'm a thinking man. I want cheerfulness and a song and a band when I feel low. Well, they charge me just the same for everything as they charge the deserving. What is middle class morality? Just an excuse for never giving me anything. Therefore, I ask you, as two gentlemen, not to play that game on me. I'm playing straight with you. I aint pretending to be deserving. I'm undeserving; and I mean to go on being undeserving. I like it; and thats the truth. Will you take advantage of a man's nature to do him out of the price of his own daughter what he's brought up and fed and clothed by the sweat of his brow until she's growed big enough to be interesting to you two gentlemen? Is five pounds unreasonable? I put it to you; and I leave it to you.

HIGGINS [*rising, and going over to Pickering*]: Pickering: if we were to take this man in hand for three months, he could choose between a seat in the Cabinet and a pop-ular pulpit in Wales.

PICKERING: What do you say to that, Doolittle?

DOOLITTLE: Not me, Governor, thank you kindly. Ive heard all the preachers and all the prime ministers—for I'm a thinking man and game for politics or religion or social reform same as all the other amusements—and I tell you it's a dog's life any way you look at it. Undeserving poverty is my line. Taking one station in society with another, it's—it's—well, it's the only one that has any ginger in it, to my taste.

HIGGINS: I suppose we must give him a fiver.

PICKERING: He'll make a bad use of it, I'm afraid.

DOOLITTLE: Not me, Governor, so help me I wont. Dont you be afraid that I'll save it and spare it and live idle on it. There wont be a penny of it left by Monday: I'll have to go to work same as if I'd never had it. It wont pauperize me, you bet. Just one good spree for myself and the missus, giving pleasure to ourselves and employment to others, and satisfaction to you to think it's not been throwed away. You couldnt spend it better.

HIGGINS [*taking out his pocket book and coming between Doolittle and the piano*]: This is irresistible. Lets give him ten. [*He offers two notes to the dustman.*]

DOOLITTLE: No, Governor. She wouldnt have the heart to spend ten; and perhaps I shouldnt either. Ten pounds is a lot of money: it makes a man feel prudent like; and then goodbye to happiness. You give me what I ask you, Governor: not a penny more, and not a penny less.

PICKERING: Why dont you marry that missus of yours? I rather draw the line at encouraging that sort of immorality.

DOOLITTLE: Tell her so, Governor: tell her so. *I*'m willing. It's me that suffers by it. Ive no hold on her. I got to be agreeable to her. I got to give her presents. I got to buy her clothes something sinful. I'm a slave to that woman, Governor, just because I'm not her lawful husband. And she knows it too. Catch her marrying me! Take my advice, Governor: marry Eliza while she's young and dont know no better. If you dont youll be sorry for it after. If you do, s h e ' l l be sorry for it after; but better her than you, because youre a man, and she's only a woman and dont know how to be happy anyhow.

HIGGINS: Pickering: if we listen to this man another minute, we shall have no convictions left. [*to Doolittle*]: Five pounds I think you said.

DOOLITTLE: Thank you kindly, Governor.

HIGGINS: Youre sure you wont take ten?

DOOLITTLE: Not now. Another time, Governor.

HIGGINS [*handing him a five-pound note*]: Here you are.

DOOLITTLE: Thank you, Governor. Good morning. [*He hurries to the door, anxious to get away with his booty. When he opens it he is confronted with a dainty and exquisitely clean young Japanese lady in a simple blue cotton kimono printed cunningly with small white jasmine blossoms. Mrs Pearce is with her. He gets out of her way deferentially and apologizes.*] Beg pardon miss.

THE JAPANESE LADY: Garn! Dont you know your own daughter?

DOOLITTLE:	}	*exclaiming*	{	Bly me! it's Eliza!
HIGGINS:	}	*simul-*	{	Whats that? This!
PICKERING:	}	*taneously*	{	By Jove!

LIZA: Dont I look silly?

MRS PEARCE [*at the door*]: Now, Mr Higgins, please dont say anything to make the girl conceited about herself.

HIGGINS [*conscientiously*]: Oh! Quite right, Mrs Pearce. [*to Eliza*]: Yes: damned silly.

MRS PEARCE: Please, sir.

HIGGINS [*correcting himself*]: I mean extremely silly.

LIZA: I should look all right with my hat on. [*She takes up her hat; puts it on; and walks across the room to the fireplace with a fashionable air.*]

HIGGINS: A new fashion, by George! And it ought to look horrible!

DOOLITTLE [*with fatherly pride*]: Well, I never thought she'd clean up as good looking as that, Governor. She's a credit to me, aint she?

LIZA: I tell you, it's easy to clean up here. Hot and cold water on tap, just as much as you like, there is. Woolly towels, there is; and a towel horse so hot, it burns your fingers. Soft brushes to scrub yourself, and a wooden bowl of soap smelling like primroses. Now I know why ladies is so clean. Washing's a treat for them. Wish they could see what it is for the like of me!

HIGGINS: I'm glad the bathroom met with your approval.

LIZA: It didnt: not all of it; and I dont care who hears me say it. Mrs Pearce knows.

HIGGINS: What was wrong, Mrs Pearce?

MRS PEARCE [*blandly*]: Oh, nothing, sir. It doesnt matter.

LIZA: I had a good mind to break it. I didnt know which way to look. But I hung a towel over it, I did.

HIGGINS: Over what?

MRS PEARCE: Over the looking-glass, sir.

HIGGINS: Doolittle: you have brought your daughter up too strictly.

DOOLITTLE: Me! I never brought her up at all, except to give her a lick of a strap now and again. Dont put it on me. Governor. She aint accustomed to it, you see: thats all. But she'll soon pick up your free-and-easy ways.

LIZA: I'm a good girl, I am; and I wont pick up no free-and-easy ways.

HIGGINS: Eliza: if you say again that youre a good girl, your father shall take you home.

LIZA: Not him. You dont know my father. All he come here for was to touch you for some money to get drunk on.

DOOLITTLE: Well, what else would I want money for? To put into the plate in church, I suppose. [*She puts out her tongue at him. He is so incensed by this that Pickering presently finds it necessary to step between them.*] Dont you give me none of your lip; and dont let me hear you giving this gentleman any of it either, or youll hear from me about it. See?

HIGGINS: Have you any further advice to give her before you go, Doolittle? Your blessing, for instance.

DOOLITTLE: No, Governor: I aint such a mug as to put up my children to all I know myself. Hard enough to hold them in without that. If you want Eliza's mind improved, Governor, you do it yourself with a strap. So long, gentlemen. [*He turns to go.*]

HIGGINS [*impressively*]: Stop. Youll come regularly to see your daughter. It's your duty, you know. My brother is a clergyman; and he could help you in your talks with her.

DOOLITTLE [*evasively*]: Certainly, I'll come, Governor. Not just this week, because I have a job at a distance. But later on you may depend on me. Afternoon, gentlemen. Afternoon, maam. [*He touches his hat to Mrs Pearce, who disdains the salutation and goes out. He winks at Higgins, thinking him probably a fellow sufferer from Mrs Pearce's difficult disposition, and follows her.*]

LIZA: Dont you believe the old liar. He'd as soon you set a bulldog on him as a clergyman. You wont see him again in a hurry.

HIGGINS: I dont want to, Eliza. Do you?

LIZA: Not me. I dont want to see him again, I dont. He's a disgrace to me, he is, collecting dust, instead of working at his trade.

PICKERING: What is his trade, Eliza?

LIZA: Talking money out of other people's pockets into his own. His proper trade's a navvy; and he works at it sometimes too—for exercise—and earns good money at it. Aint you going to call me Miss Doolittle any more?

PICKERING: I beg your pardon, Miss Doolittle. It was a slip of the tongue.

LIZA: Oh, I dont mind; only it sounded so genteel. I s h o u l d just like to take a taxi to the corner of Tottenham Court road and get out there and tell it to wait for me, just to put the girls in their place a bit. I wouldnt speak to them, you know.

PICKERING: Better wait til we get you something really fashionable.

HIGGINS: Besides, you shouldnt cut your old friends now that you have risen in the world. Thats what we call snobbery.

LIZA: You dont call the like of them my friends now, I should hope. Theyve took it out of me often enough with their ridicule when they had the chance; and now I mean to get a bit of my own back. But if I'm to have fashionable clothes, I'll wait. I should like to have some. Mrs Pearce says youre going to give me some to wear in bed at night different to what I wear in the daytime; but it do seem a waste of money when you could get something to shew. Besides, I never could fancy changing into cold things on a winter night.

MRS PEARCE [*coming back*]: Now, Eliza. The new things have come for you to try on.

LIZA: Ah-ow-oo-ooh! [*She rushes out.*]

MRS PEARCE [*following her*]: Oh, dont rush about like that, girl. [*She shuts the door behind her.*]

HIGGINS: Pickering: we have taken on a stiff job.

PICKERING [*with conviction*]: Higgins: we have.

* * *

> There seems to be some curiosity as to what Higgins's lessons to Eliza were like. Well, here is a sample: the first one.
>
> Picture Eliza, in her new clothes, and feeling her inside put out of step by a lunch, dinner, and breakfast of a kind to which it is unaccustomed, seated with Higgins and the Colonel in the study, feeling like a hospital out-patient at a first encounter with the doctors.

Higgins, constitutionally unable to sit still, discomposes her still more by striding restlessly about. But for the reassuring presence and quietude of her friend the Colonel she would run for her life, even back to Drury Lane.

HIGGINS: Say your alphabet.

LIZA: I know my alphabet. Do you think I know nothing? I dont need to be taught like a child.

HIGGINS [*thundering*]: Say your alphabet.

PICKERING: Say it, Miss Doolittle. You will understand presently. Do what he tells you; and let him teach you in his own way.

LIZA: Oh well, if you put it like that—Ahyee, bəyee, cəyee, dəyee—

HIGGINS [*with a roar of a wounded lion*]: Stop. Listen to this, Pickering. This is what we pay for as elementary education. This unfortunate animal has been locked up for nine years in school at our expense to teach her to speak and read the language of Shakespeare and Milton. And the result is Ahyee, Bə-yee, Cə-yee, Də-yee. [*to Eliza*]: Say A, B, C, D.

LIZA [*almost in tears*]: But I'm sayin it. Ahyee, Bəyee, Cə-yee—

HIGGINS: Stop. Say a cup of tea.

LIZA: A cappətə-ee.

HIGGINS: Put your tongue forward until it squeezes against the top of your lower teeth. Now say cup.

LIZA: C-c-c—I cant. C-Cup.

PICKERING: Good. Splendid, Miss Doolittle.

HIGGINS: By Jupiter, she's done it at the first shot. Pickering: we shall make a duchess of her. [*to Eliza*]: Now do you think you could possibly say tea? Not tə-yee, mind: if you ever say bə-yee cə-yee də-yee again you shall be dragged round the room three times by the hair of your head. [*fortissimo*] T, T, T, T.

LIZA [*weeping*]: I cant hear no difference cep that it sound more genteel-like when you say it.

HIGGINS: Well, if you can hear that difference, what the devil are you crying for? Pickering: give her a chocolate.

PICKERING: No, no. Never mind crying a little, Miss Doolittle: you are doing very well; and the lessons wont hurt. I promise you I wont let him drag you round the room by your hair.

HIGGINS: Be off with you to Mrs Pearce and tell her about it. Think about it. Try to do it by yourself: and keep your tongue well forward in your mouth instead of trying to roll it up and swallow it. Another lesson at half-past four this afternoon. Away with you.

Eliza, still sobbing, rushes from the room.

And that is the sort of ordeal poor Eliza has to go through for months before we meet her again on her first appearance in London society of the professional class.

ACT III

It is Mrs Higgins's at-home day. Nobody has yet arrived. Her drawing room, in a flat on Chelsea Embankment, has three windows looking on the river; and the ceiling is not so lofty as it would be in an older house of the same pretensions. The windows are open, giving access to a balcony with flower pots. If you stand with your face to the windows, you have the fireplace on your left and the door in the right-hand wall close to the corner nearest the windows.

Mrs Higgins was brought up on Morris and Burne Jones; and her room, which is very unlike her son's room in Wimpole Street, is not crowded with furniture and little tables and nicknacks. In the middle of the room there is a big ottoman; and this, with the carpet, the Morris wall-papers, and the Morris chintz window curtains and brocade covers of the ottoman and its cushions, supply all the ornament, and are much too handsome to be hidden by odds and ends of useless things. A few good oil-paintings from the exhibitions in the Grosvenor Gallery thirty years ago (the Burne Jones, not the Whistler side of them) are on the walls. The only landscape is a Cecil Lawson on the scale of a Rubens. There is a portrait of Mrs Higgins as she was when she defied fashion in her youth in one of the beautiful Rossettian costumes which, when caricatured by people who did not understand, led to the absurdities of popular estheticism in the eighteen-seventies.

In the corner diagonally opposite the door Mrs Higgins, now over sixty and long past taking the trouble to dress out of the fashion, sits writing at an elegantly simple writing-table with a bell button within reach of her hand. There is a Chippendale chair further back in the room between her and the window nearest her side. At the other side of the room, further forward, is an Elizabethan chair roughly carved in the taste of Inigo Jones. On the same side a piano in a decorated case. The corner between the fireplace and the window is occupied by a divan cushioned in Morris chintz.

It is between four and five in the afternoon.

The door is opened violently; and Higgins enters with his hat on.

MRS HIGGINS [*dismayed*]: Henry! [*scolding him*] What are you doing here today? It is my at-home day: you promised not to come. [*As he bends to kiss her, she takes his hat off, and presents it to him.*]

HIGGINS: Oh bother! [*He throws the hat down on the table.*]

MRS HIGGINS: Go home at once.

HIGGINS [*kissing her*]: I know, mother. I came on purpose.

MRS HIGGINS: But you mustnt. I'm serious, Henry. You offend all my friends: they stop coming whenever they meet you.

HIGGINS: Nonsense! I know I have no small talk; but people dont mind. [*He sits on the settee.*]

MRS HIGGINS: Oh! dont they? Small talk indeed! What about your large talk? Really, dear, you mustnt stay.

HIGGINS: I must. Ive a job for you. A phonetic job.

MRS HIGGINS: No use, dear. I'm sorry; but I cant get round your vowels; and though I like to get pretty postcards in your patent shorthand, I always have to read the copies in ordinary writing you so thoughtfully send me.

HIGGINS: Well, this isnt a phonetic job.

MRS HIGGINS: You said it was.

HIGGINS: Not your part of it. Ive picked up a girl.

MRS HIGGINS: Does that mean that some girl has picked y o u up?

HIGGINS: Not at all. I dont mean a love affair.

MRS HIGGINS: What a pity!

HIGGINS: Why?

MRS HIGGINS: Well, you never fall in love with anyone under forty-five. When will you discover that there are some rather nice-looking young women about?

HIGGINS: Oh, I cant be bothered with young women. My idea of a lovable woman is somebody as like you as possible. I shall never get into the way of seriously liking young women: some habits lie too deep to be changed. [*rising abruptly and walking about, jingling his money and his keys in his trouser pockets*] Besides, theyre all idiots.

MRS HIGGINS: Do you know what you would do if you really loved me, Henry?

HIGGINS: Oh bother! What? Marry, I suppose.

MRS HIGGINS: No. Stop fidgeting and take your hands out of your pockets. [*With a gesture of despair, he obeys and sits down again.*] Thats a good boy. Now tell me about the girl.

HIGGINS: She's coming to see you.

MRS HIGGINS: I dont remember asking her.

HIGGINS: You didnt. *I* asked her. If youd known her you wouldnt have asked her.

MRS HIGGINS: Indeed! Why?

HIGGINS: Well, it's like this. She's a common flower girl. I picked her off the kerbstone.

MRS HIGGINS: And invited her to my at-home?

HIGGINS [*rising and coming to her to coax her*]: Oh, thatll be all right. Ive taught her to speak properly; and she has strict orders as to her behaviour. She's to keep to two subjects: the weather and everybody's health—Fine day and How do you do, you know—and not to let herself go on things in general. That will be safe.

MRS HIGGINS: Safe! To talk about our health! about our insides! perhaps about our outsides! How could you be so silly, Henry?

HIGGINS [*impatiently*]: Well, she must talk about something. [*He controls himself and sits down again.*] Oh, she'll be all right: dont you fuss. Pickering is in it with me. Ive a sort of bet on that I'll pass her off as a duchess in six months. I started on her some months ago; and she's getting on like a house on fire. I shall win my bet. She has a quick ear; and she's been easier to teach than my middle-class pupils because she's had to learn a complete new language. She talks English almost as you talk French.

MRS HIGGINS: Thats satisfactory, at all events.

HIGGINS: Well, it is and it isnt.

MRS HIGGINS: What does that mean?

HIGGINS: You see, Ive got her pronunciation all right; but you have to consider not only h o w a girl pronounces, but w h a t she pronounces; and thats where—

They are interrupted by the parlour-maid, announcing guests.

THE PARLOUR-MAID: Mrs and Miss Eynsford Hill. [*She withdraws.*]

HIGGINS: Oh Lord! [*He rises; snatches his hat from the table; and makes for the door; but before he reaches it his mother introduces him.*]

Mrs and Miss Eynsford Hill are the mother and daughter who sheltered from the rain in Covent Garden. The mother is well bred, quiet, and has the habitual anxiety of straitened means. The daughter has acquired a gay air of being very much at home in society: the bravado of genteel poverty.

MRS EYNSFORD HILL [*to Mrs Higgins*]: How do you do? [*They shake hands.*]

MISS EYNSFORD HILL: How d'you do? [*She shakes.*]

MRS HIGGINS [*introducing*]: My son Henry.

MRS EYNSFORD HILL: Your celebrated son! I have so longed to meet you, Professor Higgins.

HIGGINS [*glumly, making no movement in her direction*]: Delighted. [*He backs against the piano and bows brusquely.*]

MRS EYNSFORD HILL [*going to him with confident familiarity*]: How do you do?

HIGGINS [*staring at her*]: Ive seen you before somewhere. I havnt the ghost of a notion where; but Ive heard your voice. [*drearily*] It doesnt matter. Youd better sit down.

MRS HIGGINS: I'm sorry to say that my celebrated son has no manners. You mustnt mind him.

MISS EYNSFORD HILL [*gaily*]: I dont. [*She sits in the Elizabethan chair.*]

MRS EYNSFORD HILL [*a little bewildered*]: Not at all. [*She sits on the ottoman between her daughter and Mrs Higgins, who has turned her chair away from the writing-table.*]

HIGGINS: Oh, have I been rude? I didnt mean to be.

He goes to the central window, through which, with his back to the company, he contemplates the river and the flowers in Battersea Park on the opposite bank as if they were a frozen desert.

The parlour-maid returns, ushering in Pickering.

THE PARLOUR-MAID: Colonel Pickering. [*She withdraws.*]

PICKERING: How do you do, Mrs Higgins?

MRS HIGGINS: So glad youve come. Do you know Mrs Eynsford Hill—Miss Eynsford Hill?

Exchange of bows. The Colonel brings the Chippendale chair a little forward between Mrs Hill and Mrs Higgins, and sits down.

PICKERING: Has Henry told you what weve come for?

HIGGINS [*over his shoulder*]: We were interrupted: damn it!

MRS HIGGINS: Oh Henry, Henry, really!

MRS EYNSFORD HILL [*half rising*]: Are we in the way?

MRS HIGGINS [*rising and making her sit down again*]: No, no. You couldnt have come more fortunately: we want you to meet a friend of ours.

HIGGINS [*turning hopefully*]: Yes, by George! We want two or three people. Youll do as well as anybody else.

> *The parlour-maid returns, ushering Freddy.*

THE PARLOUR-MAID: Mr Eynsford Hill.

HIGGINS [*almost audibly, past endurance*]: God of Heaven! another of them.

FREDDY [*shaking hands with Mrs Higgins*]: Ahdedo?

MRS HIGGINS: Very good of you to come. [*introducing*] Colonel Pickering.

FREDDY [*bowing*]: Ahdedo?

MRS HIGGINS: I dont think you know my son, Professor Higgins.

FREDDY [*going to Higgins*]: Ahdedo?

HIGGINS [*looking at him much as if he were a pickpocket*] I'll take my oath Ive met y o u before somewhere. Where was it?

FREDDY: I dont think so.

HIGGINS [*resignedly*]: It dont matter, anyhow. Sit down. [*He shakes Freddy's hand, and almost slings him on to the ottoman with his face to the windows; then comes round to the other side of it.*]

HIGGINS: Well, here we are, anyhow! [*He sits down on the ottoman next Mrs Eynsford Hill on her left.*] And now what the devil are we going to talk about until Eliza comes?

MRS HIGGINS: Henry: you are the life and soul of the Royal Society's soirées; but really youre rather trying on more commonplace occasions.

HIGGINS: Am I? Very sorry. [*beaming suddenly*] I suppose I am, you know. [*uproariously*] Ha, ha!

MISS EYNSFORD HILL [*who considers Higgins quite eligible matrimonially*]: I sympathize. I havnt any small talk. If people would only be frank and say what they really think!

HIGGINS [*relapsing into gloom*]: Lord forbid!

MRS EYNSFORD HILL: [*taking up her daughter's cue*]: But why?

HIGGINS: What they think they ought to think is bad enough, Lord knows; but what they really think would break up the whole show. Do you suppose it would be really agreeable if I were to come out now with what *I* really think?

MISS EYNSFORD HILL [*gaily*]: Is it so very cynical?

HIGGINS: Cynical! Who the dickens said it was cynical? I mean it wouldnt be decent.

MRS EYNSFORD HILL [*seriously*]: Oh! I'm sure you dont mean that, Mr Higgins.

HIGGINS: You see, we're all savages, more or less. We're supposed to be civilized and cultured—to know all about poetry and philosophy and art and science, and so on; but how many of us know even the meanings of these names? [*to Miss Hill*]: What do y o u know of poetry? [*to Mrs Hill*]: What do y o u know of science? [*indicating Freddy*]: What does h e know of art or science or anything else? What the devil do you imagine I know of philosophy?

MRS HIGGINS [*warningly*]: Or of manners, Henry?

THE PARLOUR-MAID [*opening the door*]: Miss Doolittle. [*She withdraws.*]

HIGGINS [*rising hastily and running to Mrs Higgins*]: Here she is, mother.

> *He stands on tiptoe and makes signs over his mother's head to Eliza to indicate to her which lady is her hostess.*

> *Eliza, who is exquisitely dressed, produces an impression of such remarkable distinction and beauty as she enters that they all rise, quite fluttered. Guided by Higgins's signals, she comes to Mrs Higgins with studied grace.*

LIZA [*speaking with pedantic correctness of pronunciation and great beauty of tone*]: How do you do, Mrs Higgins? [*She gasps slightly in making sure of the H in Higgins, but is quite successful.*] Mr Higgins told me I might come.

MRS HIGGINS [*cordially*]: Quite right: I'm very glad indeed to see you.

PICKERING: How do you do, Miss Doolittle?

LIZA [*shaking hands with him*]: Colonel Pickering, is it not?

MRS EYNSFORD HILL: I feel sure we have met before, Miss Doolittle. I remember your eyes.

LIZA: How do you do? [*She sits down on the ottoman gracefully in the place just left vacant by Higgins.*]

MRS EYNSFORD HILL [*introducing*]: My daughter Clara.

LIZA: How do you do?

CLARA [*impulsively*]: How do you do? [*She sits down on the ottoman besides Eliza, devouring her with her eyes.*]

FREDDY [*coming to their side of the ottoman*]: Ive certainly had the pleasure.

MRS EYNSFORD HILL [*introducing*]: My son Freddy.

LIZA: How do you do? [*Freddy bows and sits down in the Elizabethan chair, infatuated.*]

HIGGINS [*suddenly*]: By George, yes: it all comes back to me! [*They stare at him.*] Covent Garden! [*lamentably*] What a damned thing!

MRS HIGGINS: Henry, please! [*He is about to sit on the edge of the table.*] Dont sit on my writing-table: youll break it.

HIGGINS [*sulkily*]: Sorry.

> *He goes to the divan, stumbling into the fender and over the fire-irons on his way; extricating himself with muttered imprecations; and finishing his disastrous journey by throwing himself so impatiently on the divan that he almost breaks it. Mrs Higgins looks at him, but controls herself and says nothing.*

> *A long and painful pause ensues.*

MRS HIGGINS [*at last, conversationally*]: Will it rain, do you think?

LIZA: The shallow depression in the west of these islands is likely to move slowly in an easterly direction. There are no indications of any great change in the barometrical situation.

FREDDY: Ha! ha! how awfully funny!

LIZA: What is wrong with that, young man? I bet I got it right.

FREDDY: Killing!

MRS EYNSFORD HILL: I'm sure I hope it wont turn cold. Theres so much influenza about. It runs right through our whole family regularly every spring.

LIZA [*darkly*]: My aunt died of influenza: so they said.

MRS EYNSFORD HILL [*clicks her tongue sympathetically*]: !!!

LIZA [*in the same tragic tone*]: But it's my belief they done the old woman in.

MRS HIGGINS [*puzzled*]: Done her in?

LIZA: Y-e-e-e-es, Lord love you! Why should she die of influenza? She come through diphtheria right enough the year before. I saw her with my own eyes. Fairly blue with it, she was. They all thought she was dead; but my father he kept ladling gin down her throat til she came to so sudden that she bit the bowl off the spoon.

MRS EYNSFORD HILL [*startled*]: Dear me!

LIZA [*piling up the indictment*]: What call would a woman with that strength in her have to die of influenza? What become of her new straw hat that should have come to me? Somebody pinched it; and what I say is, them as pinched it done her in.

MRS EYNSFORD HILL: What does doing her in mean?

HIGGINS [*hastily*]: Oh, thats the new small talk. To do a person in means to kill them.

MRS EYNSFORD HILL [*to Eliza, horrified*]: You surely dont believe that your aunt was killed?

LIZA: Do I not! Them she lived with would have killed her for a hatpin, let alone a hat.

MRS EYNSFORD HILL: But it cant have been right for your father to pour spirits down her throat like that. It might have killed her.

LIZA: Not her. Gin was mother's milk to her. Besides, he'd poured so much down his own throat that he knew the good of it.

MRS EYNSFORD HILL: Do you mean that he drank?

LIZA: Drank! My word! Something chronic.

MRS EYNSFORD HILL: How dreadful for you!

LIZA: Not a bit. It never did him no harm what I could see. But then he did not keep it up regular. [*cheerfully*] On the burst, as you might say, from time to time. And always more agreeable when he had a drop in. When he was out of work, my mother used to give him four-pence and tell him to go out and not come back until he'd drunk himself cheerful and loving-like. Theres lots of women has to make their husbands drunk to make them fit to live with. [*now quite at her ease*] You see, it's like this. If a man has a bit of a conscience, it always takes him when he's sober; and then it makes him low-spirited. A drop of booze just takes that off and makes him happy. [*to Freddy, who is in convulsions of suppressed laughter*]: Here! what are you sniggering at?

FREDDY: The new small talk. You do it awfully well.

LIZA: If I was doing it proper, what was you laughing at? [*to Higgins*]: Have I said anything I oughtnt?

MRS HIGGINS [*interposing*]: Not at all, Miss Doolittle.

LIZA: Well, thats a mercy, anyhow. [*expansively*] What I always say is—

HIGGINS [*rising and looking at his watch*]: Ahem!

LIZA [*looking round at him; taking the hint; and rising*]: Well: I must go. [*They all rise. Freddy goes to the door.*] So pleased to have met you. Goodbye. [*She shakes hands with Mrs Higgins.*]

MRS HIGGINS: Goodbye.

LIZA: Goodbye, Colonel Pickering.

PICKERING: Goodbye, Miss Doolittle. [*They shake hands.*]

LIZA [*nodding to the others*]: Goodbye, all.

FREDDY [*opening the door for her*]: Are you walking across the Park, Miss Doolittle? If so—

LIZA [*with perfectly elegant diction*]: Walk! Not bloody likely. [*sensation*] I am going in a taxi. [*She goes out.*]

Pickering gasps and sits down. Freddy goes out on the balcony to catch another glimpse of Eliza.

MRS EYNSFORD HILL [*suffering from shock*]: Well, I really cant get used to the new ways.

CLARA [*throwing herself discontentedly into the Elizabethan chair*]: Oh, it's all right, mamma, quite right. People will think we never go anywhere or see anybody if you are so old-fashioned.

MRS EYNSFORD HILL: I daresay I am very old-fashioned; but I do hope you wont begin using that expression, Clara. I have got accustomed to hear you talking about men as rotters, and calling everything filthy and beastly; though I do think it horrible and unladylike. But this last is really too much. Dont you think so, Colonel Pickering?

PICKERING: Dont ask me. Ive been away in India for several years; and manners have changed so much that I sometimes dont know whether I'm at a respectable dinner-table or in a ship's forecastle.

CLARA: It's all a matter of habit. Theres no right or wrong in it. Nobody means anything by it. And it's so quaint, and gives such a smart emphasis to things that are not in themselves very witty. I find the new small talk delightful and quite innocent.

MRS EYNSFORD HILL [*rising*]: Well, after that, I think it's time for us to go.

Pickering and Higgins rise.

CLARA [*rising*]: Oh yes: we have three at-homes to go to still. Goodbye, Mrs Higgins. Goodbye, Colonel Pickering. Goodbye, Professor Higgins.

HIGGINS [*coming grimly at her from the divan, and accompanying her to the door*]: Goodbye. Be sure you try on that small talk at the three at-homes. Dont be nervous about it. Pitch it in strong.

CLARA [*all smiles*]: I will. Goodbye. Such nonsense, all this early Victorian prudery!

HIGGINS [*tempting her*]: Such damned nonsense!

CLARA: Such bloody nonsense!

MRS EYNSFORD HILL [*convulsively*]: Clara!

CLARA: Ha! ha! [*She goes out radiant, conscious of being thoroughly up to date, and is heard descending the stairs in a stream of silvery laughter.*]

FREDDY [*to the heavens at large*]: Well, I ask you—[*He gives it up, and comes to Mrs Higgins.*] Goodbye.

MRS HIGGINS [*shaking hands*]: Goodbye. Would you like to meet Miss Doolittle again?

FREDDY [*eagerly*]: Yes, I should, most awfully.

MRS HIGGINS: Well, you know my days.

FREDDY: Yes, thanks awfully. Goodbye. [*He goes out.*]

MRS EYNSFORD HILL: Goodbye, Mr Higgins.

HIGGINS: Goodbye. Goodbye.

MRS EYNSFORD HILL [*to Pickering*]: It's no use. I shall never be able to bring myself to use that word.

PICKERING: Dont. It's not compulsory, you know. Youll get on quite well without it.

MRS EYNSFORD HILL: Only, Clara is so down on me if I am not positively reeking with the latest slang. Goodbye.

PICKERING: Goodbye. [*They shake hands.*]

MRS EYNSFORD HILL [*to Mrs Higgins*]: You mustnt mind Clara. [*Pickering, catching from her lowered tone that this is not meant for him to hear, discreetly joins Higgins at the window.*] We're so poor! and she gets so few parties, poor child! She doesnt quite know. [*Mrs Higgins, seeing that her eyes are moist, takes her hand sympathetically and goes with her to the door.*] But the boy is nice. Dont you think so?

MRS HIGGINS: Oh, quite nice. I shall always be delighted to see him.

MRS EYNSFORD HILL: Thank you, dear. Goodbye. [*She goes out.*]

HIGGINS [*eagerly*]: Well? Is Eliza presentable? [*He swoops on his mother and drags her to the ottoman, where she sits down in Eliza's place with her son on her left. Pickering returns to his chair on her right.*]

MRS HIGGINS: You silly boy, of course she's not presentable. She's a triumph of your art and of her dressmaker's; but if you suppose for a moment that she doesnt give herself away in every sentence she utters, you must be perfectly cracked about her.

PICKERING: But dont you think something might be done? I mean something to eliminate the sanguinary element from her conversation.

MRS HIGGINS: Not as long as she is in Henry's hands.

HIGGINS [*aggrieved*]: Do you mean that my language is improper?

MRS HIGGINS: No, dearest: it would be quite proper—say on a canal barge, but it would not be proper for her at a garden party.

HIGGINS [*deeply injured*]: Well I must say—

PICKERING [*interrupting him*]: Come, Higgins: you must learn to know yourself. I havnt heard such language as yours since we used to review the volunteers in Hyde Park twenty years ago.

HIGGINS [*sulkily*]: Oh, well, if y o u say so, I suppose I dont always talk like a bishop.

MRS HIGGINS [*quieting Henry with a touch*]: Colonel Pickering: will you tell me what is the exact state of things in Wimpole Street?

PICKERING [*cheerfully: as if this completely changed the subject*]: Well, I have come to live there with Henry. We work together at my Indian Dialects; and we think it more convenient—

MRS HIGGINS: Quite so. I know all about that: it's an excellent arrangement. But where does this girl live?

HIGGINS: With us, of course. Where s h o u l d she live?

MRS HIGGINS: But on what terms? Is she a servant? If not, what is she?

PICKERING [*slowly*]: I think I know what you mean, Mrs Higgins.

HIGGINS: Well, dash me if *I* do! Ive had to work at the girl every day for months to get her to her present pitch. Besides, she's useful. She knows where my things are, and remembers my appointments and so forth.

MRS HIGGINS: How does your housekeeper get on with her?

HIGGINS: Mrs Pearce? Oh, she's jolly glad to get so much taken off her hands; for before Eliza came, s h e used to have to find things and remind me of my appointments. But she's got some silly bee in her bonnet about Eliza. She keeps saying 'You dont think, sir': doesnt she, Pick?

PICKERING: Yes: thats the formula. 'You dont think, sir.' Thats the end of every conversation about Eliza.

HIGGINS: As if I ever stop thinking about the girl and her confounded vowels and consonants. I'm worn out, thinking about her, and watching her lips and her teeth and her tongue, not to mention her soul, which is the quaintest of the lot.

MRS HIGGINS: You certainly are a pretty pair of babies, playing with your live doll.

HIGGINS: Playing! The hardest job I ever tackled: make no mistake about that, mother. But you have no idea how frightfully interesting it is to take a human being and change her into a quite different human being by creating a new speech for her. It's filling up the deepest gulf that separates class from class and soul from soul.

PICKERING [*drawing his chair closer to Mrs Higgins and bending over to her eagerly*]: Yes: it's enormously interesting. I assure you, Mrs Higgins, we take Eliza very seriously. Every week—every day almost—there is some new change. [*closer again*] We keep records of every stage—dozens of gramophone disks and photographs—

HIGGINS [*assailing her at the other ear*]: Yes, by George: it's the most absorbing experiment I ever tackled. She regularly fills our lives up: doesnt she, Pick?

PICKERING: We're always talking Eliza.

HIGGINS: Teaching Eliza.

PICKERING: Dressing Eliza.

MRS HIGGINS: What!

HIGGINS: Inventing new Elizas.

HIGGINS: ⎱ [*speaking* ⎰ You know, she has the most extraordinary quickness of ear:
PICKERING: ⎰ *together*] ⎱ I assure you, my dear Mrs Higgins, that girl

HIGGINS: ⎱ ⎰ just like a parrot. Ive tried her with every
PICKERING: ⎰ ⎱ is a genius. She can play the piano quite beautifully.

HIGGINS: ⎱ ⎰ possible sort of sound that a human being can make
PICKERING: ⎰ ⎱ We have taken her to classical concerts and to music

HIGGINS:	}	{ Continental dialects, African dialects, Hottentot
PICKERING:		{ halls; and its all the same to her: she plays everything
HIGGINS:	}	{ clicks, things it took me years to get hold of; and
PICKERING:		{ she hears right off when she comes home, whether it's
HIGGINS:	}	{ she picks them up like a shot, right away, as if she had
PICKERING:		{ Beethoven and Brahms or Lehar and Lionel Monckton;
HIGGINS:	}	{ been at it all her life.
PICKERING:		{ though six months ago, she'd never as much as touched a piano—

MRS HIGGINS [*putting her fingers in her ears, as they are by this time shouting one another down with an intolerable noise*]: Sh-sh-sh-sh!

> *They stop.*

PICKERING: I beg your pardon. [*He draws his chair back apologetically.*]

HIGGINS: Sorry. When Pickering starts shouting nobody can get a word in edgeways.

MRS HIGGINS: Be quiet, Henry. Colonel Pickering: dont you realize that when Eliza walked into Wimpole Street, something walked in with her?

PICKERING: Her father did. But Henry soon got rid of him.

MRS HIGGINS: It would have been more to the point if her mother had. But as her mother didnt something else did.

PICKERING: But what?

MRS HIGGINS [*unconsciously dating herself by the word*]: A problem.

PICKERING: Oh, I see. The problem of how to pass her off as a lady.

HIGGINS: I'll solve that problem. Ive half solved it already.

MRS HIGGINS: No, you two infinitely stupid male creatures: the problem of what is to be done with her afterwards.

HIGGINS: I dont see anything in that. She can go her own way, with all the advantages I have given her.

MRS HIGGINS: The advantages of that poor woman who was here just now! The manners and habits that disqualify a fine lady from earning her own living without giving her a fine lady's income! Is that what you mean?

PICKERING [*indulgently, being rather bored*]: Oh, that will be all right, Mrs Higgins. [*He rises to go.*]

HIGGINS [*rising also*]: We'll find her some light employment.

PICKERING: She's happy enough. Dont you worry about her. Goodbye. [*He shakes hands as if he were consoling a frightened child, and makes for the door.*]

HIGGINS: Anyhow, theres no good bothering now. The thing's done. Goodbye, mother. [*He kisses her, and follows Pickering.*]

PICKERING [*turning for a final consolation*]: There are plenty of openings. We'll do whats right. Goodbye.

HIGGINS [*to Pickering as they go out together*]: Lets take her to the Shakespeare exhibition at Earls Court.

PICKERING: Yes: lets. Her remarks will be delicious.

HIGGINS: She'll mimic all the people for us when we get home.

PICKERING: Ripping.

Both are heard laughing as they go downstairs.

MRS HIGGINS [*rises with an impatient bounce, and returns to her work at the writing-table. She sweeps a litter of disarranged papers out of her way; snatches a sheet of paper from her stationery case; and tries resolutely to write. At the third line she gives it up; flings down her pen; grips the table angrily and exclaims*]: Oh, men! men!! men!!!

* * *

Clearly Eliza will not pass as a duchess yet; and Higgins's bet remains unwon. But the six months are not yet exhausted; and just in time Eliza does actually pass as a princess. For a glimpse of how she did it imagine an Embassy in London one summer evening after dark. The hall door has an awning and a carpet across the sidewalk to the kerb, because a grand reception is in progress. A small crowd is lined up to see the guests arrive.

A Rolls-Royce car drives up. Pickering in evening dress, with medals and orders, alights, and hands out Eliza, in opera cloak, evening dress, diamonds, fan, flowers and all accessories. Higgins follows. The car drives off; and the three go up the steps and into the house, the door opening for them as they approach.

Inside the house they find themselves in a spacious hall from which the grand staircase rises. On the left are the arrangements for the gentlemen's cloaks. The male guests are depositing their hats and wraps there.

On the right is a door leading to the ladies' cloakroom. Ladies are going in cloaked and coming out in splendour. Pickering whispers to Eliza and points out the ladies' room. She goes into it. Higgins and Pickering take off their overcoats and take tickets for them from the attendant.

One of the guests, occupied in the same way, has his back turned. Having taken his ticket, he turns round and reveals himself as an important looking young man with an astonishingly hairy face. He has an enormous moustache, flowing out into luxuriant whiskers. Waves of hair cluster his brow. His hair is cropped closely at the back, and glows with oil. Otherwise he is very smart. He wears several worthless orders. He is evidently a foreigner, guessable as whiskered Pandour from Hungary; but in spite of the ferocity of his moustache he is amiable and genially voluble.

Recognizing Higgins, he flings his arms wide apart and approaches him enthusiastically.

WHISKERS: Maestro, maestro. [*He embraces Higgins and kisses him on both cheeks.*] You remember me?

HIGGINS: No I dont. Who the devil are you?

WHISKERS: I am your pupil: your first pupil, your best and greatest pupil. I am little Nepommuck, the marvellous boy. I have made your name famous throughout Europe. You teach me phonetic. You cannot forget ME.

HIGGINS: Why dont you shave?

NEPOMMUCK: I have not your imposing appearance, your chin, your brow. Nobody notice me when I shave. Now I am famous: they call me Hairy Faced Dick.

HIGGINS: And what are you doing here among all these swells?

NEPOMMUCK: I am interpreter. I speak 32 languages. I am indispensable at these international parties. You are great cockney specialist: you place a man anywhere in London the moment he open his mouth. I place any man in Europe.

A footman hurries down the grand staircase and comes to Nepommuck.

FOOTMAN: You are wanted upstairs. Her Excellency cannot understand the Greek gentleman.

NEPOMMUCK: Thank you, yes, immediately.

The footman goes and is lost in the crowd.

NEPOMMUCK [*to Higgins*]: This Greek diplomatist pretends he cannot speak nor understand English. He cannot deceive me. He is the son of a Clerkenwell watchmaker. He speaks English so villainously that he dare not utter a word of it without betraying his origin. I help him to pretend; but I make him pay through the nose. I make them all pay. Ha Ha! [*He hurries upstairs.*]

PICKERING: Is this fellow really an expert? Can he find out Eliza and blackmail her?

HIGGINS: We shall see. If he finds her out I lose my bet.

Eliza comes from the cloakroom and joins them.

PICKERING: Well, Eliza, now for it. Are you ready?

LIZA: Are you nervous, Colonel?

PICKERING: Frightfully. I feel exactly as I felt before my first battle. It's the first time that frightens.

LIZA: It is not the first time for me, Colonel. I have done this fifty times—hundreds of times—in my little piggery in Angel Court in my day-dreams. I am in a dream now. Promise me not to let Professor Higgins wake me; for if he does I shall forget everything and talk as I used to in Drury Lane.

PICKERING: Not a word, Higgins. [*to Eliza*]: Now, ready?

LIZA: Ready.

PICKERING: Go.

They mount the stairs, Higgins last. Pickering whispers to the footman on the first landing.

FIRST LANDING FOOTMAN: Miss Doolittle, Colonel Pickering, Professor Higgins.

SECOND LANDING FOOTMAN: Miss Doolittle, Colonel Pickering, Professor Higgins.

At the top of the staircase the Ambassador and his wife, with Nepommuck at her elbow, are receiving.

HOSTESS [*taking Eliza's hand*]: How d'ye do?

HOST [*same play*]: How d'ye do? How d'ye do, Pickering?

LIZA [*with a beautiful gravity that awes her hostess*]: How do you do? [*She passes on to the drawing room.*]

HOSTESS: Is that your adopted daughter, Colonel Pickering? She will make a sensation.

PICKERING: Most kind of you to invite her for me. [*He passes on.*]

HOSTESS [*to Nepommuck*]: Find out all about her.

NEPOMMUCK [*bowing*]: Excellency—[*He goes into the crowd.*]

HOST: How d'ye do, Higgins? You have a rival here tonight. He introduced himself as your pupil. Is he any good?

HIGGINS: He can learn a language in a fortnight—knows dozens of them. A sure mark of a fool. As a phonetician, no good whatever.

HOSTESS: How d'ye do, Professor?

HIGGINS: How do you do? Fearful bore for you this sort of thing. Forgive my part in it. [*He passes on.*]

In the drawing room and its suite of salons the reception is in full swing. Eliza passes through. She is so intent on her ordeal that she walks like a somnambulist in a desert instead of a débutante in a fashionable crowd. They stop talking to look at her, admiring her dress, her jewels, and her strangely attractive self. Some of the younger ones at the back stand on their chairs to see.

The Host and Hostess come in from the staircase and mingle with their guests. Higgins, gloomy and contemptuous of the whole business, comes into the group where they are chatting.

HOSTESS: Ah, here is Professor Higgins: he will tell us. Tell us all about the wonderful young lady, Professor.

HIGGINS [*almost morosely*]: What wonderful young lady?

HOSTESS: You know very well. They tell me there has been nothing like her in London since people stood on their chairs to look at Mrs Langtry.

Nepommuck joins the group, full of news.

HOSTESS: Ah, here you are at last, Nepommuck. Have you found out all about the Doolittle lady?

NEPOMMUCK: I have found out all about her. She is a fraud.

HOSTESS: A fraud! Oh no.

NEPOMMUCK: YES, yes. She cannot deceive me. Her name cannot be Doolittle.

HIGGINS: Why?

NEPOMMUCK: Because Doolittle is an English name. And she is not English.

HOSTESS: Oh, nonsense! She speaks English perfectly.

NEPOMMUCK: Too perfectly. Can you shew me any English woman who speaks English as it should be spoken? Only foreigners who have been taught to speak it speak it well.

HOSTESS: Certainly she terrified me by the way she said How d'ye do. I had a schoolmistress who talked like that; and I was mortally afraid of her. But if she is not English what is she?

NEPOMMUCK: Hungarian.

ALL THE REST: Hungarian!

NEPOMMUCK: Hungarian. And of royal blood. I am Hungarian. My blood is royal.

HIGGINS: Did you speak to her in Hungarian?

NEPOMMUCK: I did. She was very clever. She said 'Please speak to me in English: I do not understand French.' French! She pretends not to know the difference between Hungarian and French. Impossible: she knows both.

HIGGINS: And the blood royal? How did you find that out?

NEPOMMUCK: Instinct, maestro, instinct. Only the Magyar races can produce that air of the divine right, those resolute eyes. She is a princess.

HOST: What do you say, Professor?

HIGGINS: I say an ordinary London girl out of the gutter and taught to speak by an expert. I place her in Drury Lane.

NEPOMMUCK: Ha ha ha! Oh, maestro, maestro, you are mad on the subject of cockney dialects. The London gutter is the whole world for you.

HIGGINS [*to the Hostess*]: What does your Excellency say?

HOSTESS: Oh, of course I agree with Nepommuck. She must be a princess at least.

HOST: Not necessarily legitimate, of course. Morganatic perhaps. But that is undoubtedly her class.

HIGGINS: I stick to my opinion.

HOSTESS: Oh, you are incorrigible.

The group breaks up, leaving Higgins isolated. Pickering joins him.

PICKERING: Where is Eliza? We must keep an eye on her.

Eliza joins them.

LIZA: I dont think I can bear much more. The people all stare so at me. An old lady has just told me that I speak exactly like Queen Victoria. I am sorry if I have lost your bet. I have done my best; but nothing can make me the same as these people.

PICKERING: You have not lost it, my dear. You have won it ten times over.

HIGGINS: Let us get out of this. I have had enough of chattering to these fools.

PICKERING: Eliza is tired; and I am hungry. Let us clear out and have supper somewhere.

ACT IV

The Wimpole Street laboratory. Midnight. Nobody in the room. The clock on the mantelpiece strikes twelve. The fire is not alight: it is a summer night.

Presently Higgins and Pickering are heard on the stairs.

HIGGINS [*calling down to Pickering*]: I say, Pick: lock up, will you? I shant be going out again.

PICKERING: Right. Can Mrs Pearce go to bed? We dont want anything more, do we?

HIGGINS: Lord, no!

Eliza opens the door and is seen on the lighted landing in all the finery in which she has just won Higgins's bet for him. She comes to the hearth, and switches on the electric lights there. She is tired: her pallor contrasts strongly with her dark eyes and hair; and her expression is almost tragic. She takes off her cloak; puts her fan and gloves on the piano; and sits down on the bench, brooding and silent. Higgins, in evening dress, with overcoat and hat, comes in, carrying a smoking jacket which he has picked up downstairs. He takes off the hat and overcoat; throws them carelessly on the newspaper stand; disposes of his coat in the same way; puts on the smoking jacket; and throws himself wearily into the easy-chair at the hearth. Pickering, similarly attired, comes in. He also takes off his hat and overcoat, and is about to throw them on Higgins's when he hesitates.

PICKERING: I say: Mrs Pearce will row if we leave these things lying about in the drawing room.

HIGGINS: Oh, chuck them over the bannisters into the hall. She'll find them there in the morning and put them away all right. She'll think we were drunk.

PICKERING: We are, slightly. Are there any letters?

HIGGINS: I didnt look. [*Pickering takes the overcoats and hats and goes downstairs. Higgins begins half singing half yawning an air from La Fanciulla del Golden West. Suddenly he stops and exclaims*]: I wonder where the devil my slippers are!

*Eliza looks at him darkly; then rises suddenly and leaves the room.
Higgins yawns again, and resumes his song.
Pickering returns, with the contents of the letter-box in his hand.*

PICKERING: Only circulars, and this coroneted billet-doux for you. [*He throws the circulars into the fender, and posts himself on the hearthrug, with his back to the grate.*]

HIGGINS [*glancing at the billet-doux*]: Money-lender. [*He throws the letter after the circulars.*]

Eliza returns with a pair of down-at-heel slippers. She places them on the carpet before Higgins, and sits as before without a word.

HIGGINS [*yawning again*]: Oh Lord! What an evening! What a crew! What a silly tom-foolery! [*He raises his shoe to unlace it, and catches sight of the slippers. He stops unlacing and looks at them as if they had appeared there of their own accord.*] Oh! theyre there, are they?

PICKERING [*stretching himself*]: Well, I feel a bit tired. It's been a long day. The garden party, a dinner party, and the reception! Rather too much of a good thing. But youve won your bet, Higgins. Eliza did the trick, and something to spare, eh?

HIGGINS [*fervently*]: Thank God it's over!

> *Eliza flinches violently; but they take no notice of her; and she recovers herself and sits stonily as before.*

PICKERING: Were you nervous at the garden party? *I* was. Eliza didnt seem a bit nervous.

HIGGINS: Oh, she wasnt nervous. I knew she'd be all right. No: it's the strain of putting the job through all these months that has told on me. It was interesting enough at first, while we were at the phonetics; but after that I got deadly sick of it. If I hadnt backed myself to do it I should have chucked the whole thing up two months ago. It was a silly notion: the whole thing has been a bore.

PICKERING: Oh come! the garden party was frightfully exciting. My heart began beating like anything.

HIGGINS: Yes, for the first three minutes. But when I saw we were going to win hands down, I felt like a bear in a cage, hanging about doing nothing. The dinner was worse: sitting gorging there for over an hour, with nobody but a damned fool of a fashionable woman to talk to! I tell you, Pickering, never again for me. No more artificial duchesses. The whole thing has been simple purgatory.

PICKERING: Youve never been broken in properly to the social routine. [*strolling over to the piano*] I rather enjoy dipping into it occasionally myself: it makes me feel young again. Anyhow, it was a great success: an immense success. I was quite frightened once or twice because Eliza was doing it so well. You see, lots of the real people cant do it at all: theyre such fools that they think style comes by nature to people in their position; and so they never learn. Theres always something professional about doing a thing superlatively well.

HIGGINS: Yes: thats what drives me mad: the silly people dont know their own silly business. [*rising*] However, it's over and done with; and now I can go to bed at last without dreading tomorrow.

> *Eliza's beauty becomes murderous.*

PICKERING: I think I shall turn in too. Still, it's been a great occasion: a triumph for you. Goodnight. [*He goes.*]

HIGGINS [*following him*]: Goodnight. [*over his shoulder, at the door*] Put out the lights, Eliza; and tell Mrs Pearce not to make coffee for me in the morning: I'll take tea. [*He goes out.*]

> *Eliza tries to control herself and feel indifferent as she rises and walks across to the hearth to switch off the lights. By the time she gets there she is on the point of screaming. She sits down in Higgins's chair and holds on hard to the arms. Finally she gives way and flings herself furiously on the floor, raging.*

HIGGINS [*in despairing wrath outside*]: What the devil have I done with my slippers? [*He appears at the door.*]

LIZA [*snatching up the slippers, and hurling them at him one after the other with all her force*]: There are your slippers. And there. Take your slippers; and may you never have a day's luck with them!

HIGGINS [*astounded*]: What on earth—! [*He comes to her.*] Whats the matter? Get up. [*He pulls her up.*] Anything wrong?

LIZA [*breathless*]: Nothing wrong—with y o u. Ive won your bet for you, havnt I? Thats enough for you. I dont matter, I suppose.

HIGGINS: Y o u won my bet! You! Presumptuous insect! I won it. What did you throw those slippers at me for?

LIZA: Because I wanted to smash your face. I'd like to kill you, you selfish brute. Why didnt you leave me where you picked me out of—in the gutter? You thank God it's all over, and that now you can throw me back again there, do you? [*She crisps her fingers frantically.*]

HIGGINS [*looking at her in cool wonder*]: The creature is nervous, after all.

LIZA [*gives a suffocated scream of fury, and instinctively darts her nails at his face*]: !!

HIGGINS [*catching her wrists*]: Ah! would you? Claws in, you cat. How dare you shew your temper to me? Sit down and be quiet. [*He throws her roughly into the easy-chair.*]

LIZA [*crushed by superior strength and weight*]: Whats to become of me? Whats to become of me?

HIGGINS: How the devil do I know whats to become of you? What does it matter what becomes of you?

LIZA: You dont care. I know you dont care. You wouldnt care if I was dead. I'm nothing to you—not so much as them slippers.

HIGGINS [*thundering*]: T h o s e slippers.

LIZA [*with bitter submission*]: Those slippers. I didnt think it made any difference now.

A pause. Eliza hopeless and crushed. Higgins a little uneasy.

HIGGINS [*in his loftiest manner*]: Why have you begun going on like this? May I ask whether you complain of your treatment here?

LIZA: No.

HIGGINS: Has anybody behaved badly to you? Colonel Pickering? Mrs Pearce? Any of the servants?

LIZA: No.

HIGGINS: I presume you dont pretend that *I* have treated you badly?

LIZA: No.

HIGGINS: I am glad to hear it. [*He moderates his tone.*] Perhaps youre tired after the strain of the day. Will you have a glass of champagne? [*He moves towards the door.*]

LIZA: No. [*recollecting her manners*] Thank you.

HIGGINS [*good-humoured again*]: This has been coming on you for some days. I suppose it was natural for you to be anxious about the garden party. But thats all over now. [*He pats her kindly on the shoulder. She writhes.*] Theres nothing more to worry about.

LIZA: No. Nothing more for y o u to worry about. [*She suddenly rises and gets away from him by going to the piano bench, where she sits and hides her face.*] Oh God! I wish I was dead.

HIGGINS [*staring after her in sincere surprise*]: Why? In heaven's name, why? [*reasonably, going to her*] Listen to me, Eliza. All this irritation is purely subjective.

LIZA: I dont understand. I'm too ignorant.

HIGGINS: It's only imagination. Low spirits and nothing else. Nobody's hurting you. Nothing's wrong. You go to bed like a good girl and sleep it off. Have a little cry and say your prayers: that will make you comfortable.

LIZA: I heard your prayers. 'Thank God it's all over!'

HIGGINS [*impatiently*]: Well, d o n t you thank God it's all over? Now you are free and can do what you like.

LIZA [*pulling herself together in desperation*]: What am I fit for? What have you left me fit for? Where am I to go? What am I to do? Whats to become of me?

HIGGINS [*enlightened, but not at all impressed*]: Oh, thats whats worrying you, is it? [*He thrusts his hands into his pockets, and walks about in his usual manner, rattling the contents of his pockets, as if condescending to a trivial subject out of pure kindness.*] I shouldnt bother about it if I were you. I should imagine you wont have much difficulty in settling yourself somewhere or other, though I hadnt quite realized that you were going away. [*She looks quickly at him: he does not look at her, but examines the dessert stand on the piano and decides that he will eat an apple.*] You might marry, you know. [*He bites a large piece out of the apple and munches it noisily.*] You see, Eliza, all men are not confirmed old bachelors like me and the Colonel. Most men are the marrying sort (poor devils!); and youre not bad-looking: it's quite a pleasure to look at you sometimes—not now, of course, because youre crying and looking as ugly as the very devil; but when youre all right and quite yourself, youre what I should call attractive. That is, to the people in the marrying line, you understand. You go to bed and have a good nice rest; and then get up and look at yourself in the glass; and you wont feel so cheap.

    Eliza again looks at him speechless, and does not stir.

    The look is quite lost on him: he eats his apple with a dreamy expression of happiness, as it is quite a good one.

HIGGINS [*a genial afterthought occuring to him*]: I daresay my mother could find some chap or other who would do very well.

LIZA: We were above that at the corner of Tottenham Court Road.

HIGGINS [*waking up*]: What do you mean?

LIZA: I sold flowers. I didnt sell myself. Now youve made a lady of me I'm not fit to sell anything else. I wish youd left me where you found me.

HIGGINS [*slinging the core of the apple decisively into the grate*]: Tosh, Eliza. Dont you insult human relations by dragging all this cant about buying and selling into it. You neednt marry the fellow if you dont like him.

LIZA: What else am I to do?

HIGGINS: Oh, lots of things. What about your old idea of a florist's shop? Pickering could set you up in one: he has lots of money. [*chuckling*] He'll have to pay for all those togs you have been wearing today; and that, with the hire of the jewellery, will make a big hole in two hundred pounds. Why, six months ago you would have thought it the millennium to have a flower shop of your own. Come! youll be all right. I must clear off to bed: I'm devilish sleepy. By the way, I came down for something: I forget what it was.

LIZA: Your slippers.

HIGGINS: Oh yes, of course. You shied them at me. [*He picks them up, and is going out when she rises and speaks to him.*]

LIZA: Before you go, sir—

HIGGINS [*dropping the slippers in his surprise at her calling him* Sir]: Eh?

LIZA: Do my clothes belong to me or to Colonel Pickering?

HIGGINS [*coming back into the room as if her question were the very climax of unreason*]: What the devil use would they be to Pickering?

LIZA: He might want them for the next girl you pick up to experiment on.

HIGGINS [*shocked and hurt*]: Is t h a t the way you feel towards us?

LIZA: I dont want to hear anything more about that. All I want to know is whether anything belongs to me. My own clothes were burnt.

HIGGINS: But what does it matter? Why need you start bothering about that in the middle of the night?

LIZA: I want to know what I may take away with me. I dont want to be accused of stealing.

HIGGINS [*now deeply wounded*]: Stealing! You shouldnt have said that, Eliza. That shews a want of feeling.

LIZA: I'm sorry. I'm only a common ignorant girl; and in my station I have to be careful. There cant be any feelings between the like of you and the like of me. Please will you tell me what belongs to me and what doesnt?

HIGGINS [*very sulky*]: You may take the whole damned houseful if you like. Except the jewels. Theyre hired. Will that satisfy you? [*He turns on his heel and is about to go in extreme dudgeon.*]

LIZA [*drinking in his emotion like nectar, and nagging him to provoke a further supply*]: Stop, please. [*She takes off her jewels.*] Will you take these to your room and keep them safe? I dont want to run the risk of their being missing.

HIGGINS [*furious*]: Hand them over. [*She puts them into his hands.*] If these belonged to me instead of the jeweller, I'd ram them down your ungrateful throat. [*He perfunctorily thrusts them into his pockets unconsciously decorating himself with the protruding ends of the chains.*]

LIZA [*taking a ring off*]: This ring isnt the jeweller's: it's the one you bought me in Brighton. I dont want it now. [*Higgins dashes the ring violently into the fireplace, and turns on her so threateningly that she crouches over the piano with her hands over her face and exclaims*]: Dont you hit me.

HIGGINS: Hit you! You infamous creature, how dare you accuse me of such a thing? It is you who have hit me. You have wounded me to the heart.

LIZA [*thrilling with hidden joy*]: I'm glad. Ive got a little of my own back, anyhow.

HIGGINS [*with dignity, in his finest professional style*]: You have caused me to lose my temper: a thing that has hardly ever happened to me before. I prefer to say nothing more tonight. I am going to bed.

LIZA [*pertly*]: Youd better leave a note for Mrs Pearce about the coffee; for she wont be told by me.

HIGGINS [*formally*]: Damn Mrs Pearce; and damn the coffee; and damn you; and [*wildly*] damn my own folly in having lavished my hard-earned knowledge and the treasure of my regard and intimacy on a heartless guttersnipe. [*He goes out with impressive decorum, and spills it by slamming the door savagely.*]

> *Eliza goes down on her knees on the hearthrug to look for the ring. When she finds it she considers for a moment what to do with it. Finally she flings it down on the dessert stand and goes upstairs in a tearing rage.*

* * *

> *The furniture of Eliza's room has been increased by a big wardrobe and a sumptuous dressing-table. She comes in and switches on the electric light. She goes to the wardrobe; opens it; and pulls out a walking dress, a hat, and a pair of shoes, which she throws on the bed. She takes off her evening dress and shoes; then takes a padded hanger from the wardrobe; adjusts it carefully in the evening dress; and hangs it in the wardrobe, which she shuts with a slam. She puts on her walking shoes, her walking dress, and hat. She takes her wrist watch from the dressing-table and fastens it on. She pulls on her gloves; takes her vanity bag; and looks into it to see that her purse is there before hanging it on her wrist. She makes for the door. Every movement expresses her furious resolution.*

> *She takes a last look at herself in the glass.*

> *She suddenly puts out her tongue at herself; then leaves the room, switching off the electric light at the door.*

> *Meanwhile, in the street outside, Freddy Eynsford Hill, lovelorn, is gazing up at the second floor, in which one of the windows is still lighted.*

> *The light goes out.*

FREDDY: Goodnight, darling, darling, darling.

> *Eliza comes out, giving the door a considerable bang behind her.*

LIZA: Whatever are you doing here?

FREDDY: Nothing. I spend most nights here. It's the only place where I'm happy. Dont laugh at me, Miss Doolittle.

LIZA: Dont you call me Miss Doolittle, do you hear? Liza's good enough for me. [*She breaks down and grabs him by the shoulders.*] Freddy: you dont think I'm a heartless guttersnipe, do you?

FREDDY: Oh no, no, darling: how can you imagine such a thing? You are the loveliest, dearest—

He loses all self-control and smothers her with kisses. She, hungry for comfort, responds. They stand in one another's arms.

An elderly police constable arrives.

CONSTABLE [*scandalized*]: Now then! Now then!! Now then!!!

They release one another hastily.

FREDDY: Sorry, constable. Weve only just become engaged.

They run away.

The constable shakes his head, reflecting on his own courtship and on the vanity of human hopes. He moves off in the opposite direction with slow professional steps.

The flight of the lovers takes them to Cavendish Square. There they halt to consider their next move.

LIZA [*out of breath*]: He didnt half give me a fright, that copper. But you answered him proper.

FREDDY: I hope I havnt taken you out of your way. Where were you going?

LIZA: To the river.

FREDDY: What for?

LIZA: To make a hole in it.

FREDDY [*horrified*]: Eliza, darling. What do you mean? Whats the matter?

LIZA: Never mind. It doesnt matter now. Theres nobody in the world now but you and me, is there?

FREDDY: Not a soul.

They indulge in another embrace, and are again surprised by a much younger constable.

SECOND CONSTABLE: Now then, you two! Whats this? Where do you think you are? Move along here, double quick.

FREDDY: As you say, sir, double quick.

They run away again, and are in Hanover Square before they stop for another conference.

FREDDY: I had no idea the police were so devilishly prudish.

LIZA: It's their business to hunt girls off the streets.

FREDDY: We must go somewhere. We cant wander about the streets all night.

LIZA: Cant we? I think it'd be lovely to wander about for ever.

FREDDY: Oh, darling.

They embrace again, oblivious of the arrival of a crawling taxi. It stops.

TAXIMAN: Can I drive you and the lady anywhere, sir?

They start asunder.

LIZA: Oh, Freddy, a taxi. The very thing.

FREDDY: But, damn it, Ive no money.

LIZA: I have plenty. The Colonel thinks you should never go out without ten pounds in your pocket. Listen. We'll drive about all night; and in the morning I'll call on old Mrs Higgins and ask her what I ought to do. I'll tell you all about it in the cab. And the police wont touch us there.

FREDDY: Righto! Ripping. [*to the Taximan*]: Wimbledon Common. [*They drive off.*]

ACT V

Mrs Higgins's drawing room. She is at her writing-table as before. The parlour-maid comes in.

THE PARLOUR-MAID [*at the door*]: Mr Henry, maam, is downstairs with Colonel Pickering.

MRS HIGGINS: Well, shew them up.

THE PARLOUR-MAID: Theyre using the telephone, maam. Telephoning to the police, I think.

MRS HIGGINS: What!

THE PARLOUR-MAID [*coming further in and lowering her voice*]: Mr Henry is in a state, maam. I thought I'd better tell you.

MRS HIGGINS: If you had told me that Mr Henry was not in a state it would have been more surprising. Tell them to come up when theyve finished with the police. I suppose he's lost something.

THE PARLOUR-MAID: Yes, maam. [*going*]

MRS HIGGINS: Go upstairs and tell Miss Doolittle that Mr Henry and the Colonel are here. Ask her not to come down til I send for her.

THE PARLOUR-MAID: Yes, maam.

Higgins bursts in. He is, as the parlour-maid has said, in a state.

HIGGINS: Look here, mother: heres a confounded thing!

MRS HIGGINS: Yes, dear. Good morning. [*He checks his impatience and kisses her, whilst the parlour-maid goes out.*] What is it?

HIGGINS: Eliza's bolted.

MRS HIGGINS [*calmly continuing her writing*]: You must have frightened her.

HIGGINS: Frightened her! nonsense! She was left last night, as usual, to turn out the lights and all that; and instead of going to bed she changed her clothes and went right off: her bed wasnt slept in. She came in a cab for her things before seven this morning; and that fool Mrs Pearce let her have them without telling me a word about it. What am I to do?

MRS HIGGINS: Do without, I'm afraid, Henry. The girl has a perfect right to leave if she chooses.

HIGGINS [*wandering distractedly across the room*]: But I cant find anything. I dont know what appointments Ive got. I'm—

> *Pickering comes in. Mrs Higgins puts down her pen and turns away from the writing-table.*

PICKERING [*shaking hands*]: Good morning, Mrs Higgins. Has Henry told you? [*He sits down on the ottoman.*]

HIGGINS: What does that ass of an inspector say? Have you offered a reward?

MRS HIGGINS [*rising in indignant amazement*]: You dont mean to say you have set the police after Eliza.

HIGGINS: Of course. What are the police for? What else could we do? [*He sits in the Elizabethan chair.*]

PICKERING: The inspector made a lot of difficulties. I really think he suspected us of some improper purpose.

MRS HIGGINS: Well, of course he did. What right have you to go to the police and give the girl's name as if she were a thief, or a lost umbrella, or something? Really! [*She sits down again, deeply vexed.*]

HIGGINS: But we want to find her.

PICKERING: We cant let her go like this, you know, Mrs Higgins. What were we to do?

MRS HIGGINS: You have no more sense, either of you, than two children. Why—

> *The parlour-maid comes in and breaks off the conversation.*

THE PARLOUR-MAID: Mr Henry: a gentleman wants to see you very particular. He's been sent on from Wimpole Street.

HIGGINS: Oh, bother! I cant see anyone now. Who is it?

THE PARLOUR-MAID: A Mr Doolittle, sir.

PICKERING: Doolittle! Do you mean the dustman?

THE PARLOUR-MAID: Dustman! Oh no, sir: a gentleman.

HIGGINS [*springing up excitedly*]: By George, Pick, it's some relative of hers that she's gone to. Somebody we know nothing about. [*to the parlour-maid*]: Send him up, quick.

THE PARLOUR-MAID: Yes, sir. [*She goes.*]

HIGGINS [*eagerly, going to his mother*]: Genteel relatives! now we shall hear something. [*He sits down in the Chippendale chair.*]

MRS HIGGINS: Do you know any of her people?

PICKERING: Only her father: the fellow we told you about.

THE PARLOUR-MAID [*announcing*]: Mr Doolittle. [*She withdraws.*]

> *Doolittle enters. He is resplendently dressed as for a fashionable wedding, and might, in fact, be the bridegroom. A flower in his buttonhole, a dazzling silk hat, and patent leather shoes complete the effect. He is too concerned with the business*

he has come on to notice Mrs Higgins. He walks straight to Higgins, and accosts him with vehement reproach.

DOOLITTLE [*indicating his own person*]: See here! Do you see this? Y o u done this.

HIGGINS: Done what, man?

DOOLITTLE: This, I tell you. Look at it. Look at this hat. Look at this coat.

PICKERING: Has Eliza been buying you clothes?

DOOLITTLE: Eliza! not she. Why would she buy me clothes?

MRS HIGGINS: Good morning, Mr Doolittle. Wont you sit down?

DOOLITTLE [*taken aback as he becomes conscious that he has forgotten his hostess*]: Asking your pardon, maam. [*He approaches her and shakes her proffered hand.*] Thank you. [*He sits down on the ottoman, on Pickering's right.*] I am that full of what has happened to me that I cant think of anything else.

HIGGINS: What the dickens h a s happened to you?

DOOLITTLE: I shouldnt mind if it had only h a p p e n e d to me: anything might happen to anybody and nobody to blame but Providence, as you might say. But this is something that y o u done to me: yes, y o u, Enry Iggins.

HIGGINS: Have you found Eliza?

DOOLITTLE: Have you lost her?

HIGGINS: Yes.

DOOLITTLE: You have all the luck, you have. I aint found her; but she'll find me quick enough now after what you done to me.

MRS HIGGINS: But what has my son done to you. Mr Doolittle?

DOOLITTLE: Done to me! Ruined me. Destroyed my happiness. Tied me up and delivered me into the hands of middle class morality.

HIGGINS [*rising intolerantly and standing over Doolittle*]: Youre raving. Youre drunk. Youre mad. I gave you five pounds. After that I had two conversations with you, at half-a-crown an hour. Ive never seen you since.

DOOLITTLE: Oh! Drunk am I? Mad am I? Tell me this. Did you or did you not write a letter to an old blighter in America that was giving five million to found Moral Reform Societies all over the world, and that wanted you to invent a universal language for him?

HIGGINS: What! Ezra D. Wannafeller! He's dead. [*He sits down again carelessly.*]

DOOLITTLE: Yes: he's dead; and I'm done for. Now did you or did you not write a letter to him to say that the most original moralist at present in England, to the best your knowledge, was Alfred Doolittle, a common dustman?

HIGGINS: Oh, after your first visit I remember making some silly joke of the kind.

DOOLITTLE: Ah! you may well call it a silly joke. It put the lid on me right enough. Just give him the chance he wanted to shew that Americans is not like us: that they reckonize and respect merit in every class of life, however humble. Them words is in his blooming will, in which, Henry Higgins, thanks to your silly joking, he leaves me a share of his Predigested Cheese Trust worth three thousand a year on condition that I lecture for his Wannafeller Moral Reform World League as often as they ask me up to six times a year.

HIGGINS: The devil he does! Whew! [*Brightening suddenly*] What a lark!

PICKERING: A safe thing for you, Doolittle. They wont ask you twice.

DOOLITTLE: It aint the lecturing I mind. I'll lecture them blue in the face, I will, and not turn a hair. It's making a gentleman of me that I object to. Who asked him to make a gentleman of me? I was happy. I was free. I touched pretty nigh everybody for money when I wanted it, same as I touched you, Enry Iggins. Now I am worrited; tied neck and heels; and everybody touches m e for money. It's a fine thing for you, says my solicitor. Is it? says I. You mean it's a good thing for you, I says. When I was a poor man and had a solicitor once when they found a pram in the dust cart, he got me off, and got shut of me and got me shut of him as quick as he could. Same with the doctors: used to shove me out of the hospital before I could hardly stand on my legs, and nothing to pay. Now they finds out that I'm not a healthy man and cant live unless they looks after me twice a day. In the house I'm not let do a hand's turn for myself: somebody else must do it and touch me for it. A year ago I hadnt a relative in the world except two or three that wouldnt speak to me. Now Ive fifty, and not a decent week's wages among the lot of them. I have to live for others and not for myself: thats middle class morality. You talk of losing Eliza. Dont you be anxious: I bet she's on my doorstep by this: she that could support herself easy by selling flowers if I wasnt respectable. And the next one to touch me will be you, Enry Iggins. I'll have to learn to speak middle class language from you, instead of speaking proper English. Thats where youll come in; and I daresay thats what you done it for.

MRS HIGGINS: But, my dear Mr Doolittle, you need not suffer all this if you are really earnest. Nobody can force you to accept this bequest. You can repudiate it. Isnt that so, Colonel Pickering?

PICKERING: I believe so.

DOOLITTLE [*softening his manner in deference to her sex*]: Thats the tragedy of it, maam. It's easy to say chuck it; but I havnt the nerve. Which of us has? We're all intimidated. Intimidated, maam: thats what we are. What is there for me if I chuck it but the workhouse in my old age? I have to dye my hair already to keep my job as a dustman. If I was one of the deserving poor, and had put by a bit, I could chuck it; but then why should I, acause the deserving poor might as well be millionaires for all the happiness they ever has. They dont know what happiness is. But I, as one of the undeserving poor, have nothing between me and the pauper's uniform but this here blasted three thousand a year that shoves me into the middle class. (Excuse the expression, maam; youd use it yourself if you had my provocation.) Theyve got you every way you turn: it's a choice between the Skilly of the workhouse and the Char Bydis of the middle class; and I havnt the nerve for the workhouse. Intimidated: thats what I am. Broke. Bought up. Happier men than me will call for my dust, and touch me for their tip; and I'll look on helpless, and envy them. And thats what your son has brought me to. [*He is overcome by emotion.*]

MRS HIGGINS: Well, I'm glad youre not going to do anything foolish, Mr Doolittle. For this solves the problem of Eliza's future. You can provide for her now.

DOOLITTLE [*with melancholy resignation*]: Yes, maam: I'm expected to provide for everyone now, out of three thousand a year.

HIGGINS [*jumping up*]: Nonsense! he cant provide for her. He shant provide for her. She doesnt belong to him. I paid him five pounds for her. Doolittle: either youre an honest man or a rogue.

DOOLITTLE [*tolerantly*]: A little of both, Henry, like the rest of us: a little of both.

HIGGINS: Well, you took that money for the girl; and you have no right to take her as well.

MRS HIGGINS: Henry: dont be absurd. If you want to know where Eliza is, she is upstairs.

HIGGINS [*amazed*]: Upstairs!!! Then I shall jolly soon fetch her downstairs. [*He makes resolutely for the door.*]

MRS HIGGINS [*rising and following him*]: Be quiet, Henry. Sit down.

HIGGINS: I—

MRS HIGGINS: Sit down, dear; and listen to me.

HIGGINS: Oh very well, very well, very well. [*He throws himself ungraciously on the ottoman, with his face towards the windows.*] But I think you might have told us this half an hour ago.

MRS HIGGINS: Eliza came to me this morning. She told me of the brutal way you two treated her.

HIGGINS [*bounding up again*]: What!

PICKERING [*rising also*]: My dear Mrs Higgins, she's been telling you stories. We didnt treat her brutally. We hardly said a word to her; and we parted on particularly good terms. [*turning to Higgins*] Higgins: did you bully her after I went to bed?

HIGGINS: Just the other way about. She threw my slippers in my face. She behaved in the most outrageous way. I never gave her the slightest provocation. The slippers came bang into my face the moment I entered the room—before I had uttered a word. And used perfectly awful language.

PICKERING [*astonished*]: But why? What did we do to her?

MRS HIGGINS: I think I know pretty well what you did. The girl is naturally rather affectionate, I think. Isnt she, Mr Doolittle?

DOOLITTLE: Very tender-hearted, maam. Takes after me.

MRS HIGGINS: Just so. She had become attached to you both. She worked very hard for you, Henry. I dont think you quite realize what anything in the nature of brain work means to a girl of her class. Well, it seems that when the great day of trial came, and she did this wonderful thing for you without making a single mistake, you two sat there and never said a word to her, but talked together of how glad you were that it was all over and how you had been bored with the whole thing. And then you were surprised because she threw your slippers at you! I should have thrown the fire-irons at you.

HIGGINS: We said nothing except that we were tired and wanted to go to bed. Did we, Pick?

PICKERING [*shrugging his shoulders*]: That was all.

MRS HIGGINS [*ironically*]: Quite sure?

PICKERING: Absolutely. Really, that was all.

MRS HIGGINS: You didnt thank her, or pet her, or admire her, or tell her how splendid she'd been.

HIGGINS [*impatiently*]: But she knew all about that. We didnt make speeches to her, if thats what you mean.

PICKERING [*conscience stricken*]: Perhaps we were a little inconsiderate. Is she very angry?

MRS HIGGINS [*returning to her place at the writing-table*]: Well, I'm afraid she wont go back to Wimpole Street, especially now that Mr Doolittle is able to keep up the position you have thrust on her; but she says she is quite willing to meet you on friendly terms and to let bygones be bygones.

HIGGINS [*furious*]: Is she, by George? Ho!

MRS HIGGINS: If you promise to behave yourself, Henry, I'll ask her to come down. If not, go home; for you have taken up quite enough of my time.

HIGGINS: Oh, all right. Very well. Pick: you behave yourself. Let us put on our best Sunday manners for this creature that we picked out of the mud. [*He flings himself sulkily into the Elizabethan chair.*]

DOOLITTLE [*remonstrating*]: Now, now, Enry Iggins! Have some consideration for my feelings as a middle class man.

MRS HIGGINS: Remember your promise, Henry. [*She presses the bell-button on the writing-table.*] Mr Doolittle: will you be so good as to step out on the balcony for a moment. I dont want Eliza to have the shock of your news until she has made it up with these two gentlemen. Would you mind?

DOOLITTLE: As you wish, lady. Anything to help Henry to keep her off my hands. [*He disappears through the window.*]

The parlour-maid answers the bell. Pickering sits down in Doolittle's place.

MRS HIGGINS: Ask Miss Doolittle to come down, please.

THE PARLOUR-MAID: Yes, maam. [*She goes out.*]

MRS HIGGINS: Now, Henry: be good.

HIGGINS: I am behaving myself perfectly.

PICKERING: He is doing his best, Mrs Higgins.

A pause. Higgins throws back his head; stretches out his legs; and begins to whistle.

MRS HIGGINS: Henry, dearest, you dont look at all nice in that attitude.

HIGGINS [*pulling himself together*]: I was not trying to look nice, mother.

MRS HIGGINS: It doesnt matter, dear. I only wanted to make you speak.

HIGGINS: Why?

MRS HIGGINS: Because you cant speak and whistle at the same time.

Higgins groans. Another very trying pause.

HIGGINS [*springing up, out of patience*]: Where the devil is that girl? Are we to wait here all day?

Eliza enters, sunny, self-possessed, and giving a staggeringly convincing exhibition of ease of manner. She carries a little work-basket, and is very much at home. Pickering is too much taken aback to rise.

LIZA: How do you do, Professor Higgins? Are you quite well?

HIGGINS [*choking*]: Am I—[*He can say no more.*]

LIZA: But of course you are: you are never ill. So glad to see you again, Colonel Pickering. [*He rises hastily; and they shake hands.*] Quite chilly this morning, isnt it? [*She sits down on his left. He sits beside her.*]

HIGGINS: Dont you dare try this game on me. I taught it to you; and it doesnt take me in. Get up and come home; and dont be a fool.

> *Eliza takes a piece of needlework from her basket, and begins to stitch at it, without taking the least notice of this outburst.*

MRS HIGGINS: Very nicely put, indeed, Henry. No woman could resist such an invitation.

HIGGINS: You let her alone, mother. Let her speak for herself. You will jolly soon see whether she has an idea that I havnt put into her head or a word that I havnt put into her mouth. I tell you I have created this thing out of the squashed cabbage leaves of Covent Garden; and now she pretends to play the fine lady with me.

MRS HIGGINS [*placidly*]: Yes, dear; but youll sit down, wont you?

> *Higgins sits down again, savagely.*

LIZA [*to Pickering, taking no apparent notice of Higgins, and working away deftly*]: Will y o u drop me altogether now that the experiment is over, Colonel Pickering?

PICKERING: Oh dont. You mustnt think of it as an experiment. It shocks me, somehow.

LIZA: Oh, I'm only a squashed cabbage leaf—

PICKERING [*impulsively*]: No.

LIZA [*continuing quietly*]—but I owe so much to you that I should be very unhappy if you forgot me.

PICKERING: It's very kind of you to say so, Miss Doolittle.

LIZA: It's not because you paid for my dresses. I know you are generous to everybody with money. But it was from you that I learnt really nice manners; and that is what makes one a lady, isnt it? You see it was so very difficult for me with the example of Professor Higgins always before me. I was brought up to be just like him, unable to control myself, and using bad language on the slightest provocation. And I should never have known that ladies and gentlemen didnt behave like that if you hadnt been there.

HIGGINS: Well!!

PICKERING: Oh, thats only his way, you know. He doesnt mean it.

LIZA: Oh, *I* didnt mean it either, when I was a flower girl. It was only my way. But you see I did it; and thats what makes the difference after all.

PICKERING: No doubt. Still, he taught you to speak; and I couldnt have done that, you know.

LIZA [*trivially*]: Of course: that is his profession.

HIGGINS: Damnation!

LIZA [*continuing*]: It was just like learning to dance in the fashionable way: there was nothing more than that in it. But do you know what began my real education?

PICKERING: What?

LIZA [*stopping her work for a moment*]: Your calling me Miss Doolittle that day when I first came to Wimpole Street. That was the beginning of self-respect for me. [*She resumes her stitching.*] And there were a hundred little things you never noticed, because they came naturally to you. Things about standing up and taking off your hat and opening doors—

PICKERING: Oh, that was nothing.

LIZA: Yes: things that shewed you thought and felt about me as if I were something better than a scullery-maid; though of course I know you would have been just the same to a scullery-maid if she had been let into the drawing room. You never took off your boots in the dining room when I was there.

PICKERING: You mustnt mind that. Higgins takes off his boots all over the place.

LIZA: I know. I am not blaming him. It is his way, isnt it? But it made such a difference to me that you didnt do it. You see, really and truly, apart from the things anyone can pick up (the dressing and the proper way of speaking, and so on), the difference between a lady and a flower girl is not how she behaves, but how she's treated. I shall always be a flower girl to Professor Higgins, because he always treats me as a flower girl, and always will; but I know I can be a lady to you, because you always treat me as a lady, and always will.

MRS HIGGINS: Please dont grind your teeth, Henry.

PICKERING: Well, this is really very nice of you, Miss Doolittle.

LIZA: I should like you to call me Eliza, now, if you would.

PICKERING: Thank you. Eliza, of course.

LIZA: And I should like Professor Higgins to call me Miss Doolittle.

HIGGINS: I'll see you damned first.

MRS HIGGINS: Henry! Henry!

PICKERING [*laughing*]: Why dont you slang back at him? Dont stand it. It would do him a lot of good.

LIZA: I cant. I could have done it once; but now I cant go back to it. You told me, you know, that when a child is brought to a foreign country, it picks up the language in a few weeks, and forgets its own. Well, I am a child in your country. I have forgotten my own language, and can speak nothing but yours. Thats the real break-off with the corner of Tottenham Court Road. Leaving Wimpole Street finishes it.

PICKERING [*much alarmed*]: Oh! but youre coming back to Wimpole Street, arnt you? Youll forgive Higgins?

HIGGINS [*rising*]: Forgive! Will she, by George! Let her go. Let her find out how she can get on without us. She will relapse into the gutter in three weeks without me at her elbow.

> *Doolittle appears at the centre window. With a look of dignified reproach at Higgins, he comes slowly and silently to his daughter, who, with her back to the window, is unconscious of his approach.*

PICKERING: He's incorrigible, Eliza. You wont relapse, will you?

LIZA: No: not now. Never again. I have learnt my lesson. I dont believe I could utter one of the old sounds if I tried.

> [*Doolittle touches her on her left shoulder. She drops her work, losing her self-possession utterly at the spectacle of her father's splendour.*]

A-a-a-a-a-ah-ow-ooh!

HIGGINS [*with a crow of triumph*]: Aha! Just so. A-a-a-a-ahowooh! A-a-a-a-ahowooh! A-a-a-a-ahowooh! Victory! Victory! [*He throws himself on the diva, folding his arms, and spraddling arrogantly.*]

DOOLITTLE: Can you blame the girl? Dont look at me like that, Eliza. It aint my fault. Ive come into money.

LIZA: You must have touched a millionaire this time, dad.

DOOLITTLE: I have. But I'm dressed something special today. I'm going to St George's, Hanover Square. Your stepmother is going to marry me.

LIZA [*angrily*]: Youre going to let yourself down to marry that low common woman!

PICKERING [*quietly*]: He ought to, Eliza. [*to Doolittle*]: Why has she changed her mind?

DOOLITTLE [*sadly*]: Intimidated, Governor. Intimidated. Middle class morality claims its victim. Wont you put on your hat, Liza, and come and see me turned off?

LIZA: If the Colonel says I must, I—I'll [*almost sobbing*] I'll demean myself. And get insulted for my pains, like enough.

DOOLITTLE: Dont be afraid: she never comes to words with anyone now, poor woman! respectability has broke all the spirit out of her.

PICKERING [*squeezing Eliza's elbow gently*]: Be kind to them, Eliza. Make the best of it.

LIZA [*forcing a little smile for him through her vexation*]: Oh well, just to shew theres no ill feeling. I'll be back in a moment. [*She goes out.*]

DOOLITTLE [*sitting down beside Pickering*]: I feel uncommon nervous about the ceremony, Colonel. I wish youd come and see me through it.

PICKERING: But youve been through it before, man. You were married to Eliza's mother.

DOOLITTLE: Who told you that, Colonel?

PICKERING: Well, nobody told me. But I concluded—naturally—

DOOLITTLE: No: that aint the natural way, Colonel: it's only the middle class way. My way was always the undeserving way. But dont say nothing to Eliza. She dont know: I always had a delicacy about telling her.

PICKERING: Quite right. We'll leave it so, if you dont mind.

DOOLITTLE: And youll come to the church, Colonel, and put me through straight?

PICKERING: With pleasure. As far as a bachelor can.

MRS HIGGINS: May I come, Mr Doolittle? I should be very sorry to miss your wedding.

DOOLITTLE: I should indeed be honoured by your condescension, maam; and my poor old woman would take it as a tremenjous compliment. She's been very low, thinking of the happy days that are no more.

MRS HIGGINS [*rising*]: I'll order the carriage and get ready.

> [*The men rise, except Higgins.*]

I shant be more than fifteen minutes.

> [*As she goes to the door Eliza comes in, hatted and buttoning her gloves.*]

I'm going to the church to see your father married, Eliza. You had better come in the brougham with me. Colonel Pickering can go on with the bridegroom.

Mrs Higgins goes out. Eliza comes to the middle of the room between the centre window and the ottoman. Pickering joins her.

DOOLITTLE: Bridegroom! What a word! It makes a man realize his position, somehow. [*He takes up his hat and goes towards the door.*]

PICKERING: Before I go, Eliza, do forgive Higgins and come back to us.

LIZA: I dont think dad would allow me. Would you, dad?

DOOLITTLE [*sad but magnanimous*]: They played you off very cunning, Eliza, them two sportsmen. If it had been only one of them, you could have nailed him. But you see, there was two; and one of them chaperoned the other, as you might say. [*to Pickering*]: It was artful of you, Colonel: but I bear no malice: I should have done the same myself. I been the victim of one woman after another all my life; and I dont grudge you two getting the better of Eliza. I shant interfere. It's time for us to go, Colonel. So long, Henry. See you in St George's, Eliza. [*He goes out.*]

PICKERING [*coaxing*]: Do stay with us, Eliza. [*He follows Doolittle.*]

Eliza goes out on the balcony to avoid being alone with Higgins. He rises and joins her there. She immediately comes back into the room and makes for the door; but he goes along the balcony quickly and gets his back to the door before she reaches it.

HIGGINS: Well, Eliza, youve had a bit of your own back, as you call it. Have you had enough? and are you going to be reasonable? Or do you want any more?

LIZA: You want me back only to pick up your slippers and put up with your tempers and fetch and carry for you.

HIGGINS: I havnt said I wanted you back at all.

LIZA: Oh, indeed. Then what are we talking about?

HIGGINS: About you, not about me. If you come back I shall treat you just as I have always treated you. I cant change my nature; and I dont intend to change my manners. My manners are exactly the same as Colonel Pickering's.

LIZA: Thats not true. He treats a flower girl as if she was a duchess.

HIGGINS: And I treat a duchess as if she was a flower girl.

LIZA: I see. [*She turns away composedly, and sits on the ottoman, facing the window.*] The same to everybody.

HIGGINS: Just so.

LIZA: Like father.

HIGGINS [*grinning, a little taken down*]: Without accepting the comparison at all points, Eliza, it's quite true that your father is not a snob, and that he will be quite at home in any station of life to which his eccentric destiny may call him. [*seriously*] The great secret, Eliza, is not having bad manners or good manners or any other particular sort of manners, but having the same manners for all human souls: in short, behaving as if you were in Heaven, where there are no third-class carriages, and one soul is as good as another.

LIZA: Amen. You are a born preacher.

HIGGINS [*irritated*]: The question is not whether I treat you rudely, but whether you ever heard me treat anyone else better.

LIZA [*with sudden sincerity*]: I dont care how you treat me. I dont mind your swearing at me. I shouldnt mind a black eye: Ive had one before this. But [*standing up and facing him*] I wont be passed over.

HIGGINS: Then get out of my way; for I wont stop for you. You talk about me as if I were a motor bus.

LIZA: So you are a motor bus: all bounce and go, and no consideration for anyone. But I can do without you: dont think I cant.

HIGGINS: I know you can. I told you you could.

LIZA [*wounded, getting away from him to the other side of the ottoman with her face to the hearth*]: I know you did, you brute. You wanted to get rid of me.

HIGGINS: Liar.

LIZA: Thank you. [*She sits down with dignity.*]

HIGGINS: You never asked yourself, I suppose, whether I could do without you.

LIZA [*earnestly*]: Dont you try to get round me. Youll h a v e to do without me.

HIGGINS [*arrogant*]: I can do without anybody. I have my own soul: my own spark of divine fire. But [*with sudden humility*] I shall miss you, Eliza. [*He sits down near her on the ottoman.*] I have learnt something from your idiotic notions: I confess that humbly and gratefully. And I have grown accustomed to your voice and appearance. I like them, rather.

LIZA: Well, you have both of them on your gramophone and in your book of photographs. When you feel lonely without me, you can turn the machine on. It's got no feelings to hurt.

HIGGINS: I cant turn your soul on. Leave me those feelings; and you can take away the voice and the face. They are not you.

LIZA: Oh, you are a devil. You can twist the heart in a girl as easy as some could twist her arms to hurt her. Mrs Pearce warned me. Time and again she has wanted to leave you; and you always got round her at the last minute. And you dont care a bit for her. And you dont care a bit for me.

HIGGINS: I care for life, for humanity; and you are a part of it that has come my way and been built into my house. What more can you or anyone ask?

LIZA: I wont care for anybody that doesnt care for me.

HIGGINS: Commercial principles, Eliza. Like [*reproducing her Covent Garden pronunciation with professional exactness*] s'yollin voylets [selling violets], isn't it?

LIZA: Dont sneer at me. It's mean to sneer at me.

HIGGINS: I have never sneered in my life. Sneering doesnt become either the human face or the human soul. I am expressing my righteous contempt for Commercialism. I dont and wont trade in affection. You call me a brute because you couldnt buy a claim on me by fetching my slippers and finding my spectacles. You were a fool: I think a woman fetching a man's slippers is a disgusting sight: did I ever fetch y o u r slippers? I think a good deal more of you for throwing them in my face. No use slaving for me and then saying you want to be cared for: who cares for a slave? If you come back, come back for the sake of good fellowship; for youll get nothing else. Youve had a thousand times as much out of me as I have out of you; and if you dare to set up your little dog's tricks of fetching and carrying slippers against my creation of a Duchess Eliza, I'll slam the door in your silly face.

LIZA: What did you do it for if you didnt care for me?

HIGGINS [*heartily*]: Why, because it was my job.

LIZA: You never thought of the trouble it would make for me.

HIGGINS: Would the world ever have been made if its maker had been afraid of making trouble? Making life means making trouble. Theres only one way of escaping trouble; and thats killing things. Cowards, you notice, are always shrieking to have troublesome people killed.

LIZA: I'm no preacher: I dont notice things like that. I notice that you dont notice me.

HIGGINS [*jumping up and walking about intolerantly*]: Eliza: youre an idiot. I waste the treasures of my Miltonic mind by spreading them before you. Once for all, understand that I go my way and do my work without caring twopence what happens to either of us. I am not intimidated, like your father and your stepmother. So you can come back or go to the devil: which you please.

LIZA: What am I to come back for?

HIGGINS [*bouncing up on his knees on the ottoman and leaning over it to her*]: For the fun of it. Thats why I took you on.

LIZA [*with averted face*]: And you may throw me out tomorrow if I dont do everything you want me to?

HIGGINS: Yes; and you may walk out tomorrow if I dont do everything y o u want me to.

LIZA: And live with my stepmother?

HIGGINS: Yes, or sell flowers.

LIZA: Oh! if I only c o u l d go back to my flower basket! I should be independent of both you and father and all the world! Why did you take my independence from me? Why did I give it up? I'm a slave now, for all my fine clothes.

HIGGINS: Not a bit. I'll adopt you as my daughter and settle money on you if you like. Or would you rather marry Pickering?

LIZA [*looking fiercely round at him*]: I wouldnt marry y o u if you asked me; and youre nearer my age than what he is.

HIGGINS [*gently*]: Than he is: not 'Than what he is.'

LIZA [*losing her temper and rising*]: I'll talk as I like. Youre not my teacher now.

HIGGINS [*reflectively*]: I dont suppose Pickering would, though. He's as confirmed an old bachelor as I am.

LIZA: Thats not what I want; and dont you think it. Ive always had chaps enough wanting me that way. Freddy Hill writes to me twice and three times a day, sheets and sheets.

HIGGINS [*disagreeably surprised*]: Damn his impudence! [*He recoils and finds himself sitting on his heels.*]

LIZA: He has a right to if he likes, poor lad. And he does love me.

HIGGINS [*getting off the ottoman*]: You have no right to encourage him.

LIZA: Every girl has a right to be loved.

HIGGINS: What! By fools like that?

LIZA: Freddy's not a fool. And if he's weak and poor and wants me, may be he'd make me happier than my betters that bully me and dont want me.

HIGGINS: Can he m a k e anything of you? Thats the point.

LIZA: Perhaps I could make something of him. But I never thought of us making anything of one another; and you never think of anything else. I only want to be natural.

HIGGINS: In short, you want me to be as infatuated about you as Freddy? Is that it?

LIZA: No I dont. Thats not the sort of feeling I want from you. And dont you be too sure of yourself or of me. I could have been a bad girl if I'd liked. Ive seen more of some things than you, for all your learning. Girls like me can drag gentlemen down to make love to them easy enough. And they wish each other dead the next minute.

HIGGINS: Of course they do. Then what in thunder are we quarrelling about?

LIZA [*much troubled*]: I want a little kindness. I know I'm a common ignorant girl, and you a book-learned gentleman; but I'm not dirt under your feet. What I done [*correcting herself*] what I did was not for the dresses and the taxis: I did it because we were pleasant together and I come——came——to care for you; not to want you to make love to me, and not forgetting the difference between us, but more friendly like.

HIGGINS: Well, of course. Thats just how I feel. And how Pickering feels. Eliza: youre a fool.

LIZA: Thats not a proper answer to give me. [*She sinks on the chair at the writing-table in tears.*]

HIGGINS: It's all youll get until you stop being a common idiot. If youre going to be a lady, youll have to give up feeling neglected if the men you know dont spend half their time snivelling over you and the other half giving you black eyes. If you cant stand the coldness of my sort of life, and the strain of it, go back to the gutter. Work til youre more a brute than a human being; and then cuddle and squabble and drink til you fall asleep. Oh, it's a fine life, the life of the gutter. It's real: it's warm: it's violent: you can feel it through the thickest skin: you can taste it and smell it without any training or any work. Not like Science and Literature and Classical Music and Philosophy and Art. You find me cold, unfeeling, selfish, dont you? Very well: be off with you to the sort of people you like. Marry some senti-mental hog or other with lots of money, and a thick pair of lips to kiss you with and a thick pair of boots to kick you with. If you cant appreciate what youve got, youd better get what you can appreciate.

LIZA [*desperate*]: Oh, you a r e a cruel tyrant. I cant talk to you: you turn everything against me: I'm always in the wrong. But you know very well all the time that youre nothing but a bully. You know I cant go back to the gutter, as you call it, and that I have no real friends in the world but you and the Colonel. You know very well I couldnt bear to live with a low common man after you two; and it's wicked and cruel of you to insult me by pretending I could. You think I must go back to Wimpole Street because I have nowhere else to go but father's. But dont you be too sure that you have me under your feet to be trampled on and talked down. I'll marry Freddy, I will, as soon as I'm able to support him.

HIGGINS [*thunderstruck*]: Freddy!!! that young fool! That poor devil who couldnt get a job as an errand boy even if he had the guts to try for it! Woman: do you not understand that I have made you a consort for a king?

LIZA: Freddy loves me: that makes him king enough for me. I dont want him to work: he wasnt brought up to it as I was. I'll go and be a teacher.

HIGGINS: What'll you teach, in heaven's name?

LIZA: What you taught me. I'll teach phonetics.

HIGGINS: Ha! ha! ha!

LIZA: I'll offer myself as an assistant to that hairy-faced Hungarian.

HIGGINS [*rising in a fury*]: What! That impostor! that humbug! that toadying ignoramus! Teach him m y methods! m y discoveries! You take one step in his direction and I'll wring your neck. [*He lays hands on her.*] Do you hear?

LIZA [*defiantly non-resistant*]: Wring away. What do I care? I knew youd strike me some day.

[*He lets her go, stamping with rage at having forgotten himself, and recoils so hastily that he stumbles back into his seat on the ottoman.*]

Aha! Now I know how to deal with you. What a fool I was not to think of it before! You cant take away the knowledge you gave me. You said I had a finer ear than you. And I can be civil and kind to people, which is more than you can. Aha! [*Purposely dropping her aitches to annoy him.*] Thats done you, Enry Iggins, it az. Now I dont care t h a t [*snapping her fingers*] for your bullying and your big talk. I'll advertize it in the papers that your duchess is only a flower girl that you taught, and that she'll teach anybody to be a duchess just the same in six months for a thousand guineas. Oh, when I think of myself crawling under your feet and being trampled on and called names, when all the time I had only to lift up my finger to be as good as you, I could just kick myself.

HIGGINS [*wondering at her*]: You damned impudent slut, you! But it's better than snivelling; better than fetching slippers and finding spectacles, isnt it? [*rising*] By George, Eliza, I said I'd make a woman of you; and I have. I like you like this.

LIZA: Yes: you turn round and make up to me now that I'm not afraid of you, and can do without you.

HIGGINS: Of course I do, you little fool. Five minutes ago you were like a millstone round my neck. Now youre a tower of strength: a consort battleship. You and I and Pickering will be three old bachelors together instead of only two men and a silly girl.

Mrs Higgins returns, dressed for the wedding. Eliza instantly becomes cool and elegant.

MRS HIGGINS: The carriage is waiting, Eliza. Are you ready?

LIZA: Quite. Is the Professor coming?

MRS HIGGINS: Certainly not. He cant behave himself in church. He makes remarks out loud all the time on the clergyman's pronunciation.

LIZA: Then I shall not see you again, Professor. Goodbye. [*She goes to the door.*]

MRS HIGGINS [*coming to Higgins*]: Goodbye, dear.

HIGGINS: Goodbye, mother. [*He is about to kiss her, when he recollects something.*] Oh, by the way, Eliza, order a ham and a Stilton cheese, will you? And buy me a pair of reindeer gloves, number eights, and a tie to match that new suit of mine. You can choose the colour. [*His cheerful, careless, vigorous voice shews that he is incorrigible.*]

LIZA [*disdainfully*]: Number eights are too small for you if you want them lined with lamb's wool. You have three new ties that you have forgotten in the drawer of your washstand. Colonel Pickering prefers double Gloucester to Stilton; and you dont notice the difference. I telephoned Mrs Pearce this morning not to forget the ham. What you are to do without me I cannot imagine. [*She sweeps out.*]

MRS HIGGINS: I'm afraid youve spoilt that girl, Henry. I should be uneasy about you and her if she were less fond of Colonel Pickering.

HIGGINS: Pickering! Nonsense: she's going to marry Freddy. Ha ha! Freddy! Freddy!! Ha ha ha ha ha!!!!! [*He roars with laughter as the play ends.*]

* * *

The rest of the story need not be shewn in action, and indeed, would hardly need telling if our imaginations were not so enfeebled by their lazy dependence on the ready-mades and reach-me-downs of the ragshop in which Romance keeps its stock of 'happy endings' to misfit all stories. Now, the history of Eliza Doolittle, though called a romance because the transfiguration it records seems exceedingly improbable, is common enough. Such transfigurations have been achieved by hundreds of resolutely ambitious young women since Nell Gwynne set them the example by playing queens and fascinating kings in the theatre in which she began by selling oranges. Nevertheless, people in all directions have assumed, for no other reason than that she became the heroine of a romance, that she must have married the hero of it. This is unbearable, not only because her little drama, if acted on such a thoughtless assumption, must be spoiled, but because the true sequel is patent to anyone with a sense of human nature in general, and of feminine instinct in particular.

Eliza, in telling Higgins she would not marry him if he asked her, was not coquetting: she was announcing a well-considered decision. When a bachelor interests, and dominates, and teaches, and becomes important to a spinster, as Higgins with Eliza, she always, if she has character enough to be capable of it, considers very seriously indeed whether she will play for becoming that bachelor's wife, especially if he is so little interested in marriage that a determined and devoted woman might capture him if she set herself resolutely to do it. Her decision will depend a good deal on whether she is really free to choose; and that, again, will depend on her age and income. If she is at the end of her youth, and has no security for her livelihood, she will marry him because she must marry somebody who will provide for her. But at Eliza's age a good-looking girl does not feel that pressure: she feels free to pick and choose. She is therefore guided by her instinct in the matter. Eliza's instinct tells her not to marry Higgins. It does not tell her to give him up. It is not in the slightest doubt as to his remaining one of the strongest personal interests in her life. It would be very sorely strained if there was another woman likely to supplant her with him. But as she feels sure of him on that last point, she has no doubt at all as to her course, and would not have any, even if the difference of twenty years of age, which seems so great to youth, did not exist between them.

As our own instincts are not appealed to by her conclusion, let us see whether we cannot discover some reason for it. When Higgins excused his indifferences to young women on the ground that they had an irresistible rival in his mother, he gave the clue to his inveterate old-bachelordom. The case is uncommon only to the extent that remarkable mothers are uncommon. If an imaginative boy has a sufficiently rich mother who has intelligence, personal grace, dignity of character without harshness, and a cultivated sense of the best art of her time to enable her to make her house beautiful, she sets a standard for him against which very few women can struggle, besides effecting for him a disengagement of his affections, his sense of beauty, and his idealism from his specifically sexual impulses. This makes him a standing puzzle to the huge number of uncultivated people who have been brought up in tasteless homes by commonplace or disagreeable parents, and to whom, consequently, litera-ture, painting, sculpture, music, and affectionate personal relations come as modes of sex if they come at all. The word passion means nothing else to them; and that Higgins could have a passion for phonetics and idealize his mother instead of Eliza, would seem to them absurd and unnatural. Nevertheless, when we look round and see that hardly anyone is too ugly or disagreeable to find a wife or a husband if he or she wants one, whilst many old maids and bachelors are above the average in quality and culture, we cannot help suspecting that the disentanglement of sex from the asso-ciations with which it is so commonly confused, a disentanglement which persons of genius achieve by sheer intellectual analysis, is sometimes produced or aided by parental fascination.

Now, though Eliza was incapable of thus explaining to herself Higgins's formida-ble powers of resistance to the charm that prostrated Freddy at the first glance, she was instinctively aware that she could never obtain a complete grip on him, or come between him and his mother (the first necessity of the married woman). To put it shortly, she knew for some mysterious reason he had not the makings of a married man in him, according to her conception of a husband as one to whom she would be his nearest and fondest and warmest interest. Even had there been no mother-rival, she would still have refused to accept an interest in herself that was secondary to philo-sophic interests. Had Mrs Higgins died, there would still have been Milton and the Universal Alphabet. Landor's remark that to those who have the greatest power of lov-ing, love is a secondary affair, would not have recommended Landor to Eliza. Put that along with her resentment of Higgins's domineering superiority, and her mistrust of his coaxing cleverness in getting around her and evading her wrath when he had gone too far with his impetuous bullying, and you will see that Eliza's instinct had good grounds for warning her not to marry her Pygmalion.

And now, whom did Eliza marry? For if Higgins was a predestinate old bachelor, she was most certainly not a predestinate old maid. Well, that can be told very shortly to those who have not guessed it from the indications she has herself given them.

Almost immediately after Eliza is stung into proclaiming her considered determi-nation not to marry Higgins, she mentions the fact that young Mr Frederick Eynsford

Hill is pouring out his love for her daily through the post. Now Freddy is young, practically twenty years younger than Higgins: he is a gentleman (or, as Eliza would qualify him, a toff), and speaks like one. He is nicely dressed, is treated by the Colonel as an equal, loves her unaffectedly, and is not her master, nor ever likely to dominate her in spite of his advantage of social standing. Eliza has no use for the foolish romantic tradition that all women love to be mastered, if not actually bullied and beaten. 'When you go to women' says Nietzsche 'take your whip with you.' Sensible despots have never confined that precaution to women: they have taken their whips with them when they have dealt with men, and been slavishly idealized by the men over whom they have flourished the whip much more than by women. No doubt there are slavish women as well as slavish men; and women, like men, admire those that are stronger than themselves. But to admire a strong person and to live under that strong person's thumb are two different things. The weak may not be admired and hero-worshipped; but they are by no means disliked or shunned; and they never seem to have the least difficulty in marrying people who are too good for them. They may fail in emergencies; but life is not one long emergency: it is mostly a string of situations for which no exceptional strength is needed, and with which even rather weak people can cope if they have a stronger partner to help them out. Accordingly, it is a truth everywhere in evidence that strong people, masculine or feminine, not only do not marry stronger people, but do not shew any preference for them in selecting their friends. When a lion meets another with a louder roar 'the first lion thinks the last a bore.' The man or woman who feels strong enough for two, seeks for every other quality in a partner than strength.

The converse is also true. Weak people want to marry strong people who do not frighten them too much; and this often leads them to make the mistake we describe metaphorically as 'biting off more than they can chew'. They want too much for too little; and when the bargain is unreasonable beyond all bearing, the union becomes impossible: it ends in the weaker party being either discarded or borne as a cross, which is worse. People who are not only weak, but silly or obtuse as well, are often in these difficulties.

This being the state of human affairs, what is Eliza fairly sure to do when she is placed between Freddy and Higgins? Will she look forward to a lifetime of fetching Higgins's slippers or to a lifetime of Freddy fetching hers? There can be no doubt about the answer. Unless Freddy is biologically repulsive to her, and Higgins biologically attractive to a degree that overwhelms all her other instincts, she will, if she marries either of them, marry Freddy.

And that is just what Eliza did.

Complications ensued; but they were economic, not romantic. Freddy had no money and no occupation. His mother's jointure, a last relic of the opulence of Largelady Park, had enabled her to struggle along in Earlscourt with an air of gentility, but not to procure any serious secondary education for her children, much less give the boy a profession. A clerkship at thirty shillings a week was beneath Freddy's dignity, and extremely distasteful to him besides. His prospects consisted of a hope that if he kept up appearances somebody would do something for him. The something appeared vaguely to his imagination as a private secretaryship or a sinecure of some sort. To his mother it perhaps appeared as a marriage to some lady of means who could not resist her boy's niceness. Fancy her feelings when he married a flower girl who had become disclassed under extraordinary circumstances which were now notorious!

It is true that Eliza's situation did not seem wholly ineligible. Her father, though formerly a dustman, and now fantastically disclassed, had become extremely popular in the smartest society by a social talent which triumphed over every prejudice and every disadvantage. Rejected by the middle class, which he loathed, he had shot up at once into the highest circles by his wit, his dustmanship (which he carried like a banner), and his Nietzschean transcendence of good and evil. At intimate ducal dinners he sat on the right hand of the Duchess; and in country houses he smoked in the pantry and was made much of by the butler when he was not feeding in the dining room and being consulted by cabinet ministers. But he found it almost as hard to do all this on four thousand a year as Mrs Eynsford Hill to live in Earlscourt on an income so pitiably smaller that I have not the heart to disclose its exact figure. He absolutely refused to add the last straw to his burden by contributing to Eliza's support.

Thus Freddy and Eliza, now Mr and Mrs Eynsford Hill, would have spent a penniless honeymoon but for a wedding present of £500 from the Colonel to Eliza. It lasted a long time because Freddy did not know how to spend money, never having any to spend, and Eliza, socially trained by a pair of bachelors, wore her clothes as long as they held together and looked pretty, without the least regard to their being many months out of fashion. Still, £500 will not last two young people for ever; and they both knew, and Eliza felt as well, that they must shift for themselves in the end. She could quarter herself on Wimpole Street because it had come to be her home; but she was quite aware that she ought not to quarter Freddy there, and that it would not be good for his character if she did.

Not that the Wimpole Street bachelors objected. When she consulted them, Higgins declined to be bothered about her housing problem when that solution was so simple. Eliza's desire to have Freddy in the house with her seemed of no more importance than if she had wanted an extra piece of bedroom furniture. Pleas as to Freddy's character, and the moral obligation on him to earn his own living, were lost on Higgins. He denied that Freddy had any character, and declared that if he tried to do any useful work some competent person would have the trouble of undoing it: a procedure involving a net loss to the community, and great unhappiness to Freddy himself, who was obviously intended by Nature for such light work as amusing Eliza, which, Higgins declared, was a much more useful and honourable occupation than working in the city. When Eliza referred again to her project of teaching phonetics, Higgins abated not a jot of his violent opposition to it. He said she was not within ten years of being qualified to meddle with his pet subject; and as it was evident that the Colonel agreed with him, she felt she could not go against them in this grave matter, and that she had no right, without Higgins's consent, to exploit the knowledge he had given her; for his knowledge seemed to her as much his private property as his watch: Eliza was no communist. Besides, she was superstitiously devoted to them both, more entirely and frankly after her marriage than before it.

It was the Colonel who finally solved the problem, which had cost him much perplexed cogitation. He one day asked Eliza, rather shyly, whether she had quite given up her notion of keeping a flower shop. She replied that she had thought of it, but had put it out of her head, because the Colonel had said, that day at Mrs Higgins's, that it would never do. The Colonel confessed that when he said that, he had not quite recovered from the dazzling impression of the day before. They broke the matter to Higgins that evening. The sole comment vouchsafed by him very nearly led to a serious quarrel with Eliza. It was to the effect that she would have in Freddy an ideal errand boy.

Freddy himself was next sounded on the subject. He said he had been thinking of a shop himself; though it had presented itself to his pennilessness as a small place in which Eliza should sell tobacco at one counter whilst he sold newspapers at the opposite one. But he agreed that it would be extraordinarily jolly to go early every morning with Eliza to Covent Garden and buy flowers on the scene of their first meeting: a sentiment which earned him many kisses from his wife. He added that he had always been afraid to propose anything of the sort, because Clara would make an awful row about a step that must damage her matrimonial chances, and his mother could not be expected to like it after clinging for so many years to that step of the social ladder on which retail trade is impossible.

This difficulty was removed by an event highly unexpected by Freddy's mother. Clara, in the course of her incursions into those artistic circles which were the highest within her reach, discovered that her conversational qualifications were expected to include a grounding in the novels of Mr H.G. Wells. She borrowed them in various directions so energetically that she swallowed them all within two months. The result was a conversion of a kind quite common today. A modern Acts of the Apostles would fill fifty whole Bibles if anyone were capable of writing it.

Poor Clara, who appeared to Higgins and his mother as a disagreeable and ridiculous person, and to her own mother as in some inexplicable way a social failure, had never seen herself in either light; for, though to some extent ridiculed and mimicked in West Kensington like everybody else there, she was accepted as a rational and normal—or shall we say inevitable?—sort of human being. At worst they called her The Pusher; but to them no more than to herself had it ever occurred that she was pushing the air, and pushing it in a wrong direction. Still, she was not happy. She was growing desperate. Her one asset, the fact that her mother was what the Epsom greengrocer called a carriage lady, had no exchange value, apparently. It had prevented her from getting educated, because the only education she could have afforded was education with the Earlscourt greengrocer's daughter. It had led her to seek the society of her mother's class; and that class simply would not have her, because she was much poorer than the greengrocer, and, far from being able to afford a maid, could not afford even a housemaid, and had to scrape along at home with an illiberally treated general servant. Under such circumstances nothing could give her an air of being a genuine product of Largelady Park. And yet its tradition made her regard a marriage with anyone within her reach as an unbearable humiliation. Commercial people and professional people in a small way were odious to her. She ran after painters and novelists; but she did not charm them; and her bold attempts to pick up and practise artistic and literary talk irritated them. She was, in short, an utter failure, an ignorant, incompetent, pretentious, unwelcome, penniless, useless little snob; and though she did not admit these disqualifications (for nobody ever faces unpleasant truths of this kind until the possibility of a way out dawns on them) she felt their effects too keenly to be satisfied with her position.

Clara had a startling eyeopener when, on being suddenly wakened to enthusiasm by a girl of her own age who dazzled her and produced in her a gushing desire to take her for a model, and gain her friendship, she discovered that this exquisite apparition had graduated from the gutter in a few months time. It shook her so violently, that when Mr H.G. Wells lifted her on the point of his puissant pen, and placed her at the angle of view from which the life she was leading and the society to which she clung appeared in its true relation to real human needs and worthy social structure, he effected a conversion and a conviction of sin comparable to the most sensational feats of General Booth or Gypsy Smith. Clara's snobbery went bang. Life suddenly began to move with her. Without knowing how or why, she began to make friends and enemies. Some of the acquaintances to whom she had been a tedious or indifferent or ridiculous affliction, dropped her: others became cordial. To her amazement she found that some 'quite nice' people were saturated with Wells, and that this accessibility to ideas was the secret of their niceness. People she had thought deeply religious, and had tried to conciliate on that track with disastrous results, suddenly took an interest in her, and revealed a hostility to conventional religion which she had never conceived possible except among the most desperate characters. They made her read Galsworthy; and Galsworthy exposed the vanity of Largelady Park and finished her. It exasperated her to think that the dungeon in which she had languished for so many unhappy years had been unlocked all the time, and that the impulses she had so carefully struggled with and stifled for the sake of keeping well with society, were precisely those by which alone she could have come into any sort of sincere human contact. In the radiance of these discoveries, and the tumult of their reaction, she made a fool of herself as freely and conspicuously as when she so rashly adopted Eliza's expletive in Mrs Higgins's drawing room; for the new-born Wellsian had to find her bearings almost as ridiculously as a baby; but nobody hates a baby for its ineptitudes, or thinks the worse of it for trying to eat the matches; and Clara lost no friends by her follies. They laughed at her to her face this time; and she had to defend herself and fight it out as best she could.

When Freddy paid a visit to Earlscourt (which he never did when he could possibly help it) to make the desolating announcement that he and his Eliza were thinking of blackening the Largelady scutcheon by opening a shop, he found the little household already convulsed by a prior announcement from Clara that she also was going to work in an old furniture shop in Dover Street, which had been started by a fellow Wellsian. This appointment Clara owed, after all, to her old social accomplishment of Push. She had made up her mind that, cost what it might, she would see Mr Wells in the flesh; and she had achieved her end at a garden party. She had better luck than so rash an enterprise deserved. Mr Wells came up to her expectations. Age had not withered him, nor could custom stale his infinite variety in half an hour. His pleasant neatness and compactness, his small hands and feet, his teeming ready brain, his unaffected accessibility, and a certain fine apprehensiveness which stamped him as susceptible from his topmost hair to his tipmost toe, proved irresistible. Clara talked of nothing else for weeks and weeks afterwards. And as she happened to talk to the lady of the furniture shop, and that lady also desired above all things to know Mr Wells and sell pretty things to him, she offered Clara a job on the chance of achieving that end through her.

And so it came about that Eliza's luck held, and the expected opposition to the flower shop melted away. The shop is in the arcade of a railway station not very far from the Victoria and Albert Museum; and if you live in that neighbourhood you may go there any day and buy a buttonhole from Eliza.

Now here is a last opportunity for romance. Would you not like to be assured that the shop was an immense success, thanks to Eliza's charms and her early business experience in Covent Garden? Alas! the truth is the truth: the shop did not pay for a long time, simply because Eliza and her Freddy did not know how to keep it. True, Eliza had not to begin at the very beginning: she knew the names and prices of the cheaper flowers; and her elation was unbounded when she found that Freddy, like all youths educated at cheap, pretentious, and thoroughly inefficient schools, knew a little Latin. It was very little, but enough to make him appear to her a Porson or Bentley, and to put him at ease with botanical nomenclature. Unfortunately he knew nothing else; and Eliza, though she could count money up to eighteen shillings or so, and had acquired a certain familiarity with the language of Milton from her struggles to qualify herself for winning Higgins's bet, could not write out a bill without utterly disgracing the establishment. Freddy's power of stating in Latin that Balbus built a wall and that Gaul was divided into three parts did not carry with it the slightest knowledge of accounts or business: Colonel Pickering had to explain to him what a cheque book and a bank account meant. And the pair were by no means easily teachable. Freddy backed up Eliza in her obstinate refusal to believe that they could save money by engaging a book-keeper with some knowledge of the business. How, they argued, could you possibly save money by going to extra expense when you already could not make both ends meet? But the Colonel, after making ends meet over and over again, at last gently insisted; and Eliza, humbled to the dust by having to beg from him so often, and stung by the uproarious derision of Higgins, to whom the notion of Freddy succeeding at anything was a joke that never palled, grasped the fact that business, like phonetics, has to be learned.

On the piteous spectacle of the pair spending their evenings in shorthand schools and polytechnic classes, learning bookkeeping and typewriting with incipient junior clerks, male and female, from the elementary schools, let me not dwell. There were even classes at the London School of Economics, and a humble personal appeal to the director of that institution to recommend a course bearing on the flower business. He, being a humorist, explained to them the method of the celebrated Dickensian essay of Chinese Metaphysics by the gentleman who read an article on China and an article on Metaphysics and combined the information. He suggested that they should combine the London School with Kew Gardens. Eliza, to whom the procedure of the Dickensian gentleman seemed perfectly correct (as in fact it was) and not in the least funny (which was only her ignorance), took the advice with entire gravity. But the effort that cost her the deepest humiliation was a request to Higgins, whose pet artistic fancy, next to Milton's verse, was caligraphy, and who himself wrote a most beautiful Italian hand, that he would teach her to write. He declared that she was congenitally incapable of forming a single letter worthy of the least of Milton's words; but she persisted; and again he suddenly threw himself into the task of teaching her with a combination of stormy intensity, concentrated patience, and occasional bursts of interesting disquisition on the beauty and nobility, the august mission and destiny, of human handwriting. Eliza ended by acquiring an extremely uncommercial script which was a positive extension of her personal beauty, and spending three times as much on stationary as anyone else because certain qualities and shapes of paper became indispensable to her. She could not even address an envelope in the usual way because it made the margins all wrong.

Their commercial schooldays were a period of disgrace and despair for the young couple. They seemed to be learning nothing about flower shops. At last they gave it up as hopeless, and shook the dust of the shorthand schools, and the polytechnics, and the London School of Economics from their feet for ever. Besides, the business was in some mysterious way beginning to take care of itself. They had somehow forgotten their objections to employing other people. They came to the conclusion that their own way was the best, and that they had really a remarkable talent for business. The Colonel, who had been compelled for some years to keep a sufficient sum on current account at his bankers to make up their deficits, found that the provision was unnecessary: the young people were prospering. It is true that there was not quite fair play between them and their competitors in trade. Their week-ends in the country cost them nothing, and saved them the price of their Sunday dinners; for the motor car was the Colonel's; and he and Higgins paid the hotel bills. Mr F. Hill, florist and greengrocer (they soon discovered that there was money in asparagus; and asparagus led to other vegetables), had an air which stamped the business as classy; and in private life he was Frederick Eynsford Hill, Esquire. Not that there was any swank about him: nobody but Eliza knew that he had been christened Frederick Challoner. Eliza herself swanked like anything.

That is all. That is how it has turned out. It is astonishing how much Eliza still manages to meddle in the housekeeping at Wimpole Street in spite of the shop and her own family. And it is notable that though she never nags her husband, and frankly loves the Colonel as if she were his favourite daughter, she has never got out of the habit of nagging Higgins that was established on the fatal night when she won his bet for him. She snaps his head off on the faintest provocation, or on none. He no longer dares to tease her by assuming an abysmal inferiority of Freddy's mind to his own. He storms and bullies and derides; but she stands up to him so ruthlessly that the Colonel has to ask her from time to time to be kinder to Higgins; and it is the only request of his that brings a mulish expression into her face. Nothing but some emergency or calamity great enough to break down all likes and dislikes, and throw them both back on their common humanity—and may they be spared any such trial!—will ever alter this. She knows that Higgins does not need her, just as her father did not need her. The very scrupulousness with which he told her that day that he had become used to having her there, and dependent on her for all sorts of little services, and that he should miss her if she want away (it would never have occurred to Freddy or the Colonel to say anything of the sort) deepens her inner certainty that she is 'no more to him than them slippers'; yet she has a sense, too, that his indifference is deeper than infatuation of commoner souls. She is immensely interested in him. She has even secret mischievous moments in which she wishes she could get him alone, on a desert island, away from all ties and with nobody else in the world to consider, and just drag him off his pedestal and see him making love like any common man. We all have private imaginations of that sort. But when it comes to business, to the life that she really leads as distinguished from the life of dreams and fancies, she likes Freddy and she likes the Colonel; and she does not like Higgins and Mr Doolittle. Galatea never does quite like Pygmalion: his relation to her is too godlike to be altogether agreeable.

The End

1913

Samuel Beckett
1906–1989

Born and raised near Dublin, where his father was a well-to-do purveyor, Samuel Beckett was sent to a boarding school at the age of fourteen, and went on to receive a BA at Trinity College, Dublin, where he distinguished himself as a scholar of French and Italian. His academic distinction won him a lectureship in Paris, where he met and became the literary disciple of James Joyce, and began writing experimental poetry and fiction. After receiving his MA from Trinity College in 1931, he gave up academic life, returned to the continent, and continued to write fiction, while travelling around France and Germany, leading a vagabond existence. He settled in Paris in 1937 and subsequently became a member of the French resistance movement. At the end of the Second World War he began writing the plays that were to make him internationally famous as the first and leading practitioner of absurdist drama. His best-known plays, *Waiting for Godot* (1953), *Endgame* (1957), and *Krapp's Last Tape* (1958), repeatedly challenge conventional dramatic expectations through their depiction of bizarre vaudeville-like characters in outlandish settings, engaged in purposeless activities, exchanging frequently illogical and comically nonsensical dialogue with each other or with themselves. And in challenging traditional forms of theatre, they ultimately challenge traditional views of human existence, suggesting that it may be as illogical, as absurd, as the dramatic spectacles they portray.

Krapp's Last Tape

A late evening in the future.

Krapp's den.

> *Front centre a small table, the two drawers of which open towards audience. Sitting at the table, facing front, i.e. across from the drawers, a wearish old man: Krapp.*
>
> *Rusty black narrow trousers too short for him. Rusty black sleeveless waistcoat, four capacious pockets. Heavy silver watch and chain. Grimy white shirt open at the neck, no collar. Surprising pair of dirty boots, size ten at least, very narrow and pointed.*
>
> *White face. Purple nose. Disordered grey hair. Unshaven.*
>
> *Very near-sighted (but unspectacled). Hard of hearing.*
>
> *Crackled voice. Distinctive intonation.*
>
> *Laborious walk.*
>
> *On the table a tape-recorder with microphone and a number of cardboard boxes containing reels of recorded tapes.*
>
> *Table and immediately adjacent area in strong white light. Rest of stage in darkness.*

Krapp remains a moment motionless, heaves a great sigh, looks at his watch, fumbles in his pockets, takes out an envelope, puts it back, fumbles, takes out a small bunch of keys, raises it to his eyes, chooses a key, gets up and moves to front of table. He stoops, unlocks first drawer, peers into it, feels about inside it, takes out a reel of tape, peers at it, puts it back, locks drawer, unlocks second drawer, peers into it, feels about inside it, takes out a large banana, peers at it, locks drawer, puts keys back in his pocket. He turns, advances to edge of stage, halts, strokes banana, peels it, drops skin at his feet, puts end of banana in his mouth and remains motionless, staring vacuously before him. Finally he bites off the end, turns aside, and begins pacing to and fro at edge of stage, in the light, i.e. not more than four or five paces either way, meditatively eating banana. He treads on skin, slips, nearly falls, recovers himself, stoops and peers at skin and finally pushes it, still stooping, with his foot over the edge of the stage into pit. He resumes his pacing, finishes banana, returns to table, sits down, remains a moment motionless, heaves a great sigh, takes keys from his pockets, raises them to his eyes, chooses key, gets up and moves to front of table, unlocks second drawer, takes out a second banana, peers at it, locks drawer, puts back keys in his pocket, turns, advances to edge of stage, halts, strokes banana, peels it, tosses skin into pit, puts end of banana in his mouth and remains motionless, staring vacuously before him. Finally he has an idea, puts banana in his waistcoat pocket, the end emerging, and goes with all the speed he can muster backstage into darkness. Ten seconds. Loud pop of cork. Fifteen seconds. He comes back into light carrying an old ledger and sits down at table. He lays ledger on table, wipes his mouth, wipes his hands on the front of his waistcoat, brings them smartly together and rubs them.

KRAPP [*briskly*]: Ah! [*He bends over ledger, turns the pages, finds the entry he wants, reads.*] Box . . . thrree . . . spool . . . five. [*He raises his head and stares front. With relish.*] Spool! [*Pause.*] Spooool! [*Happy smile. Pause. He bends over table, starts peering and poking at the boxes.*] Box . . . thrree . . . thrree . . . four . . . two . . . [*with surprise*] nine! good God! . . . seven . . . ah! the little rascal! [*He takes up box, peers at it.*] Box thrree. [*He lays it on table, opens it and peers at spools inside.*] Spool . . . [*he peers at ledger*] . . . five [*he peers at spools*] . . . five . . . five! . . . ah! the little scoundrel! [*He takes out a spool, peers at it.*] Spool five. [*He lays it on table, closes box three, puts it back with the others, takes up the spool.*] Box thrree, spool five. [*He bends over the machine, looks up. With relish.*] Spooool! [*Happy smile. He bends, loads spool on machine, rubs his hands.*] Ah! [*He peers at ledger, reads entry at foot of page.*] Mother at rest at last . . . Hm . . . The black ball . . . [*He raises his head, stares blankly in front. Puzzled.*] Black ball? . . . [*He peers again at ledger, reads.*] The dark nurse . . . [*He raises his head, broods, peers again at ledger, reads.*] Slight improvement in bowel condition . . . Hm . . . Memorable . . . what? [*He peers closer.*] Equinox, memorable equinox. [*He raises his head, stares blankly front. Puzzled.*] Memorable equinox? . . . [*Pause. He shrugs his shoulders, peers again at ledger, reads.*] Farewell to—[*he turns the page*]—love.

> He raises his head, broods, bends over machine, switches on and assumes listening posture, i.e. leaning forward, elbows on table, hand cupping ear towards machine, face front.

TAPE [*strong voice, rather pompous, clearly Krapp's at a much earlier time*]: Thirty-nine today, sound as a—[*Settling himself more comfortably he knocks one of the boxes off the table, curses, switches off, sweeps boxes and ledger violently to the ground, winds tape back to beginning, switches on, resumes posture.*] Thirty-nine today, sound as a bell, apart from my old weakness, and intellectually I have now every reason to suspect at the . . . [*hesitates*] . . . crest of the wave—or thereabouts. Celebrated the awful occasion, as in recent years, quietly at the Winehouse. Not a soul. Sat before the fire with closed eyes, separating the grain from the husks. Jotted down a few notes, on the back of an envelope. Good to be back in my den, in my old rags. Have just eaten I regret to say three bananas and only with difficulty refrained from a fourth. Fatal things for a man with my condition. [*Vehemently.*] Cut 'em out! [*Pause.*] The new light above my table is a great improvement. With all this darkness round me I feel less alone. [*Pause.*] In a way. [*Pause.*] I love to get up and move about in it, then back here to . . . [*hesitates*] . . . me. [*Pause.*] Krapp.

> Pause.

The grain, now what I wonder do I mean by that, I mean . . . [*hesitates*] . . . I suppose I mean those things worth having when all the dust has—when all my dust has settled. I close my eyes and try and imagine them.

> Pause. Krapp closes his eyes briefly.

Extraordinary silence this evening, I strain my ears and do not hear a sound. Old Miss McGlome always sings at this hour. But not tonight. Songs of her girlhood, she says. Hard to think of her as a girl. Wonderful woman though. Connaught, I fancy. [*Pause.*] Shall I sing when I am her age, if I ever am? No. [*Pause.*] Did I sing as a boy? No. [*Pause.*] Did I ever sing? No.

   Pause.

Just been listening to an old year, passages at random. I did not check in the book, but it must be at least ten or twelve years ago. At that time I think I was still living on and off with Bianca in Kedar Street. Well out of that, Jesus yes! Hopeless business. [*Pause.*] Not much about her, apart from a tribute to her eyes. Very warm. I suddenly saw them again. [*Pause.*] Incomparable! [*Pause.*] Ah well . . . [*Pause.*] These old PMs are gruesome, but I often find them—[*Krapp switches off, broods, switches on*]—a help before embarking on a new . . . [*hesitates*] . . . retrospect. Hard to believe I was ever that young whelp. The voice! Jesus! And the aspirations! [*Brief laugh in which Krapp joins.*] And the resolutions! [*Brief laugh in which Krapp joins.*] To drink less, in particular. [*Brief laugh of Krapp alone.*] Statistics. Seventeen hundred hours, out of the preceding eight thousand odd, consumed on licensed premises alone. More than 20 per cent, say 40 per cent of his waking life. [*Pause.*] Plans for a less . . . [*hesitates*] . . . engrossing sexual life. Last illness of his father. Flagging pursuit of happiness. Unattainable laxation. Sneers at what he calls his youth and thanks to God that it's over. [*Pause.*] False ring there. [*Pause.*] Shadows of the opus . . . magnum. Closing with a—[*brief laugh*]—yelp to Providence. [*Prolonged laugh in which Krapp joins.*] What remains of all that misery? A girl in a shabby green coat, on a railway-station platform? No?

   Pause.

When I look——

   Krapp switches off, broods, looks at his watch, gets up, goes backstage into darkness. Ten seconds. Pop of cork. Ten seconds. Second cork. Ten seconds. Third cork. Ten seconds. Brief burst of a quavering song.

KRAPP [*sings*]:   Now the day is over,
            Night is drawing nigh-igh,
            Shadows——

   Fit of coughing. He comes back into the light, sits down, wipes his mouth, switches on, resumes his listening posture.

TAPE: —back on the year that is gone, with what I hope is perhaps a glint of the old eye to come, there is of course the house on the canal where mother lay a-dying, in the late autumn, after her long viduity [*Krapp gives a start*], and the—[*Krapp switches off, winds back tape a little, bends his ear closer to machine, switches on*]— a-dying, after her long viduity, and the——

Krapp switches off, raises his head, stares blankly before him. His lips move in the syllables of 'viduity'. No sound. He gets up, goes backstage into darkness, comes back with an enormous dictionary, lays it on table, sits down and looks up the word.

KRAPP [*reading from dictionary*]: State—or condition of being—or remaining—a widow—or widower. [*Looks up. Puzzled.*] Being—or remaining? . . . [*Pause. He peers again at dictionary. Reading.*] 'Deep weeds of viduity' . . . Also of an animal, especially a bird . . . the vidua or weaver-bird . . . Black plumage of male . . . [*He looks up. With relish.*] The vidua-bird!

> *Pause. He closes the dictionary, switches on, resumes listening posture.*

TAPE: —bench by the weir from where I could see her window. There I sat, in the biting wind, wishing she were gone. [*Pause.*] Hardly a soul, just a few regulars, nursemaids, infants, old men, dogs. I got to know them quite well—oh by appearance of course I mean! One dark young beauty I recollect particularly, all white and starch, incomparable bosom, with a big black hooded perambulator, most funereal thing. Whenever I looked in her direction she had her eyes on me. And yet when I was bold enough to speak to her—not having been introduced—she threatened to call a policeman. As if I had designs on her virtue! [*Laugh. Pause.*] The face she had! The eyes! Like . . . [*hesitates*] . . . chrysolite! [*Pause.*] Ah well . . . [*Pause.*] I was there when—[*Krapp switches off, broods, switches on again*]—the blind went down, one of those dirty brown roller affairs, throwing a ball for a little white dog, as chance would have it. I happened to look up and there it was. All over and done with, at last. I sat on for a few moments with the ball in my hand and the dog yelping and pawing at me. [*Pause.*] Moments. Her moments, my moments. [*Pause.*] The dog's moments. [*Pause.*] In the end I held it out to him and he took it in his mouth, gently, gently. A small, old, black, hard, solid rubber ball. [*Pause.*] I shall feel it, in my hand, until my dying day. [*Pause.*] I might have kept it. [*Pause.*] But I gave it to the dog.

> Pause.

Ah well . . .

> Pause.

Spiritually a year of profound gloom and indigence until that remarkable night in March, at the end of the jetty, in the howling wind, never to be forgotten, when suddenly I saw the whole thing. The vision, at last. This I fancy is what I have chiefly to record this evening, against the day when my work will be done and perhaps no place left in my memory, warm or cold, for the miracle that . . . [*hesitates*] . . . for the fire that set it alight. What I suddenly saw then was this, that the belief I had been going on all my life, namely—[*Krapp switches off impatiently, winds tape forward, switches on again*]—great granite rocks the foam flying up in the light of the lighthouse and the wind-gauge spinning like a propellor, clear to me at last that the dark I have always struggled to keep under is in reality my most—[*Krapp curses, switches off, winds tape forward, switches on again*]—unshatterable association until my dissolution of storm and night with the light of the understanding and the fire—[*Krapp curses louder, switches off, winds tape forward, switches on again*]—my face in her breasts and my hand on her. We lay there without moving. But under us all moved, and moved us, gently, up and down, and from side to side.

    Pause.

Past midnight. Never knew such silence. The earth might be uninhabited.

    Pause.

Here I end—

Krapp switches off, winds tape back, switches on again.

—upper lake, with the punt, bathed off the bank, then pushed out into the stream and drifted. She lay stretched out on the floorboards with her hands under her head and her eyes closed. Sun blazing down, bit of a breeze, water nice and lively. I noticed a scratch on her thigh and asked her how she came by it. Picking gooseberries, she said. I said again I thought it was hopeless and no good going on, and she agreed, without opening her eyes. [*Pause.*] I asked her to look at me and after a few moments—[*pause*]—after a few moments she did, but the eyes just slits, because of the glare. I bent over her to get them in the shadow and they opened. [*Pause. Low.*] Let me in. [*Pause.*] We drifted in among the flags and stuck. The way they went down, sighing, before the stem! [*Pause.*] I lay down across her with my face in her breasts and my hand on her. We lay there without moving. But under us all moved, and moved us, gently, up and down, and from side to side.

    Pause.

Past midnight. Never knew—

Krapp switches off, broods. Finally he fumbles in his pockets, encounters the banana, takes it out, peers at it, puts it back, fumbles, brings out the envelope, fumbles, puts back envelope, looks at his watch, gets up and goes backstage into darkness. Ten seconds. Sound of bottle against glass, then brief siphon. Ten seconds. Bottle against glass alone. Ten seconds. He comes back a little unsteadily into light, goes to front of table, takes out keys, raises them to his eyes, chooses key, unlocks first drawer, peers into it, feels about inside, takes out reel, peers at it, locks drawer, puts keys back in his pocket, goes and sits down, takes reel off machine, lays it on dictionary, loads virgin reel on machine, takes envelope from his pocket, consults back of it, lays it on table, switches on, clears his throat and begins to record.

KRAPP: Just been listening to that stupid bastard I took myself for thirty years ago, hard to believe I was ever as bad as that. Thank God that's all done with anyway. [*Pause*] The eyes she had! [*Broods, realizes he is recording silence, switches off, broods.*

Finally.] Everything there, everything, all the—[*Realizes this is not being recorded, switches on.*] Everything there, everything on this old muckball, all the light and dark and famine and feasting of . . . [*hesitates*] . . . the ages! [*In a shout.*] Yes! [*Pause.*] Let that go! Jesus! Take his mind off his homework! Jesus! [*Pause. Weary.*] Ah well, maybe he was right. [*Pause.*] Maybe he was right. [*Broods. Realizes. Switches off. Consults envelope.*] Pah! [*Crumples it and throws it away. Broods. Switches on.*] Nothing to say, not a squeak. What's a year now? The sour cud and the iron stool. [*Pause.*] Revelled in the word spool. [*With relish.*] Spooool! Happiest moment of the past half million. [*Pause.*] Seventeen copies sold, of which eleven at trade price to free circulating libraries beyond the seas. Getting known. [*Pause.*] One pound six and something, eight I have little doubt. [*Pause.*] Crawled out once or twice, before the summer was cold. Sat shivering in the park, drowned in dreams and burning to be gone. Not a soul. [*Pause.*] Last fancies. [*Vehemently.*] Keep 'em under! [*Pause.*] Scalded the eyes out of me reading Effie again, a page a day, with tears again. Effie . . . [*Pause.*] Could have been happy with her, up there on the Baltic, and the pines, and the dunes. [*Pause.*] Could I? [*Pause.*] And she? [*Pause.*] Pah! [*Pause.*] Fanny came in a couple of times. Bony old ghost of a whore. Couldn't do much, but I suppose better than a kick in the crutch. The last time wasn't so bad. How do you manage it, she said, at your age? I told I'd been saving up for her all my life. [*Pause.*] Went to Vespers once, like when I was in short trousers. [*Pause. Sings.*]

Now the day is over.
Night is drawing nigh-igh,
Shadows—[*coughing, then almost inaudible*]—of the evening
Steal across the sky.

[*Gasping.*] Went to sleep and fell off the pew. [*Pause.*] Sometimes wondered in the night if a last effort mightn't—[*Pause.*] Ah finish your booze now and get to your bed. Go on with this drivel in the morning. Or leave it at that. [*Pause.*] Leave it at that. [*Pause.*] Lie propped up in the dark—and wander. Be again in the dingle on a Christmas Eve, gathering holly, the red-berried. [*Pause.*] Be again on Croghan on a Sunday morning, in the haze, with the bitch, stop and listen to the bells. [*Pause.*] And so on. [*Pause.*] Be again, be again. [*Pause.*] All that old misery. [*Pause.*] Once wasn't enough for you. [*Pause.*] Lie down across her.

> *Long pause. He suddenly bends over machine, switches off, wrenches off tape, throws it away, puts on the other, winds it forward to the passage he wants, switches on, listens staring front.*

TAPE: —gooseberries, she said. I said again I thought it was hopeless and no good going on, and she agreed, without opening her eyes. [*Pause.*] I asked her to look at me and after a few moments—[*pause*]—after a few moments she did, but the eyes just slits, because of the glare. I bent over her to get them in the shadow and they opened. [*Pause. Low.*] Let me in. [*Pause.*] We drifted in among the flags and stuck. The way they went down, sighing, before the stem! [*Pause.*] I lay down across her with my face in her breasts and my hand on her. We lay there without moving. But under us all moved, and moved us, gently, up and down, and from side to side.

> *Pause. Krapp's lips move. No sound.*

Past midnight. Never knew such silence. The earth might be uninhabited.

> *Pause.*

Here I end this reel. Box—[*pause*]—three, spool—[*pause*]—five. [*Pause.*] Perhaps my best years are gone. When there was a chance of happiness. But I wouldn't want them back. Not with the fire in me now. No, I wouldn't want them back.

> *Krapp motionless staring before him. The tape runs on in silence.*

Curtain

1958

Arthur Miller
1915–2005

Born in Manhattan, Arthur Miller obtained his BA (1938) in journalism from the University of Michigan. He wrote scripts for various agencies, all the time honing his skills as a dramatist. During the Second World War, kept out of the forces by an old injury, he visited army camps to collect material for a movie; he published the journal of his tour, *Situation Normal*, in 1944. By the time he completed *All My Sons*, his first major play, in 1947, he had received many awards for his writing. *All My Sons* received the New York Drama Critics Circle Award, as did his subsequent play, *Death of a Salesman* (1949), which also won the Pulitzer Prize. His plays are generally close realistic presentations of characters trapped in webs that they have made. 'The theatre is practically a direct reflection of the preoccupations of society,' he observed. In *The Price*, which premiered on 7 February 1968 in New York City, Miller again explores the dilemma of one family, confrontations between the father and his sons of the earlier plays giving way now to filial disloyalty.

The Price

CHARACTERS

VICTOR FRANZ   GREGORY SOLOMON
ESTHER FRANZ   WALTER FRANZ

ACT I

Today. New York.

> *Two windows are seen at the back of the stage. Daylight filters through their sooty panes, which have been X'd out with fresh whitewash to prepare for the demolition of the building.*
>
> *Now daylight seeps through a skylight in the ceiling, greyed by the grimy panes. The light from above first strikes an overstuffed armchair in centre stage. It has a faded rose slipcover. Beside it on its right, a small table with a filigreed radio of the Twenties on it and old newspapers; behind it a bridge lamp. At its left an old wind-up Victrola and a pile of records on a low table. A white cleaning cloth and a mop and pail are nearby.*
>
> *The room is progressively seen. The area around the armchair alone appears to be lived-in, with other chairs and a couch related to it. Outside this area, to the sides and back limits of the room and up the walls, is the chaos of ten rooms of furniture squeezed into this one.*
>
> *There are four couches and three settees strewn at random over the floor; wing-backs, a divan, occasional chairs. On the floor and stacked against the three walls up to the ceiling are bureaus, armoires, a tall secretary, a breakfront, a long, elaborately curved serving table, end tables, a library table, desks, glass-front bookcases, bow-front glass cabinets, and so forth. Several long rolled-up rugs and some shorter ones. A long sculling oar, bedsteads, trunks. And overhead one large and one smaller crystal chandelier hang from ropes, not connected to electric wires. Twelve dining-room chairs stand in a row along a dining-room table at left.*
>
> *There is a rich heaviness, something almost Germanic, about the furniture, a weight of time upon the bulging fronts and curving chests marshalled against the walls. The room is monstrously crowded and dense, and it is difficult to decide if the stuff is impressive or merely over-heavy and ugly.*
>
> *An uncovered harp, its gilt chipped, stands alone downstage, right. At the back, behind a rather makeshift drape, long since faded, can be seen a small sink, a hot-plate, and an old icebox. Up right, a door to the bedroom. Down left, a door to the corridor and stairway, which are unseen.*
>
> *We are in the attic of a Manhattan brownstone soon to be torn down.*

> *From the down-left door, Police Sergeant Victor Franz enters in uniform. He halts inside the room, glances about, walks at random a few feet, then comes to a halt. Without expression, yet somehow stilled by some emanation from the room, he lets his gaze move from point to point, piece to piece, absorbing its sphinxlike presence.*

He moves to the harp with a certain solemnity, as toward a coffin, and, halting before it, reaches out and plucks a string. He turns and crosses to the dining-room table and removes his gun belt and jacket, hanging them on a chair which he has taken off the table, where it had been set upside down along with two others.

He looks at his watch, waiting for time to pass. Then his eye falls on the pile of records in front of the phonograph. He raises the lid of the machine, sees a record already on the turntable, cranks, and sets the tone arm on the record. Gallagher and Shean sing. He smiles at the corniness.

With the record going he moves to the long sculling oar which stands propped against furniture and touches it. Now he recalls something, reaches in behind a chest, and takes out a fencing foil and mask. He snaps the foil in the air, his gaze held by memory. He puts the foil and mask on the table, goes through two or three records on the pile, and sees a title that makes him smile widely. He replaces the Gallagher and Shean record with this. It is a Laughing Record—two men trying unsuccessfully to get out a whole sentence through their wild hysteria.

He smiles. Broader. Chuckles. Then really laughs. It gets into him; he laughs more fully. Now he bends over with laughter, taking an unsteady step as helplessness rises in him.

Esther, his wife, enters from the down-left door. His back is to her. A half-smile is already on her face as she looks about to see who is laughing with him. She starts toward him, and he hears her heels and turns.

ESTHER: What in the world is that?

VICTOR, *surprised*: Hi! *He lifts the tone arm, smiling, a little embarrassed.*

ESTHER: Sounded like a party in here!

He gives her a peck.

Of the record: What *is* that?

VICTOR, *trying not to disapprove openly*: Where'd you get a drink?

ESTHER: I told you. I went for my checkup. *She laughs with a knowing abandonment of good sense.*

VICTOR: Boy, you and that doctor. I thought he told you not to drink.

ESTHER—*laughs*: I had one! One doesn't hurt me. Everything's normal anyway. He sent you his best. *She looks about.*

VICTOR: Well, that's nice. The dealer's due in a few minutes, if you want to take anything.

ESTHER, *looking around with a sigh*: Oh, dear God—here it is again.

VICTOR: The old lady did a nice job.

ESTHER: Ya—I never saw it so clean. *Indicating the room*: Make you feel funny?

VICTOR—*shrugs*: No, not really—she didn't recognize me, imagine?

ESTHER: Dear boy, it's a hundred and fifty years. *Shaking her head as she stares about*: Huh.

VICTOR: What?

ESTHER: Time.

VICTOR: I know.

ESTHER: There's something different about it.

VICTOR: No, it's all the way it was. *Indicating one side of the room*: I had my desk on that side and my cot. The rest is the same.

ESTHER: Maybe it's that it always used to seem so pretentious to me, and kind of bourgeois. But it does have a certain character. I think some of it's in style again. It's surprising.

VICTOR: Well, you want to take anything?

ESTHER, *looking about, hesitates*: I don't know if I want it around. It's all so massive . . . where would we put any of it? That chest is lovely. *She goes to it.*

VICTOR: That was mine. *Indicating one across the room*: The one over there was Walter's. They're a pair.

ESTHER, *comparing*: Oh ya! Did you get hold of him?

VICTOR—*rather glances away, as though this had been an issue*: I called again this morning—he was in consultation.

ESTHER: Was he in the office?

VICTOR: Ya. The nurse went and talked to him for a minute—it doesn't matter. As long as he's notified so I can go ahead.

She suppresses comment, picks up a lamp.

That's probably real porcelain. Maybe it'd go in the bedroom.

ESTHER, *putting the lamp down*: Why don't I meet you somewhere? The whole thing depresses me.

VICTOR: Why? It won't take long. Relax. Come on, sit down; the dealer'll be here any minute.

ESTHER, *sitting on a couch*: There's just something so damned rotten about it. I can't help it; it always was. The whole thing is infuriating.

VICTOR: Well, don't get worked up. We'll sell it and that'll be the end of it. I picked up the tickets, by the way.

ESTHER: Oh, good. *Laying her head back*: Boy, I hope it's a good picture.

VICTOR: Better be. Great, not good. Two-fifty apiece.

ESTHER, *with sudden protest*: I don't care! I want to go somewhere. *She aborts further response, looking around.* God, what's it all about? When I was coming up the stairs just now, and all the doors hanging open . . . It doesn't seem possible . . .

VICTOR: They tear down old buildings every day in the week, kid.

ESTHER: I know, but it makes you feel a hundred years old. I hate empty rooms. *She muses.* What was that screwball's name?—rented the front parlour, remember?—repaired saxophones?

VICTOR, *smiling*: Oh—Saltzman. *Extending his hand sideways*: With the one eye went out that way.

ESTHER: Ya! Every time I came down the stairs, there he was waiting for me with his four red hands! How'd he ever get all those beautiful girls?

VICTOR—*laughs*: God knows. He must've smelled good.

She laughs, and he does.

He'd actually come running up here sometimes; middle of the afternoon—'Victor, come down quick, I got extras!'

ESTHER: And you did, too!

VICTOR: Why not? If it was free, you took it.

ESTHER, *blushing*: You never told me that.

VICTOR: No, that was before you. Mostly.

ESTHER: You dog.

VICTOR: So what? It was the Depression.

She laughs at the non sequitur.

No, really—I think people were friendlier; lot more daytime screwing in those days. Like the McLoughlin sisters—remember, with the typing service in the front bedroom? *He laughs.* My father used to say, 'In that typing service it's two dollars a copy.'

She laughs. It subsides.

ESTHER: And they're probably all dead.

VICTOR: I guess Saltzman would be—he was well along. Although—*He shakes his head, laughs softly in surprise.* Jeeze, he wasn't either. I think he was about . . . my age now. Huh!

Caught by the impact of time, they stare for a moment in silence.

ESTHER—*gets up, goes to the harp*: Well, where's your dealer?

VICTOR, *glancing at his watch*: It's twenty to six. He should be here soon.

She plucks the harp.

That should be worth something.

ESTHER: I think a lot of it is. But you're going to have to bargain, you know. You can't just take what they say . . .

VICTOR, *with an edge of protest*: *I* can bargain; don't worry, I'm not giving it away.

ESTHER: Because they *expect* to bargain.

VICTOR: Don't get depressed already, will you? We didn't even start. *I* intend to bargain, I know the score with these guys.

ESTHER—*withholds further argument, goes to the phonograph; firing up some slight gaiety*: What's this record?

VICTOR: It's a Laughing Record. It was a big thing in the Twenties.

ESTHER, *curiously*: You remember it?

VICTOR: Very vaguely. I was only five or six. Used to play them at parties. You know— see who could keep a straight face. Or maybe they just sat around laughing; I don't know.

ESTHER: That's a wonderful idea!

Their relation is quite balanced, so to speak; he turns to her.

VICTOR: You look good.

She looks at him, an embarrassed smile.

I mean it.—I *said* I'm going to bargain, why do you . . . ?

ESTHER: I believe you.—This is the suit.

VICTOR: Oh, is that it! And how much? Turn around.

ESTHER, *turning*: Forty-five, imagine? He said nobody'd buy it, it was too simple.

VICTOR, *seizing the agreement*: Boy, women are dumb; that is really handsome. See, I don't mind if you get something for your money, but half the stuff they sell is such crap . . . *Going to her*: By the way, look at this collar. Isn't this one of the ones you just bought?

ESTHER, *examines it*: No, that's an older one.

VICTOR: Well, even so. *Turning up a heel*: Ought to write to Consumers Union about these heels. Three weeks—look at them!

ESTHER: Well, you don't walk straight.—You're not going in uniform, I hope.

VICTOR: I could've murdered that guy! I'd just changed, and McGowan was trying to fingerprint some bum and he didn't want to be printed; so he swings out his arm just as I'm going by, right into my container.

ESTHER, *as though this symbolized*: Oh, God . . .

VICTOR: I gave it to that quick cleaner, he'll try to have it by six.

ESTHER: Was there cream and sugar in the coffee?

VICTOR: Ya.

ESTHER: He'll never have it by six.

VICTOR, *assuagingly*: He's going to try.

ESTHER: Oh, forget it.

Slight pause. Seriously disconsolate, she looks around at random.

VICTOR: Well, it's only a movie . . .

ESTHER: But we go out so rarely—why must everybody know your salary? I want an evening! I want to sit down in a restaurant without some drunken ex-cop coming over to the table to talk about old times.

VICTOR: It happened twice. After all these years, Esther, it would seem to me . . .

ESTHER: I know it's unimportant—but like that man in the museum; he really did— he thought you were the sculptor.

VICTOR: So I'm a sculptor.

ESTHER, *bridling*: Well, it was nice, that's all! You really do, Vic—you look distinguished in a suit. Why not? *Laying her head back on the couch*: I should've taken down the name of that scotch.

VICTOR: All scotch is chemically the same.

ESTHER: I know; but some is better.

VICTOR, *looking at his watch*: Look at that, will you? Five-thirty sharp, he tells me. People say anything. *He moves with a heightened restlessness, trying to down his irritation with her mood. His eye falls on a partly opened drawer of a chest, and he opens it and takes out an ice skate*. Look at that, they're still good! *He tests the edge with his fingernail; she merely glances at him.* They're even sharp. We ought to skate again sometime. *He sees her unremitting moodiness.* Esther, I said I would bargain!—You see?—You don't know how to drink; it only depresses you.

ESTHER: Well, it's the kind of depression I enjoy!

VICTOR: Hot diggity dog.

ESTHER: I have an idea.

VICTOR: What?

ESTHER: Why don't you leave me? Just send me enough for coffee and cigarettes.

VICTOR: Then you'd *never* have to get out of bed.

ESTHER: I'd get out. Once in a while.

VICTOR: I got a better idea. Why don't you go off for a couple of weeks with your doctor? Seriously. It might change your viewpoint.

ESTHER: I wish I could.

VICTOR: Well, do it. He's got a suit. You could even take the dog—especially the dog. *She laughs.* It's not funny. Every time you go out for one of those walks in the rain I hold my breath what's going to come back with you.

ESTHER, *laughing*: Oh, go on, you love her.

VICTOR: I love her! You get plastered, you bring home strange animals, and I 'love' them! I do not love that goddamned dog!

> *She laughs with affection, as well as with certain feminine defiance.*

ESTHER: Well, I want her!

VICTOR—*pause*: It won't be solved by a dog, Esther. You're an intelligent, capable woman, and you can't lay around all day. Even something part-time, it would give you a place to go.

ESTHER: I don't need a place to go. *Slight pause.* I'm not quite used to Richard not being there, that's all.

VICTOR: He's gone, kid. He's a grown man; you've got to do something with yourself.

ESTHER: I can't go to the same place day after day. I never could and I never will. Did you *ask* to speak to your brother?

VICTOR: I asked the nurse. Yes. He couldn't break away.

ESTHER: That son of a bitch. It's sickening.

VICTOR: Well, what are you going to do? He never had that kind of feeling.

ESTHER: What feeling? To come to the phone after sixteen years? It's common decency. *With sudden intimate sympathy*: You're furious, aren't you?

VICTOR: Only at myself. Calling him again and again all week like an idiot . . . To hell with him, I'll handle it alone. It's just as well.

ESTHER: What about his share?

> *He shifts; pressed and annoyed.*

I don't want to be a pest—but I think there could be some money here, Vic.

> *He is silent.*

You're going to raise that with him, aren't you?

VICTOR, *with a formed decision*: I've been thinking about it. He's got a right to his half, why should he give up anything?

ESTHER: I thought you'd decided to put it to him?

VICTOR: I've changed my mind. I don't really feel he owes me anything, I can't put on an act.

ESTHER: But how many Cadillacs can he drive?

VICTOR: That's why he's got Cadillacs. People who love money don't give it away.

ESTHER: I don't know why you keep putting it like charity. There's such a thing as a moral debt. Vic, you made his whole career possible. What law said that only he could study medicine—?

VICTOR: Esther, please—let's not get back on that, will you?

ESTHER: I'm not back on anything—you were even the better student. That's a real debt, and he ought to be made to face it. He could never have finished medical school if you hadn't taken care of Pop. I mean we ought to start talking the way people talk! There could be some real money here.

VICTOR: I doubt that. There are no antiques or—

ESTHER: Just because it's ours why must it be worthless?

VICTOR: Now what's that for?

ESTHER: Because that's the way we think! We do!

VICTOR, *sharply*: The man won't even come to the phone, how am I going to—?

ESTHER: Then you write him a letter, bang on his door. This *belongs* to you!

VICTOR, *surprised, seeing how deadly earnest she is*: What are you so excited about?

ESTHER: Well, for one thing it might help you make up your mind to take your retirement.

A slight pause.

VICTOR, *rather secretively, unwillingly*: It's not the money been stopping me.

ESTHER: Then what is it?

He is silent.

I just thought that with a little cushion you could take a month or two until something occurs to you that you want to do.

VICTOR: It's all I think about right now, I don't have to quit to think.

ESTHER: But nothing seems to come of it.

VICTOR: Is it that easy? I'm going to be fifty. You don't just start a whole new career. I don't understand why it's so urgent all of a sudden.

ESTHER—*laughs*: All of a sudden! It's all I've been talking about since you became eligible—I've been saying the same thing for three years!

VICTOR: Well, it's not three years—

ESTHER: It'll be three years in March! It's *three years*. If you'd gone back to school then you'd almost have your Master's by now; you might have had a chance to get into something you'd love to do. Isn't that true? Why can't you make a move?

VICTOR—*pause. He is almost ashamed*: I'll tell you the truth. I'm not sure the whole thing wasn't a little unreal. I'd be fifty-three, fifty-four by the time I could start doing anything.

ESTHER: But you always knew that.

VICTOR: It's different when you're right on top of it. I'm not sure it makes any sense now.

ESTHER, *moving away, the despair in her voice*: Well . . . . this is exactly what I tried to tell you a thousand times. It makes the same sense it ever made. But you might have twenty more years, and that's still a long time. Could do a lot of interesting things in that time. *Slight pause.* You're so young, Vic.

VICTOR: I am?

ESTHER: Sure! I'm not, but you are. God, all the girls goggle at you, what do you want?

VICTOR—*laughs emptily*: It's hard to discuss it, Es, because I don't understand it.

ESTHER: Well, why not talk about what you don't understand? Why do you expect yourself to be an authority?

VICTOR: Well, one of us is got to stay afloat, kid.

ESTHER: You want me to pretend everything is great? I'm bewildered and I'm going to act bewildered! *It flies out as though long suppressed*: I've asked you fifty times to write a letter to Walter—

VICTOR, *like a repeated story*: What's this with Walter again? What's Walter going to—?

ESTHER: He is an important scientist, and that hospital's building a whole new research division. I saw it in the paper, it's his hospital.

VICTOR: Esther, the man hasn't called me in sixteen years.

ESTHER: But neither have you called him!

> He looks at her in surprise.

Well, you haven't. That's also a fact.

VICTOR, *as though the idea were new and incredible*: What would I call him for?

ESTHER: Because, he's your brother, he's influential, and he could help—Yes, that's how people do, Vic! Those articles he wrote had a real idealism, there was a genuine human quality. I mean people do change, you know.

VICTOR, *turning away*: I'm sorry, I don't need Walter.

ESTHER: I'm not saying you have to approve of him; he's a selfish bastard, but he just might be able to put you on the track of something. I don't see the humiliation.

VICTOR, *pressed, irritated*: I don't understand why it's all such an emergency.

ESTHER: Because I don't know where in hell I am, Victor! *To her own surprise, she has ended nearly screaming. He is silent. She retracts.* I'll do anything if I know why, but all these years we've been saying, once we get the pension we're going to start to live. . . . It's like pushing against a door for twenty-five years and suddenly it opens . . . and we stand there. Sometimes I wonder, maybe I misunderstood you, maybe you like the department.

VICTOR: I've hated every minute of it.

ESTHER: I did everything wrong! I swear, I think if I demanded more it would have helped you more.

VICTOR: That's not true. You've been a terrific wife—

ESTHER: I don't think so. But the security meant so much to you I tried to fit into that; but I was wrong. God—just before coming here, I looked around at the apartment to see if we could use any of this—and it's all so ugly. It's worn and shabby and tasteless. And I have good taste! I know I do! It's that everything was always temporary with us. It's like we never were anything, we were always about-to-be. I think back to the war when any idiot was making so much money—that's when you should have quit, and I knew it, I knew it!

VICTOR: That's when I wanted to quit.

ESTHER: I only had one drink, Victor, so don't—

VICTOR: Don't change the whole story, kid. I wanted to quit, and you got scared.

ESTHER: Because you said there was going to be a Depression after the war.

VICTOR: Well, go to the library, look up the papers around 1945, see what they were saying!

ESTHER: I don't care! *She turns away—from her own irrationality.*

VICTOR: I swear, Es, sometimes you make it sound like we've had no life at all.

ESTHER: God—my mother was so right! I can never believe what I see. I knew you'd never get out if you didn't during the war—I saw it happening, and I said nothing. You know what the goddamned trouble is?

VICTOR, *glancing at his watch, as he senses the end of her revolt*: What's the goddamned trouble?

ESTHER: We can never keep our minds on money! We worry about it, we talk about it, but we can't seem to want it. I do, but you don't. I really do, Vic. I want it. Vic? *I want money*!

VICTOR: Congratulations.

ESTHER: You go to hell!

VICTOR: I wish you'd stop comparing yourself to other people, Esther! That's all you're doing lately.

ESTHER: Well, I can't help it!

VICTOR: Then you've got to be a failure, kid, because there's always going to be somebody up ahead of you. What happened? I have a certain nature; just as you do— I didn't change—

ESTHER: But you have changed. You've been walking around like a zombie ever since the retirement came up. You've gotten so vague—

VICTOR: Well, it's a decision. And I'd like to feel a little more certain about it. . . . Actually, I've even started to fill out the forms a couple of times.

ESTHER, *alerted*: And?

VICTOR, *with difficulty—he cannot understand it himself*: I suppose there's some kind of finality about it that . . . *He breaks off.*

ESTHER: But what else did you expect?

VICTOR: It's stupid; I admit it. But you look at that goddamned form and you can't help it. You sign your name to twenty-eight years and you ask yourself, Is that all? Is that it? And it is, of course. The trouble is, when I think of starting something new, that number comes up—five oh—and the steam goes out. But I'll do something. I will! *With a greater closeness to her now*: I don't know what it is; every time I think about it all—it's almost frightening.

ESTHER: What?

VICTOR: Well, like when I walked in here before . . . *He looks around*. This whole thing—it hit me like some kind of craziness. Piling up all this stuff here like it was made of gold. *He half-laughs, almost embarrassed*. I brought up every stick; damn near saved the carpet tacks. *He turns to the centre chair*. That whole way I was with him—it's inconceivable to me now.

ESTHER, *with regret over her sympathy*: Well . . . you loved him.

VICTOR: I know, but it's all words. What was he? A busted businessman like thousands of others, and I acted like some kind of a mountain crashed. I tell you the truth, every now and then the whole thing is like a story somebody told me. You ever feel that way?

ESTHER: All day, every day.

VICTOR: Oh, come on—

ESTHER: It's the truth. The first time I walked up those stairs I was nineteen years old. And when you opened that box with your first uniform in it—remember that? When you put it on the first time?—how we laughed? If anything happened you said you'd call a cop! *They both laugh*. It was like a masquerade. And we were right. That's when we were right.

VICTOR, *pained by her pain*: You know, Esther, every once in a while you try to sound childish and it—

ESTHER: I mean to be! I'm sick of the—Oh, forget it, I want a drink. *She goes for her purse*.

VICTOR, *surprised*: What's that, the great adventure? Where are you going all of a sudden?

ESTHER: I can't stand it in here, I'm going for a walk.

VICTOR: Now you cut out this nonsense!

ESTHER: I am not an alcoholic!

VICTOR: You've had a good life compared to an awful lot of people! You trying to turn into a goddamned teenager or something?

ESTHER, *indicating the furniture*: Don't talk childishness to me, Victor—not in this room! You let it lay here all these years because you can't have a simple conversation with your own brother, and I'm childish? You're still eighteen years old with that man! I mean I'm stuck, but I admit it!

VICTOR, *hurt*: Okay. Go ahead.

ESTHER—*she can't quite leave*: You got a receipt? I'll get your suit. *He doesn't move. She makes it rational*: I just want to get out of here.

VICTOR—*takes out a receipt and gives it to her. His voice is cold*: It's right off Seventh. The address is on it. *He moves from her*.

ESTHER: I'm coming back right away.

VICTOR, *freeing her to her irresponsibility*: Do as you please, kid. I mean it.

ESTHER: You were grinding your teeth again last night. Did you know that?

VICTOR: Oh! No wonder my ear hurts.

ESTHER: I wish I had a tape recorder. I mean it, it's gruesome; sounds like a lot of rocks coming down a mountain. I wish you could hear it, you wouldn't take this self-sufficient attitude.

> *He is silent, alarmed, hurt. He moves upstage as though looking at the furniture.*

VICTOR: It's okay. I think I get the message.

ESTHER, *afraid—she tries to smile and goes back toward him*: Like what?

VICTOR—*moves a chair and does a knee bend and draws out the chassis of an immense old radio*: What other message is there?

> *Slight pause.*

ESTHER, *to retrieve the contact*: What's that?

VICTOR: Oh, one of my old radios that I made. Mama mia, look at those tubes.

ESTHER, *more wondering than she feels about radios*: Would that work?

VICTOR: No, you need a storage battery. . . . *Recalling, he suddenly looks up at the ceiling.*

ESTHER, *looking up*: What?

VICTOR: One of my batteries exploded, went right through there someplace. *He points.* There! See where the plaster is different?

ESTHER, *striving for some spark between them*: Is this the one you got Tokyo on?

VICTOR, *not relenting, his voice dead*: Ya, this is the monster.

ESTHER, *with a warmth*: Why don't you take it?

VICTOR: Ah, it's useless.

ESTHER: Didn't you once say you had a lab up here? Or did I dream that?

VICTOR: Sure, I took it apart when Pop and I moved up here. Walter had that wall, and I had this. We did some great tricks up here.

> *She is fastened on him.*

> *He avoids her eyes and moves waywardly.* I'll be frank with you, kid—I look at my life and the whole thing is incomprehensible to me. I know all the reasons and all the reasons and all the reasons, and it ends up—nothing. *He goes to the harp, touches it.*

> It's strange, you know? I forgot all about it—we'd work up here all night sometimes, and it was often full of music. My mother'd play for hours down in the library. Which is peculiar, because a harp is so soft. But it penetrates, I guess.

ESTHER: You're dear. You are, Vic. *She starts toward him, but he thwarts her by looking at his watch.*

VICTOR: I'll have to call another man. Come on, let's get out of here. *With a hollow, exhausted attempt at joy*: We'll get my suit and act rich!

ESTHER: Vic, I didn't mean that I—

VICTOR: Forget it. Wait, let me put these away before somebody walks off with them. *He takes up the foil and mask.*

ESTHER: Can you still do it?

VICTOR, *his sadness, his distance clinging to him*: Oh, no, you gotta be in shape for this. It's all in the thighs—

ESTHER: Well, let me see, I never saw you do it!

VICTOR, *giving the inch*: All right, but I can't get down far enough any more. *He takes position, feet at right angles, bouncing himself down to a difficult crouch.*

ESTHER: Maybe you could take it up again.

VICTOR: Oh no, it's a lot of work, it's the toughest sport there is. *Resuming position*: Okay, just stand there.

ESTHER: Me?

VICTOR: Don't be afraid. *Snapping the tip*: It's a beautiful foil, see how alive it is? I beat Princeton with this. *He laughs tiredly and makes a tramping lunge from yards away; the button touches her stomach.*

ESTHER, *springing back*: God! Victor!

VICTOR: What?

ESTHER: You looked beautiful.

> *He laughs, surprised and half-embarrassed—when both of them are turned to the door by a loud, sustained coughing out in the corridor. The coughing increases.*
>
> *Enter Gregory Solomon. In brief, a phenomenon; a man nearly ninety but still straight-backed and the air of his massiveness still with him. He has perfected a way of leaning on his cane without appearing weak.*
>
> *He wears a worn fur-felt black fedora, its brim turned down on the right side like Jimmy Walker's—although much dustier—and a shapeless topcoat. His frayed tie has a thick knot, askew under a curled-up collar tab. His vest is wrinkled, his trousers baggy. A large diamond ring is on his left index finger. Tucked under his arm, a wrung-out leather portfolio. He hasn't shaved today.*
>
> *Still coughing, catching his breath, trying to brush his cigar ashes off his lapel in a hopeless attempt at businesslike decorum, he is nodding at Esther and Victor and has one hand raised in a promise to speak quite soon. Nor has he failed to glance with some suspicion at the foil in Victor's hand.*

VICTOR: Can I get you a glass of water?

> *Solomon gestures an imperious negative, trying to stop coughing.*

ESTHER: Why don't you sit down?

> *Solomon gestures thanks, sits in the centre armchair, the cough subsiding.*

You sure you don't want some water?

SOLOMON, *in a Russian-Yiddish accent*: Water I don't need; a little blood I could use. Thank you. *He takes deep breaths, his attention on Victor, who now puts down the foil.* Oh boy. That's some stairs.

ESTHER: You all right now?

SOLOMON: Another couple steps you'll be in heaven. Ah—excuse me, Officer, I am looking for a party. The name is . . . *He fingers in his vest.*

VICTOR: Franz.

SOLOMON: That's it, Franz.

VICTOR: That's me.

Solomon looks incredulous.

Victor Franz.

SOLOMON: So it's a policeman!

VICTOR, *grinning*: Uh huh.

SOLOMON: What do you know! *Including Esther.* You see? There's only one beauty to this lousy business, you meet all kinda people. But I never dealed with a police-man. *Reaching over to shake hands*: I'm very happy to meet you. My name is Solomon, Gregory Solomon.

VICTOR, *shaking hands*: This is my wife.

ESTHER: How do you do.

SOLOMON, *nodding appreciatively to Esther*: Very nice. *To Victor*: That's a nice-looking woman. *He extends his hands to her.* How do you do, darling. Beautiful suit.

ESTHER—*laughs*: The fact is, I just bought it!

SOLOMON: You got good taste. Congratulations, wear it in good health. *He lets go of her hand.*

ESTHER: I'll go to the cleaner dear. I'll be back soon. *With a step toward the door—to Solomon*: Will you be very long?

SOLOMON, *glancing around at the furniture as at an antagonist*: With furniture you never know, can be short, can be long, can be medium.

ESTHER: Well, you give him a good price now, you hear?

SOLOMON: Ah ha! *Waving her out*: Look, you go to the cleaner, and we'll take care everything one hundred per cent.

ESTHER: Because there's some very beautiful stuff here. I know it, but he doesn't.

SOLOMON: I'm not sixty-two years in the business by taking advantage. Go, enjoy the cleaner.

She and Victor laugh.

ESTHER, *shaking her finger at him*: I hope I'm going to like you!

SOLOMON: Sweetheart, all the girls like me, what can I do?

ESTHER, *still smiling—to Victor as she goes to the door*: You be careful.

VICTOR, *nodding*: See you later.

She goes.

SOLOMON: I like her, she's suspicious.

VICTOR, *laughing in surprise*: What do you mean by that?

SOLOMON: Well, a girl who believes everything, how you gonna trust her?

Victor laughs appreciatively.

I had a wife . . . *He breaks off with a wave of the hand.* Well, what's the difference? Tell me, if you don't mind, how did you get my name?

VICTOR: In the phone book.

SOLOMON: You don't say! The phone book.

VICTOR: Why?

SOLOMON, *cryptically*: No-no, that's fine, that's fine.

VICTOR: The ad said you're a registered appraiser.

SOLOMON: Oh yes. I am registered, I am licensed, I am even vaccinated.

> *Victor laughs.*

Don't laugh, the only thing you can do today without a licence is you'll go up the elevator and jump out the window. But I don't have to tell you, you're a policeman, you know this world. *Hoping for contact*: I'm right?

VICTOR, *reserved*: I suppose.

SOLOMON, *surveying the furniture, one hand on his thigh, the other on the chair arm in a naturally elegant position*: So. *He glances about again, and with an uncertain smile*: That's a lot of furniture. This is all for sale?

VICTOR: Well, ya.

SOLOMON: Fine, fine. I just like to be sure where we are. *With a weak attempt at a charming laugh*: Frankly, in this neighbourhood I never expected such a load. It's very surprising.

VICTOR: But I said it was a whole houseful.

SOLOMON, *with a leaven of unsureness*: Look, don't worry about it, we'll handle everything very nice. *He gets up from the chair and goes to one of the pair of chiffoniers which he is obviously impressed with. He looks up at the chandeliers. Then straight at Victor*: I'm not mixing in, Officer, but if you wouldn't mind—what is your connection? How do you come to this?

VICTOR: It was my family.

SOLOMON: You don't say. Looks like it's standing here a long time, no?

VICTOR: Well, the old man moved everything up here after the '29 crash. My uncles took over the house and they let him keep this floor.

SOLOMON, *as though to emphasize that he believes it*: I see. *He walks to the harp.*

VICTOR: Can you give me an estimate now, or do you have to—?

SOLOMON, *running a hand over the harp frame*: No-no, I'll give you right away, I don't waste a minute, I'm very busy. *He plucks a string, listens. Then bends down and runs a hand over the sounding board*: He passed away, your father?

VICTOR: Oh, long time ago—about sixteen years.

SOLOMON, *standing erect*: It's standing here sixteen years?

VICTOR: Well, we never got around to doing anything about it, but they're tearing the building down, so . . . It was very good stuff, you know—they had quite a little money.

SOLOMON: Very good, yes . . . I can see. *He leaves the harp with an estimating glance.* I was also very good; now I'm not so good. Time, you know, is a terrible thing. *He is a distance from the harp and indicates it.* That sounding board is cracked, you know. But don't worry about it, it's still a nice object. *He goes to the armoire and strokes the veneer.* It's a funny thing—an armoire like this, thirty years you couldn't give it away; it was a regular measles. Today all of a sudden, they want it again. Go figure it out. *He goes to one of the chests.*

VICTOR, *pleased*: Well, give me a good price and we'll make a deal.

SOLOMON: Definitely. You see, I don't lie to you. *He is pointing to the chest.* For instance, a chiffonier like this I wouldn't have to keep it a week. *Indicating the other chest:* That's a pair you know.

VICTOR: I know.

SOLOMON: That's a nice chairs, too. *He sits on a dining room chair, rocking to test its tightness.* I like the chairs.

VICTOR: There's more stuff in the bedroom, if you want to look.

SOLOMON: Oh? *He goes toward the bedroom.* What've you got here? *He looks into the bedroom, up and down.* I like the bed. That's a very nice carved bed. That I can sell. That's your parents' bed?

VICTOR: Yes. They may have bought that in Europe, if I'm not mistaken. They used to travel a good deal.

SOLOMON: Very handsome, very nice. I like it. *He starts to return to the centre chair, eyes roving the furniture.* Looks a very nice family.

VICTOR: By the way, that dining-room table opens up. Probably seat about twelve people.

SOLOMON, *looking at the table*: I know that. Yes. In a pinch even fourteen. *He picks up the foil.* What's this? I thought you were stabbing your wife when I came in.

VICTOR, *laughing*: No, I just found it. I used to fence years ago.

SOLOMON: You went to college?

VICTOR: Couple of years, ya.

SOLOMON: That's very interesting.

VICTOR: It's the old story.

SOLOMON: No, listen—What happens to people is always the main element to me. Because when do they call me? It's either a divorce or somebody died. So it's always a new story. I mean it's the same, but it's different. *He sits in the centre chair.*

VICTOR: You pick up the pieces.

SOLOMON: That's very good, yes. I pick up the pieces. It's a bit like you, I suppose. You must have some stories, I betcha.

VICTOR: Not very often.

SOLOMON: What are you, a traffic cop, or something . . . ?

VICTOR: I'm out in Rockaway most of the time, the airports.

SOLOMON: That's Siberia, no?

VICTOR, *laughing*: I like it better that way.

SOLOMON: You keep your nose clean.

VICTOR, *smiling*: That's it. *Indicating the furniture.* So what do you say?

SOLOMON: What I say? *Taking out two cigars as he glances about*: You like a cigar?

VICTOR: Thanks, I gave it up long ago. So what's the story here?

SOLOMON: I can see you are a very factual person.

VICTOR: You hit it.

SOLOMON: Couldn't be better. So tell me, you got some kind of paper here? To show ownership?

VICTOR: Well, no, I don't. But . . . *He half-laughs.* I'm the owner, that's all.

SOLOMON: In other words, there's no brothers, no sisters.

VICTOR: I have a brother, yes.

SOLOMON: Ah hah. You're friendly with him. Not that I'm mixing in, but I don't have to tell you that the average family they love each other like crazy, but the minute the parents die is all of a sudden a question who is going to get what and you're covered with cats and dogs—

VICTOR: There is no such problem here.

SOLOMON: Unless we're gonna talk about a few pieces, then it wouldn't bother me, but to take the whole load without a piece of paper is a—

VICTOR: All right, I'll get you some kind of statement from him; don't worry about it.

SOLOMON: That is definite; because even from high-class people you wouldn't believe the shenanigans—lawyers, college professors, television personalities—five hundred dollars they'll pay a lawyer to fight over a bookcase it's worth fifty cents—because you see, everybody wants to be number one, so . . .

VICTOR: I said I'd get you a statement. *He indicates the room.* Now what's the story?

SOLOMON: All right, so I'll tell you the story. *He looks at the dining-room table and points to it.* For instance, you mention the dining-room table. That's what they call Spanish Jacobean. Cost maybe twelve, thirteen hundred dollars. I would say—1921, '22. I'm right?

VICTOR: Probably, ya.

SOLOMON—*clears his throat*: I see you're an intelligent man, so before I'll say another word, I ask you to remember—with used furniture you cannot be emotional.

VICTOR—*laughs*: I haven't opened my mouth.

SOLOMON: I mean you're a policeman, I'm a furniture dealer, we both know this world. Anything Spanish Jacobean you'll sell quicker a case of tuberculosis.

VICTOR: Why? That table's in beautiful condition.

SOLOMON: Officer, you are talking reality; you cannot talk reality with used furniture. They don't like that style; not only they don't like it, they hate it. They same thing with that buffet there and that . . . *He starts to point elsewhere.*

VICTOR: You only want to take a few pieces, is that the ticket?

SOLOMON: Please, Officer, we're already talking too fast—

VICTOR: No-no, you're not going to walk off with the gravy and leave me with the bones. All or nothing or let's forget it. I told you on the phone it was a whole houseful.

SOLOMON: What're you in such a hurry? Talk a little bit, we'll see what happens. In a day they didn't build Rome. *He calculates worriedly for a moment, glancing again at the pieces he wants. He gets up, goes and touches the harp.* You see what I had in mind—I would give you such a knockout price for these few pieces that you—

VICTOR: That's out.

SOLOMON, *quickly*: Out.

VICTOR: I'm not running a department store. They're tearing the building down.

SOLOMON: Couldn't be better! We understand each other, so—*with his charm*—so there's no reason to be emotional. *He goes to the records.* These records go? *He picks up one.*

VICTOR: I might keep three or four.

SOLOMON, *reading a label*: Look at that! Gallagher and Shean!

VICTOR, *with only half a laugh*: You're not going to start playing them now!

SOLOMON: Who needs to play? I was on the same bill with Gallagher and Shean maybe fifty theatres.

VICTOR, *surprised*: You were an actor?

SOLOMON: An actor! An acrobat; my whole family was acrobats. *Expanding with this first opening*: You never heard 'The Five Solomons'—may they rest in peace? I was the one on the bottom.

VICTOR: Funny—I never heard of a Jewish acrobat.

SOLOMON: What's the matter with Jacob, he wasn't a wrestler?—wrestled with the Angel?

>   *Victor laughs.*

Jews been acrobats since the beginning of the world. I was a horse them days: drink, women, anything—on-the-go, on-the-go, nothing ever stopped me. Only life. Yes, my boy. *Almost lovingly putting down the record*: What do you know, Gallagher and Shean.

VICTOR, *more intimately now, despite himself, but with no less persistence in keeping to the business*: So where are we?

SOLOMON—*glancing off, he turns back to Victor with a deeply concerned look*: Tell me, what's up with crime now? It's up, hey?

VICTOR: Yeah, it's up, it's up. Look, Mr Solomon, let me make one thing clear, heh? I'm not sociable.

SOLOMON: You're not.

VICTOR: No, I'm not; I'm not a businessman, I'm not good at conversations. So let's get to a price, and finish. Okay?

SOLOMON: You don't want we should be buddies.

VICTOR: That's exactly it.

SOLOMON: So we wouldn't be buddies! *He sighs.* But just so you'll know me a little better—I'm going to show you something. *He takes out a leather folder which he flips open and hands to Victor.* There's my discharge from the British Navy. You see? 'His Majesty's Service'.

VICTOR, *looking at the document*: Huh! What were you doing in the British Navy?

SOLOMON: Forget the British Navy. What does it say the date of birth?

VICTOR: 'Eighteen . . .' *Amazed, he looks up at Solomon.* You're almost ninety?

SOLOMON: Yes, my boy. I left Russia sixty-five years ago, I was twenty-four years old. And I smoked all my life. I drinked, and I loved every women who would let me. So what do I need to steal from you?

VICTOR: Since when do people need a reason to steal?

SOLOMON: I never saw such a man in my life!

VICTOR: Oh yes you did. Now are you going to give me a figure or—?

SOLOMON—*he is actually frightened because he can't get a hook into Victor and fears losing the good pieces*: How can I give you a figure? You don't trust one word I say!

VICTOR, *with a strained laugh*: I never saw you before, what're you asking me to trust you?!

SOLOMON, *with a gesture of distrust*: But how am I going to start to talk to you? I'm sorry; here you can't be a policeman. If you want to do business a little bit you gotta believe or you can't do it. I'm . . . I'm . . . Look, forget it. *He gets up and goes to his portfolio.*

VICTOR, *astonished*: What are you doing?

SOLOMON: I can't work this way. I'm too old every time I open my mouth you should practically call me a thief.

VICTOR: Who called you a thief?

SOLOMON, *moving toward the door*: No—I don't need it. I don't want it in my shop. *Wagging a finger into Victor's face*: And don't forget it—I never gave you a price, and look what you did to me. You see? I never gave you a price!

VICTOR, *angering*: Well, what did you come here for, to do me a favour? What are you talking about?

SOLOMON: Mister, I pity you! What is the matter with you people! You're worse than my daughter! Nothing in the world you believe, nothing you respect—how can you live? You think that's such a smart thing? That's so hard, what you're doing? Let me give you a piece advice—it's not that you can't believe nothing, that's not so hard—it's that you still got to believe it. That's hard. And if you can't do that, my friend—you're a dead man! *He starts toward the door.*

VICTOR, *chastened despite himself*: Oh, Solomon, come on, will you?

SOLOMON: No-no. You got a certain problem with this furniture but you don't want to listen so how can I talk?

VICTOR: I'm listening! For Christ's sake, what do you want me to do, get down on my knees?

SOLOMON, *putting down his portfolio and taking out a wrinkled tape measure from his jacket pocket*: Okay, come here. I realize you are a factual person, but some facts are funny. *He stretches the tape measure across the depth of a piece.* What does that read? *Then turns to Victor, showing him.*

VICTOR—*comes to him, reads*: Forty inches. So?

SOLOMON: My boy, the bedroom doors in a modern apartment house are thirty, thirty-two inches maximum. So you can't get this in—

VICTOR: What about the old houses?

SOLOMON, *with a desperation growing*: All I'm trying to tell you is that my possibilities are smaller!

VICTOR: Well, can't I ask a question?

SOLOMON: I'm giving you architectural facts! Listen—*Wiping his face, he seizes on the library table, going to it.* You got there, for instance, a library table. That's a solid beauty. But go find me a modern apartment with a library. If they would build old hotels, I could sell this, but they only build new hotels. People don't live like this no more. This stuff is from another world. So I'm trying to give you a modern viewpoint. Because the price of used furniture is nothing but a viewpoint, and if you wouldn't understand the viewpoint is impossible to understand the price.

VICTOR: So what's the viewpoint—that it's all worth nothing?

SOLOMON: That's what you said, I didn't say that. The chairs is worth something, the chiffoniers, the bed, the harp—

VICTOR—*turns away from him*: Okay, let's forget it, I'm not giving you the cream—

SOLOMON: What're you jumping!

VICTOR, *turning to him*: Good God, are you going to make me an offer or not?

SOLOMON, *walking away with a hand at his temple*: Boy, oh boy, oh boy. You must've arrested a million people by now.

VICTOR: Nineteen in twenty-eight years.

SOLOMON: So what are you so hard on me?

VICTOR: Because you talk about everything but money and I don't know what the hell you're up to.

SOLOMON, *raising a finger*: We will now talk money. *He returns to the centre chair.*

VICTOR: Great. I mean you can't blame me—every time you open your mouth the price seems to go down.

SOLOMON, *sitting*: My boy, the price didn't change since I walked in.

VICTOR, *laughing*: That's even better! So what's the price?

> *Solomon glances about, his wit failed, a sunk look coming over his face.*

What's going on? What's bothering you?

SOLOMON: I'm sorry, I shouldn't have come. I thought it would be a few pieces but . . . *Sunk, he presses his fingers into his eyes.* It's too much for me.

VICTOR: Well, what'd you come for? I told you it was the whole house.

SOLOMON, *protesting*: You called me so I came! What should I do, lay down and die? *Striving again to save it*: Look, I want very much to make you an offer, the only question is . . . *He breaks off as though afraid of saying something.*

VICTOR: This is a hell of a note.

SOLOMON: Listen, it's a terrible temptation to me! But . . . *As though throwing himself on Victor's understanding*: You see, I'll tell you the truth; you must have looked in a very old phone book; a couple of years ago already I cleaned out my store. Except a few English andirons I got left, I sell when I need a few dollars. I figured I was eighty, eighty-five, it was time already. But I waited—and nothing happened—I even moved out of my apartment. I'm living in the back of the store with a hot-plate. But nothing happened. I'm still practically a hundred per cent—not a hundred, but I feel very well. And I figured maybe you got a couple nice pieces—not that the rest can't be sold, but it could take a year, year and half. For me that's a big bet. *In conflict, he looks around.* The trouble is I love to work; I love it, but— *Giving up*: I don't know what to tell you.

VICTOR: All right, let's forget it then.

SOLOMON, *standing*: What're you jumping?

VICTOR: Well, are you in or out!

SOLOMON: How do I know where I am! You see, it's also this particular furniture— the average person he'll take one look, it'll make him very nervous.

VICTOR: Solomon, you're starting again.

SOLOMON: I'm not bargaining with you!

VICTOR: Why'll it make him nervous?

SOLOMON: Because he knows it's never gonna break.

VICTOR, *not in bad humor, but clinging to his senses*: Oh come on, will you? Have a little mercy.

SOLOMON: My boy, you don't know the psychology! If it wouldn't break there is no more possibilities. For instance, you take—*crosses to table*—this table . . . Listen! *He bangs the table.* You can't move it. A man sits down to such a table he knows not only he's married, he's got to stay married—there is no more possibilities.

    Victor laughs.

You're laughing, I'm telling you the factual situation. What is the key word today? Disposable. The more you can throw it away the more it's beautiful. The car, the furniture, the wife, the children—everything has to be disposable. Because you see the main thing today is—shopping. Years ago a person, he was unhappy, didn't know what to do with himself—he'd go to church, start a revolution—*something*. Today you're unhappy? Can't figure it out? What is the salvation? Go shopping.

VICTOR, *laughing*: You're terrific, I have to give you credit.

SOLOMON: I'm telling you the truth! If they would close the stores for six months in this country there would be from coast to coast a regular massacre. With this kind of furniture the shopping is over, it's finished, there's no more possibilities, you got it, you see? So you got a problem here.

VICTOR, *laughing*: Solomon, you are one of the greatest. But I'm way ahead of you, it's not going to work.

SOLOMON, *offended*: What 'work'? I don't know how much time I got. What is so terrible if I say that? The trouble is, you're such a young fella you don't understand these things—

VICTOR: I understand very well, I know what you're up against. I am not so young.

SOLOMON, *scoffing*: What are you, forty? Forty-five?

VICTOR: I'm going to be fifty.

SOLOMON: Fifty! You're a baby boy!

VICTOR: Some baby.

SOLOMON: My God, if I was fifty . . . ! I got married I was seventy-five.

VICTOR: Go on.

SOLOMON: What are you talking about? She's still living by Eighth Avenue over there. See, that is why I like to stay liquid, because I don't want her to get her hands on this. . . . Birds she loves. She's living there with maybe a hundred birds. She gives you a plate of soup it's got feathers. I didn't work all my life for them birds.

VICTOR: I appreciate your problems, Mr Solomon, but I don't have to pay for them. *He stands.* I've got no more time.

SOLOMON, *holding up a restraining hand—desperately*: I'm going to buy it! *He has shocked himself, and glances around at the towering masses of furniture.* I mean I'll . . . *He moves, looking at the stuff.* I'll have to live, that's all, I'll make up my mind! I'll buy it.

VICTOR—*he is affected as Solomon's fear comes through to him*: We're talking about everything now.

SOLOMON, *angrily*: Everything, everything! *Going to his portfolio*: I'll figure it up, I'll give you a very nice price, and you'll be a happy man.

VICTOR, *sitting again*: That I doubt.

Solomon takes a hard-boiled egg out of the portfolio.

What's this now, lunch?

SOLOMON: You give me such an argument, I'm hungry? I'm not supposed to get too hungry.

VICTOR: Brother!

SOLOMON—*cracks the shell on his diamond ring*: You want me to starve to death? I'm going to be very quick here.

VICTOR: Boy—I picked a number!

SOLOMON: There wouldn't be a little salt, I suppose.

VICTOR: I'm not going running for salt now!

SOLOMON: Please, don't be blue. I'm going to knock you off your feet with the price, you'll see. *He swallows the egg. He now faces the furniture, and, half to himself, pad and pencil poised*: I'm going to go here like an IBM. *He starts estimating on his pad.*

VICTOR: That's all right, take it easy. As long as you're serious.

SOLOMON: Thank you. *He touches the hated buffet*: Ay, yi, yi. All right, well . . . *He jots down a figure. He goes to the next piece, jots down another figure. He goes to another piece, jots down a figure.*

VICTOR, *after a moment*: You really got married at seventy-five?

SOLOMON: What's so terrible?

VICTOR: No, I think it's terrific. But what was the point?

SOLOMON: What's the point at twenty-five? You can't die at twenty six?

VICTOR, *laughing softly*: I guess so, ya.

SOLOMON: It's the same like second-hand furniture, you see; the whole thing is a viewpoint. It's a mental world. *He jots down another figure for another piece.* Seventy-five I got married, fifty-one, and twenty-two.

VICTOR: You're kidding.

SOLOMON: I wish! *He works, jotting his estimate of each piece on the pad, opening drawers, touching everything. Peering into a dark recess, he takes out a pencil flashlight, switches it on, and begins to probe with the beam.*

VICTOR—*he has gradually turned to watch Solomon, who goes on working*: Cut the kidding now—how old are you?

SOLOMON, *sliding out a drawer*: I'm eighty-nine. It's such an accomplishment?

VICTOR: You're a hell of a guy.

SOLOMON, *smiling with the encouragement and turning to Victor*: You know, it's a funny thing. It's so long since I took on such a load like this—you forget what kind of life it puts into you. To take out a pencil again . . . it's a regular injection. Frankly, my telephone you could use for a ladle, it wouldn't interfere with nothing. I want to thank you. *He points at Victor.* I'm going to take good care of you, I mean it. I can open that?

VICTOR: Sure, anything.

SOLOMON, *going to an armoire*: Some of them had a mirror . . . *He opens the armoire, and a rolled-up fur rug falls out. It is about three by five.* What's this?

VICTOR: God knows. I guess it's a rug.

SOLOMON, *holding it up*: No-no—that's a lap robe. Like for a car.

VICTOR: Say, that's right, ya. When they went driving. God, I haven't seen that in—

SOLOMON: You had a chauffeur?

VICTOR: Ya, we had a chauffeur.

> *Their eyes meet. Solomon looks at him as though Victor were coming into focus. Victor turns away. Now Solomon turns back to the armoire.*

SOLOMON: Look at that! *He takes down an opera hat from the shelf within.* My God! *He puts it on, looks into the interior mirror.* What a world! *He turns to Victor:* He must've been some sporty guy!

VICTOR, *smiling*: You look pretty good!

SOLOMON: And from all this he could go so broke?

VICTOR: Why not? Sure. Took five weeks. Less.

SOLOMON: You don't say. And he couldn't make a comeback?

VICTOR: Well, some men don't bounce, you know.

SOLOMON—*grunts*: Hmm! So what did he do?

VICTOR: Nothing. Just sat here. Listened to the radio.

SOLOMON: But what did he do? What—?

VICTOR: Well, now and then he was making change at the Automat. Toward the end he was delivering telegrams.

SOLOMON, *with grief and wonder*: You don't say. And how much he had?

VICTOR: Oh . . . couple of million, I guess.

SOLOMON: My God. What was the matter with him?

VICTOR: Well, my mother died around the same time. I guess that didn't help. Some men just don't bounce, that's all.

SOLOMON: Listen, I can tell you bounces. I went busted 1932; then 1923 they also knocked me out; the panic of 1904, 1898 . . . But to lay down like *that* . . .

VICTOR: Well, you're different. He believed in it.

SOLOMON: What he believed?

VICTOR: The system, the whole thing. He thought it was his fault, I guess. You—you come in with your song and dance, it's all a gag. You're a hundred and fifty years old, you tell your jokes, people fall in love with you, and you walk away with their furniture.

SOLOMON: That's not nice.

VICTOR: Don't shame me, will ya?—What do you say? You don't need to look any-more, you know what I've got here.

Solomon is clearly at the end of his delaying resources. He looks about slowly; the furniture seems to loom over him like a threat or a promise. His eyes climb up to the edges of the ceiling, his hands grasping one another.

What are you afraid of? It'll keep you busy.

Solomon looks at him, wanting even more reassurance.

SOLOMON: You don't think it's foolish?

VICTOR: Who knows what's foolish? You enjoy it—

SOLOMON: Listen, I love it—

VICTOR: —so take it. You plan too much, you end up with nothing.

SOLOMON, *intimately*: I would like to tell you something. The last few months, I don't know what it is—she comes to me. You see, I had a daughter, she should rest in peace, she took her own life, a suicide. . . .

VICTOR: When was this?

SOLOMON: It was . . . 1916—the latter part. But very beautiful, a lovely face, with large eyes—she was pure like the morning. And lately, I don't know what it is—I see her clear like I see you. And every night practically, I lay down to go to sleep, so she sits there. And you can't help it, you ask yourself—what happened? What *happened*? Maybe I could have said something to her . . . maybe I *did* say something . . . it's all . . . *He looks at the furniture.* It's not that I'll die, you can't be afraid of that. But . . . I'll tell you the truth—a minute ago I mentioned I had three wives . . . *Slight pause. His fear rises.* Just this minute I realize I had four. Isn't that terrible? The first time was nineteen, in Lithuania. See, that's what I mean—it's impossible to know what's important. Here I'm sitting with you . . . and . . . and . . . *He looks around at the furniture.* What for? Not that I don't want it, I want it, but . . . You see, all my life I was a terrible fighter—you could never take nothing from me; I pushed, I pulled, I struggled in six different countries, I nearly got killed a couple times, and it's . . . It's like now I'm sitting here talking to you and I tell you it's a dream, it's a dream! You see, you can't imagine it because—

VICTOR: I know what you're talking about. But it's not a dream—it's that you've got to make decisions before you know what's involved, but you're stuck with the results anyway. Like I was very good in science—I loved it. But I had to drop out to feed the old man. And I figured I'd go on the Force temporarily, just to get us through the Depression, then go back to school. But then the war came, we had the kid, and you turn around and you've racked up fifteen years on the pension. And what you started out to do is a million miles away. Not that I regret it all— we brought up a terrific boy, for one thing; nobody's ever going to take that guy. But it's like you were saying—it's impossible to know what's important. We always agreed, we stay out of the rat race and live our own life. That was important. But you shovel the crap out the window, it comes back in under the door—it all ends up she wants, she wants. And I can't really blame her—there's just no respect for anything but money.

SOLOMON: What're you got against money?

VICTOR: Nothing, I just didn't want to lay down my life for it. But I think I laid it down another way, and I'm not even sure any more what I was trying to accomplish. I look back now, and all I can see is a long, brainless walk in the street. I guess it's the old story; do anything, but just be sure you win. Like my brother; years ago, I was living up here with the old man, and he used to contribute five dollars a month. A *month*! And a successful surgeon. But the few times he'd come around, the expression on the old man's face—you'd think God walked in. The respect, you know what I mean? The respect! And why not? Why not?

SOLOMON: Well, sure, he had the power.

VICTOR: Now you said it—if you got that you got it all. You're even lovable! *He laughs.* Well, what do you say? Give me the price.

SOLOMON—*slight pause*: I'll give you eleven hundred dollars.

VICTOR—*slight pause*: For everything?

SOLOMON, *in a breathless way*: Everything.

> *Slight pause, Victor looks around at the furniture.*

I want it so I'm giving you a good price. Believe me, you will never do better. I want it; I made up my mind.

> *Victor continues staring at the stuff. Solomon takes out a common envelope and a wad of bills.*

Here . . . I'll pay you now. *He readies a bill to start counting it out.*

VICTOR: It's that I have to split it, see—

SOLOMON: All right . . . so I'll make out a receipt for you and I'll put down six hundred dollars.

VICTOR: No-no . . . *He gets up and moves at random, looking at the furniture.*

SOLOMON: Why not? He took from you so take from him. If you want, I'll put down four hundred.

VICTOR: No, I don't want to do that. *Slight pause.* I'll call you tomorrow.

SOLOMON, *smiling*: All right; with God's help if I'm there tomorrow I'll answer the phone. If I wouldn't be . . . *Slight pause.* Then I wouldn't be.

VICTOR, *annoyed, but wanting to believe*: Don't start that again, will you?

SOLOMON: Look, you convinced me, so I want it. So what should I do?

VICTOR: *I* convinced *you*?

SOLOMON, *very distressed*: Absolutely you convinced me. You saw it—the minute I looked at it I was going to walk out.

VICTOR, *cutting him off, angered at his own indecision*: Ah, the hell with it. *He holds out his hand.* Give it to me.

SOLOMON, *wanting Victor's good will*: Please, don't be blue.

VICTOR: Oh, it all stinks. *Jabbing forth his hand*: Come on.

SOLOMON, *with a bill raised over Victor's hand—protesting*: What stinks? You should be happy. Now you can buy her a nice coat, take her to Florida, maybe—

VICTOR, *nodding ironically*: Right, right! We'll all be happy now. Give it to me.

Solomon shakes his head and counts bills into his hand. Victor turns his head and looks at the piled walls of furniture.

SOLOMON: There's one hundred; two hundred; three hundred; four hundred . . . Take my advice, buy her a nice fur coat your troubles'll be over—

VICTOR: I know all about it. Come on.

SOLOMON: So you got there four, so I'm giving you . . . five, six, seven . . . I mean it's already in the Bible, the rat race. The minute she laid her hand on the apple, that's it.

VICTOR: I never read the Bible. Come on.

SOLOMON: If you'll read it you'll see—there's always a rat race, you can't stay out of it. So you got there seven, so now I'm giving you . . .

A man appears in the doorway. In his mid-fifties, well-barbered; hatless, in a camel's-hair coat, very healthy complexion. A look of sharp intelligence on his face.

Victor, seeing past Solomon, starts slightly with shock, withdrawing his hand from the next bill which Solomon is about to lay in it.

VICTOR, *suddenly flushed, his voice oddly high and boyish*: Walter!

WALTER—*enters the room, coming to Victor with extended hand and with a reserve of warmth but a stiff smile*: How are you, kid?
Solomon has moved out of their line of sight.

VICTOR—*shifts the money to his left hand as he shakes*: God, I never expected you.

WALTER, *of the money—half-humorously*: Sorry I'm late. What are you doing?

VICTOR, *fighting a treason to himself, thus taking on a strained humorous air*: I . . . I just sold it.

WALTER: Good! How much?

VICTOR, *as though absolutely certain now he has been had*: Ah . . . eleven hundred.

WALTER, *in a dead voice shorn of comment*: Oh. Well, good. *He turns rather deliberately—but not overly so—to Solomon*: For everything?

SOLOMON—*comes to Walter, his hand extended; with an energized voice that braves everything*: I'm very happy to meet you, Doctor! My name is Gregory Solomon.

WALTER—*the look on his face is rather amused, but his reserve has possibilities of accusation*: How do you do?

He shakes Solomon's hand, as Victor raises his hand to smooth down his hair, a look of near-alarm for himself on his face.

ACT II

The action is continuous. As the curtain rises Walter is just releasing Solomon's hand and turning about to face Victor. His posture is reserved, stiffened by traditional control over a nearly fierce curiosity. His grin is disciplined and rather hard, but his eyes are warm and combative.

WALTER: How's Esther?

VICTOR: Fine. Should be here any minute.

WALTER: Here? Good! And what's Richard doing?

VICTOR: He's at MIT.

WALTER: No kidding! MIT!

VICTOR, *nodding*: They gave him a full scholarship.

WALTER, *dispelling his surprise*: What do you know. *With a wider smile, and embarrassed warmth*: You're proud.

VICTOR: I guess so. They put him in the Honours Program.

WALTER: Really. That's wonderful.—You don't mind my coming, do you?

VICTOR: No! I called you a couple of times.

WALTER: Yes, my nurse told me. What's Richard interested in?

VICTOR: Science. So far, anyway. *With security*: How're yours?

WALTER—*moving, he breaks the confrontation*: I suppose Jean turned out best—but I don't think you ever saw her.

VICTOR: I never did, no.

WALTER: The *Times* gave her quite a spread last fall. Pretty fair designer.

VICTOR: Oh? That's great. And the boys? They in school?

WALTER: They often are. *Abruptly laughs, refusing his own embarrassment*: I hardly see them, Vic. With all the unsolved mysteries of the world they're investigating the guitar. But what the hell . . . . I've given up worrying about them. *He walks past Solomon, glancing at the furniture*: I'd forgotten how much he had up here. There's your radio.

VICTOR, *smiling with him*: I know, I saw it.

WALTER, *looking down at the radio, then upward to the ceiling through which the battery once exploded. Both laugh. Then he glances with open feeling at Victor*: Long time.

VICTOR, *fending off the common emotion*: Yes. How's Dorothy?

WALTER, *cryptically*: She's all right, I guess. *He moves, glancing at things, but again with suddenness turns back*. Looking forward to seeing Esther again. She still writing poetry?

VICTOR: No, not for years now.

SOLOMON: He's got a very nice wife. We met.

WALTER, *surprised; as though at something intrusive*: Oh? *He turns back to the furniture*. Well. Same old junk, isn't it?

VICTOR, *downing a greater protest*: I wouldn't say that. Some of it isn't bad.

SOLOMON: One or two very nice things, Doctor. We came to a very nice agreement.

VICTOR, *with an implied rebuke*: I never thought you'd show up; I guess we'd better start all over again—

WALTER: Oh, no-no, I don't want to foul up your deal.

SOLOMON: Excuse me, Doctor—better you should take what you want now than we'll argue later. What did you want?

WALTER, *surprised, turning to Victor*: Oh, I didn't want anything. I came by to say hello, that's all.

VICTOR: I see. *Fending off Walter's apparent gesture with an over-quick movement toward the oar*: I found your oar, if you want it.

WALTER: Oar?

> *Victor draws it out from behind furniture. A curved-blade sweep.*

Hah! *He receives the oar, looks up its length, and laughs, hefting it.* I must have been out of my mind!

SOLOMON: Excuse me, Doctor; if you want the oar—

WALTER, *standing the oar before Solomon, whom he leaves holding on to it*: Don't get excited, I don't want it.

SOLOMON: No. I was going to say—a personal thing like this I have no objection.

WALTER, *half-laughing*: That's very generous of you.

VICTOR, *apologizing for Solomon*: I threw in everything—I never thought you'd get here.

WALTER, *with a strained over-agreeableness*: Sure, that's all right. What are you taking?

VICTOR: Nothing, really. Esther might want a lamp or something like that.

SOLOMON: He's not interested, you see; he's a modern person, what are you going to do?

WALTER: You're not taking the harp?

VICTOR, *with a certain guilt*: Well, nobody plays . . . You take it, if you like.

SOLOMON: You'll excuse me, Doctor—the harp, please, that's another story . . . .

WALTER—*laughs*—*archly amused and put out*: You don't mind if I make a suggestion, do you?

SOLOMON: Doctor, please, don't be offended, I only—

WALTER: Well, why do you interrupt? Relax, we're only talking. We haven't seen each other for a long time.

SOLOMON: Couldn't be better; I'm very sorry. *He sits, nervously pulling his cheek.*

WALTER, *touching the harp*: Kind of a pity—this was Grandpa's wedding present, you know.

VICTOR, *looking with surprise at the harp*: Say—that's right!

WALTER, *to Solomon*: What are you giving him for this?

SOLOMON: I didn't itemize—one price for everything. Maybe three hundred dollars. That sounding board is cracked, you know.

VICTOR, *to Walter*: You want it?

SOLOMON: Please, Victor, I hope you're not going to take that away from me. *To Walter*: Look, Doctor, I'm not trying to fool you. The harp is the heart and soul of the deal. I realize it was your mother's harp, but like I tried to tell—*to Victor*—you before—*to Walter*—with used furniture you cannot be emotional.

WALTER: I guess it doesn't matter. *To Victor*: Actually, I was wondering if he kept any of Mother's evening gowns, did he?

VICTOR: I haven't really gone through it all—

SOLOMON, *raising a finger, eagerly*: Wait, wait, I think I can help you. *He goes to an armoire he had earlier looked into, and opens it.*

WALTER, *moving toward the armoire*: She had some spectacular—

SOLOMON, *drawing out the bottom of a gown elaborately embroidered in gold*: Is this what you mean?

WALTER: Yes, that's the stuff!

> *Solomon blows dust off and hands him the bottom of the gown.*

Isn't that beautiful! Say, I think she wore this at my wedding! *He takes it out of the closet, holds it up.* Sure! You remember this?

VICTOR: What do you want with it?

WALTER, *drawing out another gown off the rack*: Look at this one! Isn't that something? I thought Jeannie might make something new out of the material, I'd like her to wear something of Mother's.

VICTOR—*a new, surprising idea*: Oh! Fine, that's a nice idea.

SOLOMON: Take, take—they're beautiful.

WALTER, *suddenly glancing about as he lays the gowns across a chair*: What happened to the piano?

VICTOR: Oh, we sold that while I was still in school. We lived on it for a long time.

WALTER, *very interestedly*: I never knew that.

VICTOR: Sure. And the silver.

WALTER: Of course! Stupid of me not to remember that. *He half-sits against the back of a couch. His interest is avid, and his energy immense.* I suppose you know—you've gotten to look a great deal like Dad.

VICTOR: *I* do?

WALTER: It's very striking. And your voice is very much like his.

VICTOR: I know. It has that sound to me, sometimes.

SOLOMON: So, gentlemen . . . *He moves the money in his hand.*

VICTOR, *indicating Solomon*: Maybe we'd better settle this now.

WALTER: Yes, go ahead! *He walks off, looking at the furniture.*

SOLOMON, *indicating the money Victor holds*: You got there seven—

WALTER, *oblivious of Solomon; unable, so to speak, to settle for the status quo*: Wonderful to see you looking so well.

VICTOR—*the new interruption seems odd; observing more than speaking*: You do too, you look great.

WALTER: I ski a lot; and I ride nearly every morning. . . . You know, I started to call you a dozen times this year—*He breaks off. Indicating Solomon*: Finish up, I'll talk to you later.

SOLOMON: So now I'm going to give you—*A bill is poised over Victor's hand.*

VICTOR, *to Walter*: That price all right with you?

WALTER: Oh, I don't want to interfere. It's just that I dealt with these fellows when I split up Dorothy's and my stuff last year, and I found—

VICTOR, *from an earlier impression*: You're not divorced, are you?

WALTER, *with a nervous shot of laughter*: Yes!

Esther enters on his line; she is carrying a suit in a plastic wrapper.

ESTHER, *surprised*: Walter! For heaven's sake!

WALTER, *eagerly jumping up, coming to her, shaking her hand*: How are you, Esther!

ESTHER, *between her disapproval and fascinated surprise*: What are *you* doing here?

WALTER: You've hardly changed.

ESTHER, *with a charged laugh, conflicted with herself*: Oh, go on now! *She hangs the suit on a chest handle.*

WALTER, *to Victor*: You son of a gun, she looks twenty-five!

VICTOR, *watching for Esther's reaction*: I know!

ESTHER, *flattered, and offended, too*: Oh stop it, Walter! *She sits.*

WALTER: But you do, honestly; you look marvellous.

SOLOMON: It's that suit, you see? What did I tell you, it's a very beautiful suit.

Victor laughs a little as Esther looks conflicted by Solomon's compliment.

ESTHER, *with mock-affront—to Victor*: What are you laughing at? It is. *She is about to laugh.*

VICTOR: You look so surprised, that's all.

ESTHER: Well, I'm not used to walking into all these compliments! *She bursts out laughing.*

WALTER, *suddenly recalling—eagerly*: Say! I'm sorry I didn't know I'd be seeing you when I left the house this morning—I'd have brought you some lovely Indian bracelets. I got a whole boxful from Bombay.

ESTHER, *still not focused on Walter, sizing him up*: How do you come to—?

WALTER: I operated on this big textile guy and he keeps sending me things. He sent me this coat, in fact.

ESTHER: I was noticing it. That's gorgeous material.

WALTER: Isn't it? Two gallstones.

ESTHER, *her impression lingering for the instant*: How's Dorothy?—Did I hear you saying you were—?

WALTER, *very seriously*: We're divorced, ya. Last winter.

ESTHER: I'm sorry to hear that.

WALTER: It was coming a long time. We're both much better off—we're almost friendly now. *He laughs.*

ESTHER: Oh, stop that, you dog.

WALTER, *with naive excitement*: It's true!

ESTHER: Look, I'm for the woman, so don't hand me that. *To Victor—seeing the money in his hand*: Have you settled everything?

VICTOR: Just about, I guess.

WALTER: I was just telling Victor—*to Victor*: when we split things up I—*to Solomon*: you ever hear of Spitzer and Fox?

SOLOMON: Thirty years I know Spitzer and Fox. Bert Fox worked for me maybe ten, twelve years.

WALTER: They did my appraisal.

SOLOMON: They're good boys. Spitzer is not as good as Fox, but between the two you're in good hands.

WALTER: Yes. That's why I—

SOLOMON: Spitzer is the vice president of the Appraisers' Association.

WALTER: I see. The point I'm making—

SOLOMON: I used to be president.

WALTER: Really.

SOLOMON: Oh yes. I made it all ethical.

WALTER, *trying to keep a straight face—and Victor as well*: Did you?

> *Victor suddenly bursts out laughing, which sets off Walter and Esther, and a warmth springs up among them.*

SOLOMON, *smiling, but insistent*: What's so funny? Listen, before me was a jungle—you wouldn't laugh so much. I put in all the rates, what we charge, you know—I made it a profession, like doctors, lawyers—used to be it was a regular snakepit. But today, you got nothing to worry—all the members are hundred per cent ethical.

WALTER: Well, that was a good deed, Mr Solomon—but I think you can do a little better on this furniture.

ESTHER, *to Victor, who has money in his hand*: How much has he offered?

VICTOR, *embarrassed, but braving it quite well*: Eleven hundred.

ESTHER, *distressed; with a transcendent protest*: Oh, I think that's . . . isn't that very low?

> *She looks to Walter's confirmation.*

WALTER, *familiarly*: Come on, Solomon. He's been risking his life for you every day; be generous—

SOLOMON, *to Esther*: That's a real brother! Wonderful. *To Walter*: But you can call anybody you like—Spitzer and Fox, Joe Brody, Paul Cavallo, Morris White— I know them all and I know what they'll tell you.

VICTOR, *striving to retain some assurance; to Esther*: See, the point he was making about it—

SOLOMON, *to Esther, raising his finger*: Listen to him because he—

VICTOR, *to Solomon*: Hold it one second, will you? *To Esther and Walter*: Not that I'm saying it's true, but he claims a lot of it is too big to get into the new apartments.

ESTHER, *half-laughing*: You believe that?

WALTER: I don't know, Esther, Spitzer and Fox said the same thing.

ESTHER: Walter, the city is full of big, old apartments!

SOLOMON: Darling, why don't you leave it to the boys?

ESTHER, *suppressing an outburst*: I wish you wouldn't order me around, Mr Solomon! *To Walter, protesting*: Those two bureaus alone are worth a couple of hundred dollars!

WALTER, *delicately*: Maybe I oughtn't interfere—

ESTHER: Why? *Of Solomon*: Don't let him bulldoze you—

SOLOMON: My dear girl, you're talking without a basis—

ESTHER, *slashing*: I don't like this kind of dealing, Mr Solomon! I just don't like it! *She is near tears. A pause. She turns back to Walter*: This money is very important to us, Walter.

WALTER, *chastised*: Yes. I . . . I'm sorry, Esther. *He looks about*. Well . . . if it was mine—

ESTHER: Why? It's yours as much as Victor's.

WALTER: Oh no, dear—I wouldn't take anything from this.

Pause.

VICTOR: No, Walter, you get half.

WALTER: I wouldn't think of it, kid. I came by to say hello, that's all.

Pause.

ESTHER—*she is very moved*: That's terrific, Walter. It's . . . Really, I . . .

VICTOR: Well, we'll talk about it.

WALTER: No-no, Vic, you've earned it. It's yours.

VICTOR, *rejecting the implication*: Why have I earned it? You take your share.

WALTER: Why don't we discuss it later? *To Solomon*: In my opinion—

SOLOMON, *to Victor*: So now you don't even have to split. *To Victor and Walter*: You're lucky they're tearing the building down—you got together, finally.

WALTER: I would have said a minimum of three thousand dollars.

ESTHER: That's exactly what I had in mind! *To Solomon*: I was going to say thirty-five hundred dollars.

WALTER, *to Victor; tactfully*: In that neighbourhood.

> *Silence. Solomon sits there holding back comment, not looking at Victor, blinking with protest. Victor thinks for a moment; then turns to Solomon, and there is a wide discouragement in his voice.*

VICTOR: Well? What do you say?

SOLOMON, *spreading out his hands helplessly, outraged*: What can I say? It's ridiculous. Why does he give you three thousand? What's the matter with five thousand, ten thousand?

WALTER, *to Victor, without criticism*: You should've gotten a couple of other estimates, you see, that's always the—

VICTOR: I've been calling you all week for just that reason, Walter, and you never came to the phone.

WALTER, *blushing*: Why would that stop you from—?

VICTOR: I didn't think I had the right to do it alone—the nurse gave you my messages, didn't she?

WALTER: I've been terribly tied up—and I had no intention of taking anything for myself, so I assumed—

VICTOR: But how was I supposed to know that?

WALTER, *with open self-reproach*: Yes. Well, I . . . I beg your pardon. *He decides to stop there.*

SOLOMON: Excuse me, Doctor, but I can't understand you; first it's a lot of junk—

ESTHER: Nobody called it a lot of junk!

SOLOMON: He called it a lot of junk, Esther, when he walked in here.

Esther turns to Walter, puzzled and angry.

WALTER, *reacting to her look; to Solomon*: Now just a minute—

SOLOMON: No, please. *Indicating Victor*: This is a factual man, so let's be factual.

ESTHER: Well, that's an awfully strange thing to say, Walter.

WALTER, *intimately*: I didn't mean it in that sense, Esther—

SOLOMON: Doctor, please. You said junk.

WALTER, *sharply—and there is an over-meaning of much greater anger in his tone*: I didn't mean it in that sense, Mr Solomon! *He controls himself—and, half to Esther*: When you've been brought up with things, you tend to be sick of them. . . . *To Esther*: That's all I meant.

SOLOMON: My dear man, if it was Louis Seize, Biedermeier, something like that, you wouldn't get sick.

WALTER, *pointing to a piece, and weakened by knowing he is exaggerating*: Well, there happens to be a piece right over there in Biedermeier style!

SOLOMON: Biedermeier 'style'! *He picks up his hat.* I got a hat it's in Borsolino style but it's not a Borsolino. *To Victor*: I mean he don't have to charge me to make an impression.

WALTER, *striving for an air of amusement*: Now what's that supposed to mean?

VICTOR, *with a refusal to dump Solomon*: Well, what basis do you go on, Walter?

WALTER, *reddening but smiling*: I don't know . . . it's a feeling, that's all.

ESTHER—*there is ridicule*: Well, on what basis do you take eleven hundred, dear?

VICTOR, *angered; his manly leadership is suddenly in front*: I simply felt it was probably more or less right!

ESTHER, *as a refrain*: Oh God, here we go again. All right, throw it away—

SOLOMON, *indicating Victor*: Please, Esther, he's not throwing nothing away. This man is no fool! *To Walter as well*: Excuse me, but this is not right to do to him!

WALTER, *bridling, but retaining his smile*: You going to teach me what's right now?

ESTHER, *to Victor, expanding Walter's protest*: Really! I mean.

VICTOR—*obeying her protest for want of a certainty of his own, he touches Solomon's shoulder*: Mr Solomon . . . why don't you sit down in the bedroom for a few minutes and let us talk?

SOLOMON: Certainly, whatever you say. *He gets up.* Only please, you made a very nice deal, you got no right to be ashamed. . . . *To Esther*: Excuse me, I don't want to be personal.

ESTHER—*laughs angrily*: He's fantastic!

VICTOR, *trying to get him moving again*: Whyn't you go inside?

SOLOMON: I'm going; I only want you to understand, Victor, that if it was a different kind of man—*turning to Esther*: I would say to you that he's got the money in his hand, so the deal is concluded.

WALTER: He can't conclude any deal without me, Solomon, I'm half owner here.

SOLOMON, *to Victor*: You see? What did I ask you the first thing I walked in here? 'Who is the owner'?

WALTER: Why do you confuse everything? I'm not making any claim, I merely—

SOLOMON: Then how do you come to interfere? He's got the money; I know the law!

WALTER, *angering*: Now you stop being foolish! Just stop it! I've got the best lawyers in New York, so go inside and sit down.

VICTOR, *as he turns back to escort Solomon*: Take it easy, Walter, come on, cut it out.

ESTHER, *striving to keep a light, amused tone*: Why? He's perfectly right.

VICTOR, *with a hard glance at her, moving upstage with Solomon*: Here, you better hold onto this money.

SOLOMON: No, that's yours; you hold . . .

He sways. Victor grasps his arm. Walter gets up.

WALTER: You all right?

SOLOMON—*dizzy, he grasps his head*: Yes, yes, I'm . . .

WALTER, *coming to him*: Let me look at you. *He takes Solomon's wrists, looks into his face.*

SOLOMON: I'm only a little tired, I didn't take my nap today.

WALTER: Come in here, lie down a moment. *He starts Solomon toward the bedroom.*

SOLOMON: Don't worry about me, I'm . . . *He halts and points back at his portfolio, leaning on a chest.* Please, Doctor, if you wouldn't mind—I got a Hershey's in there.

Walter hesitates to do his errand.

Helps me.

Walter unwillingly goes to the portfolio and reaches into it.

I'm a very healthy person, but a nap, you see, I have to have a . . .

Walter takes out an orange.

Not the orange—on the bottom is a Hershey's.

Walter takes out a Hershey bar.

That's a boy.

WALTER—*returns to him and helps him to the bedroom*: All right, come on . . . easy does it . . .

SOLOMON, *as he goes into the bedroom*: I'm all right, don't worry. You're very nice people.

Solomon and Walter exit into the bedroom. Victor glances at the money in his hand, then puts it on a table, setting the foil on it.

ESTHER: Why are you being so apologetic?

VICTOR: About what?

ESTHER: That old man. Was that his first offer?

VICTOR: Why do you believe Walter? He was obviously pulling a number out of a hat.

ESTHER: Well, I agree with him. Did you try to get him to go higher?

VICTOR: I don't know how to bargain and I'm not going to start now.

ESTHER: I wish you wouldn't be above everything, Victor, we're not twenty years old. We need this money.

He is silent.

You hear me?

VICTOR: I've made a deal, and that's it. You know, you take a tone sometimes—like I'm some kind of an incompetent.

ESTHER—*gets up, moves restlessly*: Well anyway, you'll get the whole amount.—God, he's certainly changed. It's amazing.

VICTOR, *without assent*: Seems so, ya.

ESTHER, *wanting him to join her*: He's so human! And he laughs!

VICTOR: I've seen him laugh.

ESTHER, *with a grin of trepidation*: Am I hearing something or is that my imagination?

VICTOR: I want to think about it.

ESTHER, *quietly*: You're not taking his share?

VICTOR: I said I would like to think . . . .

Assuming he will refuse Walter's share, she really doesn't know what to do or where to move, so she goes for her purse with a quick stride.

VICTOR, *getting up*: Where you going?

ESTHER, *turning back on him*: I want to know. Are you or aren't you taking his share?

VICTOR: Esther, I've been calling him all week; doesn't even bother to come to the phone, walks in here and smiles and I'm supposed to fall into his arms? I can't behave as though nothing ever happened, and you're not going to either! Now just take it easy, we're not dying of hunger.

ESTHER: I don't understand what you think you're upholding!

VICTOR, *outraged*: Where have you been?!

ESTHER: But he's doing exactly what you thought he should do! What do you *want*?

VICTOR: Certain things have happened, haven't they? I can't turn around this fast, kid. He's only been here ten minutes, I've got twenty-eight years to shake off my back. . . . Now sit down, I want you here. *He sits.*

She remains standing, uncertain of what to do.

Please. You can wait a few minutes for your drink.

ESTHER, *in despair*: Vic, it's all blowing away.

VICTOR, *to diminish the entire prize*: Half of eleven hundred dollars is five-fifty, dear.

ESTHER: I'm not talking about money.

Voices are heard from the bedroom.

He's obviously making a gesture, why can't you open yourself a little? *She lays her head back.* My mother was right—I can never believe anything I see. But I'm going to. That's all I'm going to do. What I see.

A chair scrapes in the bedroom.

VICTOR: Wipe your cheek, will you?

Walter enters from the bedroom.

How is he?

WALTER: I think he'll be all right. *Warmly*: God, what a pirate! *He sits*. He's eighty-nine!

ESTHER: I don't believe it!

VICTOR: He is. He showed me his—

WALTER, *laughing*: Oh, he showed you that too?

VICTOR, *smiling*: Ya, the British Navy.

ESTHER: *He* was in the British Navy?

VICTOR, *building on Walter's support*: He's got a discharge. He's not altogether phony.

WALTER: I wouldn't go that far. A guy that age, though, still driving like that . . . *As though admitting Victor was not foolish*: There is something wonderful about it.

VICTOR, *understating*: I think so.

ESTHER: What do you think we ought to do, Walter?

WALTER—slight pause. *He is trying to modify what he believes is his own overpowering force so as not to appear to be taking over. He is faintly smiling toward Victor*: There is a way to get a good deal more out of it. I suppose you know that, though.

VICTOR: Look, I'm not married to this guy. If you want to call another dealer we can compare.

WALTER: You don't have to do that; he's a registered appraiser.—You see, instead of selling it, you could make it a charitable contribution.

VICTOR: I don't understand.

WALTER: It's perfectly simple. He puts a value on it—let's say twenty-five thousand dollars, and—

ESTHER, *fascinated with a laugh*: Are you kidding?

WALTER: It's done all the time. It's a dream world but it's legal. He estimates its highest retail value, which could be put at some such figure. Then I donate it to the Salvation Army. I'd have to take ownership, you see, because my tax rate is much higher than yours so it would make more sense if I took the deduction. I pay around fifty per cent tax, so if I make a twenty-five-thousand-dollar contribution I'd be saving around twelve thousand in taxes. Which we could split however you wanted to. Let's say we split it in half, I'd give you six thousand dollars. *A pause*. It's really the only sensible way to do it, Vic.

ESTHER—*glances at Victor, but he remains silent*: Would it be costing you anything?

WALTER: On the contrary—it's found money to me. *To Victor*: I mentioned it to him just now.

VICTOR, *as though this had been the question*: What'd he say?

WALTER: It's up to you. We'd pay him an appraisal fee—fifty, sixty bucks.

VICTOR: Is he willing to do that?

WALTER: Well, of course he'd rather buy it outright, but what the hell—

ESTHER: Well, that's not his decision, is it?

VICTOR: No . . . it's just that I feel I did come to an agreement with him and I—

WALTER: Personally, I wouldn't let that bother me. He'd be making fifty bucks for filling out a piece of paper.

ESTHER: That's not bad for an afternoon.

Pause.

VICTOR: I'd like to think about it.

ESTHER: There's not much time, though, if you want to deal with *him*.

VICTOR, *cornered*: I'd like a few minutes, that's all.

WALTER, *to Esther*: Sure . . . let him think it over. *To Victor*: It's perfectly legal, if that's
what's bothering you. I almost did it with my stuff but I finally decided to keep it.
He laughs. In fact, my own apartment is so loaded up it doesn't look too different
from this.

ESTHER: Well, maybe you'll get married again.

WALTER: I doubt that very much, Esther.—I often feel I never should have.

ESTHER, *scoffing*: Why!

WALTER: Seriously. I'm in a strange business, you know. There's too much to learn
and far too little time to learn it. And there's a price you have to pay for that.
I tried awfully hard to kid myself but there's simply no time for people. Not the
way a woman expects, if she's any kind of woman. *He laughs.* But I'm doing pretty
well alone!

VICTOR: How would I list an amount like that on my income tax?

WALTER: Well . . . call it a gift.

Victor is silent, obviously in conflict. Walter sees the emotion.

Not that it is, but you could list it as such. It's allowed.

VICTOR: I see. I was just curious how it—

WALTER: Just enter it as a gift. There's no problem.

*With the first sting of a vague resentment, Walter turns his eyes away. Esther raises
her eyebrows, staring at the floor. Walter lifts the foil off the table—clearly changing
the subject.*

You still fence?

VICTOR, *almost gratefully pursuing this diversion*: No, you got to join a club and all that.
And I work weekends often. I just found it here.

WALTER, *as though to warm the mood*: Mother used to love to watch him do this.

ESTHER, *surprised, pleased*: Really?

WALTER: Sure, she used to come to all his matches.

ESTHER, *to Victor, somehow charmed*: You never told me that.

WALTER: Of course; she's the one who made him take it up. *He laughs to Victor.* She
thought it was elegant!

VICTOR: Hey, that's right!

WALTER, *laughing at the memory*: He did look pretty good too! *He spreads his jacket
away from his chest.* I've still got the wounds! *To Victor, who laughs*: Especially with
those French gauntlets she—

VICTOR, *recalling*: Say . . . ! *Looking around with an enlivened need*: I wonder where the
hell . . . *He suddenly moves toward a bureau.* Wait, I think they used to be in . . .

ESTHER, *to Walter:* French gauntlets?

WALTER: She brought them from Paris. Gorgeously embroidered. He looked like one of the musketeers.

Out of the drawer where he earlier found the ice skate, Victor takes a pair of emblazoned gauntlets.

VICTOR: Here they are! What do you know!

ESTHER, *reaching her hand out:* Aren't they beautiful!

He hands her one.

VICTOR: God, I'd forgotten all about them. *He slips one on his hand.*

WALTER: Christmas, 1929.

VICTOR, *moving his hand in the gauntlet:* Look at that, they're still soft . . . *To Walter—a little shy in asking:* How do you remember all this stuff?

WALTER: Why not? Don't you?

ESTHER: He doesn't remember your mother very well.

VICTOR: I remember her. *Looking at the gauntlet:* It's just her face; somehow I can never *see* her.

WALTER, *warmly:* That's amazing, Vic. *To Esther:* She adored him.

ESTHER, *pleased:* Did she?

WALTER: Victor? If it started to rain she'd run all the way to school with his galoshes. Her Victor—my God! By the time he could light a match he was already Louis Pasteur.

VICTOR: It's odd . . . like the harp! I can almost hear the music . . . But I can never see her face. Somehow. *For a moment, silence, as he looks across at the harp.*

WALTER: What's the problem?

Pause. Victor's eyes are swollen with feeling. He turns and looks up at Walter, who suddenly is embarrassed and oddly anxious.

SOLOMON—*enters from the bedroom. He looks quite distressed. He is in his vest, his tie is open. Without coming downstage:* Please, Doctor, if you wouldn't mind I would like to . . . *He breaks off, indicating the bedroom.*

WALTER: What is it?

SOLOMON: Just for one minute, please.

Walter stands. Solomon glances at Victor and Esther and returns to the bedroom.

WALTER: I'll be right back. *He goes rather quickly up and into the bedroom.*

A pause. Victor is sitting in silence, unable to face her.

ESTHER, *with delicacy and pity, sensing his conflicting feelings:* Why can't you take him as he is?

He glances at her.

Well you can't expect him to go into an apology, Vic—he probably sees it all differently, anyway.

> *He is silent. She comes to him.*

I know it's difficult, but he is trying to make a gesture, I think.

VICTOR: I guess he is, yes.

ESTHER: You know what would be lovely? If we could take a few weeks and go to like . . . out-of-the-way places . . . just to really break it up and see all the things that people do. You've been around such mean, petty people for so long and little ugly tricks. I'm serious—it's not romantic. We're much too suspicious of everything.

VICTOR, *staring ahead*: Strange guy.

ESTHER: Why?

VICTOR: Well, to walk in that way—as though nothing ever happened.

ESTHER: Why not? What can be done about it?

VICTOR—*slight pause*: I feel I have to say something.

ESTHER, *with a slight trepidation, less than she feels*: What can you say?

VICTOR: You feel I ought to just take the money and shut up, heh?

ESTHER: But what's the point of going backwards?

VICTOR, *with a self-bracing tension*: I'm not going to take this money unless I talk to him.

ESTHER, *frightened*: You can't bear the thought that he's decent.

> *He looks at her sharply.*

That's all it is, dear. I'm sorry, I have to say it.

VICTOR, *without raising his voice*: I can't bear that he's *decent*!

ESTHER: You throw this away, you've got to explain it to me. You can't go on blaming everything on him or the system or God knows what else! You're free and you can't make a move, Victor, and that's what's driving me crazy! *Silence. Quietly*: Now take this money.

> *He is silent, staring at her.*

You take this money! Or I'm washed up. You hear me? If you're stuck it doesn't mean I have to be. Now that's it.

> *Movements are heard within the bedroom. She straightens. Victor smooths down his hair with a slow, preparatory motion of his hand, like one adjusting himself for combat.*

WALTER—*enters from the bedroom, smiling, shaking his head. Indicating the bedroom*: Boy—we got a tiger here. What is this between you, did you know him before?

VICTOR: No. Why? What'd he say?

WALTER: He's still trying to buy it outright. *He laughs.* He talks like you added five years by calling him up.

VICTOR: Well, what's the difference, I don't mind.

WALTER, *registering the distant rebuke*: No, that's fine, that's all right. *He sits. Slight pause.* We don't understand each other, do we?

VICTOR, *with a certain thrust, matching Walter's smile*: I am a little confused, Walter . . . yes.

WALTER: Why is that?

> *Victor doesn't answer at once.*

Come on, we'll all be dead soon!

VICTOR: All right, I'll give you one example. When I called you Monday and Tuesday and again this morning—

WALTER: I've explained that.

VICTOR: But I don't make phone calls to pass the time. Your nurse sounded like I was a pest of some kind . . . it was humiliating.

WALTER—*oddly, he is over-upset*: I'm terribly sorry, she shouldn't have done that.

VICTOR: I know, Walter, but I can't imagine she takes that tone all by herself.

WALTER, *aware now of the depth of resentment in Victor*: Oh no—she's often that way. I've never referred to you like that.

> *Victor is silent, not convinced.*

Believe me, will you? I'm terribly sorry. I'm overwhelmed with work, that's all it is.

VICTOR: Well, you asked me, so I'm telling you.

WALTER: Yes! You should! But don't misinterpret that. *Slight pause. His tension has increased. He braves a smile.* Now about this tax thing. He'd be willing to make the appraisal twenty-five thousand. *With difficulty*: If you'd like, I'd be perfectly willing for you to have the whole amount I'd be saving.

> *Slight pause.*

ESTHER: Twelve thousand?

WALTER: Whatever it comes to.

> *Pause. Esther slowly looks to Victor.*

You must be near retirement now, aren't you?

ESTHER, *excitedly*: He's past it. But he's trying to decide what to do.

WALTER: Oh. *To Victor—near open embarrassment now*: It would come in handy, then, wouldn't it?

> *Victor glances at him as a substitute for a reply.*

I don't need it, that's all, Vic. Actually, I've been about to call you for quite some time now.

VICTOR: What for?

WALTER—*suddenly, with a strange quick laugh, he reaches and touches Victor's knee*: Don't be suspicious!

VICTOR, *grinning*: I'm just trying to figure it out, Walter.

WALTER: Yes, good. All right. *Slight pause.* I thought it was time we got to know one another. That's all.

Slight pause.

VICTOR: You know, Walter, I tried to call you a couple of times before this about the furniture—must be three years ago.

WALTER: I was sick.

VICTOR, *surprised*: Oh . . . Because I left a lot of messages.

WALTER: I was quite sick. I was hospitalized.

ESTHER: What happened?

WALTER—*slight pause. As though he were not quite sure whether to say it*: I broke down.

Slight pause.

VICTOR: I had no idea.

WALTER: Actually, I'm only beginning to catch up with things. I was out of commission for nearly three years. *With a thrust of success*: But I'm almost thankful for it now—I've never been happier!

ESTHER: You seem altogether different!

WALTER: I think I am, Esther. I live differently, I think differently. All I have now is a small apartment. And I got rid of the nursing homes—

VICTOR: What nursing homes?

WALTER, *with a removed self-amusement*: Oh, I owned three nursing homes. There's big money in the aged, you know. Helpless, desperate children trying to dump their parents—nothing like it. I even pulled out of the market. Fifty per cent of my time now is in City hospitals. And I tell you, I'm alive. For the first time. I do medicine, and that's it. *Attempting an intimate grin*: Not that I don't soak the rich occasionally, but only enough to live, really. *It is as though this was his mission here, and he waits for Victor's comment.*

VICTOR: Well, that must be great.

WALTER, *seizing on this minute encouragement*: Vic, I wish we could talk for weeks, there's so much I want to tell you. . . . *It is not rolling quite the way he would wish and he must pick examples of his new feelings out of the air.* I never had friends—you probably know that. But I do now, I have good friends. *He moves, sitting nearer Victor, his enthusiasm flowing.* It all happens so gradually. You start out wanting to be the best, and there's no question that you do need a certain fanaticism; there's so much to know and so little time. Until you've eliminated everything extraneous—*he smiles*—including people. And of course the time comes when you realize that you haven't merely been specializing in something—something has been specializing in you. You become a kind of instrument, an instrument that cuts money out of people, or fame out of the world. And it finally makes you stupid. Power can do that. You get to think that because you can frighten people they love you. Even that you love them.—And the whole thing comes down to fear. One night I found myself in the middle of my living room, dead drunk with a knife in my hand, getting ready to kill my wife.

ESTHER: Good Lord!

WALTER: Oh ya—and I nearly made it too! *He laughs.* But there's one virtue in going nuts—provided you survive, of course. You get to see the terror—not the screaming kind, but the slow, daily fear you call ambition, and cautiousness, and piling up the money. And really, what I wanted to tell you for some time now—is that you helped me to understand that in myself.

VICTOR: Me?

WALTER: Yes. *He grins warmly, embarrassed.* Because of what you did. I could never understand it, Vic—after all, you *were* the better student. And to stay with a job like that through all those years seemed . . . *He breaks off momentarily, the uncertainty of Victor's reception widening his smile.* You see, it never dawned on me until I got sick—that you'd made a choice.

VICTOR: A choice, how?

WALTER: You wanted a real life. And that's an expensive thing; it costs. *He has found his theme now; sees he has at last touched something in Victor. A breath of confidence comes through now.* I know I may sound terribly naive, but I'm still used to talking about anything that matters. Frankly, I didn't answer your calls this week because I was afraid. I've struggled so long for a concept of myself and I'm not sure I can make it believable to you. But I'd like to. *He sees permission to go on in Victor's perplexed eyes:* You see, I got to a certain point where . . . I dreaded my own work; I finally couldn't cut. There are times, as you know, when if you leave someone alone he might live a year or two; while if you go in you might kill him. And the decision is often . . . not quite, but almost . . . arbitrary. But the odds are acceptable, provided you think the right thoughts. Or don't think at all, which is what I managed to do till then. *Slight pause. He is no longer smiling; instead a near-embarrassment is on him.* I ran into a cluster of misjudgments. It can happen, but it never had to me, not one on top of the other. And they had one thing in common; they'd all been diagnosed by other men as inoperable. And quite suddenly the . . . the whole prospect of my motives opened up. Why had I taken risks that very competent men had declined? And the quick answer, of course, is—to pull off the impossible. Shame the competition. But suddenly I saw something else. And it was terror. In dead centre, directing my brains, my hands, my ambition—for thirty years.

> *Slight pause.*

VICTOR: Terror of what?

> *Pause.*

WALTER, *his gaze direct on Victor now:* Of it ever happening to me—*he glances at the centre chair*—as it happened to him. Overnight, for no reason, to find yourself degraded and thrown-down. *With the faintest hint of impatience and challenge:* You know what I'm talking about, don't you?

> *Victor turns away slightly, refusing commitment.*

Isn't that why you turned your back on it all?

VICTOR, *sensing the relevance to himself now:* Partly. Not altogether, though.

WALTER: Vic, we were both running from the same thing. I thought I wanted to be tops, but what it was was untouchable. I ended up in a swamp of success and bankbooks, you on civil service. The difference is that you haven't hurt other people to defend yourself. And I've learned to respect that, Vic; you simply tried to make yourself useful.

ESTHER: That's wonderful—to come to such an understanding with yourself.

WALTER: Esther, it's a strange thing; in the hospital, for the first time since we were boys, I began to feel . . . . like a brother. In the sense that we shared something. *To Victor*: And I feel I would know how to be friends now.

VICTOR—*slight pause; he is unsure*: Well fine. I'm glad of that.

WALTER—*sees the reserve but feels he has made headway and presses on a bit more urgently*: You see, that's why you're still married. That's a very rare thing. And why your boy's in such good shape. You've lived a real life. *To Esther*: But you know that better than I.

ESTHER: I don't know what I know, Walter.

WALTER: Don't doubt it, dear—believe me, you're fortunate people. *To Victor*: You know that, don't you?

VICTOR, *without looking at Esther*: I think so.

ESTHER: It's not quite as easy as you make it, Walter.

WALTER—*hesitates, then throws himself into it*: Look, I've had a wild idea—it'll probably seem absurd to you, but I wish you'd think about it before you dismiss it. I gather you haven't decided what to do with yourself now? You're retiring . . . . ?

VICTOR: I'll decide one of these days, I'm still thinking.

WALTER, *nervously*: Could I suggest something?

VICTOR: Sure, go ahead.

WALTER: We've been interviewing people for the new wing. For the administrative side. Kind of liaison people between the scientists and the board. And it occurred to me several times that you might fit in there.

    Slight pause.

ESTHER, *with a release of expectation*: That would be wonderful!

VICTOR—*slight pause. He glances at her with suppression, but his voice betrays excitement*: What could I do there, though?

WALTER, *sensing Victor's interest*: It's kind of fluid at the moment, but there's a place for people with a certain amount of science who—

VICTOR: I have no degree, you know.

WALTER: But you've had analytic chemistry, and a lot of math and physics, if I recall. If you thought you needed it you could take some courses in the evenings. I think you have enough background.—How would you feel about that?

VICTOR, *digging in against the temptation*: Well . . . I'd like to know more about it, sure.

ESTHER, *as though to press him to accept*: It'd be great if he could work in science, it's really the only thing he ever wanted.

WALTER: I know; it's a pity he never went on with it. *Turning to Victor*: It'd be perfectly simple, Vic, I'm chairman of the committee. I could set it all up—

Solomon enters. They turn to him, surprised. He seems about to say something, but in fear changes his mind.

SOLOMON: Excuse me, go right ahead. *He goes nervously to his portfolio, reaching into it—which was not his original intention.* I'm sorry to disturb you. *He takes out an orange and starts back to the bedroom, then halts, addressing Walter:* About the harp. If you'll make me a straight out-and-out sale, I would be willing to go another fifty dollars. So it's eleven fifty, and between the two of you nobody has to do any favours.

WALTER: Well, you're getting warmer.

SOLOMON: I'm a fair person! So you don't have to bother with appraisals and deduction, all right? *Before Walter can answer:* But don't rush, I'll wait. I'm at your service. *He goes quickly and worriedly into the bedroom.*

ESTHER, *starting to laugh; to Victor:* Where did you find him?

WALTER: —that wonderful? He 'made it all ethical'!

Esther bursts out laughing, and Walter with her, and Victor manages to join. As it begins to subside, Walter turns to him.

What do you say, Vic? Will you come by?

The laughter is gone. The smile is just fading on Victor's face. He looks at nothing, as though deciding. The pause lengthens, and lengthens still. Now it begins to seem he may not speak at all. No one knows how to break this puzzling silence. At last he turns to Walter with a rather quick movement of his head as though he had made up his mind to take the step.

VICTOR: I'm not sure I know what you want, Walter.

Walter looks shocked, astonished, almost unbelieving. But Victor's gaze is steady on him.

ESTHER, *with the tone of a conciliator shrouding her shock and protest:* I don't think that's being very fair, is it?

VICTOR: Why is it unfair? We're talking about some pretty big steps here. *To Walter:* Not that I don't appreciate it, Walter, but certain things have happened, haven't they? *With a half laugh:* It just seems odd to suddenly be talking about—

WALTER, *downing his resentment:* I'd hoped we could take one step at a time, that's all. It's very complicated between us, I think, and it seemed to me we might just try to—

VICTOR: I know, but you can understand it would be a little confusing.

WALTER—*unwillingly, anger peaks in his voice:* What do you find confusing?

VICTOR—*considers for a moment, but he cannot go back:* You must have some idea, don't you?

WALTER: This is a little astonishing, Victor. After all these years you can't expect to settle everything in one conversation, can you? I simply felt that with a little good will we . . . we . . . *He sees Victor's adamant poise.* Oh, the hell with it. *He goes abruptly and snatches up his coat and one of the evening gowns.* Get what you can from the old man, I don't want any of it. *He goes and extends his hand to Esther, forcing a smile.* I'm sorry, Esther. It was nice seeing you anyway.

> *Sickened, she accepts his hand.*

Maybe I'll see you again, Vic. Good luck. *He starts for the door. There are tears in his eyes.*

ESTHER, *before she can think*: Walter?

> *Walter halts and turns to her questioningly. She looks to Victor helplessly. But he cannot think either.*

WALTER: I don't accept this resentment, Victor. It simply baffles me. I don't understand it. I just want you to know how I feel.

ESTHER, *assuaging*: It's not resentment, Walter.

VICTOR: The whole thing is a little fantastic to me, that's all. I haven't cracked a book in twenty-five years, how do I walk into a research laboratory?

ESTHER: But Walter feels you have enough background—

VICTOR, *almost laughing over his quite concealed anger at her*: I know less chemistry than most high-school kids, Esther. *To Walter*: And physics, yet! Good God, Walter. *He laughs.* Where have you been?

WALTER: I'm sure you could make a place for yourself—

VICTOR: What place? Running papers from one office to another?

WALTER: You're not serious.

VICTOR: Why? Sooner or later my being your brother is not going to mean very much, is it? I've been walking a beat for twenty-eight years, I'm not qualified for anything technical. What's this all about?

WALTER: Why do you keep asking what it's about? I've been perfectly open with you, Victor!

VICTOR: I don't think you have.

WALTER: Why! What do you think I'm—?

VICTOR: Well, when you say what you said a few minutes ago, I—

WALTER: What did I say?!

VICTOR, *with a resolutely cool smile*: What a pity it was that I didn't go on with science.

WALTER, *puzzled*: What's wrong with that?

VICTOR, *laughing*: Oh, Walter, come on, now!

WALTER: But I feel that. I've always felt that.

VICTOR, *smiling still, and pointing at the centre chair; a new reverberation sounds in his voice*: There used to be a man in that chair, staring into space. Don't you remember that?

WALTER: Very well, yes. I sent him money every month.

VICTOR: You sent him five dollars every month.

WALTER: I could afford five dollars. But what's that got to do with you?

VICTOR: What it's got to do with me!

WALTER: Yes, I don't see that.

VICTOR: Where did you imagine the rest of his living was coming from?

WALTER: Victor, that was your decision, not mine.

VICTOR: My decision!

WALTER: We had a long talk in this room once, Victor.

VICTOR, *not recalling*: What talk?

WALTER, *astonished*: Victor! We came to a complete understanding—just after you moved up here with Dad. I told you then that I was going to finish my schooling come hell or high water, and I advised you to do the same. In fact, I warned you not to allow him to strangle your life. *To Esther*: And if I'm not mistaken I told you the same at your wedding, Esther.

VICTOR, *with an incredulous laugh*: Who the hell was supposed to keep him alive, Walter?

WALTER, *with a strange fear, more than anger*: Why did anyone have to? He wasn't sick. He was perfectly fit to go to work.

VICTOR: Work? In 1936? With no skill, no money?

WALTER—*outburst*: Then he could have gone on welfare! Who *was* he, some exiled royalty? What did a hundred and fifty million other people do in 1936? He'd have survived, Victor. Good God, you must know that by now, don't you?!

    Slight pause.

VICTOR—*suddenly at the edge of fury, and caught by Walter's voicing his own opinion, he turns to Esther*: I've had enough of this, Esther; it's the same old thing all over again, let's get out of here. *He starts rapidly upstage toward the bedroom.*

WALTER, *quickly*: Vic! Please! *He catches Victor, who frees his arm.* I'm not running him down. I loved him in many ways—

ESTHER, *as though conceding her earlier position*: Vic, listen—maybe you *ought* to talk about it.

VICTOR: It's all pointless! The whole thing doesn't matter to me! *He turns to go to the bedroom.*

WALTER: He exploited you!

    Victor halts, turns to him, his anger full in his face.

Doesn't that matter to you?

VICTOR: Let's get one thing straight, Walter—I am nobody's victim.

WALTER: But that's exactly what I've tried to tell you. I'm not trying to condescend.

VICTOR: Of course you are. Would you be saying any of this if I'd made a pile of money somewhere? *Dead stop.* I'm sorry, Walter, I can't take that. I made no choice; the icebox was empty and the man was sitting there with his mouth open. *Slight pause.* I didn't start this, Walter, and the whole thing doesn't interest me, but when you talk about making choices, and I should have gone with science, I have to say something.—Just because you want things a certain way doesn't make them that way. *He has ended at a point distant from Walter.*

    A slight pause.

WALTER, *with affront mixed into his trepidation*: All right then . . . . How do *you* see it?

VICTOR: Look, you've been sick, Walter, why upset yourself with all this?

WALTER: It's important to me!

VICTOR, *trying to smile—and in a friendly way*: But why? It's all over the dam. *He starts toward the bedroom again.*

ESTHER: I think he's come to you in good faith, Victor.

He turns to her angrily, but she braves his look.

I don't see why you can't consider his offer.

VICTOR: I said I'd consider it.

ESTHER, *restraining a cry*: You know you're turning it down! *In a certain fear of him, but persisting*: I mean what's so dreadful about telling the truth, can it be any worse than this?

VICTOR: What 'truth'? What are you—

Solomon *suddenly appears from the bedroom.*

ESTHER: For God's sake, *now* what?

SOLOMON: I just didn't want you to think I wouldn't make the appraisal; I will, I'll do it—

ESTHER, *pointing to the bedroom*: Will you please leave us alone!

SOLOMON, *suddenly, his underlying emotion coming through; indicating Victor*: What do you want from him? He's a policeman! I'm a dealer, he's a doctor, and he's a policeman, so what's the good you'll tear him to pieces?!

ESTHER: Well, one of us has got to leave this room, Victor.

SOLOMON: Please, Esther, let me . . . *Going quickly to Walter*: Doctor, listen to me, take my advice—stop it. What can come of this? In the first place, if you take the deduction how do you know in two, three years they wouldn't come back to you, whereby they disallow it? I don't have to tell you, the Federal Government is not reliable. I understand very well you want to be sweet to him—*to Esther*—but can be two, three years before you'll know how sweet they're going to allow him. *To Victor and Walter*: In other words, what I'm trying to bring out, my boys, is that—

ESTHER: —you want the furniture.

SOLOMON, *shouting at her*: Esther, if I didn't want it I wouldn't buy it! But what can they settle here? It's still up to the Federal Government, don't you see? If they can't settle nothing they should stop it right now! *With a look of warning and alarm in his eyes*: Now please—do what I tell you! I'm not a fool! *He walks out into the bedroom, shaking.*

WALTER, *after a moment*: I guess he's got a point, Vic. Why don't you just sell it to him; maybe then we can sit down and talk sometime. *Glancing at the furniture*: It isn't really a very conducive atmosphere.—Can I call you?

VICTOR: Sure.

ESTHER: You're both fantastic. *She tries to laugh.* We're giving this furniture away because nobody's able to say the simplest things. You're incredible, the both of you.

WALTER, *a little shamed*: It isn't that easy, Esther.

ESTHER: Oh, what the hell—I'll say it. When he went to you, Walter, for the five hundred he needed to get his degree—

VICTOR: Esther! There's no—

ESTHER: It's one of the things standing between you, isn't it? Maybe Walter can clear it up. I mean . . . Good God, is there never to be an end? *To Walter, without pause*: Because it stunned him, Walter. He'll never say it, but—*she takes the plunge*—he hadn't the slightest doubt you'd lend it to him. So when you turned him down—

VICTOR, *as though it wearies him*: Esther, he was just starting out—

ESTHER, *in effect, taking her separate road*: Not the way you told me! Please let me finish! *To Walter*: You already had the house in Rye, you were perfectly well established, weren't you?

VICTOR: So what? He didn't feel he could—

WALTER, *with a certain dread, quietly*: No, no, I . . . I could have spared the money . . . *He sits slowly.* Please, Vic—sit down, it'll only take a moment.

VICTOR: I just don't see any point in—

WALTER: No—no; maybe it's just as well to talk now. We've never talked about this. I think perhaps we have to. *Slight pause. Toward Esther*: It was despicable; but I don't think I can leave it quite that way. *Slight pause.* Two or three days afterward—*to Victor*—after you came to see me, I phoned to offer you the money. Did you know that?

Slight pause.

VICTOR: Where'd you phone?

WALTER: Here. I spoke to Dad.

Slight pause. Victor sits.

I saw that I'd acted badly, and I—

VICTOR: You didn't act badly—

WALTER, *with a sudden flight of his voice*: It was frightful! *He gathers himself against his past.* We'll have another talk, won't we? I wasn't prepared to go into all this. . . .

Victor is expressionless.

In any case . . . when I called here he told me you'd joined the Force. And I said—he mustn't permit you to do a thing like that. I said—you had a fine mind and with a little luck you could amount to something in science. That it was terrible waste. Etcetera. And his answer was—'Victor wants to help me. I can't stop him.'

Pause.

VICTOR: You told him you were ready to give me the money?

WALTER: Victor, you remember the . . . the helplessness in his voice. At that time? With Mother recently gone and everything shot out from under him?

VICTOR, *persisting*: Let me understand that, Walter; did you tell—

WALTER, *in anguish, but hewing to himself*: There are conversations, aren't there, and looking back it's impossible to explain why you said or didn't say certain things? I'm not defending it, but I would like to be understood, if that's possible. You all seemed to need each other more, Vic—more than I needed them. I was never able to feel your kind of . . . faith in him; that . . . confidence. His selfishness—which was perfectly normal—was always obvious to me, but you never seemed to notice it. To the point where I used to blame myself for a lack of feeling. You understand? So when he said that you wanted to help him, I felt somehow that it'd be wrong for me to try to break it up between you. It seemed like interfering.

VICTOR: I see.—Because he never mentioned you'd offered the money.

WALTER: All I'm trying to convey is that . . . I was never indifferent; that's the whole point. I did call here to offer the loan, but he made it impossible, don't you see?

VICTOR: I understand.

WALTER, *eagerly*: Do you?

VICTOR: Yes.

WALTER, *sensing the unsaid*: Please say what you think. It's absurd to go on this way. What do you want to say?

VICTOR—*slight pause*: I think it was all . . . very convenient for you.

WALTER, *appalled*: That's all?

VICTOR: I think so. If you thought Dad meant so much to me—and I guess he did in a certain way—why would five hundred bucks break us apart? I'd have gone on supporting him; it would have let me finish school, that's all.—It doesn't make any sense, Walter.

WALTER, *with a hint of hysteria in his tone*: What makes sense?

VICTOR: You didn't give me the money because you didn't want to.

WALTER, *hurt and quietly enraged—slight pause*: It's that simple.

VICTOR: That's what it comes to, doesn't it? Not that you had any obligation, but if you want to help somebody you do it, if you don't you don't. *He sees Walter's growing frustration and Esther's impatience.* Well, why is that so astonishing? We do what we want to do, don't we? *Walter doesn't reply. Victor's anxiety rises.* I don't understand what you're bringing this all up for.

WALTER: You don't feel the need to heal anything.

VICTOR: I wouldn't mind that, but how does this heal anything?

ESTHER: I think he's been perfectly clear, Victor. He's asking your friendship.

VICTOR: By offering me a job and twelve thousand dollars?

WALTER: Why not? What else can I offer you?

VICTOR: But why do you have to offer me anything?

> *Walter is silent, morally checked.*

It sounds like I have to be saved, or something.

WALTER: I simply felt that there was work you could do that you'd enjoy and I—

VICTOR: I haven't got the education, what are you talking about? You can't walk in with one splash and wash out twenty-eight years. There's a price people pay. I've paid it, it's all gone, I haven't got it anymore. Just like you paid, didn't you? You've got no wife, you've lost your family, you're rattling around all over the place? Can you go home and start all over again from scratch? This is where we are; now, right here, now. And as long as we are talking, I have to tell you that this is not what you say in front of a man's wife.

WALTER, *glancing at Esther, certainty shattered*: What have I said . . . ?

VICTOR, *trying to laugh*: We don't need to be saved, Walter! I've done a job that needs to be done and I think I've done it straight. You talk about being out of the rat race, in my opinion, you're in it as deep as you ever were. Maybe more.

ESTHER—*stands*: I want to go, Victor.

VICTOR: Please, Esther, he's said certain things and I don't think I can leave it this way.

ESTHER, *angrily*: Well, what's the difference?

VICTOR, *suppressing an outburst*: Because for some reason you don't understand *anything* any more! *He is trembling as he turns to Walter.* What are you trying to tell me—that it was all unnecessary? Is that it?

> *Walter is silent.*

Well, correct me, is that the message? Because that's all I get out of this.

WALTER, *toward Esther*: I guess it's impossible—

VICTOR, *the more strongly because Walter seems about to be allied with Esther*: What's impossible? . . . . What do you *want*, Walter!

WALTER—*in the pause is the admission that he indeed has not levelled yet. And there is fear in his voice*: I wanted to be of some use. I've learned some painful things, but it isn't enough to know; I wanted to act on what I know.

VICTOR: Act—in what way?

WALTER, *knowing it may be a red flag, but his honour is up*: I feel . . . I could be of help. Why live, only to repeat the same mistakes again and again? I didn't want to let the chance go by, as I let it go before.

> *Victor is unconvinced.*

And I must say, if this is as far as you can go with me, then you're only defeating yourself.

VICTOR: Like I did before.

> *Walter is silent.*

Is that what you mean?

WALTER—*hesitates, then with frightened but desperate acceptance of combat*: All right, yes; that's what I meant.

VICTOR: Well, that's what I thought.—See there's one thing about the cops—you get to learn how to listen to people, because if you don't hear right sometimes you end up with a knife in your back. In other words, I dreamed up the whole problem.

WALTER, *casting aside his caution, his character at issue*: Victor, my five hundred dollars was not what kept you from your degree! You could have left Pop and gone right on—he was perfectly fit.

VICTOR: And twelve million unemployed, what was that, my neurosis? I hypnotized myself every night to scrounge the outer leaves of lettuce from the Greek restaurant on the corner? The good parts we cut out of rotten grapefruits . . . ?

WALTER: I'm not trying to deny—

VICTOR, *leaning into Walter's face*: We were eating garbage here, buster!

ESTHER: But what is the point of—

VICTOR, *to Esther*: What are you trying to do, turn it all into a dream? *To Walter*: And perfectly fit! What about the inside of his head? The man was ashamed to go into the street!

ESTHER: But Victor, he's gone now.

VICTOR, *with a cry—he senses the weakness of his position*: Don't tell me he's gone now! *He is wracked, terribly alone before her.* He was here then, wasn't he? And a system broke down, did I invent that?

ESTHER: No, dear, but it's all different now.

VICTOR: What's different now? We're a goddamned army holding this city down and when it blows again you'll be thankful for a roof over your head! *To Walter*: How can you say that to me? I could have left him with your five dollars a month? I'm sorry, you can't brainwash me—if you got a hook in your mouth don't try to stick it into mine. You want to make up for things, you don't come around to make fools out of people. I didn't invent my life. Not altogether. You had a responsibility here and you walked on it. . . . You can go. I'll send you your half.

He is across the room from Walter, his face turned away. A long pause.

WALTER: If you can reach beyond anger, I'd like to tell you something. Vic? *Victor does not move.* I know I should have said this many years ago. But I did try. When you came to me I told you—remember I said, 'Ask Dad for money'? I did say that.

Pause.

VICTOR: What are you talking about?

WALTER: He had nearly four thousand dollars.

ESTHER: When?

WALTER: When they were eating garbage here.

Pause.

VICTOR: How do you know that?

WALTER: He'd asked me to invest it for him.

VICTOR: Invest it.

WALTER: Yes. Not long before he sent you to me for the loan.

Victor is silent.

That's why I never sent him more than I did. And if I'd had the strength of my convictions I wouldn't have sent him that!

Victor sits down in silence. A shame is flooding into him which he struggles with. He looks at nobody.

VICTOR, *as though still absorbing the fact*: He actually had it? In the bank?

WALTER: Vic, that's what he was living on, basically, till he died. What we gave him wasn't enough; you know that.

VICTOR: But he had those jobs——

WALTER: Meant very little. He lived on his money, believe me. I told him at the time, if he would send you through I'd contribute properly. But here he's got you running from job to job to feed him—I'm damned if I'd sacrifice when he was holding out on you. You can understand that, can't you?

> *Victor turns to the centre chair, shaking his head, exhales a blow of anger and astonishment.*

Kid, there's no point getting angry now. You know how terrified he was that he'd never earn anything any more. And there was just no reassuring him.

VICTOR, *with protest—it is still nearly incredible*: But he saw I was supporting him, didn't he?

WALTER: For how long, though?

VICTOR, *angering*: What do you mean, how long? He could see I wasn't walking out—

WALTER: I know, but he was sure you would sooner or later.

ESTHER: He was waiting for him to walk out.

WALTER—*fearing to inflame Victor, he undercuts the obvious answer*: Well . . . you could say that, yes.

ESTHER: I knew it! God, when do I believe what I see!

WALTER: He was terrified, dear, and . . . *To Victor*: I don't mean that he wasn't grateful to you, but he really couldn't understand it. I may as well say it, Vic—I myself never imagined you'd go that far.

> *Victor looks at him. Walter speaks with delicacy in the face of a possible explosion.*

Well, you must certainly see now how extreme a thing it was, to stick with him like that? And at such a cost to you?

> *Victor is silent.*

ESTHER, *with sorrow*: He sees it.

WALTER, *to erase it all, to achieve the reconciliation*: We could work together, Vic. I know we could. And I'd love to try it. What do you say?

> *There is a long pause. Victor now glances at Esther to see her expression. He sees she wants him to. He is on the verge of throwing it all up. Finally he turns to Walter, a new note of awareness in his voice.*

VICTOR: Why didn't you tell me he had that kind of money?

WALTER: But I did when you came to me for the loan.

VICTOR: To 'ask Dad'?

WALTER: Yes!

VICTOR: But would I have come to you if I had the faintest idea he had four thousand dollars under his ass? It was meaningless to say that to me.

WALTER: Now just a second . . . *He starts to indicate the harp.*

VICTOR: Cut it out, Walter! I'm sorry, but it's kind of insulting. I'm not five years old! What am I supposed to make of this? You knew he had that kind of money, and came here many times, you sat here, the two of you, watching me walk around in this suit? And now you expect me to—?

WALTER, *sharply*: You certainly knew he had *something*, Victor!

VICTOR: What do you want here? What do you want here!

WALTER: Well, all I can tell you is that *I* wouldn't sit around eating garbage with *that* staring me in the face! *He points to the harp.* Even then it was worth a couple hundred, maybe more. Your degree was right there. Right there, if nothing else.

>   *Victor is silent, trembling.*

But if you want to go on with this fantasy, it's all right with me. God knows I've had a few of my own.

>   *He starts for his coat.*

VICTOR: Fantasy.

WALTER: It's a fantasy, Victor. Your father was penniless and your brother a son of a bitch, and you play no part at all. I said to ask him because you could see in front of your face that he had some money. You knew it then and you certainly know it now.

VICTOR: You mean if he had a few dollars left, that—?

ESTHER: What do you mean, a few dollars?

VICTOR, *trying to retract*: I didn't know he—

ESTHER: But you knew he had something?

VICTOR, *caught; as though in a dream where nothing is explicable*: I didn't say that.

ESTHER: Then what are you saying?

VICTOR, *pointing at Walter*: Don't you have anything to say to *him*?

ESTHER: I want to understand what you're saying! You knew he had money left?

VICTOR: Not four thousand dol—

ESTHER: But enough to make out?

VICTOR, *crying out in anger and for release*: I couldn't nail him to the wall, could I? He said he had nothing!

ESTHER, *stating and asking*: But you knew better.

VICTOR: I don't know what I knew! *He has called this out, and his voice and words surprise him. He sits staring, cornered by what he senses in himself.*

ESTHER: It's a farce. It's all a goddamned farce!

VICTOR: Don't. Don't say that.

ESTHER: Farce! To stick us in a furnished room so you could send him part of your pay? Even after we were married, to go on sending him money? Put off having children, live like mice—and all the time you knew he . . . ? Victor, I'm trying to understand you. Victor?—Victor!

VICTOR, *roaring out, agonized*: Stop it! Silence. *Then*: Jesus, you can't leave everything out like this. The man was a beaten dog, ashamed to walk in the street, how do you demand his last buck—?

ESTHER: You're still saying that? The man had *four thousand dollars*!

He is silent.

It was all an act! Beaten dog!—he was a calculating liar! And in your heart you knew it!

He is struck silent by the fact, which is still ungraspable.

No wonder you're paralyzed—you haven't believed a word you've said all these years. We've been lying away our existence all these years; down the sewer, day after day after day . . . to protect a miserable cheap manipulator. No wonder it all seemed like a dream to me—it *was*; a goddamned nightmare. I knew it was all unreal, I knew it and I let it go by. Well, I can't anymore, kid. I can't watch it another day. I'm not ready to die. *She moves toward her purse.*

She sits. Pause.

VICTOR—*not going to her; he can't. He is standing yards from her.* This isn't true either.

ESTHER: We are dying, that's what's true!

VICTOR: I'll tell you what happened. You want to hear it? *She catches the lack of advocacy in his tone, the simplicity. He moves from her, gathering himself, and glances at the centre chair, then at Walter.* I did tell him what you'd said to me. I faced him with it. *He doesn't go on; his eyes go to the chair.* Not that I 'faced' him, I just told him—'Walter said to ask you.' *He stops; his stare is on the centre chair, caught by memory; in effect, the last line was addressed to the chair.*

WALTER: And what happened?

Pause.

VICTOR, *quietly*: He laughed. I didn't know what to make of it. Tell you the truth—*to Esther*—I don't think a week has gone by that I haven't seen that laugh. Like it was some kind of wild joke—because we *were* eating garbage here. *He breaks off.* I didn't know what I was supposed to do. And I went out. I went—*he sits, staring*—over to Bryant Park behind the public library. *Slight pause.* The grass was covered with men. Like a battlefield; a big open-air flophouse. And not bums—some of them still had shined shoes and good hats, busted businessmen, lawyers, skilled mechanics. Which I'd seen a hundred times. But suddenly—you know?—I saw it. *Slight pause.* There was no mercy. Anywhere. *Glancing at the chair at the head of the table*: One day you're the head of the house, at the head of the table, and suddenly you're shit. Overnight. And I tried to figure out that laugh.—How could he be holding out on me when he loved me?

ESTHER: Loved . . .

VICTOR, *his voice swelling with protest*: He loved me, Esther! He just didn't want to end up on the grass! It's not that you don't love somebody, it's that you've got to survive. We know what that feels like, don't we!

She can't answer, feeling the barb.

We do what we have to do. *With a wide gesture including her and Walter and himself*: What else are we talking about here? If he did have something left it was—

ESTHER: *'If'* he had—

VICTOR: What does that change! I know I'm talking like a fool, but what does that change? He couldn't believe in anybody any more, and it was unbearable to me! *The unlooked-for return of his old feelings seems to anger him. Of Walter*: He'd kicked him in the face; my mother—*he glances toward Walter as he speaks; there is hardly a pause*—the night he told us he was bankrupt, my mother . . . It was right on this couch. She was all dressed up—for some affair, I think. Her hair was piled up, and long earrings? And he had his tuxedo on . . . and made us all sit down; and he told us it was all gone. And she vomited. *Slight pause. His horror and pity twist in his voice.* All over his arms. His hands. Just kept on vomiting, like thirty-five years coming up. And he sat there. Stinking like a sewer. And a look came onto his face. I'd never seen a man look like that. He was sitting there, letting it dry on his hands. *Pause. He turns to Esther.* What's the difference what you know? Do *you* do everything you know?

> *She avoids his eyes, his mourning shared.*

Not that I excuse it; it was idiotic, nobody has to tell me that. But you're brought up to believe in one another, you're filled full of that crap—you can't help trying to keep it going, that's all. I thought if I stuck with him, if he could see that somebody was still . . . *He breaks off; the reason strangely has fallen loose. He sits.* I can't explain it; I wanted to . . . stop it from falling apart. I . . . *He breaks off again, staring.*

> *Pause.*

WALTER, *quietly*: It won't work, Vic.

> *Victor looks at him, then Esther does.*

You see it yourself, don't you? It's not that at all. You see that, don't you?

VICTOR, *quietly, avidly*: What?

WALTER, *with his driving need*: Is it really that something fell apart? Were we really brought up to believe in one another? We were brought up to succeed, weren't we? Why else would he respect me so and not you? What fell apart? What was here to fall apart?

> *Victor looks away at the burgeoning vision.*

Was there ever any love here? When he needed her, she vomited. And when you needed him, he laughed. What was unbearable is not that it all fell apart, it was that there was never anything here.

> *Victor turns back to him, fear on his face.*

ESTHER, *as though she herself were somehow moving under the rays of judgment*: But who . . . who can ever face that, Walter?

WALTER, *to her*: You have to! *To Victor*: What you saw behind the library was not that there was no mercy in the world, kid. It's that there was no love in this house. There was no loyalty. There was nothing here but a straight financial arrangement. That's what was unbearable. And you proceeded to wipe out what you saw.

VICTOR, *with terrible anxiety*: Wipe out—

WALTER: Vic, I've been in this box. I wasted thirty years protecting myself from that catastrophe. *He indicates the chair*: And I only got out alive when I saw that there was no catastrophe, there had never been. They were never lovers—she said a hundred times that her marriage destroyed her musical career. I saw that nothing fell here, Vic—and he doesn't follow me anymore with that vomit on his hands. I don't look high and low for some betrayal any more; my days belong to me now, I'm not afraid to risk believing in someone. All I ever wanted was simply to do science, but I invented an efficient, disaster-proof, money-maker. You—*to Esther, with a warm smile*: He could never stand the sight of blood. He was shy, he was sensitive . . . *To Victor*: And what do you do? March straight into the most violent profession there is. We invent ourselves, Vic, to wipe out what we know. You invent a life of self-sacrifice, a life of duty; but what never existed here cannot be upheld. You were not upholding something, you were denying what you knew they were. And denying yourself. And that's all that is standing between us now—an illusion, Vic. That I kicked them in the face and you must uphold them against me. But I only saw then what you see now—there was nothing here to betray. I am not your enemy. It is all an illusion and if you could walk through it, we could meet . . . *His reconciliation is on him*. You see why I said before, that in the hospital—when it struck me so that we . . . we're brothers. It was only two seemingly different roads out of the same trap. It's almost as though—*he smiles warmly, uncertain still*—we're like two halves of the same guy. As though we can't quite move ahead—alone. You ever feel that?

> *Victor is silent.*

Vic?

> *Pause.*

VICTOR: Walter, I'll tell you—there are days when I can't remember what I've got against you. *He laughs emptily, in suffering*. It hangs in me like a rock. And I see myself in a store window, and my hair going, I'm walking the streets—and I can't remember why. And you can go crazy trying to figure it out when all the reasons disappear—when you can't even hate any more.

WALTER: Because it's unreal, Vic, and underneath you know it is.

VICTOR: Then give me something real.

WALTER: What can I give you?

VICTOR: I'm not blaming you now, I'm asking you. I can understand you walking out. I've wished a thousand times I'd done the same thing. But, to come here through all those years knowing what you knew and saying nothing . . . ?

WALTER: And if I said—Victor, if I said that I did have some wish to hold you back? What would that give you now?

VICTOR: Is that what you wanted? Walter, tell me the truth.

WALTER: I wanted the freedom to do my work. Does that mean I stole your life? *Crying out and standing*: You made these choices, Victor! And that's what you have to face!

VICTOR: But, what do you face? You're not turning me into a walking fifty-year-old mistake—we have to go home when you leave, we have to look at each other. What do *you* face?

WALTER: I have offered you everything I know how to!

VICTOR: I would know if you'd come to give me something! I would know that!

WALTER, *crossing for his coat*: You don't want the truth, you want a monster!

VICTOR: You came for the old handshake, didn't you! The okay!

> *Walter halts in the doorway.*

And you end up with the respect, the career, the money, and the best of all, the thing that nobody else can tell you so you can believe it—that you're one hell of a guy and never harmed anybody in your life! Well, you won't get it, not till I get mine!

WALTER: And you? You never had any hatred for me? Never a wish to see me destroyed? To destroy me, to destroy me with this saintly self-sacrifice, this mockery of sacrifice? What will you give me, Victor?

VICTOR: I don't have it to give to you. Not any more. And you don't have it to give me. And there's nothing to give—I see that now. I just didn't want him to end up on the grass. And he didn't. That's all it was, and I don't need anything more. I couldn't work with you, Walter. I can't. I don't trust you.

WALTER: Vengeance. Down to the end. *To Esther*: He is sacrificing his life to vengeance.

ESTHER: Nothing was sacrificed.

WALTER, *to Victor*: To prove with your failure what a treacherous son of a bitch I am!—to hang yourself in my doorway!

ESTHER: Leave him, Walter—please, don't say any more!

WALTER—*humiliated by her. He is furious. He takes an unplanned step toward the door*: You quit; both of you. *To Victor as well*: You lay down and quit, and that's the long and short of all your ideology. It is all envy!

> *Solomon enters, apprehensive, looks from one to the other.*

And to this moment you haven't the guts to face it! But your failure does not give you moral authority! Not with me! I *worked* for what I made and there are people walking around who'd have been dead if I hadn't. Yes. *Moving toward the door, he points at the centre chair.* He was smarter than all of us—he saw what you wanted and he gave it to you! *He suddenly reaches out and grabs Solomon's face and laughs.* Go ahead, you old mutt—rob them blind, they love it! *Letting go, he turns to Victor.* You will never, never again make me ashamed! *He strides toward the doorway. A gown lies on the dining table, spread out, and he is halted in surprise at the sight of it.*

Suddenly Walter sweeps it up in his hands and rushes at Victor, flinging the gown at him with an outcry. Victor backs up at his wild approach.

VICTOR: Walter!

The flicker of a humiliated smile passes across Walter's face. He wants to disappear into air. He turns, hardly glancing at Victor, makes for the door, and, straightening, goes out.

VICTOR—*starts hesitatingly to the door*: Maybe he oughtn't go into the street like that—
SOLOMON, *stopping him with his hand*: Let him go.

Victor turns to Solomon uncertainly.

What can you do?
ESTHER: Whatever you see, huh.

Solomon turns to her, questioningly.

You believe what you see.
SOLOMON, *thinking she was rebuking him*: What then?
ESTHER: No—it's wonderful. Maybe that's why you're still going.

Victor turns to her. She stares at the doorway.

I was nineteen years old when I first walked up those stairs—if that's believable. And he had a brother, who was the cleverest, most wonderful young doctor . . . in the world. As he'd be soon. Somehow, some way. *She turns to the centre chair.* And a rather sweet, inoffensive gentleman, always waiting for the news to come on. . . . And next week, men we never saw or heard of will come and smash it all apart and take it all away.—So many times I thought—the one thing he wanted most was to talk to his brother, and that if they could—But he's come and he's gone. And I still feel it—isn't that terrible? It always seems to me that one little step more and some crazy kind of forgiveness will come and lift up everyone. When do you stop being so . . . foolish?
SOLOMON: I had a daughter, should rest in peace, she took her own life. That's nearly fifty years. And every night I lay down to sleep, she's sitting there. I see her clear like I see you. But if it was a miracle and she came to life, what would I say to her? *He turns back to Victor, paying out.* So you got there seven; so I'm giving you eight, nine, ten, eleven—*he searches, finds a fifty*—and there's a fifty for the harp. Now you'll excuse me—I got a lot of work here tonight. *He gets his pad and pencil and begins carefully listing each piece.*
VICTOR—*folds the money*: We could still make the picture, if you like.
ESTHER: Okay.

He goes to his suit and begins to rip the plastic wrapper off.

Don't bother.

He looks at her.

She turns to Solomon. Goodbye, Mr Solomon.

SOLOMON—*looks up from his pad*: Goodbye, dear. I like that suit, that's very nice. *He returns to his work.*

ESTHER: Thank you. *She walks out with her life.*

VICTOR—*buckles on his gun belt, pulls up his tie*: When will you be taking it away?

SOLOMON: With God's help if I'll live, first thing in the morning.

VICTOR, *of the suit*: I'll be back for this later, then. And there's my foil, and the mask, and the gauntlets. *Puts on his uniform jacket.*

SOLOMON, *continuing his work*: Don't worry, I wouldn't touch it.

VICTOR, *extending his hand*: I'm glad to have met you, Solomon.

SOLOMON: Likewise. And I want to thank you.

VICTOR: What for?

SOLOMON, *with a glance at the furniture*: Well . . . who would ever believe I would start such a thing again . . . ? *He cuts himself off.* But go, go I got a lot of work here.

VICTOR, *starting to the door, putting his cap on*: Good luck with it.

SOLOMON: Good luck you can never know till the last minute, my boy.

VICTOR, *smiling*: Right. Yes. *With a last look around at the room.* Well . . . bye-bye.

SOLOMON, *as Victor goes out*: Bye-bye, bye-bye.

> *He is alone. He has the pad and pencil in his hand, and he takes the pencil to start work again. But he looks about, and the challenge of it all oppresses him and he is afraid and worried. His hand goes to his cheek, he pulls his flesh in fear, his eyes circling the room.*

> *His eye falls on the phonograph. He goes, inspects it, winds it up, sets the tone arm on the record, and flicks the starting lever. The Laughing Record plays. As the two comedians begin their routine, his depressed expression gives way to surprise. Now he smiles. He chuckles, and remembers. Now a laugh escapes, and he nods his head in recollection. He is laughing now, and shakes his head back and forth as though to say, 'It still works!' And the laughter, of the record and his own, increase and combine. He holds his head, unable to stop laughing, and sits in the centre chair. He leans back sprawling in the chair, laughing with tears in his eyes, howling helplessly to the air.*

Slow Curtain

AUTHOR'S PRODUCTION NOTE

A fine balance of sympathy should be maintained in the playing of the roles of Victor and Walter. The actor playing Walter must not regard his attempts to win back Victor's friendship as mere manipulation. From entrance to exit, Walter is attempting to put into action what he has learned about himself, and sympathy will be evoked for him in proportion to the openness, the depth of need, the intimations of suffering with which the role is played.

This admonition goes beyond the question of theatrics to the theme of the play. As the world now operates, the qualities of both brothers are necessary to it; surely their respective psychologies and moral values conflict at the heart of the social dilemma. The production must therefore withhold judgment in favour of presenting both men in all their humanity and from their own viewpoints. Actually, each has merely proved to the other what the other has known but dared not face. At the end, demanding of one another what was forfeited to time, each is left touching the structure of his life.

The play can be performed with an intermission, as indicated at the end of Act One, if circumstances require it. But an unbroken performance is preferable.

1968

Edward Albee
b. 1928

Born in Washington, DC, Edward Albee attended a series of private schools before graduating from Choate School in Wallingford, Connecticut. He went to Trinity College, Hartford, for eighteen months, then moved to New York City, which became his home. His grim yet frequently humorous plays, usually classified as theatre of the absurd, strip their characters of their pretense and hypocrisy and force them to confront less pleasant aspects of their lives. *Who's Afraid of Virginia Woolf?* (1962) remains the most successful of his more than twenty plays. *The Zoo Story*, his first produced play, had its premiere at the Schiller Theater Werkstatt in Berlin on 28 September 1959. It received its first American production four months later at the Provincetown Playhouse in New York City on a double bill with Samuel Beckett's *Krapp's Last Tape.*

The Zoo Story

PLAYERS

PETER, *a man in his early forties, neither fat nor gaunt, neither handsome nor homely. He wears tweeds, smokes a pipe, carries horn-rimmed glasses. Although he is moving into middle age, his dress and his manner would suggest a man younger.*

JERRY, *a man in his late thirties, not poorly dressed, but carelessly. What was once a trim and lightly muscled body has begun to go to fat; and while he is no longer handsome, it is evident that he once was. His fall from physical grace should not suggest debauchery; he has, to come closest to it, a great weariness.*

> *The Scene: It is Central Park; a Sunday afternoon in summer; the present. There are two park benches, one toward either side of the stage; they both face the audience. Behind them: foliage, trees, sky. At the beginning, Peter is seated on one of the benches.*
>
> *(As the curtain rises. Peter is seated on the bench stage-right. He is reading a book. He stops reading, cleans his glasses, goes back to reading. Jerry enters.)*

JERRY: I've been to the zoo. [*Peter doesn't notice.*] I said, I've been to the zoo. MISTER, I'VE BEEN TO THE ZOO!

PETER: Hm? . . . What? . . . I'm sorry, were you talking to me?

JERRY: I went to the zoo, and then I walked until I came here. Have I been walking north?

PETER [*puzzled*]: North? Why . . . I . . . I think so. Let me see.

JERRY [*pointing past the audience*]: Is that Fifth Avenue?

PETER: Why yes; yes, it is.

JERRY: And what is that cross street there; that one, to the right?

PETER: That? Oh, that's Seventy-fourth Street.

JERRY: And the zoo is around Sixty-fifth Street; so, I've been walking north.

PETER [*anxious to get back to his reading*]: Yes; it would seem so.

JERRY: Good old north.

PETER [*lightly, by reflex*]: Ha, ha.

JERRY [*after a slight pause*]: But not due north.

PETER: I . . . well, no, not due north; but, we . . . call it north. It's northerly.

JERRY [*watches as Peter, anxious to dismiss him, prepares his pipe*]: Well, boy; you're not going to get lung cancer, are you?

PETER [*looks up, a little annoyed, then smiles*]: No, sir. Not from this.

JERRY: No, sir. What you'll probably get is cancer of the mouth, and then you'll have to wear one of those things Freud wore after they took one whole side of his jaw away. What do they call those things?

PETER [*uncomfortable*]: A prosthesis?

JERRY: The very thing! A prosthesis. You're an educated man, aren't you? Are you a doctor?

PETER: Oh, no; no. I read about it somewhere; *Time* magazine, I think. [*He turns to his book.*]

JERRY: Well, *Time* magazine isn't for blockheads.

PETER: No, I suppose not.

JERRY [*after a pause*]: Boy, I'm glad that's Fifth Avenue there.

PETER [*vaguely*]: Yes.

JERRY: I don't like the west side of the park much.

PETER: Oh. [*then, slightly wary, but interested*] Why?

JERRY [*offhand*]: I don't know.

PETER: Oh. [*He returns to his book.*]

JERRY [*He stands for a few seconds, looking at Peter, who finally looks up again, puzzled.*]: Do you mind if we talk?

PETER [*obviously minding*]: Why . . . no, no.

JERRY: Yes you do; you do.

PETER [*puts his book down, his pipe out and away, smiling*]: No, really, I don't mind.

JERRY: Yes you do.

PETER [*finally decided*]: No; I don't mind at all, really.

JERRY: It's . . . it's a nice day.

PETER [*stares unnecessarily at the sky*]: Yes. Yes, it is; lovely.

JERRY: I've been to the zoo.

PETER: Yes, I think you said so . . . . didn't you?

JERRY: You'll read about it in the papers tomorrow, if you don't see it on your TV tonight. You have TV, haven't you?

PETER: Why yes, we have two; one for the children.

JERRY: You're married!

PETER [*with pleased emphasis*]: Why, certainly.

JERRY: It isn't a law, for God's sake.

PETER: No . . . no, of course not.

JERRY: And you have a wife.

PETER [*bewildered by the seeming lack of communication*]: Yes!

JERRY: And you have children.

PETER: Yes; two.

JERRY: Boys?

PETER: No, girls . . . both girls.

JERRY: But you wanted boys.

PETER: Well . . . naturally, every man wants a son, but . . .

JERRY [*lightly mocking*]: But that's the way the cookie crumbles?

PETER [*annoyed*]: I wasn't going to say that.

JERRY: And you're not going to have any more kids, are you?

PETER [*a bit distantly*]: No. No more. [*then back, and irksome*] Why did you say that? How would you know about that?

JERRY: The way you cross your legs, perhaps; something in the voice. Or maybe I'm just guessing. Is it your wife?

PETER [*furious*]: That's none of your business! [*A silence.*] Do you understand? [*Jerry nods. Peter is quiet now.*] Well you're right. We'll have no more children.

JERRY [*softly*]: That *is* the way the cookie crumbles.

PETER [*forgiving*]: Yes . . . I guess so.

JERRY: Well, now; what else?

PETER: What were you saying about the zoo . . . that I'd read about it, or see . . . ?

JERRY: I'll tell you about it, soon. Do you mind if I ask you questions?

PETER: Oh, not really.

JERRY: I'll tell you why I do it; I don't talk to many people—except to say like: give me a beer, or where's the john, or what time does the feature go on, or keep your hands to yourself, buddy. You know—things like that.

PETER: I must say I don't . . .

JERRY: But every once in a while I like to talk to somebody, really talk; like to get to know somebody, know all about him.

PETER [*lightly laughing, still a little uncomfortable*]: And am I the guinea pig for today?

JERRY: On a sun-drenched Sunday afternoon like this? Who better than a nice married man with two daughters and . . . uh . . . a dog? [*Peter shakes his head.*] No? Two dogs. [*Peter shakes his head again.*] Hm. No dogs? [*Peter shakes his head, sadly.*] Oh, that's a shame. But you look like an animal man. CATS? [*Peter nods his head, ruefully.*] Cats! But, that can't be your idea. No, sir. Your wife and daughters? [*Peter nods his head.*] Is there anything else I should know?

PETER [*He has to clear his throat.*]: There are . . . there are two parakeets. One . . . uh . . . one for each of my daughters.

JERRY: Birds.

PETER: My daughters keep them in a cage in their bedroom.

JERRY: Do they carry disease? The birds.

PETER: I don't believe so.

JERRY: That's too bad. If they did you could set them loose in the house and the cats could eat them and die, maybe. [*Peter looks blank for a moment, then laughs.*] And what else? What do you do to support your enormous household?

PETER: I . . . uh . . . I have an executive position with a . . . a small publishing house. We . . . uh . . . we publish textbooks.

JERRY: That sounds nice; very nice. What do you make?

PETER [*still cheerful*]: Now look here!

JERRY: Oh, come on.

PETER: Well, I make around eighteen thousand a year, but I don't carry more than forty dollars at any one time . . . in case you're a . . . a holdup man . . . ha, ha, ha.

JERRY [*ignoring the above*]: Where do you live? [*Peter is reluctant.*] Oh, look; I'm not going to rob you, and I'm not going to kidnap your parakeets, your cats, or your daughters.

PETER [*too loud*]: I live between Lexington and Third Avenue, on Seventy-fourth Street.

JERRY: That wasn't so hard, was it?

PETER: I didn't mean to seem ... ah ... it's that you don't really carry on a conversation; you just ask questions. And I'm ... I'm normally ... uh ... reticent. Why do you just stand there?

JERRY: I'll start walking around in a little while, and eventually I'll sit down. [*recalling*] Wait until you see the expression on his face.

PETER: What? Whose face? Look here; is this something about the zoo?

JERRY [*distantly*]: The what?

PETER: The zoo; the zoo. Something about the zoo.

JERRY: The zoo?

PETER: You've mentioned it several times.

JERRY [*still distant, but returning abruptly*]: The zoo. Oh, yes; the zoo. I was there before I came here. I told you that. Say, what's the dividing line between upper-middle-middle-class and lower-upper-middle-class?

PETER: My dear fellow, I ...

JERRY: Don't my dear fellow me.

PETER [*unhappily*]: Was I patronizing? I believe I was; I'm sorry. But you see, your question about the classes bewildered me.

JERRY: And when you're bewildered you become patronizing?

PETER: I ... I don't express myself too well, sometimes. [*He attempts a joke on himself.*] I'm in publishing, not writing.

JERRY [*amused, but not at the humour*]: So be it. The truth is: I was being patronizing.

PETER: Oh, now; you needn't say that. [*It is at this point that Jerry may begin to move about the stage with slowly increasing determination and authority, but pacing himself, so that the long speech about the dog comes at the high point of the arc.*]

JERRY: All right. Who are your favourite writers? Baudelaire and J.P. Marquand?

PETER [*wary*]: Well, I like a great many writers; I have a considerable ... catholicity of taste, if I may say so. Those two men are fine, each in his way. [*warming up*] Baudelaire, of course ... uh ... is by far the finer of the two, but Marquand has a place ... in our ... uh ... national ...

JERRY: Skip it.

PETER: I ... sorry.

JERRY: Do you know what I did before I went to the zoo today? I walked all the way up Fifth Avenue from Washington Square; all the way.

PETER: Oh; you live in the Village! [*This seems to enlighten Peter.*]

JERRY: No, I don't. I took the subway down to the Village so I could walk all the way up Fifth Avenue to the zoo. It's one of those things a person has to do; sometimes a person has to go a very long distance out of his way to come back a short distance correctly.

PETER [*almost pouting*]: Oh, I thought you lived in the Village.

JERRY: What were you trying to do? Make sense out of things? Bring order? The old pigeonhole bit? Well, that's easy; I'll tell you. I live in a four-story brownstone rooming-house on the upper West Side between Columbus Avenue and Central Park West. I live on the top floor; rear; west. It's a laughably small room, and one of my walls is made of beaverboard; this beaverboard separates my room from another laughably small room, so I assume that the two rooms were once one room, a small room, but not necessarily laughable. The room beyond my beaverboard wall is occupied by a coloured queen who always keeps his door open; well, not always but *always* when he's plucking his eyebrows, which he does with Buddhist concentration. This coloured queen has rotten teeth, which is rare, and he has a Japanese kimono, which is also pretty rare; and he wears this kimono to and from the john in the hall, which is pretty frequent. I mean, he goes to the john a lot. He never bothers me, and he never brings anyone up to his room. All he does is pluck his eyebrows, wear his kimono and go to the john. Now, the two front rooms on my floor are a little larger, I guess; but they're pretty small, too. There's a Puerto Rican family in one of them, a husband, a wife, and some kids; I don't know how many. These people entertain a lot. And in the other front room, there's somebody living there, but I don't know who it is. I've never seen who it is. Never. Never ever.

PETER [*embarrassed*]: Why . . . why do you live there?

JERRY [*from a distance again*]: I don't know.

PETER: It doesn't sound like a very nice place . . . where you live.

JERRY: Well, no; it isn't an apartment in the East Seventies. But, then again, I don't have one wife, two daughters, two cats and two parakeets. What I do have, I have toilet articles, a few clothes, a hot plate that I'm not supposed to have, a can opener, one that works with a key, you know; a knife, two forks, and two spoons, one small, one large; three plates, a cup, a saucer, a drinking glass, two picture frames, both empty, eight or nine books, a pack of pornographic playing cards, regular deck, an old Western Union typewriter that prints nothing but capital letters, and a small strongbox without a lock which has in it . . . what? Rocks! Some rocks . . . sea-rounded rocks I picked up on the beach when I was a kid. Under which . . . weighed down . . . are some letters . . . please letters . . . please why don't you do this, and please when will you do that letters. And when letters, too. When will you write? When will you come? When? These letters are from more recent years.

PETER [*stares glumly at his shoes, then*]: About those two empty picture frames . . . ?

JERRY: I don't see why they need any explanation at all. Isn't it clear? I don't have pictures of anyone to put in them.

PETER: Your parents . . . perhaps . . . a girl friend . . .

JERRY: You're a very sweet man, and you're possessed of a truly enviable innocence. But good old Mom and good old Pop are dead . . . you know? . . . I'm broken up about it, too . . . I mean really. BUT. That particular vaudeville act is playing the cloud circuit now, so I don't see how I can look at them, all neat and framed. Besides, or, rather, to be pointed about it, good old Mom walked out on good old Pop when I was ten and a half years old; she embarked on an adulterous turn of our southern states . . . a journey of a year's duration . . . and her most constant companion . . . among others, among many others . . . was a Mr Barleycorn. At least, that's what good old Pop told me after he went down . . . came back . . . brought her body north. We'd received the news between Christmas and New Year's, you see, that good old Mom had parted with the ghost in some dump in Alabama. And, without the ghost . . . she was less welcome. I mean, what was she? A stiff . . . a northern stiff. At any rate, good old Pop celebrated the New Year for an even two weeks and then slapped into the front of a somewhat moving city omnibus, which sort of cleaned things out family-wise. Well no; then there was Mom's sister, who was given neither to sin nor the consolations of the bottle. I moved in on her, and my memory of her is slight excepting I remember still that she did all things dourly: sleeping, eating, working, praying. She dropped dead on the stairs to her apartment, my apartment then, too, on the afternoon of my high school graduation. A terribly middle-European joke, if you ask me.

PETER: Oh, my; oh, my.

JERRY: Oh, your what? But that was a long time ago, and I have no feeling about any of it that I care to admit to myself. Perhaps you can see, though, why good old Mom and good old Pop are frameless. What's your name?

PETER: I'm Peter.

JERRY: I'd forgotten to ask you. I'm Jerry.

PETER [*with a slight, nervous laugh*]: Hello, Jerry.

JERRY [*nods his hello*]: And let's see now; what's the point of having a girl's picture, especially in two frames? I have two picture frames, you remember. I never see the pretty little ladies more than once, and most of them wouldn't be caught in the same room with a camera. It's odd, and I wonder if it's sad.

PETER: The girls?

JERRY: No. I wonder if it's sad that I never see the little ladies more than once. I've never been able to have sex with, or, how is it put? . . . make love to anybody more than once. Once; that's it. . . . Oh, wait, for a week and a half, when I was fifteen . . . and I hang my head in shame that puberty was late . . . I was a h-o-m-o-s-e-x-u-a-l. I mean, I was queer . . . [*very fast*] . . . queer, queer, queer . . . with bells ringing, banners snapping in the wind. And for those eleven days, I met at least twice a day with the park superintendent's son . . . a Greek boy, whose birthday was the same as mine, except he was a year older. I think I was very much in love . . . maybe just with sex. But that was the jazz of a very special hotel, wasn't it? And now; oh, do I love the little ladies; really, I love them. For about an hour.

PETER: Well, it seems perfectly simple to me. . . .

JERRY [*angry*]: Look! Are you going to tell me to get married and have parakeets?

PETER [*angry himself*]: Forget the parakeets! And stay single if you want to. It's no business of mine. I didn't start this conversation in the . . .

JERRY: All right, all right. I'm sorry. All right? You're not angry?

PETER [*laughing*]: No, I'm not angry.

JERRY [*relieved*]: Good. [*now back to his previous tone*] Interesting that you asked me about the picture frames. I would have thought that you would have asked me about the pornographic cards.

PETER [*with a knowing smile*]: Oh, I've seen those cards.

JERRY: That's not the point. [*Laughs.*] I suppose when you were a kid you and your pals passed them around, or you had a pack of your own.

PETER: Well, I guess a lot of us did.

JERRY: And you threw them away just before you got married.

PETER: Oh, now; look here. I didn't need anything like that when I got older.

JERRY: No?

PETER [*embarrassed*]: I'd rather not talk about these things.

JERRY: So? Don't. Besides, I wasn't trying to plumb your post-adolescent sexual life and hard times; what I wanted to get at is the value difference between pornographic playing cards when you're a kid, and pornographic playing cards when you're older. It's that when you're a kid you use the cards as a substitute for a real experience, and when you're older you use real experience as a substitute for the fantasy. But I imagine you'd rather hear about what happened at the zoo.

PETER [*enthusiastic*]: Oh, yes; the zoo. [*then, awkward*] That is . . . if you . . .

JERRY: Let me tell you about why I went . . . well, let me tell you some things. I've told you about the fourth floor of the rooming-house where I live. I think the rooms are better as you go down, floor by floor. I guess they are; I don't know. I don't know any of the people on the third and second floors. Oh, wait! I do know that there's a lady living on the third floor, in the front. I know because she cries all the time. Whenever I go out or come back in, whenever I pass her door, I always hear her crying, muffled, but . . . very determined. Very determined indeed. But the one I'm getting to, and all about the dog, is the landlady. I don't like to use words that are too harsh in describing people. I don't like to. But the landlady is a fat, ugly, mean, stupid, unwashed, misanthropic, cheap, drunken bag of garbage. And you may have noticed that I very seldom use profanity, so I can't describe her as well as I might.

PETER: You describe her . . . vividly.

JERRY: Well, thanks. Anyway, she has a dog, and I will tell you about the dog, and she and her dog are the gatekeepers of my dwelling. The woman is bad enough; she leans around in the entrance hall, spying to see that I don't bring in things or people, and when she's had her midafternoon pint of lemon-flavoured gin she always stops me in the hall, and grabs ahold of my coat or my arm, and she presses her disgusting body up against me to keep me in a corner so she can talk to me. The smell of her body and her breath . . . you can't imagine it . . . and somewhere, somewhere in the back of that pea-sized brain of hers, an organ developed just enough to let her eat, drink, and emit, she has some foul parody of sexual desire. And I, Peter, I am the object of her sweaty lust.

PETER: That's disgusting. That's . . . horrible.

JERRY: But I have found a way to keep her off. When she talks to me, when she presses to my body and mumbles about her room and how I should come there, I merely say: but, Love; wasn't yesterday enough for you, and the day before? Then she puzzles, she makes slits of her tiny eyes, she sways a little and then, Peter . . . and it is at this moment that I think I might be doing some good in that tormented house . . . a simple-minded smile begins to form on her unthinkable face, and she giggles and groans as she thinks about yesterday and the day before; and she believes and relives what never happened. Then, she motions to that black monster of a dog she has, and she goes back to her room. And I am safe until our next meeting.

PETER: It's so . . . unthinkable. I find it hard to believe that people such as that really are.

JERRY [*lightly mocking*]: It's for reading about, isn't it?

PETER [*seriously*]: Yes.

JERRY: And fact is better left to fiction. You're right, Peter. Well, what I have been meaning to tell you about is the dog; I shall, now.

PETER [*nervously*]: Oh, yes; the dog.

JERRY: Don't go. You're not thinking of going, are you?

PETER: Well . . . no, I don't think so.

JERRY [*as if to a child*]: Because after I tell you about the dog, do you know what then? Then . . . then I'll tell you about what happened at the zoo.

PETER [*laughing faintly*]: You're . . . you're full of stories, aren't you?

JERRY: You don't have to listen. Nobody is holding you here; remember that. Keep that in mind.

PETER [*irritably*]: I know that.

JERRY: You do? Good. [*The following long speech, it seems to me, should be done with a great deal of action, to achieve a hypnotic effect on Peter, and on the audience, too. Some specific actions have been suggested, but the director and the actor playing Jerry might best work it out for themselves.*] ALL RIGHT. [*as if reading from a huge billboard*] THE STORY OF JERRY AND THE DOG! [*natural again*]: What I am gong to tell you has something to do with how sometimes it's necessary to go a long distance out of the way in order to come back a short distance correctly; or, maybe I only think that it has something to do with that. But, it's why I went to the zoo today, and why I walked north . . . northerly, rather . . . until I came here. All right. The dog, I think I told you, is a black monster of a beast: an oversized head, tiny, tiny ears, and eyes . . . bloodshot, infected, maybe; and a body you can see the ribs through the skin. The dog is black, all black; all black except for the bloodshot eyes, and . . . yes . . . and an open sore on its . . . *right* forepaw; that is red, too. And, oh yes; the poor monster, and I do believe it's an old dog . . . it's certainly a misused one . . . almost always has an erection . . . of sorts. That's red, too. And . . . What else? . . . oh, yes; there's a grey-yellow-white colour, too, when he bares his fangs. Like this: Grrrrrr! Which is what he did when he saw me for the first time . . . the day I moved in. I worried about that animal the very first minute I met him. Now, animals don't take to me like Saint Francis had birds hanging off him all the time. What I mean is: animals are indifferent to me . . . like people [*He smiles slightly.*] . . . most of the time. But this dog wasn't indifferent. From the very beginning he'd snarl and then go for me, to get one of my legs. Not like he was rabid, you know; he was sort of a stumbly dog, but he wasn't half-assed, either. It was a good, stumbly run; but I always got away. He got a piece of my trouser leg, look, you can see right here, where it's mended; he got that the second day I lived there; but, I kicked free and got upstairs so fast, so that was that. [*Puzzles.*] I still don't now to this day how the other roomers manage it, but you know what I think: I think it had to do only with me. Cozy. So. Anyway, this went on for over a week, whenever I came in; but never when I went out. That's funny. Or, it was funny. I could pack up and live in the street for all the dog cared. Well, I thought about it up in my room one day, one of the times after I'd bolted upstairs, and I made up my mind. I decided: First, I'll kill the dog with kindness, and if that doesn't work . . . I'll just kill him. [*Peter winces.*] Don't react, Peter; just listen. So, the next day I went out and bought a bag of hamburgers, medium rare, no catsup, no onion; and on the way home I threw away all the rolls and kept just the meat. [*Action for the following, perhaps.*] When I got back to the rooming-house the dog was waiting for me. I half opened the door that led into the entrance hall, and there he was; waiting for me. It figured. I went in, very cautiously, and I had the hamburgers, you remember; I opened the bag, and I set the meat down about twelve feet from where the dog was snarling at me. Like so! He snarled; stopped snarling; sniffed; moved slowly; then faster; then faster toward the meat. Well, when he got to it he stopped, and he looked at me. I smiled; but tentatively, you understand. He turned his face back to the hamburgers, smelled, sniffed some more, and then . . . RRRAAAAGGGGGHHHH, like that . . . he tore into them. It was as if he had never eaten anything in his life before, except like garbage. Which might very well have been the truth. I don't think the landlady ever eats anything but garbage. But. He ate all the hamburgers, almost all at once, making sounds in his throat like a woman. *Then*, when he'd finished the meat, the hamburger, and tried to eat the paper, too, he sat down and smiled. I think he smiled; I know cats do. It was a very gratifying few moments. Then BAM, he snarled and made for me again. He didn't get me this time, either. So, I got upstairs, and I lay down on my bed and started to think about the dog again. To be truthful, I was offended, and I was damn mad, too. It was six perfectly good hamburgers with not enough pork in them to make it disgusting. I was offended. But, after a while, I decided to try it for a few more days. If you think about it, this dog had what amounted to an antipathy toward me; really. And, I wondered if I mightn't overcome this antipathy. So, I tried it for five more days, but it was always the same: snarl, sniff; move; faster; stare; gobble; RAAGGGHHH; smile; snarl; BAM. Well, now; by this time Columbus Avenue was strewn with hamburger rolls and I was less offended than disgusted. So, I decided to kill the dog. [*Peter raises a hand in protest.*] Oh, don't be so alarmed, Peter; I didn't succeed. The day I tried to kill the dog I bought only one hamburger and what I thought was a murderous portion of rat poison. When I bought the hamburger I asked the man not to bother with the roll, all I wanted was the meat. I expected some reaction from him, like: we don't sell no hamburgers without rolls; or, wha' d'ya wanna do, eat it out'a ya han's? But no; he smiled benignly, wrapped up the hamburger in waxed paper, and said: A bite for ya pussycat? I wanted to say: No, not really; it's part of a plan to poison a dog I know. But, you can't say 'a dog I know' without sounding funny; so I said, a little too loud, I'm afraid, and too formally: YES, A BITE FOR MY PUSSY-CAT. People looked up. It always happens when I try to simplify things; people look up. But that's neither hither nor thither. So. On my way back to the rooming-house, I kneaded the hamburger and the rat poison together between my hands, at that point feeling as much sadness as disgust. I opened the door to the entrance hall, and there the monster was, waiting to take the offering and then jump me. Poor bastard; he never learned that the moment he took to smile before he went for me gave me time enough to get out of range. BUT, there he was; malevolence with an erection, waiting. I put the poison patty down, moved toward the stairs and watched. The poor animal gobbled the food down as usual, smiled, which made me almost sick, and then, BAM. But, I sprinted up the stairs, as usual, and the dog didn't get me, as usual. AND IT CAME TO PASS THAT THE BEAST WAS DEATHLY ILL. I knew this because he no longer attended me, and because the landlady sobered up. She stopped me in the hall the same evening of the attempted murder and confided the information that God had struck her puppy-dog a surely fatal blow. She had forgotten her bewildered lust, and her eyes were wide open for the first time. They looked like the dog's eyes. She snivelled and implored me to pray for the animal. I wanted to say to her: Madam, I have myself to pray for, the coloured queen, the Puerto Rican family, the person in the front room whom I've never seen, the woman who cries deliberately behind her closed door, and the rest of the people in all rooming-houses, everywhere; besides, Madam, I don't understand how to pray. But . . . to simplify things . . . I told her I would pray. She looked up. She said that I was a liar, and that I probably wanted the dog to die. I told her, and there was so much truth here, that I didn't want the dog to die. I didn't, and not just because I'd poisoned him. I'm afraid that I must tell you I wanted the dog to live so that I could see what our new relationship might come to. [*Peter indicates his increasing displeasure and slowly growing antagonism.*] Please understand, Peter; that sort of thing is important. You must believe me; it is important. We have to know the effect of our actions. [*another deep sigh*] Well, anyway; the dog recovered. I have no idea why, unless he was a descendant of the puppy that guarded the gates of hell or some such resort. I'm not up on my mythology. [*He pronounces the word myth-ó-logy.*] Are you? [*Peter sets to thinking, but Jerry goes on.*] At any rate, and you've missed the eight-thousand-dollar question, Peter; at any rate, the dog recovered his health and the landlady recovered her thirst, in no way altered by the bow-wow's deliverance. When I came home from a movie that was playing on Forty-second Street, a movie I'd seen, or one that was very much like one or several I'd seen, after the landlady told me puppykins was better, I was so hoping for the dog to be waiting for me. I was . . . well, how would you put it . . . enticed? . . . fascinated? . . . no, I don't think so . . . heart-shatteringly anxious, that's it; I was heart-shatteringly anxious to confront my friend again. [*Peter reacts scoffingly.*] Yes, Peter; friend. That's the only word for it. I was heart-shatteringly et cetera to confront my doggy friend again. I came in the door and advanced, unafraid, to the centre of the entrance hall. The beast was there . . . looking at me. And, you know, he looked better for his scrape with the nevermind. I stopped; I looked at him; he looked at me. I think . . . I think we stayed a long time that way . . . still, stone-statue . . . just looking at one another. I looked more into his face than he looked into mine. I mean, I can concentrate longer at looking into a dog's face than a dog can concentrate at looking into mine, or into anybody else's face, for that matter. But during that twenty seconds or two hours that we looked into each other's face, we made contact. Now, here is what I had wanted to happen: I loved the dog now, and I wanted him to love me. I had tried to love, and I had tried to kill, and both had been unsuccessful by themselves. I hoped . . . and I don't really know why I expected the dog to understand anything, much less my motivations . . . I hoped that the dog would understand. [*Peter seems to be hypnotized.*] It's just . . . it's just that . . . [*Jerry is abnormally tense, now.*] . . . it's just that if you can't deal with people, you have to make a start somewhere. WITH ANIMALS! [*much faster now, and like a conspirator*] Don't you see? A person has to have some way of dealing with SOMETHING. If not with people . . . if not with people . . . SOMETHING. With a bed, with a cockroach, with a mirror . . . no, that's too hard, that's one of the last steps. With a cockroach, with a . . . with a . . . with a carpet, a roll of toilet paper . . . no, not that, either . . . that's a mirror, too; always check bleeding. You see how hard it is to find things? With a street corner, and too many lights, all colours reflecting on the oily-wet streets . . . with a wisp of smoke, a wisp . . . of smoke . . . with . . . with pornographic playing cards, with a strongbox . . . WITH-OUT A LOCK . . . with love, with vomiting, with crying, with fury because the pretty little ladies aren't pretty little ladies, with making money with your body which is an act of love and I could prove it, with howling because you're alive; with God. How about that? WITH GOD WHO IS A COLOURED QUEEN WHO WEARS A KIMONO AND PLUCKS HIS EYEBROWS, WHO IS A WOMAN WHO CRIES WITH DETERMINATION BEHIND HER CLOSED DOOR . . . with God who, I'm told, turned his back on the whole thing some time ago . . . with . . . some day, with people. [*Jerry sighs the next word heavily.*] People. With an idea; a concept. And where better, where ever better in this humiliating excuse for a jail, where better to communicate one single, simple-minded idea than in an entrance hall? Where? It would be A START! Where better to make a beginning . . . to understand and just possibly be understood . . . a beginning of an understanding, than with . . . [*Here Jerry seems to fall into almost grotesque fatigue.*] . . . than with A DOG. Just that; a dog. [*Here there is a silence that might be prolonged for a moment or so; then Jerry wearily finishes his story.*] A dog. It seemed like a perfectly sensible idea. Man is a dog's best friend, remember. So: the dog and I looked at each other. I longer than the dog. And what I was then has been the same ever since. Whenever the dog and I see each other we both stop where we are. We regard each other with a mixture of sadness and suspicion, and then we feign indifference. We walk past each other safely; we have an understanding. It's very sad, but you'll have to admit that it is an understanding. We had made many attempts at contact, and we had failed. The dog has returned to garbage, and I to solitary but free passage. I have not returned. I mean to say, I have *gained* solitary free passage, if that much further loss can be said to be gain. I have learned that neither kindness nor cruelty by themselves, independent of each other, creates any effect beyond themselves; and I have learned that the two combined, together, at the same time, are the teaching emotion. And what is gained is loss. And what has been the result: the dog and I have attained a compromise; more of a bargain, really. We neither love nor hurt because we do not try to reach each other. And, *was* trying to feed the dog an act of love? And, perhaps, was the dog's attempt to bite me *not* an act of love? If we can so misunderstand, well then, why have we invented the word love in the first place? [*There is silence. Jerry moves to Peter's bench and sits down beside him. This is the first time Jerry has sat down during the play.*] The Story of Jerry and the Dog: the end. [*Peter is silent.*] Well, Peter? [*Jerry is suddenly cheerful.*] Well, Peter? Do you think I could sell that story to the *Reader's Digest* and make a couple of hundred bucks for *The Most Unforgettable Character I've Ever Met*? Huh? [*Jerry is animated, but Peter is disturbed.*] Oh, come on now, Peter; tell me what you think.

PETER [*numb*]: I . . . I don't understand what . . . I don't think I . . . [*now, almost tear-fully*] Why did you tell me all of this?

JERRY: Why not?

PETER: I DON'T UNDERSTAND!

JERRY [*furious, but whispering*]: That's a lie.

PETER: No. No, it's not.

JERRY [*quietly*]: I tried to explain it to you as I went along. I went slowly; it all has to do with . . .

PETER: I DON'T WANT TO HEAR ANYMORE. I don't understand you, or your landlady, or her dog. . . .

JERRY: *Her* dog! I thought it was my . . . No. No, you're right. It *is* her dog. [*Looks at Peter intently, shaking his head.*] I don't know what I was thinking about; of course you don't understand. [*in a monotone, wearily*] I don't live in your block; I'm not married to two parakeets, or whatever your setup is. I am a *permanent transient*, and my home is the sickening rooming-houses on the West Side of New York City, which is the greatest city in the world. Amen.

PETER: I'm . . . I'm sorry; I didn't meant to . . .

JERRY: Forget it. I suppose you don't quite know what to make of me, eh?

PETER [*a joke*]: We get all kinds in publishing. [*Chuckles.*]

JERRY: You're a funny man. [*He forces a laugh.*] You know that? You're a very . . . a richly comic person.

PETER [*modestly, but amused*]: Oh, now, not really [*still chuckling*].

JERRY: Peter, do I annoy you, or confuse you?

PETER [*lightly*]: Well, I must confess that this wasn't the kind of afternoon I'd anticipated.

JERRY: You mean, I'm not the gentleman you were expecting.

PETER: I wasn't expecting anybody.

JERRY: No, I don't imagine you were. But I'm here, and I'm not leaving.

PETER [*consulting his watch*]: Well, you may not be, but I must be getting home soon.

JERRY: Oh, come on; stay a while longer.

PETER: I really should get home; you see . . .

JERRY [*Tickles Peter's ribs with his fingers.*]: Oh, come on.

PETER [*He is very ticklish; as Jerry continues to tickle him his voice becomes falsetto.*]: No. I . . . OHHHHH! Don't do that. Stop, Stop. Ohhh, no, no.

JERRY: Oh, come on.

PETER [*as Jerry tickles*]: Oh, hee, hee, hee. I must go. I . . . hee, hee, hee. After all, stop, stop, hee, hee, hee, after all, the parakeets will be getting dinner ready soon. Hee, hee. And the cats are setting the table. Stop, stop, and, and . . . [*Peter is beside himself now.*] . . . and we're having . . . hee, hee . . . uh . . . ho, ho, ho. [*Jerry stops tickling Peter, but the combination of the tickling and his own mad whimsy has Peter laughing almost hysterically. As his laughter continues, then subsides, Jerry watches him, with a curious fixed smile.*]

JERRY: Peter?

PETER: Oh, ha, ha, ha, ha, ha. What? What?

JERRY: Listen, now.

PETER: Oh, ho, ho. What . . . what is it, Jerry? Oh, my.

JERRY [*mysteriously*]: Peter, do you want to know what happened at the zoo?

PETER: Ah, ha, ha. The what? Oh, yes; the zoo. Oh, ho, ho. Well, I had my own zoo there for a moment with . . . hee, hee, the parakeets getting dinner ready, and the . . . ha, ha, whatever it was, the . . .

JERRY [*calmly*]: Yes, that was very funny, Peter. I wouldn't have expected it. But do you want to hear about what happened at the zoo, or not?

PETER: Yes. Yes, by all means; tell me what happened at the zoo. Oh, my. I don't know what happened to me.

JERRY: Now I'll let you in on what happened at the zoo; but first, I should tell you why I went to the zoo. I went to the zoo to find out more about the way people exist with animals, and the way animals exist with each other, and with people too. It probably wasn't a fair test, what with everyone separated by bars from everyone else, the animals for the most part from each other, and always the people from the animals. But, if it's a zoo, that's the way it is. [*He pokes at Peter on the arm.*] Move over.

PETER [*friendly*]: I'm sorry, haven't you enough room? [*He shifts a little.*]

JERRY [*smiling slightly*]: Well, all the animals are there, and all the people are there, and it's Sunday and all the children are there. [*He pokes Peter again.*] Move over!

PETER [*patiently, still friendly*]: All right. [*He moves some more, and Jerry has all the room he might need.*]

JERRY: And it's a hot day, so all the stench is there, too, and all the balloon sellers, and all the ice cream sellers, and all the seals are barking, and all the birds are screaming. [*Pokes Peter harder.*] Move over!

PETER [*beginning to be annoyed*]: Look here, you have more than enough room! [*But he moves more, and is now fairly cramped at one end of the bench.*]

JERRY: And I am there, and it's feeding time at the lions' house, and the lion keeper comes into the lion cage, one of the lion cages, to feed one of the lions. [*Punches Peter on the arm, hard.*] MOVE OVER!

PETER [*very annoyed*]: I can't move over any more, and stop hitting me. What's the matter with you?

JERRY: Do you want to hear the story? [*Punches Peter's arm again.*]

PETER [*flabbergasted*]: I'm not so sure! I certainly don't want to be punched in the arm.

JERRY [*Punches Peter's arm again.*]: Like that?

PETER: Stop it! What's the matter with you?

JERRY: I'm crazy, you bastard.

PETER: That isn't funny.

JERRY: Listen to me, Peter. I want this bench. You go sit on the bench over there, and if you're good I'll tell you the rest of the story.

PETER [*flustered*]: But . . . whatever for? What is the matter with you? Besides, I see no reason why I should give up this bench. I sit on this bench almost every Sunday afternoon, in good weather. It's secluded here; there's never anyone sitting here, so I have it all to myself.

JERRY [*softly*]: Get off this bench, Peter; I want it.

PETER [*almost whining*]: No.

JERRY: I said I want this bench, and I'm going to have it. Now get over there.

PETER: People can't have everything they want. You should know that; it's a rule; people can have some of the things they want, but they can't have everything.

JERRY [*laughs*]: Imbecile! You're slow-witted!

PETER: Stop that!

JERRY: You're a vegetable! Go lie down on the ground.

PETER [*intense*]: Now you listen to me. I've put up with you all afternoon.

JERRY: Not really.

PETER: LONG ENOUGH. I've put up with you long enough. I've listened to you because you seemed . . . well, because I thought you wanted to talk to somebody.

JERRY: You put things well; economically, and, yet . . . oh, what is the word I want to put justice to your . . . JESUS, you make me sick . . . get off here and give me my bench.

PETER: MY BENCH!

JERRY [*pushes Peter almost, but not quite, off the bench*]: Get out of my sight.

PETER [*regaining his position*]: God da . . . mn you. That's enough! I've had enough of you. I will not give up this bench; you can't have it, and that's that. Now, go away. [*Jerry snorts but does not move.*] Go away, I said. [*Jerry does not move.*] Get away from here. If you don't move on . . . you're a bum . . . that's what you are. . . . If you don't move on, I'll get a policeman here and make you go. [*Jerry laughs, stays.*] I warn you, I'll call a policeman.

JERRY [*softly*]: You won't find a policeman around here; they're all over on the west side of the park chasing fairies down from trees or out of the bushes. That's all they do. That's their function. So scream your head off; it won't do you any good.

PETER: POLICE! I warn you, I'll have you arrested.

JERRY: You look ridiculous: a grown man screaming for the police on a bright Sunday afternoon in the park with nobody harming you. If a policeman *did* fill his quota and come sludging over this way he'd probably take you in as a nut.

PETER [*with disgust and impotence*]: Great God, I just came here to read, and now you want me to give up the bench. You're mad.

JERRY: Hey, I got news for you, as they say. I'm on your precious bench, and you're never going to have it for yourself again.

PETER [*furious*]: Look, you; get off my bench. I don't care if it makes any sense or not. I want this bench to myself; I want you OFF IT!

JERRY [*mocking*]: Aw . . . look who's mad.

PETER: GET OUT!

JERRY: No.

PETER: I WARN YOU!

JERRY: Do you know how ridiculous you look now?

PETER [*His fury and self-consciousness have possessed him.*]: It doesn't matter. [*He is almost crying.*] GET AWAY FROM MY BENCH!

JERRY: Why? You have everything in the world you want; you've told me about your home, and your family, and *your* own little zoo. You have everything, and now you want this bench. Are these the things men fight for? Tell me, Peter, is this bench, this iron and this wood, is this your honour? Is this the thing in the world you'd fight for? Can you think of anything more absurd?

PETER: Absurd? Look, I'm not going to talk to you about honour, or even try to explain it to you. Besides, it isn't a question of honour; but even if it were, you wouldn't understand.

JERRY [*contemptuously*]: You don't even know what you're saying, do you? This is probably the first time in your life you've had anything more trying to face than changing your cats' toilet box. Stupid! Don't you have any idea, not even the slightest, what other people *need*?

PETER: Oh, boy, listen to you; well, you don't need this bench. That's for sure.

JERRY: Yes; yes, I do.

PETER [*quivering*]: I've come here for years; I have hours of great pleasure, great satisfaction, right here. And that's important to a man. I'm a responsible person, and I'm a GROWNUP. This is my bench, and you have no right to take it away from me.

JERRY: Fight for it, then. Defend yourself; defend your bench.

PETER: You've *pushed* me to it. Get up and fight.

JERRY: Like a man?

PETER [*still angry*]: Yes, like a man, if you insist on mocking me even further.

JERRY: I'll have to give you credit for one thing: you *are* a vegetable, and a slightly nearsighted one, I think . . .

PETER: THAT'S ENOUGH . . .

JERRY: . . . but, you know, as they say on TV all the time—you know—and I mean this, Peter, you have a certain dignity; it surprises me . . .

PETER: STOP!

JERRY [*rises lazily*]: Very well, Peter, we'll battle for the bench, but we're not evenly matched. [*He takes out and clicks open an ugly looking knife.*]

PETER [*suddenly awakening to the reality of the situation*]: You are mad! You're stark raving mad! YOU'RE GOING TO KILL ME! [*But before Peter has time to think what to do, Jerry tosses the knife at Peter's feet.*]

JERRY: There you go. Pick it up. You have the knife and we'll be more evenly matched.

PETER [*horrified*]: No!

JERRY [*Rushes over to Peter, grabs him by the collar; Peter rises; their faces almost touch.*]: Now you pick up that knife and you fight with me. You fight for your self-respect; you fight for that goddamned bench.

PETER [*struggling*]: No! Let . . . let go of me! He . . . Help!

JERRY [*Slaps Peter on each 'fight'.*]: You fight, you miserable bastard; fight for that bench; fight for your parakeets; fight for your cats, fight for your two daughters; fight for your wife; fight for your manhood, you pathetic little vegetable. [*Spits in Peter's face.*] You couldn't even get your wife with a male child.

PETER [*Breaks away, enraged.*]: It's a matter of genetics, not manhood, you . . . you monster. [*He starts down, picks up the knife and backs off a little; he is breathing heavily.*] I'll give you one last chance; get out of here and leave me alone! [*He holds the knife with a firm arm, but far in front of him, not to attack, but to defend.*]

JERRY [*sighs heavily*]: So be it! [*With a rush he charges Peter and impales himself on the knife. Tableau: For just a moment, complete silence, Jerry impaled on the knife at the end of Peter's still firm arm. Then Peter screams, pulls away, leaving the knife in Jerry. Jerry is motionless, on point. Then he, too, screams, and it must be the sound of an infuriated and fatally wounded animal. With the knife in him, he stumbles back to the bench that Peter had vacated. He crumbles there, sitting, facing Peter, his eyes wide in agony, his mouth open.*]

PETER [*whispering*]: Oh my God, oh my God, oh my God . . . [*He repeats these words many times, very rapidly.*]

JERRY [*Jerry is dying; but now his expression seems to change. His features relax, and while his voice varies, sometimes wrenched with pain, for the most part he seems removed from his dying. He smiles.*]: Thank you, Peter. I mean that, now; thank you very much. [*Peter's mouth drops open. He cannot move; he is transfixed.*] Oh, Peter, I was so afraid I'd drive you away. [*He laughs as best he can.*] You don't know how afraid I was you'd go away and leave me. And now I'll tell you what happened at the zoo. I think . . . I think this is what happened at the zoo . . . I think. I think that while I was at the zoo I decided that I would walk north . . . northerly, rather . . . until I found you . . . or somebody . . . and I decided that I would talk to you . . . I would tell you things . . . and things that I would tell you would . . . Well, here we are. You see? Here we are. But . . . I don't know . . . could I have planned all this? No . . . no, I couldn't have. But I think I did. And now I've told you what you wanted to know, haven't I? And now you know all about what happened at the zoo. And now you will know what you'll see in your TV, and the face I told you about . . . you remember . . . the face I told you about . . . my face, the face you see right now. Peter . . . Peter? . . . Peter . . . thank you. I came unto you [*He laughs, so faintly.*] and you have comforted me. Dear Peter.

PETER [*almost fainting*]: Oh my God!

JERRY: You'd better go now. Somebody might come by, and you don't want to be here when anybody comes. ②

PETER [*does not move, but begins to weep*]: Oh my God, oh my God.

JERRY [*most faintly, now; he is very near death*]: You won't be coming back here any more, Peter; you've been dispossessed. You've lost your bench, but you've defended your honour. And Peter, I'll tell you something now; you're not really a vegetable; it's all right, you're an animal. You're an animal, too. But you'd better hurry now, Peter. Hurry, you'd better go . . . see? [*Jerry takes a handkerchief and with great effort and pain wipes the knife handle clean of fingerprints.*] Hurry away, Peter. [*Peter begins to stagger away.*] Wait . . . wait, Peter. Take your book . . . book. Right here . . . beside me . . . on your bench . . . my bench, rather. Come . . . take your book. [*Peter starts for the book, but retreats.*] Hurry . . . Peter. [*Peter rushes to the bench, grabs his book. Retreats.*] Very good, Peter . . . very good. Now . . . hurry away. [*Peter hesitates for a moment, then flees, stage-left.*] Hurry away . . . [*His eyes are closed now.*] Hurry away, your parakeets are making the dinner . . . the cats . . . are setting the table . . .

PETER [*off stage, a pitiful howl*]: OH MY GOD!

JERRY [*His eyes still closed, he shakes his head and speaks; a combination of scornful mimicry and supplication.*]: Oh . . . my . . . God. [*He is dead.*]

Curtain

Sharon Pollock
b. 1936

Playwright, actress, and director Sharon Pollock was born in Fredericton, New Brunswick. The daughter of a physician, she spent her early years in Quebec's Eastern Townships before returning to Fredericton to attend the University of New Brunswick for two years. She began her acting career in amateur theatre in New Brunswick, later moving to Calgary to join the touring company Prairie Players. Her first play, *A Compulsory Option*, won the 1971 Alberta Playwriting Competition. She has written plays for children, several radio and television scripts, and many plays for the theatre. Her early plays focus mostly on social issues; for example, *The Komagatu Maru Incident*, about a ship of Sikh immigrants that is denied permission to land in Vancouver, explores racism in the early twentieth century. Her more recent plays, such as *Doc*, focus on familial and personal conflicts. She has taught playwriting at the University of Alberta, headed the Playwrights' Colony at the Banff Centre, been playwright-in-residence at Calgary's Alberta Theatre Projects, and served as artistic director of Theatre Calgary. Based loosely on her own family background, *Doc* had its premiere at Theatre Calgary in April 1984.

Doc

THE CHARACTERS

EV, an elderly man in his seventies

CATHERINE, his daughter, in her mid-thirties

KATIE, Catherine, as a young girl

BOB, Ev's wife, Catherine's mother

OSCAR, Ev's best friend

PLAYWRIGHT NOTES

Much of the play consists of the sometimes shared, sometimes singular memories of the past, as relived by Ev and Catherine, interacting with figures from the past. Structurally, shifts in time do not occur in a linear, chronological fashion, but in an unconscious and intuitive patterning of the past by Ev and Catherine. A stage direction [*Shift*] marks these pattern changes which are often, but not always, time shifts as well. In production, music has been used to underscore the pattern shifts, however the characters' shifts from one pattern to another must be immediate. They do not 'hold' for the music. The physical blocking must accommodate this immediacy and the stage setting facilitate it.

The 'now' of the play takes place in the house in which Catherine grew up and in which Ev now lives alone. The play is most effective when the set design is not a literal one, and when props and furniture are kept to a minimum. I think of the setting as one which has the potential to explode time and space while simultaneously serving certain naturalistic demands of the play.

A kaleidoscope of memory constitutes the dialogue and action of the opening sequence. It is followed by a scene set more firmly in the 'now'. Ev is 'old' during these two segments, as he is at the opening and closing of Act II. Although Ev relives the past as a younger man, we never see Catherine any age but in her mid-thirties. She is able to speak across time to her father, to her mother, and to her younger self. Catherine and Katie blend, sharing a sense of one entity, particularly in the scenes with her father's best friend, Oscar. This should not be interpreted to mean that Catherine and Katie share one mind or are always in accord. They are often in conflict.

Oscar is first seen in the opening sequence wearing a Twenties-era hockey uniform. He is a young man about to enter medical school. Oscar's scenes with Katie cover a four-year period prior to and ending with Bob's death. In the scenes he shares with Bob and Ev there is a longer, more chronological unfolding of time. For the most part, we see him as a man in his mid-thirties.

We see Bob in her mid-twenties to mid-thirties. She wears a dressing gown which has a belt or tie at the waist, and under this she wears a slip. The material of the gown is satin or satin-like; the gown itself has the look of a tailored long dinner gown when appropriately belted. On other occasions, undone and flapping, it has the appearance of a sloppy kimono. Is it necessary to say that her descent into alcoholism, despair, and self-disgust must be carefully charted?

Ev as an old man wears glasses and a worn cardigan sweater.

There are liquor bottles on stage in Act I; they have been removed from the set in Act II. A trunk is useful on stage; it holds photos and memorabilia; as well, it provides a storage place in Act I for Oscar's hockey uniform, and the clothing into which he and Ev will change.

In some productions all characters are always on stage with the exception of Ev, who is free to exit and enter during the play, and Katie, Bob, and Oscar who exit near the end of the play. In other productions there has been a greater freedom of movement re characters' exists and entrances. The script indicates where a character 'may enter' or 'may exit'. If this is not indicated, the character must remain on stage.

ACT I

In the black there is a subtle murmuring of voices, with the odd phrase and word emerging quite clearly. They are repeats of bits and pieces of dialogue heard later in the play. The voices are those of Katie, Oscar, Bob, and the young Ev; they often speak on top of each other.

Light grows on Ev, who is seated by the open trunk. He holds an unopened letter. A match flares as Bob lights a cigarette in the background. Light grows on Bob, on Oscar who is smoothing tape on his hockey stick, and on Katie who concentrates on moving one foot back and forth slowly and rhythmically. Ev slowly closes the trunk, his focus still on the envelope he holds.

Catherine enters. She carries an overnight bag as well as her shoulder bag. She puts the overnight bag down. She sees Katie. She watches Katie for a moment, and then speaks to Katie's rhythmic movement.

CATHERINE: Up-on the carpet . . . you shall kneel . . . while the grass . . . grows in the field

Katie's motion turns into skipping as Katie turns an imaginary skipping rope and jumps to it.

Stand up straight
Upon your feet

KATIE [*speaks with Catherine. The murmuring of voices can still be heard but they are fading*]:

Choose the one you love so sweet
Now they're married wish them well
First a girl, gee that's swell

Katie's voice is growing louder, taking over from Catherine.

KATIE and CATHERINE: Seven years after, seven to come

KATIE [*alone*]:
>   Fire on the mountain kiss and run
>   [*jumps 'pepper' faster and faster*]
>   Tinker, tailor, soldier, sailor,
>   Rich man, poor man, beggar man thief

BOB: Doctor

KATIE: Doc-tor!!! [*stops skipping*]

CATHERINE [*removing her gloves*]: Daddy?

EV [*looks up from the envelope*]: Katie? [*stands up*] Is that you, Katie?

KATIE [*skipping towards Ev singing*]: La da da da daah.

Katie continues her 'la dahs' skipping away from Ev as Oscar speaks.

OSCAR: Hey, you and me, Ev.

Ev looks at the letter and sits back down.

Best friends. Ev and Oscar, Oscar and Ev—and if we weren't—I think I'd hate you.

KATIE [*stops skipping but continues*]: La dada da daaah

BOB: Why don't you open it?

OSCAR: You see, Ev—you're just too good at things.

BOB: Go on, open it.

The murmuring voices have faded out.

OSCAR: It makes people nervous.

Sound of an approaching train whistle.

It makes me nervous.

BOB: Listen.

The train whistle is growing in volume. Katie stops her 'la la la dahs'.

Your Gramma, Katie, his mother. She'd set her clock by that train. Set her clock by the junction train crossing the railway bridge into Devon. Must be what? Three-quarters of a mile of single track spanning the river? And midnight, every night, that train coming down from the junction—half-way across three-quarters of a mile of single track its whistle would split the night . . . and that night do you know what she did?

EV [*his focus on the letter*]: No.

BOB: She walked out to meet it.

EV: No.

BOB: You wanna know something, Katie?

KATIE: No.

BOB: Your father's mother, your grandmother, killed herself . . . . Katie!

KATIE: What!

BOB: She walked across the train bridge at midnight and the train hit her.

KATIE: That's an accident.

BOB: She left a letter, and the letter tells him why she did it.

KATIE: There isn't any letter.

BOB: What's that?

KATIE: Daddy?

BOB: And he won't open it cause he's afraid, he's afraid of what she wrote.

KATIE: Is that true, Daddy?

EV: No.

KATIE: Is that the letter?

EV: Your grandmother was walking across the Devon bridge—

KATIE: What for?

EV: Well—it was a kind of short cut.

BOB: Short cut?

EV: And she got caught in the middle of a span and she was hit and killed.

CATHERINE: I stayed with her once when I was little . . . I can hardly remember.

EV [*continuing to talk to Katie*]: It was after your mother had Robbie.

KATIE: Why didn't I stay with you and Robbie and Mummy?

EV: Your mother was sick so you stayed with your Gramma.

CATHERINE: Yes . . . and she made me soft-boiled runny eggs, and she'd feed me them and tell me stories about Moses in the bulrushes, and I . . . and I . . . would peel the wallpaper off behind the door, and she'd get angry.

EV: That's right.

CATHERINE: Why didn't she jump?

OSCAR: A hat trick! Ev! Everybody screaming—everybody on their feet—what's it feel like, Ev?

BOB: He doesn't care. He doesn't care about anything except his 'prac-tice' and his 'off-fice' and his 'off-fice nurse' and all those stupid, stupid people who think he's God.

EV [*to Katie*]: Don't listen to her.

BOB: You're not God.

EV: Your mother's sick.

KATIE: No she isn't.

OSCAR: God, you're good. You fly, Ev.

KATIE: Why do you keep saying she's sick?

OSCAR: You don't skate, you fly.

KATIE: She's not sick.

EV: Your mother's—

KATIE: Why do you keep saying that!

EV: Katie—

KATIE: No!

CATHERINE: For a long time I prayed to God. I asked him to make her stop. I prayed and prayed. I thought, I'm just a little girl. Why would God want to do this to a little girl? I thought it was a mistake. I thought maybe he didn't know. I don't know what I thought. I prayed and prayed. . . . Now, I don't believe in God.

KATIE: And if there is a God, then I don't like him.

EV: She isn't well.

> *Bob slowly opens a drawer, feels inside it, and runs her hand along a chair cushion. She continues to quietly, unobtrusively look for something as Katie and Ev speak.*

KATIE: Tell Robbie that. He wants to believe that. I want the truth.

EV: I'm telling you the truth.

KATIE: No! Do you know what I did yesterday? She kept going to the bathroom and going to the bathroom and I went in and looked all over and I found it. In the clothes hamper with all the dirty clothes and things. And I took it and I poured it down the sink and I went downstairs and I threw the empty bottle in the garbage so don't tell me she's sick!

BOB: It's gone.

> *Bob looks at Katie. In the following sequence, although Catherine is the speaker, Bob will act out the scene with Katie.*

CATHERINE: No. No, don't.

BOB: It's gone.

CATHERINE: No.

BOB: You.

CATHERINE: No.

BOB: You took it and I want it back.

> *Bob grabs Katie.*

I want it back.

CATHERINE: It's gone now and you can't have it.

BOB: Where? You tell me where?

CATHERINE: I poured it out.

BOB: No.

CATHERINE: Down the sink.

BOB: No.

CATHERINE: It's gone, forget it.

BOB: It's mine, I want it back!

CATHERINE: Gone.

BOB: No fair!

> *Bob struggles with Katie.*

CATHERINE: Let me go!

BOB: No right!

CATHERINE: Let me go!

BOB: You had no right!

> *Katie strikes Bob, knocking her down.*

CATHERINE: Daddy!

EV: Katie?

> *Ev gets up from his chair and moves to look for Catherine. Oscar may follow him. Ev does not see Catherine, nor she him.*

OSCAR: You know my father wishes I were you. He does. He wishes I were you. 'Oscar,' he says, 'Oscar, look at Ev—why can't you be like Ev.'

BOB: Look at what your father did.

KATIE: You lie.

OSCAR: I say nothing. There's nothing to be said. 'You got to have that killer instinct on the ice,' he says. I play goalie—what the hell's a killer instinct in a goalie? Then he says, 'Oscar,' he says, 'Oscar, you are goin' into medicine.'

EV: Katie?

OSCAR: My Dad's a doctor so I gotta be a doctor.

BOB: Your father hit me and I fell.

KATIE: You're always lying.

BOB: See?

KATIE: He didn't hit you.

BOB: See?

KATIE: I hit you!—Get away from me!

OSCAR: What's so funny is you're the one so bloody keen on medicine—you'd kill for medicine. [*laughs*] Hey Ev, kills for medicine, eh. [*laughs*]

BOB: You father's mother, your Gramma, killed herself and he's afraid to open it.

KATIE [*covers her ears*]:
> Now they're married
> wish them joy
> First a girl for a toy
> Seven year after, seven to come
> Fire on the mountain, kiss and run

> *Ev returns from his search for Catherine. Oscar follows him. Katie sees Catherine, and moves towards her, speaking the verse to her.*

> On the mountain berries sweet
> Pick as much as you can eat
> By the berries bitter bark
> Fire on the mountain break your heart.

KATIE and CATHERINE: Years to come—kiss and run—bitter bark—

> *Catherine sees Ev, who sees Catherine. Catherine speaks softly, almost to herself.*

CATHERINE: Break your heart . . .
> It's me, Daddy.

EV: Katie?

KATIE: When I was little, Daddy.

CATHERINE: It's Catherine now, call me Catherine . . . well . . . aren't you going to say anything?

EV: You're home.

CATHERINE: Ah-huh . . . a hug, a big hug, Daddy, come on.

    Catherine and Ev embrace.

  Ooh.

EV: What.

CATHERINE: How long has it been?

EV: Be ah . . .

CATHERINE: Four years, right? Medical convention in where? Vancouver, right?

EV: That's right. Vancouver.

CATHERINE: Montreal, Toronto, Calgary, Van, where haven't we met, eh?

EV: Here.

CATHERINE: Yup. Not . . . not met here.

    Catherine notices the envelope in Ev's hand.

  What're you doing with that?

EV: Oh—just goin' through things. Clearin' things out.

    Catherine, getting out a cigarette, turns away from Ev.

BOB: Katie's afraid of what she wrote.

KATIE [*to Catherine*]: Is that true?

EV: Are you here for this hoopla tomorrow?

CATHERINE: Not really.

EV: There's gonna be speeches and more speeches. I lay the cornerstone, and dinner I think.

CATHERINE: Ah-huh.

EV: I got it all written down with the times.

CATHERINE: Ah-huh.

EV: I got it downstairs. . . . You wanna take a look? . . . Not here for that, eh?

CATHERINE: No. I came home to see you.

EV: Pretty sad state of affairs when your own daughter's in town and can't attend a sod-turnin' in honour of her father.

CATHERINE: So I'll go, I'll be there.

EV: Coulda sent a telegram. Saved the air fare.

CATHERINE: Christ Daddy, don't be so stupid.

EV: Sound like your mother.

CATHERINE: I learned the four-letter words from you.

EV: Bullshit.

CATHERINE: I said I'd go, I said I'd be there. So. [*pause*] I'm proud of you, Daddy.

EV: Did you know it was a write-in campaign?

CATHERINE: Oh?

EV: The niggers from Barker's Point, the mill workers from Marysville, they're the ones got this hospital named after me. Left to the politicians God knows what they'd have called it.

CATHERINE: Well, I'm proud.

EV: Some goddamn French name I suppose—what?

CATHERINE: Proud, you must be proud having the hospital named after you.

EV: The day I first started practice, that day I was proud. Was the day after you were born. . . . There was a scarlet fever epidemic that year, you remember?

CATHERINE: No Daddy.

EV: Somebody . . . some couple came in, they were carryin' their daughter, what was she? Two, maybe three? I took her in my arms . . . could see they'd left it too late. I remember that child. I passed her back to her mother. Hold her tight, I said. Hold her tight till she goes. . . . Do you remember that woman holdin' that child in the hallway?

CATHERINE: No Daddy.

EV: No. That was you mother . . . that was your mother.

BOB: Blueberries, Katie.

EV: You were just little then.

BOB: Blueberries along the railway tracks, and every year we'd pick them and sell them. I was the youngest, and Mama was always afraid I'd get lost, but I never got lost.

Catherine looks at Bob.

Not once.

Pause.

EV: What are you thinkin'?

CATHERINE [*looks away from Bob*]: Nothing. . . . You've lost weight.

EV: Of course I lost. I damn near died. You didn't know that, did you.

CATHERINE: No. No, nobody told me.

EV: Well it was that goddamn heart man. It was him gave me a heart attack.

CATHERINE: Really?

EV: What the hell's his name?

CATHERINE: Whose?

EV: The heart man's!

CATHERINE: I wouldn't know, Daddy.

EV: Demii—no, Demsky. I go to him, I tell him I been gettin' this pain in my ticker, and he has me walkin' up and down this little set a stairs, and runnin' on treadmills. Jesus Christ, I said to him, I'm not tryin' out for a sports team, I'm here because I keep gettin' this pain in my ticker! For Christ's sake, I said, put a stethoscope to my chest before you kill me with these goddamn stairs!

CATHERINE: So how are you now?

EV: It would've served the bastard right if I'd died right there in his office—do you remember how good Valma was with your mother?

CATHERINE: I remember.

EV: Every statutory holiday your mother's killin' herself or seein' things crawlin' on the walls or some goddamn thing or other, and Valma is like a rock, isn't that right?

CATHERINE: I guess so.

EV: So I come home from Demsky's, and I get the pain in my ticker and I wait all night for it to go away, and long about four or four-thirty, I phone Valma. Valma, I say, I'm havin' a heart attack, Valma—and she drops the phone nearly breakin' my ear drum and I can't phone out and I'm damned if I'm gonna get in that car and die all alone on Charlotte Street like that foolish Hazel Arbeton—If you were livin' in town, I'd have phoned you.

CATHERINE: You couldn't if Valma dropped the phone, Daddy.

EV: I'd have phoned you first.

CATHERINE: Would you?

EV: Well if I'd known she was gonna drop that goddamn phone I would have.

CATHERINE: What about Robbie?

EV: Who?

CATHERINE: Your son—Robbie.

EV: I'm not senile, I know who the hell Robbie is, what about him?

CATHERINE: You could have phoned him.

EV: I couldn't phone anyone! I was connected to Valma and I couldn't get disconnected!

CATHERINE: Would you have phoned him if you could?

EV: He wouldn't be home.

CATHERINE: How do you know?

EV: He's never home.

CATHERINE: Do you see him much?

EV: How the hell could I if he's never home?

CATHERINE: Do you *try* to see him!

EV: Of course I try! Have you seen him, phoned him, been over to visit?

CATHERINE: For Christ's sake Daddy, I just got in.

EV: Do you write?

CATHERINE: To Robbie?

EV: Yes to Robbie! You sure as hell don't write to me!

CATHERINE: I don't have the time.

EV: Some people make time.

CATHERINE: Why don't you?

EV: I'm busy.

CATHERINE: So am I.

EV: Mn. [*pause*] Does he ever write you?

CATHERINE: No.

EV: Do you wonder why?

CATHERINE: He's busy! Everyone's busy!

EV: Bullshit. It's that woman of his.

CATHERINE: It isn't.

EV: Paula.

CATHERINE: Who's Paula?

EV: She thinks we're all crazy.

CATHERINE: Well maybe we are, who in hell's Paula?

EV: His wife!

CATHERINE: You mean Corinne.

EV: What did I say?

CATHERINE: You said Paula.

EV: Well I meant Corinne! [*pause*] Paula. Who the hell's Paula? [*pause*]

BOB: Pauline.

EV: Pauline now, that was a friend of your mother's. Died a cancer, died in your room, and where did you sleep?

CATHERINE: In this room

EV: because

CATHERINE: the maid had left

EV: and your mother nursed Pauline right through to the end. Didn't touch a drop for three months.

> *As Catherine turns away, she sees Bob.*

BOB: Not a drop for three months, Katie.

> *Pause.*

EV: Best . . . best office nurse . . . I—ever had.

CATHERINE: Who, Mummy?

EV: Not Mummy, no. Valma. She ran that office like Hitler rollin' through Poland, and good with your mother—

CATHERINE [*turns back to Ev*]: I know, forty years like a rock.

EV: That's right, like a rock, but I call her with that heart attack and she goes hysterical. I never saw that in her before. It was a surprise. It was a goddamn disappointment. She comes runnin' into the house and up the stairs and huffin' and puffin' and blue in the face and—I'm on the bathroom floor by this time. She sees that, and gets more hysterical. She's got to run next door—my phone not workin' bein' connected to her phone which she dropped breakin' my ear drum—and she phones the hospital. And then we sit—I lie, she sits—and we wait for the goddamn ambulance, her holdin' my hand and bawlin'.

CATHERINE: Poor Valma.

EV: Poor Valma be damned! If I'd had the strength I'd have killed her. I kept tellin' her two things, I said it over and over—one, you keep that Demsky away from me—and you know what she does?

CATHERINE: She is sixty-seven.

EV: I'm seventy-three, you don't see me goin' hysterical! And I'm the one havin' the heart attack!

CATHERINE: Alright.

EV: You know the first thing I lay eyes on when I wake up in that hospital bed? Well, do you!

CATHERINE: No, I don't know, no.

EV: First thing I see is that goddamn Demsky hangin' over me like a vulture. Demsky who gave me the heart attack! . . . Next death bed wish I make I sure as hell won't make it to Valma.

CATHERINE: Well . . . it wasn't a real death bed wish, Daddy. You're still here.

EV: No thanks to her!

Pause.

CATHERINE: So?

EV: So what?

CATHERINE: Jesus Daddy, so how are you now?

EV: I don't read minds, I'm not a mind reader!

CATHERINE: How are you!

EV: I'm fine.

CATHERINE: Good.

EV: What?

CATHERINE: I said good. Great. I'm glad that you're fine.

EV: Got the nitro pills . . . pop a couple of them. Slow down they say. Don't get excited, don't talk too fast, don't walk too fast, don't, don't, don't, just pop a pill.

CATHERINE: Is it hard?

EV: Is what hard?

CATHERINE: Is it hard to slow down?

EV: . . . The nurses could always tell when I'd started my rounds. They could hear my heels hittin' the floor tiles, hear me a wing away.

Oscar starts to laugh quietly.

Did I ever tell you . . .

OSCAR: That's what you call a Cuban heel, Ev.

EV: . . . 'Bout those white woman's shoes I bought on St Lawrence?

CATHERINE: For the OR.

EV: That's right. They were on sale, real cheap, but they fit my foot cause my foot is so narrow.

OSCAR: Still, a woman's shoe, Ev?

EV: A good shoe for the OR was hard to find then!

CATHERINE: So you bought two pair.

EV: And I wore them.—How did you know?

CATHERINE: You told me.

EV: I told you.

CATHERINE: Don't you remember? You and Uncle Oscar would act that whole story out. . . . Do you see Uncle Oscar? [*pause*] Daddy? [*pause*] Well . . . anyway . . . so, what was the other thing?

EV: Mn?

CATHERINE: The other thing. You kept telling Valma two things, Demsky, and what was the other?

EV: Don't tell Katie. I musta said that a dozen times. I could hear myself. You're not to tell Katie. You're not to tell Katie.

CATHERINE: Why not?

EV: Because I didn't want you to know.

CATHERINE: Why not?

EV: Because I knew, even if you did know, you wouldn't come—and my heart would've burst from that pain.

> *Catherine and Ev look at each other. Catherine looks away.*

Look at me—look at me! . . .

> *Catherine looks at Ev.*

You knew. That goddamn Valma, she told you.

CATHERINE: No—

EV: You think I don't know a lie when I hear it, I see it, right in your goddamn eyes I can see it.

CATHERINE: Alright, alright, Valma did write——

EV: Ignores every goddamn thing I tell her.

CATHERINE: You could have died, Daddy.

EV: If you gave a damn you'd have been here!

CATHERINE: I don't want to fight.

EV: You afraid?

CATHERINE: No.

EV: I'm not afraid.

CATHERINE: God.

EV: Looked death in the face in that goddamn bathroom. It's not easy starin' death down with Valma bawlin' beside you. Every bit a your bein' directed, concentrated on winnin', not lettin' go. . . . [*gets out nitro pills; unscrews top while talking; takes pill by placing it under his tongue during speech*] Hated, hated losin'! Always. Hockey, politics, surgery, never mattered to me, just had to win. Could never let go. Do you know . . . do you know I saved Billy Barnes' life by hangin' onto his hand? I would not let him go till the sulpha took hold. I hung onto his hand, and I said Billy, goddamn it, you fight! And he did. They said it was the sulpha that saved him, miracle drug in those days, but you could never convince Billy of that. 'Goddamn it, Doc, it was you!' . . . I opened his belly two or three years ago. Opened his belly and closed his belly. Inoperable carcinoma. . . . 'Are you tellin' me this thing is gonna kill me, Doc?' I reached out my hand and he took it. . . . Hung . . . onto my hand. . . .

CATHERINE: I would have come, but you didn't want me to know.

EV: But you did know, didn't you. That goddamn Valma, she told you, and you didn't come.

CATHERINE: I'm here now.

EV: Bit of free time, drop in and see the old man, eh?

CATHERINE: No.

EV: But if this ticker gives out and catches you typin', too bad.

CATHERINE: Don't.

EV: So were you workin' or weren't you workin'?

CATHERINE: I'm always working.

EV: And that's more important than your own father.

CATHERINE: Don't start.

EV: A women your age should be raisin' a family.

CATHERINE: What family did you ever raise? You were never home from one day to the next so who are you to talk to me about family?

EV: Your father, that's who. The one damn near died with no one but an office nurse by his side.

CATHERINE: Valma loves you!

EV: That's not what we're talkin' about here. We're talkin' about you and your work and your father dyin', that's what we're talkin' about!

CATHERINE: Are we?

EV: That's what I'm talking about—I don't know what the hell you're on about—I don't know what the hell you're doin' here!

CATHERINE: I just came home to see you, I wanted to see you . . . have you got any idea how hard it was for me to come home, to walk in that door, to, to come home? . . . Have you? . . . and when I leave here . . . my plane . . . could fall out of the sky, you could get another pain in your ticker, we could never talk again . . . all of the things never said, do you ever think about that?

EV: You mean dyin'?

CATHERINE: No, more than that, I mean . . . I don't know what I mean.

Pause.

EV: Are you still with that . . . . whatshisname?

CATHERINE: Sort of.

EV: What's his name?

CATHERINE: What's it matter, you never remember.

EV: What's his name? Dugan? or Dougan?

CATHERINE: That was before, years before, Daddy.

EV: You should get one and hang onto one, Katie. Then I'd remember.

CATHERINE: I . . .

EV: What?

CATHERINE: I said it's difficult to keep a relationship goin' when you're busy, right?

EV: Why don't you marry this whosits?

CATHERINE: Yeah, well. . . . Whosits talks about that.

EV: I'm still waitin' for a grandson you know.

CATHERINE: I'm too old for that.

EV: You're soon gonna be—how old are you anyway?

CATHERINE: Besides I'd only have girls.

EV: Robbie's got girls . . . girls are alright. . . . You can have girls if you want.

CATHERINE: I said I don't know if I want.

EV: But get married first.

CATHERINE: Actually—I've been thinking . . . of . . . of maybe calling it quits with whosits.

EV: Quits?

CATHERINE: Ah-huh.

EV: You're callin' it quits.

CATHERINE: The work you know. Makes it hard.

EV: I thought this was the one. What the hell was his name, Sturgeon or Stefan or—

CATHERINE: His name doesn't matter.

EV: Stupid goddamn name—an actor, an actor for Christ's sake.

CATHERINE: We're not goin' to get into whosits and me and marriage and me and kids and me, all right?

EV: You go through men like boxes of Kleenex.

CATHERINE: I don't want to talk about it!

EV: Jesus Christ, I can't keep up.

CATHERINE: No you can't! You can't even remember his name!

EV: Burgess Buchanan, that was his name! And you sat in the lounge at the Bayside and you said, 'Oh Daddy, you just got to meet him, he's such a nice fella, he's so understanding, and he's so this and he's so that and he's. . . . So explain to me what went wrong this time.

CATHERINE: Why do we always end up yelling and screaming, why do we do that?

EV: I care 'bout you! . . . I want to see you settled, Katie. Happy. I want you to write, letters, not . . . I want you close.

CATHERINE: . . . I do write somebody you know. I write Uncle Oscar . . . every once in a while . . . when the spirit moves me.

EV: Not often.

CATHERINE: No. Not often. But I do. Write letters to someone. I do make the time. I know you and he don't keep in touch any more but I like to.

EV: Not lately.

CATHERINE: No, not lately. I . . . why do you say that?

EV: He was fly-fishin'. He slipped and fell in the Miramichi with his waders on.

CATHERINE [*pause*]: No . . . Did—did you see him?

EV: At the morgue when they brought him in.

CATHERINE: I mean before. Did you see him before? Were the two of you talking?

> *Ev shakes his head.*

Why not?

EV: Too late.

CATHERINE: Now it's too late.

EV: Too late even then. Even before. Too much had been said.

CATHERINE: I wish you'd have told me.

EV: Would you have come home for him?

CATHERINE: . . . Probably not.

EV: So what difference does it make?

CATHERINE: I like to know these things. Whether I can come or not. I can't help it if I'm in the middle of things.

EV: You make sure you're always in the middle of something. It's an excuse. How old are you now?

CATHERINE: Stop asking me that.

EV: You're gonna end up a silly old woman with nothin' but a cat for company.

CATHERINE: It'll be a live-in cat which is more than you've got with Valma.

EV: If I wanted Valma here, she'd be here.

CATHERINE: So you don't want her here, eh? You like it alone. Sitting up here all alone.

EV: I'm not alone!

CATHERINE: You and Robbie, the same city, you never see Robbie!

EV: Go on! Why doncha go on! You got so goddamn much to say, why don't you say it! I am alone and it's you left me alone! My own daughter walkin' out and leavin' her father alone!

CATHERINE: How many years before you noticed my bed wasn't slept in?

EV: Don't go pointin' your finger at me! Look at yourself! What the hell do you do? Work, work, work—at what, for Christ's sake?

CATHERINE: I write! I'm good at it!

EV: Writing, eh Katie?

CATHERINE: Don't call me Katie!

EV: I'll call you by the name we gave you and that name is Katie.

CATHERINE: It's Catherine now.

EV: Oh, it's Catherine now, and you write Literature, don't you? And that means you can ignore your brother and your father and dump this Buchanan jerk and forget kids and family, but your father who gave his life to medicine because he believed in what he was doin' is an asshole!

CATHERINE: I never said that!

EV: My whole family never had a pot to piss in, lived on porridge and molasses when I was a kid.

CATHERINE: Alright!

EV: And fought for every goddamn thing I got!

CATHERINE: And it all comes down to you sitting up here alone with Gramma's letter!

EV: I am goin' through things!

CATHERINE: Why won't you open it?

EV: I know what it says.

CATHERINE: Tell me.

EV: You want it, here, take it.

> *Catherine grabs letter from Ev. She almost rips it open, but stops and turns it in her hand. Pause.*

CATHERINE: Did Gramma really walk out to meet it?

EV: It was an accident.

CATHERINE: What was Mummy?

EV: You blame me for that.

CATHERINE: No.

EV: It was all my fault, go on, say it, I know what you think.

CATHERINE: It was my fault.

EV: Oh for Christ's sake.

Ev moves away from Catherine. He sits, takes off his glasses and rubs the bridge of his nose. He looks at Catherine, then back to the glasses which he holds in his hand.

. . . Your mother . . .

CATHERINE: Yes?

EV: Your mother and I—

CATHERINE: Tell me. Explain it to me.

BOB: There were eight of us, Katie, eight of us.

OSCAR [*softly*]: Go, go.

BOB: How did my mama manage?

Oscar stands up, holding two hockey sticks. He is looking at Ev, whose back is to him. Ev puts his glasses in his pocket.

OSCAR: Go.

BOB: All older than me, all born before he went to war.

OSCAR: Go.

BOB: Him, her husband, my father, your grandfather, Katie.

OSCAR: Go. Go!

BOB: And her with the eight of us and only the pension.

OSCAR: Go!! Go!!

BOB: How did my mama manage?

Bob may exit. Shift.

OSCAR: Go!!! Go!!!

Oscar throws a hockey stick at Ev who stands, turns, plucking it out of the air at the last minute. They are catapulted back in time, rough-housing after a game.

Go!!! The Devon Terror has got the puck, out of his end, across the blue line, they're mixing it up in the corner and he's out in front, he shoots! He scores! Rahhhh!

Oscar has ended up on the floor with his hockey sweater pulled over his head. Ev, who's scored, raises his arms in acknowledgement of the crowd's 'Rah!'. Ev helps Oscar up.

You know somethin' Ev? This is the truth. Honest to God. Are you listenin'?

EV: Yeah.

Ev takes off his 'old man' sweater and hangs it on the back of a chair. During the following dialogue, Oscar changes out of his hockey clothes, putting them in the trunk. He removes a jacket, pants, and shoes for Ev, and a suit of clothes plus shoes for himself.

OSCAR: When I think of medicine I get sick. Yeah. The thought of medicine makes me ill. Physically ill. Do you think that could be my mother in me?

Ev slips out of his slippers and removes his pants. Oscar will put the pants in the trunk.

EV: Maybe.

OSCAR: My father says its my mother in me. At least she had the good sense to get out. Leaving me with him. How could she do that?

EV: I dunno. [*puts on suit jacket*]

OSCAR: The old man calls her a bitch. And now nuthin' for it but I got to go into medicine.

EV: So tell him no.

OSCAR: I can't.

EV: Stand up to him.

OSCAR: I can't.

EV: Just tell him.

OSCAR: It'd break his heart.

EV: Shit Oscar, it's your life, you can't think about that.

OSCAR: Yeah.

EV: You just gotta tell him what you really want to do . . . how does that look?

OSCAR: Great.

EV: Which is?

OSCAR: Which is what?

Oscar throws Ev a tie.

EV: What you really want to do.

OSCAR: Oh.

EV: What do you really want to do?

OSCAR: I dunno.

EV: Come on.

OSCAR: Live someplace where it's hot.

EV: Come onnn . . .

OSCAR: New Orleans, I'd like to live in New Orleans.

EV: Oscar—

OSCAR: How hot is New Orleans anyway?

EV: And *do what*—in New Orleans, Oscar?

OSCAR: Do what. I dunno. Something. Anything. Not medicine.

Oscar reties Ev's tie for him.

EV: Look, if you're gonna tell your father you don't want to do what he wants you to do, you can't just say your life's ambition is to live someplace where it's hot.

OSCAR: What if it is?

EV: That is not gonna work, Oscar.

OSCAR: You're like my Dad, Ev. The two of you. You're always . . .

EV: What?

OSCAR: Forging *ahead*.

EV: What's wrong with that? [*puts on pants*]

OSCAR: Nothing. Forging is fine. I admire forging, I do, I admire it. It's just—not for me; do you think that could be my mother in me?

EV: Forget your mother. Concentrate on what you're gonna tell your father—and New Orleans is out.

OSCAR: It's honest, don't I get points for honest?

EV: Belt?

OSCAR: No points for honest.

EV: Or suspenders?

OSCAR: What's honest, honest is nothing, nobody wants honest.

EV: Honest is good, New Orleans is bad, belt or suspenders?

OSCAR: Belt.

 Oscar throws Ev a belt.

EV: Thanks.

OSCAR: It's not fair.

EV: I don't wanna hear about fair.

OSCAR: Right.

EV: Face it, you're a lazy son of a bitch.

OSCAR: I know.

EV: You've got no drive.

OSCAR: I know.

EV: You've got no push.

OSCAR: I know.

EV: I worked my ass off last summer in construction, what did you do?

OSCAR: I lay in the sun.

EV: That's right.

OSCAR: I'm a loser.

EV: And a whiner.

OSCAR: Right. [*pause*] Why are we friends?

EV: Eh?

OSCAR: I agree with everything you say, it's the truth, what can I say? So why are we friends?—I figure it's the car and the clothes.

 Ev puts on shoes. By the end of the scene he is dressed in a suit, tie, and shoes.

EV: That's a pretty shitty thing to imply.

OSCAR: I wasn't implying, I was just wondering.

EV: You've got other qualities.

OSCAR: Name one.

EV: We grew up together.

OSCAR: Go on.

EV: So we've known each other for a long time.

OSCAR: Yeah.

EV: Since Grade One.

> *Pause.*

OSCAR: Well I figure it's the car and the clothes and the fact the old man dotes on you.

EV: Jesus Oscar.

OSCAR: Everybody knows I'm just a—

EV: Don't whine!

OSCAR: I'm not whining. I'm analyzing!

EV: I'm tryin' to help, Oscar. Now you must have some ambition, some desire, something you're at least vaguely interested in, that you could propose to your father as a kinda alternative to medicine, eh?

OSCAR: You mean apart from New Orleans.

EV: That's what I mean.

OSCAR: My mother might have gone to New Orleans.

EV: Forget your mother! Alternative to medicine! Not New Orleans!

OSCAR: Algeria.

EV: Oscar!

OSCAR: I know.

EV: I try to look out for you and it's like pissing on a forest fire.

OSCAR: I'm telling you exactly how I feel. I don't have ambitions and desires and goals in life. I don't need 'em. My old man has my whole life mapped out for me and I know what I'm supposed to do. I'm supposed to read and follow the map. That's it.

> *Ev moves away from Oscar.*

EV: There is no wardrobe and no car and no amount of dotage from your old man that would compensate a person for putting up with you!

> *Shift.*

CATHERINE: Uncle Oscar?

> *Oscar looks at Katie as if it was she who had spoken. Katie holds her shoe out to him.*

Fix my shoe.

KATIE: It's got about a million knots—but keep talking.

CATHERINE: I want to know everything.

OSCAR: Construction work in the summer, hockey in the winter, and when we went to McGill, they'd bring him home on the overnight train to play the big games, the important games—and that's how he paid his way through medical school.

KATIE: Keep talking.

OSCAR: My father was their family doctor—I was there at his house the night his brother George died from the influenza—and that left him, and his sister Millie and his Mum and Dad.

CATHERINE: My Gramma.

KATIE: What was she like?

OSCAR: Proper. United Church. Poor and proper.

Oscar gives Katie back her shoe.

That's all I remember.

Katie hits Oscar with the shoe.

KATIE: Remember more!

OSCAR: I think your father got his drive from your Gramma and you get yours from him.

KATIE: Are you saying I'm like her?

OSCAR: In some ways perhaps.

KATIE: I would never walk across a train bridge at midnight!

OSCAR: You might.

KATIE: I would not!

OSCAR: Well it was an accident she—

KATIE: What do you mean I might!

OSCAR: It was a short cut.

KATIE: I'm not like her! I would never do that!

OSCAR: It wasn't anything she did.

KATIE: I'm too smart to do that!

OSCAR: It was just something that happened.

KATIE: You don't know! You don't know anything!

OSCAR: Katie—

KATIE: Get away from me!

CATHERINE: Stop.

Shift.

EV: If you want to know about this crazy bastard—if you want to know about him—When I needed a friend at my back, in a fight, in a brawl? This silly son of a bitch in sartorial splendour has saved my ass more than once—and me his—I'm gonna tell you a story. Now listen—we used to drink at this hole in the wall, this waterin' hole for whores and medical students, eh? An' we'd sit there and nurse a beer all night and chat it up with the whores who'd come driftin' in well after midnight, towards mornin' really, and this was in winter, freeze a Frenchman's balls off—and the whores would come in off the street for a beer and we'd sit there all talkin' and jokin' around. They were nice girls these whores, all come to Montreal from Three Rivers and Chicoutimi and a lotta places I never heard tell of, and couldn't pronounce. Our acquaintance was strictly a pub acquaintance, we students preferin' to spend our money on beer thus avoidin' a medical difficulty which intimacy with these girls would most likely entail. So—this night we're stragglin' home in the cold walkin' and talkin' to a bunch a these whores, and as we pass their house, they drop off there up the steps yellin' 'Goo-night goo-night.'. . . 'Bout a block further on, someone says: 'Where the hell's Oscar?' Christ, we all start yellin': 'Where the hell's Oscar? Oscar! Oscar!' Searchin' in gutters, snowbanks, and alleys, but the bugger's gone, disappeared! Suddenly it comes to me. Surer than hell he's so pissed that he's just followed along behind the girls when they peeled off to go home and he's back there inside the cat house. So back I go. Bang on the door. This giant of a woman, uglier than sin, opens it up. Inside is all this screamin' and cryin' and poundin' and I say: 'Did a kinda skinny fellow'—and she says: 'Get that son of a bitch outa here!' 'Where is he?' I say. 'Upstairs, he's locked himself in one of the rooms with Janette! He's killin' her for Christ's sake!' She takes me up to the room, door locked, girl inside screamin' bloody murder and I can hear Oscar makin' a kinda intent diabolical ahhhhhin' and oohhhin' sound. 'Oscar! Oscar! For Christ's sake, open up!' The girl's pleadin' with him to stop, beggin' him, chill your blood to the bone to hear her. And still that aaahhhhin'! and ooohhhhhin'! Nothin' for it but I got to throw myself at the door till either it gives or my shoulder does. Finally Boom! I'm in. I can see Oscar is not. He's got Janette tied to the bed, staked right out, naked and nude. He's straddlin' her but he's fully clothed, winter hat, scarf, boots and all, and he's wieldin' his blue anatomy pencil. He's drawin' all of her vital organs, he's outlinin' them on her skin with his blue anatomy pencil. He's got her kidneys and her lungs, her trachea and her liver all traced out. Takes four of us to pull him off—me and three massive brutes who've appeared. Janette is so upset they sent her back to Rivière-du-Loup for two weeks to recover, Oscar has to turn pimp till he pays back the price of the door, and everyone swears it's the worst goddamn perversion and misuse of a whore ever witnessed in Montreal . . . what in God's name did you think you were doin' that night?

Oscar shrugs and smiles. Ev is taking out a letter and opening it as he speaks.

Jesus Christ . . . silly bastard . . .

Shift.

It's from Mum . . . the old man's been laid off.

OSCAR: She sound worried?

EV: She says go ahead with the Royal Vic.

OSCAR: The General would be closer to home.

EV: What good would that do?

OSCAR: I don't know.

EV: No money to be made in post-graduate work anywhere.

OSCAR: I thought moral support, you know, being close.

EV: The Vic's the best in the country.

OSCAR: I know that.

EV: Mum would probably kill me if I gave up the Royal Vic.

OSCAR: She definitely would. . . . What about Millie?

EV: Millie?

OSCAR: Yeah.

EV: What about her?

OSCAR: I guess she could probably help out. Get a job.

EV: There's no jobs anywhere. Besides Millie's still in school.

OSCAR: Will she quit?

EV: What the hell do you want me to do?

OSCAR: I don't want you to do anything. I just wondered if Millie would quit school to help out at home, that's all.

EV: What the hell're you tryin' to say to me? Are you sayin' I should quit?

OSCAR: No, I just meant there are hospitals closer to home.

> *Oscar may exit. Ev calls after him.*

EV: You can't be serious. The Vic's the best post-graduate training in the country. I've worked goddamn hard for it and I won't give it up—not for Mum if she asked me. Not for Millie! Not for anyone!

CATHERINE: But you did, Daddy.

> *Ev looks at Catherine.*

You gave it up for her.

EV: If . . . if you could have seen her.

> *Shift. Bob may enter. She carries a music box.*

BOB: He would step off the elevator—every nurse on the floor, 'Yes Doctor'—'No Doctor'—'Is there anything else' dramatic pause, sighhhh, 'I can *do* for you, Doctor?' Even Matron. Yes, Matron! And the goo-goo eyes—I remember those eyes.

EV: Do you know what they said?

CATHERINE: What did they say?

EV: Forget her, she is immune to the charms of the predatory male.

BOB: They were right.

EV: No fraternization between doctors and nurses on pain of dismissal.

CATHERINE: So why did you ask her?

EV: I—

BOB: He couldn't resist me—and I—

> *Bob passes Catherine the jewellery box to hold. Bob opens the box. It plays 'Smoke Gets in Your Eyes'. Bob takes out a pair of earrings and puts them on as she's speaking. The lid of the box remains up and the music box plays during the scene.*

I don't give a fig for regulation or rules, only ones I make myself. And if in the past I chose to observe that regulation, it was only because a suitable occasion to break it hadn't arisen.

EV: Be serious.

BOB: My goodness, here I am without two pennies to rub together, and I rush out and buy a new sweater for a bar date with you, and you don't call that serious?

EV: When our eyes first met over what? . . . A perforated ulcer, were you serious then?

BOB: Do you know how many floors my mama scrubbed for that sweater?

> *'Smoke Gets in Your Eyes' played by big band fades in.*

CATHERINE [*closes jewellery box*]: Was she really like that?

EV: If you could have seen her.

Oscar may enter.

OSCAR: Why risk it?

EV: Wait till you meet her.

Ev moves towards Bob, who is swaying to the music.

OSCAR: I don't need to meet her. For Christ's sake, Ev, you're . . . Ev? . . . Ev!

Ev and Bob dance to a medley of Thirties tunes. Oscar watches, drawn into that warm atmosphere. Ev and Oscar take turns cutting in on each other, as they ballroom dance with Bob. They're all very good dancers, and Oscar is as captivated as Ev by Bob. Oscar dances with Bob. She is looking over his shoulder at Ev. Shift.

KATIE [*interrupts, a sudden scream*]: Stop that! You stop it!

The dancers stop; a soft freeze.

I know things! I can figure things out!

The soft freeze breaks. Shift.

OSCAR: Have you told your mother?

EV: Not yet.

OSCAR: She had her heart set on a specialist.

EV: She'll settle for a grandson.

CATHERINE: But that's not what you got, you got me.

Shift.

KATIE: Why did he marry her?

OSCAR: He loved her.

KATIE: Why didn't you marry her?

OSCAR: She loved him.

KATIE: They didn't want to have me.

OSCAR: That isn't true.

KATIE: Did your mother want to have you?

Shift.

BOB: Your mother, ooohhh, your poor father, Ev.

EV: I know.

BOB: And Millie—you never told me about Millie.

EV: I mentioned her once or twice.

BOB: If you were only Catholic she could be a nun.

EV: Don't judge her by what you've seen tonight.

BOB: And your mother could be Pope.

EV: She liked you.

BOB: She hated me.

EV: When you get to know her, it'll be different.

BOB: I don't want to know her. Look at Millie under her thumb.

EV: Millie isn't under her thumb.

BOB: And your father.

There is a sense of intimacy, rather than irritation, between Ev and Bob.

EV: Look, you saw them for the first time for what—four or five hours—you can't make generalizations based on that.

BOB: You were there. You heard her. 'Poor Ev. Giving up the Vic.' You'd think a general practice was the end of the earth—And why've you fallen so far?

EV: She never said any of those things.

BOB: She implied I'd caught you by the oldest trick in the book.

EV: She didn't.

BOB: 'Why does a girl go into nursing?' Why to marry a doctor, of course! And Millie nodding away and your father smiling away—I wanted to stand up and scream.

EV: You're tired.

BOB: And you, you're there, way up there, the shining light, can do nothing wrong, except one thing is wrong, we are wrong!

EV: She had certain expectations, I'm not defending her, I'm just trying to explain how things are, or have been—Bob? . . . Bob!

BOB: For years she's been practising, 'I'd like you to meet my son, The Specialist.'

EV: Things haven't been that easy, you know. You've seen Dad, he's a good man but he's—when Georgie died, the old man wept on her—there was no one for her to weep on. It was hard on her losin' Georgie, and now all of her hopes for me and for Georgie are all pinned on me. . . . You can understand that.

BOB: She'll be counting the months.

EV: Let her.

Ev kisses Bob.

Again.

Ev kisses Bob.

Again.

BOB: You.

EV: You smile that smile at my Mum and she'll love you. It's a beautiful smile.

BOB: We aren't wrong, are we?

EV: We'll have a boy and we'll call him George after my brother. She'll like that.

BOB: Or William, after my brother Bill.

EV: And he'll have a beautiful smile.

BOB: And he'll have a nose like yours.

EV: And he'll . . .

Shift. Ev and Bob may exit.

CATHERINE: I notice this thing about having boys first. I mean what is that all about?

KATIE: Who was I named after?

OSCAR: Kate was your grandmother's name.

KATIE: Nobody calls me Kate.

OSCAR: That's your name.

KATIE: It's an ugly name. Why did they call me that? Couldn't they think of anything else?

OSCAR: Kate isn't ugly.

KATIE: Do I look like a Kate to you?

OSCAR: What's a Kate look like?

KATIE: Do you think names are like dogs?

OSCAR: In what way like dogs?

KATIE: I read dogs start to look like their owners or their owners start to look like their dogs. Do you think if you get an ugly name you start to look like your name?

CATHERINE: Or be like who you were named after?

> *Shift. Ev and Bob may enter. Bob carries Ev's suitcoat. Ev carries a doctor's bag. Bob will help Ev on with his jacket.*

BOB: I want to go back to work.

EV: Where would you work?

BOB: I'm an RN, I'll apply at a hospital.

EV: No.

CATHERINE: Why not?

EV: I don't want her there.

CATHERINE: Why not?

EV: A matter of policy.

CATHERINE: Whose?

EV: What about Katie?

BOB: What about her?

EV: You should be home with her.

BOB: Why?

EV: You're her mother.

BOB: You're her father, you're not home from one day to the next. What am I supposed to do, rattle around with a four-month-old baby to talk to?

EV: So get somebody in.

BOB: Let me work, Ev.

EV: I don't want you down at the hospital.

BOB: Why not?

EV: Because as a surgeon operating out of that hospital, I don't want my wife on staff. I don't want any surgeon's wife on staff. And I don't know any surgeon who wants his wife on staff.

> *Shift.*

KATIE: They were fighting last night.

OSCAR: Oh?

KATIE: Do you want to know what they were fighting about, if you don't already know.

OSCAR: How would I know?

KATIE: How do you think! Someone would tell you! Behind Daddy's back they would tell you! They would whisper.

OSCAR: That doesn't happen.

CATHERINE: Then why, Uncle Oscar, did you spend so much time talking to me if you didn't want to find out about them?

Shift.

BOB: I could work at the office. [*pours herself a drink*]

EV: No.

BOB: McQuire's wife—

EV: is a silly bitch who keeps McQuire's office in an uproar from the time she comes in in the morning till she leaves at night.

BOB: I'm not Marg McQuire.

EV: I have an office nurse, she does a good job and she needs the job and I don't intend letting her go.

BOB: I could work for someone else!

EV: I don't know what doctor would hire another doctor's wife as an office nurse.

BOB: Why not?

EV: Look, you're not just an RN anymore.

BOB: No.

EV: You're not Eloise Roberts, you're not Bob any more.

BOB: Who am I?

EV: My wife.

CATHERINE: Daddy.

EV: You're working the OR, the surgeon hits a bleeder, starts screaming for clamps, you're slow off the mark, and when the whole mess is under control, he turns round to give you shit, you take off your surgical mask and who does he see? Not a nurse, another surgeon's wife. My wife. Is he gonna give you shit?

BOB: I'm not slow off the mark in the OR.

EV: That's not the point, you're my wife, is he gonna give you shit?

BOB: That's his problem, not mine.

EV: I'm in the OR. I hit a bleeder. I scream for a clamp. I look at the nurse who's too fuckin' slow and who do I see? My wife!

BOB: I'm not slow! I'm good in the OR.

EV: That's not the point.

CATHERINE: Why don't you just say you don't want her there instead of all this bullshit?

EV: Jesus Christ I said it! I don't want her there!

Shift. Katie is holding her wrist. She speaks to Oscar.

KATIE: My father works hard! My father works really hard!

CATHERINE: I know. I know.

KATIE: You don't work as hard as my father. My father is never home. He goes to the hospital before we're up and when he comes home we're asleep.

CATHERINE: Robbie's asleep.

KATIE: I'm surprised Daddy knows who Robbie is. I'm surprised Robbie knows who Daddy is . . . I hate Robbie.

OSCAR: How did this happen?

KATIE: I dunno.

OSCAR: Yes you do.

KATIE: I'm accident-prone. Some people are you know. Accident-prone. I do dangerous things. I like doing dangerous things.

OSCAR: How did you do this?

KATIE: It was just something that happened.

OSCAR: Ah-huh.

Oscar is taping Katie's wrist.

KATIE: I do lots of things. Last Sunday when we were supposed to be in Sunday School, Robbie and I, do you know what we did?

OSCAR: Might hurt.

KATIE: Won't hurt. We went to the freight yards and played. I crawled under the train cars twice and Robbie crawled over where they're hitched together. He was too scared to crawl under. I wasn't scared.

OSCAR: You shouldn't do that.

KATIE: We decided together, Robbie and I. I didn't make him. Do you believe that?

OSCAR: What?

KATIE: That Robbie and I decided together to go to the freight yards instead of to Sunday School, do you believe that?

OSCAR: No.

KATIE: Anyway we had these gloves on. You know the ones Mummy made out of kid or leather the last time she was away? She made about a million pair. She probably gave a pair to you.

Shift.

BOB: It's not my fault if other people don't know who I am! It's not my fault if all they can see is your wife!

EV: Aren't you my wife?

BOB: That's not all I am!

EV: Don't yell at me.

BOB: Who do I yell at?

EV: Half the nurses in that goddamn hospital are lookin' for a doctor to marry so they can sit on their ass, and here you are screamin' cause you're not on your feet twelve hours a day bein' overworked and underpaid.

BOB: I am on my feet twelve hours a day!

EV: So let me get somebody in.

BOB: I feel funny with somebody in. . . . If I'm here, I feel I should be doing it.

EV: You want to get out more.

BOB: I know I'm a good nurse. I'm as good as anyone. When I'm out . . . I'm never sure what fork to use.

EV: Who gives a shit which fork you use? Whichever one comes to hand.

BOB: When you 'go out' that fork's important.

EV: Get Oscar to teach you how to play bridge. First year of university that's all he did.

BOB: I feel as if I wasted something.

Shift. Katie is still with Oscar.

KATIE: I don't know how she is supposed to get better by making gloves and painting pictures. Her pictures are awful. It costs a fortune to send her there and it never works! . . . Anyway . . . I got black all over my gloves and it wouldn't come off so I made Robbie give me his cause Mummy never gets mad at him and that's one of the reasons I hate him, and as soon as we got home do you know what he did?

CATHERINE: Told.

KATIE: He told. He said I *made* him go to the freight yards and then I *made* him change gloves. He's always telling and that's another reason I hate him.

OSCAR: You're the oldest—you should look out for Robbie.

KATIE: I'm trying to teach Robbie to look out for *himself!* I am! . . . She didn't even ask and he told. She's always saying Robbie's just like her side of the family and I'm just like Daddy's—Have you met my Uncle Bill?

OSCAR: I might have.

KATIE: Well I wouldn't want to be like her side of the family. I'd rather be like his!

Shift.

BOB: Nobody else in my family finished high school, did I tell you that?

No one is listening to Bob.

CATHERINE: Was she a good nurse, Daddy?

EV: That's not the point, Katie.

CATHERINE: Was she?

EV: I'm late for my rounds.

BOB: I was the smartest.

EV: You get some sleep now.

Ev may exit.

CATHERINE: Daddy?

BOB: And I always won, Katie! Because I played so hard! Played to win! And school— *first*, always first! 'Our valedictorian is Eloise Roberts.'

Catherine moves away from Bob, who continues speaking with the drink in her hand.

Eloise Roberts, and they called me Bob, and I could run faster and play harder and do better than any boy I ever met! And my hair? It was all the way down to there! And when I asked my Mama—Mama?—She said, we have been here since the

Seventeen Hundreds, Eloise, and in your blood runs the blood of Red Roberts! Do you know who he is? A pirate, with flamin' red hair and a flamin' red beard who harboured off a cove in PEI! A pirate! And inside of me—just bustin' to get out! To reach out! To grow! . . . And when I sat on our front porch and I looked out— I always looked *up*, cause lookin' up I saw the sky, and the sky went on forever! And I picked and sold my berries, and my Mama cleaned house for everyone all around, and my sisters and my one brother Bill, everything for one thing. For me. For Eloise Roberts. For Bob.

Shift. Ev enters, carrying his bag. He is speaking to Oscar.

EV: You know somethin'!? The goddamn health care services in this province are a laugh!

BOB: Katie?

EV: I had a woman come into my office yesterday. I've never seen her before, but she's got a lump in her breast and she's half out of her mind with worry. Surer than hell it's cancer, but there's nothin' I can do till I damn well find out it *is* cancer. So what do I have to do? I gotta take a section and ship that tissue to Saint John on the bus, for Christ's sake! And then what? I got to wait for three days to maybe a week to hear. Do you know how often I get a replay of that scenario? She's a mother or she works for a living or she's at home looking after her old man and I can't tell her what's wrong or what we have to do till I get that goddamn report back from Saint John! We need a medical laboratory in this town, and by God, I'm gonna see that we get one!

OSCAR: Have you seen Bob?

EV: When?

OSCAR: Do you know you've a son?

EV: Georgie, we're callin' him Georgie, a brother for Katie. Hell of a good-lookin' boy, have you seen him?

OSCAR: I popped into the nursery.

EV: Looks like his old man.

OSCAR: Where were you?

EV: Had a call in Keswick.

OSCAR: What the hell would take you to Keswick when your wife's in labour?

EV: I hear it went as smooth as silk.

OSCAR: Ev?

EV: . . . Frank Johnston's kid fell under a thresher.

OSCAR: Bad?

EV: Bad as it can get.

OSCAR: You . . . could have sent someone else.

EV: Frank's been a patient of mine since I started the practice. Who the hell else could I send?

OSCAR: What about Bob?

EV: Valma was with her.

OSCAR: She didn't want Valma, she wanted you.

EV: Look, I brought Frank Johnston's kid into the world—and eight hours ago I saw him out, kneelin' in a field, with the kid's blood soaking my pants. . . . And afterwards, I sat in the kitchen with his mother, and before I left, I shared a mickey of rum with Frank.

OSCAR: It was important to Bob you be here, she needed you.

> *Oscar may exit. Ev calls after him.*

EV: Well Frank Johnston needed me more!

> *Ev looks at Catherine.*

The last baby I delivered was in a tarpaper shack. They paid me seven eggs, and when the crabapples fall, the mother's bringin' some round. Would you like to talk need to that woman? . . .

> *Catherine looks away.*

She's got the best maternity care this province provides, and the best obstetrician in town. She's got a private nurse, and a baby boy. What the hell else does she want?

> *Ev carries a chair over near Bob.*

CATHERINE: She wants you.

EV: She's got me.

> *Ev sits beside Bob. Shift.*

BOB: I like Robert.

EV: I thought it was George or William.

BOB: Robbie's better.

EV: What's wrong with George?

BOB: Nothing's wrong with it, I like Robbie best.

EV: George was my brother's name.

BOB: I know.

EV: Robert George?

BOB: Robert Dann.

EV: Where the hell did you get that name?

BOB: Out of my head.

EV: Well, you can stick George in someplace, can't you?

BOB: I'm not calling him George.

EV: It's my goddamn brother's name!

BOB: I know.

EV: It means a lot to my mother.

BOB: I know.

EV: So stick it someplace!

BOB: No.

EV: Jesus Christ do you have to make an issue outa every little thing?

BOB: I don't like George.

EV: What the hell harm does it do to stick George in somewhere! Robert Dann George, George Robert Dann, George Damn Robert.

BOB: He's my son.

EV: He's our son.

BOB: So register him whatever you like.

EV: I will. [*stands up*]

BOB: I'm calling him Robbie.

EV [*returns chair to original position*]: I work my ass off. Why do I do it if it's not for her?

CATHERINE: Why?

EV: For her. Oscar?

Shift. Oscar may enter.

OSCAR: Ah-huh?

EV: What're your evenings like?

OSCAR: What're your evenings like?

EV: I'm doing rounds at night and squeezin' in house calls after that—could you drop over to see her till she comes round a bit?

OSCAR: What about my house calls?

EV: You never made a house call in your life.

OSCAR: I made one once.

EV: You lazy son of a bitch. If it weren't for the remnants of your old man's practice, you'd starve to death. What'll you do when the last of his patients die off?

OSCAR: Move someplace where it's hot.

EV: Listen, what she needs is someone to talk to, play a little golf, shit, the Medical Ball's comin' up next month, take her to that. I'm too goddamn busy.

OSCAR: When do you sleep?

EV: I don't.

OSCAR: How the hell did she ever get pregnant?

EV: I didn't say I never laid down.

Ev may exit with bag. Shift.

BOB: I want to go to New York next month. Go to New York and see the shows—do you want to do that?

Sound of Forties dance music.

OSCAR: Can Ev get away?

BOB: We'll ask.

Oscar lights Bob's cigarette.

Look around us. Look at all these pursey little lips. Look at all these doctors' wives. Do I look like that? Do I?

OSCAR: Not a bit.

BOB [*holding a glass*]: Well thas good. Look at them. . . . D'you know I joined the IODE? The IODE. I joined it. And do you wanna know what's really frightenin'? I could prolly, after a bit, I could prolly achully—forget. I could get to like the IODE. Isn't tha' frightening? . . . Isn't tha' frightening! . . . Ah, you're as bad as Everett. Whasa matter with doctors, you're a doctor, you tell me, so busy savin' lives you've forgotten how to talk? Talk!

OSCAR: The IODE eh?

BOB: Thas right . . . next year I might run as Grand Something. . . . The IODE does some very importan' work you know.

> *Oscar smiles and casually takes the glass from her.*

. . . I don't like anybody here, do you? . . .

> *Bob takes the glass back as casually, takes a drink.*

Do you know my mother . . . and all my sisters . . . and my one brother Bill who taught me how to fish—hey! We could go fishing some time if you want.

OSCAR: Bob.

BOB: Everett doesn't fish! Everett doesn't do anything except go . . . round . . .

OSCAR: Bob.

BOB: Anyway—so all these people, mother, sisters, Bill, they all worked to put me through nursing, wasn't that wonderful of them? . . . And now Ev, he lent Bill the money for something Bill thinks he wants to do and it'll all be a disaster cause it's about the tenth time he'd done it, but Ev's always giving money to his mother, so I don't care. Why should I care? But you know what I don't like? Do you?

OSCAR: What don't you like?

BOB: I don't like the cleanin' lady. Because every time . . . the cleanin' lady comes in, I think of my Mama who cleaned all around so I could go into nursing.

> *Music out; silence.*

And you want to know what's worse? My Mama's so happy I married a doctor. I'm successful you see. I made something of myself. [*moves away smiling; lifting her glass in a toast*] I married a doctor.

> *Shift. Katie carries a hairbrush.*

KATIE: Why don't you get married?

OSCAR: I'm waiting for you.

KATIE: I'm not related to you.

OSCAR: No.

KATIE: But you're always here, you're always about. . . . Do you love my mother?

OSCAR: I love you.

KATIE: Do you want to brush my hair?

OSCAR: If you want me to.

KATIE: You can if you want.

> *Katie gives Oscar the brush, and sits at his feet. He brushes her hair. She enjoys it for a moment before speaking.*

I'm named after my Gramma, but I'm not like my Gramma. . . . I know when trains are coming . . . and when they're coming, I don't go that way then. . . . Do you like brushing my hair?

OSCAR: It needs it.

KATIE: I don't care if it's messy. It's how you are inside that counts.

OSCAR: That's true.

KATIE: I'm surprised you don't know that.

CATHERINE: Did you love my mother, Uncle Oscar?

OSCAR: When your mother's not well, you should think about that.

KATIE: About what?

OSCAR: How she feels inside.

KATIE: . . . I wonder—what my father sees in you. [*grabs the hairbrush*] You're not a very good doctor. What does he see in you?

OSCAR: Katie—

KATIE: Do you like brushing my hair?

Do you like brushing my hair!

OSCAR: Katie—

KATIE: I hate you!

Katie moves away from Oscar, who follows her. Shift. Bob moves to the liquor and refills her glass. It is late, and she drinks while she waits.

BOB: Ev! . . . is that you, Ev?

Ev may enter. He will sit, his bag at his feet, with his head back and his eyes closed.

EV: Yeah.

BOB: What time is it? . . . Where were you?

EV: Just left the hospital. They brought in some kid with a ruptured spleen . . . car accident . . . took out every guard rail on that big turn on River Road . . . damn near bled out when we got him.

BOB: How is he?

EV: Mnn?

BOB: I said, how is he?

EV: Bout half a million pieces . . .

BOB: . . . Ev?

EV: What time is it?

BOB: Late.

EV: Takin' out a stomach in the mornin'.

BOB: . . . Can we talk?

EV: Talk away . . .

BOB: I let the maid go today. It wasn't working out—

EV: Medjuck call?

BOB: What?

EV: Did Sam Medjuck call?

BOB: I said I let the maid go today—

EV: Mn?

BOB [*moves to refill her drink*]: Valma phoned and said he'd called her.

EV: Christ. [*gets up; picks up his bag*]

BOB: Why would he phone Valma's looking for you?

EV: He knows her, she kids him along.

CATHERINE: Were you over at Valma's?

EV: I was takin' out a spleen!

CATHERINE: Should I believe that?

EV: I was takin' out a spleen.

BOB: I said I let the maid go today!

EV: How many's that?

BOB: She was a smarmy bitch and I fired her!

EV: I said how many's that?

> *Ev may exit.*

BOB: Where're you going?

EV [*offstage*]: House call to Medjuck's!

BOB: It's the middle of the night!

EV [*offstage*]: It's morning!

BOB: Ev! Ev!

CATHERINE: He's gone.

BOB: You'll fall asleep, Ev! You'll fall asleep and run off the road!

KATIE: Shut up Mummy!

BOB: Ev!

KATIE: Why don't you shut up and let people sleep!

BOB: Oscar!

CATHERINE: He isn't here, Mummy!

BOB: Count on Oscar!

KATIE: He's not here, Mummy!

OSCAR: When you need me you call, I'll be there.

CATHERINE: Daddy!

> *Ev may enter, isolated on stage. Music filters in, 'Auld Lang Syne'.*

EV: Buy a Packard I always say! Best goddamn car on the road!

CATHERINE: Do something.

EV: I'd be drivin' along, middle of the night—

BOB: It's seven maids, that's how many!

EV: All of a sudden, swish, swish, swish, tree branches hittin' the car, look around—

BOB: And I'll fire the next seven whenever I damn well feel like it!

CATHERINE: Daddy!

EV: Car's in the middle of a goddamn orchard.

BOB: Oscar!

EV: I've fallen asleep and failed to navigate a turn and here's me and the car travellin' through this goddamn orchard.

Bob is joined by Oscar. They dance to 'Auld Lang Syne', as Katie watches. Catherine's focus slowly switches, from her father to Bob and Oscar.

BOB: Oscar.

EV: And me without a clue in the world as to where I'm headed. Black as pitch, not a light to be seen, and me drivin' over bumps and skirtin' fences and tryin' to remember where in the hell I'm goin'. Then I catch a glimpse of this little light, almost like a low-lyin' star in the sky.

Bob kisses Oscar.

EV: . . . head for that—what the hell—could end up on Venus! Door opens and someone is standin' there—

Bob sees Katie watching.

'We've been waiting for you, Doc.'

BOB: What do you want?

EV: 'Is the coffee hot?'

BOB: What do you want!

EV: 'Melt a spoon.'

KATIE [*screams*]: Don't! You don't!

Katie launches herself at Oscar and Bob.

EV: 'We've been waitin' for you, Doc.'

Katie hits Oscar and Bob and Bob steps away from Oscar. During all the action she continues to scream.

KATIE: You! You! Get away! Get away! I hate you! I hate you! You don't! Get away!

Catherine runs to Katie and tries to restrain her.

CATHERINE: Stop. Stop. Daddy. Daddy!!

Katie collapses against Catherine.

Help me.

End of Act One

ACT II

The house is silent. Ev and Catherine are most prominent on stage. Katie is not far from Catherine. Bob and Oscar are in the background. Catherine looks at Ev, who is wearing an old cardigan and glasses. Catherine holds Gramma's letter.

CATHERINE: . . . Go on.

EV: . . . When I was little, Katie . . . when I was a kid, I saw my own father get smaller and smaller, physically smaller, cause he was nothin', no job, no . . . nothin'. I was only a kid but I saw him . . . get smaller like that. . . . Georgie now, he was the one in our family would have gone places.

CATHERINE: Haven't you 'gone places'?

EV: Seen half this province from their mother's belly to the grave.

CATHERINE: Was it worth it?

EV: . . . When that goddamn Demsky let me up, I'd wander all round that hospital. I'd look in the wards, Intensive Care. . . . You get to be my age, the only place better than a hospital for meetin' people you know is a mortuary . . . Frank Johnston died while I was there in his room. They had him hooked up to all these goddamn monitors. And do you know how they knew he was dead? Straight lines and the sound from the monitors. Nobody looked down at Frank. Just at the monitors. . . . And that is the kinda hospital they're gonna put my name on? . . . I wouldn't like to go like Frank.

CATHERINE: You won't go for ages, Daddy.

EV: If I can keep away from that Demsky I got a chance . . .

CATHERINE: Daddy?

EV: What?

CATHERINE: About Mummy.

EV: . . . If I could—I'm gonna show you somethin', I want you to see this . . . you see this, you'll understand. [*opens trunk and begins to sort through it*] Six or seven kids standin' by the car, and the car outside this Day Clinic . . . Valma and I, we were doing these check-ups and physicals and what-have-you . . . where the hell . . . we were doin' that one day a week in Minto, families a miners, poor goddamn buggers, most of 'em unemployed at the time. And this bunch a little rag-tag snotty-nosed kids, smellin' a wet wool and Javex, were impressed all to hell by the car—and Valma, out with the goddamn camera, and she took this here picture . . . it's in here, where the hell is it? [*stops looking for the snapshot*] . . . I don't care about this hospital thing, I don't care about . . . I care about those little kids! I looked into their faces, and I saw my own face when I was a kid . . . was I wrong to do that? So goddamn much misery—should I have tended my own little plot when I looked round and there was so damn much to do—so much I could do—I did do! Goddamn it, I did it! You tell me, was I wrong to do that!

> Pause. Ev is about to look again for the picture.

CATHERINE: It isn't there, Daddy.

EV: I had to rely on myself cause there was fuckin' little else to rely on, I made decisions when decisions had to be made, I chose a road, and I took it, and I never looked back.

CATHERINE: You've always been so sure of things, haven't you.

> Ev watches Catherine as she looks down at the envelope, and turns it over in her hands.

EV: . . . You're like her, Katie.

CATHERINE: Like Gramma?

EV: Like your mother. [*removes his glasses*]

CATHERINE: She always said I was just like you.

EV: Like her.

CATHERINE: Don't say that.

KATIE: Am I like Gramma, Daddy?

EV: You're like yourself, Katie.

KATIE: Why don't you open it, Daddy?

> *Katie is looking at the letter Catherine holds.*

EV: I will.

CATHERINE: When I was little I stayed with her once.

> *Catherine looks at Katie.*

EV: After your mother had Robbie.

KATIE: And I swore, and she said, 'You never say those words, Katie, only in church,' and when I dropped my prayer book I said, 'Jesus Christ, Gramma,' and she said 'Ka-Ty!'

CATHERINE: And I said, 'But we are in church, Gramma.'

> *Katie and Catherine laugh. Ev takes off the old cardigan and hangs it over his chair as he speaks.*

EV: She'd write that kinda thing in a letter. That's all that she'd write. That's what's in this letter. [*exits*]

CATHERINE [*to Katie*]: I don't want to be like her, and I don't want to be like Mummy.

KATIE [*sings to Catherine*]:

> K-K-K-Katie, my beautiful Katie,
> You're the only G-G-G-Girl that I adore
> When the M-M-M-Moon shines

[*Katie looks at a note book; she has not carried one before.*]

> I'll be waiting . . .
> K-K-K-Katie . . . Katie . . .

> *Shift. Oscar is watching Katie.*

[*to Catherine*]: Everything's down in here. I write it all down. And when I grow up, I'll have it all here.

CATHERINE: Will it be worth it?

KATIE: I used to pray to God, but I don't anymore. I write it all down in here. I was just little then and now—

> *Katie senses Oscar is watching her.*

Are you interested in this, Uncle Oscar? Cause if you aren't, why do you listen?

OSCAR: For you.

KATIE: I don't like people doing things for me. I can do things for myself . . .

> *Katie starts to write in the book, the only time she does so.*

'Now Mummy has a "medical problem" p-r-ob.' Did you know that, Uncle Oscar? Mummy has a *medical problem*—that's apart from her *personal problems*, did you know that?

OSCAR: No.

KATIE: Really?

    Shift. Ev enters with bag and suit jacket. Oscar may help him on with it.

EV: I thought you knew.

OSCAR: How the hell would I know?

EV: I'm sending her to the Royal Vic.

OSCAR: Who to?

EV: You remember Bob Green from McGill?

OSCAR: Bit quick to cut, isn't he?

EV: You never liked him.

OSCAR: Neither did you.

EV: So he's an asshole, was, is, and will be, but he's goddamn good at his job.

OSCAR: He's too quick to cut.

EV: And the best gynecologist in the country.

OSCAR: He'll have her in surgery before the ink on her train ticket dries.

EV: This is your professional opinion, is it, based on your *extensive* practice?

OSCAR: There's gotta be other options.

EV: We could go someplace where it's hot and lie in the sun till she grows a tumour the size of a melon—why don't we do that?

OSCAR: I—

EV: You wanna look at her medical records? Go talk to Barney, tell him I said to pull 'em and show you—fibrous uterus, two opinions.

OSCAR: Green'll go for radical surgery and—

EV: What the hell do you want me to do?

OSCAR: Does she know?

EV: Of course she knows! What the hell do you mean, does she know?

OSCAR: You gotta take some time with her, she's gonna need that.

EV: I got no time.

OSCAR: What's wrong with just takin' off—the two of you go just as soon as she's able.

EV: I can't.

OSCAR: Look, you lie on the sand in the sun and you relax for Christ's sake.

EV: I got patients been waitin' for a bed for months, I can't just leave 'em to whoever's on call.

OSCAR: I'll take 'em, you go.

EV: They count on me bein' there, Oscar.

OSCAR: The population of this province will not wither and die if you take a three-week vacation—I'll handle your patients.

EV: I'd go nuts doin' nothin'.

OSCAR: You're doin' it for her.

EV: I'd go nuts.

OSCAR: You're drivin' her nuts!

EV: Were that true, three weeks in the sun wouldn't change it.

OSCAR: Don't think of her as your wife—think of her as a patient who's married to an insensitive son-of-a-bitch.

EV: I was an insensitive son-of-a-bitch when she met me; I haven't changed.

OSCAR: I give up.

EV: OK, OK, I'm thinking . . . I'm thinking. . . . I'm thinking you like sand and sun, you could take her.

OSCAR: I didn't marry her.

EV: You like her.

OSCAR: I like her.

EV: She likes you.

OSCAR: Listen to yourself! You're asking me to take your wife on a three-week vacation to recover from major surgery, do you realize that?

EV: She needs to get away, I can't take the time, you can.

OSCAR: It's one thing I'm not gonna do for you.

EV: So do it for her.

OSCAR: No.

EV: It makes sense to me.

OSCAR: No.

EV: Why not?

OSCAR: No, I said no.

EV: You're the one suggested it.

OSCAR: I didn't.

Ev looks at his watch.

We're not leaving it there!

EV: Look. There's an alumnae thing in six or seven months, I can schedule around it and the three of us'll go and have one hell of a good bash, but right now I cannot get away so I'm askin' you to do me this favour. How often do I ask for a favour? Take her to one of those islands you go to, eat at the clubs, lie in the sun, and— Christ, Oscar, I got to go, so gimme an answer, yes or no? [*pause*] You make the arrangements, I'll pick up the tab.

OSCAR: Half the tab.

EV: Fifty-fifty all the way.

OSCAR: Are you sure you don't want me to check her into the Vic, observe the surgery, hang around the recovery room and generally be there?

EV: I can clear three or four days for that.

Oscar is silent. As Ev is about to leave he notices Oscar's silence and stops.

Say—how did that burn case go?

OSCAR: That was four months ago, Ev.

EV: Seems like yesterday, so how did it go?

OSCAR: Zip, kaput.

EV: What the hell did you do?

OSCAR: Did it ever occur to you that I might find Bob very attractive?

EV: I know she's attractive, hell, I married her, didn't I?

OSCAR: That she might find me very attractive?

EV: Don't let it go to your head.

OSCAR: You know rumours fly.

EV: I'm too damned busy to listen to rumours.

OSCAR: Your mother isn't. She listens. After that, she phones.

EV: Who?

OSCAR: Me. She phones me. To talk about you. She's a remnant of my old man's practice, remember?

EV: Last time I saw her she didn't—

OSCAR: When was that anyway?

EV: Oh I was over—no—ah—

OSCAR: She can't remember either. I've seen you, you son-of-a-bitch, I've seen you take time with some old biddy, you laugh, you hang onto her hand, and she leaves your office thinking she's Claudette Colbert, and has just stolen a night with you at the Ritz—and I—I get phone calls from your mother who is reduced to writing you letters and crying to me on the phone. You don't call, you don't visit, you don't . . . and now she's got it into her head that . . .

EV: What?

OSCAR: Rumours fly.

EV: So you reassure her. I gotta go, Oscar.

OSCAR: What if I can't reassure her?

EV: Then you laugh, hang onto her hand, and make Mum think she's Claudette Colbert at the Ritz.

OSCAR: It's not that simple.

> *Ev is moving away from Oscar.*

I do find Bob very attractive.

EV: Total agreement.

OSCAR: You never think for one minute there could be one iota of truth in those rumours?

EV: I just don't believe you'd do that to me.

OSCAR: How can you be so sure?

EV: I know you.

OSCAR: Better than I know myself?

EV: I must. [*speaking as he exits*] Barbados eh, or someplace like that.

> *Shift.*

BOB: I don't plan on having any more children.

CATHERINE: No more children.

BOB: I didn't plan, didn't.

CATHERINE: No children.

BOB: Don't have to plan now. All taken care of. Are you listenin' to me?

Shift. Katie and Catherine will end up together, a mirror image.

KATIE: I'll tell you what she does. What she does is, she starts doing something. Something big. That's how I can tell. She's all right for awhile—then she decides she's gonna paint all of the downstairs—or we're gonna put in new cupboards—or knock out a wall! . . . We got so many walls knocked out, the house started to fall down in the middle! Can you believe that?—And we had to get a big steel beam put through in the basement! Can you believe that?

CATHERINE: It's true.

KATIE: And before she gets finished one of those big jobs—she starts.

CATHERINE: And she never finishes. Someone else comes in, and they finish.

KATIE: But that's how I can tell when she's gonna start. And I try to figure out

CATHERINE: I ask myself

KATIE: Does the big job make her start—or does she start the big job because she knows she's gonna start?

CATHERINE: But that's how I could tell, that's the beginning.

Shift.

BOB: So . . . why does it . . . why do I feel that it matters? Two were enough, Katie and Robert, so why do I feel that it matters? I don't want any more . . . Oscar!

OSCAR: I'm here.

BOB: Does it matter?

OSCAR: Well . . . from the medical—

BOB: Medical, medical, medical, I don't wanna talk about medical.

OSCAR: It affects—

BOB: Me! Me! I'm talkin' about me! Why do I feel like, why do I feel—we didn't want any more children! I can't have any more children! Me, the part of me that's important, here, inside here—Me! That's the same. I'm the same. So . . . why do I feel that it matters?

OSCAR: It doesn't matter.

BOB: Why don't you listen? I'm trying to explain. We didn't want any more, I can't have any more, so why does it matter?

OSCAR: It doesn't matter.

BOB: It does matter! . . . I'm the same. Inside I'm the same. I'm Eloise Roberts and they called me Bob and I can run faster and do better than any boy I ever met!

OSCAR: It's all right.

BOB: No.

OSCAR: Come here.

BOB: I try to figure it out and I just keep going round.

CATHERINE: It's all right.

BOB: I need to do more, I need to . . . I need . . .

CATHERINE: Why don't you just do what you want?

BOB: Sometimes I want to scream. I just want to stand there and scream, to hit something, to reach out and smash things—and hit and smash and hit and smash and . . . and then . . . I would feel very tired and I could lie down and sleep.

OSCAR: Do you want to sleep now?

BOB: No. I'm not tired now. I want a drink now. Want a drink, and then we'll . . . what will we do?

CATHERINE: Why couldn't you leave.

BOB: Leave?

CATHERINE: Just leave!

BOB: Katie and Robbie.

CATHERINE: Did you care about them?

BOB: And your father?

Shift. Ev enters, carrying a bag. He is isolated on stage.

EV: We had the worst polio epidemic this province has seen, eleven years ago. We had an outbreak this year. You are lookin' at the attendin' physician at the present Polio Clinic—it is a building that has been condemned by the Provincial Fire Marshall, it has been condemned by the Provincial Health Officer, it has been condemned by the Victoria Public Hospital, it's infested by cockroaches, it's overrun by rats, it's the worst goddamn public building in this province! When is the government gonna stop building liquor stores and give the doctors of this province a chance to save a few fuckin' lives!

BOB: Haven't you got enough?

EV: Enough of what?

BOB: Enough! Enough everything!

EV: You're drunk.

BOB: You'll never get enough, will you?

EV: Did Valma phone?

BOB: I don't answer the phone, just let it ring and ring—

Ev starts to exit.

Where're you going?

EV: Valma's.

BOB: What for?

EV: To pick up the messages that she'd give me by phone if you'd answer the phone.

BOB: Maid could answer it. Does answer it, but she's not good with messages, no.

EV: You run them through the house so goddamn fast they don't have time to pick up a phone. Why don't you get one and keep one?

BOB: Interviewin' them gives me somethin' to do. I enjoy interviewin' them. Purpose and direction to my life! Where're you goin'?

EV [*exiting*]: Valma's.

BOB: Stay.

CATHERINE: Stay.

Ev stops.

Don't go. Sit for a little while.

There is a moment of silence.

CATHERINE: Talk.

EV: If I sit down . . . my head will start to nod.

CATHERINE: That'd be all right. She wouldn't mind. You'd be here.

Ev puts down his bag. He moves to Bob and sits beside her. He takes his hat off and takes her hand. Bob smiles and strokes Ev's hand, then holds it against her face.

BOB: Do you remember . . . sometimes I . . . we had some good times, didn't we?

EV: We can still have good times.

BOB: I don't know.

EV: You've got to get hold of things.

BOB: I try.

EV: I know I'm busy.

BOB: Always busy.

EV: I know.

BOB: If I could do something.

EV: There's the house and the kids. Just tell me what you want and I'll get it.

BOB: I can't do anything.

EV: You can.

BOB: No. There's nothing I can do.

EV: Sure there is.

Bob slowly shakes her head.

Come on . . . hey, listen, did you know the Hendersons were sellin' their camp on Miramichi?

Pause.

Well they are. What say we buy it? You'd like that, wouldn't you? You could get away from the kids and the house, do some fishin', you like fishin' don't you?

Bob nods her head.

Well, that's what we'll do. [*checks his watch*] Shit. You get to bed. Get some sleep.

[*exits*]

BOB: Can't sleep.

There is the sound of a train whistle; Bob listens to it. It fades away. Shift.

. . . Half-way across three-quarters of a mile of single track . . . its whistle would split the night, and that night . . . do you know what she did?

CATHERINE: No, and neither to you.

BOB: She walked out to meet it.

CATHERINE: And you say I'm like his side of the family, you say I'm like her?

BOB: She did.

CATHERINE: I would never do that!

> *Shift.*

KATIE: Mummy didn't like her. I could have gone to see her with Daddy, but Daddy was always too busy to go, so it was all his fault I didn't see her. . . . I guess that's true.

CATHERINE: She would phone, she would ask for me.

KATIE: But I could never think of anything to say. . . . They're the ones I'm supposed to be like, his side of the family, so it would have been nice to see her . . . was she old? . . .

> *Catherine doesn't answer.*

KATIE: Is that what she died of? . . .

> *Catherine doesn't answer.*

What did she die of, Uncle Oscar?

OSCAR: It was an accident.

CATHERINE: We know 'accidents', don't we?

KATIE: I never saw anybody dead before. I don't know if I wanted to see her dead . . . it didn't matter because they didn't take us anyway—I was a bit happy not to go because I don't like to go anywhere with Mummy when she's like that. She said Gramma was a bitch who went around saying bad things about her and Mummy was glad she was dead—and Daddy just kept getting dressed and pretended Mummy wasn't talking—You can only pretend for so long.

CATHERINE: And when they came home he went out.

KATIE: And Mummy phoned all over but he wasn't any place she could find, and . . .

CATHERINE: . . . then she tripped at the top of the stairs and she fell. I went to my bedroom as soon as that happened . . .

KATIE: . . . and Robbie screamed and cried and screamed and cried and . . .

CATHERINE: . . . the maid got up and put her to bed—she'll be leaving soon and we'll get a new one . . .

KATIE: . . . you'd think if a person kept falling down stairs it would hurt them!

CATHERINE: It never did a thing to her.

> *Shift.*

BOB: Katie! . . . Katie! You wanna know somethin'?

KATIE: No.

BOB: Your father's mother killed herself! . . .

> *Pause. Katie stares at Bob.*

You look at me . . . you look at me and what are you thinking?

KATIE: Nothing.

BOB: This isn't me you know. This isn't really me. This is someone else. . . . . What are you thinking?

KATIE: I don't think anything.

BOB: Katie!

CATHERINE: Leave her alone!

BOB: You know what your father's mother said?

CATHERINE: Leave her alone!

BOB: Do you know?

KATIE: No!

BOB: Why would a nurse—to catch a doctor, that's why. Why would he marry me, eh? Why would a brilliant young man, whole life ahead of him, why would he marry me? Eh? Do you know why? Do you know!

KATIE: No.

BOB: Why would he do that?!

KATIE: I don't know.

BOB: Answer me!

KATIE: I don't know!

BOB: No! You don't know! Nobody knows!

KATIE: I know. Inside I know. He had to.

CATHERINE: Don't.

KATIE: Inside I do know. Because of me—and that's what went wrong.

CATHERINE: He loved her and she loved him, Uncle Oscar says.

KATIE: No.

CATHERINE: That's true, Katie!

KATIE: Do you believe that?

> *Ev enters in his shirt sleeves.*

Daddy!

> *Katie runs to Ev and he puts his arms around her.*

EV: Your mother sometimes says things that she doesn't mean. She's sick and she—

KATIE: She isn't sick!

EV: She loves you.

KATIE: I don't love her.

> *Katie quickly moves away. Ev starts after her.*

EV: Yes you do.

> *Shift.*

BOB: Valma, Valma, Valma, Valma, Valma, Valma I am so sick of that woman's name. What're you and her doing, that's what I'd like to know!

EV: Nothing. [*sits*]

BOB: Oooh, you don't tell me that! I know better than that! She's like your right arm, your left arm, part of your leg!

EV: Leave Valma out of it.

BOB: I don't wanna leave Valma out of it! She'd do anything for you—put your wife to bed, get her up—why does she do that, eh? Tell me why?

EV: She's the best office nurse in the city and I couldn't run that office without her. Why the Christ don't you go to bed?

BOB: Why the Christ don't you go to bed?

EV: Go to bed.

BOB: Gonna go over to Valma's and go to bed? You don't love me, you never loved me! You never loved me.

EV: Go to bed.

BOB: You don't even see me. You look at me and there's nobody there. You don't see anybody but those stupid stupid people who think you're God. You're not God!

Catherine and Katie are together and Bob moves towards them. Bob grabs Catherine's hand.

And it's so funny . . . do you know what he's done, do you know? . . . If I . . . If I go into the liquor store, do you know what happens? They say . . . . sorry, but the Doc says no. He says . . . they're not to . . . and they don't. They don't. He tells them don't sell it to her the Doc says don't do that and they don't. But what's so funny is . . . every drunk in the city goes into that office on Saturday and they say . . . . 'Jeez Chris Doc, spent the whole cheque on booze, the old lady's gonna kill me,' and he gives them money. . . . Gives them money.

Katie moves away.

And Valma says he says maybe one of them takes it home instead of just buyin' more, can you believe that? . . . And when I go in, they say, 'The Doc says no' . . . but I don't have to worry. [*moves to refill her glass*] So long as I keep interviewin' the maids . . . I don't have to worry about a thing.

Shift.

KATIE: You don't have any family.

OSCAR: You're my family.

KATIE: I'm not related to you, and you're not related to me, you can't be family, Uncle Oscar.

Shift.

BOB [*leaves her glass*]: Hey! Do you want to know what a bastard he is?

Catherine turns her head away as Bob advances on Ev.

Well I don't care if you want to know or not—I'm gonna tell you. I put the clothes out, put the suit out for the cleaners and I went through his pockets, and do you know what I found, do you know? It was something he didn't need for me, something he wouldn't use with me, because I can't have any more, no, I've been fixed like the goddamn cat or the dog so what the hell did you have it for?

EV: If you found it, that means I didn't use it, so what the hell's your problem?

Bob runs at Ev.

BOB: You bastard!

Bob strikes at Ev's chest. He grabs her wrists.

You bastard you.

Bob attempts to strike Ev several times before collapsing against Ev's chest. He picks her up, carries her to her chair, and puts her in it. He looks down at her for a moment, then moves away, to sit isolated on the stage. Oscar joins him. Shift.

OSCAR: She tells me you're bangin' Valma.

EV: If I wanted to bang someone, it sure as hell wouldn't be Valma.

OSCAR: So who are you bangin'?

EV: Has she posted that condom story in the staff room, or is it just you she told?

OSCAR: I asked you a question.

EV: I'm not bangin' anyone! Who the hell are you bangin'! . . . I . . . I lost Jack Robinson the other night. . . . I felt so goddamn bad. I thought he was gonna make it and then everything started shuttin' down. He gets pneumonia, we get that under control, then his heart starts givin' us problems, we get that solved, then his goddamn kidneys go—I don't know why, just one thing after another. Someone was callin' his name and I couldn't do a damn thing about it . . . and I felt so bad, I thought . . . I don't want to go home, you can see what she's like so . . . you know what I did? I bought a mickey of rum and that goddamn condom and I . . . I drove around for a coupla hours. And that was it. . . . That was it.

OSCAR: Things can't go on.

EV: Don't start on that give her more time shit. Her problem's got nothin' to do with time nor work nor any other goddamn thing.

OSCAR: Her problem is the crazy son-of-a-bitch she's married to.

EV: Who the hell is crazy here? I'm the one can't keep a bottle of booze in the house, I'm the one's gotta put the fear of God in the help so they're too damn scared to buy it for her—and now she's into the vanilla or any other goddamn thing she can pour down her throat! I can't keep pills in the bag and she'd let the kids starve to death if it weren't for the maid! I'm the one goin' eighteen hours a day tryin' to hold the fuckin' fort so I can hear you say what!? . . . That I'm crazy! I'm not a goddamn machine!!! I thought if anyone would understand, it would be you . . . and you . . . [*exits*]

OSCAR: Ev. Ev!

Oscar may exit after him. Shift. Bob runs her hand along the cushion in the chair. She gets on her knees, lifts the cushion up. Catherine watches her search. Katie observes, from a distance. Bob continues her search.

BOB: Everyone has something hidden in this house. I hid it and he hides it and you hide it.

CATHERINE: Do something.

BOB: Do something. Just like your father. Do, do, do.

CATHERINE: Just stop!

BOB: Just stop. [*finds the bottle of pills*] Stop doing. [*unscrews bottle; pours pills in hand; looks at Catherine*] Stop. [*swallows pills; settles back in chair; shuts eyes*]

> *Shift. Katie slowly approaches Bob. She and Catherine stand, looking at Bob. Pause.*

KATIE: She was blue. . . . I'd never seen anybody blue before. Robbie went in the kitchen and cried. I stood at the bottom of the stairs and watched them bring her down on a stretcher. I didn't cry. . . . I don't know what she took—was it the pills that made her sleep?

CATHERINE: Uncle Oscar said.

KATIE: She was asleep all right. And really blue. I thought . . . I thought . . .

CATHERINE: Go on, you can say it.

KATIE: I thought maybe she was dead. [*moves away*] . . . and now she's going to Connecticut? Will she be better then?

> *Catherine joins Katie.*

CATHERINE: Uncle Oscar said.

KATIE: All better?

> *Catherine doesn't answer.*

I wonder . . . do you know what I wonder? I wonder, did she take the pills to sleep like she sometimes does, or did she . . .

CATHERINE: It was

KATIE: An accident? . . . Sometimes I look . . .

CATHERINE: . . . in the mirror, I look in the mirror . . .

KATIE: . . . and I see Mummy and I see . . .

CATHERINE: . . . Gramma, and Mummy and me . . .

KATIE: . . . I don't want to be like them.

> *Shift. Oscar may enter. Bob is sitting. She will get up and very carefully tie her gown. There is a certain formality, seriousness, alienation, and deliberation about her. She moves and speaks somewhat slowly. Oscar stands a distance from her, still and watching.*

BOB: You have to get hold of things. Routine's important. Get out. Get around. Do things. The IODE, Bridge. . . . The doctors' wives have this sort of club that meets on a regular basis, I . . .

OSCAR: Tired?

BOB: No. Feeling fine. How do I look?

OSCAR: Good.

> *Bob moves to another chair and sits. Oscar remains in the same position, watching her. Bob doesn't speak till seated. She does not look at Oscar.*

BOB: Leisure activity is big. Structured leisure activity. Very big. [*pause*] Painting. I paint now. You know. [*pause*] Pictures. [*pause; speaks softly*] What else? [*pause*] Gorgeous place. If you'd been there, it would have been perfect. [*pause; speaks softly*] What else. [*pause*] Psychiatrists, psychiatrists. They ask you obvious things and you give them obvious answers. It's all very obvious. . . . Obvious . . . [*softly*] what else. [*long pause; softly*] Nothing . . . nothing else . . . I can't think of . . . anything else.

> *Bob sits very still. Oscar stands watching her. Bob begins to rock back and forth very slightly and sings very softly to herself. She is not singing words, but merely making sounds. Oscar moves to her. He stands behind her looking down for a moment. He slowly places a hand on her shoulder. She reaches up and holds his hand pressing it to her shoulder. She continues to rock slightly but the words of the song can be heard. She is singing 'Auld Lang Syne'. Oscar moves around her without letting go of her hand and draws her up to dance, which they do rather formally.*

BOB [*sings*]: Should auld acquaintance be forgot
> and never brought to mind
> Should auld acquaintance
> Be forgot—and auld lang syne
> an auld lang syne m'dear
> an auld lang syne

> *Bob begins to cry but continues singing and dancing.*

> Let's drink a cup of kindness up
> For auld lang syne.

> *Shift. Ev enters. He is isolated on stage. He carries his bag, and his hat is pushed back on his head. There is an air of powerful relaxation and poise about him. He might almost be standing in a glow of golden sunshine. When he speaks Bob and Oscar stop dancing. They turn to stare at him and Oscar will step away from Bob. Bob is drawn towards Ev, who does not acknowledge her.*

EV: I say three or four of us go in together. I mean look at the situation now. A patient comes in from Durham Bridge, and has to run all over this Christless city, GP here, lab tests there, pediatrician someplace else. I've got my eye on a place on the hill. We renovate it—

BOB: Bar date with him.

EV: And we open a Medical Clinic, lab, X-ray, everything in that one building—

BOB: And you don't call that—

EV: We solicit the best specialists we can to take office space there. We give the people of this goddamn province the medical care they deserve, without havin' to run all over hell and hackety to get it!

BOB: And I laughed—and he said—and it was so funny—such a long time ago . . . .

> *Shift.*

KATIE: You lied to me.

OSCAR: When?

KATIE: People do lie to me quite a bit. They think I don't know it, but I do.

OSCAR: I didn't mean to lie.

KATIE: You didn't tell the truth.

OSCAR: What did I lie about?

KATIE: Guess—one guess?

BOB: S'funny thing.

KATIE: You promised me she'd get better, Uncle Oscar! You promised and you lied.

> *Shift. Bob lights a cigarette during her speech. By the end of her speech it is apparent she's been drinking.*

BOB: The more you do of certain things, the less it seems you do. You fill your time up, my time's filled up. I sit at these tea luncheons, s'always . . . sherry. I hate sherry. I never have any sherry. I know what they think, but that's not the reason. I just don't like sherry. No. No sherry. [*pause*] Children are important. [*pause*] And the IODE . . . I go to—and bridshe, play a lot of bridshe, I'm good at that. Win, always win. . . . I like bridshe. And ahh [*pause*] I don't really like them but—everything's working for them and everything can work for me too. I can be them. It isn't hard, I can do it. If I . . . if I want to.

> *Bob moves to drawer, opens it and feels inside. She is looking for a bottle, slowly and methodically. She becomes aware of Katie watching her.*

BOB: What do you want?

KATIE: I don't want anything.

BOB: What're you doing?

KATIE: I'm watching you.

BOB: Your father tell you to do that?

KATIE: No.

BOB: Then why are you watchin'?

KATIE: I want to remember.

BOB: Remember what?

KATIE: Remember you.

BOB: I know what you're thinking. It's all right. You can say it . . . do you want me to say it?

KATIE: No.

BOB: I'm not afraid. I can say it.

KATIE: If I were you—I wouldn't let Robbie see me like that. It makes him feel bad. He has to pretend that you're sick.

BOB: What do you pretend, Katie?

KATIE: I don't have to pretend anymore.

CATHERINE: Katie.

> *Bob stops her search, turns to Katie.*

BOB: Did you take something of mine?

KATIE: Did I?

BOB: You took something of mine and I want it back.

KATIE: You can't have it back.

BOB: I want it back!

KATIE: It's gone.

BOB: No.

KATIE: I poured it out, let go!

BOB: Give it back!

CATHERINE: Don't.

Bob and Katie struggle.

BOB: You had no right you . . .

KATIE: Let go!

BOB: No.

CATHERINE: Let her go.

BOB: Give it to me.

KATIE: Let go, let go!

BOB: You you no right!

KATIE: Go!

Katie strikes Bob, knocking her down.

I'm not gonna cry. I'm not gonna cry!

BOB: I tried. I really did try.

CATHERINE: I'm not gonna cry.

BOB: Listen.

Bob grabs Catherine's hand.

Listen Katie. I want . . . I want to tell you—when—when I was little, do you know, do you know I would sit on our front porch, and I would look up, look up at the sky, and the sky, the sky went on forever. And I just looked up. That was me, Katie. That was me.

CATHERINE: I'm holding my breath and my teeth are together and my tongue, I can feel my tongue, it presses hard on the back of my teeth and the roof of my mouth . . .

KATIE: . . . and I hang on really tight. Really tight, and then . . . I don't cry.

CATHERINE: I never cried . . . . [*to Bob*] but I couldn't listen like that.

Bob releases Catherine's hand and moves away from her. Catherine runs after her as she speaks.

CATHERINE: It's one of those things you can't do like that!

KATIE: It's better not to cry than to listen.

CATHERINE: Is it?

KATIE: It's how you keep on. It's one of the ways. I'm surprised you don't know that.

Katie moves away from Catherine, who then follows her. Shift.

EV: Close this time.

OSCAR: How close?

EV: Too damn close. We pumped her stomach and prayed. The kids spent Christmas Day at Valma's. . . . I think . . . I think the psychiatrist she sees is nuttier than she is. . . . I'm alright . . .

Ev sits in the same chair he sat in as 'Old Ev', at the start of the play. Pause.

Did you know . . . what the hell is their name . . . live over on King Street, married someone or other, moved to Toronto. . . . I'm alright. [*pause*] Some silly son of a whore didn't look close enough, she kept tellin' him she had this lump in her breast. . . . I'm alright. . . . She's got a three-month-old kid and she's come home to die. . . . Thing is no one's got around to tellin' her that's how it is. They asked me to come over and tell her . . . patients of mine . . . come home to die . . .

Oscar may exit. Pause. Ev takes Gramma's letter out of his pocket and looks at it.

EV: I'm alright . . .

Shift.

BOB: Open it! Go on, open it!

EV: You're drunk.

BOB: I'm drunk. So I'm drunk. What the hell are you, what's your excuse? What's his excuse, Katie?

EV: Leave her alone.

BOB: Why don't you open it!

EV: What for?

BOB: To see what it says.

EV: Says nothing.

BOB: Your father's mother killed herself, Katie. She walked across the train bridge at midnight and—

KATIE: That's an accident!

BOB: She left a letter and the letter tells him why she did it.

KATIE: What's in the letter, Daddy?

EV: Your Gramma—

Oscar may unobtrusively enter, and stand silently in the background.

BOB: She killed herself because of him!

KATIE: Because of you!

EV: Your Gramma loved us.

KATIE: Why don't you open it?

EV: She didn't see us so she'd write.

BOB: So open it!

EV: That's all it is.

BOB: Pretending! He's pretending!

KATIE: He is not!

BOB: He pretends a lot!

KATIE: You do!

BOB: Valma! Valma! Valma!

KATIE: I hate you!

BOB: Not afraid to say it!

KATIE: I hate you and I wish that you were dead!

CATHERINE: No.

KATIE: It's true!

CATHERINE: No.

KATIE: I wish and wish and

CATHERINE: No.

KATIE: someday you will be dead and I'll be happy!

OSCAR: It's alright, Katie!

KATIE [*to Ev*]: You all say she's sick, she isn't sick.

BOB [*to Katie*]: Katie!

KATIE: She's a drunk and that's what we should say!

BOB [*to Catherine*]: Katie!?

CATHERINE: Stop.

KATIE: And if I find her next time, I won't call for Daddy!

CATHERINE: No.

KATIE: I won't call for anyone!

CATHERINE: Stop Katie please.

KATIE [*sits*]: I'll go back downstairs and I'll sit in the kitchen and I'll pretend that I don't
    know, I'll pretend that everything's all right, I'll shut my eyes, and I'll pretend!

BOB: Katie! [*retreats*]

KATIE [*chants*]: Now they're married wish them joy

BOB: Katie. [*exits*]

KATIE [*puts hands over ears; chants louder*]:
    First a girl for a toy
    Seven years after seven years to come

BOB [*voice-over on mike, offstage*]: Katie!

KATIE [*chants louder*]: Fire on the mountain
    kiss and run
    on the mountains berries sweet

BOB [*on mike, offstage*]: Katie!

KATIE [*chants*]: Pick as much as you can eat
    By the berries bitter bark

BOB [*on mike, offstage*]: Katie!

KATIE [*chants louder*]: Fire on the mountain break your heart
    Years to come—kiss and run
    bitter bark—break your heart

Katie slowly takes her hands from her ears. There is silence. Pause.

I don't hear you! [*pause*] I don't hear you! [*pause*]! I don't!

Katie jumps up and whirls around, to look over at where she last saw Bob. Pause.

KATIE [*softly*]: I don't hear you at all.

CATHERINE: You can cry, Katie . . . it's all right to cry . . .

KATIE: Would you want to have me?

CATHERINE: Yes, yes I would.

Shift.

EV: All over now.

Ev gets up from the chair and moves to the table where Catherine left the jewellery box in Act One. He stands, looking down at it.

CATHERINE: No, Daddy.

OSCAR: When was it we played scrub hockey on the river ice. . . . Ev and Oscar, Oscar, Ev. . . . 'We're rough, we're tough, we're from Devon, that's enough' . . .

Ev lifts the lid of the music box. It plays 'Smoke Gets in Your Eyes'.

. . . driving my old man's car, watering his whisky, Ev and Oscar . . .

EV: Ever since Grade One.

OSCAR: I knew you then, and I knew you after that, and then I got to know you less and less—and here we are. . . . I said why risk it? And I saw her and knew why . . . well, she's gone now. . . . What the hell does that mean to you, Ev. That's something I want to know. What's it mean? . . . For Christ's sake, say something, say anything.

EV: There's nothing to say.

OSCAR: It shouldn't have happened.

EV: It did. [*closes the music box*]

OSCAR: She asked for goddamn little and you couldn't even give her that.

EV: You got no more idea of what she wanted that I have.

OSCAR: You never knew her and you don't know me.

EV: How can you say that? I carried you on my back since Grade One cause I liked you, I loved you, like a brother.

OSCAR: I could see it in my father, I can see it in you. You got your eyes fixed on some goddamn horizon, and while you're striding towards that, you trample on every goddamn thing around you!

EV: The biggest dream you ever had, what the hell was it? What was it, Oscar? New Orleans! New Orleans.

OSCAR: She understood what that meant.

EV: Bullshit. You been a pseudo-doctor for your old man, a pseudo-husband to my wife, and a pseudo-father to my kids! I gave you that, Oscar, like I gave you everything else cause I knew you'd never have the goddamn gumption to get it for yourself!

OSCAR: I should have taken your wife.

EV: My wife wouldn't have you!

Oscar starts to leave. Ev calls after him.

She knew you! She knew what you were! And because of that you say I killed her! It was all my fault?

Oscar stops. Ev moves to him.

Supposin' it were, her death my fault, put a figure on it, eh? Her death my fault on one side—and the other any old figure, thousand lives the figure—was that worth it?

Oscar exits.

Was it? I'm askin' you a question! Was that worth it!

Silence. Shift. Katie approaches Ev. As he removes his overcoat, he speaks to her.

What the hell do you mean?

KATIE: I don't know what I mean.

EV: Where the hell would you go?

KATIE: I don't know. Away. Away to some school.

EV: I don't want you to go.

KATIE: Send me anyway. For me, Daddy. Do it for me.

EV: What if I said no?

KATIE: You won't say no.

EV: You wanna hear me say no!

KATIE: I'm like you Daddy. I just gotta win—and you just gotta win—and if you say no—you'll have lost. [*exiting as she speaks*] I'll come back . . . every once in a while . . . I'll come back . . .

EV: Katie? [*screams*] Katie!

CATHERINE: I'm here.

Shift. Catherine and Ev are alone on stage. As Catherine speaks, Ev puts on his old cardigan, which was hanging on the back of his chair. He puts on his glasses. Catherine has Gramma's letter.

Do you remember when she gathered together all the photographs and snapshots, all the pictures of her, and she sat in the living room, and she ripped them all up? So . . . after she died, we had no pictures of her. . . . And Oscar, remember Oscar came over with one . . . it was taken at a nightclub somewhere, and she was feeding this little pig—a stupid little pig standing on the table and she—she was feeding it with a little bottle like a baby's bottle . . .

EV: Her with . . .

CATHERINE: . . . a baby bottle feeding the pig with a bottle . . .

EV [*small chuckle*]: Her and Oscar at some goddamn Caribbean nightclub feedin' a pig . . .

CATHERINE: Like a baby. She was looking up at the camera. She was smiling a bit. You could see her teeth. She didn't look happy, or unhappy. She looked like she was waiting. Just waiting.

EV: For what?

CATHERINE: I don't know. But whatever it was, she couldn't grab it.

EV: Do you know what you want?

CATHERINE: . . . Yes . . . Yes, I do.

EV: Then you grab it.

CATHERINE [*Pause; looks at Gramma's letter, which she is holding in her hand*]: What are you gonna do with this?

EV: Do you wanna open it?

CATHERINE: I can. Do you want me to?

EV: I know what's in it.

> *Pause. Catherine strikes a match. She looks at Ev.*

CATHERINE: Should I? . . . should I? . . .

> *Catherine blows the match out and gives the letter to Ev. He sits looking at it for a moment.*

EV: Burn the goddamn thing.

> *Ev holds the letter out. Catherine sets it on fire and it flares up as Ev holds it.*

CATHERINE: Be careful!

EV: I am bein' careful.

> *Ev drops the burning envelope into an ashtray. Lights are fading.*

Two minutes home and you're as bad as Valma.

CATHERINE: Bullshit, Daddy.

EV: Jesus Christ I hate to hear a woman talk like that.

> *As the lights fade to black, Catherine looks to Ev and smiles. Black except for the dying flame of the letter.*

The End

1986

Michel Tremblay

b. 1942

Born in Montreal, Michel Tremblay wrote his first play, *Le Train*, which won first prize in Radio-Canada's Young Authors' Competition, at the age of sixteen. His first staged play, *Les Belles-soeurs* (1968), revolutionized Quebec theatre with its use of *joual*, the language of working-class Montrealers, and its forthright presentation of marginalized characters. For all of its verbal comedy and abundant farce, it depicts the sheer emptiness of contemporary urban existence and the bitter alienation of the Quebec people. The play has been translated into many languages and staged throughout the world. The novels of his 'Chroniques du Plateau Mont-Royal' are semi-autobiographical fictions that further explore the world created in his plays. *For the Pleasure of Seeing Her Again*, which premiered in English on 1 October 1998 in Montreal, explores the relationship between Tremblay and his mother in the conversations between the narrator and Nana.

For the Pleasure of Seeing Her Again[1]

The stage is empty.

The narrator enters, sits down on a chair where he will stay until the end.

He can move, gesticulate, cross his arms and legs, but he should not leave the chair until the last few minutes of the play.

Nana, on the other hand, takes over the stage the minute she arrives, she fills it, dominates it, makes it her kingdom.

It is her space.

NARRATOR: Tonight, no one will rage and cry: 'My kingdom for a horse!' No ghost will come to haunt the battlements of a castle in the kingdom of Denmark where, apparently, something is rotten. Nor will anyone wring her hands and murmur: 'Leave, I do not despise you.' Three still young women will not retreat to a dacha, whispering the name of Moscow, their beloved, their lost hope. No sister will await the return of her brother to avenge the death of their father, no son will be forced to avenge an affront to his father, no mother will kill her three children to take revenge on their father. And no husband will see his doll-like wife leave him out of contempt. No one will turn into a rhinoceros. Maids will not plot to assassinate their mistress, after denouncing her lover and having him jailed. No one will fret about 'the rain in Spain!' No one will emerge from a large garbage pail to tell an absurd story. Italian families will not leave for the seashore. No soldier will return from World War II and bang on his father's bedroom door, protesting the presence of a new wife in his mother's bed. No evanescent blonde will drown. No Spanish

1 translated by Linda Gaboriau

nobleman will seduce a thousand and three women, nor will an entire family of Spanish women writhe beneath the heel of the fierce Bernarda Alba. You won't see a brute of a man rip his sweat-drenched t-shirt, shouting: 'Stella! Stella!' and his sister-in-law will not be doomed the minute she steps off the streetcar named Desire. Nor will you see a stepmother pine away for her new husband's youngest son. The plague will not descend upon the city of Thebes, and the Trojan War will not take place. No king will be betrayed by his ungrateful daughters. There will be no duels, no poisonings, no wracking coughs. No one will die, or, if someone must die, it will become a comic scene. No, there will be none of the usual theatrics. What you will see tonight is a very simple woman, a woman who will simply talk. . . . I almost said, about her life, but the lives of others will be just as important: her husband, her sons, her relatives and neighbours. Perhaps you will recognize her. You've often run into her at the theatre, in the audience and on stage, you've met her in life, she's one of you. She was born, it's true, during a specific era in this country and lived her life in a city that resembles this city, but, I am convinced, she is everywhere. She is universal. She is Rodrigue's aunt, Electra's cousin, Ivanov's sister, Caligula's stepmother, Mistress Quickly's little niece, the mother of Ham or of Clov, or perhaps of both. And when she speaks in her own words, people who speak differently will understand her, in their own words. She has existed throughout the ages and in every culture. She always has been present and always will be. I wanted the pleasure of seeing her again. The pleasure of hearing her. So she could make me laugh and cry. One more time, if I may. [*He looks towards the wings.*] Aha, I hear her coming. Get ready, she'll talk a blue streak, because words have always been her most effective weapon. [*He smiles.*] As they say in the classics: 'Hark, she cometh this way!'

Enter Nana.

She is visibly furious.

NANA: Go to your room. Right this minute! How could you do such a thing? At your age! Ten years old, you should know better! No, it's not true, how can I say that, at ten, you can't be expected to know much. Maybe you've reached the age of reason, but you're inexperienced. At ten, you're just a stupid kid, and you act like a stupid kid! But still, I thought you'd be smart enough to know not to do something like this!

NARRATOR: I didn't do it on purpose.

NANA: You didn't do it on purpose?! You threw a chunk of ice under a moving car, don't try to tell me you didn't do it on purpose! That chunk of ice didn't take off by itself.

NARRATOR: Everybody was doing it!

NANA: Listen to that! How smart can you get! Everybody was doing it! Since when do you have to act like everybody else? If everybody decides to go lick a frozen fence post, are you going to risk tearing off the tip of your tongue and lisping for the rest of your life, just to act like everybody else?

NARRATOR: If I hadn't done it—

NANA: If you hadn't done it, none of this would have happened, and I wouldn't have been so ashamed of you! Do you realize what I just went through? Eh? Do you? You don't seem very upset. There I was quietly doing my wash, pulling your father's drawers through the wringer, listening to the radio, I think I was even singing, and the doorbell rings. I didn't have time to go to the door, besides I thought it was the kid from Provost's Market who'd come to deliver the meat, so I yelled: 'C'mon in, door's not locked!' as loud as I could, hoping he'd hear me, and I kept pulling stuff through the wringer. But nothing happened, so I turned around. I thought maybe the kid from Provost's was too shy to walk through to the kitchen. . . . And what do I see burst into my dining room? A policeman! A policeman in uniform! In my own dining room! With his cap on his head and his heavy winter coat! Barefoot 'cause he had the decency to take his boots off in the hall! A policeman standing barefoot in my dining room, how do you think I felt! Of course, you're nowhere in sight, you're hiding in your room, so how was I supposed to know he'd come for you! Do you know what I thought? I thought someone had died! I thought someone was *dead!* Your father, or one of your brothers, or you! Do you know what went through my mind, eh, have you any idea? Maybe it only lasted a few seconds, who knows, but I saw a corpse, covered with a plaid blanket, cut in two by a streetcar or squashed by a bus, and that corpse was one of you! All I could see was a hand sticking out from under that blanket and I had to guess whose hand it was! Do you realize how that makes a mother feel? Eh? Answer me!

NARRATOR: You're pretty melodramatic, Ma.

NANA: Don't you talk to me like that! Just wait till a bare-socked policeman brings me back cut in two under a plaid wool blanket, young man, then we'll see which one of us is more melodramatic! I could've got my arm caught in the wringer! Right up to the elbow! Up to my armpit! Like your Aunt Gertrude!

NARRATOR: Aunt Gertrude—

NANA: Forget your Aunt Gertrude and listen to me, I haven't finished! So there I am, my jaw hanging open, facing the policeman, with one of your father's drawers caught in the wringer, spinning round and round, and I felt like the kitchen floor was about to cave in and I was going to end up downstairs, lying spreadeagle on Madame Forget's kitchen table with bits of baloney sandwiches stuck to my back!

The narrator laughs.

Don't laugh, it's not funny!

NARRATOR: Don't tell me you thought about the baloney sandwiches, Ma, you just added that now—

NANA: Maybe they weren't baloney sandwiches, but I felt them sticking to my back just the same!

NARRATOR: Ma. . . .

NANA: Shut up and listen to me! I can never get a word in edgewise around here!

The narrator shakes his head and tries not to smile.

I didn't dare ask him who had died, you hear me, I was afraid I'd collapse and die right there myself. . . . Two deaths in the family, the same day, that's one too many! But no! Nobody died! It was just . . . just that my stupid kid had been arrested like a highway robber because he was fooling around with his stupid friends, throwing chunks of ice under the cars going by! Imagine how ashamed I was! Ten years old! Ten years old and a delinquent already! Do you know what went through my mind when he told that? Any idea? Do you know what I saw?

The narrator raises his eyes to heaven.

Don't roll your eyes like that, how many times do I have to tell you, I hate it when you do that! While he was telling me about your little . . . mishap, there I was, picturing you locked up in jail for the rest of your life! I could see you, my own kid, behind bars for the rest of your days. I saw you growing up, getting married, having kids. . . . [*She realizes what she just said.*] I don't mean you got married and had kids in jail, I mean, I saw you spending the rest of your days, in and out of jail, and then. . . . Oh, now I'm all mixed up. I know you're laughing at me, and that always makes me upset! I don't feel like spending the rest of my life with a bag of oranges in one hand and a hankie in the other, every Sunday afternoon, visiting you in some jail, is that clear?

NARRATOR: It wasn't that serious, what I did, Ma, you shouldn't get all upset like that . . . and the policeman didn't come just because of the chunk of ice——

NANA: So why did he come, then, just to scare the wits out of me? Just to upset me?

NARRATOR: Didn't he tell you what happened?

NANA: Maybe he did, but he could've been speaking Chinese, I wouldn't have noticed, I was so upset. . . .

NARRATOR: Listen, I'll tell you what happened.

NANA: Make it fast. You always go into too much detail.

NARRATOR: But I don't want you to punish me. . . .

NANA: Well, I'll be the judge of that, young man, you hear me?

NARRATOR: I should have kept my mouth shut. If you didn't listen to him, you don't know what happened——

NANA [*threateningly*]: I promise I'll listen to every word you have to say.

NARRATOR: And I'm gonna get it afterwards. . . .

NANA: You were asking for it. Go on, I'm listening.

NARRATOR: Oh, God!

NANA: Don't take the Lord's name in vain! Not in front of me! How many times do I have to tell you, it's just as bad as swearing! You're looking for trouble, buster.

NARRATOR: Now I'm not so sure I want to tell you what happened.

NANA: Well, now I want to know! Let's hear it!

NARRATOR: It's true that me and my friends were throwing chunks of ice, but we weren't throwing them under the cars. We were aiming in front of the cars, before they arrived, to see how the drivers would react, to see if they'd slam on the brakes or just slow down. . . . It was only a game, Ma . . . it wasn't serious. . . . Most of the time, the drivers didn't even notice because the chunks of ice were too small. Then, when it was my turn, I chose a chunk that was a bit bigger, to make sure the guy driving down the street would see it . . . that's when Jean-Paul Jodoin held my arm. I struggled, finally pulled away from him, and the chunk of ice landed too late, it rolled under the back wheels of the car . . . and the guy thought he had run over a kid.

NANA: So that's the bit about the run-over kid! I knew there was something about a run-over kid! He got out of his car thinking he had run over a kid, and all he found was a chunk of ice! No wonder he called the cops! Can you imagine how he felt? Eh? Can you imagine what he went through, the poor guy, thinking he'd driven over the body of some poor little kid who was trying to cross the street! Maybe crawling across the street on all fours! He probably thought it was a baby who'd escaped from his mother and was crawling across the street on all fours! Good heavens! Poor man! You're lucky he didn't strangle you right on the spot! That's what I would have done, for sure, I would've driven over you with my car! And I'm not kidding! Well, believe you me, you're going to pay for this, I'm not going to forget this in a hurry!

NARRATOR: I didn't do it on purpose, Ma!

NANA: Stop saying that! If you weren't such a copycat, things like this wouldn't happen!

NARRATOR: It's the first time it's happened!

NANA: That's no excuse! Can't you think for yourself? Can't you tell when your friends are saying stupid things, when they're doing stupid things? Do I always have to be standing beside you telling you what to do, saying do this, that's fine, don't do that, it's dangerous?

NARRATOR: They'd played this game before and they said it was fun. . . .

NANA: Great, here we go again! If they told you it was fun to put your neck through the wringer, I suppose you'd believe them!

NARRATOR [*sarcastically*]: Maybe it is fun to put your neck through the wringer!

NANA: Hey, don't get smart with me! Your wisecracks aren't going to work today, I'm warning you! When I think of that poor little kid squished under the tires of that big car. . . . And the poor mother!

NARRATOR: Ma, there wasn't any run-over kid. . . .

NANA: A good thing, too! That's all I needed! A criminal in the family! The embarrassment! The relatives! The neighbours! I'd have to wear more than a little veil to Sunday mass, I'd have to wear a gas mask! Next time your friends talk about playing some stupid game, think of your poor mother who doesn't feel like wearing a gas mask to church on Sunday, just because she's ashamed of her ten year old son!

NARRATOR: Stop saying you're ashamed of me, I hate that!

NANA: You can't expect me to say I'm proud of you, there's a poor man who almost died of a heart attack because you made him think he left some kid flat as a pancake! No wonder he called the police! If it had been me, I would've taken care of you myself! And believe you me, it's not the chunk of ice that would be in bad shape! Arghh, there's no point in arguing with you, we always end up going round in circles, and there's no end to it. All I'm asking is, in the future, just think twice before you do something stupid like that! And if your friends make fun of you

'cause you don't do what they say, tell them you don't want to be a copycat, you
don't want to waste your life doing what other people tell you to do, acting like a
smart aleck, just so you can end up spending your life in Bordeaux jail!

NARRATOR: Did you really imagine me in jail?

NANA: With a skullcap on your head, and a pair of striped pyjamas! And believe me,
you were dragging your tail between your legs!

The narrator smiles.

NARRATOR: The other day, Jean-Paul Jodoin's mother asked me where I got my
imagination.

NANA: Next time, you tell her that imagination can help a person avoid a lot of trouble! I'd rather imagine the worst and be relieved, than imagine nothing, and be
surprised when trouble strikes! In the meantime, go pick up my order at Provost's,
looks like the kid went on vacation!

NARRATOR: You're not going to punish me? A little while ago, you said you were going
to punish me.

NANA: Were you scared when that guy jumped out of his car?

NARRATOR: Sure, I was.

NANA: And when the policeman showed up?

NARRATOR: Even more.

NANA: Well, that's enough punishment for today. The police, that's the worst
punishment!

She heads for the wings and pauses.

By the way, how did that guy figure out it was you who threw the chunk of ice
under his car?

NARRATOR: The other kids told on me.

She stares at him briefly.

NANA: I guess I don't have to say any more, eh? That says a lot about your friends'
solidarity!

She heads for the wings and pauses again.

If that guy takes us to court, I'll deny that you're my son, I'll say I adopted you,
that your real parents were bandits and I'm not responsible for your stupid behaviour. And don't count on me to come visiting you in Reform School!

She turns to face him.

Reform School! You know what that means? *She exits.*

NARRATOR: Need I say that the threat of Reform School hung over my entire childhood?

Nana reenters.

NANA: That's where they send stupid kids like you, the wiseguys, the tough guys, the
hotheads, the birdbrains, the copycats, and they shave their heads and stick them

in a pair of pyjamas made of burlap sacks and sentence them to hard labour! Instead of going to school, they crush stones with pickaxes, you think you'd enjoy that!? In your case, I'll tell them you prefer chunks of ice.   *She exits.*

NARRATOR: She'll be back. She's got something on her mind.

Nana returns.

NANA: Did I ever tell you what really happened to Aunt Gertrude?

NARRATOR: Yes, Ma, lots of times.

NANA: Listen to this. She was doing her wash, just like me this morning, and like me, she'd reached the point where she was pulling it through the wringer. But her washing machine wasn't as modern as mine, mine's electric, so she had to keep turning this big handle with her right hand while she slipped the wet clothes through the wringer with her left. You follow me?

She mimes the gestures she has just described.

NARRATOR: Sure, it's clear.

NANA: Good. She says she was daydreaming, I say she's crazy. Anyway. Apparently the phone rang and she wanted to finish pushing your Uncle Alfred's pyjama bottoms through the wringer before she answered, but she got all nervous—you know how she is—and she caught the tip of her left hand in the wringer. So far, it's not so bad, it happens to all of us. A little pinch, you pull your hand out, you blow on it, and you go back to work. But not her, she's so crazy she forgot to stop turning the handle with her right hand! How dumb can you get! So she keeps cranking away and the phone keeps on ringing . . . and before you know it she's put her whole arm through the wringer, and it wasn't even automatic, right up to the armpit! Can you believe it, she cranked her own arm through the wringer! She's so crazy, if it was possible, I'm sure she would've put her whole body through, and her husband would've come home from work and found her in the wet laundry basket, all wrung out, flat as a pancake! They had to stitch her up, from the tip of her indexed finger right up to her armpit! When she came over, after that, she showed us her operation, and I'm telling you, I almost lost unconsciousness, it was so ugly! Imagine, she had stitching that ran all the way up . . . through the fat part of her arm, and you know how flabby the fat part of her arm is . . . all she has to do is give it a little tap and it starts shaking like a bowl of jello. . . . She might be my sister-in-law, but I'm telling you, she's no genius. . . .   *She exits.*

NARRATOR: My Aunt Gertrude only pinched the tips of her index and middle fingers, and they were bruised for a few days—

Nana returns.

NANA: Did you believe everything I just told you?

NARRATOR: I knew there was more to come.

NANA: I'm talking to you!

NARRATOR: No, Ma, I didn't believe everything you just told me.

NANA: Good, I'm glad. You're not as gullible as I thought. Next time your friends tell you crazy stories, and they promise you the world if you do what they say, just remember the story of Aunt Gertrude. Divide everything by ten, and that'll give you an idea of how much fun is really in store for you! *She exits.*

The narrator smiles.

NARRATOR: Sometimes she was the only one who understood the point of her stories.

He takes out a copy of Patira *by Raoul de Navery, places it on his lap.*
Nana returns.

NANA: You finished it already?
NARRATOR: It doesn't take forever to read that kind of book, Ma—
NANA: But you had three of them to read.
NARRATOR: One day each, it's enough.
NANA: Beautiful books, aren't they?
NARRATOR: Hmmmm, yeah.
NANA: You don't seem so sure—
NARRATOR: Oh, they're beautiful. Real beautiful, but—
NANA: There are no buts about it! They're beautiful, period. Anyway, I loved every page of them. So don't start criticizing them in front of me, you understand?
NARRATOR: I wasn't criticizing, Ma, I didn't say anything!
NANA: You didn't say anything yet, but I can see it coming!
NARRATOR: C'mon, Ma! I told you I thought they were beautiful! But there were some things I didn't understand—
NANA: Oh, well . . . . If that's the problem. . . . What didn't you understand? Seems to me they're pretty easy to understand.
NARRATOR: The story's easy to follow, but. . . . How come, in all French novels, there are always some abandoned children?
NANA: What do you mean? Are there that many?
NARRATOR: If you ask me, yes. In *Guardian Angel Inn*, both kids have been abandoned, in *The Foundling*, little Rémi was abandoned, it's always happening in fairy tales. . . . And now, in *Patira*—
NANA: Poor little Patira, doesn't he just break your heart—
NARRATOR: Sure he does, but. . . . Do the French really go around abandoning their kids like that? Their books make it sound like the roads of France are full of abandoned children who are starving to death and filthy dirty—
NANA: They're only books—
NARRATOR: I know they're only books, but still, it seems to happen all the time—
NANA: These books take place in the past. . . . Maybe in the past, I don't know, maybe people in France abandoned their kids more than today, because they couldn't support them—
NARRATOR: Sure, but there are poor people here, too, and you don't see abandoned kids on every street corner! C'mon, people don't abandon their kids like that! I don't believe it! Didn't those people ever get arrested?

NANA: Well, as far as that goes. . . . Listen. . . . There are books where mothers abandon their babies on the church steps. Nobody can catch them that way, for sure! You can't ask a newborn baby to remember his father or his mother! Especially when the mother's an unmarried mother who dumped him there the day after he was born!

NARRATOR: I don't see how you can defend them—

NANA: I'm not defending them, I find it as awful as you do, but what can I say? I'm trying to find an explanation! You asked me a question, I'm trying to find an answer. Maybe there are lots of abandoned children in novels because it's an interesting way to start a story! We want to find out where they come from, why their parents didn't want them. . . . Take little Patira, when he's abandoned by those jugglers who raised him without even knowing where he came from, it makes you want to know where he comes from right away! So you go on reading the book! And . . . how do I know?! What kind of a question is that anyway?

NARRATOR: If you had been poor, you never would've abandoned me on the church steps!

NANA: I was poor, believe me!

NARRATOR: So, you see!

NANA: Maybe I just didn't have the guts!

NARRATOR: Ma!

NANA: C'mon, I'm just kidding! I never would've abandoned you, I wanted you too badly! But had I known—

NARRATOR: Very funny!

NANA: Anyway, things are different in France!

NARRATOR: That's what I wanted to know.

NANA: Now don't you make me say things I don't mean!

NARRATOR: You just admitted that things are different in France!

NANA: I don't mean that the French go around abandoning their kids, so don't you dare repeat that, I know you, yakety-yakking everywhere, and I'll look like a real shrew. Maybe the French only do that in their books.

NARRATOR: Aren't books supposed to be like real life?

NANA: Now you're testing my patience!

NARRATOR: I'm not testing your patience, I'm asking you a simple question!

NANA: What do you expect me to say? I'm no expert on literature! I just enjoy reading books, I like following the story and I cry when it's sad and I laugh when it's funny. I don't stop to ask myself a thousand questions after every sentence. I'd never get to the end of Chapter One! I can tell if I like a story or not, and I read it or I don't, period! What do I care if the French abandon their kids or not, as long as the story about Patira makes me cry! And believe you me, I cried so much reading *Patira*, I felt like I'd lost ten pounds by the time I finished the book, so I was very happy, you hear me!

NARRATOR: You always cry when you read.

NANA: I like sad books.

NARRATOR: Well, you got your money's worth this time!

NANA: Sure did! When poor Blanche de Coed-Queen. . . .

NARRATOR: Coëtquen, Ma.

NANA: That's what I said.

NARRATOR: You said Coed-Queen.

NANA: I got used to reading it that way, it was easier to remember. Anyway, when poor Blanche however you say it gave birth to her baby in the dungeon of the castle because her two brothers-in-law had kept her locked up there for the past six months, the heartless creeps, and when Patira arrived with his little file to saw the thick bars, and Blanche passed her baby through the cellar window, then Patira put the baby on some reeds tied together like a raft, what can I say—

NARRATOR: The whole story is kind of ridiculous—

NANA: What do you mean, ridiculous—

NARRATOR: Well, locking a poor pregnant woman up in a dungeon in the middle of winter—

NANA: Heartless creeps don't wait for warm weather, young man. They were jealous because they said she had usurped, that's the word they used, that she had usurped her title of Marquise, and they wanted to get rid of her, no matter what! They were prepared to do anything, and they did!

NARRATOR: Ma! Blanche de Coëtquen spends the *whole* winter locked up in a dungeon so damp water trickles down the walls, she sleeps on a straw mat on a wooden shelf, all she eats is black bread and stagnant water, there are floods in the spring, the cold water comes up to her chin, she can't change her clothes, she gives birth to her baby lying there in the dark on her wooden shelf, with no doctor to help her, she saws the bars of her prison with a tiny little file, she scrapes her hands so bad they're bleeding, she doesn't have any mercurochrome to put on her cuts, *and she doesn't die!*

NANA: What do you mean, she doesn't die! She certainly does die! She dies at the end of the first book, and it's so sad I thought I'd never recover!

NARRATOR: But before she dies, she's released by someone sleepwalking, she's reunited with her child *in the middle* of a fire that is devouring him and Jeanne, the crazy woman who's been taking care of him without knowing who he was, and——here we go again!——she's saved for the second time by Patira. Then she passes away peacefully, after kissing her child on the forehead and giving everyone her blessing! I mean, really!

NANA: If you didn't cry during that death, kiddo, you've got a heart of stone.

NARRATOR: Well, I guess I've got a heart of stone!

NANA: Don't say that! You're my son. No son of mine can have a heart of stone! When she realizes, just before she dies, that her hair had turned completely white while she was locked up, even though she's only *eighteen years old*, I thought I was going to die myself. . . . Don't tell me you didn't feel anything?

NARRATOR: I thought it made no sense at all. Eighteen years old and her hair's all white! C'mon!

NANA: Maybe it didn't make sense, but it was sad anyway.

NARRATOR: You see, you admit it didn't make sense!

NANA: Maybe it wouldn't have made sense in real life, but so what, it made sense in the book! And that's all that matters! All that nonsense you read, the adventures of

Biggles, and those novels by Jules Verne, and your Tintins, and the Scarlet Pimpernels, do you think all that would make sense in real life? Eh? No! But you believe it anyway.

NARRATOR: I want you to know that Jules Verne is based on science! But not this! Hey! She's locked up in a *castle*, it's not the size of Montreal, and nobody ever hears her calling for help!?

NANA: She's at the far end of the castle, in the depths of the moat, *in the dungeon*, it's explained very clearly, you have to admit that.

NARRATOR: And nobody ever goes near there!

NANA: Of course not! There are pools of water and mud, there are frogs and bugs. . . .

NARRATOR: C'mon! She could've called for help a little louder and everybody would've heard her!

NANA: People hear her when she yells, but they think it's a ghost! You're thirteen years old, don't you know how to read? They think it's the ghost of Lady Coed-Queen! There's a song about it in the book, 'n' everything! Did you skip some parts, or what?

NARRATOR: Of course not.

NANA: So you must've understood that when they hear her wailing, they're scared to death!

NARRATOR: How dumb can you get?

NANA: Okay, I think we better stop right here, or I'm going to lose my temper!

NARRATOR: Besides, doesn't that woman ever have to go to the bathroom?

NANA: What do you mean, go to the bathroom?

NARRATOR: Simon, the jailer, he brings her a pitcher of water every day, don't tell me she pees in the pitcher! And . . . where does she pooh?

NANA: Are you losing your mind? They're not about to tell us in books where people pooh!

NARRATOR: Why not? Didn't you ever wonder where she made pooh in her dungeon?

NANA: Not for one minute! I couldn't care less!

NARRATOR: Well, I care!

NANA: That figures! You and your father, you're all pee, pooh, snot, farts, and private parts, we know that! You love that kind of talk, makes you split a gut laughing! In your books by Jules Verne, do they say where people do all that?

NARRATOR: No, but when the characters are lost in the Amazon jungle, or in the back of beyond in the steppes of Russia, you can guess the answer, it's no big mystery. But her, c'mon, Ma! She spends the whole winter in a damp dungeon! She can't be constipated for six months! And if she's not constipated, and she does it in a corner of her cell, it must smell to high heaven after a few weeks, if Simon doesn't clean it up!

NANA: I refuse to let you make fun of one of my favourite books of all times, you hear me?

NARRATOR: I'm not making fun of it! I just would've liked to have that information, that's all!

NANA: Well, I wouldn't! First of all, it never even occurred to me that Blanche Coed-Queen would do such a thing! And how do you expect the author to describe that?

'She crouched in a corner and did her business. The jailer promptly arrived with a shovel and removed the little pile.' It's a novel, we don't need to know that! Last year, when you read *The Count of Monte Cristo*, and for two months straight you thought you were Edmond Dantès and wanted to take revenge on every human being you'd met in your life, did Alexandre Dumas tell you where his hero did that in **his** dungeon?

NARRATOR: No, I guess you're right.

NANA: And did you wonder?

NARRATOR: I guess not.

NANA: So, you see! You only wonder about that when it suits you! You wonder about it in *Patira* because I loved the book! You're just trying to make me mad! Well, you won't succeed! You can be so dishonest, sometimes!

NARRATOR: I'm not being dishonest, Ma, it's the first time I ever asked myself the question, that's all. Besides, the whole bit about her two brothers-in-law being jealous, I didn't believe all that. C'mon!

NANA: And why not?

NARRATOR: They never accepted her because she wasn't a real princess, and because she wasn't a real princess, she didn't deserve to belong to their family! Do *you* believe in that stuff?

NANA: Of course, I do! There are snobs everywhere! We've got one right here in this neighbourhood, a couple of blocks away, on Cartier Street! I could give you her name! But I'm a charitable soul, so I'll keep my mouth shut! She thinks she's a princess, puts on airs, struts around, dresses up like a Sunday mass day in and day out, and she forgets she came into this world under the Jacques-Cartier Bridge just like the rest of us!

NARRATOR: You didn't come into this world under the Jacques-Cartier Bridge, Ma.

NANA: You're right. I came into this world in the middle of the plains of Saskatchewan. . . . But I've been here so long I feel like a real Montrealer. . . . And believe you me, I don't think I'm a princess! That's one thing nobody can accuse me of! Unlike some people I know—

NARRATOR: Who are you talking about?

NANA: Never mind, it's not interesting.

NARRATOR: I'm interested—

NANA: Oh, I know you're interested! The minute there's a bit of gossip, you're right there. . . . Forget all that princess business, and concentrate on Patira's adventures!

NARRATOR: What is a real princess, anyway?

NANA: What do you mean, what is a real princess?

NARRATOR: I mean, what makes someone a real princess?

NANA: Well, she's the daughter of a king and a queen, it's as simple as that. You know that as well as I do.

NARRATOR: And what about her parents, how did they know they were a real king and a real queen?

NANA: It was the same for them, their parents were nobility.

NARRATOR: What does that mean, their parents were nobility?

NANA: You read French novels till they come out your ears, you must know what nobility is, don't make me waste my breath! It's people who have blue blood.

NARRATOR: Blue blood!

NANA: Right!

NARRATOR [*dubiously*]: When they cut themselves, it comes out blue!

NANA: No, it's a manner of speaking! It's an expression, their blood isn't really blue— but it's noble blood.

NARRATOR: I don't get it.

NANA: Listen. I'm no expert on French History, they taught us Canadian History out in Saskatchewan, but the way I understand it . . . when the first king of France appeared —

NARRATOR: And how did he know he was the king of France?

NANA: Listen, that's what I'm trying to explain to you! If I remember correctly, he was a Louis! They were all Louis, I think, the kings of France. . . . He must've been Louis One, or Louis the First. Anyway, the Good Lord appeared to him—

NARRATOR: The Good Lord appeared to him!

NANA: That's what they say.

NARRATOR [*jeering*]: He doesn't usually show up in person, he sends somebody else to represent him . . . like the Virgin Mary, or the angels—

NANA [*starting to lose her patience*]: Right, well, this time was special, it was for the king of France! And stop interrupting me! Anyway, apparently the Lord told him he'd been chosen to be the king of France, and from that moment on, so that everybody would recognize them, he and his descendants would have blue blood!

NARRATOR: But you told me their blood wasn't really blue!

NANA: I'm trying to explain to you that it's just an expression!

NARRATOR: Okay, but how can they know they have blue blood, if it isn't really blue?

NANA: They know, because they pass it on, from father to son! Like you, for instance, you have your father's name, well, you'd have blue blood if your father had had blue blood before you! Now do you understand?

NARRATOR: So that means Blanche de Coëtquen, when her name was still Blanche Halgan, didn't have blue blood because her father was just a ship's captain?

NANA: That's right. And since it's frowned upon for nobility—people with blue blood—to marry somebody who isn't nobility, the two Tanguy de Coed-Queen brothers can't forgive their brother for marrying the daughter of a ship's captain, instead of somebody more important.

NARRATOR: But when she married him, did her blood become blue?

NANA: No, that's the point! You don't get blue blood from your husband, you get it from your father!

NARRATOR: And their baby was born in the dungeon, I suppose his blood was half 'n' half?! That's stupid!

NANA: It's not stupid! It comes from the Good Lord!

NARRATOR: Honestly! All I'd have to do is claim that the Good Lord appeared to tell me he'd appointed me king of Canada, and then my blood would be blue?

NANA: Don't worry, if you said that, nobody would believe you!

NARRATOR: Exactly! So why did they believe him?

NANA: Because for him, it was true!

NARRATOR: It could be true for me, too!

NANA: I'm your mother, I'd know it wasn't true. Mothers know everything.

NARRATOR: Well he must've had a mother, too! And she believed him, and you say you wouldn't believe me!

NANA: How do I know, maybe he was a hero, maybe he saved his country from thieves and bandits, from the plague and dragons! And you haven't saved a darn thing!

NARRATOR: Give me time!

NANA: Okay, stop trying to get me going.

NARRATOR: You believe everything you read in your books!

NANA: Well, believe you me, it's a lot more interesting than arguing with you!

NARRATOR: It's like your stories about Aunt Gertrude, eh, Ma, you can't believe everything.

NANA: You've been asking questions since the day you were born, it's reached the point, a person doesn't know what to make up anymore!

NARRATOR: Ah ha! You just admitted it, sometimes you make things up!

NANA: If I lined up all the answers I've made up to answer all the questions you've asked since you were born, I might be a great novelist myself! And I'd make a fortune! And believe you me, we wouldn't stay cooped up on Cartier Street facing Mount-Royal Convent another day longer!

NARRATOR: What about the girls who go to the Mount-Royal Convent School, Ma, they're rich, aren't they?

NANA: I guess so! You can tell by the cars that deliver them every Sunday night!

NARRATOR: Do they have blue blood?

NANA: Of course not! Nobody has blue blood in America! Only in Europe!

NARRATOR: How come?

NANA: Don't ask me! Maybe because they've been around for longer than us. If we had been around earlier, maybe we'd have some blue bloods, too!

NARRATOR: What about your family . . . your grandparents were Cree from Saskatchewan—

NANA: On my mother's side.

NARRATOR: And they'd settled here a long time before the Europeans arrived—

NANA: I know—

NARRATOR: So how come the Good Lord never appeared to tell them they had blue blood? How come he just appeared in Europe? I don't think that's fair! There must've been a Cree somewhere who deserved to be declared noble like those guys on the other side.

NANA: It's true, actually, it's not fair. As far as that goes, you're right. But what do you expect, it comes from the Good Lord and the Cree didn't know the Lord. Or maybe he didn't know them.

NARRATOR: The Europeans are the ones who claim it comes from the Good Lord. Do we have to believe them? Did the Good Lord appear to tell you it was true, that he'd told all the first kings in Europe they had blue blood?

NANA: Listen, it all happened so long ago, somebody must've found proof, after all these years.

NARRATOR: Nobody's ever seen that proof.

NANA: Are you trying to tell me that the first one, there, Louis One, might've made all that up just to become the King of France, and that all the people who believed him were a bunch of dummies? That the kings of France were *usurpers*? Right up to the French Revolution?

NARRATOR: I don't know, I'm just asking—

NANA: That all the Louis, up to Louis . . . how many Louis were there, all together? Anyway, that they were all liars? You're such a doubting Thomas! Well, now there aren't any more kings of France. So that settles that.

NARRATOR: But there's still nobility.

NANA: Maybe—

NARRATOR: And there's still lots of blue bloods.

NANA: Not lots, but there are some left.

NARRATOR: There are lots of them in *Paris Match* magazine.

NANA: Maybe.

NARRATOR: There's even a queen in Belgium. And a brand new beautiful queen in England.

NANA: Oh yes, my pretty Princess Elizabeth who became queen so young! And her sister, Princess Margaret-Rose, too pretty for her own good! Don't you start criticizing them, you know how much I admire them! They might have blue blood, but those two girls aren't snobs, not one bit. They know how to behave, how to speak in public, and I'm telling you, they know how to wear a crown. They deserve to be noble, I can tell you that!

NARRATOR: Don't try to change the subject, Ma, I know how much you love the English royal family, you talk about them as if you'd grown up together, like they were next of kin! So, if I follow your logic, the Good Lord appeared to the first king of England, as well?

NANA: I guess so.

NARRATOR: And he told him the same thing as the other guy?

NANA: Probably, yes.

NARRATOR: In English!

NANA: If he spoke French to the other one, he must've spoken English to him! And Spanish to the King of Spain. And Italian . . . wait, is there a king of Italy?

NARRATOR: He sure speaks a lot of languages!

NANA: He's God! He's the one who invented them all at the Tower of Babel!

NARRATOR: Do you really believe all that?

NANA: I'm beginning to wonder, you know . . . I never thought about it that way. When you get right down to it, there must've been a Cree who deserved it, too.

NARRATOR: So, if we trace it back to the first king of France, nobility is something you deserve!

NANA: Right!

NARRATOR: So, Blanche de Coëtquen would've deserved to have blue blood when she married Tanguy, even if she wasn't born with it. . . .

NANA: Of course!

NARRATOR: And her two brothers-in-law, Florent and Gaël, were real bastards because they made their poor sister-in-law suffer like that!

NANA: That's what I've been trying to tell you!

NARRATOR: Blue blood or not. . . .

NANA: Right, and believe you me, I was happy when they paid for their crimes! I kissed the book, I held it to my heart—

NARRATOR: So, maybe the French Revolution was a good thing after all—

NANA: Of course, it was a good thing! I never said it wasn't! The poor people were dying of hunger while the nobility, the blue bloods, were stuffing their faces! Marie-Antoinette was gorging herself on Viennese pastry while the country was yelling their lungs out at the gates of Versailles, with their shovels, and scythes, and whips and torches! We saw the whole thing, in that film with Norma Shearer! But, wait, how come you're talking about the French Revolution all of a sudden? What's that got to do with anything?

NARRATOR: Because Raoul de Navery says the opposite in *The Treasure of the Abbey*, his sequel to *Patira*. . . . Now you're the one who skipped some parts. . . . He describes the revolutionaries as bloodthirsty monsters, they're all hunchbacks, ugly as sin, one-eyed cripples, they stink like the devil, and they kill all the poor blue bloods. . . . They're only interested in taking their place—

NANA: Now, just a minute, don't get me going again. . . . That's enough talk for this afternoon, we'll settle the problem of the French Revolution some other day. If you don't mind, we'll tackle volume two tomorrow! That's that trouble, when a person starts talking with you, there's no knowing where it will end!

NARRATOR: I wonder who I get that from—

NANA: Pardon me?

NARRATOR: I didn't say a thing—

NANA: If you didn't say a thing, you said it pretty loud, 'cause I heard you!

NARRATOR: Then why did you ask me to repeat it?

NANA: To see if you had the courage! To see if you deserved blue blood! And you flunked the test, you'll never become king, so go do the errands at Steinberg's instead, there's nothing in the house for supper. Anyway, next time I read a good book, I won't tell you! I'll keep it to myself, that way, I'll be sure to go on liking it.

She turns to exit, then turns back to him.

While you're out, you can stop by Shiller's and take these buttons back. They're too big for your father's buttonholes. And ask for my money back. If he asks any questions, just say: '*The woman* says she doesn't want them.'

NARRATOR: I hate it when you ask me to do that!

NANA: Why?

NARRATOR: Don't you think he knows it's my mother who's sent me? He's not crazy, he recognizes me!

NANA: I hope you never admitted it to him!

NARRATOR: You always told me never to lie!

NANA: Well, that's not a lie.

NARRATOR: Ma! Is it true? No. So, it's a lie.

NANA: Am I a woman or not? 'The woman says she doesn't want them'—it could be your mother or some other woman. That's what my mother used to call 'a little white lie'. Little insignificant lies we tell to protect ourselves.

NARRATOR: To protect ourselves?

NANA: Listen, if you say: 'My mother says she doesn't want them,' he won't listen and I'll never get my money back. But if you say: 'The woman says she doesn't want them,' he won't know if it's me or some other woman who stopped you on the street and asked you to do an errand for her, so he'll feel like he has to reimburse you!

NARRATOR: But he's not crazy, he knows you're the one who sent me!

NANA: I know, but I'm not crazy either! Since he can't be really sure, he'll give you the money back, it's less complicated for him and I win all down the line.

NARRATOR: Oh, my God!

NANA: Hey! What did I say! No swearing in this house!

NARRATOR: Saying, oh, my God, isn't swearing.

NANA: In my house it is! And as long as you're in my house, you follow my rules.

NARRATOR: Oh, my gosh!

NANA: That's no better, you just replace the 'sh' with a 'd' and you've got God.

NARRATOR: Oh, golly, then? Holly golly? Molly? What do you prefer?

NANA: Molly's fine. It's far enough away from Oh, my God. Now, get moving, get your gangly legs going down Mount Royal Street, and stop arguing. . . . Stop wagging your tongue and use your legs instead, it'll do you good. It'll do us both good! Here's the list for supper, I wrote everything out, and here's the buttons. Don't forget: 'The woman says she doesn't want them. . . .' [*She laughs.*] Good luck!

She exits laughing.

NARRATOR: Oh, goddamn!

She returns.

NANA: What a night! Couldn't fall asleep for the life of me! I lay there thinking. . . . Looking at the clock every ten minutes, knowing how hard it would be to get up this morning. . . . I couldn't stop thinking about that TV drama we watched together last night. You have to admit it was beautiful, 'nuff to make you cry. The sets . . . the costumes. Just like Russia last century. And such a beautiful story. . . . Really, for me to go to bed that late on a Sunday night. . . . But. . . . It's funny. . . . I don't know why . . . it's the first time I ever thought about it. . . . I lay down beside your father, and for once he wasn't snoring, for once I could've fallen asleep right away without having to smack him or shake him . . . but I was thinking about Huguette Oligny! You know, we were talking about her before we went to bed, but I couldn't stop thinking about her—that woman talked for almost two and a half hours straight, non-stop! Here we go, let me change costumes, here I am giving a party, now I've got a scene with this one, then a scene with that one. . . . She laughed, she cried, she got mad, she made up, she had love scenes, she was a flirt, she was tragic, she didn't stop once! And you told me it was all done live, like at the theatre, and that while we sat there watching her, she was performing in some studio down on Dorchester Street and they were filming it. . . . That she changed sets by ducking behind the cameras, that she changed costumes while the others were doing a scene while she was changing costumes. . . . And . . . I don't know. . . . It never occurred to me before, but . . . I guess it's because you've started to write plays you don't want me to read. . . . It's alright, don't worry, I understand, at sixteen it's normal not to want to tell your mother everything. . . . But that's not what I was thinking about, I was thinking about Huguette Oligny. . . . And I wondered. . . . Who is Huguette Oligny? You know what I mean? We always see her on TV. . . . She's always disguised as somebody else. . . . Yesterday she was a woman from Russia, last year, in that play that rhymed, you know, what's it called, she always wore the same long nightgown and it took place in Greece. . . . Anyway. Sometimes she's comical, sometimes she's amusing, she always has tons of lines to say. . . . but who is she, really? I mean, in real life? I know she's married, but when I see a picture of her in the TV guide, with her husband and kids, I don't find her as real as in 'A Month in the Country', last night. Strange, eh? I feel like she's playing some role in the photograph. We were wondering last night how she managed to learn all that by heart, two and a half hours of talk, how does she do it, but I went farther than that, I wondered . . . where was she when she learned all that by heart? I realize she must've been at home, she must have a house like everybody else, but where is she when she learns all that by heart? Is she sitting on a sofa, lying in her bed, soaking in her bath? Is she cooking supper? Doing the dishes? Is it easy? Does she find it hard? Does she have somebody help her? Does she talk out loud? Does she go over it in her head? Does she enjoy learning those lines, or does it drive her crazy? Believe me, I couldn't sleep a wink! At one point, your father woke up and I had to smack him in the back 'cause he lit up a cigarette. You know how I hate it when he smokes in bed. . . . He fell back to sleep, and I still couldn't stop thinking about it. When actors are rehearsing their plays, where do they do it? In the studio? Do they always wear their costumes? And how do they do it? How does it work? I never thought about all that before, you understand? I watch those shows as if they came out of the blue and disappeared back into the blue! I usually turn off the television set, and none of it exists anymore. No kidding! Last night I realized that the actors only exist for me when I see them on television! When Huguette Oligny finished her two and a half hour show last night, she stopped existing for us, at least, for me, even though we went on talking about her! As if your Aunt Gertrude and Uncle Alfred stopped existing when they leave the house after our Saturday night card game. Mind you, there are times when I wish they would, they drive me crazy, but that's beside the point. But what did she do last night, Huguette Oligny, when she finished taking off her makeup and changing her clothes? Did she go out with the other actors, or were they all too tired? Does she have a car? The woman who wore all those beautiful gowns, did she step on the gas to get home faster? That woman's been coming into my home since television began, and before that her voice was already here on the radio dramas and the Ford Theatre on Thursday nights, and I don't even know who she is! Then . . . it's strange, eh . . . really late, in the middle of the night, I lay there and wondered if she ever asked herself the same question about me. How crazy can you get! You know, they're there, they come into our homes every night. . . . Now don't you go thinking that I believe they can see us, you know I'm not as dumb as those people who get all dressed up to watch 'Concert Hour' on Sunday night, 'cause they think Jean Deslauriers can see them! Oh, no. But I said to myself, if I wonder who she is, does she ever wonder who I am, once in a while? I mean, not me personally, she doesn't know me, but the people who watch her spend a month in the country, or die in a Greek nightgown? Do the actors ever think about us? They can't see us, but they're staring into cameras, they know they're coming right into our homes. . . . Do they ever wonder: 'Where are they? In their living room? In the dining room? How many are there? Do they have company? Do they talk while we're saying our lines? Do they get up to go to the bathroom during the best scenes?' Or are we just like a great big empty black hole they carry on in front of, simply to earn a living? Is it clear, what I mean? I mean, they exist because we can see them, even though they're not in colour, but do we exist for them, too? Even the ones who act on stage, they might know there are people in the audience, but do they wonder what those people do after? Or does the audience stop existing for them the minute they walk out of the theatre? And the actors who work on television and on the radio, they have no contact with us, do they completely forget that we exist? You must think I'm crazy wondering about stuff like that, eh? But, you see, last night I was lying there beside my husband, thinking about Huguette Oligny, what a great actress she is, how beautiful she looks in those gowns, and I said to myself, I'd like to think that sometimes, when she's lying next to her husband, she wonders about me. I'd like to be as important in her life as she is in mine. But I guess that's too much to hope for. I don't dare ask what you think about all that, I know you want to land on the other side, part of their world, I've known that for a long time. . . . Once you're there, if you ever manage to get there, think about it and try to find an answer for me. . . . *She exits.*

NARRATOR: She never saw the wings of a theatre or a television studio, she never attended a rehearsal, a costume fitting, a preview or an opening night. She left without knowing how it all works. It's one of the greatest regrets in my life. I would have loved to introduce her to Huguette Oligny, so the possibility that Madame Oligny might think of her from time to time could exist.

Nana returns.

NANA: I'm telling you, there's no escaping that woman! Impossible! I don't know how she manages, I never see her coming, honestly, never! She cooks it up behind my back, then, I, dummy, fall right into it! Every time! And it's been going on for thirty years! More! *She always gets me to invite her to supper!* Can you tell me why? There's always some point where I hear myself say: 'Why don't you come for supper Saturday night?' Why do I say it? Do I feel obligated because her husband is your father's brother? Do I just say it to get off the phone because she talks so loud? Search me! It's a real mystery! Maybe she has hypnotical powers in her voice and I don't realize it! It just happened again, right now, do you believe it? She calls me supposedly just to say hello, I say to myself, 'Careful, it's Thursday, Saturday's right around the corner, watch out!' And sure enough! I don't know what she was rattling on about, how she roped me in, but the next thing I know, I'm saying that good goshdarn sentence, and they're coming for Saturday night supper again! I'm stuck with your aunt Gertrude, your Uncle Alfred and their boring daughter Lucille for another Saturday night supper! I know you like your cousin Lucille, but I'm telling you, that child sets my teeth on edge!

NARRATOR: She's not a child anymore, Ma.

NANA: How old are you now? Eighteen? Well, she's seventeen, it's true she's not a child anymore. Makes it all the worse!

NARRATOR: I know she bothers you because she's got some tics, but—

NANA: Tics? That kid is like a Christmas tree, blinking away non-stop! During her awkward stage, every time she left here with her parents, my face would go on twitching for hours!

NARRATOR: Ma. . . .

NANA: Ma, what?

NARRATOR: You promised you'd try not to exaggerate so much.

NANA: I tried, and I thought I was going to die of boredom! Things are never interesting enough when you describe them as is, c'mon! Just thinking about them showing up on Saturday night makes me want to pack my bags and take off for the planet Mars. How's that for an exaggeration, eh?

NARRATOR: Not bad—

NANA: If I didn't exaggerate, you'd think I was boring!

NARRATOR: That's true, but—

NANA: So don't nag me. I can see it all now. Your Uncle Alfred will take your father's place at the end of the table, and your father's too much of a coward to say anything, your uncle will light his damn pipe that smells like the devil who hasn't taken a bath since the Messiah appeared, and he'll start yakking about Fernandel! That man can only talk about one thing: *Fernandel!* Did you ever see anything like it? I ask you! Men his age, I don't know, seems to me they talk about Marilyn Monroe, or Lana Turner, or even hockey, but not him, he bends our ear about Fernandel! When he starts going on about the last Fernandel film he's seen, I don't know if you ever noticed, but I leave the room! I pretend I have to do something in the kitchen or I say I have to make a phone call, and I end up chatting with nobody at the other end of the line, but I have to do something, otherwise I'll smack him on the head! He talks like Fernandel, he imitates Fernandel's sissy gestures, and he *sings* like Fernandel! Oooff, when he starts singing with his Marseillais accent. . . . Look, just talking about it gives me hot flashes! If he tells us the story, if he acts out 'Coeur de coq' once more, I'm gonna have such a fit, they'll hear me all the way to Ausable Chasm!

They both laugh.

I'm pretty funny today, eh?

NARRATOR: Yes, you're in fine form!

NANA: No choice, otherwise I'd explode.

NARRATOR: How would you explode? Usually, you add an image—

NANA: Wait. . . . [*proud of herself*] I'd explode like a pressure cooker that was left on the burner so long, you'd all have to scrape me off the ceiling!

They laugh even harder.

Ah, that feels better! Look, your Uncle Alfred might be your father's brother, but believe you me, he's not the guy who hitched the lanterns to the fireflies' backsides!

They split a gut laughing.

It's Mr Gagnon, from Saint-Pacôme, a friend of your grandparents on your father's side, who used to say that. Funny, eh?

NARRATOR: Yeah, it's really great. I'm going to use it some day.

NANA [*more seriously*]: I'm sure you will. We should talk about that. . . . But her! THAT ONE! She's been coming to supper for thirty years now, and lately you know what she's been saying to me, as she leaves?

NARRATOR: I know, but—

NANA: 'The tea was very good.' The tea! She does me the honour of liking my tea!

NARRATOR: It's her idea of a joke, Ma—

NANA: A joke that's been going on for three years is no joke, it's sick! Her husband with Fernandel, her with her tea, and their daughter with her twitches, I'm telling you they're quite the family! I guess they don't get a few laughs every day like us!

NARRATOR: You always make roast beef when they come. . . .

NANA: People say my roast beef is the best roast beef this side of the Rockies!

NARRATOR: I know, but you always make it rare. . . . Maybe she like it well-done, I don't know. . . .

NANA: What's that supposed to mean? Did she ever say anything to you?

NARRATOR: Well, no—

NANA: Tell me the truth! Did your Aunt Gertrude ever complain about my roast beef?

NARRATOR: I told you, no. . . . I'm just saying that some people probably like it more well-done—

NANA: Well, listen to that! Would you be talking about yourself there?

NARRATOR: Well. . . .

NANA: You've hated my roast beef for eighteen years, and you never even told me!

NARRATOR: I never said I hated your roast beef, Ma. . . .

NANA: You've been eating roast beef that makes you sick for eighteen years, and you never had the courage to tell me.

NARRATOR: Ma, you've been boasting about your roast beef for so long, it's pretty hard to contradict you!

NANA: I don't believe it! He doesn't like my cooking!

She puts her hand to her heart.

He's going to kill me. How about my potatoes, are they cooked enough for you? Are my peas hot enough? Are my carrots chopped too big? Is my gravy thick enough? Maybe there's too much tea in it? Is there anything I cook right, or is it all like my roast beef, awful?!

NARRATOR: Ma, I never said I didn't like your cooking. . . . Gosh, it's hard to talk to you!

NANA: You go eat at your friend's houses where they eat baloney sandwiches day in and day out, and then, believe you me, you'll miss your mother's cooking!

NARRATOR: Ma, listen to me, please. I was just trying to say that to my taste, that's just me, you don't cook your roast beef long enough. That's all. No more, no less! It's no big deal! No tragedy!

NANA: *Well, maybe, but your father likes his beef so rare it can get up, moo, and walk away from the plate!*

NARRATOR: I know, but we don't all have to share his taste! You've just closed the oven door, and it's time to take it out again!

NANA: Now look who's exaggerating!

NARRATOR: But it's true. You put it in, what, for half an hour at 400? The outside is burnt to a crisp and inside it's still alive!

NANA: So just ask me for the end piece!

NARRATOR: Listen, when I was little, I was the youngest kid of all the families who came to dinner, so, Saturday nights, I was always the last one to be served. . . . You'd buy a huge roast beef, you'd hardly cook it, and I'd end up with the middle, you see, the middle of the roast, the least cooked, the rawest, the cow was practically still breathing in my plate. It was red, full of blood, and it tasted like a wet facecloth! I felt like there was a cow in the bathroom and you'd just gone to slice off a piece of thigh and put it in my plate!

NANA: And you never said anything.

NARRATOR: You would've killed me.

NANA: If you said it in front of other people, maybe, but—

NARRATOR: It doesn't matter, Ma, this Saturday you'll give me the end piece and we'll forget the whole thing. . . . If I'm home for supper.

NANA: What do you mean, *if* you're home for supper?

NARRATOR: Well, I don't really feel like spending another evening with Fernandel's official imitator! C'mon, Ma, I've got other things to do with my life!

NANA: First of all, that's not true, just this morning you asked me what I was making for supper Saturday night . . . and besides, you have to keep your favourite cousin Lucille company while she blinks her lights. . . .

NARRATOR: Ma, I'm eighteen years old, I'm not ten anymore, I'm a consenting adult and I can do what I want!

NANA: If you don't mind my saying so . . . you've been staying out pretty late these days . . . and hanging out with some pretty . . . strange people! You can go out when it's time for them to leave, period.

NARRATOR: And if they leave after midnight, like they usually do?

NANA [*after some hesitation*]: You'll leave along with them.

NARRATOR: And you won't say anything?

NANA [*after another hesitation*]: No.

NARRATOR: Okay!

NANA: Would you mind telling me where you go, and what you do with those weirdos, so late at night? You come home smelling of cigarettes, and you don't even smoke! I'd like to know what kind of a dive you're hanging out in!

NARRATOR: Ma!

NANA: Okay! Okay! We'll drop the subject! But you better sit there beside your cousin Lucille and mind your p's and q's.

NARRATOR: It's a deal!

NANA: You see what I mean? I feel like you just pulled the wool over my eyes, just like your Aunt Gertrude!   *She exits.*

Then returns.

Did I ever tell you about your cousin Lucille's recital?

NARRATOR: Thousands of times, Ma.

NANA: Listen to this. You'll get a kick out of it.

He raises his eyes to heaven.

Don't raise your eyes to heaven like that, you're not ten years old anymore! [*She coughs into her fist, as if about to begin a song.*] You have to realize that your Aunt Gertrude had been bending my ear about her daughter's recital for months and months! I absolutely had to attend, I absolutely had to see it, she had made Lucille's costume herself, she'd bought the material at the Shiller's in her neighbourhood. . . . Mind you, I should've realized, your Aunt Gertrude's never had good taste in clothes, but anyway. . . . It went on for months! She acted like her daughter Lucille was the first human being who had ever taken ballet lessons in the History of Humanity! The fact that she was taking her ballet lessons in an elocution school, I should've known . . . but anyway, I finally gave in and promised I'd go, she must've hypnotized me, as usual. . . . So I arrive, the night of the recital. It was in a church basement, you can imagine the atmosphere! I sit down on a hard church pew, beside your aunt who smelled so strong I felt like I was sitting in the middle of a garden of dead roses. . . . It begins with some sketch about Cinderella, with the little 8–10 year old girls. . . . Your aunt leans over and tells me this is the scene Lucille's in. I found that a bit strange 'cause your cousin Lucille was almost fifteen at the time. . . anyway, I grin and bear it. . . . Cinderella is really miserable, her stepmother and her stepsisters are really mean, she's crying her eyes out, the others leave for the ball. . . . Normally, I admit, I might've thought it was cute, I like that kinda thing, kids playacting, but that night I must've decided to hate it, so I was bored stiff. . . . I kept thinking, don't tell me Lucille's going to play Prince Charming, her mother told me she'd be wearing a dress! Then comes the moment where Cinderella's fairy godmother is supposed to appear. Cinderella is sprawled out in the cardboard pumpkins and she's crying her heart out, the mothers of the artists pull out their hankies because they think she's great, poor things, then the curtain in the background opens . . . and Lucille arrives on points, disguised like a fairy. Honestly, she was three times taller than Cinderella! And with her toeshoes, she looked like a horse trying to do ballet! Your aunt didn't dare make her a tutu 'cause she's kind of bowlegged, so she settled for these rags in blue and pink tulle, draped over a really stiff petticoat. . . . It was supposed to be chic, but it looked poorer than Cinderella's costume! It made her look like she was the one who should change her clothes to go to the ball! It was no magical apparition, it was a vision of horror! That's when your Uncle Alfred, the president of Fernandel's fan club, tries to get everyone to clap! But he's the only one clapping because only three of us in the hall realize that it's his daughter, Lucille, who's just appeared, and he looks like a damn fool! But he doesn't care how crazy he looks, the stubborn goat, he goes on clapping harder and harder! Your cousin Lucille starts to wobble on her long bowlegs, because her father won't stop clapping and she feels like she has to stay on her tiptoes till the applause stops! It was so embarrassing! It was no prima ballerina who'd appeared, for crying out loud, it was just a poor kid who'd taken a few months of ballet in an elocution school! If I'd had an axe with me, believe you me, your Uncle Alfred's arms would've grown shorter that night. He'd be imitating Fernandel with two stumps! He finally stopped clapping, but by then, there were five hundred heads turned toward us! Talk about being embarrassed! And then, Lucille, who's still tottering on her tired pins, takes a few steps, still on points, she lowers her magic wand, poof, the pumpkin turns into a carriage and she exits! That was it! I'd just attended your cousin Lucille's *recital*! She appears, poof, she waves her wand, and that's all, folks! Maybe she was on stage for a grand total of two minutes, maximum, and her career was over! Not everyone's cut out for a career on stage, you know! Your uncle was wiping his eyes, your aunt was holding her heart with both hands, and I was thinking: 'Go ahead, die a natural death, both of you, before I feel I have to kill you with my own two hands.' At intermission, I found some excuse, a bus to take or a headache, I can't remember, and I took off like a coward! Never, you hear me, never did I tell your aunt that I liked her daughter's recital! She did everything, she tried everything, but for once she didn't succeed! Maybe it's cost me tons of roast beef, and I always get roped in when she wants to be invited to supper, *but never as long as I live will I tell her I enjoyed that evening!*

NARRATOR: And you wonder why she only says tea was good when she leaves the house!

Nana freezes briefly.

NANA: Well, I'll be. . . . You. . . . Well, I never. . . .   *She exits.*

She returns.

I've changed my mind. I'm going to cook a ham Saturday night. You boil ham for ages, it should be well-done enough for you, right?   *She exits.*

NARRATOR: They never made up. I mean, my Aunt Gertrude and my mother. Because my Aunt Gertrude died suddenly of a heart attack. My mother always used to say: 'Your fat Aunt Gertrude never had time to waste away.'

Nana returns.

NANA: It could happen to me, too, you know, if you all don't start being nicer to me. You've got nothing to say? Usually, you react, when I say stupid things like that!

NARRATOR: I've learned to let you talk, it's funnier.

NANA: Well, look at that, the great twenty-year-old philosopher trying to show his mother a thing or two!

NARRATOR: I'm not trying to—

NANA [*laughing*]: You see, you're not letting me talk!

He lets out a sigh of exasperation.

Apparently he just stood there puffing on his pipe and watched her die. Your Uncle Alfred. He's a real case! I just hope he wasn't doing one of his Fernandel imitations while she was calling for help! Don't laugh.

NARRATOR: How do you know he kept puffing on his pipe while she was dying?! You weren't there.

NANA: He said so himself! He seems proud of it! Did I ever tell you how it happened? It's awful! It was a Saturday morning. Like every Saturday morning, she was on her hands and knees waxing her floor, while your Uncle Alfred stood there puffing on his pipe, watching her. Don't ask me why she always waited till Saturday morning to wash her floor, but anyway. Maybe she was hoping that some day he'd offer to help, that he'd feel sorry for her, down on her hands and knees on the linoleum, and that he'd say: 'Stop, Gertrude, let me do that.' Did I ever tell you that woman was really naive? Anyway. He says he was in the middle of telling her something. . . . Maybe she died just to avoid another description of Fernandel cutting Suzy Delair's hair. . . . Anyway. All of a sudden, she starts doing the hula on all fours. That's how he put it . . . doing the hula. I don't know how he came up with that, but anyway. He thought she was fooling around, or something, so he went on talking until she fell flat on her face in her puddle of wax. End of story. He watched her die without even realizing it. I always said he was really thick. You want a glass of milk? My stomach's hurting, again. . . .   *She exits.*

NARRATOR: She never tackled important subjects directly, she never asked a simple question when she wanted to know something or when something was bothering her. No, out of discretion or shyness, she'd make up stories, she'd beat around the bush, she'd talk a blue streak to hide her concerns, all the while keeping an eye on the person she was talking to, watching for their reactions, trying to read their expressions for a kind of understanding, I guess. An understanding she rarely found, because her ranting was often incomprehensible. People would have had to interpret her monologues, decipher her stories to understand the real meaning, but her wit submerged everything and all too often we allowed ourselves to be mesmerized by this irresistible flow of words, delighted by her punch lines, enthralled by her humour. For example, her last story, her absurd version of my Aunt Gertrude's death, had a very precise meaning which unfortunately I didn't grasp right away, I was too busy trying to understand why my mother made up a comical death for someone she had never liked, I was almost shocked by her cruelty. Until one day—it was in the spring, I remember that because it was during final exams my last year at the Graphic Arts Institute—for the first time in her life, with me at least, she opened up, all of a sudden. And for once, her monologue took the form of a confession.

Nana enters, walks over to the narrator, stands behind him, puts her arms around his shoulders.

NANA: Will you take care of your father for me when I'm gone?

Silence.

NARRATOR: Uhh . . . yes. Why are you asking me that?

NANA: I've really spoiled him, you know, and he's not always easy to get along with.

Silence.

NARRATOR: It depends on what you mean by taking care of him. I can't do everything you do. You can't expect me to give him his spoonful of Milk of Magnesia every day before he leaves for work.

NANA: Don't joke about this, I'm serious.

NARRATOR: Well, yes, I'll try, but you know that nobody will ever be able to replace you in his life, Ma!

She starts with pain, and tries to hide it.

The narrator hesitates before asking his question.

Does it really hurt?

NANA: Yes, but it will go away. It's going already. [*to change the subject*] Do you remember when I used to hold you like this when you were little?

NARRATOR: Of course, I do. But in those days, you weren't standing behind me, you were sitting down, and I was on your lap.

NANA: Hmmm, you really loved it.

NARRATOR: I still like it, you know.

She gives him a little slap on the shoulder.

NANA: You should've said so before, I've been holding back for years! When I'm gone, it'll be too late.

Heavy, embarrassed silence.

Have you thought about what will happen around the house when I'm gone?

NARRATOR: No.

NANA: You better start thinking about it, eh?

NARRATOR: I know. But I can't. It's . . . unthinkable.

NANA: Nonsense. Housekeeping isn't the end of the world. Don't worry, I'm not asking you to do the housekeeping when I'm gone. I suppose the three of you will
chip in, you, your father and your brother. . . . You'll manage, you'll see. Nobody's
irreplaceable.

NARRATOR: Yes, you are.

NANA: Oh, you're sweet. Did I ever tell you how sweet you are?

NARRATOR: Oh, no. You were more apt to tell me how stupid I was and yell your head
off at me.

NANA: You deserved it, too, you stupid kid! But behind all that couldn't you tell how
I felt about you?

NARRATOR: I guess so. But not always. Sometimes, when you got carried away about
nothing, you scared me. I used to think it wasn't normal to make such a scene over
stupid little incidents.

NANA: It's true, I can get pretty melodramatic.

NARRATOR: She finally admits it!

> *Nana smiles, stands up straight.*
>
> *He looks at her, he is smiling, too.*

NANA: I'm really worried about you, you know.

NARRATOR: Why?

NANA: I don't know. I feel as if I've managed to get all the men in my life settled,
except you.

NARRATOR: Settled?

NANA: Maybe it's not the right word. . . . Anyway. . . . What I mean is. . . . your
father's going to retire soon, he'll be able to take it easy at last, he's worked so hard
all his life. . . . Your oldest brother is a teacher, he's got a good job, even if we don't
hear from him much. Your other brother has the same trade as your father, he
earns a good living, he's got a wife and kids. . . .

NARRATOR: Ma, you're not going to start up about the wife and kids again—

NANA: No . . . I haven't talked about that for years, I realized a long time ago that you'll
never have a wife and kids, that's not what I mean, even if it is one of the things that
worries me most. . . . What I mean is what I just said, there's no other word. . . .
I don't feel as if you're settled, and that's going to be one of my greatest regrets when
I leave. . . . Not knowing what's going to happen to you. Not even being sure that
something will happen to you.

NARRATOR: Ma, please, don't worry about me. Think about yourself. For once, just
think about yourself.

NANA: I know, but what are you going to do with your life?

NARRATOR: I don't know, but for the time being, it doesn't matter.

NANA: How can you say it doesn't matter! It's *your life*!

NARRATOR: I'll manage, Ma!

NANA: It's not true! You've never managed! Never! You've always been a dreamer! Always off in your own dreamworld! Don't tell me you're going to spend the rest of your days dreaming about a life for yourself!

NARRATOR: Maybe I prefer that to being settled, as you say.

NANA: Don't say that, you'll make me even more worried! That's nonsense! Saying stuff like that at your age!

He puts his arm around her waist, places his head on her stomach.

NARRATOR: Let me live the life I want.

NANA: You know very well you're not living the life you want! You can't kid me! Don't make me lose my temper! Everything you've been doing in that school for the past three years, that's what I call marking time! Postponing things. Playing with fire! You're playing with fire, that's what you're doing! You're doing nothing to get ahead in life, just hoping that something will save you. You're waiting for someone or something to come along and save you!

NARRATOR: I'm really convinced that something or someone will come along—

NANA: Suddenly you'll realize that you're forty, fifty years old, and nothing will have happened, and—

NARRATOR: I still won't be settled—

NANA: Don't make fun of that either, I'm serious! I let you daydream too much! I encouraged you to dream too much, I let you read anything you wanted too young, I watched too many TV dramas with you, knowing perfectly well it was getting under your skin like some kind of poison—maybe you'll never end up on the other side, on the artists' side, on the side of the ones who write, who act, who dance, who make movies, the way you'd like to! Maybe you'll never make anything of your life because I let you dream too much, and it's all going to be my fault.

NARRATOR: Don't say that! I'll always be grateful to you for letting me dream, Ma! Everything I have, I got from you! I'm melodramatic, too, Ma, I love getting carried away in the long monologues I make up, and just like you, I'm willing to make fun of everything to avoid facing reality! It's not a weakness, Ma, it's a strength, and maybe that's what will save me!

NANA: If only I could believe you—

NARRATOR: Believe me, I swear it's true. If I make something of my life, I'll owe it all to you!

NANA: And if you fail?

NARRATOR: You want me to tell you something important? Listen carefully. I'm only going to say it once: I have no intention of failing. Do you hear me?

NANA: But how do you expect me to believe you? Maybe you're just saying that to comfort me, so I don't worry.

NARRATOR: Just decide to believe me!

NANA: I can't.

NARRATOR: Ma, please try, for once. . . . I'm asking you to believe in me.

She stares at him for a long moment.

NANA: Okay, I'm going to believe in you. But you know I'm capable of coming back to haunt you, if what you make of your life doesn't suit me, right?

NARRATOR: Oh, yes. If you come back to twist my toes, I'll know why and I'll change direction!

She kisses him on the forehead.

Can I tell you how empty the house is going to be without you?

NANA: Oh, if you only knew how I need to hear that. . . .

NARRATOR: The house is going to be horribly empty, Ma. We're going to miss . . . everything you did, everything you said, even the worst stuff. I'm going to miss everything, even the worst, Ma, I swear!

NANA: Even my stubbornness that used to make you so mad?

NARRATOR: Yes.

NANA: Even my unfairness?

NARRATOR: You're hardly ever unfair, Ma.

NANA: Thanks for talking about me in the present tense.

NARRATOR: You haven't left yet, Ma.

NANA: No, but believe me, I'm on my last legs.

She puts her hands on her stomach, and leans against him lightly.

NARRATOR: Is it starting again?

NANA: Yes.

NARRATOR: If you only knew how useless I feel.

NANA: When I was carrying you kids, it hurt there. The same place. The exact same place. That's what makes me the saddest. I feel like . . . I feel like I'm carrying my death. Like I'm pregnant with my own death. Like I'm preparing to give birth to my death. Do you understand? Sometimes, it's the same symptoms. I mean, when the pain starts, it hurts in the same place, a bit the same way . . . but not afterwards, not when the pain gets worse, when it becomes unbearable. You kids never hurt like that, even if all five of you were big babies. . . . I don't know how to explain it. . . . It's a presence, like being pregnant, you can feel that something is feeding off you, something that's growing, trying to kick . . . but . . . it's not life. . . . You can't . . . you can't imagine what's it's like knowing that you're carrying your own death inside you! And knowing, because it hurts in a specific place, exactly where in your body death will overcome you. . . . I look at myself the way I did when I was pregnant, twenty years after my last baby, like this, you know, with my head bent over, my hands on my belly, and I know that it's my death that's there! There, where five times—

NARRATOR: Don't talk about it, Ma, it will only make you feel bad. . . .

NANA: Don't stop me, maybe it will do me good, bring some relief . . . not from the pain, but the. . . . I don't know . . . from the weight that's made my heart so heavy since I found out.

Silence.

NANA: You know what? I would've preferred to joke about all this, as usual. . . . You know, make up a story, act crazy or dramatic. . . . I tried, at first, with the story about your Aunt Gertrude's death, but. . . . No. I can't do it anymore. You can't . . . imagine . . . the anxiety. It's as if . . . you know that expression: a sinking feeling, the sense of sinking, like a ship . . . [*She raises her arms, as if she were going to fly away.*] . . . but me, I feel as if I'm going to fly away with anxiety. The pain is horribly heavy, but I feel as if I'm going to fly away, as if I'm being lifted up, as if the fear, the fear of suffering, the fear of dying, was making me lighter. As if punishment, hell, were above us, instead of below us! Good heavens! Maybe I'm being blasphemous, without realizing it!

NARRATOR: No, don't worry, go on if it makes you feel better. . . .

NANA: I don't know if it makes me feel better! I don't know! I'm so afraid! I refuse to leave, you understand? I refuse to leave! Not because I'm afraid of death itself, but because your father needs his spoonful of Milk of Magnesia every day, and if I'm not here, he won't take it! No, that's not true. Not true. It's death I'm afraid of. I'm afraid of dying, there's no sense in trying to deny it. I'm afraid of the black hole if there's nothing, afraid of the eternal flames if there is something!

NARRATOR: You certainly won't go to hell. . . .

NANA: Well, I certainly won't go to heaven! They don't need a pain in the neck like me.

> *She almost doubles over with pain.*

Help! Help me! It hurts so bad. No, no, never mind, it's stupid of me to ask, you can't do anything for me—

NARRATOR: I don't want you to suffer like that, Ma!

NANA: It will go away. . . . It will go away. . . . It's going away already. . . .

> *The narrator gets up from his chair.*

NARRATOR: Listen, you can't leave like this. . . . I can't let you suffer like this. . . . I've prepared a surprise for you. . . .

NANA: A surprise!

> *The pain seems to subside.*

NARRATOR: Yes. Come here, I'll show you.

> *He leads her to the edge of the stage.*

Turn around.

> *Nana turns to face the back of the stage.*

Everything's possible, in the theatre, Ma, and I've prepared an exit worthy of you . . .

> *He signals.*

> *Magnificent music is heard—perhaps Händel—while from the wings and the heavens a superb trompe-l'oeil set appears, stage machinery and false perspectives, depicting the plains of Saskatchewan with a rippling lake in the background.*

NANA: Oh, how beautiful! Really, how beautiful! It looks like back home, in Saskatchewan! And look, look at the ripples on the lake, and everything!

NARRATOR: It's the stagehands, in the wings, who make it move.

She walks toward the back of the stage, then turns around.

NANA: Good heavens! It's so ugly from behind! They didn't paint both sides?

NARRATOR: It's made to be seen from the audience, Ma. . . .

NANA: Oh, right. . . . There's no point. . . . Strange, eh, I never would've imagined it that way. . . .

NARRATOR: But that's not all. . . . Come back here.

Nana returns to the edge of the stage and turns around again.

The narrator signals again and an enormous pair of angel wings holding a wicker basket descend from on high.

NANA: Oh, now I understand. That's for me, right? For my . . . departure? My . . . exit?

NARRATOR: Yes.

NANA: You're sweet. It's going to be wonderful, leaving like that! Can I go now?

NARRATOR: Of course, that's what it's here for. . . .

They walk over to the basket, the narrator opens the little door to let Nana enter.

NANA: I feel like I'm going for a balloon ride!

NARRATOR: Yes, and I promise you, there's no anxiety awaiting you up there, Ma. Anxiety doesn't come from on high!

NANA: I'm not worried about that anymore, I'm too happy!

He holds her in his arms.

NARRATOR: Don't be afraid to come back, if I do things that don't suit you. . . .

NANA: It's a promise.

The music can be heard again.

The basket begins to rise, slowly.

NARRATOR: You look good, Ma, with angel wings!

NANA: I don't know if I'm headed for heaven, but, oh, my God!, I'm having a good time!

NARRATOR: Oh, my God?

NANA: Oh, my God!

She blows kisses and waves goodbye, before disappearing into the heavens.

1998

Tomson Highway

b. 1951

Born in a tent on his father's trapline on the remote island of Maria Lake in northern Manitoba, Tomson Highway grew up in a family devoted to the art of storytelling. He attended high school in Winnipeg, then studied piano for two years at the University of Manitoba. He obtained his BA in music (1975) and then completed his courses for a second BA in general studies (1976) at the University of Western Ontario. After his graduation he devoted himself to the service of Aboriginal people, working for many First Nations social and cultural organizations. *The Rez Sisters* (1986), his first play, won the Dora Mavor Moore Award for Best Play of the Toronto Season, then toured across Canada to sold-out audiences and represented Canada at the Edinburgh Festival. His next play, *Dry Lips Oughta Move to Kapuskasing* (1989), is the flip-side to *The Rez Sisters*, featuring seven men and a female Nanabush. Highway has also written a novel, *Kiss of the Fur Queen* (1998).

The Rez Sisters

PRODUCTION NOTES

The role of Nanabush in *The Rez Sisters* is to be played by a male dancer—modern, ballet, or traditional. Stage directions for this mostly silent Nanabush are indicated very sparingly in this script. Only his most 'essential' appearances are explicitly set out.

The music for *The Rez Sisters*, in its first productions, was provided by a musician who played at least thirty different percussion instruments from drum kit to bells to rattles, etc. This is the way I find the 'soundscape' and the rhythm of this piece to be most effectively underlined.

Both Cree and Ojibway are used freely in this text for the reasons that these two languages, belonging to the same linguistic family, are very similar and that the fictional reserve of Wasaychigan Hill was a mixture of both Cree and Ojibway residents.

A NOTE ON NANABUSH

The dream world of North American Indian mythology is inhabited by the most fantastic creatures, beings, and events. Foremost among these things is the 'Trickster', as pivotal and important a figure in the Native world as Christ is in the realm of Christian mythology. 'Weesageechak' in Cree, 'Nanabush' in Ojibway, 'Raven' in others, 'Coyote' in still others, the Trickster goes by many names and many guises. In fact, he can assume any guise he chooses. Essentially a comic, clownish sort of character, he teaches us about the nature and the meaning of existence on the planet Earth; he straddles the consciousness of man and that of God, the Great Spirit.

Some say that 'Nanabush' left this continent when the white man came. We believe he is still among us—albeit a little the worse for wear and tear—having assumed other guises. Without him—and without the spiritual health of this figure—the core of Indian culture would be gone forever.

CAST OF CHARACTERS

PELAJIA PATCHNOSE, 53

PHILOMENA MOOSETAIL, 49, sister of Pelajia

MARIE-ADELE STARBLANKET, 39, half-sister of Pelajia & Philomena

ANNIE COOK, 36, sister of Marie-Adele & half-sister of the other two

EMILY DICTIONARY, 32, sister of Annie & ditto

VERONIQUE ST PIERRE, 45, sister-in-law of all the above

ZHABOONIGAN PETERSON, 24, mentally disabled adopted daughter of Veronique

NANABUSH—who plays the Seagull (the dancer in white feathers), the Nighthawk (the dancer in dark feathers), and the Bingo Master.

> *Time: Late summer, 1986*

> *Place: The Wasaychigan Hill Indian Reserve, Manitoulin Island, Ontario. (Note: 'Wasaychigan' means 'window' in Objibway.)*

ACT I

> *It is mid-morning of a beautiful late August day on the Wasaychigan Hill Indian Reserve, Manitoulin Island, Ontario. Pelajia Patchnose is alone on the roof of her house, nailing shingles on. She wears faded blue denim men's cover-alls and a baseball cap to shade her eyes from the sun. A brightly-coloured square cushion belonging to her sister, Philomena Moosetail, rests on the roof beside her. The ladder to the roof is off-stage.*

PELAJIA: Philomena. I wanna go to Toronto.

PHILOMENA [*from offstage*]: Oh, go on.

PELAJIA: Sure as I'm sitting away up here on the roof of this old house. I kind of like it up here, though. From here, I can see half of Manitoulin Island on a clear day. I can see the chimneys, the tops of apple trees, the garbage heap behind Big Joey's dumpy little house. I can see the seagulls circling over Marie-Adele Starblanket's white picket fence. Boats on the North Channel I wish I was on, sailing away somewhere. The mill at Espanola, a hundred miles away . . . and that's with just a bit of squinting. See? If I had binoculars, I could see the superstack in Sudbury. And if I were Superwoman, I could see the CN Tower in Toronto. Ah, but I'm just plain old Pelajia Rosella Patchnose and I'm here in plain, dusty, boring old Wasaychigan Hill . . . Wasy . . . waiting . . . waiting . . . nailing shining shingles with my trusty silver hammer on the roof of Pelajia Rosella Patchnose's little two-bedroom welfare house. Philomena. I wanna go to Toronto.

Philomena Moosetail comes up the ladder to the roof with one shingle and obviously hating it. She is very well-dressed, with a skirt, nylons, even heels, completely impractical for the roof.

PHILOMENA: Oh, go on.

PELAJIA: I'm tired, Philomena, tired of this place. There's days I wanna leave so bad.

PHILOMENA: But you were born here. All your poop's on this reserve.

PELAJIA: Oh, go on.

PHILOMENA: You'll never leave.

PELAJIA: Yes, I will. When I'm old.

PHILOMENA: You're old right now.

PELAJIA: I got a good 30 years to go . . .

PHILOMENA: . . . and you're gonna live every one of them right here beside me . . .

PELAJIA: . . . maybe 40 . . .

PHILOMENA: . . . here in Wasy. [*tickles Pelajia on the breasts*] Chiga-chiga-chiga.

PELAJIA [*yelps and slaps Philomena's hand away*]: Oh, go on. It's not like it used to be.

PHILOMENA: Oh, go on. People change, places change, time changes things. You expect to be young and gorgeous forever?

PELAJIA: See? I told you I'm not old.

PHILOMENA: Oh, go on. You.

PELAJIA: 'Oh, go on. You.' You bug me like hell when you say that.

PHILOMENA: You say it, too. And don't give me none of this 'I don't like this place. I'm tired of it.' This place is too much inside your blood. You can't get rid of it. And it can't get rid of you.

PELAJIA: Four thirty this morning, I was woken by . . .

PHILOMENA: Here we go again.

PELAJIA: . . . Andrew Starblanket and his brother, Matthew. Drunk. Again. Or sounded like . . .

PHILOMENA: Nothing better to do.

PELAJIA: . . . fighting over some girl. Heard what sounded like a baseball bat landing on somebody's back. My lawn looks like the shits this morning.

PHILOMENA: Well, I like it here. Myself, I'm gonna go to every bingo and I'm gonna hit every jackpot between here and Espanola and I'm gonna buy me that toilet I'm dreaming about at night . . . big and wide and very white . . .

PELAJIA: Aw-ni-gi-naw-ee-dick.[1]

PHILOMENA: I'm good at bingo.

PELAJIA: So what! And the old stories, the old language. Almost all gone . . . was a time Nanabush and Windigo and everyone here could rattle away in Indian fast as Bingo Betty could lay her bingo chips down on a hot night.

---

1 Oh, go on. (Ojibway)

PHILOMENA: Pelajia Rosella Patchnose. The sun's gonna drive you crazy.

[*And she descends the ladder.*]

PELAJIA: Everyone here's crazy. No jobs. Nothing to do but drink and screw each other's wives and husbands and forget about our Nanabush.

From off stage Philomena screams. She fell down the ladder.

Philomena! [*as she looks over the edge of the roof*] What are you doing down there?

PHILOMENA: What do you think? I fell.

PELAJIA: Bring me some of them nails while you're down there.

PHILOMENA [*whining and still from offstage, from behind the house*]: You think I can race up and down this ladder? You think I got wings?

PELAJIA: You gotta wear pants when you're doing a man's job. See? You got your skirt ripped on a nail and now you can see your thighs. People gonna think you just came from Big Joey's house.

PHILOMENA [*She comes up the ladder in a state of disarray.*] Let them think what they want. That old cow Gazelle Nataways . . . always acting like she thinks she's still a spring chicken. She's got them legs of hers wrapped around Big Joey day and night . . .

PELAJIA: Philomena. Park your tongue. My old man has to go the hundred miles to Espanola just to get a job. My boys. Gone to Toronto. Only place educated Indian boys can find decent jobs these days. And here I sit all broken-hearted.

PHILOMENA: Paid a dime and only farted.

PELAJIA: Look at you. You got dirt all over your backside. [*turning her attention to the road in front of her house and standing up for the first and only time*] And dirt roads! Years now that old chief's been making speeches about getting paved roads 'for my people' and still we got dirt roads all over.

PHILOMENA: Oh, go on.

PELAJIA: When I win that jackpot next time we play bingo in Espanola . . .

PHILOMENA [*examining her torn skirt, her general state of disarray, and fretting over it*]: Look at this! Will you look at this! Ohhh!

PELAJIA: . . . I'm gonna put that old chief to shame and build me a nice paved road right here in front of my house. Jet black. Shiny. Make my lawn look real nice.

PHILOMENA: My rib-cage!

PELAJIA: And if that old chief don't wanna make paved roads for all my sisters around here . . .

PHILOMENA: There's something rattling around inside me!

PELAJIA: . . . I'm packing my bags and moving to Toronto. [*sits down again*]

PHILOMENA: Oh, go on. [*She spies Annie Cook's approach a distance up the hill.*] Why, I do believe that cloud of dust over there is Annie Cook racing down the hill, Pelajia.

PELAJIA: Philomena. I wanna go to Toronto.

PHILOMENA: She's walking mighty fast. Must be excited about something.

PELAJIA: Never seen Annie Cook walk slow since the day she finally lost Eugene to Marie-Adele at the church 19 years ago. And even then she was walking a little too fast for a girl who was supposed to be broken-heart . . . [*stopping just in time and laughing*] . . . heart-broken.

Annie Cook pops up the top of the ladder to the roof.

ANNIE [*all cheery and fast and perky*]: Halloooo! Watchyou doing up here?
PELAJIA: There's room for only so much weight up here before we go crashing into my kitchen, so what do you want?
ANNIE: Just popped up to say hi.
PELAJIA: And see what we're doing?
ANNIE: Well . . .
PELAJIA: Couldn't you see what we're doing from up where you were?
ANNIE [*confidentially, to Philomena*]: Is it true Gazelle Nataways won the bingo last night?
PHILOMENA: Annie Cook, first you say you're gonna come with me and then you don't even bother showing up. If you were sitting beside me at that bingo last night you would have seen Gazelle Nataways win that big pot again with your own two eyes.
ANNIE: Emily Dictionary and I went to Little Current to listen to Fritz the Katz.
PELAJIA: What in God's name kind of a band might that be?
ANNIE: Country rock. My favourite. Fritz the Katz is from Toronto.
PELAJIA: Fritzy . . . ritzy . . . Philomena! Say something.
PHILOMENA: My record player is in Espanola getting fixed.
ANNIE: That's nice.
PHILOMENA: Good.
ANNIE: Is it true Gazelle Nataways plans to spend her bingo money to go to Toronto with . . . with Big Joey?
PHILOMENA: Who wants to know? Emily Dictionary?
ANNIE: I guess so.
PELAJIA: That Gazelle Nataways gonna leave all her babies behind and let them starve to death?
ANNIE: I guess so. I don't know. I'm asking you.
PELAJIA and PHILOMENA: We don't know.
ANNIE: I'm on my way to Marie-Adele's to pick her up.
PELAJIA: Why? Where you gonna put her down?

Pelajia and Philomena laugh.

ANNIE: I mean, we're going to the store together. To the post office. We're going to pick up a parcel. They say there's a parcel for me. They say it's shaped like a record. And they say it's from Sudbury. So it must be from my daughter, Ellen . . .
PELAJIA and PHILOMENA: . . . 'who lives with this white guy in Sudbury' . . .
ANNIE: How did you know?
PHILOMENA: Everybody knows.

ANNIE: His name is Ray<u>mond</u>. Not <u>Ray</u>mond. But Ray<u>mond</u>. Like in Bon Bon.

> [*Philomena tries out 'bon bon' to herself.*]
> He's French.

PELAJIA: Oh?

ANNIE: Garage mechanic. He fixes cars. And you know, talking about Frenchmen, that old priest is holding another bingo next week and when I win . . . [*to Philomena*]: Are you going?

PELAJIA: Does a bear shit in the woods?

ANNIE: . . . When I win, I'm going to Espanola and play the bingo there. Emily Dictionary says that Fire Minklater can give us a ride in her new car. She got it through Ray<u>mond</u>'s garage. The bingo in Espanola is bigger. And it's better. And I'll win. And then I'll go to Sudbury, where the bingos are even bigger and better. And then I can visit my daughter, Ellen . . .

PELAJIA: . . . 'Who lives with this white guy in Sudbury' . . .

ANNIE: . . . and go shopping in the record stores and go to the hotel and drink beer quietly—not noisy and crazy like here—and listen to the live bands. It will be so much fun. I hope Emily Dictionary can come with me.

PHILOMENA: It's true. I've been thinking . . .

PELAJIA: You don't say.

PHILOMENA: It's true. The bingos here are getting kind of boring . . .

ANNIE: That old priest is too slow and sometimes he gets the numbers all mixed up and the pot's not big enough.

PHILOMENA: And I don't like the way he calls the numbers. [*nasally*] B 12, O 64.

ANNIE: When Little Girl Manitowabi won last month . . .

PHILOMENA: She won just enough to take a taxi back to Buzwah.

ANNIE: That's all.

> *Both Annie and Philomena pause to give a quick sigh of yearning.*

PHILOMENA: Annie Cook, I want that big pot.

ANNIE: We all want big pots.

PELAJIA: Start a revolution!

PHILOMENA and ANNIE: Yes!

ANNIE: All us Wasy women. We'll march up the hill, burn the church hall down, scare the priest to death, and then we'll march all the way to Espanola, where the bingos are bigger and better . . .

PHILOMENA: We'll hold big placards!

ANNIE: They'll say: 'Wasy women want bigger bingos!'

PELAJIA: And one will say: 'Annie Cook Wants Big Pot!'

PHILOMENA: . . . and the numbers at those bingos in Espanola go faster and the pots get bigger by the week. Oh, Pelajia Patchnose, I'm getting excited just thinking about it!

ANNIE: I'm going.

PELAJIA: You are, are you?

ANNIE: Yes. I'm going. I'm running out of time. I'm going to Marie-Adele's house and then we'll walk to the store together and pick up the parcel—I'm sure there'll be a letter in it, and Marie-Adele is expecting mail, too—and we'll see if Emily Dictionary is working today and we'll ask her if Fire Minklater has her new car yet so we can go to Espanola for that big pot. [*She begins to descend the ladder.*]

PELAJIA: Well, you don't have much to do today, do you?

ANNIE: Well. Toodle-oo! [*And she pops down the ladder and is gone.*]

PELAJIA: Not bad for someone who was in such a hurry to get her parcel. She talks faster than she walks. [*Noticing how dejected and abandoned Philomena looks, she holds up her hammer.*] Bingo money. Top quality. $24.95.

PHILOMENA: It's true. Bingos here in Wasy are getting smaller and smaller all the time. Especially now when the value of the dollar is getting lesser and lesser. In the old days, when Bingo Betty was still alive and walking these dirt roads, she'd come to every single bingo and she'd sit there like the Queen of Tonga, big and huge like a roast beef, smack-dab in the middle of the bingo hall. One night, I remember, she brought two young cousins from the city—two young women, dressed real fancy, like they were going to Sunday church—and Bingo Betty made them sit one on her left, with her three little bingo cards, and one on her right, with her three little ones. And Bingo Betty herself sat in the middle with 27 cards. Twenty seven cards! Amazing.

[*Pelajia starts to descend the ladder, and Philomena, getting excited, steps closer and closer to the edge of the roof.*]

And those were the days when they still used bingo chips, not these dabbers like nowadays, and everyone came with a little margarine container full of these bingo chips. When the game began they started calling out the numbers, Bingo Betty was all set, like a horse at the race-track in Sudbury, you could practically see the foam sizzling and bubbling between her teeth. Bingo Betty! Bingo Betty with her beady little darting eyes, sharp as needles, and her roly-poly jiggledy-piggledy arms with their stubby little claws would go: chiga-chiga-chiga-chiga-chiga-chiga arms flying across the table smooth as angel's wings chiga-chiga-chiga-chiga-chiga-chiga-woosh! Cousin on the left chiga-chiga, cousin on the right chiga, chiga-eeee! [*She narrowly misses falling off the roof and cries out in terror.*]

PELAJIA: Philomena!

PHILOMENA [*scrambling on hands and knees to Pelajia, and coming to rest in this languorous pose, takes a moment to regain her composure and catch her breath*]: And you know, to this very day, they say that on certain nights at the bingo here in Wasy, they say you can see Bingo Betty's ghost, like a mist, hovering in the air above the bingo tables, playing bingo like it's never been played before. Or since.

PELAJIA: Amazing! She should have gone to Toronto.

Black-out.

The same day, same time, in Wasaychigan Hill. Marie-Adele Starblanket is standing alone outside her house, in her yard, by her 14-post white picket fence. Her house is down the hill from Pelajia Patchnose's, close to the lake. A seagull watches her from a distance away. He is the dancer in white feathers. Through this whole section, Nanabush (i.e. Nanabush in the guise of the seagull), Marie-Adele, and Zhaboonigan play 'games' with each other. Only she and Zhaboonigan Peterson can see the spirit inside the bird and can sort of (though not quite) recognize him for who he is. A doll belonging to a little girl lies on the porch floor. Marie-Adele throws little stones at the seagull.

MARIE-ADELE: Awus! Wee-chee-gis. Ka-tha pu-g'wun-ta oo-ta pee-wee-sta-ta-gu-mik-si. Awus! Neee. U-wi-nuk oo-ma kee-tha ee-tee-thi-mi-soo-yin holy spirit chee? Awus! Hey, maw ma-a oop-mee tay-si-thow u-wu seagull bird. I-goo-ta poo-goo ta-poo. Nu-gu-na-wa-pa-mik. Nu-gu-na-wa-pa-mik.

NANABUSH: As-tum.

MARIE-ADELE: Neee. Moo-tha ni-gus-kee-tan tu-pi-mi-tha-an. Moo-tha oo-ta-ta-gwu-na n'tay-yan. Chees-kwa. [*Pause.*] Ma-ti poo-ni-mee-see i-goo-ta wee-chi-gi-seagull bird come shit on my fence one more time and you and anybody else look like you cook like stew on my stove. Awus![2]

Veronique St Pierre 'passes by' with her adopted daughter Zhaboonigan Peterson.

VERONIQUE: Talking to the birds again, Marie-Adele Starblanket?

MARIE-ADELE: Aha. Veronique St Pierre. How are you today?

VERONIQUE: Black Lady Halked's sister-in-law Fire Minklater, Fire Minklater's husband, just bought Fire Minklater a car in Sudbury.

MARIE-ADELE: New?

VERONIQUE: Used. They say he bought it from some Frenchman, some garage. Cray-<u>on</u>.

MARIE-ADELE: Ray<u>mond</u>.

VERONIQUE: These Frenchmen are forever selling us their used cars. And I'm sure that's why Black Lady Halked has been baring those big yellow teeth of hers, smiling all over the reserve recently. She looks like a hound about to pounce on a mouse, she smiles so hard when she smiles. I'd like to see her smile after plastic surgery. Anyway. At the bingo last night she was hinting that it wouldn't be too long before she would be able to go to the bingo in Espanola more frequently. Unfortunately, a new game started and you know how Black Lady Halked has to concentrate when she plays bingo—her forehead looks like corduroy, she concentrates so hard—so I didn't get a chance to ask her what she meant. So. Fire Minklater has a used car. Imagine! Maybe I can make friends with her again. NO! I wouldn't be caught dead inside her car. Not even if she had a brand-new Cadillac. How are your children? All 14 of them.

2 MARIE-ADELE: Go away! You stinking thing. Don't come messing around here for nothing. Go away! Neee. Who the hell do you think you are, the Holy Spirit? Go away! Hey, but he won't fly away, this seagull bird. He just sits there. And watches me. Watches me.
NANABUSH: Come.
MARIE-ADELE: Neee. I can't fly away. I have no wings. Yet. [*Pause.*] Will you stop shitting all over the place you stinking seagull bird etc. (Cree)
(Note: 'Neee' is a very common Cree expression with the approximate meaning of 'Oh you.')

MARIE-ADELE: Okay, I guess.

VERONIQUE: Imagine. And all from one father. Anyway. Who will take care of them after you . . . ahem . . . I mean . . . when you go to the hospital?

MARIE-ADELE: Eugene.

ZHABOONIGAN: Is he gentle?

MARIE-ADELE: Baby-cakes. How are you?

ZHABOONIGAN: Fine. [*giggles*]

VERONIQUE: She's fine. She went berry-picking yesterday with the children.

ZHABOONIGAN: Where's Nicky?

MARIE-ADELE: Nicky's down at the beach.

ZHABOONIGAN: Why?

MARIE-ADELE: Taking care of Rose-Marie.

ZHABOONIGAN: Oh.

MARIE-ADELE: Yup.

ZHABOONIGAN: Me and Nicky, ever lots of blueberries!

MARIE-ADELE: Me and Nicky picked lots of blueberries.

ZHABOONIGAN: I didn't see you there.

MARIE-ADELE: When?

ZHABOONIGAN: Before today.

MARIE-ADELE: How come Nicky didn't come home with any?

ZHABOONIGAN: Why?

> *Marie-Adele shrugs. Zhaboonigan imitates this, and then pretends she is stuffing her mouth with berries.*

MARIE-ADELE: Aw, yous went and made pigs of yourselves.

ZHABOONIGAN: Nicky's the pig.

MARIE-ADELE: Neee.

ZHABOONIGAN: Are you going away far?

MARIE-ADELE: I'm not going far.

ZHABOONIGAN: Oh. Are you pretty?

> *Marie-Adele, embarrassed for a moment, smiles and Zhaboonigan smiles, too.*

MARIE-ADELE: You're pretty, too.

> [*Zhaboonigan tugs at Marie-Adele's shoelaces.*]

Oh, Zhaboonigan. Now you have to tie it up. I can't bend too far cuz I get tired.

> *Zhaboonigan tries to tie the shoelaces with great difficulty. When she finds she can't she throws her arms up and screams.*

ZHABOONIGAN: Dirty trick! Dirty trick!   [*She bites her hand and hurts herself.*]

MARIE-ADELE: Now, don't get mad.

VERONIQUE: Stop it. Stop it right now.

ZHABOONIGAN: No! No!

MARIE-ADELE: Zha. Zha. Listen. Listen.

ZHABOONIGAN: Stop it! Stop it right now!

MARIE-ADELE: Come on Zha. You and I can name the koo-koos-suk.[3] All 14 of them.
ZHABOONIGAN: Okay. Here we go.

Marie-Adele leads Zhaboonigan over to the picket fence and Veronique follows them.

ZHABOONIGAN [*to Veronique*]: No.

Veronique retreats, obviously hurt.

MARIE-ADELE [*taking Zhaboonigan's hand and counting on the 14 posts of her white picket fence*]: Simon, Andrew, Matthew, Janie, Nicky, Ricky, Ben, Mark, Ron, Don, John, Tom, Pete, and Rose-Marie. There.

Underneath Marie-Adele's voice, Zhaboonigan has been counting.

ZHABOONIGAN: One, two, three, four, five, six, seven, eight, nine, ten, eleven, twelve, thirteen, fourteen. [*giggles*]
MARIE-ADELE: Ever good counter you, Zhaboonigan.
ZHABOONIGAN: Yup.
VERONIQUE: This reserve, sometimes I get so sick of it. They laugh at me behind my back, I just know it. They laugh at me and Pierre St Pierre because we don't have any children of our own. 'Imagine, they say, she's on her second husband already and she still can't have children!' They laugh at Zhaboonigan Peterson because she's crazy, that's what they call her. They can't even take care of their own people, they'd rather laugh at them. I'm the only person who would take Zhaboonigan after her parents died in that horrible car crash near Manitowaning on Saturday November 12 1964 may they rest in peace. [*She makes a quick sign of the cross without skipping a beat.*] I'm the only one around here who is kind enough. And they laugh at me. Oh, I wish I had a new stove, Marie-Adele. My stove is so old and broken down, only two elements work anymore and my oven is starting to talk back at me.
MARIE-ADELE: Get it fixed.
VERONIQUE: You know that Pierre St Pierre never has any money. He drinks it all up. [*She sighs longingly.*] Some day! Anyway. Zhaboonigan here wanted to go for a swim so I thought I'd walk her down—drop by and see how you and the children are doing—it will do my weak heart good, I was saying to myself.
MARIE-ADELE: Awus!

As she throws a pebble at the seagull on the stone, Veronique, for a second, thinks it's her Marie-Adele is shooing away. There is a brief silence broken after awhile by Zhaboonigan's little giggle.

VERONIQUE: Anyway, I was walking down by that Big Joey's shameless little shack just this morning when guess who pokes her nose out the window but Gazelle Nataways—the nerve of that woman. I couldn't see inside but I'm sure she was only half-dressed, her hairdo was all mixed up and she said to me: 'Did you know,

1322 | A Collection of Plays

Veronique St Pierre, that Little Girl Manitowabi told me her daughter, June Bug
McLeod, just got back from the hospital in Sudbury where she had her tubes tied
and told her that THE BIGGEST BINGO IN THE WORLD is coming to Toronto?'

MARIE-ADELE: When?

VERONIQUE: I just about had a heart attack.

MARIE-ADELE: When?

VERONIQUE: But I said to Gazelle anyway: Is there such a thing as a BIGGEST BINGO
IN THE WORLD? And she said: Yes. And she should know about these things
because she spends all her waking and sleeping hours just banging about in bed
with the biggest thing on Manitoulin Island, I almost said.

MARIE-ADELE: This bingo. When?

VERONIQUE: She didn't know. And now that I think of it, I don't know whether to
believe her. After all, who should believe a woman who wrestles around with dirt
like Big Joey all night long leaving her poor babies to starve to death in her empty
kitchen? But if it's true, Marie-Adele, if it's true that THE BIGGEST BINGO IN THE
WORLD is coming to Toronto I'm going and I want you to come with me.

MARIE-ADELE: Well . . . .

VERONIQUE: I want you to come shopping with me and help me choose my new stove
after I win.

MARIE-ADELE: Hang on . . . .

VERONIQUE: They have good stoves in Toronto.

MARIE-ADELE: Let's find out for sure. Then we start making plans.

VERONIQUE: Maybe we should go back and ask that Gazelle Nataways about this. If
she's sure.

MARIE-ADELE: Maybe we should go and ask June Bug McLeod herself.

VERONIQUE: We can't walk to Buzwah and I'm too old to hitch-hike.

MARIE-ADELE: There's Eugene's van. He'll be home by six.

VERONIQUE: I want to find out NOW. But what if people see us standing at Big
Joey's door?

MARIE-ADELE: What do you mean? We just knock on the door, march right in, ask
the bitch, and march right out again.

VERONIQUE: Zhaboonigan dear, wait for me over there. [*She waits until Zhaboonigan
is safely out of earshot and then leans over to Marie-Adele in a conspiratorial whisper.*]
Anyway. You must know, Marie-Adele, that there's all kinds of women who come
streaming out of that house at all hours of the day and night. I might be considered one of them. You know your youngest sister, Emily Dictionary, was seen staggering out of that house in the dead of night two nights ago?

MARIE-ADELE: Veronique St Pierre, what Emily Dictionary does is Emily's business.

Annie Cook enters, walking fast and comes to a screeching halt.

ANNIE: Hallooooo! Whatchyou doin'?

VERONIQUE [*giving Annie the baleful eye*]: How are you?

ANNIE: High as a kite. Just kidding. Hi, Zha.

ZHABOONIGAN: Hi. [*giggles. She runs toward Marie-Adele, bumping into Annie en route.*]

ANNIE: Hey, Marie-Adele.

ZHABOONIGAN: Marie-Adele. How's your cancer? [*giggles and scurries off laughing*]

VERONIQUE: Shkanah, Zhaboonigan, sna-ma-bah . . .[4]

MARIE-ADELE: Come on, before the post office closes for lunch.

VERONIQUE: You didn't tell me you were going to the store.

ANNIE: Well, we are. [*to Marie-Adele*]: Hey, is Simon in? I'm sure he's got my Ricky Skaggs album. You know the one that goes [*sings*] 'Honeee!' [*calling into the house*] Yoo-hoo, Simon!

MARIE-ADELE: He's in Espanola with Eugene.

VERONIQUE: Expecting mail, Annie Cook?

ANNIE: A parcel from my daughter, Ellen, who lives with this white guy in Sudbury . . .

VERONIQUE: So I've heard.

ANNIE: And my sister here is expecting a letter, too.

VERONIQUE: From whom?

ANNIE: From the doctor, about her next check-up.

VERONIQUE: When?

MARIE-ADELE: We don't know when. Or where. Annie, let's go.

ANNIE: They say it's shaped like a record.

VERONIQUE: Maybe there'll be news in that parcel about THE BIGGEST BINGO IN THE WORLD! [*shouts toward the lake, in a state of great excitement*] Zhaboonigan! Zhaboonigan! We're going to the store!

ANNIE: THE BIGGEST BINGO IN THE WORLD?

VERONIQUE: In Toronto. Soon. Imagine! Gazelle Nataways told me. She heard about it from Little Girl Manitowabi over in Buzwah who heard about it from her daughter June Bug McLeod who just got back from the hospital in Sudbury where she had her tubes tied I just about had a heart attack!

ANNIE: Toronto?

MARIE-ADELE: We gotta find out for sure.

ANNIE: Right.

MARIE-ADELE: We could go to Big Joey's and ask Gazelle Nataways except Veronique St Pierre's too scared of Gazelle.

VERONIQUE: I am not.

ANNIE: You are too.

MARIE-ADELE: We could wait and borrow Eugene's van . . .

VERONIQUE: I am not.

ANNIE: . . . drive over to Buzwah . . .

MARIE-ADELE: . . . and ask June Bug McLeod . . .

ANNIE: . . . but wait a minute! . . .

MARIE-ADELE and ANNIE: Maybe there IS news in that parcel about this BIGGEST BINGO IN THE WORLD!

MARIE-ADELE: Come on.

VERONIQUE [*shouting toward the lake*]: Zhaboonigan! Zhaboonigan!

4 Shush, Zhaboonigan, don't say that. (Ojibway)

ANNIE: And here I was so excited about the next little bingo that old priest is holding next week. Toronto! Oh, I hope it's true!

VERONIQUE: Zhaboonigan! Zhaboonigan! Zhaboonigan! Dammit! We're going to the store!

And the 'march' to the store begins, during which Nanabush, still in the guise of the seagull, follows them and continues to play tricks, mimicking their hand movements, the movement of their mouths, etc. The three women appear each in her own spot of light at widely divergent points on the stage area.

ANNIE: When I go to THE BIGGEST BINGO IN THE WORLD, in Toronto, I will win. For sure, I will win. If they shout the B 14 at the end, for sure I will win. The B 14 is my lucky number after all. Then I will take all my money and I will go to every record store in Toronto. I will buy every single one of Patsy Cline's records, especially the one that goes [*sings*] 'I go a-walking, after midnight,' oh I go crazy every time I hear that one. Then I will buy a huge record player, the biggest one in the whole world. And then I will go to all the taverns and all the night clubs in Toronto and listen to the live bands while I drink beer quietly—not noisy and crazy like here—I will bring my daughter Ellen and her white guy from Sudbury and we will sit together. Maybe I will call Fritz the Katz and he will take me out. Maybe he will hire me as one of his singers and I can [*sings*] 'Oooh,' in the background while my feet go [*shuffles her feet from side to side*] while Fritz the Katz is singing and the lights are flashing and the people are drinking beer and smoking cigarettes and dancing. Ohhh, I could dance all night with that Fritz the Katz. When I win, when I win THE BIGGEST BINGO IN THE WORLD!

MARIE-ADELE: When I win THE BIGGEST BINGO IN THE WORLD, I'm gonna buy me an island. In the North Channel, right smack-dab in the middle—eem-shak min-stik[5]—the most beautiful island in the world. And my island will have lots of trees—great big bushy ones—and lots and lots and lots of sweetgrass. MMMMM! And there's gonna be pine trees and oak trees and maple trees and big stones and little stonelets—neee—and, oh yeah, this real neat picket fence, real high, long and very, very, very white. No bird shit. Eugene will live there and me and all my Starblanket kids. Yup, no more smelly, stinky old pulp and paper mill in Espanola for my Eugene—pooh!—my 12 Starblanket boys and my two Starblanket girls and me and my Eugene all living real nice and comfy right there on Starblanket Island, the most beautiful incredible goddamn island in the whole goddamn world. Een-shak min-stik! When I win THE BIGGEST BINGO IN THE WORLD!

VERONIQUE: Well, when I win the BIGGEST BINGO IN THE WORLD. No! After I win THE BIGGEST BINGO IN THE WORLD, I will go shopping for a brand-new stove. In Toronto. At the Eaton Centre. A great big stove. The kind Madame Benoit has. The kind that has the three different compartments in the oven alone. I'll have the biggest stove on the reserve. I'll cook for all the children on the reserve. I'll adopt all of Marie-Adele Starblanket's 14 children and I will cook for them. I'll even cook

5 A great big island. (Cree)

for Gazelle Nataways' poor starving babies while she's lolling around like a pig in Big Joey's smelly, sweaty bed. And Pierre St Pierre can drink himself to death for all I care. Because I'll be the best cook on all of Manitoulin Island! I'll enter competitions. I'll go to Paris and meet what's-his-name Cordon Bleu! I'll write a cookbook called 'The Joy of Veronique St Pierre's Cooking' and it will sell in the millions! And I will become rich and famous! Zhaboonigan Peterson will wear a mink while she eats steak tartare-de-frou-frou! Madame Benoit will be so jealous she'll suicide herself. Oh, when I win THE BIGGEST BINGO IN THE WORLD.

Zhaboonigan comes running in from swimming, 'chasing' after the other three women, counting to herself and giggling.

ZHABOONIGAN: One, two, three, four, five, six, seven, eight, nine, ten, eleven, twelve, thirteen, fourteen.

At the store. Annie Cook, Marie-Adele Starblanket, Veronique St Pierre, and Zhaboonigan Peterson have arrived. Emily Dictionary makes a sudden appearance, carrying a huge bag of flour on her shoulder. She is one tough lady, wearing cowboy boots, tight blue jeans, a black leather jacket—all three items worn to the seams—and she sports one black eye.

EMILY: [*in a loud, booming voice that paralyzes all movement in the room while she speaks*]: Zhaboonigan Peterson! What in Red Lucifer's name ever possessed you to be hangin' out with a buncha' dizzy old dames like this?

Bag of flour hits the floor with a 'doof'.

MARIE-ADELE: Emily. Your eye.

EMILY: Oh, bit of a tussle.

VERONIQUE: With who?

EMILY: None of your goddamn business.

MARIE-ADELE: Emily, please.

ANNIE [*following Emily about the store while Veronique tries, in vain, to hear what she can*]: I wasn't able to find out from Pelajia Patchnose or Philomena Moosemeat if Gazelle Nataways is going to Toronto this weekend with . . . Big Joey . . . they didn't know . . . Gazelle did win the bingo last night though.

EMILY: Aw shit. Veronique St Pierre, you old bag. Is it true Gazelle Nataways is takin' off for Toronto with that hunk Big Joey?

VERONIQUE: It WAS you coming out of that house two nights ago. I walked by as quickly as I could . . .

EMILY: . . . shoulda come out and nailed your big floppy ears to the door . . .

VERONIQUE: . . . and I would have called the police but I was too scared Big Joey might come after me and Zhaboonigan later . . .

EMILY: . . . yeah, right.

ZHABOONIGAN: Yeah, right.

VERONIQUE: . . . and I have a weak heart, you know? Who hit you? Big Joey? Or Gazelle Nataways?

EMILY: The nerve of this woman.

VERONIQUE: Well?

EMILY [*calls Zhaboonigan, who is behind the counter, on the floor, playing with the merchandise*]: Zhaboonigan Peterson! Where in Red Lucifer's name is that dozy pagan?

VERONIQUE: You keep hanging around that house and you're gonna end up in deep trouble. You don't know how wicked and vicious those Nataways women can get. They say there's witchcraft in their blood. And with manners like yours, Emily Dictionary, you'd deserve every hex you got.

EMILY: Do I know this woman? Do I know this woman?

VERONIQUE: [*During this speech, Marie-Adele and Annie sing 'Honeee' tauntingly.*] I'm sorry I have to say this in front of everyone like this but this woman has just accused my daughter of being a pagan. I didn't call her Zhaboonigan. The people on this reserve, who have nothing better to do with their time than call each other names, they called her that. Her name is Marie-Adele. Marie-Adele Peterson. You should talk. I should ask you where in Red . . . Red . . . whatever, you got a circus of a name like Emily Dictionary.

> *Emily grabs Veronique and throws her across the room. Veronique goes flying right into Pelajia, who has entered the store during the latter part of this speech.*

PELAJIA: Veronique St Pierre! Control yourself or I'll hit you over the head with my hammer.

VERONIQUE [*blows a 'raspberry' in Pelajia's face*]: Bleah!

ANNIE: No, Pelajia, no.

EMILY: Go ahead, Pelajia. Make my day.

ANNIE: Down, put it down.

PHILOMENA [*as she comes scurrying into the store*]: I have to use the toilet. [*running to Emily*] I have to use the toilet. [*and goes scurrying into the toilet*]

ANNIE [*to Pelajia*]: Remember, that's Veronique St Pierre and if you get on the wrong side of Veronique St Pierre she's liable to spread rumours about you all over kingdom come and you'll lose every bit of respect you got on this reserve. Don't let those pants you're wearing go to your head.

PELAJIA [*catching Annie by the arm as she tries to run away*]: Annie Cook! You got a mouth on you like a helicopter.

ANNIE: Veronique's mad at you, Emily, because you won't tell her what happened the other night at Big Joey's house. And she's jealous of Gazelle Nataways because Gazelle won the bingo again last night and she hopes you're the one person on this reserve who has the guts to stand up to Gazelle.

VERONIQUE [*making a lunge at Annie, who hides behind Emily*]: What's that! What's that! Ohhh! Ohhh!

ANNIE: Leave me alone, you old snoop. All I wanna know is is this big bingo really happening in Toronto.

VERONIQUE: Annie Cook. You are a little suck.

EMILY [*to Veronique*]: Someday, someone oughta stick a great big piece of shit into that mouth of yours.

PELAJIA [*to Emily*]: And someday, someone ought to wash yours out with soap.

PHILOMENA [*Throwing the toilet door open, she sits there in her glory, panties down to her ankles.*]: Emily Dictionary. You come back to the reserve after all these years and you strut around like you own the place. I know Veronique St Pierre is a pain in the ass but I don't care. She's your elder and you respect her. Now shut up, all of you, and let me shit in peace.

> And slams the washroom door. Veronique, scandalized by this, haughtily walks through toward the door, bumping into Pelajia en route.

PELAJIA: Philomena. Get your bum out here. Veronique St Pierre is about to lose her life. [*She raises her hammer at Veronique.*]

VERONIQUE [*to Pelajia*]: Put that hammer away. And go put a skirt on, for heaven's sake, you look obscene in those tight pants.

ANNIE: Hit her. Go on. Hit the bitch. One good bang is all she needs.

EMILY: Yeah, right. A gang-bang is more like it.

> And a full-scale riot breaks out, during which the women throw every conceivable insult at each other. Emily throws open the toilet door and Philomena comes stomping out, pulling her panties on and joining the riot. All talk at the same time, quietly at first, but then getting louder and louder until they are all screaming.

PHILOMENA [*to Annie*]: What a slime. Make promises and then you go do something else. And I always have to smile at you. What a slime. [*to Emily*]: All that tough talk. I know what's behind it all. You'll never be big enough to push me around. [*to Marie-Adele*]: Fourteen kids! You look like a wrinkled old prune already. [*to Pelajia*]: At least I'm a woman. [*to Veronique*]: Have you any idea how, just how offensive, how obnoxious you are to people? And that halitosis. Pooh! You wouldn't have it if you didn't talk so much.

EMILY [*to Philomena*]: So damned bossy and pushy and sucky. You make me sick. Always wanting your own way. [*to Veronique*]: Goddamned trouble-making old crow. [*to Pelajia*]: Fuckin' self-righteous old bitch. [*to Marie-Adele*]: Mental problems, that's what you got, princess. I ain't no baby. I'm the size of a fuckin' church. [*to Annie*]: You slippery little slut. Brain the size of a fuckin pea. Fuck, man, take a Valium.

VERONIQUE [*to Emily*]: You have no morals at all. You sick pervert. You should have stayed where you came from, where all the other perverts are. [*to Pelajia*]: Slow turtle. Talk big and move like Jell-o. [*to Annie*]: Cockroach! [*to Philomena*]: You big phony. Flush yourself down that damned toilet of yours and shut up. [*to Marie-Adele*]: Hasn't this slimy little reptile [*referring to Annie*] ever told you that sweet little Ellen of hers is really Eugene's daughter? Go talk to the birds in Sudbury and find out for yourself.

PELAJIA [*to Veronique*]: This reserve would be a better place without you. I'm tired of dealing with people like you. Tired. [*to Marie-Adele*]: You can't act that way. This here's no time to be selfish. You spoiled brat. [*to Philomena*]: You old fool. I thought you were coming back to help me and here you are all trussed up like a Thanksgiving turkey, putting on these white lady airs. [*to Annie*]: Annie Cook. Move to Kapuskasing! [*to Emily*]: 'Fuck, fuck, fuck!' Us women got no business talking like that.

MARIE-ADELE [*to Pelajia*]: You don't have all the answers. You can't fix everything. [*to Annie*]: White guys. Slow down a minute and see how stupid you look. [*to Emily*]: Voice like a fog-horn. You ram through everything like a truck. You look like a truck. [*to Veronique*]: Some kind of insect, sticking insect claws into everybody's business. [*to Philomena*]: Those clothes. You look like a giant Kewpie doll. You make me laugh.

ANNIE [*to Marie-Adele*]: You always make me feel so . . . small . . . like a little pig or something. You're no better than me. [*to Philomena*]: Why can't you go to bingo by yourself, you big baby? At least I got staying power. Piss off. [*to Veronique*]: Sucking off everybody else's life like a leech because you got nothing of your own. Pathetic old coot. Just buzz off. [*to Emily*]: You call me names. I don't call you names. You think you're too smart. Shut up. [*to Pelajia*]: 'Queen of the Indians,' you think that's what you are. Well, that stupid hammer of yours doesn't scare me. Go away. Piss me off.

> *Then Pelajia lifts her hammer with a big loud 'Woah'! And they come to a sudden dead stop. Pause. Then one quick final volley, all at once, loudest of all.*

PHILOMENA [*to Annie*]: You slimy buck-toothed drunken worm!

EMILY [*to Veronique*]: Fuckin' instigator!

VERONIQUE [*to Marie-Adele*]: Clutching, clinging vine!

PELAJIA [*to Veronique*]: Evil no-good insect!

MARIE-ADELE [*to Veronique*]: Maggot-mouthed vulture!

ANNIE [*to Philomena*]: Fat-assed floozy, get off the pot!

> *Marie-Adele, stung to the quick, makes a vicious grab for Veronique by the throat. In a split-second, all freeze. Lights out in store interior. Lights on on Zhaboonigan, who has run out in fright during the riot, outside the store. Nanabush, still in his guise as the seagull, makes a grab at Zhaboonigan. Zhaboonigan begins talking to the bird.*

ZHABOONIGAN: Are you gentle? I was not little. Maybe. Same size as now. Long ago it must be? You think I'm funny? Shhh. I know who you are. There, there. Boys. White boys. Two. Ever nice white wings, you. I was walking down the road to the store. They ask me if I want ride in car. Oh, I was happy I said, 'Yup.' They took me far away. Ever nice ride. Dizzy. They took all my clothes off me. Put something up inside me here. [*pointing to her crotch, underneath her dress*] Many, many times. Remember. Don't fly away. Don't go. I saw you before. There, there. It was a. Screwdriver. They put the screwdriver inside me. Here. Remember. Ever lots of blood. The two white boys. Left me in the bush. Alone. It was cold. And then.

Remember. Zhaboonigan. Everybody calls me Zhaboonigan. Why? It means needle. Zhaboonigan. Going-through-thing. Needle Peterson. Going-through-thing Peterson. That's me. It was a screwdriver. Nice. Nice. Nicky Ricky Ben Mark. [*as she counts, with each name, feathers on the bird's wing*] Ever nice. Nice white birdie you.

> *During this last speech, Nanabush goes through agonizing contortions. Then lights change instantly back to the interior of the store. The six women spring back into action. Philomena stomps back into the toilet.*

MARIE-ADELE [*to Veronique*]: Fine. And the whole reserve knows the only reason you ever adopted Zhaboonigan is for her disability cheque.

ANNIE: You fake saint.

> *Annie, Marie-Adele, and Emily start pushing Veronique, round-robin, between the three of them, laughing tauntingly until Veronique is almost reduced to tears.*

VERONIQUE [*almost weeping*]: Bastards. The three of you.

> *Marie-Adele grabs Veronique by the throat and lifts her fist to punch her in the face. But the exertion causes her body to weaken, almost to the point of collapse, from her illness. At this point, Philomena emerges from the toilet.*

PHILOMENA [*crinkling her nose*]: Emily. Your toilet.

WOMEN: Shhhh.

MARIE-ADELE [*holding her waist, reeling, barely audible*]: Oh, shit.

PHILOMENA: I can't get it to flush.

WOMEN: Shhhh.

PELAJIA [*rushing to Marie-Adele*]: Marie-Adele. You're not well.

MARIE-ADELE [*screams*]: Don't touch me.

> *Complete silence from all while Marie-Adele weaves and struggles to keep herself from collapsing. Annie scurries offstage, to the back part of the store, where the post office would be.*

EMILY [*to Veronique*]: You f'in' bitch!

PHILOMENA: What did I just tell you? Who did that to your eye?

VERONIQUE: Big Joey.

EMILY [*to Veronique*]: Look here, you old buzzard. I'll tell you a few things. You see this fist? You see these knuckles? You wanna know where they come from? Ten years. Every second night for 10 long ass-fuckin' years that goddamn Yellowknife asshole Henry Dadzinanare come home to me so drunk his eyes was spittin' blood like Red Lucifer himself and he'd beat me purple.

VERONIQUE: I wish I'd been there to see it all.

EMILY: Yeah, scumbag. I wish you'd been there to watch me learn to fight back like you've never seen a woman fight for her life before. Take a look at this eye. I earned it, Veronique St Pierre, I earned it.

PHILOMENA: Henry Dadzinanare, Big Joey. They're all the same. Emily, use your brains.

EMILY: Use my brains. Yeah, right. I used them alright the night he came at me with an axe and just about sank it into my spine, I grabbed one bag, took one last look at the kids, and walked out of his life forever.

ANNIE [*from offstage*]: And she took the bus to San Francisco.

PHILOMENA: And gets herself mixed up with a motorcycle gang, for God's sake.

EMILY [*now addressing all in the room*]: Rosabella Baez, Hortensia Colorado, Liz Jones, Pussy Commanda. And me. The best. 'Rose and the Rez Sisters', that's us. And man, us sisters could weave knuckle magic.

VERONIQUE: So why did you bother coming back?

PHILOMENA: You stay out of this.

EMILY: Come back to the Rez for a visit, get all wedged up with that hunk Big Joey one night . . . [*grunts*]

PHILOMENA: I give up.

EMILY: . . . and I was hooked. Couldn't leave. Settlin' back on a couple beers with Big Joey the other night when Gazelle Nataways come sashayin' in like she's got half the Rez squished down the crack of her ass. She was high. I was high. Hell, we were all high. Get into a bit of a discussion, when she gets me miffed and I let fly, she let fly, Big Joey let fly, misses that nympho and lands me one in the eye instead.

VERONIQUE: So it was Big Joey.

EMILY: Damn rights. And that's as close as he got cuz I put him out for the night right then and there. Just one of these. [*brandishing her fist*] One. That's all it took.

Veronique runs off to look for Zhaboonigan.

ANNIE and PHILOMENA [*Philomena with exasperation, Annie with adulation, from off-stage*]: Emily Dictionary.

ANNIE: You're amazing!

EMILY: Not Dictionary. Dadzinanare. Henry Dadzinanare. The man who made me learn to fight back. Never let a man raise one dick hair against me since.

VERONIQUE [*calling out to Zhaboonigan*]: Zhaboonigan. Don't you be talking to the birds like that again. You're crazy enough as it is.

ANNIE [*as she comes running back in from the post office with her parcel, already unwrapped, and two letters, one for herself, already unfolded, and one still in its envelope*]: See? I told you. It's a record. Patsy Cline.

PHILOMENA: Never mind Patsy Cline.

ANNIE [*as she hands Marie-Adele the letter in the envelope*]: Hey, Marie-Adele.

EMILY: Read your friggin' letter, Annie Cook.

ANNIE: Listen to this.

Zhaboonigan walks back in as Annie reads her own letter very haltingly.

Dear Mom: Here is the record you wanted. I thought you'd like the picture of Patsy Cline on the cover. [*Annie shows off her record.*] See? It's Patsy Cline. [*returns to her letter*] I also thought you might like to know that there is a bingo called THE BIGGEST BINGO IN THE WORLD. Can you fu . . . ture that?

EMILY [*who has been looking over Annie's shoulder*]: Feature. Feature.

ANNIE: Can you . . . feature . . . that? . . . that's coming to Toronto. The jackpot is $500,000. It's on Saturday, September 8. Ray<u>mond</u>'s Mom was in Toronto. Aunt Philomena will hit the roof when she hears this. Much love, your daughter Ellen. [*Annie announces once more.*]

> *There is a brief electric silence followed by an equally electric scream from all the women. Even Zhaboonigan screams. Excitement takes over completely.*

VERONIQUE: So it's true! It's true!

PHILOMENA: The Espanola bingo. Piffle. Mere piffle.

VERONIQUE: My new stove!

PHILOMENA: My new toilet! White! Spirit white!

EMILY [*grabbing Zhaboonigan and dancing around the room with her*]: I'd take the money, come back to the Rez, beat the shit out of Gazelle Nataways and take you down to Frisco with me. Whaddaya think?

ZHABOONIGAN: Yup.

MARIE-ADELE [*in the background, where she has been reading her letter quietly to herself*]: September 10.

ANNIE [*taking the letter from Marie-Adele*]: Look, Pelajia. Marie-Adele's tests are in Toronto just two days after THE BIGGEST.

> *There is a brief embarrassed silence.*

MARIE-ADELE: Kill two birds with one stone. [*to Nanabush*]: I wanna go. [*to Pelajia and Philomena*]: I wanna go.

VERONIQUE: Goood!

EMILY [*mimicking Veronique*]: Goood! Now how the hell are you guys gonna get down to Toronto? You're all goddamn welfare cases.

ANNIE: Fire Minklater.

VERONIQUE: Mary, mother of Jesus! I refuse, I absolutely refuse to be seen anywhere near that sorceress! We'll chip in and rent a car.

EMILY: Zhaboonigan Peterson here gonna chauffeur you down?

ZHABOONIGAN: Yup.

VERONIQUE: Don't you make fun of my daughter.

EMILY: What kind of stove you gonna buy, Veronique St Pierre? Westinghouse? Electrolux? Yamaha? Kawasaki?

VERONIQUE: Oh my god, Marie-Adele, I never thought about it. They will have so many stoves in Toronto, I'll get confused.

ANNIE: If you go to Toronto and leave Wasy for even one day, Emily, you'll lose Big Joey forever . . .

VERONIQUE: To that witch!

ANNIE: . . . and then whose thighs will you have to wrestle around with in the dead of night? You'll dry up, get all puckered up and pass into ancient history.

EMILY: Annie Cook. I don't know what the fuck you're yatterin' on about now but I'd like to hear you say two words of French to that white guy in Sudbury you're so damn proud of.

ANNIE: Oh my god, Marie-Adele, she's right. I won't know what to say to this Raymond. I've never met him. I can't speak French. All I can say in French is Raymond and Bon Bon and I don't even know what that means. I can't go and live with them, not even after I win THE BIGGEST BINGO IN THE WORLD. What am I gonna do?

[*She collapses on the floor and rolls around for a bit.*]

EMILY: And Philomena Moosemeat's so fulla shit she'd need five toilets to get it all out.

PHILOMENA [*going at Emily*]: And just who do you think you're talking to, Miss Dictionary, just who the hell do you think you're talking to?

With a resounding belly butt from Emily, they begin to wrestle.

PELAJIA [*banging her hammer on the counter*]: Alright, alright. It's obvious we've got a problem here.

EMILY [*throwing Philomena off to the side*]: I'll say.

MARIE-ADELE: It's true. None of us has any money.

But Veronique, standing behind Pelajia, winks at the others and makes a hand motion indicating that Pelajia, for one, does have money. All the other women slowly surround Pelajia. But Pelajia catches the drift and quickly collects herself to meet the onslaught. During Pelajia's speech, the women respond at periodic intervals with a 'yoah' and 'hmmm,' etc., as when a chief speaks at a council meeting.

PELAJIA: I say we all march down to the Band Office and ask the Band Council for a loan that will pay for the trip to this bingo. I know how to handle that tired old chief. He and I have been arguing about paved roads for years now. I'll tell him we'll build paved roads all over the reserve with our prize money. I'll tell him the people will stop drinking themselves to death because they'll have paved roads to walk on. I'll tell him there'll be more jobs because the people will have paved roads to drive to work on. I'll tell him the people will stop fighting and screwing around and Nanabush will come back to us because he'll have paved roads to dance on. There's enough money in there for everyone, I'll say. And if he doesn't lend us the money. I'll tell him I'm packing my bags and moving to Toronto tomorrow.

EMILY: That oughta twist his arm but good.

PELAJIA: And if he still says no, I'll bop him over the head with my hammer and we'll attack the accountant and take the money ourselves. Philomena, we're going to Toronto!

The seven women have this grand and ridiculous march to the band office, around the set and all over the stage area, with Pelajia leading them forward heroically, her hammer just a-swinging in the air. Nanabush trails merrily along in the rear of the line. They reach the 'band office'—standing in one straight line square in front of the audience. The 'invisible' chief 'speaks': cacophonous percussion for about seven beats, the women listening more and more incredulously. Finally, the percussion comes to a dead stop.

PELAJIA: No?

> *Pelajia raises her hammer to hit the 'invisible' chief, Nanabush shrugs a 'don't ask me, I don't know,' Emily fingers a 'fuck you, man.' Blackout. End of Act I.*

ACT II

> *All seven women are holding a meeting in the basement of Pelajia Patchnose's house. This is a collection of chairs and stools off to the side of the stage area. The only light comes from an old, beat-up trilight pole lamp. Some have tea, Emily and Annie a beer.*

VERONIQUE: We should have met at the priest's house.

PELAJIA: No! We're gonna work this out on our own. Right here. Emily Dictionary, you chair. [*And she lends Emily her hammer.*]

VERONIQUE: She's good at ordering people around.

PHILOMENA: Shut up.

EMILY: First. When are we leaving? [*She bangs the hammer regularly throughout the meeting.*]

VERONIQUE: How much is the trip going to cost?

EMILY: When are we leaving?

PHILOMENA: How long to Toronto?

ANNIE: Four hours.

EMILY: When are we leaving?

PHILOMENA: The only human being who can make it in four hours is Annie Cook.

VERONIQUE: I'm not dying on the highway.

PHILOMENA: Eight hours.

PELAJIA: No way we're gonna stop at every toilet on the highway.

MARIE-ADELE: Six hours. Eugene's driven there.

VERONIQUE: Maybe we can borrow his van.

ANNIE: Maybe we can borrow Big Joey's van. [*a quick little aside to Pelajia*]: Hey, can I have another beer?

PELAJIA: No.

VERONIQUE: What about Gazelle Nataways?

EMILY: We're gonna borrow his van, not his buns, for Chris'sakes.

MARIE-ADELE: The only thing we have to pay for is the gas.

ANNIE: Philomena's got gas.

EMILY: Right! Six hours. Eugene's van.

MARIE-ADELE: We still don't know when we're leaving.

PHILOMENA: Bingo's on Saturday night.

ANNIE: Leave Saturday morning.

VERONIQUE: Oh! I'll be so tired for the bingo. I'll get confused. Wednesday. Rest on Thursday.

ANNIE: And rest again on Friday? Too much resting. I can't go for that.

PELAJIA: And we can't afford such a long stay.

PHILOMENA: Where are we gonna stay?

EMILY: Whoa!

Pause.

PELAJIA: Friday night.

EMILY: Right. Leave Friday night. Next.

PHILOMENA: Coming home right after the bingo.

MARIE-ADELE: And leave me behind? Remember my tests Monday morning.

EMILY: Right. Monday noon, we come back. Next.

VERONIQUE: Don't go so fast. My mind is getting confused.

EMILY: Goood! Next.

MARIE-ADELE: Where are we gonna stay?

ANNIE: The Silver Dollar!

MARIE-ADELE: You can't stay there.

ANNIE: There's rooms upstairs.

PELAJIA: You wanna sleep in a whorehouse?

VERONIQUE: Zhaboonigan! Don't listen to this part.

PELAJIA: There's room at my son's.

PHILOMENA: Two washrooms! He's got a wonderful education.

EMILY: Next.

VERONIQUE: Who's going to drive?

ANNIE: Emily. She can drive anything.

VERONIQUE: I believe it.

ANNIE: But I can drive, too.

VERONIQUE: Oh my god.

ANNIE: Long as I don't have to drive in the city. You drive the city.

VERONIQUE: Me?

ANNIE and MARIE-ADELE: No!

PELAJIA: Long as you don't drive too fast, Annie Cook.

PHILOMENA: And we'll pack a lunch for the trip and then eat in restaurants. Chinese.

PELAJIA: Can't afford it. We chip in, buy groceries and cook at my son's.

VERONIQUE: I'll give $10.

EMILY: You old fossil. You want us to starve?

PHILOMENA: $50 a day. Each.

EMILY: Philomena Moosemeat! That's $50 times seven people times four days. That's over a $1,000 worth of groceries.

VERONIQUE: Imagine!

MARIE-ADELE: Okay. Veronique St Pierre. You cook. $20 apiece. Right?

EMILY: Right. Next.

PHILOMENA: Anybody writing this down?

ANNIE: I'm gonna go to Sam the Recordman.

MARIE-ADELE: I'll make the grocery list.

PELAJIA: How much for gas?

VERONIQUE [*still in dreamland over the groceries*]: $1,000!

PHILOMENA [*flabbergasted*]: Nooo! You goose.

ANNIE: $40.

EMILY: $150. Period. Next.

PELAJIA: We got 10 days to find this money.

MARIE-ADELE: What's it cost to get into the bingo?

VERONIQUE: All the Indians in the world will be there!

PHILOMENA: $50.

ANNIE: And we're gonna be the only Indians there.

PELAJIA: Silence.

> [*There is a long, thoughtful silence, broken only after awhile by a scream from Zhaboonigan. Nanabush has knocked her off her stool. The women laugh.*]

Can't think of anything else.

PHILOMENA: Add it up. [*She hands a pencil to Emily.*]

EMILY [*calculates*]: $1,400. You guys need $200 each.

VERONIQUE: Where am I going to get $400?

EMILY: Make it. End of meeting.

And the women start their fundraising activities with a vengeance. The drive is underlined by a wild rhythmic beat from the musician, one that gets wilder and wilder with each successive beat, though always underpinned by this persistent, almost dance-like pulse. The movement of the women covers the entire stage area, and like the music, gets wilder and wilder, until by the end it is as if we are look-ing at an insane eight-ring circus, eight-ring because through all this, Nanabush, as the seagull, has a holiday, particularly with Marie-Adele's lines of laundry, as Marie-Adele madly strings one line of laundry after another all over the set, from Pelajia's roof to Emily's store, etc. For the garage sale, Annie sells off Pelajia's lamp, chairs, etc., so that Pelajia's 'basement' simply dissolves into the madness of the fund-raising drive.

Beat one.

Pelajia is hammering on the roof.
Emily is at the store cash register and rings up each sale as Annie, Philomena, Marie-Adele, Zhaboonigan, and Veronique stand shoulder to shoulder and pass the following from one side of the stage to the other:
seven large sacks marked 'FLOUR'
two giant tubs marked 'LARD'
one bushel of apples

Beat two.

Zhaboonigan brings small table on and puts it stage left.
Annie brings table on and puts it stage right.
Philomena brings a basket full of beer bottles to centre and empties it. She has a baby attached to her.

Veronique comes on with cloth and Windex and starts 'cleaning windows' rhythmically, listening to whatever gossip she can hear.
Marie-Adele strings two lines of clothing across the stage.
Pelajia hammers on her roof.
Emily brings on several empty beer cases and fills them with Philomena's bottles.

Beat three.

Zhaboonigan brings in six quarts of blueberries and then takes over window cleaning from Veronique.
Annie brings on basket of old clothes and a broken kitchen chair.
Philomena brings on another basket full of beer bottles, empties it. She now has two babies attached to her, like a fungus.
Emily fills beer cases rapidly, expertly.
Pelajia gets down off roof, hammering everything until she is on hands and knees, hammering the floor.
Marie-Adele strings third and fourth lines of laundry across the stage.
Veronique comes in burdened with seven apple pies and puts them on Annie's table.

Beat four.

Pelajia hammers as she crawls across the floor.
Zhaboonigan washes windows like a person possessed.
Emily runs and rings up a sale on the cash register and then brings on more empty beer cases and loads them up.
Philomena brings on a third load of bottles. Three babies are now attached to her.
Annie brings on an old trilight pole lamp and an old record player, which she opens and stacks alongside the rest of her stuff.
Annie and Emily sing a line of their song with very bad harmony.
Marie-Adele strings fifth and sixth lines of laundry across stage.
Veronique comes on with seven loaves of bread and puts them neatly by the pies.

Beat five.

Pelajia hammers as she crawls across the floor, hammering everything in sight. The women protect their poor feet.
Zhaboonigan washes windows even faster; she's starting to cry.
Emily and Philomena work together filling the empty beer cases as fast as they can.
Emily runs to the register, rings in seven sales and sings a bit of song with Annie, better this time. Philomena now has four kids attached to her body.
Annie comes on with a small black and white TV with rabbit ears and an old toaster.
Veronique comes on with six dozen buns and dumps them out of their tins all over the table.
Pelajia hammers faster and faster.
Zhaboonigan is now working like a maniac and is sobbing.
Marie-Adele strings seventh and eight lines of laundry across the stage.

Beat six.

Emily goes to cash register and tallies their earnings; she works the register with tremendous speed and efficiency all this beat.
Zhaboonigan continues washing windows.
Philomena sticks a sign in beer bottles: World's Biggest Bottle Drive. She now has five babies attached to her.
Veronique sticks a sign on her table: World's Biggest Bake Sale.
Annie sticks a sign up around her stuff: World's Biggest Garage Sale.
Marie-Adele sticks a sign up on Zha's table: Big Blueberries and Laundry While You Wait.
Pelajia begins hammering the air. She may have lost her marbles.

Beat seven.

EMILY: Whoa!

The 'music' comes to a sudden stop. The women all collapse. The women look at each other. They then quickly clear the stage of everything they've brought on as Pelajia speaks, consulting her list. By the end of Pelajia's speech, the stage area is clear once more, except for a microphone stand that one of the women has brought on as part of the 'clean-up' activities.

PELAJIA: Bottle drive. Ten cents a bottle, 24 bottles a case, equals two dollars and 40 cents. 777 bottles collected divided by 24 is 32 cases and nine singles that's 32 times $2.40 equals $77.70. Blueberries equals $90. Good pickin' Zha and the Starblanket kids. Washing windows at $5.00 a house times 18 houses. Five eights are 40, carry the four and add the five is 90 bucks less two on account of that cheap Gazelle Nataways only gave three dollars. That's $88. Household repairs is four roofs including the Chief's and one tiled floor is $225. Garage sale brung in $246.95, the bake sale equals $83 after expenses, we make 110 bucks on doing laundry, 65 bucks babysitting, 145 from Emily doing a double shift at the store and I have generously donated $103 from my savings. That brings us to a grand total of $1233.75. So!

Emily and Annie move forward as the music starts up. They are lit only by tacky floor flood-lighting, and are, in effect, at the Anchor Inn, Little Current. Emily speaks into the microphone.

EMILY: Thank-you. Thank-you, ladies and gentlemen. I thank you very much. And now for the last song of the night, ladies and gents, before we hit the road. A song that's real special to me in my heart. A song I wrote in memory of one Rosabella Baez, a Rez Sister from way back. And Rose baby, if you're up there tonight, I hope you're listenin' in. Cuz it's called: 'I'm Thinkin' of You.' Here goes . . .

Emily and Annie grab their microphones; Emily sings lead, Annie sings backup. And it's 'country' to the hilt.

I'm thinkin' of you every moment,
As though you were here by my side;
I'll always remember the good times,
So darlin' please come back to me.

I'm dreamin' of you every night,
That we were together again;
If time can heal up our partin'
Then love can remove all this pain.

> *Instrumental—dance break*

If love is the secret of livin',
Then give me that love, shinin' light;
When you are again by my side,
Then livin' will once more be right.

> *The audience claps. Emily says, 'Thank-you.' And then she and Annie join the other women, who have, during the song, loaded themselves, their suitcases, and their lunches into the 'van'. This van consists of three battered old van seats stuck to the walls of the theatre, on either side and up high. The back seat is on the 'stage left' side of the theatre and the other two are on the other side, the middle seat of the van towards the back of the theatre, the front seat, complete with detachable steering wheel, just in front and 'stage right' of the stage area. Each seat is lit by its own light.*

EMILY: How much did me and Annie take in singin' at the Anchor Inn?

PELAJIA: $330 at the door.

MARIE-ADELE: Solid packed house, eh? Shoulda charged more.

ANNIE: Fifty bucks for the oom-chi-cha machine. Twenty bucks for Ronnie's guitar. That's our only costs.

EMILY: Ha! We're laughin'.

> A capella *reprise of a verse of their song, which fades into the highway sounds, and they drive, for a few moments, in silence.*

> *In the van, driving down the highway to Toronto, at night. The women have intimate conversations, one on one, while the rest are asleep or seated at the other end of the van. Annie is driving. Emily sits beside her listening to her Walkman, while Marie-Adele is 'leaning' over Annie's shoulder from her place in the middle seat. Veronique sits beside Marie-Adele, sleeping. Pelajia and Philomena are in the very back seat with Zhaboonigan between them.*

MARIE-ADELE: Nee, Annie, not so fast.

> [*Pause. Annie slows down.*]

So. You couldn't get Ellen and <u>Raymond</u> to come along? I'd like to meet this <u>Raymond</u> someday.

ANNIE [*angrily insisting on the correct pronunciation*]: Ray<u>mond</u>! Ellen says he's got a whole library full of cassette tapes.

MARIE-ADELE: Annie. You ever think about getting married again?

ANNIE: Not really. I can hear the band at the Silver Dollar already.

MARIE-ADELE: Do you still think about . . . Eugene?

ANNIE: What're you talkin' about? Of course, I think about him, he's my brother-in-law, ain't he?

MARIE-ADELE: He made his choice.

ANNIE: Yeah. He picked you.

MARIE-ADELE: Annie. I never stole him off you.

ANNIE: Drop dead. Shit! I forgot to bring that blouse. I mean. In case I sing. Shit.

MARIE-ADELE: If I'm gone and Eugene if he starts drinkin' again. I see you going for him.

ANNIE: Why would I bother? I had my chance 20 years ago. Christ!

MARIE-ADELE: Twenty years ago, I was there.

ANNIE: Why would I want 14 kids for?

MARIE-ADELE: That's exactly what I'm scared of. I don't want them kids to be split up. You come near Eugene you start drinking messing things up me not here I come back and don't matter where you are . . . .

ANNIE: I don't want him. I don't want him. I don't want him. I don't want him. I don't want him.

EMILY: Put us all in the fuckin' ditch!

PELAJIA: Hey, watch your language up there.

ANNIE: Shit! I don't care. There's nothing more to say about it. Why don't you take your pills and go to sleep.

Pelajia and Philomena begin talking.

PHILOMENA: September 8 again.

PELAJIA: Hmmm? What about September 8?

PHILOMENA: You don't remember?

PELAJIA: What?

PHILOMENA: How could you?

PELAJIA: Mama died?

PHILOMENA: No! Remember?

PELAJIA: I can't remember. Got so much on my mind. So many things to forget.

ZHABOONIGAN [*to Philomena*]: You like me?

PHILOMENA: Yes, Zhaboonigan. I like you.

ZHABOONIGAN: I like the birdies.

PHILOMENA: You like talking to the birdies?

ZHABOONIGAN: Yup. [*She falls asleep.*]

PHILOMENA: Zhaboonigan . . . sometimes I wonder . . .

PELAJIA: It's dark . . . warm . . . quiet . . . .

PHILOMENA: Toronto. Had a good job in Toronto. Yeah. Had to give it all up. Yeah. Cuz mama got sick. Philomena Margaret Moosetail. Real live secretary in the garment district. He'd come in and see my boss. Nice man, I thought. That big, red, fish-tail Caddy. Down Queen Street. He liked me. Treated me like a queen. Loved me. Or I thought he did. I don't know. Got pregnant anyway. Blond, blue-eyed, six foot two. And the way he smelled. God! His wife walks in on us.

[*Long silence.*]

He left with her.

[*Long silence.*]

I don't even know to this day if it was a boy or a girl. I'm getting old. That child would be . . . 28 . . . 28 years old. September 8. You know what I'm gonna do with that money if I win? I'm gonna find a lawyer. Maybe I can find that child. Maybe I wouldn't even have to let him . . . her . . . know who I am. I just . . . want to see . . . who . . .

PELAJIA: I hope you win.

> *Annie and Emily, at the front of the van with Annie driving, are laughing and singing, 'I'm a little Indian who loves fry bread'. From time to time, they sneak each other a sip of this little bottle of whisky Annie has hidden away inside her purse.*

I'm a little Indian who loves fry bread,
Early in the morning and when I go to bed;
Some folks say I'm crazy in the head,
Cuz I'm a little Indian who loves fry bread.

Now, some folks say I've put on a pound or two,
My jeans don't fit the way they used to do;
But I don't care, let the people talk,
Cuz if I don't get my fry bread, you'll hear me squawk.

ANNIE: So tell me. What's it like to go to a big bar like . . . I mean like . . . the Silver Dollar.

EMILY: Lotta Nishnawbs.[6]

ANNIE [*disappointed*]: Yeah? Is the music good?

EMILY: Country rock.

ANNIE [*screams gleefully*]: Yee-haw! Maybe the band will ask me up to sing, eh? I'll sing something fast.

EMILY: You would, too.

ANNIE [*sings real fast*]: 'Well, it's 40 below and I don't give a fuck, got a heater in my truck and I'm off to the rodeo. Woof!' Something like that.

EMILY: Yup. That's pretty fast.

ANNIE: Hey. Maybe Fritz the Katz will be there. Never know. Might get laid, too, eh? Remember Room 20 at the Anchor Inn? Oh, that Fritz! Sure like singin' with him. Crazy about the way . . .

[*Emily starts singing Patsy Cline's famous 'Crazy . . . crazy for feelin' so lonely . . .' all the way through Annie's next speech.*]

. . . he stands there with his guitar and his 10-gallon hat. Is that what you call them hats? You know the kind you wear kind of off to the side like this? That's what he

6 Indians. (Ojibway)

does. And then he winks at me. [*sings*] 'Crazy . . .' Oooh, I love, just love the way the lights go woosh woosh in your eyes and kinda' wash over your body. Me standing there shuffling my feet side to side, dressed real nice and going [*sings*] 'Oooh darlin' . . .' with my mike in my hand just so. Oh! And the sound of that band behind me. And Fritz. [*sings*] 'Crazy, crazy for feelin' so lonely . . .'

EMILY: Yeah. You look good on stage.

ANNIE: Yeah?

EMILY: How come you're so keen on that guy anyway?

ANNIE: Sure Veronique St Pierre isn't just pretending to be asleep back there?

Emily and Marie-Adele check Veronique in the middle seat.

MARIE-ADELE: Nah. Out like a lamp.

EMILY: Hey! We'll get her drunk at the Silver Dollar and leave her passed out under some table. Take two beers to do that.

ANNIE: Hey. Too bad Big Joey had to come back from Toronto before we got there, eh?

EMILY: Man! That dude's got buns on him like no other buns on the face of God's entire creation. Whooo! No to mention a dick that's bigger than a goddamn breadbox.
[*Annie screams gleefully.*]
How about Fritz? What's his look like?

ANNIE [*after an awkward pause*]: He's Jewish, you know.

EMILY [*laughing raucously*]: World's first Jewish country singer!

ANNIE: Don't laugh. Those Jews make a lot of money, you know.

EMILY: Not all of them.

ANNIE: Fritz buys me jeans and things. I'm gonna be one of them Jewish princesses.

EMILY: What's wrong with being an Indian princess?

ANNIE: Aw, these white guys. They're nicer to their women. Not like Indian guys. Screw you, drink all your money, and leave you flat on your ass.

EMILY: Yeah, right. Apple Indian Annie. Red on the outside. White on the inside.

ANNIE: Emily!

EMILY: Keep your eye on the road.

ANNIE: Good ol' highway 69.

EMILY: Hey. Ever 69 with Fritz?

MARIE-ADELE: Neee.

ANNIE: White guys don't make you do things to them. You just lie there and they do it all for you. Ellen's real happy with her Raymond. You can tell the way she sounds on the phone. Maybe someday I'll just take off with a guy like Fritz.

EMILY: Then what? Never come back to the rez?
[*Annie is cornered. Emily then slaps her playfully on the arm.*]
Hey. Know what?
[*sings*]

When I die, I may not go to heaven,
I don't know if they let Indians in;
If they don't, just let me go to Wasy, lord,
Cuz Wasy is as close as I've been.

ANNIE: Lots of white people at this Silver Dollar?

EMILY: Sometimes. Depends.

ANNIE: How much for beer there?

EMILY: Same as up here. Nah! Don't need money, Annie Cook. You just gotta know how to handle men. Like me and the Rez Sisters down in Frisco.

ANNIE: Yeah?

EMILY: I'll take care of them.

ANNIE: Maybe we can find a party, eh? Maybe with the band.

EMILY: Whoa! Slow down, Annie Cook! Easy on the gas!

MARIE-ADELE: Annie!

Pow. Black-out. They have a flat tire.

The flat tire. Everything now happens in complete darkness.

VERONIQUE: Bingo!

PHILOMENA: What was that? What happened?

ANNIE: I don't know. Something just went 'poof'!

EMILY: Alright. Everybody out. We got a fuckin' flat.

They all climb out of the van.

VERONIQUE: Oh my god! We'll never get to the bingo.

ZHABOONIGAN: Pee pee.

PELAJIA: I can't fix a flat tire.

ANNIE: Emily can.

PELAJIA: Get the jack. Spare tire.

ANNIE: Philomena's wearing one.

ZHABOONIGAN: Pee pee.

PHILOMENA: This is all your fault, Annie Cook.

MARIE-ADELE: It's in the back.

ANNIE: So what do we do?

PELAJIA: What's the matter with Zha?

PHILOMENA: Gotta make pee pee.

VERONIQUE: I knew there was something wrong with this van the moment I set eyes on it. I should have taken the bus.

PHILOMENA: Oh shut up. Quack, quack, quack.

ANNIE: Don't look at me. It's not my fault the tires are all bald.

PHILOMENA: Nobody's blaming you.

ANNIE: But you just did.

PHILOMENA: Quack, quack, quack.

VERONIQUE: Where are we?

ANNIE: The Lost Channel. This is where you get off.

VERONIQUE [*groans*]: Ohhh!

EMILY: Yeah, right.

PHILOMENA: Shhh!

PELAJIA: Jack's not working too well.

EMILY: Okay. Everybody. Positions.

VERONIQUE: Not me. My heart will collapse.

EMILY: You wanna play bingo?

VERONIQUE [*groans*]: Ohhh!

ANNIE: Hurry up! Hurry up!

EMILY: Okay. One, two, three lift.

Everybody lifts and groans.

PELAJIA: Put the jack in there.

All lift, except Marie-Adele and Zha, who wander off into the moonlight darkness. Dim light on them.

ZHABOONIGAN: Ever dark.

MARIE-ADELE: You'll be fine, Zhaboonigan.

Suddenly, a nighthawk—Nanabush, now in dark feathers—appears, darting in the night.

ZHABOONIGAN: The birdies!

MARIE-ADELE: Yes, a birdie.

ZHABOONIGAN: Black wings!

Marie-Adele begins talking to the bird, almost if she were talking to herself. Quietly, at first, but gradually—as the bird begins attacking her—growing more and more hysterical, until she is shrieking, flailing, and thrashing about insanely.

MARIE-ADELE: Who are you? What do you want? My children? Eugene? No! Oh no! Me? Not yet. Give me time. Please. Don't. Please don't. Awus! Get away from me. Eugene! Awus! You fucking bird! Awus! Awus! Awus! Awus!

And she has a total hysterical breakdown.

Zhaboonigan, at first, attempts to scare the bird off by running and flailing her arms at it. Until the bird knocks her down and she lies there on the ground, watching in helpless astonishment and abject terror. Underneath Marie-Adele's screams, she mumbles to herself, sobbing.

ZHABOONIGAN: One, two, three, four, five, six, seven . . . Nicky Ricky Ben Mark . . . eight, nine, ten, eleven, twelve . . . [*until the other women come running. Total darkness again.*]

EMILY: What the . . .

ANNIE: Marie-Adele!

PELAJIA: Stop her! Hold her!

VERONIQUE: What's happening?

PHILOMENA: Marie-Adele. Now, now . . . come . . . come . . .

EMILY [*in the background*]: Stop that fucking screaming will ya, Marie-Adele!

PHILOMENA: Emily. There's no need to talk to her like that now.

PELAJIA: Help us get her in the van.

PHILOMENA: Come . . . come, Marie-Adele . . . everything's fine . . . you'll be fine . . . come . . . shhh . . . shhh . . .

> *And they ease Marie-Adele back into the van. Once all is beginning to settle down again:*

PELAJIA: Everything okay now?

PHILOMENA: Yes. She's fine now.

PELAJIA: Emily, take over.

VERONIQUE: Yes. I don't trust that Annie Cook. Not for one minute.

EMILY: All set?

MARIE-ADELE: What time is it?

PELAJIA: Twenty after four.

ANNIE: Oh! We're over two hours behind schedule. Hurry up. Hurry up.

VERONIQUE: I'll be exhausted for the bingo tomorrow night. Maybe I should just take 15 cards.

EMILY: You can rest your heart. And your mouth. All day tomorrow. All set? [*And she starts up the van. The van lights come back on.*]

> *The dialogues resume. Marie-Adele now sits in the front with Emily, who is driving. Zhaboonigan sits between them. Pelajia and Philomena are now in the middle seat, Annie and Veronique in the back.*

EMILY: You scared the shit out of me out there.

[*silence*]

Don't do that again.

[*silence*]

Feeling better now?

[*silence*]

MARIE-ADELE: I could be really mad, just raging mad just wanna tear his eyes out with my nails when he walks in the door and my whole body just goes 'k-k-k-k'. . . . He doesn't talk when something goes wrong with him, he doesn't talk, shuts me out, just disappears. Last night he didn't come home. Again, it happened. I couldn't sleep. You feel so ugly. He walks in this morning. Wanted to be alone, he said. The curve of his back, his breath on my neck. 'Adele, ki-sa-gee-ee-tin oo-ma,'[7] making love, always in Indian, only. When we still could. I can't even have him inside me anymore. It's still growing there. The cancer. Pelajia, een-pay-seek-see-yan.[8]

PELAJIA: You know one time, I knew this couple where one of them was dying and the other one was angry at her for dying. And she was mad because he was gonna be there when she wasn't and she had so much left to do. And she'd lie there in bed and tell him to do this and do that and he'd say 'Okay, okay.' And then he'd go

---

7 Adele, I love you. (Cree)
8 Pelajia, I'm scared to death. (Cree)

into the kitchen and say to me, 'She's so this and she's so that and she's so damned difficult.' And I watched all this going on. That house didn't have room for two such angry people. But you know, I said to her, 'You gotta have faith in him and you gotta have faith in life. He loves you very much but there's only so much he can do. He's only human.' There's only so much Eugene can understand, Marie-Adele. He's only human.

EMILY: Fuckin' right. Me and the Rez Sisters, okay? Cruisin' down the coast highway one night. Hum of the engine between my thighs. Rose. That's Rosabella Baez, leader of the pack. We were real close, me and her. She was always thinkin' real deep. And talkin' about bein' a woman. An Indian woman. And suicide. And alcohol and despair and how fuckin' hard it is to be an Indian in this country.

[*Marie-Adele shushes her gently.*]

No goddamn future for them, she'd say. And why, why, why? Always carryin' on like that. Chris'sakes. She was pretty heavy into the drugs. Guess we all were. We had a fight. Cruisin' down the coast highway that night. Rose in the middle. Me and Pussy Commanda off to the side. Big 18-wheeler come along real fast and me and Pussy Commanda get out of the way. But not Rose. She stayed in the middle. Went head-on into that truck like a fly splat against a windshield. I swear to this day I can still feel the spray of her blood against my neck. I drove on. Straight into daylight. Never looked back. Had enough gas money on me to take me far as Salt Lake City. Pawned my bike off and bought me a bus ticket back to Wasy. When I got to Chicago, that's when I got up the nerve to wash my lover's dried blood from off my neck. I loved that woman, Marie-Adele, I loved her like no man's ever loved a woman. But she's gone. I never wanna go back to San Francisco. No way, man.

MARIE-ADELE [*comforting the crying Emily*]: You should get some rest. Let Annie take over.

EMILY: I'll be fine. You go to sleep. Wake you up when we get to Toronto.

Emily puts her Walkman on and starts to sing along quietly to 'Blue Kentucky Girl' by Emmylou Harris with its 'I swear I love you . . .' while Marie-Adele leans her head against the 'window' and falls asleep.

After a few moments, Zhaboonigan, who has been dozing off between Emily and Marie-Adele in the front seat, pokes her head up and starts to sing along off-key. Then she starts to play with Emily's hair.

EMILY [*shrugging Zhaboonigan's hand off*]: Don't bug me. My favourite part's comin' up.

Initiated by Zhaboonigan, they start playing 'slap.' The game escalates to the point where Emily almost bangs Zhaboonigan over the head with her elbow.

EMILY: Yeah, right. You little retard.

[*Mad at this, Zhaboonigan hits Emily in the stomach.*]

Don't hit me there, you little. . . . Hey, man, like ummm . . . I'm sorry, Zha.

ZHABOONIGAN: Sorry.

EMILY [*Emily feels her belly thoughtfully. After a brief silence*]: You gonna have kids someday, Zha?

ZHABOONIGAN: Ummm . . . buy one.

EMILY: Holy! Well, kids were alright. Aw geez, Zha, that man treated me real bad. Ever been tied to a bed post with your arms up like this? Whoa! [*grabbing the steering wheel*] Maybe you should drive.

ZHABOONIGAN: Scary.

EMILY: Aw, don't be scared. Fuck.

ZHABOONIGAN: Fuck.

EMILY: Zhaboonigan Peterson! Your ma'll give me a black eye.

> *Zhaboonigan turns her head toward the back seat, where Veronique sits sleeping, and says one more time, really loud.*

ZHABOONIGAN: Fuck!

EMILY: Shhh! Look, Zha. You don't let any man bother you while we're down in T.O. You just stick close to me.

ZHABOONIGAN: Yup.

EMILY: We're sisters, right? Gimme five.

[*They slap hands.*]

Alright. Bingo!!!

> *Instantly, the house lights come on full blast. The Bingo Master—the most beautiful man in the world—comes running up the centre aisle, cordless mike in hand, dressed to kill: tails, rhinestones, and all. The entire theatre is now the bingo palace. We are in: Toronto!!!!*

BINGO MASTER: Welcome, ladies and gentlemen, to the biggest bingo the world has ever seen! Yes, ladies and gentlemen, tonight, we have a very special treat for you. Tonight, ladies and gentlemen, you will be witness to events of such gargantuan proportions, such cataclysmic ramifications, such masterly and magnificent manifestations that your minds will reel, your eyes will nictitate, and your hearts will palpitate erratically.

Because tonight, ladies and gentlemen, you will see the biggest, yes, ladies and gentlemen, the very biggest prizes ever known to man, woman, beast, or appliance. And the jackpot tonight? The jackpot, ladies and gentlemen, is surely the biggest, the largest, the hugest, and the most monstrous jackpot ever conceived of in the entire history of monstrous jackpots as we know them. $500,000! Yes, ladies and gentlemen, $500,000 can be yours this very night! That's half a million—A HALF MILLION SMACKEROOS!!! IF you play the game right.

And all you have to do, ladies and gentlemen, is reach into your programs and extract the single bingo card placed therein. Yes, ladies and gentlemen, the single bingo card placed therein, which bingo card will entitle you to one chance at winning the warm-up game for a prize of $20. $20! And all you have to do is poke holes in that single bingo card. Yes, ladies and gentlemen, just poke holes in that single bingo card and bend the numbers backward as the numbers are called. And don't forget the free hole in the middle of the card. Twenty dollars, ladies and gentlemen, that's one line in any direction. That means, of course, ladies and gentlemen, that the first person to form one line, just one straight line in any direction on their card, will be the very lucky winner of the $20 prize. $20! Are you ready, ladies and gentlemen? Are you ready? Then let the game begin! Under the G 56. Etc. . . .

The audience plays bingo, with the seven women, who have moved slowly into the audience during the Bingo Master's speech, playing along. Until somebody in the audience shouts, 'Bingo!'

BINGO MASTER: Hold your cards, ladies and gentlemen, bingo has been called.

The Bingo Master and the assistant stage manager check the numbers and the prize money is paid out.

BINGO MASTER: And now for the game you've all been waiting for, ladies and gentlemen. Now for the big game. Yes, ladies and gentlemen, get ready for THE BIGGEST BINGO IN THE WORLD! For the grand jackpot prize of $500,000! Full house, ladies and gentlemen, full house! Are you ready? Are you ready? Then let the game begin!

The house lights go out. And the only lights now are on the bingo balls bouncing around in the bingo machine—an eery, surreal sort of glow—and on the seven women who are now playing bingo with a vengeance on centrestage, behind the Bingo Master, where a long bingo table has magically appeared with Zhaboonigan at the table's centre banging a crucifix Veronique has bought along for good luck. The scene is lit so that it looks like 'The Last Supper'.

The women face the audience. The bingo table is covered with all the necessary accoutrements: bags of potato chips, cans of pop, ashtrays (some of the women are smoking), etc. The Bingo Master calls out number after number—but not the B 14—with the women improvising responses. These responses—Philomena has 27 cards!—grow more and more raucous: 'B 14? Annie Cook? One more number to go! The B 14! Where is that B 14? Gimme that B 14! Where the fuck is that B 14?!!!' etc. Until the women have all risen from the table and come running downstage, attacking the bingo machine and throwing the Bingo Master out of the way. The women grab the bingo machine with shouts of: 'Throw this fucking machine into the lake! It's no damn good!' etc. And they go running down centre aisle with it and out of the theatre. Bingo cards are flying like confetti. Total madness and mayhem. The music is going crazy.

And out of this chaos emerges the calm, silent image of Marie-Adele waltzing romantically in the arms of the Bingo Master. The Bingo Master says 'Bingo' into her ear. And the Bingo Master changes, with sudden bird-like movements, into the nighthawk, Nanabush in dark feathers. Marie-Adele meets Nanabush.

During this next speech, the other women, one by one, take their positions around Marie-Adele's porch, some kneeling, some standing. The stage area, by means of 'lighting magic', slowly returns to its Wasaychigan Hill appearance.

MARIE-ADELE: U-wi-nuk u-wa? U-wi-nuk u-wa? Eugene? Neee. U-wi-nuk ma-a oo-ma kee-tha? Ka. Kee-tha i-chi-goo-ma so that's who you are . . . at rest upon the rock . . . the master of the game . . . the game . . . it's me . . . nee-tha . . . come . . . come . . . don't be afraid . . . as-tum . . . come . . . to . . . me . . . ever soft wings . . . beautiful soft . . . soft . . . dark wings . . . here . . . take me . . . as-tum . . . as-tum . . . pee-na-sin . . . wings . . . here . . . take me . . . take . . . me . . . with . . . pee-na-sin . . .[9]

As Nanabush escorts Marie-Adele into the spirit world, Zhaboonigan, uttering a cry, makes a last desperate attempt to go with them. But Emily rushes after and catches her at the very last split second. And the six remaining women begin to sing the Ojibway funeral song. By the beginning of the funeral song, we are back at the Wasaychigan Hill Indian Reserve, at Marie-Adele's grave.

WOMEN:
Wa-kwing, wa-kwing,
Wa-kwing nin wi-i-ja;
Wa-kwing, wa-kwing,
Wa-kwing nin wi-i-ja.[10]

At Marie-Adele's grave. During Pelajia's speech, the other women continue humming the funeral song until they fade into silence. Pelajia drops a handful of earth on the grave.

PELAJIA: Well, sister, guess you finally hit the big jackpot. Best bingo game we've ever been to in our lives, huh? You know, life's like that, I figure. When all is said and done. Kinda' silly, innit, this business of living? But. What choice do we have? When some fool of a being goes and puts us Indians plunk down in the middle of this old earth, dishes out this lot we got right now. But. I figure we gotta make the most of it while we're here. You certainly did. And I sure as hell am giving it one good try. For you. For me. For all of us. Promise. Really. See you when that big bird finally comes for me.[*whips out her hammer one more time, holds it up in the air and smiles*] And my hammer.

Back at the store in Wasaychigan Hill. Emily is tearing open a brand-new case of the small cans of Carnation milk, takes two cans out and goes up to Zhaboonigan with them.

9 MARIE-ADELE: Who are you? Who are you? Eugene? Nee. Then who are you really? Oh. It's you, so that's who you are . . . at rest upon the rock . . . the master of the game . . . the game . . . it's me . . . me . . . come . . . come . . . don't be afraid . . . come . . . come . . . to . . . me . . . ever . . . soft wings . . . beautiful soft . . . soft . . . darkwings . . . here . . . take me . . . come . . . come . . . come and get me . . . wings here . . . take me . . . take . . . me . . . with . . . come and get me . . . (Cree)
10 WOMEN: Heaven, heaven, heaven, I'm going there; Heaven, heaven, heaven, I'm going there. (Ojibway)

EMILY: See, Zha? The red part up here and the white part down here and the pink flowers in the middle?

ZHABOONIGAN: Oh.

EMILY: Carnation milk.

ZHABOONIGAN: Carnation milk.

EMILY: And it goes over here where all the other red and white cans are, okay?

ZHABOONIGAN: Yup.

Zhaboonigan rushes to Emily and throws her arms around her affectionately. Emily is embarrassed and struggles to free herself. Just then, Annie enters. She's lost some of her speed and frenetic energy. There's obviously something wrong with her.

ANNIE: Halloo! Whatchyou doing.

EMILY: Red Lucifer's whiskers! It's Annie Cook.

ANNIE: Well, we seem to have survived the biggest bingo in the world, eh? Well . . . ummm . . . not all of us . . . not Marie-Adele . . . but she knew she was . . . but we're okay. [*laughs*] . . . us? . . .

EMILY: Annie Cook. Sometimes you can be so goddamn ignorant. [*pause*] Too bad none of us won, eh.

ANNIE: Philomena Moosemeat won $600. That's something.

EMILY: Yup. That's one helluva jazzy toilet she's got there, eh?

ANNIE: She's got eight-ply toilet paper. Dark green. Feels like you're wiping your ass with moss!

EMILY: Holy!

ANNIE: I'm singing back-up for Fritz weekends. 25 bucks a gig. That's something, eh?

EMILY: Katz's whore . . .

ANNIE: What?

EMILY: You heard me.

ANNIE: The Katz's what?

EMILY: Chris'sakes. Wake up.

ANNIE: I love him, Emily.

EMILY: You been drinkin'.

ANNIE: Please, come with me tonight.

EMILY: Have to wait for the old buzzard to come pick up this dozy daughter of hers and that's not 'til seven.

ANNIE: Okay?

EMILY: Alright. But we're comin' right back to the Rez soon as the gig's over. Hear?

ANNIE: Thanks. Any mail today?

EMILY: Sorry.

ANNIE: That's okay. See you at seven. [*And she exits.*]

ZHABOONIGAN: Why . . . why . . . why do you call me that?

EMILY: Call you what?

ZHABOONIGAN: Dozy dotter.

Awkward silence, broken after awhile by Zhaboonigan's little giggle.

EMILY: Look, Zha. Share a little secret with you, okay?

ZHABOONIGAN: Yup.

EMILY: Just you and me, promise?

ZHABOONIGAN: Yup.

EMILY: Gazelle Nataways'll see fit to kill . . . but I'm gonna have a baby.

ZHABOONIGAN [*drops the Carnation milk cans she's been holding all this time and gasps*]:
Ohhh! Big Joey!

EMILY [*in exasperation*]: This business of having babies . . .

> *And the last we see of them is Zhaboonigan playfully poking Emily in the belly and
> Emily slapping Zhaboonigan's hand away.*

> *At Eugene Starblanket's house. Veronique St Pierre is sitting on the steps, glowing
> with happiness, looking up at the sky as though looking for seagulls. She sees none so
> she picks up the doll that lies under her chair and cradles it on her lap as though it
> were a child. At this point, Annie Cook enters.*

ANNIE: Halloo! [*surprised to see Veronique sitting there*] Veronique St Pierre. What are
you doing here?

VERONIQUE: Annie Cook. Haven't you heard I'm cooking for Eugene and the children
these days? It's been four days since the funeral as you know may she rest in peace
[*makes a quick sign of the cross without missing beat*] but I was the only person on
this reserve who was willing to help with these 14 little orphans.

ANNIE: That's nice. But I came to see if Simon Star . . .

VERONIQUE: The stove is so good. All four elements work and there is even a timer for
the oven. As I was saying to Black Lady Halked at the bingo last night, 'Now I don't
have to worry about burning the fried potatoes or serving the roast beef half-raw.'

ANNIE: Well, I was about to . . .

VERONIQUE: Yes, Annie Cook. I bought a roast beef just yesterday. A great roast beef.
Almost 16 pounds. It's probably the biggest roast beef that's been seen on this
reserve in recent years. The meat was so heavy that Nicky, Ricky, Ben, and Mark
had to take turns carrying it here for me. Oh, it was hard and slippery at first, but
I finally managed to wrestle it into my oven. And it's sitting in there at this very
moment just sizzling and bubbling with the most succulent and delicious juices.
And speaking of succulent and delicious juices, did you come to call on Eugene?
Well, Eugene's not home.

ANNIE: Yeah, right. I came to see if Simon had that new record.

VERONIQUE: Why?

ANNIE: I'm singing in Little Current tonight and I gotta practise this one song.

VERONIQUE [*contemptuously*]: That Ritzie Ditzie character.

ANNIE: It's Fritz the Katz, Veronique St Pierre. FREDERICK STEPHEN KATZ. He's a very
fine musician and a good teacher.

VERONIQUE: Teacher?! Of what?! As I was saying to Little Girl Manitowabi and her
daughter June Bug McLeod at the bingo last night, 'You never know about these
non-Native bar-room types.' I said to them, 'We have enough trouble right here

on this reserve without having our women come dragging these shady white characters into the picture.' Before you know it, you will end up in deep trouble and bring shame and disrespect on the name of Pelajia Patchnose and all your sisters, myself included.

ANNIE: Myself included, my ass! Veronique St Pierre. I wish you would shut that great big shitty mouth of yours at least once a year!

VERONIQUE [*stunned into momentary silence. Then*]: Simon Starblanket is not at home. [*With this, she bangs the doll down viciously.*]

ANNIE: Good day, Veronique St Pierre. [*And exits.*]

Veronique, meanwhile, just sits there in her stunned state, mouth hanging open and looking after the departing Annie.

On Pelajia Patchnose's roof. As at the beginning of the play, Pelajia is alone, nailing shingles on. But no cushion this time.

PELAJIA: Philomena. Where are those shingles?

PHILOMENA [*from offstage*]: Oh, go on. I'll be up in just a minute.

PELAJIA [*coughs*]: The dust today. It's these dirt roads. Dirt roads all over. Even the main street. If I were chief around here, that's the very first thing I would do is . . .

PHILOMENA [*coming up the ladder with one shingle and the most beautiful pink, lace-embroidered, heart-shaped pillow you'll ever see*]: Oh, go on. You'll never be chief.

PELAJIA: And why not?

PHILOMENA: Because you're a woman.

PELAJIA: Bullshit! If that useless old chief of ours was a woman, we'd see a few things get done around here. We'd see our women working, we'd see our men working, we'd see our young people sober on Saturday nights, and we'd see Nanabush dancing up and down the hill on shiny black paved roads.

Annie Cook pops up at the top of the ladder.

ANNIE: Pelajia for chief! I'd vote for you.

PHILOMENA: Why, Annie Cook. You just about scared me off the edge of this roof.

PELAJIA: Someday, we'll have to find you a man who can slow you down. So what do you want this time, Annie Cook?

ANNIE: Well, to tell you the truth, I came to borrow your record player, Philomena Moosemeat . . . I mean, Moosetail. I'm going to practise this one song for tonight. Emily Dictionary is coming to Little Current to watch me sing with the band.

PELAJIA: It's back from Espanola.

PHILOMENA [*to Pelajia*]: Pelajia Rosella Patchnose! [*to Annie*]: It's still not working very well. There's a certain screeching, squawking noise that comes out of it every time you try to play it.

PELAJIA: That's okay, Philomena. There's a certain screechy, squawky noise that comes out of Annie Cook every time she opens her mouth to sing anyway.

PHILOMENA: Yes, Annie Cook. You can borrow it. But only for one night.

ANNIE: Good. Hey, there's a bingo in Espanola next week and Fire Minklater is driving up in her new car. There might be room. [*to Philomena*]: Would you like to go?

PELAJIA: Does a bear shit in the woods?

PHILOMENA [*glares at Pelajia first*]: Yes. [*then quickly to Annie*]: Make . . . make sure you don't leave me behind.

ANNIE: I'll make sure. Well. Toodle-oo! [*And she pops down the ladder again, happy, now that she's finally got her record player.*]

PELAJIA: That Annie Cook. Records and bingo. Bingo and records.

PHILOMENA: You know, Pelajia, I'd like to see what this Fritz looks like. Maybe he IS the man who can slow her down, after all.

PELAJIA: Foolishness! Annie Cook will be walking fast right up until the day she dies and gets buried beside the two of us in that little cemetery beside the church.

PHILOMENA: Oh, go on.

> [*Pause. As Philomena sits down beside her sister, leaning with her elbow on her heart-shaped pillow.*]

So, Pelajia Patchnose. Still thinking about packing your bags and shipping off to Toronto?

PELAJIA: Well . . . oh . . . sometimes, I'm not so sure I would get along with him if I were to live down there. I mean my son Tom. He was telling me not to play so much bingo.

PHILOMENA: His upstairs washroom. Mine looks just like it now.

PELAJIA: Here we go again.

PHILOMENA: Large shining porcelain tiles in hippity-hoppity squares of black and white . . . so clean you can see your own face, like in a mirror, when you lean over to look into them. It looks so nice. The shower curtains have a certain matching blackness and whiteness to them—they're made of a rich, thick plasticky sort of material—and they're see-through in parts. The bathtub is beautiful, too. But the best, the most wonderful, my absolute most favourite part is the toilet bowl itself. First of all, it's elevated, like on a sort of . . . pedestal, so that it makes you feel like . . . the Queen . . . sitting on her royal throne, ruling her Queendom with a firm yet gentle hand. And the bowl itself—white, spirit white—is of such a shape, such an exquisitely soft, perfect oval shape that it makes you want to cry. Oh!!! And it's so comfortable you could just sit on it right up until the day you die!

> *After a long, languorous pause, Philomena snaps out of her reverie when she realizes that Pelajia, all this time, has been looking at her disbelievingly and then contemptuously. Pelajia cradles her hammer as though she'd like to bang Philomena's head with it. Philomena delicately starts to descend the ladder. The last we see of her is her Kewpie-doll face. And beside it, the heart-shaped pillow, disappearing like a setting sun behind the edge of the roof. Once she's good and gone, Pelajia dismisses her.*

PELAJIA: Oh, go on!

[*Then she pauses to look wistfully at the view for a moment.*]

Not many seagulls flying over Eugene Starblanket's house today.

And returns once more to her hammering on the roof as the lights fade into black-out. Split seconds before complete black-out, Nanabush, back once more in his guise as the seagull, 'lands' on the roof behind the unaware and unseeing Pelajia Patchnose. He dances to the beat of the hammer, merrily and triumphantly.

End of Play

1988

Glossary of Critical Terms

Fiction

ALLEGORY a story in which the events and characters are symbolic of another order of meaning, in a frame of reference outside that of the fictional world, the way slaying a dragon may symbolize defeating the devil.

CHARACTER a name (or title) and a set of qualities that make up a fictional person.

COMEDY the story of a person's rise to a higher station in life through education or improvement of personality.

DESIGN the shape of a story when it is considered as a completed object rather than an ongoing process.

DIALOGUE the parts of a story in which the words of characters are reported directly.

FABULATION fiction that violates normal probabilities to make some point about the nature of existence.

FACT a thing that has been done, or a true statement.

FANTASY a story of events that violate our sense of natural possibilities in this world; the more extreme the violation, the more *fantastic* the story is said to be.

FICTION something made up, usually a made-up story.

HISTORY the events of the past, or a retelling of those events in the form of a story; the most factual kind of fiction.

IRONY the result of some difference in the point of view or values of a character in fiction and those of the narrator or reader.

JUXTAPOSITION the way episodes or elements of a plot are located next to one another to contribute to the design of a story.

METAFICTION a kind of fabulation that calls into question the nature of fiction itself.

METAPHOR a method of conveying rich and complex thoughts by linking different images and ideas.

NARRATION the parts of a story that summarize events and conversations.

NARRATOR the person who tells a story.

PATHOS the emotion generated by the story of a character's fall or persecution through no fault of his or her own.

PICARESQUE a word used to describe a kind of story that blends comedy and satire to narrate the adventures of a rogue through a low or debased version of contemporary reality.

PLOT the order of events in a story as an ongoing process.

POINT OF VIEW the voice and vision through which the events of a story reach the reader.

REALISM a mode of fiction that is not specifically factual but presents a world recognizably bound by the same laws as the world of the author.

REPETITION a means of drawing attention to the thematic point by presenting certain features or elements of a story more than once.

ROMANCE a story that is neither wildly fantastic nor bound by the conventions of realism, but that offers a heightened version of reality.

SATIRE a story that offers a world that is debased in relation to the world of the author.

STORY a complete sequence of events, as told about a single character or a group of characters.

STREAM OF CONSCIOUSNESS a technique of narrative fiction in which the thoughts of a character are entirely open to the reader, usually being presented as a flow of ideas and feelings apparently without logical organization.

SYMBOL a particular object or event in a story that acquires thematic value through its function or the way it is presented.

THEME   the ideas, values, or feelings that are developed or questioned in a work of fiction.

TONE   the way in which attitudes are conveyed through language without being presented directly as statements, as in sarcasm.

TRAGEDY   the story of a character's fall from a high position through some flaw of personality.

Poetry

ACCENT   the rhythm of alternating light and heavy (soft and loud) sounds in verse. (*See also* stress.)

ALLITERATION   the use of the same sound at the beginning of two or more words in the same line (or two adjacent lines) of verse.

ANIMATION   the endowment of inanimate objects with some of the qualities of living creatures. (*Compare* personification.)

ASSONANCE   the repetition of vowel sounds in two or more words in the same line (or adjacent lines).

BALLAD   a poem that tells a story, usually meant to be sung.

BLANK VERSE   unrhymed iambic pentameter lines. (*See also* foot; line.)

CAESURA   the point or points within a line of verse where a pause is noticeable.

CONCEIT   an elaborate and sometimes far-fetched metaphor.

DESCRIPTION   in poetry, the use of visual images and appeals to other senses. (*Compare* imagery.)

DRAMA   the quality of poetry that is like theatrical drama, requiring the reader to grasp the nature of speaker, listener, and situation.

DRAMATIC MONOLOGUE   a poem in which a single speaker addresses remarks to one or more listeners at some significant moment in the speaker's life.

END-STOPPED   describing a line of verse that ends where one would normally pause in speech or punctuate in writing.

ENJAMBMENT   the use of run-on lines in verse. (*See* run-on line.)

FEMININE RHYME   a rhyme of two words that end in unaccented syllables (e.g., *yellow* and *fellow*), in which two rhyming sounds are required.

FOOT   a unit of metre or rhythm. Five kinds of metrical foot are normally recognized: the iamb (da-*dum*), the anapest (da-da-*dum*), the trochee (*dum*-da), the dactyl (*dum*-da-da), and the spondee (*dum*-*dum*). (*See* metre.)

FREE VERSE   unrhymed lines in which no particular metre is maintained. (*See* metre.)

HEROIC COUPLET   a rhymed pair of iambic pentameter lines, both of which are typically end-stopped, with a period or other full stop at the end of the second line. (*See* end-stopped.)

IMAGERY   the use in poetry of sensory details (*images*), such as sounds, scents, tastes, textures, and especially sights. (*Compare* description.)

IRONY   a deliberate gap or disparity between the language in which a thing is discussed and the language usually considered appropriate for that particular subject.

LINE   the line of verse as it is normally printed on a page. Lines may be divided into feet and labelled according to the number of feet per line. In English metrical verse the most common lines are pentameter (five feet) and tetrameter (four feet). (*See* foot; metre.)

MEDITATION   in poetry, the movement from images to ideas.

METAPHOR   the discovery and presentation of likeness or similarity in different things — a major resource of poetical expression.

METRE   the rhythm of a piece of poetry, determined by the kind and number of feet in a line. (*See* foot.)

METRICS   the aspect of poetry that has to do with sound rather than sense.

NARRATION   the quality of poetry that is like fiction, requiring the reader to follow shifts in time and space, and to observe significant details, in order to understand a poem as a kind of story.

NARRATOR   the character who tells a story.

PERSONIFICATION the endowment of non-human things or creatures with distinctly human qualities. (*Compare* animation.)

PUN a word used in a context in which it carries two conflicting meanings.

RHYME a sound pattern in which both vowel and consonant sounds at the end of words match (as in *rhyme* and *chime*), especially when these words come at the ends of nearby lines.

RUN-ON LINE a line of verse that ends where one would not normally pause in speech or punctuate in writing.

SCANSION the act of determining the metrical structure and rhyme scheme of a poem. (*See* metre.)

SIMILE a kind of metaphor in which the likeness of two things is made explicit by such words as *like, as, so.* (*See* metaphor.)

SITUATION in a narrative or dramatic poem, the circumstances of the character or speaker.

SONNET a verse form featuring intricate rhyming, typically consisting of fourteen iambic pentameter lines.

STANZA a regularly repeated metrical pattern of the same number of lines in groups throughout a poem, sometimes including repeated patterns of rhyme as well.

STRESS the ways in which verse sounds are accented. Three types of stress are recognized in poetry: *grammatical stress*, which is the normal pronunciation of a word or phrase; *rhetorical stress*, which involves a change in pronunciation to emphasize some part of the meaning of an utterance; and *poetical stress*, the regular rhythm established in metrical verse.

SYMBOL an extension of metaphor in which one thing is implicitly discussed by means of the explicit discussion of something else.

TACT a reader's ability to observe the conventions operating in any particular poem and to pay attention to the idiom of every poet.

Drama

ABSURDIST DRAMA a mode of drama that does not provide any rational source of explanation for the behaviour and fate of its characters and thus expresses the possibility that human existence may be meaningless.

BLOCKING the arrangement of characters on stage during any particular moment in the production of a play.

CHARACTER a dramatic being, known by name, word, and deed.

CHORIC CHARACTER a character who takes part in the action of a play but is not directly involved in the outcome of the action, and thus can provide commentary upon it.

CHORIC COMMENTARY commentary upon characters and events of a play provided either by a chorus or by choric characters.

CHORUS (*or* CHORAGOS) a group of characters who comment upon the action of a play but do not take part in it.

CLOSET DRAMA drama written to be read either privately or aloud in a small group, rather than performed on stage.

COMEDY the dramatization of a hero's and heroine's change in fortune (from frustration to satisfaction) brought about not only by the effort of the hero and heroine themselves but also by some element of chance, coincidence, or luck.

COSTUME a piece of physical apparel worn by actors to create a visual illusion appropriate to the characters they are pretending to be.

CUE a word, phrase, or statement in the text of a play that provides explicit or implicit information relevant to the theatrical production of the play.

DIALOGUE a specialized form of conversation in drama that is designed to convey everything about the imaginative world of a play as well as to provide all the cues necessary for production of the play.

DISCOVERY a change from ignorance to knowledge on the part of a dramatic hero and/or heroine, which brings about a significant change in the fortune of the hero and/or heroine. (*Compare* reversal.)

DRAMA   imitative action created through the words of imaginary beings talking to one another rather than to a reader or spectator.

DRAMATIC UNIT   a segment of the scenario that is determined by the entrance or exit of a character or group of characters. (*See* scenario.)

EXPOSITION   dialogue at the beginning of a play that includes background information about characters and events in the imaginative world of a play.

GESTURE   a physical movement made by actors appropriate to the attitudes and intentions of the characters they are pretending to be.

INTERACTION   verbal and physical deeds performed by dramatic characters in relation to one another.

INTONATION   the particular manner (including pronunciation, rhythm, and volume) in which actors deliver the lines of the characters they are pretending to be.

MEDITATIVE DRAMA   a form of drama that is primarily concerned with representing the internalized thoughts and feelings of its characters.

NARRATION   an element in drama that is like the act of storytelling in that it tells about characters and events, or comments upon characters and events, rather than showing them directly. (*See also* choric commentary; exposition; reported action; retrospection.)

NATURALISTIC DRAMA   a mode of drama that embodies a view of humans as being influenced by psychological, social, and economic forces beyond their control and comprehension.

PACING   the tempo of activity on stage during any particular moment in the production of a play.

PERSUASIVE DRAMA   a form of drama that uses dialogue, plot, and character primarily as a means of testing ideas, expounding ideas, or demonstrating the superiority of one set of ideas over another.

PLOT   a specialized form of experience that consists of a wholly interconnected system of events, deliberately selected and arranged to fulfill both the imaginative and the theatrical purposes of a play. (*Compare* scenario.)

PROP   any physical item (apart from costume and set) that is used by actors on stage during the production of a play.

REPORTED ACTION   action taking place during the time of the play that is reported by one or more of the characters rather than presented directly.

REPRESENTED ACTION   action taking place during the time of the play that is presented directly rather than reported by one or more of the characters.

RETROSPECTION   post-expository dialogue in which characters survey, explore, and attempt to understand action that has taken place well before the time of the play.

REVERSAL   an incident or sequence of incidents that goes contrary to the expectations of a hero and/or heroine. (*Compare* discovery.)

ROMANCE   a mode of drama that uses characters and events to present an intensified but not completely idealized view of human excellence.

SATIRE   a mode of drama that uses characters and events to present an intensified but not completely negative view of human imperfection.

SCENARIO   action that is presented directly and thus embodies everything that takes place in the imaginative world of a play (i.e. the plot).

SCRIPT   the text of a play interpreted as a set of cues for theatrical production.

SET   a physical construction placed on stage to represent an interior or exterior location in the imaginative world of a play.

SOLILOQUY   lines spoken by a character but meant to represent his or her unspoken thoughts and feelings.

SPECTACLE   sights and sounds of performance by means of which the imaginative world of a play is brought to life in the theatre. (*See also* blocking; costume; gesture; intonation; pacing; prop; set.)

TRAGEDY   the dramatization of a hero's or heroine's change in fortune (from prosperity to catastrophe) brought about by some great error in judgment on the part of the hero or heroine.

TRAGICOMEDY   a mode of drama that does not embody a clear-cut pattern of catastrophe or rebirth (as in tragedy or comedy) or present clear-cut images of good or evil (as in romance or satire), and thus presents an ambiguous and problematic view of human experience. (*See also* absurdist drama; naturalistic drama.)

Acknowledgements

EDWARD ALBEE *The Zoo Story*. Copyright © 1959, renewed 1987 by Edward Albee. Reprinted by permission of William Morris Endeavor Entertainment, UC on behalf of the author.

MARGARET ATWOOD 'At the tourist centre in Boston', 'Death of a Young Son by Drowning', Variations on the Word *LOVE*, Variations on the Word *SLEEP*, and 'Interlunar', from *Selected Poems 1966–1984* by Margaret Atwood. Copyright © 1990 Oxford University Press Canada. Reprinted by permission of the publisher. • 'The Door', from *The Door* by Margaret Atwood. Copyright © 2007, published by McClelland & Stewart Ltd. Used with permission of the publisher.

W.H. AUDEN 'Who's Who', 'As I Walked Out One Evening', 'Lullaby', 'Musée des Beaux Arts', 'In Memory of W.B. Yeats', and 'The Unknown Citizen', from *Collected Poems*, edited by Edward Mendelson (London: Faber and Faber, 1991), reprinted by permission of the publisher.

MARGARET AVISON 'Snow', 'New Year's Poem', 'The Swimmer's Moment', 'Butterfly Bones: Sonnet Against Sonnets', 'In a Season of Unemployment', and 'We the Poor Who Are Always with Us', from *Always Now: The Collected Poems* (in three volumes) by Margaret Avison. Copyright © Margaret Avison 2003, reprinted by permission of the Porcupine's Quill.

JOHN BARTH 'Lost in the Funhouse', from *Lost in the Funhouse* by John Barth. Copyright © 1967 by The Atlantic Monthly Company. Used by permission of Doubleday, a division of Random House, Inc.

SAMUEL BECKETT *Krapp's Last Tape* by Samuel Beckett. Copyright © 1958 by the Estate of Samuel Beckett. Used by permission of Grove/Atlantic, Inc.

ELIZABETH BISHOP 'The Map', 'First Death in Nova Scotia', 'In the Waiting Room', and 'One Art', from *The Complete Poems: 1927–1979* by Elizabeth Bishop.

ELIZABETH BOWEN 'The Demon Lover', from *The Collected Stories of Elizabeth Bowen* by Elizabeth Bowen. Copyright © 1981 by Curtis Brown Limited, Literary Executors of the Estate of Elizabeth Bowen. Used by permission of Alfred A. Knopf, a division of Random House, Inc.

DIONNE BRAND 'Islands Vanish', from *Land to Light On* by Dionne Brand. Copyright © 1997, published by McClelland & Stewart Ltd. Used with permission of the publisher. • 'Poem I', 'Poem II', and 'Poem III', from *thirsty* by Dionne Brand. Copyright © 2002, published by McClelland & Stewart Ltd. Used with permission of the publisher.

ROBERT BRINGHURST 'Essay on Adam', 'The Stonecutter's Horses', and 'Leda and the Swan', from *Selected Poems* by Robert Bringhurst. Copyright © Robert Bringhurst. Reprinted with the permission of Gaspereau Press Limited, Printers & Publishers.

MORLEY CALLAGHAN 'A Cap for Steve' appears in *The Complete Stories, Volume One*, by Morley Callaghan, pages 96–110, published by Exile Editions, © 2003.

GEOFFREY CHAUCER excerpt from the 'General Prologue' and 'The Miller's Tale', from *The Riverside Chaucer*, 3rd edn, edited by Larry D. Benson. Copyright © 1987 Heinle/Arts & Sciences, a part of Cengage Learning, Inc. Reproduced by permission. www.cengage.com/permissions.

JOHN CHEEVER 'The Swimmer', from *The Stories of John Cheever* by John Cheever. Copyright © 1978 by John Cheever. Used by permission of Alfred A. Knopf, a division of Random House, Inc.

GEORGE ELLIOTT CLARKE 'Look Homeward, Exile', 'Bees' Wings', and 'Blank Sonnet', from *Whylah Falls*, published in 2000 by Polestar, an imprint of Raincoast Books, reprinted by permission. • 'Le Tombeau de Bishop', 'Paris Annapolis', and 'Burning Poems', from *Blue*, published in 2001 by Polestar, an imprint of Raincoast Books, reprinted by permission.

E.E. CUMMINGS 'Buffalo Bill's', copyright © 1923, 1951, 1991 by the Trustees for the E.E. Cummings Trust. • Copyright © 1976 by George James Firmage, 'my father moved through dooms of love'. • Copyright © 1940, 1968, 1991 by the Trustees for the E.E. Cummings Trust, 'somewhere i have never travelled, gladly beyond'. Copyright © 1931, 1959, 1991 by the Trustees for the E.E. Cummings Trust. • Copyright © 1979 by George James Firmage, 'Spring is like a perhaps hand.' Copyright © 1923, 1925, 1951, 1953, 1991 by the Trustees for the E.E. Cummings Trust. • Copyright © 1976 by George James Firmage. 'pity this busy monster, manunkind'. Copyright © 1944, 1972, 1991 by the Trustees for the E.E. Cummings Trust, from *Complete Poems: 1904–1962* by E.E. Cummings, edited by George J. Firmage. Used by permission of Liveright Publishing Corporation.

T.S. ELIOT 'The Love Song of J. Alfred Prufrock', 'The Hollow Men', 'Journey of the Magi', and 'Marina', from *Collected Poems 1909–1962* (London: Faber and Faber, 1963), reprinted by permission of Faber and Faber Ltd.

LOUISE ERDRICH 'Fleur', from *Tracks* by Louise Erdrich. Copyright © 1988 by Louise Erdrich. Reprinted by arrangement with Henry Holt and Company, LLC.

WILLIAM FAULKNER 'A Rose for Emily', from *Collected Stories of William Faulkner* by William Faulkner. Copyright 1930 and renewed 1958 by William Faulkner. Used by permission of Random House, Inc.

ROBERT FROST 'Mending Wall', 'After Apple-Picking', 'Design', 'Provide, Provide', 'Stopping by Woods on a Snowy Evening', and 'Birches', from *The Poetry of Robert Frost*, edited by Edward Connery Lathem. Copyright 1923, 1930, 1939, 1947, 1969 by Henry Holt and Company, copyright 1936, 1951, 1958 by Robert Frost, copyright 1964, 1967, 1975 by Lesley Frost Ballantine. Reprinted by arrangement with Henry Holt and Company, LLC.

MAVIS GALLANT 'The Ice Wagon Going Down the Street', from *Home Truths* by Mavis Gallant. Copyright © 1956, 1959, 1963, 1965, 1968, 1971, 1975, 1976, 1977, 1978, 1981 by Mavis Gallant. Originally appeared in *The New Yorker*. Reprinted by permission of Georges Borchardt, Inc., on behalf of the author.

ERNEST HEMINGWAY 'A Clean, Well-Lighted Place', from *The Short Stories of Ernest Hemingway*. Reprinted with the permission of Scribner, a Division of Simon & Schuster, Inc. Copyright © 1933 by Charles Scribner's Sons. Copyright renewed © 1961 by Mary Hemingway.

TOMSON HIGHWAY *The Rez Sisters*, published by Fitzhenry & Whiteside.

HENRIK IBSEN *Hedda Gabler*, from *Henrik Ibsen: Four Major Plays*, translated by James McFarlane and Jens Arup, published by Oxford University Press. By permission of Oxford University Press, Inc.

THOMAS KING 'Borders', from *One Good Story, That One* (HarperCollins, 1993; New Edition, 1999). Copyright © 1993 Dead Dog Café Productions Inc. Reprinted with permission of the author.

A.M. KLEIN 'Soiree of Velvel Kleinburger', 'The Rocking Chair', and 'Portrait of the Poet as Landscape', from *Complete Poems*, edited by Zailig Pollock (Toronto: University of Toronto Press, 1990), reprinted by permission of the publisher.

ROBERT KROETSCH 'The Poet's Mother', from *Completed Field Notes: The Long Poems of Robert Kroetsch* by Robert Kroetsch (McClelland & Stewart, 1989). Copyright © 1989 Robert Kroetsch. Reprinted with permission of the author. • 'Hornbook #43' and 'Hornbook #45', from *The Hornbooks of Rita K* by Robert Kroetsch (The University of Alberta Press, 2001). Copyright © 2001 Robert Kroetsch. Reprinted with permission of the author.

MARGARET LAURENCE 'A Bird in the House', from *A Bird in the House* by Margaret Laurence. Copyright © 1963, 1964, 1965, 1966, 1967, 1970. Published by McClelland & Stewart Ltd. Used with permission of the publisher.

IRVING LAYTON 'The Cold Green Element', 'Berry Picking', 'Whatever Else Poetry Is Freedom', and 'Keine Lazarovitch 1870–1959', from *The Collected Poems of Irving Layton* by Irving Layton, published by McClelland & Stewart Ltd. Used with permission of the publisher.

DORIS LESSING 'A Sunrise on the Veld'. Copyright © 1973 Doris Lessing. Reprinted by kind permission of Jonathan Clowes Ltd, London, on behalf of Doris Lessing.

ROBERT LOWELL 'To Speak of Woe That Is in Marriage', 'Skunk Hour', 'Water', and 'For the Union Dead', from *Selected Poems* by Robert Lowell, published by Farrar, Straus and Giroux.

ALISTAIR MACLEOD 'The Boat', from *Island: The Collected Stories of Alistair MacLeod* by Alistair MacLeod. Copyright © 2000. Published by McClelland & Stewart Ltd. Used with permission of the publisher.

BERNARD MALAMUD 'The Magic Barrel', from *The Magic Barrel* by Bernard Malamud, published by Farrar, Straus and Giroux.

ROY MIKI 'make it new', 'attractive', 'subversion in tokyo', and 'on the sublime', from *Surrender* (Toronto: The Mercury Press, 2001).

ARTHUR MILLER *The Price*. Copyright © 1968 by Arthur Miller and Ingeborg M. Miller, Trustee. Used by permission of Viking Penguin, a division of Penguin Group (USA) Inc.

ROHINTON MISTRY 'The Collectors', from *Tales from Firozsha Baag* by Rohinton Mistry. Copyright © 1987. Published by McClelland & Stewart Ltd. Used with permission of the publisher.

MARIANNE MOORE 'Poetry', from *The Poems of Marianne Moore* by Marianne Moore, edited by Grace Schulman. Copyright © 2003 by Marianne Craig Moore, Executor of the Estate of Marianne Moore. Used by permission of Viking Penguin, a division of Penguin Group (USA) Inc. • 'The Fish', from *The Collected Poems of Marianne Moore* by Marianne Moore, reprinted with the permission of Scribner, a Division of Simon & Schuster, Inc. Copyright © 1935 Marianne Moore; copyright renewed © 1963 Marianne Moore and T.S. Eliot. Copyright © 1944 Marianne Moore; copyright renewed © 1972 Marianne Moore. • 'A Jelly-Fish', from *The Complete Poems of Marianne Moore* by Marianne Moore. Copyright © 1959 by Marianne Moore, © renewed 1987 by Lawrence E. Brinn and Louise Crane, Executors of the Estate of Marianne Moore. Used by permission of Viking Penguin, a division of Penguin Group (USA) Inc. • 'Nevertheless', from *The Collected Poems of Marianne Moore* by Marianne Moore, reprinted with the permission of Scribner, a Division of Simon & Schuster, Inc. Copyright © 1935 Marianne Moore; copyright renewed © 1963 Marianne Moore and T.S. Eliot. Copyright © 1944 Marianne Moore; copyright renewed © 1972 Marianne Moore.

BHARATI MUKHERJEE 'The Lady from Lucknow', originally published in *Darkness*. Copyright © 1985 by Bharati Mukherjee. Reprinted by permission of the author.

ALICE MUNRO 'Family Furnishings', from *Hateship, Friendship, Courtship, Loveship, Marriage* by Alice Munro. Copyright © 2001. Published by McClelland & Stewart Ltd. Used with permission of the publisher.

FLANNERY O'CONNOR 'Everything That Rises Must Converge', from *The Complete Stories* by Flannery O'Connor, published by Farrar, Straus and Giroux.

MICHAEL ONDAATJE 'Bearhug', 'Letters and Other Worlds', 'Elizabeth', and 'The Cinnamon Peeler', reprinted by permission of the author.

P.K. PAGE 'The Stenographers', 'Photos of a Salt Mine', 'Arras', 'The New Bicycle', and 'Deaf-mute in a Pear Tree', from *The Hidden Room* (in two volumes) by P.K. Page, reprinted by permission of the Porcupine's Quill. Copyright © P.K. Page, 1997.

SYLVIA PLATH 'Sheep in Fog', 'Daddy', 'Kindness', 'Edge', and 'Worlds', from *Collected Poems*, edited by Ted Hughes (London: Faber and Faber, 1981), reprinted by permission of the publisher.

SHARON POLLOCK *Doc*. Copyright © 1984 Sharon Pollock, revised edition copyright © 2003 Sharon Pollock. Reprinted by permission of Broadview Press.

E.J. PRATT 'The Shark', 'Erosion', 'One Hour of Life', 'Silences', and 'The Dead', from *E.J. Pratt: The Complete Poems*, edited by Sandra Djwa and R.J. Moyles (Toronto: University of Toronto Press, 1989), reprinted by permission of the publisher.

ADRIENNE RICH 'The Afterwake', 'Novella', 'Night-Pieces: For a Child', and 'Moving in Winter', from *Collected Early Poems: 1950–1970* by Adrienne Rich. Copyright © 1993 by Adrienne Rich.

Index

After Apple-Picking (Frost), 563–4
After Long Silence (Yeats), 560
Afterwake, The (Rich), 665–6
[A happy lover who has come] (Tennyson), 515
ALBEE, EDWARD, 735, 1207–24
Among School Children (Yeats), 556–9
Anecdote of the Jar (Stevens), 572
Antigone (Watson), 189–95
Araby (Joyce), 111–14
Arras (Page), 642–3
As I Walked Out One Evening (Auden), 608–9
At the Long Sault: May 1660 (Lampman), 550–2
At the Tourist Centre in Boston (Atwood), 675
attractive (Miki), 682–4
ATWOOD, MARGARET, 674–81
AUDEN, W.H., 607–14
Auguries of Innocence (Blake), 481–4
AVISON, MARGARET, 652–6

Babylon Revisited (Fitzgerald), 137–51
BARTH, JOHN, 272–87
Bartleby, the Scrivener (Melville), 47–72
[Batter my heart, three-personed God; for you] (Donne), 436
Bearhug (Ondaatje), 688
[Because I could not stop for death] (Dickinson), 534–5
BECKETT, SAMUEL, 1141–8
Bees' Wings (Clarke), 708
Berry Picking (Layton), 631–2
Birches (Frost), 564–6
Bird in the House, A (Laurence), 259–71
BISHOP, ELIZABETH, 624–9
Bishop Orders His Tomb at Saint Praxed's Church, The (Browning), 520–3
BLAKE, WILLIAM, 477–84
Blank Sonnet (Clarke), 708–9
Boat, The (MacLeod), 309–21
Borders (King), 328–36
BOWEN, ELIZABETH, 159–63

BRAND, DIONNE, 701–6
Bride Comes to Yellow Sky, The (Crane), 102–10
Bright Star (Keats), 505
BRINGHURST, ROBERT, 693–700
BROWNING, ROBERT, 516–24
Buffalo Bill 's (cummings), 602
Burning Poems (Clarke), 711
Butterfly Bones; or Sonnet against Sonnets (Avison), 654

CALLAGHAN, MORLEY, 168–75
Canonization, The (Donne), 432–3
Canterbury Tales, The (Chaucer), 401–427
Cap for Steve, A (Callaghan), 168–75
CHAUCER, GEOFFREY, 401–427
CHEEVER, JOHN, 205–13
Chimney-Sweeper, The (Blake), 479
CHOPIN, KATE, 72–74
Cinnamon Peeler, The (Ondaatje), 692–3
Circus Animals' Desertion, The (Yeats), 560–1
City of the End of Things, The (Lampman), 547–9
CLARKE, GEORGE ELLIOTT, 706–11
Clean, Well-Lighted Place, A (Hemingway), 164–7
Clod and the Pebble, The (Blake), 478–9
Cold Green Element, The (Layton), 630–1
Collectors, The (Mistry), 336–53
Composed upon Westminster Bridge, September 3, 1802 (Wordsworth), 492
Convergence of the Twain, The (Hardy), 539–40
Coronet, The (Marvell), 450
CRANE, STEPHEN, 102–10
Crossing Brooklyn Ferry (Whitman), 525–30
CUMMINGS, E.E., 602–6

Daddy (Plath), 670–2
Dalliance of the Eagles, The (Whitman), 532
[Dark house, by which once more I stand] (Tennyson), 514

Darkling Thrush, The (Hardy), 538

Days of the Unicorns, The (Webb), 663–4

Deaf-Mute in the Pear Tree (Page), 645–6

[Death, be not proud, though some have callèd thee] (Donne), 436

Death of a Young Son by Drowning (Atwood), 676

Death of Tennyson, The (Lampman), 547

Deed, The (Pratt), 580–1

Delight in Disorder (Herrick), 437

Demon Lover, The (Bowen), 159–63

Design (Frost), 566

DICKINSON, EMILY, 532–6

Doc (Pollock), 735, 1225–80

Dolls, The (Yeats), 381–2, 554

DONNE, JOHN, 380–1, 430–6

Do Not Go Gentle into That Good Night (Thomas), 637

Door, The (Atwood), 680–1

During Wind and Rain (Hardy), 541–2

[Earth has not anything to show more fair] (Wordsworth), 492

Edge (Plath), 673

ELIOT, T.S., 591–601

Elizabeth (Ondaatje), 690–2

Epistle IV: To Richard Boyle, Earl of Burlington (Pope), 470–77

ERDRICH, LOUISE, 353–62

Erosion (Pratt), 578

Essay on Adam (Bringhurst), 694

Everything That Rises Must Converge (O'Connor), 248–58

Fair Singer, The (Marvell), 449–50

Family Furnishings (Munro), 288–308

FAULKNER, WILLIAM, 151–58

Fern Hill (Thomas), 637–9

First Death in Nova Scotia (Bishop), 625–6

Fish, The (Moore), 589–90

FITZGERALD, F. SCOTT, 137–51

Flea, The (Donne), 380–1, 434

Fleur (Erdrich), 353–62

Flowers by the Sea (Williams), 584

Force that through the Green Fuse Drives the Flower, The (Thomas), 635–6

For the Pleasure of Seeing Her Again (Tremblay), 1281–1311

For the Union Dead (Lowell), 650–1

FROST, ROBERT, 562–7

GALLANT, MAVIS, 231–47

Garden, The (Marvell), 447–9

Garden Party, The (Mansfield), 126–36

GILMAN, CHARLOTTE PERKINS, 75–87

God's Grandeur (Hopkins), 543

Good Morrow, The (Donne), 431

Hap (Hardy), 537

HARDY, THOMAS, 537–42

HAWTHORNE, NATHANIEL, 21–34

Hedda Gabler (Ibsen), 734–5, 961–1021

HEMINGWAY, ERNEST, 164–7

HERRICK, ROBERT, 437–8

High-Toned Old Christian Woman, A (Stevens), 575–6

HIGHWAY, TOMSON, 1312–53

Hollow Men, The (Eliot), 596–9

Holy Sonnets (Donne), 436

HOPKINS, GERARD MANLEY, 543–5

Hornbook #43 (Kroetsch), 659

Hornbook #45 (Kroetsch), 659–60

Hornbooks of Rita K., The (Kroetsch), 659–60

How Soon Hath Time (Milton), 440

IBSEN, HENRIK, 734–5, 960–1021

Ice Wagon Going Down the Street, The (Gallant), 231–47

I Hear America Singing (Whitman), 530

[I heard a fly buzz — when I died —] (Dickinson), 536

Importance of Being Earnest, The (Wilde), 734, 1022–65

[I'm 'wife'— I've finished that] (Dickinson), 533–4

In a Season of Unemployment (Avison), 654–5

[I never hear the word 'escape'] (Dickinson), 535–6

In Memoriam (Tennyson), 514–6

In Memory of W.B. Yeats (Auden), 611–13

Interlunar (Atwood), 678–9

In the Waiting Room (Bishop), 626–9

In Time of 'The Breaking of Nations' (Hardy), 542

[I on my horse, and Love on me doth try] (Sidney), 383–3

Islands Vanish (Brand), 701–3

It Is a Beauteous Evening, Calm and Free (Wordsworth), 376

I Wandered Lonely as a Cloud (Wordsworth), 485

Jellyfish, A (Moore), 591
Journey of the Magi (Eliot), 599–600
JOYCE, JAMES, 110–114

KEATS, JOHN, 497–506
Keine Lazarovitch 1870–1959 (Layton), 634
Kindness (Plath), 672
KING, THOMAS, 328–36
King Lear (Shakespeare), 733–4, 780–894
KLEIN, A.M., 614–24
Krapp's Last Tape (Beckett), 735, 1142–8
KROETSCH, ROBERT, 656–60

La Belle Dame Sans Merci (Keats), 503–5
Lady from Lucknow, The (Mukherjee), 321–27
Lady of Shalott, The (Tennyson), 507–11
Lake Isle of Innisfree, The (Yeats), 553
Lamb, The (Blake), 478
Lament (Webb), 662
LAMPMAN, ARCHIBALD, 393–5, 546–52
Landscape with the Fall of Icarus (Williams), 586–7
Last Words of My English Grandmother, The (Williams), 584–5
LAURENCE, MARGARET, 259–71
LAWRENCE, D.H., 115–26, 372, 373
LAYTON, IRVING, 630–4
LEACOCK, STEPHEN, 90–102
Leda and the Swan (Bringhurst), 699–700
Leda and the Swan (Yeats), 556
LESSING, DORIS, 225–31
Le Tombeau de Bishop (Clarke), 709
Letters & Other Worlds (Ondaatje), 688–90
Lines Composed a few miles above Tintern Abbey (Wordsworth), 493–6
London (Blake), 480–1
Look Homeward, Exile (Clarke), 707
Lost in the Funhouse (Barth), 272–87
Love Song of J. Alfred Prufrock, The (Eliot), 592–6
LOWELL, ROBERT, 646–51
Lullaby (Auden), 609–10
Lycidas (Milton), 440–4

MACLEOD, ALISTAIR, 308–21
Magic Barrel, The (Malamud), 213–25
make it new (Miki), 681–2

MALAMUD, BERNARD, 213–25
MANSFIELD, KATHERINE, 126–36
Map, The (Bishop), 624–5
Marina (Eliot), 600–1
Marine Excursion of the Knights of Pythias, The (Leacock), 90–102
MARVELL, ANDREW, 446–50
Marvell's Garden (Webb), 660–1
MELVILLE, HERMAN, 47–72
Mending Wall (Frost), 562–3
MIKI, ROY, 681–7
MILLER, ARTHUR, 735, 1148–1207
Miller's Prologue and Tale, The (Chaucer), 401–427
MILTON, JOHN, 439–45
MISTRY, ROHINTON, 336–53
MOORE, MARIANNE, 587–91
Moving in Winter (Rich), 666
MUKHERJEE, BHARATI, 321–27
MUNRO, ALICE, 288–308
Musée des Beaux Arts (Auden), 610–11
my father moved through dooms of love (cummings), 604–6
My Kinsman, Major Molineux (Hawthorne), 21–34
My Last Duchess (Browning), 519–20
[My mistress' eyes are nothing like the sun] (Shakespeare), 430

Nevertheless (Moore), 590–1
New Bicycle, The (Page), 644
New Year's Poem (Avison), 652–3
Night-Pieces: For a Child (Rich), 667
[No more be grieved at that which thou hast done] (Shakespeare), 428
Novella (Rich), 666
[Not marble nor the gilded monuments] (Shakespeare), 429
[Now fades the last long streak of snow] (Tennyson), 515–6

O'CONNOR, FLANNERY, 247–58
Ode: Intimations of Immortality from Recollections of Early Childhood (Wordsworth), 486–91
Ode on a Grecian Urn (Keats), 500–1
Ode to a Nightingale (Keats), 497–500
Ode to Autumn (Keats), 502
Oedipus Rex (Sophocles), 733, 737–79
Of Modern Poetry (Stevens), 576

ONDAATJE, MICHAEL, 687–93
One Art (Bishop), 629
One Hour of Life (Pratt), 578
On Shakespeare (Milton), 439
On the Sonnet (Keats), 506
on the sublime (Miki), 686–7
Oxen, The (Hardy), 541
Ox-Tamer, The (Whitman), 531–2

PAGE, P.K., 639–46
Painted Door, The (Ross), 176–89
Paris Annapolis (Clarke), 710
Photos of a Salt Mine (Page), 641–2
Piano, The (Lawrence), 372, 373
Pied Beauty (Hopkins), 544
pity this busy monster (cummings), 606
PLATH, SYLVIA, 669–74
POE, EDGAR ALLAN, 34–47
Poetry (Moore), 588
Poet's Mother, The (Kroetsch), 656–8
POLLOCK, SHARON, 1224–80
POPE, ALEXANDER, 451–77
Porphyria's Lover (Browning), 523–4
Portrait of the Poet as Landscape (Klein), 367,
    619–24
PRATT, E.J., 577–81
Price, The (Miller), 735, 1149–1207
Provide, Provide (Frost), 567
Purloined Letter, The (Poe), 34–47
Pygmalion (Shaw), 735, 1066–1141

Railway Station, The (Lampman), 393–5, 546
Rape (Rich), 668
Rape of the Lock, The (Pope), 451–70
Red Wheelbarrow, The (Williams), 374–5,
    583
Refusal to Mourn the Death, by Fire, of a
    Child in London, A (Thomas), 636
Relic, The (Donne), 435
Rez Sisters, The (Highway), 735, 1312–53
RICH, ADRIENNE, 665–8
ROBERTS, CHARLES G.D., 87–89
Rocking Chair, The (Klein), 618
Rocking-Horse Winner, The (Lawrence),
    115–26
Rose for Emily, A (Faulkner), 152–8
ROSS, SINCLAIR, 176–89

Sailing to Byzantium (Yeats), 559

School for Scandal, The (Sheridan), 734,
    895–960
Second Coming, The (Yeats), 555–6
SHAKESPEARE, WILLIAM, 379–80, 427–30,
    780–894
[Shall I compare thee to a summer's day?]
    (Shakespeare), 427–8
Shark, The (Pratt), 577–8
SHAW, GEORGE BERNARD, 735; 1065–1141
Sheep in Fog (Plath), 669
SHERIDAN, ROBERT BRINSLEY, 894–960
Sick Rose, The (Blake), 479
SIDNEY, PHILIP, 382–3
Sight in Camp in the Daybreak Grey and
    Dim, A (Whitman), 531
Silences (Pratt), 579–80
[Since brass, nor stone, nor earth, nor
    boundless sea] (Shakespeare), 429
Skunk Hour (Lowell), 647–8
Snow (Avison), 652
Snow Man, The (Stevens), 575
Soirée of Velvel Kleinburger (Klein), 615–17
Soliloquy of the Spanish Cloister (Browning),
    517–18
somewhere i have never travelled
    (cummings), 603–4
Songs of Experience (Blake), 478–81
Songs of Innocence (Blake), 478
SOPHOCLES, 733, 737–79
Spring and All (Williams), 582–3
Spring and Fall: To a Young Child (Hopkins),
    545
Spring is like a perhaps hand (cummings),
    602–3
Stenographers, The (Page), 639–40
STEVENS, WALLACE, 568–76
Stonecutter's Horses, The (Bringhurst),
    369–71, 694–8
Stopping by Woods on a Snowy Evening
    (Frost), 566–7
Story of an Hour, The (Chopin), 73–74
Strayed (Roberts), 87–89
subversion in tokyo (Miki), 684–6
[Success is counted sweetest] (Dickinson), 533
Sunday Morning (Stevens), 568–71
Sunrise on the Veld, A (Lessing), 225–31
Sun Rising, The (Donne), 431–2
Swimmer, The (Cheever), 205–13
Swimmer's Moment, The (Avison), 653